W9-BSY-480

WITHDRAWN

FACTS ABOUT THE PRESIDENTS

Eighth Edition

Other Reference Titles by

H. W. Wilson

Joseph Nathan Kane

Janet Podell

FACTS ABOUT THE PRESIDENTS

A COMPILATION OF BIOGRAPHICAL AND HISTORICAL INFORMATION

Eighth Edition

The H.W. Wilson Company

New York • Dublin

2009

Printed in the United States of America

ISBN 978-0-8242-1087-8

Library of Congress Cataloging-in-Publication Data

Kane, Joseph Nathan, 1899–2002.
    Facts about the presidents : a compilation of biographical and historical information / Joseph Nathan Kane, Janet Podell.—8th ed.
        p. cm.
    Includes index.
    ISBN 978-0-8242-1087-8 (alk. paper)
    1. Presidents—United States—History—Miscellanea. 2. Presidents—United States—Biography—Miscellanea. I. Podell, Janet. II. Title.
    E176.1.K3 2009
    973.09'9—dc22

                                                                    2008056016

Cover: Main photo (Barack Obama) courtesy of the White House. Portraits, from top, of George Washington, Thomas Jefferson, Abraham Lincoln, and Franklin Delano Roosevelt all courtesy of The Library of Congress.

The H. W. Wilson Company
950 University Avenue
Bronx, NY 10452

Visit H.W. Wilson's Web site: www.hwwilson.com

Contents

Preface

The Presidents of the United States, from George Washington to Barack Obama, are the subjects of continuing popular interest and scholarly research. Countless books have been published about these forty-three men—individual biographies, collective biographies, academic studies, political analyses, and pictorial histories. Since 1959, readers seeking essential facts about the Presidents and their administrations have been able to turn to *Facts About the Presidents*, a compilation that presents, in one volume, data about the Presidents' lives, backgrounds, and terms in office, as well as information about the presidency in history, tradition, and law.

Facts About the Presidents comprises two parts. Part I contains a separate chapter for each President, in chronological order. Each chapter has a general profile showing the President's dates in office, dates of birth and death, and his religious, ethnic, educational, and occupational background; a section on his parents, siblings, marriages, and children; and reference material on the relevant elections, congressional sessions, cabinet members, Supreme Court appointments, and Vice President, together with highlights of the President's life and administration. In this eighth edition, Part I also features more than 200 images depicting the Presidents, Vice Presidents, and First Ladies, as well as the people, places, and events associated with each administration.

Part II presents material in a comparative format, with collective data and statistics on the Presidents, presidential elections, and the offices of the presidency and vice presidency.

The information in the eighth edition has been brought up to date as of February 2009. Should further research bring to light primary sources that contradict any of the material in *Facts About the Presidents*, the publishers would appreciate being notified.

In preparing this book, I have been fortunate to have as my editors Paul McCaffrey, Ken Partridge, and Rich Stein of the General Reference Department at the H.W. Wilson Company, to whom I give hearty thanks. I am the lucky beneficiary of the excellent research and proofreading skills of my mother, Diane Kopperman Podell, Professor Emerita of the B. Davis Schwartz Library, C.W. Post Campus, Long Island University, who has helped me enormously in this project as in many others. In gratitude for this help, but even more for her constant support, wise advice, generous spirit, and selfless love over the years, I am happy to dedicate this book to her.

Janet Podell
March 2009

Part I

Biographical Data

Courtesy of The Library of Congress

George Washington

Date of birth—Feb. 22, 1732 (Feb. 11 on Julian calendar)

Place of birth—Pope's Creek, Westmoreland County, Va.

Education—Unknown; basic literacy and mathematical skills

Religion—Episcopalian

Ancestry—English

Career—Surveyor, planter, soldier, colonial legislator, delegate to Continental Congress, commander in chief of Continental Army, president of Constitutional Convention

Political party—Federalist

State represented—Virginia

Term of office—Apr. 30, 1789–Mar. 4, 1797

Term served—7 years, 308 days

Administration—1st, 2nd

Congresses—1st, 2nd, 3rd, 4th

Age at inauguration—57 years, 67 days

Lived after term—2 years, 285 days

Occupation after term—Planter; held rank of lieutenant general and commander in chief of the nation's armies

Date of death—Dec. 14, 1799

Age at death—67 years, 295 days

Place of death—Mount Vernon, near Alexandria, Va.

Burial place—Family vault, Mount Vernon, Va.

FAMILY

FATHER

Name—Augustine Washington

Date of birth—1694

Place of birth—Westmoreland, Va.

First marriage—Jane Butler, Apr. 20, 1715 (d. Nov. 24, 1728)

Second marriage—Mary Ball, Mar. 6, 1731

Occupation—Farmer, planter, iron exporter, sheriff, justice of the peace

Date of death—Apr. 12, 1743

Place of death—King George County, Va.

Age at death—About 49 years

Augustine Washington was the grandson of John Washington, who immigrated to the colony of Virginia from the north of England circa 1657, and the son of Lawrence and Mildred Warner Washington, who died when their children were young. (Mildred Warner Washington was a descendant of King Edward III of England.)

Like his father and grandfather, Augustine was prominent in the colonial government, serving as justice of the peace and sheriff; he ran a plantation using slave labor and went into business as an iron manufacturer and exporter after ore was found on his land. He is known to have been prone to lawsuits. He is reported to have been a distant and preoccupied father, often away from home. His first wife, Jane Butler, was about 15 years old at the time of their marriage in 1715 and about 28 when she died; they had four children together. With his second wife, Mary Ball, he had six children.

George Washington was 11 years old when Augustine died unexpectedly of a stomach disorder. In some 20,000 surviving letters and other documents written by George Washington, Augustine Washington is mentioned a total of three times.

MOTHER

Name at birth—Mary Ball

Date of birth—1708

Place of birth—Lancaster County, Va.

Marriage—Augustine Washington, Mar. 6, 1731

Date of death—Aug. 25, 1789

Place of death—Near Fredericksburg, Va.

Age at death—81 years

Mary Washington's grandfather, William Ball, abandoned his English estate during England's Civil War, circa 1650, and fled to Virginia, where he became a wealthy tobacco grower. Mary was the product of the marriage of his son Joseph, a widower, to a widow named Johnson; from their first marriages, she had numerous half-siblings. Her father died when she was a toddler, her mother when she was 12.

At the age of 35, after some 13 years of marriage, Mary Washington was left a widow with four sons and a daughter. George, the eldest, rebelled against her overbearing manner and spent long visits with his married half-brothers. He learned surveying and became a soldier only because she vetoed his plan to join the British Navy. She also refused to relinquish to him the property that he had inherited from his father. Although he supported her financially during all his adult life, including the years when he was serving as commander in chief of the Continental Army and as President, she pestered him for money and embarrassed him by petitioning Virginia's legislature for a pension she did not need.

Mary Washington died of breast cancer in her eighties. She was not much mourned by President Washington and her grave had no marker until 1894, when a group of Virginia women paid for a marble shaft with the legend "Mary the mother of Washington."

SIBLINGS

Augustine Washington was the father of ten children, four by his first wife and six by his second wife. George Washington was his fifth child and the firstborn of Mary Ball Washington.

Children of Jane Butler Washington and Augustine Washington

Butler Washington, b. 1716, d. 1716

Lawrence Washington, b. 1718, d. July 26, 1752

Augustine Washington, b. 1720, d. May 1762

Jane Washington, b. 1722, d. Jan. 17, 1735

Children of Mary Ball Washington and Augustine Washington

George Washington, b. Feb. 22, 1732, d. Dec. 14, 1799

Elizabeth ("Betty") Washington, b. June 20, 1733, d. Mar. 31, 1797

Samuel Washington, b. Nov. 16, 1734, d. Dec. 1781

John Augustine Washington, b. Jan. 13, 1736, d. Feb. 1787

Charles Washington, b. May 2, 1738, d. Sept. 1799

Mildred Washington, b. June 21, 1739, d. Oct. 23, 1740

MARRIAGE

Married—Martha Dandridge Custis

Date of marriage—Jan. 6, 1759

Place of marriage—New Kent County, Va.

Courtesy of The Library of Congress

George Washington and his family

Age of wife at marriage—27 years, 199 days

Age of husband at marriage—26 years, 318 days

Years married—40 years, 342 days

CHILDREN

George Washington had no children of his own. He was stepfather to Martha Park Custis (known as Patsy) and John Parke Custis, Martha Washington's two surviving children from her first marriage (she had had two other children who died very young). Patsy died at the age of 17 during an epileptic seizure. John Parke Custis served during the Revolutionary War as Washington's aide-de-camp and died of camp fever shortly after the war ended, leaving four little children. The Washingtons took into their household the two youngest of these grandchildren—a three-year-old girl, Eleanor Parke Custis, known as Nelly, and an infant boy, George Washington Parke Custis, known as Wash—and acted as parents to both.

George Washington's will bequeathed to his stepgrandson a piece of land on the Potomac River. Wash Custis built on it a mansion he called Arlington. It eventually passed to his daughter Mary Ann and her husband, army officer Robert E. Lee. During the Civil War, while Lee was commanding the armies of the Confederacy, the property was confiscated by the Union Army; the mansion was used as a headquarters and the surrounding parkland as a burial ground. The estate is now Arlington National Cemetery, the nation's chief military cemetery.

THE PRESIDENT'S WIFE

Name at birth—Martha Dandridge

Date of birth—June 21, 1731

Place of birth—New Kent County, Va.

Mother—Frances Jones Dandridge

Father—Colonel John Dandridge

Father's occupation—Planter

First marriage—Daniel Parke Custis, June 1749, Dandridge estate, New Kent County, Va. (d. July 8, 1757)

Second marriage—George Washington, January 6, 1759, Custis estate, New Kent County, Va.

Children from first marriage—Daniel Parke Custis, b. 1751, d. 1754; Frances Parke Custis, b.1753, d. 1757; John Parke Custis, b. 1754, d. 1781; Martha Parke ("Patsy") Custis, b. 1756, d. 1773

Children from second marriage—None

Religion—Episcopalian

Date of death—May 22, 1802

Age at death—70 years, 355 days

Place of death—Mount Vernon, near Alexandria, Va.

Burial place—Mount Vernon, Va.

Years older than the president—246 days

Years she survived the President—2 years, 159 days

Martha Washington grew up in Virginia on a small plantation and at the age of 17 married a wealthy planter twice her age, with whom she had four children. She was widowed at 26 and married George Washington less than two years later. They were in their forties when the Continental Congress asked George to lead the war of independence against Britain. From 1775 until the war's

Courtesy of The Library of Congress

Martha Washington, wife of George Washington

end, Martha joined her husband each year in the army's winter camp, where she spent her time doing what she could to ease the suffering of sick and freezing soldiers, sewing shirts and knitting socks for them, patching their torn clothes, and encouraging other officers' wives to do likewise.

Martha Washington outlived two husbands, all four of her children, and numerous siblings, nieces, and nephews, but succeeded in maintaining her equanimity and amiability. "I am still determined to be cheerful and happy in whatever situation I may be," she once wrote to her friend Mercy Warren, "for I have also learned from experience that the greater part of our happiness or misery depends on our dispositions and not on our circumstances. We carry the seeds of the one or the other about with us in our minds, wherever we go."

THE FIRST LADY

The wife of the nation's first President was known as Lady Washington even before her husband took office. She never occupied the White House in Washington, D.C., as it had not been completed during George Washington's administration. The seat of government at the time of his first inauguration was at New York City, where the Washingtons lived first in a mansion on Franklin Square and then in a mansion on Broadway. They were assisted by a secretary, Tobias Lear, and a steward, Sam Fraunces, who ran a staff of 14 servants. (Fraunces was the proprietor of the famous Fraunces Tavern, where Washington had escaped an assassination attempt during the Revolutionary War.) When the capital was transferred to Philadelphia in 1790, the Washingtons lived in a house owned by Robert Morris, the Revolution's financier. The government did not furnish the President's House, and the expense of furnishing was borne by the Washingtons.

Martha Washington set a precedent for the treatment of First Ladies in May 1789 when she traveled from Mount Vernon to New York City to join her husband, who had been inaugurated a few weeks earlier. Though most of her journey was made as a private citizen, when she reached New Jersey she boarded the presidential barge and was conveyed by American sailors across New York Bay to Manhattan, where she was

greeted by a 13-gun salute and cries of "Long live Lady Washington!" This was the first time that the spouse of a President was accorded public honors.

THE WASHINGTONS AND THEIR GUESTS

Although Martha Washington was never consulted by her husband in matters of government, she was his partner in matters of state ceremony and entertainment, though like all First Ladies she received no compensation for the services she performed. The Washingtons hosted weekly receptions for dignitaries and members of Congress, with the President holding one reception for men on Tuesday afternoons and his wife holding a mixed-sex "drawing room" on Friday evenings. The practice of calling on socially important people and receiving them in turn was observed punctiliously by the Washingtons: the President maintained regular calling hours twice a week and received visitors every day but Sunday, while Mrs. Washington made it her practice to return all calls within three days. To her near relatives she confided her longing to be at home in Mount Vernon with her husband. She carried out her ceremonial tasks as a matter of duty, since she had been, as she once expressed it, "taught by the great example which I have so long before me never to oppose my private wishes to the public will."

MARTHA WASHINGTON ESTABLISHED NEW YEAR'S RECEPTION

The New Year's Day reception, a presidential tradition for 140 years, was established by Martha Washington on January 1, 1790, when she received guests in her house in Philadelphia. Except in time of war and national mourning, the custom continued until the Hoover administration abolished it in 1930.

ASSESSMENT OF MARTHA WASHINGTON BY A CONTEMPORARY

Martha Washington's successor as First Lady, Abigail Adams, was known as a shrewd judge of character. After meeting Martha in

1789, Mrs. Adams wrote: "Mrs. Washington is one of those unassuming characters which create Love & Esteem. A most becoming pleasentness sits upon her countenance & an unaffected deportment which renders her the object of veneration and respect."

IMPORTANT DATES IN THE PRESIDENT'S LIFE

1749, licensed as surveyor by College of William and Mary

July 20, 1749, official surveyor, Culpeper County, Va.

Nov. 6, 1752, appointed adjutant of one of Virginia's four militia districts, with rank of major

Mar. 15, 1754, lieutenant-colonel of Virginia regiment

June 5, 1754, colonel of Virginia regiment

May 10, 1755, appointed aide-de-camp (a volunteer position without rank) by General Braddock in French and Indian War

July 9, 1755, two horses were shot under him and four bullets pierced his coat in battle near Fort Duquesne, Pa.; withdrew remnants of Braddock's defeated army at the Monongahela to Fort Cumberland

Aug. 14, 1755, appointed by the legislature colonel of the Virginia regiment and commander in chief of the Virginia forces protecting the frontier against the French and Indians

1755–1758, engaged in recruiting and organizing troops for colonial defense

1758, commanded successful expedition to Fort Duquesne

July 24, 1758, elected to House of Burgesses from Frederick County

Dec. 1758, resigned commission as colonel of the Virginia regiment and commander in chief of the Virginia forces

1758, resided at Mount Vernon, Va.

Oct. 1770, justice of the peace for Fairfax County

Aug. 1773, delegate to the Williamsburg Convention

Aug. 1774, member, First Virginia Provincial Convention

Aug. 5, 1774, elected delegate to First Continental Congress

Sept. 5, 1774, attended first session of Continental Congress at Philadelphia, Pa.

Mar. 25, 1775, Second Virginia Provincial Congress selected Washington to attend Second Continental Congress

June 15, 1775, Congress elected Washington as general and commander in chief of the Army of the United Colonies

July 3, 1775, assumed command at Cambridge, Mass.

Mar. 17, 1776, Boston evacuated by the British

Aug. 27, 1776, Battle of Long Island

Oct. 28, 1776, Battle of White Plains

Dec. 25, 1776, recrossed Delaware River

Dec. 26, 1776, Battle of Trenton

Jan. 3, 1777, Battle of Princeton

Sept. 11, 1777, Battle of Brandywine

Oct. 4, 1777, Battle of Germantown

Dec. 19, 1777, winter headquarters established at Valley Forge

Oct. 19, 1781, Cornwallis surrendered at Yorktown, Va.

May 8, 1783, dinner with Lord Carleton after conference; Washington received 17-gun salute

June 19, 1783, elected President General of the Society of the Cincinnati

Sept. 3, 1783, Treaty of Peace signed

Nov. 2, 1783, issued Farewell Orders to the armies

Nov. 25, 1783, reoccupied New York City after British occupation

Dec. 4, 1783, bade farewell to his officers at Fraunces' Tavern

Dec. 23, 1783, surrendered his commission as commander in chief to Congress; returned to private life

May 25, 1787, delegate from Virginia to the Federal Convention; elected president unanimously

Feb. 4, 1789, unanimously elected President of the United States for 1789–1793 term

Apr. 30, 1789, inaugurated President at Federal Hall, New York City

June 1, 1789, signed first act of Congress

Aug. 25, 1789, his mother, Mary Ball Washington, died at Fredericksburg, Va.

Dec. 5, 1792, unanimously reelected President

Mar. 4, 1793, inaugurated at Philadelphia, Pa., as President of the United States for a second term

Sept. 18, 1793, laid cornerstone of the Capitol at Washington, D.C.

Sept. 17, 1796, issued Farewell Address

Mar. 3, 1797, expiration of his second term as President

July 11, 1798, President John Adams appointed him lieutenant general and commander in chief of all the armies of the United States

July 13, 1798, accepted appointment

ELECTIONS

THE ELECTION OF 1789

The date of the first election was established on September 13, 1788, by the Continental Congress. The first Wednesday in January 1789 was fixed by Congress as the date for the choosing of electors by the several states. The first Wednesday in February 1789 was fixed as the day on which the electors would vote.

When the first electors cast their ballots, there were no political organizations or political parties in existence. Each elector had to vote for two persons. The person who received the majority of votes was elected President, and the person with the next highest number became Vice President. No distinction was made between votes for President and Vice President until 1804.

The method of balloting and selecting the candidate is governed by Article 2, Section 1, Paragraph 3 of the Constitution:

The Electors shall meet in their respective States, and vote by Ballot for two persons, of whom one at least shall not be an Inhabitant of the same State with themselves. And they shall make a List of all the Persons voted for, and of the Number of Votes for each; which List they shall sign and certify, and transmit sealed to the Seat of the Government of the United States, directed to the President of the Senate. The President of the Senate shall, in the Presence of the Senate and the House of Representatives, open all the Certificates, and the Votes shall then be counted. The Person having the greatest Number of Votes shall be the President, if such a number be a Majority of the whole Number of Electors appointed; and if there be more than one who have such Majority, and have an equal number of Votes, then the House of Representatives shall immediately chuse by Ballot one of them for President; and if no Person has a Majority, then from the five highest on the List, the said House shall in like Manner chuse the President. But in chusing the President, the Votes shall be taken by States, the Representation from each State having one Vote; A quorum for this purpose shall consist of a Member or Members from two-thirds of the States, and a Majority of all the States shall be necessary to a Choice. In every Case, after the Choice of the President, the Person having the greatest Number of Votes of the Electors shall be the Vice President. But if there should remain two or more who have equal Votes, the Senate shall chuse from them by Ballot the Vice President.

It was the intention of the Continental Congress that the newly formed government should convene on "the first Wednesday in March next" (March 4, 1789) at Federal Hall, New York City. Only 8 of the 26 senators and 13 of the 65 representatives presented themselves on that date, and it was not until April 6, 1789, that a quorum was present. John Langdon, President of the Senate, received, opened, and counted the votes of the electors.

George Washington received one vote from each of the 69 electors from the 10 states and was the unanimous choice for President. The votes were cast by the states as follows: Massachusetts 10, Pennsylvania 10, Virginia 10, Connecticut 7, South Carolina 7, Maryland 6, New Jersey 6, Georgia 5, New Hampshire 5, and Delaware 3.

A committee from both houses was appointed to meet him: John Langdon of New Hampshire, Charles Carroll of Maryland, and William Samuel Johnson of Connecticut, representing the Senate; and Elias Boudinot of

New Jersey, Richard Bland Lee of Virginia, Thomas Tudor Tucker of South Carolina, Egbert Benson of New York, and John Laurance of New York, representing the House.

Charles Thomson was appointed to notify George Washington that he had been elected President and Sylvanus Bourn was appointed to notify John Adams that he had been elected Vice President.

On April 14, 1789, Charles Thomson, secretary of the Continental Congress, notified George Washington of his election, and on April 16, 1789, Washington left his home at Mount Vernon, Va., for the capital.

FULL ELECTORAL VOTE NOT CAST IN 1789

On February 4, 1789, the first presidential electors—a total of 69—met in their respective states to cast their ballots. The electors of five states—Connecticut, Delaware, Georgia, New Jersey, and South Carolina—had been chosen by the state legislatures. Three states—Maryland, Pennsylvania, and Virginia—held popular elections. Massachusetts had a system combining popular election and appointment by the legislature. New Hampshire held a popular election, but none of the electors received a majority, and the electors finally chosen were those named by the state Senate.

Had all of the electors qualified, a total of 91 votes, instead of 69, would have been cast. New York had not yet chosen its 8 electors even though the seat of the new government was in New York. Consequently, New York's vote was not cast. The weather delayed the votes of 4 electors, 2 from Maryland and 2 from Virginia. Since North Carolina and Rhode Island had not yet ratified the Constitution, they did not cast their 7 and 3 votes respectively. Thus, 22 of the 91 possible votes were not cast.

ADAMS ELECTED VICE PRESIDENT

Each elector cast 1 of his 2 votes for Washington, who thus received 69 of the 138 votes. The other 69 were divided among eleven other candidates; John Adams of Massachusetts, the candidate with the greatest number, became Vice President. The other candidates were John Jay of New York, Robert Hanson Harrison of Maryland, John Rutledge of South Carolina, John Hancock of Massachusetts, George Clinton of New York, Samuel Huntington of Connecticut, John Milton of Georgia, James Armstrong of Pennsylvania, Edward Telfair of Georgia, and Benjamin Lincoln of Massachusetts.

Adams received 34 votes as follows: Conn. 5 (of the 7 votes); Mass. 10; N.H. 5; N.J. 1 (of the 6 votes); Pa. 8 (of the 10 votes); Va. 5 (of the 10 votes). The other candidates received the following votes:

Jay—Del. 3; N.J. 5 (of the 6 votes); Va. 1 (of the 10 votes)

Harrison—Md. 6

Rutledge—S.C. 6 (of the 7 votes)

Hancock—Pa. 2 (of the 10 votes); S.C. 1 (of the 7 votes); Va. 1 (of the 10 votes)

Courtesy of The Library of Congress

Washington at a reception in his honor

Clinton—Va. 3 (of the 10 votes)
Huntington—Conn. 2 (of the 7 votes)
Milton—Ga. 2 (of the 5 votes)
Armstrong—Ga. 1 (of the 5 votes)
Lincoln—Ga. 1 (of the 5 votes)
Telfair—Ga. 1 (of the 5 votes)

THE ELECTION OF 1792

Before the conclusion of George Washington's four-year term, it was necessary to elect a President for the second administration. George Washington and John Adams, who were known as Federalists, were advocates of a strong central government. Those in accord with their principles wanted them reelected for a second term of four years.

Naturally, not all of the ideas and plans advocated by them were acceptable to everyone. Those who differed were known as Democratic-Republicans or Republicans. As the Democratic-Republicans were a minority group, they realized the futility of organizing to oppose Washington's reelection and did not oppose him.

The schedule for the choosing of presidential electors in 1792 was not the same as the schedule that had been in force in 1789. Congress, in March of 1792, adopted a new plan that allowed the states to choose electors during the 34 days preceding the first Wednesday in December, on which day the electors in each state would convene and cast their ballots. These ballots, sealed, were to be forwarded to Congress before the first Wednesday in January and counted on the second Wednesday in February.

When the count was complete, George Washington had received 132 of the 264 electoral votes cast, a unanimous election. The second highest vote, 77 out of a possible 132, was for John Adams of Massachusetts, who was thus reelected Vice President. The remaining electoral votes were cast for George Clinton of New York (50), Thomas Jefferson of Virginia (4), and Aaron Burr of New York (1).

INAUGURATIONS

FIRST TERM

April 30, 1789

George Washington took the oath of office as President of the United States on Thursday, April 30, 1789, outdoors, on the balcony of the Senate Chamber at Federal Hall, Wall and Nassau Streets, New York City. The oath was administered by Robert R. Livingston, Chancellor of New York State. The Bible on which Washington took his oath was borrowed from St. John's Lodge, Free and Accepted Masons. His hand rested on Psalm 127:1 when he took the oath. He then proceeded to the Senate Chamber to deliver his inaugural address. After the ceremony, he was escorted to the President's House by a troop of cavalry, assistants, a committee of Representatives, and a committee of the Senate.

The evening celebration was opened and closed by 13 skyrockets and 13 cannon.

A weekly, the U.S. *Chronicle* of May 21, 1789, recorded:

The President of the United States on the day of his inauguration, appeared dressed in a complete suit of Homespun Cloaths; the cloth was of a fine fabric, and as handsomely finished, as any European superfine cloth. A circumstance, which must be considered as not only highly flattering to our manufacturers in particular, but interesting to our countrymen in general. His Excellency the Vice President appeared also in a suit of American manufacture and several members of both Houses are distinguished by the same token of attention to the manufacturing interests of their country.

After Chancellor Robert R. Livingston administered the oath of office to George Washington on April 30, 1789, he proclaimed, "Long live George Washington, the President of the United States."

The first inaugural ball was held Thursday, May 7, 1789, in the Assembly Rooms on the east side of Broadway, a little above Wall Street, New York City. It was attended by

President Washington, Vice President Adams, the French and Spanish ministers, Chancellor Livingston, Baron von Steuben, General Knox, John Jay, Alexander Hamilton, and the majority of the House of Representatives and the Senate. Fans which were decorated with a medallion portrait of President George Washington in profile were presented as souvenirs to the ladies. Martha Washington did not attend, as she did not arrive in the city until the end of May.

SECOND TERM

March 4, 1793

The government having moved from New York City to Philadelphia, George Washington took the oath of office for his second term on Monday, March 4, 1793, in the Senate Chamber, Federal Hall, Philadelphia, Pa. Washington was the first President to be inaugurated at Philadelphia and the first inaugurated on March 4th. The oath was administered by William Cushing of Massachusetts, Associate Justice of the Supreme Court.

THE VICE PRESIDENT

Name—John Adams (1st V.P.)
Political party—Federalist
State represented—Massachusetts
Term of office—Apr. 21, 1789–Mar. 4, 1797
Age at inauguration—53 years, 173 days

Occupation after term—President of the United States

For further biographical information, see the chapter on John Adams, 2nd President, on page 27.

Courtesy of The Library of Congress

Washington delivering his inaugural address in April 1789, at the old city hall in New York, New York.

CABINET

FIRST TERM

March 4, 1789–March 3, 1793

State—John Jay, N.Y., Secretary for Foreign Affairs under the Confederation, continued to act at the request of President Washington until Thomas Jefferson assumed office; Thomas Jefferson, Va., Sept. 26, 1789, entered upon duties Mar. 22, 1790

Treasury—Alexander Hamilton, N.Y., Sept. 11, 1789

War—Henry Knox, Mass., Sept. 12, 1789

Attorney General—Edmund Randolph, Va., Sept. 26, 1789, entered upon duties Feb. 2, 1790

Postmaster General—Samuel Osgood, Mass., Sept. 26, 1789; Timothy Pickering, Pa., Aug. 12, 1791, entered upon duties Aug. 19, 1791

SECOND TERM

March 4, 1793–March 3, 1797

State—Thomas Jefferson, Va., continued from preceding administration; Edmund Randolph, Va., Jan. 2, 1794; Timothy Pickering, Pa. (secretary of war), ad interim August 20, 1795; Timothy Pickering, Pa., Dec. 10, 1795

Treasury—Alexander Hamilton, N.Y., continued from preceding administration; Oliver Wolcott, Jr., Conn., Feb. 2, 1795

War—Henry Knox, Mass., continued from preceding administration; Timothy Pickering, Pa., Jan. 2, 1795; Timothy Pickering, Pa. (secretary of state), ad interim Dec. 10, 1795 to Feb. 5, 1796; James McHenry, Md., Jan. 27, 1796, entered upon duties Feb. 6, 1796

Attorney General—Edmund Randolph, Va., continued from preceding administration; William Bradford, Pa., Jan. 27, 1794, entered upon duties Jan. 29, 1794; Charles Lee, Va., Dec. 10, 1795

Postmaster General—Timothy Pickering, Pa., continued from preceding administration; Timothy Pickering, Pa., recommissioned June 1, 1794; Joseph Habersham, Ga., Feb. 25, 1795

CONGRESS

FIRST CONGRESS

March 4, 1789–March 3, 1791

First session—Mar. 4, 1789–Sept. 29, 1789 (210 days)

Second session—Jan. 4, 1790–Aug. 12, 1790 (221 days)

Third session—Dec. 6, 1790–Mar. 3, 1791 (88 days)

Vice President—John Adams, Mass.

President pro tempore of the Senate —John Langdon, N.H., elected Apr. 6, 1789

Secretary of the Senate—Samuel Allyne Otis, Mass., elected Apr. 6, 1789

Speaker of the House—Frederick Augustus Conrad Muhlenberg, Pa., elected Apr. 1, 1789

Clerk of the House—John Beckley, Va., elected Apr. 1, 1789

SECOND CONGRESS

March 4, 1791–March 3, 1793

First session—Oct. 24, 1791–May 8, 1792 (197 days)

Second session—Nov. 5, 1792–Mar. 12, 1793 (119 days)

Special session of the Senate—Mar. 4, 1791 (1 day only)

Vice President—John Adams, Mass.

President pro tempore of the Senate—Richard Henry Lee, Va., elected Apr. 18, 1792; John Langdon, N.H., elected Nov. 5, 1792, and Mar. 1, 1793

Secretary of the Senate—Samuel Allyne Otis, Mass.

Speaker of the House—Jonathan Trumbull, Conn., elected Oct. 24, 1791

Clerk of the House—John Beckley, Va., reelected Oct. 24, 1791

THIRD CONGRESS

March 4, 1793–March 3, 1795

First session—Dec. 2, 1793–June 9, 1794 (190 days)

Second session—Nov. 3, 1794–Mar. 3, 1795 (121 days)

Special session of the Senate—Mar. 4, 1793 (1 day only)

Vice President—John Adams, Mass.

President pro tempore of the Senate—Ralph Izard, S.C., elected May 31, 1794; Henry Tazewell, Va., elected Feb. 20, 1795 (Samuel Livermore, N.H., was elected Feb. 20, 1795, but declined)

Secretary of the Senate—Samuel Allyne Otis, Mass.

Speaker of the House—Frederick Augustus Conrad Muhlenberg, Pa., elected Dec. 2, 1793

Clerk of the House—John Beckley, Va., reelected Dec. 2, 1793

FOURTH CONGRESS

March 4, 1795–March 3, 1797

First session—Dec. 7, 1795–June 1, 1796 (177 days)

Second session—Dec. 5, 1796–Mar. 3, 1797 (89 days)

Special session of the Senate—June 8, 1795–June 26, 1795 (19 days)

Vice President—John Adams, Mass.

President pro tempore of the Senate—Henry Tazewell, Va., elected Dec. 7, 1795; Samuel Livermore, N.H., elected May 6, 1796; William Bingham, Pa., elected Feb. 16, 1797

Secretary of the Senate—Samuel Allyne Otis, Mass.

Speaker of the House—Jonathan Dayton, N.J., elected Dec. 7, 1795

Clerk of the House—John Beckley, Va., reelected Dec. 7, 1795

APPOINTMENTS TO THE SUPREME COURT

Chief Justices

John Jay, N.Y., Sept. 26, 1789 (newly created seat)

John Rutledge, S.C., July 1, 1795 (temporarily replaced John Jay). Rutledge was never confirmed as Chief Justice, although he presided over the Court in August 1795. Congress was in recess when he was commissioned. After it reconvened, the Senate rejected his nomination, on December 15, 1795.

Oliver Ellsworth, Conn., Mar. 4, 1796 (replaced John Rutledge)

Associate Justices

John Rutledge, S.C., Sept. 26, 1789 (newly created seat; resigned in 1791, to take South Carolina judgeship)

William Cushing, Mass., Sept. 27, 1789 (newly created seat)

Robert Hanson Harrison, Md., Sept. 28, 1789 (newly created seat; died before taking office)

James Wilson, Pa., Sept. 29, 1789 (newly created seat)

John Blair, Va., Sept. 30, 1789 (newly created seat)

James Iredell, N.C., Feb. 10, 1790 (replaced Robert Hanson Harrison)

Thomas Johnson, Md., Aug. 5, 1791 (replaced John Rutledge)

William Paterson, N.J., Mar. 4, 1793 (replaced Thomas Johnson)

Samuel Chase, Md., Jan. 27, 1796 (replaced John Blair)

William Cushing was commissioned as Chief Justice on January 27, 1796, but declined to serve, continuing as Associate Justice.

IMPORTANT DATES IN THE PRESIDENCY

Apr. 1, 1789, first quorum, House of Representatives

Apr. 6, 1789, first quorum, U.S. Senate

June 1, 1789, first congressional act approved "to regulate the time and manner of administering certain oaths"

July 4, 1789, first tariff act, placing duties on imports to protect domestic industries

July 20, 1789, first federal navigation act, imposing duty on the tonnage of vessels

July 27, 1789, State Department created as Department of Foreign Affairs

Aug. 4, 1789, first federal bond issue authorized to fund domestic and state debt

Aug. 7, 1789, Department of War created

Sept. 2, 1789, Treasury Department established

Sept. 13, 1789, first loan to the U.S. government negotiated by Alexander Hamilton with New York banks

Sept. 22, 1789, Post Office Department created

Sept. 24, 1789, Judiciary Act passed

Sept. 24, 1789, Office of Attorney General established

Sept. 25, 1789, first ten amendments to the Constitution enacted by Congress

Sept. 29, 1789, first Congress adjourned after 210-day session

Nov. 21, 1789, twelfth state ratified the Constitution

Feb. 1, 1790, first session of U.S. Supreme Court

Mar. 1, 1790, first U.S. census authorized

Apr. 10, 1790, first patent law passed

May 29, 1790, Rhode Island adopted Constitution (last of the original thirteen to sign)

May 31, 1790, first copyright law signed

July 16, 1790, Congress passed act locating future seat of government in District of Columbia

Aug. 9, 1790, *Columbia*, under Captain Robert Gray, returned to Boston, completing first trip around the world under U.S. flag

Jan. 10, 1791, Vermont ratified Constitution

Feb. 25, 1791, Bank of the United States chartered

Mar. 3, 1791, District of Columbia established

Mar. 3, 1791, first internal revenue act

Mar. 4, 1791, Vermont admitted as the 14th state

Mar. 4, 1791, Arthur St. Clair appointed commander in chief of federal troops

Apr. 7, 1791–June 12, 1791, George Washington made tour of the South

Nov. 4, 1791, General St. Clair surprised and defeated by Indians at Wabash River

Dec. 15, 1791, Bill of Rights, first ten amendments to the Constitution, ratified

Mar. 1, 1792, presidential succession bill enacted

Mar. 1, 1792, Secretary of State Jefferson announced the adoption of the first ten amendments (Bill of Rights)

Apr. 2, 1792, U.S. Mint established; coinage of various denominations authorized

Courtesy of The Library of Congress

Washington entering Trenton, New Jersey, in 1789

Apr. 5, 1792, Washington vetoed apportion-ment bill

June 1, 1792, Kentucky admitted as the 15th state

Sept. 27, 1792, peace treaty signed with Wabash and Illinois Indians

Oct. 13, 1792, cornerstone of White House laid

Mar. 4, 1793, second inauguration, held at Philadelphia, Pa.

Apr. 22, 1793, neutrality proclamation issued by Washington

Sept. 18, 1793, cornerstone of Capitol laid

Mar. 14, 1794, Eli Whitney patented cotton gin

July–Nov. 1794, Whisky Rebellion in western Pennsylvania

Aug. 20, 1794, General Wayne defeated Miami Indians at Fallen Timbers, Ohio

Nov. 19, 1794, Jay's Treaty with Great Brit-ain signed to settle terms of peace, amity, commerce, navigation, boundaries, and extradition

Feb. 7, 1795, Eleventh Amendment to Consti-tution ratified

Sept. 5, 1795, treaty of peace and amity with Algiers signed

May 19, 1796, first national game law approved

May 31, 1796, treaty with Six Nations con-cluded

June 1, 1796, Tennessee admitted as the 16th state

Sept. 17, 1796, George Washington issued his Farewell Address

Nov. 4, 1796, treaty of peace, friendship, and navigation with Tripoli signed

ADDITIONAL DATA ON WASHINGTON

GEORGE WASHINGTON

—was the only President who was inaugu-rated in two cities (New York City, April 30, 1789, and Philadelphia, Pa., March 4, 1793).

—was the only President who did not live in Washington, D.C.

—was the first and only President unani-mously elected (twice).

—was the first President to serve a second term.

—was the first President to refuse a third term.

—was the first President born in Virginia.

—was the first President whose mother was alive when he was inaugurated.

—was the first President to marry a widow.

—was the first President whose mother was a second wife.

WASHINGTON WAS BORN ON FEBRUARY 11

George Washington was born on February 11, 1731, and celebrated his first nineteen birthdays on February 11.

An act of the British Parliament in 1750 discarded the Julian calendar and adopted the Gregorian calendar in its stead for Great Britain and the colonies. In the Julian calen-dar, the first day of the year had been March 25, but in the year 1751 the year ended on December 31 and the days between January and March 24 were omitted from the calen-dar. This legal year contained only 282 days. The period from January 1 to March 24 was dated 1752.

Thus George Washington was nineteen years old on February 11, 1750, but his twen-tieth birthday was on February 11, 1752, not 1751.

Since the vernal equinox had been dis-placed by 11 days in the Julian calendar, it was ordered that the difference be removed by the omission of 11 days from September 1752. There were no days dated September 3 to 13 inclusive; the day after September 2 was September 14. This required the addition of 11 days to compensate, and in 1753 George Washington celebrated his birthday on Feb-ruary 22 instead of on February 11.

BAPTISM

George Washington was baptized April 5, 1732 (1731 Old Style). His godfathers were Beverley Whiting and Captain Christopher Brooks and his godmother was Mrs. Mildred Gregory.

WASHINGTON OPERATED A FERRY

George Washington loaned $3,750 to Captain John Posey, who was unable to repay the amount and turned over his land, including a ferry and fishery, to Washington. Washington then ran the fishery, shipping fish in his own boats and selling them along the Atlantic seaboard.

The ferry, which he operated from 1769 to 1790, crossed the Potomac at a spot about a mile wide, landing at what is now Marshall Hall, Md. The schedule of rates as set up by the Virginia General Assembly was one shilling for an adult and a horse.

The rates were: for every coach, wagon, or chariot and driver, the same price as for six horses; for every four-wheeled chaise or phaeton and driver, the same price as for four horses; for every two-wheeled riding carriage, the same price as for two horses; for every hogshead of tobacco, the same price as for one horse; for every head of neat cattle, the same price as for one horse, and for every sheep, hog, goat, or lamb, the same price as for one horse.

The ferry was abandoned in October 1790, a year and a half after Washington had become President. He submitted his reasons for discontinuing the service to the General Assembly, which acceded to his request to be permitted to abandon the ferry service.

WASHINGTON ESCAPED KIDNAPPERS

Prior to George Washington's inauguration, while he was still commander in chief of the army, an attempt was made to kidnap or kill him. Involved in the conspiracy were the Tory governor of New York, William Tryon, the Tory mayor of New York City, David Matthews, and many others, including Thomas Hickey, one of Washington's bodyguards. Hickey was tried before a court-martial, which found him guilty. On June 28, 1776, Hickey was hanged on a field near the Bowery Lane in the presence of 20,000 persons.

The episode is recorded in General George Washington's orderly book on June 28, 1776, as follows: "The unhappy Fate of Thomas Hickey, executed this day for Mutiny, Sedition and Treachery; the General hopes it will be a warning to every soldier, in the Army, to avoid those crimes and all others, so disgraceful to the character of a soldier and pernicious to his country, whose pay he receives and bread he eats."

WASHINGTON DISAPPROVED OF SWEARING

A General Order issued August 3, 1776, by General George Washington from his headquarters at New York stated:

The General is sorry to be informed that the foolish and wicked practice of profane cursing and swearing, a vice heretofore little known in an American army, is growing into fashion. He hopes the officers will, by example as well as influence, endeavor to check it, and that both they and the men will reflect, that we can have little hope of the blessing of Heaven on our arms, if we insult it by our impiety and folly. Added to this, it is a vice so mean and low, without any temptation, that every man of sense and character detests and despises it.

HONORARY DEGREES FOR WASHINGTON

The formal education of George Washington ceased before he was seventeen years of age; however, he did much studying on his own. Although he lacked a college degree, five of the country's foremost colleges conferred honorary degrees upon him.

The first degree was the honorary degree of Doctor of Laws, awarded by Harvard in 1776. Yale followed suit in 1781. The University of Pennsylvania made a similar award in 1783. Washington College of Chestertown, Md., and Brown University also conferred the honorary LL.D. degree in 1789 and 1790 respectively.

WASHINGTON REJECTED MONARCHY

The suggestion made by Colonel Lewis Nicola in a letter to General George Washington to the effect that Washington become king brought a stinging rebuke from the general. His answer from Newburgh, N.Y., dated May 22, 1782, follows:

With a mixture of great surprise and astonishment I have read with attention the Sentiments you have submitted to my perusal. Be assured Sir, no occurrence in the course of of the War, has given me more painful sensations than your information of there being such ideas existing in the Army as you have expressed, and I must view them with abhorrence, and reprehend them with severity. For the present, the communication of them will rest in my bosom, unless some further agitation of the matter, shall make a disclosure necessary. I am much at a loss to conceive what part of my conduct could have given encouragement to an address which to me seems big with the greatest mischiefs that can befall my Country. If I am not deceived in the knowledge of myself, you could not have found a person to whom your schemes are more disagreeable: at the same time in justice to my own feelings I must add, that no Man possesses a more sincere wish to see ample justice done to the Army than I do, and as far as my powers and influence, in a constitutional way extend, they shall be employed to the utmost of my abilities to effect it, should there be any occasion. Let me conjure you then, if you have any regard for your Country, concern for yourself or posterity, or respect for me, to banish these thoughts from your Mind, and never communicate, as from yourself, or any one else, a sentiment of the like Nature.

WASHINGTON RAISED MULES

Although the exportation of full-blooded jacks from Spain was prohibited, Charles III of Spain sent George Washington two jacks and two jennets with a Spanish caretaker. They arrived at Boston on October 26, 1785. Only one of the jacks survived the trip; it was named Royal Gift by Washington and was used to breed heavy mules for draft purposes.

A Maltese jack sent by Lafayette to George Washington was named the Knight of Malta. It was used to breed lighter and nimbler mules for saddle and carriage use.

JOHN LANGDON, PRESIDENT OF THE SENATE PRO TEMPORE, NOTIFYING WASHINGTON OF HIS ELECTION

New York
6 April, 1789
Sir,

I have the honor to transmit to your Excellency the information of your unanimous election to the office of President of the United States of America. Suffer me, Sir, to indulge the hope, that so auspicious a mark of public confidence will meet your approbation, and be considered as a pledge of the affection and support you are to expect from a free and enlightened people.

I am, Sir, with sentiments of respect, &c.

JOHN LANGDON

GEORGE WASHINGTON'S LETTER TO JOHN LANGDON, PRESIDENT OF THE SENATE PRO TEMPORE, ACCEPTING THE OFFICE OF PRESIDENT

Mount Vernon, Va.
April 14, 1789
Sir,

I had the honor to receive your official communication by the hand of Mr. Secretary Thomson, about one o'clock this day. Having concluded to obey the important and flattering call of my country, and having been impressed with an idea of the expediency of my being with Congress at as early a period as possible, I propose to commence my journey on Thursday morning which will be the day after tomorrow.

I have the honor to be with sentiments of esteem, Sir,

Your most obedient servant,

G. WASHINGTON

WASHINGTON BORROWED MONEY TO GO TO HIS FIRST INAUGURATION

Although George Washington was one of the richest men of his time, he was "land-poor" and was obliged to borrow money to finance his trip to New York. He received a loan of 600 pounds from Richard Conway of

Alexandria, Va., to whom he had written the following letter on March 4, 1789, from his home at Mount Vernon:

Dear Sir,

Never till within these two years have I experienced the want of money. Short crops, and other causes not entirely within my control, make me feel it now very sensibly. To collect money without the intervention of Suits (and these are tedious) seems impracticable—and Land, which I have offered for sale, will not command Cash at an undervalue, if at all. Under this statement, I am inclined to do what I never expected to be driven to, that is, to borrow money on Interest. Five hundred pounds would enable me to discharge what I owe in Alexandria, etc., and to leave the State (if it shall not be in my power to remain home in retirement) without doing this, would be exceedingly disagreeable to me. Having thus fully and candidly explained myself, permit me to ask if it is in your power to supply me with the above or smaller Sum. Any security you may best like I can give, and you may be assured, that it is no more my inclination than it can be yours, to let it remain long unpaid.

WASHINGTON ARRIVED IN NEW YORK BY BOAT

Thirteen pilots, all dressed in white sailor costume, rowed the barge that conveyed George Washington from Elizabeth Town, N.J., to New York City for his inauguration. The barge had a 47-foot keel and carried two flags astern. It came out of the Kill van Kull into New York Bay, passed the Battery, and proceeded up the Hudson River to Murray's wharf at the foot of Wall Street.

A brief parade was held through Queen Street to the Franklin House. The order of march was as follows: 1, a troop of horse; 2, artillery and those remaining of the Legion under arms; 3, off-duty military officers in uniform; 4, the President's Guard, composed of the Grenadiers of the First Regiment; 5, the President, the governor, and their suites; 6, the principal officers of the state; 7, the mayor of New York and the Corporation of New York; 8, the clergy; 9, the citizens.

WASHINGTON'S FIRST TERM 57 DAYS SHORT

As George Washington did not take the oath of office until April 30, 1789, his first term was 57 days shorter than it would have been had the inauguration taken place on March 4 as originally intended.

THE FIRST PRESIDENTIAL MANSION

George Washington lived at No. 1 Cherry Street, New York City, from April 23, 1789, to February 23, 1790. This residence has been referred to as the first presidential mansion. Residences were not supplied for our earliest Presidents.

CONGRESS IN SESSION AT NEW YORK AND PHILADELPHIA

The only Congress to meet at New York City was the First Congress. It held two sessions, the first from March 4, 1789, to September 29, 1789 (210 days), the second from January 4, 1790, to August 12, 1790 (221 days). A quorum was not present, however, until April 6, 1789.

The first session of Congress to meet at Philadelphia, Pa., was the third session of the First Congress, which was held from December 6, 1790, to March 3, 1791 (88 days). The first session of the Sixth Congress, from December 2, 1799, to May 14, 1800 (164 days), was the last time Congress met at Philadelphia.

"HIS HIGHNESS, GEORGE WASHINGTON"?

The committee appointed by the United States Senate on Thursday, April 23, 1789, to decide on the proper form of address for the President of the United States reported on Thursday, May 14, 1789, "that in the opinion of the committee it will be proper thus to address the President: His Highness, the President of the United States of America, and Protector of their Liberties."

SENATORS' TERMS DETERMINED BY DRAWING LOTS

In accordance with the constitutional provision regarding senatorial terms (Article 1, section 3), the Senate decided on May 14, 1789,

> that three papers of an equal size, numbered 1, 2 and 3, be, by the Secretary, rolled up and put into a box, and drawn by Mr. Langdon, Mr. Wingate, Mr. Dalton, in behalf of the respective classes, in which each of them are placed; and that the classes shall vacate their seats in the Senate, according to the order of numbers drawn for them, beginning with Number 1.

> And that when Senators shall take their seats from States that have not yet appointed Senators, they shall be placed by lot in the foregoing classes, but in such manner as shall keep the classes as nearly equal as may be in numbers.

The senators in Class 1, who drew six-year terms, were John Langdon of New Hampshire, William Samuel Johnson of Connecticut, Robert Morris of Pennsylvania, John Henry of Maryland, Ralph Izard of South Carolina, and James Gunn of Georgia.

Those in Class 2, who drew four-year terms, were Paine Wingate of New Hampshire, Caleb Strong of Massachusetts, William Paterson of New Jersey, Richard Bassett of Delaware, Richard Lee of Virginia, Pierce Butler of South Carolina, and William Few of Georgia.

Those in Class 3, who drew two-year terms, were Tristram Dalton of Massachusetts, Oliver Ellsworth of Connecticut, Jonathan Elmer of New Jersey, William Maclay of Pennsylvania, George Read of Delaware, Charles Carroll of Maryland, and William Grayson of Virginia.

New York, North Carolina, and Rhode Island were not included in the original selection as their senators were still unrepresented at the time of the drawing.

THE FIRST ACT OF CONGRESS

An Act to Regulate the Time and Manner of Administering Certain Oaths

Section 1. Be it enacted by the Senate and Representatives of the United States of America in Congress assembled, That the Oath or Affirmation required by the sixth article of the Constitution of the United States, shall be administered in the form following, to wit, "I, A.B., do solemnly swear or affirm (as the case may

Washington Crossing the Delaware *by Emanuel Leutze*

be) that I will support the Constitution of the United States!" The said oath or affirmation shall be administered within three days after the passing of this act, by any one member of the Senate, to the President of the Senate, and by him to all the members, and to the Secretary; and by the Speaker of the House of Representatives to all members who have not taken a similar oath, by virtue of a particular resolution of the said House, and to the Clerk: And in case of the absence of any member from the service of either House, at the same time prescribed for taking said oath or affirmation, the same shall be administered to such member when he shall appear to take his seat.

Section 2. And be it further enacted, That at the first session of Congress after every general election of Representatives, the oath or affirmation aforesaid, shall be administered by any one member of the House of Representatives to the Speaker; and by him to all the members present, and to the Clerk, previous to entering on any other business; and to the members who shall afterward appear, previous to taking their seats. The President of the Senate for the time being, shall also administer the oath or affirmation to each Senator who shall hereafter be elected, previous to taking his seat; and in any future case of a President of the Senate, who shall not have taken said oath or affirmation, the same shall be administered to him by any one member of the Senate.

Section 3. And be it further enacted, That the members of the several State legislatures, at the next session of the said legislature respectively, and all executive and judicial officers of the several States, who have been heretofore chosen or appointed, or who shall be chosen or appointed, before the first day of August next, and who shall then be in office, shall within one month thereafter, take the same oath or affirmation, except where they shall have taken it before; which may be administered by any person authorized by the law of the State in which such office shall be holden, to administer oaths. And the members of the several State legislatures, and all

executive and judicial officers of the several States, who shall be chosen or appointed after the said first day of August, shall, before they proceed to execute the duties of their respective offices, take the foregoing oath or affirmation which shall be administered by the person or persons who by the law of the State shall be authorized to administer the oath of office; and the person or persons so administering the oath hereby required to be taken, shall cause a record or certificate thereof to be made in the same manner as, by the law of the State, he or they shall be directed to record or certify the oath of office.

Section 4. And be it further enacted, That all officers appointed, or hereafter to be appointed, under the authority of the United States, shall before they act in their respective offices, take the same oath or affirmation, which shall be administered by the person or persons who shall be authorized by law to administer to such officers their respective oaths of office; and such officers shall incur the same penalties in case of failure, as shall be imposed by law in case of failure in taking their respective oaths of office.

Section 5. And be it further enacted, That the Secretary of the Senate, and the Clerk of the House of Representatives for the time being, shall, at the time of taking the oath or affirmation aforesaid, each take an oath or affirmation in the words following, to wit, "I, A.B., Secretary of the Senate, or Clerk of the House of Representatives (as the case may be) of the United States of America, do solemnly swear or affirm that I will truly and faithfully discharge the duties of my office to the best of my knowledge and abilities."

FREDERICK AUGUSTUS MUHLENBERG
Speaker of the House of Representatives

JOHN ADAMS
Vice President of the United States and
President of the Senate
Approved June 1, 1789

GEORGE WASHINGTON
President of the United States
(1 Stat. L. 23)

THE FIRST PRESIDENTIAL APPOINTMENT

The first presidential appointment was made by George Washington in June 1789, when he nominated William Short to be chargé d'affaires in Paris during the temporary absence of the United States minister to France, Thomas Jefferson. The Senate received the letter of nomination on June 16 and confirmed the appointment after polling its members by secret ballot.

THE FIRST REJECTION OF A PRESIDENTIAL APPOINTEE

The first presidential appointee rejected by the Senate was Benjamin Fishbourn of Georgia, who was nominated by George Washington for the position of naval officer of the port of Savannah, Ga. Fishbourn had served valiantly in the storming of Stony Point and had held numerous important positions in Georgia. He was rejected on August 5, 1789, by a secret ballot of Congress because the two Georgia senators, William Few and James Gunn, had not been consulted. On August 6, Washington nominated Lachlan McIntosh in his place. On August 7, the President wrote to Congress: "Permit me to submit to your consideration whether on occasions where the propriety of Nominations appear questionable to you, it would not be expedient to communicate that circumstance to me, and thereby avail yourselves of the information which led me to make them, and which I would with pleasure lay before you."

TEN CONSTITUTIONAL AMENDMENTS ENACTED

The first ten amendments to the Constitution, known as the Bill of Rights, were passed by Congress on September 25, 1789. As Vermont had become a state before the ratification of the Constitution was completed, it was necessary to have 11 of the 14 states ratify the amendments. On December 15, 1791, Virginia became the eleventh state to ratify the first ten amendments.

THE FIRST PRESIDENTIAL TOURS

President George Washington made the first presidential tour through the New England states from October 15 to November 13, 1789. He traveled in a hired coach accompanied by Major William Jackson, his aide-de-camp; Tobias Lear, his private secretary; six servants; nine horses; and a luggage wagon. He went as far north as Kittery, Maine (then part of Massachusetts). As Rhode Island and Vermont had not yet joined the new government, he did not visit those states. Washington's first tour of the southern states was made from April 7 to June 12, 1791, during which time he left Mount Vernon, his estate in Virginia, on a 1,887-mile trip that took him north through Philadelphia, south through Virginia and the Carolinas into Georgia, and back to Mount Vernon.

THE FIRST PRESIDENTIAL PROCLAMATION

The first presidential proclamation was made by George Washington on January 24, 1791, from New York City, at that time the capital. He directed surveyors "to survey and limit a part of the territory of ten miles square on both sides of the river Potomac, so as to comprehend Georgetown, in Maryland, and extend to the Eastern Branch."

THE FIRST PRESIDENTIAL THANKSGIVING PROCLAMATION

By the President of the United States of America.

Whereas it is the duty of all nations to acknowledge the providence of Almighty God, to obey his will, to be grateful for his benefits, and humbly to implore his protection and favor—and Whereas both Houses of Congress have by their joint committee requested me "to recommend to the People of the United States a day of public thanksgiving and prayer, to be observed by acknowledging with grateful hearts the many signal favors of Almighty God, especially by affording them an opportunity to establish a form of government for their safety and happiness";

Now, therefore, I do recommend and assign Thursday, the 26th day of November next, to be devoted by the People of these States to the service of that great and glorious Being who is the beneficent Author of all the good that was, that is, or that will be—That we may then all unite in rendering unto him our sincere and humble thanks—for his kind care and protection of the People of this country previous to their becoming a Nation—for the signal and manifold mercies and the favorable interpositions of his providence, which we experienced in the course and conclusion of the late war—for the great degree of tranquillity, union and plenty, which we have since enjoyed—for the peaceful and rational manner in which we have been enabled to establish constitutions of government for our safety and happiness, and particularly the national One now lately instituted—for the civil and religious liberty with which we are blessed and the means we have of acquiring and diffusing useful knowledge; and in general for all the great and various favors which he hath been pleased to confer upon us.

And also that we may then unite in most humbly offering our prayers and supplications to the great Lord and Ruler of Nations, and beseech him to pardon our national and other transgressions—to enable us all, whether in public or private stations, to perform our several and relative duties properly and punctually—to render our national Government a blessing to all the People by constantly being a Government of wise, just, and constitutional laws, discreetly and faithfully executed and obeyed—to protect and guide all Sovereigns and Nations (especially such as have shown kindness to us) and to bless them with good Government, peace, and concord—to promote the knowledge and practice of true religion and virtue, and the increase of science among them and us—and generally to grant unto all mankind such a degree of temporal prosperity as he alone knows to be best.

Given under my hand at the City of New York the third day of October in the year of our Lord 1789.

GEORGE WASHINGTON

THE FIRST PRESIDENTIAL VETO

During his two terms of office, George Washington vetoed only two bills. His action on the first veto, dated April 5, 1792, was explained in the following letter to the members of the House of Representatives:

I have maturely considered the act passed by the two Houses entitled "An act for an apportionment of Representatives among the several States according to the first enumeration," and I return it to your House, wherein it originated, with the following objections.

First. The Constitution has prescribed that Representatives shall be apportioned among the several States according to their respective numbers, and there is no one proportion or divisor which, applied to the respective numbers of the States, will yield the number and allotment of representatives proposed by the bill.

Second. The Constitution has also provided that the number of representatives shall not exceed 1 for every 30,000, which restriction is by the context and by fair and obvious construction to be applied to the separate and respective members of the States; and the bill has allotted to eight of the States more than 1 for every 30,000.

His only other veto, dated February 28, 1797, rejected a bill to reduce the cavalry force of the army.

WASHINGTON'S CONSULTATION OF THE CABINET

Washington, like the Presidents who succeeded him, made frequent requests to the members of his cabinet for their opinions on the conduct of government affairs. One of his letters, sent from Philadelphia to his cabinet members on April 18, 1793, during the French revolutionary wars, is reproduced herewith:

Sir,

The posture of affairs in Europe, particularly between France and Great Britain, places the United States in a delicate situation, and requires much consideration of the measures which will be proper for them to observe in the war between those powers. With a view to forming a general plan of conduct for the executive, I have stated and enclosed sundry questions to be considered preparatory to a meeting at my house to-morrow, where I shall expect to see you at nine o'clock, and to receive the result of your reflections thereon.

Quest. 1. Shall a proclamation issue for the purpose of preventing interferences of the citizens of the United States between France and Great Britain, &c.? Shall it contain a declaration of neutrality or not? What shall it contain?

2. Shall a minister from the republic of France be received?

3. If received, shall it be absolutely or with qualifications, and if with qualifications, of what kind?

4. Are the United States obliged by good faith to consider the treaties heretofore made with France as applying to the present situation of the parties? May they either renounce them or hold them suspended until the government of France shall be established?

5. If they have the right, is it expedient to do either? and which?

6. If they have an option, would it be a breach of neutrality to consider the treaties in operation?

7. If the treaties are to be considered as now in operation, is the guaranty in the treaty of alliance applicable to a defensive war only, or to a war, either offensive or defensive?

8. Does the war in which France is engaged appear to be offensive or defensive on her part? or of a mixed or equivocal character?

9. If of a mixed or equivocal character, does the guaranty in any event apply to such a war?

10. What is the effect of a guaranty, such as that to be found in the treaty of alliance between the United States and France?

11. Does any article in either of the treaties prevent ships of war, other than privateers, of the powers opposed to France, from coming into the ports of the United States to act as convoys to their own mer-

chantmen? Or does it lay any other restraints upon them more than would apply to the ships of war of France?

12. Should the future regent of France send a minister to the United States, ought he to be received?

13. Is it necessary or advisable to call together the two houses of Congress with a view to the present posture of European affairs? If it is, what should be the particular objects of such call?

THE FIRST PRESIDENTIAL COMMISSION

The first presidential commission was appointed by Washington to deal with the rebellious elements in Washington and Allegheny counties, Pennsylvania (the Whiskey Rebellion). In his proclamation to Congress on August 7, 1794, he said: "I do hereby command all persons, being insurgents as aforesaid, on or before the first day of September next to disperse and retire peacefully to their respective abodes." In his sixth annual report, on November 19, 1794, he declared: "The report of the commissioners marks their firmness and abilities, and must unite all virtuous men, by shewing that the means of conciliation have been exhausted."

THE FIRST PRESIDENTIAL AMNESTY

The first presidential amnesty, or pardon to insurrectionists, was extended by George Washington on July 10, 1795. He granted "a full, free, and entire pardon" to most of the people who had participated in the Whisky Rebellion, conditional upon their signing an oath of allegiance to the United States.

WASHINGTON DECLINED A THIRD TERM

Washington's second term of office expired on March 3, 1797. On September 17, 1796, he issued his "Farewell Address," which was not delivered orally but released to the press. It was addressed to "Friends and Fellow Citizens" and began:

The period for a new election of a citizen to administer the Executive Government of the United States being not far distant, and the time actually arrived when your thoughts must be employed in designating the person who is to be clothed with that important trust, it appears to me proper, especially as it may conduce to a more distinct expression of the public voice, that I should now apprise you of the resolution I have formed to decline being considered among the number of those out of whom a choice is to be made. . . .

WASHINGTON APPOINTED LIEUTENANT-GENERAL

On July 11, 1798, Secretary of War James McHenry delivered a letter from President John Adams to George Washington appointing Washington, with the advice and consent of the Senate, "Lieutenant-General and Commander-in-Chief of all the armies raised or to be raised for the service of the United States."

Washington's reply, dated July 13, 1798, from Mount Vernon, Va., was read in the Senate on July 18. He accepted

with the reserve only that I shall not be called into the field until the Army is in a situation to require my presence, or it becomes indispensable by the urgency of circumstances. I take the liberty also to

mention, that I must decline having my acceptance considered as drawing after it any immediate charge upon the public, or that I can receive any emoluments annexed to the appointment, before entering into a situation to incur expense.

WASHINGTON LEFT HUGE ESTATE

George Washington was one of our richest Presidents. At the time of his death, his estate was valued at more than half a million dollars.

In his last will and testament, dated July 9, 1799, he listed his assets. His land holdings, exceeding 33,000 acres, consisted of 23,341 acres in Virginia, 5,000 acres in Kentucky, 3,051 acres in the Northwest Territory, 1,119 acres in Maryland, 1,000 acres in New York, 234 acres in Pennsylvania, and other property in Virginia and Washington, D.C., valued at $489,135. He also listed his stocks as worth $25,212. He valued his livestock, which consisted of 640 sheep, 329 cows, 42 mules, 20 working horses, pigs, etc., at $15,653. The value of these three items— acreage, stocks, and livestock—was estimated at $530,000.

Mount Rushmore, with Washington at left

WASHINGTON OWNED LAND IN WASHINGTON, D.C.

On October 3, 1798, George Washington acquired two lots in the federal city (now Washington, D.C.). He described his purchase in his last will and testament as follows:

> The two lots near the Capitol in Square 634, cost me $963 only, but in this price I was favoured on condition that I should build two brick houses, three storys high each;—without this reduction, the selling price of these lots would have cost me about $1,350. These lots with the buildings thereon when completed will stand me in $15,000 at least.

WASHINGTON'S SWORDS

In his will George Washington bequeathed five swords, one to each of his five nephews, with the admonition that none of these weapons should be unsheathed by the future owners for the purpose of shedding blood, "except it be for self-defence or in defence of their country and its rights and in the latter case to keep them unsheathed and prefer falling with them in their hands to the relinquishment thereof."

"FIRST IN WAR, FIRST IN PEACE, FIRST IN THE HEARTS OF HIS COUNTRYMEN"

This famous phrase was part of the "Funeral Oration Upon George Washington" delivered December 26, 1799, before the houses of Congress by General Henry Lee.

General Lee was familiarly known as "Light-Horse Harry" and during the Revolutionary War commanded Lee's Legion, three troops of light cavalry which harassed the British lines. He was the father of Robert E. Lee, the Confederate general.

FIRST TOWN NAMED FOR WASHINGTON

The first town named for George Washington was Forks of Tar River, N.C., which changed its name to Washington in 1775. The town was originally formed November 20, 1771, by James Bonner, who owned all the land on which it was situated.

Washington, Ga., incorporated Jan. 23, 1780, was the first town incorporated with the name of Washington.

FIRST STAMP DEPICTING A PRESIDENT

The first President depicted on a United States postage stamp was George Washington, whose likeness appeared on the ten-cent black 1847, to take effect July 1, 1847. The stamps were produced by Rawdon, Wright, Hatch & Edson. The issue was declared invalid as of July 1, 1851. (Some of the local postmasters' provisional stamps, however, bore a likeness of Washington.)

MOUNT VERNON NEUTRAL TERRITORY

In the Civil War, George Washington's home at Mount Vernon (named for Admiral Vernon, under whom George's brother Lawrence served in the attack on Cartagena) was treated as neutral territory by arrangement between both sides. No armed soldiers ever invaded the home.

FURTHER READING

Brookhiser, Richard. *Founding Father: Rediscovering George Washington*. 1996.

Ellis, Joseph J. *His Excellency: George Washington*. 2004.

Flexner, James T. *George Washington*. 1965.

———. *George Washington and the New Nation*. 1972.

———. *George Washington: Anguish and Farewell*. 1972.

Freeman, Douglas S. *Washington*. 7 vols. 1948–54.

Hirschfeld, Fritz. *George Washington and Slavery*. 1997.

McDonald, Forrest. *The Presidency of George Washington*. Rev. ed. 1988.

Wills, Garry. *Cincinnatus: George Washington and the Enlightenment*. 1984.

Courtesy of The Library of Congress

John Adams

John Adams

Date of birth—Oct. 30, 1735

Place of birth—Braintree (now Quincy), Mass.

Education—Schooled by local teachers; bachelor's degree, Harvard College, Cambridge, Mass., B.A., July 16, 1755; private study in law office, Worcester, Mass.

Religion—Unitarian

Ancestry—English

Career—Lawyer, colonial legislator, delegate to Continental Congress, delegate to state constitutional convention, minister to France, the Netherlands, and Great Britain

Political party—Federalist

State represented—Massachusetts

Term of office—Mar. 4, 1797–Mar. 4, 1801

Term served—4 years

Administration—3rd

Congresses—5th, 6th

Age at inauguration—61 years, 125 days

Lived after term—25 years, 122 days

Occupation after term—Writer, delegate to state constitutional convention

Date of death—July 4, 1826

Age at death—90 years, 247 days

Place of death—Quincy, Mass.

Burial place—First Unitarian Church, Quincy, Mass.

FAMILY

FATHER

Name—John Adams

Date of birth—Feb. 8, 1691

Marriage—Oct. 31, 1734

Occupation—Farmer, shoemaker, harness-maker; church deacon, tithingman; tax collector, city councilman

Date of death—May 25, 1761

Age at death—70 years, 106 days

MOTHER

Name at birth—Susanna Boylston

Date of birth—Mar. 5, 1699

First marriage—John Adams, Oct. 31, 1734 (d. May 25, 1761)

Second marriage—John Hall, 1766

Date of death—Apr. 17, 1797

Age at death—98 years, 43 days

SIBLINGS

John Adams was the oldest in a family of three boys.

Children of John Adams and Susanna Boylston Adams

John Adams, b. Oct. 30, 1735, d. July 4, 1826
Peter Boylston Adams, b. Oct. 16, 1738, d. June 2, 1823
Elihu Adams, b. May 29, 1741, d. Mar. 18, 1776

MARRIAGE

Married—Abigail Smith

Date of marriage—Oct. 25, 1764

Place of marriage—Weymouth, Mass.

Age of wife at marriage—19 years, 348 days

Age of husband at marriage—28 years, 360 days

Years married—54 years, 3 days

CHILDREN

Abigail Amelia Adams, b. July 14, 1765, Braintree, Mass.; m. June 12, 1786, William Stephens Smith; d. Aug. 15, 1813

John Quincy Adams, b. July 11, 1767, Braintree, Mass.; m. July 26, 1797, Louisa Catherine Johnson; d. Feb. 23, 1848, Washington, D.C.

Susanna Adams, b. Dec. 28, 1768, Boston, Mass.; d. Feb. 4, 1770

Charles Adams, b. May 29, 1770, Boston, Mass.; m. Aug. 29, 1795, Sarah Smith; d. Nov. 30, 1800

Thomas Boylston Adams, b. Sept. 15, 1772, Quincy, Mass.; m. May 16, 1805, Ann Harod; d. Mar. 13, 1832

THE PRESIDENT'S WIFE

Name at birth—Abigail Smith

Date of birth—Nov. 11, 1744

Place of birth—Weymouth, Mass.

Mother—Elizabeth Quincy Smith

Father—William Smith

Father's occupation—Congregational minister

Marriage—John Adams, Oct. 25, 1764, Weymouth, Mass.

Children—Abigail Amelia Adams, b. July 14, 1765, d. Aug. 15, 1813; John Quincy Adams, b. July 11, 1767, d. Feb. 23, 1848; Susanna Adams, b. Dec. 28, 1768, d. Feb. 4, 1770; Charles Adams, b. May 29, 1770, d. Nov. 30, 1800; Thomas Boylston Adams, b. Sept. 15, 1772, d. Mar. 13, 1832

Date of death—Oct. 28, 1818

Age at death—73 years, 351 days

Place of death—Quincy, Mass.

Burial place—Quincy, Mass.

Years younger than the President—9 years, 12 days

Years the President survived her—7 years, 249 days

Courtesy of The Library of Congress

Abigail Adams, wife of John Adams

THE FIRST LADY

Abigail Adams, the first President's wife to live in the Executive Mansion, did not move to Washington, D.C., until November 1800, when the President's House was ready for occupancy. A New Year's reception was held there in 1801, the first reception at the White House. As Adams's term of office expired on March 3, 1801, Mrs. Adams resided at the Executive Mansion less than four months. She maintained the same strict etiquette as Martha Washington. She preferred the climate of New England to that of the capital, however, and she maintained her interests in Quincy, Mass., anticipating the time when her husband's term would be completed.

Abigail Adams was a lively, acutely observant correspondent, and her letters are treasured by historians.

IMPORTANT DATES IN THE PRESIDENT'S LIFE

1755, taught school at Worcester, Mass.

1758, admitted to the bar, practiced at Boston, Mass.

1768, member of Massachusetts legislature

Sept. 5, 1774, delegate to First Continental Congress

Nov. 28, 1774, member of revolutionary Provincial Congress of Massachusetts

May 10, 1775, delegate to Second Continental Congress

June 1775, proposed George Washington as leader of the American Army

1776, one of committee of five to draft the Declaration of Independence

Aug. 2, 1776, signed Declaration of Independence; head of War Department

Apr. 8, 1778, reached Paris as Commissioner to France, superseding Silas Deane

Sept. 1, 1779, member of Massachusetts Constitutional Convention

Dec. 29, 1780, minister to the Netherlands; negotiated loan and Treaty of Amity and Commerce

May 14, 1785, minister to England (served until 1788)

Apr. 21, 1789, inaugurated Vice President at New York City

Apr. 21, 1789–Mar. 4, 1797, Vice President under George Washington

Mar. 4, 1797–Mar. 4, 1801, President

Mar. 4, 1801, retired to Quincy, Mass.

Nov. 15, 1820, member of Second Constitutional Convention of Massachusetts

ELECTIONS

THE ELECTION OF 1796

After he had served his second four-year term, George Washington declined a third term for the presidency. This left the field wide open for numerous candidates.

The elections of 1789 and 1792 were contests between individuals rather than contests between political groups and factions. In 1796, the growth of political parties began.

The strong central-government contingent in Congress, to whom the designation "Federalists" was applied, had been in power eight years during Washington's two administrations. They met in a congressional caucus to discuss policy, plans, and procedure. They pledged their support in the 1796 election to John Adams of Massachusetts and Thomas Pinckney of South Carolina, whose views coincided with theirs. Since the majority favored this selection, no balloting was undertaken.

Courtesy of The Library of Congress

Leaders of the Continental Congress—John Adams, Samuel Morris, Alexander Hamilton, and Thomas Jefferson

At about the same time, the anti-Federalist group of congressmen convened and mutually agreed to support Jefferson and Burr. They were known as the Republicans, or Democratic-Republicans, and opposed the establishment of a central government more powerful than the states.

The Constitution did not provide for these congressional caucuses. The system, which flourished until 1824, was not typical or representative of the views of the country since it perpetuated the rule of those in power. Less important members of the factions had nothing to say about the selection of candidates and the people had no choice whatsoever.

Since the electors voted for the President and Vice President, they were the powerful influence in determining the presidential elections. As each state was sovereign unto itself, there was no uniform method of selecting the electors. Each state enacted its own law. Some electors were chosen by popular vote, some by designation of state legislatures, and some by other methods.

The electors, once chosen, were not legally bound to cast their ballots for a designated candidate, but only one dared break faith with the powers that placed them in nomination. At first, the votes of individuals were counted so that states could have had divided votes. Later, states voted as a unit, the political candidate with the greatest number of votes receiving the entire state electoral vote.

The electoral vote of 1796 consisted of 276 votes from sixteen states. The votes were divided among a total of thirteen names.

George Washington received two votes even though he was not a candidate. Two of the candidates were brothers—Thomas Pinckney and Charles Cotesworth Pinckney, both of South Carolina.

John Adams received 71 votes, a plurality, and was elected President of the United States. The candidate receiving the next highest number of votes was Thomas Jefferson of Virginia, who had 68 votes and was elected Vice President.

The framers of the Constitution had not foreseen the development of political parties—they imagined the electors choosing from among individual candidates solely on the basis of merit—and they did not anticipate a situation in which the President represented one political party and his Vice President stood for a rival party. Adams was a Federalist, Jefferson a Democratic-Republican, and their political philosophies were utterly at odds. This inadequacy in the law was later corrected. The votes were cast as follows:

John Adams, Mass., 71
Thomas Jefferson, Va., 68
Thomas Pinckney, S.C., 59
Aaron Burr, N.Y., 30
Samuel Adams, Mass., 15
Oliver Ellsworth, Conn., 11
George Clinton, N.Y., 7
John Jay, N.Y., 5
James Iredell, N.C., 3
John Henry, Md., 2
Samuel Johnston, N.C., 2

Courtesy of The Library of Congress

John Adams proposing George Washington for Commander-in-Chief of the American Army

George Washington, Va., 2
Charles Cotesworth Pinckney, S.C., 1

Total number of votes: 276

INAUGURATION

March 4, 1797

John Adams, the first Vice President to be elevated to the presidency, was the only president besides George Washington to be inaugurated at Philadelphia. He was the first President to whom the oath of office was administered by a Chief Justice. On Satur-day, March 4, 1797, in the Chamber of the House of Representatives in Federal Hall, the oath was administered to John Adams by Oliver Ellsworth, Chief Justice of the United States. Adams was driven to the inauguration in a gilded coach drawn by six white horses.

THE VICE PRESIDENT

Name—Thomas Jefferson (2nd V.P.)
Political party—Democratic-Republican
State represented—Virginia
Term of office—Mar. 4, 1797–Mar. 4, 1801
Age at inauguration—53 years, 325 days

Occupation after term—President of the United States

For further biographical information, see the chapter on Thomas Jefferson, 3rd President, on page 39.

CABINET

March 4, 1797–March 3, 1801

State—Timothy Pickering, Pa., continued from preceding administration (requested to resign May 10, 1800, but declined to resign and was dismissed May 12, 1800); Charles Lee, Va. (Attorney General), ad interim May 13, 1800; John Marshall, Va., May 13, 1800; entered upon duties June 6, 1800; John Marshall, Va. (Chief Justice of the United States), ad interim Feb. 4, 1801, to Mar. 3, 1801

Treasury—Oliver Wolcott, Jr., Conn., continued from preceding administration; Samuel Dexter, Mass., Jan. 1, 1801

War—James McHenry, Md., continued from preceding administration; Benjamin Stoddert, Md. (Secretary of the Navy), ad interim June 1, 1800, to June 12, 1800; Samuel Dexter, Mass., May 13, 1800; entered upon duties June 12, 1800; Samuel Dexter, Mass. (Secretary of the Treasury), ad interim Jan. 1, 1801

Attorney General—Charles Lee, Va., continued from preceding administration

Postmaster General—Joseph Habersham, Ga., continued from preceding administration

Navy—Benjamin Stoddert, Md., May 21, 1798; entered upon duties June 18, 1798

CONGRESS

FIFTH CONGRESS

March 4, 1797–March 3, 1799

First session—May 15, 1797–July 10, 1797 (57 days)

Second session—Nov. 13, 1797–July 16, 1798 (246 days)

Third session—Dec. 3, 1798–Mar. 3, 1799 (91 days)

Special session of the Senate—Mar. 4, 1797 (one day only); July 17, 1798–July 19, 1798 (3 days)

Vice President—Thomas Jefferson, Va.

President pro tempore of the Senate —William Bradford, R.I., elected July 6, 1797; Jacob Read, S.C., elected Nov. 22, 1797; Theodore Sedgwich, Mass., elected June 27, 1798; John Laurance, N.Y., elected Dec. 6, 1798; James Ross, Pa., elected Mar. 1, 1799

Secretary of the Senate—Samuel Allyne Otis, Mass.

Speaker of the House—Jonathan Dayton, N.J., reelected May 15, 1797; George Dent, Md., elected speaker pro tempore for Apr. 20, 1798, and again for May 28, 1798

Clerk of the House—John Beckley, Va., Jonathan Williams Condy, Pa., elected May 15, 1797

SIXTH CONGRESS

March 4, 1799–March 3, 1801

First session—Dec. 2, 1799–May 14, 1800 (164 days)

Second session—Nov. 17, 1800–Mar. 3, 1801 (107 days)

Vice President—Thomas Jefferson, Va.

President pro tempore of the Senate —Samuel Livermore, N.H., elected Dec. 2, 1799; Uriah Tracy, Conn., elected May 14, 1800; John Eager Howard, Md., elected Nov. 21, 1800; James Hillhouse, Conn., elected Feb. 28, 1801

Secretary of the Senate—Samuel Allyne Otis, Mass.

Speaker of the House—Theodore Sedgwick, Mass., elected Dec. 2, 1799

Clerk of the House—Jonathan Williams Condy, Pa., reelected Dec. 2, 1799, resigned Dec. 4, 1799; John Holt Oswald, Pa., elected Dec. 9, 1799

APPOINTMENTS TO THE SUPREME COURT

Chief Justice

John Marshall, Va., Jan. 31, 1801 (replaced Oliver Ellsworth)

Associate Justices

Bushrod Washington, Va., Sept. 29, 1798 (replaced James Wilson)

Alfred Moore, N.C., Dec. 10, 1799 (replaced James Iredell)

IMPORTANT DATES IN THE PRESIDENCY

May 10, 1797, first naval vessel, *United States,* launched, Philadelphia, Pa.

June 14, 1797, exportation of arms prohibited

Sept. 20, 1797, Frigate *Constitution* ("Old Ironsides") launched

Jan. 8, 1798, Adams informed Congress that Eleventh Amendment had been adopted

Apr. 7, 1798, Mississippi Territory created

Apr. 25, 1798, "Hail Columbia" first sung in theater

Apr. 30, 1798, Navy Department created

June 25, 1798, Alien Act passed

July 1798, yellow fever epidemic in Philadelphia; many officials moved to Trenton, N.J.

July 9, 1798–Sept. 30, 1800, conflict with France

July 11, 1798, U.S. Marine Corps created

July 13, 1798, Lieutenant General George Washington accepted office as commander in chief

July 14, 1798, Sedition Act passed

July 16, 1798, U.S. Public Health Service established

Oct. 2, 1798, treaty with Cherokee Indians

Nov. 16, 1798, governor of Kentucky signed law declaring the Alien and Sedition Acts unconstitutional

Dec. 21, 1798, Virginia resolution similarly declared the Alien and Sedition Act unconstitutional

Jan. 14, 1799, Senate impeachment trial of Senator William Blount of Tennessee concluded; charges dismissed for want of jurisdiction (first impeachment proceedings against a U.S. senator)

Feb. 25, 1799, first federal forestry legislation to acquire timber lands for the U.S. Navy

Dec. 14, 1799, death of George Washington

Apr. 4, 1800, federal bankruptcy act passed

Apr. 24, 1800, Library of Congress established

June 15, 1800, capital moved to District of Columbia

Sept. 3, 1800, treaty with Napoleon Bonaparte

Oct. 1, 1800, Spain ceded Louisiana back to France by secret treaty of San Ildefonso

Nov. 17, 1800, first session of Congress at Washington, D.C.

Jan. 31, 1801, John Marshall began thirty-four-year period as Chief Justice of the Supreme Court

ADDITIONAL DATA ON ADAMS

JOHN ADAMS

—was the first President born in Massachusetts.

—was the first President whose son was inaugurated President.

—was the second President whose mother was alive when he was inaugurated.

—was the first President to reside at Washington, D.C. When he moved into the President's House on November 1, 1800, it was not completed and not a single apartment was finished.

—was the first President to have children of his own. He had three sons and two daughters.

—was the first President to have a Chief Justice of the Supreme Court administer the oath to him. He was sworn in on March 4, 1797, by Chief Justice Oliver Ellsworth.

—was the only President who was inaugurated at Philadelphia both as President and Vice President. On March 4, 1793, he was inaugurated as Vice President with George Washington as President, and on March 4, 1797, he was inaugurated President with Thomas Jefferson as his Vice President.

—was the first President to reach the age of 90.

ADAMS MARRIED BY FATHER-IN-LAW

The marriage of John Adams to Abigail Smith on October 25, 1764, at Weymouth, Mass., was performed by the father of the bride, the Reverend William Smith, a Congregational minister.

ADAMS SWORN IN AS WASHINGTON'S VICE PRESIDENT

John Adams entered upon his duties as Vice President of the United States on Tuesday, April 21, 1789, nine days before George Washington was inaugurated.

John Langdon of New Hampshire, who was president pro tempore of the Senate, introduced him to the senators as follows, "Sir: I have it in charge from the Senate to introduce you to the chair of this House; and, also to congratulate you on your appointment to the office of Vice President of the United States of America." He then conducted the Vice President to the chair, and John Adams addressed the Senate.

On Wednesday, June 3, 1789, the oath of office was administered to John Adams, who, in turn, administered the oath to the Senate members. The oath, "[name] do solemnly swear or affirm (as the case may be) that I will support the Constitution of the United States," was required by "an act to regulate the time and manner of administering certain oaths," June 1, 1789 (1 Sat. L. 23), Chapter One, Statute One.

A bust portrait of President John Adams, with garland and curtain, framed by the arms of sixteen states

citizens of another state or subjects of any foreign state, was passed by Congress on March 4, 1794, and proposed to the legislatures of the several states by the Third Congress on March 5, 1794. The twelfth state to ratify, making the amendment effective, was Delaware. Although Delaware ratified it on January 23, 1795, it was not until January 8, 1798, that the Secretary of State certified that the amendment had been made a part of the Constitution. This was because the states were dilatory in notifying the central government.

SECRETARY OF THE NAVY APPOINTED BY ADAMS

The Secretary of War was in charge of both the army and the navy, until May 21, 1798, when President John Adams appointed Benjamin Stoddert as the first Secretary of the Navy.

APPOINTMENT OF A GENERAL AUTHORIZED

An act of May 28, 1798 (1 Stat. L. 558), "an act authorizing the President of the United States to raise a provisional army," empowered the President

to appoint, by and with the advice and consent of the Senate, a commander of the army which may be raised by virtue of this act, and who being commissioned as lieutenant-general may be authorized to command the armies of the United States, and shall be entitled to the following pay and emoluments, viz.: two-hundred-and-fifty dollars monthly pay, fifty dollars monthly allowance for forage, when the same shall not be provided by the United States, and forty rations per day, or money in lieu thereof at the current price; who shall have authority to appoint, from time to time, such number of aides not exceeding four, and secretaries not exceeding two, as he may judge proper, each to have the rank, pay and emoluments of a lieutenant-colonel.

The oath as administered at present is, "I do solemnly swear (or affirm) that I will support and defend the constitution of the United States against all enemies, foreign and domestic; that I will bear true faith and allegiance to the same; that I take this obligation freely, without any mental reservation or purpose of evasion, and that I will well and faithfully discharge the duties of the office on which I am about to enter. So help me God."

Adams made an inaugural address after being sworn in as Vice President. He spoke about the successful formation of the federal union, the adoption of the federal Constitution, and the auspicious circumstances under which the new government came into operation "under the presidency of him who had led the American armies to victory and conducted by those who had contributed to achieve Independence."

ELEVENTH AMENDMENT ENACTED

The eleventh amendment to the Constitution, providing that federal judicial authority shall not extend to suits against a state by

CONGRESS IN SESSION AT WASHINGTON

The first Congress to meet at Washington, D.C., was the Sixth Congress; the second session opened on November 17, 1800, and lasted until March 3, 1801 (107 days). The House of Representatives did not have a quorum until November 18, and the Senate did not have a quorum until November 21. On November 22, 1800, President John Adams read his fourth annual address to Congress.

ADAMS APPOINTED "MIDNIGHT JUDGES"

On February 13, 1801, Congress passed "an act to provide for the more convenient organization of the Courts of the United States" (2 Stat. L. 89). It provided for the appointment of eighteen new judges. President John Adams sat at his desk until midnight, March 3, 1801, signing the appointments of Federalists to public office.

The law was repealed during Jefferson's term and the judges lost their offices. The act of April 29, 1802, "an act to amend the Judicial System of the United States," voided the appointments.

ADAMS DEFEATED FOR REELECTION

John Adams was the first President of the United States who was defeated for reelection. After completing his term, 1797–1801, John Adams hoped to be reelected, but the electors decided otherwise.

Thomas Jefferson received 73 electoral votes and so did Aaron Burr; the decision was referred to the House of Representatives, which made Jefferson President and Burr Vice President. John Adams received 65 electoral votes, Charles Cotesworth Pinckney 64 votes, and John Jay 1 vote.

ADAMS RECALLED SON

On January 31, 1801, John Adams recalled his son, John Quincy Adams, from his post as Minister to Prussia to prevent President-elect Thomas Jefferson from dismissing him. On April 26, 1801, the recall reached John Quincy Adams, who returned to Philadelphia, Pa., on September 4, 1801.

Adams' letter to Secretary of State John Marshall stated:

I request you would cause to be prepared letters for me to sign, to the King of Prussia recalling Mr. John Quincy Adams as minister plenipotentiary from his court. . . . I wish you to make out one letter to go by the way of Hamburg, another by Holland, a third by France, a fourth through Mr. King in England, a fifth, if you please, by way of Bremen or Stettin, or any channel most likely to convey it soon. It is my opinion this minister ought to be recalled from Prussia. . . . Besides, it is my opinion that it is my duty to call him home.

ABSENCE AT INAUGURATION OF SUCCESSOR

John Adams set a precedent by not attending the inauguration of his successor. When Thomas Jefferson was inaugurated on March 4, 1801, Adams absented himself, possibly because he did not wish to witness the success of his political rival, or possibly because he was not invited. His son, John Quincy Adams, likewise refused to attend the inauguration services for Andrew Jackson. Andrew Johnson and Richard Nixon also followed this example.

FATHER AND SON PRESIDENTS

John Adams and John Quincy Adams were the first father and son to be inaugurated Presidents of the United States. They each served one term. John Adams lived to see his son sworn in as President.

ADAMS'S LAST WORDS

The last words attributed to John Adams were made by him without a full knowledge of the facts. Adams's last words were reported to have been "Thomas Jefferson still survives." He had not learned, nor had he any means of knowing, that Thomas Jefferson had died the same morning at 9:50 A.M. on July 4, 1826, the fiftieth anniversary of the Declaration of Independence.

ADAMS SUPPLIED VITAL INFORMATION

In a letter dated March 11, 1809, from Quincy, Mass., in response to a request for biographical material, John Adams wrote to Skelton Jones:

I was born in Quincy on the 19th of October 1735. . . .

The Fourth of March 1801. The causes of my retirement are to be found in the writings of Freneau, Markoe, Ned Church, Andrew Brown, Paine, Callender, Hamilton, Cobbett and John Ward Fenno and many others, but more especially in the circular letters of Members of Congress from the southern and middle States. Without a complete collection of all these libels, no faithful history of the last twenty years can ever be written, nor any adequate account given of the causes of my retirement from public life.

I have one head, four limbs and five senses, like any other man, and nothing peculiar in any of them.

I have been married forty-four years. To Miss Abigail Smith on the 25th of October 1764 in her father's house at Weymouth, the next town to his, and by her father who was a clergyman.

I have no miniature, and have been too much abused by painters ever to sit for any one again.

EXTRACT FROM FIRST LETTER FROM THE WHITE HOUSE BY A PRESIDENT (JOHN ADAMS TO ABIGAIL ADAMS)

President's House, Washington City
2 November, 1800
My Dearest Friend,

We arrived here last night, or rather yesterday, at one o'clock, and here we dined and slept. . . . Before I end my letter, I pray heaven to bestow the best of blessings on this house, and on all that shall hereafter inhabit it. May none but honest and wise men ever rule under this roof! I shall not attempt a description of it. You will form the best idea of it from inspection. . . .

I am, with unabated confidence and affection, yours,

JOHN ADAMS

MRS. ADAMS'S IMPRESSION OF THE WHITE HOUSE (A LETTER TO HER DAUGHTER)

Washington
21 November, 1800
My Dear Child:

I arrived here on Sunday last, and without meeting with any accident worth noticing, except losing ourselves when we left Baltimore, and going eight or nine miles on the Frederick road, by which means we were obliged to go the other eight through woods, where we wandered two hours without finding a guide, or the path. . . . The house is made habitable, but there is not a single apartment finished. . . . withinside, except the plastering has been done since Briesler came. We have not the least fence, yard, or other convenience, without, and the great unfinished audience room I make a drying-room of, to hang up the clothes in. The principal stairs are not up, and will not be this winter. . . .

Affectionately your mother,

A. ADAMS

FURTHER READING

Adams, Charles F. *John Adams.* 2 vols. Rev. ed. 1980.

Brown, Ralph A. *The Presidency of John Adams.* 1975.

Ellis, Joseph J. *The Character and Legacy of John Adams.* 1993.

Ferling, John E. *John Adams: A Life.* 1992.

Handler, Edward. *America and Europe in the Political Thought of John Adams.* 1964.

McCullough, David G. *John Adams.* 2001

Morse, John T. *John Adams.* 1972.

Taylor, Robert J. ed. *Papers of John Adams.* 4 vols. 1977.

Courtesy of The Library of Congress

Thomas Jefferson

Date of birth—Apr. 13, 1743

Place of birth—Shadwell, Goochland County, now Albemarle County, Va.

Education—Attended schools of Rev. William Douglas, Northam, Va., and Rev. James Maury, Fredericksville, Va.; College of William and Mary, Williamsburg, Va., graduated Apr. 25, 1762; private study in Virginia law office of George Wythe, 1762–1767

Religion—Christian (no specific denomination)

Ancestry—Scottish, English, Welsh

Career—Lawyer, colonial legislator, delegate to Continental Congress and state constitutional convention, author of the Declaration of Independence, state legislator, governor of Virginia, minister to France, Secretary of State, Vice President

Political party—Democratic-Republican

State represented—Virginia

Term of office—Mar. 4, 1801–Mar. 4, 1809

Term served—8 years

Administration—4th, 5th

Congresses—7th, 8th, 9th, 10th

Age at inauguration—57 years, 325 days

Lived after term—17 years, 122 days

Occupation after term—Founder and rector, University of Virginia

Date of death—July 4, 1826

Age at death—83 years, 82 days

Place of death—Monticello, near Charlottesville, Va.

Burial place—Monticello, Va.

FAMILY

FATHER

Name—Peter Jefferson

Date of birth—Feb. 29, 1708

Marriage—Jane Randolph, Oct. 2, 1739

Occupation—Farmer, planter, soldier, surveyor, mapmaker, magistrate, colonial legislator, justice of the peace

Date of death—Aug. 17, 1757

Age at death—49 years, 170 days

MOTHER

Name at birth—Jane Randolph

Date of birth—Feb. 9, 1720

Place of birth—London, England

Marriage—Peter Jefferson, Oct. 2, 1739

Date of death—Mar. 31, 1776

Age at death—56 years, 50 days

SIBLINGS

Thomas Jefferson was the third child in a family of ten.

Children of Peter Jefferson and Jane Randolph Jefferson

Jane Jefferson, b. June 27, 1740, d. Oct. 1, 1765

Mary Jefferson, b. Oct. 1, 1741, d. 1760

Thomas Jefferson, b. Apr. 13, 1743, d. July 4, 1826

Elizabeth Jefferson, b. Nov. 4, 1744, d. Feb. 1774

Martha Jefferson, b. May 29, 1746, d. Sept. 3, 1811

Peter Field Jefferson, b. Oct. 16, 1748, d. Nov. 29, 1748

—— Jefferson (son), b. Mar. 9, 1750, d. Mar. 9, 1750

Lucy Jefferson, b. Oct. 10, 1752, d. 1811

Anna Scott Jefferson, twin, b. Oct. 1, 1755

Randolph Jefferson, twin, b. Oct. 1, 1755, d. Aug. 7, 1815

MARRIAGE

Married—Martha Wayles Skelton

Date of marriage—Jan. 1, 1772

Place of marriage—Wayles estate, Williamsburg, Va.

Age of wife at marriage—23 years, 74 days

Age of husband at marriage—28 years, 263 days

Years married—10 years, 248 days

FIRST WIDOWER TO BECOME PRESIDENT

Thomas Jefferson was the first widower to become President of the United States. His wife, Martha Wayles Skelton, died 18 years, 179 days before he was inaugurated. Jefferson never remarried and was a widower 43 years, 301 days. Four of his six children died before he became President.

CHILDREN

Children of Thomas Jefferson and Martha Wayles Skelton Jefferson

Martha Washington Jefferson, b. Sept. 27, 1772, Charlottesville, Va.; m. Feb. 23, 1790, Thomas Mann Randolph; d. Oct. 10, 1836

Jane Randolph Jefferson, b. Apr. 3, 1774; d. Sept. 1775

—— Jefferson (son), b. May 28, 1777; d. June 14, 1777

Mary ("Marie," "Polly") Jefferson, b. Aug. 1, 1778; m. Oct. 13, 1797, John Wayles Eppes; d. Apr. 17, 1804

Lucy Elizabeth Jefferson, b. Nov. 3, 1780, Richmond, Va.; d. Apr. 15, 1781

Lucy Elizabeth Jefferson, b. May 8, 1782; d. Nov. 17, 1785, Eppington, Va.

Possible children of Thomas Jefferson and Sally Hemings

Thomas Corbin Woodson, b. 1790; d. 1880

Harriet Hemings, b. Oct. 5, 1795; d. Dec. 1797

Beverly (William) Hemings, b. Apr. 1, 1798; d. after 1822

Thenia Jefferson Hemings, b. Dec. 7, 1799; d. 1802

Harriet Hemings, b. May 1801; d. 1876

Madison (James) Hemings, b. Jan. 19, 1805; d. Nov. 28, 1877

Eston (Thomas) Hemings, b. May 21, 1808; d. circa 1856, Ross County, Ohio

Sally Hemings, a slave in Thomas Jefferson's household, was the half-sister of Jefferson's wife Martha. Jefferson's father-in-law, John Wayles, was the father of both Martha and Sally—Martha by his wife, Martha Eppes Wayles, and Sally by Betty Hemings, a woman who was one of his slaves. Betty Hemings herself is thought to have been the child of an Englishman and an African slave woman, and Sally was the last of six children she had with John Wayles. Sally was born in Virginia in July 1773.

After the death of Wayles, their owner, Betty and Sally Hemings moved to Jefferson's estate. They nursed Jefferson's wife during her final illness, and when Jefferson's nine-year-old daughter Polly traveled to France to live with her father, she was accompanied by Sally, who was then fourteen.

Sally gave birth to seven children, died in 1835, and was buried somewhere near Monticello; her gravesite is unknown. Speculation about the paternity of her children began during her lifetime and centered on Thomas Jefferson, although claims were also made for his sister's sons, Samuel and Peter Carr. The children of Sally Hemings handed down to their descendants an oral tradition stating that the father was Jefferson, but this was not considered sufficient proof by the Monticello Association, a group of Jefferson descendants that organizes family reunions. In recent years, some biographers have attributed to Jefferson and Hemings a close relationship that lasted for decades.

In November 1998, the journal *Nature* published the results of a DNA study made by a British laboratory. The authors of the study obtained blood samples from male descendants of Thomas Jefferson's uncle, Field Jefferson; male descendants of the Carr brothers; and male descendants of Thomas Woodson and Eston Hemings, two of Sally Hemings's children. They compared the Y-chromosomes in the DNA of these blood samples, since these chromosomes are passed down through the male line. No match was found for Thomas Woodson's descendants. In the case of the descendants of Eston Hemings, there was no match with the Carr brothers, but one descendant had Y-chromosomes that matched those of the Jeffersons.

Since the study did not conclusively prove that Thomas Jefferson was the father of Eston Hemings—only that he was a definite possibility—advocates on both sides of the debate have used the results to bolster their own beliefs.

THE PRESIDENT'S WIFE

Name at birth—Martha Wayles

Date of birth—Oct. 19, 1748

Place of birth—Charles City County, Va.

Mother—Martha Eppes Wayles

Father—John Wayles

Father's occupation—Lawyer, planter

First marriage—Bathurst Skelton (d.)

Second marriage—Thomas Jefferson, Jan. 1, 1772, Wayles estate, Williamsburg, Va.

Children from first marriage——— Skelton (son), b. Nov. 7, 1767; d. June 10, 1771

Children from second marriage—Martha Washington Jefferson, b. Sept. 27, 1772, d. Oct. 10, 1836; Jane Randolph Jefferson, b. Apr. 3, 1774, d. Sept. 1775; —— Jefferson (son), b. May 28, 1777, d. June 14, 1777; Mary ("Marie," "Polly") Jefferson, b. Aug. 1, 1778, d. Apr. 17, 1804; Lucy Elizabeth Jefferson, b. Nov. 3, 1780, d. Apr. 15, 1781; Lucy Elizabeth Jefferson, b. May 8, 1782, d. Nov. 17, 1785

Date of death—Sept. 6, 1782

Age at death—33 years, 322 days

Place of death—Monticello, near Charlottesville, Va.

Burial place—Monticello, Va.

Years younger than the president—5 years, 189 days

Years the President survived her—43 years, 301 days

JEFFERSON'S HOSTESSES AT THE WHITE HOUSE

Thomas Jefferson had been a widower for about 18 years when he entered the White House. The duties of mistress of the White House were assumed by his daughters; one was Martha Washington Jefferson, the wife of Thomas Mann Randolph, and the other was Marie Jefferson, the wife of John Wayles Eppes. The unhealthy situation of the city of Washington, which was low and marshy, engendered disease, and his daughters preferred not to bring their children to the capital city. Dolley Madison, wife of Secretary of State James Madison, generally presided at functions in the absence of Jefferson's daughters.

IMPORTANT DATES IN THE PRESIDENT'S LIFE

1757, inherited land and slaves after death of his father and took over responsibilities as head of the family

1760–1762 student, College of William and Mary

Apr. 1767, admitted to the bar

1769, began building of home at Monticello

May 11, 1769, member of Virginia House of Burgesses (served until 1774)

Nov. 26, 1770, moved to Monticello

Apr. 1773, attended meeting of Committee of Correspondence

Aug. 1774, published influential pamphlet *A Summary View of the Rights of British America*

Mar. 1775, deputy delegate to Continental Congress, Philadelphia, Pa.

June 21–July 31, Oct. 2–Dec. 28, 1775, delegate to Continental Congress

Aug. 1775, Virginia convention, Richmond

May 15–Sept. 2, 1776, delegate to Continental Congress

June 10–July 2, 1776, chairman of committee to prepare Declaration of Independence

Oct. 11–Dec. 14, 1776, Virginia General Assembly, Williamsburg

June 1, 1779, elected governor of Virginia

June 2, 1780, reelected governor

Monticello, home of Thomas Jefferson, Charlottesville, Virginia

Courtesy of The Library of Congress

June 3, 1781, resigned governorship; offered post as Peace Commissioner by Continental Congress but declined appointment

June 15, 1781, empowered to negotiate treaty of peace with Great Britain

June 1783, drafted constitution for Virginia

May 7, 1784, appointed minister plenipotentiary to France

Mar. 10, 1785, elected by Congress to succeed Benjamin Franklin as minister to France; presented credentials to King of France on May 14

June 1785, left Paris for London

1786–1787, diplomatic missions in Paris and London

Oct. 12, 1787, reelected minister for three-year term; appointment subject to revocation by Congress

1789, prepared Charter of Rights for France

Sept. 26, 1789, confirmed as Secretary of State

Oct. 22–Nov. 23, 1789, returned from France on the *Clermont,* disembarking at Norfolk, Va.

Mar. 22, 1790–Dec. 31, 1793, secretary of state

Jan. 1797, elected president of Philosophical Society

Mar. 4, 1797–Mar. 4, 1801, Vice President under John Adams

1800, prepared *Parliamentary Manual*

Mar. 4, 1801–Mar. 4, 1805, President (1st term)

May 2, 1803, Louisiana Purchase treaty signed

Mar. 4, 1805–Mar. 4, 1809, President (2nd term)

Sept. 1814, sold his library to Library of Congress

Mar. 29, 1819–1826, founder and rector of University of Virginia

Nov. 12, 1822, injured in fall (left forearm broken and wrist bones dislocated)

ELECTIONS

THE ELECTION OF 1800

By the nation's fourth national election, the loosely knit political groups had begun to organize. The Federalists, still advocating a strong central government with only such political power for the various states as was absolutely necessary, began to encounter apparent dissatisfaction with their policies. The Federalist congressmen, in a congressional caucus which met in a Senate chamber, decided to support Adams for a second term with Charles Cotesworth Pinckney of South Carolina as a running mate. Since both the President and the Vice President were elected by the same ballot, one faction of the

Federalists, led by Alexander Hamilton, hoped that Pinckney would receive the presidency and that Adams with the second greatest number of votes might become Vice President.

The Democratic-Republicans, believing that the states should yield to the federal government only that which was necessary, denounced the federal caucus but continued to work under it. At a congressional caucus held in Philadelphia, Pa., the Democratic-Republicans placed their hopes on Thomas Jefferson of Virginia and Aaron Burr of New York. At this caucus they adopted the first national platform ever formulated by a political party.

The electors were chosen in the various states, by various methods, in November and early December 1800. The electoral votes were opened in Congress on February 11, 1801. Of the 276 votes cast, 73 were cast for Thomas Jefferson and 73 for Aaron Burr, both Democratic-Republicans. The Federalists cast 65 votes for John Adams, 64 votes for Charles Cotesworth Pinckney, and 1 vote for John Jay of New York.

Inasmuch as both Jefferson and Burr had each received 73 votes and tied for first place, the election was immediately referred to the House of Representatives to decide which candidate would be the President and which would be the Vice President. Since both candidates were members of the same political faction, it was not a contest of political factions but of personalities.

The balloting to decide the tie began in the House on February 11. The representatives did not vote individually but by state groups, each state being entitled to one vote. On the first ballot, Jefferson had eight states and Burr six states, with Maryland and Vermont equally divided. As a majority was required, further ballots were taken. On February 17, the thirty-sixth ballot was taken to arrive at a choice. Ten states voted for Jefferson, four for Burr, and two voted blank. Jefferson was declared elected President and Burr his Vice President.

THE ELECTION OF 1804

In 1804, after Jefferson had served four years, the Democratic-Republicans found Vice President Aaron Burr no longer accept-able. He had presided impartially over the Senate, and disgruntled members of his own party felt that Burr was guilty of catering to the Federalists. When the congressional caucus was held on February 25, 1804, the Democratic-Republicans decided to support Jefferson for a second term as President. However, they withdrew their support of Burr and favored George Clinton, governor of New York for 18 years, to supplant him as Vice President.

The Federalists, whose party strength was waning, held no congressional caucus and threw their support to Charles Cotesworth Pinckney of South Carolina for President and Rufus King of New York for Vice President.

Jefferson won a clear-cut victory and was elected President for a second term, carrying George Clinton with him as Vice President. He received 162 of the 176 electoral votes.

The election of 1804 was the first in which separate votes were cast for the President and the Vice President. This change in election procedure, authorized by the Twelfth Amendment to the Constitution, went into effect September 25, 1804, and superseded Article II, Section 1, paragraph three of the Constitution. The bill was passed by the Senate on December 3, 1803, by a vote of 22 yeas to 10 nays, and by the House of Representatives on December 9, 1803, by a vote of 83 yeas to 42 nays, with the speaker, Nathaniel Macon of North Carolina, casting the deciding vote to make the necessary two-thirds majority. The amendment was submitted to the states, was ratified by three fourths of them, and was declared in force on September 25, 1804. Connecticut, Delaware, Massachusetts, and New Hampshire rejected the amendment.

1804 ELECTORAL VOTE

There were 176 electoral votes from 17 states.

Jefferson received 92.05 percent (162 votes—15 states) as follows: Ga. 6; Ky. 8; Md. 9 (of the 11 votes); Mass. 19; N.H. 7; N.J. 8; N.Y. 19; N.C. 14; Ohio 3; Pa. 20; R.I. 4; S.C. 10; Tenn. 5; Vt. 6; Va. 24.

Pinckney received 7.95 percent (14 votes—2 states) as follows: Conn. 9; Del. 3; Md. 2 (of the 11 votes).

INAUGURATIONS

FIRST TERM

March 4, 1801

Thomas Jefferson was the first President to take the oath of office at Washington, D.C. It was a fair day and he walked to the Capitol from Mrs. Conrad's boarding house, one block away, accompanied by a group of riflemen, artillerymen, and civilians. The oath was administered on Wednesday, March 4, 1801, by Chief Justice John Marshall in the Senate Chamber in the Capitol. Only the north wing of the Capitol building had been completed and the center was unfinished. Jefferson delivered his inaugural address in a voice so soft that he was scarcely audible to any but the two men who flanked him, Marshall and Vice President Burr. President John Adams had driven out of the city at dawn, refusing to attend the inauguration of his successor to witness what he considered the dissolution of the republic.

SECOND TERM

March 4, 1805

Thomas Jefferson took the oath of office for his second term on Monday, March 4, 1805, in the Senate Chamber. Chief Justice John Marshall administered the oath. In the evening, a ceremony in the East Room of the Executive Mansion was attended by a large crowd which caused much disorder.

THE VICE PRESIDENTS

FIRST TERM

Name—Aaron Burr (3rd V.P.)
Date of birth—Feb. 6, 1756
Place of birth—Newark, N.J.
Political party—Democratic-Republican
State represented—New York
Term of office—Mar. 4, 1801–Mar. 4, 1805
Age at inauguration—45 years, 26 days
Occupation after term—Lawyer
Date of death—Sept. 14, 1836
Age at death—80 years, 220 days
Place of death—Staten Island, N.Y.
Burial place—Princeton Cemetery, Princeton, N.J.

ADDITIONAL DATA ON BURR

1772, graduated College of New Jersey, now Princeton University, Princeton, N.J. (he was the son of a clergyman who had been the college's second President)
1773, studied theology at Litchfield, Conn.
1775, joined Continental Army, distinguishing himself at Quebec, Monmouth, and New Haven
Mar. 10, 1779, resigned because of ill health

Courtesy of The Library of Congress

Aaron Burr, first Vice President to Thomas Jefferson

Apr. 17, 1782, admitted to the bar; practiced in Albany, N.Y.
1783, moved to New York City
1784, New York State Assembly
1789–1790, Attorney General of New York
1791, commissioner on Revolutionary claims
Mar. 4, 1791–Mar. 3, 1797, U.S. Senate (from New York)
1798–1799, New York State Assembly

1800, led the Democratic-Republicans to control of New York State legislature and turned the Tammany Society into a statewide political force

1801, New York State Constitutional Convention

Mar. 4, 1801–Mar. 4, 1805, Vice President of the United States

1804, unsuccessful candidate for governor of New York

1804, killed Alexander Hamilton in duel (July 11); fled to South Carolina; completed term as Vice President

1807, arrested and tried for treason, accused of attempting to form a republic in the Southwest of which he was to be the head; acquitted

1808, went to Europe

1812, resumed law practice, New York City

SECOND TERM

Name—George Clinton (4th V.P.)

Political party—Democratic-Republican

State represented—New York

Term of office—Mar. 4, 1805–Mar. 4, 1809 —

Age at inauguration—65 years, 221 days

Occupation after term—Vice President under James Madison

For additional data on Clinton, see the section on the Vice President in the chapter on James Madison, 4th President.

Courtesy of The Library of Congress

George Clinton, second Vice President to Thomas Jefferson

CABINET

FIRST TERM

March 4, 1801–March 3, 1805

State—John Marshall, Va. (Chief Justice of the United States) for one day, Mar. 4, 1801, and for a special purpose; Levi Lincoln, Mass. (Attorney General), ad interim Mar. 5, 1801; James Madison, Va., Mar. 5, 1801; entered upon duties May 2, 1801

Treasury—Samuel Dexter, Mass., continued from preceding administration to May 6, 1801; Albert Gallatin, Pa., May 14, 1801

War—Henry Dearborn, Mass., Mar. 5, 1801

Attorney General—Levi Lincoln, Mass., Mar. 5, 1801 to Dec. 31, 1804

Postmaster General—Joseph Habersham, Ga., continued from preceding administration; Gideon Granger, Conn., Nov. 28, 1801

Navy—Benjamin Stoddert, Md., continued from preceding administration; Henry Dearborn, Mass. (Secretary of War), ad interim Apr. 1, 1801; Robert Smith, Md., July 15, 1801; entered upon duties July 27, 1801

SECOND TERM

March 4, 1805–March 3, 1809

State—James Madison, Va., continued from preceding administration

Treasury—Albert Gallatin, Pa., continued from preceding administration

War—Henry Dearborn, Mass., continued from preceding administration; John Smith (chief clerk), ad interim Feb. 17, 1809

Attorney General—John Breckenridge, Ky., Aug. 7, 1805, died Dec. 14, 1806; Caesar Augustus Rodney, Del., Jan. 20, 1807

Postmaster General—Gideon Granger, Conn., continued from preceding administration

Navy—Robert Smith, Md., continued from preceding administration

CONGRESS

SEVENTH CONGRESS

March 4, 1801–March 3, 1803

First session—Dec. 7, 1801–May 3, 1802 (148 days)

Second session—Dec. 6, 1802–Mar. 3, 1803 (88 days)

special session—Mar. 4, 1801–Mar. 5, 1801 (2 days)

Vice President—Aaron Burr, N.Y.

President pro tempore of the Senate—Abraham Baldwin, Ga., elected Dec. 7, 1801, Apr. 17, 1802; Stephen Row Bradley, Vt., elected Dec. 14, 1802; Feb. 25, 1803; Mar. 2, 1803

Secretary of the Senate—Samuel Allyne Otis, Mass.

Speaker of the House—Nathaniel Macon, N.C., elected Dec. 7, 1801

Clerk of the House—John Holt Oswald, Pa., John Beckley, Va., elected Dec. 7, 1801

EIGHTH CONGRESS

March 4, 1803–March 3, 1805

First session—Oct. 17, 1803–Mar. 27, 1804 (163 days)

Second session—Nov. 5, 1804–Mar. 3, 1805 (119 days)

Vice President—Aaron Burr, N.Y.

President pro tempore of the Senate—John Brown, Ky., elected Oct. 17, 1803, Jan. 23, 1804; Jesse Franklin, N.C., elected Mar. 10, 1804; Joseph Anderson, Tenn., elected Jan. 15, 1805, Feb. 28, 1805, Mar. 2, 1805

Secretary of the Senate—Samuel Allyne Otis, Mass.

Speaker of the House—Nathaniel Macon, N.C., reelected Oct. 17, 1803

Clerk of the House—John Beckley, Va., reelected Oct. 17, 1803

NINTH CONGRESS

March 4, 1805–March 3, 1807

First session—Dec. 2, 1805–Apr. 21, 1806 (141 days)

Second session—Dec. 1, 1806–Mar. 3, 1807 (93 days)

Special session of the Senate—Mar. 4, 1805–Mar. 6, 1805 (3 days)

Vice President—George Clinton, N.Y.

President pro tempore of the Senate—Samuel Smith, Md., elected Dec. 2, 1805; Mar. 18, 1806; Mar. 2, 1807

Courtesy of U.S. National Archives and Records Administration

The Declaration of Independence

46

Secretary of the Senate—Samuel Allyne Otis, Mass.

Speaker of the House—Nathaniel Macon, reelected Dec. 2, 1805

Clerk of the House—John Beckley, Va., reelected Dec. 2, 1805

TENTH CONGRESS

March 4, 1807–March 3, 1809

First session—Oct. 26, 1807–Apr. 25, 1808 (182 days)

Second session—Nov. 7, 1808–Mar. 3, 1809 (117 days)

Vice President—George Clinton, N.Y.

President pro tempore of the Senate —Samuel Smith, elected Apr. 16, 1808; Stephen Row Bradley, Vt., elected Dec. 28, 1808; John Milledge, Ga., elected Jan. 30, 1809

Secretary of the Senate—Samuel Allyne Otis, Mass.

Speaker of the House—Joseph Bradley Varnum, Mass., elected Oct. 26, 1807

Clerk of the House—John Beckley, Va.; Patrick Magruder, Md., elected Oct. 26, 1807

APPOINTMENTS TO THE SUPREME COURT

Associate Justices

William Johnson, S.C., Mar. 26, 1804 (replaced Alfred Moore)

(Henry) Brockholst Livingston, N.Y., Nov. 10, 1806 (replaced William Paterson)

Thomas Todd, Ky., Mar. 3, 1807 (newly created seat)

IMPORTANT DATES IN THE PRESIDENCY

June 10, 1801, Tripoli declared war against the United States

Feb. 6, 1802, war declared against Tripoli

Mar. 16, 1802, Army engineer corps created

Mar. 16, 1802, United States Military Academy authorized; opened July 4, 1802

Feb. 24, 1803, *Marbury* v. *Madison*— Supreme Court decision declaring portion of Judiciary Act of 1789 unconstitutional

Mar. 1, 1803, Ohio admitted as 17th state

Apr. 30, 1803, Louisiana Purchase made from France for $15 million

May 2, 1803, Louisiana Purchase treaty signed

Oct. 31, 1803, Captain Bainbridge of the *Philadelphia* ran on a reef pursuing Tripoli cruiser and was captured

Dec. 20, 1803, France formally ceded Louisiana to United States

Feb. 3, 1804, Lieutenant Decatur, aboard the *Philadelphia,* defeated Tripolitans

Mar. 12, 1804, Judge John Pickering impeached and removed from office in trial begun Mar. 3, 1803 (first impeachment of a federal judge)

May 14, 1804, Lewis and Clark left St. Louis, Mo., on their expedition to the Pacific

July 12, 1804, Alexander Hamilton killed by Aaron Burr in a duel

Sept. 25, 1804, Twelfth Amendment to the Constitution ratified

Jan. 11, 1805, Michigan Territory created

Mar. 1, 1805, Supreme Court Justice Samuel Chase acquitted in impeachment trial begun Nov. 30, 1804 (first impeachment proceedings against a Supreme Court justice)

June 4, 1805, treaty of peace and amity signed with Tripoli

Nov. 15, 1805, Lewis and Clark reached Pacific Ocean

Mar. 29, 1806, Cumberland road construction to Ohio authorized

Nov. 13, 1806, Lieutenant Zebulon Pike discovered Colorado peak later named for him

Mar. 26, 1807, Territory of Orleans established

May 22, 1807–Oct. 20, 1807, trial of Aaron Burr at Richmond, Va., for conspiracy

June 1807, American ship *Chesapeake* fired upon by British *Leopard*; *Chesapeake* searched and British deserters seized

Aug. 7, 1807, Robert Fulton's steamboat *Clermont* made trip on Hudson River

Dec. 22, 1807, Embargo Act against international commerce and forbidding the docking of American ships at foreign ports

Jan. 1, 1808, law prohibiting importation of African slaves became effective

Nov. 10, 1808, Osage Treaty signed

Feb. 3, 1809, Illinois Territory established

Mar. 1, 1809, trade with Great Britain and France prohibited by non-intercourse act

ADDITIONAL DATA ON JEFFERSON

THOMAS JEFFERSON

—was the second President born in Virginia.

—was the second President to marry a widow.

—was the first widower inaugurated President.

—was the first President inaugurated in Washington, D.C.

—was the first President who had been a governor of a state.

—was the first President to have served in a cabinet.

—was the first President whose parents had twins.

—was the first President elected by the House of Representatives.

—was the first President who had served as Secretary of State.

JEFFERSON ADVOCATED RELIGIOUS FREEDOM

One of Jefferson's greatest achievements was the bill establishing religious freedom which was drawn up by him and enacted by the Legislature of Virginia in 1779. This bill served as the basis for the Federal Constitution's First Amendment.

Section 2 stated:

We the General Assembly of Virginia do enact that no man shall be compelled to frequent or support any religious worship, place, or ministry whatsoever, nor shall be enforced, restrained, molested, or burthened in his body or goods, or shall otherwise suffer, on account of his religious opinions or belief; but that all men shall be free to profess, and by argument to maintain, their opinions in matters of religion, and that the same shall in no wise diminish, enlarge, or affect their civil capacities.

JEFFERSON ADVOCATED DECIMAL SYSTEM OF CURRENCY

In April 1784 Thomas Jefferson wrote an important document entitled "Notes on the Establishment of a Money Unit and of a Coinage for the United States." The paper concluded:

My proposition then, is, that our notation of money shall be decimal, descending *ad libitum* of the person noting; that the Unit of this notation shall be a Dollar; that coins shall be accommodated to it from ten dollars to the hundredth of a dollar; and that, to set this on foot, the resolutions be adopted which were proposed in the notes only substituting an *enquiry into the fineness of the coins* in lieu of *an assay of them.*

GOVERNOR ELECTED PRESIDENT

Thomas Jefferson was the first governor of a state to be elected President. He was governor of Virginia from 1779 to 1781.

VICE PRESIDENT DEFEATED PRESIDENT

Thomas Jefferson was the first and last Vice President to defeat a President. In the election of 1800, Thomas Jefferson of Virginia and Aaron Burr of New York received 73 electoral votes, the election being decided in Jefferson's favor by the House of Representatives. Accordingly, Aaron Burr was made the Vice President. President John Adams received only 65 electoral votes and was defeated in his quest for reelection.

JEFFERSON AT THE EXECUTIVE MANSION

The White House, which at the time of Jefferson's inauguration was called the President's House, was not fully completed. Jefferson described it as "a great stone house, big enough for two emperors, one pope and the grand lama in the bargain." Jefferson did not move into the official residence until March 19, 1801. Before leaving the White House in 1809, he oversaw the addition of east and west wings to the mansion and decorated it with imported French furniture.

TROOPS REVIEWED FROM THE WHITE HOUSE

Thomas Jefferson held the first presidential review of military forces from his residence at the White House. On July 4, 1801, he reviewed the Marines, who were led by the Marine Band.

HAND-SHAKING INTRODUCED

On July 4, 1801, President Jefferson held a reception in the Blue Room at the White House which was attended by about one hundred guests. Jefferson introduced the custom of having the guests shake hands instead of bowing stiffly, as had been the custom under Presidents Washington and Adams.

JEFFERSON SUBMITTED ANNUAL ADDRESS IN WRITING

When Thomas Jefferson prepared his first annual message to Congress, he sent it to that body on December 8, 1801, instead of addressing both houses in person as Washington and Adams had done. On the same date, he wrote the presiding officer of each house. The following letter was included with the message for the Senate.

Sir:

The circumstances under which we find ourselves at this place rendering inconvenient the mode heretofore practiced of making by personal address the first communications between the legislative and executive branches, I have adopted that by

message, as used on all subsequent occasions through the session. In doing this I have had principal regard to the convenience of the Legislature, to the economy of their time, to their relief from the embarrassment of immediate answers on subjects not yet fully before them, and to the benefits thence resulting to the public affairs. Trusting that a procedure founded in these motives will meet their approbation, I beg leave through you, sir, to communicate the inclosed message, with the documents accompanying it, to the honorable the Senate, and pray you to accept for yourself and them the homage of my high respect and consideration.

TH. JEFFERSON

CHEESE PRESENTED TO JEFFERSON

On January 1, 1802, a cart pulled by six horses delivered a 1,235-pound cheese made at West Chester, Mass., to the White House. It was addressed, "The greatest cheese in America for the greatest man in America."

UNITED STATES DOUBLED ITS AREA

The Louisiana Purchase contract, dated April 30, 1803, and signed on May 2, 1803, increased the territory of the United States by approximately 846,000 square miles, practically doubling the area of the nation. Jefferson bought from Napoleon an area which was to become the entire states or substantial parts of Arkansas, Colorado, Iowa, Kansas, Louisiana, Minnesota, Missouri, Montana, Nebraska, North Dakota, Oklahoma, South Dakota, and Wyoming. The purchase price was $11,250,000, and the United States also assumed claims of Americans against France estimated at about $3,750,000.

TWELFTH AMENDMENT ENACTED

The Twelfth Amendment to the Constitution, altering the method of electing the President and the Vice President by the electoral college, was passed by Congress on December 9, 1803 and was proposed to the legislatures of the several states on December 12, 1803. Ratified by all the states except Connecticut,

Delaware, Massachusetts, and New Hampshire, it was declared ratified by the Secretary of State on September 25, 1804.

The text of the amendment follows:

The electors shall meet in their respective states and vote by ballot for President and Vice-President, one of whom, at least, shall not be an inhabitant of the same state with themselves; they shall name in their ballots the persons voted for as President, and in distinct ballots the person voted for as Vice-President, and they shall make distinct lists of all persons voted for as President, and of all persons voted for as Vice-President, and of the number of votes for each, which lists they shall sign and certify, and transmit sealed to the seat of the government of the United States directed to the President of the Senate;—The President of the Senate shall, in presence of the Senate and House of Representatives, open all the certificates and the votes shall then be counted;—The person having the greatest number of votes for President, shall be the President, if such number be a majority of the whole number of Electors appointed; and if no person have such majority, then from the persons having the highest numbers not exceeding three on the list of those voted for as President, the House of Representatives shall choose immediately, by ballot, the President. But in choosing the President, the votes shall be taken by states, the representation from each state having one vote; a quorum for this purpose shall consist of a member or members from two-thirds of the states, and a majority of all the states shall be necessary to a choice. (And if the House of Representatives shall not choose a President whenever the right of choice shall devolve upon them, before the fourth day of March next following, then the Vice-President shall act as President, as in the case of the death or other constitutional disability of the President.) The person having the greatest number of votes as Vice-President, shall be the Vice-President, if such number be a majority of the whole number of Electors appointed, and if no person have a majority, then from the two highest numbers on the list, the Senate shall choose the Vice-President; a quorum for the purpose shall consist of two-thirds of the whole number of Senators, and a majority of the whole number shall be necessary to a choice. But no person constitutionally ineligible to the office of President shall be eligible to that of Vice-President of the United States.

Declaration of Independence *by John Trumbull*

JEFFERSON ASSERTED PRESIDENT'S IMMUNITY TO COURTS

The lawyers defending Aaron Burr, who had been indicted for high treason, attempted to issue a *duces tecum* subpoena on June 10, 1807, on President Jefferson. In a letter to United States Attorney George Hay, dated June 20, 1807, President Jefferson wrote:

Let us apply the Judge's own doctrine to the case of himself and his brethren. The Sheriff of Henrico summons him from the bench to quell a riot somewhere in his county. The Federal judge is by the general law a part of the *posse* of the state sheriff. Would the judge abandon major duties to perform lesser ones? Again, the court of Orleans or Maine commands by subpoenas the attendance of all judges of the Supreme Court. Would they abandon their posts as judges and the interest of millions committed to them to serve the purposes of a single individual? The leading principle of our constitution is the independence of the legislature, executive and judiciary of each other; and none are more jealous of this than the judiciary. But would the executive be independent of the judiciary if he were subject to the commands of the latter and to imprisonment for disobedience; if the several courts could bandy him from pillar to post, keep him constantly trudging from north to south, and east to west, and withdraw him entirely from his constitutional duties?

JEFFERSON SIGNED FIRST EMBARGO ACT

President Jefferson signed the first embargo act. It was passed December 22, 1807 (2 Stat. L. 451), by a vote of 82 to 44. Intended to prevent the United States from being drawn into the war between Britain and France, the act placed "an embargo on all ships and vessels in the ports and harbors of the United States" and required all American ships to refrain from international commerce. The act, signed by President Jefferson, stopped all foreign trade. It was repealed on March 1, 1809. A later act was substituted which stopped trade with England and France.

JEFFERSON WROTE HIS OWN EPITAPH

Thomas Jefferson wrote the epitaph to be placed over his grave. He made no mention of his presidency. The inscription reads: "Here was buried Thomas Jefferson, author of the Declaration of American Independence, of the statute of Virginia for religious freedom, and father of the University of Virginia."

FIRST CHILD BORN IN THE WHITE HOUSE

James Madison Randolph, the grandson of President Thomas Jefferson, was the first child born in the White House. He was born January 17, 1806, and died January 23, 1834. His parents were Thomas Mann Randolph and Martha Jefferson Randolph, the daughter of President Jefferson.

FURTHER READING

Bernstein, R. B. *Thomas Jefferson.* 2003.

Boorstin, Daniel J. *The Lost World of Thomas Jefferson.* 1960.

Bowers, Claude G. *Jefferson in Power.* 1936.

———. *Jefferson and Hamilton.* 1953.

Ellis, Joseph J. *American Sphinx: The Character of Thomas Jefferson.* 1997.

Foner, Philip S., ed. *Basic Writings of Thomas Jefferson.* 1944.

Parton, James. *Life of Thomas Jefferson.* 1971.

Peterson, Merrill D. *The Jefferson Image in the American Mind.* 1960.

———. *Thomas Jefferson and the New Nation.* 1970.

Courtesy of The Library of Congress

James Madison

Date of birth—Mar. 16, 1751

Place of birth—Port Conway, Va.

Education—Attended Donald Robertson's school, King and Queen County, Va; tutored by Rev. Thomas Martin at home; College of New Jersey, now Princeton University, Princeton, N.J., bachelor's degree, Sept. 25, 1771, and postgraduate studies in Hebrew and philosophy, 1771–1772; intermittent private law studies

Religion—Episcopalian

Ancestry—English

Career—Lawyer, delegate to state constitutional convention, state legislator, member of state council and executive council, delegate to Continental Congress, delegate to Constitutional Convention, chief author of the Constitution, U.S. congressman, author of the Virginia Resolutions, U.S. Secretary of State

Political party—Democratic-Republican

State represented—Virginia

Term of office—Mar. 4, 1809–Mar. 4, 1817

Term served—8 years

Administration—6th, 7th

Congresses—11th, 12th, 13th, 14th

Age at inauguration—57 years, 353 days

Lived after term—19 years, 116 days

Occupation after term—Rector, University of Virginia; delegate to state constitutional convention

Date of death—June 28, 1836

Age at death—85 years, 104 days

Place of death—Montpelier, near Charlottesville, Va.

Burial place—Family plot, Montpelier, Va.

FAMILY

FATHER

Name—James Madison

Date of birth—Mar. 27, 1723

Marriage—Nelly Rose Conway, Sept. 15, 1749

Occupation—Farmer, planter, commander of King's militia; church vestryman, tax collector, sheriff, city lieutenant, county magistrate, justice of the peace; active in Revolution

Date of death—Feb. 27, 1801

Age at death—77 years, 337 days

MOTHER

Name at birth—Nelly Rose Conway

Date of birth—Jan. 9, 1731

Marriage—James Madison, Sept. 15, 1749

Date of death—Feb. 11, 1829

Age at death—98 years, 33 days

SIBLINGS

James Madison was the oldest of twelve children.

Children of James Madison and Nelly Rose Conway Madison

James Madison, b. Mar. 16, 1751, d. June 28, 1836

Francis Madison, b. June 18, 1753

Ambrose Madison, b. Jan. 27, 1755, d. Oct. 1793

Catlett Madison, b. Feb. 10, 1758, d. Mar. 18, 1758

Nelly Conway Madison, b. Feb. 14, 1760, d. 1802

William Madison, b. May 5, 1752, d. July 20, 1843

Sarah Madison, b. Aug. 17, 1764

Elizabeth Madison, b. Feb. 19, 1768

Reuben Madison, b. Sept. 19, 1771
Frances Taylor Madison, b. Oct. 4, 1774
—— Madison
Eli Madison
One child stillborn

MARRIAGE

Married—Dorothea ("Dolley") Dandridge Payne

Date of marriage—Sept. 15, 1794

Place of marriage—Harewood, Jefferson County, Va.

Age of wife at marriage—26 years, 118 days

Age of husband at marriage—43 years, 183 days

Years married—41 years, 286 days

CHILDREN

None

THE PRESIDENT'S WIFE

Name at birth—Dorothea ("Dolley") Dandridge

Date of birth—May 20, 1768

Place of birth—Area now in Guilford County, N.C.

Mother—Mary Coles Payne

Father—John Payne

Father's occupation—Farmer, planter

First marriage—John Todd, Jan. 7, 1790, Philadelphia, Pa. (d. 1793)

Second marriage—James Madison, Sept. 15, 1794, Jefferson County, Va.

Children from first marriage—John Payne Todd, 1792 (d. 1852); William Temple Todd, 1793 (d. 1793)

Children from second marriage—None

Date of death—July 12, 1849

Age at death—81 years, 53 days

Place of death—Washington, D.C.

Burial place—Montpelier, near Charlottesville, Va.

Years younger than the President—17 years, 65 days

Years she survived the President—13 years, 14 days

Dolley Madison, wife of James Madison

THE FIRST LADY

On March 4, 1809, Dolley Madison became the first First Lady to attend her husband's inauguration and the first to preside over the inaugural ball.

Mrs. Madison had a warm, vivacious personality and was an extraordinarily popular member of Washington society. She arrived at the White House with a fund of experience, having often served as hostess for the widowed President Jefferson.

MRS. MADISON VOTED SEAT IN HOUSE OF REPRESENTATIVES

When the elderly Dolley Madison was observed seated in the visitors' gallery of the House of Representatives, Romulus Saunders, a representative from North Carolina, introduced a resolution to grant Mrs. Madison a seat within the House. The measure was immediately and unanimously passed.

The widow of President Madison wrote a letter dated January 9, 1844, which was read in the House the following day. She stated:

Permit me to thank you, gentlemen, as the Committee on the part of the House of Representatives, for the great gratification you have this day conferred on me, by the delivery of the favor from that honorable body allowing me a seat within its hall. I shall be ever proud to recollect it, as a token of their remembrance, collectively and individually, of one who had gone before us.

IMPORTANT DATES IN THE PRESIDENT'S LIFE

1763–1767, attended Donald Robertson's school, King and Queen County, Va.

1767–1768, private instruction from the Reverend Thomas Martin

1769–1772, student at Princeton (graduated 1771); then took one-year post-graduate course

1772–1774, in ill health, continued studies at home

Dec. 1774, member of "Committee of Safety"

Oct. 1775, commissioned a colonel in the Orange County militia; brief service consisted of drilling, target practice, and recruiting

May 6, 1776, delegate to Williamsburg convention which declared for independence and set up state government

1776, drafted Virginia guarantee of religious liberty and helped write state constitution

1776–1777, member of Virginia legislature

1777, elected to Virginia State Council

Jan. 14, 1778, member of executive council to direct Virginia's activities in the Revolution

Dec. 14, 1779, elected by Virginia legislature to Continental Congress

Mar. 20, 1780–Feb. 25, 1783, member of Continental Congress

1784–1786, member of Virginia legislature

1786–1788, member of Continental Congress

Feb.–Apr. 1787, attended Congress at New York

May 2, 1787, left for Federal Convention at Philadelphia where he proposed the "Virginia Plan"

Sept. 1787, began writing essays on constitutional government for *The Federalist*

June 2, 1788, member of Virginia Ratification Convention

Mar. 4, 1789–Mar. 3, 1797, U.S. House of Representatives (from Virginia)

1794, declined Washington's invitation to join mission to France and position as Secretary of State

1799–1800, member of Virginia legislature

May 2, 1801–Mar. 3, 1809, Secretary of State under Jefferson

Mar. 4, 1809–Mar. 4, 1813, President (1st term)

Mar. 4, 1813–Mar. 4, 1817, President (2nd term)

1817, retired to estate at Montpelier, Va.

1826, rector, University of Virginia

1829, delegate to Virginia Constitutional Convention

ELECTIONS

THE ELECTION OF 1808

After he had served two terms (1801–1809) as President, Jefferson carried out the policy established by George Washington and refused to be a candidate for a third term. Jefferson favored James Monroe of Virginia as his successor, but the Democratic-Republican caucus decided in favor of James Madison, also of Virginia.

The Federalists, again without a congressional caucus, put up the same candidate, Charles Cotesworth Pinckney of South Carolina, whom they had unsuccessfully run in 1804.

For the vice presidency, the Democratic-Republican votes were split among four candidates: George Clinton of New York (who had served under Jefferson), John Langdon of New Hampshire, James Madison, and James Monroe.

The Federalist candidate for the vice presidency was Rufus King of New York, who had been Pinckney's running mate in 1804.

The presidential electors cast their ballots in their respective states on December 7, 1808. The results were informally tallied and were announced in newspapers on January 4, 1809, several weeks before the official count by Congress.

1808 ELECTORAL VOTE

There were 175 electoral votes from 17 states.

Madison received 69.71 percent (122 votes—12 states) as follows: Ga. 6; Ky. 7; Md. 9 (of the 11 votes); N.J. 8; N.Y. 13 (of the 19 votes); N.C. 11 (of the 14 votes); Ohio 3; Pa. 20; S.C. 10; Tenn. 5; Vt. 6; Va. 24.

Pinckney received 26.86 percent (47 votes—5 states) as follows: Conn. 9; Del. 3; Md. 2 (of the 11 votes); Mass. 19; N.H. 7; N.C. 3 (of the 14 votes); R.I. 4.

Clinton received 3.43 percent (6 votes—of the 19 N.Y. votes).

For the vice presidency Clinton received 113 votes as follows: Ga. 6; Ky. 7; Md. 9 (of the 11 votes); N.J. 8; N.Y. 13 (of the 19 votes); N.C. 11 (of the 14 votes); Pa. 20; S.C. 10; Tenn. 5; Va. 24.

King, the Federalist, received 47 votes as follows: Conn. 9; Del. 3; Md. 2 (of the 11 votes); Mass. 19; N.H. 7; N.C. 3 (of the 14 votes); R.I. 4.

The other Democratic-Republican candidates for the vice presidency received the following votes:

Langdon—Ohio 3; Vt. 6
Madison—N.Y. 3 (of the 19 votes)
Monroe—N.Y. 3 (of the 19 votes)

THE ELECTION OF 1812

After James Madison had served one term, the Democratic-Republicans in May 1812 chose to support him for a second term. George Clinton had died on April 20 while serving as Vice President and the party favored John Langdon of New Hampshire for that office. Langdon, however, declined to run because of his age (71), and Elbridge Gerry of Massachusetts was then selected for the vice presidency.

The Federalists in caucus at New York City decided to support the nomination of De Witt Clinton of New York and Jared Ingersoll of Pennsylvania.

The electors' sealed ballots were opened and counted by Congress on February 10, 1813.

1812 ELECTORAL VOTE

There were 217 electoral votes from 18 states.

Madison received 58.99 percent (128 votes—11 states) as follows: Ga. 8; Ky. 12; La. 3; Md. 6 (of the 11 votes); N.C. 15; Ohio 7; Pa. 25; S.C. 11; Tenn. 8; Vt. 8; Va. 25.

Clinton received 41.01 percent (89 votes—7 states) as follows: Conn. 9; Del. 4; Md. 5 (of the 11 votes); Mass. 22; N.H. 8; N.J. 8; N.Y. 29; R.I. 4.

Gerry received 131 votes for the vice presidency as follows: Ga. 8; Ky. 12; La. 3; Md. 6 (of the 11 votes); Mass. 2 (of the 22 votes); N.H. 1 (of the 8 votes); N.C. 15; Ohio 7; Pa. 25; S.C. 11; Tenn. 8; Vt. 8; Va. 25.

Ingersoll received 86 votes for the vice presidency as follows: Conn. 9; Del. 4; Md. 5 (of the 11 votes); Mass. 20 (of the 22 votes); N.H. 7 (of the 8 votes); N.J. 8; N.Y. 29; R.I. 4.

INAUGURATIONS

FIRST TERM

March 4, 1809

James Madison took the oath of office on Saturday, March 4, 1809. It was administered by Chief Justice John Marshall in the Chamber of the House of Representatives. Madison was the first President whose complete costume was made in the United States. He wore a jacket of oxford cloth which came from Hartford, Conn., and merino wool breeches fashioned from cloth made at the farm of Chancellor Robert R. Livingston of New York. He wore silk stockings and black shoes which were made in Massachusetts.

This was the first inauguration at which the First Lady was present.

The inaugural ball, held at Long's Hotel on Capitol Hill, was the first one at Washington, D.C. Dancing started at 7 P.M., and Dolley Madison presided.

SECOND TERM

March 4, 1813

Madison took his second oath of office on Thursday, March 4, 1813. It was administered by Chief Justice John Marshall in the Chamber of the House of Representatives. The inaugural ball was held at Long's Hotel.

THE VICE PRESIDENTS

FIRST TERM

Name—George Clinton (4th V.P.)

Date of birth—July 26, 1739

Place of birth—Little Britain, N.Y.

Political party—Democratic-Republican

State represented—New York

Term of office—Mar. 4, 1809–Apr. 20, 1812

Age at inauguration—69 years, 221 days

Occupation after term—Died in office, Apr. 20, 1812

Date of death—Apr. 20, 1812

Age at death—72 years, 268 days

Place of death—Washington, D.C.

Burial place—Kingston, N.Y.

ADDITIONAL DATA ON CLINTON

1755, admitted to the bar; practiced in Little Britain, N.Y.

1758, lieutenant of Rangers in expedition against Fort Frontenac

1759, clerk of Court of Common Pleas

1765, district attorney; surveyor of New Windsor, N.Y.

1768, New York State Assembly

Courtesy of The Library of Congress

George Clinton, first Vice President to James Madison

1774, New York Committee of Correspondence

May 13, 1775–July 8, 1776, Continental Congress

1775, brigadier general of militia, appointed by George Washington

Mar. 25, 1777, brigadier general, appointed by Congress

1777–1795, governor of New York

1788, president of state convention which ratified federal Constitution

1796, unsuccessful candidate for Vice President

1800–1801, New York State Assembly

1801–1804, governor of New York

Mar. 4, 1805–Mar. 4, 1809, Vice President under Thomas Jefferson

Mar. 4, 1809–Apr. 20, 1812, Vice President under James Madison

VICE PRESIDENT CLINTON UNSUCCESSFUL IN THREE PREVIOUS ELECTIONS

George Clinton of New York, who was elected Vice President under Thomas Jefferson (second term, 1805–1809) and under James Madison (first term, 1809–1813), had been unsuccessful in three previous elections. In 1789 he received three votes for the vice presidency; in 1793 he received fifty electoral votes; and in 1797 he received seven electoral votes.

SECOND TERM

Name—Elbridge Gerry (5th V.P.)

Date of birth—July 17, 1744

Place of birth—Marblehead, Mass.

Political party—Democratic-Republican

State represented—Massachusetts

Term of office—Mar. 4, 1813–Nov. 23, 1814

Age at inauguration—68 years, 230 days

Occupation after term—Died in office

Date of death—Nov. 23, 1814

Age at death—70 years, 129 days

Place of death—Washington, D.C.

Burial place—Washington, D.C.

ADDITIONAL DATA ON GERRY

1762, graduated from Harvard College, Cambridge, Mass.

1772–1775, colonial House of Representatives

1776–1781, member of Continental Congress

1776, signer of Declaration of Independence

1782–1785, member of Continental Congress

1787, delegate to Constitutional Convention at Philadelphia

Mar. 4, 1789–Mar. 3, 1793, U.S. House of Representatives (from Massachusetts)

1797, diplomatic mission to France with Marshall and Pinckney

1801, unsuccessful candidate for governor of Massachusetts

1810–1811, governor of Massachusetts

1812, unsuccessful candidate for reelection as governor

Mar. 4, 1813–Nov. 23, 1814, Vice President under James Madison

THE GERRYMANDER

The only Vice President whose name has been adopted as part of the English language was Elbridge Gerry. On February 11, 1812, when he was the governor of the Commonwealth of Massachusetts, he signed an act which rearranged the senatorial districts so that the Federalists were massed together in one or two districts, leaving the other districts controlled by a safe majority of Democratic-Republicans.

It is claimed that when Gilbert Stuart, the painter, saw a colored map of the redistricting hanging in the Boston office of Benjamin Russell, Federalist editor of the *Columbian Centinel,* he added a few strokes and said, "This will do for a salamander." Russell said, "Call it a gerrymander." Thus the word was

Courtesy of The Library of Congress

Eldridge Gery, second Vice President to Madison

born which became a Federalist war cry, even though Governor Gerry had not sponsored the bill and had signed it reluctantly.

BOTH OF MADISON'S VICE PRESIDENTS DIED IN OFFICE

James Madison was the only President whose administration suffered the death of two Vice Presidents.

George Clinton, who had served four years during the second term of Thomas Jefferson and 3 years and 47 days during the first term of James Madison, died in Washington, D.C., on April 20, 1812, at the age of 72.

On May 12, 1812, a Democratic-Republican caucus decided upon Senator John Langdon of New Hampshire as the party's vice presidential nominee. He received 64 of the 82 votes cast, but refused to accept the nomination because of his age (71). A second caucus nominated Elbridge Gerry of Massachusetts, who received 74 of the 77 votes cast. Gerry, who was over 68 and thus only 3 years younger than Langdon, was elected Vice President to serve during Madison's second term, 1813–1817. But he did not live to complete the term. He died on November 23, 1814, at the age of 70, having served one year and 264 days. (Langdon, who died September 18, 1819, at the age of 78, survived Gerry by almost five years.)

VICE PRESIDENT BURIED AT WASHINGTON, D.C.

Elbridge Gerry was the only Vice President to be buried at Washington, D.C. He was buried in the Washington Parish Burial Ground, better known as the Congressional Cemetery, comprising about thirty acres of ground on the north bank of the Anacostia River.

CABINET

FIRST TERM

March 4, 1809–March 3, 1813

State—Robert Smith, Md., Mar. 6, 1809; James Monroe, Va., Apr. 2, 1811; entered upon duties Apr. 6, 1811

Treasury—Albert Gallatin, Pa., continued from preceding administration

War—John Smith (chief clerk), ad interim, continued from preceding administration; William Eustis, Mass., Mar. 7, 1809; entered upon duties Apr. 8, 1809; served to Dec. 31, 1812; James Monroe, Va. (Secretary of State), ad interim Jan. 1, 1813; John Armstrong, N.Y., Jan. 13, 1813; entered upon duties Feb. 5, 1813

Attorney General—Caesar Augustus Rodney, Del., continued from preceding administration, resigned Dec. 5, 1811; William Pinkney, Md., Dec. 11, 1811; entered upon duties Jan. 6, 1812

Postmaster General—Gideon Granger, Conn., continued from preceding administration

Navy—Robert Smith, Md., continued from preceding administration; Charles Washington Goldsborough (chief clerk), ad interim Mar. 8, 1809; Paul Hamilton, S.C., Mar. 7, 1809; entered upon duties May 15, 1809; served to Dec. 31, 1812; Charles Washington Goldsborough (chief clerk), ad interim Jan. 7, 1813, to Jan. 18, 1813; William Jones, Pa., Jan. 12, 1813; entered upon duties Jan. 19, 1813

SECOND TERM

March 4, 1813–March 3, 1817

State—James Monroe, Va., continued from preceding administration; James Monroe (Secretary of War), ad interim Oct. 1, 1814; James Monroe, Va., Feb. 28, 1815

Treasury—Albert Gallatin, Pa., continued from preceding administration; William Jones, Pa. (Secretary of the Navy), performed the duties of the Secretary of the Treasury during the absence of Gallatin in Europe (Apr. 21, 1813 to Feb. 9, 1814); George Washington Campbell, Tenn., Feb. 9, 1814; Alexander James Dallas, Pa., Oct. 6, 1814; entered upon duties Oct. 14, 1814; William Harris Crawford, Ga., Oct. 22, 1816

War—John Armstrong, N.Y., continued from preceding administration; James Monroe, Va. (Secretary of State), ad interim Aug. 30, 1814; James Monroe, Sept. 27, 1814; entered upon duties Oct. 1, 1814; James Monroe (Secretary of State), ad interim Mar. 1, 1815; Alexander James Dallas, Pa. (Secretary of the Treasury), ad interim Mar. 14, 1815, to Aug. 8, 1815; William Harris Crawford, Ga., Aug. 1, 1815; entered upon duties Aug. 8, 1815; George Graham (chief clerk), ad interim Oct. 22, 1816 to close of administration

Attorney General—William Pinkney, Md., continued from preceding administration; Richard Rush, Pa., Feb. 10, 1814, entered upon duties Feb. 11, 1814

Postmaster General—Gideon Granger, Conn., continued from preceding administration; Return Jonathan Meigs, Jr., Ohio, Mar. 17, 1814; entered upon duties Apr. 11, 1814

Navy—William Jones, Pa., continued from preceding administration; Benjamin Homans (chief clerk), ad interim Dec. 2, 1814; Benjamin Williams Crowninshield, Mass., Dec. 19, 1814; entered upon duties Jan. 16, 1815

CONGRESS

ELEVENTH CONGRESS

March 4, 1809–March 3, 1811

First session—May 22, 1809–June 28, 1809 (38 days)

Second session—Nov. 27, 1809–May 1, 1810 (156 days)

Third session—Dec. 3, 1810–Mar. 3, 1811 (91 days)

Special session of the Senate—Mar. 4, 1809–Mar. 7, 180 (4 days)

Vice President—George Clinton, N.Y.

President pro tempore of the Senate —Andrew Gregg, Pa., elected June 26, 1809; John Gaillard, S.C., elected Feb. 28, 1810, reelected Apr. 17, 1810; John Pope, Ky., elected Feb. 23, 1811

Secretary of the Senate—Samuel Allyne Otis, Mass.

Speaker of the House—Joseph Bradley Varnum, Mass., reelected May 22, 1809

Clerk of the House—Patrick Magruder, Md., reelected May 22, 1809

TWELFTH CONGRESS

March 4, 1811–March 3, 1813

First session—Nov. 4, 1811–July 6, 1812 (245 days)

Second session—Nov. 2, 1812–Mar. 3, 1813 (122 days)

Vice President—George Clinton, N.Y., died Apr. 20, 1812

President pro tempore of the Senate —William Harris Crawford, Ga., elected Mar. 24, 1812

Secretary of the Senate—Samuel Allyne Otis, Mass.

Speaker of the House—Henry Clay, Ky., elected Nov. 4, 1811

Clerk of the House—Patrick Magruder, Md., reelected Nov. 4, 1811

THIRTEENTH CONGRESS

March 4, 1813–March 3, 1815

First session—May 24, 1813–Aug. 2, 1813 (71 days)

Second session—Dec. 6, 1813–Apr. 18, 1814 (134 days)

Third session—Sept. 19, 1814–Mar. 3, 1815 (166 days)

Vice President—Elbridge Gerry, Mass., died Nov. 23, 1814

President pro tempore of the Senate —Joseph Bradley Varnum, Mass., elected Dec. 6, 1813; John Gaillard, S.C., elected Apr. 18, 1814; Nov. 25, 1814, upon the death of Vice President Elbridge Gerry

Secretary of the Senate—Samuel Allyne Otis, Mass., died Apr. 22, 1814; Charles Cutts, N.H., elected Oct. 11, 1814

Speaker of the House—Henry Clay, Ky., reelected May 24, 1813; resigned from Congress Jan. 19, 1814; Langdon Cheves, S.C., elected Jan. 19, 1814

Clerk of the House—Patrick Magruder, Md., reelected May 24, 1813; resigned Jan. 28, 1815; Thomas Dougherty, Ky., elected Jan. 30, 1815

FOURTEENTH CONGRESS

March 4, 1815–March 3, 1817

First session—Dec. 4, 1815–Apr. 30, 1816 (148 days)

Second session—Dec. 2, 1816–Mar. 3, 1817 (92 days)

Vice President—Elbridge Gerry died during session of preceding Congress

President pro tempore of the Senate —John Gaillard, S.C.

Secretary of the Senate—Charles Cutts, N.H.

Speaker of the House—Henry Clay, Ky., elected Dec. 4, 1815

Clerk of the House—Thomas Dougherty, Ky., reelected Dec. 4, 1815

APPOINTMENTS TO THE SUPREME COURT

Associate Justices

Levi Lincoln, Mass., Jan. 7, 1811 (declined to serve)

John Quincy Adams, Mass., Feb. 22, 1811 (declined to serve)

Joseph Story, Mass., Nov. 18, 1811 (replaced William Cushing)

Gabriel Duvall, Md., Nov. 18, 1811 (replaced Samuel Chase)

IMPORTANT DATES IN THE PRESIDENCY

Sept. 30, 1809, General W. H. Harrison negotiated treaty with Indians for three million acres

1810–1811, British and French naval blockades during Napoleonic wars continued to harass American shipping

Nov. 7, 1811, General W. H. Harrison defeated Indian attackers at battle of Tippecanoe

Jan. 12, 1812, arrival in New Orleans, La., of first steamboat to travel from Pittsburgh, Pa., to New Orleans

Mar. 4, 1812, first war bond issue authorized

Apr. 20, 1812, death of George Clinton, first Vice President to die in office

Apr. 30, 1812, Louisiana admitted as the 18th state

June 4, 1812, Missouri Territory organized

June 18, 1812, war declared against Great Britain

June 30, 1812, first interest-bearing treasury notes authorized

Aug. 16, 1812, without firing a shot, General William Hull surrendered Detroit and Michigan Territory to the British under General Brock

Aug. 19, 1812, *Constitution,* under Captain Isaac Hull, defeated and burned the British *Guerrière* off Nova Scotia

Sept. 4, 1812, Captain Zachary Taylor defended Fort Harrison against Indian attack

Oct. 25, 1812, *United States,* under Captain Decatur, defeated the *Macedonian*

Mar. 25, 1813, *Essex,* on cruise around Cape Horn, engaged in first U.S. naval encounter in the Pacific Ocean

June 1, 1813, Commander James Lawrence, who said "Don't give up the ship," fatally wounded in combat between the *Chesapeake* and the British warship *Shannon*

Sept. 10, 1813, Oliver Hazard Perry's naval victory on Lake Erie

Aug. 24, 1814, British captured Washington, D.C.

Sept. 11, 1814, defeat of British on Lake Champlain

Sept. 13, 1814, "Star Spangled Banner" composed by Francis Scott Key as he watched the British attack on Fort McHenry at Baltimore

Dec. 24, 1814, peace treaty signed with Great Britain

1815, treaties with Algiers, Tripoli, and Tunis

Jan. 8, 1815, battle of New Orleans

Jan. 30, 1815, Thomas Jefferson's library purchased for Library of Congress

July 4, 1815, cornerstone of first monument to George Washington laid at Baltimore, Md.

1815, public debt of the United States exceeded $100 million for the first time

Dec. 11, 1816, Indiana admitted as the 19th state

Feb. 5, 1817, first gas light company incorporated, Baltimore, Md.

ADDITIONAL DATA ON MADISON

JAMES MADISON

—was the third President born in Virginia.

—was the third President whose mother was alive when he was inaugurated.

—was the third President to marry a widow.

—was the first President who had been a Congressman.

—was the first President to lead the nation in war (1812).

—was the first President regularly to wear trousers instead of knee breeches.

—was the last surviving signer of the Constitution.

CONSCIENCE FUND ESTABLISHED

In 1811, during Madison's administration, the "Conscience Fund" was started by an unknown person who sent an anonymous letter containing five dollars, since he had, he claimed, defrauded the government of that sum. Other deposits received that year increased the total to $250. No further deposits were received until 1827 when $6 was forwarded anonymously. For statistical and accounting purposes, the funds are listed by the government as "miscellaneous receipts."

WHITE HOUSE WEDDING

The first wedding in the White House took place March 29, 1812, when Mrs. Lucy Payne Washington, a sister of Mrs. James Madison and the widow of George Steptoe Washington, was married to Justice Thomas Todd of the United States Supreme Court.

JEWISH DIPLOMATIC REPRESENTATIVE APPOINTED

During James Madison's administration, Mordecai Manuel Noah was appointed United States Consul with diplomatic powers to Tunis. He served from 1813 to 1816 and was the first Jewish diplomatic representative of the United States.

MADISON AT SCENE OF BATTLE

President James Madison was the first President to face enemy gunfire while in office and the first and only President to exercise in battle his authority as commander in chief.

During the War of 1812, a force of 5,400 British troops commanded by Major General Robert Ross landed at Benedict, Md., on the Patuxent River on August 19, 1814, and advanced on the American capital, 40 miles to the northwest. Five days later, at Bladensburg, Md., the British encountered and completely routed an American force of militia and marines under the incompetent command of Major General William H. Winder. President James Madison was at the scene of battle and at one point took command of the only American force left on the field, Commodore Joshua Barney's naval battery, known as "Barney's Battery," in an unsuccessful attempt to forestall the capture of Washington by the British.

MADISON FLED FROM THE CAPITAL

On August 24, 1814, the British entered Washington, D.C., and found the officials of the government had fled. On August 24 and 25 the British burned the Capitol, the White House, and numerous other buildings. The damage might have been more extensive had the British known how completely the defenders had been routed. Unable to understand the lack of defense at the Capitol, the British officers feared that they were being drawn too far away from their ships and supplies and were walking into a trap. Afraid of being cut off, the British force withdrew to their base.

MADISON MOVED TO OCTAGON HOUSE

After the British had burned the White House in 1814, Colonel John Taylor dispatched a courier offering President Madison the use of his home, the Octagon House. For more than a year, Madison made it his official residence. The building, known as the

Courtesy of The Library of Congress

The Octagon House, Washington, D.C.

Octagon House, was not octagon-shaped. It had two rectangular wings connected by a circular tower.

MRS. MADISON'S ACCOUNT OF THE BRITISH INVASION OF WASHINGTON

One of the most anxious periods in the life of a First Lady is described by Dolley Madison in a letter to her sister:
Tuesday, August 23, 1814
Dear Sister:
My husband left me yesterday to join General Winder. He enquired anxiously whether I had the courage or firmness to remain in the President's House until his return, on the morrow, or succeeding day, and on my assurance that I had no fear but for him and the success of our army, he left me, beseeching me to take care of myself and of the Cabinet papers, public and private. I have since received two dispatches from him, written with a pencil; the last is alarming, because he desires that I should be ready at a moment's warning, to enter my carriage and leave the city; that the enemy seemed stronger than had been reported, and that it might happen that they would reach the city with intention to destroy it. . . . I am accordingly ready; I have pressed as many Cabinet papers into trunks as to fill one carriage; our private property must be sacrificed, as it is impossible to procure wagons for its transportation. I am determined not to go myself, until I see Mr. Madison safe, and he can accompany me—as I hear of much hostility toward him. . . . Disaffection stalks around us. My friends and acquaintances are all gone, even Colonel C. with his hundred men, who were stationed as a guard in this enclosure. . . . French John (a faithful domestic) with his usual activity and resolution offers to spike the cannon at the gate, and lay a train of powder which would blow up the British, should they enter the house. To the last proposition, I positively objected, without being able, however, to make him understand why all advantages in war may not be taken.
Wednesday morning, twelve o'clock—
Since sunrise, I have been turning my spyglass in every direction and watching with unwearied anxiety, hoping to discover the approach of my dear husband and his friends; but, alas, I can descry only groups of military

wandering in all direction, as if there was a lack of arms, or of spirits, to fight for their own firesides.

Three o'clock—

Will you believe it, my sister, we have had a battle, or a skirmish, near Bladensburg, and I am still here within sound of the cannon! Mr. Madison comes not; may God protect him! Two messengers, covered with dust, come to bid me fly; but I wait for him. . . . At this late hour a wagon has been procured; I have filled it with the plate and most valuable portable articles belonging to the house; whether it will reach its destination, the Bank of Maryland, or fall into the hands of British soldiery, events must determine. Our kind friend, Mr. Carroll, has come to hasten my departure, and is in a very bad humor with me because I insist on waiting until the large picture of General Washington is secured: and it requires to be unscrewed from the wall. This process was found too tedious for these perilous moments; I have ordered the frame to be broken and the canvas taken out; it is done, and the precious portrait placed in the hands of two gentlemen of New York for safe-keeping. And now, dear sister, I must leave this house or the retreating army will make me a prisoner in it, by filling up the road I am directed to take. When I shall again write to you, or where I shall be tomorrow, I cannot tell!

FURTHER READING

Banning, Lance. *The Sacred Fire of Liberty.* 1995.

Brant, Irving. *James Madison and American Nationalism.* 1968.

———. *The Fourth President.* 1970.

Ketchum, Ralph L. *James Madison.* 1971.

Koch, Adrienne. *Jefferson and Madison.* 1950.

Labunski, Richard. *James Madison and the Struggle for the Bill of Rights.* 2006.

Padover, Saul K., ed. *The Complete Madison: His Basic Writings.* 1971.

Rakove, Jack N. *James Madison and the Creation of the American Republic.* 1990.

Stagg, J. C. A. *Mr. Madison's War.* 1983.

Courtesy of The Library of Congress

Drawing shows the ruins of the U.S. Capitol following British attempts to burn the building.

Courtesy of The Library of Congress

James Monroe

Date of birth—Apr. 28, 1758

Place of birth—Westmoreland County, Va.

Education—Campbelltown Academy, Washington Parish, Va.; College of William and Mary, Williamsburg, Va., 1774–1776; private law study under Thomas Jefferson

Religion—Episcopalian

Ancestry—Scottish

Career—Lawyer, officer in Continental Army, military commissioner of Virginia, state legislator, member of state council, delegate to Continental Congress, U.S. senator; minister to France, Great Britain, and Spain; governor of Virginia, Secretary of State, Secretary of War

Political party—Democratic-Republican

State represented—Virginia

Term of office—Mar. 4, 1817–Mar. 4, 1825

Term served—8 years

Administration—8th, 9th

Congresses—15th, 16th, 17th, 18th

Age at inauguration— 58 years, 310 days

Lived after term—6 years, 122 days

Occupation after term—Writer, regent of University of Virginia, chairman of state constitutional convention

Date of death—July 4, 1831

Age at death—73 years, 67 days

Place of death—New York, N.Y.

Burial place—Marble Cemetery, New York, N.Y.; removed in 1858 to Hollywood Cemetery, Richmond, Va.

FAMILY

FATHER

Name—Spence Monroe

Marriage—Elizabeth Jones, 1752

Occupation—Farmer, carpenter; circuit judge; active in Revolution

Date of death—1774

MOTHER

Name at birth—Elizabeth Jones

Marriage—Spence Monroe, 1752

SIBLINGS

James Monroe was the oldest of five children.

Children of Spence Monroe and Elizabeth Jones Monroe

James Monroe, b. Apr. 28, 1758, d. July 4, 1831

Andrew Monroe, d. 1826

Spence Monroe

Joseph Jones Monroe, b. 1764, d. Aug. 5, 1824

Elizabeth Monroe

MARRIAGE

Married—Elizabeth Kortright

Date of marriage—Feb. 16, 1786

Place of marriage—New York, N.Y.

Age of wife at marriage—17 years, 231 days

Age of husband at marriage—27 years, 294 days

Years married—44 years, 219 days

CHILDREN

Eliza Kortright Monroe, b. Dec. 1786; m. Oct. 17, 1808, George Hay; d. 1835, Paris, France

J. S. Monroe (son), b. May 1799; d. Sept. 28, 1801

Maria Hester Monroe, b. 1803; m. Mar. 9, 1820, Samuel Lawrence Gouverneur in White House, Washington, D.C.; d. 1850, Oak Hill, Va.

THE PRESIDENT'S WIFE

Name at birth—Elizabeth Kortright

Date of birth—June 30, 1768

Place of birth—New York, N.Y.

Mother—Hannah Aspinwall Kortright

Father—Captain Lawrence Kortright

Father's occupation—Former officer in British Army

Marriage—James Monroe, Feb. 16, 1786, New York, N.Y.

Children—Eliza Kortright Monroe, b. Dec. 1786, d. 1835; J. S. Monroe (son), b. May 1799, d. Sept. 28, 1801; Maria Hester Monroe, b. 1803, d. 1850

Date of death—Sept. 23, 1830

Age at death—62 years, 85 days

Place of death—Oak Hill, near Leesburg, Va.

Burial place—Richmond, Va.

Years younger than the President—10 years, 63 days

Years the President survived her—284 days

Courtesy of The Library of Congress

Elizabeth Monroe, wife of James Monroe

THE FIRST LADY

Mrs. Monroe had accompanied her husband to his posts in England and France and was familiar with political life. She became the First Lady in 1817 and was an amiable hostess. Her health failed in later years, however, and she secluded herself from the throng. She discontinued the custom of returning calls.

IMPORTANT DATES IN THE PRESIDENT'S LIFE

1776, left College of William and Mary to join the army

Sept. 28, 1775, second lieutenant, Third Virginia Regiment, under General Hugh Mercer

June 24, 1776, first lieutenant

Sept. 16, 1776, wounded at Battle of Harlem Heights, N.Y.

Oct. 28, 1776, fought at White Plains, N.Y.

Dec. 26, 1776, wounded at Trenton, N.J.; promoted to rank of captain by General George Washington for "bravery under fire"

Sept. 11, 1777, fought at Brandywine, Pa.

Oct. 4, 1777, fought at Germantown, Pa.

Nov. 20, 1777, volunteer aide with rank of major on staff of General Lord Stirling

June 28, 1778, fought at Monmouth, N.J.

1780, military commissioner for Virginia, with rank of lieutenant colonel (appointed by Governor Thomas Jefferson)

Dec. 20, 1780, resigned

1780, elected to Virginia Legislature

1781–1783, on Governor Jefferson's council

Oct. 21, 1782, member of Virginia House of Delegates

Dec. 13, 1783–1786, member of Continental Congress

17—, resumed study of law in office of Thomas Jefferson

Oct. 1786, admitted to the bar of the Courts of Appeal and Chancery; practiced at Fredericksburg, Va.

1786, member of Virginia Assembly

June 2, 1788, delegate to Virginia state convention to ratify the Federal Constitution

Nov. 9, 1790–May 27, 1794, U.S. Senate (from Virginia); sworn in Dec. 6, 1790

May 28, 1794–Dec. 30, 1796, minister plenipotentiary to France (appointed by Washington)

1799–1803, governor of Virginia

Jan. 12–July 12, 1803, minister plenipotentiary to France (appointed by Jefferson)

Apr. 18, 1803, minister plenipotentiary to England

Feb. 14, 1804, headed diplomatic mission to Spain

May 21, 1805, left Spanish court for London

May 12, 1806, commissioner to negotiate treaty with England

1808, returned to the United States

1810, member of Virginia Assembly

1811, governor of Virginia

Apr. 6, 1811–Mar. 3, 1817, Secretary of State under Madison

Aug. 30, 1814, Secretary of War, ad interim

Sept. 27, 1814, Secretary of War

Mar. 1, 1815, Secretary of War, ad interim

Mar. 4, 1817–Mar. 4, 1821, President (1st term)

Mar. 5, 1821–Mar. 4, 1825, President (2nd term)

Mar. 1825, retired to his farm at Loudoun County, Va.

1826, regent, University of Virginia, Charlottesville

Oct. 5, 1829, chairman of Virginia Constitutional Convention, Richmond

1831, moved to New York City

ELECTIONS

THE ELECTION OF 1816

After Madison had served two full terms, the Democratic-Republican party was divided between William Harris Crawford and James Monroe, the latter securing the party endorsement by a vote of 65 to 54. James Monroe's running mate was Daniel D. Tompkins of New York. Burr and other extremists denounced the caucus system. They declared that Virginia was trying to dominate the presidential succession.

The Federalists made no nominations but supported Rufus King of New York for the presidency. Their electoral vote for the vice presidency was split among four candidates— John Eager Howard of Maryland, James Ross of Pennsylvania, John Marshall of Virginia, and Robert Goodloe Harper of Maryland.

1816 ELECTORAL VOTE

There were 217 electoral votes from 19 states.

Monroe received 84.33 percent (183 votes— 16 states) as follows: Ga. 8; Ind. 3; Ky. 12; La. 3; Md. 8; N.H. 8; N.J. 8; N.Y. 29; N.C. 15; Ohio 8; Pa. 25; R.I. 4; S.C. 11; Tenn. 8; Vt. 8; Va. 25.

King received 15.67 percent (34 votes—3 states) as follows: Conn. 9; Del. 3; Mass. 22.

For the vice presidency Tompkins received 183 votes.

The Federalist candidates for the vice presidency received the following votes:

Howard—Mass. 22

Ross—Conn. 5 (of the 9 votes)

Marshall—Conn. 4 (of the 9 votes)

Harper—Del. 3

THE ELECTION OF 1820

James Monroe was so popular during his first term, 1817–1821, that an "era of good feeling" swept the nation, and the Federalist Party went into permanent eclipse. All of the 232 electors, with only one exception, voted for Monroe, the Democratic-Republican incumbent, for a second term. William Plumer, Sr., of New Hampshire, one of the electors, cast his vote for John Quincy Adams in protest against a unanimous election. He was not opposed to Monroe, but evidently felt that no one other than George Washington should have the honor of a unanimous election. (Some sources, however, maintain that he opposed the Virginia dynasty of presidents.)

The electoral vote for Vice President was split among five candidates: Daniel D. Tompkins of New York (seeking reelection), Richard Stockton of New Jersey, Daniel Rodney of Delaware, Robert Goodloe Harper of Maryland, and Richard Rush of Pennsylvania.

The number of electors chosen was 235, but three electors died and their respective states—Mississippi, Pennsylvania, and Tennessee—did not choose to replace them and as a result they failed to cast full electoral votes for President and Vice President. The electoral ballots were opened in Congress on February 14, 1821.

1820 ELECTORAL VOTE

There were 235 electoral votes from 24 states.

Monroe received 99.57 percent (231 votes—24 states) as follows: Ala. 3; Conn. 9; Del. 4; Ga. 8; Ill. 3; Ind. 3; Ky. 12; La. 3; Me. 9; Md. 11; Mass. 15; Miss. 2; Mo. 3; N.H. 7 (of the 8 votes); N.J. 8; N.Y. 29; N.C. 15; Ohio 8; Pa. 24; R.I. 4; S.C. 11; Tenn. 7; Vt. 8; Va. 25.

Adams received 43 percent (1 vote—of the 9 N.H. votes).

For the vice presidency Tompkins received 218 votes as follows: Ala. 3; Conn. 9; Ga. 8; Ill. 3; Ind. 3; Ky. 12; La. 3; Me. 9; Md. 10 (of the 11 votes); Mass. 7 (of the 15 votes); Miss. 2; Mo. 3; N.H. 7 (of the 8 votes); N.J. 8; N.Y. 29; N.C. 15; Ohio 8; Pa. 24; R.I. 4; S.C. 11; Tenn. 7; Vt. 8; Va. 25.

The other candidates for the vice presidency received the following votes:

Stockton—Mass. 8 (of the 15 votes)

Rodney—Del. 4

Harper—Md. 1 (of the 11 votes)

Rush—N.H. 1 (of the 8 votes)

INAUGURATIONS

FIRST TERM

March 4, 1817

James Monroe took his oath of office on Tuesday, March 4, 1817. It was administered by Chief Justice John Marshall on the platform erected on the east portico of the Capitol. As a result of a controversy between the Senate and the House of Representatives over the distribution of seats, it was decided that the inaugural be held outdoors. This was the first outdoor inaugural.

Monroe rode to the Capitol accompanied by an escort of citizens. After the ceremonies, he went to the Octagon House, at Eighteenth Street and New York Avenue, where he resided as the White House had been burned by the British during Madison's administration. He was accompanied by an escort of Marines, Georgia riflemen, artillerymen, and two companies of infantry from Alexandria, Va.

In the evening a reception was held at Davis' Hotel.

SECOND TERM

March 5, 1821

As March 4, 1821 fell on a Sunday, Monroe did not take office until Monday, March 5. Because of snow and rain, Monroe took his oath of office in the Chamber of the Hall of Representatives. The oath was administered to him by Chief Justice John Marshall. This was the first postponement of an inauguration.

The Marine Band played, introducing a new trend followed in all later inaugurations.

THE VICE PRESIDENT

Name—Daniel D. Tompkins (6th V.P.)

Date of birth—June 21, 1774

Place of birth—Fox Meadows (now Scarsdale), N.Y.

Political party—Democratic-Republican

State represented—New York

Term of office—Mar. 4, 1817–Mar. 4, 1825

Age at inauguration—42 years, 256 days

Occupation after term—Lawyer

Date of death—June 11, 1825

Age at death—50 years, 355 days

Place of death—Tompkinsville, Staten Island, N.Y.

Burial place—New York City

ADDITIONAL DATA ON TOMPKINS

1795, graduated from Columbia College

1797, admitted to bar; practiced in New York City

1801, delegate to New York State Constitutional Convention

1803, member of New York State Assembly

1804, elected to U.S. House of Representatives, but resigned before commencement of term to accept appointment as associate justice of New York Supreme Court

Courtesy of The Library of Congress

Daniel D. Tompkins, Vice President to James Monroe

1807, resigned from Supreme Court

1807–1817, governor of New York

Mar. 4, 1817–Mar. 4, 1825, Vice President under James Monroe

1821, president of New York State Constitutional Convention

CABINET

FIRST TERM

March 4, 1817–March 3, 1821

State—John Graham (chief clerk), ad interim Mar. 4, 1817; Richard Rush, Pa. (Attorney General), ad interim Mar. 10, 1817; John Quincy Adams, Mass., Mar. 5, 1817; entered upon duties Sept. 22, 1817

Treasury—William Harris Crawford, Ga., recommissioned Mar. 5, 1817

War—George Graham (chief clerk), ad interim Mar. 4, 1817; John Caldwell Calhoun, S.C., Oct. 8, 1817; entered upon duties Dec. 10, 1817

Attorney General—Richard Rush, Pa., continued from preceding administration to Oct. 30, 1817; William Wirt, Va., Nov. 13, 1817; entered upon duties Nov. 15, 1817

Postmaster General—Return Jonathan Meigs, Jr., Ohio, continued from preceding administration

Navy—Benjamin Williams Crowninshield, Mass., continued from preceding administration; John Caldwell Calhoun (Secretary of War), ad interim Oct. 1, 1818; Smith Thompson, N.Y., Nov. 9, 1818; entered upon duties Jan. 1, 1819

SECOND TERM

March 4, 1821–March 3, 1825

State—John Quincy Adams, Mass., continued from preceding administration

Treasury—William Harris Crawford, Ga., continued from preceding administration

War—John Caldwell Calhoun, S.C., continued from preceding administration

Attorney General—William Wirt, Va., continued from preceding administration

Postmaster General—Return Jonathan Meigs, Jr., Ohio, continued from preceding administration; John McLean, Ohio, commissioned June 26, 1823, commission to take effect July 1, 1823

Navy—Smith Thompson, N.Y., continued from preceding administration; John Rodgers (Commodore, United States Navy and President of the Board of Navy Commissioners), ad interim Sept. 1, 1823; Samuel Lewis Southard, N.J., Sept. 16, 1823

CONGRESS

FIFTEENTH CONGRESS

March 4, 1817–March 3, 1819

First session—Dec. 1, 1817–Apr. 20, 1818 (141 days)

Second session—Nov. 16, 1818–Mar. 3, 1819 (108 days)

Special session of the Senate—Mar. 4, 1817 (one day only)

Vice President—Daniel D. Tompkins, N.Y.

President pro tempore of the Senate —John Gaillard, S.C., elected Mar. 6, 1817, special session; Mar. 31, 1818; James Barbour, Va., elected Feb. 15, 1819

Secretary of the Senate—Charles Cutts, N.H.

Speaker of the House—Henry Clay, Ky., reelected Dec. 1, 1817

Clerk of the House—Thomas Dougherty, Ky., reelected Dec. 1, 1817

SIXTEENTH CONGRESS

March 4, 1819–March 3, 1821

First session—Dec. 6, 1819–May 15, 1820 (162 days)

Second session—Nov. 13, 1820–Mar. 3, 1821 (111 days)

Vice President—Daniel D. Tompkins, N.Y.

President pro tempore of the Senate —James Barbour, Va.; John Gaillard, S.C., elected Jan. 25, 1820

Secretary of the Senate—Charles Cutts, N.H.

Speaker of the House—Henry Clay, Ky., reelected Dec. 6, 1819; resigned as Speaker Oct. 28, 1820; John W. Taylor, N.Y., elected Nov. 15, 1820

Clerk of the House—Thomas Dougherty, Ky., reelected Dec. 6, 1819

SEVENTEENTH CONGRESS

March 4, 1821–March 3, 1823

First session—Dec. 3, 1821–May 8, 1822 (157 days)

Second session—Dec. 2, 1822–Mar. 3, 1823 (92 days)

Vice President—Daniel D. Tompkins, N.Y.

President pro tempore of the Senate —John Gaillard, S.C., elected Feb. 1, 1822; Feb. 19, 1823

Secretary of the Senate—Charles Cutts, N.H.

Speaker of the House—Philip Pendleton Barbour, Va., elected Dec. 4, 1821

Clerk of the House—Thomas Dougherty, Ky., reelected Dec. 4, 1821; died 1822; Matthew St. Clair Clarke, Pa., elected Dec. 3, 1822

EIGHTEENTH CONGRESS

March 4, 1823–March 3, 1825

First session—Dec. 1, 1823–May 27, 1824 (178 days)

Second session—Dec. 6, 1824–Mar. 3, 1825 (88 days)

Vice President—Daniel D. Thompkins, N.Y.

President pro tempore of the Senate —John Gaillard, S.C., elected May 21, 1824

Secretary of the Senate—Charles Cutts, N.H.

Speaker of the House—Henry Clay, Ky., elected Dec. 1, 1823

Clerk of the House—Matthew St. Clair Clarke, Pa., reelected Dec. 1, 1823

APPOINTMENTS TO THE SUPREME COURT

Associate Justice

Smith Thompson, N.Y., Sept. 1, 1823 (replaced Brockholst Livingston)

IMPORTANT DATES IN THE PRESIDENCY

1817, Rush-Bagot agreement with Great Britain, which eliminated fortifications on the Canadian-U.S. border

July 4, 1817, Erie Canal construction began

Nov. 1817, first Seminole war began

Dec. 10, 1817, Mississippi admitted as the 20th state

Apr. 4, 1818, legislation established flag of the United States

May 28, 1818, Andrew Jackson captured Pensacola, Fla.

Oct. 19, 1818, treaty with Chickasaw Indians

Dec. 3, 1818, Illinois admitted as the 21st state

1819, financial panic

1819, *McCulloch v. Maryland* and Dartmouth College cases—Supreme Court affirmed its power to set aside acts of state legislatures if unconstitutional

Feb. 22, 1819, Florida purchased from Spain

May 22, 1819, *Savannah,* first American steamship to cross the Atlantic Ocean, left Savannah, Ga.

Dec. 14, 1819, Alabama admitted as the 22nd state

Mar. 3, 1820, Missouri Compromise—Maine admitted as a separate state; Missouri admitted as slave state; slavery prohibited in Louisiana Purchase north of 36°30'

Mar. 15, 1820, Maine admitted as the 23rd state

May 1820, first high school opened, Boston, Mass.

May 31, 1821, first Catholic cathedral dedicated, Baltimore, Md.

Aug. 10, 1821, Missouri admitted as the 24th state

Dec. 2, 1823, Monroe Doctrine proclaimed

1824, Clay's "American system" proposed— higher protective tariff and internal improvements in transportation

1824, *Gibbons v. Ogden* case—Supreme Court declared a state law unconstitutional

Aug. 15, 1824, Lafayette landed in United States to begin tour

ADDITIONAL DATA ON MONROE

JAMES MONROE

—was the fourth President born in Virginia.

—was the first President who was inaugurated on March 5 (March 4 was a Sunday).

—was the first President who had been a senator.

—was the last of the Virginia regime of Presidents (Washington, Jefferson, Madison, Monroe).

—was the first President whose daughter was married in the White House.

MONROE RODE ON STEAMBOAT

The first President to ride on a steamboat was James Monroe, who sailed on the *Savannah* on May 11, 1819, on an all-day excursion to Tybee Light from Savannah, Ga. The *Savannah* was accompanied by the steamboat *Alatamaha* and two barges. Sails were used for part of the trip. The presidential party included John Caldwell Calhoun, Secretary of War; Major General Edmund Pendleton Gaines, Monroe's private secretary; General David Bradie Mitchell; Major General Floyd; General Benjamin Huger of South Carolina; General John M'Intosh; and Colonel James Marshall.

SENATOR ELECTED PRESIDENT

James Monroe was the first senator to become President of the United States. He served as senator from Virginia from November 9, 1790 to May 27, 1794, filling the vacancy caused by the death of William Grayson on March 12, 1790.

THE MONROE DOCTRINE

Extract from President Monroe's Annual Message, Washington, D.C., December 2, 1823:

The citizens of the United States cherish sentiments the most friendly in favor of the liberty and happiness of their fellowmen on that side of the Atlantic. In the wars of the European powers, in matters relating to themselves, we have never taken any part, nor does it comport with our policy to do so. It is only when our rights are invaded, or seriously menaced, that we resent injuries or make preparations for our defence. With the movements in this hemisphere, we are, of necessity, more immediately connected, and by causes which must be obvious to all enlightened and impartial observers. The political system of the allied powers is essentially different, in this respect, from that of America. This difference proceeds from that which exists in their respective Governments. And to the defence of our own, which has been achieved by the loss of so much blood and

Courtesy of The Library of Congress

Uncle Sam, as armed soldier, standing between European powers (Britain, France, Germany, Spain, and Portugal) and Nicaragua and Venezuela

treasure, and matured by the wisdom of their most enlightened citizens, and under which we have enjoyed unexampled felicity, this whole nation is devoted. . . . We owe it, therefore, to candor and to the amicable relations existing between the United States and those powers, to declare, that we should consider any attempt on their part to extend their system to any portion of this hemisphere, as dangerous to our peace and safety. With the existing colonies or dependencies of any European power, we have not interfered, and shall not interfere. But, with the Governments who have declared their independence, and maintained it, and whose independence we have, on great consideration, and on just principles, acknowledged, we could not view any interposition for the purpose of oppressing them, or controlling, in any other manner, their destiny, by any European power, in any other light than as the manifestation of an unfriendly disposition towards the United States. In the war between those new Governments and Spain, we declared our neutrality at the time of their recognition, and to this we have adhered, and shall continue to adhere, provided no change shall occur, which, in the judgement of the competent authorities of this Government, shall make a corresponding change on the part of the United States, indispensable to their security.

AFRICA HONORED MONROE

Upper Guinea, West Africa, was acquired by the American Colonization Society, founded in 1817 for the purpose of colonizing free blacks from the United States. On August 15, 1824, the name of the country was changed to Liberia and its capital city was named Monrovia in honor of President James Monroe.

FURTHER READING

Ammon, Harry. *James Monroe: The Quest for National Identity.* 1971.

Hamilton, S. M., ed. *The Writings of James Monroe.* 1969.

Morgan, George. *The Life of James Monroe.* 1969.

Courtesy of The Library of Congress

James Monroe's tomb, near Richmond, Virginia

Courtesy of The Library of Congress

John Quincy Adams

Date of birth—July 11, 1767

Place of birth—Braintree (now Quincy), Mass.

Education—Tutored at home by parents and John Adams's law clerks; Passy Academy, Paris, France, 1778; Latin school, Amsterdam, the Netherlands, 1780; Leyden University, 1781–1782; private study under Rev. John Shaw, Haverhill, Mass.; Harvard College, Cambridge, Mass., bachelor's degree, July 18, 1787; private study in law office of Theophilus Parsons, Newburyport, Mass.

Religion—Unitarian

Ancestry—English

Career—Lawyer; minister to the Netherlands, Portugal, Prussia, Russia, and Great Britain; state senator, U.S. senator, treaty negotiator, Secretary of State

Political party—Democratic-Republican

State represented—Massachusetts

Term of office—Mar. 4, 1825–Mar. 4, 1829

Term served—4 years

Administration—10th

Congresses—19th, 20th

Age at inauguration—57 years, 236 days

Lived after term—18 years, 356 days

Occupation after term—U.S. congressman from Massachusetts

Date of death—Feb. 23, 1848

Age at death—80 years, 227 days

Place of death—Washington, D.C.

Burial place—First Unitarian Church, Quincy, Mass.

FAMILY

FATHER

Name—John Adams

Date of birth—Oct. 30, 1735,

Place of birth—Braintree, Mass.

Marriage—Abigail Smith, Oct. 25, 1764, Weymouth, Mass.

Occupation—Teacher, farmer, lawyer; diplomat, founder of the Republic, framer of the Constitution, Vice President of the United States, President of the United States; active in Revolution

Date of death—July 4, 1826

Place of death—Quincy, Mass.

Age at death—90 years, 247 days

MOTHER

Name at birth—Abigail Smith

Date of birth—Nov. 11, 1744

Place of birth—Weymouth, Mass.

Marriage—John Adams, Oct. 25, 1764, Weymouth, Mass.

Date of death—Oct. 28, 1818

Place of death—Quincy, Mass.

Age at death—73 years, 351 days

SIBLINGS

John Quincy Adams was the second child in a family of five.

Children of John Adams and Abigail Smith Adams

Abigail Adams, b. July 14, 1765, d. Aug. 15, 1813

John Quincy Adams, b. July 11, 1767, d. Feb. 23, 1848

Susanna Adams, b. Dec. 28, 1768, d. Feb. 4, 1770

Charles Adams, b. May 29, 1770, d. Nov. 30, 1800

Thomas Boylston Adams, b. Sept. 15, 1772, d. Mar. 12, 1832

MARRIAGE

Married—Louisa Catherine Johnson

Date of marriage—July 26, 1797

Place of marriage—London, England

Age of wife at marriage—22 years, 164 days

Age of husband at marriage—30 years, 15 days

Years married—50 years, 212 days

CHILDREN

George Washington Adams, b. Apr. 13, 1801, Berlin, Germany; d. Apr. 30, 1829, on steamer in Long Island Sound, lost at sea

John Adams, b. July 4, 1803, Boston, Mass.; m. Feb. 25, 1828, Mary Catherine Hellen in the White House, Washington, D.C.; d. Oct. 23, 1834, Washington, D.C.

Charles Francis Adams, b. Aug. 18, 1807, Boston, Mass.; m. Sept. 3, 1829, Abigail Brown Brooks; d. Nov. 21, 1886, Boston, Mass.

Louisa Catherine Adams, b. 1811, St. Petersburg, Russia; d. 1812

THE PRESIDENT'S WIFE

Name at birth—Louisa Catherine Johnson

Date of birth—Feb. 12, 1775

Place of birth—London, England

Mother—Catherine Nuth Johnson

Father—Joshua Johnson

Father's occupation—U.S. Consul

Marriage—John Quincy Adams, July 26, 1797

Children—George Washington Adams, b. Apr. 13, 1801, d. Apr. 30, 1829; John Adams, b. July 4, 1803, d. Oct. 23, 1834; Charles Francis Adams, b. Aug. 18, 1807, d. Nov. 21, 1886; Louisa Catherine Adams, b. 1811, d. 1812

Date of death—May 14, 1852

Age at death—77 years, 91 days

Place of death—Washington, D.C.

Burial place—Quincy, Mass.

Years younger than the President—7 years, 216 days

Years she survived the President—4 years, 80 days

Courtesy of The Library of Congress

Louisa Catherine Adams, wife of John Quincy Adams

THE FIRST LADY

Under Louisa Catherine Johnson Adams, the hospitality of the White House was warm and sincere. The frugality and severity of the two previous administrations gave way to an era of gracious living in which the choicest foods and the rarest wines were always served.

Louisa Adams was the first First Lady born outside the boundaries of the United States. She was born in London, England, where her father was posted as the U.S. consul. She was also the first First Lady to write her autobiography. It was published privately in 1825 under the title *Adventures of a Nobody.*

IMPORTANT DATES IN THE PRESIDENT'S LIFE

1778, attended school at Paris

Aug. 1779, returned to the United States

1780, made fourth trip across Atlantic

1780, attended school at Amsterdam, Holland; entered University of Leyden

July 1781, accompanied Francis Dana, minister to Russia, as his private secretary

1782, made a six-month trip alone to Sweden, Denmark, northern Germany, and France

Sept. 3, 1783, present at signing of Treaty of Paris

1785, secretary to his father, John Adams, minister to Great Britain

1785, returned to the United States

1786, entered Harvard College

1787, graduated from Harvard College; entered on study of law in office of Theophilus Parsons

July 1790, admitted to the bar; practiced in Boston, Mass.

1791–17—, wrote pamphlets and articles under the pseudonymns of Publicola, Marcellus, Columbus, etc.

May 30, 1794, appointed minister to the Netherlands by George Washington

1796, minister plenipotentiary to Portugal

June 1, 1797, minister plenipotentiary to Prussia

Mar. 14, 1798, commissioned to make a commercial treaty with Sweden (mission terminated when Jefferson became President)

1801, resumed law practice, Boston, Mass.

1802, member of Massachusetts Senate

Mar. 4, 1803–June 8, 1808, U.S. Senate (from Massachusetts)

1805, professor of rhetoric and belles lettres, Harvard College

1807, broke with Federalist Party in his support of President Jefferson's embargo act

1808, resigned from Senate when Massachusetts legislature chose James Lloyd to succeed him

1809–1814, minister to Russia

1811, nominated to Supreme Court, but declined

1814, sent by President Madison to negotiate terms of peace with England (War of 1812); commissioners met at Ghent in Aug. 1814; signed Treaty of Ghent, Dec. 24, 1814

1815, Adams, Clay, and Gallatin negotiated a commercial treaty with England (completed July 13)

1815–1817, minister to England

Sept. 22, 1817–Mar. 3, 1825, Secretary of State

Mar. 4, 1825–Mar. 4, 1829, President

1828, unsuccessful candidate for reelection

1829, retired to farm

Mar. 4, 1831–Feb. 23, 1848, U.S. House of Representatives (from Massachusetts)

1834, unsuccessful candidate for governor of Massachusetts as nominee of the Anti-Masonic party

1846, paralysis; confined at home four months

1848, paralysis, second attack, in Speaker's Room, House of Representatives

Courtesy of The Library of Congress

Birthplace of John Quincy Adams, Quincy, Mass.

ELECTIONS

THE ELECTION OF 1824

The last of the congressional caucuses met in 1824 in the chamber of the House of Representatives. William Harris Crawford of Georgia was chosen as the Democratic-Republican presidential candidate.

The selection was not popular with the various state legislatures, which asserted themselves and decided that they were no longer bound to endorse the congressional choices. The legislature of Tennessee placed Andrew Jackson in nomination on July 22, 1822, and other state legislatures proposed their choices. Ultimately, there were four candidates—Crawford, Jackson, John Quincy Adams, and Henry Clay—each representing a different faction of the Democratic-Republican Party.

Well before the electoral votes were counted, it became clear that no candidate for the presidency was likely to receive a majority, and that the House would be required, in accordance with the Constitution, to decide the outcome. The House prepared for that eventuality by passing a resolution on January 18, 1825, establishing the procedures it would employ. The votes were counted on February 9 and the majority was indeed absent. Crawford then withdrew, leaving three contenders.

Twenty-four tellers, one from each state, were appointed to examine the ballots in the House. Clay's supporters threw their strength to Adams, with the result that Adams was elected. Adams received 13 votes, Jackson 7 votes, and Crawford 4 votes.

It is misleading to say that the popular vote was won by Andrew Jackson. As this was the first year in which there was widespread recording of popular votes, the figures are considered dubious. There was no popular polling at all in 6 of the 24 states, and the ballots in the remaining 18 states did not present a uniform set of candidate choices.

1824 POPULAR VOTE

Andrew Jackson, Tenn., 153,544
John Quincy Adams, Mass., 108,740
William Harris Crawford, Ga., 47,136

Henry Clay, Ky., 46,618

1824 ELECTORAL VOTE

There were 261 electoral votes from 24 states.

Jackson received 37.93 percent (99 votes—11 states) as follows: Ala. 5; Ill. 2 (of the 3 votes); Ind. 5; La. 3 (of the 5 votes); Md. 7 (of the 11 votes); Miss. 3; N.J. 8; N.Y. 1 (of the 36 votes); N.C. 15; Pa. 28; S.C. 11; Tenn. 11.

Adams received 32.18 percent (84 votes—7 states) as follows: Conn. 8; Del. 1 (of the 3 votes); Ill. 1 (of the 3 votes); La. 2 (of the 5 votes); Me. 9; Md. 3 (of the 11 votes); Mass. 15; N.H. 8; N.Y. 26 (of the 36 votes); R.I. 4; Vt. 7.

Crawford received 15.71 percent (41 votes—3 states) as follows: Ga. 9; Del. 2 (of the 3 votes); Md. 1 (of the 11 votes); N.Y. 5 (of the 36 votes); Va. 24.

Clay received 14.18 percent (37 votes—3 states) as follows: Ky. 14; Mo. 3; Ohio 16; N.Y. 4 (of the 36 votes).

VICE PRESIDENTIAL CANDIDATES

There were six vice presidential candidates: John Caldwell Calhoun of South Carolina, Nathan Sanford of New York, Nathaniel Macon of North Carolina, Andrew Jackson of Tennessee, Martin Van Buren of New York, and Henry Clay of Kentucky. Since one elector failed to cast his vote, the total number of votes was 260 instead of 261.

Calhoun received 182 votes as follows: Ala. 5; Del. 1 (of the 3 votes); Ill. 3; Ind. 5; Ky. 7 (of the 14 votes); La. 5; Md. 10 (of the 11 votes); Me. 9; Mass. 15; Miss. 3; N.H. 7; N.J. 8; N.Y 29 (of the 36 votes); N.C. 15; Pa. 28; R.I. 3; S.C. 11; Tenn. 11; Vt. 7.

Sanford received 30 votes as follows: Ky. 7 (of the 14 votes); N.Y. (of the 36 votes); Ohio 16.

Macon received the 24 Va. votes.

Jackson received 13 votes as follows: Conn. 8; Md. 1 (of the 11 votes); Mo. 3; N.H. 1.

Van Buren received the 9 Ga. votes.

Clay received 2 of the 3 Del. votes.

INAUGURATION

March 4, 1825

John Quincy Adams took the oath of office on Friday, March 4, 1825, at noon in the Hall of the House of Representatives. The oath was administered by Chief Justice John Marshall. Adams was accompanied to the Capitol by a military escort. After the ceremony, he returned to his residence at 1333 F Street, where a reception was held; later he went to the White House.

An inaugural ball was held that evening at Louis Carusi's Assembly Room, known also as the City Assembly Rooms.

THE VICE PRESIDENT

Name—John Caldwell Calhoun (7th V.P.)

Political party—Democratic-Republican

State represented—South Carolina

Term of office—Mar. 4, 1825–Mar. 4, 1829

Age at inauguration—42 years, 351 days

Occupation after term—Vice President under Andrew Jackson

For additional data on John Caldwell Calhoun, see the section on the Vice President in the chapter on Andrew Jackson, 7th President.

Courtesy of The Library of Congress

John Caldwell Calhoun, Vice President to John Quincy Adams

CABINET

March 4, 1825–March 3, 1829

State—Daniel Brent (chief clerk), ad interim Mar. 4, 1825; Henry Clay, Ky., Mar. 7, 1825

Treasury—Samuel Lewis Southard, N.J. (Secretary of the Navy), ad interim Mar. 7, 1825; Richard Rush, Pa., Mar. 7, 1825; entered upon duties Aug. 1, 1825

War—James Barbour, Va., Mar. 7, 1825; Samuel Lewis Southard, N.J., Secretary of the Navy, ad interim May 26, 1828; Peter Buell Porter, N.Y., May 26, 1828; entered upon duties June 21, 1828

Attorney General—William Wirt, Va., continued from preceding administration

Postmaster General—John McLean, Ohio, continued from preceding administration

Navy—Samuel Lewis Southard, N.J., continued from preceding administration

CONGRESS

NINETEENTH CONGRESS

March 4, 1825–March 3, 1827

First session—Dec. 5, 1825–May 22, 1826 (169 days)

Second session—Dec. 4, 1826–Mar. 3, 1827 (90 days)

Special session of the Senate—Mar. 4, 1825–Mar. 9, 1825

Vice President—John Caldwell Calhoun, S.C.

President pro tempore of the Senate —John Gaillard, S.C., elected Mar. 9, 1825, special session; Nathaniel Macon, N.C., elected May 20, 1826; Jan. 2, 1827; and Mar. 2, 1827

Secretary of the Senate—Charles Cutts, N.H.; Walter Lowrie, Pa., elected Dec. 12, 1825

Speaker of the House—John W. Taylor, N.Y., elected Dec. 5, 1825

Clerk of the House—Matthew St. Clair Clarke, Pa., reelected Dec. 5, 1825

TWENTIETH CONGRESS

March 4, 1827–Mar 3, 1829

First session—Dec. 3, 1827–May 26, 1828 (175 days)

Second session—Dec. 1, 1828–Mar. 3, 1829 (93 days)

Vice President—John Caldwell Calhoun, S.C.

President pro tempore of the Senate —Samuel Smith, Md., elected May 15, 1828

Secretary of the Senate—Walter Lowrie, Pa., reelected Dec. 10, 1827

Speaker of the House—Andrew Stevenson, Va., elected Dec. 3, 1827

Clerk of the House—Matthew St. Clair Clarke, Pa., reelected Dec. 3, 1827

APPOINTMENTS TO THE SUPREME COURT

Associate Justice

Robert Trimble, Ky., May 9, 1826 (replaced Thomas Todd)

IMPORTANT DATES IN THE PRESIDENCY

June 17, 1825, Bunker Hill Monument cornerstone laid by General Lafayette

Oct. 26, 1825, Erie Canal opened for traffic

Mar. 24, 1826, General Congress of South American States convened at Panama

July 4, 1826, John Adams and Thomas Jefferson died

1828, South Carolina Exposition on nullification of federal tariffs

July 4, 1828, construction of Baltimore and Ohio Railroad begun

ADDITIONAL DATA ON ADAMS

JOHN QUINCY ADAMS

—was the first President whose father had signed the Declaration of Independence.

—was the first President whose father had been President.

—was the second President born in Massachusetts.

—was the first President who had been elected a member of Phi Beta Kappa.

—was the first President to wear long trousers at his inauguration.

—was the President least interested in clothes. It is said that he wore the same hat ten years.

—was the first President elected without receiving a plurality of either the popular votes or the votes of the electoral college.

—was the first and only President to have a son whose given name was George Washington.

—was the first President whose son was married in the White House.

—was the first President who was married abroad.

ADAMS THE SON OF A PRESIDENT

John Quincy Adams was the first President whose father had also been President. Like his father, he served only one term.

FORMER PRESIDENTS STILL LIVING

When John Quincy Adams took the oath of office as President of the United States on March 4, 1825, all of the former presidents, with the exception of George Washington, were living: John Adams, Thomas Jefferson, James Madison, and James Monroe.

ADAMS SUFFERED WORST DEFEAT

The most badly defeated presidential candidate, excluding those nominated by the minor parties, was John Quincy Adams. In the election of 1820, he received only one electoral vote, which was cast by an elector from New Hampshire, whereas James Monroe received 231 of the 232 electoral votes.

PRESIDENT BECAME CONGRESSMAN

After serving as President, John Quincy Adams became a congressman. He represented the Plymouth, Mass., district, serving as a Whig congressman in the 22nd and the eight succeeding congresses, from March 4, 1831, to February 23, 1848, when he died. He served ten days less than seventeen years.

FURTHER READING

Adams, James T. *The Adams Family*. 1930.

Allen, David G., ed. *Diary of John Quincy Adams*. 1981.

Bemis, Samuel F. *John Quincy Adams and the Foundations of American Foreign Policy*. 1949.

———. *John Quincy Adams and the Union*. 1956.

Hargreaves, Mary W. M. *The Presidency of John Quincy Adams*. Rev. ed. 1988.

Hecht, Marie B. *John Quincy Adams*. 1972.

Miller, William Lee. *Arguing About Slavery: The Great Battle in the United States Congress*. 1996.

Nagel, Paul C. *John Quincy Adams: A Public Life, a Private Life*. 1997.

Wheelan, Joseph. *Mr. Adams' Last Crusade: John Quincy Adams' Extraordinary Post-Presidential Life in Congress*. 2008.

Courtesy of the United States Senate

Andrew Jackson

Date of birth—Mar. 15, 1767

Place of birth—Waxhaw, S.C.

Education—Attended schools of Dr. William Humphries, Rev. James White Stephenson, and Robert McCulloch; private study in law offices of Spruce McCay and John Stokes, Salisbury, N.C.

Religion—Presbyterian

Ancestry—Scotch-Irish

Career—Lawyer, delegate to state constitutional convention, U.S. congressman, U.S. senator, justice of state superior court, state senator, Army general in War of 1812 and First Seminole War, military governor of Florida

Political party—Democratic (Democratic-Republican)

State represented—Tennessee

Term of office—Mar. 4, 1829–Mar. 4, 1837

Term served—8 years

Administration—11th, 12th

Congresses—21st, 22nd, 23rd, 24th

Age at inauguration—61 years, 354 days

Lived after term—8 years, 96 days

Occupation after term—Retired

Date of death—June 8, 1845

Age at death—78 years, 85 days

Place of death—The Hermitage, near Nashville, Tenn.

Burial place—The Hermitage, Tenn.

FAMILY

FATHER

Name—Andrew Jackson

Place of birth—Ireland

Marriage—Elizabeth Hutchinson

Occupation—Linen weaver (in Ireland), farmer

Date of death—Mar. 1767

MOTHER

Name at birth—Elizabeth Hutchinson

Place of birth—Ireland

Marriage—Andrew Jackson

Date of death—November 1781

Place of death—Charleston, S.C.

SIBLINGS

Andrew Jackson was the third child in a family of three.

Children of Andrew Jackson and Elizabeth Hutchinson Jackson

Hugh Jackson, b. 1762, d. May 29, 1779
Robert Jackson, b. 1765, d. Aug. 6, 1781
Andrew Jackson, b. Mar. 15, 1767, d. June 8, 1845

MARRIAGE

Married—Rachel Donelson Robards

Date of marriage—Aug. 1791, Natchez, Miss. (second ceremony, Jan. 17, 1794, Nashville, Tenn.)

Age of wife at marriage—24 years

Age of husband at marriage—24 years

Years married—37 years

Rachel Donelson married Captain Lewis Robards March 1, 1785. In 1790 the legislature of Virginia granted Robards the right to sue for divorce—a grant which she mistakenly assumed was a divorce. She married Jackson in 1791, learned later that the proceeding had not been completed, and was remarried to Jackson in 1794 after Robards had received the divorce decree (September 27, 1793, Court of Quarter Sessions, Mercer County, Ky.).

CHILDREN

Andrew Jackson, Jr. (adopted child, one of Mrs. Jackson's twin nephews), b. 1809; m. 1831 Sarah Yorke; d. 1865

THE PRESIDENT'S WIFE

Name at birth—Rachel Donelson

Date of birth—June 15 (?), 1767

Place of birth—Halifax County, Va.

Mother—Rachel Stockley Donelson

Father—Colonel John Donelson

Father's occupation—Surveyor

First marriage—Lewis Robards, March 1, 1785 (div. September 27, 1793)

Second marriage—Andrew Jackson

Children—Andrew Jackson, Jr. (adopted child, one of twin sons born to the wife of Severn Donelson, Mrs. Jackson's brother), b. 1809, d. 1865

Date of death—Dec. 22, 1828

Age at death—61 years, 190 days

Place of death—The Hermitage, near Nashville, Tenn.

Burial place—The Hermitage, Tenn.

Years younger than the President—92 days

Years the President survived her—16 years, 168 days

Courtesy of The Library of Congress

Rachel Jackson, wife of President Andrew Jackson

HOSTESSES AT THE WHITE HOUSE

As Rachel Donelson Robards Jackson had died of a heart attack before her husband was inaugurated, President Jackson assigned the duties of hostess at the White House to his wife's niece, Emily Donelson, who was the wife of Andrew Jackson Donelson, the President's aide-de-camp and private secretary. Their four children were all born in the White House. She contracted tuberculosis and in 1836 returned to her home in Tennessee. Also serving at various times as hostess was Sarah Yorke Jackson, wife of Andrew Jackson's adopted son Andrew Jackson, Jr.

IMPORTANT DATES IN THE PRESIDENT'S LIFE

1784, studied law, Salisbury, N.C.

1787, fought first duel (with Waightstill Avery)

Nov. 21, 1787, admitted to the bar; practiced in McLeanville, N.C., and Tennessee

Oct. 1788, solicitor of western district of North Carolina (comprising what is now Tennessee)

Jan. 1796, delegate to Tennessee State Constitutional Convention, Knoxville

Dec. 5, 1796–Mar. 3, 1797, U.S. House of Representatives (from Tennessee)

Nov. 1797–Apr. 1798, U.S. Senate (from Tennessee)

1798–July 24, 1804, judge, Supreme Court of Tennessee

1801, major general of militia for western district of Tennessee

1804, moved to the Hermitage, near Nashville, Tenn.; engaged in planting and mercantile pursuits

May 30, 1806, killed Charles Dickinson in duel

1807, Tennessee state senator and lawyer

1812, commander of Tennessee militia; served against Creek Indians

1812–1814, major general of volunteers

Aug. 30, 1813, expedition against Creek Indians who massacred garrison at Fort Mims, Ala.

Sept. 4, 1813, wounded in affray with the brothers Thomas Hart Benton and Jesse Benton

Mar. 27, 1814, defeated Creek Indians at Horseshoe Bend of the Tallapoosa

Apr. 19, 1814, commissioned brigadier general, U.S. Army

May 1, 1814, promoted to major general, U.S. Army

Aug. 9, 1814, negotiated treaty with the Creek Indians

Sept. 9, 1814, began first Florida campaign

Nov. 7, 1814, captured Pensacola and Fort Michael; British retreated

Jan. 8, 1815, defeated British under General Pakenham at Battle of New Orleans, not aware that a peace treaty had been signed at Ghent

Feb. 27, 1815, received thanks of Congress; awarded a gold medal by resolution

Mar. 24, 1815, fined $1,000 by Judge Dominick A. Hall for contempt of court

Dec. 26, 1817, ordered by Secretary of War Calhoun to attack the Seminoles

Mar. 1818, in an incursion into Spanish Florida, defeated the Seminoles and captured St. Marks and Pensacola, in the process, nearly precipitating a war with Great Britain; John Quincy Adams was his sole defender in Monroe's Cabinet

Mar. 10–July 18, 1821, governor of Florida

July 20, 1822, nominated for President by Tennessee legislature

Mar. 4, 1823–Oct. 14, 1825, U.S. Senator (from Tennessee); resigned

1824, unsuccessful candidate for the presidency; won plurality of electoral votes, but House of Representatives chose John Quincy Adams

Mar. 4, 1829–Mar. 4, 1837, President

June 26, 1833, LL.D. degree conferred by Harvard

Courtesy of The Library of Congress

Andrew Jackson during the Battle of New Orleans

ELECTIONS

THE ELECTION OF 1828

Andrew Jackson's supporters claimed that the caucus system defeated the purposes of the Constitution, which envisaged electors voting as they pleased, and that the power of selection had passed from the electors to an extra-legal body. They argued that the popular vote showed that the congressional caucus was not representative of the wishes of the people.

In 1828 a new policy was instituted. It was the first election in which the nominations were all made by state legislatures instead of congressional caucuses. It was also the first in which the popular vote was a real factor in the selection of electors.

The Democratic-Republicans, known also as Republicans or Democrats, were split into factions. Jackson's supporters (who tended more and more to call themselves Democrats) felt that he had been deprived of the election in 1825 and were determined to elect him in 1828. It was not only a personal matter, but a geographical struggle as well. The Adams-Clay adherents (who soon joined the remaining Federalists to form the National Republican Party) nominated two candidates from the North, John Quincy Adams of Massachusetts and Richard Rush of Pennsylvania. The Democrats nominated two from the South, Jackson of Tennessee and John Caldwell Calhoun of South Carolina. Jackson carried 15 of the 24 states.

1828 POPULAR VOTE

Jackson-Calhoun faction (Democratic Party), 647,286

Adams-Clay faction (Federalist or National Republican Party), 508,064

1828 ELECTORAL VOTE

There were 261 electoral votes from 24 states.

Jackson received 68.20 percent (178 votes—15 states) as follows: Ala. 5; Ga. 9; Ill. 3; Ind. 5; Ky. 14; La. 5; Me. 1 (of the 9 votes); Md. 5 (of the 11 votes); Miss. 3; Mo. 3; N.Y. 20 (of the 36 votes); N.C. 15; Ohio 16; Pa. 28; S.C. 11; Tenn. 11; Va. 24.

For the vice presidency Calhoun received 171 votes and William Smith (also of South Carolina) received 7 votes.

Adams received 31.80 percent (84 votes—9 states) as follows: Conn. 8; Del. 3; Me. 8 (of the 9 votes); Md. 6 (of the 11 votes); Mass. 15; N.H. 8; N.J. 8; N.Y. 16 (of the 36 votes); R.I. 4; Vt. 7.

For the vice presidency Rush received 83 votes.

THE ELECTION OF 1832

The election of 1832 was the first in which all the candidates were nominated by conventions. Four were held, three of them at the same location, the Atheneum in Baltimore, Md.

The earliest one—and thus the first national nominating convention ever to meet—took place on September 26, 1831, when Anti-Masonic Party delegates met in Baltimore to cast their votes into an open ballot box. The winner was William Wirt of Maryland.

The National Republicans (soon to evolve into the Whigs) met in Baltimore in December 1831 and nominated Henry Clay of Kentucky.

The Democratic-Republicans (soon to be known as the Democrats) convened in Baltimore in May 1832. This convention established a number of precedents. It was the first to enact the two-thirds rule, requiring successful nominees to obtain two-thirds of the vote (a rule that remained valid until 1936); the first to apportion delegates based on the state's electoral voting in the previous election; the first to renominate an incumbent President (Andrew Jackson); and the first to be controlled by a single politician (again Jackson, who used his power to influence the selection of delegates and compel them to vote as he wished in choosing Martin Van Buren for the vice presidency).

A pro-nullification group of Democrats calling themselves the Independent Party met at Charleston, S.C., in November 1832, and nominated John Floyd of Virginia.

CANDIDATES

Democratic (Democratic-Republican) Party (1st Convention)

May 21–23, 1832, The Athenaeum and the Universalist Church, Baltimore, Md.

P: Andrew Jackson, Tenn.
VP: Martin Van Buren, N.Y.

Jackson was not formally nominated; rather, the delegates expressed their agreement with Jackson's previous nominations by various state legislatures.

This convention was held by the "Republican Delegates from the Several States." The party which today bears the name Democratic was then known officially as the Republican Party (a name that had come down from the time of Jefferson) and popularly as the Democratic-Republican Party, or simply the Democratic Party. In the early national conventions, the designations "Democratic" and "Republican" were often used

Andrew Jackson on horseback

interchangeably, but by 1840 the designation "Republican" had been dropped entirely and the official name of the party became the Democratic Party.

At the convention of 1832 a two-thirds majority was necessary for a choice. Since the Democrats were unanimous in the choice of Andrew Jackson for a second term, there was no opposition to his renomination. The sole purpose of this convention was to select a vice presidential candidate to replace John Caldwell Calhoun, who had long had a running feud with Jackson, and whom Jackson had repudiated. Martin Van Buren of New York received 208 of the 283 votes cast and was nominated Vice President on the first ballot. Other vice presidential nominees were Philip Pendleton Barbour of Virginia, who received 49 votes, and Richard Mentor Johnson of Kentucky, who received 26 votes.

National Republican Party

December 12–15, 1831, The Athenaeum, Baltimore, Md.

P: Henry Clay, Ky.
VP: John Sergeant, Pa.

Clay was nominated unanimously on the first ballot by 168 delegates from 18 states.

This anti-Jackson political faction, although not fully crystallized as a political party, defined the issues of the campaign as the tariff, internal improvements, the renewal of the charter of the Bank of the United States, and the resettling of the Cherokee Indians. The National Republicans gradually began to call themselves Whigs, and by 1834 the name was in general use.

Anti-Masonic Party

Sept. 26–28, 1831, The Athenaeum, Baltimore, Md.

P: William Wirt, Md.
VP: Amos Ellmaker, Pa.

Wirt was nominated on the first ballot. Candidates for nomination and the votes they received:
William Wirt, Md., 108
Richard Rush, Pa., 1
Total number of votes: 111 (2 votes not cast)
Number necessary for nomination: 84
Nomination made unanimous

This was the first national nominating convention at which candidates were placed in nomination by delegates, a procedure that was later adopted by all political parties. The delegates represented 13 states. The party had been formed in 1827 in western New York. A national convention, held at Philadelphia, Pa., September 11–18, 1830, was attended by 96 delegates from 10 states, but no nominations were made at that time.

Independent Party

November 20, 1832, Charleston, S.C.

P: John Floyd, Va.
VP: Henry Lee, Mass.

South Carolina cast its 11 electoral votes for this newly formed party—the nullification faction of the Democratic Party—which maintained that states had the right to veto or nullify federal legislation and executive orders.

1832 POPULAR VOTE

Democratic (Democratic-Republican) Party, 701,780
National Republican Party, 484,205
Anti-Masonic Party, 100,715
Other, 7,273

1832 ELECTORAL VOTE

There were 286 electoral votes from 24 states.

Jackson received 76.57 percent (219 votes—16 states) as follows: Ala. 7; Ga. 11; Ill. 5; Ind. 9; La. 5; Me. 10; Md. 3 (of the 8 votes); Miss. 4; Mo. 4; N.H. 7; N.J. 8; N.Y. 42; N.C. 15; Ohio 21; Pa. 30; Tenn. 15; Va. 23.

Clay received 17.13 percent (49 votes—6 states) as follows: Conn. 8; Del. 3; Ky. 15; Md. 5 (of the 8 votes); Mass. 14; R.I. 4.

Floyd received 3.85 percent (1 state): S.C. 11.

Wirt received 2.45 percent (1 state): Vt. 7.

For the vice presidency Martin Van Buren received 189 votes and William Wilkins of Pennsylvania received 30 votes, the Democratic vote for the vice presidency being divided.

INAUGURATIONS

FIRST TERM

March 4, 1829

Like his father, John Adams, John Quincy Adams, the outgoing President, refused to participate in the inaugural ceremonies of his successor. Andrew Jackson took the oath of office on Wednesday, March 4, 1829, on the east portico of the White House. The oath was administered by Chief Justice John Marshall. The ceremonies ended with the firing of cannon.

It was a warm and spring-like day. Andrew Jackson was an imposing figure as he rode down Pennsylvania Avenue leading a parade which included war veterans, many of whom had fought in the Revolution. As Jackson was in mourning for his wife, who had died on December 22, 1828, no ceremonies were planned. In the evening a reception was held for the public at the White House. A crowd of 20,000 people jammed the building, ruining rugs, furniture, and glassware, and causing thousands of dollars' worth of damage. It was a boisterous reception. Jackson was a man of the people, the first President not descended from an old aristocratic family.

SECOND TERM

March 4, 1833

Andrew Jackson took the oath of office for his second term on Monday, March 4, 1833, in the House of Representatives. John Marshall, the Chief Justice, administered the oath (the ninth presidential oath administered by him).

THE VICE PRESIDENTS

FIRST TERM

Name—John Caldwell Calhoun (7th V.P.)

Political party—Democratic-Republican

State represented—South Carolina

Term of office—Mar. 4, 1829–Dec. 28, 1832

Age at inauguration—46 years, 351 days

Occupation after term—U.S. Senate (from South Carolina), U.S. Secretary of State

Date of death—Mar. 31, 1850

Age at death—68 years, 13 days

Place of death—Washington, D.C.

Burial place—Charleston, S.C.

ADDITIONAL DATA ON CALHOUN

1804, graduated from Yale College

1807, admitted to the bar; practiced in Abbeville, S.C.

1808–1809, South Carolina House of Representatives

Mar. 4, 1811–Nov. 3, 1817, U.S. House of Representatives (from South Carolina)

Dec. 10, 1817–Mar. 3, 1825, Secretary of War

Mar. 4, 1825–Mar. 4, 1829, Vice President under John Quincy Adams

Mar. 4, 1829–Dec. 28, 1832, Vice President under Andrew Jackson

Dec. 29, 1832–Mar. 3, 1843, U.S. Senate
  (from South Carolina)
Mar. 6, 1844–Mar. 6, 1845, Secretary of State
Nov. 26, 1845–Mar. 31, 1850, U.S. Senate
  (from South Carolina)

FIRST VICE PRESIDENT BORN A CITIZEN OF THE UNITED STATES

John Caldwell Calhoun, Vice President under John Quincy Adams and Andrew Jackson, was the first Vice President not born a British subject. He was born on March 18, 1782, near Calhoun Mills, Abbeville District, S.C.

VICE PRESIDENT RESIGNED TO BECOME SENATOR

John Caldwell Calhoun, Vice President from March 4, 1825, to December 28, 1832, resigned to become a senator from South Carolina. He had been elected to the United States Senate on December 12, 1832, to fill the vacancy caused by the resignation of Robert Young Hayne, who became governor of South Carolina. Calhoun was reelected in 1834 and 1840 and served from December 29, 1832, until his resignation, effective March 3, 1843. He later served as secretary of state and afterward was reelected to the Senate, where he served from November 26, 1845, until his death in Washington, D.C., on March 31, 1850.

Courtesy of The Library of Congress

John Caldwell Calhoun, first Vice President to Andrew Jackson

SECOND TERM

Name—Martin Van Buren (8th V.P.)

Political party—Democratic (Democratic-Republican)

State represented—New York

Term of office—Mar. 4, 1833–Mar. 4, 1837

Age at inauguration—50 years, 89 days

Occupation after term—President of the United States

For further biographical information, see the chapter on Martin Van Buren, 8th President, on page 101.

Courtesy of The Library of Congress

Martin Van Buren, second Vice President to Andrew Jackson

CABINET

FIRST TERM

March 4, 1829–March 3, 1833

State—James Alexander Hamilton, N.Y., ad interim Mar. 4, 1829; Martin Van Buren, N.Y., Mar. 6, 1829, entered upon duties Mar. 28, 1829; Edward Livingston, La., May 24, 1831

Treasury—Samuel Delucenna Ingham, Pa., Mar. 6, 1829; Asbury Dickins (chief clerk), ad interim June 21, 1831; Louis McLane, Del., Aug. 8, 1831

War—John Henry Eaton, Tenn., Mar. 9, 1829; Philip G. Randolph (chief clerk), ad interim June 20, 1831; Roger Brooke Taney, Md. (Attorney General), ad interim July 21, 1831; Lewis Cass, Ohio, Aug. 1, 1831; entered upon duties Aug. 8, 1831

Attorney General—John Macpherson Berrien, Ga., Mar. 9, 1829–June 22, 1831; Roger Brooke Taney, Md., July 20, 1831

Postmaster General—John McLean, Ohio, continued from preceding administration; William Taylor Barry, Ky., Mar. 9, 1829, entered upon duties Apr. 6, 1829

Navy—Charles Hay (chief clerk), ad interim Mar. 4, 1829; John Branch, N.C., Mar. 9, 1829; John Boyle (chief clerk), ad interim May 12, 1831; Levi Woodbury, N.H., May 23, 1831

Peggy O'Neale, the wife of Secretary of War John Eaton, was not accepted by Washington society. Although Jackson championed her, the wives of other Cabinet members refused to entertain Mrs. Eaton. The dissension within the administration was such that Jackson often preferred to consult his "kitchen cabinet."

SECOND TERM

March 4, 1833–March 3, 1837

State—Edward Livingston, La., continued from preceding administration; Louis McLane, Del., May 29, 1833; John Forsyth, Ga., June 27, 1834, entered upon duties July 1, 1834

Treasury—Louis McLane, Del., continued from preceding administration; William John Duane, Pa., May 29, 1833, entered upon duties June 1, 1833; Roger Brooke Taney, Md., Sept. 23, 1833; McClintock Young (chief clerk), ad interim June 25, 1834; Levi Woodbury, N.H., June 27, 1834, entered upon duties July 1, 1834

War—Lewis Cass, Ohio, continued from preceding administration; Carey A. Harris, Tenn. (Commissioner of Indian Affairs), ad interim Oct. 5, 1836; Benjamin Franklin Butler, N.Y., commissioned Mar. 3, 1837, ad interim

Attorney General—Roger Brooke Taney, Md., continued from preceding administration to Sept. 23, 1833; Benjamin Franklin Butler, N.Y., Nov. 15, 1833; entered upon duties Nov. 18, 1833

Postmaster General—William Taylor Barry, Ky., continued from preceding administration; Amos Kendall, Ky., May 1, 1835

Navy—Levi Woodbury, N.H., continued from preceding administration; Mahlon Dickerson, N.J., June 30, 1834

CONGRESS

TWENTY-FIRST CONGRESS

March 4, 1829–March 3, 1831

First session—Dec. 7, 1829–May 31, 1830 (176 days)

Second session—Dec. 6, 1830–Mar. 3, 1831 (88 days)

Special session of the Senate—Mar. 4, 1829–Mar. 17, 1829 (14 days)

Vice President—John Caldwell Calhoun, S.C.

President pro tempore of the Senate —Samuel Smith, Md., elected Mar. 13, 1829, special session; May 29, 1830; Mar. 1, 1831

Secretary of the Senate—Walter Lowrie, Pa., reelected Dec. 14, 1829

Speaker of the House—Andrew Stevenson, Va., reelected Dec. 7, 1829

Clerk of the House—Matthew St. Clair Clarke, Pa., reelected Dec. 7, 1829

TWENTY-SECOND CONGRESS

March 4, 1831–March 3, 1833

First session—Dec. 5, 1831–July 16, 1832 (225 days)

Second session—Dec. 3, 1832–Mar. 2, 1833 (91 days)

Vice President—John Caldwell Calhoun, S.C., resigned Dec. 28, 1832, having been elected senator

President pro tempore of the Senate —Littleton Waller Tazewell, Va., elected July 9, 1832; Hugh Lawson White, Tenn., elected Dec. 3, 1832

Secretary of the Senate—Walter Lowrie, Pa., reelected Dec. 9, 1831

Speaker of the House—Andrew Stevenson, Va., reelected Dec. 5, 1831

Clerk of the House—Matthew St. Clair Clarke, Pa., reelected Dec. 5, 1831

TWENTY-THIRD CONGRESS

March 4, 1833–March 3, 1835

First session—Dec. 2, 1833–June 30, 1834 (211 days)

Second session—Dec. 1, 1834–Mar. 3, 1835 (93 days)

Vice President—Martin Van Buren, N.Y.

President pro tempore of the Senate —Hugh Lawson White, Tenn.; George Poindexter, Miss., elected June 28, 1834; John Tyler, Va., elected Mar. 3, 1835

Secretary of the Senate—Walter Lowrie, Pa., reelected Dec. 9, 1833

Speaker of the House—Andrew Stevenson, Va., reelected Dec. 2, 1833; resigned from the House June 2, 1834; John Bell, Tenn., elected June 2, 1834

Clerk of the House—Matthew St. Clair Clarke, Pa.; Walter S. Franklin, Pa., elected Dec. 2, 1833

TWENTY-FOURTH CONGRESS

March 4, 1835–March 3, 1837

First session—Dec. 7, 1835–July 4, 1836 (211 days)

Second session—Dec. 5, 1836–Mar. 3, 1837 (89 days)

Vice President—Martin Van Buren, N.Y.

President pro tempore of the Senate —William Rufus Devane King, Ala., elected July 1, 1836; Jan. 28, 1837

Secretary of the Senate—Walter Lowrie, Pa., reelected Dec. 15, 1835; resigned Dec. 5, 1836; Asbury Dickens, N.C., elected Dec. 12, 1836

Speaker of the House—James Knox Polk, Tenn., elected Dec. 7, 1835

Clerk of the House—Walter S. Franklin, Pa., reelected Dec. 7, 1835

APPOINTMENTS TO THE SUPREME COURT

Chief Justice

Roger Brooke Taney, Md., Mar. 15, 1836 (replaced John Marshall)

Associate Justices

John McLean, Ohio, Mar. 7, 1829 (replaced Robert Trimble)

Henry Baldwin, Pa., Jan. 6, 1830 (replaced Bushrod Washington)

James Moore Wayne, Ga., Jan. 9, 1835 (replaced William Johnson)

Philip Pendleton Barbour, Va., Mar. 15, 1836 (replaced Gabriel Duvall)

IMPORTANT DATES IN THE PRESIDENCY

Aug. 9, 1829, "Stourbridge Lion," first locomotive for railroad use, in service

Oct. 17, 1826, Delaware River and Chesapeake Bay canal formally opened

1830, Webster-Hayne debates on states' rights

1830, Indian Removal Act

June 8, 1830, *Vincennes,* first warship to circumnavigate the world, returned to New York City

1832, Jackson vetoed renewal of charter of the Bank of the United States

1832, Georgia defied Supreme Court decision upholding U.S. Treaty with Cherokees

Apr. 6, 1832, Black Hawk War began

June 28, 1832, cholera epidemic broke out at New York City

July 4, 1832, "America" first sung publicly, Boston, Mass.

Aug. 2, 1832, Black Hawk War ended

Nov. 24, 1832, South Carolina declared federal tariff acts null and void; compromise reached to save Union sent to Charleston and action was suspended

Dec. 1832, Jackson issued Proclamation on Nullification, in which he warned, "Disunion by armed force is treason"

Dec. 28, 1832, Vice President Calhoun resigned

1833, Jackson removed Government deposits from Bank of the United States

Mar. 20, 1833, treaty with Siam signed—first treaty with a Far Eastern nation

Jan. 29, 1834, President ordered War Department to quell riot at Chesapeake and Ohio Canal, near Williamsport, Ind.

Mar. 28, 1834, Senate voted to censure President for removing public deposits from Bank of the United States

June 21, 1834, McCormick's reaper patented

June 24, 1834, appointment of Roger B. Taney as Secretary of the Treasury rejected by Senate—first rejection of cabinet appointee

Jan. 8, 1835, U.S. government paid off the Federal debt; it was the first time the debt had been relieved, and its being retired ushered in a period of prosperity

Nov. 2, 1835, Second Seminole War begun by Osceola

Dec. 16, 1835, fire in New York City destroyed 600 buildings

Mar. 1, 1836, Texas declaration of independence

Mar. 6, 1836, slaughter of defenders of the Alamo

Apr. 21, 1836, Texans defeated Mexicans at San Jacinto battlefield

May 14, 1836, Wilkes expedition to the South Seas authorized

June 15, 1836, Arkansas admitted as the 25th state

July 4, 1836, Wisconsin Territory organized

July 11, 1836, Jackson issued "specie circular" requiring payment for public lands in coin

Jan. 26, 1837, Michigan admitted as the 26th state

Mar. 3, 1837, United States recognized independence of Texas

Mar. 16, 1837, Senate passed resolution expunging its 1834 censure of President

ADDITIONAL DATA ON JACKSON

ANDREW JACKSON

—was the first President born in a log cabin.

—was the first President born in South Carolina.

—was the second President whose birthplace was a matter of dispute. It was variously claimed that his birthplace was Union County, N.C.; Berkeley County, Va.; Augusta County, Va. (now W.Va.); York County, Pa.; England; Ireland; and on the high seas. However, Waxhaw, S.C., is now generally accepted.

—was the first President born west of the Allegheny Mountains.

—was the first President who had been a prisoner of war.

—was the first President to marry a woman who had been divorced.

—was the first President to receive a plurality of popular votes but fail to win the election (although the recorded 1824 popular vote is not considered accurate).

—was the second widower inaugurated President.

—was the first President whose candidacy was launched at a national nominating convention.

—was the first President who was a resident of a state other than his native state.

—was the first President to ride on a railroad train.

—could, most likely, have been elected for a third term, but as none of his predecessors had served more than two terms he refused to be a candidate again and supported Van Buren for the presidency.

JACKSON A WAR PRISONER

Jackson was only 13 when he joined the Continental Army, in which he served as a messenger. In April 1781, he and his older brother Robert were captured by the British and forced to march 40 miles to Camden, S.C., where they were incarcerated for two weeks in a POW camp; his brother died of smallpox not long after their release. Jackson thereafter bore permanent scars on his head and left hand, marking the places where a British officer had slashed him with a sword for refusing to clean his boots. His widowed mother died that same year of cholera, caught while she was tending other American POWs; his eldest brother, Hugh, had died of heat exhaustion after the Battle of Stono Ferry. Jackson thus lost his entire remaining family in the Revolution.

ANDREW JACKSON, DUELIST

There are many estimates of the number of brawls and duels in which Andrew Jackson is believed to have participated. Some sources maintain that the figure approximates one hundred.

History records one duel in which Andrew Jackson killed his opponent. Charles Dickinson, one of the best pistol shots in the United States, made derogatory remarks about Mrs. Jackson. Andrew Jackson challenged him to a duel. They met on May 30, 1806, at Harrison's Mills on Red River in Logan County, Ky. They stood 24 feet apart with pistols pointed downwards. At the signal, Dickinson fired first, breaking some of Jackson's ribs and grazing his breastbone. Jackson, without flinching, maintained his position and fired. His shot proved mortal. Dickinson's bullet remained permanently in Jackson's chest.

In 1813, Andrew Jackson was wounded in a gun battle at Nashville, Tenn., by a bullet fired by Jesse Benton. It was feared that Jackson's arm would have to be amputated. In 1832, an operation was performed and the bullet which had been imbedded in Jackson's arm for 20 years was removed.

NOMINATION OF VAN BUREN NOT CONFIRMED BY THE SENATE

President Andrew Jackson's nomination of Martin Van Buren to the post of minister to Great Britain in August 1831 was not confirmed by the Senate. Indeed, the deciding vote against Van Buren's appointment was cast by Vice President Calhoun, who had been repudiated by the President in 1831. Van Buren therefore relinquished his post and returned from England.

Jackson's Memorial, Lafayette Park (i.e. Square), Washington, D.C.

JACKSON DENOUNCED NULLIFICATION ATTEMPT

South Carolina assembled in convention passed an ordinance that declared:

> The several acts and parts of acts of the Congress of the United States, purporting to be laws for the imposing of duties and imposts on the importation of foreign commodities, and now having actual operation and effect within the United States, and more especially two acts for the same purposes, passed on the 29th of May 1828, and on the 14th of July 1832, are unauthorized by the Constitution of the United States, and violate the true meaning and intent thereof, and are null and void, and no law.

President Jackson issued a proclamation on December 10, 1832, in which he stated, in part:

> I consider, then, the power to annul a law of the United States, assumed by one state, incompatible with the existence of the Union, contradicted expressly by the letter of the Constitution, unauthorized by its spirit, inconsistent with every principle on which it was founded, and destructive of the great object for which it was formed.

The dispute ended in a compromise which provided for gradual reduction of the tariff, and South Carolina withdrew the ordinance. However, before the compromise was reached, the President had begun to mobilize federal troops and signaled that if South Carolina seceded he planned to hang John C. Calhoun, who had resigned as Vice President to become U.S. senator from South Carolina.

FIRST TRAIN TRIP BY A PRESIDENT

On June 6, 1833, President Jackson took the stagecoach from Washington, D.C., to Ellicott's Mill, Md., where he boarded a Baltimore and Ohio train for Baltimore, Md. It was a pleasure trip. (John Quincy Adams, however, had made a trip on the same line a few months earlier, when he was no longer President.)

HARVARD CONFERRED LL.D. ON JACKSON

The honorary degree of LL.D. was conferred on President Andrew Jackson by Harvard, Cambridge, Mass., on June 26, 1833. A distinguished alumnus, former President John Quincy Adams, expressed his disapproval of the award on June 18, to Josiah Quincy, president of Harvard College:

> As myself an affectionate child of our alma mater, I would not be present to witness her disgrace in conferring her highest literary honors upon a barbarian who could not write a sentence of grammar and hardly could spell his own name.

PRESIDENT JACKSON CENSURED

The first President to draw the censure of the Senate was Andrew Jackson, who displeased the Senate by opposing the recharter of the Bank of the United States. On December 11, 1833, the Senate directed Jackson to produce a bank document that he had read to his cabinet, but he refused, retorting that Constitution did not empower the Senate to require of a president "an account of any communication, either verbally or in writing, made to the heads of departments acting as a cabinet council." On March 28, 1834, by a vote of 26 to 20, the Senate passed a resolution declaring that Jackson "in the last executive proceedings in relation to the public revenue, has assumed upon himself authority and power not conferred by the Constitution and laws, but in derogation of both."

PRESIDENT JACKSON'S PROTEST

The Senate's censure of President Jackson prompted first presidential protest, signed on April 15, 1834. The protest concluded:

> To the end that the resolution of the Senate may not be hereafter drawn into precedent with the authority of silent acquiescence on the part of the Executive department, and to the end also that my motives and views in the Executive proceedings denounced in that resolution may be known to my fellow-citizens, to the world, and to all posterity, I respectfully request that this message and protest may be entered at length on the journals of the Senate.

The Senate, however, ordered his message not to be entered in the journal.

A motion expunging the censure resolution was passed by the Senate three years later, on March 16, 1837.

SENATE REJECTED JACKSON CABINET APPOINTEE

The first cabinet appointee rejected by the Senate was Roger Brooke Taney of Frederick, Md., who was proposed by President Andrew Jackson for Secretary of the Treasury. He was rejected by a vote of 28 to 18 on June 24, 1834.

JACKSON ESCAPED ASSASSINATION

The first attempt upon the life of a President was made January 30, 1835, upon President Andrew Jackson in the rotunda of the Capitol while he attended the funeral services for Representative Warren Ransom Davis of South Carolina. As Jackson was about to go to the portico, Richard Lawrence, a mentally unbalanced house painter, fired two pistols at him from a distance of only six feet. Both weapons misfired and Jackson was unhurt.

Lawrence was tried April 11, 1835, in the United States Circuit Court at Washington, D.C., and was committed to jail and mental hospitals for life. He suffered from chronic monomania and was found insane at the time of his act.

JACKSON APPOINTED CATHOLIC CHIEF JUSTICE

The first Roman Catholic Chief Justice of the Supreme Court of the United States was Roger Brooke Taney of Frederick, Md., who was appointed on March 28, 1836, by President Andrew Jackson to succeed John Marshall.

Courtesy of The Library of Congress

The Hermitage, Jackson's tomb, and Andrew J. Donelson's residence, 12 miles from Nashville, Tennessee.

JACKSON REFUNDED TAXES

A surplus of $37 million accumulated during President Jackson's administration. On June 23, 1836, Congress voted to permit the government to disburse all but $5 million to the states in proportion to their representation in Congress. About $28 million was distributed in three installments. The panic of 1837 caused a sudden shift in government finances, and revenues decreased to such an extent that payments of the balance were discontinued.

JACKSON'S KITCHEN CABINET

While feuding for most of his first term with those Cabinet members who were adherents of Vice President Calhoun, Jackson had a coterie of advisers who met with him unofficially in the kitchen or rear of the White House to discuss public affairs. Referred to as "Jackson's kitchen cabinet," they held no government positions and had no official standing. Among those who were in this group were Andrew Jackson Donelson, his private secretary; Amos Kendall of Kentucky, later Postmaster General; General Duff Green, editor of the *United States Telegraph*; Francis P. Blair, editor of the Washington, D.C., *Globe*; Isaac Hill, Senator from New Hampshire; and Major William B. Lewis of Nashville, Tenn.

EXTRACT FROM JACKSON'S WILL

June, 1843
The Hermitage

First, I bequeath my body to the dust whence it comes, and my soul to God who gave it, hoping for a happy immortality through the atoning merits of our Lord, Jesus Christ, the Saviour of the world. My desire is, that my body be buried by the side of my dear departed wife, in the garden at the Hermitage, in the vault prepared in the garden, and all expenses paid by my executor hereafter named. . . .

JACKSON WILLED HIS PISTOLS TO GENERAL ARMSTRONG

The famous pistols carried by Jackson are mentioned in his last will and testament:

As a memento of my high regard for Gen'l. Robert Armstrong as a gentleman, patriot and soldier, as well as for his meritorious military services under my command during the late British and Indian war, and remembering the gallant bearing of him and his gallant little band at Enotochopco Creek, when, falling desperately wounded, he called out— "My brave fellows, some may fall, but save the cannon"—as a memento of all these things, I give and bequeath to him my case of pistols and sword worn by me throughout my military career, well satisfied that in his hands they will never be disgraced—that they will never be used or drawn without occasion, nor sheathed but with honour.

JACKSON'S FINE RETURNED

On March 24, 1815, Judge Hall of the United States District Court at New Orleans fined Andrew Jackson $1,000 for contempt in declaring martial law during the defense of New Orleans. On January 8, 1844, the House of Representatives voted (158 to 28) to return the $1,000 with interest at 6 percent.

FURTHER READING

Cole, Donald B. *The Presidency of Andrew Jackson*. 1993.

Curtis, James C. *Andrew Jackson and the Search for Vindication*. 1976.

Marszalek, John. *The Petticoat Affair*. 1997.

Meacham, Jon. *American Lion: Andrew Jackson in the White House*. 2008.

Remini, Robert V. *Andrew Jackson and the Course of American Empire 1767–1821*. 1978.

———. *Andrew Jackson and the Course of American Freedom 1822–1832*. 1981.

———. *Andrew Jackson and the Course of American Democracy 1833–1845*. 1984.

Schlesinger, Arthur M. *The Age of Jackson*. 1945.

Courtesy of The Library of Congress

Martin Van Buren

Date of birth—Dec. 5, 1782

Place of birth—Kinderhook, N.Y.

Education—Attended public schoolhouse; Kinderhook Academy, N.Y.; private study at law offices of Francis Sylvester, Kinderhook, N.Y., 1796–1802, and William P. Van Ness, New York, N.Y., 1802

Religion—Dutch Reformed

Ancestry—Dutch

Career—Lawyer, county surrogate, state senator, state attorney general, U.S. senator, governor of New York, Secretary of State, Vice President

Political party—Democratic (Democratic-Republican)

State represented—New York

Term of office—Mar. 4, 1837–Mar. 4, 1841

Term served—4 years

Administration—13th

Congresses—25th, 26th

Age at inauguration—54 years, 89 days

Lived after term—21 years, 142 days

Occupation after term—Presidential candidate; active in Free Soil Party

Date of death—July 24, 1862

Age at death—79 years, 231 days

Place of death—Kinderhook, N.Y.

Burial place—Kinderhook Cemetery, Kinderhook, N.Y.

FAMILY

FATHER

Name—Abraham Van Buren

Date of birth—Feb. 17, 1737

Place of birth—Albany, N.Y.

Marriage— Maria Hoes Van Alen, 1776

Occupation—Farmer, innkeeper, tavern-keeper, captain in 7th Regiment, Albany County Militia; town clerk

Date of death—Apr. 8, 1817

Age at death—80 years, 40 days

MOTHER

Name at birth—Maria Hoes Van Alen

Date of birth—1747(?) (baptized Jan. 16, 1747)

First marriage—Johannes Van Alen (d.)

Second marriage—Abraham Van Buren, 1776

Date of death—Feb. 16, 1817 (or 1818)

SIBLINGS

Martin Van Buren was the third child in a family of five. He also had three half-siblings from his mother's first marriage.

Children of Abraham Van Buren and Maria Hoes Van Alen Van Buren

Derike (or Dirckie) Van Buren, b. 1777, d. Oct. 18, 1865

Hannah (or Jannetje) Van Buren, baptized Jan. 16, 1780

Martin Van Buren, b. Dec. 5, 1782, d. July 24, 1862

Lawrence Van Buren, baptized Jan. 8, 1786, d. July 1, 1868

Abraham Van Buren, baptized May 11, 1788, d. Oct. 30, 1836

Children of Johannes Van Alen and Maria Hoes Van Alen

James Isaac Van Alen, b. 1776, d. Dec. 23, 1870(?)

Two others, names unknown

MARRIAGE

Married—Hannah Hoes

Date of marriage—Feb. 21, 1807

Place of marriage—Catskill, N.Y.

Age of wife at marriage—23 years, 350 days

Age of husband at marriage—24 years, 78 days

Years married—11 years, 349 days

CHILDREN

Abraham Van Buren, b. Nov. 27, 1807, Kinderhook, N.Y.; m. Sarah Angelica Singleton, Nov. 27, 1838; d. Mar. 15, 1873, New York, N.Y.

John Van Buren, b. Feb. 18, 1810, Hudson, N.Y.; m. Elizabeth Van der Poel, June 22, 1841; d. Oct. 13, 1866, at sea

Martin Van Buren, b. Dec. 20, 1812; d. Mar. 19, 1855, Paris

Smith Thompson Van Buren, b. Jan. 16, 1817; m. Ellen King James, June 18, 1842; m. Henrietta Irving, Feb. 1, 1855; d. 1876

THE PRESIDENT'S WIFE

Name at birth—Hannah Hoes

Date of birth—Mar. 8, 1783

Place of birth—Kinderhook, N.Y.

Mother—Maria Quakenboss Hoes

Father—John Hoes

Marriage—Martin Van Buren, Feb. 21, 1807, Catskill, N.Y.

Children—Abraham Van Buren, b. Nov. 27, 1807, d. Mar. 15, 1873; John Van Buren, b. Feb. 18, 1810, d. Oct. 13, 1866; Martin Van Buren, b. Dec. 20, 1812, d. Mar. 19, 1855; Smith Thompson Van Buren, b. Jan. 16, 1817, d. 1876

Date of death—Feb. 5, 1819

Age at death—35 years, 334 days

Place of death—Albany, N.Y.

Burial place—Kinderhook, N.Y.

Years younger than the President—93 days

Years the President survived her—43 years, 169 days

Courtesy of The Library of Congress

Hannah Van Buren, wife of Martin Van Buren

HOSTESS AT THE WHITE HOUSE

Hannah Van Buren died about 19 years before Martin Van Buren became President. The mistress of the White House during his administration was Angelica Van Buren, the wife of Abraham Van Buren, President Van Buren's son and private secretary.

Hannah Hoes Van Buren has the distinction of being the first wife of a President to be born a citizen of the United States, rather than a British subject.

IMPORTANT DATES IN THE PRESIDENT'S LIFE

1796–1802, worked in law office of Francis Sylvester

1802, studied law in New York City with William P. Van Ness

1803, admitted to the bar; practiced in Kinderhook, N.Y.

1807, counselor of Supreme Court, N.Y.

Feb. 20, 1808, appointed surrogate of Columbia County, N.Y., by Governor Tompkins (his first public office)

1809, moved to Hudson, N.Y.

1813–1820, New York State Senate

1815–1819, attorney general, New York State

Mar. 4, 1821–Dec. 20, 1828, U.S. Senate (from New York); resigned

Aug. 28, 1821, delegate to 3rd New York State constitutional convention

Jan. 1, 1829–Mar. 12, 1829, governor of New York; resigned

Mar. 28, 1829–May 23, 1831, Secretary of State under Jackson; resigned

June 25, 1831, appointed minister to Great Britain

Jan. 25, 1832, U.S. Senate rejected his nomination; returned to United States

Mar. 4, 1833–Mar. 4, 1837, Vice President under Andrew Jackson

Mar. 4, 1837–Mar. 4, 1841, President

1840, unsuccessful Democratic nominee for reelection to the presidency; defeated in his own state

1844, unsuccessful Democratic candidate for nomination; received highest number of votes but not two-thirds majority

1848, unsuccessful Free Soil nominee for the presidency, not receiving any electoral votes; withdrew from public life; returned to his home, Lindenwald, at Kinderhook, N.Y.

ELECTIONS

THE ELECTION OF 1836

Since Congress had yet to establish a nationwide, uniform Election Day, the legislatures of the different states appointed a variety of voting days during the 34 days preceding the meeting of the electors, which was mandated for the first Wednesday in December. The polls opened in New Jersey, Pennsylvania, and Ohio on November 4, and in Rhode Island as late as November 23, with the polls in many places remaining open for several days to accommodate travelers.

CANDIDATES

Democratic (Democratic-Republican) Party (2nd Convention)

May 20–22, 1835, First Presbyterian Church, Baltimore, Md.

P: Martin Van Buren, N.Y.

VP: Richard Mentor Johnson, Ky.

Martin Van Buren was nominated on the first ballot with 265 votes. Nomination made unanimous

Whig Party (state convention)

December 14, 1835, Harrisburg, Pa.

P: William Henry Harrison, Ohio

VP: Francis Granger, N.Y.

The Anti-Masons and others opposed to Van Buren rallied to Harrison's support at this and other state conventions which confirmed Harrison's nomination. But the Whig Party (which had absorbed the short-lived National Republican Party) held no national convention and its electoral votes were divided among four presidential candidates.

1836 POPULAR VOTE

Democratic (Democratic-Republican) Party, 762,678

Whig Party, 735,561

Presidential candidates:

William Henry Harrison, Ohio

Hugh Lawson White, Tenn.

Daniel Webster, Mass.

Willie Person Mangum, N.C.

Vice presidential candidates:

Francis Granger, N.Y.
John Tyler, Va.
William Smith, Ala.

1836 ELECTORAL VOTE

There were 294 electoral votes from 26 states.

Van Buren received 57.82 percent (170 votes—15 states) as follows: Ala. 7; Ark. 3; Conn. 8; Ill. 5; La. 5; Me. 10; Mich. 3; Miss. 4; Mo. 4; N.H. 7; N.Y. 42; N.C. 15; Pa. 30; R.I. 4; Va. 23.

Harrison received 24.83 percent (73 votes—7 states) as follows: Del. 3; Ind. 9; Ky. 15; Md. 10; N.J. 8; Ohio 21; Vt. 7.

White received 8.85 percent (26 votes—2 states) as follows: Ga. 11; Tenn. 15.

Webster received 4.76 percent (1 state): Mass. 14.

Mangum received 3.74 percent (1 state): S.C. 11.

For the vice presidency Johnson received 147 votes, Granger 77 votes, Tyler 47 votes, and Smith 23 votes. Since no candidate had a majority, the election devolved upon the Senate, and Johnson was elected by a vote of 33 to 16.

INAUGURATION

March 4, 1837

Martin Van Buren took the oath of office on Saturday, March 4, 1837, on the east portico of the White House. Chief Justice Roger Brooke Taney administered the oath. As Van Buren and Jackson rode to the Capitol in a beautiful phaeton built from wood obtained from the frigate *Constitution*, they were accompanied by cavalry and infantry, as well as delegations from political organizations.

For several hours crowds visited the White House to greet the new President and pay their respects to Andrew Jackson.

This inauguration was in one respect a political curiosity. The Chief Justice of the United States Supreme Court, whose earlier appointments as Secretary of the Treasury and Associate Justice had not been confirmed by the Senate, swore in as President of the United States a man whose appointment as United States minister to Great Britain had likewise not been approved by the Senate.

THE VICE PRESIDENT

Name—Richard Mentor Johnson (9th V.P.)

Date of birth—Oct. 17, 1780

Place of birth—Floyd's Station, Ky.

Political party—Democratic (Democratic-Republican)

State represented—Kentucky

Term of office—Mar. 4, 1837–Mar. 4, 1841

Age at inauguration—56 years, 138 days

Occupation after term—Retired; served in Kentucky legislature

Date of death—Nov. 19, 1850

Age at death—70 years, 33 days

Place of death—Frankfort, Ky.

Burial place—Frankfort, Ky.

Courtesy of The Library of Congress

Richard Johnson, Vice President to Martin Van Buren

ADDITIONAL DATA ON JOHNSON

1802, admitted to the bar; practiced at Great Crossings, Ky.

1804–1807, Kentucky House of Representatives

Mar. 4, 1807–Mar. 3, 1819, U.S. House of Representatives (from Kentucky)

1813, served during term as colonel in Kentucky Volunteers; commanded regiment under General William Henry Harrison in the expedition and engagements in lower Canada in 1813; participated in the Battle of the Thames, Oct. 5, 1813

Apr. 4, 1818, by resolution of Congress he was presented with a sword in recognition of "the daring and distinguished valor displayed by himself and the regiment of volunteers under his command in charging and essentially contributing to vanquish the combined British and Indian forces" in the battle

1819, Kentucky House of Representatives

Dec. 10, 1819–Mar. 3, 1829, U.S. Senate (from Kentucky)

Mar. 4, 1829–Mar. 3, 1837, U.S. House of Representatives (from Kentucky)

1836, elected Vice President by the Senate

Mar. 4, 1837–Mar. 4, 1841, Vice President under Martin Van Buren

1840, 1844, unsuccessful Democratic candidate for Vice President

1850, Kentucky House of Representatives

A monument in Frankfort, Ky., identifies Johnson as the slayer of Tecumseh, commander of the Native American confederate forces at the Battle of the Thames, Oct. 5, 1813.

FIRST VICE PRESIDENT ELECTED BY THE SENATE

In the election of 1836, Richard Mentor Johnson of Kentucky received 147 of the 294 electoral votes for the vice presidency; Francis Granger of New York, 77 votes; John Tyler of Virginia, 47 votes; and William Smith of Alabama, 23 votes. There was no choice for Vice President by the people; the election devolved upon the Senate of the United States. Johnson received 33 votes, Granger received 16 votes, and Johnson was declared the elected Vice President.

The Twelfth Amendment to the Constitution provided that:

> If no person have a majority, then from the two highest numbers on the list, the Senate shall choose the Vice President; a quorum for the purpose shall consist of two thirds of the whole number of Senators, and a majority of the whole number shall be necessary to a choice.

CABINET

March 4, 1837–March 3, 1841

State—John Forsyth, Ga., continued from preceding administration

Treasury—Levi Woodbury, N.H., continued from preceding administration

War—Benjamin Franklin Butler, N.Y., ad interim, continued from preceding administration; Joel Roberts Poinsett, S.C., Mar. 7, 1837; entered upon duties Mar. 14, 1837

Attorney General—Benjamin Franklin Butler, N.Y., continued from preceding administration; Felix Grundy, Tenn., July

5, 1838, to take effect Sept. 1, 1838; Henry Dilworth Gilpin, Pa., Jan 11, 1840

Postmaster General—Amos Kendall, Ky., continued from preceding administration; John Milton Niles, Conn., May 19, 1840, to take effect May 25, 1840; entered upon duties May 26, 1840

Navy—Mahlon Dickerson, N.J., continued from preceding administration; James Kirke Paulding, N.Y., June 25, 1838, to take effect "after the 30th instant," entered upon duties July 1, 1838

CONGRESS

TWENTY-FIFTH CONGRESS

March 4, 1837–March 3, 1839

First session—Sept. 4, 1837–Oct. 16, 1837 (43 days)

Second session—Dec. 4, 1837–July 9, 1838 (218 days)

Third session—Dec. 3, 1838–Mar. 3, 1839 (91 days)

Special session of the Senate—Mar. 4, 1837–Mar. 10, 1837 (7 days)

Vice President—Richard Mentor Johnson, Ky.

President pro tempore of the Senate —William Rufus Devane King, Ala., elected Mar. 7, 1837, special session; Oct. 13, 1837; July 2, 1838; Feb. 25, 1839

Secretary of the Senate—Asbury Dickens, N.C., reelected Sept. 11, 1837

Speaker of the House—James Knox Polk, Tenn., reelected Sept. 4, 1837

Clerk of the House—Walter S. Franklin, Pa., reelected Sept. 4, 1837, died Sept. 20, 1838; Hugh A. Garland, Va., elected Dec. 3, 183

TWENTY-SIXTH CONGRESS

March 4, 1839–March 3, 1841

First session—Dec. 2, 1839–July 21, 1840 (233 days)

Second session—Dec. 7, 1840–Mar. 3, 1841 (87 days)

Vice President—Richard Mentor Johnson, Ky.

President pro tempore of the Senate —William Rufus Devane King, Ala., reelected July 3, 1840; Mar. 3, 1841

Secretary of the Senate—Asbury Dickens, N.C., reelected Dec. 9, 1839

Speaker of the House—Robert Mercer Taliaferro Hunter, Va., elected Dec. 9, 1839

Clerk of the House—Hugh A. Garland, Va., reelected Dec. 21, 1839

APPOINTMENTS TO THE SUPREME COURT

Associate Justices

William Smith, Ala., Mar. 8, 1837 (declined to serve)

John Catron, Tenn., Mar. 8, 1837 (newly created seat)

John McKinley, Ala., Apr. 22, 1837 (newly created seat)

Peter Vivian Daniel, Va., Mar. 3, 1841 (replaced Philip Pendleton Barbour)

IMPORTANT DATES IN THE PRESIDENCY

Mar. 6, 1837, General Jesup concluded agreement with Seminole Indian chiefs

Mar. 17, 1837, Republic of Texas adopted constitution

Spring 1837, financial panic of 1837

June 17, 1837, rubber patent obtained by Charles Goodyear

July 29, 1837, Chippewa treaty signed

Aug. 25, 1837, Texas petition for annexation refused

Oct. 12, 1837, $10 million in Treasury notes authorized to relieve economic distress

Oct. 21, 1837, Osceola, Seminole chief, seized while under flag of truce

Dec. 25, 1837, Seminoles defeated by General Zachary Taylor at Okeechobee swamp

Jan. 5, 1838, Van Buren issued neutrality proclamation in Great Britain–Canada dispute

Jan. 8, 1838, Alfred Vail transmitted telegraph message using dots and dashes

Jan. 26, 1838, Osceola died in prison

Jan. 26, 1838, Tennessee forbade liquor sales

Apr. 25, 1838, boundary treaty with Texas signed

June 12, 1838, Iowa territorial government authorized

Aug. 18, 1838, Charles Wilkes left Hampton Roads, Va., on scientific expedition to the South Seas

Winter, 1838–1839, Cherokees removed from the South to Oklahoma, on the "Trail of Tears"

Feb. 23, 1839, express service organized, Boston, Mass.

Mar. 3, 1839, President authorized to send troops to Maine to protect frontiersmen in Aroostook War

Feb. 1, 1840, Baltimore College of Dental Surgery, first dental school incorporated

July 4, 1840, independent treasury system created; subtreasuries established in New York, Boston, Charleston, and St. Louis

ADDITIONAL DATA ON VAN BUREN

MARTIN VAN BUREN

—was the first President born in New York.

—was the third widower inaugurated President.

—was the first President not born a British subject.

—was the first President whose son died in a foreign country.

—was the only President to have had a bilingual upbringing. As a boy he spoke both Dutch and English.

—was the eighth President and eighth Vice President of the United States.

—lived to see eight Presidents from eight different states succeed him.

—was the last Vice President until the late twentieth century to be elected to succeed the President under whom he served. The only other Vice Presidents similarly elected—not counting those who succeeded to the presidency and were then elected in their own right—were John Adams in 1796, Thomas Jefferson in 1800, and George Bush in 1988.

—brought his four sons with him when he went to the White House in 1837. They were 20, 25, 27, and 30 years of age.

FIRST PRESIDENT BORN AN AMERICAN CITIZEN

The first President born a citizen of the United States and therefore never a British subject was Martin Van Buren, born December 5, 1782.

VAN BUREN CHANGED JOBS

In fourteen weeks Martin Van Buren held three important positions. On December 20, 1828, he gave up the office of United States senator. Eleven days later, he was governor of New York State. Sixty-four days later, he was made secretary of state under President Andrew Jackson, resigning the governorship on March 12 and assuming his new post on March 28.

VAN BUREN WAS O.K.

The expression "O.K." or "Okay" was solidified as part of the English language because Martin Van Buren was born in Kinderhook, N.Y. He was known by the nickname of "Old Kinderhook," and the O.K. Club of New York City, a Democratic organization formed in 1840, was named for him. A rage for abbreviations swept New York and Boston around that time. The Democrats' use of "O.K." as their slogan won a permanent place in the language to mean "all correct," in comic spelling, "oll korrect."

VAN BUREN SOUGHT REELECTION

Martin Van Buren, who served as President from 1837 to 1841, made three unsuccessful attempts to be reelected. He was renominated by the Democrats in 1840 but was defeated by the Whig candidate, William Henry Harrison. Van Buren won in only 7 of the 26 states.

In the 1844 convention, he received 146 of the 266 votes on the first nominating ballot, but the two-thirds rule was in effect and 177 votes were required for choice. He could not muster sufficient strength and the nomination was captured on the ninth ballot by a "dark horse," James Knox Polk, who had the support of former President Andrew Jackson.

The Democrats did not consider him as their candidate in 1848, but the party's anti-slavery faction formed the Free Soil Party and ran Van Buren for President. In this election, his fourth candidacy, he received not a single electoral vote and less than 11 percent of the popular vote.

FURTHER READING

Alexander, H. M. *The American Talleyrand: The Career and Contemporaries of Martin Van Buren.* 1962.

Cole, Donald B. *Martin Van Buren and the American Political System.* 1984.

Niven, John. *Martin Van Buren.* 1983.

Remini, Robert V. *Martin Van Buren and the Making of the Democratic Party.* 1959.

Shepard, Edward M. *Martin Van Buren.* 1983.

Wilson, Major. *The Presidency of Martin Van Buren.* 1985.

Courtesy of The Library of Congress

The Martin Van Buren residence in Kinderhook, New York

Courtesy of The Library of Congress

W. H. Harrison

William Henry Harrison

Date of birth—Feb. 9, 1773

Place of birth—Berkeley, Charles City County, Va.

Education—Tutored; Hampden-Sydney College, Hampden-Sydney, Va., 1787–1790; medical apprentice, Dr. Andrew Leiper, Richmond, Va., 1790; University of Pennsylvania Medical School, Philadelphia, Pa., 1791

Religion—Episcopalian

Ancestry—English

Career—Army officer, secretary of Northwest Territory, territorial delegate to U.S. House, governor of Indiana Territory, Army general in War of 1812, U.S. representative, state senator, U.S. senator, minister to Colombia

Political party—Whig

State represented—Ohio

Term of office—Mar. 4, 1841–Apr. 4, 1841

Term served—32 days

Administration—14th

Congresses—27th

Age at inauguration—68 years, 23 days

Date of death—Apr. 4, 1841 (died in office)

Age at death—68 years, 54 days

Place of death—Washington, D.C.

Burial place—William Henry Harrison Memorial State Park, North Bend, Ohio

FAMILY

FATHER

Name—Benjamin Harrison V

Date of birth—Apr. 5, 1726,

Place of birth—Berkeley, Va.

Marriage—Elizabeth Bassett, 1748

Occupation—Planter; Virginia legislator (House of Burgesses, Speaker of the House of Delegates), member of Continental Congress, governor of Virginia; active in Revolution, signer of Declaration of Independence

Date of death—Apr. 24, 1791

Place of death—City Point, Va.

Age at death—65 years, 19 days

MOTHER

Name at birth—Elizabeth Bassett

Date of birth—Dec. 13, 1730

Place of birth—Berkeley, Va.

Marriage—Benjamin Harrison, 1748

Date of death—1792

Place of death—Berkeley, Va.

Age at death—62 years

SIBLINGS

William Henry Harrison was the seventh child in a family of seven.

Children of Benjamin Harrison and Elizabeth Bassett Harrison

Elizabeth Harrison, b. 1751
Ann Harrison, b. May 21, 1753, d. 1821
Benjamin Harrison, b. 1755, d. 1799
Lucy Harrison, d. 1809
Carter Bassett Harrison, d. Apr. 18, 1808
Sarah Harrison, b. 1770, d. 1812
William Henry Harrison, b. Feb. 9, 1773, d. Apr. 4, 1841

Courtesy of The Library of Congress

William Henry Harrison's residence, "Berkeley," in Charles City, Virginia

MARRIAGE

Married—Anna Tuthill Symmes

Date of marriage—Nov. 25, 1795

Place of marriage—North Bend, Ohio

Age of wife at marriage—20 years, 123 days

Age of husband at marriage—22 years, 289 days

Years married—45 years, 130 days

CHILDREN

Elizabeth Bassett Harrison, b. Sept. 29, 1796, Fort Washington, Ohio; m. June 29, 1814, John Cleves Short; d. Sept. 26, 1846

John Cleves Symmes Harrison, b. Oct. 28, 1798, Vincennes, Ind.; m. Sept. 29, 1819, Clarissa Pike; d. Oct. 30, 1830

Lucy Singleton Harrison, b. Sept. 1800, Richmond, Va.; m. Sept. 30, 1819, David K. Este; d. Apr. 7, 1826, Cincinnati, Ohio

William Henry Harrison, b. Sept. 3, 1802, Vincennes, Ind.; m. Feb. 18, 1824, Jane Findlay Irwin; d. Feb. 6, 1838, North Bend, Ohio

John Scott Harrison, b. Oct. 4, 1804, Vincennes, Ind.; m. 1824, Lucretia Knapp Johnson; m. Aug. 12, 1831, Elizabeth Ramsey Irwin; d. May 25, 1878, Point Farm, Ind.

Benjamin Harrison, b. 1806, Vincennes, Ind.; m. Louisa Bonner; m. Mary Raney; d. June 9, 1840

Mary Symmes Harrison, b. Jan. 22, 1809, Vincennes, Ind.; m. Mar. 5, 1829, John Henry Fitzhugh Thornton; d. Nov. 16, 1842

Carter Bassett Harrison, b. Oct. 26, 1811, Vincennes, Ind.; m. June 16, 1836, Mary Anne Sutherland; d. Aug. 12, 1839

Anna Tuthill Harrison, b. Oct. 28, 1813, Cincinnati, Ohio; m. June 16, 1836, William Henry Harrison Taylor, d. July 5, 1845

James Findlay Harrison, b. 1814, North Bend, Ohio; d. 1817, North Bend, Ohio

THE PRESIDENT'S WIFE

Name at birth—Anna Tuthill Symmes

Date of birth—July 25, 1775

Place of birth—Morristown, N.J.

Mother—Anna Tuthill Symmes (d. July 17, 1776)

Stepmothers—Mary Henry Halsey Symmes; Susanna Livingston Symmes

Father—John Cleves Symmes

Father's occupation—Judge, landowner

Education—Clinton Academy, Easthampton, N.Y.; Mrs. Graham's Boarding School for Young Ladies, New York, N.Y.

Marriage—William Henry Harrison Nov. 25, 1795, North Bend, Ohio

Children—Elizabeth Bassett Harrison, b. Sept. 29, 1796, d. Sept. 26, 1846; John Cleves Symmes Harrison, b. Oct. 28, 1798, d. Oct. 30, 1830; Lucy Singleton Harrison, b. Sept. 1800, d. Apr. 7, 1826, Cincinnati, Ohio; William Henry Harrison, b. Sept. 3, 1802, d. Feb. 6, 1838; John Scott Harrison, b. Oct. 4, 1804, d. May 25, 1878; Benjamin Harrison, b. 1806, d. June 9, 1840; Mary Symmes Harrison, b. Jan. 22, 1809, d. Nov.

Courtesy of The Library of Congress

Anna Harrison, wife of William Henry Harrison

16, 1842; Carter Bassett Harrison, b. Oct. 26, 1811, d. Aug. 12, 1839; Anna Tuthill Harrison, b. Oct. 28, 1813, d. July 5, 1845; James Findlay Harrison, b. 1814, d. 1817

Date of death—Feb. 25, 1864

Age at death—88 years, 215 days

Place of death—North Bend, Ohio

Burial place—North Bend, Ohio

Years younger than the President—2 years, 166 days

Years she survived the President—22 years, 327 days

THE FIRST LADY

Anna Symmes Harrison, the wife of William Henry Harrison, was taken ill one month before the inauguration and did not accompany her husband to Washington. Mrs. Harrison intended to follow later, but her husband died before she arrived. Harrison's daughter-in-law, Mrs. Jane Irwin Harrison, the wife of Colonel William Henry Harrison, Jr., accompanied the President to Washington and acted temporarily as mistress of the White House. There was practically no social activity at the White House in the short time Harrison presided there.

IMPORTANT DATES IN THE PRESIDENT'S LIFE

1791, enrolled in the medical school of the University of Pennsylvania

Aug. 1791, left school to join Army

Aug. 16, 1791, commissioned ensign in the First Infantry by General George Washington

June 2, 1792, commissioned a second lieutenant

1793, aide-de-camp under General Anthony Wayne

1793, general orders issued thanking him and others for their part in expedition that erected Fort Recovery

June 30, 1794, served in Indian war

Aug. 20, 1794, fought in Battle of Miami Rapids

May 15, 1797, promoted to captain; given command of Fort Washington

June 1, 1798, resigned with rank of captain

1798–1799, secretary of the Northwest Territory (appointed at $1,200 a year by President John Adams; resigned in Oct. 1799)

Mar. 4, 1799–May 14, 1800, U.S. House of Representatives (delegate from the Territory Northwest of the River Ohio)

1800–1813, territorial governor of Indiana and superintendent of Indian Affairs (appointed by President John Adams; reappointed by Presidents Jefferson and Madison)

Nov. 7, 1811, defeated Indians under the Prophet, brother of Chief Tecumseh, at Tippecanoe, on the Wabash River (American casualties: 108 killed and wounded)

Courtesy of The Library of Congress

William Henry Harrison leading an attack at the Battle of Tippecanoe, Nov. 6, 1811

1811, complimented by President Madison; votes of thanks extended to him by legislatures of Kentucky and Indiana

Aug. 22, 1812, commissioned major general of Kentucky militia in War of 1812

Sept. 2, 1812, commissioned brigadier general in U.S. Army

Mar. 2, 1813, commissioned major general in chief command of the Northwest

Oct. 5, 1813, defeated the British and Indians in Battle of the Thames (Ontario), in which Tecumseh was killed

May 31, 1814, resigned from U.S. Army

1814, appointed head commissioner to treat with the Indians

Oct. 8, 1816–Mar. 3, 1819, U.S. House of Representatives (from Ohio)

Mar. 24, 1818, received gold medal from Congress for his victory at the battle of the Thames

Dec. 6, 1819–1821, member of Ohio Senate

1822, unsuccessful candidate for U.S. House of Representatives

Mar. 4, 1825–May 20, 1828, U.S. Senate (from Ohio)

May 24, 1828–Sept. 26, 1829, envoy extraordinary and minister plenipotentiary to Colombia

1829, retired to his farm at North Bend, Ohio

1829–1836, county recorder, clerk of county court, president of county agricultural society

Nov. 8, 1836, unsuccessful Whig candidate for the presidency

Mar. 4–Apr. 4, 1841, President

ELECTIONS

THE ELECTION OF 1840

Since Congress had yet to establish a nationwide, uniform Election Day, the legislatures of the different states appointed a variety of voting days during the 34 days preceding the meeting of the electors, which was mandated for the first Wednesday in December. The polls in Pennsylvania and Ohio opened as early as October 30, 1840, and in North Carolina as late as November 12; South Carolina's electors were not chosen by its legislature until the end of November.

CANDIDATES

Whig Party

Dec. 4–7, 1839, Zion Lutheran Church, Harrisburg, Pa.

P: William Henry Harrison, Ohio
VP: John Tyler, Va.

Harrison was nominated on the second ballot. Candidates for nomination and the votes they received on the first and second ballots:

Henry Clay, Ky., 103, 90
William Henry Harrison, Ohio, 94, 148
Winfield Scott, N.J., 57, 16

This was the first national convention to adopt the unit rule by which all the votes of a state delegation are cast for the candidate who receives a majority of the state's votes. There were 254 delegates from 22 states.

On May 4–5, 1840, the nomination was approved at a meeting of young Whigs at Baltimore, Md.

Democratic (Democratic-Republican) Party (3rd Convention)

May 5–7, 1840, Hall of the Musical Association, Baltimore, Md.

P: Martin Van Buren, N.Y.

Nomination unanimous on the first ballot. The nomination for the vice presidency was not made at this convention. Each state proposed its own nominee. Candidates running on the Democratic ticket included the following:

Richard Mentor Johnson, Ky.
Littleton Waller Tazewell, Va.
James Knox Polk, Tenn.
The nomination was accorded to Johnson.

Liberty (Abolitionist) Party

Nov. 13, 1839, Warsaw, N.Y.

P: James Gillespie Birney, N.Y.
VP: Francis Julius Lemoyne, Pa.

Both candidates declined the nomination, and on April 1, 1840, another nominating convention was held at Albany, N.Y.:

P: James Gillespie Birney, N.Y.
VP: Thomas Earle, Pa.

This newly formed political party advocated abolition of slavery in the District of Columbia, as well as abolition of interstate slave trade, and generally opposed slavery to the fullest extent within constitutional powers.

At this "national" convention, the name Liberty Party was adopted. The nominees declined the nomination, but more than 7,000 votes were cast for them in the popular election.

1840 POPULAR VOTE

Whig Party, 1,275,016
Democratic (Democratic-Republican) Party, 1,129,102
Liberty (Abolitionist) Party

1840 ELECTORAL VOTE

There were 294 electoral votes from 26 states.

Harrison received 79.60 percent (234 votes—19 states) as follows: Conn. 8; Del. 3; Ga. 11; Ind. 9; Ky. 15; La. 5; Me. 10; Md. 10; Mass. 14; Mich. 3; Miss. 4; N.J. 8; N.Y. 42; N.C. 15; Ohio 21; Pa. 30; R.I. 4; Tenn. 15; Vt. 7.

Van Buren received 20.40 percent (60 votes—7 states) as follows: Ala. 7; Ark. 3; Ill. 5; Mo. 4; N.H. 7; S.C. 11; Va. 23.

For the vice presidency the 60 Democratic votes were divided as follows: Johnson received 48 votes, Tazewell received 11 votes, and Polk received 1 vote.

INAUGURATION

March 4, 1841

William Henry Harrison took the oath of office on Thursday, March 4, 1841, on the east portico of the Capitol. He was 68 years and 23 days old. The oath was administered by Chief Justice Taney. Harrison rode a white horse to the Capitol, refusing to wear hat or coat despite the cold and stormy weather. He read his 8,578-word inaugural address, the longest on record, taking about one hour and 45 minutes.

After the ceremony, he led the inaugural parade to the White House. Numerous floats depicting log cabins and cider barrels were highlights of the parade. Great crowds flocked to the White House.

In the evening, Harrison attended three inaugural balls: one known as the "Native American Inaugural Ball"; another on Louisiana Avenue in a converted theatre known as the new Washington Assembly Room; and the third the People's Tippecanoe Ball at Carusi's Saloon between 10th and 11th Streets on C Street, attended by a thousand people who paid 10 dollars each.

Harrison caught cold at the ceremonies and was prostrated by a chill on March 27, 1841. He died of pleurisy fever (pneumonia) at 1:30 A.M. on Sunday April 4, 1841.

THE VICE PRESIDENT

Name—John Tyler (10th V.P.)

Political party—Whig (originally Democratic)

State represented—Virginia

Term of office—Mar. 4, 1841–Apr. 6, 1841

Age at inauguration—50 years, 340 days

Occupation after term—President of the United States

For further biographical information, see the chapter on John Tyler, 10th President, on page 121.

Courtesy of The Library of Congress

John Tyler, Vice President to William Henry Harrison

CABINET

March 4, 1841–April 4, 1841

State—J. L. Martin (chief clerk), ad interim Mar. 4, 1841; Daniel Webster, Mass., Mar. 5, 1841

Treasury—McClintock Young (chief clerk), ad interim Mar. 4, 1841; Thomas Ewing, Ohio, Mar. 5, 1841

War—John Bell, Tenn., Mar. 5, 1841

Attorney General—John Jordan Crittenden, Ky., Mar. 5, 1841

Postmaster General—Selah Reeve Hobbie, N.Y. (first assistant Postmaster General), ad interim Mar. 4, 1841; Francis Granger, N.Y., Mar. 6, 1841, entered upon duties Mar. 8, 1841

Navy—John D. Simms (chief clerk), ad interim Mar. 4, 1841; George Edmund Badger, N.C., Mar. 5, 1841

CONGRESS

TWENTY-SEVENTH CONGRESS

March 4, 1841–March 3, 1843

First session—May 31, 1841–Sept. 13, 1841 (106 days)

Second session—Dec. 6, 1841–Aug. 31, 1842 (269 days)

Third session—Dec. 5, 1842–Mar. 3, 1843 (89 days)

Special session of the Senate—Mar. 4, 1841–Mar. 15, 1841 (12 days)

Vice President—John Tyler, Va. (succeeded to the presidency on Apr. 4, 1841, on the death of William Henry Harrison)

President pro tempore of the Senate—William Rufus Devane King, Ala., elected Mar. 4, 1841, special session; Samuel Lewis Southard, N.J., elected Mar. 11, 1841; Willie Person Mangum, N.C., elected May 31, 1842

Secretary of the Senate—Asbury Dickens, N.C., reelected June 7, 1841

Speaker of the House—John White, Ky., elected May 31, 1841

Clerk of the House—Hugh A. Garland, Va., continued from preceding Congress; Matthew St. Clair Clarke, Pa., elected May 31, 1841

Courtesy of The Library of Congress

An untitled woodcut apparently created for use on broadsides or banners during the Whigs' "log cabin" campaign of 1840

IMPORTANT DATES IN THE PRESIDENCY

Mar. 9, 1841, decision by Supreme Court freed Negroes taken from Spanish ship *Amistad* after they had seized the ship (defense argued by John Quincy Adams)

Mar. 12, 1841, British minister made formal demand for release of Alexander McLeod, Canadian deputy sheriff involved in death of American citizen during Canadian rebellion (1837)

Mar. 17, 1841, Claims Convention signed with Peru

Mar. 27, 1841, steam fire-engine publicly tested, New York, N.Y.

ADDITIONAL DATA ON HARRISON

WILLIAM HENRY HARRISON

—was the first President to die in office. He died on April 4, 1841, in the White House.

—was the first President whose father had been a governor of a state (Virginia).

—was the second President who was a resident of a state other than his native state.

—was the fifth President born in Virginia.

—was the last President born before the American Revolution. He was born February 9, 1773.

—was the second President whose father had been a signer of the Declaration of Independence.

—was the first and only President who studied to become a doctor. He was regularly enrolled in the Medical Department of the University of Pennsylvania and completed 16 weeks of a 32-week course.

—served the shortest term as President, from March 4, 1841, to April 4, 1841.

—was the only President whose grandson (Benjamin Harrison) also became a President.

—was the first President to lie in state in the White House.

HARRISON ARRIVED BY TRAIN

William Henry Harrison was the first President-elect to arrive by railroad at Washington, D.C., for his inauguration. Harrison left Baltimore, Md., February 9, 1841, on his 68th birthday. He boarded a Baltimore and Ohio Railroad train and arrived at Washington, D.C., where he registered at Gadsby's Hotel.

HARRISON'S PROPHETIC FAREWELL

In a speech delivered January 26, 1841, at Cincinnati, Ohio, Harrison said: "Gentlemen and fellow citizens. . . . Perhaps this may be the last time I may have the pleasure of speaking to you on earth or seeing you. I will bid you farewell, if forever, fare thee well."

Courtesy of The Library of Congress

The tomb of William Henry Harrison, North Bend, Ohio

FATHERS OF HARRISON AND TYLER BOTH VIRGINIA STATESMEN

The Whig ticket of 1840 featured two candidates from Virginia whose fathers—Benjamin Harrison V and John Tyler, Sr.—had much in common, and who indeed were political rivals. Both had been active in the Revolution. Both were wealthy planters who served in Virginia's House of Delegates. Both of them were elected Speaker of the House of Delegates, with Tyler succeeding Harrison as Speaker in 1781 and Harrison defeating Tyler in a contest for the speakership some years later. Both ran for the same seat in the House of Delegates in 1784, with Harrison losing to Tyler. Both became governors of the state of Virginia, Benjamin Harrison V from 1781 to 1784 and John Tyler, Sr., from 1808 to 1811.

HARRISON'S FAMILY IN OFFICE

Benjamin Harrison of Virginia, one of the signers of the Declaration of Independence and a member of the Continental Congress from 1774 to 1778, was the father of William Henry Harrison.

Carter Bassett Harrison of Virginia, who served in the Third, Fourth, and Fifth Congresses from March 4, 1793, to March 3, 1799, was a brother of William Henry Harrison.

John Scott Harrison, a Whig representative from Ohio in the 34th and 35th Congresses from March 4, 1853, to March 3, 1857, was a son of William Henry Harrison.

Benjamin Harrison, a Republican senator from March 4, 1881, to March 3, 1887, and President of the United States from March 4, 1889, to March 3, 1893, was a grandson of William Henry Harrison.

FURTHER READING

Cleaves, Freeman. *Old Tippecanoe.* 1939.

Goebel, Dorothy. *William Henry Harrison.* 1974.

Owens, Robert M. *Mr. Jefferson's Hammer: William Henry Harrison and the Origins of American Indian Policy.* 2007.

Peterson, Norma Lois. *The Presidencies of William Henry Harrison and John Tyler.* 1989.

John Tyler

Date of birth—Mar. 29, 1790

Place of birth—Charles City County, Va.

Education—Preparatory division, College of William and Mary, Williamsburg, Va.; College of William and Mary, graduated July 4, 1807; private law study with father and cousin and at law office of Edmund Randolph, Richmond, Va.

Religion—Episcopalian

Ancestry—English

Career—Lawyer, state legislator, member of state council, U.S. congressman, governor of Virginia, U.S. senator, Vice President

Political party—Whig (originally Democratic)

State represented—Virginia

Term of office—Apr. 6, 1841–Mar. 4, 1845 (Tyler succeeded to the presidency on the death of William Henry Harrison)

Term served—3 years, 332 days

Administration—14th

Congresses—27th, 28th

Age at inauguration—51 years, 8 days

Lived after term—16 years, 320 days

Occupation after term—Lawyer, chancellor of College of William and Mary, delegate to Virginia secession convention, delegate to Confederate Provisional Congress

Date of death—Jan. 18, 1862

Age at death—71 years, 295 days

Place of death—Richmond, Va.

Burial place—Hollywood Cemetery, Richmond, Va.

FAMILY

FATHER

Name—John Tyler

Date of birth—Feb. 28, 1747

Place of birth—Yarmouth, James City County, Va.

Marriage—Mary Marot Armistead, 1776, Weyanoke, Va.

Occupation—Planter, soldier, lawyer; Virginia legislator (Speaker of House of Delegates), state and federal judge, governor of Virginia; active in Revolution

Date of death—Jan. 6, 1813

Place of death—Charles City County, Va.

Age at death—65 years, 312 days

MOTHER

Name at birth—Mary Marot Armistead

Date of birth—1761

Marriage—John Tyler, 1776, Weyanoke, Va.

Date of death—Apr. 1797

Age at death—36 years

SIBLINGS

John Tyler was the sixth child in a family of eight.

Children of John Tyler and Mary Marot Armistead Tyler

Anne Contesse Tyler, b. 1778, d. June 12, 1803

Elizabeth Armistead Tyler, b. 1780, d. 1824

Martha Jefferson Tyler, b. 1782, d. 1855

Maria Henry Tyler, b. 1784, d. 1843

Wat Henry Tyler, b. 1788, d. July 1862

John Tyler, b. Mar. 29, 1790, d. Jan. 18, 1862

William Tyler, d. 1856

Christianna Booth Tyler, b. 1795, d. 1842

MARRIAGES

First marriage

Married—Letitia Christian

Date of marriage—Mar. 29, 1813

Place of marriage—New Kent County, Va.

Age of wife at marriage—22 years, 137 days

Age of husband at marriage—23 years

Years married—20 years, 165 days

Second marriage

Married—Julia Gardiner

Date of marriage—June 26, 1844

Place of marriage—New York, N.Y.

Age of wife at marriage—24 years, 53 days

Age of husband at marriage—54 years, 89 days

Years married—17 years, 206 days

PRESIDENT TYLER REMARRIED

John Tyler was the first President to marry while in office. After the death of his first wife, he remained a widower for a little over twenty-one months. He married Julia Gardiner on June 26, 1844, at the Church of the Ascension, New York, N.Y.

CHILDREN

Children of John Tyler and Letitia Christian Tyler

Mary Tyler, b. Apr. 15, 1815; m. Dec. 14, 1835, Henry Lightfoot Jones; d. June 17, 1848

Robert Tyler, b. Sept. 9, 1816; m. Sept. 12, 1839, Elizabeth Priscilla Cooper; d. Dec. 3, 1877

John Tyler, b. Apr. 27, 1819; m. Oct. 25, 1838, Martha Rochelle; d. Jan. 26, 1896

Letitia Tyler, b. May 11, 1821; m. James A. Semple; d. Dec. 28, 1907

Elizabeth Tyler, b. July 11, 1823; m. Jan. 31, 1842, William Nevison Waller at the White House, Washington, D.C.; d. June 1, 1850

Courtesy of The Library of Congress

John Tyler's Sherwood Forest residence in Charles City, Virginia

Anne Contesse Tyler, b. Apr. 1825; d. July 1825

Alice Tyler, b. Mar. 23, 1827; m. 1850, Rev. Henry Mandeville Denison; d. June 8, 1854

Tazewell ("Taz") Tyler, b. Dec. 6, 1830; m. Dec. 1857, Nannie Bridges (div. 1873); d. Jan. 8, 1874

Children of John Tyler and Julia Gardiner Tyler

David Gardiner ("Gardie") Tyler, b. July 12, 1846, Charles City County, Va.; m. June 6, 1894, Mary Morris Jones; d. Sept. 5, 1927, Richmond, Va.

John Alexander Tyler, b. Apr. 7, 1848; m. Sarah Gardiner; d. Sept. 1, 1883

Julia Tyler, b. Dec. 25, 1849; m. June 26, 1869, William H. Spencer; d. May 8, 1871

Lachlan Tyler, b. Dec. 2, 1851; m. Georgia Powell; d. Jan. 26, 1902, New York, N.Y.

Lyon Gardiner Tyler, b. Aug. 1853, Charles City County, Va.; m. Nov. 14, 1878, Annie Baker Tucker; m. Sept. 12, 1923, Susan Ruffin; d. Feb. 12, 1935, Charles City County, Va.

Robert Fitzwalter Tyler, b. Mar. 12, 1856; m. Fannie Glinn; d. Dec. 30, 1927, Richmond, Va.

Pearl Tyler, b. June 20, 1860; m. Major William Mumford Ellis; d. June 30, 1947, Elliston, Va.

THE PRESIDENT'S WIVES

First Wife

Name at birth—Letitia Christian

Date of birth—Nov. 12, 1790

Place of birth—Cedar Grove, New Kent County, Va.

Mother—Mary Brown Christian

Father—Colonel Robert Christian

Father's occupation—Planter

Marriage—John Tyler, Mar. 29, 1813, New Kent County, Va.

Children—Mary Tyler, b. Apr. 15, 1815, d. June 17, 1848; Robert Tyler, b. Sept. 9, 1816, d. Dec. 3, 1877; John Tyler, b. Apr. 27, 1819, d. Jan. 26, 1896; Letitia Tyler, b. May 11, 1821, d. Dec. 28, 1907; Elizabeth Tyler, b. July 11, 1823, d. June 1, 1850; Anne Contesse Tyler, b. Apr. 1825, d. July 1825; Alice Tyler, b. Mar. 23, 1827, d. June 8, 1854; Tazewell Tyler, b. Dec. 6, 1830, d. Jan. 8, 1874

Date of death—Sept. 10, 1842

Age at death—51 years, 302 days

Place of death—White House, Washington, D.C.

Burial place—Cedar Grove, Va.

Years younger than the President—228 days

Years the President survived her—19 years, 130 days

Second wife

Name at birth—Julia Gardiner

Date of birth—May 4, 1820

Place of birth—Gardiner's Island, N.Y.

Mother—Juliana McLachlan Gardiner

Father—David Gardiner

Father's occupation—U.S. Senate (from New York)

Education—Chegary Institute, New York, N.Y.

Marriage—John Tyler, June 26, 1844, New York, N.Y.

Children—David Gardiner Tyler, b. July 12, 1846, d. Sept. 5, 1927; John Alexander Tyler, b. Apr. 7, 1848, d. Sept. 1, 1883; Julia Tyler, b. Dec. 25, 1849, d. May 8, 1871;

Courtesy of The Library of Congress

Julia Tyler, second wife of John Tyler.

Lachlan Tyler, b. Dec. 2, 1851, d. Jan. 26, 1902; Lyon Gardiner Tyler, b. Aug. 1853, d. Feb. 12, 1935; Robert Fitzwalter Tyler, b. Mar. 12, 1856, d. Dec. 30, 1927; Pearl Tyler, b. June 20, 1860, d. June 30, 1947.

Date of death—July 10, 1889

Age at death—69 years, 67 days

Place of death—Richmond, Va.

Burial place—Richmond, Va.

Years younger than the President—30 years, 36 days

Years she survived the President—27 years, 173 days

FIRST LADIES

Letitia Christian Tyler was still suffering from the effects of a paralytic attack when her husband became President. As she was unable to act as mistress of the White House, Priscilla Cooper Tyler, the wife of their eldest son, acted in that capacity.

During the 17 months that Letitia Tyler was the First Lady, she appeared in public at the White House only once. On January 31, 1842, she attended the marriage of her daughter Elizabeth to William Nevinson Waller. Less than eight months later, on September 10, 1842, Mrs. Tyler died.

President Tyler married again on June 26, 1844. His second wife, Julia Gardiner Tyler, was in the White House only a little more than eight months, but she had been a famous belle and was known as the "Lady Presidentress." She was known for her entertainments, which mimicked those of the court of Louis Philippe of France, and for dancing the polka in public in the White House.

IMPORTANT DATES IN THE PRESIDENT'S LIFE

1807, graduated from College of William and Mary, which he had entered at age of 12

1809, admitted to the bar; practiced in Charles City County, Va.

1811–1816, member of Virginia House of Delegates

1813, captain of a military company

1816, member of Virginia Council of State

Dec. 16, 1817–Mar. 3, 1821, U.S. House of Representatives (from Virginia)

1820, declined renomination because of ill health

18–, rector and chancellor of College of William and Mary

1823–1825, Virginia House of Delegates

Dec. 1, 1825–1827, Governor of Virginia

Mar. 4, 1827–Feb. 29, 1836, member of U.S. Senate (from Virginia); resigned

1829, 1830, delegate to Virginia constitutional conventions

Mar. 3, 1835–July 1, 1836, president pro tempore of the Senate

1836, unsuccessful candidate for Vice President on Whig ticket

1838, president of Virginia African Colonization Society

1839, member of Virginia State House of Delegates

Mar. 4, 1841–Apr. 4, 1841, Vice President under William Henry Harrison

Apr. 6, 1841–Mar. 4, 1845, President (succeeded to office at death of Harrison)

1844, proposed as presidential candidate by secessionist Democratic convention

1859, chancellor of College of William and Mary

Mar. 1, 1861, member of Virginia secession convention

July 20, 1861, delegate to Confederate Provisional Congress

INAUGURATION

April 6, 1841

John Tyler was the first Vice President to succeed to the presidency through the death of a President. He was at Williamsburg, Va., when he received the news that President William Henry Harrison had died on April 4, 1841. Fletcher Webster, chief clerk of the Department of State and son of Daniel Webster, Secretary of State, delivered the note to Tyler at his home. Tyler returned to Washington, D.C., on April 6, 1841, at 4 A.M. At 12 noon on April 6 the oath was administered by William Cranch, Chief Justice of the United States Circuit Court of the District of Columbia, at the Indian Queen Hotel, Washington, D.C. Tyler held a cabinet meeting in the afternoon. On April 14, 1841, he moved into the White House.

CABINET

April 6, 1841–March 3, 1845

State—Daniel Webster, Mass., continued from preceding administration; Hugh Swinton Legaré, S.C. (Attorney General), ad interim May 9, 1843; William S. Derrick (chief clerk), ad interim June 21, 1843; Abel Parker Upshur, Va. (Secretary of the Navy), ad interim June 24, 1843; Abel Parker Upshur, Va., July 24, 1843; John Nelson, Md. (Attorney General), ad interim Feb. 29, 1844; John Caldwell Calhoun, S.C., Mar. 6, 1844; entered upon duties Apr. 1, 1844

Treasury—Thomas Ewing, Ohio, continued from preceding administration; McClintock Young (chief clerk), ad interim Sept. 13, 1841; Walter Forward, Pa., Sept. 13, 1841; McClintock Young (chief clerk), ad interim Mar. 1, 1843; John Canfield Spencer, N.Y., Mar. 3, 1843; entered upon duties Mar. 8, 1843; McClintock Young (chief clerk), ad interim May 2, 1844; George Mortimer, Bibb, Ky., June 15, 1844; entered upon duties July 4, 1844

War—John Bell, Tenn., continued from preceding administration; Albert M. Lea, Md. (chief clerk), ad interim Sept. 12, 1841; John Canfield Spencer, N.Y., Oct. 12, 1841; James Madison Porter, Pa., Mar. 8, 1843; William Wilkins, Pa., Feb. 15, 1844; entered upon duties Feb. 20, 1844

Attorney General—John Jordan Crittenden, Ky., continued from preceding administration; Hugh Swinton Legaré, S.C., Sept. 13, 1841; entered upon duties Sept. 20, 1841; John Nelson, Md., July 1, 1843

Postmaster General—Francis Granger, N.Y., continued from preceding administration; Selah Reeve Hobbie, N.Y. (first assistant), ad interim Sept. 14, 1841; Charles Anderson Wickliffe, Ky., Sept. 13, 1841; entered upon duties Oct. 13, 1841

Navy—George Edmund Badger, N.C., continued from preceding administration; John D. Simms (chief clerk), ad interim Sept. 11, 1841; Abel Parker Upshur, Va., Sept. 13, 1841; entered upon duties Oct. 11, 1841; David Henshaw, Mass., July 24, 1843; Thomas Walker Gilmer, Va., Feb. 15, 1844; entered upon duties Feb. 19, 1844; Lewis Warrington (captain, United States Navy), ad interim Feb. 29, 1844; John Young Mason, Va., Mar. 14, 1844; entered upon duties Mar. 26, 1844

CONGRESS

TWENTY-EIGHTH CONGRESS

March 4, 1843–March 3, 1845

First session—Dec. 4, 1843–June 17, 1844 (196 days)

Second session—Dec. 2, 1844–Mar. 3, 1845 (92 days)

Vice President—John Tyler succeeded to the presidency on Apr. 4, 1841, on the death of William Henry Harrison. The office of Vice President was vacant for the remainder of the term.

President pro tempore of the Senate —Willie Person Mangum, N.C.

Secretary of the Senate—Asbury Dickens, N.C., reelected Dec. 11, 1843

Speaker of the House—John Winston Jones, Va., elected Dec. 4, 1843

Clerk of the House—Matthew St. Clair Clarke, Pa., continued from preceding Congress; Caleb J. McNulty, Ohio, elected Dec. 6, 1843; dismissed from office Jan. 18, 1845; Benjamin Brown French, N.H., elected Jan. 18, 1845

APPOINTMENTS TO THE SUPREME COURT

Associate Justice

Samuel Nelson, N.Y., Feb. 13, 1845 (replaced Smith Thompson)

IMPORTANT DATES IN THE PRESIDENCY

Aug. 13, 1841, independent treasury act repealed

Sept. 11, 1841, cabinet resigned, except Secretary of State

1842, gold discovered, San Fernando Mission, Calif.

Feb. 1, 1842, Coast Guard commandant appointed

Feb. 15, 1842, adhesive postage stamps used, New York, N.Y.

Feb. 21, 1842, sewing machine patented, J. J. Greenough

Mar. 31, 1842, Henry Clay resigned after 36 years in Congress

June 10, 1842, Wilkes Expedition returned

Aug. 9, 1842, Webster-Ashburton treaty with Great Britain signed, settling Maine boundary

Aug. 14, 1842, end of Seminole War announced by Colonel Worth

Aug. 22, 1842, northeastern boundary treaty ratified by the Senate

Aug. 26, 1842, start of fiscal year changed from Jan. 1 to July 1

Aug. 30, 1842, tariff placed upon opium imports

Aug. 31, 1842, Bureau of Medicine and Surgery of the Navy authorized

Oct. 18, 1842, underwater cable laid in New York Harbor

Nov. 22, 1842, Mount Saint Helens, Wash., erupted

Mar. 3, 1843, Congress appropriated $30,000 to test the telegraph

May 2, 1843, organization of Oregon government attempted

June 17, 1843, Bunker Hill monument dedicated

Nov. 13, 1843, Mount Rainier, Wash., erupted

Feb. 28, 1844, explosion on warship *Princeton* killed the Secretary of State and the Secretary of the Navy, among others

May 25, 1844, first news dispatch sent by telegraph to Baltimore *Patriot*

June 15, 1844, Charles Goodyear obtained patent on vulcanized rubber

July 3, 1844, treaty of peace, amity, and commerce signed with China

Jan. 23, 1845, uniform election day established

Mar. 1, 1845, annexation of Texas by joint resolution of Congress

Mar. 3, 1845, first legislation passed over a presidential veto

Mar. 3, 1845, Florida admitted as the 27th state

ADDITIONAL DATA ON TYLER

JOHN TYLER

—was the sixth President born in Virginia.

—was the first President whose wife died while he was in office.

—was the first Vice President elevated to the presidency through the death of a Chief Executive. He was elected as a Whig to the vice presidency and took office March 4, 1841. Upon the death of President William Henry Harrison, Tyler took the oath of office as President of the United States on April 6, 1841.

—was the first President to marry while in office. He remarried on June 26, 1844.

—was the first President to marry on his birthday.

SENATOR TYLER OPPOSED STATE MANDATE

Tyler refused to obey a resolution of the Virginia legislature demanding that he vote for the Benton resolution, and resigned his seat in the Senate on February 29, 1836.

President Jackson had removed Secretary of the Treasury Duane for refusing to check out the deposits in the United States Bank, and for this action he had been censured by

126

the Senate. Senator Thomas Hart Benton of Missouri moved to have the Senate expunge the censure.

THREE PRESIDENTS SERVED IN SAME YEAR

Martin Van Buren completed his four-year term on March 3, 1841. On March 4, 1841, William Henry Harrison was inaugurated. Harrison died on April 4, 1841, and on April 6, 1841, John Tyler was inaugurated President, the third President in one year.

TYLER PROCLAIMED MEMORIAL FOR HARRISON

On April 13, 1841, one week after his succession to the presidency, John Tyler issued a proclamation recommending:

to the people of the United States of every religious denomination that, according to their several modes and forms of worship, they observe a day of fasting and prayer by such religious services as may be suitable on the occasion; and I recommend Friday the 14th of May next, for that purpose. . . .

TYLER CABINET RESIGNED

On September 9, 1841, President Tyler vetoed a bill "to provide for the better collection, safekeeping, and disbursement of the public revenues by means of a corporation to be styled the Fiscal Corporation of the United States." This action was disapproved of by his cabinet, and the secretaries of the Treasury, War, and Navy, as well as the Attorney General and the Postmaster General, resigned. The only cabinet member who retained his post was Secretary of State Daniel Webster.

PRESIDENTIAL COMMISSION OPPOSED

The first President requested by Congress to justify the creation of a presidential commission was John Tyler. The House of Representatives on February 7, 1842, passed a resolution

that the President of the United States inform this House under what authority the commission, consisting of George Poindexter and others, for the investiga-

Courtesy of The Library of Congress

Awful explosion of the "peace-maker" on board the U.S. Steam Frigate Princeton

tions of the concerns of the New York Customs House was raised, what were the purposes and objects of said commission . . . and out of what fund the said expenditures have been or are to be paid.

In a letter dated February 9, 1842, Tyler cited the authority vested in the President of the United States "to take care that the laws be faithfully executed and to give to Congress from time to time information on the state of the Union."

TYLER'S GRANDDAUGHTER BORN IN WHITE HOUSE

The first girl born in the White House was Letitia Christian Tyler, the daughter of Robert Tyler, and the granddaughter of President John Tyler. She was born in 1842.

TYLER ESCAPED DEATH ABOARD THE *PRINCETON*

About four hundred visitors, including President Tyler, the members of the Cabinet, the diplomatic corps, members of Congress, and their families visited the U.S.S. *Princeton,* the first propeller-driven warship, on February 28, 1844. She proceeded from Alexandria, Va., down the Potomac River. Below Fort Washington, the ship's "Peacemaker," a ten-ton gun, fifteen feet long with a twelve-inch bore, fired a 25-pound ball.

On the return trip, when the ship was about fifteen miles below Washington, D.C., the gun was fired again, with a 25-pound charge. Although the gun had been tested at 49 pounds and had frequently been fired successfully with a 30-pound charge, it exploded and burst at the breech. Thomas Walker Gilmer, Secretary of the Navy; Abel Parker Upshur, Secretary of State; Commodore Kennon of the *Princeton*; David Gardiner, a former state senator of New York; Virgil Maxcy, a former United States chargé d'affaires in Belgium; and Tyler's servant were killed. Seventeen seamen were wounded and many others were stunned, including Captain Robert Field Stockton of the *Princeton*. President Tyler was below decks when the explosion took place. Also on board was David Gardiner's daughter Julia, whom the President would marry about four months later.

The bodies were brought to the Executive Mansion and the coffins were placed in the East Room. Because the explosion was an accident the captain and the officers were exonerated from blame.

CONGRESS OVERRODE VETO

The first legislation passed over a President's veto was an act (S. 66, 2 sess. 28 Cong.) "relating to revenue cutters and steamers." It provided that no revenue cutter could be built unless an appropriation was first made by law. President Tyler vetoed the bill, on the grounds a contract for two revenue cutters had already been let, one to a firm in Richmond, Va., and the other to a Pittsburgh, Pa., contractor. He vetoed the bill on February 20, 1845. It was reconsidered by the Senate and House on March 3, 1845. The former passed it without debate over his veto, 41 to 1, and the House by a vote of 127 to 30.

ATTEMPT TO IMPEACH TYLER

John Minor Botts, representative from Virginia, introduced a resolution on January 10, 1843, charging "John Tyler, Vice President acting as President" of corruption, malconduct in office, high crimes, and misdemeanors. The nine charges were rejected and the resolution was not accepted, by a vote of 83 ayes to 127 nays. (*Congressional Globe,* Jan. 10, 1843)

TYLER PRESIDED AT PEACE CONFERENCE

Former President Tyler was president of the peace conference that met in secret session from February 4 to February 27, 1861, at Washington, D.C., in a late attempt to avert the Civil War. A report presented to the delegates at the conference on February 15 was adopted February 26. The conference was attended by 133 commissioners from 22 states. The free states represented were Connecticut, Illinois, Indiana, Iowa, Kansas, Maine, Massachusetts, New Hampshire, New Jersey, New York, Ohio, Pennsylvania, Rhode Island, Vermont, and Wisconsin, and the slave states represented were Delaware, Kentucky, Maryland, Missouri, North Carolina, Tennessee, and Virginia.

The report of the conference was submitted to Congress, which considered it and finally rejected it.

TYLER IN CONFEDERATE CONGRESS

John Tyler served as a member of the Confederate States Congress. On August 1, 1861, he was a delegate to the Provisional Congress of the Confederate States. He was elected a member of the House of Representatives of the permanent Confederate Congress on November 7, 1861, but never took his seat, as he died January 18, 1862, at Richmond, Va., before the Congress assembled.

TYLER'S DEATH IGNORED

When former President John Tyler died at Richmond, Va., on January 18, 1862, the government made no announcement or proclamation of his death and no official notice of his demise was taken.

GOVERNMENT AUTHORIZED TYLER MONUMENT FIFTY YEARS AFTER HIS DEATH

On March 4, 1911, Congress authorized the erection of a monument to Tyler's memory and on August 24, 1912, appropriated $10,000 for it. It was completed June 9, 1915, and dedicated October 12, 1915, at Hollywood Cemetery, Cherry and Albemarle Streets,

Richmond, Va. Five senators and five congressmen represented the United States at the ceremonies.

TYLER HONORED HIS HORSE

In Sherwood, Charles City County, Va., John Tyler had a grave dug for his horse, The General, over which was the following inscription:

Here lies the body of my good horse, The General. For twenty years he bore me around the circuit of my practice, and in all that time he never made a blunder. Would that his master could say the same! John Tyler.

FURTHER READING

Chitwood, Oliver P. *John Tyler.* 1964.

Crapol, Edward P. *John Tyler, the Accidental President.* 2006.

Peterson, Norma Lois. *The Presidencies of William Henry Harrison and John Tyler.* 1989.

Seager, Robert. *And Tyler Too.* 1963.

Courtesy of The Library of Congress

Tombstone of John Tyler

Courtesy of The Library of Congress

James Knox Polk

Date of birth—Nov. 2, 1795

Place of birth—Near Pineville, Mecklenburg County, N.C.

Education—Attended schools of Rev. Robert Henderson, Columbia, N.C., 1813, and Samuel P. Black, Murfreesboro, N.C. 1814–1816; University of North Carolina, Chapel Hill, N.C., bachelor's degree with honors, June 4, 1818; private study in law office of Felix Grundy, Nashville, Tenn.

Religion—Presbyterian at birth; became a Methodist

Ancestry—Scotch-Irish

Career—Lawyer, officer in militia cavalry, state legislator, U.S. congressman, Speaker of the House, governor of Tennessee

Political party—Democratic

State represented—Tennessee

Term of office—Mar. 4, 1845–Mar. 4, 1849

Term served—4 years

Administration—15th

Congresses—29th, 30th

Age at inauguration—49 years, 122 days

Lived after term—103 days

Occupation after term—Retired because of illness

Date of death—June 15, 1849

Age at death—53 years, 225 days

Place of death—Nashville, Tenn.

Burial place—Polk Place, Nashville, Tenn.; remains removed in 1893 to the State Capitol Grounds, Nashville, Tenn.

FAMILY

FATHER

Name—Samuel Polk

Date of birth—July 5, 1772

Place of birth—Tryon, N.C.

Marriage—Jane Knox, Dec. 25, 1794, Mecklenburg County, N.C.

Occupation—Farmer, planter, surveyor, land speculator, businessman, newspaper founder, bank director; magistrate

Date of death—Nov. 5, 1827

Place of death—Maury County, Tenn.

Age at death—55 years, 123 days

MOTHER

Name at birth—Jane Knox

Date of birth—Nov. 15, 1776

Marriage—Samuel Polk, Dec. 25, 1794, Mecklenburg County, N.C.

Date of death—Jan. 11, 1852

Place of death—Maury County, Tenn.

Age at death—75 years, 57 days

SIBLINGS

James Knox Polk was the oldest child in a family of ten.

Children of Samuel Polk and Jane Knox Polk

James Knox Polk, b. Nov. 2, 1795, d. June 15, 1849

Jane Maria Polk, b. Jan. 14, 1798, d. Oct. 11, 1876

Lydia Eliza Polk, b. Feb. 17, 1800, d. May 29, 1864

Franklin Ezekiel Polk, b. Aug. 23, 1802, d. Jan. 21, 1831

Marshall Tate Polk, b. Jan. 17, 1805, d. Apr. 12, 1831

John Lee Polk, b. Mar. 23, 1807, d. Sept. 28, 1831

Naomi Tate Polk, b. July 2, 1809, d. Aug. 6, 1836

Ophelia Clarissa Polk, b. Sept. 6, 1812, d. Apr. 18, 1851

William Hawkins Polk, b. May 24, 1815, d. Dec. 16, 1862

Samuel Wilson Polk, b. Oct. 17, 1817, d. Feb. 24, 1839

MARRIAGE

Married—Sarah Childress

Date of marriage—Jan. 1, 1824

Place of marriage—Murfreesboro, Tenn.

Age of wife at marriage— 20 years, 119 days

Age of husband at marriage—28 years, 60 days

Years married—25 years, 165 days

CHILDREN

None

THE PRESIDENT'S WIFE

Name at birth—Sarah Childress

Date of birth—Sept. 4, 1803

Place of birth—Murfreesboro, Tenn.

Mother—Elizabeth Whitsitt Childress

Father—Captain Joel Childress

Father's occupation—Planter

Education—Moravian Female Academy, Salem, N.C.

Marriage—James Knox Polk, Jan. 1, 1824, Murfreesboro, Tenn.

Children—None

Occupation—Personal secretary and political advisor to James K. Polk

Date of death—Aug. 14, 1891

Age at death—87 years, 344 days

Place of death—Nashville, Tenn.

Burial place—Nashville, Tenn.

Years younger than the President—7 years, 306 days

Years she survived the President—42 years, 60 days

Courtesy of The Library of Congress

Sarah Polk, wife of James K. Polk

THE FIRST LADY

As Sarah Childress Polk had no children, her interests were not divided and her entire time was devoted to her husband. She was a capable mistress of the White House, and had the crumbling interiors refurbished and redecorated. She was renowned for her glittering parties, receptions, and open houses. A devout Presbyterian, she banned dancing, considering it undignified, but she permitted entertainments such as juggling in the White House. She was famous for her intelligence and wit, and was highly respected even by her husband's political foes. She was her husband's partner in every respect, and although she did not profess feminist ideas, she was recognized favorably for her contributions to the presidency.

IMPORTANT DATES IN THE PRESIDENT'S LIFE

1806, family moved to Tennessee, settling in what is now Maury County

1818, graduated from University of North Carolina

1820, admitted to the bar; practiced at Columbia, Tenn.

1821–1823, chief clerk of Tennessee Senate

1823–1825, Tennessee House of Representatives

Mar. 4, 1825–Mar. 3, 1839, U.S. House of Representatives (from Tennessee)

Dec. 7, 1835–Mar. 3, 1839, Speaker of the House of Representatives

1839–1841, governor of Tennessee

Mar. 4, 1845–Mar. 4, 1849, President

1849, declined to be a candidate for reelection; retired to Nashville

---

ELECTIONS

THE ELECTION OF 1844

Since Congress had yet to establish a nationwide, uniform Election Day, the legislatures of the different states appointed a variety of voting days during the 34 days preceding the meeting of the electors, which was mandated for the first Wednesday in December. The polls opened in Pennsylvania and Ohio on November 1, in most other states on November 4, in New York on November 5, and in Delaware and Vermont on November 12.

On January 23, 1845, Congress passed on act appointing as Election Day the first Tuesday after the first Monday in November of every even-numbered year. As a result, the date has varied between November 2 and November 8.

The first Tuesday after the first Monday was decided upon in order to eliminate the possibility of an Election Day falling on the first day of November, a day often inconvenient to merchants balancing their books for the month. Monday also was found objectionable as, prior to the establishment of good roads, it often took more than a day for the voter to reach the polling place. As this might have necessitated voters' leaving their homes on Sunday, the Christian day of rest, it was found preferable to have Election Day fall on Tuesday instead of on Monday.

CANDIDATES

Democratic Party (4th Convention)

May 27–30, 1844, Odd Fellows' Hall, Baltimore, Md.

P: James Knox Polk, Tenn.

VP: George Mifflin Dallas, Pa.

Polk received his first votes on the eighth ballot. Candidates for nomination and the votes they received on the first and eighth ballots:

Martin Van Buren, N.Y., 146, 104

Lewis Cass, Mich., 83, 114

Richard Mentor Johnson, Ky., 24, 0

John Caldwell Calhoun, S.C., 6, 2

James Buchanan, Pa., 4, 2

Levi Woodbury, N.H., 2, 0

John Stewart, Conn., 1, 0

James Knox Polk, Tenn., 0, 44

Total number of votes: 266

Number necessary for nomination: 177

Polk was nominated unanimously on the ninth ballot.

Silas Wright of New York was nominated for the vice presidency, receiving 258 votes, while Levi Woodbury of New Hampshire received 8 votes. Wright declined the nomination and George Mifflin Dallas became the nominee.

Whig Party

May 1, 1844, Universalist Church, Baltimore, Md.

P: Henry Clay, Ky.

VP: Theodore Frelinghuysen, N.J.

Clay was nominated on the first ballot by acclamation.

Liberty Party

Aug. 30, 1843, Buffalo, N.Y.

P: James Gillespie Birney, N.Y.
VP: Thomas Morris, Ohio

National Democratic Tyler party

May 27–28, 1844, Calvert Hall, Baltimore, Md.

P: John Tyler, Va.
VP: None

A group of Democrats opposed to the nominations of the major parties endeavored to establish a separate ticket and party. A committee was appointed to nominate a vice presidential candidate.

1844 POPULAR VOTE

Democratic Party, 1,337,243
Whig Party, 1,299,062
Liberty Party, 62,300

1844 ELECTORAL VOTE

There were 275 electoral votes from 26 states.

Polk received 61.82 percent (170 votes—15 states) as follows: Ala. 9; Ark. 3; Ga. 10; Ill. 9; Ind. 12; La. 6; Me. 9; Mich. 5; Miss. 6; Mo. 7; N.H. 6; N.Y. 36; Pa. 26; S.C. 9; Va. 17.

Clay received 38.18 percent (105 votes—11 states) as follows: Conn. 6; Del. 3; Ky. 12; Md. 8; Mass. 12; N.J. 7; N.C. 11; Ohio 23; R.I. 4; Tenn. 13; Vt. 6.

INAUGURATION

March 4, 1845

James Knox Polk took the oath of office on Tuesday, March 4, 1845, on the east portico of the Capitol. Chief Justice Taney administered the oath. Although it rained, Polk delivered his inaugural address outdoors, and a large military parade took place. This was the first presidential inauguration reported by telegraph. Samuel F. B. Morse, using a telegraph key installed on the platform, sent the news by wire to Baltimore, Md. Two inaugural balls were held.

Courtesy of The Library of Congress

The inauguration of James K. Polk

THE VICE PRESIDENT

Name—George Mifflin Dallas (11th V.P.)
Date of birth—July 10, 1792
Place of birth—Philadelphia, Pa.
Political party—Democratic
State represented—Pennsylvania
Term of office—Mar. 4, 1845–Mar. 4, 1849
Age at inauguration—52 years, 237 days
Occupation after term—U.S. minister to Great Britain
Date of death—Dec. 31, 1864
Place of death—Philadelphia, Pa.
Age at death—72 years, 174 days
Burial place—Philadelphia, Pa.

ADDITIONAL DATA ON DALLAS

1810, graduated from Princeton
1813, admitted to the bar
1813, private secretary to U.S. minister to Russia, Albert Gallatin
1815–1817, solicitor of the U.S. Bank
1817, deputy attorney general of Philadelphia
1829, mayor of Philadelphia
1829–1831, U.S. district attorney, eastern district of Pennsylvania

Courtesy of The Library of Congress

George Mifflin Dallas, Vice President to James K. Polk

Dec. 13, 1831–Mar. 3, 1833, U.S. Senate (from Pennsylvania)
1833–1835, attorney general of Pennsylvania
Mar. 7, 1837–July 29, 1839, minister to Russia
Mar. 4, 1845–Mar. 4, 1849, Vice President under James Knox Polk
Feb. 4, 1856–May 16, 1861, U.S. minister to Great Britain

CABINET

March 4, 1845–March 3, 1849

State—John Caldwell Calhoun S.C., continued from preceding administration; James Buchanan, Pa., Mar. 6, 1845; entered upon duties Mar. 10, 1845

Treasury—George Mortimer Bibb, Ky., continued from preceding administration; Robert James Walker, Miss., Mar. 6, 1845; entered upon duties Mar. 8, 1845

War—William Wilkins, Pa., continued from preceding administration; William Learned Marcy, N.Y., Mar. 6, 1845; entered upon duties Mar. 8, 1845

Attorney General—John Nelson, Md., continued from preceding administration; John Young Mason, Va., Mar. 6, 1845; entered upon duties Mar. 11, 1845; Nathan Clifford, Me., Oct. 17, 1846; resigned Mar. 18, 1848; Isaac Toucey, Conn., June 21, 1848; entered upon duties June 29, 1848

Postmaster General—Charles Anderson Wickliffe, Ky., continued from preceding administration; Cave Johnson, Tenn., Mar. 6, 1845

Navy—John Young Mason, Va., continued from preceding administration; George Bancroft, Mass., Mar. 10, 1845; John Young Mason, Va., Sept. 9, 1846

CONGRESS

TWENTY-NINTH CONGRESS

March 4, 1845–March 3, 1847

First session—Dec. 1, 1845–Aug. 10, 1846 (253 days)

Second session—Dec. 7, 1846–Mar. 3, 1847 (87 days)

Special session of the Senate—Mar. 4, 1845–Mar. 20, 1845 (17 days)

Vice President—George Mifflin Dallas, Pa.

President pro tempore of the Senate—Ambrose Hundley Sevier, Ark., served Dec. 27, 1845 (one day); David Rice Atchison, Mo., elected Aug. 8, 1846; Jan. 11, 1847; Mar. 3, 1847

Secretary of the Senate—Asbury Dickens, N.C., reelected Dec. 9, 1845

Speaker of the House—John Wesley Davis, Ind., elected Dec. 1, 1845

Clerk of the House—Benjamin Brown French, N.H., reelected Dec. 2, 1845

THIRTIETH CONGRESS

March 4, 1847–March 3, 1849

First session—Dec. 6, 1847–Aug. 14, 1848 (254 days)

Second session—Dec. 4, 1848–Mar. 3, 1849 (90 days)

Vice President—George Mifflin Dallas, Pa.

President pro tempore of the Senate—David Rice Atchison, Mo., elected Feb. 2, 1848; June 1, 1848; June 26, 1848; July 29, 1848; Dec. 26, 1848; Mar. 2, 1849

Secretary of the Senate—Asbury Dickens, N.C., reelected Dec. 13, 1847

Speaker of the House—Robert Charles Winthrop, Mass., elected Dec. 6, 1847

Clerk of the House—Benjamin Brown French, N.H., Thomas Jefferson Campbell, Tenn., elected Dec. 7, 1847

APPOINTMENTS TO THE SUPREME COURT

Associate Justices

Levi Woodbury, N.H., Sept. 20, 1845 (replaced Joseph Story)

Robert Cooper Grier, Pa., Aug. 4, 1846 (replaced Henry Baldwin)

IMPORTANT DATES IN THE PRESIDENCY

Oct. 10, 1845, United States Naval Academy opened

Dec. 29, 1845, Texas admitted as the 28th state

1846, Howe patented sewing machine

Mar. 4, 1846, Michigan legislature abolished death penalty (first state to do so)

Apr. 25, 1846, first skirmish in Mexican War

May 8, 1846, Battle of Palo Alto

May 9, 1846, Battle of Resaca de la Palma

May 13, 1846, United States formally declared war against Mexico

June 15, 1846, treaty concluded with Great Britain establishing Oregon boundary on the 49th parallel; in force Aug. 1846

Aug. 8, 1846, defeat in Senate of Wilmot proviso calling for exclusion of slavery from any territory acquired from Mexico

Sept. 24, 1846, Battle of Monterrey

Dec. 28, 1846, Iowa admitted as the 29th state

1847, conquest of California by American forces

Feb. 23, 1847, Battle of Buena Vista

Mar. 29, 1847, General Winfield Scott captured Vera Cruz

Apr. 18, 1847, Battle of Cerro Gordo

May 5, 1847, American Medical Association organized

Sept. 8, 1847, Battle of Molino del Rey

Sept. 13, 1847, Battle of Chapultepec

Sept. 14, 1847, fall of Mexico City to General Scott

Jan. 24, 1848, gold discovered in California by James W. Marshall; beginning of gold rush which reached its height in 1849

Feb. 2, 1848, treaty of Guadalupe Hidalgo signed with Mexico; Mexico recognized Rio Grande as boundary and ceded, for $15 million, territory that became California, New Mexico, Arizona, Nevada, Utah, and parts of Colorado and Wyoming

Mar. 10, 1848, treaty of Guadalupe Hidalgo ratified by Senate

Mar. 25, 1848, treaty of Guadalupe Hidalgo ratified by Mexican government

May 29, 1848, Wisconsin admitted as the 30th state

May 30, 1848, treaty ratifications formally exchanged

June 12, 1848, American troops evacuated Mexico City

July 4, 1848, President Polk laid cornerstone of the Washington Monument

July 19–20, 1848, women's rights convention, Seneca Falls, N.Y.

Aug. 14, 1848, Oregon admitted as a territory

Mar. 3, 1849, Department of Interior created

ADDITIONAL DATA ON POLK

JAMES KNOX POLK

—was the first President born in North Carolina.

—was the third President who was resident of a state other than his native state.

—was the second President to lead the nation in war.

—was the fourth President whose mother was alive when he was inaugurated.

—was the first President who was survived by his mother.

NEWS OF POLK'S NOMINATION TELEGRAPHED

The first use of the telegraph in politics occurred on May 29, 1844, when news was flashed to Washington, D.C., from Baltimore, Md., that Polk had been nominated for the presidency on the Democratic ticket. The Washington *National Intelligencer* reported:

During the whole day, a crowd of persons, including a number of Members of Congress, were in attendance at the Capitol to receive the reports by telegraph of news from Baltimore, which were made at successive intervals with striking despatch and accuracy, and were received by the auditors, as the responses of the ancient Oracle may be supposed to have been, with emotions corresponding to the

Courtesy of The Library of Congress

Tomb of President James K. Polk, Nashville, Tennessee

various and opposite sentiments of those comprising the assembly. Whatever variety of impression the news made upon the auditory, however, there was but one sentiment concerning the telegraph itself, which was that of mingled delight and wonder.

Twenty minutes after Polk had been nominated, a telegram was sent to the convention from Washington, D.C.:

The Democratic members of Congress to their Democratic brethren in convention assembled. Three cheers for James K. Polk.

POLK THE FIRST "DARK HORSE" NOMINATED

Polk was not even considered as a candidate for the presidency at the Democratic national convention, held at Odd Fellows' Hall, Baltimore, Md., from May 27 to May 30, 1844. His name was not mentioned during the first seven ballots and not a single vote was cast for him. A stalemate existed between former President Martin Van Buren and Lewis Cass of Michigan. On the eighth ballot (May 29, 1844), Polk was suggested as a compromise candidate and received 44 votes, while Van Buren had 104 votes and Cass 114. Two votes each were also cast for Buchanan and Calhoun. On the ninth ballot, amid indescribable confusion, the convention stampeded for Polk. State after state that had supported Van Buren or Cass cast its votes for Polk, and before the final tally his nomination was declared unanimous, as he had received 266 of the 266 votes cast.

POLK AN EARLY SURVIVOR OF SURGERY

Polk was sickly as a child, suffering recurrent bouts of abdominal pain and debilitation. In 1812, at the age of 17, he was taken to Dr. Ephraim McDowell in Danville, Kentucky, a 250-mile journey from his home. The diagnosis was gallstone, and after a period of regaining strength, Dr. McDowell had him given brandy, strapped to a bare wooden table, and held down by assistants while he performed surgery. The art was in its infancy: antisepsis and anesthesia were unknown. Dr. McDowell's operation was successful, however, and Polk survived, improved in health, and went on to become, as he himself said, "the hardest working person" in America. Dr. McDowell is enshrined in Statuary Hall in the Capitol.

POLK THE FIRST PRESIDENT WHO HAD BEEN A SPEAKER OF THE HOUSE

James Knox Polk was the first Speaker of the House of Representatives who became a President of the United States. He served as Speaker of the 24th Congress (first session,

One of several campaign banners Nathaniel Currier is known to have produced for the Democrats in 1844

December 7, 1835 to July 4, 1836, 211 days; second session, December 5, 1836 to March 3, 1837, 89 days). He also served as Speaker of the 25th Congress (first session, September 4, 1837 to October 16, 1837, 43 days; second session, December 4, 1837 to July 9, 1838, 218 days; and third session, December 3, 1838 to March 3, 1839, 91 days).

POLK RELIEVED AT CONCLUSION OF PRESIDENTIAL TERM

President Polk made the following notation in his diary on February 13, 1849:

I am heartily rejoiced that my term is so near its close. I will soon cease to be a servant and become a sovereign. As a private citizen, I will have no one but myself to serve, and will exercise a part of the sovereign power of the country. I am sure I will be happier in this condition than in the exalted station I now hold.

Under the date of Sunday, March 4, 1849, Polk wrote in his diary:

I feel exceedingly relieved that I am now free from all public cares. I am sure I shall be a happier man in my retirement than I have been during the four years I have filled the highest office in the gift of my countrymen.

138

FURTHER READING

Bergeron, Paul H. *The Presidency of James K. Polk.* Rev. ed. 1988.

———., ed. *Correspondence of James K. Polk: 1833–1834.* 1972.

Cutler, Wayne., ed. *Correspondence of James K. Polk: 1837–1838.* 1977.

Leonard, Thomas M. *James K. Polk: A Clear and Unquestionable Destiny.* 2000.

McCoy, Charles A. *Polk and the Presidency.* 1973.

Sellers, Charles. *James Knox Polk, Jacksonian, 1795–1843.* 1957.

———. *James Knox Polk, Continentalist, 1843–1846.* 1967.

Courtesy of The Library of Congress

Zachary Taylor

Zachary Taylor

Date of birth—Nov. 24, 1784

Place of birth—Montebello, Orange County, Va.

Education—Various local teachers in Kentucky

Religion—Episcopalian

Ancestry—English

Career—Army officer, rising to general in Mexican War

Political party—Whig

State represented—Louisiana

Term of office—Mar. 4, 1849–July 9, 1850

Term served—1 year, 127 days

Administration—16th

Congresses—31st

Age at inauguration—64 years, 100 days

Date of death—July 9, 1850 (died in office)

Age at death—65 years, 227 days

Place of death—Washington, D.C.

Burial place—Louisville, Ky.

FAMILY

FATHER

Name—Richard Taylor

Date of birth—Apr. 3, 1744

Place of birth—Orange County, Va.

Marriage—Sarah Dabney Strother, Aug. 20, 1779

Occupation—Farmer, planter, soldier (lieutenant colonel), port collector, justice of the peace, county magistrate, delegate to two state constitutional conventions, Kentucky state legislator, presidential elector; active in Revolution

Date of death—Jan. 19, 1829

Place of death—Near Lexington, Ky.

Age at death—84 years, 291 days

MOTHER

Name at birth—Sarah Dabney Strother

Date of birth—Dec. 14, 1760

Marriage—Richard Taylor, Aug. 20, 1779

Date of death—Dec. 13, 1822

Age at death—61 years, 364 days

SIBLINGS

Zachary Taylor was the third child in a family of nine.

Children of Richard Taylor and Sarah Dabney Strother Taylor

Hancock Taylor, b. Jan. 29, 1781, d. Mar. 20, 1841

William Dabney Strother Taylor, b. 1782, d. June 3, 1808

Zachary Taylor, b. Nov. 24, 1784, d. July 9, 1850

George Taylor, b. 1790, d. Sept. 1829

Elizabeth Lee Taylor, b. Jan. 14, 1792, d. Apr. 22, 1845

Joseph Pannill Taylor, b. May 4, 1796, d. June 29, 1864

Strother Taylor

Sarah Strother Taylor, b. June 11, 1799, d. Sept. 6, 1851

Emily Taylor, b. June 30, 1801, d. Nov. 30, 1842

MARRIAGE

Married—Margaret Mackall Smith

Date of marriage—June 21, 1810

Place of marriage—Near Louisville, Ky.

Age of wife at marriage—21 years, 273 days

Age of husband at marriage—25 years, 209 days

Years married—40 years, 18 days

CHILDREN

Anne Margaret Mackall Taylor, b. Apr. 9, 1811, Jefferson County, Ky.; m. Sept. 20, 1829, Robert Crooke Wood, Prairie du Chien, Michigan Territory; d. Dec. 2, 1875, Freiburg, Germany

Sarah Knox Taylor, b. Mar. 6, 1814, Fort Knox, Indiana Territory; m. June 17, 1835, Jefferson Davis, near Lexington, Ky.; d. Sept. 15, 1835, near St. Francisville, La.

Octavia Pannel Taylor, b. Aug. 16, 1816, Jefferson County, Ky.; d. July 8, 1820, Bayou Sara, La.

Margaret Smith Taylor, b. July 27, 1819, Jefferson County, Ky.; d. Oct. 22, 1820, Bayou Sara, La.

Mary Elizabeth ("Betty") Taylor, b. Apr. 20, 1824, Jefferson County, Ky.; m. Dec. 5, 1848, William Wallace Smith Bliss, Baton Rouge, La.; m. Feb. 11, 1858, Philip Pendleton Dandridge; d. July 26, 1909, Winchester, Va.

Richard Taylor, b. Jan. 27, 1826, near Louisville, Ky.; m. Feb. 10, 1851, Louise Marie Myrthé Bringier, New Orleans, La.; d. Apr. 12, 1879, New York, N.Y.

THE PRESIDENT'S WIFE

Name at birth—Margaret Mackall Smith

Date of birth—Sept. 21, 1788

Place of birth—Calvert County, Md.

Mother—Ann Mackall Smith

Father—Walter Smith

Father's occupation—Planter

Marriage—Zachary Taylor, June 21, 1810

Children—Anne Margaret Mackall Taylor, b. Apr. 9, 1811, d. Dec. 2, 1875; Sarah Knox Taylor, b. Mar. 6, 1814, d. Sept. 15, 1835; Octavia Pannel Taylor, b. Aug. 16, 1816, d. July 8, 1820; Margaret Smith Taylor, b. July 27, 1819, d. Oct. 22, 1820; Mary Elizabeth ("Betty") Taylor, b. Apr. 20, 1824, d. July 26, 1909; Richard Taylor, b. Jan. 27, 1826, d. Apr. 12, 1879

Date of death—Aug. 18, 1852

Age at death—63 years, 331 days

Place of death—near Pascagoula, Miss.

Burial place—Louisville, Ky.

Years younger than the President—3 years, 301 days

Years she survived the President—2 years, 40 days

THE FIRST LADY

Margaret Smith Taylor preferred to live a quiet, simple life, avoiding all gaiety and excitement. She refused to appear at public functions. She was about 61 years of age when her husband became President, on March 4, 1849. She was in ill health and her youngest daughter, Mary Elizabeth, who was married to William Wallace Bliss, acted as White House hostess for her. The First Lady, who had traveled from one military post to another during her husband's years in the army, was looking forward to his retirement from public life, but he became ill on July 4, 1850, and died five days later, having served about sixteen months of his term.

IMPORTANT DATES IN THE PRESIDENT'S LIFE

May 3, 1808, appointed first lieutenant, 7th Infantry

Nov. 30, 1810, appointed captain

July 1, 1811, in charge of Fort Knox at Vincennes in Indian territory

Sept. 1812, defended Fort Harrison against Tecumseh

Sept. 5, 1812, brevet rank of major conferred for gallant conduct at the defense of Fort Harrison

May 15, 1814, major, 26th Infantry

June 15, 1815, after the War of 1812, retained as captain of the 7th Infantry; declined and received honorable discharge

May 17, 1816, reinstated as major, 3rd Infantry

The Battle of Buena Vista, February 23, 1847

Apr. 20, 1819, lieutenant colonel, 4th Infantry

1821, stationed at Cantonment Bay, St. Louis, Mo.

Nov. 9, 1822, established Fort Jesup, La.

Dec. 1822, in charge of Cantonment Robertson near Baton Rouge, La.

May 1828, commanded Fort Snelling, unorganized territory, Minnesota

July 18, 1829, commanded Fort Crawford, Michigan territory (now Wisconsin)

Apr. 4, 1832, colonel, First Regiment

Aug. 2, 1832, Indians defeated at Bad Axe, ending the Black Hawk War

Dec. 25, 1837, brevet brigadier general for distinguished service at the battle of Okeechobee against the Seminole Indians

June 17, 1844, assumed command of Fort Jesup

Apr. 24, 1846, Mexicans crossed Rio Grande, clashed with a scouting party

May 8, 1846, Mexicans routed, battle of Palo Alto

May 9, 1846, Mexicans routed, Resaca de la Palma

May 18, 1846, Mexican army fled Matamoros, which was occupied without bloodshed

May 28, 1846, brevet major general for his zealous and distinguished services in Mexico

June 29, 1846, general of the line

July 18, 1846, received thanks of Congress "for the fortitude, skill, enterprise and courage which have distinguished the recent operations on the Rio Grande"

Sept. 25, 1846, Monterrey surrendered; Mexicans left city

Feb. 23, 1847, defeated Santa Anna at battle of Buena Vista (La Angostura)

July 18, 1848, nominated for the presidency by the Whigs

Jan. 31, 1849, resigned from the army

Mar. 4, 1849–July 9, 1850, President

ELECTIONS

THE ELECTION OF 1848

November 7, 1848

CANDIDATES

Whig Party

June 7–9, 1848, Museum Building, Philadelphia, Pa.

P: Zachary Taylor, La.

VP: Millard Fillmore, N.Y.

Taylor was nominated on the fourth ballot. Candidates for nomination and the votes they received on the first and fourth ballots:

Zachary Taylor, La., 111, 171
Henry Clay, Ky., 97, 32
Winfield Scott, N.J., 43, 63
Daniel Webster, Mass., 22, 14
John Middleton Clayton, Del., 4, 0
John McLean, Ohio, 2, 0
Total number of votes:
First ballot: 279
Fourth ballot: 280
Number necessary for nomination: 140

Democratic Party (5th Convention)

May 22–26, 1848, Universalist Church, Baltimore, Md.

P: Lewis Cass, Mich.
VP: William Orlando Butler, Ky.

Cass was nominated on the fourth ballot. Candidates for nomination and the number of votes they received on the first and fourth ballots:

Lewis Cass, Mich., 125, 179
James Buchanan, Pa., 55, 33
Levi Woodbury, N.H., 53, 33
John Caldwell Calhoun, S.C., 9, 0
William Jenkins Worth, N.Y., 6, 1
George Mifflin Dallas, Pa., 3, 0
William Orlando Butler, Ky., 0, 3
Total number of votes:
First ballot: 251
Fourth ballot: 254
Number necessary for nomination: 168

Free Soil (Democratic) Party

Aug. 9–10, 1848, Buffalo, N.Y.

P: Martin Van Buren, N.Y.
VP: Charles Francis Adams, Mass.

Van Buren was nominated by acclamation on the first ballot with votes cast as follows:

Martin Van Buren, N.Y., 154
John Parker Hale, N.H., 129

This party, formed by the antislavery element of the Democratic Party, was supported by the Liberty Party. Their campaign slogan was "Free Soil, Free Speech, Free Labor, Free Men." They were not abolitionists, but were opposed to the extension of slavery.

Free Soil (Barnburners—Liberty Party)

Oct. 20, 1847, Buffalo, N.Y.

P: John Parker Hale, N.H.
VP: Leicester King, Ohio

John Parker Hale withdrew from the race after Martin Van Buren defeated him in the balloting for the nomination of the Free Soilers in August 1848.

National Liberty Party

June 14–15, 1848, Buffalo, N.Y

P: Gerrit Smith, N.Y.
VP: Charles C. Foote, Mich.

Smith was nominated on the first ballot. Candidates for nomination and the votes they received:

Gerrit Smith, N.Y., 99
Beriah Green, N.Y., 2
Frederick Douglass, 1
Amos A. Sampson, 1
Charles C. Foote, Mich., 1

1848 POPULAR VOTE

Whig Party, 1,360,099
Democratic Party, 1,220,544
Free Soil (Democratic) Party, 291,263
National Liberty Party, 2,733

1848 ELECTORAL VOTE

There were 290 electoral votes from 30 states.

Courtesy of The Library of Congress

Campaign portrait of Zachary Taylor for the Whig party

Taylor received 56.21 percent (163 votes—15 states) as follows: Conn. 6; Del. 3; Fla. 3; Ga. 10; Ky. 12; La. 6; Md. 8; Mass. 12; N.J. 7; N.Y. 36; N.C. 11; Pa. 26; R.I. 4; Tenn. 13; Vt. 6.

Cass received 43.79 percent (127 votes—15 states) as follows: Ala. 9; Ark. 3; Ill. 9; Ind. 12; Iowa 4; Me. 9; Mich. 5; Miss. 6; Mo. 7; N.H. 6; Ohio 23; S.C. 9; Tex. 4; Va. 17; Wis. 4.

INAUGURATION

March 5, 1849

Zachary Taylor took the oath of office on the east portico of the Capitol on Monday, March 5, 1849, as March 4 fell on a Sunday, the second time in inaugural history. One hundred marshals escorted the presidential carriage from Willard's Hotel to the Capitol.

Thirty thousand persons witnessed the inauguration. After a parade lasting one hour, a reception was held in the afternoon at the White House. Three different inaugural balls were held, each attended by President Taylor.

THE VICE PRESIDENT

Name—Millard Fillmore (12th V.P.)

Political party—Whig

State represented—New York

Term of office—Mar. 4, 1849–July 9, 1850

Age at inauguration—49 years, 56 days

Occupation after term—President of the United States

For further biographical information, see the chapter on Millard Fillmore, 13th president, on page 151.

Courtesy of The Library of Congress

Millard Fillmore, Vice President to Zachary Taylor

CABINET

March 4, 1849–July 9, 1850

State—James Buchanan, Pa., continued from preceding administration; John Middleton Clayton, Del., Mar. 7, 1849

Treasury—Robert James Walker, Miss., continued from preceding administration; McClintock Young (chief clerk), ad interim

Mar. 6, 1849; William Morris Meredith, Pa., Mar. 8, 1849

War—William Learned Marcy, N.Y., continued from preceding administration; Reverdy Johnson, Md. (Attorney General), ad interim Mar. 8, 1849; George Washington Crawford, Ga., Mar. 8, 1849; entered upon duties Mar. 14, 1849

Attorney General—Isaac Toucey, Conn., continued from preceding administration; Reverdy Johnson, Md., Mar. 8, 1849

Postmaster General—Cave Johnson, Tenn., continued from preceding administration; Selah Reeve Hobbie, N.Y. (first assistant Postmaster General), ad interim Mar. 6, 1849; Jacob Collamer, Vt., Mar. 8, 1849

Navy—John Young Mason, Va., continued from preceding administration; William Ballard Preston, Va., Mar. 8, 1849

Interior—Thomas Ewing, Ohio, Mar. 8, 1849

Courtesy of The Library of Congress

The inauguration of Zachary Taylor

CONGRESS

THIRTY-FIRST CONGRESS

March 4, 1849–March 3, 1851

First session—Dec. 3, 1849–Sept. 30, 1850 (302 days)

Second session—Dec. 2, 1850–Mar. 3, 1851 (92 days)

Special session of the Senate—Mar. 5, 1849–Mar. 23, 1849 (19 days)

Vice President—Millard Fillmore, N.Y. (succeeded to the presidency on July 9, 1850, on the death of Zachary Taylor)

President pro tempore of the Senate—David Rice Atchison, Mo., elected Mar. 5, 1849, and Mar. 16, 1849, special session; William Rufus Devane King, Ala., elected May 6, 1850; July 11, 1850

Secretary of the Senate—Asbury Dickens, N.C.

Speaker of the House—Howell Cobb, Ga., elected Dec. 22, 1849

Clerk of the House—Thomas Jefferson Campbell, Tenn., reelected Jan. 11, 1850; died Apr. 13, 1850; Richard Montgomery Young, Ill., elected Apr. 17, 1850

IMPORTANT DATES IN THE PRESIDENCY

Dec. 20, 1849, treaty with Hawaiian Islands

1850, private mint authorized, Mt. Ophir, Calif.

Apr. 19, 1850, Clayton-Bulwer treaty with Great Britain ratified

Aug.–Sept. 1850, measures constituting Clay Compromise of 1850 passed, providing for admission of California as free state; formation of territories of New Mexico and Utah, with option on slavery at time of admission as states; abolition of slave trade in District of Columbia; drastic fugitive slave bill

ADDITIONAL DATA ON TAYLOR

ZACHARY TAYLOR

—was the seventh President born in Virginia.

—was the first President who had not served in the United States Congress or the Continental Congress.

—was the first President whose political party did not enjoy a majority in the Senate.

—was the second President inaugurated on March 5 (March 4 was a Sunday).

—was the fourth President who was a resident of a state other than his native state.

—was the second President to die in office.

—was the second President to die in the White House.

TAYLOR THE THIRD PRESIDENT BORN AFTER REVOLUTION

Zachary Taylor was the third President born after the Revolutionary War. The two Presidents who preceded him in office were also born after the war and after Taylor.

The final draft of the treaty of peace was made on September 3, 1783. Taylor, the twelfth President, was born November 24, 1784, about six years before John Tyler (March 29, 1790), the tenth President, and about eleven years before James Knox Polk (November 2, 1795), the eleventh President.

TAYLOR THE FIRST PRESIDENT REPRESENTING A STATE WEST OF THE MISSISSIPPI

Zachary Taylor of Louisiana was the first President elected from a state west of the Mississippi River. He was, however, born in Virginia.

TAYLOR UNWITTINGLY REFUSED LETTER OF NOMINATION

The reason attributed to Zachary Taylor's not answering the letter sent by the Whigs notifying him at Baton Rouge, La., of his nomination for the presidency was that it arrived "postage due." Taylor refused to accept all unpaid mail. At that time, the Post Office carried "collect letters" which could be sent without the prepayment of postage.

BALLOTLESS PRESIDENT ELECTED

Zachary Taylor was too busy soldiering to vote. He served in the War of 1812, in the Indian wars against the Sauk and Fox nations under Chief Black Hawk and against the Seminoles, and in the war with Mexico. He never stayed in one place long enough to qualify as a voter, and being in the army, had not voted for 40 years. His first vote was cast when he was 62 years of age.

CLAY TRIED FIFTH TIME FOR THE PRESIDENCY

Henry Clay's fifth attempt for the Whig Party nomination was made in 1848 at the Philadelphia convention. He failed to secure the necessary number of votes and the nomination was won by Zachary Taylor, who also won the election. At the Baltimore convention in 1840, Clay had tried in vain for the Whig Party nomination, the nominee that year being William Henry Harrison, who was elected President.

On three other occasions, Henry Clay was a presidential nominee, losing the election each time. He was defeated for the presidency

Courtesy of The Library of Congress

The Clay Compromise of 1850

in 1824 by John Quincy Adams, in 1832 by Andrew Jackson, and in 1844 by James Knox Polk.

Henry Clay made numerous speeches while he was a Senator from Kentucky stating that he was opposed to secession or separation from the union and advocating compromise measures. William Preston, a member of the Kentucky legislature, told Clay that his views would interfere with his chances of becoming President. Clay answered: "Sir, I would rather be right than be President."

TAYLOR'S SON-IN-LAW

Jefferson Davis, who eloped with and married Sarah Knox Taylor in 1835, had incurred the animosity of her father, Zachary Taylor, while serving under his military command. Davis, who had been promoted to the rank of first lieutenant in the First Dragoons on March 4, 1833, "for gallant service," was not the same hardbitten type of soldier as "Old Rough and Ready." In June 1846, after the outbreak of the Mexican War, Davis resigned from Congress, in which he represented Mississippi, and took command of the First Regiment of Mississippi Riflemen. He served under his father-in-law during the three-day siege of Monterrey and greatly distinguished himself, as he did later at Buena Vista.

HORSE PASTURED ON WHITE HOUSE LAWN

When Zachary Taylor moved into the White House, he had his favorite mount, Whitey, accompany him. The horse that had served the general in the Mexican War at Buena Vista, Palo Alto, and other battles was given the freedom of the White House lawn. When President Taylor was buried, old Whitey followed his master's body in the funeral procession.

INTERIOR DEPARTMENT ESTABLISHED

On March 3, 1849, "an act to establish the Home Department" was passed. On March 8, 1849, Thomas Ewing of Ohio was appointed Secretary; he served until July 23, 1850. The name of the department was later changed to the Department of Interior. It is concerned principally with the management, conservation, and development of the natural resources of the United States. These resources include the public lands and the federal range, water and power resources, oil, gas, and other mineral resources, certain foreign resources, fish and wildlife resources, and the national park system.

WAS ATCHISON PRESIDENT?

Many people have claimed that David Rice Atchison was President of the United States.

As March 4, 1849 fell on a Sunday, Zachary Taylor did not take his oath of office as President until Monday, March 5, 1849. Polk's four-year term ended at noon on March 4, 1849. Vice President George Mifflin Dallas resigned as president of the Senate on Friday, March 2, 1849, and Senator David Rice Atchison of Missouri was elected president of the Senate pro tempore on March 2. He was nominated by Thomas Hart Benton.

Atchison presided over the Senate the following day and late into the night. On March 5, he was again elected president of the Senate pro tempore for the purpose of administering the oath of office to the senators-elect.

Article II of the Constitution contains the following provision:

> In Case of the Removal of the President from Office, or of his Death, Resignation, or Inability to discharge the Powers and Duties of the said Office, the Same shall devolve on the Vice President, and the Congress may by Law provide for the Case of Removal, Death, Resignation or Inability, both of the President and the Vice President, declaring what Officer shall then act as President, and such Officer shall act accordingly, until the Disability be removed, or a President shall be elected.

Although Atchison was never a Vice President and never lived in the White House, and signed no acts of Congress, many insist that he was President of the United States for one day.

He died in 1886 and Missouri appropriated $15,000 for his monument, which bears this inscription: "David Rice Atchison, 1807–1886. President of U.S. one day. Lawyer, statesman and jurist."

148

FURTHER READING

Bauer, K. J. *Zachary Taylor: Soldier, Planter, Statesman of the Old Southwest.* 1985.

Eisenhower, John S. D. *Zachary Taylor: The 12th President, 1849-1850 (The American Presidents).* 2008.

Hamilton, Holman. *Zachary Taylor.* 2 vols. 1952.

Smith, Elbert B. *The Presidencies of Zachary Taylor and Millard Fillmore.* Rev. ed. 1988.

Millard Fillmore

Date of birth—Jan. 7, 1800

Place of birth—Summerhill, Cayuga County, N.Y.

Education—Received basic local instruction; apprentice cloth-dresser; self-taught through library reading; classes at academy in New Hope, N.Y.; private studies at law offices of Judge Walter Wood, Montville, N.Y., and of Asa Rice and Joseph Clary, Buffalo, N.Y.

Religion—Unitarian

Ancestry—English

Career—Lawyer, state legislator, U.S. congressman, state comptroller, Vice President

Political party—Whig

State represented—New York

Term of office—July 10, 1850–Mar. 4, 1853 (Fillmore succeeded to the presidency on the death of Zachary Taylor)

Term served—2 years, 236 days

Administration—16th

Congresses—31st, 32nd

Age at inauguration—50 years, 184 days

Lived after term—21 years, 4 days

Occupation after term—Chancellor of University of Buffalo, president of Buffalo Historical Society, presidential candidate

Date of death—Mar. 8, 1874

Age at death—74 years, 60 days

Place of death—Buffalo, N.Y.

Burial place—Forest Lawn Cemetery, Buffalo, N.Y.

FAMILY

FATHER

Name—Nathaniel Fillmore

Date of birth—Apr. 19, 1771

Place of birth—Bennington, Vt.

First marriage—Phoebe Millard, c. 1796 (d. May 2, 1831)

Second marriage—Eunice Love, May 2, 1834

Occupation—Tenant farmer; magistrate, justice of the peace

Date of death—Mar. 28, 1863

Place of death—East Aurora, N.Y.

Age at death—91 years, 343 days

MOTHER

Name at birth—Phoebe Millard

Date of birth—1780

Place of birth—Pittsfield, Mass.

Marriage—Nathaniel Fillmore, c. 1796

Date of death—May 2, 1831

Age at death—About 51 years

SIBLINGS

Millard Fillmore was the second child in a family of nine.

Children of Nathaniel Fillmore and Phoebe Millard Fillmore

Olive Armstrong Fillmore, b. Dec. 16, 1797

Millard Fillmore, b. Jan. 7, 1800, d. Mar. 8, 1874

Cyrus Fillmore, b. Dec. 22, 1801

Almon Hopkins Fillmore, b. Apr. 13, 1806, d. Jan. 17, 1830

Calvin Turner Fillmore, b. July 9, 1810

Julia Fillmore, b. Aug. 29, 1812

Darius Ingraham Fillmore, b. Nov. 16, 1814, d. Mar. 9, 1837

Charles De Witt Fillmore, b. Sept. 23, 1817, d. 1854

Phoebe Maria Fillmore, b. Nov. 23, 1819, d. July 2, 1843

MARRIAGES

First marriage

Married—Abigail Powers
Date of marriage—Feb. 5, 1826
Place of marriage—Moravia, N.Y.
Age of wife at marriage—27 years, 329 days
Age of husband at marriage—26 years, 29 days
Years married—27 years, 53 days

Second marriage

Married—Caroline Carmichael McIntosh
Date of marriage—Feb. 10, 1858
Place of marriage—Albany, N.Y.
Age of wife at marriage—44 years, 112 days
Age of husband at marriage—58 years, 34 days
Years married—16 years, 36 days

CHILDREN

Children of Millard Fillmore and Abigail Powers Fillmore

Millard Powers Fillmore, b. Apr. 25, 1828, Aurora, N.Y.; d. Nov. 15, 1889, Buffalo, N.Y.
Mary Abigail Fillmore, b. Mar. 27, 1832, Buffalo, N.Y.; d. July 26, 1854, Aurora, N.Y.

Children of Millard Fillmore and Caroline Carmichael McIntosh Fillmore

None

THE PRESIDENT'S WIVES

Courtesy of The Library of Congress

Abigail Fillmore, first wife of Millard Fillmore

First wife

Name at birth—Abigail Powers
Date of birth—Mar. 13, 1798
Place of birth—Stillwater, N.Y.
Mother—Abigail Newland Powers
Father—Reverend Lemuel Powers
Father's occupation—Baptist clergyman
Education—Self-taught through reading
Marriage—Millard Fillmore, Feb. 5, 1826, Moravia, N.Y.
Children—Millard Powers Fillmore, b. Apr. 25, 1828, d. Nov. 15, 1889; Mary Abigail Fillmore, b. Mar. 27, 1832, d. July 26, 1854
Occupation—Schoolteacher
Date of death—Mar. 30, 1853
Age at death—55 years, 17 days
Place of death—Washington, D.C.
Burial place—Buffalo, N.Y.
Years older than the President—1 year, 300 days
Years the President survived her—20 years, 343 days

Second wife

Name at birth—Caroline Carmichael
Date of birth—Oct. 21, 1813
Place of birth—Morristown, N.J.
Mother—Temperance Blachley Carmichael
Father—Charles Carmichael
First marriage—Ezekiel C. McIntosh (d.)

Second marriage—Millard Fillmore, Feb. 10, 1858, Albany, N.Y.

Children—None

Date of death—Aug. 11, 1881

Age at death—67 years, 294 days

Place of death—Buffalo, N.Y.

Burial place—Buffalo, N.Y.

Years younger than the President—13 years, 287 days

Years she survived the President—7 years, 156 days

THE FIRST LADY

Abigail Powers Fillmore met her future husband at an academy in New Hope, N.Y., where she was a teacher and he was a 17-year-old student attending classes in his spare time. She was well known for her love of books.

Mrs. Fillmore was an invalid by the time her husband succeeded to the presidency. Her daughter, Mary Abigail Fillmore, assumed the functions of First Lady. Mrs. Fillmore died less than a month after her husband ended his term of office, having contracted a chill while attending the inauguration of President Franklin Pierce.

IMPORTANT DATES IN THE PRESIDENT'S LIFE

18—, attended primitive rural schools and was self-instructed

1815, apprenticed to wool carder and cloth-dresser

1818, taught school at Scott, N.Y.

1823, admitted to the bar; practiced in East Aurora, N.Y.

1829–1831, New York State Assembly (Anti-Masonic party)

1830, moved to Buffalo, N.Y.

Mar. 4, 1833–Mar. 3, 1835, U.S. House of Representatives (from New York)

Mar. 4, 1837–Mar. 3, 1843, U.S. House of Representatives (from New York)

1842, declined to be a candidate for renomination to U.S. House seat

1844, unsuccessful Whig candidate for governor of New York

1846, commanded a corps of Home Guard during the Mexican War

1846, named chancellor of the University of Buffalo (served until his death)

Jan. 1, 1848–Feb. 20, 1849, New York State Controller

Mar. 4, 1849–July 9, 1850, Vice President under Zachary Taylor

July 10, 1850–Mar. 4, 1853, President (succeeded to office at death of Taylor)

June 1852, unsuccessful aspirant for Whig presidential nomination

Nov. 1856, unsuccessful candidate for the presidency on the American ("Know-Nothing") Party and the Whig Party tickets

1862–1867, president of Buffalo Historical Society

INAUGURATION

July 10, 1850

Millard Fillmore, succeeding President Zachary Taylor, who died on July 9, 1850, was the second Vice President to succeed to the presidency on the death of a President. At noon on Wednesday, July 10, 1850, Judge William Cranch, Chief Justice of the United States Circuit Court of the District of Columbia, administered the oath to Fillmore in the Hall of Representatives.

CABINET

July 10, 1850–March 3, 1853

State—John Middleton Clayton, Del., continued from preceding administration; Daniel Webster, Mass., July 22, 1850 (died Oct. 24, 1852); Charles Magill Conrad, La. (secretary of war), ad interim Oct. 25, 1852; Edward Everett, Mass., Nov. 6, 1852

Treasury—William Morris Meredith, Pa., continued from preceding administration; Thomas Corwin, Ohio, July 23, 1850

War—George Washington Crawford, Ga., continued from preceding administration; Samuel J. Anderson (chief clerk), ad interim July 23, 1850; Winfield Scott (major general, U.S. Army), ad interim July 24, 1850; Charles Magill Conrad, La., Aug. 15, 1850

Attorney General—Reverdy Johnson, Md., continued from preceding administration; served to July 22, 1850; John Jordan Crittenden, Ky., July 22, 1850; entered upon duties Aug. 14, 1850

Postmaster General—Jacob Collamer, Vt., continued from preceding administration; Nathan Kelsey Hall, N.Y., July 23, 1850; Samuel Dickinson Hubbard, Conn., Aug. 31, 1852; entered upon duties Sept. 14, 1852

Navy—William Ballard Preston, Va., continued from preceding administration; Lewis Warrington (captain, U.S. Navy), ad interim July 23, 1850; William Alexander Graham, N.C., July 22, 1850; entered upon duties Aug. 2, 1850; John Pendleton Kennedy, Md., July 22, 1852; entered upon duties July 26, 1852

Interior—Thomas Ewing, Md., continued from preceding administration; Daniel C. Goddard (chief clerk), ad interim July 23, 1850; Thomas McKean Thompson McKennan, Pa., Aug. 15, 1850; Daniel C. Goddard (chief clerk), ad interim Aug. 27, 1850; Alexander Hugh Holmes Stuart, Va., Sept. 12, 1850; entered upon duties Sept. 16, 1850

CONGRESS

THIRTY-SECOND CONGRESS

March 4, 1851–March 3, 1853

First session—Dec. 1, 1851–Aug. 31, 1852 (275 days)

Second session—Dec. 6, 1852–Mar. 3, 1853 (88 days)

Special session of the Senate—Mar. 4, 1851–Mar. 13, 1851 (10 days)

Vice President—Millard Fillmore (succeeded to the presidency on July 9, 1850, on the death of Zachary Taylor)

President pro tempore of the Senate—William Rufus Devane King, Ala., resigned as president pro tempore on Dec. 20, 1852; David Rice Atchison, Mo., elected Dec. 20, 1852

Secretary of the Senate—Asbury Dickens, N.C.

Speaker of the House—Linn Boyd, Ky., elected Dec. 1, 185

Clerk of the House—Richard Montgomery Young, Ill.; John Wien Forney, Pa., elected Dec. 1, 1851

APPOINTMENTS TO THE SUPREME COURT

Associate Justice

Benjamin Robbins Curtis, Mass., Sept. 22, 1851 (replaced Levi Woodbury)

IMPORTANT DATES IN THE PRESIDENCY

Sept. 9, 1850, California admitted as the 31st state

Sept. 11, 1850, first American performance of Jenny Lind, "the Swedish Nightingale," at New York City

Sept. 18, 1850, fugitive slave law enacted, making recovery of runaway slaves the responsibility of the federal government

July 4, 1851, cornerstone laid for the south House extension of the Capitol

Dec. 5, 1851, General Louis Kossuth, an architect of the Hungarian revolution of 1848, arrived; celebration at New York City, Dec. 6, where he was proclaimed a champion of liberty

Dec. 24, 1851, Capitol at Washington, D.C., partly destroyed by fire

1852, Harriet Beecher Stowe published *Uncle Tom's Cabin*, the novel that kept slavery a burning issue

Nov. 1852, Commodore Matthew C. Perry sent on expedition to open the ports of Japan to commerce

Mar. 2, 1853, Washington Territory created out of northern part of Oregon

Mar. 3, 1853, federal assay office building authorized

ADDITIONAL DATA ON FILLMORE

MILLARD FILLMORE

—was the second President born in New York.

—was the second President whose father was alive when he was inaugurated.

—was the second President to remarry.

—was the fourth President to marry a widow.

—was the first President to have a stepmother.

BOOKS FOR THE PRESIDENT

According to contemporary reports, when President Millard Fillmore took office the White House had no books, not even a Bible. His wife, Abigail Powers Fillmore, a former schoolteacher and a voracious reader, converted a large room on the second floor into a library, and the appropriation act of March 3, 1851 (9 Stat. L. 613) authorized "for purchase of books for a library at the Executive Mansion two hundred and fifty dollars to be expended under the direction of the President of the United States."

Courtesy of The Library of Congress

Print shows the American delegation, under the command of Matthew C. Perry, presenting a letter from President Fillmore to the Japanese, requesting the establishment of diplomatic and trade relations.

FILLMORE'S REPLY TO BIOGRAPHER

Fillmore wrote as follows to L. J. Cisti on January 4, 1855:

In compliance with your request I have frankly stated the facts connected with my early history, and as no man is responsible for the circumstances of his birth, they furnish nothing of which he should be ashamed or proud, and therefore while they require no apology they can justify no boasting. I need hardly add that this letter is not intended for publication.

FILLMORE DECLINED HONORARY DEGREE

Oxford University, through its chancellor, the Earl of Derby, offered to confer the honorary degree of Doctor of Civil Law (D.C.L.) on Millard Fillmore. He refused the honor, stating, "I had not the advantage of a classical education and no man should, in my judgment, accept a degree he cannot read."

FILLMORE SOUGHT RENOMINATION AND REELECTION

Millard Fillmore served until the completion of the term ending March 3, 1853. He was an aspirant for the presidential nomination at the Whig convention held in Baltimore, Md., in June 1852, but the Whigs nominated General Winfield Scott.

Four years later, Fillmore was nominated for the presidency by the anti-immigrant, anti-Catholic American Party (the "Know-

Courtesy of The Library of Congress

A large woodcut proof for a campaign banner or poster for the Native American party's 1856 presidential candidate

Nothing" Party) but was defeated in the election. He received approximately 875,000 votes against 1,341,000 for John Charles Frémont, the first presidential candidate of the newly formed Republican Party, and 1,838,000 for James Buchanan, the Democrat, who was elected.

The platform adopted by the American Party on February 21, 1856, at Philadelphia, Pa., contained the following section:

Americans must rule America; and to this end native-born citizens should be selected for all state, federal, and municipal offices of government employment, in preference to all others. A change in the laws of naturalization, making a continued residence of twenty-one years, of all not heretofore provided for, an indispensable requisite for citizenship hereafter, and excluding all paupers and persons convicted of crime from landing upon our shores; but no interference with the vested rights of foreigners.

FURTHER READING

Barre, W. L. *The Life and Public Services of Millard Fillmore.* 1971.

Rayback, Robert J. *Millard Fillmore.* 1959.

Smith, Elbert B. *The Presidencies of Zachary Taylor and Millard Fillmore.* 1988.

Courtesy of The Library of Congress

Franklin Pierce

Date of birth—Nov. 23, 1804

Place of birth—Hillsborough, N.H. (now Hillsboro)

Education—Attended public school at Hillsborough, N.H.; Hancock Academy, Hancock, N.H., 1818–1820; Francestown Academy, Francestown, N.H., 1820; Bowdoin College, Brunswick, Me., bachelor's degree., Sept. 1, 1824; private study in law offices of John Burnham, Hillsborough, N.H., Levi Woodbury, Portsmouth, N.H., Samuel Howe, Northampton, Mass., and Edmund Parker, Amherst, N.H.

Religion—Episcopalian

Ancestry—English

Career—Lawyer, state legislator and House speaker, U.S. congressman, U.S. senator, delegate to state constitutional convention, chairman of state Democratic party, U.S. district attorney, Army general in Mexican War

Political party—Democratic

State represented—New Hampshire

Term of office—Mar. 4, 1853–Mar. 4, 1857

Term served—4 years

Administration—17th

Congresses—33rd, 34th

Age at inauguration—48 years, 101 days

Lived after term—12 years, 218 days

Occupation after term—Retired; traveled

Date of death—Oct. 8, 1869

Age at death—64 years, 319 days

Place of death—Concord, N.H.

Burial place—Old North Cemetery, Concord, N.H.

FAMILY

FATHER

Name—Benjamin Pierce

Date of birth—Dec. 25, 1757

Place of birth—Chelmsford, Mass.

First marriage—Elizabeth Andrews, May 24, 1787 (b. 1768; d. Aug. 13, 1788)

Second marriage—Anna Kendrick, Feb. 1, 1790

Occupation—Soldier (brigadier general in Revolution), farmer, innkeeper and tavern owner; sheriff, delegate to state constitutional convention, New Hampshire state legislator, presidential elector, member of governor's council, governor of New Hampshire

Date of death—Apr. 1, 1839

Age at death—81 years, 97 days

Benjamin Pierce was descended from Thomas Pierce, who came to Charleston, Mass., from England circa 1634. The family name was pronounced "purse."

MOTHER

Name at birth—Anna Kendrick

Date of birth—1768

Marriage—Benjamin Pierce, Feb. 1, 1790

Date of death—Dec. 1838

Age at death—70 years

SIBLINGS

Franklin Pierce was the seventh child of his father, the sixth of eight children of a second marriage.

Children of Benjamin Pierce and Elizabeth Andrews Pierce

Elizabeth Andrews Pierce, b. Aug. 9, 1788; d. Mar. 27, 1855

Children of Benjamin Pierce and Anna Kendrick Pierce

Benjamin Kendrick Pierce, b. Aug. 29, 1790; d. Aug. 1, 1850

Nancy M. Pierce, b. Nov. 2, 1792; d. Aug. 27, 1837

John Sullivan Pierce, b. Nov. 5, 1796; d. Mar. 13, 1824

Harriet B. Pierce, b. 1800; d. Nov. 24, 1837

Charles Grandison Pierce, b. 1803; d. June 15, 1828

Franklin Pierce, b. Nov. 23, 1804; d. Oct. 8, 1869

Charlotte Pierce

Henry Dearborn Pierce, b. Sept. 19, 1812; d. 1880

MARRIAGE

Married—Jane Means Appleton

Date of marriage—Nov. 10, 1834

Place of marriage—Amherst, Mass.

Age at wife at marriage—28 years, 243 days

Age of husband at marriage—29 years, 352 days

Years married—29 years, 22 days

CHILDREN

Franklin Pierce, b. Feb. 2, 1836, Hillsborough, N.H.; d. Feb. 5, 1836, Hillsborough, N.H.

Frank Robert Pierce, b. Aug. 27, 1839, Concord, N.H.; d. Nov. 14, 1843, Concord, N.H.

Benjamin Pierce, b. Apr. 13, 1841, Concord, N.H.; d. Jan. 6. 1853, near Andover, Mass.

President Pierce's firstborn child lived only a few days. His second died at the age of four, of typhoid fever. The last child, known as Bennie, was killed in a train wreck, which both his parents survived.

THE PRESIDENT'S WIFE

Name at birth—Jane Means Appleton

Date of birth—Mar. 12, 1806

Place of birth—Hampton, N.H.

Mother—Elizabeth Means Appleton

Father—Jesse Appleton

Father's occupation—Congregational minister; president of Bowdoin College

Marriage—Franklin Pierce, Nov. 10, 1834, Amherst, Mass.

Children—Franklin Pierce, b. Feb. 2, 1836, d. Feb. 5, 1836; Frank Robert Pierce, b. Aug. 27, 1839, d. Nov. 14, 1843; Benjamin Pierce, b. Apr. 13, 1841, d. Jan. 6. 1853

Date of death—Dec. 2, 1863

Age at death—57 years, 265 days

Place of death—Andover, Mass.

Burial place—Concord, N.H.

Years younger than the President—1 year, 109 days

Years the President survived her—5 years, 310 days

Courtesy of The Library of Congress

Jane Pierce, wife of Franklin Pierce

THE FIRST LADY

When Jane Appleton Pierce became mistress of the White House on March 4, 1853, she entered upon her duties with a troubled heart. Less than two months before the inauguration, her youngest and only surviving child had been killed in a railroad accident. All three children had died before reaching their teens. Her grief was so great that she lost interest in other matters. Always resentful of the demands that political life made on her husband—he had turned down a series of opportunities at her request—she chose to believe that her son's death was connected to her husband's election as President. She wore black while in the White House and did not take on the responsibilities of hostess until New Year's Day, 1855. Up to that time, her place was filled by her uncle's wife, Abby Kent Means. Mrs. Means was assisted by Varina Davis, the second wife of Jefferson Davis, Secretary of State (and later president of the Confederacy).

IMPORTANT DATES IN THE PRESIDENT'S LIFE

Sept. 1, 1824, graduated from Bowdoin College, Brunswick, Me.

Sept. 1827, admitted to the bar; practiced at Hillsborough, N.H.

June 3, 1829–1833, served in New Hampshire House of Representatives

1832, speaker, New Hampshire House of Representatives

Mar. 4, 1833–Mar. 3, 1837, served in U.S. House of Representatives (from New Hampshire)

Mar. 4, 1837–Feb. 28, 1842, served in U.S. Senate (from New Hampshire)

1842, resigned to practice law at Concord, N.H.

1845, declined appointment to vacant U.S. Senate seat; declined Democratic Party nomination for governor

1846, declined appointment as U.S. Attorney General under President Polk

1847, enlisted as private in Mexican War

Feb. 16, 1847, became colonel of 9th Regiment, Infantry

Mar. 3, 1847, commissioned brigadier general

May 27, 1847, sailed for Mexico City

June 28, 1847, landed in Vera Cruz, Mexico

Aug. 19, 1847, injured at Contreras when horse became frightened

Sept.–Dec. 1847, in Mexico City

Sept. 13, 1847, served at Chapultepec

Mar. 20, 1848, resigned from army

1848, declined second nomination for governor by state Democratic Party

Courtesy of The Library of Congress

Franklin Pierce during the Mexican-American War

Nov. 6, 1850, member and president of New Hampshire Fifth State Constitutional Convention

1852, Democratic nominee for the presidency

Jan. 6, 1853, railway car accident took the life of his only remaining child

Mar. 4, 1853–Mar. 4, 1857, President

1856, unsuccessful candidate for Democratic nomination for the presidency

Nov. 1857, made European tour, visiting Portugal, Spain, France, Switzerland, Italy, Austria, Germany, Belgium, and England

May 1860, received one complimentary vote at Democratic convention

ELECTIONS

THE ELECTION OF 1852

November 2, 1852

CANDIDATES

Democratic Party (6th Convention)

June 1–5, 1852, Maryland Institute Hall, Baltimore, Md.

P: Franklin Pierce, N.H.
VP: William Rufus Devane King, Ala.

Pierce was nominated on the forty-ninth ballot. Candidates for nomination and the votes they received on the first and forty-ninth ballots:
Lewis Cass, Mich., 116, 2
James Buchanan, Pa., 93, 0
William Learned Marcy, N.Y., 27, 0
Stephen Arnold Douglas, Ill., 20, 2
Joseph Lane, Ore., 13, 0
Samuel Houston, Tex., 8, 1
John B. Weller, Calif., 4, 0
Henry Dodge, Wis., 3, 0
William Orlando Butler, Ky., 2, 1
Daniel Stevens Dickinson, N.Y., 1, 1
Franklin Pierce, N.H., 0, 282
Total number of votes:
First ballot: 287
Forty-ninth ballot: 289

Whig Party

June 17–20, 1852, Maryland Institute Hall, Baltimore, Md.

P: Winfield Scott, N.J.
VP: William Alexander Graham, N.C.

Scott was nominated on the fifty-third ballot. Candidates for nomination and the votes they received on the first and fifty-third ballots:
Millard Fillmore, N.Y., 133, 112
Winfield Scott, N.J., 131, 159
Daniel Webster, Mass., 29, 21
Total number of votes:
First ballot: 293
Fifty-third ballot: 292

Free Soil (Democratic) Party

Aug. 11, 1852, Pittsburgh, Pa.

P: John Parker Hale, N.H.
VP: George Washington Julian, Ind.

1852 POPULAR VOTE

Democratic Party, 1,601,274
Whig Party, 1,386,580
Free Soil Party, 155,825

1852 ELECTORAL VOTE

There were 296 electoral votes from 31 states.

Pierce received 85.81 percent (254 votes—27 states) as follows: Ala. 9; Ark. 4; Calif. 4; Conn. 6; Del. 3; Fla. 3; Ga. 10; Ill. 11; Ind. 13; Iowa 4; La. 6; Me. 8; Md. 8; Mich. 6; Miss. 7; Mo. 9; N.H. 5; N.J. 7; N.Y. 35; N.C. 10; Ohio 23; Pa. 27; R.I. 4; S.C. 8; Tex. 4; Va. 15; Wis. 5.

Scott received 14.19 percent (42 votes—4 states) as follows: Ky. 12; Mass. 13; Tenn. 12; Vt. 5.

INAUGURATION

March 4, 1853

Franklin Pierce was inaugurated on Friday, March 4, 1853, and took the oath of office on the east portico of the Capitol. A raw northeasterly wind blew over the fast-melting snow.

The oath was administered by Chief Justice Taney. In taking the oath, Pierce availed himself of an option provided in Article II, section 1 of the Constitution. Instead of the usual "I do solemnly swear," he said, "I do solemnly affirm." He was the only President to "affirm" instead of "swear." (His objection to "swear" was a religious one, based on Matthew 5:34–7.)

Pierce delivered his 3,319-word inaugural address without reference to notes. More than 80,000 spectators flocked to Washington, but as it commenced to snow during the ceremonies, only about 15,000 remained to hear the address.

The cost of putting up and taking down the grandstand in front of the Capitol was $322, including the pay of 16 extra policemen.

A reception was held at the White House. The inaugural ball at Jackson Hall was canceled because Pierce was in mourning for his 11-year-old son, who had been killed in a railroad accident on January 6. Mrs. Pierce did not go to Washington for the inauguration.

THE VICE PRESIDENT

Name—William Rufus Devane King (13th V.P.)

Date of birth—Apr. 7, 1786

Place of birth—Sampson County, N.C.

Mother—Margaret King

Father—William King

Father's occupation—Planter

Political party—Democratic

State represented—Alabama

Term of office—Mar. 24, 1853–Apr. 18, 1853

Age at inauguration—66 years, 331 days

Occupation after term—Died in office

Date of death—Apr. 18, 1853

Age at death—67 years, 11 days

Place of death—Cahaba, Ala.

Burial place—Selma, Ala.

ADDITIONAL DATA ON KING

1803, graduated from the University of North Carolina, Chapel Hill, N.C.

1806, admitted to bar; practiced in Clinton, N.C.

1807–1809, served in North Carolina House of Commons

1810, city solicitor, Wilmington, N.C.

Mar. 4, 1811–Nov. 4, 1816, served in U.S. House of Representatives (from North Carolina)

1816–1818, secretary of U.S. legation, Naples, Italy, and subsequently of U.S. legation, St. Petersburg, Russia

1819, served as delegate to Alabama's constitutional convention prior to statehood

Courtesy of The Library of Congress

William King, Vice President to Franklin Pierce

Dec. 14, 1819–Apr. 15, 1844, served in U.S. Senate (from Alabama)

1836–1841, president pro tempore of the Senate

1844–1846, minister to France

1846, defeated for reelection to the Senate

July 1, 1848–Dec. 20, 1852, appointed by Alabama governor to vacant Senate seat; served as chairman of Senate Foreign Relations Committee

1850, elected by Senate as its presiding officer after Vice President Millard Fillmore succeeded to the presidency

Mar. 24, 1853–Apr. 18, 1853, Vice President under Franklin Pierce

163

VICE PRESIDENT KING SERVED IN BOTH HOUSES AND REPRESENTED TWO STATES

Prior to his election as Vice President, King served in both houses of Congress. In each house he represented a different state. He was a representative from North Carolina from March 4, 1811, to November 4, 1816, and a senator from Alabama from December 14, 1819, to April 15, 1844, and again from July 1, 1848, to December 20, 1852.

KING POSSIBLY THE FIRST GAY VICE PRESIDENT

During his lifetime, King was reputed to be homosexual. For some years, while he was serving in the Senate, he lived with James Buchanan, congressman from Pennsylvania (and later President of the United States). Their surviving correspondence suggests that they were in an intimate relationship.

VICE PRESIDENT KING NEVER SERVED

After his election as Vice President, William Rufus Devane King went to Cuba. He was suffering from tuberculosis and hoped that his health would improve in Cuba's tropical climate. On March 24, 1853, he had the oath of office administered to him in Havana, Cuba, by William L. Sharkey, United States Consul at Havana. This was permitted by a special act of Congress. Of all the Presidents and Vice Presidents, King was the first and only one to take the oath in a foreign country.

King's illness continued to worsen, and he returned to the United States aboard the U.S. Navy steamship *Fulton*. He died at his Alabama estate on April 18, 1853. As the first session of the 33rd Congress was not held until December 5, 1853, he never performed any of the duties of his office and therefore never presided over the Senate. He was not replaced, and President Pierce served the remainder of his term without a Vice President.

CABINET

March 4, 1853–March 3, 1857

State—William Hunter (chief clerk), ad interim Mar. 4, 1853; William Learned Marcy, N.Y., Mar. 7, 1853

Treasury—Thomas Corwin, Ohio, continued from preceding administration; James Guthrie, Ky., Mar. 7, 1853

War—Charles Magill Conrad, La., continued from preceding administration; Jefferson Davis, Miss., Mar. 7, 1853; Samuel Cooper (adjutant general, U.S. Army), ad interim Mar. 3, 1857

Attorney General—John Jordan Crittenden, Ky., continued from preceding administration; Caleb Cushing, Mass., Mar. 7, 1853

Postmaster General—Samuel Dickinson Hubbard, Conn., continued from preceding administration; James Campbell, Pa., Mar. 7, 1853

Navy—John Pendleton Kennedy, Md., continued from preceding administration; James Cochran Dobbin, N.C., Mar. 7, 1853

Interior—Alexander Hugh Holmes Stuart, Va., continued from preceding administration; Robert McClelland, Mich., Mar. 7, 1853

CONGRESS

THIRTY-THIRD CONGRESS

March 4, 1853–March 3, 1855

First session—Dec. 5, 1853–Aug. 7, 1854

(246 days)

Second session—Dec. 4, 1854–Mar. 3, 1855 (90 days)

Special session of the Senate—Mar. 4, 1853–Apr. 11, 1853 (38 days)

Vice President—William Rufus Devane King, Ala. (died Apr. 18, 1853)

President pro tempore of the Senate —David Rice Atchison, Mo., elected Mar. 4, 1853; Lewis Cass, Mich., elected Dec. 4, 1854, for one day only; Jesse David Bright, Ind., elected Dec. 5, 1854

Secretary of the Senate—Asbury Dickens, N.C.

Speaker of the House—Linn Boyd, Ky., reelected Dec. 5, 1853

Clerk of the House—John Wien Forney, Pa., reelected Dec. 5, 1853

THIRTY-FOURTH CONGRESS

March 4, 1855–March 3, 1857

First session—Dec. 3, 1855–Aug. 18, 1856 (260 days)

Second session—Aug. 21, 1856–Aug. 30, 1856 (10 days)

Third session—Dec. 1, 1856–Mar. 3, 1857 (93 days)

Vice President—Vacant

President pro tempore of the Senate —Jesse David Bright, Ind., reelected June 11, 1856; Charles Edward Stuart, Mich., served June 5, 1856; elected June 9, 1856; resigned June 11, 1856; James Murray Mason, Va., served Jan. 5, 1856, elected Jan. 6, 1857

Secretary of the Senate—Asbury Dickens, N.C.

Speaker of the House—Nathaniel Prentice Banks, Mass., elected Feb. 2, 1856

Clerk of the house—John Wien Forney, Pa.; William Cullom, Tenn., elected Feb. 4, 1856

APPOINTMENTS TO THE SUPREME COURT

Associate Justice

John Archibald Campbell, Ala., Mar. 22, 1853 (replaced John McKinley)

IMPORTANT DATES IN THE PRESIDENCY

May 31, 1853, Elisha Kent Kane expedition to Arctic left New York City

July 14, 1853, President Pierce opened Crystal Palace Exposition, New York, N.Y.

1854, Republican Party formed

Mar. 8, 1854, Perry's treaty with Japan ratified, opening Japanese ports to American trade

May 22, 1854, Congress enacted Kansas-Nebraska Act permitting state option on slavery, nullifying the Missouri Compromise and supporting pro-slavery forces in Kansas

June 30, 1854, Gadsden Purchase treaty proclaimed; United States acquired border territory from Mexico

Courtesy of The Library of Congress

Delivering of the American presents at Yokuhama

165

Oct. 1854, Ostend Manifesto, issued by U.S. ministers to England, France, and Spain, urged American acquisition of Cuba from Spain by purchase or force

1855, first postal directory published
Sept. 4, 1856, first American flag flown in Japan by Consul General Townsend Harris
1857, financial panic

ADDITIONAL DATA ON PIERCE

FRANKLIN PIERCE

—was the first President born in New Hampshire.

—was the first President born in the nineteenth century (November 23, 1804).

—was the only President to affirm rather than swear the oath of office.

—was the only elected President who sought but did not win renomination.

PIERCE A "DARK HORSE" CANDIDATE

Franklin Pierce, the Democratic nominee for President in 1852, was not considered as a candidate until the thirty-fifth ballot, when Virginia cast fifteen votes for him. On the forty-eight ballot, he received 55 votes. On the forty-ninth ballot, there was a sudden surge in his favor and he received 283 of the 289 votes cast, thereby winning the nomination.

PIERCE DEFEATED GENERAL SCOTT

Franklin Pierce carried 27 of the 31 states and defeated General Winfield Scott, the Whig party nominee. Pierce, a brigadier general in the Mexican War, had served under General Scott and was with him during his march to and capture of Mexico City on September 14, 1847. Pierce enlisted in the war as a private and was enrolled in a company of volunteers organized at Concord, N.H. He was commissioned a colonel in the Ninth Regiment, and on March 3, 1847, was commissioned a brigadier general in the volunteer army.

PIERCE NOT RENOMINATED

Pierce has the dubious distinction of being the only President elected to office who was not renominated by his party for a second term. The Democratic Party convention held in Cincinnati, Ohio, June 2–6, 1856, did not endorse Pierce. He was named on the first ballot, but more votes were received by James Buchanan. On the seventeenth ballot Buchanan received the nomination, which was declared unanimous.

FULL CABINET RETAINED

Franklin Pierce was the only President to retain the same cabinet for four years without any changes, replacements, resignations, or vacancies due to illness or death. His seven cabinet members remained in office until the completion of his term on March 3, 1857.

133 BALLOTS TO ELECT SPEAKER

The 34th Congress assembled on Monday, December 3, 1855, to elect a Speaker of the House of Representatives. It was not until the 133rd ballot, on February 2, 1856, that Nathaniel Prentice Banks of Massachusetts was elected Speaker.

Courtesy of The Library of Congress

Birthplace of Franklin Pierce, Hillsboro, N.H.

PIERCE'S HEALTH

During his early years in Congress, Pierce lived in a boardinghouse in Washington, D.C., his wife having remained at home in New Hampshire during her first pregnancy. Like other congressmen in the same position, he became a drinker and carouser, and developed a tendency to alcoholism that plagued him for the rest of his life. His drinking increased markedly after the death of his last remaining child a few weeks before his inauguration. He died of stomach inflammation caused by consumption of alcohol.

FURTHER READING

Gara, Larry. *The Presidency of Franklin Pierce.* 1991.

Hawthorne, Nathaniel. *The Life of Franklin Pierce.* 1852.

Nichols, Roy Franklin. *Franklin Pierce: Young Hickory of the Granite Hills.* 1931.

Wallner, Peter A. Franklin Pierce: New Hampshire's Favorite Son. 2004

———. *Franklin Pierce: Martyr for the Union.* 2007.

Courtesy of The Library of Congress

James Buchanan

James Buchanan

Date of birth—Apr. 23, 1791

Place of birth—Cove Gap, Pa.

Education—Attended local schools; Old Stone Academy, Mercersburg, Pa.; Dickinson College, Carlisle, Pa., graduated Sept. 27, 1809; private study in law office of James Hopkins, Lancaster, Pa.

Religion—Presbyterian

Ancestry—Scotch-Irish

Career—Lawyer, volunteer in War of 1812, state legislator, U.S. congressman, minister to Russia and Great Britain, U.S. senator, Secretary of State

Political party—Democratic

State represented—Pennsylvania

Term of office—Mar. 4, 1857–Mar. 4, 1861

Term served—4 years

Administration—18th

Congresses—35th, 36th

Age at inauguration—65 years, 315 days

Lived after term—7 years, 89 days

Occupation after term—Writing

Date of death—June 1, 1868

Age at death—77 years, 39 days

Place of death—Lancaster, Pa.

Burial place—Woodward Hill Cemetery, Lancaster, Pa.

FAMILY

FATHER

Name—James Buchanan

Date of birth—1761

Place of birth—County Donegal, Ireland

Marriage—Elizabeth Speer, Apr. 16, 1788

Occupation—Farmer, storekeeper; magistrate, justice of the peace

Date of death—June 11, 1821

Age at death—60 years

MOTHER

Name at birth—Elizabeth Speer

Date of birth—1767

Marriage—James Buchanan, Apr. 16, 1788

Date of death—May 14, 1833

Place of death—Greensburg, Pa.

Age at death—66 years

SIBLINGS

James Buchanan was the second child in a family of eleven.

Children of James Buchanan and Elizabeth Speer Buchanan

Mary Buchanan, b. 1789, d. 1791

James Buchanan, b. Apr. 23, 1791, d. June 1, 1868

Jane Buchanan, b. 1793, d. 1839

Maria Buchanan, b. 1795, d. 1849

Sarah Buchanan, b. 1798, d. 1825

Elizabeth Buchanan, b. 1800, d. 1801

Harriet Buchanan, b. 1802, d. 1840

John Buchanan, b. 1804, d. 1804

William Speer Buchanan, b. Nov. 14, 1805, d. Dec. 19, 1826

George Washington Buchanan, b. 1808, d. Nov. 13, 1832

Edward Young Buchanan, b. May 30, 1811, d. Jan. 20, 1895

MARRIAGE

President Buchanan was one of two Presidents to enter the White House as a bachelor and the only one to remain unmarried. The other bachelor President, Grover Cleveland, married during the first of his two terms in office.

BUCHANAN WAS ENGAGED TO MARRY

In the summer of 1819, James Buchanan, twenty-eight, was engaged to twenty-three-year-old Ann Caroline Coleman, the daughter of Robert Coleman of Lancaster, Pa., a wealthy iron-mill owner who accused Buchanan of being a fortune hunter. While on a visit in Philadelphia, Pa., she took an overdose of laudanum and died there on December 9, 1819. She was buried December 12, 1819, in St. James Episcopal churchyard at Lancaster, Pa.

BUCHANAN POSSIBLY THE FIRST GAY PRESIDENT

Some historians believe that President Buchanan did not marry because he was homosexual. During his years in the Senate he shared an apartment in Washington, D.C., with fellow congressman Rufus William Devane King, who became Vice President under Franklin Pierce. Their surviving correspondence suggests that they were in an intimate relationship.

HOSTESS AT THE WHITE HOUSE

Since James Buchanan was a bachelor, Harriet Lane, the daughter of his sister Jane Lane, served as mistress of the White House during his administration. Her mother had died when she was seven and her father when she was nine. During her uncle's presidential term, she married Henry Elliott Johnston of Baltimore, Md.

IMPORTANT DATES IN THE PRESIDENT'S LIFE

1807, entered junior class Dickinson College

Nov. 17, 1812, admitted to bar; practiced at Lancaster, Pa.

1814, served in company of dragoons under Major Charles Sterret Ridgely of Baltimore in War of 1812

Dec. 6, 1814–Oct. 1815, Pennsylvania House of Representatives

1816, unsuccessful candidate for U.S. House of Representatives

18–, became a Jacksonian Democrat when Federalist Party went out of existence

Mar. 4, 1821–Mar. 3, 1831, U.S. House of Representatives (from Pennsylvania)

Jan. 4, 1832–Aug. 5, 1833, U.S. Minister to Russia

Dec. 6, 1834–Mar. 5, 1845, U.S. Senate (from Pennsylvania)

May 29, 1844, unsuccessful aspirant to Democratic presidential nomination

Mar. 6, 1845–Mar. 6, 1849, Secretary of State in cabinet of President Polk

May 25, 1848, unsuccessful aspirant to Democratic presidential nomination

1849, retired to Wheatland, his 22-acre estate near Lancaster, Pa.

June 4, 1852, unsuccessful aspirant to Democratic presidential nomination

Apr. 11, 1853, envoy extraordinary and minister plenipotentiary to Great Britain

Oct. 1854, coauthor (with U.S. ministers to France and Spain) of pro-slavery Ostend Manifesto calling for immediate acquisition of Cuba

Mar. 4, 1857–Mar. 4, 1861, President

ELECTIONS

THE ELECTION OF 1856

November 4, 1856

CANDIDATES

Democratic Party (7th Convention)

June 2–6, 1856, Smith and Nixon's Hall, Cincinnati, Ohio

P: James Buchanan, Pa.
VP: John Cabell Breckinridge, Ky.

Buchanan was nominated on the seventeenth ballot, receiving all of the 296 votes cast. Candidates for nomination and the votes they received on the first ballot:

James Buchanan, Pa., $135^1/_2$

Franklin Pierce, N.H., $122^1/_2$

Stephen Arnold Douglas, Ill., 33

Lewis Cass, Mich., 5

Nomination made unanimous

Republican Party (1st Convention)

June, 17–19, 1856, Music Fund Hall, Philadelphia, Pa.

P: John Charles Frémont, Calif.
VP: William Lewis Dayton, N.J.

Frémont was nominated on the first official ballot. Candidates for nomination and the votes they received on the first informal and the first official ballots:

John Charles Frémont, Calif., 359, 520

John McLean, Ohio, 190, 37

Charles Sumner, Mass., 2, 0

Nathaniel Prentice Banks, Mass., 1, 0

William Henry Seward, N.Y., 1, 1

Total number of votes:

First informal ballot: 553

First official ballot: 558

Nomination made unanimous

The antislavery factions of the Whigs and the Free Democratic parties formed the Republican Party. (The name "Republican" had been applied to the earlier Democratic-Republican Party, which developed into the present Democratic Party.)

JAMES BUCHANAN,
DEMOCRATIC CANDIDATE FOR PRESIDENT OF THE UNITED STATES.

Courtesy of The Library of Congress

Campaign poster for James Buchanan

American (Know-Nothing) Party

Feb. 22, 1856, National Hall, Philadelphia, Pa.

P: Millard Fillmore, N.Y.
VP: Andrew Jackson Donelson, Tenn.

The American Party started as more of a secret society than a political party. Membership was divided into three degrees. The first included members who were American-born and were wholly unconnected with the Roman Catholic Church. They were obliged to vote as the society dictated. The second degree included members who were permitted to hold office inside the organization. The third degree was composed of members who were eligible for office outside the organization. At this convention, the secret features were eliminated and nominations were made.

Whig Party (the "Silver Grays")

Sept. 17, 1856, Baltimore, Md.

P: Millard Fillmore, N.Y.
VP: Andrew Jackson Donelson, Tenn.

The Whig Party lost its power in 1852. Its few remaining adherents—conservative "Old Line" Whigs known as "Silver Grays"—supported the candidates of the American Party in 1856. Most of the southern Whigs had joined the Democrats, and most of the antislavery northern Whigs eventually joined the Republican Party.

North American Party

June 12, 1856, New York, N.Y.

P: Nathaniel Prentice Banks, Mass.
VP: William Freame Johnson, Pa.

The North Americans broke away from the American Party. Their nominees later declined and their support was given to the Republican party.

1856 POPULAR VOTE

Democratic Party, 1,838,169

Republican Party, 1,341,264

American Party, 874,534

1856 ELECTORAL VOTE

There were 296 electoral votes from 31 states.

Buchanan received 58.79 percent (174 votes—19 states) as follows: Ala. 9; Ark. 4; Calif. 4; Del. 3; Fla. 3; Ga. 10; Ill. 11; Ind. 13; Ky. 12; La. 6; Miss. 7; Mo. 9; N.J. 7; N.C. 10; Pa. 27; S.C. 8; Tenn. 12; Tex. 4; Va. 15.

Frémont received 38.51 percent (114 votes—11 states) as follows: Conn. 6; Iowa 4; Me. 8; Mass. 13; Mich. 6; N.H. 5; N.Y. 35; Ohio 23; R.I. 4; Vt. 5; Wis. 5.

Fillmore received 2.70 percent (1 state): Md. 8.

INAUGURATION

March 4, 1857

James Buchanan was inaugurated on Wednesday, March 4, 1857, the oath of office being administered by Chief Justice Taney on the east portico of the Capitol.

A big parade containing impressive floats attracted great crowds. Models of battleships, the Goddess of Liberty, and historical scenes were depicted on the floats.

A special building to accommodate six thousand persons was erected at a cost of $15,000 on Judiciary Square for the inaugural ball. The building, which contained two rooms, one for dancing and one for the supper, was 235 feet long, 77 feet wide, and 20 feet high, and had a white ceiling studded with gold stars. The walls were red, white, and blue. The music was furnished by an orchestra of 40. Refreshments were lavish. At the supper, 400 gallons of oysters were consumed, 60 saddles of mutton, 4 saddles of venison, 125 tongues, 75 hams, 500 quarts of chicken salad, 500 quarts of jellies, 1,200 quarts of ice cream, and a cake four feet high. More than $3,000 was spent for wine.

THE VICE PRESIDENT

Name—John Cabell Breckinridge (14th V.P.)

Date of birth—Jan. 21, 1821

Place of birth—Near Lexington, Ky.

Political party—Democratic

State represented—Kentucky

Term of office—Mar. 4, 1857–Mar. 4, 1861

Age at inauguration—36 years, 42 days

Occupation after term—Military service in Confederate Army, Confederate Secretary of War, lawyer

Date of death—May 17, 1875

Age at death—54 years, 116 days

Place of death—Lexington, Ky.

Burial place—Lexington, Ky.

ADDITIONAL DATA ON BRECKINRIDGE

1839, graduated from Centre College, Danville, Ky.

1840, admitted to the bar; practiced at Lexington, Ky.

1847–1848, major, Third Kentucky Volunteers, in Mexican War

Courtesy of The Library of Congress

John C. Breckinridge, Vice President to James Buchanan

1849, Kentucky State House of Representatives

Mar. 4, 1851–Mar. 3, 1855, U.S. House of Representatives (from Kentucky)

Mar. 4, 1857–Mar. 4, 1861, Vice President under James Buchanan

1860, unsuccessful candidate for President on the Southern Democratic ticket

Mar. 4, 1861–Dec. 4, 1861, U.S. Senate (from Kentucky); expelled by resolution

1862, served in Confederate army as brigadier general at Bowling Green; later major general

May 18–July 27, 1862, defended Vicksburg

Jan. 1863, at Battle of Murfreesboro

May 14, 1863, at Battle of Jackson, Miss.

Jan.–Apr. 1865, Secretary of War in cabinet of Confederate States

1865, escaped to Europe

1867, returned to Lexington, Ky.; resumed law practice

YOUNGEST VICE PRESIDENT

John Cabell Breckinridge of Kentucky, who served as Vice President under President James Buchanan, was the youngest man to become Vice President. He was inaugurated on March 4, 1857, when he was 36 years, 1 month, and 11 days old.

CABINET

March 4, 1857–March 3, 1861

State—William Learned Marcy, N.Y., continued from preceding administration; Lewis Cass, Mich., Mar. 6, 1857; William Hunter (chief clerk), ad interim Dec. 15, 1860; Jeremiah Sullivan Black, Pa., Dec. 17, 1860

Treasury—James Guthrie, Ky., continued from preceding administration; Howell Cobb, Ga., Mar. 6, 1857; Isaac Toucey, Conn. (secretary of the Navy), ad interim Dec. 10, 1860; Philip Francis Thomas, Md., Dec. 12, 1860; John Adams Dix, N.Y., Jan. 11, 1861; entered upon duties Jan. 15, 1861

War—Samuel Cooper (adjutant-general, U.S. Army), ad interim Mar. 4, 1857; John Buchanan Floyd, Va., Mar. 6, 1857; Joseph Holt, Ky. (Postmaster General), ad interim Jan. 18, 1861

Attorney General—Caleb Cushing, Mass., continued from preceding administration; Jeremiah Sullivan Black, Pa., Mar. 6, 1857; entered upon duties Mar. 11, 1857; Edwin

McMasters Stanton, Pa., Dec. 20, 1860; entered upon duties Dec. 22, 1860

Postmaster General—James Campbell, Pa., continued from preceding administration; Aaron Venable Brown, Tenn., Mar. 6, 1857; died Mar. 8, 1859; Horatio King, Me. (first assistant Postmaster General), ad interim Mar. 9, 1859; Joseph Holt, Ky., Mar. 14, 1859; Horatio King, Me. (first assistant Postmaster General), ad interim Jan. 1, 1861; Horatio King, Me., Feb. 12, 1861

Navy—James Cochran Dobbin, N.C., continued from preceding administration; Isaac Toucey, Conn., Mar. 6, 1857

Interior—Robert McClelland, Mich., continued from preceding administration; Jacob Thompson, Miss., Mar. 6, 1857; entered upon duties Mar. 10, 1857; Moses Kelly (chief clerk), ad interim Jan. 10, 1861

CONGRESS

THIRTY-FIFTH CONGRESS

March 4, 1857–March 3, 1859

First session—Dec. 7, 1857–June 14, 1858 (189 days)

Second session—Dec. 6, 1858–Mar. 3, 1859 (88 days)

Special sessions of the Senate—Mar. 4, 1857–Mar. 14, 1857 (11 days); June 15, 1858–June 16, 1858 (2 days)

Vice President—John Cabell Breckinridge, Ky.

President pro tempore of the Senate— James Murray Mason, Va., elected Mar. 4, 1857, special session; Thomas Jefferson Rusk, Tex., elected Mar. 14, 1857, special session; Benjamin Fitzpatrick, Ala., elected Dec. 7, 1857; Mar. 29, 1858; June 14, 1858; Jan. 25, 1859

Secretary of the Senate—Asbury Dickens, N.C.

Speaker of the House—James Lawrence Orr, S.C., elected Dec. 7, 1857

Clerk of the House—William Cullom, Tenn.; James Cameron Allen, Ill., elected Dec. 7, 1857

THIRTY-SIXTH CONGRESS

March 4, 1859–March 3, 1861

First session—Dec. 5, 1859–June 25, 1860 (202 days)

Second session—Dec. 3, 1860–Mar. 3, 1861 (93 days)

Special sessions of the Senate—Mar. 4, 1859–Mar. 10, 1859 (7 days); June 26, 1860–June 28, 1860 (3 days)

Vice President—John Cabell Breckinridge, Ky.

Courtesy of The Library of Congress

James Buchanan's inaugural procession

President pro tempore of the Senate —Benjamin Fitzpatrick, Ala., elected Mar. 9, 1859, special session; Dec. 19, 1859; Feb. 20, 1860; June 26, 1860, special session; Jesse David Bright, Ind., elected June 12, 1860; Solomon Foot, Vt., elected Feb. 16, 1861

Secretary of the Senate—Asbury Dickens, N.C.,

Speaker of the House—William Pennington, N.J., elected Feb. 1, 1860

Clerk of the House—James Cameron Allen, Ill.; John Wien Forney, Pa., elected Feb. 3, 1860

APPOINTMENTS TO THE SUPREME COURT

Associate Justice

Nathan Clifford, Me., Jan. 12, 1858 (replaced Benjamin Robbins Curtis)

IMPORTANT DATES IN THE PRESIDENCY

1857, U.S. troops sent to Utah territory to restore federal authority and quell rebellion led by Brigham Young

Mar. 6, 1857, Chief Justice Taney announced Dred Scott decision, rendering the Missouri Compromise unconstitutional

1858, pro-slavery Lecompton Constitution defeated in Kansas

May 11, 1858, Minnesota admitted as the 32nd state

Aug.–Oct. 1858, Lincoln-Douglas debates

Aug. 5, 1858, Atlantic cable completed

Aug. 16, 1858, James Buchanan and Queen Victoria exchanged greetings by means of the Atlantic cable

Feb. 14, 1859, Oregon admitted as the 33rd state

Aug. 27, 1859, oil discovered in Pennsylvania

Oct. 16, 1859, the federal arsenal at Harper's Ferry, Va. (now W.Va.), raided by John Brown in an attempt to provoke a slave revolt

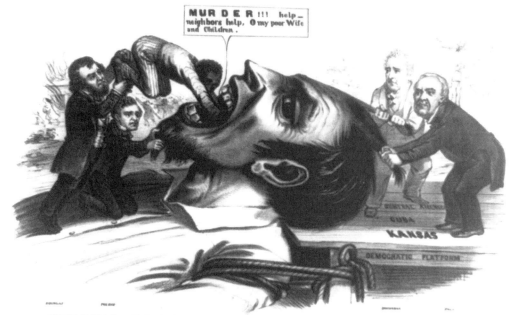

FORCING SLAVERY DOWN THE THROAT OF A FREESOILER

Courtesy of The Library of Congress

Political cartoon: "Forcing slavery down the throat of a freesoiler"

Apr. 3, 1860, Pony Express service began between St. Joseph, Mo., and Sacramento, Calif.

Sept. 20, 1860, Prince of Wales arrived at Detroit, Mich., from Canada, traveling as Baron Renfrew

Dec. 1860–Feb. 1861, futile compromise attempts to save the Union

Dec. 20, 1860, South Carolina seceded from the Union

Dec. 26, 1860, Major Robert Anderson, commander of troops in Charleston Harbor, S.C., removed his garrison from Fort Moultrie to Fort Sumter

Jan.–Feb. 1861, secession of Mississippi, Florida, Alabama, Georgia, Louisiana, Texas

Jan. 9, 1861, *Star of the West* fired on by South Carolina troops from Morris Island and Fort Moultrie as the unarmed Union supply ship attempted to enter Charleston Harbor

Jan. 29, 1861, Kansas admitted as the 34th state

Feb. 4, 1861, delegates from seceding states met at Montgomery, Ala.

Feb. 8, 1861, Confederate States of America organized

ADDITIONAL DATA ON BUCHANAN

JAMES BUCHANAN

—was the first President born in Pennsylvania.

—was the only President to remain a bachelor.

FIRST NATIONAL REPUBLICAN PLATFORM

At its first convention, which opened in Philadelphia, Pa., on June 2, 1856, the newly formed Republican Party adopted the following platform:

This convention of delegates, assembled in pursuance of a call addressed to the people of the United States, without regard to past political differences or divisions, who are opposed to the repeal of the Missouri Compromise, to the policy of the present administration, to the extension of slavery into free territory; in favor of admitting Kansas as a free State, of restoring the action of the Federal Government to the principles of Washington and Jefferson, and who purpose to unite in presenting candidates for the offices of President and Vice-President, do resolve as follows:

Resolved, that the maintenance of the principles promulgated in the Declaration of Independence and embodied in the Federal Constitution is essential to the preservation of our republican institutions, and that the Federal Constitution, the rights of the States, and the Union of the States, shall be preserved.

Resolved, That with our Republican fathers we hold it to be a self-evident truth that all men are endowed with the inalienable rights to life, liberty, and the pursuit of happiness, and that the primary object and ulterior designs of our Federal Government were to secure these rights to all persons within its exclusive jurisdiction; that our Republican fathers, when they had abolished slavery in all of our national territory, ordained that no person should be deprived of life, liberty, or property without due process of law, it becomes our duty to maintain this provision of the Constitution against all attempts to violate, for the purpose of establishing slavery in any territory of the United States, by positive legislation, prohibiting its existence or extension therein. That we deny the authority of Congress, or of a territorial Legislature, of any individual or association of individuals, to give legal existence to slavery in any Territory of the United States, while the present constitution shall be maintained.

Resolved, That the Constitution confers upon Congress sovereign power over the Territories of the United States for their government, and that in the exercise of this power it is both the right and the duty of Congress to prohibit in the Territories those twin relics of barbarism—polygamy and slavery.

Resolved, That while the Constitution of the United States was ordained and established by the people in order to form a more perfect union, establish justice, insure domestic tranquillity, provide for the common defense, and secure the blessings of liberty, and contains ample provision for the protection of the life, liberty and property of every citizen, the dearest constitutional rights of the people of Kansas have been fraudulently and violently taken from them; their territory has been invaded by an armed force; spurious and pretended legislative, judicial and executive officers have been set over them, by whose usurped authority, sustained by the military power of the Government, tyrannical and unconstitutional laws have been enacted and enforced; the rights of the people to keep and bear arms have been infringed; test oaths of an extraordinary and entangling nature have been imposed as a condition of exercising the right of suffrage and holding office; the right of an accused person to a speedy and public trial by an impartial jury has been denied; the right of the people to be secure in their persons, houses, papers, and effects against unreasonable searches and seizures has been violated; they have been deprived of life, liberty, and property without due process of law; the freedom of speech and of the press has been abridged; the right to choose their representatives has been made of no effect; murders, robberies, and arsons have been instigated and encouraged, and the offenders have been allowed to go unpunished;—that all of these things have been done with the knowledge, sanction, and procurement of the present administration, and that for this high crime against the Constitution, the Union, and humanity, we arraign the administration, the President, his advisers, agents, supporters, apologists, and accessories, either before or after the facts, before the country and before the world, and that it is our fixed purpose to bring the actual perpetrators of these atrocious outrages and their accomplices to a sure and condign punishment hereafter.

Resolved, That Kansas should be immediately admitted as a State of the Union, with her present free Constitution, as at once the most effectual way of securing to her citizens the enjoyment of the rights and privileges to which they are entitled, and of ending the civil strife now raging in her territory.

Resolved, That the highwayman's plea, that "might makes right," embodied in the Ostend circular, was in every respect unworthy of American diplomacy, and would bring shame and dishonor upon any government or people that gave it their sanction.

Resolved, That a railroad to the Pacific Ocean by the most central and practicable route, is imperatively demanded by the interests of the whole country and that the Federal Government ought to render immediate and efficient aid in its construction, and, as an auxiliary thereto, the immediate construction of an emigrant route on the line of the railroad.

Resolved, That appropriations by Congress for the improvement of rivers and harbors, of a national character, required for the accommodation and security of our existing commerce, are authorized by the Constitution, and justified by the obligation of Government to protect the lives and property of its citizens.

BUCHANAN TIRED OF PRESIDENCY

Buchanan, in a letter to Mrs. James Knox Polk on September 19, 1859, wrote:

I am now in my sixty-ninth year and am heartily tired of my position as president. I shall leave it in the beginning of March 1861, should a kind Providence prolong my days until that period, with much greater satisfaction than when entering on the duties of the office.

FURTHER READINGS

Auchampaugh, Philip G. *James Buchanan and His Cabinet on the Eve of Secession.* 1965.

Baker, Jean H. *James Buchanan (The American Presidents).* 2004.

Klein, Philip S. *President James Buchanan.* 1960.

Moore, John. ed. *The Works of James Buchanan.* 12 vols. 1908–1911.

Courtesy of The Library of Congress

Abraham Lincoln

Date of birth—Feb. 12, 1809

Place of birth—Hodgenville, Hardin County (now Larue County), Ky.

Education—Sporadic attendance at the intermittent public schools; self-taught through reading

Religion—Christian (no specific denomination)

Ancestry—English

Career—Store clerk, soldier, postmaster, rail-splitter, surveyor, lawyer, state legislator, U.S. congressman

Political party—Republican

State represented—Illinois

Term of office—Mar. 4, 1861–Apr. 15, 1865

Term served—4 years, 42 days

Administration—19th, 20th

Congresses—37th, 38th, 39th

Age at inauguration—52 years, 20 days

Lived after term—Died in office

Date of death—Apr. 15, 1865

Age at death—56 years, 62 days

Place of death—Washington, D.C.

Burial place—Oak Ridge Cemetery, Springfield, Ill.

FAMILY

FATHER

Name—Thomas Lincoln

Date of birth—Jan. 6, 1778

Place of birth—Rockingham County, Va.

First marriage— Nancy Hanks, June 12, 1806, Beechland, Ky.

Second marriage—Sarah Bush Johnston

Occupation—Farmer, soldier, carpenter, woodcutter, wheelwright, laborer

Date of death—Jan. 17, 1851

Place of death—Coles County, Ill.

Age at death—73 years, 11 days

MOTHER

Name at birth—Nancy Hanks

Date of birth—Feb. 5, 1784

Place of birth—Campbell County, Va.

Marriage—Thomas Lincoln, June 12, 1806, Beechland, Ky.

Date of death—Oct. 5, 1818

Place of death—Spencer County, Ind.

Age at death—34 years, 242 days

STEPMOTHER

Name at birth—Sarah Bush

Date of birth—Dec. 12, 1788

Place of birth—Hardin County, Ky.

First marriage—Daniel Johnston, Mar. 13, 1806 (d. Oct. 1818)

Second marriage—Thomas Lincoln, Dec. 2, 1819, Elizabethtown, Ky.

Children from first marriage—Four children

Children from second marriage—None

Date of death—Apr. 10, 1869

Place of death—Charleston, Ill.

Age at death—80 years, 119 days

SIBLINGS

Abraham Lincoln was the second child of his father's first wife.

Children of Thomas Lincoln and Nancy Hanks Lincoln

Nancy ("Sarah") Lincoln, b. Feb. 10, 1807, d. Jan. 20, 1828

Abraham Lincoln, b. Feb. 12, 1809, d. Apr. 15, 1865

Abraham Lincoln with his family, Mrs. Lincoln, Robert, and Thaddeus sitting around dinner table

Thomas Lincoln, b. 1811, d. 1813

MARRIAGE

Married—Mary Todd

Date of marriage—Nov. 4, 1842

Place of marriage—Springfield, Ill.

Age of wife at marriage—23 years, 326 days

Age of husband at marriage—33 years, 265 days

Years married—22 years, 162 days

CHILDREN

Robert Todd Lincoln, b. Aug. 1, 1843, Springfield, Ill.; m. Sept. 24, 1868, Mary Harlan, Washington, D.C.; d. July 25, 1926, Manchester, Vt.

Edward Baker Lincoln, b. Mar. 10, 1846, Springfield, Ill.; d. Feb. 1, 1850, Springfield, Ill.

William Wallace Lincoln, b. Dec. 21, 1850, Springfield, Ill.; d. Feb. 20, 1862, at the White House, Washington, D.C.

Thomas ("Tad") Lincoln, b. Apr. 4, 1853, Springfield, Ill.; d. July 15, 1871, Chicago, Ill.

THE PRESIDENT'S WIFE

Name at birth—Mary Todd

Date of birth—Dec. 13, 1818

Place of birth—Lexington, Ky.

Mother—Eliza Ann Parker Todd

Father—Robert Smith Todd

Father's occupation—Banker, manufacturer, merchant, farmer

Education—John Ward's academy and Mme. Mentelle's school, Lexington, Ky.

Marriage—Abraham Lincoln, Nov. 4, 1842, Springfield, Ill.

Children—Robert Todd Lincoln, b. Aug. 1, 1843, d. July 25, 1926; Edward Baker Lincoln, b. Mar. 10, 1846, d. Feb. 1, 1850; William Wallace Lincoln, b. Dec. 21, 1850, d. Feb. 20, 1862; Thomas ("Tad") Lincoln, b. Apr. 4, 1853, d. July 15, 1871

Date of death—July 16, 1882

Age at death—63 years, 215 days

Place of death—Springfield, Ill.

Burial place—Springfield, Ill.

Years younger than the President—9 years, 304 days

Years she survived the President—17 years, 92 days

THE FIRST LADY

Mary Todd Lincoln served as hostess of the White House in a very simple and quiet manner. The war years placed a pall on social functions and much of her time was devoted to war work. Nevertheless, Mrs. Lincoln, whose family had founded the city of Lexington, Kentucky, spent extravagant sums in pursuit of her goal of turning the Executive Mansion into an American palace. She was an intelligent, energetic woman who always tried to embody the ideals of nineteenth-century femininity—being a steadfast mother and a loyal, submissive wife—but the rigid codes of female conduct in her time placed restrictions on her outspoken ways and independent nature.

LINCOLN'S WIFE AND THE SOUTH

Mary Todd Lincoln, born in Lexington, Ky., was the subject of much speculation. Her patriotism was questioned by many.

Her brother, George Rogers Clark Todd, was a surgeon in the Confederate army.

Her half-brother, Samuel Briggs Todd, a soldier in the Confederate army, was killed at the battle of Shiloh, Tenn., April 6–7, 1862. Another half-brother, David H. Todd, an officer, died from wounds received at Vicksburg, Miss., and another, Alexander H. Todd, was killed at Baton Rouge, La., August 20, 1862.

The husband of Emilie, her half-sister, was Confederate Brigadier General Ben Hardin Helm, killed on September 20, 1863, at Chickamauga, Ga.

Two other brothers-in-law were also in the Confederate service.

Courtesy of The Library of Congress

Mary Todd Lincoln, wife of Abraham Lincoln

President Lincoln appeared before the Senate members of the Committee on the Conduct of the War, and made this statement:

I, Abraham Lincoln, President of the United States, appear of my own volition before this committee of the Senate, to say I, of my own knowledge, know that it is untrue that any of my family hold treasonable relations with the enemy.

MRS. LINCOLN COMMITTED

In 1875 a Court of Inquest ordered that Mrs. Lincoln "be committed to a state hospital for the insane." She was confined to the Bellevue Place Sanatorium, a private institution at Batavia, Ill., from May 20, 1875, to September 10, 1875.

IMPORTANT DATES IN THE PRESIDENT'S LIFE

1816, family moved from Kentucky to Indiana

July 1827, hired to operate a ferry across the Anderson River in Spencer County, Ind.

Apr. 1828, hired to pilot a flatboat from Rockport, Ind., to New Orleans, La.

Mar. 1, 1830, family moved from Indiana to Illinois

Mar. 1831, hired to build a flatboat at Sangamon Town, Ill., and take a load of produce to New Orleans

1832, volunteer, Sangamon Rifle Co., Richland, Ill.; reenlisted as private; mustered out June 16; returned to New Salem, Ill.; unsuccessful in general merchandise business with partner

Aug. 6, 1832, unsuccessful candidate for Illinois legislature

Mar. 6, 1833, received saloon license to dispense liquor at Springfield, Ill. (Berry and Lincoln)

May 7, 1833, appointed postmaster, New Salem, Ill.

Dec. 7, 1835–Feb. 7, 1836, Illinois General Assembly

1837, moved to Springfield, Ill.

Mar. 1, 1837, admitted to the bar

Mar. 4, 1847–Mar. 3, 1849, U.S. House of Representatives (only Whig elected from Illinois)

Feb. 8, 1855, unsuccessful Whig candidate for senator from Illinois

June 19, 1856, unsuccessful aspirant to the Republican vice presidential nomination

Aug.–Oct. 1858, Lincoln-Douglas debates in Illinois (senatorial campaign)

Nov. 2, 1858, unsuccessful candidate for senator from Illinois on Republican ticket

May 18, 1860, nominated for the presidency

Nov. 6, 1860, elected as first Republican President

Courtesy of The Library of Congress

Lincoln taking the oath at his second inauguration, March 4, 1865

Mar. 4, 1861–Mar. 4, 1865, President (first term)

Nov. 19, 1863, delivered Gettysburg Address

Nov. 8, 1864, reelected President

Mar. 4, 1865, inaugurated President for second term ending Mar. 4, 1869

Apr. 14, 1865, assassinated at Ford's Theater, Washington, D.C.; died at 7:22 A.M., Apr. 15

ELECTIONS

THE ELECTION OF 1860

November 6, 1860

CANDIDATES

Republican Party (2nd Convention)

May 16–18, 1860, the Wigwam, Chicago, Ill.

P: Abraham Lincoln, Ill.

VP: Hannibal Hamlin, Me.

Lincoln was nominated on the third ballot. Before the third ballot was completed, a shift in votes brought Lincoln's total to 364 votes. Candidates for nomination and the votes they received on the first and third ballots:

William Henry Seward, N.Y., $173^1/_2$, 180

Abraham Lincoln, Ill., 102, $231^1/_2$

Simon Cameron, Pa., $50^1/_2$, 0

Salmon Portland Chase, Ohio, 49, $24^1/_2$

Edward Bates, Mo., 48, 22

William Lewis Dayton, N.J., 14, 1

John McLean, Ohio, 12, 5

Jacob Colamer, Vt., 10, 0

Benjamin Franklin Wade, Ohio, 3, 0

John Charles Frémont, Calif., 1, 0

John M. Read, Pa., 1, 0

Charles Sumner, Mass., 1, 0

Cassius Marcellus Clay, Ky., 0, 1

Total number of votes: 465

Number necessary for nomination: 233

Democratic Party (8th Convention)

April 23–28, 30, and May 1–3, 1860, the Hall of the South Carolina Institute, Charleston, S.C.

P: No nomination made

VP: No nomination made

Candidates for nomination and the votes they received on the first and fifty-seventh ballots:

Stephen Arnold Douglas, Ill., $145^1/_2$, $151^1/_2$

Robert Mercer Taliaferro Hunter, Va., 42, 16

James Guthrie, Ky., 35, $65^1/_2$

Andrew Johnson, Tenn., 12, 0

Daniel Stevens Dickinson, N.Y., 7, 4

Joseph Lane, Ore., 6, 14

Isaac Toucey, Conn., $2^1/_2$, 0

Jefferson Davis, Miss., $1^1/_2$, 1

Franklin Pierce, N.H., 1, 0

Total number of votes:

First ballot: $252^1/_2$

Fifty-seventh ballot: 252

Number necessary for nomination: 202

Unable to reach a decision on the fifty-seventh ballot, the convention adjourned to meet at Baltimore, Md., on June 18, 1860.

Democratic Party (Northern or Douglas Democrat)

June 18–23, 1860, Front Street Theatre, Baltimore, Md.

P: Stephen Arnold Douglas, Ill.

VP: Herschel Vespasian Johnson, Ga.

Douglas was nominated on the second ballot. Candidates for nomination and the votes they received on the first and second ballots:

Stephen Arnold Douglas, Ill., $173^1/_2$, $181^1/_2$

James Guthrie, Ky., 9, $5^1/_2$

John Cabell Breckinridge, KY., 5, $7^1/_2$

Horatio Seymour, N.Y., 1, 0

Thomas Stanhope Bocock, Va., 1, 0

Daniel Stevens Dickinson, N.Y., $^1/_2$, 0

Henry Alexander Wise, Va., $^1/_2$, 0

Total number of votes:

First ballot: $190^1/_2$

Second ballot: $194^1/_2$

Nomination made unanimous

National Democratic Party (Independent Democratic Party)

June 23, 1860, Maryland Institute Hall, Baltimore, Md.

P: John Cabell Breckinridge, Ky.

VP: Joseph Lane, Ore.

Breckinridge was nominated on the first ballot. Candidates for nomination and the votes they received:

John Cabell Breckinridge, Ky., 81

Daniel Stevens Dickinson, N.Y., 24

Total number of votes: 105

Nomination made unanimous

This segment seceded from the Democratic Party and pledged the new party to a Pacific railroad, the acquisition of Cuba, the enforcement of the Fugitive Slave Law, and the admission of territories as states when their populations were adequate, with or without slavery as their constitutions provided.

Southern Democratic Party (Southern or Breckinridge Democrats)

June 28, 1860, Market Hall, Baltimore, Md.

P: John Cabell Breckinridge, Ky.

VP: Joseph Lane, Ore.

This party declared that it was the right and duty of Congress to protect slavery in the territories whenever the owners chose to take slaves to the territories.

Constitutional Union Party (formerly the American Party)

May 9–10, 1860, Presbyterian Church, Baltimore, Md.

P: John Bell, Tenn.

VP: Edward Everett, Mass.

Bell was nominated on the second ballot. Candidates for nomination and the votes they received on the first and second ballots:

John Bell, Tenn., $68^1/_2$, 138

Samuel Houston, Tex., 57, 69

John Jordan Crittenden, Ky., 28, 1

Edward Everett, Mass., 25, $9^1/_2$

William Alexander Graham, N.C., 24, $18^1/_2$

John McLean, Ohio, 19, 1

William Cabell Rives, Va., 13, 0

John Minor Botts, Va., $9^1/_2$, $5^1/_2$

William Lewis Sharkey, 7, 8$\frac{1}{2}$

William Leftwich Goggin, Va., 3, 2

Total number of votes:

First ballot: 254

Second ballot: 253

Number necessary for nomination: 138

This party tried to ignore the slavery question. It favored "the constitution of the country, the union of the states and the enforcement of the laws."

1860 POPULAR VOTE

Republican Party, 1,866,452

Democratic Party (Northern Democrats), 1,375,157

Democratic Party (Southern Democrats), 847,953

Constitutional Union Party, 590,631

1860 ELECTORAL VOTE

There were 303 electoral votes from 33 states.

Lincoln received 59.41 percent (180 votes—18 states) as follows: Calif. 4; Conn. 6; Ill. 11; Ind. 13; Iowa 4; Me. 8; Mass. 13; Mich. 6; Minn. 4; N.H. 5; N.J. 4 (of the 7 votes); N.Y. 35; Ohio 23; Ore. 3; Pa. 27; R.I. 4; Vt. 5; Wis. 5.

Breckinridge received 23.76 percent (72 votes—11 states) as follows: Ala. 9; Ark. 4; Del. 3; Fla. 3; Ga. 10; La. 6; Md. 8; Miss. 7; N.C. 10; S.C. 8; Tex. 4.

Bell received 12.87 percent (39 votes—3 states) as follows: Ky. 12; Tenn. 12; Va. 15.

Douglas received 3.96 percent (12 votes—1 state) as follows: Mo. 9; N.J. 3 (of the 7 votes).

THE ELECTION OF 1864

November 8, 1864

CANDIDATES

Republican Party (National Union) (3rd Convention)

June 7–8, 1864, Front Street Theatre, Baltimore, Md.

P: Abraham Lincoln, Ill.

VP: Andrew Johnson, Tenn.

Courtesy of The Library of Congress

Abraham Lincoln on horseback in front of his home in Springfield, Illinois, at the close of the campaign with Senator Douglas

Abraham Lincoln was nominated on the first ballot. Candidates for nomination and the votes they received:

Abraham Lincoln, Ill., 484

Ulysses Simpson Grant, Ill., 22

Total number of votes: 506

Nomination made unanimous

Democratic Party (9th Convention)

August 29–31, 1864, the Amphitheatre, Chicago, Ill.

P: George Brinton McClellan, N.Y.

VP: George Hunt Pendleton, Ohio

George Brinton McClellan was nominated on the first ballot. Candidates for nomination and the votes they received:

George Brinton McClellan, N.J., 202$\frac{1}{2}$

Thomas Hart Seymour, Conn., 23$\frac{1}{2}$

Total number of votes: 226

Number necessary for nomination: 151

Nomination made unanimous

Independent Republican Party

May 31, 1864, Cleveland, Ohio

P: John Charles Frémont, Calif.

VP: John Cochrane, N.Y.

A one-term principle was advocated by this faction of the Republican Party. Later, the candidates withdrew and supported the Republican Party nominations.

1864 POPULAR VOTE

Republican Party, 2,213,635
Democratic Party, 1,805,237

1864 ELECTORAL VOTE

There were 233 electoral votes from 25 states.

Lincoln received 90.99 percent (212 votes—22 states) as follows: Calif. 5; Conn. 6; Ill. 16; Ind. 13; Iowa 8; Kan. 3; Me. 7; Md. 7; Mass. 12; Mich. 8; Minn. 4; Mo. 11; Nev. 2; N.H. 5; N.Y. 33; Ohio 21; Ore. 3; Pa. 26; R.I. 4; Vt. 5; W.Va. 5; Wis. 8.

McClellan received 9.01 percent (21 votes—3 states) as follows: Del. 3; Ky. 11; N.J. 7.

Eleven Confederate states with 80 votes did not vote: Ala. 8; Ark. 5; Fla. 3; Ga. 9; La. 7; Miss. 7; N.C. 9; S.C. 6; Tenn. 10; Tex. 6; Va. 10.

INAUGURATIONS

FIRST TERM

March 4, 1861

Abraham Lincoln was inaugurated on Monday, March 4, 1861, on the east portico of the Capitol. It was the seventh time that Chief Justice Taney had administered the oath of office to a President.

Outgoing President Buchanan greeted the incoming President by saying, "If you are as happy, my dear sir, on entering this house as I am on leaving it and returning home, you are the happiest man on earth."

Lincoln was the first President whose military escort was really a guard instead of an honorary escort.

The intense feeling between the North and the South marred the occasion, but a large military parade seemed to lend assurance to the nervous populace. After the ceremonies, Lincoln returned to the White House to watch the parade. One of the floats carried 34 young girls, each one representing a state in the union. As the float passed in front of Lincoln, the girls rushed over to him and he kissed all of them.

Lincoln did not attend the inaugural ball, which was held in a frame building called, for the occasion, "The White Muslin Palace of Aladdin."

SECOND TERM

March 4, 1865

Lincoln was inaugurated on Saturday, March 4, 1865, on the east portico of the Capitol. The oath was administered by Chief Justice Salmon Portland Chase. The morning was stormy, but the weather cleared by afternoon.

Lincoln's second inaugural address, long famed as a masterpiece of rhetoric, contained the moving "with malice toward none, with charity for all" phrase that embodied his attitude of forgiveness.

This was the first inauguration in which Americans of African descent participated. African-American civic associations and a battalion of black soldiers formed part of the Lincoln escort. For security reasons, Lincoln did not ride in the military procession to the Capitol. Enthusiasm gripped the people, for the war was drawing to a close.

At the inaugural ball, held on Monday, March 6, Mrs. Lincoln wore a white silk and lace dress with a headdress, an ensemble that cost more than $2,000.

Andrew Johnson's inauguration as Vice President took place in the Senate chamber. Johnson was barely recovered from a bout with typhoid fever, and to give himself strength he had doctored himself with liquor. He arrived in the chamber with his face flushed and his balance unsteady. Before taking the oath, he delivered a peculiar harangue in which he stressed his lowly origin. Although this was the most humiliating event that had ever occurred at an inauguration, Johnson was not disgraced. Even his enemies forgave him, since it was known that he was not a habitual drunkard.

THE VICE PRESIDENTS

Hannibal Hamlin, first Vice President to Abraham Lincoln

FIRST TERM

Name—Hannibal Hamlin (15th V.P.)

Date of birth—Aug. 27, 1809

Place of birth—Paris, Me.

Political party—Republican (after 1856)

State represented—Maine

Term of office—Mar. 4, 1861–Mar. 4, 1865

Age at inauguration—51 years, 189 days

Occupation after term—U.S. Senate (from Maine), U.S. minister to Spain

Date of death—July 4, 1891

Age at death—81 years, 311 days

Place of death—Bangor, Me.

Burial place Bangor, Me.

Additional Data on Hamlin

18–, attended local schools and Hebron Academy; worked on farm until of age

18–, served one year as compositor

1833, admitted to bar; practiced in Hampden, Penobscot County, Me.

1836–1840, Maine House of Representatives; served as Speaker 1837, 1839, and 1840

1840, unsuccessful candidate for U.S. House of Representatives

Mar. 4, 1843–Mar. 3, 1847, U.S. House of Representatives (from Maine)

1846, unsuccessful Anti-slavery Democratic candidate for U.S. Senate (from Maine)

1848, Maine House of Representatives

June 8, 1848–Jan. 7, 1857, U.S. Senate (from Maine)

Jan. 8, 1857–Feb. 20, 1857, governor of Maine

Mar. 4, 1857–Jan. 17, 1861, U.S. Senate (from Maine)

Mar. 4, 1861–Mar. 4, 1865, Vice President under Abraham Lincoln

1864, enlisted as a private in Maine State Guard for sixty-day period

1865–1866, collector of the port of Boston; resigned

Mar. 4, 1869–Mar. 3, 1881, U.S. Senate (from Maine)

1881–1882, U.S. minister to Spain

1882, engaged in agricultural pursuits

SECOND TERM

Name—Andrew Johnson (16th V.P.)

Political party—Democratic (elected Vice President on Republican ticket)

State represented—Tennessee

Term of office—Mar. 4, 1865–Apr. 15, 1865

Andrew Johnson second Vice President to Abraham Lincoln

Age at inauguration—56 years, 65 days

Occupation after term—President of the United States

For further biographical information, see the chapter on Andrew Johnson, 17th President, on page 203.

CABINET

FIRST TERM

March 4, 1861–March 3, 1865

State—Jeremiah Sullivan Black, Pa., continued from preceding administration; William Henry Seward, N.Y., Mar. 5, 1861

Treasury—John Adams Dix, N.Y., continued from preceding administration; Salmon Portland Chase, Ohio, Mar. 5, 1861; entered upon duties Mar. 7, 1861; George Harrington, D.C. (assistant secretary), ad interim July 1, 1864; William Pitt Fessenden, Me., July 1, 1864; entered upon duties July 5, 1864

War—Joseph Holt, Ky., continued from preceding administration; Simon Cameron, Pa., Mar. 5, 1861; entered upon duties Mar. 11, 1861; Edwin McMasters Stanton, Pa., Jan. 15, 1862; entered upon duties Jan. 20, 1862

Attorney General—Edwin McMasters Stanton, Pa., continued from preceding administration; Edward Bates, Mo., Mar. 5, 1861; James Speed, Ky., Dec. 2, 1864; entered upon duties Dec. 5, 1864

Postmaster General—Horatio King, Me.; continued from preceding administration; Montgomery Blair, D.C., Mar. 5, 1861; entered upon duties Mar. 9, 1861; William Dennison, Ohio, Sept. 24, 1864; entered upon duties Oct. 1, 1864

Navy—Isaac Toucey, Conn., continued from preceding administration; Gideon Welles, Conn., Mar. 5, 1861; entered upon duties Mar. 7, 1861

Interior—Moses Kelly (chief clerk), ad interim Mar. 4, 1861; Caleb Blood Smith, Ind., Mar. 5, 1861; John Palmer Usher, Ind. (assistant secretary), ad interim Jan. 1, 1863; John Palmer Usher, Ind., Jan. 8, 1863

SECOND TERM

March 4, 1865–April 15, 1865

State—William Henry Seward, N.Y., continued from preceding administration

Treasury—George Harrington, D.C. (assistant secretary), ad interim Mar. 4, 1865; Hugh McCulloch, Ind., Mar. 7, 1865; entered upon duties Mar. 9, 1865

War—Edwin McMasters Stanton, Pa., continued from preceding administration

Attorney General—James Speed, Ky., continued from preceding administration

Postmaster General—William Dennison, Ohio, continued from preceding administration

Navy—Gideon Welles, Conn., continued from preceding administration

Interior—John Palmer Usher, Ind., continued from preceding administration

CONGRESS

THIRTY-SEVENTH CONGRESS

March 4, 1861–March 3, 1863

First session—July 4, 1861–Aug. 6, 1861 (34 days)

Second session—Dec. 2, 1861–July 17, 1862 (228 days)

Third session—Dec. 1, 1862–Mar. 3, 1863 (93 days)

Special session of the Senate—Mar. 4, 1861–Mar. 28, 1861 (24 days)

Vice President—Hannibal Hamlin, Me.

President pro tempore of the Senate—Solomon Foot, Vt., elected Mar. 23, 1861; July 18, 1861; Jan. 15, 1862; Mar. 31, 1862; June 19, 1862; Feb. 18, 1863

Secretary of the Senate—Asbury Dickens, N.C.; John Wien Forney, Pa., elected July 15, 1861; William Hickey (chief clerk), appointed Mar. 22, 1861, "to serve during the present infirmity of the secretary"

Speaker of the House—Galusha Aaron Grow, Pa., elected July 4, 1861

Clerk of the House—John Wien Forney, Pa., Emerson Etheridge, Tenn., elected July 4, 1861

THIRTY-EIGHTH CONGRESS

March 4, 1863–March 3, 1865

First session—Dec. 7, 1863–July 4, 1864 (209 days)

Second session—Dec. 5, 1864–Mar. 3, 1865 (89 days)

Special session of the Senate—Mar. 4, 1863–Mar. 14, 1863 (11 days)

Vice President—Hannibal Hamlin, Me.

President pro tempore of the Senate —Solomon Foot, Vt., elected Mar. 4, 1863, special session; Dec. 18, 1863; Feb. 23, 1864;

Mar. 11, 1864; Apr. 11, 1864; Daniel Clark, N.H., elected Apr. 26, 1864; Feb. 9, 1865

Secretary of the Senate—John Wien Forney, Pa.

Speaker of the House—Schuyler Colfax, Ind., elected Dec. 7, 1863

Clerk of the House—Emerson Etheridge, Tenn., Edward McPherson, Pa., elected Dec. 8, 1863

THIRTY-NINTH CONGRESS

March 4, 1865–March 3, 1867

First session—Dec. 4, 1865–July 28, 1866 (237 days)

Second session—Dec. 3, 1866–Mar. 3, 1867 (91 days)

Special session of the Senate—Mar. 4, 1865–Mar. 11, 1865 (8 days)

Vice President—Andrew Johnson, Tenn. (succeeded to the presidency on Apr. 15, 1865, on the death of Abraham Lincoln)

President pro tempore of the Senate —Lafayette Sabine Foster, Conn., elected Mar. 7, 1865, special session, "to serve in the absence of the Vice President"; Benjamin Franklin Wade, Ohio, elected Mar. 2, 1867

Secretary of the Senate—John Wien Forney, Pa.

Speaker of the House—Schuyler Colfax, Ind., reelected Dec. 4, 1865

Clerk of the House—Edward McPherson, Pa., reelected Dec. 4, 1865

APPOINTMENTS TO THE SUPREME COURT

Chief Justice

Salmon Portland Chase, Ohio, Dec. 6, 1864 (replaced Roger Brooke Taney)

Associate Justices

Noah Haynes Swayne, Ohio, Jan. 24, 1862 (replaced John McLean)

Samuel Freeman Miller, Iowa, July 16, 1862 (replaced Peter Vivian Daniel)

David Davis, Ill., Oct. 17, 1862 (replaced John Archibald Campbell)

Stephen Johnson Field, Calif., Mar. 10, 1863 (newly created seat)

IMPORTANT DATES IN THE PRESIDENCY

Feb. 1861, plot to assassinate President-elect

Lincoln at Baltimore, Md.

Apr.–June 1861, secession of Virginia, Arkansas, North Carolina, Tennessee

Apr. 12, 1861, first attack in Civil War at Fort Sumter, S.C.

Apr. 15, 1861, President Lincoln issued call for 75,000 volunteers

Apr. 19, 1861, riot at Baltimore, Md.

May 3, 1861, call for 42,034 volunteers for three years

June 3, 1861, first battle in Civil War, Philippi, Va. (now W.Va.)

July 21, 1861, First Battle of Bull Run

Aug. 16, 1861, proclamation prohibiting intercourse between loyal and seceding states

Nov. 8, 1861, *Trent* affair—Confederate agents Mason and Slidell taken from British steamer *Trent* by Union ship

Mar. 9, 1862, battle between *Monitor* and *Merrimac*

Mar. 11, 1862, President Lincoln assumed command of the Army and the Navy

Apr. 6–7, 1862, Battle of Shiloh

Apr. 16, 1862, slavery abolished in the District of Columbia

May 15, 1862, act to establish Department of Agriculture approved

May 20, 1862, Homestead Act approved

July 2, 1862, Morrill land-grant college act approved

Aug. 30, 1862, Second Battle of Bull Run

Sept. 17, 1862, Battle of Antietam

Sept. 22, 1862, preliminary Emancipation Proclamation issued (a warning that unless hostilities ceased and the secessionist states soon returned to the Union, the slaves would be freed)

Jan. 1, 1863, Emancipation Proclamation issued

Feb. 25, 1863, national banking system created

May 1–4, 1863, Battle of Chancellorsville

June 1863, occupation of Mexico by French troops led to American protests

Courtesy of The Library of Congress

Abraham Lincoln and Mary Todd Lincoln greeting Union generals, Cabinet members, and others at a reception

June 19, 1863, West Virginia admitted as the 35th state

July 1–3, 1863, Battle of Gettysburg

July 4, 1863, surrender of Vicksburg

Sept. 19–20, 1863, Battle of Chickamauga

Nov. 19, 1863, Lincoln delivered Gettysburg Address

Nov. 24–25, 1863, Battle of Chattanooga

May 5–7, 1864, Battle of the Wilderness

June 19, 1864, U.S. warship *Kearsarge* sank the British-built Confederate ship *Alabama,* which had preyed upon American vessels

Sept. 2, 1864, General Sherman captured Atlanta

Oct. 31, 1864, Nevada admitted as the 36th state

Nov. 15, 1864, burning of Atlanta; beginning of Sherman's march to the sea

Apr. 3, 1865, evacuation of Richmond

Apr. 9, 1865, General Robert E. Lee surrendered to General Ulysses S. Grant at Appomattox Courthouse, Va.

ADDITIONAL DATA ON LINCOLN

ABRAHAM LINCOLN

—was the first President born in Kentucky.

—was the third President to die in office.

—was the first President assassinated.

—was the only elected President to hold office during a civil war. His authority was not recognized in eleven states.

—was the fifth President who was a resident of a state other than his native state.

—was the first President to obtain a patent.

FIRST PRESIDENT BORN OUTSIDE ORIGINAL THIRTEEN STATES

Abraham Lincoln was the first President born beyond the boundaries of the original thirteen states. He was born near Hodgenville, in Hardin County, now Larue County, Ky.

LINCOLN ENLISTED AS A SOLDIER

On April 16, 1832, Governor John Reynolds called the Illinois militia to duty. When the notice reached New Salem on April 19, 1832, Lincoln gave up his job as a clerk and enlisted. On April 21, 1832, he was elected captain of his company.

The call for troops was issued as follows:

Your Country Requires Your Services

The Indians have assumed a hostile attitude and have invaded the State in violation of the treaty of last summer. The British band of Sacs and other hostile Indians, headed by Black Hawk, are in possession of the Rock River country, to the great terror of the frontier inhabitants. . . . No citizen ought to remain inactive when his country is invaded and the helpless part of the community are in danger.

His company was enrolled at Beardstown, Ill., in state service on April 28 and into federal service on May 9. When mustered out on May 27, Lincoln reenlisted as a private in Captain Elijah Iles's company. This enlist-ment expired June 16, while Lincoln was at Fort Wilbourn, and he reenlisted in the company under the command of Captain Jacob M. Early. On July 10, he was mustered out of service at White Water, Wis.

LINCOLN A PATENTEE

On March 10, 1849, Abraham Lincoln of Springfield, Ill., applied for a patent on "a new and improved manner of combining adjustable buoyant air chambers with a steamboat or other vessel for the purpose of enabling their draught of water to be readily lessened to enable them to pass over bars, or through shallow water, without discharging their cargoes."

The Patent Office awarded Lincoln U.S. Patent No. 6,469 on May 22, 1849. This was the first and only patent obtained by a President. It was never put into practical use.

"LINCOLN'S LOST SPEECH"

The Kansas-Nebraska Bill which became a law May 30, 1854, provided that the two new territories could determine whether they wanted to be free states or slave states. This act repealed the Missouri Compromise, an act of Congress passed in February 1820, which had admitted Missouri as a slave state and prohibited the extension of slavery to the remainder of the Louisiana territory north of the 36° 30' line.

Slavery agitators sacked the town of Lawrence, Kan., on May 21, 1856. Lives were lost, homes burned, printing presses destroyed. The slavery question aroused the nation, and when the Illinois Republican Party held its first convention at Bloomington, Ill. on May 29, 1856, Lincoln was called upon to speak. His denunciation of slavery thrilled the newspaper reporters, and they listened instead of taking notes. As no verbatim account exists, this speech is known as "Lincoln's Lost Speech."

LINCOLN DEFEATED IN RACE FOR VICE PRESIDENTIAL NOMINATION

On June 19, 1856, at the first Republican Party convention, held at Philadelphia, Pa., Abraham Lincoln ran for the vice presidential nomination. He received 110 votes (Illinois 33, Indiana 26, California 12, Pennsylvania 11, New Hampshire 8, Massachusetts 7, Michigan 5, New York 3, Ohio 2, Rhode Island 2, and Maine 1). He was defeated on the first ballot, as William Lewis Dayton of New Jersey received 253 votes. Another candidate for the office of Vice President was Nathaniel Prentice Banks of Massachusetts, who received 46 votes.

LINCOLN'S MODESTY

Abraham Lincoln, considered one of our greatest Presidents, was an extremely modest man. In Lincoln's letter to Thomas J. Pickett, of Rock Island, Ill., dated April 16, 1859. he wrote: "I do not think myself fit for the Presidency. I certainly am flattered, and grateful that some partial friends think of me in that connection."

FIRST CONVENTION BUILDING ERECTED

The first building especially constructed to house a political convention was the Wigwam on Lake Street, Chicago, Ill., built for the second Republican Party convention, which met May 16–18, 1860. The main floor was reserved for delegates. A balcony was provided for spectators. The building was equipped with telegraph equipment. The Wigwam, decorated with flags, flowers, evergreens, and statuary, accommodated 10,000 persons. William Boyington was the architect.

LINCOLN SUPPORTERS PACKED THE WIGWAM

The Republican convention of 1860 was the first to which the general public was admitted. While the supporters of William Henry Seward of New York were parading through the city with a brass band prior to the time set for nominating, the followers of Abraham Lincoln of Illinois filled the spectators' seats in the convention hall, leaving only a few places for the thousands of Seward followers seeking admission.

LINCOLN NOT EXPECTED TO WIN NOMINATION

Reporting the prospects of the various candidates at the Republican convention of 1860, the Washington, D.C., *Evening Star* of May 16, 1860, said: "Lincoln is urged by the delegates from Illinois, but his alleged want of administrative ability is the objection raised against him. After a complimentary vote for him, Illinois will likely go for [Edward] Bates."

KENTUCKY IGNORED FAVORITE SONS

Kentucky cast its 12 electoral votes in the election of 1860 for John Bell of Tennessee despite the fact that the two other presidential candidates, Abraham Lincoln and John Cabell Breckinridge, were born in Kentucky.

LINCOLN'S BEARD

Abraham Lincoln was the first President to wear a beard, which he began to grow shortly after his election in 1860. Many of his supporters had suggested that he would look more dignified with a beard, that it would soften his somewhat harsh appearance, and while he was campaigning he received the following letter:

Westfield, Chautauqua Co., N.Y.

October 15, 1860

Hon. A B Lincoln

Dear Sir

I am a little girl 11 years old, but want you should be President of the United States very much so I hope you wont think me very bold to write to such a great man as you are.

Have you any little girls about as large as I am if so give them my love and tell her to write me if you cannot answer this letter. I have got four brothers and part of them will vote for you any way and if you will let your whiskers grow I will try to get the rest of them to vote for you. You would look a great deal better for your face is so thin. All the ladies like whiskers and they would tease their husbands to vote for you and then you would be President.

GRACE BEDELL

Lincoln replied to her letter as follows:

Private
Springfield, Ill.
Oct. 19, 1860
Miss Grace Bedell
Westfield, N.Y.
My dear little Miss:

Your very agreeable letter of the 15th is received. I regret the necessity of saying I have no daughters. I have three sons, one seventeen, one nine, and one seven years of age. They, with their mother, constitute my whole family. As to the whiskers, having never worn any, do you not think people would call it a piece of silly affectation if I were to begin it now?

Your very sincere well-wisher,

A. LINCOLN

Legend has it that when the train bearing Lincoln to the White House stopped at a station near Westfield, Lincoln told the assembled crowd about his correspondent. He asked if she was present. When she came forward, he picked her up, kissed her, and told the crowd, "She wrote me that she thought I'd look better if I wore whiskers."

However, some modern historians cast a cold eye on the story of the little girl and Lincoln's beard. They think that the President-elect, who was a minority president, and possibly some of his political advisers calculated that the beard would predispose the populace to view him as a kind and wise man.

LINCOLN'S ADIEU TO SPRINGFIELD, ILLINOIS

On February 11, 1861, from the rear of the railroad car transporting him to Washington, D.C., for his inauguration, President-elect Lincoln made a prophetic speech to his fellow Springfield townsfolk who had gathered in the morning rain to bid him farewell. His speech as reported is as follows:

My friends: No one, not in my situation, can appreciate my feeling of sadness at this parting. To this place, and the kindness of these people, I owe everything. . . . Here my children have been born, and one is buried. I now leave, not knowing when or whether I may return, with a task before me greater than that which rested on Washington.

ATTEMPT MADE TO ASSASSINATE LINCOLN IN 1861

An attempt to assassinate Lincoln was made in 1861. Lincoln's inaugural train left Springfield, Ill., on February 11, 1861, bound for Washington, D.C., but scheduled to make several intermediate stops. The conspirators planned to kill him at the Calvert Street Depot, Baltimore, Md. A commotion was to be staged that would engage the attention of the police, during which time an assassin would carry out the murder. The plot was discovered and the crime prevented by Allan Pinkerton, a detective assigned to guard Lincoln. The President-elect arrived safely in Washington nine days before the inauguration.

FIVE FORMER PRESIDENTS ALIVE WHEN LINCOLN WAS INAUGURATED

When President Abraham Lincoln took the oath of office on March 4, 1861, as the sixteenth President of the United States, five former Presidents of the United States were alive: Martin Van Buren, John Tyler, Millard Fillmore, Franklin Pierce, and James Buchanan.

KENTUCKY PRESIDENTS OF 1861

Abraham Lincoln, inaugurated President of the United States on March 4, 1861, was born in Hodgenville, Hardin County, Ky., on February 12, 1809.

Jefferson Davis, chosen President of the Confederate States of America by the provisional Confederate congress on February 18, 1861, was born in Fairview, Todd County (formerly Christian County), Ky., on June 3, 1808.

CONFEDERATE STATES ADOPT CONSTITUTION

During President Lincoln's first term, the first formal attempts at a united secession government were made when the Constitution of the Confederate States of America was

Troops led by Union general Terry fighting Confederates, Jan. 15th, 1865

adopted by the seceding southern states on March 11, 1861, at Montgomery, Ala. It contained the following preamble:

> We, the people of the Confederate States, each State acting in its sovereign and independent character, in order to form a permanent federal government, establish justice, insure domestic tranquillity, and secure the blessings of liberty to ourselves and our posterity—invoking the favor and guidance of Almighty God—do ordain and establish this Constitution for the Confederate States of America.

CHARLES FRANCIS ADAMS APPOINTED AMBASSADOR TO GREAT BRITAIN

President Lincoln appointed Charles Francis Adams as envoy extraordinary and minister plenipotentiary to Great Britain on March 20, 1861. Adams was the third member of his family to receive this coveted appointment. His father, President John Quincy Adams, and his grandfather, President John Adams, had also served as ambassadors to Great Britain.

LINCOLN'S FIRST CALL FOR TROOPS, APRIL 15, 1861

Whereas, the laws of the United States have been for some time past, and now are, opposed, and the execution thereof obstructed, in the States of South Carolina, Georgia, Alabama, Florida, Mississippi, Louisiana, and Texas, by combinations too powerful to be suppressed by the ordinary course of judicial proceedings, or by the powers vested in the marshals by law; now, therefore, I, Abraham Lincoln, President of the United States, in virtue of the power in me vested by the Constitution and the laws, have thought fit to call forth the Militia of the several States of the Union to the aggregate number of 75,000, in order to suppress said combinations, and to cause the laws to be duly executed.

The details for this object will be immediately communicated to the State authorities through the War Department. I appeal to all loyal citizens to favor, facilitate, and aid, this effort to maintain the honor, the integrity, and existence, of our national Union, and the perpetuity of popular government, and to redress wrongs already long enough endured. I deem it proper to say that the first service assigned to the forces hereby called forth will probably be to repossess the forts, places, and property which have been seized from the Union; and in every event the utmost care will be observed, consistently with the objects aforesaid, to avoid any devastation, any destruction of, or interference with property, or any disturbance of peaceful citizens of any part of the country; and I hereby command the persons composing the combinations aforesaid, to disperse and retire peacefully to their respective abodes, within twenty days from this date.

Deeming that the present condition of public affairs presents an extraordinary occasion, I do hereby, in virtue of the power in me vested by the Constitution, convene both houses of Congress. The Senators and Representatives are, therefore, summoned to assemble at their respective chambers at twelve o'clock, noon, on Thursday, the fourth day of July next, then and there to consider and determine such measures as, in their wisdom, the public safety and interest may seem to demand.

In witness whereof, I have hereunto set my hand, and caused the seal of the United States to be affixed.

Done at the City of Washington, this fifteenth day of April, in the year of our Lord, one thousand eight hundred and sixty-one, of the Independence of the United States the eighty-fifth.

FIRST PRESIDENTIAL EXECUTIVE ORDER

The first presidential executive order to be numbered was Order No. 1, signed by President Lincoln on October 20, 1862. This order established a provisional court in Louisiana. It was not the first executive order issued by a President, but the first one in the files of the Department of State.

THE EMANCIPATION PROCLAMATION

The Emancipation Proclamation, issued by President Lincoln as a war measure, did not free all the slaves. The complete abolition of slavery everywhere in the United States was brought about by the Thirteenth Amendment, ratified on December 18, 1865.

Lincoln's preliminary proclamation of September 22, 1862, declared that slavery was to be abolished in those states which should be in rebellion against the government on January 1, 1863. The seceding states controlled by the Confederate armies (Alabama, Arkansas, Florida, Georgia, Mississippi, North Carolina, South Carolina, Texas, and parts of Louisiana and Virginia) of course ignored the warning, and on January 1, 1863, Lincoln issued his Emancipation Proclamation.

The document, which freed the slaves in all Confederate territory occupied by Union troops—it did not affect loyal districts and could not be enforced in Confederate-held areas—proclaimed the policy of the United States on the question of slavery:

Whereas, on the twenty-second day of September, in the year of our Lord one thousand eight hundred and sixty-two, a Proclamation was issued by the President of the United States, containing among other things the following, to wit:

Courtesy of The Library of Congress

The text of the Emancipation Proclamation

"That on the first day of January, in the year of our Lord one thousand eight hundred and sixty-three, all persons held as slaves within any State, or designated part of a State, the people whereof shall then be in rebellion against the United States, shall be then, thenceforth and forever free, and the Executive Government of the United States, including the military and naval authorities thereof, will recognize and maintain the freedom of such persons, and will do no act or acts to repress such persons, or any of them, in any efforts they may make for their actual freedom.

"That the Executive will, on the first day of January aforesaid, by proclamation, designate the States and parts of States, if any, in which the people thereof respectively shall then be in rebellion against the United States, and the fact that any State, or the people thereof, shall on that day be in good faith represented in the Congress of the United States by members chosen thereto at elections wherein a majority of the qualified voters of such State shall have participated, shall, in the absence of strong countervailing testimony, be deemed conclusive evidence that such State and the people thereof are not then in rebellion against the United States."

Now, therefore, I, Abraham Lincoln, President of the United States, by virtue of the power in me vested as Commander-in-Chief of the Army and Navy of the United States in time of actual armed rebellion against the authority and government of the United States, and as a fit and necessary war measure for suppressing said rebellion, do, on this first day of January, in the year of our Lord, one thousand eight hundred and sixty-three, and in accordance with my purpose so to do, publicly proclaim for the full period of one hundred days from the day of first above mentioned order, and designate, as the States and parts of States wherein the people thereof respectively are this day in rebellion against the United States the following, to wit:

ARKANSAS, TEXAS, LOUISIANA (except the Parishes of St. Bernard, Plaquemines, Jefferson, St. John, St. Charles, St. James, Ascension, Assumption, Terre Bonne, Lafourche, St. Mary, St. Martin, and Orleans, including the City of New Orleans), MISSISSIPPI, ALABAMA, FLORIDA, GEORGIA, SOUTH CAROLINA, NORTH CAROLINA and VIRGINIA (except the forty-eight counties designated as West Virginia, and also the counties of Berkeley, Accomac, Northhampton, Elizabeth City, York, Princess Anne, and Norfolk, including the cities of Norfolk and Portsmouth), and which excepted parts are, for the present, left precisely as if this Proclamation were not issued.

And by virtue of the power and for the purpose aforesaid, I do order and declare that ALL PERSONS HELD AS SLAVES within said designated States and parts of States ARE, AND HENCEFORWARD SHALL BE FREE! and that the Executive Government of the United States, including the military and naval authorities thereof, will recognize and maintain the freedom of said persons. And I hereby enjoin upon the people so declared to be free, to abstain from all violence, unless in necessary self-defense, and I recommend to them that in all cases, when allowed, they labor faithfully for reasonable wages.

And I further declare and make known that such persons of suitable condition will be received into the armed service of the United States to garrison forts, positions, stations and other places, and to man vessels of all sorts in said service.

And upon this act, sincerely believed to be an act of justice, warranted by the Constitution, upon military necessity, I invoke the considerate judgment of mankind and the gracious favor of Almighty God.

In testimony whereof I have hereunto set my name, and caused the seal of the United States to be affixed.

Done at the City of Washington, this first day of January, in the year of our Lord one thousand eight hundred and sixty-three, and of the Independence of the United States the eighty-seventh.

ABRAHAM LINCOLN
By the President

WILLIAM H. SEWARD
Secretary of State

LINCOLN PROCLAIMED ANNUAL THANKSGIVING DAY

Thanksgiving Day proclamations had been issued on numerous earlier occasions. Governor William Bradford in 1621 proclaimed a day for the Massachusetts colonists to offer thanks to God for their lives, their food, their clothing, etc. During the Revolutionary War, numerous days of thanksgiving were appointed for prayer and fasting by the Continental Congress. November 26, 1789, was set aside by President Washington to thank God for the newly formed government and the blessings which accompanied it. Other Thanksgiving days were set aside to commemorate special occasions such as the conclusion of a war.

The first of the national Thanksgiving Day proclamations was issued by Abraham Lincoln in 1863, on October 3, the month and day of George Washington's first Thanksgiving Day proclamation. President Andrew Johnson continued the custom, which was followed by the succeeding Presidents until, under President Franklin Delano Roosevelt, Congress fixed the date as the fourth Thursday in November.

An extract from Lincoln's Thanksgiving Day proclamation of October 3, 1863, follows:

I do, therefore, invite my fellow-citizens in every part of the United States, and also those who are at sea and those who are sojourning in foreign lands, to set apart and observe the last Thursday of November next [November 26] as a day of thanksgiving and praise to our beneficent Father who dwelleth in the heavens. And I recommend to them that, while offering up the ascriptions justly due to Him for singular deliverances and blessings, they do also, with humble penitence for our national perverseness and disobedience, commend to His tender care all

those who have become widows, orphans, mourners, or sufferers in the lamentable civil strife in which we are unavoidably engaged, and fervently implore the interposition of the almighty hand to heal the wounds of the nation, and to restore it, as soon as may be consistent with the Divine purposes, to the full enjoyment of peace, harmony, tranquillity, and union.

LINCOLN'S GETTYSBURG ADDRESS

Delivered on November 19, 1863, this immortal address commemorated the battle fought at Gettysburg, July 1–3, 1863:

Fourscore and seven years ago our fathers brought forth on this continent a new nation, conceived in liberty, and dedicated to the proposition that all men are created equal.

Now we are engaged in a great civil war, testing whether that nation, or any nation so conceived and so dedicated, can long endure. We are met on a great battlefield of that war. We have come to dedicate a portion of that field as a final resting place for those who here gave their lives that the nation might live. It is altogether fitting and proper that we should do this.

But, in a larger sense we cannot dedicate—we cannot consecrate—we cannot hallow—this ground. The brave men, living and dead, who struggled here, have consecrated it far above our poor power to add or detract. The world will little note nor long remember what we say here, but it can never forget what they did here. It is for us, the living, rather, to be dedicated here to the unfinished work which they who fought here have thus far so nobly advanced. It is rather for us to be here dedicated to the great task remaining before us—that from these honored dead we take increased devotion to that cause for which they gave the last full measure of devotion; that we here highly resolve that these dead shall not have died in vain; that this nation under God, shall have a new birth of freedom; and the government of the people, by the people, for the people, shall not perish from the earth.

Courtesy of The Library of Congress

Lincoln delivers his address at the dedication of the Gettysburg National Cemetery

AMNESTY PROCLAMATIONS

An amnesty proclamation to citizens of the Confederate states was issued by President Abraham Lincoln on December 8, 1863. He issued a similar proclamation on March 26, 1864.

President Andrew Johnson issued supplementary proclamations on May 29, 1865; September 27, 1867; July 4, 1868; and December 25, 1868.

REPUBLICAN FACTION DISAPPROVED OF SECOND TERM

Although Lincoln was chosen unanimously on the first ballot at the Republican convention of 1864, not all the Republicans had favored his candidacy for a second term. A group of Republican dissenters held a convention at Cleveland, Ohio, on May 31, 1864, and nominated John Charles Frémont for the presidency and John Cochrane of New York for the vice presidency. Both nominees withdrew on September 21, 1864, urging the reelection of Abraham Lincoln.

LINCOLN WATCHED CIVIL WAR BATTLE

On July 12, 1864, Lincoln visited Fort Stevens, Washington, D.C., which was being defended by three brigades (6th Corps) of the Army of the Potomac under Major General Horatio Gates Wright against an attack led by Lieutenant General Jubal Anderson Early of the 2nd Corps, Army of the Confederacy. Captain Oliver Wendell Holmes acted as the President's guide. Lincoln watched the battle from the parapet of the fort, heedless of the danger. Three additional brigades reinforced the defenders, and the tide of battle changed.

LINCOLN WON 1864 SOLDIER VOTE

In the 1864 election, Lincoln received 77.5 percent of the soldier vote, compared with 22.5 percent cast for Major General George Brinton McClellan, former general in chief of the armies of the United States and commander of the Army of the Potomac. The vote was 116,887 for Lincoln and 33,748 for McClellan.

The states that provided for soldier votes were California, Iowa, Kentucky, Maine, Maryland, Michigan, New Hampshire, Ohio, Pennsylvania, Vermont, and Wisconsin. No provision was made allowing soldiers to vote in Connecticut, Delaware, Illinois, Indiana, Massachusetts, Missouri, Nevada, New Jersey, New York, Oregon, Rhode Island, or West Virginia. The votes of Kansas and Minnesota soldiers were not counted as they arrived too late.

The 1864 election was the first in which the army vote was tabulated.

LINCOLN'S LETTER TO MRS. BIXBY

Perhaps the most famous letter in American literature was Lincoln's letter to Mrs. Lydia Bixby of Boston, written at the request of Governor Andrew of Massachusetts. The letter, dated November 21, 1864, was sent to Adjutant General Schouler, who delivered it on November 25 to Mrs. Bixby. It reads:

I have been shown in the files of the War Department a statement of the Adjutant General that you are the mother of five sons who have died gloriously on the field of battle. I feel how weak and fruitless must be any word of mine which should attempt to beguile you from the grief of a loss so overwhelming. But I cannot refrain from tendering you the consolation that may be found in the thanks of the republic they died to save. I pray that our Heavenly Father may assuage the anguish of your bereavement, and leave you only the cherished memory of the loved and lost, and the solemn pride that must be yours to have laid so costly a sacrifice upon the altar of freedom.

Yours very sincerely and respectfully,

A. LINCOLN

The reports upon which Lincoln based his consoling letter were inaccurate. Charles N. Bixby was killed at the second battle of Fredericksburg, May 3, 1863. Henry Cromwell Bixby, first reported missing and later as killed, was captured and honorably discharged on December 19, 1864. Edward Bixby deserted from Company C, 1st Massachusetts Heavy Artillery, and went to sea to escape the penalty of desertion. Oliver Cromwell Bixby was killed in action in the Crater fight before Petersburg, Va., on July 30, 1864. George Way Bixby was captured on July 30, 1864, and deserted to the enemy at Salisbury, N.C.

THIRTEENTH AMENDMENT ENACTED

The Thirteenth Amendment to the Constitution, prohibiting slavery, was passed by Congress on January 31, 1865. It was proposed to the legislatures of the several states by the 38th Congress on February 1, 1865. It was rejected by Delaware and Kentucky and was conditionally ratified by Alabama and Mississippi. Texas took no action. The twenty-seventh state to ratify, making it effective, was Georgia, on December 6, 1865. The amendment was declared ratified by the Secretary of State on December 18, 1865.

This amendment was the first of the three Civil War amendments.

LINCOLN MET CONFEDERATE COMMISSIONERS

The conference of February 3, 1865, between President Lincoln and the Confederate peace commissioners—Alexander Hamilton Stephens, Vice President of the Confederate States; Robert Mercer Taliaferro Hunter, Confederate States senator; and John Archibald Campbell, assistant secretary of war of the Confederate States—was held at Hampton Roads, Va., aboard the *River Queen,* a steamer of 536 tons, hired by the Quartermaster General of the War Depart-

ment from George N. Power at $24 per day. A second conference was held on March 23, 1865, aboard the same steamer.

LINCOLN ASSASSINATED

The first assassination of a President was the murder of Lincoln on Good Friday, April 14, 1865, by John Wilkes Booth, an actor and Southern sympathizer. President Lincoln drove to Ford's Theatre on Tenth Street, between E and F streets, Washington, D.C., with Mrs. Lincoln, Major Henry Reed Rathbone, and Clara Harris, Rathbone's fiancée. They were viewing a performance of *Our American Cousin,* a three-act comedy by Tom Taylor starring Laura Keene, when at about 10:30 P.M. Booth fired the fatal shot. Lincoln was carried across the street to William Petersen's boarding house at 453 Tenth Street, and put in the room of William Clark, a boarder. He died at 21 minutes 55 seconds past 7 A.M. on April 15, 1865.

Booth, who fled after the crime, was shot April 26, 1865, in a barn by Sergeant Boston Corbett.

FUNERAL PROCESSION AND INTERMENT

Abraham Lincoln was the first President to lie in state at the United States Capitol rotunda. His body was taken first to the White House, where it remained from April 15 to April 18, after which it was removed to the Capitol rotunda, where it was displayed from April 19 to April 20. On April 21, it was taken to the railroad station, whence it was conveyed to Springfield, Ill.

The funeral procession took 12 days, stops along the route being made at Baltimore, Harrisburg, Philadelphia, New York City, Albany, Utica, Syracuse, Cleveland, Columbus, Indianapolis, and Chicago so that people could pay their respects, before the train arrived at Springfield, Ill. Lincoln was buried on May 4, 1865, in Oak Ridge Cemetery, Springfield.

Lincoln was moved 17 times from the night of April 14, 1865, when he was carried from Ford's Theatre to the Petersen house across the street, until his body was finally laid to rest in a solid block of concrete in Lincoln tomb at Springfield in 1901.

The assassination of President Lincoln by John Wilkes Booth, at Ford's Theatre, Washington, D.C., April 14th, 1865

THIEVES TRIED TO STEAL LINCOLN'S BODY

On November 7, 1876, a gang of thieves and counterfeiters broke into Lincoln's tomb at Springfield, Ill., tore open the sarcophagus and partially pulled out the Lincoln casket. They intended to cart the casket by wagon, bury it in the sand dunes of Indiana, and demand $200,000 for its return. They intended also to demand the freedom of Benjamin Boyd, an engraver of counterfeit plates, who was confined in the penitentiary at Joliet, Ill. A Pinkerton detective to whom they had confided their plans agreed to help them. Instead he notified the Secret Service, worked with the conspirators, and gave the signal that enabled the Secret Service to make the arrests. As there was no penalty at that time for such an offense, they were charged with breaking the lock and sentenced to serve a year in the penitentiary. The next legislature enacted a law which made body-stealing punishable by imprisonment for from one to ten years.

LINCOLN'S SON AT THE SCENE OF THREE ASSASSINATIONS

Robert Todd Lincoln, Lincoln's oldest son, who was in Washington, D.C., the night his father was shot at Ford's Theatre, was summoned to the house across the street to which the wounded President was carried.

On July 2, 1881, Lincoln, then secretary of war in President Garfield's cabinet, went to the railroad station at Washington to tell the President that pressure of business prevented him from accompanying the President to Elberon, N.J. When Lincoln arrived at the station, Garfield had just been shot by Charles J. Guiteau.

Twenty years later, Lincoln received an invitation from President William McKinley to meet him on September 6, 1901, at the Pan American Exposition at Buffalo, N.Y. When Lincoln arrived there, he saw a group gathered about the President, who had just been mortally wounded by Leon Czolgosz.

FURTHER READING

Basler, Roy P. *The Lincoln Legend.* 1935.

————. *Abraham Lincoln, His Speeches and Writings.* 1946.

Catton, Bruce. *Two Roads to Sumter.* 1963.

Donald, David Herbert. *Lincoln.* 1995.

Hay, John. *Lincoln and the Civil War in the Diaries and Letters of John Hay.* Rev. ed. 1939.

McPherson, James M. *Tried by War: Abraham Lincoln as Commander in Chief.* 2008.

Nevins, Allan. *The Emergence of Lincoln.* 2 vols. 1950.

Paludan, Phillip S. *The Presidency of Abraham Lincoln.* 1994.

Sandburg, Carl. *Abraham Lincoln: The Prairie Years.* 2 vols., 1926.

————. *Abraham Lincoln: The War Years.* 2 vols., 1939.

White, Ronald C., Jr. *A. Lincoln: A Biography.* 2009.

Courtesy of The Library of Congress

Andrew Johnson

Date of birth—Dec. 29, 1808

Place of birth—Raleigh, N.C.

Education—No formal education; self-taught in simple reading; taught to read and write by his wife; apprentice tailor, Wake County, N.C., 1822

Religion—Christian (no specific denomination)

Ancestry—English, Scottish, Irish

Career—Tailor, alderman, mayor, state legislator, state senator, U.S. congressman, governor of Tennessee, U.S. senator, military governor, Vice President

Political party—Democratic (elected Vice President on Republican [National Union] ticket)

State represented—Tennessee

Term of office—Apr. 15, 1865–Mar. 4, 1869 (Johnson succeeded to the presidency on the death of Abraham Lincoln)

Term served—3 years, 323 days

Administration—20th

Congresses—39th, 40th

Age at inauguration—56 years, 107 days

Lived after term—6 years, 149 days

Occupation after term—U.S. Senate (from Tennessee)

Date of death—July 31, 1875

Age at death—66 years, 214 days

Place of death—Carter's Station, Tenn.

Burial place—Andrew Johnson National Cemetery, Greeneville, Tenn.

FAMILY

FATHER

Name—Jacob Johnson

Date of birth—Apr. 1778

Marriage—Mary McDonough, Sept. 9, 1801 (date of marriage bond)

Occupation—Soldier (captain in state militia), sexton, jack-of-all-trades (porter, constable, miller, horse tender, barbeque caterer, town bell-ringer)

Date of death—Jan. 4, 1812

Place of death—Raleigh, N.C.

Age at death—33 years

MOTHER

Name at birth—Mary McDonough

Date of birth—July 17, 1783

First marriage—Jacob Johnson, Sept. 9, 1801 (date of marriage bond)

Second marriage—Turner Dougherty

Date of death—Feb. 13, 1856

Age at death—72 years, 211 days

SIBLINGS

Andrew Johnson was the third child in a family of three.

Children of Jacob Johnson and Mary McDonough Johnson

William Johnson, b. 1804

—— Johnson (daughter), d. in infancy

Andrew Johnson, b. Dec. 29, 1808, d. July 31, 1875

MARRIAGE

Married—Eliza McCardle

Date of marriage—May 17, 1827

Place of marriage—Greeneville, Tenn.

Age of wife at marriage—16 years, 225 days

Age of husband at marriage—18 years, 139 days

Years married—48 years, 75 days

CHILDREN

Martha Johnson, b. Oct. 25, 1828, Greeneville, Tenn.; m. Dec. 13, 1855, David Trotter Patterson, Greeneville, Tenn.; d. July 10, 1901, Greeneville, Tenn.

Charles Johnson, b. Feb. 19, 1830, Greeneville, Tenn.; d. Apr. 4, 1863, near Nashville, Tenn.

Mary Johnson, b. May 8, 1832, Greeneville, Tenn.; m. Apr. 7, 1852, Daniel Stover; m. William R. Brown; d. Apr. 19, 1883, Bluff City, Tenn.

Robert Johnson, b. Feb. 22, 1834, Greeneville, Tenn.; d. Apr. 22, 1869, Greeneville, Tenn.

Andrew Johnson, b. Aug. 5, 1852, Greeneville, Tenn.; m. Bessie May Rumbough; d. Mar. 12, 1879, Elizabethtown, Tenn.

THE PRESIDENT'S WIFE

Name at birth—Eliza McCardle

Date of birth—Oct. 4, 1810

Place of birth—Leesburg, Tenn.

Mother—Sarah Phillips McCardle

Father—John McCardle

Father's occupation—Shoemaker

Marriage—Andrew Johnson, May 17, 1827, Greeneville, Tenn.

Children—Martha Johnson, b. Oct. 25, 1828, d. July 10, 1901; Charles Johnson, b. Feb. 19, 1830, d. Apr. 4, 1863; Mary Johnson, b. May 8, 1832, d. Apr. 19, 1883; Robert Johnson, b. Feb. 22, 1834, d. Apr. 22, 1869; Andrew Johnson, b. Aug. 5, 1852, d. Mar. 12, 1879

Date of death—Jan. 15, 1876

Age at death—65 years, 103 days

Place of death—Greene County, Tenn.

Burial place—Greeneville, Tenn.

Years younger than the President—1 year, 279 days

Years she survived the President—168 days

Courtesy of The Library of Congress

Eliza Johnson, wife of Andrew Johnson

THE FIRST LADY

Eliza McCardle Johnson was an invalid when Andrew Johnson became President on April 15, 1865. Their daughter, Martha Johnson Patterson, the wife of Senator David Trotter Patterson, acted as White House hostess. Another daughter, Mary Johnson Stover, the wife of Daniel Stover, also acted in this capacity.

IMPORTANT DATES IN THE PRESIDENT'S LIFE

Feb. 18, 1822, bound out as an apprentice to a tailor, James J. Selby, Wake County, N.C.

1824, opened tailor shop, Laurens, S.C.

1828, became leader of a workingmen's party which he organized; elected alderman of Greeneville, Tenn.; reelected in 1829

1830–1833, mayor of Greeneville, Tenn. (three terms)

1833, trustee of Rhea Academy

Oct. 5, 1835, nominated himself for the Tennessee legislature; elected; served two years

1837, opposed bond issue and was defeated for reelection

1839, reelected to legislature

Oct. 4, 1841, elected to Tennessee Senate

Mar. 4, 1843–Mar. 3, 1853, U.S. House of Representatives (from Tennessee)

Oct. 3, 1853, elected governor of Tennessee

1855, reelected governor

Oct. 8, 1857–Mar. 4, 1862, U.S. Senate (from Tennessee)

Mar. 4, 1862–Mar. 3, 1865, military governor of Tennessee with rank of brigadier general of volunteers (appointed by President Lincoln)

1864, nominated as vice presidential candidate by National Union Party at Baltimore, Md.

Mar. 4, 1865–Apr. 15, 1865, Vice President under Abraham Lincoln

Apr. 15, 1865–Mar. 4, 1869, President (succeeded to office at death of Lincoln)

Mar. 13, 1868, impeachment trial in U.S. Senate

May 26, 1868, acquitted

1868, unsuccessful candidate for nomination to the presidency on the Democratic ticket

1869, unsuccessful candidate for U.S. Senate (from Tennessee)

1872, unsuccessful candidate for U.S. House of Representatives (from Tennessee)

1874, elected to U.S. Senate

Mar. 4–July 31, 1875, U.S. Senate

INAUGURATION

April 15, 1865

The death of Lincoln profoundly shocked the nation. The oath of office as Lincoln's successor was quietly administered to Andrew Johnson at 10 A.M., on Saturday, April 15, 1865, at the Kirkwood House, Washington, D.C. Chief Justice Chase went to Johnson's suite to administer the oath.

The following is an extract from Johnson's inaugural address:

I have long labored to ameliorate and elevate the condition of the great mass of the American people. Toil and an honest advocacy of the great principles of free government have been my lot. Duties have been mine; consequences are God's. This has been the foundation of my political creed, and I feel that in the end the government will triumph and that these great principles will be permanently established.

CABINET

April 15, 1865–March 3, 1869

State—William Henry Seward, N.Y., continued from preceding administration

Treasury—Hugh McCulloch, Ind., continued from preceding administration

War—Edwin McMasters Stanton, Pa., continued from preceding administration; suspended Aug. 12, 1867; Ulysses Simpson Grant (General of the Army), ad interim Aug. 12, 1867; Edwin McMasters Stanton,

Pa., reinstated Jan. 13, 1868 to May 26, 1868, John McAllister Schofield, Ill., May 28, 1868; entered upon duties June 1, 1868

Attorney General—James Speed, Ky., continued from preceding administration; J. Hubley Ashton, Pa. (assistant attorney general), acting, July 17, 1866; Henry Stanbery, Ohio, July 23, 1866; Orville Hickman Browning, Ill. (secretary of the Interior), ad interim Mar. 13, 1868; William Maxwell

Evarts, N.Y., July 15, 1868; entered upon duties July 20, 1868

Postmaster General—William Dennison, Ohio, continued from preceding administration; Alexander Williams Randall, Wis. (first assistant Postmaster General), ad interim July 17, 1866; Alexander Williams Randall, Wis., July 25, 1866

Navy—Gideon Welles, Conn., continued from preceding administration

Interior—John Palmer Usher, Ind., continued from preceding administration; James Harlan, Iowa, May 15, 1865; Orville Hickman Browning, Ill., July 27, 1866, appointment to take effect Sept. 1, 1866

Courtesy of The Library of Congress

Andrew Johnson taking the oath of office in the small parlor of the Kirkwood House Hotel, Washington, D.C.

CONGRESS

FORTIETH CONGRESS

March 4, 1867–March 3, 1869

First session—Mar. 4, 1867–Mar. 30, 1867; July 3, 1867–July 20, 1867; Nov. 21, 1867–Dec. 1, 1867 (274 days)

Second session—Dec. 2, 1867–July 27, 1868; Sept. 21, 1868, for 1 day only; Oct. 16, 1868, for 1 day only; Nov. 10, 1868, for 1 day only (345 days)

Third session—Dec. 7, 1868–Mar. 3, 1869 (87 days)

Special session of the Senate—Apr. 1, 1867–Apr. 20, 1867 (20 days)

Vice President—Andrew Johnson (succeeded to the presidency on Apr. 15, 1865, on the death of Abraham Lincoln)

President pro tempore of the Senate—Benjamin Franklin Wade, Ohio

Secretary of the Senate—John Wien Forney, Pa., resigned, effective June 4, 1868; George Congdon Gorham, Calif., elected June 4, 1868

Speaker of the House—Schuyler Colfax, Ind., reelected Mar. 4, 1867; resigned Mar. 3, 1869, having been elected Vice President; Theodore Medad Pomeroy, N.Y., elected Mar. 3, 1869

Clerk of the House—Edward McPherson, Pa., reelected Mar. 4, 1867

IMPORTANT DATES IN THE PRESIDENCY

Apr. 26, 1865, General Joseph E. Johnston surrendered at Durham Station, N.C., to General William T. Sherman

May 10, 1865, Confederate President Jefferson Davis captured by federal troops

May 26, 1865, General Edmund Kirby-Smith, commander of Trans-Mississippi Department, surrendered at New Orleans, La., to Major General E. S. Canby (last major Confederate commander to surrender)

Dec. 18, 1865, Thirteenth Amendment to the Constitution ratified, abolishing slavery

1867, Reconstruction Acts passed despite President Johnson's opposition

Mar. 1, 1867, Nebraska admitted as the 37th state

Mar. 2, 1867, Tenure of Office Act passed, prohibiting President from removing cabinet officers without Senate approval

Mar. 30, 1867, Territory of Alaska ceded by treaty with Russia

Aug. 1867, Secretary of War Edwin M. Stanton, a Radical Republican, removed from office by President Johnson, who appointed General U.S. Grant in Stanton's stead

Feb. 1868, U. S. Grant defied President Johnson by turning over office of Secretary of War to Edwin Stanton

Feb. 21, 1868, President removed Edwin Stanton from office and appointed General Lorenzo Thomas as Secretary of War

Feb. 24, 1868, House of Representatives passed an 11-count impeachment of President Johnson

May 26, 1868, President Johnson acquitted at impeachment trial before U.S. Senate

July 28, 1868, Fourteenth Amendment to the Constitution ratified, establishing rights of citizens

ADDITIONAL DATA ON JOHNSON

ANDREW JOHNSON

—was the second President born in North Carolina.

—was the sixth President who was a resident of a state other than his native state.

—married at a younger age than any other President.

—was the first President to be impeached. (He was acquitted.)

—was the first President whose early background was not military or legal.

JOHNSON TAUGHT ABC's BY HIS WIFE

Andrew Johnson never attended school and was practically illiterate when he met Eliza McCardle, whom he married on May 17, 1827. He was about 17 years of age when she taught him how to read and write.

JOHNSON DEFIED ENEMIES

Several threats were made against the life of Andrew Johnson while he was campaigning for a second term as governor of Tennessee. While addressing an enthusiastic crowd, Johnson, it is recorded, drew a pistol and laid it on the table so that everyone could see it. He addressed his audience as follows:

Fellow-citizens, I have been informed that part of the business to be transacted on the present occasion is the assassination of the individual who now has the honor of addressing you. I beg respectfully to propose that this be the first business in order. Therefore if any man has come here tonight for the purpose indicated, I do not say to him let him speak, but let him shoot.

JOHNSON DEFENDED THE UNION

Senator Andrew Johnson of Tennessee made a stirring pro-Union speech on the floor of the Senate on December 18, 1860. He said:

I am in the Union, and intend to stay in it. I intend to hold on to the Union, and the guarantees under which the Union has grown; and I do not intend to be driven from it, nor out of it, by . . . unconstitutional enactments.

The following day, Johnson said:

Then, let us stand by the Constitution; and in preserving the Constitution we shall save the Union; and in saving the Union we save this, the greatest government on earth.

"WHAT WILL THE ARISTOCRATS DO?"

When Andrew Johnson was told that he, a former tailor, had been nominated on the same ticket with Abraham Lincoln, a former rail splitter, it is reported that he said, "What will the aristocrats do?"

DAY OF MOURNING FOR LINCOLN

On April 25, 1865, President Johnson issued the following proclamation:

Thursday, the 25th of May next, [is] to be observed, wherever in the United States the flag of the country may be respected, as a day of humiliation and mourning, and I recommend my fellow-citizens then to assemble in their respective places of worship, there to unite in solemn service to Almighty God in memory of the good man who has been removed, so that all shall be occupied at the same time in contemplation of his virtues and in sorrow for his sudden and violent end.

On April 29, 1865, President Johnson issued a further proclamation changing the date to Thursday, June 1, 1865, as his attention had since been called to "the fact that the day aforesaid is sacred to large numbers of Christians as one of rejoicing for the ascension of the Saviour."

GOVERNMENT OFFERED REWARDS FOR ARREST

On May 2, 1865, President Andrew Johnson issued a proclamation offering rewards for the arrest of the persons presumed to be connected with the assassination of President Lincoln and the attempted assassination of William H. Seward, Secretary of State. The rewards were $100,000 for Jefferson Davis, $25,000 for Clement C. Clay, $25,000 for Jacob Thompson, $25,000 for George N. Sanders, $25,000 for Beverley Tucker, and $10,000 for William C. Cleary.

AMNESTY PROCLAMATION

On May 29, 1865, President Andrew Johnson issued the following amnesty proclamation:

I hereby grant to all persons who have, directly or indirectly, participated in the existing rebellion, except as hereinafter excepted, amnesty and pardon, with restoration of all rights of property, except as to slaves and except in cases where legal proceedings under the laws of the United States providing for the confiscation of property of persons engaged in rebellion have been instituted; but upon the condition, nevertheless, that every such person shall take and subscribe the following oath (or affirmation) and thenceforward keep and maintain said oath inviolate, and which oath shall be registered for permanent preservation and shall be of the tenor and effect following, to wit: "I, . . . do hereby solemnly swear (or affirm), in presence of Almighty God, that I will henceforth faithfully support, protect, and defend the Constitution of the United States and the Union of the States thereunder, and that I will in like manner abide by and faithfully support all laws and proclamations which have been made during the existing rebellion with reference to the emancipation of slaves. So help me God."

EXTRACT OF PROCLAMATION OF PEACE, APRIL 2, 1866

Whereas there now exists no organized armed resistance of misguided citizens or others to the authority of the United States in the States of Georgia, South Carolina, Virginia, North Carolina, Tennessee, Alabama, Louisiana, Arkansas, Mississippi, and Florida, and the laws can be sustained and enforced therein by the proper civil authority, State or Federal, and the people of said States are well and loyally disposed and have conformed or will conform in their legislation to the condition of affairs growing out of the amendment to the Constitution of the United States prohibiting slavery within the limits and jurisdiction of the United States; and . . .

Whereas the people of the several beforementioned States have, in the manner aforesaid, given satisfactory evidence that they acquiesce in this sovereign and important resolution of national unity; and . . .

Whereas it is believed to be a fundamental principle of government that people who have revolted and who have been overcome and subdued must either be dealt with so as to induce them voluntarily to become friends or else they must be held by absolute military power or devastated so as to prevent them from ever again doing harm as enemies, which last-named policy is abhorrent to humanity and to freedom; and . . .

Whereas the observance of political equality, as a principle of right and justice, is well calculated to encourage the people of the aforesaid States to be and become more and more constant and persevering in their renewed allegiance; and . . .

Whereas the policy of the Government of the United States from the beginning of the insurrection to its overthrow and final suppression has been in conformity with the principles herein set forth and enumerated:

Now, therefore, I, Andrew Johnson, President of the United States, do hereby proclaim and declare that the insurrection which heretofore existed in the States of Georgia, South Carolina, Virginia, North Carolina, Tennessee, Alabama, Louisiana, Arkansas, Mississippi, and Florida is at an end and is henceforth to be so regarded.

CIVIL RIGHTS LEGISLATION ENACTED

The first session of the 39th Congress passed an "act to protect all persons in the United States in their Civil Rights and furnish the means of their vindication" on April 9, 1866 (14 Stat. L. 27).

This first civil rights act provided that "citizens of every race and color, without regard to any previous condition of slavery or involuntary servitude . . . shall have the same right, in every State and Territory in the United States to make and enforce contracts, to sue, be parties, and give evidence, to inherit, purchase, lease, sell, hold and convey real and personal property and to full and equal benefit of all laws and proceedings for the security of person and property, as is enjoyed by white citizens, and shall be subject to like punishment, pains and penalties, and to none other, any law, statute, ordinance, regulation or custom, to the contrary notwithstanding."

Native Americans were not covered by the legislation.

THE CRUEL UNCLE AND THE VETOED BABES IN THE WOOD.

Courtesy of The Library of Congress

A cartoon Johnson shown holding the hands of two children depicted as 'civil rights' and 'bureau', from Frank Leslie's illustrated paper.

FOURTEENTH AMENDMENT ENACTED

The Fourteenth Amendment to the Constitution, decreeing citizenship "for all persons born or naturalized in the United States" and declaring that states shall not deprive any person of "life, liberty, or property without due process of law," was passed by Congress June 13, 1866. It was proposed to the legislatures of the several states by the Thirty-ninth Congress on June 16, 1866. It received the support of 23 Northern states. California took no action. It was rejected by Delaware, Kentucky, Maryland, and ten Southern states, which later ratified it. The twenty-eighth state to ratify it, making it effective, was Louisiana, which ratified it on July 9, 1868 (the same day on which South Carolina ratified it). The amendment was declared ratified by the Secretary of State on July 28, 1868.

VISIT OF A QUEEN

Andrew Johnson was the first President to receive the visit of a queen. Queen Emma, widow of King Kamehameha IV of the Sandwich Islands (Hawaii), sailed from England on the Cunard ship *Java* and arrived in New

York City on August 8, 1866. She was received on August 14, 1866, by President Johnson and introduced to dignitaries.

IMPEACHMENT PROCEEDINGS

Johnson's attempt to carry out Lincoln's policies of reconstruction and reconciliation brought him into bitter conflict with the Radical Republicans in Congress.

The Tenure of Office Act of March 2, 1867, prohibited the President from removing a cabinet officer without Senate approval. On August 12, 1867, in defiance of this act, President Johnson dismissed a cabinet officer, Secretary of War Edwin McMasters Stanton, a Radical Republican. The President appointed General of the Army Ulysses Simpson Grant to act ad interim.

The Senate declared Stanton's removal from office illegal and in its session of January 13, 1868, ordered Stanton reinstated. Grant returned to his army duties and Stanton again returned to head the War Department.

On February 21, 1868, President Johnson replaced Stanton with Brevet Major General Lorenzo Thomas, to whom he wrote: "You are hereby authorized and empowered to act as Secretary of War ad interim, and will immediately enter upon the discharge of the duties pertaining to that office."

Impeachment proceedings were instituted against President Johnson by the House of Representatives on February 24, 1868, with the following resolution: "Resolved: that Andrew Johnson be impeached of high crimes and misdemeanors." The charges brought against him were usurpation of the law, corrupt use of the veto power, interference at elections, and misdemeanors.

The trial began formally on March 13, 1868, with Chief Justice Salmon Portland Chase of the Supreme Court of the United States presiding in the Senate chambers.

Associate Justice Samuel Nelson of the Supreme Court administered the following oath to the Chief Justice: "I do solemnly swear that in all things appertaining to the trial of the impeachment of Andrew Johnson, President of the United States, now pending, I will do impartial justice according to the Constitution and laws. So help me God." This oath was then administered by the Chief Justice to the fifty-four members of the Senate.

The vote on the eleventh article was guilty 35, not guilty 19 (May 16, 1868). The vote on the second article was guilty 35, not guilty 19

Courtesy of The Library of Congress

The Senate as a court of impeachment for the trial of Andrew Johnson

(May 26, 1868). The proceedings terminated on May 26, 1868, with the acquittal of Johnson by one vote, a two-thirds vote being necessary for conviction.

JOHNSON'S FEUD WITH GRANT

President Johnson wrote an angry letter to General Grant, who had given up his ad interim appointment as Secretary of War and returned to his army duties, thereby allowing Stanton to return to the War Department. Johnson accused Grant of violating his word.

Grant replied that he considered Congress the final authority and that he had never given the President any intimation that he would disobey the law. He concluded his letter dated February 3, 1868, by stating:

And now, Mr. President, when my honor as a soldier and integrity as a man have been so violently assailed, pardon me for saying that I can but regard this whole matter from beginning to end as an attempt to involve me in a resistance of law for which you hesitated to assume the responsibility, and thus destroy my character before the country.

When Grant was inaugurated President of the United States on March 4, 1869, Johnson refused to ride with him to his inaugural and therefore did not witness Grant's induction into office.

PRESIDENT BECOMES SENATOR

The first President to become a senator after his term of office was Andrew Johnson. He was elected senator from Tennessee and served from March 4, 1875, until his death on July 31, 1875. He had made an unsuccessful attempt to become a senator in 1869, and another unsuccessful attempt in 1872 to win a seat as a representative in the 43rd Congress.

When Johnson took his seat in the 44th Congress he was one of 74 senators. Only 14 of these senators had taken part in his trial of 1868. Twelve of them had voted "guilty" and two of them "not guilty."

FURTHER READING

Benedict, Michael L. *A Compromise of Principle*. 1974.

Bowers, Claude G. *The Tragic Era*. 1929.

Dewitt, David M. *The Impeachment and Trial of Andrew Johnson*. 1967.

McKitrick, Eric L. *Andrew Johnson and Reconstruction*. 1960.

Means, Howard. *The Avenger Takes His Place: Andrew Johnson and the 45 Days That Changed the Nation*. 2006.

Steele, Robert V. P. *The First President Johnson*. 1968.

Trefousse, Hans Louis. *Andrew Johnson: A Biography*. 1989.

Courtesy of The Library of Congress

Ulysses Simpson Grant

Name at birth—Hiram Ulysses Grant

Date of birth—Apr. 27, 1822

Place of birth—Point Pleasant, Ohio

Education—Attended local schools in Georgetown, Ohio; Maysville Seminary, Maysville, Ky., 1836–1837; Presbyterian Academy, Ripley, Ohio, 1838–1839; U.S. Military Academy, West Point, N.Y., graduated July 1, 1843

Religion—Methodist

Ancestry—English, Scottish

Career—U.S. Army officer, rising to general in Civil War; Secretary of War

Political party—Republican

State represented—Illinois

Term of office—Mar. 4, 1869–Mar. 4, 1877

Term served—8 years

Administration—21th, 22nd

Congresses—41st, 42nd, 43rd, 44th

Age at inauguration—46 years, 311 days

Lived after term—8 years, 141 days

Occupation after term—Traveling and writing

Date of death—July 23, 1885

Age at death—63 years, 87 days

Place of death—Mount McGregor, N.Y.

Burial place—Grant's Tomb, New York, N.Y.

FAMILY

FATHER

Name—Jesse Root Grant

Date of birth—Jan. 23, 1794

Place of birth—Near Greensburgh, Pa.

Marriage—Hannah Simpson, June 24, 1821, Point Pleasant, Ohio

Occupation—Leather tanner, factory manager, livery stable owner, merchant; postmaster

Date of death—June 29, 1873

Place of death—Covington, Ky.

Age at death—79 years, 157 days

MOTHER

Name at birth—Hannah Simpson

Date of birth—Nov. 23, 1798

Place of birth—Montgomery County, Pa.

Marriage—Jesse Root Grant, June 24, 1821, Point Pleasant, Ohio

Date of death—May 11, 1883

Place of death—Jersey City, N.J.

Age at death—84 years, 169 days

SIBLINGS

Ulysses Simpson Grant was the oldest child in a family of six.

Children of Jesse Root Grant and Hannah Simpson Grant

Ulysses Simpson Grant, b. Apr. 27, 1822, d. July 23, 1885

Samuel Simpson Grant, b. Sept. 23, 1825, d. Sept. 13, 1861

Clara Rachel Grant, b. Dec. 11, 1828, d. Mar. 6, 1865

Virginia Paine Grant, b. Feb. 20, 1832, d. Mar. 28, 1881

Orville Lynch Grant, b. May 15, 1835, d. Aug. 5, 1881

Mary Frances Grant, b. July 30, 1839, d. Jan. 23, 1898

MARRIAGE

Married—Julia Boggs Dent

Date of marriage—Aug. 22, 1848

Place of marriage—St. Louis, Mo.

Age of wife at marriage—22 years, 208 days

Age of husband at marriage—26 years, 117 days

Years married—36 years, 335 days

CHILDREN

Frederick Dent Grant, b. May 30, 1850, St. Louis, Mo.; m. Oct. 20, 1874, Ida Maria Honoré, Chicago, Ill.; d. Apr. 11, 1912, New York, N.Y.

Ulysses Simpson ("Buck") Grant, b. July 22, 1852, Bethel, Ohio; m. Nov. 1, 1880, Fannie Josephine Chaffee, New York, N.Y.; m. July 12, 1913, America Workman Wills, San Diego, Calif.; d. Sept. 25, 1929, San Diego, Calif.

Ellen Wrenshall ("Nellie") Grant, b. July 4, 1855, Wistonwisch, Mo.; m. May 21, 1874, Algernon Charles Frederick Sartoris at the White House, Washington, D.C.; m. July 4, 1912, Franklin Hatch Jones, Cobourg, Ontario, Canada; d. Aug. 30, 1922, Chicago, Ill.

Jesse Root Grant, b. Feb. 6, 1858, St. Louis, Mo.; m. Sept. 21, 1880, Elizabeth Chapman, San Francisco, Calif.; m. Aug. 26, 1918, Lillian Burns Wilkins, New York, N.Y., d. June 8, 1934, Los Altos, Calif.

THE PRESIDENT'S WIFE

Name at birth—Julia Boggs Dent

Date of birth—Jan. 26, 1826

Place of birth—St. Louis, Mo.

Mother—Ellen Wrenshall Dent

Father—Frederick Dent

Father's occupation—Judge

Education—Boarding school, St. Louis, Mo.

Marriage—Ulysses Simpson Grant, Aug. 22, 1848, St. Louis, Mo.

Children—Frederick Dent Grant, b. May 30, 1850, d. Apr. 11, 1912; Ulysses Simpson Grant, b. July 22, 1852, d. Sept. 25, 1929; Ellen Wrenshall ("Nellie") Grant, b. July 4, 1855, d. Aug. 30, 1922; Jesse Root Grant, b. Feb. 6, 1858, d. June 8, 1934

Date of death—Dec. 14, 1902

Age at death—76 years, 322 days

Place of death—Washington, D.C.

Burial place—New York, N.Y.

Years younger than the President—3 years, 274 days

Years she survived the President—17 years, 144 days

Courtesy of The Library of Congress

Julia Grant, wife of Ulysses Grant

THE FIRST LADY

Julia Dent Grant, wife of President Grant, was very much admired as a White House hostess. In keeping with the fashion of the time, her dinners often extended to 29 courses, which her plump figure showed.

She was decidedly a political force. One of her coups, for instance, was to obtain the friendship of Hamilton Fish, and to influence his appointment as Secretary of State. She urged her husband to veto the Finance Bill, saying he would be hanged in effigy no matter what he did, so he should do what was morally right. Julia Grant was a supporter of women's rights and became a friend of Susan B. Anthony, who supported President Grant rather than Victoria Woodhull, the first woman to run for the presidency.

IMPORTANT DATES IN THE PRESIDENT'S LIFE

1829–1839, worked on his father's farm

July 1, 1839–July 1, 1843, U.S. Military Academy

July 1, 1843, graduated from U.S. Military Academy (21st in class of 39); brevet second lieutenant, 4th Infantry

1846, served under Generals Zachary Taylor and Winfield Scott in Mexican War

Sept. 8, 1847, brevet first lieutenant for gallant and meritorious conduct in battle of Molino del Rey

Sept. 13, 1847, brevet captain for gallant conduct in the battle of Chapultepec

Sept. 16, 1847, commissioned first lieutenant of Fourth Infantry

Aug. 5, 1853, commissioned captain of Fourth Infantry

July 31, 1854, resigned from army

1854, farming and real estate business, St. Louis, Mo.

1860, worked in his father's hardware and leather store, Galena, Ill.

April 19, 1861, commander of a company of Illinois volunteers

May 17, 1861, brigadier general, U.S. Volunteers

June 17, 1861, commissioned by Governor Yates of Illinois as colonel of the 21st Illinois Infantry Regiment

Apr. 6–7, 1862, Battle of Shiloh (bloodiest battle fought on North American continent to that time)

Feb. 16, 1862, major general, U.S. Volunteers

July 4, 1863, captured Vicksburg; major general, U.S. Army

Nov. 24–25, 1863, Battle of Chattanooga, Union victory that prepared the way for invasion of Georgia

Dec. 17, 1863, received thanks of Congress and a gold medal

Mar. 9, 1864, commissioned lieutenant general, commander in chief of U.S. Army

June 8, 1864, unsuccessful candidate for the Republican nomination for President

1864–1865, siege of Richmond

Apr. 2, 1865, Lee retreats from Richmond

Apr. 9, 1865, received Lee's surrender at Appomattox, Va.

July 25, 1866, commissioned general of the army by Congress (first award of the title "general of the army")

Aug. 12, 1867–Jan. 13, 1868, Secretary of War, ad interim

Mar. 4, 1869–Mar. 4, 1873, President (first term)

Mar. 4, 1873–Mar. 4, 1877, President (second term)

1877–1879, toured the world

1880, visited the Southern United States, Cuba, and Mexico

1880, unsuccessful candidate for the presidential nomination on the Republican ticket

Dec. 24, 1883, injured hip in fall; afterwards always walked with cane

1884, failure of Grant and Ward, New York bankers, wiped out his fortune

1885, wrote his memoirs, which were completed four days before he died; family derived about $500,000 from royalties

Apr. 2, 1885, baptized a Methodist by the Reverend John Philip Newman

Courtesy of The Library of Congress

General Grant at his headquarters in Cold Harbor, Virginia

ELECTIONS

THE ELECTION OF 1868

November 3, 1868

CANDIDATES

Republican Party (Union-Republican Party) (4th Convention)

May 20–21, 1868, Crosby's Opera House, Chicago, Ill.

P: Ulysses Simpson Grant, Ill.
VP: Schuyler Colfax, Ind.
First ballot: Ulysses Simpson Grant, Ill., 650
Nomination made unanimous

Democratic Party (10th Convention)

July 4–9, 1868, Tammany Hall, New York City

P: Horatio Seymour, N.Y.
VP: Francis Preston Blair, Jr., Mo.

Forty-seven nominations were made. Seymour was nominated on the twenty-second ballot; the nomination was declared unanimous before the final vote was recorded. Candidates for nomination and the votes they received on the first ballot:

George Hunt Pendleton, Ohio, 105
Andrew Johnson, Tenn., 65
Sanford Elias Church, N.Y., 34
Winfield Scott Hancock, Pa., $33^1/_2$
Asa Packer, Pa., 26
James Edward English, Conn., 16
James Rood Doolittle, Wis., 13
Joel Parker, N.J., 13
Reverdy Johnson, Md., $8^1/_2$
Thomas Andrews Hendricks, Ind., $2^1/_2$
Francis Preston Blair, Mo., $^1/_2$
Total number of votes: 317
Number necessary for nomination: 212

1868 POPULAR VOTE

Republican Party, 3,012,833
Democratic Party, 2,703,249

1868 ELECTORAL VOTE

There were 294 electoral votes from 34 states.

Grant received 72.79 percent (214 votes—26 states) as follows: Ala. 8; Ark. 5; Calif. 5; Conn. 6; Fla. 3; Ill. 16; Ind. 13; Iowa 8; Kan. 3; Me. 7; Mass. 12; Mich. 8; Minn. 4; Mo. 11; Neb. 3; Nev. 3; N.H. 5; N.C. 9; Ohio 21; Pa. 26; R.I. 4; S.C. 6; Tenn. 10; Vt. 5; W. Va. 5; Wis. 8.

Seymour received 27.21 percent (80 votes—8 states) as follows: Del. 3; Ga. 9; Ky. 11; La. 7; Md. 7; N.J. 7; N.Y. 33; Ore. 3.

Three states with 26 votes were not represented in the balloting: Miss. 10; Tex. 6; Va. 10.

THE ELECTION OF 1872

November 5, 1872

CANDIDATES

Republican Party (5th Convention)

June 5–6, 1872, Academy of Music, Philadelphia, Pa.

P: Ulysses Simpson Grant, Ill.
VP: Henry Wilson, Mass.
First ballot: Ulysses Simpson Grant, Ill., 752
Nomination made unanimous

Liberal Republican Party

May 1, 1872, Industrial (Music) Hall, Cincinnati, Ohio

P: Horace Greeley, N.Y.
VP: Benjamin Gratz Brown, Mo.

Greeley was nominated on the sixth ballot. Candidates for nomination and the votes they received on the first and sixth ballots:

Charles Francis Adams, Mass., 203, 187
Horace Greeley, N.Y., 147, 482
Lyman Trumbull, Ill., 108, 21
David Davis, Ill., $92^1/_2$, 6
Benjamin Gratz Brown, Mo., 95, 0
Andrew Gregg Curtin, Pa., 62, 0
Salmon Portland Chase, Ohio, $2^1/_2$, 0
Total number of votes:

First ballot: 689

Sixth ballot: 682

The Liberal Republicans recognized the equality of all men; pledged the party to union, enfranchisement; demanded amnesty for former Confederates, states' rights, reform of the civil service, a modest tariff, and maintenance of public credit.

Independent Liberal Republican Party (Opposition Party)

June 21, 1872, Fifth Avenue Hotel, New York, N.Y.

P: William Slocum Groesbeck, Ohio
VP: Frederick Law Olmsted, N.Y.

This nomination was made by members of the Liberal Republican Party opposed to the nomination of Greeley and Brown.

Democratic Party (11th Convention)

July 9–10, 1872, Ford's Opera House, Baltimore, Md.

P: Horace Greeley, N.Y.
VP: Benjamin Gratz Brown, Mo.

Greeley was nominated on the first ballot. Candidates for nomination and the votes they received:

Horace Greeley, N.Y., 686
Jeremiah Sullivan Black, Pa., 21
James Asheton Bayard, Del., 16
William Slocum Groesbeck, Ohio, 2
Blank votes: 7
Total number of votes: 725
Nomination made unanimous

Straight-out Democratic Party

Sept. 3, 1872, Louisville, Ky.

P: Charles O'Conor, N.Y.
VP: Charles Francis Adams, Mass.

This party was opposed to the fusion of the Democrats with the Liberal Republicans. O'Conor declined the nomination but was not permitted to withdraw.

Prohibition Party

Feb. 22, 1872, Opera House, Columbus, Ohio

P: James Black, Pa.
VP: John Russell, Mich.

This party, formed in 1869 at Chicago, Ill., endorsed prohibition, woman suffrage, a direct popular vote for President and Vice President, sound currency, the encouragement of immigration, and a reduction in transportation rates.

People's Party (Equal Rights Party)

May 10, 1872, Apollo Hall, New York, N.Y.

P: Victoria Claflin Woodhull, N.Y.
VP: Frederick Douglass

This party was formed by unauthorized delegates, seceders, and others who bolted from the National Woman Suffrage Association convention. The Equal Rights Party convention was attended by 500 delegates from 26 states and 4 territories.

Labor Reform Party

Feb. 21–22, 1872, Columbus, Ohio

P: David Davis, Ill.
VP: Joel Parker, N.J.

Davis was nominated on the third ballot. Candidates for nomination and the votes they received on the first and third ballots:

John White Geary, Pa., 69, 0
Horace H. Day, N.Y., 59, 3
David Davis, Ill., 47, 201
Wendell Phillips, Mass., 13, 0
John McCauley Palmer, Ill., 8, 0
Joel Parker, N.J., 7, 0
George Washington Julian, Ind., 6, 0

Both candidates declined the nomination.

Liberal Republican Convention of Colored Men

Sept. 25, 1872, Weissiger Hall, Louisville, Ky.

P: Horace Greeley, N.Y.
VP: Benjamin Gratz Brown, Mo.

National Working Men's Convention

May 23, 1872, New York, N.Y.

P: Ulysses Simpson Grant, Ill.
VP: Henry Wilson, Mass.

Delegates from 31 states attended.

1872 POPULAR VOTE

Republican Party, 3,597,132
Democratic Party and Liberal Republican Party, 2,834,079
Straight-Out Democratic Party, 29,489
Prohibition Party, 5,608

1872 ELECTORAL VOTE

There were 352 electoral votes from 35 states. The returns of two states—Arkansas and Louisiana—were disputed and not counted.

Grant received 81.205 percent (286 votes—29 states) as follows: Ala. 10; Calif. 6; Conn. 6; Del. 3; Fla. 4; Ill. 21; Ind. 15; Iowa 11; Kan. 5; Me. 7; Mass. 13; Mich. 11; Minn. 5; Miss. 8; Neb. 3; Nev. 3; N.H. 5; N.J. 9; N.Y. 35; N.C. 10; Ohio 22; Ore. 3; Pa. 29; R.I. 4; S.C. 7; Vt. 5; Va. 11; W.Va. 5; Wis. 10.

Greeley died on November 29, 1872, three weeks after the election. The six states he had carried—Georgia, Kentucky, Maryland, Missouri, Tennessee, and Texas—split their electoral votes among the following: Thomas Andrews Hendricks of Indiana, Benjamin Gratz Brown of Missouri, Charles Jones Jenkins of Georgia, and David Davis of Illinois.

Hendricks received 11.93 percent (42 votes—4 states) as follows: Ky. 8 (of the 12 votes); Md. 8; Mo. 6 (of the 15 votes); Tenn. 12; Tex. 8.

Brown received 5.14 percent (18 votes—2 states) as follows: Ga. 6 (of the 11 votes); Ky. 4 (of the 12 votes); Mo. 8 (of the 15 votes).

Jenkins received 2 votes (of the 11 Ga. votes).

Davis received 1 vote (of the 15 Mo. votes).

Greeley received 3 votes (of the 11 Ga. votes), but by House resolution they were not counted.

The electoral vote for the vice presidency was divided, as the party lines were not solidly for one candidate. Nine individuals received electoral votes: Henry Wilson of Massachusetts, Benjamin Gratz Brown of Missouri, Alfred Holt Colquitt of Georgia (Democrat), George Washington Julian of Indiana (Liberal Republican), John McCauley Palmer of Illinois (Democrat), Thomas E. Bramlette of Kentucky (Democrat), William

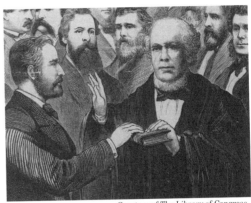

Courtesy of The Library of Congress

Chief Justice Salmon P. Chase administers the oath of office to Ulysses Grant.

Slocum Groesbeck of Ohio (Democrat), Willis Benson Machen of Kentucky (Democrat), and Nathaniel Prentiss Banks of Massachusetts (Liberal Republican).

Wilson received 81.25 percent (268 votes—29 states) as follows: Ala. 10; Calif. 6; Conn. 6; Del. 3; Fla. 4; Ill. 21; Ind. 15; Iowa 11; Kan. 5; Me. 7; Mass. 13; Mich. 11; Minn. 5; Miss. 8; Neb. 3; Nev. 3; N.H. 5; N.J. 9; N.Y. 35; N.C. 10; Ohio 22; Ore. 3; Pa. 29; R.I. 4; S.C. 7; Vt. 5; Va. 11; W.Va. 5; Wis. 10.

Brown received 13.35 percent (47 votes—4 states) as follows: Ga. 5 (of the 11 votes); Ky. 8 (of the 12 votes); Md. 8; Mo. 6 (of the 15 votes); Tenn. 12; Tex. 8.

Colquitt received 5 votes (of the 11 Ga. votes).

Julian received 5 votes (of the 15 Mo. votes).

Palmer received 3 votes (of the 15 Mo. votes).

Bramlette received 3 votes (of the 12 Ky. votes).

Groesbeck received 1 vote (of the 15 Mo. votes).

Machen received 1 vote (of the 12 Ky. votes).

Banks received 1 vote (of the 11 Ga. votes).

INAUGURATIONS

FIRST TERM

March 4, 1869

Ulysses Simpson Grant took the oath of office on Thursday, March 4, 1869, on the east portico of the Capitol. Eight full divisions of troops participated in the parade, the most impressive inauguration that had yet been seen.

Retiring President Johnson refused to attend the inauguration. He stayed with his cabinet until noon and then left the city.

The inaugural ball was held in a newly finished section of the Treasury Building. Errors in the checking room caused guests to wait hours to reclaim their possessions. It was reported that costly jewels were stolen.

SECOND TERM

March 4, 1873

Grant took the oath of office for his second term on Tuesday, March 4, 1873. The oath was administered by Chief Justice Chase.

The parade was marred by a near-blizzard. The thermometer registered zero, causing marchers great discomfort, and several West Point cadets lost consciousness because of the cold. The inaugural ball was held at Judiciary Square in a temporary building so cold that the guests wore their coats while dancing. The valves on the musicians' wind instruments froze, and fingering became difficult on the strings.

THE VICE PRESIDENTS

FIRST TERM

Name—Schuyler Colfax (17th V.P.)
Date of birth—Mar. 23, 1823
Place of birth—New York, N.Y.
Political party—Republican
State represented—Indiana
Term of office—Mar. 4, 1869–Mar. 4, 1873
Age at inauguration—45 years, 346 days
Occupation after term—Retired; lecturer
Date of death—Jan. 13, 1885
Age at death—61 years, 296 days
Place of death—Mankato, Minn.
Burial place—South Bend, Ind.

ADDITIONAL DATA ON COLFAX

1836, moved to Indiana

1841, appointed deputy auditor of St. Joseph County, Ind.

1845, acquired interest in South Bend *Free Press,* changed its name to St. Joseph Valley *Register*

1850, member, Indiana state constitutional convention

1850, unsuccessful Whig candidate for Congress

Mar. 4, 1855–Mar. 3, 1869, U.S. House of Representatives (from Indiana)

Courtesy of The Library of Congress

Schuyler Colfax, Vice President to Ulysses S. Grant

Dec. 7, 1863–Mar. 3, 1869, Speaker, U.S. House of Representatives

Mar. 4, 1869–Mar. 4, 1873, Vice President under Ulysses S. Grant

1872, unsuccessful candidate for vice presidential renomination

1873, charged with corruption in Crédit Mobilier scandal, but completely exonerated

COLFAX PRESIDED OVER BOTH HOUSES

Schuyler Colfax was the first officer to preside over both houses of Congress. He was Speaker of the House of Representatives in the 38th, 39th, and 40th Congresses (December 7, 1863–November 10, 1868). As Vice President under President Grant, he presided over the Senate from March 4, 1869, to March 3, 1873.

SECOND TERM

Name—Henry Wilson (18th V.P.)
Name at birth—Jeremiah Jones Colbaith
Date of birth—Feb. 16, 1812
Place of birth—Farmington, N.H.
Political party—Republican
State represented—Massachusetts
Term of office—Mar. 4, 1873–Nov. 22, 1875
Age at inauguration—61 years, 16 days
Occupation after term—Died in office
Date of death—Nov. 22, 1875
Age at death—63 years, 279 days
Place of death—Washington, D.C.
Burial place—Natick, Mass.

ADDITIONAL DATA ON WILSON

18—, educated in common schools
1822–33, worked on farm
1833, adopted name of Henry Wilson legally
1833, moved to Massachusetts; learned shoe-maker's trade

Courtesy of The Library of Congress

Henry Wilson, second Vice President to Ulysses Grant

1841–1842, Massachusetts House of Representatives
1844–1846, Massachusetts Senate
1848–1851, owner and editor of Boston *Republican*
1850–1852, Massachusetts Senate
1852, president of Free Soil National Convention at Pittsburgh, Pa.; unsuccessful candidate for Congress on Free Soil ticket
1853, delegate to Massachusetts state constitutional convention
Jan. 31, 1855–Mar. 3, 1873, U.S. Senate (from Massachusetts)
1861, commanded 22nd Regiment, Massachusetts Volunteer Infantry
Mar. 4, 1873–Nov. 22, 1875, Vice President under Ulysses S. Grant

CABINET

FIRST TERM

March 4, 1869–March 3, 1873

State—William Henry Seward, N.Y., continued from preceding administration; Elihu Benjamin Washburne, Ill., Mar. 5, 1869; Hamilton Fish, N.Y., Mar. 11, 1869; entered upon duties Mar. 17, 1869

Treasury—Hugh McCulloch, Ind., continued from preceding administration; John F. Hartley, Me. (assistant secretary), ad interim Mar. 5, 1869; George Sewall Boutwell, Mass., Mar. 11, 1869

War—John McAllister Schofield, Ill., continued from preceding administration; John Aaron Rawlins, Ill., Mar. 11, 1869; William Tecumseh Sherman, Ohio, Sept. 9, 1869; entered upon duties Sept. 11, 1869; William Worth Belknap, Iowa, Oct. 25, 1869; entered upon duties Nov. 1, 1869

Attorney General—William Maxwell Evarts, N.Y., continued from preceding administration; J. Hubley Ashton, Pa. (assistant attorney general); acting, Mar. 5, 1869; Ebenezer Rockwood Hoar, Mass., Mar. 5, 1869; entered upon duties Mar. 11, 1869; Amos Tappan Akerman, Ga., June 23, 1870; entered upon duties July 8, 1870;

George Henry Williams, Ore., Dec. 14, 1871; to take effect Jan. 10, 1872

Postmaster General—St. John B. L. Skinner, N.Y. (first assistant Postmaster General), ad interim Mar. 4, 1869; John Angel James Creswell, Md., Mar. 5, 1869

Navy—William Faxon, Conn. (assistant secretary), ad interim Mar. 4, 1869; Adolph Edward Borie, Pa., Mar. 5, 1869; entered upon duties Mar. 9, 1869; George Maxwell Robeson, N.J., June 25, 1869

Interior—William Tod Otto, Ind. (assistant secretary), ad interim Mar. 4, 1869; Jacob Dolson Cox, Ohio, Mar. 5, 1869; entered upon duties Mar. 9, 1869; Columbus Delano, Ohio, Nov. 1, 1870

SECOND TERM

March 4, 1873–March 3, 1877

State—Hamilton Fish, N.Y., continued from preceding administration; recommissioned Mar. 17, 1873

Treasury—George Sewall Boutwell, Mass., continued from preceding administration; William Adams Richardson, Mass., Mar. 17, 1873; Benjamin Helm Bristow, Ky., June 2, 1874; entered upon duties June 4, 1874; Charles F. Conant, N.H. (assistant secretary), ad interim June 21, 1876–June 30, 1876; Lot Myrick Morrill, Me., June 21, 1876; entered upon duties July 7, 1876

War—William Worth Belknap, Iowa, continued from preceding administration; recommissioned Mar. 17, 1873; George Maxwell Robeson, N.J. (secretary of the Navy), ad interim Mar. 2, 1876; Alphonso Taft, Ohio, Mar. 8, 1876; entered upon duties Mar. 11, 1876; James Donald Cameron, Pa., May 22, 1876; entered upon duties June 1, 1876

Attorney General—George Henry Williams, Ore., continued from preceding

administration; recommissioned Mar. 17, 1873; Edward Pierrepont, N.Y., Apr. 26, 1875; to take effect May 15, 1875; Alphonso Taft, Ohio, May 22, 1876; entered upon duties June 1, 1876

Postmaster General—John Angel James Creswell, Md., continued from preceding administration; recommissioned Mar. 17, 1873; James William Marshall, Va., July 3, 1874; entered upon duties July 7, 1874; Marshall Jewell, Conn., Aug. 24, 1874; entered upon duties Sept. 1, 1874; James Noble Tyner, Ind., July 12, 1876

Navy—George Maxwell Robeson, N.J., continued from preceding administration; recommissioned Mar. 17, 1873

Interior—Columbus Delano, Ohio, continued from preceding administration; recommissioned Mar. 17, 1873; Benjamin Rush Cowen, Ohio (assistant secretary), ad interim Oct. 1, 1875; Zachariah Chandler, Mich., Oct. 19, 1875

CONGRESS

FORTY-FIRST CONGRESS

March 4, 1869–March 3, 1871

First session—Mar. 4, 1869–Apr. 10, 1869 (38 days)

Second session—Dec. 6, 1869–July 15, 1870 (222 days)

Third session—Dec. 5, 1870–Mar. 3, 1871 (89 days)

Special session of the Senate—Apr. 12, 1869–Apr. 22, 1869 (11 days)

Vice President—Schuyler Colfax, Ind.

President pro tempore of the Senate —Henry Bowen Anthony, R.I., elected Mar. 23, 1869; Apr. 9, 1869; May 28, 1870; July 1, 1870; July 14, 1870

Secretary of the Senate—George Congdon Gorham, Calif.

Speaker of the House—James Gillespie Blaine, Me., elected Mar. 4, 1869

Clerk of the House—Edward McPherson, Pa., reelected Mar. 5, 1869

FORTY-SECOND CONGRESS

March 4, 1871–March 3, 1873

First session—Mar. 4, 1871–Apr. 20, 1871 (48 days)

Second session—Dec. 4, 1871–June 10, 1872 (190 days)

Third session—Dec. 2, 1872–Mar. 3, 1873 (92 days)

Special session of the Senate—May 10, 1871–May 27, 187 (18 days)

Vice President—Schuyler Colfax, Ind.

President pro tempore of the Senate —Henry Bowen Anthony, R.I., elected Mar. 10, 1871; Apr. 17, 1871; May 23, 1871, special session; Dec. 21, 1871; Feb. 23, 1872; June 8, 1872; Dec. 4, 1872; Dec. 13, 1872; Dec. 20, 1872; Jan. 24, 1873

Secretary of the Senate—George Congdon Gorham, Calif.

Speaker of the House—James Gillespie Blaine, Me., reelected Mar. 4, 1871

Clerk of the House—Edward McPherson, Pa., reelected Mar. 4, 1871

FORTY-THIRD CONGRESS

March 4, 1873–March 3, 1875

First session—Dec. 1, 1873–June 23, 1874 (204 days)

Second session—Dec. 7, 1874–Mar. 3, 1875 (87 days)

Special session of the Senate—Mar. 4, 1873–Mar. 26, 1873 (22 days)

Vice President—Henry Wilson, Mass.

President pro tempore of the Senate —Matthew Hale Carpenter, Wis., elected Mar. 12, 1873; Mar. 26, 1873; special session; Dec. 11, 1873, Dec. 23, 1874; Henry Bowen Anthony, R.I., elected Jan. 25, 1875; Feb. 15, 1875

Secretary of the Senate—George Congdon Gorham, Calif.

Speaker of the House—James Gillespie Blaine, Me., reelected Dec. 1, 1873

Clerk of the House—Edward McPherson, Pa., reelected Dec. 1, 1873

FORTY-FOURTH CONGRESS

March 4, 1875–March 3, 1877

First session—Dec. 6, 1875–Aug. 15, 1876 (254 days)

Second session—Dec. 4, 1876–Mar. 3, 1877 (90 days)

Special session of the Senate—Mar. 5, 1875–Mar. 24, 1875 (20 days)

Vice President—Henry Wilson, Mass.; died Nov. 22, 1875

President pro tempore of the Senate —Thomas White Ferry, Mich., elected Mar. 9, 1875; special session; Dec. 20, 1875

Secretary of the Senate—George Congdon Gorham, Calif.

Speaker of the House—Michael Crawford Kerr, Ind., elected Dec. 6, 1875; died Aug. 19, 1876; Samuel Jackson Randall, Pa., elected Dec. 4, 1876

Clerk of the House—Edward McPherson, Pa.; George Madison Adams, Ky., elected Dec. 6, 1875

APPOINTMENTS TO THE SUPREME COURT

Chief Justice

Morrison Remick Waite, Ohio, Jan. 21, 1874

(replaced Salmon Portland Chase)

Associate Justices

Edwin McMasters Stanton, Pa., Dec. 20, 1869 (did not serve)

William Strong, Pa., Feb. 18, 1870 (replaced Robert Cooper Grier)

Joseph Philo Bradley, N.J., Mar. 21, 1870 (newly created seat)

Ward Hunt, N.Y., Dec. 11, 1872 (replaced Samuel Nelson)

IMPORTANT DATES IN THE PRESIDENCY

May 10, 1869, ceremonies at Promontory, Utah, to celebrate junction of Pacific railroads and start of transcontinental service

Sept. 24, 1869, Black Friday financial panic

Dec. 9, 1869, Knights of Labor formed at Philadelphia, Pa.

Mar. 30, 1870, Fifteenth Amendment to the Constitution ratified

June 22, 1870, Department of Justice created

May 8, 1871, Treaty of Washington signed with Great Britain to provide for settlement of boundary and fishery disputes and *Alabama* claims

Oct. 8–9, 1871, Chicago fire; 300 killed, 90,000 homeless

1872, revelation of Crédit Mobilier stock scandal involving several members of Congress

Jan. 1, 1872, Civil Service Act became effective

Aug. 25, 1872, international commission, in Geneva Award, directed Great Britain to pay United States $15.5 million to compensate for damages caused by Confederate *Alabama,* built in England despite British neutrality

Feb. 1873, Congress demonetized silver, causing a drop in the value of silver

Sept. 18, 1873, start of financial panic of 1873

Nov. 18, 1874, National Women's Christian Temperance Union organized at Cleveland, Ohio

Mar. 10, 1876, Alexander Graham Bell transmitted sound of the human voice on telephone

May 10, 1876, International Centennial Exposition opened, Philadelphia, Pa. (to Nov. 10)

June 25, 1876, General Custer's command destroyed by Indians under Sitting Bull at Little Big Horn River, Mont.

Aug. 1, 1876, Colorado admitted as the 38th state

ADDITIONAL DATA ON GRANT

ULYSSES SIMPSON GRANT

—was the first President born in Ohio.

—was the seventh President who was a resident of a state other than his native state.

—was the first President whose parents were both alive when he was inaugurated.

GRANT CHANGED HIS NAME

Ulysses Simpson Grant was given the name Hiram Ulysses Grant when he was born. Not liking the acronym formed by his initials—HUG—he transposed it to Ulysses Hiram Grant. When he applied to Representative Thomas Lyon Hamer in 1839 for an appointment to West Point, the congressman

made an error and listed Grant as Ulysses Simpson Grant (Simpson being his mother's maiden name). Grant accepted this accidental change in his name.

GRANT RECEIVED CIGARS

General Grant is reputed to have smoked 20 cigars daily. The cigar habit was acquired after the battle of Fort Donelson, Tenn., February 13–16, 1862. It is reported that General Grant gave the following explanation to General Horace Porter:

> I had been a light smoker previous to the attack on Donelson. . . . In the accounts published in the papers, I was repre-

Lieutenant General Grant, commander of all the Union Armies

sented as smoking a cigar in the midst of the conflict; and many persons, thinking, no doubt, that tobacco was my chief solace, sent me boxes of the choicest brands. . . . As many as ten thousand were soon received. I gave away all I could get rid of, but having such a quantity on hand I naturally smoked more than I would have done under ordinary circumstances, and I have continued the habit ever since.

GRANT ACQUIRED NICKNAME

General Grant's letter to Confederate General Simon Bolivar Buckner dated February 16, 1862, dictating the terms for the surrender of Fort Donelson, earned him the nickname "Unconditional Surrender" Grant. Grant wrote:

Yours of this date proposing armistice, and appointment of commissioners to settle terms of capitulation is just received. No terms except an unconditional and immediate surrender can be accepted. I propose to move immediately upon your works.

LINCOLN PROMOTED GRANT

On March 9, 1864, President Lincoln in the presence of the entire cabinet in the cabinet chamber at the Executive Mansion pre-

sented Grant, then a major general, with his commission as lieutenant general in command of all the Union armies. Lincoln spoke briefly and Grant replied with a short prepared speech.

On July 25, 1866, Grant was appointed a general with four stars, a rank he relinquished when he became President.

SURRENDER OF LEE ANNOUNCED BY GRANT

On April 9, 1865, the surrender of General Lee was announced in the following terse communication to the secretary of war by General Grant:
Hon. E. M. Stanton
Secretary of War,
Washington.

General Lee surrendered the Army of Northern Virginia this afternoon on terms proposed by myself. The accompanying additional correspondence will show the conditions fully.

U. S. GRANT, LT. GEN.

GRANT'S RELUCTANT OPPONENT

Horatio Seymour, the Democratic presidential nominee in 1868, was perhaps the most reluctant candidate ever nominated. He knew that the standard bearer of the party would be blamed for the Civil War and that the opposition candidate was Grant, the most popular hero of the war. Seymour refused to be a candidate, but on the twenty-second ballot he was unanimously chosen. He received 80 electoral votes compared with 214 for Grant.

FIFTEENTH AMENDMENT RATIFIED

The Fifteenth Amendment to the Constitution, which declares that the right of suffrage shall not be denied to citizens "on account of race, color or previous condition of servitude," was passed by Congress February 26, 1869. It was proposed to the legislatures of the several states by the 40th Congress on February 27, 1869. It was not acted on by Tennessee and was rejected by California, Delaware, Kentucky, Maryland, and Oregon. New York rescinded its ratification on January 5, 1870. New Jersey rejected it in 1870, but ratified it in 1871. The twenty-eighth state to ratify it, making it effective, was Georgia, on February 2, 1870. The amendment was declared ratified by the secretary of state on March 30, 1870.

WOMAN PRESIDENTIAL CANDIDATE

The first woman presidential candidate was Victoria Claflin Woodhull, who was nominated on May 10, 1872, at a convention held at Apollo Hall, New York City, by a group of seceders and unauthorized delegates attending the National Woman Suffrage Association convention at Steinway Hall, New York City. The group adopted the name People's Party (also known as the National Radical Reformers and later as the Equal Rights Party). About 500 delegates, representing 26 states and 4 territories, were present at the convention. Mrs. Woodhull was nominated by Judge Carter of Cincinnati, Ohio.

AFRICAN-AMERICAN VICE PRESIDENTIAL CANDIDATE

The first African-American vice presidential candidate was Frederick Douglass, who was nominated with Victoria Claflin Woodhull at the People's Party (Equal Rights Party) convention held on May 10, 1872, at Apollo Hall, New York City.

CATHOLIC NOMINATED FOR PRESIDENCY

Charles O'Conor of New York, a Catholic, was nominated for the presidency at the Democratic convention at Louisville, Ky., by a wing of the Democrats who refused to accept the nomination of Horace Greeley made at Baltimore, Md. O'Conor declined the nomination on August 31, 1872, but was listed as a candidate nevertheless, and he received approximately 30,000 votes from 23 states.

GRANT RECEIVED HAWAIIAN KING

The first reigning king to visit the United States was David Kalakaua, king of the Sandwich Islands (Hawaii), who was received by President Ulysses Simpson Grant at the White House on December 15, 1874. Con-gress tendered him a reception on December 18, 1874. Grant arranged for a treaty of reciprocity, which was concluded January 30, 1875, with ratification being effected at Washington, D.C., on June 3, 1875. The king came to the United States on the U.S.S. *Benicia* and returned on the U.S.S. *Pensacola.*

GRANT REINSTATED AS GENERAL

General Grant suffered great financial reverses after his term of office and was almost destitute. To relieve this situation, Congress passed legislation restoring former president Grant to his old military status as general. On March 3, 1885, Congress passed an act (23 Stat. L. 434) to authorize an additional appointment on the retired list of the Army—from among those who had been generals commanding the armies of the United States or generals in chief of said army—of one person with the rank and full pay of general.

GRANT WROTE "BEST SELLER"

One of the best-paying books of its time and still high on the all-time list was President Grant's *Memoirs.* Royalties amounted to an estimated $500,000. He never saw his book in type, as he died four days after he had completed the manuscript. Encouraged by Mark Twain, publishers brought it out in book form in 1885.

WHY GRANT WAS BURIED IN NEW YORK CITY

Grant was born in Ohio, represented Illinois, served eight years in Washington, D.C., and spent many years in military service. On June 24, 1885, shortly before his death, Grant wrote a note in longhand (he was unable to speak) and handed it to his son, who crumpled and disposed of it. The note said, in effect: "I would prefer this (West Point) above others but for the fact that my wife could not be placed beside me there. Galena, or some place in Illinois, because from that state I received my first general commission. New York City, because the people of that city befriended me in my need."

On June 16, 1885, Grant went from New York City to Mount McGregor, N.Y., where he died on July 23, 1885. He was buried Sat-

Courtesy of Richard Stein

Grant's Tomb in New York, New York

urday, August 8, 1885, in Riverside Park, New York City. On April 27, 1897, his tomb was dedicated.

WANT OF MUSICAL KNOWLEDGE

President Grant claimed that he knew only two tunes. One was "Yankee Doodle" and the other wasn't.

FURTHER READING

Catton, Bruce. *Grant Moves South.* 1960.
———. *Grant Takes Command.* 1969.
Hesseltine, William B. *Ulysses S. Grant, Politician.* Rev. ed. 1957.
McFeely, William S. *Grant.* 1981.
Perret, Geoffrey. *Ulysses S. Grant: Soldier and President.* 1997.

Simon, John Y., ed. *The Papers of Ulysses S. Grant.* 12 vols., 1960.
Simpson, Brooks D. *Let Us Have Peace: Ulysses S. Grant and the Politics of War and Reconstruction, 1861–1868.* 1991.
———. *Ulysses S. Grant: Triumph over Adversity.* 2000.

Courtesy of The Library of Congress

Rutherford Birchard Hayes

Date of birth—Oct. 4, 1822

Place of birth—Delaware, Ohio

Education—Attended school in Delaware, Ohio; Norwalk (Methodist) Academy, Norwalk, Ohio; Webb Preparatory School, Middletown, Conn.; Kenyon College, Gambier, Ohio, bachelor's degree (valedictorian), Aug. 3, 1842; Harvard Law School, Cambridge, Mass., LL.B., Jan. 1845

Religion—Christian (no specific denomination, though baptized Presbyterian)

Ancestry—Scottish, English

Career—Lawyer, city solicitor, general in Civil War, U.S. congressman, governor of Ohio

Political party—Republican

State represented—Ohio

Term of office—Mar. 4, 1877–Mar. 4, 1881

Term served—4 years

Administration—23rd

Congresses—45th, 46th

Age at inauguration—54 years, 151 days

Lived after term—11 years, 319 days

Occupation after term—Philanthropic activities

Date of death—Jan. 17, 1893

Age at death—70 years, 105 days

Place of death—Fremont, Ohio

Burial place—Spiegel Grove State Park, Fremont, Ohio

FAMILY

FATHER

Name—Rutherford Hayes

Date of birth—Jan. 4, 1787

Place of birth—Brattleboro, Vt.

Marriage—Sophia Birchard, Sept. 13, 1813

Occupation—Farmer, storekeeper, distiller

Date of death—July 20, 1822

Place of death—Delaware, Ohio

Age at death—35 years, 197 days

MOTHER

Name at birth—Sophia Birchard

Date of birth—Apr. 15, 1792

Place of birth—Wilmington, Vt

Marriage—Rutherford Hayes, Sept. 13, 1813

Date of death—Oct. 30, 1866

Place of death—Columbus, Ohio

Age at death—74 years, 198 days

SIBLINGS

Rutherford Birchard Hayes was the fifth child in a family of five.

Children of Rutherford Hayes and Sophia Birchard Hayes

—— Hayes (son), b. Aug. 14, 1814, d. Aug. 14, 1814

Lorenzo Hayes, June 9, 1815, d. Jan. 20, 1825

Sarah Sophia Hayes, b. July 10, 1817, d. Oct. 9, 1821

Fanny Arabella Hayes, b. Jan. 20, 1820, d. July 16, 1856

Rutherford Birchard Hayes, b. Oct. 4, 1822, d. Jan. 17, 1893

MARRIAGE

Married—Lucy Ware Webb

Date of marriage—Dec. 30, 1852

Place of marriage—Cincinnati, Ohio

Age of wife at marriage—21 years, 124 days

Age of husband at marriage—30 years, 87 days

Years married—40 years, 18 days

CHILDREN

Birchard Austin Hayes, b. Nov. 4, 1853, Cincinnati, Ohio; m. Dec. 30, 1886, Mary Nancy Sherman, Norwalk, Ohio; d. Jan. 24, 1926, Toledo, Ohio

James Webb Cook Hayes, b. Mar. 20, 1856, Cincinnati, Ohio; m. Sept. 30, 1912, Mary Otis Miller, Fremont, Ohio; d. July 26, 1934, Fremont, Ohio

Rutherford Platt Hayes, b. June 24, 1858, Cincinnati, Ohio; m. Oct. 24, 1894, Lucy Hayes Platt, Columbus, Ohio; d. July 31, 1927, Tampa, Fla.

Joseph Thompson Hayes, b. Dec. 21, 1861, Cincinnati, Ohio; d. June 24, 1863, near Charleston, W. Va.

George Crook Hayes, b. Sept. 29, 1864, Chillicothe, Ohio; d. May 24, 1866, Chillicothe, Ohio

Fanny Hayes, b. Sept. 2, 1867, Cincinnati, Ohio; m. Sept. 1, 1897, Harry Eaton Smith, Fremont, Ohio; d. Mar. 18, 1950, Lewiston, Me.

Scott Russell Hayes, b. Feb. 8, 1871, Columbus, Ohio; m. Sept. 1912, Maude Anderson; d. May 6, 1923, Croton-on-Hudson, N.Y.

Manning Force Hayes, b. Aug. 1, 1873, Fremont, Ohio; d. Aug. 28, 1874, Fremont, Ohio

THE PRESIDENT'S WIFE

Name at birth—Lucy Ware Webb

Date of birth—Aug. 28, 1831

Place of birth—Chillicothe, Ohio

Mother—Maria Cook Webb

Father—James Webb

Father's occupation—Physician

Education—Wesleyan Female Seminary, Cincinnati, Ohio, graduated 1850

Married—Rutherford Birchard Hayes, Dec. 30, 1852, Cincinnati, Ohio

Children—Birchard Austin Hayes, b. Nov. 4, 1853, d. Jan. 24, 1926; James Webb Cook Hayes, b. Mar. 20, 1856, d. July 26, 1934; Rutherford Platt Hayes, b. June 24, 1858, d. July 31, 1927; Joseph Thompson Hayes, b. Dec. 21, 1861, d. June 24, 1863; George Crook Hayes, b. Sept. 29, 1864, d. May 24, 1866; Fanny Hayes, b. Sept. 2, 1867, d. Mar. 18, 1950; Scott Russell Hayes, b. Feb. 8, 1871, d. May 6, 1923; Manning Force Hayes, b. Aug. 1, 1873, d. Aug. 28, 1874

Date of death—June 25, 1889

Age at death—57 years, 301 days

Place of death—Fremont, Ohio

Burial place—Fremont, Ohio

Years younger than the President—8 years, 328 days

Years the President survived her—3 years, 206 days

Courtesy of The Library of Congress

Lucy Hayes, wife of Rutherford B. Hayes

THE FIRST LADY

Lucy Ware Webb Hayes, the first First Lady to graduate from college, was a woman whose strong opinions on social issues were informed by her adherence to Methodism. Early in her marriage, she encouraged her husband, then a young lawyer, to defend runaway slaves in court and gave employment in her household to freed slaves. During the Civil War she journeyed to a military hospital to nurse Hayes after he was wounded, leaving her little children at home, and later made repeated visits to his army camp, where she cared for sick soldiers under the supervision of her brother, the regiment's doctor. In the White House she was known for generous gestures, especially toward the staff; the traditional Easter egg roll on the White House lawn got its start in 1878 when she opened the grounds to the neighborhood children. In 1880 she was named national president of the Woman's Home Missionary Society, a Methodist social-welfare organization. She was also a prominent member of the Women's Christian Temperance Union, earning the nickname "Lemonade Lucy" from disgruntled Washingtonians who resented her decision to serve only soft drinks. It was her custom to start the day with a morning prayer service in the White House.

SILVER WEDDING ANNIVERSARY AT WHITE HOUSE

President Hayes and his wife celebrated their silver wedding anniversary on December 31, 1877, in the White House. Reverend

Courtesy of The Library of Congress

Rutherford and Lucy Hayes

Dr. Lorenzo Dow McCabe of Ohio Wesleyan University, who had united them in marriage on December 30, 1852, reenacted the ceremony at their silver anniversary.

IMPORTANT DATES IN THE PRESIDENT'S LIFE

Aug. 1842, graduated from Kenyon College

Jan. 1845, graduated from Harvard Law School, LL.B. degree

Mar. 10, 1845, admitted to the bar, Marietta, Ohio; practiced in Sandusky (now Fremont), Ohio

1849, moved to Cincinnati; practiced law

1857–1861, city solicitor of Cincinnati

June 27, 1861, commissioned major, 23rd Regiment, Ohio Volunteer Infantry

Sept. 19, 1861, appointed judge advocate general

Oct. 24, 1861, lieutenant colonel

Sept. 14, 1862, wounded in left arm at South Mountain

Oct. 24, 1862, colonel

1862, detailed to act as brigadier general in command of Kanawha division

July 1863, checked Confederate raid led by John Morgan

1864, commanded brigade under General Crook

July 1864, with Colonel Milligan ordered to charge superior force; Milligan fell and Hayes conducted retreat

Sept. 1864, second Battle of Winchester

Sept. 22, 1864, routed enemy at Fisher's Hill

Oct. 9, 1864, brigadier general of volunteers

Oct. 19, 1864, Battle of Cedar Creek; badly stunned when his horse was killed

Mar. 3, 1865, breveted major general of volunteers "for gallant and distinguished services during the campaign of 1864 in West Virginia and particularly at the battles of Fisher's Hill and Cedar Creek"

Mar. 4, 1865–July 20, 1867, U.S. House of Representatives (from Ohio)

June 8, 1865, resigned from Army

Jan. 13, 1868, governor of Ohio

1872, unsuccessful candidate for election to Congress; declined appointment as U.S. treasurer at Cincinnati

Jan. 10, 1876–Mar. 2, 1877, governor of Ohio

Mar. 4, 1877–Mar. 4, 1881, President

1880, declined to run for a second term

ELECTIONS

THE ELECTION OF 1876

November 7, 1876

Republican Party (6th Convention)

June 14–16, 1876, Exposition Hall, Cincinnati, Ohio

P: Rutherford Birchard Hayes, Ohio

VP: William Almon Wheeler, N.Y.

Hayes was nominated on the seventh ballot. Candidates for nomination and the votes they received on the first and seventh ballots:

James Gillespie Blaine, Me., 285, 351

Oliver Hazard Perry Throck Morton, Ind., 124, 0

Benjamin Helm Bristow, Ky., 113, 21

Roscoe Conkling, N.Y., 99, 0

Rutherford Birchard Hayes, Ohio, 61, 384

John Frederick Hartranft, Pa., 58, 0

Marshall Jewell, Conn., 11, 0

William Almon Wheeler, N.Y., 3, 0

Total number of votes

First ballot: 754

Seventh ballot: 756

Number necessary for nomination: 379

Democratic Party (12th Convention)

June 27–29, 1876, Merchant's Exchange, St. Louis, Mo.

P: Samuel Jones Tilden, N.Y.

VP: Thomas Andrews Hendricks, Ind.

Tilden was nominated on the second ballot. Candidates for nomination and the votes they received on the first and second ballots:

Samuel Jones Tilden, N.Y., $403^1/_2$, 508

Thomas Andrews Hendricks, Ind., $133^1/_2$, 85

Winfield Scott Hancock, Pa., 77, 60

William Allen, Ohio, 56, 54

Thomas Francis Bayard, Del., 31, 11

Joel Parker, N.J., 18, 18

James Overton Broadhead, Mo., 16, 0

Allen Granberry Thurman, Ohio, 3, 2

Total number of votes: 738

Number necessary for nomination: 492

Greenback Party (Independent Party)

May 16–18, 1876, Academy of Music, Indianapolis, Ind.

P: Peter Cooper, N.Y.

VP: Samuel Fenton Cary, Ohio

The Greenback Party was organized November 25, 1874, at Indianapolis, Ind. It advocated withdrawal of all national and state bank currency and substitution of paper currency issued by the government. Newton Booth of California, was nominated for the vice presidency but declined.

Prohibition Party (National Prohibition Reform Party)

May 17, 1876, Halle's Hall, Cleveland, Ohio

P: Green Clay Smith, Ky.

VP: Gideon Tabor Stewart, Ohio

American National Party

June 9, 1875, Pittsburgh, Pa.

P: James B. Walker, Ill.

VP: Donald Kirkpatrick, N.Y.

1876 POPULAR VOTE

Republican Party, 4,036,298

Democratic Party, 4,300,590

Greenback Party, 81,737

Prohibition Party, 9,522

American National Party, 2,636

DISPUTED ELECTION DECIDED BY ELECTORAL COMMISSION

It was not until March 2, 1877, that the nation knew who would be inaugurated President of the United States on Monday, March 5, 1877.

Courtesy of The Library of Congress

The inauguration of Rutherford B. Hayes

Tilden had won a majority of the popular votes, but neither candidate had the requisite 185 electoral votes—Tilden had 184 and Hayes had 165. Twenty votes were in dispute: the votes of three Southern states with "carpetbag" governments (Florida, Louisiana, and South Carolina) were claimed by both parties, and an elector of a fourth state (Oregon) was found ineligible. When the electoral college met in December 1876 there was a conflict as to which electors should be certified. The Constitution provided that the votes should be counted in the presence of both houses of Congress. But the Republican-controlled Senate and the Democratic-controlled House could not agree on how the votes were to be counted. To end the deadlock congressional leaders suggested a compromise: decision by a bipartisan electoral commission consisting of seven Republicans, seven Democrats, and one independent. Unexpectedly, the independent (Supreme Court Justice David Davis) retired, and a Republican (Justice Bradley) was substituted.

The count, begun on February 1, was not completed until March 2. The commission, which voted strictly on partisan lines (eight to seven in favor of all Hayes electors), consisted of the following members:

Justices of the Supreme Court

Nathan Clifford (President of the Commission), Me., Democrat; Samuel Freeman Miller, Iowa, Republican; Stephen Johnson Field, Calif., Democrat; William Strong, Pa., Republican; Joseph Philo Bradley, N.J., Republican

U.S. Senators

George Franklin Edmunds, Vt., Republican; Oliver Hazard Perry Thock Morton, Ind., Republican; Frederick Theodore Frelinghuysen, N.J., Republican; Thomas Francis Bayard, Del., Democrat; Allen Granberry Thurman, Ohio, Democrat

U.S. Congressmen

Henry B. Payne, Ohio, Democrat; Eppa Hunton, Va., Democrat; Josiah Gardner Abbott, Mass., Democrat; James Abram Garfield, Ohio, Republican; George Frisbie Hoar, Mass., Republican

According to most historians, the Democrats agreed to accept the decision of the electoral commission only in return for a promise that all troops would be withdrawn from the carpetbag states, thereby ending the Reconstruction governments and giving the Democrats control in the South.

1876 ELECTORAL VOTE

There were 369 electoral votes from 38 states.

Hayes received 50.14 percent (185 votes—21 states) as follows: Calif. 6; Colo. 3; Fla. 4; Ill. 21; Iowa, 11; Kans. 5; La. 8; Me. 7; Mass. 13; Mich. 11; Minn. 5; Neb. 3; Nev. 3; N.H. 5; Ohio 22; Ore. 3; Pa. 29; R.I. 4; S.C. 7; Vt. 5; Wis. 10.

Tilden received 49.86 percent (184 votes—17 states) as follows: Ala. 10; Ark. 6; Conn. 6; Del. 3; Ga. 11; Ind. 15; Ky. 12; Md. 8; Miss. 8; Mo. 15; N.J. 9; N.Y. 35; N.C. 10; Tenn. 12; Tex. 8; Va. 11; W.Va. 5.

INAUGURATION

March 5, 1877

Rutherford Birchard Hayes took the oath of office on Monday, March 5, 1877, the oath being administered by Chief Justice Morrison Remick Waite at the east end of the Capitol.

As March 4 for the third time in the history of the republic fell on a Sunday, and as this was the most disputed election in history, Hayes took the oath of office privately on Saturday, March 3, in the Red Room of the White House. This was the first time that a President-elect had taken the oath in the White House.

A torchlight parade was held Monday night and a reception followed at the Willard Hotel, Washington, D.C. No inaugural parade or inaugural ball was held.

THE VICE PRESIDENT

Name—William Almon Wheeler (19th V.P.)

Date of birth—June 30, 1819

Place of birth—Malone, N.Y.

Political party—Republican

State represented—New York

Term of office—Mar. 4, 1877–Mar. 4, 1881

Age at inauguration—57 years, 247 days

Occupation after term—Lawyer

Date of death—June 4, 1887

Age at death—67 years, 339 days

Place of death—Malone, N.Y.

Burial place—Malone, N.Y.

ADDITIONAL DATA ON WHEELER

1838, student, University of Vermont, Burlington, Vt.

1845, admitted to bar; practiced in Malone, N.Y.

1846–1849, district attorney for Franklin County, N.Y.

1850–1851, New York State Assembly

1858–1859, New York State Senate

Mar. 4, 1861–Mar. 3, 1863, U.S. House of Representatives (from New York)

1867–1868, delegate to state constitutional conventions

Courtesy of The Library of Congress

William Wheeler, Vice President to Rutherford B. Hayes

Mar. 4, 1869–Mar. 3, 1877, U.S. House of Representatives (from New York)

Mar. 4, 1877–Mar. 4, 1881, Vice President under Rutherford B. Hayes

1881, resumed law practice

CABINET

March 4, 1877–March 3, 1881

State—Hamilton Fish, N.Y., continued from preceding administration; William Maxwell Evarts, N.Y., Mar. 12, 1877

Treasury—Lot Myrick Morrill, Me., continued from preceding administration; John Sherman, Ohio, Mar. 8, 1877; entered upon duties Mar. 10, 1877

War—James Donald Cameron, Pa., continued from preceding administration; George Washington McCrary, Iowa, Mar. 12, 1877; Alexander Ramsey, Minn., Dec. 10, 1879; entered upon duties Dec. 12, 1879

Attorney General—Alphonso Taft, Ohio, continued from preceding administration; Charles Devens, Mass., Mar. 12, 1877

Postmaster General—James Noble Tyner, Ind., continued from preceding administration; David McKendree Key, Tenn., Mar. 12, 1877; resigned June 1, 1880; served to Aug. 24, 1880; Horace Maynard, Tenn., June 2, 1880; entered upon duties Aug. 25, 1880

Navy—George Maxwell Robeson, N.J., continued from preceding administration; Richard Wigginton Thompson, Ind., Mar. 12, 1877; Alexander Ramsey, Minn. (secretary of war), ad interim Dec. 20, 1880; Nathan Goff, Jr., W. Va., Jan. 6, 1881

Interior—Zachariah Chandler, Mich., continued from preceding administration; Carl Schurz, Mo., Mar. 12, 1877

CONGRESS

FORTY-FIFTH CONGRESS

March 4, 1877–March 3, 1879

First session—Oct. 15, 1877–Dec. 3, 1877 (50 days)

Second session—Dec. 3, 1877–June 20, 1878 (200 days)

Third session—Dec. 2, 1878–Mar. 3, 1879 (92 days)

Special session of the Senate—Mar. 5, 1877–Mar. 17, 1877 (13 days)

Vice President—William Almon Wheeler, N.Y.

The cabinet of Rutherford B Hayes

Courtesy of The Library of Congress

President pro tempore of the Senate
—Thomas White Ferry, Mich., elected Mar. 5, 1877, special session of the Senate; Feb. 26, 1878; Apr. 17, 1878; Mar. 3, 1879

Secretary of the Senate—George Congdon Gorham, Calif.

Speaker of the House—Samuel Jackson Randall, Pa., reelected Oct. 15, 1877

Clerk of the House—George Madison Adams, Ky., reelected Oct. 15, 1877

FORTY-SIXTH CONGRESS

March 4, 1879–March 3, 1881

First session—Mar. 18, 1879–July 1, 1879 (106 days)

Second session—Dec. 1, 1879–June 16, 1880 (199 days)

Third session—Dec. 6, 1880–Mar. 3, 1881 (88 days)

Vice President—William Almon Wheeler, N.Y.

President pro tempore of the Senate
—Allen Granberry Thurman, Ohio

Secretary of the Senate—George Congdon Gorham, Mass.; John C. Burch, Tenn.; elected Mar. 24, 1879

Speaker of the House—Samuel Jackson Randall, Pa., reelected Mar. 18, 1879

Clerk of the House—George Madison Adams, Ky., reelected Mar. 18, 1879

APPOINTMENTS TO THE SUPREME COURT

Associate Justices

John Marshall Harlan, Ky., Nov. 29, 1877 (replaced David Davis)

William Burnham Woods, Ga., Dec. 21, 1880 (replaced William Strong)

IMPORTANT DATES IN THE PRESIDENCY

Feb. 12, 1877, first news dispatch telephoned to *Boston Globe*

Apr. 24, 1877, President Hayes withdrew federal troops from New Orleans, La.

May 10, 1877, opening ceremonies of the Permanent Exhibition, Philadelphia, Pa.

July 21, 1877, troops from Philadelphia, Pa., clashed with railroad strikers at Pittsburgh, Pa. (labor halt by railroad workers was the first significant nationwide strike)

Oct. 4, 1877, surrender of Chief Joseph ended war with Idaho Indians who were attempting to resettle in Canada

Feb. 19, 1878, Thomas Alva Edison obtained phonograph patent

Feb. 21, 1878, first telephone directory issued at New Haven, Conn.

Feb. 28, 1878, Bland-Allison Act permitting limited coinage of silver passed over presidential veto

Oct. 4, 1878, first Chinese embassy officials received by President Hayes

Jan. 1, 1879, resumption of specie payment—redemption of paper money in coin

Feb. 15, 1879, act passed to permit women to practice before U.S. Supreme Court

Mar. 3, 1879, Belva Ann Lockwood admitted to practice before U.S. Supreme Court

Mar. 3, 1879, office of U.S. Geological Survey director authorized

Oct. 21, 1879, first electric incandescent lamp of practical value invented by Edison

Nov. 1, 1879, Indian school opened at Carlisle, Pa.

Nov. 4, 1879, James and John Ritty granted patent on the cash register

1880, New York City (not including Brooklyn) became the first U.S. city with population of a million (1,206,299 shown in the 1880 census report)

Mar. 10, 1880, first Salvation Army services in U.S. held by Commissioner George Scott Railton and seven women at New York City

July 20, 1880, Egyptian obelisk, "Cleopatra's Needle," arrived at New York City

ADDITIONAL DATA ON HAYES

RUTHERFORD BIRCHARD HAYES

—was the second President born in Ohio.

—was the first President sworn in on March 3 in a private ceremony at the White House.

—was the third President inaugurated on March 5.

ABOLITION OF SEX DISCRIMINATION IN LAW PRACTICE BEFORE SUPREME COURT

President Hayes on February 15, 1879, signed "an act to relieve certain legal disabilities of women." It provided that any woman member of the bar of good moral character who had practiced for three years before a state Supreme Court was eligible for admittance to practice before the Supreme Court of the United States. The first woman admitted to practice before the Supreme Court was Belva Ann Bennett Lockwood.

HAYES VISITED THE WEST COAST

The first President in office to visit the West Coast was Hayes. He attended a reunion of the 23rd Ohio Regiment on September 1, 1880, at the Opera House, Canton, Ohio, and left from there for the West Coast. On September 8, 1880, he arrived at San Francisco, Calif. He stopped at the Palace Hotel in the same suite occupied by former President Grant on September 20, 1879, on his return from his world tour. Hayes returned to his home in Fremont, Ohio, on November 1, 1880. On the tour he was accompanied by his wife, his sons Birchard and Rutherford, General Sherman and his daughter, General and Mrs. Mitchell, and other friends.

TECHNOLOGICAL ADVANCES DURING HAYES'S TERM

Stymied politically because of the way he had achieved office, President Hayes was unable to push legislation through a Democrat-controlled Congress. However, technological advances continued apace during Hayes's term of office. The first telephone in the White House was installed by Alexander Graham Bell himself, and at the President's request Thomas Edison demonstrated one of his new inventions, the phonograph.

HAYES CONTENT ON RETIREMENT

President Hayes wrote a letter to Guy Bryan on January 1, 1881 in which he said, "Nobody ever left the Presidency with less regret, less disappointment, fewer heartburnings, or more general content with the result of his term (in his own heart, I mean) than I do." (Guy Bryan of Texas, a descendant of Stephen F. Austin, had been a classmate of Hayes at Kenyon College.)

HAYES ESCAPED INJURY

After President Garfield's inauguration on March 4, 1881, former President Hayes left Washington on a special train of the Baltimore and Potomac Railroad. A few miles out of Baltimore, Md., his train collided with another and the former President was thrown several feet out of his chair. Two people were killed and twenty were seriously injured in the collision. The train was delayed 24 hours. Hayes was with a party of friends in the fifth car. The three preceding cars contained the Cleveland City Troop, which had marched in the inaugural parade.

FURTHER READING

Hoogenboom, Ari. *The Presidency of Rutherford B. Hayes.* Rev. ed. 1988.

———. *Rutherford B. Hayes: Warrior and President.* 1995.

Howells, William D. *Sketch of the Life and Character of Rutherford B. Hayes.* 1876.

Morris, Roy Jr. *Fraud of the Century: Rutherford B. Hayes, Samuel Tilden, and the Stolen Election of 1876.* 2003.

Williams, Charles R. *Life of Rutherford Birchard Hayes.* 2 vols., 1914.

Courtesy of The Library of Congress

James Abram Garfield

Date of birth—Nov. 19, 1831

Place of birth—Orange, Ohio

Education—District school, Orange Township, Ohio; Geauga Seminary, Chester, Ohio, 1849–1850; Western Reserve Eclectic Institute, Hiram, Ohio, 1851–1854; Williams College, Williamstown, Mass., graduated with honors, Aug. 6, 1856; independent law study

Religion—Disciples of Christ

Ancestry—English, French

Career—Teacher, lawyer, state senator, general in Civil War, U.S. congressman

Political party—Republican

State represented—Ohio

Term of office—Mar. 4, 1881–Sept. 19, 1881

Term served—199 days

Administration—24th

Congresses—47th

Age at inauguration—49 years, 105 days

Lived after term—Died in office

Date of death—Sept. 19, 1881

Age at death—49 years, 304 days

Place of death—Elberon, N.J.

Burial place—Lake View Cemetery, Cleveland, Ohio

FAMILY

FATHER

Name—Abram Garfield

Date of birth—Dec. 28, 1799

Marriage—Eliza Ballou, Feb. 3, 1820, Zanesville, Ohio

Occupation—Farmer, canal constructor

Date of death—May 8, 1833

Place of death—Otsego County, Ohio

Age at death—33 years, 126 days

MOTHER

Name at birth—Eliza Ballou

Date of birth—Sept. 21, 1801

Place of birth—Richmond, N.H.

Marriage—Abram Garfield, Feb. 3, 1820, Zanesville, Ohio

Date of death—Jan. 21, 1888

Place of death—Mentor, Ohio

Age at death—86 years, 122 days

Courtesy of The Library of Congress

James Garfield and family in library

GARFIELD'S MOTHER WITNESSED INAUGURATION

Elizabeth Ballou Garfield was the first mother of a President to witness the inauguration of her son. The first act of President Garfield after his inauguration was to kiss his mother. Mrs. Garfield was also the first mother of a President to live at the White House.

SIBLINGS

James Abram Garfield was the fifth child in a family of five.

Children of Abram Garfield and Eliza Ballou Garfield

Mehitabel Garfield, b. Jan. 28, 1821
Thomas Garfield, b. Oct. 16, 1822
Mary Garfield, b. Oct. 19, 1824, d. Nov. 4, 1884
James Ballou Garfield, b. Oct. 21, 1826, d. Jan. 8, 1829
James Abram Garfield, b. Nov. 19, 1831, d. Sept. 19, 1881

MARRIAGE

Married—Lucretia Rudolph
Date of marriage—Nov. 11, 1858
Place of marriage—Hiram, Ohio
Age of wife at marriage—26 years, 206 days
Age of husband at marriage—26 years, 357 days
Years married—22 years, 312 days

CHILDREN

Eliza Arabella ("Trot") Garfield, b. July 3, 1860, Hiram, Ohio; d. Dec. 3, 1863, Hiram, Ohio

Harry Augustus Garfield, b. Oct. 11, 1863, Hiram, Ohio; m. June 14, 1888, Belle Hartford Mason, Williamstown, Mass.; d. Dec. 12, 1942, Williamstown, Mass.

James Rudolph Garfield, b. Oct. 17, 1865, Hiram, Ohio; m. Dec. 30, 1890, Helen Newell, Chicago, Ill.; d. Mar. 24, 1950, Cleveland, Ohio

Mary ("Molly") Garfield, b. Jan. 16, 1867, Washington, D.C.; m. June 14, 1888, Joseph Stanley-Brown, Mentor, Ohio; d. Dec. 30, 1947, Pasadena, Calif.

Irvin McDowell Garfield, b. Aug. 3, 1870, Hiram, Ohio; m. Oct. 16, 1906, Susan Emmons, Falmouth, Mass.; d. July 18, 1951, Boston, Mass.

Abram Garfield, b. Nov. 21, 1872, Washington, D.C.; m. Oct. 14, 1897, Sarah Granger Williams, Cleveland, Ohio; m. Apr. 12, 1947, Helen Grannis Matthews, Cleveland, Ohio; d. Oct. 16, 1958, Cleveland, Ohio

Edward Garfield, b. Dec. 25, 1874, Hiram, Ohio; d. Oct. 25, 1876, Washington, D.C.

THE PRESIDENT'S WIFE

Name at birth—Lucretia Rudolph
Date of birth—Apr. 19, 1832
Place of birth—Hiram, Ohio
Mother—Arabella Green Mason Rudolph
Father—Zebulon Rudolph
Father's occupation—Farmer, carpenter
Education—Geauga Seminary, Chester, Ohio; Western Reserve Eclectic Institute, Hiram, Ohio
Marriage—James Abram Garfield, Nov. 11, 1858, Hiram, Ohio
Children—Eliza Arabella Garfield, b. July 3, 1860, d. Dec. 3, 1863; Harry Augustus Garfield, b. Oct. 11, 1863, d. Dec. 12, 1942; James Rudolph Garfield, b. Oct. 17, 1865, d. Mar. 24, 1950; Mary ("Molly") Garfield, b. Jan. 16, 1867, d. Dec. 30, 1947; Irvin McDowell Garfield, b. Aug. 3, 1870, d. July 18, 1951; Abram Garfield, b. Nov. 21, 1872,

Courtesy of The Library of Congress

Lucretia Garfield, wife of James Garfield

242

d. Oct. 16, 1958; Edward Garfield, b. Dec. 25, 1874, d. Oct. 25, 1876

Occupation—Schoolteacher

Date of death—Mar. 14, 1918

Age at death—85 years, 329 days

Place of death—Pasadena, Calif.

Burial place—Cleveland, Ohio

Years younger than the President—151 days

Years she survived the President—36 years, 176 days

THE FIRST LADY

Lucretia ("Crete") Rudolph Garfield was First Lady of the land for less than seven months. She and her future husband were fellow students at two different schools in Ohio; at Western Reserve Eclectic Institute (now Hiram College), he was her tutor. They were both teachers for some years before and after their marriage.

IMPORTANT DATES IN THE PRESIDENT'S LIFE

1841, worked on farm; supported widowed mother

18—, attended district school three months every winter

1848, driver, helmsman, carpenter on Ohio canals

1849–1850, attended Geauga Seminary, Chester, Ohio

1849, taught one term in district school in Solon, Ohio

1851–1854, attended Western Reserve Eclectic Institute, Hiram, Ohio (now Hiram College)

1854–1856, attended Williams College

1857–1861, president of Western Reserve Eclectic Institute; taught Latin, Greek, higher mathematics, history, philosophy, English literature, and English rhetoric

1859, member, Ohio state senate

1860, admitted to the bar

Aug. 21, 1861, commissioned lieutenant colonel of 42nd Regiment, Ohio Volunteer Infantry

Nov. 27, 1861, promoted to colonel

Dec. 14, 1861, ordered into field at Big Sandy Valley (in charge of 18th Brigade)

Jan. 10, 1862, defeated Confederate forces under General Marshall at Paintville, Ky.

Jan. 11, 1862, promoted to brigadier general of volunteers

1862, commanded brigade at Shiloh but was not ordered into fighting until the second day, when the battle was over

1862, developed camp fever; relieved of command and given leave to recuperate

Feb. 1863, appointed chief of staff under General Rosecrans

Mar. 4, 1863–Nov. 8, 1880, U.S. House of Representatives (from Ohio) (elected in 1862 while in military service)

Sept. 19, 1863, promoted to major general of volunteers

Dec. 5, 1863, resigned from army to take seat in House of Representatives

1877, moved to Mentor, Ohio

1877, member of the Electoral Commission created by act of Congress approved Jan. 29, 1877, to decide the contests in the various states in the disputed Tilden-Hayes election of 1876

Jan. 13, 1880, elected by Ohio legislature to U.S. Senate for term beginning Mar. 4, 1881

June 8, 1880, nominated for the presidency at the Republican convention at Chicago

Nov. 4, 1880, elected President

Nov. 8, 1880, resigned from House of Representatives

Dec. 23, 1880, declined senatorial election, having been elected President

Mar. 4, 1881–Sept. 19, 1881, President

July 2, 1881, shot by Charles J. Guiteau while passing through the railroad depot, Washington, D.C.

Sept. 19, 1881, died from effects of the wound at Elberon, N.J.

ELECTIONS

THE ELECTION OF 1880

November 2, 1880

CANDIDATES

Republican Party (7th Convention)

June 2–5, 7–8, 1880, Exposition Hall, Chicago, Ill.

P: James Abram Garfield, Ohio
VP: Chester Alan Arthur, N.Y.

Garfield was nominated on the thirty-sixth ballot. Candidates for nomination and the votes they received on the first and thirty-sixth ballots:
Ulysses Simpson Grant, Ill., 304, 306
James Gillespie Blaine, Me., 284, 42
John Sherman, Ohio, 93, 3
George Franklin Edmunds, Vt., 34, 0
Elihu Benjamin Washburne, Ill., 30, 5
William Windom, Minn., 10, 0
James Abram Garfield, Ohio, 0, 399
Total number of votes: 755
Number necessary for nomination: 378

Democratic Party (13th Convention)

June 22–24, 1880, Music Hall, Cincinnati, Ohio

P: Winfield Scott Hancock, Pa.
VP: William Hayden English, Ind.

Hancock was nominated on the second ballot. Candidates for nomination and the votes they received on the first and second ballots:
Winfield Scott Hancock, Pa., 171, 705

Thomas Francis Bayard, Del., 153$^1/_2$, 2

Henry B. Payne, Ohio, 81, 0

Allen Granberry Thurman, Ohio, 68$^1/_2$, 0

Stephen Johnson Field, Calif., 65, 0

William Ralls Morrison, Ill., 62, 0

Thomas Andrews Hendricks, Ind., 49$^1/_2$, 30

Samuel Jones Tilden, N.Y., 38, 1
Thomas Ewing, Ohio, 10, 0
Horatio Seymour, N.Y., 8, 0
Samuel Jackson Randall, Pa., 6, 0
William Austin Hamilton Loveland, Colo., 5, 0

Joseph Ewing McDonald, Ind., 2, 0
George Brinton McClellan, N.J., 2, 0
Jeremiah Sullivan Black, Pa., 1, 0
James Edward English, Conn., 1, 0
Hugh Judge Jewett, Ohio, 1, 0
George Van Ness Lothrop, Mich., 1, 0
Joel Parker, N.J., 1, 0
Total number of votes
First ballot: 726$^1/_2$
Second ballot: 738
Number necessary for nomination: 492

Greenback Labor Party (National Party)

June 9–11, 1880, Exposition Hall, Chicago, Ill.

P: James Baird Weaver, Iowa
VP: Benjamin J. Chambers, Tex.

Weaver was nominated on the first ballot. Candidates for nomination and the votes they received:

James Baird Weaver, Iowa, 224$^1/_2$

Hendrick Bradley Wright, Pa., 126$^1/_2$
Stephen Devalson Dillaye, N.Y., 119
Benjamin Franklin Butler, Mass., 95
Solon Chase, Me., 89
Edward Phelps Allis, Wis., 41
Alexander Campbell, Ill., 21
Total number of votes: 716
Nomination made unanimous

Prohibition Party (National Prohibition Reform Party)

June 17, 1880, Halle's Hall, Cleveland, Ohio

P: Neal Dow, Me.
VP: Henry Adams Thompson, Ohio

Candidates were nominated by acclamation.

American Party

P: John Wolcott Phelps, Vt.
VP: Samuel Clarke Pomeroy, Kan.

This was an Anti-Masonic party.

1880 POPULAR VOTE
Republican Party, 4,454,416
Democratic Party, 4,444,952

Greenback Labor Party (National Party), 308,578

Prohibition Party, 10,305

American Party, 700

1880 ELECTORAL VOTE

There were 369 electoral votes from 38 states.

Garfield received 57.99 percent (214 votes—19 states) as follows: Calif. 1 (of the 6 votes); Colo. 3; Conn. 6; Ill. 21; Ind. 15; Iowa 11; Kan. 5; Me. 7; Mass. 13; Mich. 11; Minn. 5; Neb. 3; N.H. 5; Ohio 22; Ore. 3; Pa. 29; R.I. 4; Vt. 5; Wis. 10.

Hancock received 42.01 percent (155 votes—19 states) as follows: Ala. 10; Ark. 6; Calif. 5 (of the 6 votes); Del. 3; Fla. 4; Ga. 11; Ky. 12; La. 8; Md. 8; Miss. 8; Mo. 15; Nev. 3; N.J. 9; N.C. 10; S.C. 7; Tenn. 12; Tex. 8; Va. 11; W.Va. 5.

INAUGURATION

March 4, 1881

James Abram Garfield took the oath of office on Friday, March 4, 1881. Chief Justice Morrison Remick Waite administered the oath.

A heavy snowstorm, accompanied by strong winds, and the damp, penetrating cold kept the crowds down to a minimum. Despite the weather, about fifteen to twenty thousand people were in the two-and-a-half-hour parade. In the evening, a fireworks display thrilled the city.

The inaugural ball was held in the Hall of the Smithsonian Institution. An electric lamp, which was a great attraction to many of the guests, hung over the main entrance. The music was supplied by 150 musicians, members of the German Orchestra of Philadelphia under the direction of William Stoll, Jr., and the United States Marine Band under John Philip Sousa.

Those who attended the inaugural ball for President Garfield held at the Smithsonian Institution paid five dollars for tickets. Those who paid one dollar extra were entitled to a supper, which was served in a temporary building. The bill of fare consisted of pickled oysters, chicken salad, roast turkey, roast ham, roast beef, beef tongues, ice cream,

Courtesy of The Library of Congress

James Garfield taking the oath of office

water ices, assorted cakes, jellies, rolls, bread and butter, tea, coffee, lemonade, fruits, and relishes.

The caterers prepared 50 hams, 1,500 pounds of turkey, 100 gallons of oysters, 200 gallons of chicken salad, 150 gallons of ice cream, 50 gallons of water ices, 50 gallons of jelly, 350 pounds of butter, 15,000 cakes, 200 gallons of coffee, and 2,000 biscuits.

THE VICE PRESIDENT

Name—Chester Alan Arthur (20th V.P.)

Political party—Republican

State represented—New York

Term of office—Mar. 4, 1881–Sept. 19, 1881

Age at inauguration—50 years, 150 days

Occupation after term—President

For further biographical information, see the chapter on Chester Alan Arthur, 21st President, on page 251.

CABINET

March 4, 1881–September 19, 1881

State—William Maxwell Evarts, N.Y., continued from preceding administration; James Gillespie Blaine, Me., Mar. 5, 1881; entered upon duties Mar. 7, 1881

Treasury—Henry Flagg French, Mass. (assistant secretary), ad interim Mar. 4, 1881; William Windom, Minn., Mar. 5, 1881; entered upon duties Mar. 8, 1881

War—Alexander Ramsey, Minn., continued from preceding administration; Robert Todd Lincoln, Ill., Mar. 5, 1881; entered upon duties Mar. 11, 1881

Attorney General—Charles Devens, Mass., continued from preceding administration;

Wayne McVeagh, Pa., Mar. 5, 1881; entered upon duties Mar. 7, 1881

Postmaster General—Horace Maynard, Tenn., continued from preceding administration; Thomas Lemuel James, N.Y., Mar. 5, 1881; entered upon duties Mar. 8, 1881

Navy—Nathan Goff, Jr., W.Va., continued from preceding administration; William Henry Hunt, La., Mar. 5, 1881; entered upon duties Mar. 7, 1881

Interior—Carl Schurz, Mo., continued from preceding administration; Samuel Jordan Kirkwood, Iowa, Mar. 5, 1881; entered upon duties Mar. 8, 1881

CONGRESS

FORTY-SEVENTH CONGRESS

March 4, 1881–March 3, 1883

First session—Dec. 5, 1881–Aug. 8, 1882 (247 days)

Second session—Dec. 4, 1882–Mar. 3, 1883 (90 days)

Special session of the Senate—Mar. 4, 1881–May 20, 1881 (77 days); Oct. 10, 1881–Oct. 29, 1881 (20 days)

Vice President—Chester Alan Arthur, N.Y. (succeeded to the presidency on Sept. 19, 1881, on the death of James Abram Garfield)

President pro tempore of the Senate —Thomas Francis Bayard, Del., elected Oct. 10, 1881; David Davis, Ill., elected Oct. 13, 1881, resigned Mar. 3, 1883; George Franklin Edmunds, Vt., elected Mar. 3, 1883

Secretary of the Senate—John C. Burch, Tenn., died July 28, 1881; Francis Edwin Shober (chief clerk), N.C., appointed acting secretary by resolution of Oct. 24, 1881

Speaker of the House—Joseph Warren Keifer, Ohio, elected Dec. 5, 1881

Clerk of the House—George Madison Adams, Ky., Edward McPherson, Pa., elected Dec. 5, 1881

APPOINTMENTS TO THE SUPREME COURT

Associate Justice

Stanley Matthews, Ohio, May 12, 1881 (replaced Noah Haynes Swayne)

IMPORTANT DATES IN THE PRESIDENCY

Apr. 9, 1881, Post Office Department discovery of fraudulent payments for mail services caused several resignations

May 16, 1881, Senators Roscoe Conkling and Thomas Collier Platt of New York resigned because of a disagreement with President Garfield over federal appointments in New York

May 21, 1881, American Red Cross organized

ADDITIONAL DATA ON GARFIELD

JAMES ABRAM GARFIELD

—was the third President born in Ohio.
—was the first President whose mother was present at his inauguration.
—was the fourth President to die in office.
—was the second President assassinated.
—was the sixth President whose mother was alive when he was inaugurated.
—was the first President to review an inaugural parade from a stand in front of the White House.
—was the second President who was survived by his mother.
—was the first left-handed President.

GARFIELD DISPERSED HECKLERS

In 1863, General James Abram Garfield, speaking in favor of abolition at Chestertown, Md., was besieged by a barrage of eggs. Garfield stopped his speech and said, "I have just come from fighting brave rebels at Chickamauga; I shall not flinch before cowardly rebels." He continued his speech and his opponents dispersed.

GARFIELD CALMED THE MOB

Fifty thousand angry citizens answered a call to assemble at the Custom House, New York City, on April 15, 1865, ready to take the law into their own hands to avenge the death of President Lincoln. Two men in the crowd who expressed sentiments against the martyred President were attacked; one was killed, the other severely injured. About ten thousand people prepared to march to the office of the New York *World* crying "Vengeance!" A telegram that arrived from Washington stating "Seward is dying" stopped the march for a moment. Garfield, then visiting New York as a member of Congress, lifted his arm and in a loud voice addressed the mob:

Fellow-citizens! Clouds and darkness are round about Him! His pavilion is dark waters and thick clouds of the skies! Justice and judgment are the establishment of His throne! Mercy and truth shall go before His face! Fellow-citizens! God reigns and the Government at Washington still lives!

The crowd was deeply moved by Garfield's words and the threatened riot never occurred.

NOMINATION OF GARFIELD

At the Republican convention of 1880, on the first ballot, not one vote was cast for Garfield. The party was divided into two factions: "Stalwarts," who supported former President U.S. Grant, and "Half-Breeds," supporters of James G. Blaine, the "Plumed Knight" who served as U.S. senator from Maine. On the second, third, fourth, and fifth ballots, a delegate from Pennsylvania cast his vote for Garfield. A delegate from Alabama joined him on the sixth and seventh ballots. On the eighth ballot, Garfield lost the Alabama vote. The ninth, tenth, and eleventh ballots saw delegates from Massachusetts and one from Pennsylvania casting their votes for Garfield. The Massachusetts delegates did not vote for Garfield on the twelfth and thirteenth ballots but the Pennsylvania delegate still voted for Garfield. The next five ballots saw Garfield dropped from the running. He did not receive a single vote in the fourteenth, fifteenth, sixteenth, seventeenth, or eighteenth ballots.

The delegate from Pennsylvania brought Garfield back into the running, casting one vote for him in the nineteenth, twentieth, twenty-first, and twenty-second ballots. The next eight ballots, the twenty-third to the thirtieth, saw Garfield's strength double. Instead of one vote from Pennsylvania, he received two. The next three ballots, the thirty-first to the thirty-third, witnessed a drop in Garfield's strength. He managed to keep only one vote, that from Pennsylvania.

The thirty-fourth vote showed that the persistent delegate from Pennsylvania was a great strategist, because Wisconsin added 16 votes to his, giving Garfield 17 votes. The next ballot, the thirty-fifth, showed Garfield with 50 votes. On the next ballot, when Senator Blaine switched his support to Garfield, he received 399 of the 756 votes, which gave him the Republican nomination for the presidency. This was the largest number of ballots cast at a Republican convention up to that time.

Garfield was the only presidential nominee who was present in the convention hall to see himself nominated. Garfield was the leader of the Ohio delegation, which originally supported Secretary of the Treasury John Sherman for the presidency rather than declaring either for the Stalwarts or the Half-Breeds.

GARFIELD CAMPAIGNED IN GERMAN AS WELL AS IN ENGLISH

Garfield studied Latin and Greek at Williams College and chose German as an elective study. The latter language was of great help to him in his campaign for the German-American vote. On October 18, 1880, a delegation of about 500 German-Americans from Cleveland, Ohio, visited General Garfield at Mentor, Ohio. He welcomed them in German, "*Wilkommen alle*," and often used the German language in campaigning.

TEN THOUSAND VOTES DETERMINED THE PRESIDENCY

A plurality of about one tenth of 1 percent of the popular vote enabled Garfield to become President of the United States.

Garfield received 4,454,416 votes; Hancock, the Democratic candidate, received 4,444,952 votes. With a plurality of 9,464 votes Garfield won 214 of the electoral votes, as compared with 155 for Hancock.

GARFIELD QUALIFIED FOR THREE FEDERAL POSITIONS AT THE SAME TIME

On November 2, 1880, Garfield qualified for three federal positions. He was a congressman from Ohio, having taken office in the House of Representatives on March 4, 1863, and having served in the 38th Congress and the eight succeeding Congresses. On January 13, 1880, while he was serving in the House of Representatives, he was elected by the legislature of Ohio to serve in the United States Senate for the term beginning March 4, 1881. On November 2, 1880, Garfield was elected President of the United States. On that date, he was President-elect, senator-elect, and a member of the House of Representatives (the first member elected President while serving in the House).

As the senatorial and presidential terms began on the same day, Garfield surrendered his seat and never sat in the Senate. (John Sherman served in his place.) On November 8, 1880, Garfield resigned from the House and on March 4, 1881, he was inaugurated President of the United States.

GARFIELD JUDGES GARFIELD

Garfield said:

I do not care what others say and think about me. But there is one man's opinion which I very much value, and that is the opinion of James Garfield. Others I need not think about. I can get away from them, but I have to be with him all the time. He is with me when I rise up and when I lie down; when I eat and talk; when I go out and come in. It makes a great difference whether he thinks well of me or not.

GARFIELD ASSASSINATED

Garfield was shot on July 2, 1881, at the Baltimore and Potomac Railway Depot, Washington, D.C., by Charles Julius Guiteau, a disappointed office-seeker who had

Courtesy of The Library of Congress

The assassination of James Garfield

wanted to be appointed United States consul at Paris. The President survived 80 days, during which time his only official act was the signing of an extradition paper. On September 6, 1881, Garfield was taken to Elberon, N.J., to recuperate, but he died there of blood poisoning on September 19, 1881. He had three funerals, one at Elberon, N.J., another at Washington, D.C., where his body rested in state for three days, and the third at Cleveland, Ohio, where he was buried.

Guiteau was tried on November 14, 1881. The verdict was rendered on January 25, 1882, and he was hanged at the jail at Washington, D.C., on June 30, 1882.

PRESIDENT GARFIELD'S LAST LETTER

August 11, 1881
Dear Mother:

Don't be disturbed by conflicting reports about my condition. It is true I am still weak and on my back, but I am gaining every day and need only time and patience to bring me through. Give my love to all the relatives and friends and especially to sisters Hetty and Mary.

Your loving son,
JAMES ABRAM GARFIELD

Mrs. Eliza Garfield
Hiram, Ohio.

FURTHER READING

Ackerman, Kenneth D. *The Dark Horse: The Surprise Election and Political Murder of President James A. Garfield*. 2003.

Doenecke, Justus D. *The Presidencies of James A. Garfield and Chester A. Arthur*. 1981.

Leech, Margaret. *The Garfield Orbit*. 1978.

Peskin, Allan. *Garfield: A Biography*. 1999.

Smith, Theodore C. *The Life and Letters of James Abram Garfield*. 2 vols., 1968

Courtesy of The Library of Congress

Chester Alan Arthur

Date of birth—Oct. 5, 1829

Place of birth—Fairfield, Vt.

Education—Attended public school at Union Village (now Greenwich), N.Y.; the Lyceum, Schenectady, N.Y.; Union College, Schenectady, N.Y., graduated July 1848; private law study in Ballston Spa, N.Y., and at law office of E. D. Culver, New York, N.Y.

Religion—Episcopalian

Ancestry—Scotch-Irish, English

Career—Teacher, lawyer, inspector general and quartermaster general in state militia in Civil War, state Republican chairman, customhouse collector of Port of New York, Vice President

Political party—Republican

State represented—New York

Term of office—Sept. 20, 1881–Mar. 4, 1885 (Arthur succeeded to the presidency on the death of James Abram Garfield)

Term served—3 years, 166 days

Administration—24th

Congresses—47th, 48th

Age at inauguration—51 years, 350 days

Lived after term—1 year, 260 days

Occupation after term—Lawyer

Date of death—Nov. 18, 1886

Age at death—57 years, 44 days

Place of death—New York, N.Y.

Burial place—Rural Cemetery, Albany, N.Y.

FAMILY

FATHER

Name—William Arthur

Date of birth—Dec. 5, 1796

Place of birth—County Antrim, Ireland

Marriage—Malvina Stone, Apr. 12, 1821, Dunham, Quebec, Canada

Occupation—Teacher, author, editor, Baptist minister

Date of death—Oct. 27, 1875

Place of death—Newtonville, N.Y.

Age at death—78 years, 326 days

MOTHER

Name at birth—Malvina Stone

Date of birth—Apr. 29, 1802

Place of birth—Berkshire, Vt.

Marriage—William Arthur, Apr. 12, 1821, Dunham, Quebec, Canada

Date of death—Jan. 16, 1869

Place of death—Newtonville, N.Y.

Age at death—66 years, 262 days

SIBLINGS

Chester Alan Arthur was the fifth child and the oldest son in a family of nine.

Children of William Arthur and Malvina Stone Arthur

Regina Malvina Arthur, b. Mar. 8, 1822, d. Nov. 15, 1910

Jane Arthur, b. Mar. 14, 1824, d. Apr. 15, 1842

Almeda Arthur, b. Jan. 22, 1826, d. Mar. 26, 1899

Ann Eliza Arthur, b. Jan. 1, 1828, d. Apr. 10, 1915

Chester Alan Arthur, b. Oct. 5, 1829, d. Nov. 18, 1886

Malvina Arthur, b. 1832, d. Jan. 16, 1920

William Arthur, b. May 28, 1834, d. Feb. 27, 1915

George Arthur, b. May 24, 1836, d. Mar. 8, 1838

Mary Arthur, b. June 5, 1841, d. Jan. 8, 1917

MARRIAGE

Married—Ellen Lewis Herndon

Date of marriage—Oct. 25, 1859

Place of marriage—New York, N.Y.

Age of wife at marriage—22 years, 56 days

Age of husband at marriage—30 years, 20 days

Years married—20 years, 79 days

CHILDREN

William Lewis Herndon Arthur, b. Dec. 10, 1860, New York, N.Y.; d. July 7, 1863, Englewood, N.J.

Chester Alan Arthur, b. July 25, 1864, New York, N.Y.; m. May 8, 1900, Myra Townsend Fithian Andrews, Montreux, Switzerland; m. Nov. 3, 1934, Rowena Dashwood Graves, Colorado Springs, Colo.; d. July 17, 1937, Colorado Springs, Colo.

Ellen Herndon Arthur, b. Nov. 21, 1871; m. Charles Pinkerton; d. Sept. 6, 1915, Mount Kisco, N.Y.

THE PRESIDENT'S WIFE

Name at birth—Ellen Lewis Herndon

Date of birth—Aug. 30, 1837

Place of birth—Culpeper Court House, Va.

Mother—Frances Elizabeth Hansbrough Herndon

Father—William Lewis Herndon

Father's occupation—Captain, U.S. Navy

Marriage—Chester Alan Arthur, Oct. 25, 1859, New York, N.Y.

Children—William Lewis Herndon Arthur, b. Dec. 10, 1860, d. July 7, 1863; Chester Alan Arthur, b. July 25, 1864, d. July 17, 1937; Ellen Herndon Arthur, b. Nov. 21, 1871, d. Sept. 6, 1915

Date of death—Jan. 12, 1880

Age at death—42 years, 135 days

Place of death—New York, N.Y.

Burial place—Albany, N.Y.

Years younger than the President—7 years, 329 days

Years the President survived her—6 years, 310 days

Courtesy of The Library of Congress

Ellen Arthur, wife of Chester Arthur

HOSTESS AT THE WHITE HOUSE

President Arthur's wife, Ellen Herndon Arthur, died before her husband's election as Vice President. As Arthur's daughter, Ellen, was only 10 years of age when he succeeded to the presidency, the duties of mistress of the White House were assumed by his sister, Mary Arthur McElroy of Albany, N.Y.

IMPORTANT DATES IN THE PRESIDENT'S LIFE

1845–1848, taught school at Schaghticoke, north of Albany, N.Y., during winter vacations from college

1848, graduated from Union College

1851–1852, taught school in North Pownal, Vt.

1852–1853, principal of academy in Cohoes, N.Y.

1854, admitted to the bar; practiced at New York, N.Y.

1857, judge advocate of Second Brigade, New York State Militia

1861, appointed engineer-in-chief on the staff of Governor Morgan with the rank of brigadier-general, New York State Militia

July 10–Dec. 31, 1862, quartermaster-general with the rank of brigadier-general

1863, resumed practice of law at New York, N.Y.

Nov. 24, 1871–July 11, 1878, collector of the Port of New York (appointed by President Grant)

July 11, 1878, removed as collector by executive order issued by President Hayes

1878, resumed practice of law at New York, N.Y.

1880, delegate from New York to Republican National Convention at Chicago, Ill., to name Grant for a third term

Nov. 5, 1880, nominated for the vice presidency

Mar. 4, 1881–Sept. 19, 1881, Vice President under James Abram Garfield

Sept. 20, 1881–Mar. 4, 1885, President (succeeded to the presidency on the death of Garfield)

June 6, 1884, unsuccessful candidate for presidential nomination on the Republican ticket

INAUGURATION

September 20, 1881

Chester Alan Arthur, who succeeded to the presidency upon the death of President Garfield, took the oath of office at his residence, 123 Lexington Avenue, New York, N.Y., at 2 A.M. on September 20, 1881. (Garfield had died at 10:30 P.M. on September 19.) The oath was administered by New York Supreme Court Justice John R. Brady.

The oath was repeated on Thursday, September 22, 1881, in the Vice President's room at the Capitol, where it was administered by Chief Justice Morrison Remick Waite in the presence of former Presidents Hayes and Grant.

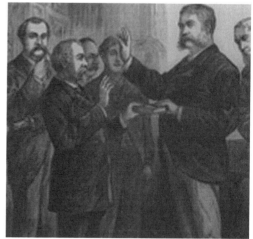

The inauguration of Chester Arthur

CABINET

September 20, 1881–March 3, 1885

State—James Gillespie Blaine, Me., continued from preceding administration; Frederick Theodore Frelinghuysen, N.J., Dec. 12, 1881; entered upon duties Dec. 19, 1881

Treasury—William Windom, Minn., continued from preceding administration; Charles James Folger, N.Y., Oct. 27, 1881; entered upon duties Nov. 14, 1881; died Sept. 4, 1884; Charles E. Coon, N.Y. (assistant secretary), ad interim Sept. 4, 1884; Henry Flagg French, Mass. (assistant secretary), ad interim Sept. 8, 1884; Charles E. Coon, N.Y. (assistant secretary), ad interim Sept. 15, 1884; Walter Quintin Gresham, Ind., Sept. 24, 1884; Henry Flagg French, Mass. (assistant secretary), ad interim Oct. 29, 1884; Hugh McCulloch, Ind., Oct. 28, 1884; entered upon duties Oct. 31, 1884

War—Robert Todd Lincoln, Ill., continued from preceding administration

Attorney General—Wayne MacVeagh, Pa., continued from preceding administration; Samuel Field Phillips, N.C. (solicitor general), ad interim Nov. 14, 1881; Benjamin Harris Brewster, Pa., Dec. 19, 1881; entered upon duties Jan. 3, 1882

Postmaster General—Thomas Lemuel James, N.Y., continued from preceding administration; recommissioned Oct. 27, 1881; Timothy Otis Howe, Wis., Dec. 20, 1881; entered upon duties Jan. 5, 1882, died Mar. 25, 1883; Frank Hatton, Iowa (first assistant postmaster general), ad interim Mar. 26 1883; Walter Quintin Gresham, Ind., Apr. 3, 1883; entered upon duties Apr. 11, 1883; Frank Hatton, Iowa (first assistant postmaster general), ad interim Sept. 25, 1884; Frank Hatton, Iowa, Oct. 14, 1884

Navy—William Henry Hunt, La.., continued from preceding administration; William Eaton Chandler, N.H., Apr. 12, 1882; entered upon duties Apr. 17, 1882

Interior—Samuel Jordan Kirkwood, Iowa, continued from preceding administration; Henry Moore Teller, Colo., Apr. 6, 1882; entered upon duties Apr. 17, 1882

CONGRESS

FORTY-EIGHTH CONGRESS

March 4, 1883–March 3, 1885

First session—Dec. 3, 1883–July 7, 1884 (218 days)

Second session—Dec. 1, 1884–Mar. 3, 1885 (93 days)

Vice President—Chester Alan Arthur succeeded to the presidency on Sept. 19, 1881, on the death of James Abram Garfield; the office was vacant for the remainder of the term.

President pro tempore of the Senate—George Franklin Edmunds, Vt., reelected Jan. 14, 1884

Secretary of the Senate—Francis Edwin Shober (chief clerk), N.C.; Anson George McCook, N.Y., elected Dec. 18, 1883

Speaker of the House—John Griffin Carlisle, Ky., elected Dec. 3, 1883

Clerk of the House—Edward McPherson, Pa., John Bullock Clark, Jr., Mo., elected Dec. 4, 1883

APPOINTMENTS TO THE SUPREME COURT

Associate Justices

Horace Gray, Mass., Dec. 20, 1881 (replaced Nathan Clifford)

Roscoe Conkling, N.Y., Feb. 1882 (declined appointment)

Samuel Blatchford, N.Y., Mar. 22, 1882
(replaced Ward Hunt)

IMPORTANT DATES IN THE PRESIDENCY

May 22, 1882, treaty of peace, amity, commerce, and navigation signed with Korea

Aug. 5, 1882, exclusion act passed restricting Chinese immigration

Mar. 9, 1883, Civil Service Commission organized

Nov. 18, 1883, standard time adopted

1884, United States granted exclusive right to establish coaling and repair station at Pearl Harbor, Oahu, Hawaii, by Hawaiian king

May 17, 1884, establishment of territorial government in Alaska (formed from territory ceded to the United States by Russia by treaty of March 30, 1867)

Dec. 1884, treaty with Nicaragua for construction of a canal (it was never built, but the idea was later realized in the form of the Panama Canal)

Dec. 16, 1884, President Arthur pressed a button at Washington, D.C., to open the World's Industrial and Cotton Centennial Exposition at New Orleans, La.

Feb. 21, 1885, Washington monument dedicated, Washington, D.C.

ADDITIONAL DATA ON ARTHUR

CHESTER ALAN ARTHUR

—was the first President born in Vermont.
—was the eighth President who was a resident of a state other than his native state.
—was the fourth widower inaugurated President.

THREE PRESIDENTS IN ONE YEAR

In 1881, for the second time in American history, there were three Presidents in one year. Rutherford Birchard Hayes concluded his term on March 3, 1881. On March 4, 1881, James Abram Garfield was inaugurated President. Garfield died September 19, 1881, on which date Chester Alan Arthur, his Vice President, became President.

In 1841, the three Presidents of the United States had been Martin Van Buren, William Henry Harrison, and John Tyler.

FURTHER READING

Doenecke, Justus D. *The Presidencies of James A. Garfield and Chester A. Arthur.* 1981.

Howe, George F. *Chester A. Arthur.* 1935.
Reeves, Thomas C. *Gentleman Boss.* 1975.

Courtesy of The Library of Congress

Grover Cleveland

Name at birth—Stephen Grover Cleveland

Date of birth—Mar. 18, 1837

Place of birth—Caldwell, N.J.

Education—Tutored at home to age 11; academy at Fayetteville, N.Y.; Clinton Liberal Institute, Clinton, N.Y., 1850–1851; Fayetteville academy 1851–1853; private study at law office of Rogers, Bowen, and Rogers, Buffalo, N.Y.

Religion— Presbyterian

Ancestry—English, Irish

Career—Lawyer, assistant district attorney, sheriff, mayor of Buffalo, governor of New York

Political party—Democratic

State represented—New York

Term of office—Mar. 4, 1885–Mar. 4, 1889

Term served—4 years

Administration—25th

Congresses—49th, 50th

Age at inauguration—47 years, 351 days

Lived after term—19 years, 112 days

Occupation after term—President 1893–1897; thereafter, trustee of Princeton University

Date of death—June 24, 1908

Age at death—71 years, 98 days

Place of death—Princeton, N.J.

Burial place—Princeton, N.J.

FAMILY

FATHER

Name—Richard Falley Cleveland

Date of birth—June 19, 1804

Place of birth—Norwich, Conn.

Marriage—Anne Neal, Sept. 10, 1829, Baltimore, Md.

Occupation—Teacher, Congregational minister, district secretary of missionary organization

Date of death—Oct. 1, 1853

Place of death—Holland Patent, N.Y.

Age at death—49 years, 104 days

MOTHER

Name at birth—Anne Neal

Date of birth—Feb. 4, 1806

Place of birth—Baltimore, Md.

Marriage—Richard Falley Cleveland, Sept. 10, 1829, Baltimore, Md.

Date of death—July 19, 1882

Place of death—Holland Patent, N.Y.

Age at death—76 years, 165 days

SIBLINGS

Grover Cleveland was the fifth child in a family of nine.

Children of Richard Falley Cleveland and Anne Neal Cleveland

Anna Neal Cleveland, b. July 9, 1830, d. 1909

William Neal Cleveland, b. Apr. 7, 1832, d. Jan. 15, 1906

Mary Allen Cleveland, b. Nov. 16, 1833, d. July 28, 1914

Richard Cecil Cleveland, b. July 31, 1835, d. Oct. 22, 1872

(Stephen) Grover Cleveland, b. Mar. 18, 1837, d. June 24, 1908

Margaret Louise Falley Cleveland, b. Oct. 28, 1838, d. Mar. 5, 1932

Lewis Frederick Cleveland, b. May 2, 1841, d. Oct. 22, 1872

Susan Sophia Cleveland, b. Sept. 2, 1843, d. Nov. 4, 1938

Rose Elizabeth Cleveland, b. June 13, 1846, d. Nov. 26, 1918

MARRIAGE

Married—Frances Clara Folsom

Date of marriage—June 2, 1886

Place of marriage—White House, Washington, D.C.

Age of wife at marriage—21 years, 316 days

Age of husband at marriage—49 years, 76 days

Years married—22 years, 22 days

CHILDREN

Ruth Cleveland, b. Oct. 3, 1891, New York, N.Y.; d. Jan. 7, 1904, Princeton, N.J.

Esther Cleveland, b. Sept. 9, 1893, in White House, Washington, D.C.; m. Mar. 14, 1918, William Sydney Bence Bosanquet, London, England; d. June 26, 1980

Marion Cleveland, b. July 7, 1895, Buzzards Bay, Mass.; m. Nov. 28, 1917, William Stanley Dell, Princeton, N.J.; m. July 25, 1926, John Harlan Amen, Tamworth, N.H.; d. June 18, 1977, New York City

Richard Folsom Cleveland, b. Oct. 28, 1897, Princeton, N.J.; m. June 20, 1923, Ellen Douglas Gailor, Memphis, Tenn.; m. 1943, Jessie Maxwell Black; d. Jan. 10, 1974, Baltimore, Md.

Francis Grover Cleveland, b. July 18, 1903, Buzzards Bay, Mass.; m. June 20, 1925, Alice Erdman, Princeton, N.J. (d. 1992); d. Nov. 8, 1995, Wolfeboro, N.H.

Ruth Cleveland, the President's first child, was born between her father's terms in office. The "Baby Ruth," a popular candy bar, was named for her.

Esther Cleveland, the President's second child, was the first child of a President to be born in the White House.

THE PRESIDENT'S WIFE

Name at birth—Frances Clara Folsom

Date of birth—July 21, 1864

Place of birth—Folsomville, N.Y.

Mother—Emma Cornelia Harmon Folsom

Father—Oscar Folsom

Father's occupation—Lawyer

Education—Wells College, Aurora, N.Y., B.A., June 1885

First marriage—Grover Cleveland, June 2, 1886, White House, Washington, D.C. (d. June 24, 1908)

Second marriage—Thomas Jex Preston, Jr., Feb. 10, 1913, Princeton, N.J.

Children from first marriage—Ruth Cleveland, b. Oct. 3, 1891, d. Jan. 7, 1904; Esther Cleveland, b. Sept. 9, 1893; Marion Cleveland, b. July 7, 1895, d. June 15, 1977; Richard Folsom Cleveland, b. Oct. 28, 1897, d. Jan. 10, 1974; Francis Grover Cleveland, b. July 18, 1903, d. Nov. 8, 1995

Children from second marriage—None

Date of death—Oct. 29, 1947; Baltimore, Md.

Age at death—83 years, 100 days

Place of death—Baltimore, Md.

Burial place—Princeton, N.J.

Courtesy of The Library of Congress

Frances Cleveland, wife of Grover Cleveland

Years younger than the President—27 years, 125 days

Years she survived the President—39 years, 137 days

THE FIRST LADY

Before President Cleveland's marriage to Frances Folsom, his sister, Rose Elizabeth Cleveland, acted as White House hostess.

Frances Cleveland was the first First Lady to have a baby during her husband's term in office. She gave birth to their second child, Esther, in the White House on September 9, 1893, and to their third child, Marion, on July 7, 1896. The Clevelands' eldest child was born during the hiatus between Grover Cleveland's two nonconsecutive terms. Two more children were born after he left office.

FIRST PRESIDENT'S WIDOW TO REMARRY

On February 10, 1913, Frances Cleveland married Thomas Jex Preston, Jr., a professor of archaeology at Princeton University. She was the first wife of a President to remarry after his death.

IMPORTANT DATES IN THE PRESIDENT'S LIFE

Oct. 5, 1853, appointed assistant teacher, New York Institution for the Blind

1855, hired to edit the *American Shorthorn Handbook*

1855–1858, clerk and copyist for a Buffalo, N.Y., law firm

1859, admitted to the bar

Nov. 1862, elected ward supervisor, Buffalo, N.Y.

1863–1865, assistant district attorney of Erie County, N.Y.

1865, unsuccessful candidate for district attorney

1871–1873, sheriff of Erie County

1882, mayor of Buffalo

Jan. 1, 1883–Jan. 6, 1885, governor of New York

July 11, 1884, nominated for the presidency by the Democratic convention at Chicago, Ill.

Mar. 4, 1885–Mar. 4, 1889, President (first term)

June 5, 1888, nominated for the presidency by the Democratic convention at St. Louis, Mo.

Nov. 6, 1888, defeated in election by Republican candidate, Benjamin Harrison

Mar. 4, 1889, returned to law practice

June 2, 1892, nominated for the presidency by the Democratic convention at Chicago

Mar. 4, 1893–Mar. 4, 1897, President (second term)

Oct. 15, 1901, trustee of Princeton University

ELECTIONS

THE ELECTION OF 1884

November 4, 1884

CANDIDATES

Democratic Party (14th Convention)

July 8–11, 1884, Exposition Hall, Chicago, Ill.

P: Grover Cleveland, N.Y.
VP: Thomas Andrews Hendricks, Ind.

Cleveland was nominated on the second ballot. Candidates for nomination and the votes they received on the first and second ballots:

Grover Cleveland, N.Y., 392, 683

Thomas Francis Bayard, Del., 170, $81\frac{1}{2}$

Allen Granberry Thurman, Ohio, 88, 4

Samuel Jackson Randall, Pa., 78, 4

Joseph Ewing McDonald, Ind., 56, 2

John Griffin Carlisle, Ky., 27, 0

Roswell Pettibone Flower, N.Y., 4, 0

George Hoadly, Ohio, 3, 0

Thomas Andrews Hendricks, Ind., 1, $45\frac{1}{2}$

Samuel Jones Tilden, N.Y., 1, 0

Total number of votes: 820

Number necessary for nomination: 547

Republican Party (8th Convention)

June 3–6, 1884, Exposition Hall, Chicago, Ill.

P: James Gillespie Blaine, Me.
VP: John Alexander Logan, Ill.

Blaine was nominated on the fourth ballot. Candidates for nomination and the votes they received on the first and fourth ballots:

James Gillespie Blaine, Me., $334^1/_2$, 541
Chester Alan Arthur, N.Y., 278, 207
George Franklin Edmunds, Vt., 93, 41
John Alexander Logan, Ill., $63^1/_2$, 7
John Sherman, Ohio, 30, 0
Joseph Roswell Hawley, Conn., 13, 15
Robert Todd Lincoln, Ill., 4, 2
William Tecumseh Sherman, Mo., 2, 0
Total number of votes:
First ballot: 818
Fourth ballot: 813

Number necessary for nomination: 411

Anti-Monopoly Party

May 14, 1884, Hershey Music Hall, Chicago, Ill.

P: Benjamin Franklin Butler, Mass.
VP: Absolom Madden West, Miss.

Butler was nominated on the first ballot. Candidates for nomination and the votes they received:
Benjamin Franklin Butler, Mass., 124
Allen Granberry Thurman, Ohio, 7
Solon Chase, Me., 1

This political group was formed as The Anti-Monopoly Organization of the United States. West was not nominated at the convention. His nomination was decided by a committee appointed to negotiate with other political parties.

Greenback Party (National Greenback Labor Party)

May 28–29, 1884, English's Opera House, Indianapolis, Ind.

P: Benjamin Franklin Butler, Mass.
VP: Absolom Madden West, Miss.

Butler was nominated on the first ballot. Candidates for nomination and the votes they received:
Benjamin Franklin Butler, Mass., 323
Jesse Harper, Ill., 98
Solon Chase, Me., 2

Edward Phelps Allis, Wis., 1
Total number of votes: 424

The Greenback and Anti-Monopoly parties endorsed the same candidates.

Prohibition Party

July 23–24, 1884, Lafayette Hall, Pittsburgh, Pa.

P: John Pierce St. John, Kan.
VP: William Daniel, Md.

American Prohibition Party

June 19, 1884, Chicago, Ill.

P: Samuel Clarke Pomeroy, Kan.
VP: John A. Conant, Conn.

Equal Rights Party

September 20, 1884, San Francisco, Calif.

P: Belva Ann Bennett Lockwood, D.C.
VP: Marietta Lizzie Bell Stow, Calif.

This convention was held by the Woman's Rights Party or Female Suffragettes. Suffrage for women was its principal aim, but it also endorsed equal property rights for women, the discouragement of trade in liquor, and the distribution of public lands to settlers only.

1884 POPULAR VOTE

Democratic Party, 4,874,986
Republican Party, 4,851,981
Greenback Party and Anti-Monopoly Party, 175,370
Prohibition Party, 150,369

Grover Cleveland delivering his inaugural address

1884 ELECTORAL VOTE

There were 401 electoral votes from 38 states.

Cleveland received 54.61 percent (219 votes—20 states) as follows: Ala. 10; Ark. 7; Conn. 6; Del. 3; Fla. 4; Ga. 12; Ind. 15; Ky. 13; La. 8; Md. 8; Miss. 9; Mo. 16; N.J. 9; N.Y. 36; N.C. 11; S.C. 9; Tenn. 12; Tex. 13; Va. 12; W.Va. 6.

Blaine received 45.39 percent (182 votes—18 states) as follows: Calif. 8; Colo. 3; Ill. 22; Iowa 13; Kan. 9; Me. 6; Mass. 14; Mich. 13; Minn. 7; Neb. 5; Nev. 3; N.H. 4; Ohio 23; Ore. 3; Pa. 30; R.I. 4; Vt. 4; Wis. 11.

INAUGURATION

March 4, 1885

Grover Cleveland took the oath of office on his mother's Bible on Wednesday, March 4, 1885, on the east portico of the Capitol. The oath was administered by Chief Justice Morrison Remick Waite. The President reviewed the parade from the White House.

THE VICE PRESIDENT

Name—Thomas Andrews Hendricks (21st V.P.)

Date of birth—Sept. 7, 1819

Place of birth—Muskingum County, Ohio

Political party—Democratic

State represented—Indiana

Term of office—Mar. 4, 1885–Nov. 25, 1885

Age at inauguration—65 years, 178 days

Occupation after term—Died in office

Date of death—Nov. 25, 1885

Age at death—66 years, 79 days

Place of death—Indianapolis, Ind.

Burial place—Indianapolis, Ind.

ADDITIONAL DATA ON HENDRICKS

1841, graduated from Hanover College, Hanover, Ind.

1843, admitted to bar; practiced at Shelbyville, Ind.

1848, Indiana State House of Representatives

1849, Indiana State Senate

1851, member, Indiana State Constitutional Convention

Mar. 4, 1851–Mar. 3, 1855, U.S. House of Representatives (from Indiana)

1854, unsuccessful candidate for reelection

1855–1859, commissioner, General Land Office

Courtesy of The Library of Congress

Thomas Andrews Hendricks, Vice President to Grover Cleveland

1860, unsuccessful candidate for governor of Indiana

Mar. 4, 1863–Mar. 3, 1869, U.S. Senate (from Indiana)

1873–1877, governor of Indiana

1876, unsuccessful candidate for Vice President on Democratic ticket with Tilden

Mar. 4, 1885–Nov. 25, 1885, Vice President under Grover Cleveland

CABINET

March 4, 1885–March 3, 1889

State—Frederick Theodore Frelinghuysen, N.J., continued from preceding administration; Thomas Francis Bayard, Del., Mar. 6, 1885

Treasury—Hugh McCulloch, Ind., continued from preceding administration; Daniel Manning, N.Y., Mar. 6, 1885; entered upon duties Mar. 8, 1885; Charles Stebbins Fairchild, N.Y., Apr. 1, 1887

War—Robert Todd Lincoln, Ill., continued from preceding administration; William Crowninshield Endicott, Mass., Mar. 6, 1885

Attorney General—Benjamin Harris Brewster, Pa., continued from preceding administration; Augustus Hill Garland, Ark., Mar. 6, 1885; entered upon duties Mar. 9, 1885

Postmaster General—Frank Hatton, Iowa, continued from preceding administration; William Freeman Vilas, Wis., Mar. 6, 1885; Donald McDonald Dickinson, Mich., Jan. 16, 1888

Navy—William Eaton Chandler, N.H., continued from preceding administration; William Collins Whitney, N.Y., Mar. 6, 1885

Interior—Merritt L. Josly, Ill. (assistant secretary), ad interim Mar. 4, 1885; Lucius Quintus Cincinnatus Lamar, Miss., Mar. 6, 1885; Henry Lowndes Muldrow, Miss. (first assistant secretary), ad interim Jan. 11, 1888; William Freeman Vilas, Wis., Jan. 16, 1888

Agriculture—Norman Jay Colman, Mo., Feb. 13, 1889

CONGRESS

FORTY-NINTH CONGRESS

March 4, 1885–March 3, 1887

First session—Dec. 7, 1885–Aug. 5, 1886 (242 days)

Second session—Dec. 6, 1886–March 3, 1887 (88 days)

Special session of the Senate—Mar. 4, 1885–Apr. 2, 188 (30 days)

Vice President—Thomas Andrews Hendricks, Ind., died Nov. 25, 1885

President pro tempore of the Senate—John Sherman, Ohio; elected Dec. 7, 1885; resigned effective Feb. 26, 1887; John James Ingalls, Kan., elected Feb. 25, 1887

Courtesy of The Library of Congress

Grover Cleveland's cabinet: Front row, left to right: Thomas F. Bayard, Cleveland, Daniel Manning, Lucius Q. C. Lamar. Back row, left to right: William F. Vilas, William C. Whitney, William C. Endicott, Augustus H. Garland

Secretary of the Senate—Anson George McCook, N.Y.

Speaker of the House—John Griffin Carlisle, Ky., reelected Dec. 7, 1885

Clerk of the House—John Bullock Clark, Mo., reelected Dec. 7, 1885

FIFTIETH CONGRESS

March 4, 1887–March 3, 1889

First session—Dec. 5, 1887–Oct. 20, 1888 (321 days)

Second session—Dec. 3, 1888–Mar. 3, 1889 (91 days)

Vice President—Thomas Andrews Hendricks, Ind., died Nov. 25, 1885

President pro tempore of the Senate —John James Ingalls, Ky.

Secretary of the Senate—Anson George McCook, N.Y.

Speaker of the House—John Griffin Carlisle, Ky., reelected Dec. 5, 1887

Clerk of the House—John Bullock Clark, Jr., Mo., reelected Dec. 5, 1887

APPOINTMENTS TO THE SUPREME COURT

Chief Justice

Melville Weston Fuller, Ill., July 20, 1888 (replaced Morrison Remick Waite)

Associate Justice

Lucius Quintus Cincinnatus Lamar, Miss., Jan. 15, 1888 (replaced William Burnham Woods)

IMPORTANT DATES IN THE PRESIDENCY

Apr. 8, 1885, U.S. marines landed at Panama

May 17, 1885, Apache chief Geronimo on warpath in Arizona and New Mexico

Sept. 3, 1885, Naval War College opened at Newport, R.I.

Jan. 19, 1886, Presidential Succession Act approved

Mar. 22, 1886, first Interstate Commerce Commission appointed

May 4, 1886, outbreak of Haymarket Square riot in Chicago, Ill.; violence erupted at demonstration calling for an eight-hour working day; 11 persons were killed and more than 100 wounded

May 17, 1886, act passed providing for commissioning of graduates of U.S. Military Academy as second lieutenants

Oct. 28, 1886, dedication of the Statue of Liberty

Dec. 1886, American Federation of Labor organized

Feb. 4, 1887, Interstate Commerce Act approved (first federal controls on business)

Feb. 23, 1887, importation of opium from China prohibited

Aug. 9, 1887, Colorado troops battled Ute Indians

May 30, 1888, Massachusetts first state to adopt the Australian ballot

Feb. 1889, Department of Agriculture established as executive department

Courtesy of The Library of Congress

The Statue of Liberty, partly clouded by smoke from military and naval salute marking the President's arrival at Liberty Island

ADDITIONAL DATA ON CLEVELAND

GROVER CLEVELAND

—was the first President born in New Jersey.

—was the only President who was defeated for reelection and later reelected, thus serving two nonconsecutive terms (March 4, 1885–March 3, 1889 and March 4, 1893–March 3, 1897).

—was the second President married while in office.

—was the only President married in the White House.

—was the first President whose wife gave birth during his term in office.

—was the first President to have a child born in the White House.

—was the ninth President who was a resident of a state other than his native state.

—was the first President elected after the Civil War who had not taken an active part in the conflict.

—was the first Democratic President elected after the Civil War.

CLEVELAND CHANGED NAME

Grover Cleveland was originally named Stephen Grover Cleveland, for Stephen Grover, the minister of the First Presbyterian Church at Caldwell, N.J., from 1787 to 1837. This was the position to which Cleveland's father was appointed. Cleveland dropped his first name, Stephen, in his youth.

CLEVELAND PURCHASED SUBSTITUTE FOR MILITARY SERVICE DURING THE CIVIL WAR

Since the age of 16, Cleveland had been working to support his widowed mother and younger sisters and brothers. He was admitted to the bar in 1859 and three years later his political activities earned him appointment as assistant district attorney for Erie Country, N.Y. But in 1863, Cleveland's name was one of the first to be drawn in Buffalo under the Conscription Act that Congress had passed in March of that year.

As an antiwar Democrat and as his family's principal means of support, and inasmuch as he likely did not want to leave behind the career in politics and law that now beckoned, Cleveland faced a choice between two legal means of avoiding military service. He could buy his way out for the sum of $300, which was called "commutation," or he might find a substitute. Cleveland chose the latter course of action, paying a 32-year-old Polish immigrant $150 to take the future President's place in the ranks of the Union armies. (Popular resentment of the commutation clause brought about its repeal by Congress in 1864.)

CLEVELAND HANGED CRIMINALS

On January 1, 1871, Grover Cleveland took office as sheriff of the Erie County Jail, Buffalo, N.Y. Instead of delegating disagreeable tasks, such as hangings, to others, he personally carried out the duties of his office. On September 6, 1872, he superintended the hanging of Patrick Morrissey, convicted of stabbing his mother.

The Buffalo *Express* on September 7, 1872, reported that "the sheriff [Cleveland] stood at the gallows with his right hand on the rod attached to the trap bolt, and at fourteen minutes past twelve, Mr. Emerick gave the signal."

On February 14, 1873, Cleveland took charge also of the hanging of Jack Gaffney, a gambler, convicted of shooting and killing a man during a card game at Buffalo.

CLEVELAND'S TWO BROTHERS PERISHED IN FIRE AT SEA

On October 22, 1872, the S.S. *Missouri* of the Atlantic Mail Line bound from New York City to Havana, Cuba, burned at sea. Over eighty lives were lost, including Cleveland's two brothers: Richard Cecil Cleveland, aged 37, and Lewis Frederick Cleveland, aged 31. Grover Cleveland at that time was sheriff of Erie County.

RELIGIOUS ISSUE IN THE CAMPAIGN OF 1884

A few days before the election, on October 29, 1884, a delegation of Protestant clergymen met the Republican candidate at the Fifth Avenue Hotel in New York City. One of the ministers, Dr. Samuel Dickinson Burchard, made a speech in which he referred to the Democrats as the party of "rum, Romanism, and rebellion." In his reply, Blaine failed to disavow this insult to the Catholic Church and the Democratic party, and his subsequent denials of anti-Catholic bigotry came too late. As a result Blaine lost many votes in New York, which had been expected to vote Republican, and he failed to carry that key state. Since a few hundred more votes would have carried the state for Blaine—Cleveland's New York plurality was less than 1,200—the religious issue played a significant part in the election.

CLEVELAND'S ILLICIT PATERNITY AN ISSUE IN THE CAMPAIGN OF 1884

Because he had been a staunch reformer and opponent of the Tammany Hall machine while serving as governor of New York, the Democratic presidential candidate was called "Grover the Good" by his supporters. His Republican opponent, on the other had, was tainted by involvement in the railroad scandals that occurred during President Grant's term of office. However, less than two weeks after Cleveland had won his party's nomination, a Buffalo newspaper revealed that the bachelor candidate was the father of an 11-year-old son.

Cleveland never denied the accusation, although his paternity was not established fact. The mother of the boy, Maria C. Halpin, had been a worker in a Buffalo department store in the early 1870s, when Cleveland was sheriff of Erie County. She had sexual relationships with a number of men, most of whom were married, and when she gave birth in September 1874, Cleveland volunteered to accept paternity for the child in order to

Courtesy of The Library of Congress

Illustration shows a woman holding a baby that is crying out "I want my pa" as Grover Cleveland passes.

spare the other men embarrassment. The boy, named Oscar Folsom Cleveland, was placed in an orphanage after Mrs. Halpin became a heavy drinker, with Cleveland paying for his support; he was later adopted, and Mrs. Halpin remarried.

Blaine's supporters effectively exploited the issue by popularizing a chant:

Ma, Ma, where's my Pa?

Gone to the White House, ha ha ha!

In the end, though, Cleveland partisans had the last word on the subject when they chanted:

Hurrah for Maria,

Hurrah for the kid,

We voted for Grover

And we're damn glad we did.

PRESIDENT MARRIED IN WHITE HOUSE

President Cleveland became the first President to be married in the White House when he married his ward, Frances Folsom (the daughter of his deceased law partner), on June 2, 1886. At 21 years old, she was the youngest woman to be First Lady.

FURTHER READING

Ford, Henry J. *The Cleveland Era.* 1919.

Jeffers, H. P. *An Honest President: The Life and Presidencies of Grover Cleveland.* 2000.

Merrill, Horace S. *The Bourbon Leader.* 1957.

Nevins, Allan. *Grover Cleveland.* Rev. ed. 1966.

Tugwell, Rexford G. *Grover Cleveland.* 1968.

Welch, Richard E. *The Presidencies of Grover Cleveland.* Rev. ed. 1988.

Courtesy of The Library of Congress

Benjamin Harrison

Date of birth—Aug. 20, 1833

Place of birth—North Bend, Ohio

Education—Tutored at home, attended local school; Farmer's College, Cincinnati, Ohio, 1847–1850; Miami University, Oxford, Ohio, bachelor's degree, June 24, 1852; private study at law office of Storer and Gwynne, Cincinnati, Ohio, 1852–1854

Religion—Presbyterian

Ancestry—English

Career—Lawyer, city attorney, Army general in Civil War, state supreme court reporter, member of Mississippi River Commission, U.S. senator

Political party—Republican

State represented—Indiana

Term of office—Mar. 4, 1889–Mar. 4, 1893

Term served—4 years

Administration—26th

Congresses—51st, 52nd

Age at inauguration—55 years, 196 days

Lived after term—8 years, 9 days

Occupation after term—Lawyer, teacher

Date of death—Mar. 13, 1901

Age at death—67 years, 205 days

Place of death—Indianapolis, Ind.

Burial place—Crown Hill Cemetery, Indianapolis, Ind.

FAMILY

FATHER

Name—John Scott Harrison

Date of birth—Oct. 4, 1804

Place of birth—Vincennes, Ind.

First marriage—Lucretia Knapp Johnson, 1824 (b. Sept. 16, 1804, d. Feb. 6, 1830)

Second marriage—Elizabeth Ramsey Irwin

Occupation—Farmer; U.S. congressman from Ohio

Date of death—May 25, 1878, North Bend, Ohio

Age at death—73 years, 233 days

MOTHER

Name at birth—Elizabeth Ramsey Irwin

Date of birth—July 18, 1810

Place of birth—Mercersburg, Pa.

Married—Aug. 12, 1831

Date of death—Aug. 15, 1850

Age at death—40 years, 28 days

SIBLINGS

Benjamin Harrison was the fifth of his father's thirteen children, the second of ten children of a second marriage.

Children of John Scott Harrison and Lucretia Knapp Johnson Harrison

Elizabeth Short Harrison, b. 1825, d. May 12, 1904

William Henry Harrison, b. Mar. 9, 1827, d. Sept. 15, 1829

Sarah Lucretia Harrison, b. 1829

Children of John Scott Harrison and Elizabeth Ramsey Irwin Harrison

Archibald Irwin Harrison, b. June 9, 1832, d. Dec. 16, 1870

Benjamin Harrison, b. Aug. 20, 1833, d. Mar. 13, 1901

Mary Jane Irwin Harrison, b. July 5, 1835, d. Sept. 14, 1867

Anna Symmes Harrison, b. Aug. 23, 1837, d. Aug. 26, 1838

John Irwin Harrison, b. June 25, 1839, d. Oct. 25, 1839

Carter Bassett Harrison, b. Sept. 26, 1840, d. Dec. 6, 1905

Anna Symmes Harrison, b. Nov. 4, 1842, d. Mar. 26, 1926

John Scott Harrison, b. Nov. 16, 1844, d. Jan. 10, 1926

James Friedlay Harrison, b. Feb. 14, 1847, d. Jan. 3, 1848

James Irwin Harrison, b. Oct. 7, 1849, d. Aug. 25, 1850

MARRIAGES

First marriage

Married—Caroline Lavinia Scott

Date of marriage—Oct. 20, 1853

Place of marriage—Oxford, Ohio

Age of wife at marriage—21 years, 19 days

Age of husband at marriage—20 years, 61 days

Years married—39 years, 5 days

Second marriage

Married—Mary Scott Lord Dimmick

Date of marriage—Apr. 6, 1896

Place of marriage—New York, N.Y.

Age of wife at marriage—37 years, 341 days

Age of husband at marriage—62 years, 229 days

Years married—4 years, 341 days

CHILDREN

Children of Benjamin Harrison and Caroline Lavinia Scott Harrison

Russell Benjamin Harrison, b. Aug. 12, 1854, Oxford, Ohio; m. Jan. 9, 1884, Mary Angeline Saunders, Omaha, Neb.; d. Dec. 12, 1936, Indianapolis, Ind.

Mary Scott Harrison, b. Apr. 3, 1858; m. Nov. 5, 1884, James Robert McKee, Indianapolis, Ind.; d. Oct. 28, 1930, Greenwich, Conn.

Children of Benjamin Harrison and Mary Scott Lord Dimmick Harrison

Elizabeth Harrison, b. Feb. 21, 1897, Indianapolis, Ind.; m. Apr. 6, 1921, James Blaine Walker, New York, N.Y.; d. Dec. 25, 1955

HARRISON'S DAUGHTER WAS YOUNGER THAN HIS GRANDCHILDREN

On February 21, 1897, Mary Scott Lord Dimmick Harrison, Harrison's second wife, bore the former President a daughter. The child was younger than Harrison's four grandchildren. Harrison's son, Russell Benjamin Harrison, had two children: Marthena, born January 18, 1888, and William Henry, born August 10, 1896. His daughter, Mary Scott Harrison McKee, had two children: Benjamin Harrison McKee, born in 1887, and Mary Lodge McKee, born in 1888.

Courtesy of The Library of Congress

President Benjamin Harrison and his family

THE PRESIDENT'S WIVES

First wife

Name at birth—Caroline Lavinia Scott

Date of birth—Oct. 1, 1832

Place of birth—Oxford, Ohio

Mother—Mary Potts Neal Scott

Father—John Witherspoon Scott

Father's occupation—Presbyterian minister

Education—Oxford Female Seminary, Oxford, Ohio

Marriage—Benjamin Harrison, Oct. 20, 1853, Oxford, Ohio

Children—Russell Benjamin Harrison, b. Aug. 12, 1854, d. Dec. 12, 1936; Mary Scott Harrison, b. Apr. 3, 1858, d. Oct. 28, 1930

Date of death—Oct. 25, 1892

Age at death—60 years, 24 days

Place of death—Washington, D.C.

Burial place—Indianapolis, Ind.

Years older than the President—323 days

Years the President survived her—8 years, 139 days

Second wife

Name at birth—Mary Scott Lord

Date of birth—Apr. 30, 1858

Place of birth—Honesdale, Pa.

Mother—Elizabeth Scott Lord

Father—Russell Farnham Lord

Father's occupation—Engineer and manager, Delaware and Hudson Canal Co.

Education—Mrs. Moffatt's School, Princeton, N.J.; Elmira College, Elmira, N.Y.

First marriage—Walter Erskine Dimmick (d. Jan. 14, 1882)

Second marriage—Benjamin Harrison, Apr. 6, 1896, New York, N.Y.

Children from second marriage—Elizabeth Harrison, b. Feb. 21, 1897, d. Dec. 25, 1955

Date of death—Jan. 5, 1948

Age at death—89 years, 250 days

Place of death—New York, N.Y.

Burial place—Indianapolis, Ind.

Years younger than the President—24 years, 253 days

Years she survived the President—46 years, 298 days

Courtesy of The Library of Congress

Caroline Harrison, first wife of Benjamin Harrison

Courtesy of The Library of Congress

Mary Scott Harrison, second wife of Benjamin Harrison

THE FIRST LADY

Caroline Scott Harrison was the first President General of the National Society of the Daughters of the American Revolution, organized on October 11, 1890, and incorporated on December 2, 1895. She was also the founder in 1889 of the White House presidential china collection, now displayed in the China Room. In 1890 she initiated the first plan to enlarge the White House, though it was never carried out.

Caroline Scott Harrison became an invalid during her years in the White House and died before the end of her husband's term. While she was ill, the social events at the White House were supervised by the First Lady's widowed niece, Mary Scott Lord Dimmick, who lived at the White House for two years. After President Harrison left office, he married Mrs. Dimmick at St. Thomas's Protestant Episcopal Church, New York City. Thus, though Benjamin Harrison's second wife had fulfilled the duties of a First Lady, she was never the mistress of the White House in her own right.

IMPORTANT DATES IN THE PRESIDENT'S LIFE

1853, admitted to the bar, practiced at Cincinnati, Ohio

1854, started law practice, Indianapolis, Ind.

1855, established law partnership with William Wallace, Indianapolis

1860, reporter of decisions, Indiana Supreme Court

July 14, 1862, commissioned second lieutenant of Indiana Volunteers

July 1862–June 1865, formed Company A of the 70th Regiment, Indiana Volunteer Infantry, and was made captain; at the organization of the regiment was commissioned colonel; went with regiment to Kentucky and served until June 1865

1864–1868, served as reporter of Indiana Supreme Court while still in military service

Jan. 23, 1865, breveted brigadier general

June 8, 1865, honorable discharge from army

1876, unsuccessful candidate for governor of Indiana

1879, member, Mississippi River Commission

Mar. 4, 1881–Mar. 3, 1887, U.S. Senate (from Indiana)

Mar. 4, 1889–Mar. 4, 1893, President

1892, unsuccessful candidate for a second term—defeated by Cleveland

1900, practiced law, served in Paris as chief attorney for the Republic of Venezuela in the Venezuela–Great Britain boundary dispute

ELECTIONS

THE ELECTION OF 1888

November 6, 1888

CANDIDATES

Republican Party (9th Convention)

June 19–23, 25, 1888, Civic Auditorium, Chicago, Ill.

P: Benjamin Harrison, Ind.
VP: Levi Parsons Morton, N.Y.

Harrison was nominated on the eighth ballot. Candidates for nomination and the votes they received on the first and eighth ballots:

John Sherman, Ohio, 229, 118
Walter Quintin Gresham, Ind., 107, 59
Chauncey Mitchell Depew, N.Y., 99, 0
Benjamin Harrison, Ind., 85, 544
Russell Alexander Alger, Mich., 84, 100
William Boyd Allison, Iowa, 72, 0
James Gillespie Blaine, Me., 35, 5
John James Ingalls, Kan., 28, 0

Darwin Phelps, Pa., 25, 0
Jeremiah McLain Rusk, Wis., 25, 0
Edwin Henry Fitler, Pa., 24, 0
Joseph Roswell Hawley, N.C., 13, 0
Robert Todd Lincoln, Ill., 3, 0
William McKinley, Ohio, 2, 4
Total number of votes:
First ballot: 831
Eighth ballot: 830
Number necessary for nomination: 416

Democratic Party (15th Convention)

June 5–7, 1888, Exposition Building, St. Louis, Mo.

P: Grover Cleveland, N.Y.
VP: Allen Gransberry Thurman, Ohio
   Cleveland was nominated on the first ballot by acclamation.

Total number of votes: 822

Prohibition Party

May 30–31, 1888, Tomlinson Hall, Indianapolis, Ind.

P: Clinton Bowen Fisk, N.J.
VP: John Anderson Brooks, Mo.
   Fisk was nominated by acclamation.

Union Labor Party

May 15–17, 1888, Cincinnati, Ohio

P: Alson Jennes Streeter, Ill.
VP: Charles E. Cunningham, Ark. (Samuel Evans of Texas declined the nomination.)
   The Union Labor Party was organized February 22, 1887, at Cincinnati, Ohio.
   Delegates to the convention came from the Knights of Labor, Agricultural Wheelers, Corngrowers, Homesteadry, Farmers' Alliances, Greenbackers, and Grangers.

United Labor Party

May 15–17, 1888, Grand Opera House, Cincinnati, Ohio

P: Robert Hall Cowdery, Ill.
VP: William H. T. Wakefield, Kan.
   This party, an outgrowth of the Henry George movement of 1886, nominated its first national ticket in 1888.

American Party

Aug. 14–15, 1888, Grand Army Hall, Washington, D.C.

P: James Langdon Curtis, N.Y.
VP: Peter Dinwiddie Wigginton, Calif.
   Curtis was nominated on the first ballot. Candidates for nomination and the votes they received:
James Langdon Curtis, N.Y., 45
Abram Stevens Hewitt, N.Y., 15
James Scott Negley, Pa., 4
Nomination made unanimous
   James R. Greer of Tennessee was nominated for Vice President but declined.

Equal Rights Party

May 15, 1888, Des Moines, Iowa

P: Belva Ann Bennett Lockwood, D.C.
VP: Alfred Henry Love, Pa.
   Love declined the nomination and Charles Stuart Wells was substituted.

Industrial Reform Party

Feb. 22–23, 1888, Washington, D.C.

P: Albert E. Redstone, Calif.
VP: John Colvin, Kan.

1888 POPULAR VOTE

Democratic Party, 5,537,857
Republican Party, 5,447,129
Prohibition Party, 249,506
Union Labor Party, 146,935
United Labor Party, 2,818
American Party, 1,612

1888 ELECTORAL VOTE

   There were 401 electoral votes from 38 states.
Harrison received 58.10 percent (233 votes— 20 states) as follows: Calif. 8; Colo. 3; Ill. 22; Ind. 15; Iowa 13; Kan. 9; Me. 6; Mass. 14; Mich. 13; Minn. 7; Neb. 5; N.H. 4; N.Y. 36; Ohio 23; Ore. 3; Pa. 30; R.I. 4; Vt. 4; Wis. 11.
Cleveland received 41.90 percent (168 votes—18 states) as follows: Ala. 10; Ark. 7; Conn. 6; Del. 3; Fla. 4; Ga. 12; Ky. 13; La. 8; Md. 8; Miss. 9; Mo. 16; N.J. 9; N.C. 11; S.C. 9; Tenn. 12; Tex. 13; Va. 12; W.Va. 6.

INAUGURATION

March 4, 1889

Benjamin Harrison took the oath of office on Monday, Mar. 4, 1889. The oath was administered by Chief Justice Melville Weston Fuller on the east portico of the Capitol. Despite the torrential rains and strong winds, Harrison rode to the Capitol in an open carriage and delivered his inaugural address.

A parade that continued after dark was marred by the inclement weather. The fireworks exhibition scheduled for the evening was abandoned.

The inaugural ball, attended by more than 12,000 persons, was held in the Pension Office, 5th and F Streets, Washington, D.C. An orchestra of one hundred provided the music. The menu included blue points on ice. The hot foods consisted of bouillon in cups, steamed oysters, oysters à la poulette, chicken croquettes, sweetbread pâté à la reine, and terrapin, Philadelphia style. The cold foods were assorted roll sandwiches, mayonnaise of chicken, lobster salad, cold tongue en Bellevue, cold ham à la Montmorency, boned turkey à la Américaine, breast of quail à la Cicéron, pâté de foie gras à la Harrison, terrine of game à la Morton. The desserts were ice cream, orange water ice, Roman punch, pyramid of nougat renaissance, beehive of bon-bons Republican, Pavilion Rustic, and assorted fancy cakes. Fruits, other desserts, and coffee were also available.

THE VICE PRESIDENT

Name—Levi Parsons Morton (22nd V.P.)

Date of birth—May 16, 1824

Place of birth—Shoreham, Vt.

Political party—Republican

State represented—New York

Term of office—Mar. 4, 1889–Mar. 4, 1893

Age at inauguration—64 years, 292 days

Occupation after term—Governor of New York

Date of death—May 16, 1920

Age at death—96 years

Place of death—Rhinebeck, N.Y.

Burial place—Rhinebeck, N.Y.

ADDITIONAL DATA ON MORTON

1838–1840, clerk, general store, Enfield, Mass.

1840–1841, taught school, Boscawen, N.H.

1845, mercantile pursuits, Hanover, N.H.

1854, dry goods business, New York City

1863, banker, New York City

1876, unsuccessful candidate for U.S. Congress

1878, Commissioner, Paris Exposition

Courtesy of The Library of Congress

Levi Morton, Vice President to Benjamin Harrison.

Mar. 4, 1879–Mar. 21, 1881, U.S. House of Representatives (from New York)

Aug. 5, 1881–May 14, 1885, U.S. minister to France

Mar. 4, 1889–Mar. 4, 1893, Vice President under Benjamin Harrison

1895–1897, governor of New York

CABINET

March 4, 1889–March 3, 1893

State—Thomas Francis Bayard, Del., continued from preceding administration; James Gillespie Blaine, Me., Mar. 5, 1869; entered upon duties Mar. 7, 1889; William Fisher Wharton, Mass. (assistant secretary), ad interim June 4, 1892; John Watson Foster, Ind., June 29, 1892; William Fisher Wharton, Mass. (assistant secretary), ad interim Feb. 23, 1893

Treasury—Charles Stebbins Fairchild, N.Y., continued from preceding administration; William Windom, Minn., Mar. 5, 1889; entered upon duties Mar. 7, 1889; Alvred Bayard Nettleton, Minn. (assistant secretary), ad interim Jan. 30, 1891; Charles Foster, Ohio, Feb. 24, 1891

War—William Crowninshield Endicott, Mass., continued from preceding administration; Redfield Proctor, Vt., Mar. 5, 1889; Lewis Addison Grant, Minn. (assistant secretary), ad interim Dec. 6, 1891; Stephen

Benton Elkins, W.Va., Dec. 22, 1891; entered upon duties Dec. 24, 1891

Attorney General—Augustus Hill Garland, Ark., continued from preceding administration; William Henry Harrison Miller, Ind., Mar. 5, 1889

Postmaster General—Donald McDonald Dickinson, Mich., continued from preceding administration; John Wanamaker, Pa., Mar. 5, 1889

Navy—William Collins Whitney, N.Y., continued from preceding administration; Benjamin Franklin Tracy, N.Y., Mar. 5, 1889

Interior—William Freeman Vilas, Wis., continued from preceding administration; John Willock Noble, Mo., Mar. 5, 1889; entered upon duties Mar. 7, 1889

Agriculture—Norman Jay Colman, Mo., continued from preceding administration; Jeremiah McLain Rusk, Wis., Mar. 5, 1889; entered upon duties Mar. 7, 1889

Courtesy of The Library of Congress

Benjamin Harrison's cabinet

CONGRESS

FIFTY-FIRST CONGRESS

March 4, 1889–March 3, 1891

First session—Dec. 2, 1889–Oct. 1, 1890 (304 days)

Second session—Dec. 1, 1890–Mar. 2, 1891 (93 days)

Special session of the Senate—Mar. 4, 1889–Apr. 2, 188 (30 days)

Vice President—Levi Parsons Morton, N.Y.

President pro tempore of the Senate —John James Ingalls, Kan., elected Mar. 7, 1889; and Apr. 2, 1889, special sessions of the Senate; Feb. 28, 1890 and Apr. 3, 1890; Charles Frederick Manderson, Neb., elected Mar. 2, 1891

Secretary of the Senate—Anson George McCook, N.Y.

Speaker of the House—Thomas Brackett Reed, Me., elected Dec. 2, 1889

Clerk of the House—John Bullock Clark, Jr., Mo., Edward McPherson, Pa., elected Dec. 2, 1889

FIFTY-SECOND CONGRESS

March 4, 1891–March 3, 1893

First session—Dec. 7, 1891–Aug. 5, 1892 (251 days)

Second session—Dec. 5, 1892–Mar. 3, 1893 (89 days)

Vice President—Levi Parsons Morton, N.Y.

President pro tempore of the Senate —Charles Frederick Manderson, Neb.

Secretary of the Senate—Anson George McCook, N.Y.

Speaker of the House—Charles Frederick Crisp, Ga., elected Dec. 8, 1891

Clerk of the House—Edward McPherson, Pa., continued from preceding Congress; James Kerr, Pa., elected Dec. 8, 1891

APPOINTMENTS TO THE SUPREME COURT

Associate Justices

David Josiah Brewer, Kan., Dec. 18, 1889 (replaced Stanley Matthews)

Henry Billings Brown, Mich., Dec. 29, 1890 (replaced Samuel Freeman Miller)

George Shiras, Jr., Pa., July 26, 1892 (replaced Joseph Philo Bradley)

Howell Edmunds Jackson, Tenn., Feb. 18, 1893 (replaced Lucius Quintus Cincinnatus Lamar)

IMPORTANT DATES IN THE PRESIDENCY

Apr. 22, 1889, Oklahoma opened to settlers

May 31, 1889, Johnstown flood

Oct. 2, 1889, Pan American Conference

Nov. 2, 1889, North Dakota and South Dakota admitted to the Union as the 39th and 40th states

Nov. 8, 1889, Montana admitted as the 41st state

Nov. 11, 1889, Washington admitted as the 42nd state

July 2, 1890, Sherman Antitrust Act enacted

July 3, 1890, Idaho admitted as the 43rd state

July 10, 1890, Wyoming admitted as the 44th state

July 14, 1890, Sherman Silver Purchase Act passed

ADDITIONAL DATA ON HARRISON

BENJAMIN HARRISON

—was the fourth President born in Ohio.

—was the first President who was the grandson of a President.

—was the tenth President who was a resident of a state other than his native state.

—was the third President to remarry.

—was the fifth President to marry a widow.

—was the second President whose wife died while he was in office.

GRANDSON OF A PRESIDENT

Benjamin Harrison was the only grandson of a President to become President. The twenty-third President was a grandson of William Henry Harrison, the ninth President, who took office on March 4, 1841 and died on April 4, 1841.

HARRISON PRECEDED AND FOLLOWED BY CLEVELAND

Benjamin Harrison was the only President who was preceded and succeeded by the same man. When Grover Cleveland retired from office on March 4, 1889, Harrison was sworn in and when Harrison retired on March 4, 1893, Grover Cleveland took the oath of office for a second time.

TWO CABINET OFFICERS WITH SAME NAME

Benjamin Harrison was the only President who had two secretaries in his cabinet with the same last name. For a period of eight months, from June 29, 1892, to February 23, 1893, he had two secretaries named Foster. One was Charles Foster of Ohio, Secretary of the Treasury from February 24, 1891, to March 3, 1893; the other was John Watson Foster of Indiana, Secretary of State from June 29, 1892, to February 23, 1893.

SIX STATES ADMITTED

More states were admitted into the United States during Benjamin Harrison's administration than in any other. The states were (39–40) North Dakota and South Dakota, November 2, 1889; (41) Montana, November 8, 1889; (42) Washington, November 11, 1889; (43) Idaho, July 3, 1890; and (44) Wyoming, July 10, 1890.

HARRISON HAD FIRST BILLION-DOLLAR CONGRESS

The first Congress to appropriate a billion dollars was the 52nd Congress (March 4, 1891 to March 3, 1893), which appropriated $507,376,397.52 in the first session for the fiscal year 1893, and $519,535,293.31 in the second session for the fiscal year 1894. The appropriations included the postal service items payable from postal revenues and estimated permanent annual appropriations including sinking-fund requirements.

FURTHER READING

Harrison, B. *Public Papers and Addresses of Benjamin Harrison.* Rev. ed. 1969.

Sievers, Harry J. *Benjamin Harrison.* 3 vols., 1959–1968.

Socolofsky, Homer E. *The Presidency of Benjamin Harrison.* Rev. ed. 1988.

Grover Cleveland

Term of office—Mar. 4, 1893–Mar. 4, 1897
Administration—27th
Congresses—53rd, 54th
Age at inauguration—55 years, 351 days

Lived after term—11 years, 112 days
For additional biographical information about Grover Cleveland, see the chapter on his first term on page 257.

ELECTIONS

THE ELECTION OF 1892

November 8, 1892

CANDIDATES

Democratic Party (16th Convention)

June 21–23, 1892, in a specially constructed building, Chicago, Ill.

P: Grover Cleveland, N.Y.
VP: Adlai Ewing Stevenson, Ill.

Cleveland was nominated on the first ballot. Candidates for nomination and the votes they received:

Grover Cleveland, N.Y., $617^1/_3$

David Bennett Hill, N.Y., 114

Horace Boies, Iowa, 103

Arthur Pue Gorman, Md., $36^1/_2$

Adlai Ewing Stevenson, Ill., $16^2/_3$

John Griffin Carlisle, Ky., 14

William Ralls Morrison, Ill., 3

James Edwin Campbell, Ohio, 2

Robert Emory Pattison, Pa., 1

William Eustis Russell, Mass., 1

William Collins Whitney, N.Y., 1

Total number of votes: $909^1/_2$

Number necessary for nomination: 607

Nomination made unanimous

Republican Party (10th Convention)

June 7–10, 1892, Industrial Exposition Building, Minneapolis, Minn.

P: Benjamin Harrison, Ind.

VP: Whitelaw Reid, N.Y.

Harrison was nominated on the first ballot. Candidates for nomination and the votes they received:

Benjamin Harrison, Ind., $535^1/_6$

James Gillespie Blaine, Me., $182^1/_6$

William McKinley, Ohio, 182

Thomas Brackett Reed, Me., 4

Robert Todd Lincoln, Ill., 1

Total number of votes: $904^1/_3$

Number necessary for nomination: 453

People's Party of America

July 2–5, 1892, Convention Hall Coliseum, Omaha, Neb.

P: James Baird Weaver, Iowa
VP: James Gaven Field, Va.

Weaver was nominated on the first ballot. Candidates for nomination and the votes they received:

James Baird Weaver, Iowa, 995

James Henderson Kyle, S.D., 265

Seymour Frank Norton, Ill., 1

Mann Page, Va., 1

——Stanford, 1

Total number of votes: 1,263; nomination made unanimous

The People's Party (formed by members of the Farmers' Alliance and other industrial unions) was organized May 19, 1891, at a national convention at Cincinnati, Ohio. The first presidential candidates were nominated in 1892. The People's Party later developed into the Populist Party.

Prohibition Party

June 29–30, 1892, Music Hall, Cincinnati, Ohio

P: John Bidwell, Calif.
VP: James Britton Cranfill, Tex.

Bidwell was nominated on the first ballot. Candidates for the nomination and the votes they received:
John Bidwell, Calif., 590
Gideon Stewart, Ohio, 179
W. Jennings Demarest, N.Y., 139
Total number of votes: 908

Socialist Labor Party

Aug. 28, 1892, New York City

P: Simon Wing, Mass.
VP: Charles Horatio Matchett, N.Y.

The Social Democratic Workmen's Party of North America, which was formed July 4, 1874, changed its name to the Socialist Labor Party of North America in 1877, at which time it held a national convention at Newark, N.J. No presidential candidates were nominated until 1892 when the party appeared on the ballot in six states.

1892 POPULAR VOTE

Democratic Party, 5,556,918
Republican Party, 5,176,108
People's Party (Populists), 1,041,028
Prohibition Party, 264,138
Socialist Labor Party, 21,512

1892 ELECTORAL VOTE

There were 444 electoral votes from 44 states.

Courtesy of The Library of Congress

Grover Cleveland's second inauguration

Cleveland received 62.39 percent (277 votes—23 states) as follows: Ala. 11; Ark. 8; Calif. 8 (of the 9 votes); Conn. 6; Del. 3; Fla. 4; Ga. 13; Ill. 24; Ind. 15; Ky. 13; La. 8; Md. 8; Mich. 5 (of the 14 votes); Miss. 9; Mo. 17; N.J. 10; N.Y. 36; N.C. 11; N.D. 1 (of the 3 votes); Ohio 1 (of the 23 votes); S.C. 9; Tenn. 12; Tex. 15; Va. 12; W.Va. 6; Wis. 12.

Harrison received 32.66 percent (145 votes—16 states) as follows: Calif. 1 (of the 9 votes); Iowa 13; Me. 6; Mass. 15; Mich. 9 (of the 14 votes); Minn. 9; Mont. 3; Neb. 8; N.H. 4; N.D. 1 (of the 3 votes); Ohio 22 (of the 23 votes); Ore. 3 (of the 4 votes); Pa. 32; R.I. 4; S.D. 4; Vt. 4; Wash. 4; Wyo. 3.

Weaver received 4.95 percent (22 votes—4 states) as follows: Colo. 4; Idaho 3; Kan. 10; Nev. 3; N.D. 1 (of the 3 votes); Ore. 1 (of the 4 votes).

The North Dakota vote was divided evenly among the three candidates.

INAUGURATION

March 4, 1893

Grover Cleveland took the oath of office for the second time on Saturday, March 4, 1893, on the east portico of the Capitol. Chief Justice Melville Weston Fuller administered the oath.

On March 3, 1893, it rained, and at midnight snow and rain began to fall. March 4 was clear, but the ground was covered with one inch of moist snow. Cleveland made an address before taking the oath of office. The inaugural parade lasted about six hours. An inaugural ball was held at the Pension Office, but the fireworks display was postponed until March 6.

THE VICE PRESIDENT

Name—Adlai Ewing Stevenson (23rd V.P.)
Date of birth—Oct. 23, 1835
Place of birth—Christian County, Ky.
Political party—Democratic
State represented—Illinois
Term of office—Mar. 4, 1893–Mar. 4, 1897
Age at inauguration—57 years, 132 days
Occupation after term—Politics
Date of death—June 14, 1914
Age at death—78 years, 234 days
Place of death—Chicago, Ill.
Burial place—Bloomington, Ill.

ADDITIONAL DATA ON STEVENSON

1852, moved to Bloomington, Ill.
1858, admitted to bar, practiced in Metamora, Ill.
1860, master in chancery, four years
1865, District Attorney, three years
Mar. 4, 1875–Mar. 3, 1877, U.S. House of Representatives (from Illinois)
1876, unsuccessful candidate for reelection to Congress
Mar. 4, 1879–Mar. 3, 1881, U.S. House of Representatives
1880, unsuccessful candidate for reelection to Congress
1885–1889, first assistant postmaster general

Courtesy of The Library of Congress

Adlai Stevenson, Vice President to Grover Cleveland

Mar. 4, 1893–Mar. 4, 1897, Vice President under Grover Cleveland
1900, unsuccessful candidate for Vice President
1908, unsuccessful candidate for governor of Illinois; retired from public and political activities

CABINET

March 4, 1893–March 3, 1897

State—William Fisher Wharton, Mass. (assistant secretary), ad interim, continued from preceding administration; Walter Quintin Gresham, Ill., Mar. 6, 1893 (died May 28, 1895); Edwin Fuller Uhl, Mich. (assistant secretary), ad interim May 28, 1895; Alvey Augustus Adee, D. C. (second assistant secretary), ad interim May 31, 1895; Edwin Fuller Uhl, Mich. (assistant secretary), ad interim June 1, 1895; Richard Olney, Mass., June 8, 1895; entered upon duties June 10, 1895

Treasury—Charles Foster, Ohio, continued from preceding administration; John Griffin Carlisle, Ky., Mar. 6, 1893

War—Stephen Benton Elkins, W.Va., continued from preceding administration; Daniel Scott Lamont, N.Y., Mar. 6, 1893

Attorney General—William Henry Harrison Miller, Ind., continued from preceding administration; Richard Olney, Mass., Mar. 6, 1893; Judson Harmon, Ohio, June 8, 1895; entered upon duties June 11, 1895

Postmaster General—John Wanamaker, Pa., continued from preceding administration; Wilson Shannon Bissell, N.Y., Mar. 6, 1893; William Lyne Wilson, W.Va., Mar. 1, 1895; entered upon duties April 4, 1895

Navy—Benjamin Franklin Tracy, N.Y., continued from preceding administration; Hilary Abner Herbert, Ala., Mar. 6, 1893

Interior—John Willock Noble, Mo., continued from preceding administration; Hoke Smith, Ga., Mar. 6, 1893; John Merriman Reynolds, Pa. (assistant secretary), ad interim Sept. 1, 1896; David Rowland Francis, Mo., Sept. 1, 1896; entered upon duties Sept. 4, 1896

Agriculture—Jeremiah McLain Rusk, Wis., continued from preceding administration; Julius Sterling Morton, Neb., Mar. 6, 1893

CONGRESS

FIFTY-THIRD CONGRESS

March 4, 1893–March 3, 1895

First session—Aug. 7, 1893–Nov. 3, 1893 (89 days)

Second session—Dec. 4, 1893–Aug. 28, 1894 (268 days)

Third session—Dec. 3, 1894–Mar. 3, 1895 (97 days)

Special session of the Senate—Mar. 4, 1893–Apr. 15, 1893 (43 days)

Vice President—Adlai Ewing Stevenson, Ill.

President pro tempore of the Senate —Charles Frederick Manderson, Neb., resigned as president pro tempore Mar. 22, 1893; Isham Green Harris, Tenn., elected Mar. 22, 1893; Matt Whitaker Ransom, N.C., elected Jan. 7, 1895, resigned as president pro tempore Jan. 10, 1895; Isham Green Harris, Tenn., elected Jan. 10, 1895

Secretary of the Senate—Anson George McCook, N.Y., William Ruffin Cox, N.C., elected Apr. 6, 1893

Speaker of the House—Charles Frederick Crisp, Ga., reelected Aug. 7, 1893

Clerk of the House—James Kerr, Pa., elected Aug. 7, 1893

FIFTY-FOURTH CONGRESS

March 4, 1895–March 3, 1897

First session—Dec. 2, 1895–June 11, 1896 (193 days)

Second session—Dec. 7, 1896–Mar. 3, 1897 (87 days)

Vice President—Adlai Ewing Stevenson, Ill.

President pro tempore of the Senate —William Pierce Frye, Me., elected Feb. 7, 1896

Secretary of the Senate—William Ruffin Cox, N.C.

Speaker of the House—Thomas Brackett Reed, Me., elected Dec. 2, 1895

Clerk of the House—James Kerr, Pa.; Alexander McDowell, Pa., elected Dec. 2, 1895

APPOINTMENTS TO THE SUPREME COURT

Associate Justices

Edward Douglass White, La., Feb. 19, 1894 (replaced Samuel Blatchford)

Rufus William Peckham, N.Y., Dec. 9, 1895 (replaced Howell Edmunds Jackson)

IMPORTANT DATES IN THE PRESIDENCY

1893, financial panic

The second cabinet of Grover Cleveland

May 1, 1893, World's Columbian Exposition (Chicago World's Fair) opened by President Cleveland

Oct. 30, 1893, Sherman Silver Purchase Act repealed

May 1894, President Cleveland sent federal troops to Chicago, Ill., to stop obstruction of mail by Pullman Company strikers

July 4, 1894, Hawaii made a republic

Aug. 18, 1894, Carey Act passed, providing for land reclamation by irrigation

Feb. 24, 1895, Cuban revolt against Spanish rule began

May 20, 1895, income tax declared unconstitutional

Dec. 17, 1895, Cleveland's message to Congress denounced Great Britain's refusal to arbitrate with Venezuela in territorial dispute between Venezuela and British Guinea

Jan. 4, 1896, Utah admitted as the 45th state

ADDITIONAL DATA ON CLEVELAND

CLEVELAND STAGED COMEBACK

Grover Cleveland was inaugurated on March 4, 1885, as the twenty-second President. He was a candidate for reelection in 1888 for the 1889–1893 term but was defeated by Benjamin Harrison, who received 233 of the 401 electoral votes. In 1892 Harrison was a candidate for reelection for the 1893–1897 term but he was defeated by Cleveland, who received 277 of the 444 electoral votes. Cleveland was inaugurated on March 4, 1893. As Cleveland served two non-consecutive terms, he is referred to by most authorities as the twenty-second and the twenty-fourth President.

CLEVELAND RECEIVED PLURALITY VOTE THREE TIMES

In the 1884 election Cleveland received 4,874,986 votes while Blaine received 4,851,981. In 1888, Cleveland received 5,540,309 votes, about 100,000 more than Harrison, but Cleveland was not elected as the electoral vote was in Harrison's favor. In 1892, Cleveland received the popular vote plurality for the third time—5,556,918 votes

283

compared with 5,176,108 for Harrison. As he also received the greater electoral vote he was elected President for the second time.

CLEVELAND AND THE GEORGE WASHINGTONS

When Grover Cleveland looked over the roster of the 53rd Congress, which took office with him on March 4, 1893, he found that eight congressmen had *"George Washington"* as their given names:

George Washington Smith, Murphysboro, Ill.
George Washington Fithian, Newton, Ill.
George Washington Ray, Norwich, N.Y.
George Washington Houk, Dayton, Ohio
George Washington Hulick, Batavia, Ohio
George Washington Wilson, London, Ohio
George Washington Shell, Laurens, S.C.
George Washington Murray, Sumter, S.C.

SURGERY PERFORMED ON CLEVELAND

In 1893 President Cleveland was afflicted with cancer of the mouth, the growth necessitating the removal of his upper left jaw. The operation was performed without any publicity on July 1, 1893, aboard Commodore E. C. Benedict's yacht *Oneida* on Long Island Sound. Dr. Joseph Decatur Bryant was the chief surgeon. In a second secret operation, on July 17, other parts of the growth were removed and the President was fitted with an artificial jaw of vulcanized rubber. By August 7 he had recovered sufficiently to address the Congress.

FEDERAL TROOPS DISPATCHED TO MAINTAIN ORDER

Without the request of Governor John Peter Altgeld of Illinois, President Cleveland dispatched federal troops from Fort Sheridan to Chicago, Ill., on July 4, 1894, to maintain order and insure the transportation of mail during the strike of the employees of the Pullman Palace Car Company and the sympathetic strike of railway workers.

Courtesy of The Library of Congress

William McKinley

Date of birth—Jan. 29, 1843

Place of birth—Niles, Ohio

Education—Attended public schools at Niles, Ohio, and Poland, Ohio; Poland Academy, Poland, Ohio; Allegheny College, Meadville, Pa., left before graduation; private study at law office of Judge Charles E. Glidden, Youngstown, Ohio; Albany Law School, Albany, N.Y., 1866–1867

Religion—Methodist

Ancestry—Scotch-Irish

Career—Army officer in Civil War, lawyer, county prosecutor, U.S. congressman, governor of Ohio

Political party—Republican

State represented—Ohio

Term of office—Mar. 4, 1897–Sept. 14, 1901

Term served—4 years, 194 days

Administration—28th, 29th

Congresses—55th, 56th, 57th

Age at inauguration—54 years, 34 days

Lived after term—Died in office

Date of death—Sept. 14, 1901

Age at death—58 years, 228 days

Place of death—Buffalo, N.Y.

Burial place—Adjacent to Westlawn Cemetery, Canton, Ohio

FAMILY

FATHER

Name—William McKinley

Date of birth—Nov. 15, 1807

Place of birth—Pine Township, Pa.

Marriage—Nancy Campbell Allison, Jan. 6, 1829

Occupation—Iron manufacturer

Date of death—Nov. 24, 1892

Place of death—Canton, Ohio

Age at death—85 years, 9 days

MOTHER

Name at birth—Nancy Campbell Allison

Date of birth—Apr. 22, 1809

Place of birth—near Lisbon, Ohio

Marriage—William McKinley, Jan. 6, 1829

Date of death—Dec. 12, 1897

Place of death—Canton, Ohio

Age at death—88 years, 234 days

SIBLINGS

William McKinley was the seventh child in a family of nine.

Children of William McKinley and Nancy Campbell Allison McKinley

David Allison McKinley, b. 1829, d. Sept. 18, 1892

Anna McKinley, b. 1832, d. July 29, 1890

James McKinley, d. Oct. 11, 1889

Mary McKinley

Helen Minerva McKinley

Sarah Elizabeth McKinley

William McKinley, b. Jan. 29, 1843, d. Sept. 14, 1901

Abbie Celia McKinley

Abner McKinley, b. Nov. 27, 1849, d. June 11, 1904

MARRIAGE

Married—Ida Saxton

Date of marriage—Jan. 25, 1871

Place of marriage—Canton, Ohio

Age of wife at marriage—23 years, 231 days

Age of husband at marriage—27 years, 361 days

Years married—30 years, 232 days

CHILDREN

Katherine McKinley, b. Jan. 25, 1872, d. July 25, 1875

Ida McKinley, b. Mar. 31, 1873, d. Aug. 22, 1873

THE PRESIDENT'S WIFE

Name at birth—Ida Saxton

Date of birth—June 8, 1847

Place of birth—Canton, Ohio

Mother—Catherine Dewalt Saxton

Father—James Asbury Saxton

Father's occupation—Banker

Education—Brook Hall Seminary, Media, Pa.

Marriage—William McKinley, Jan. 25, 1871, Canton, Ohio

Children—Katherine McKinley, b. Jan. 25, 1872, d. July 25, 1875; Ida McKinley, b. Mar. 31, 1873, d. Aug. 22, 1873

Date of death—May 26, 1907
—

Age at death—59 years, 352 days

Place of death—Canton, Ohio

Burial place—Canton, Ohio

Years younger than the President—4 years, 130 days

Years she survived the President—5 years, 254 days

Courtesy of The Library of Congress

Ida KcKinley, wife of William McKinley

THE FIRST LADY

Ida Saxton McKinley had been an invalid for many years before coming to the White House. She was an epileptic and had a seizure at the second inaugural ball. The President was noted for his tender affection and great devotion toward his ailing wife.

IMPORTANT DATES IN THE PRESIDENT'S LIFE

1860–1861, taught at Kerr District School, Poland, Ohio, then worked as post office clerk

June 11, 1861, enlisted as a private in the 23rd Regiment, Ohio Volunteer Infantry

Sept. 10, 1861, Battle of Carnifax Ferry, his first engagement

Apr. 15, 1862, promoted to commissary sergeant

Sept. 17, 1862, Battle of Antietam

Sept. 24, 1862, commissioned second lieutenant

Feb. 7, 1863, promoted to first lieutenant

July 25, 1864, promoted to captain

Mar. 13, 1865, breveted major of volunteers for gallant and meritorious services at battles of Opequan, Fisher's Hill, and Cedar Creek July 26, 1865, honorable discharge with rank of captain

1865–1867, studied law

Mar. 1867, admitted to the bar; practiced at Canton County, Ohio

1869–1871, prosecuting attorney, Stark County, Ohio

Mar. 4, 1877–Mar. 3, 1883, U.S. House of Representatives (from Ohio)

Mar. 4, 1883, presented credentials as a member-elect to the 48th Congress (served to May 27, 1884, when he was succeeded by Jonathan Hasson Wallace, who contested his election)

Mar. 4, 1885–Mar. 3, 1891, U.S. House of Representatives (from Ohio)

June 1888, received two complimentary votes for nomination to the presidency on the Republican ticket

1890, McKinley Tariff Act passed by Congress

1890, unsuccessful candidate for reelection to Congress

Jan. 11, 1892–Jan. 13, 1896, governor of Ohio

June 1892, unsuccessful candidate for Republican nomination for the presidency

Nov. 1896, nominated as presidential candidate on Republican ticket

Mar. 4, 1897–Mar. 4, 1900, President (first term)

Mar. 4, 1901, inaugurated President (second term)

Sept. 6, 1901, shot by anarchist while attending Pan American Exposition, Buffalo, N.Y.

Sept. 14, 1901, died from wound

ELECTIONS

THE ELECTION OF 1896

November 3, 1896

CANDIDATES

Republican Party (11th Convention)

June 16–18, 1896, at a specially built auditorium, St. Louis, Mo.

P: William McKinley, Ohio
VP: Garret Augustus Hobart, N.J.

McKinley was nominated on the first ballot.

Candidates for nomination and the votes they received:

William McKinley, Ohio, 666$\frac{1}{2}$

Thomas Brackett Reed, Me., 84$\frac{1}{2}$

Matthew Stanley Quay, Pa., 61$\frac{1}{2}$

Levi Parsons Morton, N.Y., 58

William Boyd Allison, Iowa, 35$\frac{1}{2}$

James Donald Cameron, Pa., 1

Total number of votes: 907

Nomination made unanimous

Democratic Party (17th Convention)

July 7–11, 1896, the Coliseum, Chicago, Ill.

P: William Jennings Bryan, Neb.

VP: Arthur Sewall, Me.

Bryan was nominated on the fifth ballot. Candidates for nomination and the votes they received on the first and fifth ballots:

Richard Parks Bland, Mo., 235, 11

William Jennings Bryan, Neb., 137, 652

Robert Emory Pattison, Pa., 97, 95

Joseph Clay Stiles Blackburn, Ky., 82, 0

Horace Boies, Iowa, 67, 0

John McLean, Ohio, 54, 0

Claude Matthews, Ind., 37, 0

Benjamin Ryan Tillman, S.C., 17, 0

Sylvester Pennoyer, Ore., 8, 0

Henry Moore Teller, Colo., 8, 0

Adlai Ewing Stevenson, Ill., 6, 8

William Eustis Russell, Mass., 2, 0

James Edwin Campbell, Pa., 1, 0

David Bennett Hill, N.Y., 1, 1

David Turpie, Ind., 0, 1

Total number of votes:

First ballot: 752

Fifth ballot: 768

Number necessary for nomination: 512

Candidates were nominated by acclamation.

Populist Party (People's Party, Middle-of-the-Road Party)

July 22–25, 1896, the Auditorium, St. Louis, Mo.

P: William Jennings Bryan, Neb.
VP: Thomas Edward Watson, Ga.

Bryan was nominated on the first ballot. Candidates for nomination and the votes they received:

William Jennings Bryan, Neb., 1042
Seymour Frank Norton, Ill., 321
Eugene Victor Debs, Ind., 8
Ignatius Donnelly, Minn., 3
Jacob Sechler Coxey, Ohio, 1

At this convention, the nomination for Vice President was made before the nomination for President.

National Democratic Party (Sound Money Democratic Party)

Sept. 2–3, 1896, Indianapolis, Ind.

P: John McAuley Palmer, Ill.
VP: Simon Bolivar Buckner, Ky.

Palmer was nominated on the first ballot. Candidates for nomination and the votes they received:

John McAuley Palmer, Ill., $763^1/_4$

Edward Stuyvesant Bragg, Wis., $124^1/_2$

Prohibition Party

May 27–28, 1896, Exhibition Hall, Pittsburgh, Pa.

P: Joshua Levering, Md.
VP: Hale Johnson, Ill.

Socialist Labor Party

July 4–10, 1896, Grand Central Palace, New York, N.Y.

P: Charles Horatio Matchett, N.Y.
VP: Matthew Maguire, N.J.

National Party

May 28, 1896, Pittsburgh, Pa.

P: Charles Eugene Bentley, Neb.
VP: James Haywood Southgate, N.C.

This group bolted from the Prohibition Party and formed a new party advocating a financial plan favoring the free and unlimited coinage of both silver and gold at a ratio of 16 to 1.

National Silver Party (Bi-Metallic League)

July 23–25, 1896, Exposition Building, St. Louis, Mo.

P: William Jennings Bryan, Neb.
VP: Arthur Sewall, Me.

Candidates were nominated by acclamation.

1896 POPULAR VOTE

Republican Party, 7,104,779
Democratic Party, 6,502,925
Populist Party (People's Party), 222,583
National Democratic Party, 133,148
Prohibition Party, 132,007
Socialist Labor Party, 36,274
National Party, 13,969

1896 ELECTORAL VOTE

There were 447 electoral votes from 45 states.

McKinley received 60.63 percent (271 votes—23 states) as follows: Calif. 8 (of the 9 votes); Conn. 6; Del. 3; Ill. 24; Ind. 15; Iowa 13; Ky. 12 (of the 13 votes); Me. 6; Md. 8; Mass. 15; Mich. 14; Minn. 9; N.H. 4; N.J. 10; N.Y. 36; N.D. 3; Ohio 23; Ore. 4; Pa. 32; R.I. 4; Vt. 4; W.Va. 6; Wis. 12.

Bryan received 39.37 percent (176 votes—22 states) as follows: Ala. 11; Ark. 8; Calif. 1 (of the 9 votes); Colo. 4; Fla. 4; Ga. 13; Idaho 3; Kan. 10; Ky. 1 (of the 13 votes); La. 8; Miss. 9; Mo. 17; Mont. 3; Neb. 8; Nev. 3; N.C. 11; S.C. 9; S.D. 4; Tenn. 12; Tex. 15; Utah 3; Va. 12; Wash. 4; Wyo. 3.

For the vice presidency the electoral votes were divided as follows: Hobart, McKinley's Republican running-mate, received 271 votes. Sewall, Bryan's Democratic running-mate, received 149 votes. Watson, Bryan's Populist running-mate, received 27 votes.

THE ELECTION OF 1900

November 6, 1900

CANDIDATES

Republican Party (12th Convention)

June 19–21, 1900, Exposition Auditorium, Philadelphia, Pa.

P: William McKinley, Ohio
VP: Theodore Roosevelt, N.Y.
First ballot: William McKinley, Ohio, 926
   Nomination made unanimous

Democratic Party (18th Convention)

July 4–6, 1900, Convention Hall, Kansas City, Mo.

P: William Jennings Bryan, Neb.
VP: Adlai Ewing Stevenson, Ill.
First ballot: William Jennings Bryan, Neb., 936
   Nomination made unanimous

Prohibition Party

June 27–28, 1900, Chicago, Ill.

P: John Granville Woolley, Ill.
VP: Henry Brewer Metcalf, R.I.
   Woolley was nominated on the first ballot. Candidates for nomination and the votes they received:
John Granville Wooley, Ill., 380
Silas Comfort Swallow, Pa., 329

Social-Democratic Party

Mar. 6–7, 1900, Indianapolis, Ind.

P: Eugene Victor Debs, Ind.
VP: Job Harriman, Calif.
   This party was later known as the Socialist Party.

People's Party (Populist—Middle-of-the-Road, Anti-Fusionist faction)

May 9–10, 1900, Robinson's Opera House, Cincinnati, Ohio

P: Wharton Barker, Pa.
VP: Ignatius Donnelly, Minn.
   Barker was nominated on the second ballot. Candidates for nomination and the votes they received on the first and second ballots:
Milford Wryarson Howard, Ala., 326 $^6/_{10}$, 336
Wharton Barker, Pa., 323 $^4/_{10}$, 370

Ignatius Donnelly, Minn., 70, 7
Seymour Frank Norton, Ill., 3, 2
Total number of votes:
First ballot: 723
Second ballot: 715
Nomination made unanimous

Socialist Labor Party

June 2–8, 1900, Grand Central Palace, New York City

P: Joseph Francis Malloney, Mass.
VP: Valentine Remmel, Pa.
   Malloney was nominated on the first ballot. Candidates for nomination and the votes they received:
Joseph Francis Malloney, Mass., 60
Valentine Remmel, Pa., 17
W. B. Hammond, Minn., 1

Union Reform Party

Sept. 3, 1900, Baltimore, Md.

P: Seth Hockett Ellis, Ohio
VP: Samuel T. Nicholson, Pa.
   This party was organized Mar. 1, 1899, at Cincinnati, Ohio, by Silver Republicans, Populists, Socialist Labor Party members, Liberty Party members, and others.

United Christian Party

May 1–2, 1900, Rock Island, Ill.

P: Jonah Fitz Randolph Leonard, Iowa
VP: David H. Martin, Pa.
   The original nominees, Silas Comfort Swallow, Pa., and John Granville Woolley, Ill., declined the nominations.

People's Party (Populist—Fusionist faction)

May 9–10, 1900, in a tent, Sioux Falls, S.D.

P: William Jennings Bryan, Neb.
VP: Adlai Ewing Stevenson, Ill.
   Candidates were nominated by acclamation.

Silver Republican Party

July 5–6, 1900, the Auditorium, Kansas City, Mo.

P: William Jennings Bryan, Neb.
VP: Adlai Ewing Stevenson, Ill.
   Charles Arnette Towne was nominated Vice President but declined the nomination.

This party favored bimetallism, a graduated income tax, and the direct election of senators. It opposed the importation of Asian labor.

National Party

Sept. 5, 1900, Carnegie Lyceum, New York, N.Y.

P: Donelson Caffery, La.
VP: Archibald Murray Howe, Mass.
Both candidates refused the nomination.

1900 POPULAR VOTE

Republican Party, 7,207,923
Democratic Party, 6,358,138
Prohibition Party, 208,914
Social-Democratic Party, 87,814
People's Party (Populist—Middle-of-the-Road, Anti-Fusionist faction), 50,373

Socialist Labor Party, 39,739
Union Reform Party, 5,700
United Christian Party, 5,500

1900 ELECTORAL VOTE

There were 447 electoral votes from 45 states.

McKinley received 65.33 percent (292 votes—28 states) as follows: Calif. 9; Conn. 6; Del. 3; Ill. 24; Ind. 15; Iowa 13; Kan. 10; Me. 6; Md. 8; Mass. 15; Mich. 14; Minn. 9; Neb. 8; N.H. 4; N.J. 10; N.Y. 36; Ohio 23; Ore. 4; Pa. 32; R.I. 4; S.D. 4; Utah 3; Vt. 4; Wash. 4; W.Va. 6; Wis. 12; Wyo. 3.

Bryan received 34.67 percent (155 votes—17 states) as follows: Ala. 11; Ark. 8; Colo. 4; Fla. 4; Ga. 13; Idaho 3; Ky. 13; La. 8; Miss. 9; Mo. 17; Mont. 3; Nev. 3; N.C. 11; S.C. 9; Tenn. 12; Tex. 15; Va. 12.

INAUGURATIONS

FIRST TERM

March 4, 1897

William McKinley took the oath of office on Thursday, March 4, 1897, on the east portico of the Capitol. The oath was administered by Chief Justice Melville Weston Fuller. It was a mild day that seemed to promise an early spring, and the ceremonies were climaxed by an impressive parade.

SECOND TERM

March 4, 1901

President McKinley took his second oath of office on Monday, March 4, 1901, on the east portico of the Capitol. Chief Justice Melville Weston Fuller again administered the oath. The inaugural parade was even larger than the one held during his first inauguration.

Drenched by showers, many spectators left to avoid the downpour. The fireworks scheduled for the evening were postponed because of the rain.

Courtesy of The Library of Congress

William McKinley's inauguration

THE VICE PRESIDENTS

Garret Augustus Hobart, first Vice President to McKinley

FIRST TERM

Name—Garret Augustus Hobart (24th V.P.)
Date of birth—June 3, 1844
Place of birth—Long Branch, N.J.
Political party—Republican
State represented—New Jersey
Term of office—Mar. 4, 1897–Nov. 21, 1899
Age at inauguration—52 years, 274 days
Occupation after term—Died in office
Date of death—Nov. 21, 1899
Age at death—55 years, 171 days
Place of death—Paterson, N.J.
Burial place—Paterson, N.J.

ADDITIONAL DATA ON HOBART

1863, graduated from Rutgers College, New Brunswick, N.J.
18–, taught school
1865, clerk for grand jury, Passaic County, N.J.

1869, admitted to the bar; practiced in Paterson, N.J.
1871–1872, city counsel, Paterson, N.J.
1872, counsel, Board of Freeholders
1872–1876, New Jersey state assembly
1874, speaker, New Jersey state assembly
1876–1882, New Jersey state senate
1881–1882, president, New Jersey state senate
Mar. 4, 1897–Nov. 21, 1899, Vice President under William McKinley

SECOND TERM

Name—Theodore Roosevelt (25th V.P.)
Political party—Republican
State represented—New York
Term of office—Mar. 4, 1901–Sept. 14, 1901
Age at inauguration—42 years, 128 days
Occupation after term—President of the United States

For further biographical information, see the chapter on Theodore Roosevelt, 26th President, on page 299.

Theodore Roosevelt, second Vice President to McKinley

CABINET

FIRST TERM

March 4, 1897–March 3, 1901

State—Richard Olney, Mass., continued from preceding administration; John Sherman, Ohio, Mar. 5, 1897; William Rufus Day, Ohio, Apr. 26, 1898; entered upon duties Apr. 28, 1898; Alvey Augustus Adee (second assistant secretary), ad interim Sept. 17, 1898; John Hay, D.C., Sept. 20, 1898; entered upon duties Sept. 30, 1898

Treasury—John Griffin Carlisle, Ky., continued from preceding administration; Lyman Judson Gage, Ill., Mar. 5, 1897

War—Daniel Scott Lamont, N.Y., continued from preceding administration; Russell Alexander Alger, Mich., Mar. 5, 1897; Elihu Root, N.Y., Aug. 1, 1899

Attorney General—Judson Harmon, Ohio, continued from preceding administration; Joseph McKenna, Calif., Mar. 5, 1897; entered upon duties Mar. 7, 1897; John Kelvey Richards, Ohio (solicitor general), ad interim Jan. 26, 1898; John William Griggs, N.J., Jan. 25, 1898; entered upon duties Feb. 1, 1898

Postmaster General—William Lyne Wilson, W.Va., continued from preceding administration; James Albert Gary, Md., Mar. 5, 1897; Charles Emory Smith, Pa., Apr. 21, 1898

Navy—Hilary Abner Herbert, Ala., continued from preceding administration; John Davis Long, Mass., Mar. 5, 1897

Interior—David Rowland Francis, Mo., continued from preceding administration; Cornelius Newton Bliss, N.Y., Mar. 5, 1897; Ethan Allen Hitchcock, Mo., Dec. 21, 1898; entered upon duties Feb. 20, 1899

Agriculture—Julius Sterling Morton, Neb., continued from preceding administration; James Wilson, Iowa, Mar. 5, 1897

—

President McKinley, far left, with his first cabinet

SECOND TERM

March 4, 1901–September 14, 1901

State—John Hay, D.C., continued from preceding administration; recommissioned Mar. 5, 1901

Treasury—Lyman Judson Gage, Ill., continued from preceding administration; recommissioned Mar. 5, 1901

War—Elihu Root, N.Y., continued from preceding administration; recommissioned Mar. 5, 1901

Attorney General—John William Griggs, N.J., continued from preceding administration; recommissioned Mar. 5, 1901; John Kelvey Richards, Ohio (solicitor general), ad interim Apr. 1, 1901; Philander Chase

Knox, Pa., Apr. 5, 1901; entered upon duties Apr. 10, 1901

Postmaster General—Charles Emory Smith, Pa., continued from preceding administration; recommissioned Mar. 5, 1901

Navy—John Davis Long, Mass., continued from preceding administration; recommissioned Mar. 5, 1901

Interior—Ethan Allen Hitchcock, Mo., continued from preceding administration; recommissioned Mar. 5, 1901

Agriculture—James Wilson, Iowa, continued from preceding administration; recommissioned Mar. 5, 1901

CONGRESS

FIFTY-FIFTH CONGRESS

March 4, 1897–March 3, 1899

First session—Mar. 15, 1897–July 24, 1897 (131 days)

Second session—Dec. 6, 1897–July 8, 1898 (215 days)

Third session—Dec. 5, 1898–Mar. 3, 1899 (89 days)

Special session of the Senate—Mar. 4, 1897–Mar. 10, 1897 (7 days)

Vice President—Garret Augustus Hobart, N.J.

President pro tempore of the Senate —William Pierce Frye, Me.

Secretary of the Senate—William Ruffin Cox, N.C.

Speaker of the House—Thomas Brackett Reed, Me., reelected Mar. 15, 1897

Clerk of the House—Alexander McDowell, Pa., reelected Mar. 15, 1897

FIFTY-SIXTH CONGRESS

March 4, 1899–March 3, 1901

First session—Dec. 4, 1899–June 7, 1900 (186 days)

Second session—Dec. 3, 1900–Mar. 3, 1901 (91 days)

Vice President—Garret Augustus Hobart, N.J., died Nov. 21, 1899; office vacant for remainder of term

President pro tempore of the Senate —William Pierce Frye, Me.

Secretary of the Senate—William Ruffin Cox, N.C.; Charles Goodwin Bennett, N.Y., elected Jan. 29, 1900

Speaker of the House—David Bremner Henderson, Iowa, elected Dec. 4, 1899

Clerk of the House—Alexander McDowell, Pa., reelected Dec. 4, 1899

FIFTY-SEVENTH CONGRESS

March 4, 1901–March 3, 1903

First session—Dec. 2, 1901–July 1, 1902 (212 days)

Second session—Dec. 1, 1866–Mar. 3, 1903 (93 days)

Special session of the Senate—Mar. 4, 1901–Mar. 9, 190 (6 days)

Vice President—Theodore Roosevelt, N.Y. (succeeded to the presidency on Sept. 14, 1901, on the death of William McKinley; office vacant for remainder of term)

President pro tempore of the Senate —William Pierce Frye, Me., reelected Mar. 7, 1901

Secretary of the Senate—Charles Goodwin Bennett, N.Y.

Speaker of the House—David Bremner Henderson, Iowa, elected Dec. 2, 1901

Clerk of the House—Alexander McDowell, Pa., elected Dec. 2, 1901

APPOINTMENTS TO THE SUPREME COURT

Associate Justice

Joseph McKenna, Calif., Jan. 21, 1898 (replaced Stephen Johnson Field)

IMPORTANT DATES IN THE PRESIDENCY

Feb. 15, 1898, battleship U.S.S. *Maine* blown up in Havana harbor

Apr. 23, 1898, President McKinley issued call for 125,000 volunteers to serve two years

Apr. 25, 1898, United States declared war against Spain

May 1, 1898, Commodore Dewey, commander of Asiatic squadron, destroyed Spanish fleet at Manila Bay in the Philippines

June 10, 1898, U.S. Marines landed in Cuba at Guantánamo Bay

July 1, 1898, United States Expeditionary Force at Manila

Courtesy of The Library of Congress

The destruction of the USS Maine, *February 15, 1898*

July 1, 1898, first balloon destroyed by enemy gunfire, Santiago, Cuba

July 3, 1898, Spain's Caribbean fleet defeated at Santiago, Cuba

July 7, 1898, Hawaii annexed to the United States by act of Congress (first island territory annexed)

Aug. 12, 1898, peace protocol signed

Nov. 8, 1898, South Dakota voters approved initiative and referendum

Dec. 10, 1898, Treaty of Paris signed: Spain freed Cuba and ceded Puerto Rico, Guam, and the Philippines to the United States, receiving $20 million in payment for the Philippines; the United States established as a world power

Feb. 4, 1899, Filipino insurgents started unsuccessful guerrilla war against United States to gain recognition of independence

Mar. 3, 1899, George Dewey made Admiral of the Navy

Apr. 11, 1899, Philippines, Puerto Rico, and Guam formally acquired by the United States

Dec. 2, 1899, American Samoa acquired by treaty

1900, Gold Standard Act passed by Congress

Sept. 8, 1900, Galveston, Tex., hurricane

Nov. 3–10, 1900, first automobile show, New York City

ADDITIONAL DATA ON McKINLEY

WILLIAM McKINLEY

—was the fifth President born in Ohio.
—was the seventh President whose mother was alive when he was inaugurated.
—was the fifth President to die in office.
—was the third President assassinated.
—was the second Ohio-born President to be assassinated.
—was the fifth Ohio-born President elected within 28 years.

McKINLEY CAMPAIGNED BY TELEPHONE

William McKinley was the first President to use the telephone for campaign purposes. In 1896 he telephoned 38 of his campaign managers in as many states from his residence at Canton, Ohio, on matters pertaining to his campaign.

McKINLEY REJECTED TRADE PROTECTIONISM

For much of his political career, McKinley was the nation's foremost advocate of high tariffs. The son of a pig-iron manufacturer, he devoutly believed that protectionist policies were needed to develop strong domestic industries. The Tariff Act of 1890 that bore his name pushed tariffs to record highs, and in 1897 he persuaded Congress to pass the Dingley Tariff, the highest ever. At the dawn of the twentieth century, however, the nation was a young world power with vast productive capacities, and new markets for trade were becoming available in Asia as well as Europe.

In a speech at Buffalo, New York, on September 5, 1901, the President called for reciprocal trade agreements among commercial

Courtesy of The Library of Congress

The assassination of President McKinley

partners that would facilitate lowered trade restrictions and that might create a "universal brotherhood of man" through the fair structuring of international commerce. Although McKinley might have had the political clout to force Congress to accept tariff reform, he was fatally shot by the anarchist Leon Czolgosz the day after delivering his speech on trade reciprocity.

McKINLEY ASSASSINATED

President McKinley was shot on September 6, 1901, at the Pan American Exposition, Buffalo, N.Y., by Leon Czolgosz, a factory worker who was an anarchist. Czolgosz fired two shots from a pistol hidden in his handkerchief. McKinley died on September 14, 1901. Czolgosz was tried in the Supreme Court of New York and was convicted. He was electrocuted on October 29, 1901, at Auburn State Prison, Auburn, N.Y.

FURTHER READING

Glad, Paul W. *McKinley, Bryan, and the People.* 1964.

Gould, Lewis L. *The Presidency of William McKinley.* 1980.

Leech, Margaret *In the Days of McKinley.* 1959.

Morgan, H. W. *William McKinley and His America.* 1963.

Courtesy of The Library of Congress

Theodore Roosevelt

Theodore Roosevelt

Date of birth—Oct. 27, 1858

Place of birth—New York, N.Y.

Education—Tutored at home; studied in Dresden, Germany, summer 1873; Harvard College, Cambridge, Mass., bachelor's degree, magna cum laude, June 30, 1880; Columbia Law School, 1880–1881

Religion—Dutch Reformed Church

Ancestry—Dutch, Scottish, French, English

Career—Officer in state national guard, state legislator, member of U.S. Civil Service Commission, New York City police commissioner, Army colonel in Spanish-American War, assistant Secretary of the Navy, governor of New York, Vice President

Political party—Republican

State represented—New York

Term of office—Sept. 14, 1901–Mar. 4, 1909 (Roosevelt succeeded to the presidency on the death of William McKinley.)

Term served—7 years, 171 days

Administration—29th, 30th

Congresses—57th, 58th, 59th, 60th

Age at inauguration—42 years, 322 days

Lived after term—9 years, 309 days

Occupation after term—Writer, big-game hunter, political leader

Date of death—Jan. 6, 1919

Age at death—60 years, 71 days

Place of death—Oyster Bay, N.Y.

Burial place—Young's Memorial Cemetery, Oyster Bay, N.Y.

FAMILY

FATHER

Name—Theodore Roosevelt

Date of birth—Sept. 22, 1831

Place of birth—New York, N.Y.

Marriage—Martha Bulloch, Dec. 22, 1853, Roswell, Ga.

Occupation—Glass importer, merchant; philanthropist, civic activist

Date of death—Feb. 9, 1878

Place of death—New York, N.Y.

Age at death—46 years, 140 days

MOTHER

Name at birth—Martha Bulloch

Date of birth—July 8, 1834

Place of birth—Hartford, Conn.

Marriage—Theodore Roosevelt, Dec. 22, 1853, Roswell, Ga.

Date of death—Feb. 14, 1884

Place of death—New York, N.Y.

Age at death—49 years, 221 days

SIBLINGS

Theodore Roosevelt was the second of four children.

Children of Theodore Roosevelt and Martha Bulloch Roosevelt

Anna Roosevelt, b. Jan. 7, 1855, d. Aug. 25, 1931

Theodore Roosevelt, b. Oct. 27, 1858, d. Jan. 6, 1919

Elliott Roosevelt, b. Feb. 28, 1860, d. Aug. 14, 1894

Corinne Roosevelt, b. Sept. 17, 1861, d. Feb. 17, 1933

MARRIAGES

First marriage

Married—Alice Lee

Date of marriage—Oct. 27, 1880

Place of marriage—Brookline, Mass.
Age of wife at marriage—19 years, 82 days
Age of husband at marriage—22 years
Years married—3 years, 110 days

Second marriage

Married—Edith Kermit Carow
Date of marriage—Dec. 2, 1886
Place of marriage—London, England
Age of wife at marriage—25 years, 118 days
Age of husband at marriage—28 years, 36 days
Years married—32 years, 35 days

CHILDREN

Children of Theodore Roosevelt and Alice Lee Roosevelt
Alice Lee Roosevelt, b. Feb. 12, 1884, New York, N.Y.; m. Feb. 17, 1906, Nicholas Longworth, at the White House, Washington, D.C.; d. Feb. 20, 1980, Washington, D.C.

Children of Theodore Roosevelt and Edith Kermit Carow Roosevelt
Theodore Roosevelt, b. Sept. 13, 1887, Oyster Bay, N.Y.; m. June 20, 1910, Eleanor Butler Alexander, New York, N.Y.; d. July 12, 1944, Normandy, France
Kermit Roosevelt, b. Oct. 10, 1889, Oyster Bay, N.Y.; m. June 11, 1914, Belle Wyatt Willard, Madrid, Spain; d. June 4, 1943, on active military duty in Alaska
Ethel Carow Roosevelt, b. Aug. 13, 1891, Oyster Bay, N.Y.; m. Apr. 4, 1913, Dr. Richard Derby, Oyster Bay, N.Y.; d. Dec. 10, 1977, Oyster Bay, N.Y.
Archibald ("Archie") Bulloch Roosevelt, b. Apr. 9, 1894, Washington, D.C.; m. Apr. 14, 1917, Grace Stackpole Lockwood, Boston, Mass.; d. Oct. 13, 1979, Hobe Sound, Fla.
Quentin Roosevelt, b. Nov. 19, 1897, Washington, D.C.; d. July 14, 1918, shot down in aerial combat in France

THE PRESIDENT'S WIVES

First wife

Name at birth—Alice Hathaway Lee
Date of birth—July 29, 1861
Place of birth—Chestnut Hill, Mass.
Mother—Caroline Haskell Lee
Father—George Cabot Lee
Marriage—Theodore Roosevelt, Oct. 27, 1880, Brookline, Mass.
Children—Alice Lee Roosevelt, b. Feb. 12, 1884, d. Feb. 20, 1980
Date of death—Feb. 14, 1884
Age at death—22 years, 192 days
Place of death—New York, N.Y.
Burial place—Cambridge, Mass.
Years younger than the President—2 years, 283 days
Years the President survived her—34 years, 326 days

Courtesy of The Library of Congress

Alice Hathaway Lee, first wife of Theodore Roosevelt

Second wife

Name at birth—Edith Kermit Carow

Date of birth—Aug. 6, 1861

Place of birth—Norwich, Conn.

Mother—Gertrude Elizabeth Tyler Carow

Father—Charles Carow

Education—Miss Comstock's School, New York, N.Y.

Marriage—Theodore Roosevelt, Dec. 2, 1886, London, England

Children—Theodore Roosevelt, b. Sept. 13, 1887, d. July 12, 1944; Kermit Roosevelt, b. Oct. 10, 1889, d. June 4, 1943; Ethel Carow Roosevelt, b. Aug. 13, 1891, d. Dec. 10, 1977; Archibald Bulloch Roosevelt, b. Apr. 9, 1894, d. Oct. 13, 1979; Quentin Roosevelt, b. Nov. 19, 1897, d. July 14, 1918

Date of death—Sept. 30, 1948

Age at death—87 years, 45 days

Place of death—Oyster Bay, N.Y.

Burial place—Oyster Bay, N.Y.

Years younger than the President—2 years, 293 days

Years she survived the President—29 years, 267 days

Courtesy of The Library of Congress

Edith Roosevelt, second wife of Theodore Roosevelt

THE FIRST LADY

When Theodore Roosevelt succeeded to the presidency, Edith Kermit Carow, his second wife, became the First Lady of the land. The White House was a lively place because of the activities of the President's children—four sons and two daughters. During Roosevelt's administration, Alice Lee Roosevelt, the daughter of the President by his first wife, Alice Lee, was married to Nicholas Longworth, a congressman from Ohio, at the White House.

IMPORTANT DATES IN THE PRESIDENT'S LIFE

1880, graduated from Harvard

1880–1881, attended Columbia University Law School

1882–1884, New York State Assembly

1884–1886, at his North Dakota ranch

1886, returned to New York City; unsuccessful candidate for mayor

May 13, 1889–1895, U.S. Civil Service Commission (appointed by President Harrison)

May 6, 1895, president of New York City Board of Police Commissioners

Apr. 19, 1897, appointed assistant secretary of the Navy

1898, resigned Navy post; organized first regiment U.S. volunteer cavalry, known as "Roosevelt's Rough Riders"

May 6, 1898, lieutenant colonel

July 11, 1898, colonel

Sept. 15, 1898, mustered out of service

1899–1901, governor of New York

1900, nominated as vice presidential candidate on Republican ticket

Mar. 4, 1901–Sept. 14, 1901, Vice President under William McKinley

Sept. 14, 1901, succeeded to the presidency on the death of President McKinley; took oath of office at Buffalo, N.Y.

1904, nominated for another term as President on the Republican ticket

Mar. 4, 1905–Mar. 4, 1909, President (second term)

1906, awarded Nobel Prize for services in connection with Russo-Japanese peace treaty

June 1908, received three complimentary votes at Republican nominating convention

1909, on African hunting and scientific expedition outfitted by the Smithsonian Institution

1910, special ambassador from the United States at the funeral of King Edward VII of England

June 1912, unsuccessful candidate for Republican nomination for the presidency

Aug. 1912, organized Progressive ("Bull Moose") Party; nominated for presidency

Oct. 1913–May 1914, explored River of Doubt in South America

1916, declined nomination by the Progressive Party as presidential candidate

1916–1919, engaged in literary pursuits

Courtesy of The Library of Congress

Theodore Roosevelt at the head of his "Rough Riders"

ELECTIONS

THE ELECTION OF 1904

November 8, 1904

CANDIDATES

Republican Party (13th Convention)

June 21–23, 1904, the Coliseum, Chicago, Ill.

P: Theodore Roosevelt, N.Y.
VP: Charles Warren Fairbanks, Ind.
First ballot: Theodore Roosevelt, N.Y., 994
Nomination made unanimous

Democratic Party (19th Convention)

July 6–9, 1904, the Coliseum, St. Louis, Mo.

P: Alton Brooks Parker, N.Y.
VP: Henry Gassaway Davis, W. Va.

Parker was nominated on the first ballot. Candidates for nomination and the votes they received:
Alton Brooks Parker, N.Y., 679

William Randolph Hearst, N.Y., 181
Francis Marion Cockrell, Mo., 42
Richard Olney, Mass., 38
Edward C. Wall, Wis., 27
George Gray, Del., 12
John Sharp Williams, Miss., 8
Robert Emory Pattison, Pa., 4
Nelson Appleton Miles, Mass., 3
George Brinton McClellan, N.J., 3
Charles Arnette Towne, Minn., 2
Bird Sim Coler, N.Y., 1
Total number of votes: 1,000
Number necessary for nomination: 667
Nomination made unanimous

Socialist Party

May 1–6, 1904, Brand's Hall, Chicago, Ill.

P: Eugene Victor Debs, Ind.
VP: Benjamin Hanford, N.Y.

Debs was nominated by acclamation on the first ballot.

This was the first nominating convention of the Socialist Party, which was formed March 25, 1900, at Indianapolis, Ind., by a group of secessionists from the Socialist Labor Party.

Prohibition Party

June 30, 1904, Indianapolis, Ind.

P: Silas Comfort Swallow, Pa.
VP: George W. Carroll, Tex.

People's Party (Populist Party)

July 4, 1904, Springfield, Ill.

P: Thomas Edward Watson, Ga.
   VP: Thomas Henry Tibbles, Neb.

Socialist Labor Party

July 2–8, 1904, New York, N.Y.

P: Charles Hunter Corregan, N.Y.
VP: William Wesley Cox, Ill.

Continental Party

Aug. 31, 1904, Chicago, Ill.

P: Austin Holcomb, Ga.
VP: A. King, Mo.

United Christian Party

May 2, 1904, St. Louis, Mo.

A platform was adopted, but no nominations were made for President or Vice President.

1904 POPULAR VOTE

Republican Party, 7,623,486
Democratic Party, 5,077,911
Socialist Party, 402,283
Prohibition Party, 258,536
People's Party, 117,183
Socialist Labor Party, 31,249
Continental Party, 1,000

1904 ELECTORAL VOTE

There were 476 electoral votes from 45 states.

Roosevelt received 70.60 percent (336 votes—32 states) as follows: Calif. 10; Colo. 5; Conn. 7; Del. 3; Idaho 3; Ill. 27; Ind. 15; Iowa 13; Kan. 10; Me. 6; Md. 1 (of the 8 votes); Mass. 16; Mich. 14; Minn. 11; Mo. 18; Mont. 3; Neb. 8; Nev. 3; N.H. 4; N.J. 12; N.Y. 39; N.D. 4; Ohio 23; Ore. 4; Pa. 34; R.I. 4; S.D. 4; Utah 3; Vt. 4; Wash. 5; W.Va. 7; Wis. 13; Wyo. 13.

Parker received 29.40 percent (140 votes—13 states) as follows: Ala. 11; Ark. 9; Fla. 5; Ga. 13; Ky. 13; La. 9; Md. 7 (of the 8 votes); Miss. 10; N.C. 12; S.C. 9; Tenn. 12; Tex. 18; Va. 12.

INAUGURATIONS

FIRST TERM

September 14, 1901

After the death of President McKinley, Theodore Roosevelt took the oath of office on Saturday, September 14, 1901, at 3:32 P.M., at the residence of Ansley Wilcox at Buffalo, N.Y. The oath was administered by Judge John R. Hazel of the United States District Court.

Courtesy of The Library of Congress

Theodore Roosevelt at his inauguration

303

SECOND TERM

March 4, 1905

President Roosevelt took the oath of office Saturday, March 4, 1905, on the east portico of the Capitol. Chief Justice Melville Weston Fuller administered the oath. A spectacular parade from 3:00 P.M. to 6:15 P.M. was witnessed by more than 200,000 visitors. Although it was very windy, Roosevelt delivered his inaugural address bareheaded, the first President to do so.

THE VICE PRESIDENT

Name—Charles Warren Fairbanks (26th V.P.)

Date of birth—May 11, 1852

Place of birth—Unionville Center, Ohio

Political party—Republican

State represented—Indiana

Term of office—Mar. 4, 1905–Mar. 4, 1909

Age at inauguration—52 years, 297 days

Occupation after term—Lawyer

Date of death—June 4, 1918

Age at death—66 years, 24 days

Place of death—Indianapolis, Ind.

Burial place—Indianapolis, Ind.

ADDITIONAL DATA ON FAIRBANKS

1872, graduated from Ohio Wesleyan University, Delaware, Ohio

1874, admitted to the bar in Ohio; practiced in Indianapolis, Ind.

1892, unsuccessful candidate for election to U.S. Senate (from Indiana)

Mar. 4, 1897–Mar. 3, 1905, U.S. Senate (from Indiana)

Mar. 4, 1905–Mar. 4, 1909, Vice President under Theodore Roosevelt

Courtesy of The Library of Congress

Charles Warren Fairbanks, Vice President to Theodore Roosevelt

1916, unsuccessful candidate for vice presidency on Republican ticket headed by Charles Evans Hughes

1916, resumed law practice, Indianapolis

CABINET

FIRST TERM

September 14, 1901–March 3, 1905

State—John Hay, D.C., continued from preceding administration

Treasury—Lyman Judson Gage, Ill., continued from preceding administration; Leslie Mortier Shaw, Iowa, Jan. 9, 1902; entered upon duties Feb. 1, 1902

War—Elihu Root, N.Y., continued from preceding administration; William Howard Taft, Ohio, Jan. 11, 1904, to take effect Feb. 1, 1904

Attorney General—Philander Chase Knox, Pa., continued from preceding administra-

The first cabinet of Theodore Roosevelt

tion; recommissioned Dec. 16, 1901; William Henry Moody, Mass., July 1, 1904

Postmaster General—Charles Emory Smith, Pa., continued from preceding administration; Henry Clay Payne, Wis., Jan. 9, 1902; Robert John Wynne, Pa., Oct. 10, 1904

Navy—John Davis Long, Mass., continued from preceding administration; William Henry Moody, Mass., Apr. 29, 1902; entered upon duties May 1, 1902; Paul Morton, Ill., July 1, 1904

Interior—Ethan Allen Hitchcock, Mo., continued from preceding administration

Agriculture—James Wilson, Iowa, continued from preceding administration

Commerce and Labor—George Bruce Cortelyou, N.Y., Feb. 16, 1903; Victor Howard Metcalf, Calif., July 1, 1904

SECOND TERM

March 4, 1905–March 3, 1909

State—John Hay, D.C., continued from preceding administration; recommissioned Mar. 6, 1905; died July 1, 1905; Francis Butler Loomis, Ohio (assistant secretary), ad interim July 1–18, 1905; Elihu Root, N.Y., July 7, 1905; entered upon duties July 19, 1905; Robert Bacon, N.Y., Jan. 27, 1909

Treasury—Leslie Mortier Shaw, Iowa, continued from preceding administration; recommissioned Mar. 6, 1905; George Bruce Cortelyou, N.Y., Jan. 15, 1907, to take effect Mar. 4, 1907

War—William Howard Taft, Ohio, continued from preceding administration; recommissioned Mar. 6, 1905; Luke Edward Wright, Tenn., June 29, 1908; entered upon duties July 1, 1908

Attorney General—William Henry Moody, Mass., continued from preceding administration; recommissioned Mar. 6, 1905; Charles Joseph Bonaparte, Md., Dec. 12, 1906; entered upon duties Dec. 17, 1906

Postmaster General—Robert John Wynne, Pa., continued from preceding administration; George Bruce Cortelyou, N.Y., Mar. 6,

1905; George von Lengerke Meyer, Mass.,
Jan. 15, 1907, to take effect Mar. 4, 1907

Navy—Paul Morton, Ill., continued from pre-
ceding administration; recommissioned
Mar. 6, 1905; Charles Joseph Bonaparte,
Md., July 1, 1905; Victor Howard Metcalf,
Calif., Dec. 12, 1906; entered upon duties
Dec. 17, 1906; Truman Handy Newberry,
Mich., Dec. 1, 1908

Interior—Ethan Allen Hitchcock, Mo., continued from preceding administration;

recommissioned Mar. 6, 1905; James
Rudolph Garfield, Ohio, Jan. 15, 1907, to
take effect Mar. 4, 1907

Agriculture—James Wilson, Iowa, continued from preceding administration; recommissioned Mar. 6, 1905

Commerce and Labor—Victor Howard
Metcalf, Calif., continued from preceding
administration; recommissioned Mar. 6,
1905; Oscar Solomon Straus, N.Y., Dec. 12,
1906; entered upon duties Dec. 17, 1906

CONGRESS

FIFTY-EIGHTH CONGRESS

March 4, 1903–March 3, 1905

First session—Nov. 9, 1903–Dec. 7, 1903
(29 days)

Second session—Dec. 7, 1903–May 7, 1904
(144 days)

Third session—Dec. 5, 1904–Mar. 3, 1905
(89 days)

Special session of the Senate—Mar. 5,
1903–Mar. 19, 1903 (14 days)

Vice President—None (Theodore Roosevelt
succeeded to the presidency on the death of
William McKinley on Sept. 14, 1901)

President pro tempore of the Senate
—William Pierce Frye, Me.

Secretary of the Senate—Charles Goodwin Bennett, N.Y.

Speaker of the House—Joseph Gurney
Cannon, Ill., elected Nov. 9, 1903

Clerk of the House—Alexander McDowell,
Pa., reelected Nov. 9, 1903

FIFTY-NINTH CONGRESS

March 4, 1905–March 3, 1907

First session—Dec. 4, 1905–June 30, 1906
(209 days)

Second session—Dec. 3, 1906–Mar. 3, 1907
(91 days)

Special session of the Senate—Mar. 4,
1905–Mar. 18, 1905 (14 days)

Vice President—Charles Warren Fairbanks, Ind.

President pro tempore of the Senate
—William Pierce Frye, Me.

Secretary of the Senate—Charles Goodwin Bennett, N.Y.

Speaker of the House—Joseph Gurney
Cannon, Ill., reelected Dec. 4, 1905

Clerk of the House—Alexander McDowell,
Pa., reelected Dec. 4, 1905

SIXTIETH CONGRESS

March 4, 1907–March 3, 1909

First session—Dec. 2, 1907–May 30, 1908
(181 days)

Second session—Dec. 7, 1908–Mar. 3, 1909
(87 days)

Vice president—Charles Warren Fairbanks, Ind.

President pro tempore of the Senate
—William Frye, Me., reelected Dec. 5,
1907

Secretary of the Senate—Charles Goodwin Bennett, N.Y.

Speaker of the House—Joseph Gurney
Cannon, Ill., reelected Dec. 2, 1907

Clerk of the House—Alexander McDowell,
Pa., reelected Dec. 2, 1907

APPOINTMENTS TO THE SUPREME COURT

Associate Justices

Oliver Wendell Holmes, Mass., Dec. 4, 1902
(replaced Horace Gray)

William Rufus Day, Ohio, Feb. 23, 1903
(replaced George Shiras)

William Henry Moody, Mass., Dec. 12, 1906
(replaced Henry Billings Brown)

IMPORTANT DATES IN THE PRESIDENCY

Sept. 18, 1901, commission form of government adopted, Galveston, Tex.

Dec. 11, 1901, first wireless signal received from Europe

1902, President used Sherman Anti-Trust Act to initiate legal action against a rail monopoly; the government won its case in 1904

May 12, 1902, Pennsylvania coal strike begun

May 20, 1902, Cuban republic inaugurated

June 17, 1902, Newlands Reclamation Act passed, making federal funds available for irrigation projects

Dec. 14, 1902, laying of Pacific cable began at San Francisco, Calif.

Dec. 19, 1902, U.S. intervention in Venezuelan dispute with European nations

Feb. 14, 1903, Department of Commerce and Labor created

Mar. 19, 1903, reciprocity treaty with Cuba ratified

Oct. 17, 1903, Alaska boundary award made

Nov. 3, 1903, encouraged by the President, Panamanian rebels declared their independence from Colombia

Nov. 6, 1903, Republic of Panama recognized

Nov. 18, 1903, Isthmian Canal Convention; Panama ceded Canal Zone strip ten miles wide through lease and sale to United States

Dec. 17, 1903, Wright brothers' airplane flight, Kitty Hawk, N.C.

Feb. 26, 1904, Panama Canal Zone formally acquired by the United States

March 14, 1904, Supreme Court upheld Sherman Anti-trust Act, dissolving Northern Securities Company (railroad trust organized by J. P. Morgan)

Apr. 30, 1904, President Roosevelt opened Louisiana Purchase Exposition, St. Louis, Mo.

Dec. 6, 1904, President Roosevelt issued corollary to the Monroe Doctrine, defending American intervention in Latin America to stop European aggression

Sept. 5, 1905, Russo-Japanese peace treaty signed, Portsmouth, N.H.

Mar. 1906, Congress passed Hepburn Act, which awarded greater powers to the Interstate Commerce Commission

Apr. 18–20, 1906, San Francisco earthquake

June 30, 1906, federal Pure Food and Drug Act passed

1907, financial panic

1907, Inland Waterways Commission established

1907, White House Conference on Conservation

Courtesy of The Library of Congress

The Wright Brothers take flight at Kitty Hawk, N.C.

Oct. 18, 1907, Fourth Hague Convention signed by 32 nations

Nov. 16, 1907, Oklahoma admitted as the 46th state

Dec. 16, 1907, Great White Fleet, an array of American battleships, left on around-the-world cruise; fleet commander was Rear Admiral Robley D. "Fighting Bob" Evans until he fell ill and was succeeded by Rear Admiral Charles S. Sperry

1907–1908, "gentlemen's agreement" with Japan—Japanese declared they would issue no passports to laborors wishing to emigrate to the United States

1908, Bureau of Investigation created to conduct investigations for the Justice Department

Oct. 1, 1908, Henry Ford introduced the Model T

Feb. 9, 1909, first narcotics prohibition act passed

Feb. 22, 1909, Great White Fleet completed voyage

ADDITIONAL DATA ON ROOSEVELT

THEODORE ROOSEVELT

—was the third President born in New York.
—was the fourth President to remarry.
—was the first President to win a Nobel Peace Prize.
—was the youngest President at the time he took office.

DOUBLE TRAGEDY IN THE ROOSEVELT FAMILY

Thursday, February 14, 1884, was a day of tragedy for Assemblyman Theodore Roosevelt. On that day, at Roosevelt's home in New York City, his mother died of typhoid fever and his wife, Alice, died of Bright's disease.

On February 16, 1884, two hearses were driven from his mother's residence in New York City to the Fifth Avenue Presbyterian Church, where services were conducted by Rev. John Hall, prior to interment in Greenwood Cemetery, Brooklyn, N.Y.

THE YOUNGEST PRESIDENT

Theodore Roosevelt was the youngest man to take the oath of office as Chief Executive. He was a little more than 42 years and 10 months old when sworn in.

ROOSEVELT RODE IN AUTOMOBILE AND AIRPLANE

The first President to ride in an automobile was Theodore Roosevelt, who was a passenger in a purple-lined Columbia Electric Victoria on a trip through Hartford, Conn., on August 22, 1902. Twenty carriages followed the presidential automobile during its tour of the city.

After his term of office, Roosevelt again pioneered when he took a ride in an airplane on October 11, 1910, at St. Louis, Mo. The plane was piloted by Archie Hoxsey. Roosevelt was the first of the Presidents to fly in an airplane.

ROOSEVELT APPOINTED COMMERCE AND LABOR SECRETARY

On February 16, 1903, Theodore Roosevelt appointed George B. Cortelyou Secretary of Commerce and Labor, the first man to hold that office.

LINCOLN'S RING WORN BY ROOSEVELT

Prior to the inauguration, Secretary of State John Hay gave the President a ring that had been worn by Abraham Lincoln and taken off his hand after his death. After the ceremonies, Roosevelt returned the ring to Hay. (John Hay had been Lincoln's private secretary.)

ROOSEVELT VISITED A FOREIGN COUNTRY

Theodore Roosevelt was the first President to visit a foreign country during his term of office. He traveled to Panama on the U.S.S. *Louisiana.* After visiting Panama from November 14 to 17, 1906, he went to Puerto Rico.

PEACE PRIZE TO ROOSEVELT

The first American recipient of a Nobel Prize was Theodore Roosevelt, to whom the $40,000 prize was awarded in 1906 for his services in concluding the treaty of peace between Russia and Japan at the end of the Russo-Japanese War.

ROOSEVELT SUBMERGED IN SUBMARINE

Theodore Roosevelt was the first President to submerge in a submarine. On Friday, August 25, 1905, he went aboard the submarine *Plunger,* commanded by Lieutenant Charles Preston Nelson, in Long Island Sound, off Oyster Bay, N.Y. The *Plunger* submerged to a depth of 20 feet in water from 30 to 40 feet deep, remaining stationary for about 55 minutes. Roosevelt operated the controls. At one time, the lights were turned off and the *Plunger* operated in complete darkness.

ASSASSINATION OF ROOSEVELT ATTEMPTED

When Theodore Roosevelt was leaving the Hotel Gilpatrick in Milwaukee, Wis., on October 14, 1912, about 8 P.M., en route to the Auditorium to make a speech during his "Bull Moose" campaign for the presidency, John Nepomuk Schrank, a saloon keeper, attempted to assassinate him. Roosevelt was shot in the chest.

Although the bullet tore through his coat and his shirt was covered with blood, Roosevelt said, "I will deliver this speech or die, one or the other." He began, "Friends, I shall ask you to be very quiet and please excuse me from making you a very long speech. I'll do the best I can, but, you see, there is a bullet in my body. But, it's nothing. I'm not hurt badly." He spoke about fifty minutes and then went to the hospital.

The assassin was opposed to the former President's attempt to capture a third term. Five alienists decided Schrank was suffering from insane delusions, and on November 13, 1912, he was declared insane. He was committed to the Northern State Hospital for the Insane at Oshkosh, Wis., and died September 15, 1943, at Central State Hospital, Waupun, Wis.

ROOSEVELT WAS AWARDED MEDAL OF HONOR

On January 16, 2001, more than a century after the Rough Riders charged up Kettle Hill in the battle for Cuba's San Juan Heights, President William Jefferson Clinton awarded the Medal of Honor to the man who led the charge, Colonel Theodore Roosevelt, and cited him posthumously for bravery in an action that may well have changed the course of the Spanish-American War. Roosevelt would have been pleased: "I am entitled to the Medal of Honor and I want it," he wrote after the battle, but the War Department, which he had criticized in a widely reprinted letter, disappointed him. The Roosevelt family reopened the matter in connection with the centennial of the charge, in 1998, and a thorough review of the case resulted in the posthumous award. The family announced that the medal would be on permanent display in the Roosevelt Room at the White House, complementing the former President's Nobel Peace Prize.

Courtesy of The Library of Congress

Teddy Roosevelt's famous smile

FURTHER READING

Brands, H. W. *T. R.: The Last Romantic.* 1997.

Chessman, G. W. *Theodore Roosevelt and the Politics of Power.* 1969.

Gould, Lewis L. *The Presidency of Theodore Roosevelt.* 1991.

Harbaugh, William H. *Power and Responsibility.* 1961.

———. *The Life and Times of Theodore Roosevelt.* 1963.

Hawley, Joshua David. *Theodore Roosevelt: Preacher of Righteousness.* 2008.

Miller, Nathan. *Theodore Roosevelt: A Life.* 1992.

Morris, Edmund. *The Rise of Theodore Roosevelt.* 1979.

Mowry, George E. *Theodore Roosevelt and the Progressive Movement.* 1946.

Courtesy of The Library of Congress

William Howard Taft

Date of birth—Sept. 15, 1857

Place of birth—Cincinnati, Ohio

Education—District school, Cincinnati, Ohio; Woodward High School, Cincinnati, Ohio, graduated June 5, 1874; Yale College, New Haven, Conn., graduated (salutatorian) June 27, 1878; University of Cincinnati Law School, graduated May 1, 1880

Religion—Unitarian

Ancestry—English

Career—Lawyer, assistant county prosecutor, tax collector, assistant county solicitor, judge of Cincinnati Superior Court, U.S. solicitor general, judge of Sixth U.S. Circuit Court, law professor and law school dean, commissioner and governor-general of the Philippines, Secretary of War

Political party—Republican

State represented—Ohio

Term of office—Mar. 4, 1909–Mar. 4, 1913

Term served—4 years

Administration—31st

Congresses—61st, 62nd

Age at inauguration—51 years, 170 days

Lived after term—17 years, 4 days

Occupation after term—Chief Associate Justice, U.S. Supreme Court

Date of death—Mar. 8, 1930

Age at death—72 years, 174 days

Place of death—Washington, D.C.

Burial place—Arlington National Cemetery, Arlington, Va.

FAMILY

FATHER

Name—Alphonso Taft

Date of birth—Nov. 5, 1810

Place of birth—East Townshend, Vt.

First marriage—Fanny Phelps, Aug. 29, 1841, Townshend, Vt. (b. Mar. 28, 1823, West Townshend, Vt.; d. June 2, 1852, Cincinnati, Ohio)

Second marriage—Louise Maria Torrey, Dec. 26, 1853, Millbury, Mass

Occupation—Lawyer; justice of state supreme court, U.S. ambassador to Hungary, U.S. Secretary of War, U.S. Attorney General

Date of death—May 21, 1891

Place of death—San Diego, Calif.

Age at death—80 years, 197 days

MOTHER

Name at birth—Louise Maria Torrey

Date of birth—Sept. 11, 1827

Place of birth—Boston, Mass.

Marriage—Alphonso Taft, Dec. 26, 1853, Millbury, Mass.

Date of death—Dec. 8, 1907

Place of death—Millbury, Mass.

Age at death—80 years, 88 days

SIBLINGS

William Howard Taft was the seventh of his father's ten children, the second of five children of a second marriage.

Children of Alphonso Taft and Fanny Phelps Taft

Charles Phelps Taft, b. Dec. 21, 1843, d. Dec. 31, 1929

Peter Rawson Taft, b. May 12, 1846, d. June 4, 1889

Mary Taft, b. 1848 (died in infancy)

Alphonso Taft, b. 1850, d. June 2, 1851

Alphonso Taft, b. 1851, d. 1852

Children of Alphonso Taft and Louise Maria Torrey Taft

Samuel Davenport Taft, b. Feb. 1855, d. Apr. 8, 1856

William Howard Taft, b. Sept. 15, 1857, d. Mar. 8, 1930

Henry Waters Taft, b. May 27, 1859, d. Aug. 11, 1945

Horace Dutton Taft, b. Dec. 28, 1861, d. Jan. 28, 1943

Frances Louise Taft, b. July 18, 1865, d. Jan. 5, 1950

MARRIAGE

Married—Helen Herron

Date of marriage—June 19, 1886

Place of marriage—Cincinnati, Ohio

Age of wife at marriage—25 years, 168 days

Age of husband at marriage—28 years, 277 days

Years married—43 years, 262 days

SILVER WEDDING CELEBRATION

President and Mrs. Taft celebrated their silver wedding anniversary at the White House on June 9, 1911, with a night garden party for about 5,000 guests. The members of the House of Representatives presented them with a $1,700 solid silver service and the members of the Senate gave them compote dishes.

CHILDREN

Robert Alphonso Taft, b. Sept. 8, 1889, Cincinnati, Ohio; m. Oct. 17, 1914, Martha Wheaton Bowers, Washington, D.C.; d. July 31, 1953, New York, N.Y.

Helen Herron Taft, b. Aug. 1, 1891, Cincinnati, Ohio; m. July 19, 1920, Frederick Johnson Manning, Murray Bay, Canada; d. Feb. 1987, Philadelphia, Pa.

Charles Phelps Taft, b. Sept. 20, 1897, Cincinnati, Ohio; m. Oct. 6, 1917, Eleanor Kellogg Chase, Waterbury, Conn.; d. June 24, 1983, Cincinnati, Ohio

THE PRESIDENT'S WIFE

Name at birth—Helen ("Nellie") Herron

Date of birth—Jan. 2, 1861

Place of birth—Cincinnati, Ohio

Mother—Harriet Collins Herron

Father—John Williamson Herron

Father's occupation—Judge, lawyer (partner of Rutherford B. Hayes)

Education—Miss Nourse's school, Cincinnati, Ohio; Miami University, Oxford, Ohio; studied music, Cincinnati, Ohio

Marriage—William Howard Taft, June 19, 1886, Cincinnati, Ohio

Children—Robert Alphonso Taft, b. Sept. 8, 1889, d. July 31, 1953; Helen Herron Taft, b. Aug. 1, 1891, d. Feb. 1987; Charles Phelps Taft, b. Sept. 20, 1897, d. June 24, 1983

Date of death—May 22, 1943

Age at death—82 years, 140 days

Place of death—Washington, D.C.

Burial place—Arlington National Cemetery, Arlington, Va.

Courtesy of The Library of Congress

Helen Taft, wife of William Howard Taft

Years younger than the President—3 years, 109 days

Years she survived the President—13 years, 75 days

THE FIRST LADY

Helen Herron Taft was a suffragist and greatly interested in politics. She said of her partnership with her husband, "I always had the satisfaction of knowing almost as much as he about the politics and intricacies of any situation." She attended many political and official conferences with the President.

Helen Herron Taft was the first President's wife to write a commercially published book: *Recollections of Full Years* was published in 1914 by Dodd, Mead & Company, New York City.

She was also the first wife to ride with a President from the Capitol to the White House after his inauguration (March 4, 1909).

In 1909, Mrs. Taft suffered a stroke, leaving her partly paralyzed and unable to speak for a time. She was too proud to let the public know of her illness and retreated temporarily to the Taft summer home in Beverley, Mass. When she returned to the White House, the President tried to conceal his political problems from her, and wrote to Theodore Roosevelt, his rival, that his duties were "heavier to bear because of Mrs. Taft's condition."

By 1911, however, she had recovered, and the Tafts celebrated their silver wedding anniversary with a lavish reception. In 1912, Mrs. Taft led a fund-raising drive for a memorial to victims of the *Titanic*.

IMPORTANT DATES IN THE PRESIDENT'S LIFE

June 5, 1874, graduated from Woodward High School, Cincinnati, Ohio

June 27, 1878, graduated from Yale College

May 1, 1880, graduated from law school, University of Cincinnati

May 5, 1880, admitted to the bar

1880–1881, law reporter on Cincinnati newspapers

1881–1882, assistant prosecuting attorney, Cincinnati, Ohio

1887, assistant city solicitor, Cincinnati

Mar. 7, 1887–Feb. 1890, judge, Superior Court of Cincinnati

Feb. 4, 1890–1892, U.S. Solicitor General

Mar. 17, 1892–1900, U.S. Federal Circuit Court

1896–1900, dean, University of Cincinnati Law School

Mar. 13, 1900–1901, president of Philippines Commission

July 4, 1901, appointed governor-general of Philippine Islands

1902, arranged with Pope Leo XIII for the purchase of Roman Catholic lands in the Philippines

Feb. 1, 1904–June 1908, secretary of war

1907, government mission to Cuba, Panama, and Philippine Islands

1907, provisional governor of Cuba

June 22, 1912, nominated for the presidency by the Republican Party

Apr. 1, 1913–1921, professor of law, Yale

June 30, 1921–Feb. 3, 1930, chief justice, U.S. Supreme Court

ELECTIONS

THE ELECTION OF 1908

November 3, 1908

CANDIDATES

Republican Party (14th Convention)

June 16–19, 1908, the Coliseum, Chicago, Ill.

P: William Howard Taft, Ohio

VP: James Schoolcraft Sherman, N.Y.

Taft was nominated on the first ballot. Candidates for nomination and the votes they received:

William Howard Taft, Ohio, 702

Philander Chase Knox, Pa., 68

Charles Evans Hughes, N.Y., 67

Joseph Gurney Cannon, Ill., 58
Charles Warren Fairbanks, Ind., 40
Robert Marion La Follette, Wis., 25
Joseph Benson Foraker, Ohio, 16
Theodore Roosevelt, N.Y., 3
Total number of votes: 979
Nomination made unanimous

Democratic Party (20th Convention)

July 8–10, 1908, Civic Auditorium, Denver, Colo.

P: William Jennings Bryan, Neb.
VP: John Worth Kern, Ind.

Bryan was nominated on the first ballot. Candidates for nomination and the votes they received:
William Jennings Bryan, Neb., 888
George Gray, Del., 59
John Albert Johnson, Minn., 46
Total number of votes: 993

Socialist Party

May 10–17, 1908, Brand's Hall, Chicago, Ill.

P: Eugene Victor Debs, Ind.
VP: Benjamin Hanford, N.Y.

Debs was nominated on the first ballot. Candidates for nomination and the votes they received:
Eugene Victor Debs, Ind., 159
James F. Carey, Mass., 16
Carl D. Thompson, Wis., 14
A. M. Simons, Ill., 9
Nomination made unanimous

Prohibition Party

July 15–16, 1908, Columbus, Ohio

P: Eugene Wilder Chafin, Ill.
VP: Aaron Sherman Watkins, Ohio

Chafin was nominated on the third ballot. Candidates for nomination and the votes they received on the third ballot:
Eugene Wilder Chafin, Ill., 636
William B. Palmer, Mo., 451

Independence Party

July 29, 1908, Chicago, Ill.

P: Thomas Louis Hisgen, Mass.
VP: John Temple Graves, Ga.

Hisgen was nominated on the third ballot. Candidates for nomination and the votes they received on the third ballot:

Courtesy of The Library of Congress

Taft's inauguration

Thomas Louis Hisgen, Mass., 83
Milford W. Howard, Ala., 38
John Temple Graves, Ga., 7
William Randolph Hearst, N.Y., 2

People's Party (Populist Party)

Apr. 2–3, 1908, St. Louis, Mo.

P: Thomas Edward Watson, Ga.
VP: Samuel Williams, Ind.

Watson was nominated on the first ballot.

Socialist Labor Party

July 2–5, 1908, New York, N.Y.

P: August Gillhaus, N.Y.
VP: Donald L. Munro, Va.

Martin R. Preston of Nevada, convicted of killing a man in 1905 and serving a 25-year term in a Nevada penitentiary, was unanimously nominated even though he was also ineligible as he was under constitutional age. Gillhaus was selected later.

United Christian Party

May 1, 1908, Rock Island, Ill.

P: Daniel Braxton Turner, Ill.
VP: Lorenzo S. Coffin, Iowa

1908 POPULAR VOTE

Republican Party, 7,678,908
Democratic Party, 6,409,104
Socialist Party, 420,793

Prohibition Party, 253,840
Independence Party, 82,872
People's Party (Populist Party), 29,100
Socialist Labor Party, 14,021
United Christian Party, 400

1908 ELECTORAL VOTE

There were 483 electoral votes from 46 states.

Taft received 66.46 percent (321 votes—29 states) as follows: Calif. 10; Conn. 7; Del. 3; Idaho 3; Ill. 27; Ind. 15; Iowa 13; Kan. 10; Me. 6; Md. 2 (of the 8 votes); Mass. 16; Mich. 14; Minn. 11; Mo. 18; Mont. 3; N.H. 4; N.J. 12; N.Y. 39; N.D. 4; Ohio 23; Ore. 4; Pa. 34; R.I. 4; S.D. 4; Utah 3; Vt. 4; Wash. 5; W.Va. 7; Wis. 13; Wyo. 3.

Bryan received 33.54 percent (162 votes—17 states) as follows: Ala. 11; Ark. 9; Colo. 5; Fla. 5; Ga. 13; Ky. 13; La. 9; Md. 6 (of the 8 votes); Miss. 10; Neb. 8; Nev. 3; N.C. 12; Okla. 7; S.C. 9; Tenn. 12; Tex. 18; Va. 12.

INAUGURATION

March 4, 1909

William Howard Taft took the oath of office on Thursday, March 4, 1909, in the Senate Chamber. The oath was to have been administered on the east portico of the Capitol, but as a blizzard was raging the ceremonies were held indoors. The oath was administered by Chief Justice Melville Weston Fuller. It was the sixth time Justice Fuller had officiated in this capacity.

Ice forming on trees cracked branches and made transportation so hazardous that incoming trains were prevented from entering the city. Most of the inaugural parade was disbanded; only a small part of the planned parade was held. Mrs. Taft set a precedent by riding to the White House with her husband.

Instead of riding back to the White House with the new President, former President Roosevelt went directly to the railroad station from which he left the city.

THE VICE PRESIDENT

Name—James Schoolcraft Sherman (27th V.P.)

Date of birth—Oct. 24, 1855

Place of birth—Utica, N.Y.

Political party—Republican

State represented—New York

Term of office—Mar. 4, 1909–Oct. 30, 1912

Age at inauguration—53 years, 131 days

Occupation after term—Died in office

Date of death—Oct. 30, 1912

Age at death—57 years, 6 days

Place of death—Utica, N.Y.

Burial place—Utica, N.Y.

ADDITIONAL DATA ON SHERMAN

1878, graduated from Hamilton College, Clinton, N.Y.

Courtesy of The Library of Congress

James Sherman, Vice President to William H. Taft

1880, admitted to the bar; practiced in Utica, N.Y.

1884, mayor of Utica, N.Y.

Mar. 4, 1887–Mar. 3, 1891, U.S. House of Representatives (from New York)

1890, unsuccessful candidate for reelection

Mar. 4, 1893–Mar. 3, 1909, U.S. House of Representatives (from New York)

Mar. 4, 1909–Oct. 30, 1912, Vice President under William Howard Taft

1912, Republican nominee for Vice President

VICE PRESIDENT RENOMINATED BUT DIED BEFORE ELECTION

James Schoolcraft Sherman of New York was elected Vice President to serve with President Taft from March 4, 1909 to March 3, 1913. In June 1912 he was renominated by the Republicans for a second term, but he died on October 30, 1912, six days before the election. The eight electoral votes which would have been cast for him had he lived were transferred to Nicholas Murray Butler, nominated by the Republican National Committee.

CABINET

March 4, 1909–March 3, 1913

State—Roger Bacon, N.Y., continued from preceding administration; Philander Chase Knox, Pa., Mar. 5, 1909

Treasury—George Bruce Cortelyou, N.Y., continued from preceding administration; Franklin MacVeagh, Ill., Mar. 5, 1909; entered upon duties Mar. 8, 1909

War—Luke Edward Wright, Tenn., continued from preceding administration; Jacob McGavock Dickinson, Tenn., Mar. 5, 1909, entered upon duties Mar. 12, 1909; Henry Lewis Stimson, N.Y., May 16, 1911; entered upon duties May 22, 1911

Attorney General—Charles Joseph Bonaparte, Md., continued from preceding administration; George Woodward Wickersham, N.Y., Mar. 5, 1909

Postmaster General—George von Lengerke Meyer, Mass., continued from preceding administration; Frank Harris Hitchcock, Mass., Mar. 5, 1909

Navy—Truman Handy Newberry, Mich., continued from preceding administration; George von Lengerke Meyer, Mass., Mar. 5, 1909

Interior—James Rudolph Garfield, Ohio, continued from preceding administration; Richard Achilles Ballinger, Wash., Mar. 5, 1909; Walter Lowrie Fisher, Ill., Mar. 7, 1911

Agriculture—James Wilson, Iowa, continued from preceding administration; recommissioned Mar. 5, 1909

Commerce and Labor—Oscar Solomon Straus, N.Y., continued from preceding administration; Charles Nagel, Mo., Mar. 5, 1909

CONGRESS

SIXTY–FIRST CONGRESS

March 4, 1909–March 3, 1911

First session—Mar. 15, 1909–Aug. 5, 1909 (144 days)

Second session—Dec. 6, 1909–June 25, 1910 (202 days)

Third session—Dec. 5, 1910–Mar. 3, 1911 (89 days)

Special session of the Senate—Mar. 4, 1909–Mar. 6, 190 (3 days)

Vice President—James Schoolcraft Sherman, N.Y.

President pro tempore of the Senate —William Pierce Frye, Me.

Secretary of the Senate—Charles Goodwin Bennett, N.Y.

Clerk of the House—Alexander McDowell, Pa., reelected Mar. 15, 1909

Speaker of the House— Joseph Gurney Cannon, Ill.

SIXTY–SECOND CONGRESS

March 4, 1911–March 3, 1913

First session—Apr. 4, 1911–Aug. 22, 1911 (141 days)

Second session—Dec. 4, 1911–Aug. 26, 1912 (267 days)

Third session—Dec. 2, 1912–Mar. 3, 1913 (92 days)

Vice President—James Schoolcraft Sherman, N.Y., died Oct. 30, 1912

President pro tempore of the Senate —William Pierce Frye, Me., resigned as president pro tempore Apr. 27, 1911; Charles Curtis, Kan., elected to serve Dec.

4–12, 1911; Augustus Octavius Bacon, Ga., elected to serve Jan. 15–17, Mar. 11–12, Apr. 8, May 10, May 30–June 3, June 13–July 5, Aug. 1–10, and Aug. 27–Dec. 15, 1912; Jan. 5–18 and Feb. 2–15, 1913; Jacob Harold Gallinger, N.H., elected to serve Feb. 12–14, Apr. 26–27, May 7, July 6–31, Aug. 12–26, 1912, Dec. 16, 1912–Jan. 4, 1913, Jan. 19–Feb. 1, and Feb. 16–Mar. 3, 1913; Henry Cabot Lodge, Mass., elected to serve Mar. 25–26, 1912; Frank Bosworth Brandegee, Conn., elected to serve May 25, 1912

Secretary of the Senate—Charles Goodwin Bennett, N.Y.

Speaker of the House—Champ Clark, Mo., elected Apr. 4, 1911

Clerk of the House—Alexander McDowell, Pa., South Trimble, Ky., elected Apr. 4, 1911

APPOINTMENTS TO THE SUPREME COURT

Chief Justice

Edward Douglass White, La., Dec. 19, 1910 (served as Associate Justice, 1894–1910; replaced Melville Weston Fuller)

Associate Justices

Horace Harmon Lurton, Tenn., Dec. 20, 1909 (replaced Rufus William Peckham)

Charles Evans Hughes, N.Y., May 2, 1910 (replaced David Josiah Brewer)

Willis Van Devanter, Wyo., Dec. 16, 1910 (replaced William Henry Moody)

Joseph Rucker Lamar, Ga., Dec. 17, 1910 (replaced Edward Douglass White)

Mahlon Pitney, N.J., Mar. 13, 1912 (replaced John Marshall Harlan)

IMPORTANT DATES IN THE PRESIDENCY

Apr. 6, 1909, Peary discovered the North Pole

July 30, 1909, Army officer, B. D. Foulois, made first transcontinental flight

Aug. 2, 1909, U.S. purchased its first airplane

Aug. 11, 1909, first radio SOS from an American ship

Feb. 8, 1910, Boy Scouts of America incorporated

June 1, 1910, Atlantic fisheries dispute settled by the Hague

June 25, 1910, postal savings bank authorized

Jan. 3, 1911, postal banks established

Jan. 6, 1911, "Flying Fish," first successful hydroplane, flown

Feb. 15, 1911, U.S. Commerce Court opened

March 25, 1911, Triangle Shirtwaist Co. fire caused 146 deaths and new demands for workplace safety

May 15, 1911, Supreme Court ordered the Standard Oil trust dissolved

Oct. 18, 1911, keel of *Jupiter,* first electrically propelled vessel of U.S. Navy, laid

Jan. 6, 1912, New Mexico admitted as the 47th state

Feb. 14, 1912, Arizona admitted as the 48th state

Aug. 14, 1912, Marines sent to Nicaragua, when that nation defaulted on loans

Jan. 1, 1913, parcel post service began

Feb. 25, 1913, Sixteenth Amendment to the Constitution ratified, giving Congress the power to collect taxes on income

Mar. 4, 1913, Department of Commerce and Labor reorganized as two departments

ADDITIONAL DATA ON TAFT

WILLIAM HOWARD TAFT

—was the sixth President born in Ohio.

—was the first to become chief justice of the United States Supreme Court.

—was the first President who had been a member of a cabinet after the Civil War.

—was the first cabinet member other than a secretary of state to become President.

TAFT AT YALE

William Howard Taft stood second in scholarship in the Yale class of 1878, which consisted of 132 graduates. On graduation day, he was 20 years and 285 days old. He was 5 feet $10^3/_4$ inches tall and weighed 225 pounds. The average weight of his classmates was 151 pounds.

SIXTEENTH AMENDMENT ENACTED

The Sixteenth Amendment to the Constitution, granting income tax power to the Federal Government "without apportionment among the several states and without regard to census," was passed by Congress on July 12, 1909. It was proposed to the legislatures of the several states by the Sixty-first Congress on July 12, 1909, and was ratified by all the states except Connecticut, Florida, Pennsylvania, Rhode Island, Utah, and Virginia. Delaware, New Mexico, and Wyoming all ratified it on February 3, 1913, making it effective. The amendment was declared ratified by the Secretary of State on February 25, 1913.

JAPANESE CHERRY TREES PLANTED

In 1909 Mrs. Taft was instrumental in securing eighty Japanese cherry trees from various nurseries, all that were available at that time. These were planted along the banks of the Potomac River in West Potomac Park.

On December 10, 1909, a shipment of two thousand additional trees, the gift of the City of Tokyo to the City of Washington, reached Seattle, Washington. They were transported to Washington, D.C., but proved diseased. Three thousand more trees replaced them and were planted by Mrs. Taft on March 27, 1912, and by Viscountess Chinda, the wife of the Japanese ambassador, around the Tidal Basin and along Riverside Drive in East and West Potomac Parks.

TAFT OPENED BASEBALL SEASON

William Howard Taft was the first President to pitch a ball to open the baseball season. On April 14, 1910, he threw out the first ball in the American League game between the Washington Senators and the Philadelphia Athletics. The Senators, with Walter Johnson pitching, won the game 3–0. A crowd of 12,226 broke all previous attendance records.

FIRST PRESIDENT OF FORTY-EIGHT STATES

The forty-eighth state admitted to the United States was Arizona, which became a state on February 14, 1912, during the Taft administration. President Taft thus became the first President of the 48 states that comprised the Union until 1959.

PRESIDENT BECAME CHIEF JUSTICE

President Taft was the first and only President of the United States to become a chief justice of the Supreme Court of the United States. Taft was appointed by President Warren G. Harding on June 30, 1921, and he resigned on February 3, 1930, a few weeks before his death.

TAFT BURIED IN ARLINGTON CEMETERY

The first President buried in the National Cemetery at Arlington, Va., was William Howard Taft, interred March 11, 1930.

Courtesy of the Library of Congress

Taft's gravesite at Arlington National Cemetery, Virginia

FURTHER READING

Anderson, Donald F. *William Howard Taft.* 1973.

Burton, David Henry. *The Learned Presidency: Theodore Roosevelt, William Howard Taft, Woodrow Wilson.* 1988.

Coletta, Paolo E. *The Presidency of William Howard Taft.* Rev. ed. 1988.

Pringle, Henry F. *The Life and Times of William Howard Taft.* 2 vols., 1939.

Severn, William. *William Howard Taft: The President Who Became Chief Justice.* 1970.

Courtesy of The Library of Congress

Woodrow Wilson

Name at birth—Thomas Woodrow Wilson

Date of birth—Dec. 29, 1856

Place of birth—Staunton, Va.

Education—Tutored at home to age 12; private school, Columbia, S.C.; Davidson College, 1873–1874; College of New Jersey, now Princeton University, bachelor's degree, June 18, 1879; University of Virginia Law School, 1879–1880; private law studies; Johns Hopkins University, Baltimore, Md., Ph.D. in political science, 1886

Religion—Presbyterian

Ancestry—Scotch-Irish, English, Scottish

Career—College professor, historian and political scientist, president of Princeton University, governor of New Jersey

Political party—Democratic

State represented—New Jersey

Term of office—Mar. 4, 1913–Mar. 4, 1921

Term served—8 years

Administration—32nd, 33rd

Congresses—63rd, 64th, 65th, 66th

Age at inauguration—56 years, 65 days

Lived after term—2 years, 337 days

Occupation after term—None; ill

Date of death—Feb. 3, 1924

Age at death—67 years, 36 days

Place of death—Washington, D.C.

Burial place—National Cathedral, Washington, D.C.

FAMILY

FATHER

Name—Joseph Ruggles Wilson

Date of birth—Feb. 28, 1822

Place of birth—Steubenville, Ohio

Marriage—Jessie Janet Woodrow, June 7, 1849, Chillicothe, Ohio

Occupation—Teacher, Presbyterian minister, university and seminary professor, church officer

Date of death—Jan. 21, 1903

Place of death—Princeton, N.J.

Age at death—80 years, 327 days

MOTHER

Name at birth—Jessie Janet Woodrow

Date of birth—Dec. 20, 1826

Place of birth—Carlisle, England

Marriage—Joseph Ruggles Wilson, June 7, 1849, Chillicothe, Ohio

Date of death—Apr. 15, 1888

Place of death—Clarksville, Tenn.

Age at death—61 years, 116 days

SIBLINGS

Woodrow Wilson was the third child in a family of four.

Children of Joseph Ruggles Wilson and Jessie Janet Woodrow Wilson

Marion Wilson, b. 1850

Annie Josephine Wilson, b. 1854, d. Sept. 15, 1916

(Thomas) Woodrow Wilson, b. Dec. 28, 1856, d. Feb. 3, 1924

Joseph Ruggles Wilson, b. 1866

MARRIAGES

First marriage

Married—Ellen Louise Axson

Date of marriage—June 24, 1885

Place of marriage—Savannah, Ga.

Age of wife at marriage—25 years, 40 days

Age of husband at marriage—28 years, 177 days

Years married—29 years, 43 days

Second marriage

Married—Edith Bolling Galt

Date of marriage—Dec. 18, 1915

Place of marriage—Washington, D.C.

Age of wife at marriage—43 years, 64 days

Age of husband at marriage—58 years, 354 days

Years married—8 years, 47 days

CHILDREN

Children of Woodrow Wilson and Ellen Louise Axson Wilson

Margaret Woodrow Wilson, b. Apr. 30, 1886, Gainesville, Ga; d. Feb. 12, 1944, Pondicherry, India

Jessie Woodrow Wilson, b. Aug. 28, 1887, Gainesville, Ga.; m. Nov. 25, 1913, Francis Bowres Sayre at the White House, Washington D.C.; d. Jan. 15, 1933, Cambridge, Mass.

Eleanor Randolph Wilson, b. Oct. 16, 1889, Middletown, Conn.; m. May 7, 1914, William Gibbs McAdoo, at the White House, Washington, D.C.; d. Apr. 5, 1967, Montecito, Calif.

Children of Woodrow Wilson and Edith Bolling Galt Wilson

None

THE PRESIDENT'S WIVES

First wife

Name at birth—Ellen Louise Axson

Date of birth—May 15, 1860

Place of birth—Savannah, Ga.

Mother—Margaret Hoyt Axson

Father—Samuel Edward Axson

Father's occupation—Presbyterian minister

Education—Private schools; Female Seminary, Rome, Ga.; attended Art Students' League, New York, N.Y.

Marriage—Woodrow Wilson, June 24, 1885, Savannah, Ga.

Children—Margaret Woodrow Wilson, b. Apr. 30, 1886, d. Feb. 12, 1944; Jessie Woodrow Wilson, b. Aug. 28, 1887, d. Jan. 15, 1933; Eleanor Randolph Wilson, b. Oct. 16, 1889, d. Apr. 5, 1967

Occupation—Painter, housing activist

Date of death—Aug. 6, 1914

Age at death—54 years, 83 days

Place of death—Washington, D.C.

Burial place—Rome, Ga.

Courtesy of The Library of Congress

Ellen Wilson, first wife of Woodrow Wilson

Years younger than the President—3 years, 137 days

Years the President survived her—9 years, 181 days

Second wife

Name at birth—Edith Bolling

Date of birth—Oct. 15, 1872

Place of birth—Wytheville, Va.

Mother—Sallie White Bolling

Father—William Holcombe Bolling

Father's occupation—Judge

Education—Martha Washington College, Abington, Va.; Powell's School, Richmond, Va.

First marriage—Norman Galt, Apr. 30, 1896, Wytheville, Va. (d. Jan. 28, 1908)

Second marriage—Woodrow Wilson, Dec. 18, 1915, Washington, D.C.

Children—None

Occupation—Owner of jewelry store

Date of death—Dec. 28, 1961

Age at death—89 years, 64 days

Place of death—Washington, D.C.

Burial place—Washington, D.C.

Years younger than the President—15 years, 291 days

Years she survived the President—37 years, 328 days

THE FIRST LADIES

Ellen Louise Axson Wilson died on August 6, 1914, having served only 17 months as First Lady of the land. A daughter, Margaret, took over the functions of hostess of the White House, serving until December 18, 1915, when President Wilson married Edith Bolling Galt. After Wilson suffered a para-

Courtesy of The Library of Congress

Edith Wilson, second wife of Woodrow Wilson

lytic attack on September 26, 1919, social activities at the White House were suspended for the balance of his term.

During the time of President Wilson's incapacity, from October 1919 to April 1920, Edith Wilson controlled all access to the President and kept him sequestered. She maintained that his mental functions were unimpaired. The President was not shown any document she did not wish him to see, and she was his only spokesperson. In the spring of 1920 the President improved slightly, but Mrs. Wilson continued to supervise his activities closely. Although the public was not told the full extent of Wilson's illness, reports of Mrs. Wilson's power emerged in the press, and one reporter called her "the finest argument for suffrage."

IMPORTANT DATES IN THE PRESIDENT'S LIFE

1856, family moved to Augusta, Ga.

1870, family moved to Columbia, S.C.

1873, entered Davidson College, Davidson, N.C.

1874, withdrew from college because of ill health

Sept. 1875, entered the College of New Jersey (now Princeton)

June 18, 1879, graduated from Princeton

Oct. 2, 1879, entered University of Virginia Law School

1880, left school because of ill health

1882, admitted to the bar

1882–1883, practiced law at Atlanta, Ga., with partner, Edward I. Renick

1885, taught history and political science at Bryn Mawr College, Bryn Mawr, Pa.; published *Congressional Government*

June 1886, received Ph.D degree in political science from Johns Hopkins University

1888–1890, taught at Wesleyan University, Middletown, Conn.

1890–1902, professor of jurisprudence and political economy, Princeton University

June 9, 1902, unanimously elected president of Princeton University

Oct. 25, 1902–Oct. 23, 1910, president of Princeton University

Sept. 15, 1910, nominated by the Democrats as candidate for governor of New Jersey

Jan. 7, 1911–Mar. 1, 1913, governor of New Jersey

July 2, 1912, nominated by the Democrats for the presidency

Nov. 5, 1912, elected President

Mar. 4, 1913–Mar. 4, 1921, President

Dec. 8, 1915, married Edith Bolling Galt at Washington, D.C.

Dec. 4, 1918, sailed for Europe to attend Peace Conference at Paris

Jan. 18, 1919, addressed opening session of Paris Peace Conference

Feb. 1919, returned to United States

Mar. 1919, sailed for Europe

June 28, 1919, signed peace treaty with Germany at Versailles, France

July 8, 1919, returned to United States

Sept. 26, 1919, collapsed; suffered paralytic stroke at Pueblo, Colo.

Oct. 2, 1919, stroke paralyzed his left arm and leg

Oct. 4, 1919, complete physical breakdown

Dec. 10, 1920, awarded Nobel Peace Prize

Mar. 4, 1921, after inauguration of his successor retired to his Washington, D.C., residence, where his health continued to deteriorate

ELECTIONS

THE ELECTION OF 1912

November 5, 1912

CANDIDATES

Democratic Party (21st Convention)

June 25–29, July 1–2, 1912, Fifth Maryland Regiment Armory, Baltimore, Md.

P: Woodrow Wilson, N.J.
VP: Thomas Riley Marshall, Ind.

Wilson was nominated on the forty-sixth ballot. Candidates for nomination and the votes they received on the first and forty-sixth ballots:

Champ Clark, Mo., 440$^1/_2$, 84

Woodrow Wilson, N.J., 324, 990

Judson Harmon, Ohio, 148, 0

Oscar Wilder Underwood, Ala., 117$^1/_2$, 12

Thomas Riley Marshall, Ind., 31, 0

Simeon Eben Baldwin, Conn., 22, 0

George Sebastian Silzer, N.J., 2, 0

William Jennings Bryan, Neb., 1, 0

Number necessary for nomination: 545

Total number of votes: 1,086

Progressive Party ("Bull Moose" Party)

Aug. 5–7, 1912, the Coliseum, Chicago, Ill.

P: Theodore Roosevelt, N.Y.
VP: Hiram Warren Johnson, Calif.

Roosevelt was nominated by acclamation on the first ballot.

The Progressive Party was organized June 19, 1912, by Roosevelt supporters who seceded from the Republican party after the nomination of Taft. The nickname "Bull Moose" was derived from Roosevelt's comparison of his own strength with that of a bull moose.

Republican Party (15th Convention)

June 18–22, 1912, the Coliseum, Chicago, Ill.

P: William Howard Taft, Ohio
VP: James Schoolcraft Sherman, N.Y.

Taft was nominated on the first ballot. Candidates for nomination and the votes they received:

William Howard Taft, Ohio, 561

Theodore Roosevelt, N.Y., 107

Robert Marion La Follette, Wis., 41

Albert Baird Cummins, Iowa, 17

Charles Evans Hughes, N.Y., 2

Total number of votes: 728

Of the 1,078 delegates present, 344 did not vote.

John Schoolcraft Sherman, the vice presidential nominee, died on Oct. 30, 1912. He was replaced by Nicholas Murray Butler, N.Y.

Socialist Party

May 12–18, 1912, Tomlinson Hall, Indianapolis, Ind.

P: Eugene Victor Debs, Ind.
VP: Emil Seidel, Wis.

Debs was nominated on the first ballot. Candidates for nomination and the votes they received:

Eugene Victor Debs., Ind., 163
Emil Seidel, Wis., 56
Charles Edward Russell, 54
    Nomination made unanimous

Prohibition Party

July 10–12, 1912, Atlantic City, N.J.

P: Eugene Wilder Chafin, Ill.
VP: Aaron Sherman Watkins, Ohio

Chafin was nominated by acclamation on the first ballot.

Socialist Labor Party

Apr. 7–10, 1912, New York, N.Y.

P: Arthur Elmer Reimer, Mass.
VP: August Gillhaus, N.Y.

1912 POPULAR VOTE

Democratic Party, 6,293,454
Progressive Party, 4,119,538
Republican Party, 3,484,980
Socialist Party, 900,672
Prohibition Party, 206,275
Socialist Labor Party, 28,750

1912 ELECTORAL VOTE

There were 531 electoral votes from 48 states.

Wilson received 81.92 percent (435 votes—40 states) as follows: Ala. 12; Ariz. 3; Ark. 9; Calif. 2 (of the 13 votes); Colo. 6; Conn. 7; Del. 3; Fla. 6; Ga. 14; Idaho 4; Ill. 29; Ind. 15; Iowa 13; Kan. 10; Ky. 13; La. 10; Me. 6; Md. 8; Mass. 18; Miss. 10; Mo. 18; Mont. 4; Neb. 8; Nev. 3; N.H. 4; N.J. 14; N.M. 3; N.Y. 45; N.C. 12; N.D. 5; Ohio 24; Okla. 10; Ore. 5; R.I. 5; S.C. 9; Tenn. 12; Tex. 20; Va. 12; W.Va. 8; Wis. 13; Wyo. 3.

Roosevelt received 16.57 percent (88 votes—6 states) as follows: Calif. 11 (of the 13 votes); Mich. 15; Minn. 12; Pa. 38; S.D. 5; Wash. 7.

Taft received 1.51 percent (8 votes—2 states) as follows: Utah 4; Vt. 4.

The Republican electoral votes for the vice presidency were transferred to Butler after the death of Sherman.

THE ELECTION OF 1916

November 7, 1916

CANDIDATES

Democratic Party (22nd Convention)

June 14–16, 1916, the Coliseum, St. Louis, Mo.

P: Woodrow Wilson, N.J.
VP: Thomas Riley Marshall, Ind.

First ballot: Woodrow Wilson, N.J., 1,093

    Candidates were nominated by acclamation.

Republican Party (16th Convention)

June 7–10, 1916, the Coliseum, Chicago, Ill.

P: Charles Evans Hughes, N.Y.
VP: Charles Warren Fairbanks, Ind.

Hughes was nominated on the third ballot. Candidates for nomination and the votes they received on the first and third ballots:

Charles Evans Hughes, N.Y., $253^1/_2$, $949^1/_2$
John Wingate Weeks, Mass., 105, 3
Elihu Root, N.Y., 103, 0
Albert Baird Cummins, Iowa, 85, 0
Theodore Elijah Burton, Ohio, $77^1/_2$, 0
Charles Warren Fairbanks, Ind., $74^1/_2$, 0
Laurence Yates Sherman, Ill., 66, 0
Theodore Roosevelt, N.Y., 65, $18^1/_2$
Philander Chase Knox, Pa., 36, 0
Henry Ford, Mich., 32, 0
Martin Grove Brumbaugh, Pa., 29, 0
Robert Marion La Follette, Wis., 25, 3
William Howard Taft, Ohio, 14, 0
Thomas Coleman Du Pont, Del., 12, 5
Frank Bartlett Willis, Ohio, 4, 0
William Edgar Borah, Idaho, 2, 0

Samuel Walker McCall, Mass., 1, 0
Henry Cabot Lodge, Mass., 0, 7
Total number of votes:
First ballot: 984$^1/_2$
Third ballot: 986

Socialist Party

Mar. 10–11, 1916, Chicago, Ill.

P: Allan Louis Benson, N.Y.
VP: George Ross Kirkpatrick, N.J.

Ballots sent by mail to state organizations were counted at this meeting, which served in place of a national convention. The ballots were cast as follows:
Allan Louis Benson, N.Y., 16,639
James Hudson Maurer, Pa., 12,264
Arthur Lesueur, N.D., 3,495

Prohibition Party

July 19–21, 1916, St. Paul, Minn.

P: James Franklin Hanly, Ind.
VP: Ira Landrith, Tenn.

Socialist Labor Party

Apr. 29–30, May 1–3, 1916, New York, N.Y.

P: Arthur Elmer Reimer, Mass.
VP: Caleb Harrison, Ill.

Progressive Party

June 7–10, 1916, Auditorium, Chicago, Ill.

P: Theodore Roosevelt, N.Y.
VP: John Milliken Parker, La.

Roosevelt declined the nomination. In accord with his wishes, the Republican candidate, Hughes, was endorsed. The Progressive Party went out of existence before the election.

Courtesy of The Library of Congress

Woodrow Wilson, delivering his first inauguaral address

1916 POPULAR VOTE

Democratic Party, 9,129,606
Republican Party, 8,538,221
Socialist Party, 585,113
Prohibition Party, 220,506
Socialist Labor Party, 13,403

1916 ELECTORAL VOTE

There were 531 electoral votes from 48 states.

Wilson received 52.17 percent (277 votes—30 states) as follows: Ala. 12; Ariz. 3; Ark. 9; Calif. 13; Colo. 6; Fla. 6; Ga. 14; Idaho 4; Kan. 10; Ky. 13; La. 10; Md. 8; Miss. 10; Mo. 18; Mont. 4; Neb. 8; Nev. 3; N.H. 4; N.M. 3; N.C. 12; N.D. 5; Ohio 24; Okla. 10; S.C. 9; Tenn. 12; Tex. 20; Utah 4; Va. 12; Wash. 7; W.Va. 1 (of the 8 votes); Wyo. 3.

Hughes received 47.83 percent (254 votes—18 states) as follows: Conn. 7; Del. 3; Ill. 29; Ind. 15; Iowa 13; Me. 6; Mass. 18; Mich. 15; Minn. 12; N.J. 14; N.Y. 45; Ore. 5; Pa. 38; R.I. 5; S.D. 4; Vt. 4; W.Va. 7 (of the 8 votes); Wis. 13.

INAUGURATIONS

FIRST TERM

March 4, 1913

Woodrow Wilson took the oath of office on Tuesday, March 4, 1913, on the east portico of the Capitol. The oath was administered by Chief Justice Edward Douglass White. The day was cold and disagreeable.

SECOND TERM

March 5, 1917

Woodrow Wilson took the oath of office Monday, March 5, 1917, as March 4 fell on Sunday for the fifth time in the history of the country. Chief Justice Edward Douglass White again administered the oath to him.

THE VICE PRESIDENT

Name—Thomas Riley Marshall (28th V.P.)

Date of birth—Mar. 14, 1854

Place of birth—North Manchester, Ind.

Political party—Democratic

State represented—Indiana

Term of office—Mar. 4, 1913–Mar. 4, 1921

Age at inauguration—58 years, 355 days

Occupation after term—Lawyer, government official, writer

Date of death—June 1, 1925

Age at death—71 years, 79 days

Place of death—Washington, D.C.

Burial place—Indianapolis, Ind.

ADDITIONAL DATA ON MARSHALL

1873, graduated from Wabash College, Crawfordsville, Ind.

1875, admitted to the bar in Ohio; practiced at Columbia City, Ind.

1909–1913, governor of Indiana

Mar. 4, 1913–Mar. 4, 1921, Vice President under Woodrow Wilson

1922–1923, member of Federal Coal Commission

Courtesy of The Library of Congress

Thomas Marshall, Vice President to Woodrow Wilson

CABINET

FIRST TERM

March 4, 1913–March 3, 1917

State—Philander Chase Knox, Pa., continued from preceding administration; William Jennings Bryan, Neb., Mar. 5, 1913; Robert Lansing, N.Y. (counselor), ad interim June 9, 1915; Robert Lansing, N.Y., June 23, 1915

Treasury—Franklin MacVeagh, Ill., continued from preceding administration; William Gibbs McAdoo, N.Y., Mar. 5, 1913; entered upon duties Mar. 6, 1913

War—Henry Lewis Stimson, N.Y., continued from preceding administration; Lindley Miller Garrison, N.J., Mar. 5, 1913; Hugh Lenox Scott (United States Army), ad interim Feb. 12, 1916; served Feb. 11–Mar. 8, 1916; Newton Diehl Baker, Ohio, Mar. 7, 1916; entered upon duties Mar. 9, 1916

Attorney General—George Woodward Wickersham, N.Y., continued from preceding administration; James Clark McReynolds, Tenn., Mar. 5, 1913; entered upon duties Mar. 6, 1913; Thomas Watt Gregory, Tex., Aug. 29, 1914; entered upon duties Sept. 3, 1914

Postmaster General—Frank Harris Hitchcock, Mass., continued from preceding administration; Albert Sidney Burleson, Tex., Mar. 5, 1913

Navy—George von Lengerke Meyer, Mass., continued from preceding administration; Josephus Daniels, N.C., Mar. 5, 1913

Interior—Walter Lowrie Fisher, Ill., continued from preceding administration; Franklin Knight Lane, Calif., Mar. 5, 1913

Agriculture—James Wilson, Iowa, continued from preceding administration; David Franklin Houston, Mo., Mar. 5, 1913; entered upon duties Mar. 6, 1913

Commerce—Charles Nagel, Mo. (secretary of Commerce and Labor), continued from preceding administration; William Cox Redfield, N.Y., Mar. 5, 1913

Labor—Charles Nagel, Mo. (secretary of Commerce and Labor), continued from preceding administration; William Bauchop Wilson, Pa., Mar. 5, 1913

SECOND TERM

March 4, 1917–March 3, 1921

State—Robert Lansing, N.Y., continued from preceding administration; Frank Lyon Polk, N.Y. (under secretary), ad interim Feb. 14, 1920–Mar. 13, 1920; Bainbridge Colby, N.Y., Mar. 22, 1920; entered upon duties Mar. 23, 1920

Treasury—William Gibbs McAdoo, N.Y., continued from preceding administration; Carter Glass, Va., Dec. 6, 1918; entered upon duties Dec. 16, 1918; David Franklin Houston, Mo., Jan. 31, 1920; entered upon duties Feb. 2, 1920

War—Newton Diehl Baker, Ohio, continued from preceding administration

Attorney General—Thomas Watt Gregory, Tex., continued from preceding administration; Alexander Mitchell Palmer, Pa., Mar. 5, 1919

Postmaster General—Albert Sidney Burleson, Tex., continued from preceding administration; recommissioned Jan. 24, 1918

Navy—Josephus Daniels, N.C., continued from preceding administration

Interior—Franklin Knight Lane, Calif., continued from preceding administration; John Barton Payne, Ill., Feb. 28, 1920; entered upon duties Mar. 13, 1920

Agriculture—David Franklin Houston, Mo., continued from preceding administration; Edwin Thomas Meredith, Iowa, Jan. 31, 1920; entered upon duties Feb. 2, 1920

Commerce—William Cox Redfield, N.Y., continued from preceding administration; Joshua Willis Alexander, Mo., Dec. 11, 1919; entered upon duties Dec. 16, 1919

Labor—William Bauchop Wilson, Pa., continued from preceding administration

Woodrow Wilson, far left, with his cabinet

CONGRESS

SIXTY-THIRD CONGRESS

March 4, 1913–March 3, 1915

First session—Apr. 7, 1913–Dec. 1, 1913 (239 days)

Second session—Dec. 1, 1913–Oct. 24, 1914 (328 days)

Third session—Dec. 7, 1914–Mar. 3, 1915 (87 days)

Special session of the Senate—Mar. 4, 1913–Mar. 17, 1913 (13 days)

Vice President—Thomas Riley Marshall, Ind.

President pro tempore of the Senate —James Paul Clarke, Ark., elected Mar. 13, 1913

Secretary of the Senate—Charles Goodwin Bennett, N.Y., James Marion Baker, S.C., elected Mar. 13, 1913

Speaker of the House—Champ Clark, Mo., reelected Apr. 7, 1913

Clerk of the House—South Trimble, Ky., reelected Apr. 7, 1913

SIXTY-FOURTH CONGRESS

March 4, 1915–March 3, 1917

First session—Dec. 6, 1915–Sept. 8, 1916 (278 days)

Second session—Dec. 4, 1916–Mar. 3, 1917 (90 days)

Vice President—Thomas Riley Marshall, Ind.

President pro tempore of the Senate —James Paul Clarke, Ark., reelected Dec. 6, 1915, died Oct. 1, 1916; Willard Saulsbury, Del., elected Dec. 14, 1916

Secretary of the Senate—James Marion Baker, S.C.

Speaker of the House—Champ Clark, Mo., reelected Dec. 6, 1915

Clerk of the House—South Trimble, Ky., reelected Dec. 6, 1915

SIXTY-FIFTH CONGRESS

March 4, 1917–March 3, 1919

First session—Apr. 2, 1917–Oct. 6, 1917 (188 days)

Second session—Dec. 3, 1917–Nov. 21, 1918 (354 days)

Third session—Dec. 2, 1918–Mar. 3, 1919 (92 days)

Special session of the Senate—Mar. 5, 1917–Mar. 16, 1917

Vice President—Thomas Riley Marshall, Ind.

President pro tempore of the Senate —Willard Saulsbury, Del.

Secretary of the Senate—James Marion Baker, S.C.

Speaker of the House—Champ Clark, Mo., reelected Apr. 2, 1917

Clerk of the House—South Trimble, Ky., reelected Apr. 2, 1917

SIXTY-SIXTH CONGRESS

March 4, 1919–March 3, 1921

First session—May 19, 1919–Nov. 19, 1919 (185 days)

Second session—Dec. 1, 1919–June 5, 1920 (188 days)

Third session—Dec. 6, 1920–Mar. 3, 1921 (88 days)

Vice President—Thomas Riley Marshall, Ind.

President pro tempore of the Senate —Albert Baird Cummins, Iowa, elected May 19, 1919

Secretary of the Senate—James Marion Baker, S.C.; George Andrew Sanderson, Ill., elected May 19, 1919

Speaker of the House—Frederick Huntington Gillett, Mass., elected May 19, 1919

Clerk of the House—South Trimble, Ky.; William Tyler Page, Md., elected May 19, 1919

APPOINTMENTS TO THE SUPREME COURT

Associate Justices

James Clark McReynolds, Tenn., Aug. 29, 1914 (replaced Horace Harmon Lurton)

Louis Dembitz Brandeis, Mass., June 1, 1916 (replaced Joseph Rucker Lamar)

John Hessin Clarke, Ohio, July 24, 1916 (replaced Charles Evans Hughes)

IMPORTANT DATES IN THE PRESIDENCY

May 31, 1913, Seventeenth Amendment to the Constitution ratified (direct election of senators)

Oct. 3, 1913, the President signed the tariff bill relaxing the protectionist tariff duties that the Taft administration had promoted

Dec. 23, 1913, Federal Reserve Act

Apr. 22, 1914, Vera Cruz taken by U.S. Navy

Aug. 3, 1914, World War I began

Aug. 15, 1914, Panama Canal admitted commercial traffic

Sept. 26, 1914, Federal Trade Commission established

Oct. 15, 1914, Clayton Anti-trust Act passed

Nov. 23, 1914, U.S. troops withdrawn from Vera Cruz

Jan. 25, 1915, New York to San Francisco transcontinental telephone demonstration

Feb. 20, 1915, Panama-Pacific Exposition opened, San Francisco, Calif.

May 7, 1915, sinking of *Lusitania* by German submarine

Oct. 19, 1915, United States recognized de facto government of Carranza in Mexico

Feb. 28, 1916, treaty signed with Haitian government for United States to assume protectorate over Haiti

Mar. 1916, General Pershing with 6,000 troops sent to Mexico in pursuit of revolutionary Francisco ("Pancho") Villa

July 17, 1916, Federal Farm Loan Act signed

Aug. 4, 1916, Danish West Indies (Virgin Islands) bought from Denmark for $25 million

Sept. 1, 1916, Keating-Owen Child Labor Act signed

Sept. 3, 1916, Adamson Act established eight-hour-day on railroads

Courtesy of The Library of Congress

Soldiers in the trenches of World War I

Sept. 7, 1916, Senate ratified treaty to purchase Danish West Indies (Virgin Islands)

Nov. 1916, Jeannette Rankin of Montana elected as first congresswoman

Mar. 18, 1917, three unarmed U.S. merchant ships sunk by German submarines

Mar. 19, 1917, Supreme Court ruled that Congress has the power to deal with wages and hours of work of railroad employees in interstate commerce

Apr. 6, 1917, United States declared war against Germany

June 8, 1917, advance unit of American Expeditionary Force landed at Liverpool, England

July 28, 1917, War Industries Board created

Dec. 7, 1917, United States declared war against Austria-Hungary

Dec. 26, 1917, railroads placed under government operation

Jan. 8, 1918, Wilson outlined his "fourteen points" to Congress

Nov. 11, 1918, armistice signed at 5 A.M.

Dec. 1918, President arrived in France for peace conference

Jan. 29, 1919, Eighteenth Amendment to the Constitution ratified (prohibition of liquor manufacture, sale, and transportation)

June 28, 1919, Treaty of Versailles signed

Nov. 19, 1919, Treaty of Versailles rejected by the Senate

Courtesy of The Library of Congress

The Signing of Peace in the Hall of Mirrors, Versailles, France, June 28, 1919

Jan. 13, 1920, first meeting of League of Nations called; United States not represented

June 10, 1920, Federal Water Power Act approved

Aug. 26, 1920, Nineteenth Amendment to the Constitution ratified (woman suffrage)

Feb. 22, 1921, first transcontinental airmail flight from San Francisco to New York

ADDITIONAL DATA ON WILSON

WOODROW WILSON

—was the eighth President born in Virginia.

—was the second Democratic President since the Civil War.

—was the first President who majored in history and government at college.

—was the first President with a doctoral degree.

—was the first President who had been president of a major university.

—was the fourth President inaugurated on March 5 (March 4 was a Sunday).

—was the eleventh President who was a resident of a state other than his native state.

—was the third President whose wife died while he was in office.

—was the fifth President to remarry.

—was the sixth President to marry a widow.

—was the third President married while in office.

—was the only President who had two daughters who married in the White House.

EXTRAORDINARY POLITICAL RISE OF WILSON

Within two years and 170 days, Woodrow Wilson rose from a citizen who had never held public office to President of the United States. Wilson had never been a candidate for political office until September 15, 1910, when the Democrats nominated him for governor of New Jersey. He took office on January 17, 1911, and served two years. On July 2, 1912, he was nominated as the Democratic candidate for the presidency; on November 5, 1912, he was elected; and on March 4, 1913, he took office as President.

THE "BIG THREE" ELECTION

Before World War I, the leading college football powers in America were Harvard, Princeton, and Yale, and sportswriters dubbed these colleges the "Big Three." Accordingly, when the presidential election of 1912 matched Woodrow Wilson (Princeton, class of 1879), William Howard Taft (Yale, class 1878), and Theodore Roosevelt (Harvard, class of 1880), it became widely known as the "Big Three" election.

President Taft, the Republican, received 3,484,980 popular votes, and former President Roosevelt, running as a Progressive, received 4,119,53 votes; their combined total was 7,604,518 votes. Receiving 6,293,454 votes, Wilson, the Democrat, had a plurality. He was elected with 435 electoral votes to Roosevelt's 88 votes and Taft's 8 votes. Wilson was the only President who simultaneously defeated two other Presidents in one election.

WILSON APPOINTED NAMESAKE TO CABINET

Woodrow Wilson was the first President to have a cabinet member with the same last name as his own—Secretary of Labor William Bauchop Wilson of Pennsylvania, who took office on March 5, 1913. In 1961, President John F. Kennedy appointed Robert Francis Kennedy (his brother) to the post of Attorney General.

WILSON APPOINTED FIRST SECRETARY OF LABOR

The work of Secretary of Commerce and Labor was divided into two separate departments with the passing of a law by the Sixty-second Congress. On March 15, 1913, President Wilson appointed William Cox Redfield as Secretary of Commerce and William Bauchop Wilson as Secretary of Labor.

WILSON HELD FIRST PRESS CONFERENCE

The first presidential press conference was held on March 15, 1913, eleven days after his inauguration, by President Wilson at the Executive Offices in the White House. Newsmen who covered White House news were invited, and about 125 attended. The meeting was suggested by Joseph Patrick Tumulty, Wilson's private secretary. Previously news conferences had been limited to selected and favored newsmen.

WILSON EARNED DOCTORATE

Woodrow Wilson was the first President who had earned a doctoral degree. His thesis, *Congressional Government, a Study in American Politics,* earned him his doctorate from Johns Hopkins University in 1886. The work contained 333 pages and was published October 7, 1884, by Houghton Mifflin Company, Boston, Mass. It ran to 15 editions.

SEVENTEENTH AMENDMENT ENACTED

The Seventeenth Amendment to the Constitution, providing for direct election of United States senators, was passed by Congress on May 13, 1912. It was proposed to the legislatures of the several states by the 62nd Congress on May 16, 1912, and adopted by all the states except Alabama, Delaware, Florida, Georgia, Kentucky, Louisiana, Maryland, Mississippi, Rhode Island, South Carolina, Utah, and Virginia. The thirty-sixth state to ratify, making it effective, was Connecticut, on April 8, 1913. The amendment was declared ratified by the Secretary of State on May 31, 1913.

WILSON APPOINTED BRANDEIS

The first Jewish associate justice of the Supreme Court was Louis Dembitz Brandeis, appointed on January 28, 1916, by President Woodrow Wilson. The nomination was confirmed by the Senate on June 1, 1916, and Brandeis was sworn in on June 3, 1916. He served until February 13, 1939.

WILSON INTENDED TO RESIGN

Wilson wrote to Secretary of State Robert Lansing on November 5, 1916, two days prior to his reelection:

What would it be my duty to do were Mr. [Charles Evans] Hughes to be elected? Four months would elapse before he could take charge of the affairs of the government, and during those four months I would be without such moral backing from the nation as would be necessary to steady and control our relations with other governments. I would be known to be the rejected, not the accredited, spokesman of the country; and yet the accredited spokesman would be without legal authority to speak for the nation. Such a situation would be fraught with the gravest dangers. The direction of the foreign policy of the government would in effect have been taken out of my hands and yet its new definition would be impossible until March.

I feel that it would be my duty to relieve the country of the perils of such a situation at once. The course I have in mind is dependent upon the consent and cooperation of the Vice President; but if I could gain his consent to the plan, I would ask your permission to invite Mr. Hughes to become Secretary of State and would then join the Vice President in resigning, and thus open to Mr. Hughes the immediate succession to the presidency.

The election of Woodrow Wilson and Thomas Riley Marshall for a second term made this drastic action unnecessary.

FINAL COUNT CHANGED RESULTS

The early returns of the election of November 7, 1916, indicated that Wilson had been defeated and that Charles Evans Hughes had been elected President. Many newspapers carried the news of Wilson's defeat. When the votes of California were finally tabulated, Hughes lost the state by approximately 4,000 votes—a loss that insured the election of Wilson.

WILSON'S FOURTEEN POINTS

The fourteen points which President Wilson announced to Congress in January 1918 as necessary for world peace were the following:

1. Open treaties openly arrived at through international diplomacy
2. Freedom of the seas
3. Free international trade
4. Reduction of national armaments
5. Impartial adjustment of colonial claims
6. Evacuation of Russian territory
7. Evacuation of Belgium
8. Evacuation of French territory and return of Alsace-Lorraine to France
9. Readjustment of Italian frontiers
10. Autonomy for Austria and Hungary
11. Evacuation of Rumania, Serbia, and Montenegro, and security for the Balkan States
12. Self-determination for the peoples of the Turkish empire
13. Independence for Poland
14. Formation of a "general association of nations"

WILSON VISITED EUROPE

Woodrow Wilson was the first President of the United States to cross the Atlantic while in office. He left Washington, D.C., December 4, 1918, and sailed on the transport U.S.S. *George Washington* from Hoboken, N.J. He arrived at Brest, France, on December 13,

Courtesy of The Library of Congress

League of Nations Assembly—September 1, 1928, Geneva, Switzerland

1918. He left there on February 15, 1919, and landed at Boston, Mass., on February 24, 1919.

Wilson made a second trip, leaving Hoboken, N.J., on March 5, 1919, arriving March 13, 1919, at Brest, from which city he sailed on June 29, 1919, returning to Hoboken on July 8, 1919.

The trips were made to further the peace negotiations after World War I.

WILSON USED RADIO PHONE

The first President to use radio equipment was Woodrow Wilson. On his way home from France in the summer of 1919, on board the U.S.S. *George Washington*, President Wilson made phone calls to his aides in Washington, D.C., using radio equipment installed on the ship by the Research Laboratory of the General Electric Company. He attempted to broadcast a speech to American troops aboard other ships but did not stand close enough to the microphone, and the speech could not be heard.

WILSON INCAPACITATED BY A STROKE

On September 4, 1919, President Wilson embarked on a strenuous speaking tour, hoping to encourage public support for his League of Nations plan as embodied in the Treaty of Versailles. The stress of his advocacy efforts injured his health, already weakened by a 1918 attack of influenza. On October 2, in Washington, D.C., he suffered a stroke that left him paralyzed on the left side and barely able to speak. He nonetheless refused to allow the Vice President to serve in his stead and carried out the duties of the presidency from his sickroom as best he could, with the assistance of his wife, who placed herself in charge of deciding which matters were important enough to require his attention. The cabinet continued to meet unofficially until April 13, 1920, when, after a six-month hiatus, the President called a cabinet meeting at his White House study. Wilson never fully recovered from the stroke, began to lose his eyesight after the end of his term, and died of a second stroke in 1924.

CABINET MEETINGS NOT CALLED

After his stroke, Wilson issued no calls for cabinet meetings. The first cabinet meeting he held after September 2, 1919, was called on April 13, 1920, the meeting taking place in the President's study in the White House instead of the cabinet room. The cabinet, however, met unofficially without call.

EIGHTEENTH AMENDMENT ENACTED

The Eighteenth Amendment to the Constitution, prohibiting the manufacture, sale, or transportation of intoxicating liquors, was passed by Congress on December 18, 1917, and proposed to the legislatures of the several states by the 65th Congress. It was ratified by a total of 36 states on January 16, 1919, when Missouri, Nebraska, and Wyoming voted approval. On January 29, 1919, it was declared by the Secretary of State to have been ratified and on January 16, 1920, it went into effect. It was repealed December 5, 1933, by ratification of the Twenty-first Amendment.

NINETEENTH AMENDMENT ENACTED

More than 40 years before the adoption of the woman suffrage amendment, a resolution in favor of suffrage for women had been introduced by Senator Aaron Augustus Sargent of California. The resolution, introduced on June 10, 1878, at the request of Susan Brownell Anthony, had failed to pass.

The Nineteenth Amendment to the Constitution, guaranteeing suffrage for women, was passed by Congress on June 4, 1919. It was proposed to the legislatures of the several states on June 5, 1919, by the Sixty-sixth Congress. There was no action by Alabama, Florida, or North Carolina. It was rejected by Delaware, Georgia, Louisiana, Maryland, Mississippi, South Carolina and Virginia. The thirty-sixth state to ratify, making it effective, was Tennessee, on August 18, 1920. Later, the Tennessee House rescinded its ratification. The amendment was declared ratified by the Secretary of State on August 26, 1920. Connecticut ratified it later, on September 14, 1920, and Vermont on February 8, 1921.

Demonstrators for women's suffrage

WILSON APPOINTED WOMAN AS SUB-CABINET MEMBER

Wilson created a precedent when he appointed a woman as a sub-cabinet member. On June 26, 1920, he appointed Annette Abbott Adams as assistant attorney general, a post which she held until August 15, 1921.

ELECTION RETURNS BROADCAST

Election returns were broadcast for the first time on August 31, 1920, when WWJ of Detroit, Mich., broadcast the results of congressional and county primaries.

WILSON THE SECOND PRESIDENT TO RECEIVE NOBEL PRIZE

Woodrow Wilson was the second President to receive the Nobel Prize for Peace, the first having been awarded to President Theodore Roosevelt. On December 10, 1920, at Christiania, Norway, the 1919 prize was presented to President Wilson and received by Albert Schmedeman, the American Minister to Norway. The prize carried with it a gift of 150,000 kroner, then worth about $29,100.

WILSON BURIED IN WASHINGTON, D.C.

The only President buried in Washington, D.C., is Woodrow Wilson, interred on February 5, 1924, in the National Cathedral (the Protestant Episcopal Cathedral of Saints Peter and Paul).

FURTHER READING

Auchincloss, Louis. *Woodrow Wilson*. 2000.

Bailey, Thomas A. *Woodrow Wilson and the Lost Peace*. 1963.

———. *Woodrow Wilson and the Great Betrayal*. 1972.

Clements, Kendrick A. *The Presidency of Woodrow Wilson*. 1992.

Cooper, John M. *The Warrior and the Priest*. 1983.

Devlin, Patrick. *Too Proud to Fight*. 1974.

Heckscher, August. *Woodrow Wilson*. 1991.

Link, Arthur S. *Wilson*. 1947.

———. *Woodrow Wilson and the Progressive Era, 1910–1917*. 1954.

———. *Woodrow Wilson: A Profile*. 1968.

Maynard, W. Barksdale. *Woodrow Wilson: Princeton to the Presidency*. 2008.

Courtesy of The Library of Congress

Warren Gamaliel Harding

Date of birth—Nov. 2, 1865

Place of birth—Corsica (now Blooming Grove), Ohio

Education—Public schools, Corsica, Ohio; Ohio Central College, Iberia, Ohio, B.S., 1882

Religion—Baptist

Ancestry—English, Scottish, Irish, Dutch

Career—Insurance salesman, reporter, newspaper publisher, state senator, state lieutenant governor, U.S. senator

Political party—Republican

State represented—Ohio

Term of office—Mar. 4, 1921–Aug. 2, 1923

Term served—2 years, 151 days

Administration—34th

Congresses—67th

Age at inauguration—55 years, 122 days

Lived after term—Died in office

Date of death—Aug. 2, 1923

Age at death—57 years, 273 days

Place of death—San Francisco, Calif.

Burial place—Marion Cemetery, Marion, Ohio (His body and that of his wife were reinterred Dec. 21, 1927.)

FAMILY

FATHER

Name—George Tryon Harding

Date of birth—June 12, 1843

Place of birth—Corsica (now Blooming Grove), Ohio

First marriage—Phoebe Elizabeth Dickerson, May 7, 1864, Galion, Ohio (d. 1910)

Second marriage—Eudora Adella Kelley Luvisi, Nov. 23, 1911, Anderson, Ind. (b. Sept. 25, 1868, near Bartonia, Ind.; div. 1916; d. July 24, 1955, Union City, Ind.)

Third marriage—Mary Alice Severns, Aug. 12, 1921, Monroe, Mich. (b. Nov. 13, 1869, Marion, Ohio; d. Nov. 19, 1928, Santa Ana, Calif.)

Occupation—Farmer, soldier, teacher, homeopathic physician, realtor, trader, insurance salesman, newspaper owner

Date of death—Nov. 19, 1928

Place of death—Santa Ana, Calif.

Age at death—84 years, 160 days

MOTHER

Name at birth—Phoebe Elizabeth Dickerson

Date of birth—Dec. 21, 1843

Place of birth—near Corsica, Ohio

Marriage—George Tryon Harding, May 7, 1864, Galion, Ohio

Date of death—May 20, 1910

Age at death—66 years, 159 days

SIBLINGS

Warren Gamaliel Harding was the oldest of eight children.

Children of George Tryon Harding and Phoebe Elizabeth Dickerson Harding

Warren Gamaliel Harding, b. Nov. 2, 1865, d. Aug. 2, 1923

Charity Malvina Harding, b. Mar. 1, 1867, d. Nov. 2, 1951

Mary Clarissa Harding, b. Apr. 26, 1868, d. Oct. 29, 1913

Eleanor Priscilla Harding, b. Nov. 11, 1872, d. Nov. 9, 1878

Charles Alexander Harding, b. Apr. 8, 1874, d. Nov. 9, 1878

Abigail Victoria Harding, b. May 31, 1875, d. Mar. 21, 1935

George Tryon Harding, b. Mar. 11, 1878, d. Jan. 13, 1934

Phoebe Caroline Harding, b. Oct. 21, 1879, d. Oct. 21, 1951

MARRIAGE

Married—Florence Kling DeWolfe

Date of marriage—July 8, 1891

Place of marriage—Marion, Ohio

Age of wife at marriage—30 years, 327 days

Age of husband at marriage—25 years, 248 days

Years married—32 years, 25 days

CHILDREN

Harding and his wife had no children, but Harding was the father of a daughter by Nan Britton, one of his two long-term mistresses.

(The other was Carrie Fulton Phillips, wife of Harding's close friend James Phillips.) Britton's and Harding's daughter, named Elizabeth Ann Christian, was born on October 22, 1919, in Asbury Park, N.J. President Harding periodically sent money for his daughter's support, entrusting the job to Secret Service agents. When, after Harding's death, his executors refused to provide further money, Britton wrote an exposé, *The President's Daughter,* which she dedicated to unwed mothers and their innocent children. The book was published in 1927 and became a bestseller.

Florence Harding had a son from her early marriage to Henry A. DeWolfe, but he was not an important part of her life with Warren Harding. When he was four years old, she gave him to her parents to adopt.

THE PRESIDENT'S WIFE

Name at birth—Florence Kling

Date of birth—Aug. 15, 1860

Place of birth—Marion, Ohio

Mother—Louisa M. Bouton Kling

Father—Amos H. Kling

Father's occupation—Banker, merchant

Education—Cincinnati Conservatory of Music

First marriage—Henry Atherton DeWolfe, Mar. 1880, Marion, Ohio (div. 1886)

Second marriage—Warren Gamaliel Harding, July 8, 1891, Marion, Ohio

Children from first marriage—(Eugene) Marshall DeWolfe (b. Sept. 22, 1880, d. 1915)

Children from second marriage—None

Occupation—Circulation manager at Harding's newspaper

Date of death—Nov. 21, 1924

Age at death—64 years, 98 days

Place of death—Marion, Ohio

Burial place—Marion, Ohio

Courtesy of The Library of Congress

Florence Harding, wife of Warren Harding

Years older than the President—5 years, 79 days

Years she survived the President—1 year, 111 days

THE FIRST LADY

In their early years together, Florence Kling DeWolfe Harding ran her husband's newspaper. An industrious woman gifted with a keen understanding of politics, she was said to harbor greater ambitions for her husband and his political career than he did, and for that reason she was sometimes called "the Duchess."

IMPORTANT DATES IN THE PRESIDENT'S LIFE

1879–1882, attended Ohio Central College, Iberia, Ohio

1882, taught school

1883, in insurance business

Nov. 26, 1884, with two others purchased Marion, Ohio, *Star* for $300

1895, county auditor, Marion, Ohio (his first political office)

1899–1903, Ohio Senate

1904–1905, lieutenant governor of Ohio

1910, unsuccessful Republican candidate for governor of Ohio

Mar. 4, 1915–Jan. 13, 1921, U.S. Senate (from Ohio)

Mar. 4, 1921–Aug. 2, 1923, President

ELECTIONS

THE ELECTION OF 1920

November 2, 1920

CANDIDATES

Republican Party (17th Convention)

June 8–12, 1920, the Coliseum, Chicago, Ill.

P: Warren Gamaliel Harding, Ohio

VP: Calvin Coolidge, Mass.

Harding was nominated on the tenth ballot. Candidates for nomination and the votes they received on the first and tenth ballots:

Leonard Wood, Mass., $287^1/_2$, 156

Frank Orren Lowden, Ill., $211^1/_2$, 11

Hiram Johnson, Calif., $133^1/_2$, $80^4/_5$

William Cameron Sproul, Pa., 84, 0

Nicholas Murray Butler, N.Y., $69^1/_2$, 2

Warren Gamaliel Harding, Ohio, $65^1/_2$, $692^1/_5$

Calvin Coolidge, Mass., 34, 5

Robert Marion La Follette, Wis., 24, 24

Peter Conley Pritchard, Tenn., 21, 0

Miles Poindexter, Wash., 20, 0

Howard Sutherland, W.Va., 17, 0

Thomas Coleman Du Pont, Del., 7, 0

Herbert Clark Hoover, Calif., $5^1/_2$, $9^1/_2$

William Edgar Borah, Idaho, 2, 0

Charles Beecher Warren, Mich., 1, 0

William Harrison Hays, Ind., 0, 1

Irving Luther Lenroot, Wis., 0, 1

Philander Chase Knox, Pa., 0, 1

Total number of votes: 984

Nomination made unanimous

Democratic Party (23rd Convention)

July 28–30, July 1–3, 5–6, 1920, Civic Auditorium, San Francisco, Calif.

P: James Middleton Cox, Ohio

VP: Franklin Delano Roosevelt, N.Y.

Cox was nominated on the forty-fourth ballot. Candidates for nomination and the votes they received on the first and forty-fourth ballots:

William Gibbs McAdoo, Calif., 266, 267

Alexander Mitchell Palmer, Pa., 256, 1

James Middleton Cox, Ohio, 134, $732^1/_2$

Alfred Emanuel Smith, N.Y., 109, 0

Edward Irving Edwards, N.J., 42, 0

Thomas Riley Marshall, Ind., 37, 52

Robert Latham Owen, Okla., 33, 34

John William Davis, W.Va., 32, 0

Edwin Thomas Meredith, Iowa, 27, 0

Carter Glass, Va., $26^1/_2$, $1^1/_2$

Homer Stille Cummings, Conn., 25, 1

Furnifold McLendel Simmons, N.C., 24, 0

James Watson Gerard, N.Y., 21, 0
John Sharp Williams, Miss., 20, 0
Gilbert Monell Hitchcock, Neb., 18, 0
Champ [James Beauchamp] Clark, Mo., 9, 0
Francis Burton Harrison, N.Y., 6, 0
Alfred M. Wood, Mass., 4, 0
William Jennings Bryan, Neb., 1, 0
Bainbridge Colby, N.Y., 1, 0
Josephus Daniels, N.C., 1, 0
William Randolph Hearst, N.Y., 1, 0

Oscar Wilder Underwood, Ala., $^1/_2$, 0

Total number of votes: 1094
Number necessary for nomination: 729
On the forty-fourth ballot the rules were suspended and Cox was declared nominated unanimously.

Socialist Party

May 8–14, 1920, Finnish Socialist Hall, New York, N.Y.

P: Eugene Victor Debs, Ind.
VP: Seymour Stedman, Ill.

Debs did not appear at the convention. Convicted under the 1917 Espionage Statute for making a speech that was deemed subversive of the war effort, he was serving a 10-year sentence in a federal prison in Atlanta, Ga.

Farmer Labor Party

July 13–15, 1920, Carmen's Hall, Chicago, Ill.

P: Parley Parker Christensen, Utah
VP: Maximilian Sebastian Hayes, Ohio

Christensen was nominated on the second ballot. Candidates for nomination and the votes they received on the first and second ballots:

Dudley Field Malone, N.Y., 166 $^8/_{10}$, 174$^6/_{10}$

Parley Parker Christensen, Utah, 121$^1/_{10}$, 193$^5/_{10}$

Eugene Victor Debs, Ind., 68, 0

Henry Ford, Mich., 12$^3/_{10}$, 0

Lynn Joseph Frazier, N.D., 12$^3/_{10}$, 9

Herbert Bigelow, $^5/_{10}$, 0

Louis Freeland Post, Ill., 1$^2/_{10}$, 0

The Farmer Labor Party was formed July 13, 1920, at Chicago, Ill., from the National Labor Party.

Courtesy of The Library of Congress

President Harding taking the oath administered by Chief Justice White, March 4, 1921, Washington, D.C.

Prohibition Party

July 21–22, 1920, Lincoln, Neb.

P: Aaron Sherman Watkins, Ohio
VP: David Leigh Colvin, N.Y.

Socialist Labor Party

May 5–10, 1920, New York, N.Y.

P: William Wesley Cox, Mo.
VP: August Gillhaus, N.Y.

Single Tax Party

July 12–14, 1920, Chicago, Ill.

P: Robert Colvin Macauley, Pa.
VP: R. G. Barnum, Ohio

American Party

P: James Edward Ferguson, Tex.

The American Party was formed August 14, 1919, at Fort Worth, Tex., by a group of Democrats. On April 21, 1920, former Governor Ferguson announced his candidacy at Temple, Tex.

1920 POPULAR VOTE

Republican Party, 16,152,200
Democratic Party, 9,147,353
Socialist Party, 919,799
Farmer Labor Party, 265,411
Prohibition Party, 189,408
Socialist Labor Party, 31,715
Single Tax Party, 5,837

1920 ELECTORAL VOTE

There were 531 electoral votes from 48 states.

Harding received 76.08 percent (404 votes—37 states) as follows: Ariz. 3; Calif. 13; Colo. 6; Conn. 7; Del. 3; Idaho 4; Ill. 29; Ind. 15; Iowa 13; Kan. 10; Me. 6; Md. 8; Mass. 18; Mich. 15; Minn. 12; Mo. 18; Mont. 4; Neb. 8; Nev. 3; N.H. 4; N.J. 14; N.M. 3; N.Y. 45; N.D. 5; Ohio 24; Okla. 10; Ore. 5; Pa. 38; R.I. 5; S.D. 5; Tenn. 12; Utah 4; Vt. 4; Wash. 7; W.Va. 8; Wis. 13; Wyo. 3.

Cox received 23.92 percent (127 votes—11 states) as follows: Ala. 12; Ark. 9; Fla. 6; Ga. 14; Ky. 13; La. 10; Miss. 10; N.C. 12; S.C. 9; Tex. 20; Va. 12.

INAUGURATION

March 4, 1921

Warren Gamaliel Harding took the oath of office on Friday, March 4, 1921, on the east portico of the Capitol. Chief Justice Edward Douglass White administered the oath.

Accompanied by outgoing President Woodrow Wilson, he rode to the Capitol in an automobile, the first President to ride thus to his inaugural. This inauguration was also the first one described over radio. Another innovation was the use of an amplifying public address system so that the assembled crowds could hear the proceedings.

THE VICE PRESIDENT

Name—Calvin Coolidge (29th V.P.)

Political party—Republican

State represented—Massachusetts

Term of office—Mar. 4, 1921–Aug. 3, 1923

Age at inauguration—48 years, 243 days

Occupation after term—President of the United States

For further biographical information, see the chapter on Calvin Coolidge, 30th President, on page 351.

Courtesy of The Library of Congress

Calvin Coolidge, Vice President to Warren Harding

CABINET

March 4, 1921–August 2, 1923

State—Bainbridge Colby, N.Y., continued from preceding administration; Charles

Evans Hughes, N.Y., Mar. 4, 1921, entered upon duties Mar. 5, 1921

Treasury—David Franklin Houston, Mo., continued from preceding administration; Andrew William Mellon, Pa., Mar. 4, 1921; entered upon duties Mar. 5, 1921

War—Newton Diehl Baker, Ohio, continued from preceding administration; John Wingate Weeks, Mass., Mar. 5, 1921

Attorney General—Alexander Mitchell Palmer, Pa., continued from preceding administration; Harry Micajah Daugherty, Ohio, Mar. 5, 1921

Postmaster General—Albert Sidney Burleson, Tex., continued from preceding administration; William Harrison Hays, Ind., Mar. 5, 1921; Hubert Work, Colo., Mar. 4, 1922; Harry Stewart New, Ind., Feb. 27, 1923; entered upon duties Mar. 5, 1923

Navy—Josephus Daniels, N.C., continued from preceding administration; Edwin Denby, Mich., Mar. 5, 1921

Interior—John Barton Payne, Ill., continued from preceding administration; Albert Bacon Fall, N.M., Mar. 5, 1921; Hubert Work, Colo., Feb. 27, 1923; entered upon duties Mar. 5, 1923

Agriculture—Edwin Thomas Meredith, Iowa, continued from preceding administration; Henry Cantwell Wallace, Iowa, Mar. 5, 1921

Commerce—Joshua Willis Alexander, Mo., continued from preceding administration; Herbert Clark Hoover, Calif., Mar. 5, 1921

Labor—William Bauchop Wilson, Pa., continued from preceding administration; James John Davis, Pa., Mar. 5, 1921

CONGRESS

SIXTY–SEVENTH CONGRESS

March 4, 1921–March 3, 1923

First session—Apr. 11, 1921–Nov. 23, 1921 (227 days)

Second session—Dec. 5, 1921–Sept. 22, 1922 (292 days)

Third session—Nov. 20, 1922–Dec. 4, 1922 (15 days)

Fourth session— Dec. 4, 1922–Mar. 3, 1923 (90 days)

Special session of the Senate—Mar. 4, 1921–Mar. 15, 1921

Vice President—Calvin Coolidge, Mass.

Courtesy of The Library of Congress

Harding, third from right, shown with members of his cabinet.

President pro tempore of the Senate
—Albert Baird Cummins, Iowa, reelected Mar. 7, 1921

Secretary of the Senate—George Andrew Sanderson, Ill., reelected Mar. 7, 1921

Speaker of the House—Frederick Huntington Gillett, Mass., reelected Apr. 11, 1921

Clerk of the House—William Tyler Page, Md.

SIXTY–EIGHTH CONGRESS

March 4, 1923–March 3, 1925

First session—Dec. 3, 1923–June 7, 1924 (188 days)

Second session—Dec. 1, 1924–Mar. 3, 1925 (93 days)

Vice President—Calvin Coolidge, Mass., succeeded to the presidency on the death of Warren Gamaliel Harding on Aug. 2, 1923; office vacant for the remainder of the term

President pro tempore of the Senate
—Albert Baird Cummins, Iowa

Secretary of the Senate—George Andrew Sanderson, Ill., reelected Dec. 17, 1923

Speaker of the House—Frederick Huntington Gillett, Mass.

Clerk of the House—William Tyler Page, Md.

APPOINTMENTS TO THE SUPREME COURT

Chief Justice

William Howard Taft, Ohio, June 30, 1921 (replaced Edward Douglass White)

Associate Justices

George Sutherland, Utah, Sept. 5, 1922 (replaced John Hessin Clarke)

Pierce Butler, Minn., Dec. 21, 1922 (replaced William Rufus Day)

Edward Terry Sanford, Tenn., Jan. 29, 1923 (replaced Mahlon Pitney)

IMPORTANT DATES IN THE PRESIDENCY

1921, President ordered the release of Eugene V. Debs from prison

Mar. 28, 1921, Nevada first state to authorize executions by lethal gas

Apr. 11, 1921, Iowa enacted first state cigarette tax

May 3, 1921, West Virginia approved first state sales tax

May 19, 1921, first immigration quota act passed

June 10, 1921, U.S. Budget Bureau created

June 20, 1921, first congresswoman to preside over the House of Representatives, Mrs. Alice M. Robertson of Oklahoma, announced the vote on an appropriation.

June 27, 1921, U.S. Comptroller General appointed

July 21, 1921, battleship sunk by an airplane in demonstration at Hampton Roads, Va.

Nov. 11, 1921, dedication of the Tomb of the Unknown Soldier at Arlington, Va.

Nov. 12, 1921, conference on the limitation of armaments at Washington, D.C.; nine nations represented

Mar. 29, 1922, Five-power Limitation on Naval Armaments Treaty (France, Great Britain, Italy, Japan, United States)

June 16, 1922, helicopter flight by H. A. Berliner demonstrated to U.S. Bureau of Aeronautics

Oct. 3, 1922, first woman senator, Rebecca L. Felton of Georgia, appointed

Oct. 27, 1922, Navy Day celebrated for the first time as an annual holiday

Jan. 23, 1923, first woman elected to Congress to serve in the place of her husband, Mrs. Mae Ella Nolan of California, took office

ADDITIONAL DATA ON HARDING

WARREN GAMALIEL HARDING

—was the seventh President born in Ohio.

—was the sixth President elected from Ohio.

—was the second President elected while a senator.

—was the sixth President to die in office.

—was the fourth Ohioan to die in office.

—was the first newspaper publisher elected to the presidency.

—was the second President to marry a woman who had been divorced.

—was the fourth President whose father was alive when he was inaugurated.

—was the first President who was survived by his father.

—was the first President to ride to his inauguration in an automobile.

THE SMOKE-FILLED ROOM

The 1920 Republican convention in Chicago, Ill., was unable to decide upon a candidate after the first day of balloting (June 11, 1920), and it did not seem likely that an amicable decision would be reached by the contenders and their adherents. On June 12, 1920, Senator Harding received 692 $^1/_5$ votes on the tenth ballot, a total that won him the nomination.

On Sunday, June 13, 1920, the New York *Times* carried the headline "Prophesied How Harding Would Win—Daugherty, His Campaign Manager, Said Fifteen Tired Men Would Put Him Over." The story stated that Harry Micajah Daugherty, the Ohio lawyer and politician who managed Harding's campaign, had said shortly before the presidential primaries in Ohio:

At the proper time after the Republican National Convention meets some fifteen men, bleary-eyed with loss of sleep and perspiring profusely with the excessive heat, will sit down in seclusion around a big table. I will be with them and will

Courtesy of The Library of Congress

The Tomb of the Unknown Soldier in Arlington National Cemetery, Virginia

present the name of Senator Harding to them, and before we get through they will put him over.

In the small hours of June 12, a group of senators and party leaders met in a room at the Blackstone Hotel. Daugherty's prediction had come true.

THREE NEWSPAPERMEN PRESIDENTIAL NOMINEES IN 1920

Three of the presidential candidates in 1920 were active newspapermen. Warren Gamaliel Harding, the Republican candidate, was the editor and publisher of the Marion, Ohio, *Star*. James Middleton Cox, the Democratic candidate, became the owner and publisher of the Dayton, Ohio, *Daily News* in 1898 and later acquired other newspapers. Robert C. Macauley, the candidate of the Single Tax party, was a reporter on the *Philadelphia Inquirer*.

The funeral of President Harding

PRESIDENTIAL ELECTION RETURNS BROADCAST

Presidential election returns were communicated by radio for the first time on November 2, 1920, when Leo H. Rosenberg of station KDKA, Pittsburgh, Pa., broadcast the results of the Harding-Cox election.

HARDING ELECTED WHILE SERVING IN THE SENATE

Warren Gamaliel Harding of Ohio, elected to the presidency on November 2, 1920, was the first senator in office to be elected President. He resigned from the Senate on January 13, 1921.

HARDING HAD A RADIO

Warren Gamaliel Harding was the first President to have a radio. On February 8, 1922, he had a vacuum tube detector and two-stage amplifier receiving set installed in a bookcase in his study on the second floor of the White House.

HARDING BROADCAST SPEECH

The first President to broadcast over the radio was Warren Gamaliel Harding, whose speech at the dedication of the Francis Scott Key Memorial at Fort McHenry, Baltimore, Md., on June 14, 1922, was transmitted by WEAR (now WFBR), Baltimore, Md. His voice was carried over telephone wires to the studio from which it was broadcast. President Harding's World Court speech on June 21, 1923, at St. Louis, Mo., was transmitted over KSD, St. Louis, Mo., and WEAF, New York, N.Y.

On November 5, 1921, a message from President Harding had been broadcast from Washington, D.C., to 28 countries. It was sent in code over the RCA 25,000-volt station at Rocky Point, N.Y.

HARDING VISITED ALASKA AND CANADA

President Harding was the first President to visit Alaska and Canada during his term of office. He sailed on the U.S.S. *Henderson,* a naval transport, and visited Metlakahtla, Alaska, on July 8, 1923, and Vancouver, British Columbia, on July 26, 1923.

CABINET MEMBER CONVICTED IN TEAPOT DOME CASE

The first cabinet member convicted of a crime was Albert Bacon Fall, Secretary of the Interior during the Harding administration. On October 25, 1929, after a trial in the District of Columbia Supreme Court, Fall was found guilty by Justice William Hitz of having received and accepted a bribe of $100,000 from Edward Laurence Doheny in connection with the Elk Hills Naval Oil Reserve in California. The bribe had been given with a view to influencing Fall to grant valuable oil leases to Doheny's Pan-American Petroleum and Transport Company. Also involved were the Teapot Dome oil reserves in Wyoming, which Fall had secretly leased to Harry F. Sinclair. On November 1, 1929, Fall was sentenced to one year in prison and a $100,000 fine.

DEATH AND BURIAL

The first and only time that both a President and his wife died during the period for which the President had been elected was the term of March 4, 1921–March 4, 1925. President Harding died August 2, 1923, and his wife died November 21, 1924.

On December 20, 1927, their bodies were removed from the vault in Marion Cemetery to an $800,000 mausoleum ($500,000 for the memorial, $300,000 for the ground and landscaping). The mausoleum was dedicated on June 16, 1931.

FURTHER READING

Adams, Samuel H. *Incredible Era*. 1939.

Bagby, Wesley M. *The Road to Normalcy*. 1968.

Dean, John W. *Warren G. Harding (The American Presidents Series)*. 2004.

Mee, Charles C. *The Ohio Gang*. 1981.

Murray, Robert K. *The Harding Era*. 1969.

Russell, Francis. *The Shadow of Blooming Grove*. 1969.

Courtesy of The Library of Congress

Calvin Coolidge

Name at birth—John Calvin Coolidge

Date of birth—July 4, 1872

Place of birth—Plymouth, Vt.

Education—Public schools, Plymouth, Vt.; Black River Academy, Ludlow, graduated 1890; St. Johnsbury Academy, Ludlow, Vt., 1891; Amherst College, Amherst, Mass., bachelor's degree, cum laude, June 26, 1895; private studies at law office of John C. Hammond and Henry P. Field, Northampton, Mass.

Religion—Congregationalist

Ancestry—English, Scottish, Welsh

Career—Lawyer, city councilman, city solicitor, state legislator, mayor, state senator and senate president, state lieutenant governor, governor of Massachusetts, Vice President

Political party—Republican

State represented—Massachusetts

Term of office—Aug. 3, 1923–Mar. 4, 1929 (Coolidge succeeded to the presidency on the death of Warren Gamaliel Harding.)

Term served—5 years, 214 days

Administration—34th, 35th

Congresses—68th, 69th, 70th

Age at inauguration—51 years, 30 days

Lived after term—3 years, 307 days

Occupation after term—Writer, columnist

Date of death—Jan. 5, 1933

Age at death—60 years, 185 days

Place of death—Northampton, Mass.

Burial place—Notch Cemetery, Plymouth Notch, Plymouth, Vt.

FAMILY

FATHER

Name—John Calvin Coolidge

Date of birth—Mar. 31, 1845

Place of birth—Plymouth, Vt.

First marriage—Victoria Josephine Moore, May 6, 1868, Plymouth, Vt. (d. Mar. 14, 1885)

Second marriage—Caroline Athelia Brown Coolidge, Sept. 9, 1891 (b. Jan. 22, 1857; d. May 18, 1920, Plymouth, Vt.)

Occupation—Farmer, soldier, storekeeper, notary public, carpenter, cabinetmaker, buggy maker, mason, blacksmith; school superintendent, deputy sheriff, selectman, tax collector, road commissioner, Vermont state legislator, Vermont state senator

Date of death—Mar. 18, 1926

Place of death—Plymouth, Vt.

Age at death—80 years, 352 days

MOTHER

Name at birth—Victoria Josephine Moore

Date of birth—Mar. 14, 1846

Place of birth—Pinney Hollow, Vt.

Marriage—John Calvin Coolidge, May 6, 1868, Plymouth, Vt.

Date of death—Mar. 14, 1885

Place of death—Plymouth, Vt.

Age at death—39 years

SIBLINGS

Calvin Coolidge was the older of two children of his father's first marriage.

Children of John Calvin Coolidge and Victoria Josephine Moore Coolidge

Calvin Coolidge, b. July 4, 1872, d. Jan. 5, 1933

Abigail Gratia Coolidge, b. Apr. 15, 1875, d. Mar. 6, 1890

MARRIAGE

Married—Grace Anna Goodhue

Date of marriage—Oct. 4, 1905

Place of marriage—Burlington, Vt.

Age of wife at marriage—26 years, 274 days

Age of husband at marriage—33 years, 92 days

Years married—27 years, 93 days

CHILDREN

John Coolidge, b. Sept. 7, 1906, Northampton, Mass.; m. Sept. 23, 1929, Florence Trumbull, Plainville, Conn.; d. May 31, 2000, Lebanon, N.H.

Calvin Coolidge, b. Apr. 13, 1908, Northampton, Mass., d. July 7, 1924, Washington, D.C.

Calvin Coolidge, Jr., was 16 years old when he died of blood poisoning. During a summer tennis game, which he played in sneakers worn without socks, he developed a blister on his toe that became infected. He died during his father's campaign for reelection.

THE PRESIDENT'S WIFE

Name at birth—Grace Anna Goodhue

Date of birth—Jan. 3, 1879

Place of birth—Burlington, Vt.

Mother—Lemira Barrett Goodhue

Father—Andrew Issachar Goodhue

Education—University of Vermont, bachelor of philosophy degree, 1902

Marriage—Calvin Coolidge, Oct. 4, 1905, Burlington, Vt.

Children—John Coolidge, b. Sept. 7, 1906, d. May 31, 2000; Calvin Coolidge, b. Apr. 13, 1908, d. July 7, 1924

Occupation—Teacher of deaf students

Date of death—July 8, 1957

Age at death—78 years, 186 days

Place of death—Northampton, Mass.

Burial place—Plymouth, Vt.

Years younger than the President—6 years, 183 days

Years she survived the President—24 years, 184 days

Courtesy of The Library of Congress

Grace Coolidge, wife of Calvin Coolidge

THE FIRST LADY

Grace Goodhue Coolidge assumed the modern social role, appearing frequently beside her husband, her friendly charm a contrast to his famous taciturnity. She met the press regularly, entertained, and publicized her domestic concerns. She wore notably stylish fashions and had a rapier wit. She had been a teacher at a school for deaf children and was the first First Lady to receive an honorary degree, from Boston University. Although President Coolidge made clear his disapproval of his wife's participation in politics, he was conscious of her popularity and charm, and promoted them to his advantage.

IMPORTANT DATES IN THE PRESIDENT'S LIFE

June 26, 1895, graduated from Amherst College

July 2, 1897, admitted to the bar; practiced in Northampton, Mass.

1899, City Council, Northampton, Mass.

1900–1901, city solicitor, Northampton, Mass.

June 1903–Jan. 1, 1904, clerk of the courts, Hampshire County, Northampton, Mass.

1907–1908, Massachusetts House of Representatives

1909, resumed law practice, Northampton, Mass.

1910–1911, mayor, Northampton, Mass.

1912–1915, Massachusetts Senate

1914–1915, president of Massachusetts Senate

1916–1918, lieutenant governor of Massachusetts

Nov. 27, 1918, president of Nonotuck Savings Bank, Northampton, Mass.

1919–1920, governor of Massachusetts

1919, settled Boston police strike

Mar. 4, 1921–Aug. 3, 1923, Vice President under Warren G. Harding

Aug. 3, 1923, succeeded to the presidency on the death of Harding

Nov. 1924, nominated for another term as President on the Republican ticket

Mar. 4, 1925–Mar. 4, 1929, President (second term)

1928, declined to be a candidate for renomination

1929, published his autobiography

1930–1932, president of American Antiquarian Society

1930, conducted syndicated newspaper column

ELECTIONS

THE ELECTION OF 1924

November 4, 1924

CANDIDATES

Republican Party (18th Convention)

June 10–12, 1924, Municipal Auditorium, Cleveland, Ohio

P: Calvin Coolidge, Mass.
VP: Charles Gates Dawes, Ill.

Coolidge was nominated on the first ballot. Candidates for nomination and the votes they received:
Calvin Coolidge, Mass., 1065
Robert Marion La Follette, Wis., 34
Hiram Johnson, Calif., 10
Total number of votes: 1109
Nomination made unanimous

Democratic Party (24th Convention)

June 24–28, 30, July 1–5, 7–9, 1924, Madison Square Garden, New York, N.Y.

P: John William Davis, W.Va.
VP: Charles Wayland Bryan, Neb.

Davis was nominated on the one hundred and third ballot. Candidates for nomination and the votes they received on the first and one hundred and third ballots:

William Gibbs McAdoo, Calif., 431½, 11½

Alfred Emanuel Smith, N.Y., 241, 7½

James Middleton Cox, Ohio, 59, 0

Byron Patrick Harrison, Miss., 43½, 0

Oscar Wilder Underwood, Ala., 42½, 102½

George Sebastian Silzer, N.J., 38, 0

John William Davis, W.Va., 31, 844

Samuel Moffett Ralston, Ind., 30, 0

Woodbridge Nathan Ferris, Mich., 30, 0

Carter Glass, Va., 25, 23

Albert Cabell Ritchie, Md., 22½, 0

Joseph Taylor Robinson, Ark., 21, 20

Jonathan McMillan Davis, Kan., 20, 0

Charles Wayland Bryan, Neb., 18, 0

Fred Herbert Brown, N.H., 17, 0

William Ellery Sweet, Colo., 12, 0

William Saulsbury, Del., 7, 0

John Benjamin Kendrick, Wyo., 6, 0

Houston Thompson, 1, 0

Thomas James Walsh, Mont., 0, 58

Edwin Thomas Meredith, Iowa, 0, 15$^{1}/_{2}$

James Watson Gerard, N.Y., 0, 7

Cordell Hull, Tenn., 0, 1

Total number of votes:

First ballot: 1096

One hundred and third ballot: 1090

Number necessary for nomination: 731

This was the longest nomination convention of a major political party. Sixty candidates were nominated for the presidency.

Progressive Party

July 4, 1924, Municipal Auditorium, Cleveland, Ohio

P: Robert Marion La Follette, Wis.
VP: Burton Kendall Wheeler, Mont.

Prohibition Party

June 4–6, 1924, Columbus, Ohio

P: Herman Preston Faris, Mo.
VP: Marie Caroline Brehm, Calif.

Faris was nominated on the first ballot. Candidates for nomination and the votes they received:

Herman Preston Faris, Mo., 82

A. P. Gouttey, Wash., 40

William Frederick Varney, N.Y., 2

A. P. Gouttey was nominated for the vice presidency but declined.

Socialist Labor Party

May 10–13, 1924, New York, N.Y.

P: Frank T. Johns, Ore.
VP: Verne L. Reynolds, N.Y.

Socialist Party

July 6–8, 1924, Hotel Winton, Cleveland, Ohio

P: Robert Marion La Follette, Wis.
VP: Burton Kendall Wheeler, Mont.

The national committee was authorized at this convention to name a suitable vice presidential candidate at a later date. Wheeler was endorsed on July 22, 1924.

Workers Party (Communist Party)

July 11, 1924, St. Paul, Minn.

P: William Zebulon Foster, Ill.

VP: Benjamin Gitlow, N.Y.

American Party

June 3–4, 1924, Columbus, Ohio

P: Gilbert Owen Nations, D.C.
VP: Charles Hiram Randall, Calif.

Commonwealth Land Party

Feb. 9, 1924, Engineering Society Building, New York, N.Y.

P: William J. Wallace, N.J.
VP: John Cromwell Lincoln, Ohio

Farmer Labor Party

June 17–19, 1924, Convention Hall, St. Paul, Minn.

P: Duncan McDonald, Ill.
VP: William Bouck, Wash.

Both candidates withdrew in July and the party supported the candidates of the Communist Party.

Greenback Party

July 9, 1924, Indianapolis, Ind.

P: John Zahnd, Ind.
VP: Roy M. Harrop, Neb.

1924 POPULAR VOTE

Republican Party, 15,725,016
Democratic Party, 8,386,503
Progressive Party, 4,822,856
Prohibition Party, 57,520
Socialist Labor Party, 36,428
Workers Party (Communist Party), 36,386
American Party, 23,967
Commonwealth Land Party, 1,582

1924 ELECTORAL VOTE

There were 531 electoral votes from 48 states.

Coolidge received 71.94 percent (382 votes—35 states) as follows: Ariz. 3; Calif. 13; Colo. 6; Conn. 7; Del. 3; Idaho 4; Ill. 29; Ind. 15; Iowa 13; Kan. 10; Ky. 13; Me. 6; Md. 8; Mass. 18; Mich. 15; Minn. 12, Mo. 18; Mont. 4; Neb. 8; Nev. 3; N.H. 4; N.J. 14; N.M. 3; N.Y. 45; N.D. 5; Ohio 24; Ore. 5; Pa. 38; R.I. 5; S.D. 5; Utah 4; Vt. 4; Wash. 7; W.Va. 8; Wyo. 3.

Davis received 25.61 percent (136 votes—12 states) as follows: Ala. 12; Ark. 9; Fla. 6; Ga. 14; La. 10; Miss. 10; N.C. 12; Okla. 10; S.C. 9; Tenn. 12; Tex. 20; Va. 12.

La Follette received 2.45 percent (1 state): Wis. 13.

INAUGURATIONS

FIRST TERM

August 3, 1923

Calvin Coolidge, who succeeded to the presidency on the death of President Harding, took the oath of office as President at the family homestead at Plymouth, Vt., at 2:47 A.M. on August 3, 1923. The oath was administered to him by his father, Colonel John Calvin Coolidge, a notary public. The ceremony, which took place in the sitting room by the light of a kerosene lamp, was witnessed by Mrs. Coolidge, Senator Dale Porter Hinman, and Coolidge's stenographer and chauffeur.

The oath was repeated on Tuesday, August 21, 1923, by Calvin Coolidge in his suite at the Willard Hotel, Washington, D.C. It was administered by Justice Adolph August Hoehling of the District of Columbia Supreme Court.

SECOND TERM

March 4, 1925

Calvin Coolidge took the oath of office on Wednesday, March 4, 1925, on the east portico of the Capitol. The oath was adminis-

Courtesy of The Library of Congress

Coolidge delivers his second inaugural address.

tered by Chief Justice William Howard Taft. This was the first time that a former President administered the oath to a President-elect.

The 41-minute inaugural speech was broadcast by 25 radio stations and heard by an audience estimated at 22,800,000.

THE VICE PRESIDENT

Name—Charles Gates Dawes (30th V.P.)

Date of birth—Aug. 27, 1865

Place of birth—Marietta, Ohio

Political party—Republican

State represented—Illinois

Term of office—Mar. 4, 1925–Mar. 4, 1929

Age at inauguration—59 years, 189 days

Occupation after term—U.S. ambassador to Great Britain, government official, banker

Date of death—Apr. 23, 1951

Age at death—85 years, 239 days

Place of death—Evanston, Ill.

Burial place—Chicago, Ill.

ADDITIONAL DATA ON DAWES

1884, graduated from Marietta College, Marietta, Ohio

1886, admitted to the bar; practiced in Lincoln, Neb.

Courtesy of The Library of Congress

Charles Dawes, Vice President to Calvin Coolidge

1892, published *The Banking System of the United States*

1898–1901, U.S. comptroller of the currency

1902–1925, officer, Chicago, Ill., banks

1911, wrote the first of many musical compositions, a popular piano score entitled "Melody in A Major" (later retitled "It's All in the Game").

June 11, 1917, commissioned major of Seventeenth Engineers, U.S. Army

July 16, 1917, commissioned lieutenant colonel

Sept. 27, 1917, chief of supply procurement on staff of commander in chief of American Expeditionary Forces

Jan. 16, 1918, commissioned colonel

Oct. 15, 1918, commissioned brigadier general

1918, member, Liquidation Commission, American Expeditionary Forces

Aug. 31, 1919, resigned from Army

1919, awarded Distinguished Service Medal of the United States for "exceptionally meritorious and distinguished services"; French Legion of Honor and Croix de Guerre with Palm; British Order of the Bath; Italian Order of St. Maurice and St. Lazarus; Belgian Order of Leopold

June 1920, unsuccessful candidate for Republican presidential nomination

1921, director of the U.S. Bureau of the Budget

1921–1926, brigadier general, Officers' Reserve Corps

1923, president of German reparations commission, which worked out the "Dawes Plan"

Mar. 4, 1925–Mar. 4, 1929, Vice President under Calvin Coolidge

1925, recipient, with Sir Austen Chamberlain, of Nobel Peace Prize

June 1928, received four votes for Republican presidential nomination

1929–1932, ambassador to Great Britain

1930, delegate, London Naval Conference

Feb.–June 1932, president, Reconstruction Finance Corporation

June 1932, resumed banking business

June 1932, received one vote for Republican presidential nomination

1939, wrote *Journal as Ambassador to Great Britain*

1950, wrote *A Journal of the McKinley Years*

CABINET

FIRST TERM

August 3, 1923–March 3, 1925

State—Charles Evans Hughes, N.Y., continued from preceding administration

Treasury—Andrew William Mellon, Pa., continued from preceding administration

War—John Wingate Weeks, Mass., continued from preceding administration

Attorney General—Harry Micajah Daugherty, Ohio, continued from preceding administration; Harlan Fiske Stone, N.Y., Apr. 7, 1924; entered upon duties Apr. 9, 1924

Postmaster General—Harry Stewart New, Ind., continued from preceding administration

Navy—Edwin Denby, Mich., continued from preceding administration; Curtis Dwight Wilbur, Calif., Mar. 18, 1924

Interior—Hubert Work, Colo., continued from preceding administration

Agriculture—Henry Cantwell Wallace, Iowa, continued from preceding administra-tion; died Oct. 25, 1924; Howard Mason Gore, W.Va. (assistant secretary), ad interim Oct. 26, 1924 to Nov. 22, 1924; Howard Mason Gore. W.Va., Nov. 21, 1924; entered upon duties Nov. 22, 1924

Commerce—Herbert Clark Hoover, Calif., continued from preceding administration

Labor—James John Davis, Pa., continued from preceding administration

SECOND TERM

March 4, 1925–March 3, 1929

State—Charles Evans Hughes, N.Y., contin-ued from preceding administration; Frank Billings Kellogg, Minn., Feb. 16, 1925; entered upon duties Mar. 5, 1925

Treasury—Andrew William Mellon, Pa., continued from preceding administration

War—John Wingate Weeks, Mass., contin-ued from preceding administration; Dwight Filley Davis, Mo., Oct. 13, 1925; entered upon duties Oct. 14, 1925

Attorney General—James Montgomery Beck, Pa., (solicitor general), ad interim Mar. 4, 1925 to Mar. 16, 1925; John Garibaldi Sargent, Vt., Mar. 17, 1925; entered upon duties Mar. 18, 1925

Postmaster General—Harry Stewart New, Ind., continued from preceding administra-tion; recommissioned Mar. 5, 1925

Navy—Curtis Dwight Wilbur, Calif., contin-ued from preceding administration

Coolidge, first row center, with members of his cabinet

Interior—Hubert Work, Colo., continued from preceding administration; Roy Owen West, Ill., ad interim July 25, 1928, to Jan. 21, 1929; Roy Owen West, Ill., Jan. 21, 1929

Agriculture—Howard Mason Gore, W.Va., continued from preceding administration; William Marion Jardine, Kan., Feb. 18, 1925; entered upon duties Mar. 5, 1925

Commerce—Herbert Clark Hoover, Calif., continued from preceding administration; William Fairfield Whiting, Mass., ad interim Aug. 21, 1928 to Dec. 11, 1928; William Fairfield Whiting, Mass., Dec. 11, 1928

Labor—James John Davis, Pa., continued from preceding administration

CONGRESS

SIXTY-NINTH CONGRESS

March 4, 1925–March 3, 1927

First session—Dec. 7, 1925–July 3, 1926 (209 days); Nov. 10, 1926 (The Senate met subsequent to adjournment for the purpose of sitting as a court of impeachment; adjourned sine die the same day; court of impeachment adjourned to Dec. 13, 1926, when, on request of House managers, impeachment proceedings were dismissed.)

Second session—Dec. 6, 1926–March 3, 1927 (88 days)

Special session of the Senate—Mar. 4, 1925–Mar. 18, 1925

Vice President—Charles Gates Dawes, Ill.

President pro tempore of the Senate —Albert Baird Cummins, Iowa; George Higgins Moses, N.H., elected Mar. 6, 1925

Secretary of the Senate—George Andrew Sanderson, Ill., reelected Mar. 6, 1925, died Apr. 24, 1925; Edwin Pope Thayer, Ind., elected Dec. 7, 1925

Speaker of the House—Nicholas Ohio, elected Dec, 7. 1925

Clerk of the House—William Tyler Page, Md., reelected Dec. 7, 1925

SEVENTIETH CONGRESS

March 4, 1927–March 3, 1929

First session—Dec. 5, 1927–May 29, 1928 (177 days)

Second session—Dec. 3, 1928–Mar. 3, 1929 (91 days)

Vice President—Charles Gates Dawes, Ill.

President pro tempore of the Senate —George Higgins Moses, N.H., reelected Dec. 15, 1927

Secretary of the Senate—Edwin Pope Thayer, Ind., reelected Dec. 15, 1927

Speaker of the House—Nicholas Longworth, Ohio, reelected Dec. 5, 1927

Clerk of the House—William Tyler Page, Md., reelected Dec. 5, 1927

APPOINTMENTS TO THE SUPREME COURT

Associate Justice

Harlan Fiske Stone, N.Y., Feb. 5, 1925 (replaced Joseph McKenna)

IMPORTANT DATES IN THE PRESIDENCY

1923–1924, Teapot Dome oil scandal of Harding administration revealed in Senate investigations

May 15, 1924, soldier bonus bill vetoed, later passed over veto by both Houses of Congress

May 26, 1924, immigration bill signed reducing quotas established in 1921

June 2, 1924, citizenship granted to non-citizen American Indians born in the United States

July 1, 1924, regular airmail transcontinental service established

July 1, 1924, U.S. Foreign Service created

Dec. 17, 1924, diesel electric locomotive placed in service

Jan. 5, 1925, first woman governor, Nellie Tayloe Ross, took office in Wyoming

Mar. 23, 1925, Tennessee enacted law making it unlawful to teach theory of evolution

Mar. 16, 1926, liquid fuel rocket flown

Apr. 6, 1926, Tacna-Arica Conference between Chile and Peru held at Washington, D.C.

May 9, 1926, Richard E. Byrd and Floyd Bennett made first flight over North Pole

May 31, 1926, Sesquicentennial Exposition opened, Philadelphia, Pa.

June 14, 1926, Board of Mediation appointed to succeed Railroad Labor Board

July 2, 1926, Distinguished Flying Cross authorized

Feb. 23, 1927, U.S. Radio Commission created

Mar. 5, 1927, marines sent to China to protect Western property during civil war

May 20, 1927, Lindbergh's transatlantic solo flight

Jan. 15, 1929, Kellogg-Briand peace pact ratified by U.S. Senate

---

ADDITIONAL DATA ON COOLIDGE

CALVIN COOLIDGE

—was the second President born in Vermont.

—was the twelfth President who was a resident of a state other than his native state.

—was the fifth President whose father was alive when he was inaugurated.

—was the first President sworn in by his father (in 1923).

—was the first President whose inaugural ceremonies were broadcast.

—was the first President sworn in by a former President (in 1925).

COOLIDGE BORN ON INDEPENDENCE DAY

Calvin Coolidge was born on July 4, 1872, at Plymouth, Vt., on the ninety-sixth anniversary of the Declaration of Independence.

PRESIDENTIAL CANDIDATES POSED FOR NEWSREELS

The first films of presidential candidates were seen by movie spectators in September 1924. On August 11, 1924, Theodore W. Case and Lee De Forest took motion pictures on the grounds of the White House of President Calvin Coolidge, Republican candidate for reelection. On the same day they photographed Senator Robert Marion La Follette, Progressive Party candidate, who posed on the steps of the Capitol. Later, movies were taken of John William Davis, Democratic presidential nominee, at Locust Valley, N.Y.

LIKENESS OF COOLIDGE ON COINS

The first coin bearing the likeness of a living President was the 1926 Sesquicentennial half dollar, the obverse of which bore the heads of Presidents George Washington and Calvin Coolidge. The reverse depicted the Liberty Bell. The net coinage was 141,120 pieces struck at the mint at Philadelphia, Pa.

FURTHER READING

Abels, Jules. *In the Time of Silent Cal.* 1969.

Ferrell, Robert H. *The Presidency of Calvin Coolidge*. 1998.

McCoy, Donald R. *Calvin Coolidge*. 1967.

Sobel, Robert. *Coolidge: An American Enigma*. 1998.

White, William A. *A Puritan in Babylon*. 1938.

Courtesy of The Library of Congress

31st PRESIDENT

Herbert Clark Hoover

Date of birth—Aug. 10, 1874

Place of birth—West Branch, Iowa

Education—West Branch Free School, West Branch, Iowa; Friends Pacific Academy, Newberg, Ore., 1885–1887; business school, Salem, Ore.; Stanford University, Stanford, Calif., bachelor of arts degree in geology, May 29, 1895

Religion—Society of Friends (Quaker)

Ancestry—Swiss-German, English

Career—Mining engineer, relief administrator during World War I, member of federal and international economic organizations, Secretary of Commerce

Political party—Republican

State represented—California

Term of office—Mar. 4, 1929–Mar. 4, 1933

Term served—4 years

Administration—36th

Congresses—71st, 72nd

Age at inauguration—54 years, 206 days

Lived after term—31 years, 231 days

Occupation after term—Special reorganization commissions, writing

Date of death—Oct. 20, 1964

Age at death—90 years, 71 days

Place of death—New York, N.Y.

Burial place—West Branch, Iowa

FAMILY

FATHER

Name—Jesse Clark Hoover

Date of birth—Sept. 2, 1846

Place of birth—West Milton, Ohio

Marriage—Hulda Randall Minthorn, Mar. 12, 1870

Occupation—Blacksmith, owner of farm implement business

Date of death—Dec. 13, 1880

Place of death—West Branch, Iowa

Age at death—34 years, 112 days

MOTHER

Name at birth—Hulda Randall Minthorn

Date of birth—May 4, 1848

Place of birth—Burgersville, Ontario, Canada

Marriage—Jesse Clark Hoover, Mar. 12, 1870

Date of death—Feb. 22, 1884

Place of death—West Branch, Iowa

Age at death—35 years, 294 days

SIBLINGS

Herbert Clark Hoover was the second child in a family of three.

Children of Jesse Clark Hoover and Hulda Randall Minthorn Hoover

Theodore Jesse Hoover, b. Jan. 28, 1871; d. Feb. 4, 1955

Herbert Clark Hoover, b. Aug. 10, 1874; d. Oct. 20, 1964

Mary ("May") Hoover, b. Sept. 1, 1876; d. June 7, 1953

MARRIAGE

Married—Lou Henry

Date of marriage—Feb. 10, 1899

Place of marriage—Monterey, Calif.

Age of wife at marriage—24 years, 318 days

Age of husband at marriage—24 years, 184 days

Years married—44 years, 331 days

CHILDREN

Herbert Clark Hoover, Jr., b. Aug. 4, 1903, London, England; m. June 25, 1925, Margaret Eva Watson, Palo Alto, Calif.; d. July 9, 1969, Pasadena, Calif.

Allan Henry Hoover, b. July 17, 1907, London, England; m. Mar. 17, 1937, Margaret Coberly, Los Angeles, Calif.; d. Nov. 8, 1993

THE PRESIDENT'S WIFE

Name at birth—Lou Henry

Date of birth—Mar. 29, 1874

Place of birth—Waterloo, Iowa

Mother—Florence Ida Weed Henry

Father—Charles Delano Henry

Father's occupation—Banker

Education—Stanford University, Stanford, Calif., bachelor's degree, 1898

Marriage—Herbert Clark Hoover, Feb. 10, 1899, Monterey, Calif.

Children—Herbert Clark Hoover, Jr., b. Aug. 4, 1903, d. July 9, 1969; Allan Henry Hoover, b. July 17, 1907, d. Nov. 8, 1993

Occupation—Relief administrator

Date of death—Jan. 7, 1944

Age at death—69 years, 284 days

Place of death—New York, N.Y.

Burial place—Alta Mesa Cemetery, Palo Alto, Calif.; reinterred Nov. 1, 1964, West Branch, Iowa

Years older than the President—134 days

Courtesy of The Library of Congress

Lou Hoover, wife of Herbert Hoover

THE FIRST LADY

Lou Henry Hoover was the first woman to major in geology at what is now Stanford University, and was co-translator with her husband of Georgius Agricola's sixteenth-century book *De re metallica,* published in 1912. She accompanied him around the globe on his engineering jobs and government administration positions, running their large household and assisting in his work. From her years as a cabinet wife, she had numerous personal friends in Washington, D.C., and as a result White House social functions under the Hoovers were more friendly than formal. Lou Hoover was also a leader in the Girl Scout movement and other organizations.

IMPORTANT DATES IN THE PRESIDENT'S LIFE

1884, sent to Newberg, Ore., to live with an uncle after both parents had died

1891–1895, worked his way through college; held summer jobs with Geological Survey of Arkansas and U.S. Geological Survey

1895, graduated from Stanford University

1895–1913, mining engineer, consultant in North America, Europe, Asia, Africa, and Australia

1899, went to China with his bride

1900, took part in defense of Tientsin in Boxer outbreak

1914–1915, chairman of American Relief Committee in London

1915–1918, chairman of Commission for Relief in Belgium

Aug. 1917–June 1919, U.S. food administrator

1919, chairman of Supreme Economic Conference, Paris

1920, chairman of European Relief Council

1920, complimentary votes at Republican nominating convention

1921–1928, secretary of commerce under Presidents Harding and Coolidge

1922, coal administration

June 14, 1928, nominated for the presidency by the Republican convention at Kansas City, Mo.

Mar. 4, 1929–Mar. 4, 1933, President

Nov. 8, 1932, defeated for reelection by Democratic candidate, Franklin Delano Roosevelt

1946, appointed coordinator of European food program by President Truman

1947–1949, 1953–1955, chairman of Commission on Organization of the Executive Branch of the Government (Hoover Commission on administrative reform)

ELECTIONS

THE ELECTION OF 1928

November 6, 1928

CANDIDATES

Republican Party (19th Convention)

June 12–15, 1928, Civic Auditorium, Kansas City, Mo.

P: Herbert Clark Hoover, Calif.
VP: Charles Curtis, Kan.

Hoover was nominated on the first ballot. Candidates for nomination and the votes they received:

Herbert Clark Hoover, Calif., 837
Frank Orren Lowden, Ill., 74
Charles Curtis, Kan., 64
James Eli Watson, Ind., 45
George William Norris, Neb., 24
Guy Despard Goff, W.Va., 18
Calvin Coolidge, Mass., 17
Charles Gates Dawes, Ill., 4
Charles Evans Hughes, N.Y., 1
Total number of votes: 1,089
Nomination made unanimous

Democratic Party (25th Convention)

June 26–29, 1928, Sam Houston Hall, Houston, Tex.

P: Alfred Emanuel Smith, N.Y.
VP: Joseph Taylor Robinson, Ark.

Smith was nominated on the first ballot. Candidates for nomination and the votes they received:

Alfred Emanuel Smith, N.Y., $849^2/_3$

Walter Franklin George, Ga., $52^1/_2$

James Alexander Reed, Mo., 52

Cordell Hull, Tenn., $50^5/_6$

Jesse Holman Jones, Tex., 43

Richard Cannon Watts, S.C., 18

Byron Patton Harrison, Miss., $8^1/_2$

Evans Woollen, Ind., 7

Alvin Victor Donahey, Ohio, 5

William Augustus Ayres, Kan., 3

Atlee Pomerene, Ohio, 3

Gilbert Monell Hitchcock, Neb., 2

Theodore Gilmore Bilbo, Miss., 1

Total number of votes: $1,097^1/_2$

Number necessary for nomination: 733
Nomination made unanimous

Socialist Party

Apr. 13–17, 1928, Finnish Socialist Hall and Manhattan Opera House, New York, N.Y.

P: Norman Mattoon Thomas, N.Y.
VP: James Hudson Maurer, Pa.

Workers Party (Communist Party)

May 25–26, 1928, Mecca Temple and Central Opera House, New York, N.Y.

P: William Zebulon Foster, Ill.
VP: Benjamin Gitlow, N.Y.

Socialist Labor Party

May 12–14, 1928, New York, N.Y.

P: Verne L. Reynolds, Mich.

VP: Jeremiah D. Crowley, N.Y.

Frank T. Johns of Oregon was nominated for the presidency, but lost his life endeavoring to effect a rescue. On May 22, 1928, Reynolds was nominated in his place.

Prohibition Party

July 10–12, 1928, Chicago, Ill.

P: William Frederick Varney, N.Y.

VP: James Arthur Edgerton, Va.

Varney was nominated on the second ballot. Candidates for nomination and the votes they received on the first and second ballots:

William Frederick Varney, N.Y., 52, 68

Herbert Clark Hoover, Calif., 42, 45

Farmer Labor Party

July 10–11, 1928, Chicago, Ill.

P: Frank Elbridge Webb, Calif.

VP: Will Vereen, Ga.

Senator George William Norris of Nebraska was nominated for the presidency, but declined the nomination.

Greenback Party

P: John Zahnd, Ind.

VP: Wesley Henry Bennington, Ohio

The party filed no ticket. The candidates were write-in candidates.

1928 POPULAR VOTE

Republican Party, 21,392,190
Democratic Party, 15,016,443
Socialist Party, 267,420
Workers Party (Communist Party), 48,770
Socialist Labor Party, 21,603
Prohibition Party, 20,106
Farmer Labor Party, 6,390

1928 ELECTORAL VOTE

There were 531 electoral votes from 48 states.

Hoover received 83.62 percent (444 votes—40 states) as follows: Ariz. 3; Calif. 13; Colo. 6; Conn. 7; Del. 3; Fla. 6; Idaho 4; Ill. 29; Ind. 15; Iowa. 13; Kan. 10; Ky. 13; Me. 6; Md. 8; Mich. 15; Minn. 12; Mo. 18; Mont. 4; Neb. 8; Nev. 3; N.H. 4; N.J. 14; N.M. 3; N.Y. 45; N.C. 12; N.D. 5; Ohio 24; Okla. 10; Ore. 5; Pa. 38; S.D. 5; Tenn. 12; Tex. 20; Utah 4; Vt. 4; Va. 12; Wash. 7; W.Va. 8; Wis. 13; Wyo. 3.

Smith received 16.38 percent (87 votes—8 states) as follows: Ala. 12; Ark. 9; Ga. 14; La. 10; Mass. 18; Miss. 10; R.I. 5; S.C. 9.

INAUGURATION

March 4, 1929

Herbert Clark Hoover took his oath of office on Monday, March 4, 1929, on the east portico of the Capitol. A crowd of about 50,000 witnessed the ceremony.

At 1:08 P.M. Chief Justice William Howard Taft administered the oath of office. Twenty years before, on March 4, 1909, the same oath had been administered to Taft by Chief Justice Edward Douglass White.

The dirigible *Los Angeles,* four blimps, and thirty airplanes flew over the city. Rain fell in the afternoon. At 8 P.M. a fireworks display thrilled the crowds. At 9 P.M. the largest inaugural ball up to that time was held at the Washington Auditorium. The ball was opened by an Indian orchestra from Tulsa, Okla. The reigning woman at the ball was Mrs. Gann, sister of Vice President Curtis.

Courtesy of The Library of Congress

Hoover delivers his inaugural address.

THE VICE PRESIDENT

Name—Charles Curtis (31st V.P.)
Date of birth—Jan. 25, 1860
Place of birth—Topeka, Kan.
Political party—Republican
State represented—Kansas
Term of office—Mar. 4, 1929–Mar. 4, 1933
Age at inauguration—69 years, 38 days
Occupation after term—Lawyer
Date of death—Feb. 8, 1936
Age at death—76 years, 14 days
Place of death—Washington, D.C.
Burial place—Topeka, Kan.

ADDITIONAL DATA ON CURTIS

1881, admitted to the bar; practiced in Topeka, Kan.
1885–1889, prosecuting attorney, Shawnee County, Kan.
Mar. 4, 1893–Jan. 28, 1907, U.S. House of Representatives (from Kansas)
Jan. 29, 1907–Mar. 3, 1913, U.S. Senate (from Kansas)
Dec. 4–12, 1911, president pro tempore of the Senate
1912, unsuccessful candidate for reelection to Senate

Courtesy of The Library of Congress

Charles Curtis, Vice President to Herbert Hoover

Mar. 4, 1915–Mar. 3, 1929, U.S. Senate
1924, elected majority leader of the Senate
Mar. 4, 1929–Mar. 4, 1933, Vice President under Herbert Hoover
1932, unsuccessful candidate for reelection as Vice President
1933–1936, practiced law in Washington, D.C.

CABINET

March 4, 1929–March 3, 1933

State—Frank Billings Kellogg, Minn., continued from preceding administration; Henry Lewis Stimson, N.Y., Mar. 4, 1929; entered upon duties Mar. 29, 1929

Treasury—Andrew William Mellon, Pa., continued from preceding administration; Ogden Livingston Mills, N.Y., Feb. 10, 1932; entered upon duties Feb. 13, 1932

War—Dwight Filley Davis, Mo., continued from preceding administration; James William Good, Ill., Mar. 5, 1929; entered upon duties Mar. 6, 1929; Patrick Jay Hurley, Okla., Dec. 9, 1929

Attorney General—John Garibaldi Sargent, Vt., continued from preceding administration; William De Witt Mitchell, Minn., Mar. 5, 1929; entered upon duties Mar. 6, 1929

Postmaster General—Harry Stewart New, Ind., continued from preceding administration; Walter Folger Brown, Ohio, Mar. 5, 1929; entered upon duties Mar. 6, 1929

Navy—Curtis Dwight Wilbur, Calif., continued from preceding administration; Charles Francis Adams, Mass., Mar. 5, 1929

Interior—Roy Owen West, Ill., continued from preceding administration; Ray Lyman Wilbur, Calif., Mar. 5, 1929

Agriculture—William Marion Jardine, Kan., continued from preceding administration; Arthur Mastick Hyde, Mo., Mar. 5, 1929; entered upon duties Mar. 6, 1929

Commerce—William Fairfield Whiting, Mass., continued from preceding adminis-

tration; Robert Patterson Lamont, Ill., Mar. 5, 1929; Roy Dikeman Chapin, Mich., ad interim Aug. 8, 1932–Dec. 14, 1932; Roy Dikeman Chapin, Mich., Dec. 14, 1932

Labor—James John Davis, Pa., continued from preceding administration; William Nuckles Doak, Va., Dec. 8, 1930; entered upon duties Dec. 9, 1930

CONGRESS

SEVENTY–FIRST CONGRESS

March 4, 1929–March 3, 1931

First session—Apr. 15, 1929–Nov. 22, 1929 (222 days)

Second session—Dec. 2, 1929–July 3, 1930 (214 days)

Third session—Dec. 1, 1930–Mar. 3, 1931 (93 days)

Special sessions of the Senate—Mar. 4, 1929–Mar. 5, 1929 (2 days); July 7, 1930–July 21, 1930 (15 days)

Vice President—Charles Curtis, Kan.

President pro tempore of the Senate —George Higgins Moses, N.H.

Secretary of the Senate—Edwin Pope Thayer, Ind.

Speaker of the House—Nicholas Longworth, Ohio, reelected Apr. 15, 1929

President Hoover, seated third from right, pictured with his cabinet.

Clerk of the House—William Tyler Page, Md. reelected Apr. 15, 1929

SEVENTY–SECOND CONGRESS

March 4, 1931–March 3, 1933

First session—Dec. 7, 1931–July 16, 1932 (223 days)

Second session—Dec. 5, 1932–Mar. 3, 1933 (89 days)

Vice President—Charles Curtis, Kan.

President pro tempore of the Senate —George Higgins Moses, N.H.

Secretary of the Senate—Edwin Pope Thayer, Ind.

Speaker of the House—John Nance Garner, Tex., elected Dec. 7, 1931

Clerk of the House—South Trimble, Ky., elected Dec. 7, 1931

APPOINTMENTS TO THE SUPREME COURT

Chief Justice

Charles Evans Hughes, N.Y., Feb. 13, 1930 (replaced William Howard Taft)

Associate Justices

Owen Josephus Roberts, Pa., May 20, 1930 (replaced Edward Terry Sanford)

Benjamin Nathan Cardozo, N.Y., Mar. 2, 1932 (replaced Oliver Wendell Holmes)

IMPORTANT DATES IN THE PRESIDENCY

Feb. 14, 1929, gangland massacre in Chicago

Mar. 16, 1929, Indiana taxed chain stores

May 16, 1929, first Moving Picture Academy "Oscars" awarded

June 15, 1929, Agricultural Marketing Act established Farm Board to encourage cooperatives and dispose of surpluses

July 10, 1929, new small-size dollar bills issued

Oct. 25, 1929, former cabinet member A. B. Fall convicted

Oct. 29, 1929, stock market crash preceding Great Depression

Nov. 19–27, 1929, White House conference on depression

Nov. 28, 1929, Richard Byrd made South Pole flight

Feb. 10, 1930, Grain Stabilization Corporation authorized

Mar. 26, 1930, Inter-American highway appropriation bill enacted

June 17, 1930, protectionist Hawley-Smoot Tariff signed

July 1, 1930, streamlined submarine *Nautilus* commissioned

July 21, 1930, Veterans Administration created

Sept. 17, 1930, Boulder (later Hoover) Dam begun

Feb. 14, 1931, Airmail Flyer's Medal of Honor authorized

Mar. 3, 1931, "Star Spangled Banner" adopted as national anthem

June 1931, Hoover moratorium on German debts arranged

July 1, 1931, Harold Gatty and Wiley Post completed airplane flight around the world

Sept. 26, 1931, keel laid for the *Ranger*, first aircraft carrier

Dec. 15, 1931, Maria Norton of New Jersey appointed chairman of House committee (first woman to head congressional committee)

Jan. 1932, unemployment figures reach 12 million

Jan. 7, 1932, Non-Recognition Doctrine propounded by Stimson

Jan. 12, 1932, Hattie Caraway of Arkansas elected U.S. senator (first woman to hold Senate office by election rather than appointment)

Jan. 22, 1932, Reconstruction Finance Corporation created

May 21, 1932, Amelia Earhart Putnam completed first transatlantic solo flight by a woman

May–July 1932, "bonus army" march on Washington, D.C., by unemployed veterans; routed by force

Feb. 6, 1933, Twentieth ("Lame Duck") Amendment to the Constitution ratified

ADDITIONAL DATA ON HOOVER

HERBERT CLARK HOOVER

—was the first President born in Iowa.

—was the thirteenth President who was a resident of a state other than his native state.

—was the first President to have served in a cabinet other than as secretary of state or war.

—was the first President to have been an engineer.

—was the last President whose term of office ended on March 3.

FIRST PRESIDENT BORN WEST OF THE MISSISSIPPI

Herbert Clark Hoover, born August 10, 1874, at West Branch, Iowa, was the first President born west of the Mississippi River. His wife, Lou Henry Hoover, born March 29, 1874, at Waterloo, Iowa, was the second President's wife born west of the Mississippi.

ASTEROID NAMED FOR HOOVER

The first asteroid named for an American President was Hooveria. It was discovered in March 1920 by Professor Johann Palisan of the University of Vienna, Austria, and named for Herbert Hoover. At that time, Hoover was not yet President; he was engaged in providing food for distressed European countries.

NOTIFICATION OF NOMINATION TELEVISED

Presidential nomination notification ceremonies were televised for the first time at the Assembly Chamber, Albany, N.Y., on Wednesday, August 22, 1928, when Democratic candidate Alfred Emanuel Smith was notified of his nomination. The pictures were transmitted by television to Schenectady, N.Y., and sent out by short wave over 2XAF and 2XAD by the General Electric Company.

HUGHES REAPPOINTED TO SUPREME COURT

President Hoover established a precedent when he appointed as Chief Justice of the Supreme Court Charles Evans Hughes, who served February 13, 1930, to July 1, 1941. This was Hughes's second appointment to the Court, a distinction accorded no other person. He was appointed an associate justice of the Supreme Court by President Taft, serving from May 2, 1910, to June 10, 1916, when he resigned. He became the Republican nominee for President in 1916 and was defeated by Woodrow Wilson. Afterward he served as secretary of state (1921–1925), as a member of the Hague Tribunal (1926–1930), and as a judge on the Permanent Court of International Justice (1928–1930).

ABSOLUTE MONARCH VISITED HOOVER

The first absolute monarch to visit the United States was King Prajadhipok of Siam. He arrived in New York City, April 1931, accompanied by his wife, Queen Rambai Barni, and the royal entourage. President Hoover received them on April 29, 1931. They crossed into the United States on April 19, 1931 at Portal, N.D., from Canada. This was not, however, the king's first visit to the United States. As a prince he had arrived at New York City from England on September 22, 1924, for a short visit.

TWENTIETH AMENDMENT ENACTED

The Twentieth Amendment to the Constitution, known as the "lame duck amendment," which provided that "the terms of the President and the Vice President shall end at noon on the 20th day of January," was proposed to the states on March 2, 1932, by the Seventy-second Congress. Virginia was the first state to ratify the amendment when a joint resolution was passed March 4, 1932, although the State Department resolutions were not mailed until March 8, 1932. The amendment was ratified on January 23, 1933, by Georgia, Missouri, Ohio, and Utah (the thirty-sixth state) and certified by the Secretary of State on February 6, 1933; but in accordance with Section 5, the amendment did not take effect until October 15, 1933. By October 15, 1933, the amendment had been ratified by all the states.

The Amendment follows:

Section 1. The terms of the President and Vice President shall end at noon on the 20th day of January, and the terms of Senators and Representatives at noon on the 3rd day of January, of the years in which such terms would have ended if this article had not been ratified; and the terms of their successors shall then begin.

Section 2. The Congress shall assemble at least once in every year, and such meeting shall begin at noon on the 3rd day of January, unless they shall by law appoint a different day.

Section 3. If, at the time fixed for the beginning of the term of the President, the President elect shall have died, the Vice President elect shall become President. If a President shall not have been chosen before the time fixed for the beginning of his term, or if the President elect shall have failed to qualify, then the Vice President elect shall act as President until a President shall have qualified; and the Congress may by law provide for the case wherein neither a President elect nor a Vice President elect shall have qualified, declaring who shall then act as President, or the manner in which one who is to act shall be selected, and such person shall act accordingly until a President or Vice President shall have qualified.

Section 4. The Congress may by law provide for the case of the death of any of the persons from whom the House of Representatives may choose a President whenever the right of choice shall have devolved upon them, and for the case of the death of any of the persons from whom the Senate may choose a Vice President whenever the right of choice shall have devolved upon them.

Section 5. Sections 1 and 2 shall take effect on the 15th day of October following the ratification of this article.

Section 6. This article shall be inoperative unless it shall have been ratified as an amendment to the Constitution by the legislatures of three-fourths of the several States within seven years from the date of its submission.

HOOVER HONORED

President Hoover was one of the most honored Presidents in our history. He received more than 50 honorary degrees from American universities, more than 25 honorary degrees from foreign universities, the freedom of more than a dozen cities, and more than 70 medals and awards, in addition to about a hundred miscellaneous honors.

On January 13, 1958, General Mark Wayne Clark, president of the Citadel, South Carolina State Military College, bestowed the honorary degree of doctor of laws on the former President at the Citadel. It was the eighty-third degree that he received, one for each year of his life. He was honored as "engineer, humanitarian and statesman."

On April 25, 1958, the University of the State of New York, at the eighty-ninth convocation of the Board of Regents, awarded him an honorary degree, which he received in absentia while recovering from a gall-bladder operation.

HOOVER, ENGINEER

A survey conducted in 1964 as part of the one hundredth anniversary of the School of Engineering and Applied Science of Columbia

University named Herbert Clark Hoover and Thomas Alva Edison as the two greatest engineers in the history of the United States.

HOOVER LIVED THIRTY-ONE YEARS AFTER TERM

Herbert Clark Hoover lived longer after his term of office than any other President—31 years and 231 days. He was not, however, the oldest former President at the time of his death, nor was he the youngest upon completion of his presidential term.

HOOVER NATIONAL HISTORIC SITE

On August 12, 1965, Congress enacted a law (79 Stat. L. 119) "to establish the Herbert Hoover National Historical Site" near West Branch, Iowa (President Hoover's birthplace), and appropriated $1,650,00 for land acquisition and development.

HOOVER HAD DESK TELEPHONE

The first President to have a telephone on his desk was Herbert Clark Hoover, who had it installed March 27, 1929. Previously, there had been a telephone in a booth in a room adjoining the President's office and another one in his study on the second floor.

HOOVER TRANSLATED BOOK ON METALS

De Re Metallica (1556), a book in Latin on mining and metallurgy by Georgius Agricola, was translated by Herbert Clark Hoover and Lou Henry Hoover and published in 1912 by *The Mining Magazine*, Salisbury House, London, England. The translation contained 672 pages, including introductory matter, and had 289 woodcut illustrations.

FURTHER READING

Barber, William J. *From New Era to New Deal*. 1985.

Burner, David. *Herbert Hoover: A Public Life*. 1978.

Fausold, Martin L. *The Presidency of Herbert C. Hoover*. 1985.

Hamilton, David E. *From New Day to New Deal: American Farm Policy from Hoover to Roosevelt, 1928–1933*. 1991.

Leuchtenburg, William E. *Herbert Hoover: The American Presidents Series: The 31st President, 1929-1933*. 2009.

Nash, George H. *The Life of Herbert Hoover: The Engineer, 1874–1914*. 1983.

———. *The Humanitarian, 1914–1917*. 1988.

———. *Master of Emergencies, 1917–1918*. 1996.

Courtesy of The Library of Congress

Franklin Delano Roosevelt

Date of birth—Jan. 30, 1882

Place of birth—Hyde Park, N.Y.

Education—Private tutors; Groton School, Groton, Mass., 1896–1900; Harvard College, Cambridge, Mass., bachelor's degree, June 24, 1903; Columbia Law School, 1904–1907

Religion—Episcopalian

Ancestry—Dutch, French

Career—Lawyer, state senator, assistant Secretary of the Navy, governor of New York

Political party—Democratic

State represented—New York

Term of office—Mar. 4, 1933–Apr. 12, 1945

Term served—12 years, 39 days

Administration—37th, 38th, 39th, 40th

Congresses—73rd, 74th, 75th, 76th, 77th, 78th, 79th

Age at inauguration—51 years, 33 days

Lived after term—Died in office

Date of death—Apr. 12, 1945

Age at death—63 years, 72 days

Place of death—Warm Springs, Ga.

Burial place—Family plot, Hyde Park, N.Y.

FAMILY

FATHER

Name—James Roosevelt

Date of birth—July 16, 1828

Place of birth—Hyde Park, N.Y.

First marriage—Rebecca Brien Howland, 1853 (b. Jan. 15, 1831; d. Aug. 21, 1876, age 45 years, 218 days)

Second marriage—Sara Delano, Oct. 7, 1880, Hyde Park, N.Y.

Occupation—Gentleman farmer, lawyer, financier, owner of coal mine, vice president of Delaware and Hudson Railroad; church vestryman and senior warden, civic activist

Date of death—Dec. 8, 1900

Place of death—New York, N.Y.

Age at death—72 years, 145 days

MOTHER

Name at birth—Sara Delano

Date of birth—Sept. 21, 1854

Place of birth—Newburgh, N.Y.

Marriage—James Roosevelt, Oct. 7, 1880, Hyde Park, N.Y.

Date of death—Sept. 7, 1941

Place of death—Hyde Park, N.Y.

Age at death—86 years, 351 days

SIBLINGS

Franklin Delano Roosevelt was a second son, the only child of his father's second marriage.

Children of James Roosevelt and Rebecca Brien Howland Roosevelt

James Roosevelt, b. Mar. 27, 1854; d. May 7, 1927

Children of James Roosevelt and Sara Delano Roosevelt

Franklin Delano Roosevelt, b. Jan. 30, 1882; d. Apr. 12, 1945

MARRIAGE

Married—(Anna) Eleanor Roosevelt

Date of marriage—Mar. 17, 1905

Place of marriage—New York, N.Y.

Age of wife at marriage—20 years, 157 days

Age of husband at marriage—23 years, 46 days

Years married—40 years, 26 days

CHILDREN

Anna Eleanor Roosevelt, b. May 3, 1906, New York, N.Y.; m. June 5, 1926, Curtis Bean Dall, Hyde Park, N.Y.; m. Jan. 18, 1935, John Boettiger, New York, N.Y.; m. Nov. 11, 1952, James Addison Halsted, Malibu, Calif.; d. Dec. 1, 1975, New York, N.Y.

James Roosevelt, b. Dec. 23, 1907, New York, N.Y.; m. June 4, 1930, Betsy Cushing, Brookline, Mass.; m. Apr. 14, 1941, Romelle Theresa Schneider, Beverly Hills, Calif.; m. July 1, 1956, Gladys Irene Owens, Los Angeles, Calif.; d. Aug. 13, 1991, Newport Beach, Calif.

Franklin Roosevelt, b. Mar. 18, 1909; d. Nov. 8, 1909

Elliott Roosevelt, b. Sept. 23, 1910, New York, N.Y.; m. Jan. 16, 1932, Elizabeth Browning Donner, Bryn Mawr, Pa.; m. July 22, 1933, Ruth Josephine Googins, Burlington, Iowa; m. Dec. 3, 1944, Faye Emerson, Grand Canyon, Ariz.; m. Mar. 15, 1951, Minnewa Bell Ross, Miami Beach, Fla.; d. Oct. 27, 1990, Scottsdale, Ariz.

Franklin Delano Roosevelt, Jr., b. Aug. 17, 1914, Campobello, New Brunswick, Canada; m. June 30, 1937, Ethel Du Pont, Wilmington, Del.; m. Aug. 31, 1949, Suzanne Perrin, New York, N.Y.; m. July 1, 1970, Felicia Schiff Warburg Sarnoff, New York, N.Y.; m. May 6, 1977, Patricia Luisa Oakes; d. Aug. 17, 1988

John Aspinwall Roosevelt, b. Mar. 13, 1916, Washington, D.C.; m. June 18, 1938, Anne Lindsay Clark, Nahant, Mass.; m. Oct. 22, 1965, Irene Boyd McAlpin; d. Apr. 27, 1981, New York, N.Y.

THE PRESIDENT'S WIFE

Name at birth—(Anna) Eleanor Roosevelt

Date of birth—Oct. 11, 1884

Place of birth—New York, N.Y.

Mother—Anna Livingston Hall Roosevelt

Father—Elliott Roosevelt

Father's occupation—Sportsman

Education—Tutors; Allenwood School, London, England

Marriage—Franklin Delano Roosevelt, Mar. 17, 1905, New York, N.Y.

Children—Anna Eleanor Roosevelt, b. May 3, 1906, d. Dec. 1, 1975; James Roosevelt, b. Dec. 23, 1907, d. Aug. 13, 1991; Franklin Roosevelt, b. Mar. 18, 1909, d. Nov. 8, 1909; Elliott Roosevelt, b. Sept. 23, 1910, d. Oct. 27, 1990; Franklin Delano Roosevelt, Jr., b. Aug. 17, 1914, d. Aug. 17, 1988; John Aspinwall Roosevelt, b. Mar. 13, 1916, d. Apr. 27, 1981

Occupation—Social worker, political and social activist

Date of death—Nov. 7, 1962

Age at death—78 years, 27 days

Place of death—New York, N.Y.

Courtesy of The Library of Congress

Eleanor Roosevelt, wife of Franklin Roosevelt

Burial place—Family plot, Hyde Park, N.Y.

Years younger than the President—2 years, 254 days

Years she survived the President—17 years, 209 days

THE FIRST LADY

Mrs. Franklin Delano Roosevelt, born Anna Eleanor Roosevelt, daughter of Elliott Roosevelt, President Theodore Roosevelt's younger brother, was active in civic affairs. As a young girl she worked as a volunteer in a settlement house, and after her marriage she assisted her husband in his rising political career.

During her husband's administration she established a precedent as a First Lady famous in her own right, though not without subjecting herself to much controversy and criticism. Engaging actively in public life, she traveled extensively, making numerous speeches and reporting her observations in the press. The first news conference held in the White House by a President's wife was held March 6, 1933, by Eleanor Roosevelt in the Red Room. It was attended by 35 newspaper women.

After the death of her husband, Eleanor Roosevelt continued to travel widely at home and abroad, to write about her experiences, and to devote herself to humanitarian interests both national and international. In 1945, 1947–1952, and 1961, she served as a United States delegate to the United Nations General Assembly; from 1946 to 1951, she was head of the U.N. Commission on Human Rights. Known almost as well in foreign countries as in her own, she was often referred to as "the First Lady of the world."

FIRST PRESIDENT'S WIFE TO TRAVEL IN AN AIRPLANE

On March 6, 1934, Eleanor Roosevelt left Miami, Fla., in a commercial airplane to visit Puerto Rico and the Virgin Islands in a 2,836-mile trip. Stops were also made at Port au Prince, Haiti, and Nuevitas, Cuba. Mrs. Roosevelt returned to the United States on March 16, 1934. This was the first airplane trip made by the wife of a President.

IMPORTANT DATES IN THE PRESIDENT'S LIFE

1900–1904, student at Harvard

1904–1907, student at Columbia Law School

1907, admitted to the bar

1907–1910, practiced in New York City with firm of Carter, Ledyard and Milburn

Nov. 8, 1910, elected to N.Y. Senate

Jan. 1, 1911–Mar. 17, 1913, first public office—New York State Senate (from Dutchess County)

Nov. 5, 1912, reelected to N.Y. Senate

1913–1920, assistant secretary of the Navy

1914, unsuccessful in Democratic primaries for U.S. Senate (from New York)

July–Sept. 1918, in Europe on army inspection

Jan. 1919, in Europe in charge of demobilization

July 1920, received Democratic nomination for the vice presidency at San Francisco, Calif., convention as running mate of James M. Cox

Nov. 1920, defeated for the vice presidency

1920, returned to New York law practice with firm of Emmet, Marvin and Roosevelt

1920–1928, vice president of Fidelity and Deposit Company

Aug. 1921, stricken with infantile paralysis at summer home, Campobello, New Brunswick, Canada

1924, member of law firm of Roosevelt and O'Connor

1929–1933, governor of New York

Mar. 4, 1933–Jan. 19, 1937, President (first term)

Jan. 20, 1937–Jan. 19, 1941, President (second term) (first President to take office on the new date specified by the Twentieth Amendment)

Jan. 20, 1941–Jan. 19, 1945, President (third term)

Jan. 20, 1945–Apr. 12, 1945, President (fourth term)

ELECTIONS

THE ELECTION OF 1932

November 8, 1932

CANDIDATES

Democratic Party (26th Convention)

June 27–July 2, 1932, Chicago Stadium, Chicago, Ill.

P: Franklin Delano Roosevelt, N.Y.
VP: John Nance Garner, Tex.

Roosevelt was nominated on the fourth ballot. Candidates for nomination and the votes they received on the first and fourth ballots:

Franklin Delano Roosevelt, N.Y., $666^1/_4$, 945

Alfred Emanuel Smith, N.Y., $201^3/_4$, $190^1/_2$

John Nance Garner, Tex., $90^1/_4$, 0

George White, Ohio, 52, 3

Melvin Alvah Traylor, Ill., $42^1/_4$, 0

Harry Flood Byrd, Va., 25, 0
James Alexander Reed, Mo., 24, 0
William Henry Murray, Okla., 23, 0

Albert Cabell Ritchie, Md., 21, $3^1/_2$

Newton Diehl Baker, Ohio, $8^1/_2$, $5^1/_2$

James Middleton Cox, Ohio, 0, 1
Total number of votes:
First ballot: 1,154

Fourth ballot: $1,148^1/_2$

Number necessary for nomination: 766

Republican Party (20th Convention)

June 14–16, 1932, Chicago Stadium, Chicago, Ill.

P: Herbert Clark Hoover, Calif.
VP: Charles Curtis, Kan.

Hoover was nominated on the first ballot. Candidates for nomination and the votes they received:

Herbert Clark Hoover, Calif., $1,126^1/_2$

John James Blaine, Wis., 13

Calvin Coolidge, Mass., $4^1/_2$

Joseph Irwin France, Md., 4
Charles Gates Dawes, Ill., 1

James Wolcott Wadsworth, N.Y., 1
Total number of votes: 1,150
Nomination made unanimous

Socialist Party

May 20–24, 1932, Municipal Auditorium, Milwaukee, Wis.

P: Norman Mattoon Thomas, N.Y.
VP: James Hudson Maurer, Pa.

Communist Party

May 28, 1932, People's Auditorium, Chicago, Ill.

P: William Zebulon Foster, Ill.
VP: James William Ford, N.Y.

Prohibition Party

July 5–7, 1932 at Indianapolis, Ind.

P: William David Upshaw, Ga.
VP: Frank Stewart Regan, Ill.

Liberty Party

Aug. 17, 1932, St. Louis, Mo.

P: William Hope Harvey, Ark.
VP: Frank B. Hemenway, Wash.

Socialist Labor Party

Apr. 30–May 2, 1932, Cornish Arms Hotel, New York, N.Y.

P: Verne L. Reynolds, N.Y.
VP: John W. Aiken, Mass.

Eric Hass of New York, nominated for President, was too young to qualify and declined.

Farmer Labor Party

Apr. 26–27, 1932, Omaha, Neb.

P: Frank Elbridge Webb, Calif.
VP: Jacob Sechler Coxey, Ohio

The executive committee replaced Webb with Coxey on July 10, 1932. Julius J. Reiter of Minnesota was named for Vice President.

Jobless Party

Aug. 17, 1932, Crevecoeur Speedway, St. Louis, Mo.

P: James Renshaw Cox, Pa.
VP: V. C. Tisdal, Okla.

Franklin D. Roosevelt campaigning for president

Candidates were nominated by acclamation.

National Party

June 26, 1932, Indianapolis, Ind.

P: Seymour E. Allen, Mass.
　Allen declined the nomination.

1932 POPULAR VOTE

Democratic Party, 22,821,857
Republican Party, 15,761,845
Socialist Party, 881,951
Communist Party, 102,785
Prohibition Party, 81,869
Liberty Party, 53,425
Socialist Labor Party, 33,276
Farmer Labor Party, 7,309

1932 ELECTORAL VOTE

There were 531 electoral votes from 48 states.
Roosevelt received 88.89 percent (472 votes—42 states) as follows: Ala. 11; Ariz. 3; Ark. 9; Calif. 22; Colo. 6; Fla. 7; Ga. 12; Idaho 4; Ill. 29; Ind. 14; Iowa 11; Kan. 9; Ky. 11; La.

10; Md. 8; Mass. 17; Mich. 19; Minn. 11; Miss. 9; Mo. 15; Mont. 4; Neb. 7; Nev. 3; N.J. 16; N.M. 3; N.Y. 47; N.C. 13; N.D. 4; Ohio 26; Okla. 11; Ore. 5; R.I. 4; S.C. 8; S.D. 4; Tenn. 11; Tex. 23; Utah 4; Va. 11; Wash. 8; W.Va. 8; Wis. 12; Wyo. 3.
Hoover received 11.11 percent (59 votes–6 states) as follows: Conn. 8; Del. 3; Me. 5; Nev. 4; Pa. 36; Vt. 3.

THE ELECTION OF 1936

November 3, 1936

CANDIDATES

Democratic Party (27th Convention)

June 23–27, 1936, Convention Hall, Philadelphia, Pa.

P: Franklin Delano Roosevelt, N.Y.
VP: John Nance Garner, Tex.
　Franklin Delano Roosevelt was renominated by acclamation and no vote was taken.

Republican Party (21st Convention)

June 9–12, 1936, Municipal Auditorium, Cleveland, Ohio

P: Alfred Mossman Landon, Kan.
VP: Frank Knox, Ill.
　Landon was nominated on the first ballot. Candidates for nomination and the votes they received:
Alfred Mossman Landon, Kan., 984
William Edgar Borah, Idaho, 19
Total number of votes: 1,003
Number necessary for nomination: 502

Union Party

June 19, 1936

P: William Lemke, N.D.
VP: Thomas Charles O'Brien, Mass.

Socialist Party

May 22–26, 1936, Municipal Auditorium, Cleveland, Ohio

P: Norman Mattoon Thomas, N.Y.
VP: George A. Nelson, Wis.

Communist Party

June 24–28, 1936, New York, N.Y.

P: Earl Russell Browder, Kan.
VP: James William Ford, N.Y.

Prohibition Party

May 5–7, 1936, Niagara Falls, N.Y.

P: David Leigh Colvin, N.Y.
VP: Alvin York, Tenn.

York declined the nomination and the executive committee nominated Claude A. Watson of California.

Socialist Labor Party

Apr. 25–28, 1936, Cornish Arms Hotel, New York, N.Y.

P: John W. Aiken, Mass.
VP: Emil F. Teichert, N.Y.

National Greenback Party (formerly the National Independent Party; renamed in 1934)

Apr. 6, 1936, Indianapolis, Ind.

P: John Zahnd, Ind.
VP: Florence Garvin, R.I.

1936 POPULAR VOTE

Democratic Party, 27,476,673
Republican Party, 16,679,583
Union Party, 892,793
Socialist Party, 187,720
Communist Party, 80,159
Prohibition Party, 37,847
Socialist Labor Party, 12,777

1936 ELECTORAL VOTE

There were 531 electoral votes from 48 states.
Roosevelt received 94.49 percent (523 votes—46 states—all states except Maine and Vermont).
Landon received 1.51 percent (8 votes—2 states) as follows: Me. 5; Vt. 3.

THE ELECTION OF 1940

November 5, 1940

CANDIDATES

Democratic Party (28th Convention)

July 15–18, 1940, Chicago Stadium, Chicago, Ill.

P: Franklin Delano Roosevelt, N.Y.

VP: Henry Agard Wallace, Iowa

Roosevelt was nominated on the first ballot. Candidates for nomination and the votes they received:
Franklin Delano Roosevelt, N.Y., 946 13/30
James Aloysius Farley, N.Y., 72 9/10
John Nance Garner, Tex., 61
Millard Evelyn Tydings, Md., $9^1/_2$
Cordell Hull, Tenn., 5 2/3
Number necessary for nomination: 551
Roosevelt was nominated by acclamation.

Republican Party (22nd Convention)

June 24–28, 1940, Convention Hall, Philadelphia, Pa.

P: Wendell Lewis Willkie, N.Y.
VP: Charles Linza McNary, Ore.

Willkie was nominated unanimously on the sixth ballot. Candidates for nomination and the votes they received on the first ballot:
Thomas Edmund Dewey, N.Y., 360
Robert Alphonso Taft, Ohio, 189
Wendell Lewis Willkie, N.Y., 105
Arthur Hendrick Vandenberg, Mich., 76
Arthur Horace James, Pa., 74
Joseph William Martin, Mass., 44
Frank Ernest Gannett, N.Y., 33
Henry Styles Bridges, N.H., 28
Arthur Capper, Kan., 18
Herbert Clark Hoover, Calif., 17
Charles Linza McNary, Ore., 13
Harlan John Bushfeld, S.D., 9
Total number of votes:
First ballot: 1,000
Sixth ballot: 998
Number necessary for nomination: 501

Socialist Party

Apr. 6–8, 1940, National Press Club Auditorium, Washington, D.C.

P: Norman Mattoon Thomas, N.Y.
VP: Maynard C. Krueger, Ill.

Thomas was nominated unanimously on the first ballot.

Prohibition Party

May 8–10, 1940, Chicago, Ill.

P: Roger Ward Babson, Mass.
VP: Edgar V. Moorman, Ill.

Communist Party (Workers Party)

May 30, June 1–2, 1940, Royal Windsor Hotel, New York, N.Y.

P: Earl Russell Browder, Kan.
VP: James William Ford, N.Y.

Socialist Labor Party

Apr. 27–30, 1940, Cornish Arms Hotel, New York, N.Y.

P: John W. Aiken, Mass.
VP: Aaron M. Orange, N.Y.

Greenback Party

July 4, 1940, Indianapolis, Ind.

P: John Zahnd, Ind.
VP: James Elmer Yates, Ariz.

Anna Milburn of Washington was nominated for the presidency but declined.

1940 POPULAR VOTE

Democratic Party, 27,243,466
Republican Party, 22,304,755
Socialist Party, 99,557
Prohibition Party, 57,812
Communist Party (Workers Party), 46,251
Independent Democrats (Ga.), 22,428
Progressives (Calif.), 16,506
Socialist Labor Party, 9,458
Independent Republicans (Miss.), 4,550
Industrial Party (Minn.), 2,553
Independent Government Party (Pa.), 1,518
Labor Party of Maryland, 657
Miscellaneous, 5,701

1940 ELECTORAL VOTE

There were 531 electoral votes from 48 states.
Roosevelt received 84.56 percent (449 votes—38 states) as follows: Ala. 11; Ariz. 3; Ark. 9; Calif. 22; Conn. 8; Del. 3; Fla. 7; Ga. 12; Idaho 4; Ill. 29; Ky. 11; La. 10; Md. 8; Mass. 17; Minn. 11; Miss. 9; Mo. 15; Mont. 4; Nev. 3; N.H. 4; N.J. 16; N.M. 3; N.Y. 47; N.C. 13; Ohio 26; Okla. 11; Ore. 5; Pa. 36; R.I. 4; S.C. 8; Tenn. 11; Tex. 23; Utah 4; Va. 11; Wash. 8; W.Va. 8; Wis. 12; Wyo. 3.
Willkie received 15.44 percent (82 votes—10 states) as follows: Colo. 6; Ind. 14; Iowa 11; Kan. 9; Me. 5; Mich. 19; Neb. 7; N.D. 4; S.D. 4; Vt. 3.

THE ELECTION OF 1944

November 7, 1944

CANDIDATES

Democratic Party (29th Convention)

July 19–21, 1944, Chicago Stadium, Chicago, Ill.

P: Franklin Delano Roosevelt, N.Y.
VP: Harry S. Truman, Mo.

Roosevelt was nominated on the first ballot. Candidates for nomination and the votes they received:
Franklin Delano Roosevelt, N.Y., 1,086
Harry Flood Byrd, Va., 89
James Aloysius Farley, N.Y., 1
Total number of votes: 1,176
Number necessary for nomination: 589

Republican Party (23rd Convention)

June 26–28, 1944, Chicago Stadium, Chicago, Ill.

P: Thomas Edmund Dewey, N.Y.
VP: John William Bricker, Ohio

Dewey was nominated on the first ballot. Candidates for nomination and the votes they received:
Thomas Edmund Dewey, N.Y., 1,056
Douglas MacArthur, Wis., 1
Total number of votes: 1,057
Number necessary for nomination: 529

Socialist Party

June 2–4, 1944, Berkshire Hotel, Reading, Pa.

P: Norman Mattoon Thomas, N.Y.
VP: Darlington Hoopes, Pa.

Prohibition Party

Nov. 12, 1943, Indianapolis, Ind.

P: Claude A. Watson, Calif.
VP: Andrew Johnson, Ky.

F. C. Carrer of Maryland was chosen as vice presidential nominee but did not accept.

Socialist Labor Party

Apr. 29–May 2, 1944, Cornish Arms Hotel, New York, N.Y.

P: Edward A. Teichert, Pa.
VP: Arla A. Albaugh, Ohio

American First Party

Aug. 30, 1944, Detroit, Mich.

P: Gerald Lyman Kenneth Smith, Mich.
VP: Henry A. Romer, Ohio

Communist Party

May 19–22, 1944, Riverside Plaza Hotel, New York, N.Y.

No candidates were nominated though Roosevelt was favored.

1944 POPULAR VOTE

Democratic Party, 25,602,505
Republican Party, 22,006,278
Texas Regulars (Tex.), 135,439
Socialist Party, 80,518
Prohibition Party, 74,758
Socialist Labor Party, 45,336
Blank votes (Mass.), 49,328
Regular Democrats (Miss.), 9,964

Independent Republicans (Miss.), 7,859
Southern Democrats (S.C.), 7,799
Independent Democrats (Ga.), 3,373
Miscellaneous, 2,527

1944 ELECTORAL VOTE

There were 531 electoral votes from 48 states.

Roosevelt received 81.36 percent (432 votes—36 states) as follows: Ala. 11; Ariz. 4; Ark. 9; Calif. 25; Conn. 8; Del. 3; Fla. 8; Ga. 12; Idaho 4; Ill. 28; Ky. 11; La. 10; Md. 8; Mass. 16; Mich. 19; Minn. 11; Miss. 9; Mo. 15; Mont. 4; Nev. 3; N.H. 4; N.J. 16; N.M. 4; N.Y. 47; N.C. 14; Okla. 10; Ore. 6; Pa. 35; R.I. 4; S.C. 8; Tenn. 12; Tex. 23; Utah 4; Va. 11; Wash. 8; W.Va. 8.

Dewey received 18.64 percent (99 votes—12 states) as follows: Colo. 6; Ind. 13; Iowa 10; Kan. 8; Me. 5; Neb. 6; N.D. 4; S.D. 4; Vt. 3; Wis. 12; Wyo. 3.

INAUGURATIONS

FIRST TERM

March 4, 1933

Franklin Delano Roosevelt took the oath of office on Saturday, March 4, 1933, on the east portico of the Capitol. Chief Justice Charles Evans Hughes administered the oath.

A reception was held for about 50 diplomatic missions and a standup luncheon for about 2,000 persons. The inaugural ball was held at the Washington Auditorium, Washington, D.C. Rosa Ponselle sang "The Star Spangled Banner." The ball was attended by Mrs. Roosevelt but not by the President.

SECOND TERM

January 20, 1937

Franklin Delano Roosevelt took his second oath of office on Wednesday, January 20, 1937. The oath was administered by Chief Justice Charles Evans Hughes. This was the first inauguration held on January 20. The

Courtesy of The Library of Congress

Roosevelt delivers his first inaugural address.

day was seasonably cold. Electric pads were used to keep the President and the Chief Justice warm.

THIRD TERM

January 20, 1941

Franklin Delano Roosevelt took his third oath of office on Monday, January 20, 1941. The oath was administered by Chief Justice Charles Evans Hughes. A buffet luncheon was served to invited guests. Despite the cold weather, there was an impressive parade.

Mrs. Sara Delano Roosevelt, who had been the first mother of a President to witness her son's second inauguration, also witnessed the third. Because of the two-term limitation set by the Twenty-second Amendment, no other mother will have that distinction.

FOURTH TERM

January 20, 1945

Franklin Delano Roosevelt took his fourth oath of office on Saturday, January 20, 1945. The oath was administered by Chief Justice Harlan Fiske Stone on the south portico of the White House, a location used for the third time since 1829. President Roosevelt, bareheaded and without an overcoat, delivered a six-minute address.

A light snow had fallen on the night preceding the inauguration, and on inauguration day the thermometer registered one degree above freezing. The sky was overcast and one of the smallest crowds in recent times witnessed the ceremonies. A canvas mat was spread on the lawn for the diplomats, high government officials, and the press. A crowd of about two thousand spectators gathered beyond the south fence. Roosevelt's 13 grandchildren were present.

THE VICE PRESIDENTS

FIRST AND SECOND TERMS

Vice President—John Nance Garner (32nd V.P.)

Date of birth—Nov. 22, 1868

Place of birth—near Detroit, Red River County, Tex.

Political party—Democratic

State represented—Texas

Term of office—Mar. 4, 1933–Jan. 19, 1941

Age at inauguration—64 years, 102 days

Occupation after term—Retired, farmer

Date of death—Nov. 7, 1967

Age at death—98 years, 351 days

Place of death—Uvalde, Tex.

Burial place—Uvalde, Tex.

ADDITIONAL DATA ON GARNER

1890, admitted to bar; practiced in Uvalde County, Tex.

1893–1896, judge, Uvalde County, Tex.

1898–1902, Texas House of Representatives

Mar. 4, 1903–Mar. 3, 1933, U.S. House of Representatives (from Texas)

Courtesy of The Library of Congress

John Nance Garner, first Vice President to Franklin Roosevelt

Dec. 7, 1931, elected Speaker of U.S. House of Representatives

Nov. 8, 1932, reelected to 73rd Congress and elected Vice President

Mar. 4, 1933–Jan. 19, 1941, Vice President under Franklin D. Roosevelt

1941, retired to private life

On November 8, 1932, John Nance Garner was elected as a representative to the 73rd Congress and also as Vice President under President Roosevelt. Garner had been elected as a Democrat to the 58th Congress and the 15 succeeding Congresses and served from March 4, 1903, to March 3, 1933. He resigned from the 73rd Congress on March 3, 1933, the day before his inauguration as Vice President.

THIRD TERM

Vice President—Henry Agard Wallace (33rd V.P.)

Date of birth—Oct. 7, 1888

Place of birth—Adair County, Iowa

Political party—Democratic

State represented—Iowa

Term of office—Jan. 20, 1941–Jan. 19, 1945

Age at inauguration—52 years, 105 days

Occupation after term—U.S. Secretary of Commerce, presidential candidate, editor, plant breeder

Date of death—Nov. 18, 1965

Age at death—77 years, 42 days

Place of death—Danbury, Conn.

Burial place—Glendale Cemetery, Des Moines, Iowa

Additional Data on Wallace

1910, graduated from Iowa State College, Ames

1910–1924, editorial staff, *Wallace's Farmer*

1913–1933, bred high-yielding strains of corn

Courtesy of The U.S. Department of Agriculture

Henry Wallace, second Vice President to Franklin Roosevelt

1924–1929, editor, *Wallace's Farmer*

1927, chairman, Agricultural Round Table, Williamsburg, Va.

1929–1933, editor, *Iowa Homestead* and *Wallace's Farmer*

1929, delegate, International Conference of Agricultural Economists, South Devon, England

Mar. 4, 1933–Sept. 2, 1940, secretary of agriculture

Jan. 20, 1941–Jan. 19, 1945, Vice President under Franklin D. Roosevelt

1944, failed to receive Democratic nomination for second term as Vice President

Mar. 2, 1945–Sept. 20, 1946, secretary of commerce

1948, unsuccessful candidate for the presidency on Progressive Party ticket

FOURTH TERM

Vice President—Harry S. Truman (34th V.P.)

Political party—Democratic

State represented—Missouri

Term of office—Jan. 20, 1945–Apr. 12, 1945 (82 days)

Age at inauguration—60 years, 257 days

Occupation after term—President

For further biographical information, see the chapter on Harry S. Truman, 33rd President, on page 399.

Courtesy of The Library of Congress

Harry Truman, third Vice President to Franklin Roosevelt

CABINET

FIRST TERM

March 4, 1933–January 20, 1937

State—Cordell Hull, Tenn., Mar. 4, 1933

Treasury—William Hartman Woodin, N.Y., Mar. 4, 1933; Henry Morgenthau, Jr., N.Y. (under secretary), ad interim Jan. 1, 1934–Jan. 8, 1934; Henry Morgenthau, Jr., N.Y., Jan. 8, 1934

War—George Henry Dern, Utah, Mar. 4, 1933; died Aug. 27, 1936; Harry Hines Woodring, Kan. (assistant secretary), ad interim Sept. 25, 1936–May 6, 1937

Attorney General—Homer Stille Cummings, Conn., Mar. 4, 1933

Postmaster General—James Aloysius Farley, N.Y., Mar. 4, 1933

Navy—Claude Augustus Swanson, Va., Mar. 4, 1933

Interior—Harold Le Claire Ickes, Ill., Mar. 4, 1933

Agriculture—Henry Agard Wallace, Iowa, Mar. 4, 1933

Commerce—Daniel Calhoun Roper, S.C., Mar, 4, 1933

Labor—Frances Perkins, N.Y., Mar. 4, 1933

SECOND TERM

January 20, 1937–January 20, 1941

State—Cordell Hull, Tenn., continued from preceding administration

Treasury—Henry Morgenthau, Jr., N.Y., continued from preceding administration

War—Harry Hines Woodring, Kan. (assistant secretary), ad interim Sept. 25, 1936–May 6, 1937; Harry Hines Woodring, Kan.,

May 6, 1937; Henry Lewis Stimson, N.Y., July 10, 1940

Attorney General—Homer Stille Cummings, Conn., continued from preceding administration; Frank Murphy, Mich., ad interim Jan. 2, 1939–Jan. 17, 1939; Frank Murphy, Mich., Jan. 17, 1939; Robert Houghwout Jackson, N.Y., Jan. 18, 1940

Postmaster General—James Aloysius Farley, N.Y., continued from preceding administration; recommissioned Jan. 22, 1937; Frank Comerford Walker, Pa., Sept. 10, 1940

Navy—Claude Augustus Swanson, Va., continued from preceding administration; died July 7, 1939; Charles Edison, N.J. (acting secretary), Aug. 5, 1939–Dec. 30, 1939; (assistant secretary) ad interim Dec. 30, 1939–Jan. 11, 1940; Jan. 11, 1940–July 9, 1940; Frank Knox, Ill., July 10, 1940

Interior—Harold Le Claire Ickes, Ill., continued from preceding administration

Agriculture—Henry Agard Wallace, Iowa, continued from preceding administration; Claude Raymond Wickard, Ind., Aug. 27, 1940; entered upon duties Sept. 5, 1940

Commerce—Daniel Calhoun Roper, S.C., continued from preceding administration; Harry Lloyd Hopkins, N.Y., ad interim Dec. 24, 1938–Jan. 23, 1939; Harry Lloyd Hopkins, N.Y., Jan. 23, 1939; Jesse Holman Jones, Tex., Sept. 16, 1940; entered upon duties Sept. 19, 1940

Labor—Frances Perkins, N.Y., continued from preceding administration

THIRD TERM

January 20, 1941–January 20, 1945

State—Cordell Hull, Tenn., continued from preceding administration; Edward Reilly Stettinius, Va., Nov. 30, 1944; entered upon duties Dec. 1, 1944

Treasury—Henry Morgenthau, Jr., N.Y., continued from preceding administration

War—Henry Lewis Stimson, N.Y., continued from preceding administration

Attorney General—Robert Houghwout Jackson, N.Y., continued from preceding administration; Francis Biddle, Pa., Sept. 5, 1941

Postmaster General—Frank Comerford Walker, Pa., continued from preceding

administration; recommissioned Jan. 27, 1941

Navy—Frank Knox, Ill., continued from preceding administration; died Apr. 28, 1944; James Vincent Forrestal, N.Y., May 18, 1944

Interior—Harold Le Claire Ickes, Ill., continued from preceding administration

Agriculture—Claude Raymond Wickard, Ind., continued from preceding administration

Commerce—Jesse Holman Jones, Tex., continued from preceding administration

Labor—Frances Perkins, N.Y., continued from preceding administration

FOURTH TERM

January 20, 1945–April 12, 1945

State—Edward Reilly Stettinius, Va., continued from preceding administration

Treasury—Henry Morgenthau, Jr., N.Y., continued from preceding administration

War—Henry Lewis Stimson, N.Y., continued from preceding administration

Attorney General—Francis Biddle, Pa., continued from preceding administration

Postmaster General—Frank Comerford Walker, Pa., continued from preceding administration; recommissioned Feb. 6, 1945

Navy—James Vincent Forrestal, N.Y., continued from preceding administration

Interior—Harold Le Claire Ickes, Ill., continued from preceding administration

Agriculture—Claude Raymond Wickard, Ind., continued from preceding administration

Commerce—Jesse Holman Jones, Tex., continued from preceding administration; Henry Agard Wallace, Iowa, Mar. 1, 1945; entered upon duties Mar. 2, 1945

Labor—Frances Perkins, N.Y., continued from preceding administration

CONGRESS

SEVENTY-THIRD CONGRESS

March 4, 1933–January 3, 1935

First session—Mar. 9, 1933–June 16, 1933 (99 days)

Second session—Jan. 3, 1934–June 18, 1934 (167 days)

Special session of the Senate—Mar. 4, 1933–Mar. 6, 1933 (3 days)

Vice President—John Nance Garner, Tex.

President pro tempore of the Senate —Key Pittman, Nev., elected Mar. 9, 1933

Secretary of the Senate—Edwin Alexander Halsey, Va., elected Mar. 9, 1933

Speaker of the House—Henry Thomas Rainey, Ill., elected Mar. 9, 1933; died Aug. 19, 1934

Clerk of the House—South Trimble, Ky., reelected Mar. 9, 1933

SEVENTY-FOURTH CONGRESS

January 3, 1935–January 3, 1937

First session—Jan. 3, 1935–Aug. 26, 1935 (236 days)

Second session—Jan. 3, 1936–June 20, 1936 (170 days)

Vice President—John Nance Garner, Tex.

President pro tempore of the Senate —Key Pittman, Nev., reelected Jan. 7, 1935

Secretary of the Senate—Edwin Alexander Halsey, Va.

Speaker of the House—Joseph Wellington Byrns, Tenn., elected Jan. 3, 1935, died June 4, 1936; William Brockman Bankhead, Ala., elected June 4, 1936

Clerk of the House—South Trimble, Ky., reelected Jan. 3, 1935

SEVENTY-FIFTH CONGRESS

January 3, 1937–January 3, 1939

First session—Jan. 5, 1937–Aug. 21, 1937 (229 days)

Second session—Nov. 15, 1937–Dec. 21, 1937 (37 days)

Third session—Jan. 3, 1938–June 16, 1938 (165 days)

Vice President—John Nance Garner, Tex.

President pro tempore of the Senate —Key Pittman, Nev.

Secretary of the Senate—Edwin Alexander Halsey, Va.

Speaker of the House—William Brockman Bankhead, Ala., reelected Jan. 5, 1937

Clerk of the House—South Trimble, Ky., reelected Jan. 5, 1937

SEVENTY-SIXTH CONGRESS

January 3, 1939–January 3, 1941

First session—Jan. 3, 1939–Aug. 5, 1939 (215 days)

Second session—Sept. 21, 1939–Nov. 3, 1939 (44 days)

Third session—Jan. 3, 1940–Jan. 3, 1941 (366 days)

Vice President—John Nance Garner, Tex.

President pro tempore of the Senate —Key Pittman, Nev.; died Nov. 10, 1940; William Henry King, Utah, elected Nov. 19, 1940

Secretary of the Senate—Edwin Alexander Halsey, Va.

Speaker of the House—William Brockman Bankhead, Ala., reelected Jan. 3, 1939, died Sept. 15, 1940; Samuel Taliaferro Rayburn, Tex., elected Sept. 16, 1940

Clerk of the House—South Trimble, Ky., reelected Jan. 3, 1939

SEVENTY-SEVENTH CONGRESS

January 3, 1941–January 3, 1943

First session—Jan. 3, 1941–Jan. 2, 1942 (365 days)

Second session—Jan. 5, 1942–Dec. 16, 1942 (346 days)

Vice Presidents—John Nance Garner, Tex.; Henry Agard Wallace, Iowa, Jan. 20, 1941

President pro tempore of the Senate
—Pat Harrison, Miss., elected Jan. 6,
1941; died June 22, 1941; Carter Glass, Va.,
elected July 10, 1941

Secretary of the Senate—Edwin Alexander Halsey, Va.

Speaker of the House—Samuel Taliaferro Rayburn, Tex., reelected Jan. 3, 1941

Clerk of the House—South Trimble, Ky., reelected Jan. 3, 1941

SEVENTY-EIGHTH CONGRESS

January 3, 1943–January 3, 1945

First session—Jan. 6, 1943–Dec. 21, 1943 (350 days)

Second session—Jan. 10, 1944–Dec. 19, 1944 (345 days)

Vice President—Henry Agard Wallace, Iowa

President pro tempore of the Senate
—Carter Glass, Va.

Secretary of the Senate—Edwin Alexander Halsey, Va.

Speaker of the House—Samuel Taliaferro Rayburn, Tex., reelected Jan. 6, 1943

Clerk of the House—South Trimble, Ky., reelected Jan. 6, 1943

SEVENTY-NINTH CONGRESS

January 3, 1945–January 3, 1947

First session—Jan. 3, 1945–Dec. 21, 1945 (353 days))

Courtesy of The Library of Congress

President Roosevelt gives report to Congress, 1945.

Second session—Jan. 14, 1946–Aug. 2, 1946 (201 days)

Vice Presidents—Henry Agard Wallace, Iowa; Harry S. Truman, Mo., Jan. 20, 1945, succeeded to the presidency on the death of Franklin Delano Roosevelt on Apr. 12, 1945

President pro tempore of the Senate
—Kenneth McKellar, Tenn., elected Jan. 6, 1945

Secretary of the Senate—Edwin Alexander Halsey, Va., died Jan. 29, 1945; Leslie L. Biffle, Ark., elected Feb. 8, 1945

Speaker of the House—Samuel Taliaferro Rayburn, Tex., reelected Jan. 3, 1945

Clerk of the House—South Trimble, Ky., reelected Jan. 3, 1945, died Nov. 23, 1946

APPOINTMENTS TO THE SUPREME COURT

Chief Justice

Harlan Fiske Stone, N.Y., July 3, 1941 (replaced Charles Evans Hughes)

Associate Justices

Hugo LaFayette Black, Ala., Oct. 4, 1937 (replaced Willis Van Devanter)

Stanley Forman Reed, Ky., Jan. 31, 1938 (replaced George Sutherland)

Felix Frankfurter, Mass., Jan. 20, 1939 (replaced Benjamin Nathan Cardozo)

William Orville Douglas, Conn., Apr. 17, 1939 (replaced Louis Dembitz Brandeis)

William Francis Murphy, Mich., Jan. 18, 1940 (replaced Pierce Butler)

James Francis Byrnes. S.C., July 8, 1941 (replaced James Clark McReynolds)

Robert Houghwout Jackson, N.Y., July 11, 1941 (replaced Harlan Fiske Stone)

Wiley Blount Rutledge, Iowa, Feb. 15, 1943 (replaced James Francis Byrnes)

IMPORTANT DATES IN THE PRESIDENCY

Mar. 4, 1933, Good Neighbor policy in Latin American relations announced

Mar. 5–13, 1933, bank holiday

Mar. 9–June 16, 1933, "Hundred Days" congressional session in which New Deal recovery measures were enacted

Mar. 31, 1933, Civilian Conservation Corps created

May 12, 1933, Agricultural Adjustment Act passed

May 12, 1933, Federal Emergency Relief Act approved

May 18, 1933, Tennessee Valley Authority established

June 5, 1933, gold repeal joint resolution canceled clauses in debts, taking United States completely off gold standard

June 13, 1933, Home Owners Loan Corporation created

June 16, 1933, Federal Deposit Insurance Corporation created

June 16, 1933, Farm Credit Administration authorized

June 16, 1933, National Recovery Administration and Public Works Administration created by National Industrial Recovery Act

Nov. 16, 1933, United States recognized Soviet Union

Dec. 5, 1933, Twenty-first Amendment to the Constitution ratified (repeal of Prohibition)

Mar. 24, 1934, Philippine Independence Act, providing for independence in 1946

June 6, 1934, Securities and Exchange Commission authorized

June 12, 1934, Reciprocal Tariff Act passed

June 19, 1934, Federal Communications Commission created

June 27, 1934, Railway Pension Act passed

June 28, 1934, Federal Housing Administration authorized

Apr. 8, 1935, Works Progress Administration established

May 27, 1935, National Industrial Recovery Act declared unconstitutional

1935, Bureau of Investigation became Federal Bureau of Investigation under J. Edgar Hoover, with broad powers to police all violations of Federal law, except those assigned to other Federal agencies

July 5, 1935, Wagner Labor Relations Act passed

Aug. 1935, Neutrality Act passed

Aug. 14, 1935, Social Security Act passed

Aug. 26, 1935, Federal Power Commission established under Public Utility Holding Act

Jan. 6, 1936, Agricultural Adjustment Act declared unconstitutional

Feb. 29, 1936, Soil Conservation and Domestic Allotment Act passed

Jan.–June 1937, CIO sit-down strikes

Feb. 5, 1937, U.S. Supreme Court controversy started with Roosevelt's "court packing" recommendations

Apr. 12, 1937, U.S. Supreme Court sanctioned power of Congress to regulate labor relations of persons engaged in interstate commerce

Courtesy of The Library of Congress

"Migrant Mother," by Dorothea Lange, one of the representative photos of the Great Depression

May 24, 1937, Supreme Court held Social Security Act of Aug. 14, 1935 constitutional

July 22, 1937, Senate rejected President's Supreme Court "packing" plan by vote of 70 to 20

Sept. 2, 1937, Wagner-Steagall Housing Act passed

Oct.–Nov. 1937, business recession

Feb. 16, 1938, second Agricultural Adjustment Act passed

June 24, 1938, Food, Drug and Cosmetic Act passed

June 25, 1938, Fair Labor Standards Act passed

Apr. 3, 1939, Administrative Reorganization Act passed

Apr. 30, 1939, opening of New York World's Fair

Sept. 1, 1939, Germany invaded Poland

Sept. 3, 1939, Great Britain and France declared war on Germany; World War II started

Sept. 5, 1939, United States proclaimed its neutrality in European War

May 10, 1940, Churchill became Prime Minister of England

June 27, 1940, national emergency declared

June 28, 1940, Alien Registration Act passed

Sept. 3, 1940, Roosevelt announced trade of fifty over-age destroyers to Great Britain in exchange for air bases

Sept. 16, 1940, Selective Training and Service Act approved

Oct. 16, 1940, registration for selective service, ages 21 to 35

Oct. 28, 1940, Italy invaded Greece

Jan. 6, 1941, "Four Freedoms" enunciated in State of Union message

Mar. 11, 1941, Lend-Lease Act passed

June 22, 1941, Germany invaded Russia

July 7, 1941, Roosevelt announced occupation of Iceland by U.S. troops on invitation of Icelandic government

July 26, 1941, General MacArthur appointed commander of U.S. forces in the Philippines

Aug. 14, 1941, Atlantic Charter—eight-point statement of principles for peace—issued jointly by United States and Great Britain

Sept. 29, 1941, three-power Moscow conference; United States and Great Britain agreed to send U.S.S.R. large supplies of war material

Dec. 7, 1941, Japan attacked Hawaii, Guam, and the Philippines

Dec. 8, 1941, United States declared war against Japan

Dec. 11, 1941, Germany and Italy declared war against the United States; hours later the United States declared war against both countries

Dec. 12, 1941, Guam captured (first American possession to fall into enemy hands)

Dec. 22, 1941, Prime Minister Churchill arrived in the United States on a battleship; returned by airplane Jan. 14, 1942

Mar. 17, 1942, General MacArthur in command of Allied forces in Australia and the southwest Pacific

Apr. 9, 1942, fall of Bataan, P.I.

Oct.–Dec. 1942, Allied invasion of North Africa

Nov. 3, 1942, United States severed relations with Vichy government of France

Nov. 13, 1942, American naval victory at Guadalcanal

Dec. 2, 1942, self-sustained nuclear chain reaction demonstration, Chicago, Ill.

Jan. 14–24, 1943, Churchill and Roosevelt conferred in North Africa

Sept.–Dec. 1943, invasion of Italy

Prime Minister Winston Churchill, President Franklin D. Roosevelt, and Marshal Joseph Stalin at the palace in Yalta, where the "Big Three" met

Nov. 28–Dec. 1, 1943, Churchill, Stalin, and Roosevelt conferred at Teheran, Iran

June 6, 1944, D-Day invasion of France by Allies

June 22, 1944, Servicemen's Readjustment Act (G.I. Bill of Rights) approved

July 1944, United Nations Monetary and Financial Conference, Bretton Woods, N.H.

Aug.–Oct. 1944, Dumbarton Oaks conference on a postwar international organization; proposals served as basis for United Nations charter

Feb. 4–11, 1945, Churchill, Stalin, Roosevelt conferred at Yalta in the Crimea

ADDITIONAL DATA ON ROOSEVELT

FRANKLIN DELANO ROOSEVELT

—was the fourth President born in New York.

—was the eighth President whose mother was alive when he was inaugurated.

—was the first President whose mother could have voted for him for the presidency.

—was the third Democratic President since the Civil War.

—was the first President elected for a third term (and also a fourth term).

—was the first and only President inaugurated twice on Saturday (March 4, 1933, and Jan. 20, 1945).

—was the first defeated vice presidential nominee to win election as President.

—was the first President with a physical disability.

—was the seventh President to die in office.

—was the fourth President to die a natural death in office.

F.D.R. RELATED TO ELEVEN FORMER PRESIDENTS

Genealogists have shown that President Franklin Delano Roosevelt was related by blood or through marriage to eleven former Presidents: Washington, John Adams, Madison, John Quincy Adams, Van Buren, William Henry Harrison, Taylor, Grant, Benjamin Harrison, Theodore Roosevelt, and Taft.

ROOSEVELT FLEW TO ACCEPT NOMINATION AT CONVENTION

The first nominating convention at which a presidential nominee made a speech of acceptance was the Democratic convention held at Chicago, Ill., July 1932, when Governor Franklin Delano Roosevelt of New York accepted the nomination and addressed the delegates.

Roosevelt was also the first presidential candidate to fly to a political convention to make his acceptance speech. He chartered a 10-passenger tri-motor airplane for his party and flew from Albany, N.Y., to Chicago on July 2.

ASSASSINATION OF ROOSEVELT ATTEMPTED

An attempt on the life of President Roosevelt was made on February 15, 1933, at Miami, Fla., by Giuseppe Zangara, a bricklayer. His shot killed Anton Joseph Cermak, mayor of Chicago, Ill., who was with the President. Cermak died on March 6, 1933. Zangara's shots wounded five other persons. Zangara was electrocuted on March 20, 1933, at the Florida State Prison, Raiford, Fla.

ELECTORS INVITED TO INAUGURAL

Presidential electors generally became forgotten people after they cast their ballots. The 531 electors, of whom all but 59 were Democrats, were invited by President-elect Roosevelt to attend his inaugural at Washington, D.C., on March 4, 1933. This was the first time the electoral college was invited to witness an inaugural.

WOMAN APPOINTED TO CABINET

Roosevelt established a precedent when he appointed a woman to the presidential cabinet. He appointed Frances Perkins Secretary of Labor. She served from March 4, 1933, to

June 30, 1945. Prior to the appointment Frances Perkins had been industrial commissioner for New York.

ROOSEVELT APPOINTED WOMAN MINISTER

On April 12, 1933, President Roosevelt appointed the first woman to represent the United States as a minister to a foreign country. The appointee was Ruth Bryan Owen, the eldest daughter of William Jennings Bryan, who was appointed Envoy Extraordinary and Minister Plenipotentiary to Denmark and Iceland. Her nomination was confirmed by the Senate without even the customary formality of reference to a committee.

U.S.S.R. RECOGNIZED

Recognition of the Union of Soviet Socialist Republics was effected November 16, 1933, between President Roosevelt and Maksim Maksimovich Litvinov, the Soviet People's Commissar for Foreign Affairs. The first Soviet representative to the United States was Alexander Antonovich Troyanovsky, who was accredited as Russian ambassador from January 8, 1934, to June 22, 1938. The first ambassador from the United States to the U.S.S.R. was William Christian Bullitt, who was appointed by President Roosevelt and served from November 21, 1933, until August 25, 1936.

TWENTY-FIRST AMENDMENT ENACTED

The Twenty-first Amendment was the first amendment ratified by conventions in the several states. The first twenty amendments were ratified by state legislatures.

This amendment, which repealed the eighteenth, was proposed by the 72nd Congress on February 20, 1933. Ratification was completed on December 5, 1933, when the thirty-sixth state, Utah, approved the amendment. On this date the secretary of state announced that it had been adopted by the necessary number of states.

ROOSEVELT CONDUCTED RELIGIOUS SERVICES

The first President to conduct divine services as commander in chief of the U.S. Navy was President Franklin Delano Roosevelt, on Easter Sunday, April 1, 1934. He read from the Book of Common Prayer of the Episcopal Church while on the quarterdeck of the *Nourmahal,* east of Key West, Fla. The services were attended by the crew of the U.S.S. *Nourmahal* and the U.S.S. *Ellis* destroyer.

PRESIDENT ROOSEVELT CONCEALED HIS DISABILITY

In 1921, when he was 39, Franklin Delano Roosevelt suffered an attack of poliomyelitis that caused paralysis in his legs. Though a rehabilitation program restored some of his mobility, he continued to rely on crutches and wheelchairs for the rest of his life, a fact that he was at pains to conceal from the public out of concern that voters would not accept a leader with a physical infirmity. In 1938 he helped to found the March of Dimes, an organization that raised funds for polio research and rehabilitation, and in his first annual message as governor of New York he called on the state "to give the same care to removing the physical handicaps of its citizens as it now gives to their mental development."

Courtesy of The Library of Congress

Franklin Delano Roosevelt and Herbert Hoover in convertible automobile on their way to the U.S. Capitol for Roosevelt's inauguration, March 4, 1933

PRESIDENT ROOSEVELT RECORD TRAVELER

Franklin Delano Roosevelt established numerous precedents in the field of traveling while he was President of the United States.

He was the first President to visit South America while in office. On July 10, 1934, he stopped at Cartagena, Colombia. Prior to this visit, President Enrique Olaya Herrara of Colombia had visited President Roosevelt on board the cruiser U.S.S. *Houston*.

He was also the first President to go through the Panama Canal, passing through it on July 11, 1934, on the U.S.S. *Houston*. He was greeted at Balboa, Panama, by President Harmodio Arias and Foreign Secretary Arosemena of Panama.

Roosevelt was also the first President to visit Hawaii. He landed on July 25, 1934, at Hilo, Hawaii, where he was greeted by Governor Joseph Poindexter.

These three "firsts" took place while Roosevelt was President. Other Presidents had made similar trips either before or after their terms of office.

ROOSEVELT BROADCAST FROM A FOREIGN COUNTRY

The first President to broadcast from a foreign country was Franklin Delano Roosevelt, whose speech on July 10, 1934, from Cartagena, Colombia, South America, was relayed to New York and transmitted over the combined WEAF, WJZ, and WABC networks.

F.D.R. ORIGINATED A MYSTERY STORY

President Roosevelt was an avid reader of detective stories and contemplated writing one, but was stymied when he sought the solution. He propounded the question, "How can a man disappear with five million dollars in negotiable form and not be traced?"

Six writers submitted solutions, each constituting a separate chapter in the 202-page book, "The President's Mystery Story," published in 1935, by Farrar & Rinehart. The preface was written by Fulton Oursler and the various chapters by Anthony Abbot (pseudonym of Fulton Oursler), Samuel Hopkins Adams, John Erskine, Rupert Hughes, S. S. Van Dine (pseudonym of Willard Huntington Wright), and Rita Weiman. The story was also published in the November issue of *Liberty* magazine.

PRESIDENT AND VICE PRESIDENT OUT OF THE COUNTRY

While President Roosevelt was aboard the U.S.S. *Houston* on his vacation, Vice President John Nance Garner sailed for Japan from Seattle, Wash., on October 16, 1936, on the *President Grant*. This was the first time that both President and Vice President were simultaneously out of the country. Under the act of succession of January 19, 1886, Cordell Hull, secretary of state, acted as President. Technically, President Roosevelt was on United States soil as he was on a United States naval ship.

VETO READ TO CONGRESS

The first veto message read directly by a President was the Patman bonus bill veto, read May 22, 1935, by President Roosevelt to a joint session of Congress. The bill provided for the immediate payment to veterans of the payable 1935 face value of their adjusted service certificates. Within an hour after the veto, the House voted 322 to 98 to override it. The original vote on the measure had been 318 to 90. The following day the Senate voted 54 to 40 to override the veto. The original vote had been 55 to 33. The 54 to 40 vote was short of the two-thirds vote needed to override the veto.

OFFICIAL FLAG FOR VICE PRESIDENT

The first flag for a Vice President was established on February 7, 1936, by Executive Order No. 7,285, signed by President Roosevelt. The flag was designed with the seal of the United States and a blue star in each corner on a field of white. The Navy had previously created a flag for the Vice President, but its use by other governmental departments was optional.

PENSIONS TO PRIVATE WORKERS

The first pension payments by the United States Government to workers in private industry were mailed on July 13, 1936, when checks totaling $901.56 were sent to 18 retired railroad employees, in accordance with the Railroad Retirement Act of August 29, 1935 (49 Stat. L. 967), which appropriated $46,685,000 "to establish a retirement system for employees of carriers subject to the Interstate Commerce Act, and for other purposes."

WORST REPUBLICAN DEFEAT

The most humbling defeat in recent times was suffered in 1936 by the Republican candidate, Alfred Mossman Landon of Kansas, who carried only 2 states, Maine and Vermont. He received 8 electoral votes. Franklin Delano Roosevelt carried 46 states, receiving 523 electoral votes.

In 1912, William Howard Taft received only 8 electoral votes. The other 523 electoral votes were divided between Woodrow Wilson (435 votes) and Theodore Roosevelt (88 votes).

ROOSEVELT RODE ON DIESEL

President Roosevelt was the first President to ride on a Diesel train. On October 23, 1937, he rode on a Diesel train on the Baltimore and Ohio Railroad from Washington, D.C., to New York City. He was en route to his home at Hyde Park, N.Y.

ROOSEVELT HONORED BY FOREIGN POSTAGE STAMP

Although the United States Postal Laws and Regulations forbid placing the picture of a living President on postage stamps, these laws do not apply outside the United States. In 1938, Guatemala issued a souvenir sheet of four stamps to commemorate the second term of President Jorge Ubico. One of the stamps, a four-cent carmine-and-sepia stamp, bore a picture of Franklin Delano Roosevelt.

ROOSEVELT ON TELEVISION

The first President to appear on television was Franklin Delano Roosevelt, who spoke on April 30, 1939, at the opening ceremonies of the New York World's Fair from the Federal Building on the Exposition Grounds overlooking the Court of Peace. The proceedings were telecast by the National Broadcasting Company.

ROOSEVELT RECEIVED KING AND QUEEN OF ENGLAND

The first King and Queen of England to visit the United States were King George VI and Queen Elizabeth, who arrived by way of Canada, crossing the international border on the night of June 7, 1939, at the Suspension Bridge Station, Niagara Falls, N.Y. At an outdoor picnic arranged by President Roosevelt, the King and Queen were served hot dogs. They visited New York City and Washington, D.C., and recrossed the border on the morning of June 12, 1939, bound for Halifax, Nova Scotia, whence they sailed on June 15, 1939.

FIRST THIRD-TERM PRESIDENT

Franklin Delano Roosevelt was the first and only President to be elected for a third term. He received 27,243,466 of the 49,815,312 votes cast on November 5, 1940, carrying 38 of the 48 states and winning 449 of the 531 electoral votes. His opponent, Wendell Lewis Willkie, the Republican candidate, received 22,304,755 votes and 82 electoral votes.

Roosevelt was reelected for a fourth term in 1944, definitively shattering the two-term tradition of all former Presidents. The ratification of the Twenty-second Amendment in 1951, however, limited the terms of future President's to two.

ROOSEVELT GODFATHER TO PRINCE GEORGE

The first President to become a godfather to a member of the British royal family was President Roosevelt. On August 4, 1942, the Duke of Kent, youngest brother of King George VI, served as proxy for President Roosevelt at the christening of his son, Michael George Charles Franklin, Prince George of Kent, who was born July 4, 1942.

ROOSEVELT BROADCAST IN FRENCH

Franklin Delano Roosevelt was the first President to broadcast in a foreign language. On November 7, 1942, he addressed the French people in their own language from Washington, D.C., at the same time that the

American Army was taking part in the invasion of French territorial possessions in North Africa.

ROOSEVELT LEFT THE UNITED STATES IN WARTIME

President Roosevelt was the first President to leave the confines of the United States in wartime. His itinerary on a 16,965-mile trip follows: January 9, 1943, left Washington, D.C., by train; January 10, 1943, arrived at Miami, Fla., and flew to Trinidad, B.W.I.; January 11, flew from Trinidad to Belém, Brazil; January 12–13, flew to Bathurst, Gambia; January 14, arrived at Casablanca in newly liberated Morocco, where he met with Churchill; January 21, drove to Rabat and Port Lyautey and back to Casablanca; January 24, drove from Casablanca to Marrakesh; January 25, flew from Marrakesh to Bathurst; January 27, flew from Bathurst to Roberts Field, Liberia, and back to Bathurst before taking off for Brazil; January 28, arrived at Natal; January 29, flew from Natal to Trinidad; January 30, flew from Trinidad to Miami; left Miami by train and arrived at Washington, D.C., January 31, 1943.

President Roosevelt later in 1943 conferred with Churchill and Stalin in Teheran. Roosevelt's final foreign trip, undertaken only months before his death, was to Yalta in the Soviet Union in 1945, where he again met Churchill and Stalin, toward the conclusion of World War II.

FIRST BLACK PRESIDENTS TO VISIT THE UNITED STATES

The first president of an African country to visit the United States was President Edwin Barclay of Liberia, who addressed the United States Senate on May 27, 1943, the day following his arrival.

On October 14, 1943, President Elie Lescot of Haiti, former Minister to the United States, arrived for a brief visit.

ROOSEVELT PRESENTED MEDAL

On June 21, 1943, President Roosevelt presented the first Medal of Honor to a soldier who had already received a Distinguished Service Cross in World War II. It was awarded to Gerry Kisters of Bloomington,

Ind., for heroism in the Sicily campaign. In May 1943 General George Catlett Marshall had awarded him the Distinguished Service Cross for bravery in Africa.

ROOSEVELT VISITED OTTAWA

On August 25, 1943, President Franklin Delano Roosevelt arrived at Ottawa, Ontario, the capital of Canada, by train from Quebec, where he had conferred with Winston Churchill. Roosevelt was the first President of the United States to make an official visit to the Canadian capital while in office.

The Earl of Athlone, Governor-General of Canada, acting as Chancellor of the University of London, conferred an honorary doctor of laws degree (LL.D.) on Roosevelt at Government House, Ottawa, on August 25, 1943.

CABINET MEMBER ADDRESSED CONGRESS

Secretary of State Cordell Hull, who reported to President Roosevelt on the tripartite conference at Moscow for the maintenance of peace and security in the postwar world, established a precedent by making a further report to Congress on November 18, 1943. The two houses of Congress, being in recess, assembled to hear him. Technically, it was not a joint session.

MOST FIRST PITCHES

Of all the Presidents, Franklin Delano Roosevelt threw out the most first pitches at major league baseball games, doing so a total of eleven times while President. He also was the first President to throw the inaugural pitch at baseball's All-Star Game, which he did on July 7, 1937, at Griffith Park in Washington, D.C.

DEMOCRATIC VICTORIES

Franklin Delano Roosevelt won four consecutive elections, as many as the Democrats had won between the time of Abraham Lincoln and Herbert Hoover.

In 1884 Grover Cleveland defeated James Gillespie Blaine.

In 1892 Grover Cleveland defeated Benjamin Harrison.

In 1912 Woodrow Wilson defeated William Howard Taft.

In 1916 Woodrow Wilson defeated Charles Evans Hughes.

ENTIRE DIVISION CITED

The first presidential citation to an entire division was made on March 15, 1945, to the 101st Airborne Division, the heroes of Bastogne, by General Dwight David Eisenhower. For 10 days—December 18–27, 1944—the men had withstood overwhelming odds. When the Germans demanded their surrender, General Anthony McAuliffe replied in one word: "Nuts!"

FURTHER READING

Burns, James M. *Roosevelt: The Lion and the Fox.* 1956.

———. *Roosevelt: The Soldier of Freedom.* 1970.

Dallek, Robert. *Franklin D. Roosevelt and American Foreign Policy, 1932–1945.* 1979.

Davis, Kenneth S. *F.D.R.: The Beckoning of Destiny.* 1972.

———. *F. D. R.: The New York Years 1928–1933.* 1985.

———. *F.D.R.: The New Deal Years 1933–1937.* 1986.

Freidel, Frank B. *Franklin D. Roosevelt.* 1974.

Goodwin, Doris Kearns. *No Ordinary Time; Franklin and Eleanor Roosevelt: The Home Front in World War II.* 1994.

Lash, Joseph F. *Eleanor and Franklin.* 1971.

Smith, Jean Edward. *FDR.* 2007.

Ward, Geoffrey C. *A First-Class Temperament: The Emergence of Franklin Roosevelt.* 1989.

Courtesy of The Library of Congress

Harry S. Truman

Date of birth—May 8, 1884

Place of birth—Lamar, Mo.

Education—Tutored by his mother; attended public schools, Independence, Mo.; studied piano; Independence High School, graduated 1901; Kansas City Law School, 1923–1925

Religion—Baptist

Ancestry—English, Irish, German

Career—Bank and mailroom clerk, farmer, Army officer in World War I, haberdasher, county administrative judge, U.S. senator, Vice President

Political party—Democratic

State represented—Missouri

Term of office—Apr. 12, 1945–Jan. 20, 1953 (Truman succeeded to the presidency on the death of Franklin Delano Roosevelt.)

Term served—7 years, 283 days

Administration—40th, 41st

Congresses—79th, 80th, 81st, 82nd

Age at inauguration—60 years, 339 days

Lived after term—19 years, 340 days

Occupation after term—Retired; writer

Date of death—Dec. 26, 1972

Age at death—88 years, 232 days

Place of death—Independence, Mo.

Burial place—Independence, Mo.

FAMILY

FATHER

Name—John Anderson Truman

Date of birth—Dec. 5, 1851

Place of birth—Jackson County, Mo.

Marriage—Martha Ellen Young, Dec. 28, 1881, Grandview, Mo.

Occupation—Farmer, livestock dealer, watchman, road overseer

Date of death—Nov. 3, 1914

Place of death—Kansas City, Mo.

Age at death—62 years, 333 days

MOTHER

Name at birth—Martha Ellen Young

Date of birth—Nov. 25, 1852

Place of birth—Jackson County, Mo.

Marriage—John Anderson Truman, Dec. 28, 1881, Grandview, Mo.

Date of death—July 26, 1947

Place of death—Grandview, Mo.

Age at death—94 years, 243 days

SIBLINGS

Harry S. Truman was the oldest of three children.

Children of John Anderson Truman and Martha Ellen Young Truman

Harry S. Truman, b. May 8, 1884; d. Dec. 26, 1972

John Vivian Truman, b. Apr. 25, 1886; d. July 8, 1965, Grand View, Mo.

Mary Jane Truman, b. Aug. 12, 1889; d. Nov. 3, 1978, Grand View, Mo.

MARRIAGE

Married—Elizabeth Virginia ("Bess") Wallace

Date of marriage—June 28, 1919

Place of marriage—Independence, Mo.

Age of wife at marriage—34 years, 135 days

Age of husband at marriage—35 years, 51 days

Years married—53 years, 181 days

CHILDREN

(Mary) Margaret Truman, b. Feb. 17, 1924, Independence, Mo.; m. Apr. 21, 1956, Clifton Daniel, Independence, Mo.; d. Jan. 29, 2008, Chicago, Ill.

Margaret Truman made frequent appearances as a concert singer and a television performer and went on to become a best-selling novelist of murder mysteries having the nation's capital as their setting. She also wrote a biographical book, *First Ladies* (1995).

THE PRESIDENT'S WIFE

Name at birth—Elizabeth Virginia ("Bess") Wallace

Date of birth—Feb. 13, 1885

Place of birth—Independence, Mo.

Mother—Madge Gates Wallace

Father—David Willock Wallace

Father's occupation—Farmer, businessman, customs officer

Education—High school, Independence, Mo.; Barstow School for Girls, Kansas City, Mo.

Marriage—Harry S. Truman, June 28, 1919, Independence, Mo.

Children—(Mary) Margaret Truman, b. Feb. 17, 1924, d. Jan. 29, 2008

Occupation—Husband's Senate secretary

Date of death—Oct. 18, 1982

Age at death—97 years, 247 days

Place of death—Independence, Mo.

Burial place—Independence, Mo.

Years younger than the President—281 days

Years she survived the President—9 years, 296 days

Courtesy of The Library of Congress

Elizabeth "Bess" Truman, wife of Harry Truman

THE FIRST LADY

During her husband's administration Bess Wallace Truman, in contrast to her predecessor, was very retiring and endeavored to keep out of the public eye as much as possible. Mrs. Truman was well known to an intimate group of friends in Washington, however, as she had been her husband's secretary while he was a senator.

IMPORTANT DATES IN THE PRESIDENT'S LIFE

1886, moved to Harrisonville, Mo.

1888, moved to farm at Grandview, Mo.

Dec. 28, 1890, moved to Independence, Mo.

1895, worked at Clinton Drug Store, earning three dollars a week

1901, graduated from high school

1901, worked in mail room of *Kansas City Star*

1902, timekeeper for contractor working for Santa Fe Railroad

1903–1905, worked at National Bank of Commerce, Kansas City, Mo.

Truman in uniform in France during World War I

1905, worked at Union National Bank, Kansas City, Mo.

June 14, 1905, joined National Guard of Missouri as charter member of Battery B

1906–1917, worked as partner on his father's farm

1917, helped organize 2nd Missouri Field Artillery, and later 129th Field Artillery, 35th Division

June 22, 1917, commissioned a first lieutenant

Sept. 26, 1917, first lieutenant, Field Artillery

1917, went to School of Fire; did regular battery duty and ran the regimental canteen

Mar. 1918, recommended for promotion

Mar. 30, 1918, overseas with the Division School Detail; sailed on S.S. *George Washington*

Apr. 20–June 18, 1918, Second Corps Artillery School at Chantillon-sur-Seine

June 1918, rejoined regiment as a captain; made adjutant, Second Battalion

July 5, 1918, regiment sent to Artillery School at Coëtquidan, France

July 11, 1918, ordered to command Battery D, 129th Field Artillery

Aug. 15, 1918, ordered to front

Aug. 18, 1918, arrived in Vosges Mountains in Alsace, France

Sept. 12–16, 1918, at St. Mihiel

Sept. 26–Oct. 3, 1918, at Meuse-Argonne, France

Oct. 8–Nov. 7, 1918, at Sommedieu, France

Nov. 7–11, 1918, at second phase of Meuse-Argonne offensive, France

Apr. 20, 1919, returned to New York

May 6, 1919, discharged, as major

1919–1921, haberdashery business, Kansas City, Mo.

1922–1924, judge, county court, Jackson County, Mo. (administrative, not judicial, position)

1923–1925, studied law at Kansas City Law School

1924, unsuccessful candidate for reelection as judge

1926–1934, presiding judge, county court, Jackson County, Mo.

Jan. 3, 1935–Jan. 17, 1945, U.S. Senate (from Missouri)

1941–1944, chairman of Special Senate Committee to Investigate the National Defense Program ("Truman Committee")

July. 1944, nominated as vice presidential candidate on Democratic ticket

Jan. 20, 1945–Apr. 12, 1945, Vice President under Franklin D. Roosevelt

Apr. 12, 1945, succeeded to the presidency on the death of President Roosevelt

July 1948, nominated for another term as President on Democratic ticket

Nov. 1948, won election, upsetting all polls

Jan. 20, 1949–Jan. 19, 1953, President (second term)

ELECTIONS

THE ELECTION OF 1948

November 2, 1948

Democratic Party (30th Convention)

July 12–14, 1948, Convention Hall, Philadelphia, Pa.

P: Harry S. Truman, Mo.

VP: Alben William Barkley, Ky.

Truman was nominated on the first ballot. Candidates for nomination and the votes they received:

Harry S. Truman, Mo., 947$^1/_2$

Richard Brevard Russell, Ga., 263

Paul Vories McNutt, Ind., $^1/_2$

Total number of votes: 1,211

Number necessary for nomination: 606

Republican Party (24th Convention)

June 21, 1948, Convention Hall, Philadelphia, Pa.

P: Thomas Edmund Dewey, N.Y.

VP: Earl Warren, Calif.

Dewey was nominated unanimously on the third ballot. Candidates for nomination and the votes they received on the first ballot:

Thomas Edmund Dewey, N.Y., 434

Robert Alphonso Taft, Ohio, 224

Harold Edward Stassen, Minn., 157

Arthur Hendrick Vandenberg, Mich., 62

Earl Warren, Calif., 59

Dwight Herbert Green, Ill., 56

Alfred Herbert Driscoll, N.J., 35

Raymond Earl Baldwin, Conn., 19

Joseph William Martin, Mass., 18

Carroll Reece, Tenn., 15

Douglas MacArthur, Wis., 11

Everett McKinley Dirksen, Ill., 1

Total number of votes: 1,091

Number necessary for nomination: 548

States' Rights Democratic Party ("Dixiecrat" Party)

July 17, 1948, Birmingham, Ala.

P: (James) Strom Thurmond, S.C.

VP: Fielding Lewis Wright, Miss.

Thurmond was nominated by acclamation on the first ballot. This party was organized by Southern dissidents who opposed Truman's civil rights program.

Progressive Party

July 23–25, 1948, Convention Hall, Philadelphia, Pa.

P: Henry Agard Wallace, Iowa

VP: Glen Hearst Taylor, Idaho

This newly organized party adopted the same name as the political party organized in 1912 to support the candidacy of Theodore Roosevelt. Wallace attracted the support of left-wing Democrats and others who favored negotiations with the Soviet Union to settle the cold war, and his party was charged with domination by Communists.

Socialist Party

May 7–9, 1948, Knights of Malta Hall and Berkshire Hall, Reading, Pa.

P: Norman Mattoon Thomas, N.Y.

VP: Tucker Powell Smith, Mich.

Prohibition Party

June 26–28, 1947, Winona Lake, Ind.

P: Claude A. Watson, Calif.

VP: Dale Learn, Pa.

Socialist Labor Party

May 1–3, 1948, Cornish Arms Hotel, New York, N.Y.

P: Edward A. Teichert, Pa.

VP: Stephen Emery, N.Y.

This party was listed in Minnesota, New York, and Pennsylvania as the Industrial Government Party.

Socialist Workers Party (Trotskyites)

July 2–3, 1948, Irving Plaza Hall, New York, N.Y.

P: Farrell Dobbs, N.Y.

VP: Grace Carlson, Minn.

This party was founded December 31, 1937 at Chicago, Ill. No presidential ticket was named until March 3, 1948. The thirteenth annual convention ratified the selection of the candidates.

Christian Nationalist Party

Aug. 20–22, 1948, Keel Auditorium, St. Louis, Mo.

P: Gerald Lyman Kenneth Smith, Mo.

VP: Henry A. Romer, Ohio

Greenback Party

Indianapolis, Ind.

P: John G. Scott, N.Y.

VP: Granville B. Leeke, Ind.

The nominations were made by mail referendum vote.

Vegetarian Party

July 7, 1948, Hotel Commodore, New York, N.Y.

P: John Maxwell, Ill.

VP: Symon Gould, N.Y.

This was the first convention of the American Vegetarian party.

John Maxwell was born in Kent, England, and was therefore constitutionally barred from becoming President.

1948 POPULAR VOTE

Democratic Party, 24,105,695

Republican Party, 21,969,170

States' Rights Democratic Party ("Dixiecrat" Party), 1,169,021

Progressive Party, 1,156,103

Socialist Party, 139,009

Prohibition Party, 103,216

Socialist Labor Party, 29,061

Socialist Workers Party, 13,613

1948 ELECTORAL VOTE

There were 531 electoral votes from 48 states.

Truman received 57.06 percent (303 votes—28 states) as follows: Ariz. 4; Ark. 9; Calif. 25; Colo. 6; Fla. 8; Ga. 12; Idaho 4; Ill. 28; Iowa 10; Ky. 11; Mass. 16; Minn. 11; Mo. 15; Mont. 4; Nev. 3; N.M. 4; N.C. 14; Ohio 25; Okla. 10; R.I. 4; Tenn. 11 (of the 12 votes); Tex. 23; Utah 4; Va. 11; Wash. 8; W.Va. 8; Wis. 12; Wyo. 3.

Dewey received 35.59 percent (189 votes—16 states) as follows: Conn. 8; Del. 3; Ind. 13; Kan. 8; Me. 5; Md. 8; Mich. 19; Neb. 6; N.H. 4; N.J. 16; N.Y. 47; N.D. 4; Ore. 6; Pa. 35; S.D. 4; Vt. 3.

Thurmond received 7.35 percent (39 votes—4 states) as follows: Ala. 11; La. 10; Miss. 9; S.C. 8; Tenn. 1 (of the 12 votes).

INAUGURATIONS

Courtesy of the Harry S. Truman Library and Museum

The inauguration of Harry S. Truman

FIRST TERM

April 12, 1945

Harry S. Truman took the oath of office at 7:09 P.M., on Thursday, April 12, 1945, in the Cabinet Room at the White House. The oath was administered by Chief Justice Harlan Fiske Stone.

SECOND TERM

January 20, 1949

President Truman took the oath of office on Thursday, January 20, 1949. It was administered by Chief Justice Frederick Moore Vinson. This was the first presidential inauguration in which a rabbi participated. Rabbi Samuel Thurman of the United Hebrew Temple of St. Louis, Mo., who had been Grand Chaplain of the Missouri Grand Lodge of Masons when Truman was Grand Master, delivered a prayer.

There was a brilliant and cloudless sky and the air was clear and crisp. The thermometer hovered between 30° and 40°. About 44,000 persons in the specially constructed grandstand witnessed the three-hour parade, which was seven and a half miles long. The ceremonies and parade were viewed by about a million persons in Washington. This was the first televised presidential inaugural, and it was estimated that ten million persons watched the ceremony on television. An estimated 100,000,000 listeners heard the proceedings on radio. The honor guard was Battery D, the unit in which the President had served during World War I. Over seven hundred airplanes, led by five B-36's, participated in a display of aerial power.

A reception was held at the National Gallery of Art for 7,500 to 10,000 guests, and an inaugural ball was held at the National Guard Armory.

As the White House was undergoing repairs, the President temporarily occupied Blair House.

THE VICE PRESIDENT

Name—Alben William Barkley (35th V.P.)

Date of birth—Nov. 24, 1877

Place of birth—Near Lowes, Graves County, Ky.

Political party—Democratic

State represented—Kentucky

Term of office—Jan. 20, 1949–Jan. 20, 1953

Age at inauguration—71 years, 57 days

Occupation after term—U.S. senator

Date of death—Apr. 30, 1956

Age at death—78 years, 157 days

Place of death—Lexington, Va.

Burial place—Paducah, Ky.

ADDITIONAL DATA ON BARKLEY

1897, graduated from Marvin College, Clinton, Ky.

1901, admitted to bar; practiced in Paducah, Ky.

1905–1909, prosecuting attorney, McCracken County, Ky.

1909–1913–Mar. 3, 1927, U.S. House of Representatives (from Kentucky)

Mar. 4, 1927–Jan. 19, 1949, U.S. Senate (from Kentucky)

1937–1947, Democratic majority leader of Senate

Courtesy of the Library of Congress

Alben William Barkley, Vice President to Harry Truman

1947–1948, Democratic minority leader of Senate

Jan. 20, 1949–Jan. 20, 1953, Vice President under Harry S. Truman

Jan. 3, 1955–April 30, 1956, U.S. Senate (from Kentucky)

CABINET

FIRST TERM

April 12, 1945–January 20, 1949

State—Edward Reilly Stettinius, Va., continued from preceding administration; James Francis Byrnes, N.C., July 2, 1945; entered upon duties July 3, 1945; George Catlett Marshall, Pa., Jan. 8, 1947; entered upon duties Jan. 21, 1947

Treasury—Henry Morgenthau, Jr., N.Y., continued from preceding administration; Frederick Moore Vinson, Ky., July 18, 1945; entered upon duties July 23, 1945; John Wesley Snyder, Mo., June 12, 1946; entered upon duties June 25, 1946

Defense—James Vincent Forrestal, N.Y., July 26, 1947; entered upon duties Sept. 17, 1947

War—Henry Lewis Stimson, N.Y., continued from preceding administration; Robert Porter Patterson, N.Y., Sept. 26, 1945; entered upon duties Sept. 27, 1945; Kenneth Clairborne Royall, N.C., July 21, 1947; entered upon duties July 25, 1947; served until Sept. 17, 1947

Attorney General—Francis Biddle, Pa., continued from preceding administration; Thomas Campbell Clark, Tex., June 15, 1945; entered upon duties July 1, 1945

Postmaster General—Frank Comerford Walker, Pa., continued from preceding administration; Robert Emmet Hannegan, Mo., May 8, 1945; entered upon duties July 1, 1945; Jesse Monroe Donaldson, Mo., Dec. 16, 1947

Navy—James Vincent Forrestal, N.Y., continued from preceding administration; served until Sept. 17, 1947

Interior—Harold Le Claire Ickes, Ill., continued from preceding administration;

Julius Albert Krug, Wis., Mar. 6, 1946; entered upon duties Mar. 18, 1946

Agriculture—Claude Raymond Wickard, Ind., continued from preceding administration; Clinton Presba Anderson, N.M., June 2, 1945; entered upon duties June 30, 1945; Charles Franklin Brannan, Colo., May 29, 1948; entered upon duties June 2, 1948

Commerce—Henry Agard Wallace, Iowa, continued from preceding administration; William Averell Harriman, N.Y., ad interim Sept. 28, 1946–Jan. 28, 1947; William Averell Harriman, Jan. 28, 1947; Charles Sawyer, Ohio, May 6, 1948

Labor—Frances Perkins, N.Y., continued from preceding administration; Lewis Baxter Schwellenbach, Wash., June 1, 1945; entered upon duties July 1, 1945; died June 10, 1948; Maurice Joseph Tobin, Mass., ad interim Aug. 13, 1948

Courtesy of the Harry S. Truman Library and Museum

Truman and his cabinet discuss the Japanese surrender

SECOND TERM

January 20, 1949–January 20, 1953

State—Dean Gooderham Acheson, Conn., Jan. 21, 1949

Treasury—John Wesley Snyder, Mo., continued from preceding administration

Defense—James Vincent Forrestal, N.Y., continued from preceding administration; Louis Arthur Johnson, W.Va., Mar. 28, 1949; George Catlett Marshall, Pa., Sept. 21, 1950; Robert Abercrombie Lovett, N.Y., Sept. 17, 1951

Attorney General—Thomas Campbell Clark, Tex., continued from preceding administration; James Howard McGrath, R.I., Aug. 19, 1949; entered upon duties Aug. 24, 1949

Postmaster General—Jesse Monroe Donaldson, Mo., continued from preceding administration; recommissioned Feb. 8, 1949

Interior—Julius Albert Krug, Wis., continued from preceding administration; Oscar Littleton Chapman, Colo. (under secretary), ad interim Dec. 1, 1949–Jan. 19, 1950; Oscar Littleton Chapman, Jan. 19, 1950

Agriculture—Charles Franklin Brannan, Colo., continued from preceding administration

Commerce—Charles Sawyer, Ohio, continued from preceding administration

405

Labor—Maurice Joseph Tobin, Mass., ad interim continued from preceding administration

CONGRESS

EIGHTIETH CONGRESS

January 3, 1947–January 3, 1949

First session—Jan. 3, 1947–Dec. 19, 1947 (351 days)

Second session—Jan. 6, 1948–Dec. 31, 1948 (361 days)

Vice President—Harry S. Truman (succeeded to the presidency on Apr. 12, 1945, on the death of Franklin Delano Roosevelt)

President pro tempore of the Senate—Arthur Hendrick Vandenberg, Mich., elected Jan. 4, 1947

Secretary of the Senate—Carl August Loeffler, Pa., elected Jan. 4, 1947

Speaker of the House— Joseph William Martin, Jr., Mass., elected Jan. 3, 1947

Clerk of the House—John Andrews, Mass., elected Jan. 3, 1947

EIGHTY–FIRST CONGRESS

January 3, 1949–January 3, 1951

First session—Jan. 3, 1949–Oct. 19, 1949 (290 days)

Second session—Jan. 3, 1950–Jan. 2, 1951 (365 days)

Vice President—Alben William Barkley, Ky.

President pro tempore of the Senate—Kenneth Douglas McKellar, Tenn., elected Jan. 3, 1949

Secretary of the Senate—Leslie L. Biffle, Ark., elected Jan. 3, 1949

Speaker of the House— Samuel Taliaferro Rayburn, Tex., elected Jan. 3, 1949

Clerk of the House—Ralph R. Roberts, Ind., elected Jan. 3, 1949

EIGHTY–SECOND CONGRESS

January 3, 1951–January 3, 1953

First session—Jan. 3, 1951–Oct. 20, 1951 (291 days)

Second session—Jan. 8, 1952–July 7, 1952 (182 days)

Vice President—Alben William Barkley, Ky.

President pro tempore of the Senate—Kenneth Douglas McKellar, Tenn., elected Jan. 3, 1951

Secretary of the Senate—Leslie L. Biffle, Ark., elected Jan. 3, 1951

Speaker of the House— Samuel Taliaferro Rayburn, Tex., elected Jan. 3, 1951

Clerk of the House—Ralph R. Roberts, Ind., elected Jan. 3, 1951

APPOINTMENTS TO THE SUPREME COURT

Chief Justice

Frederick Moore Vinson, Ky., June 21, 1946 (replaced Harlan Fiske Stone)

Associate Justices

Harold Hitz Burton, Ohio, Oct. 1, 1945 (replaced Owen Josephus Roberts)

Thomas Campbell Clark, Tex., Aug. 24, 1949 (replaced William Francis Murphy)

Sherman Minton, Ind., Oct. 12, 1949 (replaced Wiley Blount Rutledge)

IMPORTANT DATES IN THE PRESIDENCY

May 7, 1945, V-E Day—Germans unconditionally surrendered to Allied forces

June 26, 1945, United Nations charter signed at San Francisco

July 16, 1945, first atomic bomb detonated, Alamogordo, N.M.

July 17–Aug. 2, 1945, President Truman attended tripartite conference near Potsdam, Germany, establishing a Council of Foreign Ministers representing the United States, France, Great Britain, China, and the U.S.S.R.

Aug. 6, 1945, U.S. Air Force dropped atomic bomb on Hiroshima, Japan, first use of atomic energy in war

Aug. 9, 1945, second atomic bomb dropped on Nagasaki, Japan

Aug. 14, 1945, Japan surrendered

Sept. 2, 1945, V-J Day—Japanese accepted surrender terms aboard U.S.S. *Missouri*

July 4, 1946, Philippine Republic established

Aug. 1, 1946, Atomic Energy Commission created

Aug. 2, 1946, Legislative Reorganization Act passed

Courtesy of The Library of Congress

The explosion of the second atomic bomb at Nagasaki, Japan

Nov. 1946, Republicans won control of House and Senate

Feb. 10, 1947, Big Four treaty signed after New York meeting of foreign ministers, Dec. 1946

1947, Central Intelligence Agency created, replacing Office of Strategic Services; purpose of CIA declared foreign intelligence gathering only

Apr. 12, 1947, United Nations granted United States trusteeship of Pacific Islands formerly held by Japan

May 15, 1947, Congress approved "Truman Doctrine"—aid to Greece and Turkey to combat communism

May–June 1947, Congress passed Labor-Management Relations Act (Taft-Hartley Law) and overrode presidential veto

June 14, 1947, peace treaties with Bulgaria, Hungary, Italy, and Rumania ratified by the Senate

July 18, 1947, Presidential Succession Act passed

July 26, 1947, National Military Establishment created, with services integrated under Secretary of Defense

Apr. 1, 1948, Soviets began Berlin blockade; United States and Great Britain set up airlift of food and coal to West Berlin

Apr. 2, 1948, Congress passed foreign aid bill establishing Economic Cooperation Administration (known as European Recovery Program or Marshall Plan)

Apr. 30, 1948, Organization of American States formed at the ninth International Conference of American States at Bogotá, Colombia, by 21 member countries

May 14, 1948, President officially recognized the new state of Israel

May 25, 1948, first union contract with sliding wage scale negotiated by General Motors and United Auto Workers

Nov. 2, 1948, President won election; Democrats regained control of Congress

Apr. 4, 1949, North Atlantic treaty signed by twelve nations, Washington, D.C.

Apr. 8, 1949, United States, Great Britain, and France agreed to establish West German republic

July 25, 1949, President signed NATO Pact (effective Aug. 24); asked for arms for Europe

Sept. 19, 1949, soft-coal strike called by John L. Lewis

Sept. 30, 1949, Berlin blockade ended

Oct. 1, 1949, United Steel Workers began strike against steel industry

Oct. 14, 1949, Communist leaders convicted of violation of Smith act

Oct. 26, 1949, minimum wage bill raised salaries to 75 cents an hour

June 25, 1950, North Korean Communists crossed 38th Parallel, invading Republic of Korea; United Nations requested support for South Korea

July 3, 1950, U.S. troops and North Koreans in battle

July 8, 1950, General MacArthur named commander in chief of United Nations troops in Korea

Aug. 27, 1950, Army seized railroads to prevent strike

Oct. 7, 1950, U.S. First Cavalry made first crossing of the 38th Parallel in Korea

Nov. 1, 1950, attempted assassination of President Truman by two Puerto Rican nationalists

Nov. 26, 1950, Communist Chinese entered Korean War; forced U.S. troops back

Dec. 16, 1950, President proclaimed state of national emergency

Feb. 26, 1951, Twenty-second Amendment ratified (limiting Presidents to two terms)

Apr. 11, 1951, General MacArthur relieved of Far Eastern command because of failure to heed presidential directives

Sept. 12, 1951, Tripartite Security Treaty signed at San Francisco, Calif. (United States, Australia, and New Zealand)

Sept. 4, 1951, first transcontinental television broadcast

Apr. 8, 1952, President Truman ordered seizure of steel mills to prevent a strike

May 23, 1952, railroads under army control since Aug. 27, 1950, restored to owners after signing of union contract

May 25, 1952, atomic artillery shell fired in Nevada

June 2, 1952, seizure of steel mills declared illegal by Supreme Court

July 25, 1952, Puerto Rico became a U.S. commonwealth

Nov. 1, 1952, first U.S. hydrogen bomb detonated, Eniwetok, Marshall Islands

ADDITIONAL DATA ON TRUMAN

HARRY S. TRUMAN

—was the first President born in Missouri.

—was the ninth President whose mother was alive when he assumed office.

—was the fourth Democratic President since the Civil War.

HARRY "S" TRUMAN

The initial "S" in President Harry S. Truman's name has no special significance and is not an abbreviation of any name. It is said to have been chosen by his parents to avoid a display of favoritism, since his paternal grandfather's name was Shippe (Anderson Shippe Truman) and his maternal grandfather's name was Solomon Young.

TRUMAN WITNESSED OATH-TAKING OF SUPREME COURT JUDGE

President Truman was the first President to witness the swearing in of one of his Supreme Court appointees. On October 1, 1945, he attended the swearing-in ceremony of Harold Hitz Burton in the Supreme Court Chamber.

TRUMAN PRESENTED MEDAL TO CONSCIENTIOUS OBJECTOR

A unique medal presentation ceremony was held on October 12, 1945, when President Truman presented a medal of honor to a conscientious objector, the first time such an award was made. The recipient was Private Desmond T. Doss of Lynchburg, Va., whose acts of heroism and outstanding bravery as a medical corpsman on Okinawa between April 29 and May 21, 1945, earned him this signal distinction.

TRUMAN THIRTY-THIRD-DEGREE MASON

Truman was the only President to attain the thirty-third and last degree of the Supreme Council of the Scottish Rite for the Southern jurisdiction, which honor was accorded him on October 19, 1945, at the House of the Temple, Washington, D.C. Harding was nominated but died before the degree was conferred.

TRUMAN TRAVELED IN SUBMARINE

President Truman was the first President to travel underwater in a modern submarine. He embarked at Key West, Fla., on November 21, 1946, in the U-2513, a captured German submarine. The submarine submerged off Key West during naval exercises. (President Theodore Roosevelt went underwater in the *Plunger* on August 25, 1905, off Oyster Bay, N.Y.)

TWENTY-SECOND AMENDMENT

The Twenty-second Amendment, which limited the presidential term to two four-year terms, was proposed by Congress on March 26, 1947. It became effective on February 26, 1951, when the thirty-sixth state, Nevada, ratified it.

The amendment follows:

No person shall be elected to the office of the President more than twice, and no person who has held the office of President, or acted as President, for more than two years of a term to which some other person was elected President shall be elected to the office of the President more than once. But this article shall not apply to any person holding the office of President when this Article was proposed by the Congress, and shall not prevent any person who may be holding the office of President, or acting as President, during the term within this article

becomes operative from holding the office of President or acting as President during the remainder of such term.

TRUMAN TELECAST ADDRESS FROM WHITE HOUSE

The first presidential address telecast from the White House was delivered on October 5, 1947, by President Truman. He spoke about food conservation and the world food crisis, proposing meatless Tuesdays and eggless and poultryless Thursdays. The speech was relayed to New York City, Schenectady, N.Y., and Philadelphia, PA.

ASSASSINATION ATTEMPT MADE ON TRUMAN

President Truman escaped assassination on November 1, 1950, when at 2:15 P.M. Oscar Collazo and Griselio Torresola, two Puerto Rican nationalists, tried to shoot their way into Blair House. Leslie Coffelt of Arlington, Va., a White House guard, was killed and two others wounded. Torresola was killed and Collazo was wounded.

One hour after the shooting, President Truman dedicated a memorial to British Field Marshal Sir John Dill at the Arlington National Cemetery.

On July 24, 1952, Collazo was sentenced to die on August 1, 1952, but his sentence was commuted to life imprisonment.

PRESS CONFERENCE TAPED

The first presidential press conference recorded on tape was held at the White House on January 25, 1951. It was recorded for the White House archives by the United States Army Signal Corps unit permanently attached to the White House to handle communications. Portions were released by consent of President Truman.

TRUMAN RECEIVED FIRST WOMAN AMBASSADOR

President Truman was the first President to receive officially a woman ambassador from a foreign country. On May 12, 1952, he received the letter of credence from Her Excellency Shrimati Vijaya Lakshmi Pandit, ambassador of India.

FORMER PRESIDENT ADDRESSED THE SENATE

Senator Clairborne Pell (D–R.I.) introduced a resolution in the Senate that was enacted October 1, 1963 (*Congressional Quarterly Almanac,* 19:378, 1963). The Pell resolution stated that "former Presidents of the United States shall be entitled to address the Senate upon giving appropriate notice of their intentions to the Presiding Officer."

The first former President to address the Senate was Harry S. Truman, whose presence in the Senate was acknowledged on May 8, 1964, his eightieth birthday. Truman replied in a brief sixty-eight word speech.

FURTHER READING

Caute, David. *The Great Fear.* 1978.

Hamby, Alonzo L. *Beyond the New Deal: Harry S. Truman and American Liberalism.* 1978.

———. *Man of the People: A Life of Harry S. Truman.* 1995.

McCoy, Donald R. *The Presidency of Harry S. Truman.* Rev. ed. 1988.

McCullough, David G. *Truman.* 1992.

Miller, Merle. *Plain Speaking.* 1974.

Ross, Irwin. *The Loneliest Campaign.* 1968.

Walton, Richard J. *Henry Wallace, Harry Truman and the Cold War.* 1976.

Courtesy of The Library of Congress

Dwight David Eisenhower

Name at birth—David Dwight Eisenhower

Date of birth—Oct. 14, 1890

Place of birth—Denison, Tex.

Education—Public schools, Abilene, Kans.; Abilene High School, graduated 1909; United States Military Academy, West Point, N.Y., graduated June 12, 1915; Command and General Staff School, Fort Leavenworth, Kans., 1925–1926; Army War College, 1928–1929

Religion—Presbyterian (born River Brethren)

Ancestry—Swiss-German

Career—Army officer, rising to Supreme Allied Commander and five-star general in World War II; president of Columbia University, supreme commander of North Atlantic Treaty Organization

Political party—Republican

State represented—New York

Term of office—Jan. 20, 1953–Jan. 20, 1961

Term served—8 years

Administration—42nd, 43rd

Congresses—83rd, 84th, 85th, 86th

Age at inauguration—62 years, 98 days

Lived after term—8 years, 67 days

Occupation after term—Retired; author

Date of death—Mar. 28, 1969

Age at death—78 years, 165 days

Place of death—Washington, D.C.

Burial place—Abilene, Kan.

FAMILY

FATHER

Name—David Jacob Eisenhower

Date of birth—Sept. 23, 1863

Place of birth—Elizabethville, Pa.

Marriage—Ida Elizabeth Stover, Sept. 23, 1885, Hope, Kan.

Occupation—Creamery mechanic, storekeeper, manager of gas company, director of employee savings for group of public utilities

Date of death—May 10, 1942

Place of death—Abilene, Kan.

Age at death—79 years, 168 days

MOTHER

Name at birth—Ida Elizabeth Stover

Date of birth—May 1, 1862

Marriage—David Jacob Eisenhower, Sept. 23, 1885, Hope, Kan.

Place of birth—Mount Sidney, Va.

Date of death—Sept. 11, 1946

Place of death—Abilene, Kan.

Age at death—84 years, 133 days

SIBLINGS

Dwight David Eisenhower was the third of seven sons.

Children of David Jacob Eisenhower and Ida Elizabeth Stover Eisenhower

Arthur Bradford Eisenhower, b. Nov. 11, 1886; d. Jan. 26, 1958

Edgar Newton Eisenhower, b. Jan. 19, 1889; d. July 12, 1971

Dwight David Eisenhower, b. Oct. 14, 1890; d. Mar. 28, 1969

Roy Jacob Eisenhower, b. Aug. 9, 1892; d. June 17, 1942

Paul A. Eisenhower, b. May 12, 1894; d. Mar. 16, 1895

Earl Dewey Eisenhower, b. Feb. 1, 1898; d. Dec. 18, 1968

Milton Stover Eisenhower, b. Sept. 15, 1899, d. May 2, 1985

MARRIAGE

Married—Marie ("Mamie") Geneva Doud

Date of marriage—July 1, 1916

Place of marriage—Denver, Colo.

Age of wife at marriage—19 years, 229 days

Age of husband at marriage—25 years, 260 days

Years married—52 years, 270 days

CHILDREN

Dwight Doud Eisenhower, b. Sept. 24, 1917, Denver, Colo.; d. Jan. 2, 1920, Camp Meade, Md.

John Sheldon Doud Eisenhower, b. Aug. 3, 1922, Denver, Colo.; m. June 10, 1947, Barbara Jean Thompson, Fort Monroe, Va.

THE PRESIDENT'S WIFE

Name at birth—Marie Geneva ("Mamie") Doud

Date of birth—Nov. 14, 1896

Place of birth—Boone, Iowa

Mother—Elivera Carlson Doud

Father—John Sheldon Doud

Father's occupation—Meat packer

Marriage—Dwight David Eisenhower, July 1, 1916, Denver, Colo.

Children—Dwight Doud Eisenhower, b. Sept. 24, 1917, d. Jan. 2, 1920; John Sheldon Doud Eisenhower, b. Aug. 3, 1922

Date of death—Nov. 1, 1979

Age at death—82 years, 350 days

Place of death—Washington, D.C.

Burial place—Abilene, Kan.

Years younger than the President—6 years, 30 days

Years she survived the President—10 years, 218 days

THE FIRST LADY

Mamie Geneva Doud Eisenhower was reserved, dignified, and unassuming, avoiding unnecessary publicity. As an Army wife for 37 years, she grew accustomed to entertaining groups of influential people, a talent she drew on as the White House hostess. She suffered from Ménière's syndrome, an inner-ear disorder that produces vertigo, and her resulting shaky balance gave rise to erroneous rumors that she was an alcoholic.

Courtesy of The Library of Congress

Marie "Mamie" Eisenhower, wife of Dwight Eisenhower

IMPORTANT DATES IN THE PRESIDENT'S LIFE

1909, graduated from Abilene High School, Abilene, Kan.

June 12, 1915, graduated from U.S. Military Academy (61st in class of 164, 95th in deportment); commissioned second lieutenant of infantry; assigned to 19th Infantry, San Antonio, Tex.

1918, commanded 6,000 men at Tank Training Center at Camp Colt, near Gettysburg, Pa.; served at army training post in World War I, but did not go overseas

July 2, 1920, promoted to permanent rank of major; ordered to Fort Meade, Md., graduated from Infantry Tank School

1925–1926, Command and General Staff School, Fort Leavenworth, Kan.; graduated first in class of 275

1935–1939, major; assistant to General MacArthur in the Philippines

Feb. 1942, chief, War Plans Division of War Department General Staff

June 25, 1942, appointed commanding general, European Theatre of Operations

Nov. 8, 1942, appointed commander in chief of Allied forces in North Africa

Feb. 1943, full general (temporary rank)

July–Dec. 1943, directed invasions of Sicily and Italy

Dec. 24, 1943, appointed supreme commander, Allied Expeditionary Force

June 6, 1944, directed D-Day invasion of Normandy

Dec. 20, 1944, General of the Army (temporary rank)

May 7, 1945, accepted surrender of German Army at Rheims (V-E Day)

May–Nov. 1945, commander of U.S. occupation forces in Europe

Nov. 19, 1945–Feb. 7, 1948, chief of staff, U.S. Army; first chief of staff under unification of armed services in 1947

Feb. 7, 1948, retired from active duty in the Army

June 7, 1948, appointed president of Columbia University

Dec. 16, 1950, granted indefinite leave of absence from Columbia University to serve as commander of NATO forces in Europe

June 1952, resigned from the Army

July 1952, received Republican presidential nomination

Nov. 4, 1952, elected President

Jan. 20, 1953–Jan. 20, 1957, President (first term)

Sept. 24, 1955, suffered heart attack at Denver, Colo.

June 9, 1956, underwent emergency ileitis operation

Aug. 22, 1956, renominated by Republicans

Nov. 6, 1956, elected President for second term

Jan. 20, 1957–Jan. 20, 1961, President (second term)

Jan. 21, 1957, inaugurated for second term (took oath of office in private ceremony on Sunday, Jan. 20)

Nov. 25, 1957, suffered mild stroke, but recovered rapidly

1961, retired to Gettysburg farm

Mar. 22, 1961, rank as General of the Army restored

1963, published *Mandate for Change, 1953–1956*

1965, published *Waging Peace, 1956–1961*

1967, published *At Ease*

ELECTIONS

THE ELECTION OF 1952

November 4, 1952

CANDIDATES

Republican Party (25th Convention)

July 7–11, 1952, International Amphitheatre, Chicago, Ill.

P: Dwight David Eisenhower, N.Y.

VP: Richard Milhous Nixon, Calif.

Eisenhower was nominated on the first ballot. Candidates for nomination and the votes they received:

Dwight David Eisenhower, N.Y., 845

Robert Alphonso Taft, Ohio, 280

Earl Warren, Calif., 77

Douglas MacArthur, Wis., 4

Total number of votes: 1,206

Number necessary for nomination: 604

Nomination made unanimous

Democratic Party (31st Convention)

July 21–26, 1952, International Amphitheatre, Chicago, Ill.

P: Adlai Ewing Stevenson, Ill.

VP: John Jackson Sparkman, Ala.

Stevenson was nominated on the third ballot. Candidates for nomination and the votes they received on the first and third ballots:

Estes Kefauver, Tenn., 340, 275$^1/_2$

Adlai Ewing Stevenson, Ill., 273, 617$^1/_2$

Richard Brevard Russell, Ga., 268, 261

William Averell Harriman, N.Y., $123^1/_2$, 0

Robert Samuel Kerr, Okla., 65, 0

Alben William Barkley, Ky., $48^1/_2$, $67^1/_2$

Paul Andrew Dever, Mass., $37^1/_2$, $^1/_2$

Hubert Horatio Humphrey, Minn., 26, 0

James William Fulbright, Ark., 22, 0

James Edward Murray, Mont., 12, 0

Harry S. Truman, Mo., 6, 0

Oscar Ross Ewing, Ind., 4, 3

Paul Howard Douglas, Ill., 3, 3

William Orville Douglas, Va., $^1/_2$, 0

Total number of votes:

First ballot: 1,229

Third ballot: 1,228

Number necessary for nomination: 616

Nomination made unanimous

Progressive Party

July 4–6, 1952, International Amphitheatre, Chicago, Ill.

P: Vincent William Hallinan, Calif.
VP: Charlotta A. Bass, N.Y.

Prohibition Party

Nov. 13–15, 1951, Indianapolis, Ind.

P: Stuart Hamblen, Calif.
VP: Enoch Arden Holtwick, Ill.

Socialist Labor Party

May 3–5, 1952, Henry Hudson Hotel, New York, N.Y.

P: Eric Hass, N.Y.
VP: Stephen Emery, N.Y.

Socialist Party

May 30, June 1–2, 1952, Hotel Hollenden, Cleveland, Ohio

P: Darlington Hoopes, Pa.
VP: Samuel Herman Friedman, N.Y.

Socialist Workers Party

July 20, 1952, New York, N.Y.

P: Farrell Dobbs, N.Y.
VP: Myra Tanner Weiss, N.Y.

America First Party

Aug. 25, 1952, Kansas City, Mo.

P: Douglas MacArthur, Wis.
VP: Harry Flood Byrd, Va.

Courtesy of The Library of Congress

Eisenhower campaigns in Baltimore, Maryland, in September 1952.

American Labor Party

Aug. 28, 1952, City Center Casino, New York, N.Y.

P: Vincent William Hallinan, Calif.
VP: Charlotta A. Bass, N.Y.

The party endorsed the candidates of the Progressive Party.

American Vegetarian Party

P: Daniel J. Murphy, Calif.
VP: Symon Gould, N.Y.

Church of God Party

July 2–8, 1952, Moses Tabernacle, Nashville, Tenn.

P: Homer Aubrey Tomlinson, N.Y.
VP: Willie Isaac Bass, N.C.

The Church of God Party was organized July 4, 1952, at the forty-sixth annual general assembly of the Church of God in Christ, Nashville, Tenn.

Constitution Party

Aug. 31, 1952, Philadelphia, Pa.

P: Douglas MacArthur, Wis.
VP: Harry Flood Byrd, Va.

Greenback Party

P: Frederick C. Proehl, Wash.
VP: Edward J. Bedell, Ind.

The candidates were nominated by referendum. Ballots were mailed to all dues-paying members.

Poor Man's Party

P: Henry B. Krajewski, N.J.
VP: Frank Jenkins, N.J.

1952 POPULAR VOTE

Republican Party, 33,778,963
Democratic Party, 27,314,992
South Carolina Republicans (separate set of electors), 158,289
Progressive Party, 135,007
Prohibition Party, 72,769
Socialist Labor Party, 30,376
Socialist Party, 19,685
Christian Nationalists, 13,883
Socialist Workers Party, 10,306
Poor Man's Party, 4,203
Oregon Independent, 3,665
Constitution Party, 3,089
People's Party of Connecticut, 1,466
Social Democrats, 504
America First Party, 233
Scattering, 4,489

1952 ELECTORAL VOTE

There were 531 electoral votes from 48 states.

Eisenhower received 83.24 percent (442 votes—39 states) as follows: Ariz. 4; Calif. 32; Colo. 6; Conn. 8; Del. 3; Fla. 3; Idaho 4; Ill. 27; Ind. 13; Iowa 10; Kan. 8; Me. 5; Md. 9; Mass. 16; Mich. 20; Minn. 11; Mo. 13; Mont. 4; Neb. 6; Nev. 3; N.H. 4; N.J. 16; N.M. 4; N.Y. 45; N.D. 4; Ohio 25; Okla. 8; Ore. 6; Pa. 32; R.I. 4; S.D. 4; Tenn. 11; Tex. 24; Utah 4; Vt. 3; Va. 12; Wash. 9; Wis. 12; Wyo. 3.

Stevenson received 16.76 percent (89 votes—9 states) as follows: Ala. 11; Ark. 8; Ga. 12; Ky. 10; La. 10; Miss. 8; N.C. 14; S.C. 8; W.Va. 8.

THE ELECTION OF 1956

November 6, 1956

CANDIDATES

Republican Party (26th Convention)

Aug. 20–23, 1956, the Cow Palace, San Francisco, Calif.

P: Dwight David Eisenhower, N.Y.

VP: Richard Milhous Nixon, Calif.

Eisenhower was nominated by acclamation on the first ballot.
Total number of votes: 1,323
Number necessary for nomination: 662

Democratic Party (32nd Convention)

Aug. 13–17, 1956, International Amphitheatre, Chicago, Ill.

P: Adlai Ewing Stevenson, Ill.
VP: Estes Kefauver, Tenn.

Stevenson was nominated on the first ballot. Candidates for nomination and the votes they received:

Adlai Ewing Stevenson, Ill., 905$^1/_2$
William Averell Harriman, N.Y., 210
Lyndon Baines Johnson, Tex., 80
William Stuart Symington, Mo., 45$^1/_2$
Albert Benjamin Chandler, Ky., 36$^1/_2$
James Curran Davis, Ga., 33
John Stewart Battle, Va., 32$^1/_2$
George Bell Timmerman, Jr., S.C., 23$^1/_2$
Frank John Lausche, Ohio, 5$^1/_2$
Total number of votes: 1,372
Number necessary for nomination: 686$^1/_2$

Liberal Party

Sept. 11, 1956, Manhattan Center, New York, N.Y.

P: Adlai Ewing Stevenson, Ill.
VP: Estes Kefauver, Tenn.

States' Rights Party

Oct. 15, 1956, Mosque Auditorium, Richmond, Va.

P: Thomas Coleman Andrews, Va.
VP: Thomas Harold Werdel, Calif.

The candidates were nominated by acclamation.

Prohibition Party

Sept. 4–6, 1955, Milford, Ind.

P: Enoch Arden Holtwick, Ill.
VP: Herbert Charles Holdridge, Calif.

Holdridge resigned February 15, 1956, and the national committee substituted Edward M. Cooper of California.

417

Socialist Labor Party

May 5–7, 1956, Henry Hudson Hotel, New York, N.Y.

P: Eric Hass, N.Y.
VP: Georgia Cozzini, Wis.

Texas Constitution Party

P: William Ezra Jenner, Ind.
VP: Joseph Bracken Lee, Utah

Socialist Workers Party

Aug. 19, 1956, Adelphi Hall, New York, N.Y.

P: Farrell Dobbs, N.Y.
VP: Myra Tanner Weiss, N.Y.

American Third Party

P: Henry Krajewski, N.J.
VP: Ann Marie Yezo, N.J.

Socialist Party

June 8–10, 1956, Chicago, Ill.

P: Darlington Hoopes, Pa.
VP: Samuel Herman Friedman, N.Y.

Pioneer Party

Nov. 26–27, 1955, Milwaukee, Wis.

P: William Langer, N.D.
VP: Burr McCloskey, Ill.

American Vegetarian Party

July 6, 1956, Los Angeles, Calif.

P: Herbert M. Shelton, Calif.
VP: Symon Gould, N.Y.

Greenback Party

P: Frederick C. Proehl, Wash.
VP: Edward Kirby Meador, Mass.

The candidates were nominated by referendum. Ballots were mailed to all dues-paying members.

States' Rights Party of Kentucky

P: Harry Flood Byrd, Va.
VP: William Ezra Jenner, Ind.

South Carolinians for Independent Electors

P: Harry Flood Byrd, Va.

Constitution Party

Aug. 28, 1956, Fort Worth, Tex.

Seventy-five delegates from seventeen states favored Thomas Coleman Andrews, Va., and Thomas Harold Werdel, Calif., who were to be nominated by the States' Rights party.

Christian National Party

P: Gerald Lyman Kenneth Smith

1956 POPULAR VOTE

Republican Party, 35,581,003
Democratic Party, 25,738,765
Liberal Party, 292,557
States' Rights Party, 109,961
Prohibition Party, 41,937
Socialist Labor Party, 41,159
Texas Constitution Party, 30,999
Socialist Workers Party, 5,549
Conservative Party (N.J.), 5,317
Black and Tan Grand Old Party (Miss.), 4,313
Industrial Government (N.Y.), 2,080
Militant Workers (Pa.), 2,035
American Third Party, 1,829
Socialist Party, 846
American Party, 483
Virginia Social Democrats, 444
New Party (N.M.), 364

1956 ELECTORAL VOTE

There were 531 electoral votes from 48 states.

Eisenhower received 86.06 percent (457 votes—41 states) as follows: Ariz. 4; Calif. 32; Colo. 6; Conn. 8; Del. 3; Fla. 10; Idaho 4; Ill. 27; Ind. 13; Iowa 10; Kan. 8; Ky. 10; La. 10; Me. 5; Md. 9; Mass. 16; Mich. 20; Minn. 11; Mont. 4; Neb. 6; Nev. 3; N.H. 4; N.J. 16; N.M. 4; N.Y. 65; N.D. 4; Ohio 25; Okla. 8; Ore. 6; Pa. 32; R.I. 4; S.D. 4; Tenn. 11; Tex. 24; Utah 4; Vt. 3; Va. 12; Wash. 9; W.Va. 8; Wis. 12; Wyo. 3.

Stevenson received 13.75 percent (73 votes—7 states) as follows: Ala. 10 of the 11 votes); Ark. 8; Ga. 12; Miss. 8; Mo. 13; N.C. 14; S.C. 8.

Stevenson did not receive all 74 Democratic votes; one vote went to Walter Burgwyn Jones of Alabama.

Jones received 00.19 percent (1 of the 11 Ala. votes).

INAUGURATIONS

FIRST TERM

January 20, 1953

Dwight David Eisenhower took the oath of office on Tuesday, January 20, 1953. The oath was administered by Chief Justice Frederick Moore Vinson.

Before delivering his inaugural address, the President offered a prayer, the text of which follows:

> My friends, before I begin the expression of these thoughts that I deem appropriate to this moment, would you permit me the privilege of uttering a little private prayer of my own. And I ask that you bow your heads. Almighty God, as we stand here at this moment my future associates in the Executive branch of Government join me in beseeching that Thou will make full and complete our dedication to the service of the people in this throng, and their fellow citizens everywhere. Give us, we pray, the power to discern clearly right from wrong and allow all our words and actions to be governed thereby, and by the laws of this land. Especially we pray that our concern shall be for all the people regardless of station, race or calling. May cooperation be permitted and be the mutual aim of those who, under the concepts of our Constitution, hold to different political faiths; so that all may work for the good of our beloved country and Thy glory. Amen.

The two-and-a-half-hour inaugural parade was witnessed by an estimated one million persons, of whom 60,000 were in the grandstand in seats ranging in price from $3 to $15, according to location. About 22,000 servicemen and servicewomen and 5,000 civilians were in the parade, which included 50 state and organization floats costing $100,000. There were also 65 musical units, 350 horses, 3 elephants, an Alaskan dog team, and the 280-millimeter atomic cannon.

In addition to a governors' reception for 3,000 invited guests, there were two inaugural festivals, one at the Uline Arena for 11,000 persons, and one at the Capitol Theater for 3,500 persons. Tickets ranged in price from $3 to $12. Forty stars of stage, screen, and TV participated in the celebration.

In the evening two inaugural balls were held, one at the National Guard Armory and the other at the gymnasium of McDonough Hall at Georgetown University.

SECOND TERM

January 20, 1957

As January 20, 1957, fell on a Sunday, President Eisenhower took the oath of office in a private White House ceremony.

On Monday, January 21, 1957, he repeated the oath at the inaugural ceremonies held on the east portico of the White House. The oath was administered by Chief Justice Earl Warren.

In the afternoon 750,000 spectators watched a three-and-a-half-hour parade over a three-mile route. Marching in the parade were 17,000 people, including 11,757 in military service. There were 47 marching units, 52 bands, and 10 drum and bugle corps. The highlight of the parade was a mammoth float—408 feet long and mounted on 164 wheels—which introduced the theme "Liberty and Strength Through Consent of the Governed."

Four inaugural balls were held in the evening at the Armory, the Mayflower Hotel, the Statler Hotel, and the Sheraton-Park Hotel.

THE VICE PRESIDENT

Name—Richard Milhous Nixon (36th V.P.)
Political party—Republican

State represented—California
Term of office—Jan. 20, 1953–Jan. 20, 1961

Age at inauguration—40 years, 11 days

Occupation after term—Lawyer, President of the United States

For further biographical information, see the chapter on Richard Milhous Nixon, 37th President, on page 461

Courtesy of The Library of Congress

Richard Nixon, Vice President to Dwight Eisenhower

CABINET

FIRST TERM

January 20, 1953–January 20, 1957

State—John Foster Dulles, N.Y., Jan. 21, 1953

Treasury—George Magoffin Humphrey, Ohio, Jan. 21, 1953

Defense—Charles Erwin Wilson, Mich., Jan. 28, 1953

Attorney General—Herbert Brownell, Jr., N.Y., Jan. 21, 1953

Postmaster General—Arthur Ellsworth Summerfield, Mich., Jan. 21, 1953

Interior—Douglas McKay, Ore., Jan. 21, 1953; Frederick Andrew Seaton, Neb., June 8, 1956

Agriculture—Ezra Taft Benson, Utah, Jan. 21, 1953

Commerce—Sinclair Weeks, Mass., Jan. 21, 1953

Labor—Martin Patrick Durkin, Ill., Jan. 21, 1953; James Paul Mitchell, N.J., Oct. 9, 1953

Health, Education, and Welfare—Oveta Culp Hobby, Tex., Apr. 11, 1953; Marion Bayard Folson, Ga., Aug. 1, 1955

SECOND TERM

January 20, 1957–January 20, 1961

State—John Foster Dulles, N.Y., continued from preceding administration; Christian Archibald Herter, Mass., Apr. 22, 1959

Treasury—George Magoffin Humphrey, Ohio, continued from preceding administration; Robert Bernerd Anderson, Tex., July 29, 1957

Defense—Charles Erwin Wilson, Mich., continued from preceding administration; Neil Hosler McElroy, Ohio, Oct. 9, 1957; Thomas Sovereign Gates, Jr., Pa., Dec. 2, 1959

Attorney General—Herbert Brownell, Jr., N.Y., continued from preceding administration; William Pierce Rogers, N.Y., Jan. 27, 1958

Postmaster General—Arthur Ellsworth Summerfield, Mich., continued from preceding administration

Interior—Frederick Andrew Seaton, Neb., continued from preceding administration

Agriculture—Ezra Taft Benson, Utah, continued from preceding administration

Commerce—Sinclair Weeks, Mass., continued from preceding administration; Lewis Lichtenstein Strauss, N.Y., Nov. 13, 1958, not confirmed, Senate rejected appointment June 18, 1959; Frederick Henry Mueller, Mich., Aug. 10, 1959

Labor—James Paul Mitchell, N.J., continued from preceding administration

Health, Education, and Welfare—Marion Bayard Folsom, Ga., continued from preceding administration; Arthur Sherwood Flemming, Ohio, Aug. 1, 1958

CONGRESS

EIGHTY-THIRD CONGRESS

January 3, 1953–January 3, 1955

First session—Jan. 3, 1953–Aug. 3, 1953 (213 days)

Second session—Jan. 6, 1954–Dec. 2, 1954 (331 days)

Vice President—Richard Milhous Nixon, Calif.

President pro tempore of the Senate —Styles Bridges, N.H., elected Jan. 3, 1953

Secretary of the Senate—Felton McLellan Johnston, Miss., elected Jan. 3, 1953

Speaker of the House—Joseph William Martin, Mass., elected Jan. 3, 1953

Clerk of the House—Lyle O. Snader, Ill., elected Jan. 3, 1953

EIGHTY–FOURTH CONGRESS

January 3, 1955–January 3, 1957

First session—Jan. 5, 1955–Aug. 2, 1955 (210 days)

Second session—Jan. 3, 1956–July 27, 1956 (207 days)

Vice President—Richard Milhouse Nixon, Calif.

President pro tempore of the Senate —Walter Franklin George, Ga., elected Jan. 5, 1955

Secretary of the Senate—Felton McLellan Johnston Miss., elected Jan. 5, 1955

Speaker of the House—Samuel Taliaferro Rayburn, Tex., elected Jan. 5, 1955

Clerk of the House—Ralph R. Roberts, Ind., elected Jan. 5, 1955

EIGHTY–FIFTH CONGRESS

January 3, 1957–January 3, 1959

First session—Jan. 3, 1957–Aug. 30, 1957 (239 days)

Second session—Jan. 7, 1958–Aug. 24, 1958 (230 days)

Vice President—Richard Milhous Nixon, Calif.

President pro tempore of the Senate —Carl Hayden, Ariz., elected Jan. 3, 1957

Secretary of the Senate—Felton McLellan Johnston, Miss., elected Jan. 3, 1957

Speaker of the House—Samuel Taliaferro Rayburn, Tex., elected Jan. 3, 1957

Clerk of the House—Ralph R. Roberts, Ind., elected Jan. 3, 1957

EIGHTY–SIXTH CONGRESS

January 3, 1959–January 3, 1961

First session—Jan. 7, 1959–Sept. 15, 1959 (252 days)

Second session—Jan. 6, 1960–Sept. 1, 1960 (240 days)

Vice President—Richard Milhous Nixon, Calif.

President pro tempore of the Senate —Carl Hayden, Ariz., elected Jan. 3, 1959

Secretary of the Senate—Felton McLellan Johnston, Miss., elected Jan. 5, 1959

Speaker of the House—Samuel Taliaferro Rayburn, Tex., elected Jan. 7, 1959

Clerk of the House—Ralph R. Roberts, Ind., elected Jan. 7, 1959

APPOINTMENTS TO THE SUPREME COURT

Chief Justice

Earl Warren, Calif., Oct. 5, 1953 (replaced Frederick Moore Vinson)

Associate Justices

John Marshall Harlan II, N.Y., Mar. 28, 1955 (replaced Robert Houghwout Jackson)

William Joseph Brennan, Jr., N.J., Oct. 16, 1956 (replaced Sherman Minton)

Charles Evans Whittaker, Mo., Mar. 25, 1957 (replaced Stanley Forman Reed)

Potter Stewart, Ohio, Oct. 14, 1958 (replaced Harold Hitz Burton)

IMPORTANT DATES IN THE PRESIDENCY

June 19, 1953, execution of atomic spies Julius and Ethel Rosenberg, first spies sentenced to death by a U.S. civil court and the first executed for treason in peacetime

July 27, 1953, Korean war ended with signing of armistice calling for demilitarized zone and voluntary repatriation of prisoners

Jan. 21, 1954, first atomic submarine, *Nautilus,* launched, Groton, Conn.

Mar. 1, 1954, five representatives wounded in House of Representatives by shots fired by Puerto Rican nationalists

Apr. 22–June 17, 1954 Army-McCarthy hearings arising out of Senator McCarthy's charges of subversive activities

May 17, 1954, Supreme Court declared racial segregation in schools unconstitutional

July 21, 1954, Geneva agreement signed to end war in Indochina after French withdrawal

Aug. 24, 1954, Communist party outlawed, but party membership not made a crime

Sept. 1, 1954, social security coverage extended to 10 million additional persons (farmers, professional people, etc.)

Sept. 3, 1954, death penalty for peacetime espionage authorized

Courtesy of the National Archives and Records Administration

United Nations forces withdraw from North Korea at the conclusion of the Korean Conflict.

Sept. 8, 1954, Southeast Asia defense treaty (SEATO) signed

Oct. 25, 1954, first telecast of a cabinet meeting

Dec. 2, 1954, Senate voted condemnation of Senator McCarthy for conduct during Senate hearings

Jan. 28, 1955, Congress approved presidential request to allow U.S. forces to defend Formosa against Communist aggression

Feb. 7, 1955, U.S. Seventh fleet helped evacuation of Communist-threatened Tachen Islands, near Formosa (Taiwan)

Apr. 12, 1955, Salk vaccine against polio declared "safe, effective, and potent"

Apr. 21, 1955, U.S. occupation of Germany ended; troops remained on contractual basis

May 31, 1955, Supreme Court reaffirmed principle of school integration, ordering gradual compliance by local authorities

Sept. 24, 1955, President suffered heart attack

Dec. 5, 1955, AFL-CIO merger

Mar. 12, 1956, manifesto issued by southern senators and representatives pledging use of all legal means to reverse Supreme Court integration ruling

July 19, 1956, United States withdrew offers to finance construction of Aswan Dam in Egypt, precipitating Egyptian seizure of Suez canal

Oct. 31, 1956, President, deploring Anglo-French-Israeli attack on Egypt, promised that United States would not be involved

Mar. 9, 1957, Eisenhower Doctrine bill signed, authorizing use of U.S. forces to assist Middle East nations threatened by Communist aggression

Sept. 9, 1957, Congress approved establishment of Civil Rights Commission

Sept. 19, 1957, first underground nuclear explosion, Nevada proving grounds

Sept. 24, 1957, President sent federal troops to Little Rock, Ark., high school to enforce integration of black students

Oct. 4, 1957, launching of first Soviet Sputnik set off demand for greater American efforts in defense and technology

1957–1958, business recession; over 5 million unemployed before reversal of downward trend

Jan. 31, 1958, launching of Explorer I, first American satellite

May 13, 1958, Vice President Nixon, on Latin American tour, attacked by anti-U.S. demonstrators

July–Oct. 1958, U.S. troops in Lebanon at request of Lebanese government threatened by United Arab Republic infiltration

July 29, 1958, National Aeronautics and Space Administration established

Sept. 1958, closing of schools in which integration had been ordered in Arkansas and Virginia

Jan. 1, 1959, rebel forces loyal to Fidel Castro occupied Havana, forcing the abdication of President Fulgencio Batista

Jan. 3, 1959, Alaska proclaimed 49th state

Mar. 18, 1959, President signed act admitting Hawaii as the 50th state

May 7, 1960, United States admitted that U-2 plane shot down in U.S.S.R. had been on intelligence mission

May 16, 1960, collapse of East-West summit conference in Paris after U-2 incident

Sept. 20, 1960, opening of UN General Assembly in New York attended by world leaders

Jan. 3, 1961, President severed diplomatic relations with Cuba

ADDITIONAL DATA ON EISENHOWER

DWIGHT DAVID EISENHOWER

—was the first President born in Texas.

—was the fourteenth President who was a resident of a state other than his native state.

—was the first President to serve a constitutionally limited term (as provided by the Twenty-second Amendment).

—was the first President of 49 (and later 50) states.

—was the first President to serve with three congresses in which both chambers were controlled by an opposing party.

EISENHOWER CHANGED NAME

The Eisenhower family Bible records the birth of President Eisenhower's mother and father and his two brothers, Arthur and Edgar. The entry for a third son is "D. Dwight Eisenhower," the "D" an abbreviation for David. Later, David Dwight Eisenhower reversed his names.

EISENHOWER WON HIS WINGS

President Eisenhower learned to pilot an airplane when he was a lieutenant colonel in the Philippines on the staff of General Douglas MacArthur. His first solo flight was made on May 19, 1937. On November 30, 1939, he received pilot's license number 93,258. He was the first President licensed to pilot an airplane.

EISENHOWER RESIGNED AS GENERAL

On July 18, 1952, about a week after his nomination as the presidential candidate on the Republican ticket, General Eisenhower resigned as General of the Army, forfeiting an annual pension of $19,542 (later increased to $22,943), an office at government expense, and a staff of eight aides including a colonel, a lieutenant colonel, a major, and five enlisted men.

INCOMING STAFF ATTENDED CHURCH SERVICE

The first occasion on which an entire official family attended church services with an incoming President took place on January 20,

Courtesy of the Library of Congress

General Eisenhower gives orders to American paratroopers in England during World War II.

1953, when President-elect Eisenhower and his staff attended a preinaugural service at the National Presbyterian Church on Connecticut Avenue, Washington, D.C. The Reverend Edward L. R. Elson, pastor of the church, conducted the service.

EISENHOWER BECAME COMMUNICANT

President Eisenhower was the first President to take the complete action from baptism to confirmation and full communicant membership in a church subsequent to his inauguration.

The President was received into the membership of the National Presbyterian Church of Washington, D.C., by baptism and confession of faith before the session of the church early on Sunday morning February 1, 1953, and thereafter on the same day participated as a church member in the service of Holy Communion.

EISENHOWER APPOINTED GRANDSONS TO POSITIONS HELD BY THEIR GRANDFATHERS

John Foster Dulles of New York, who served as Secretary of State under President Eisenhower from January 21, 1953, until April 1959, was the grandson of John Watson Foster of Indiana, who served as Secretary of State under Benjamin Harrison from June 29, 1892, to February 22, 1893.

John Marshall Harlan, who took office on March 28, 1955, as an Associate Justice of the Supreme Court, was a grandson of John Marshall Harlan, who served in the same capacity from November 29, 1877, to October 14, 1911.

NEW CABINET POST CREATED

Legislation enacted March 12, 1953 (67 Stat. L. 631), effective April 11, 1953, provided for a new cabinet department, the Department of Health, Education, and Welfare. The first secretary was Oveta Culp Hobby of Houston, Tex. No provision was made to include the secretary in the presidential succession.

DIRECT QUOTATIONS PERMITTED

The first presidential press conference in which direct quotations were allowed to be used was attended by 161 reporters on December 16, 1953, at the White House. The 35-minute press conference with President Eisenhower was held from 10:31 A.M. to 11:05 A.M. The entire conference was printed in some newspapers, and it was also broadcast. The White House also released a tape recording for use on radio and television.

PRESIDENTIAL NEWS CONFERENCE TELEVISED

The first presidential news conference to be recorded by both newsreels and television was held January 19, 1955, when reporters questioned President Eisenhower about Communist China and Formosa (Taiwan), national security, the imprisonment of American fliers, trade with the Communists, and other subjects. The conference was filmed by Fox Movietone News and the National Broadcasting Company, which pooled the telecast with the other networks. The program was held until officially released.

PAY OF VICE PRESIDENT AND OTHER OFFICIALS INCREASED

On March 2, 1955, President Eisenhower signed the congressional-judicial pay bill granting federal employees the highest salaries ever paid to government officials. The pay of congressmen was increased from $15,000 to $22,500 a year, and the pay of the Vice President and Speaker of the House from $30,000 to $35,000.

The salary of the chief justice was raised from $25,500 to $35,000; associated justices, from $25,500 to $35,000; higher court judges, from $17,500 to $25,000; lower court judges, from $15,000 to $22,500; deputy attorney generals, from $17,500 to $21,000; and solicitor general, from $17,500 to $20,500 a year.

EISENHOWER TELECAST IN COLOR

President Dwight David Eisenhower was the first President telecast in color. He addressed the fortieth class reunion of the class of 1915 of the United States Military Academy at West Point, N.Y., on June 6, 1955. The film was shown June 7, 1955, from 11 A.M. to noon on NBC's *Home Show*.

EISENHOWER STRICKEN WITH HEART ATTACK AND OTHER ILLNESSES

The first presidential candidate to have suffered a heart attack was President Eisenhower. The attack occurred on September 24, 1955, while the President was on vacation at Denver, Colo. His first steps after the illness were taken on October 25, 1955, at the Fitzsimons Army Hospital at Denver. On February 29, 1956, he announced that he would be available for a second term.

During his administration, President Eisenhower was operated upon for ileitis and also suffered a very slight stroke.

PRESIDENTIAL INAUGURAL CEREMONIES ACT

The presidential inaugural ceremonies act was an act "to provide for the maintenance of public order and the protection of life and property in connection with the presidential inaugural ceremonies," passed by joint resolution on August 6, 1956 (70 Stat. L. 1049). The act empowered the inaugural committee to make arrangements and plans for the inauguration.

EISENHOWER SUBMERGED IN ATOMIC SUBMARINE

President Eisenhower was the first President to submerge in an atomic-powered submarine. He was aboard the *Seawolf* on September 26, 1957, when the submarine submerged five miles southwest of Brentons Reef, off Newport, R.I., and remained sixty feet below the surface for about 15 minutes. (Eisenhower had submerged twice before in a submarine—at Panama after World War I.)

PRESIDENT OF FIFTY STATES

Two new states were added to the Union while Eisenhower was President. On January 3, 1959, Alaska was proclaimed the 49th state, after the population voted 5 to 1 in favor of statehood. Hawaii became the 50th state on March 18, 1959, when the President signed an act of Congress admitting it to the Union.

Both the new states (the first since 1912) were separated by great distances from the other forty-eight. Hawaii had been proposed for statehood as early as 1937, but at that time the idea of a state so far away seemed impractical. Modern developments in air travel and communications, as well as the necessity of defending both territories during World War II, helped resolve these doubts.

EISENHOWER MAKES HOLE-IN-ONE

Former President Eisenhower made a hole-in-one on the 104-yard par-three thirteenth hole at the Seven Lake Country Club, Palm Springs, Calif., on February 6, 1968, in a foursome with Lee Freeman Gosden, George Allen, and Leigh Battson.

EISENHOWER'S COMMISSION RESTORED

Legislation was enacted by Congress on March 14, 1961, to restore the five-star rank of General of the Army to former President Dwight David Eisenhower, retroactive to December 20, 1944, the day he was first promoted to that rank. The legislation was approved by voice vote and signed by President John Fitzgerald Kennedy on March 24, 1961.

Eisenhower did not go on the military payroll, for he drew the annual presidential pension of $25,000, plus $50,000 for office expenses and staff.

FURTHER READING

Ambrose, Stephen E. *Eisenhower: Soldier, General of the Army, President-Elect, 1890–1952.* 1984.

———. *Eisenhower: The President.* 1984.

Brendon, Piers. *Ike: His Life and Times.* 1986.

Burke, Robert Frederick. *Dwight D. Eisenhower, Hero and Politician.* 1986.

Irving, David J. C. *The War Between the Generals.* 1981.

D'Este, Carlo. *Eisenhower: A Soldier's Life.* 2002.

Lyon, Peter. *Eisenhower: Portrait of the Hero.* 1974.

Parmet, Herbert S. *Eisenhower and the American Crusades.* 1972.

Courtesy of The Library of Congress

John Fitzgerald Kennedy

Date of birth—May 29, 1917

Place of birth—Brookline, Mass.

Education—Dexter School, Brookline, Mass.; Riverdale Country Day School, New York, N.Y.; Canterbury School, New Milford, Conn.; Choate School, Wallingford, Conn., graduated 1935; London School of Economics, summer 1935; Princeton University, 1935; Harvard College, Cambridge, Mass., bachelor of science degree in political science, cum laude, June 20, 1940

Religion—Roman Catholic

Ancestry—Irish

Career—Naval officer in World War II, journalist, U.S. congressman, U.S. senator, author

Political party—Democratic

State represented—Massachusetts

Term of office—Jan. 20, 1961–Nov. 22, 1963

Term served—2 years, 306 days

Administration—44th

Congresses—87th, 88th

Age at inauguration—43 years, 236 days

Lived after term—Died in office

Date of death—Nov. 22, 1963

Age at death—46 years, 177 days

Place of death—Dallas, Tex.

Burial place—Arlington National Cemetery, Va.

FAMILY

FATHER

Name—Joseph Patrick Kennedy

Date of birth—Sept. 6, 1888

Place of birth—East Boston, Mass.

Marriage—Rose Elizabeth Fitzgerald, Oct. 7, 1914

Occupation—Bank examiner, investment banker, financier, stock manipulator, wartime shipyard manager, liquor distributor, real estate executive, movie studio executive; chairman of Securities and Exchange Commission, U.S. ambassador to Great Britain

Date of death—Nov. 18, 1969

Place of death—Hyannis Port, Mass.

Age at death—81 years, 73 days

MOTHER

Name at birth—Rose Elizabeth Fitzgerald

Date of birth—July 22, 1890

Place of birth—Boston, Mass.

Marriage—Joseph Patrick Kennedy, Oct. 7, 1914

Date of death—January 22, 1995

SIBLINGS

John Fitzgerald Kennedy was the second child in a family of nine.

Children of Joseph Patrick Kennedy and Rose Fitzgerald Kennedy

Joseph Patrick Kennedy, Jr., b. July 25, 1915; d. August 12, 1944

John Fitzgerald Kennedy, b. May 29, 1917; d. Nov. 22, 1963

Rosemary Kennedy, b. Sept. 13, 1918; d. Jan. 7, 2005

Kathleen Kennedy, b. Feb. 20, 1920; d. May 13, 1948

Eunice Mary Kennedy, b. July 10, 1921

Patricia Kennedy, b. May 6, 1924, d. Sept. 17, 2006

Robert Francis Kennedy, b. Nov. 20, 1925; d. June 6, 1968

Jean Ann Kennedy, b. Feb. 20, 1928

Edward Moore Kennedy, b. February 22, 1932

MARRIAGE

Married—Jacqueline Lee Bouvier

Date of marriage—Sept. 12, 1953

Place of marriage—Newport, R.I.

Age of wife at marriage—24 years, 46 days

Age of husband at marriage—36 years, 106 days

Years married—10 years, 71 days

CHILDREN

—— Kennedy (daughter), b. 1956; d. 1956 (stillborn, unnamed; buried in Kennedy family plot in Holyhood Cemetary, Brookline, Mass.; reinterred Dec. 4, 1963, Arlington National Cemetary, Va.)

Caroline Bouvier Kennedy, b. Nov. 27, 1957, New York City; m. July 1986, Edwin Schlossberg, Hyannis Port, Mass.

John Fitzgerald Kennedy, Jr., b. Nov. 25, 1960, Washington, D.C.; m. Sept. 1995, Carolyn Bessette; d. July 16, 1999, off Massachusetts coast

Patrick Bouvier Kennedy, b. Aug. 7, 1963, Otis Air Force Base, Mass.; d. Aug. 9, 1963, Boston, Mass. (Buried in Kennedy family plot in Holyhood Cemetery, Brookline, Mass.; reinterred Dec. 4, 1963, Arlington National Cemetery, Va.)

THE PRESIDENT'S WIFE

Name at birth—Jacqueline Lee Bouvier

Date of birth—July 28, 1929

Place of birth—Southampton, N.Y.

Mother—Janet Norton Lee Bouvier

Father—John Vernou ("Jack") Bouvier III

Father's occupation—Stockbroker

Stepfather—Hugh D. Auchincloss (div. from Maria Chrapovitsky and Nina Gore Vidal; m. Janet Bouvier in 1942 after her divorce from Jack Bouvier)

Stepfather's occupation—Stockbroker

Education—Holton-Arms School, Washington, D.C., 1942–1944; Miss Porter's School, Farmington, Conn., 1944–1947; junior year at the Sorbonne, Paris, France; George Washington University, Washington, D.C., bachelor of arts degree, 1951

First marriage—John Fitzgerald Kennedy, Sept. 12, 1953, Newport, R.I.

Second marriage—Aristotle Socrates Onassis, Oct. 20, 1968, Skorpios, Greece

Children from first marriage—Daughter (stillborn), 1956; Caroline Bouvier Kennedy, b. Nov. 27, 1957; John Fitzgerald Kennedy, Jr., b. Nov. 25, 1960, d. July 16, 1999; Patrick Bouvier Kennedy, b. Aug. 7, 1963, d. Aug. 9, 1963

Children from second marriage—None

Occupation—Book editor, architectural and cultural preservationist

Date of death—May 19, 1994

Place of death—New York, N.Y.

Burial place—Arlington, Va.

Years younger than the President—12 years, 60 days

Years she survived the President—30 years, 178 days

THE FIRST LADY

When she was in the White House Jacqueline Bouvier Kennedy, a painter, art collector, and linguist, had a marked influence on American taste. After attending several fashionable private schools, she made her debut in Newport, R.I., and later studied at Vassar College, the Sorbonne in Paris, and George Washington University in Washington, D.C. For a year she was the Washington *Times-Herald's* "Inquiring Camera Girl"—a position involving both photography and reporting—and she also wrote feature stories for the paper.

As First Lady, Mrs. Kennedy restored the Interior of the White House with authentic art and furnishings of America's past, and when the restoration was complete she appeared on a nationwide televised tour of

Jacqueline Kennedy, wife of John F. Kennedy

In her later years, Jackie Kennedy Onassis became a book editor in New York, N.Y.

MRS. KENNEDY VOTED SPECIAL FUNDS

On December 11, 1963 (77 Stat. L. 348), Congress voted Mrs. Kennedy office space for one year and a staff of her own choice for the same period at a combined salary of not more than $50,000, as well as funds to defray funeral expenses.

In addition, she was entitled to receive the yearly pension of $10,000 granted to widows of Presidents for life or until they marry, and free mailing privileges for life. She and her children were also provided with Secret Service protection for a period of two years, later increased to four. In 1968, Secret Service protection for all Presidents' widows was extended until death or remarriage, and for Presidents' children until the age of 16.

PRESIDENT'S WIDOW REMARRIED

On October 20, 1968, Jacqueline Kennedy married Aristotle Socrates Onassis in a Greek Orthodox ceremony in the chapel of the Little Virgin, on the island of Skorpios, off the Greek coast. She was the second President's widow to remarry.

the White House, displaying and discussing its art treasures. This televised tour had an effect upon American decorating fashions. Mrs. Kennedy's hair and dress styles, too, were copied by many women.

Mrs. Kennedy also accompanied the President on official trips to Europe and to Latin America in 1961. On both tours she was acclaimed by her hosts for her charm and her command of foreign languages.

IMPORTANT DATES IN THE PRESIDENT'S LIFE

1923–1935, attended public and private schools in Massachusetts, New York, and Connecticut

Fall 1935, entered Princeton, but withdrew after one term owing to illness

May 29, 1938, at age of 21 received $1 million trust fund established by his father

1939, visited France, Poland, Russia, Turkey, Palestine, Balkans

June 20, 1940, graduated from Harvard College, B.S. cum laude

Sept. 1941, ensign, U.S. Navy

Aug. 2, 1943, his torpedo boat, PT-109, rammed by Japanese destroyer *Amagiri*

1944, awarded Purple Heart and Navy and Marine Corps Medal

Apr. 1945, honorable discharge from U.S. Navy

1945, newspaper correspondent (covered UN Conference at San Francisco, British elections, Potsdam meeting, etc.)

Nov. 5, 1946, elected to U.S. House of Representatives (from Massachusetts); reelected in 1948 and 1950

1951, visited Britain, France, Italy, Spain, West Germany, Yugoslavia

Nov. 4, 1952, elected to U.S. Senate (from Massachusetts); reelected in 1958

Oct. 21, 1954, spinal operation

Feb. 1955, second spinal operation

Aug. 17, 1956, defeated for Democratic vice presidential nomination by Estes Kefauver

May 6, 1957, awarded Pulitzer Prize for biography *Profiles in Courage*

July 13, 1960, nominated for presidency on first ballot at Democratic convention

Nov. 8, 1960, elected President, defeating Richard M. Nixon

Jan. 20, 1961, inaugurated President

Nov. 22, 1963, assassinated in Dallas, Tex.

ELECTIONS

THE ELECTION OF 1960

November 8, 1960

CANDIDATES

Democratic Party (33rd Convention)

July 11–15, 1960, Los Angeles Memorial Sports Arena and the Coliseum, Los Angeles, Calif.

P: John Fitzgerald Kennedy, Mass.
VP: Lyndon Baines Johnson, Tex.

Kennedy was nominated on the first ballot. Candidates for nomination and the votes they received:

John Fitzgerald Kennedy, Mass., 806
Lyndon Baines Johnson, Tex., 409
(William) Stuart Symington, Mo., 86
Adlai Ewing Stevenson, Ill., $79^1/_2$
Robert Baumle Meyner, N.J., 43
Hubert Horatio Humphrey, Minn., $41^1/_2$
George Armistead Smathers, Fla., 30
Ross Barnett, Miss., 23
Herschel Gellel Loveless, Iowa, $1^1/_2$
Edmund Gerald Brown, Calif., $^1/_2$
Orval Eugene Faubus, Ark., $^1/_2$
Albert Dean Rossellini, Wash., $^1/_2$
Total number of votes: 1,521
Number necessary for nomination: 761

Republican Party (27th Convention)

July 25–28, 1960, International Amphitheatre, Chicago, Ill.

P: Richard Milhous Nixon, Calif.
VP: Henry Cabot Lodge, Mass.
Total number of votes: 1,331
Number necessary for nomination: 666
Nixon was nominated by acclamation.

National States' Rights Party

Mar. 19–20, 1960, Dayton, Ohio

P: Orval Eugene Faubus, Ark.

Courtesy of The Library of Congress

The 1960 Democratic National Convention in Los Angeles

VP: John Geraerdt Crommelin, Ala.
Faubus was nominated against his wishes.

Socialist Labor Party

May 7–9, 1960, Henry Hudson Hotel, New York, N.Y.

P: Eric Hass, N.Y.
VP: Georgia Cozzini, Wis.

Prohibition Party

Sept. 1–3, 1959, Winona Lake, Ind.

P: Rutherford Losey Decker, Mo.
VP: Earle Harold Munn, Mich.

Socialist Workers Party

P: Farrell Dobbs, N.Y.
VP: Myra Tanner Weiss, N.Y.

Conservative Party of New Jersey

P: Joseph Bracken Lee, Utah
VP: Kent H. Courtney, La.
Barry Morris Goldwater of Arizona declined the nomination.

Conservative Party of Virginia

P: C. Benton Coiner, Va.

VP: Edward M. Silverman, Va.

Constitution Party (Texas)

P: Charles Loten Sullivan, Miss.
VP: Merritt Barton Curtis, Washington, D.C.

Constitution Party (Washington)

Apr. 20–21, 1960, Indianapolis, Ind.

P: Merritt Barton Curtis, Washington, D.C.
VP: B. N. Miller

Greenback Party

P: Whitney Hart Slocomb, Calif.
VP: Edward Kirby Meador, Mass.
  The candidates were selected by mail referendum.

Independent Afro-American Party

P: Clennon King, Ga.
VP: Reginald Carter, Ga.

Socialist Party

May 28–30, 1960, Washington, D.C.

No candidates named

Tax Cut Party (America First Party; American Party)

P: Lar Daly, Ill.
VP: Merritt Barton Curtis, Washington, D.C.

Theocratic Party

May 21, 1960, Fulton, Mo.

P: Homer Aubrey Tomlinson, N.Y.
VP: Raymond L. Teague, Alaska
  The Theocratic Party was organized March 21, 1960, at the Church of God in Christ, Fulton, Mo.

Vegetarian Party

P: Symon Gould, N.Y.
VP: Christopher Gian-Cursio, Fla.

1960 POPULAR VOTE

Democratic Party, 34,227,096
Republican Party, 34,107,646
National States' Rights Party, 214,195
Byrd unpledged Democrats (Miss.), 116,248
Socialist Party, 46,478
Prohibition Party, 45,919
Socialist Workers Party, 39,541

Courtesy of the John F. Kennedy Library

President Kennedy delivers his inaugural address.

Constitution Party (Tex.), 18,169
Conservative Party of New Jersey, 8,708
Conservative Party of Virginia, 4,204
Tax Cut Party (Mich.), 1,767
Independent Afro-American Party (Ala.), 1,485
Constitution Party (Wash.), 1,401
Industrial Government Party (Minn.), 962
Independent American Party (Mich.), 539
Write-in-votes, 1,064
Scattering, 963

1960 ELECTORAL VOTE

  There were 537 electoral votes from 50 states.

Kennedy received 56.43 percent (303 votes—22 states) as follows: Ala. 5 (of the 11 votes); Ark. 8; Conn. 8; Del. 3; Ga. 12; Hawaii 3; Ill. 27; La. 10; Md. 9; Mass. 16; Mich. 20; Minn. 11; Mo. 13; Nev. 3; N.J. 16; N.M. 4; N.Y. 45; N.C. 14; Pa. 32; R.I. 4; S.C. 8; Tex. 24; W.Va. 8.

Nixon received 40.78 percent (219 votes–26 states) as follows: Alaska 3; Ariz. 4; Calif. 32; Colo. 6; Fla. 10; Idaho 4; Ind. 13; Iowa 10; Kan. 8; Ky. 10; Me. 5; Mont. 4; Neb. 6; N.H. 4; N.D. 4; Ohio 25; Okla. 7 (of the 8 votes); Ore. 6; S.D. 4; Tenn. 11; Utah 4; Vt. 3; Va. 12; Wash. 9; Wis. 12; Wyo. 3.

Byrd received 2.79 percent (15 votes—2 states) as follows: Ala. 6 (of the 11 votes); Miss. 8; Okla. 1 (of the 8 votes).

INAUGURATION

January 20, 1961

At 12:51 p.m., on January 20, 1961, John Fitzgerald Kennedy took the oath of office as the thirty-fifth President of the United States on a platform erected on the newly renovated east front of the United States Capitol. The oath was administered by Chief Justice Earl Warren.

The ceremonies began at 12:20 P.M. with an invocation by Cardinal Richard Cushing of Boston. Prayers were also offered by Archbishop Iakovos, Primate of the Greek Orthodox Church of North and South America; the Reverend John Barclay of the Central Christian Church; and Rabbi Nelson Glueck, president of the Hebrew Union College, Cincinnati, Ohio. Marian Anderson sang "The Star-Spangled Banner," and Robert Frost recited one of his poems, "The Gift Outright." (Frost had also prepared prefatory verses for the occasion but was unable to read them because of the wind and sun-glare.)

The President's 1,355-word inaugural address was very well received. Among the more eloquent passages was the memorable appeal:

And so, my fellow Americans, ask not what your country can do for you—ask what you can do for your country. My fellow citizens of the world: ask not what America will do for you, but what together we can do for the freedom of man.

The day was cold (22°), clear, and sunny, with occasional blasts of icy wind. Washington was covered with eight inches of snow, which had fallen the previous night, but the inaugural route was cleared for the parade led by the President. More than 32,000 marchers participated. Included in the procession were an array of missiles and a truck bearing a duplicate of the PT boat that Kennedy had commanded in the Pacific during World War II, with eight surviving members of its 12-man crew.

Five inaugural balls were held in the evening at the Mayflower Hotel, the Statler Hotel, the Shoreham Hotel, the Sheraton Park Hotel, and the National Guard Armory.

More than 4,000 Secret Service agents, policemen, plainclothesmen, and troops were assigned to protect the incoming and outgoing Presidents.

THE VICE PRESIDENT

Name—Lyndon Baines Johnson (37th V.P.)

Political party—Democratic

State represented—Texas

Term of office—Jan. 20, 1961–Nov. 22, 1963

Age at inauguration—52 years, 146 days

Occupation after term—President of the United States

For further biographical information, see chapter on Lyndon Baines Johnson, 36th President, on page 444.

Courtesy of The Library of Congress

Lyndon Johnson, Vice President to John F. Kennedy

434

CABINET

January 20, 1961–Nov. 22, 1963

State—(David) Dean Rusk, N.Y., Jan. 21, 1961

Treasury—C. (Clarence) Douglas Dillon, N.J., Jan. 21, 1961

Defense—Robert Strange McNamara, Mich., Jan. 21, 1961

Attorney General—Robert Francis Kennedy, Mass., Jan. 21, 1961

Postmaster General—(James) Edward Day, Calif., Jan. 21, 1961; John A. Gronouski, Wis., Sept. 30, 1963

Interior—Stewart Lee Udall, Ariz., Jan. 21, 1961

Agriculture—Orville Lothrop Freeman, Minn., Jan. 21, 196

Commerce—Luther Hartwell Hodges, N.C., Jan. 21, 1961

Labor—Arthur Joseph Goldberg, Ill., Jan. 21, 1961; (William) Willard Wirtz, Ill., Sept. 25, 1962

Health, Education, and Welfare—Abraham Alexander Ribicoff, Conn., Jan. 21, 1961; Anthony Joseph Celebrezze, Ohio, July 31, 1962

CONGRESS

EIGHTY-SEVENTH CONGRESS

January 3, 1961–January 3, 1963

First session—Jan. 3, 1961–Sept. 27, 1961 (268 days)

Second session—Jan. 10, 1962–Oct. 13, 1962 (277 days)

Vice President—Lyndon Baines Johnson, Tex.

President pro tempore of the Senate —Carl Hayden, Ariz.

Secretary of the Senate—Felton McLellan Johnston, Miss.

Speaker of the House—Samuel Taliaferro Rayburn, Tex. (died Nov. 16, 1961); John William McCormack, Mass.

Clerk of the House—Ralph R. Roberts, Ind.

EIGHTY-EIGHTH CONGRESS

January 3, 1963–January 3, 1965

First session—Jan. 9, 1963–Dec. 30, 1963 (256 days))

Courtesy of The Library of Congress

President Kennedy with cabinet members

435

Second session—Jan. 7, 1964–Oct. 3, 1964 (270 days)

Vice President—Lyndon Baines Johnson, Tex., succeeded to the presidency on the death of John Fitzgerald Kennedy on Nov. 22, 1963.

President pro tempore of the Senate —Carl Hayden, Ariz.

Secretary of the Senate—Felton McLellan Johnston, Miss.

Speaker of the House—John William McCormack, Mass.

Clerk of the House—Ralph R. Roberts, Ind.

APPOINTMENTS TO THE SUPREME COURT

Associate Justices

Byron Raymond White, Colo., Apr. 16, 1962 (replaced Charles E. Whittaker)

Arthur Joseph Goldberg, Ill., Oct. 1, 1962 (replaced Felix Frankfurter)

IMPORTANT DATES IN THE PRESIDENCY

Jan. 25, 1961, first live television press conference by a President

Mar. 1, 1961, Peace Corps created by executive order

Mar. 6, 1961, President established a Committee on Equal Employment Opportunity, with Vice President Johnson as chairman

Mar. 29, 1961, residents of District of Columbia granted the right to vote for President by the twenty-third Amendment

Apr. 12, 1961, first man in space, Soviet Major Yuri Gagarin, orbited earth

Apr. 17–20, 1961, failure of Bay of Pigs invasion, Cuba

May 1961, "Freedom Riders"—integrated groups sponsored by the Congress on Racial Equality—boarded southbound buses to challenge segregation in interstate bus facilities

May 5, 1961, first U.S. astronaut, Commander Alan Bartlett Shepard, reached 116.5-mile altitude in space

May 5, 1961, minimum-wage bill raised hourly rate from $1.00 to $1.25 over a two-year period

June 3–4, 1961, President conferred with Premier Khrushchev in Vienna

June 5, 1961, Communist party ordered to register as agent of a foreign power by Supreme Court

July 25, 1961, United States warned that interference with West Berlin access would be considered an aggressive act

Aug. 5–17, 1961, charter of the Alliance for Progress, for Latin American economic aid and development, drafted and approved by Inter-American Economic and Social Council at Punta del Este, Uruguay

Aug. 13, 1961, East Germany built wall to close border between East and West Berlin

Sept. 4, 1961, President signed Foreign Assistance Act of 1961, setting up the Agency for International Development as the chief U.S. aid agency

Jan. 25, 1962, President called for reciprocal tariff reductions in new trade expansion act

Courtesy of the John F. Kennedy Library

Kennedy speaks in front of the Berlin Wall, June 26, 1963.

436

Feb. 7, 1962, almost total embargo placed on trade with Cuba

Feb. 20, 1962, first U.S. astronaut in orbit; Lieutenant Colonel John Herschel Glenn, Jr., orbited earth three times

Mar. 26, 1962, Supreme Court restricted rural domination of state legislatures

Apr. 11, 1962, President denounced rise in steel prices

Apr. 13, 1962, steel price rise rescinded

May 12, 1962, U.S. naval and ground forces ordered to Laos

May 28, 1962, worst one-day market slide since 1929, but sharp recovery on following day

June 25, 1962, Supreme Court declared public school prayers unconstitutional

Sept. 30–Oct. 1, 1962, segregationists staged fifteen-hour riot on University of Mississippi campus to prevent enrollment of African-American student; two persons killed

Oct. 22, 1962, President announced imposition of "quarantine" on Cuba because of construction by Russians of nuclear missile bases

Oct. 28, 1962, Soviet Premier Krushchev agreed to halt construction of missile bases in Cuba and to remove Soviet rockets under United Nations supervision

Nov. 20, 1962, blockade of Cuba lifted

Jan. 14, 1963, tax cuts to bolster economy recommended in President's State of the Union message

May 7, 1963, *Telstar II*, communications satellite, launched

June 11, 1963, Governor Wallace of Alabama, faced by National Guards troops, allowed two African-American students to enter University of Alabama

June 12, 1963, President's Advisory Council on the Arts established by executive order

June 17, 1963, Supreme Court decision declared required reading of Bible verses in public schools unconstitutional

June 19, 1963, strong civil rights legislation urged by President

June 20, 1963, agreement for a direct communication link with Soviet Union ("hot line") signed at Geneva

July 25, 1963, United States, Great Britain, and Soviet Union agreed on limited nuclear test treaty, effective Oct. 10

Aug. 16, 1963, United States and Canada completed agreement to arm Canadian air defense systems with nuclear warheads under United States control

Aug. 28, 1963, civil rights march on Washington, D.C., by 200,000 persons, mostly African-Americans

Sept. 24, 1963, Senate ratified treaty banning nuclear weapons tests in atmosphere, in outer space, and under water (but not underground tests)

Nov. 1, 1963, President Diem and brother Ngo Dinh Nhu assassinated in Vietnam coup

Nov. 22, 1963, President assassinated in Dallas, Tex.

ADDITIONAL DATA ON KENNEDY

JOHN FITZGERALD KENNEDY

—was the first President born in the twentieth century.

—was the first President who was a Roman Catholic.

—was the first President inaugurated on the new east front of the U.S. Capitol.

—was the first President survived by both his parents.

—was the first President whose inauguration was celebrated with five inaugural balls.

—was the first President whose inaugural parade was shown on color television.

—was the first President to hold a press conference on live television.

—was the first President to have won the Pulitzer Prize.

—was the first President who had served in the U.S. Navy.

—was the second President buried in Arlington National Cemetery, Va.

—was the fourth President assassinated.

—was the eighth President to die in office.

FIFTH HARVARD COLLEGE GRADUATE PRESIDENT

John Fitzgerald Kennedy was the fifth President of the United States who was a graduate of Harvard College (June 20, 1940). Other chief executives of the United States who were Harvard alumni were John Adams (July 16, 1755), John Quincy Adams (July 18, 1787), Theodore Roosevelt (June 30, 1880), and Franklin Delano Roosevelt (June 24, 1903).

Rutherford Birchard Hayes, who graduated from Kenyon College, received his law degree in 1845 from the Harvard Law School. George Walker Bush, who graduated from Yale College, received his M.B.A. degree in 1975 from Harvard.

KENNEDY, AUTHOR AND PULITZER PRIZE WINNER

John Fitzgerald Kennedy achieved distinction as a commentator on public affairs with his book *Why England Slept,* an account of England's slowness to rearm in the 1930s in the face of growing Nazi aggressiveness. It was published in 1940, when Kennedy was twenty-three years old, and was regarded as a thoughtful study.

In 1945, working as a newspaper correspondent, he covered the UN Conference in San Francisco for the Chicago *Herald-American* and the Potsdam Conference and the British elections for International News Service.

While convalescing in a hospital from a spinal operation, Kennedy wrote *Profiles in Courage,* which was published in 1956 and for which he received the Pulitzer Prize for biography on May 6, 1957. It is a biographical work chronicling decisive moments in the lives of John Quincy Adams, Daniel Webster, Sam Houston, George Norris, and other political figures.

Many of Kennedy's speeches have been printed in collections—*The Strategy of Peace, To Turn the Tide,* etc.

KENNEDY A HERO IN NAVAL ACTION

John Fitzgerald Kennedy, who enlisted in the U.S. Navy in September 1941, assumed command on April 25, 1943, of PT-109, a gas-

Courtesy of the National Archive and Records Administration

Kennedy debates Richard Nixon during the 1960 presidential race.

oline-engine torpedo boat, 80 feet long with a beam of 20 feet 8 inches. The 38-ton boat had a draft of 5 feet, carried a complement of 17 men, and made the speed of 41 knots. Its armament consisted of four 21-inch torpedoes.

While attached to a convoy in the Blackett Strait in the Solomon Islands, the PT boat was rammed and cut in half by the Japanese destroyer *Amagiri* on August 2, 1943.

For his heroism in rescuing members of his crew, he was presented with the Navy and Marine Corps Medal in 1944 by Captain Frederick L. Conklin, the citation having been signed by Admiral William Frederick Halsey. Another version of the citation, signed by Secretary of the Navy James V. Forrestal, said:

> For extremely heroic conduct as Commanding Officer of Motor Torpedo Boat 109 following the collision and sinking of that vessel in the Pacific War Theater on August 1–2, 1943. Unmindful of personal danger, Lieutenant (then Lieutenant, Junior Grade) Kennedy unhesitatingly braved the difficulties and hazards of darkness to direct rescue operations, swimming many hours to secure aid and food after he had succeeded in getting his crew ashore. His outstanding courage, endurance and leadership contributed to the saving of several lives and were in keeping with the highest traditions of the United States Naval Service.

A youngster in Ashland, Wis., asked Kennedy how he had become a war hero. He replied, "It was involuntary; they sank my boat."

KENNEDY-NIXON DEBATES

The first presidential candidate debate series on television was the Nixon-Kennedy debate series during the 1960 presidential campaign. It gave the voting public a closer look at the two major candidates and the issues. The first of four debates was held September 26, 1960, in a Chicago studio; the second, October 7, 1960, in a Washington, D.C. studio; the third, October 13, 1960 (Kennedy in New York City, Nixon in Hollywood, Calif.); and the fourth, October 21, 1960, in a New York studio.

THE YOUNGEST ELECTED PRESIDENT

John Fitzgerald Kennedy was the youngest presidential nominee elected, and the youngest man elected to the office, but he was not the youngest President.

Kennedy was 43 years and 236 days old when he was inaugurated President. He was 2 years and 257 days younger than Theodore Roosevelt was when he was inaugurated for his second term, but Roosevelt was 279 days younger when he became President through succession.

Theodore Roosevelt, who was inaugurated Vice President of the United States, succeeded to the presidency on September 14, 1901, after the assassination of President William McKinley. Roosevelt was 42 years and 322 days old when he became President. He became a candidate for a second term and was sworn in March 4, 1905, when he was 46 years and 12 days old.

HOUSE SPEAKER ADMINISTERED OATH

The first Speaker of the House of Representatives to administer the oath of office to a Vice President of the United States was Sam Rayburn, who on January 20, 1961, administered the oath of office to Vice President Lyndon Baines Johnson.

NEW CONGRESSIONAL APPORTIONMENT

A new apportionment of the 435 seats in the House of Representatives was made on the basis of the decennial census of the population (1960).

In the new apportionment, 9 states gained a total of 19 seats: Arizona, Hawaii, Maryland, Michigan, New Jersey, Ohio, and Texas each gained 1 seat; Florida gained 4 seats; California gained 8 seats. Sixteen states lost a total of 21 seats: Alabama, Illinois, Iowa, Kansas, Kentucky, Maine, Minnesota, Mississippi, Missouri, Nebraska, North Carolina, and West Virginia each lost 1 seat; Arkansas, Massachusetts, and New York each lost 2 seats; Pennsylvania lost 3 seats.

The resulting apportionment was as follows: Alabama 8, Alaska 1, Arizona 3, Arkansas 4, California 38, Colorado 4, Connecticut 6, Delaware 1, Florida 12, Georgia 10, Hawaii 2, Idaho 2, Illinois 24, Indiana 11, Iowa 7, Kansas 5, Kentucky 7, Louisiana 8, Maine 2, Maryland 8, Massachusetts 12, Michigan 19, Minnesota 8, Mississippi 5, Missouri 10, Montana 2, Nebraska 3, Nevada 1, New Hampshire 2, New Jersey 15, New Mexico 2, New York 41, North Carolina 11, North Dakota 2, Ohio 24, Oklahoma 6, Oregon 4, Pennsylvania 27, Rhode Island 2, South Carolina 6, South Dakota 2, Tennessee 9, Texas 23, Utah 2, Vermont 1, Virginia 10, Washington 7, West Virginia 5, Wisconsin 10, Wyoming 1.

TWENTY-THIRD AMENDMENT RATIFIED

The Twenty-third Amendment, granting the citizens of the District of Columbia the right to vote in presidential elections, was enacted by the 86th Congress and sent to the states for ratification on June 16, 1960. The first state to ratify was Hawaii, on June 23, 1960. The required number of votes (38) was reached on March 29, 1961, when New Hampshire, Kansas, and Ohio ratified. The Secretary of State formally declared the amendment a part of the Constitution on April 3, 1961.

Section 1 of the amendment follows:

The District constituting the seat of Government of the United States shall appoint in such manner as the Congress may direct:

A number of electors of President and Vice President equal to the whole number of Senators and Representatives in Congress to which the District would be entitled if it were a State, but in no event more than the least populous State; they shall be in addition to those appointed by the States, but they shall be considered, for the purpose of the election of President and Vice President, to be electors appointed by a State; and they shall meet in the District and perform such duties as provided by the twelfth article of amendment.

The first primary election was held May 5, 1964.

BROTHER APPOINTED TO CABINET

President Kennedy was the first President to appoint a brother to cabinet rank. On January 21, 1961, Robert Francis Kennedy was sworn in as Attorney General of the United States.

STATE DINNER AT MOUNT VERNON

The first state dinner held at Mount Vernon was tendered to Mohammed Ayub Khan, the President of Pakistan, on July 11, 1961, by President Kennedy. Mount Vernon, George Washington's Virginia home, is an historic site maintained by the Mount Vernon Ladies' Association of the Union. (A luncheon—not a state dinner—was held there on October 19, 1926, for Queen Marie of Rumania.)

Although state dinners are usually held at the White House, this was not the first time one had been held at another place. During the Truman administration, when the White House was undergoing renovation, several official state dinners were held at the Carlton Hotel, Washington, D.C.

BROTHER SERVED IN SENATE

President Kennedy was the first President to have a brother in the Senate. His brother Edward Moore Kennedy was elected November 6, 1962, to fill the unexpired senatorial term of the President. (After the election of John Fitzgerald Kennedy to the presidency in 1960, Benjamin A. Smith II was appointed to occupy his senatorial seat on an interim basis until the 1962 election.) Edward Moore Kennedy was reelected November 3, 1964.

Another brother, Robert Francis Kennedy, was elected to the U.S. Senate from New York in 1964 and served from January 4, 1965, to June 6, 1968, when he was assassinated while campaigning for the Democratic nomination for President.

WHITE HOUSE PATRONAGE OF THE ARTS

In their few years in the White House both President Kennedy and his wife did much to foster public interest in literature and the arts. Their own interest was shown at the very outset by the participation of the poet Robert Frost in the inaugural services. At the request of the President and Mrs. Kennedy a company of actors performed at the White House in scenes from Shakespeare, and the cellist Pablo Casals and other musicians performed string quartets at the White House on several occasions. The published list of invited guests at the White House, including many distinguished writers, artists, and musicians, betokened the same interest in cultural matters. It was largely through the interest shown by President and Mrs. Kennedy that the French authorities consented to lend Leonardo da Vinci's "Mona Lisa," one of the treasures of the Louvre, for display in Washington, D.C., and New York City. The President's cultural interest was shown at the governmental level by his appointment of August Heckscher as Special Consultant on the Arts and by the executive order establishing the President's Advisory Council on the Arts, comprising heads of federal departments and agencies concerned with the arts, as well as 30 private citizens.

PRESIDENTIAL MEDAL OF FREEDOM

On February 22, 1963, President Kennedy changed the name of the Medal of Freedom, originated by President Truman in 1945, to the Presidential Medal of Freedom and announced that it would be conferred annually as the highest civilian honor on persons "who have contributed to the quality of American life." The medal, redesigned by President and Mrs. Kennedy, is a white star with gold eagles and 13 silver stars on a blue field. The names of the 29 Americans and two foreigners (Jean Monnet and Pablo Casals) who were to receive the medal in 1963 were announced by President Kennedy on July 4, 1963, but he did not live to make the presentations. (The medals were presented by President Johnson on December 6, 1963. President Johnson also made two posthumous awards, one to the late President John Fitzgerald Kennedy and the other to the late Pope John XXIII.)

KENNEDY WITNESSED POLARIS FIRING

The first President to witness the firing of a Polaris missile was President John Fitzgerald Kennedy. On November 16, 1963, aboard the U.S.S. *Observation Island,* 32 miles off Cape Canaveral, Fla., Kennedy watched the firing from the submerged nuclear submarine, the U.S.S. *Andrew Jackson.* The Polaris A-2 missile broke through the surface of the water and headed on a 1,500 mile flight into the Caribbean.

KENNEDY ASSASSINATED

On November 22, 1963, while riding in an automobile procession from Love Field to the Trade Mart, Dallas, Tex., along streets lined with cheering spectators, President Kennedy was struck in the back of the right shoulder near the neck and in the back of the head by two rifle shots, apparently fired from a sixth-floor window in a building overlooking the route of the procession. The wounds caused immediate unconsciousness and despite the efforts of a team of surgeons at Parkland Memorial Hospital, he was pronounced dead within less than an hour.

Another shot, believed to be the second of the three that were fired, severely wounded the Governor of Texas, John Bowden Connally, Jr., who was sitting on a jump seat directly in front of the President. Mrs. Kennedy, Mrs. Connally, and a Secret Service Agent were also in the automobile, in addition to the chauffeur. Vice President and Mrs. Johnson were in another automobile in the motorcade.

The accused assassin of the President, Lee Harvey Oswald, was arrested after he shot and killed a Dallas police officer, J. D. Tippitt. Two days later, Oswald himself was shot and killed in the Dallas Police Station by Jack Ruby (Rubenstein), a local nightclub owner.

The Warren Commission, a seven-man panel headed by the Chief Justice, conducted an investigation of the assassination of the President immediately after the event and concluded that Oswald had acted alone and was probably unstable. However, later investigations, among them an inquiry by a Select Committee of the House of Representatives, raised the possibility of a second gunman. Various theories of conspiracy have been propounded, but because of the paucity of hard evidence in the case and the plethora of bizarre or suspicious circumstances, no single account of the Kennedy assassination has gained wide acceptance.

Courtesy of the Library of Congress

President and Mrs. Kennedy in Dallas, Texas, shortly before his assassination

441

KENNEDY COFFIN DISPLAYED IN CAPITOL ROTUNDA

John Fitzgerald Kennedy was the sixth President to lie in state in the Capitol Rotunda. The others were Lincoln, Garfield, McKinley, Harding, and Taft. The black-draped catafalque used to support the coffin of Abraham Lincoln was used for the Kennedy coffin.

THE GREATEST SIMULTANEOUS EXPERIENCE IN AMERICAN HISTORY

The assassination of President Kennedy and the events that followed until his interment in Arlington Cemetery have been described by a historian of the assassination as "the greatest simultaneous experience in American history." The events of the four days were witnessed on television by what was probably the largest mass audience in history, and the television coverage was extraordinarily full, including the reproduction of a film taken by a bystander showing the fatally wounded President slump into his wife's lap, views of the automobiles in the procession racing to the hospital, the swearing in of President Johnson in the presidential plane, the removal of the late President's coffin from the plane in Washington, the lying in state in the Capitol Rotunda, and the funeral services, procession, and burial at Arlington.

FUNERAL AND BURIAL

One of the greatest assemblages of foreign dignitaries to attend funeral services in the United States met at St. Matthew's Cathedral, Washington, D.C., on November 25, 1963, to pay their respects at the funeral of President Kennedy.

The President was interred at Arlington National Cemetery with full military honors as befitted a war hero and commander in chief of the United States Armed Forces. (William Howard Taft had been the only President previously buried in this national shrine.)

The foreign dignitaries who attended the funeral represented 102 countries. Among the many distinguished mourners were Prince Philip, representing Queen Elizabeth of Great Britain; Frederika, Queen of the Hellenes; Crown Princess Beatrix of The Netherlands; Baudouin I, King of the Belgians; Haile Selassie I, Emperor of Ethiopia; President Charles de Gaulle of France; and President Eamon de Valera of Ireland. Other dignitaries who attended were from the United Nations, the European Coal and Steel Community, the European Atomic Energy Commission, and the Organization of American States.

In the funeral procession, precedence was established by alphabetical order of countries.

THE KENNEDY MEMORIAL LIBRARY

The John Fitzgerald Kennedy Library, which houses the President's papers and memorabilia, is located in Boston near the University of Massachusetts campus. As President, Kennedy had planned to donate his papers to a memorial library; two weeks after his assassination a private corporation was formed to develop and carry out this idea. Contributions from the American people provided some of the funding for the project. A building designed by I. M. Pei was constructed to house the museum, two auditoriums, and the collection of research materials. The Kennedy Library was dedicated on October 20, 1979. It is now administered by the

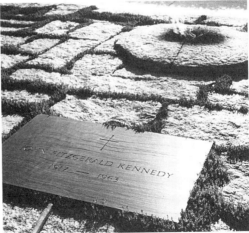

Courtesy of The Library of Congress

The eternal flame commemorating John F. Kennedy at Arlington National Cemetery, Virginia

National Archives and Records Service. In addition to many items relating to Kennedy's years in the White House, his sailing sloop— the *Victura*—and a collection of materials about Ernest Hemingway, one of the President's favorite authors, are on display.

CENTER FOR THE PERFORMING ARTS

A joint resolution of Congress, enacted January 23, 1964 (78 Stat. L. 4), renamed the National Cultural Center the John F. Kennedy Center for the Performing Arts.

CARRIER NAMED FOR KENNEDY

A contract for building an attack aircraft carrier to be named for President Kennedy was awarded in April 1964 to the Newport News Shipbuilding and Dry Dock Company, Newport News, Va. The U.S.S. *John F. Kennedy* (CVA-67) was laid down on October 22, 1964. On May 27, 1967, she was christened by President Kennedy's daughter, Caroline Kennedy, at Newport News and was launched into the James River. The carrier, which was 1,057.5 feet long and had an 83,000-ton displacement, was commissioned September 7, 1968. The complement consisted of 2,600 enlisted men and 120 officers. The first captain was Earl Preston Yates.

PRESIDENT'S BROTHER ASSASSINATED

On June 5, 1968, Senator Robert Francis Kennedy was shot by Sirhan Bishara Sirhan at the Ambassador Hotel, Los Angeles, Calif. He died the following day, June 6, 1968.

FURTHER READING

Beschloss, Michael. *The Crisis Years: Kennedy and Khrushchev, 1960–1963.* 1991.

Dallek, Robert: *John F. Kennedy: An Unfinished Life, 1917-1963.* 2003.

Fairlie, Henry. *The Kennedy Promise.* 1973.

Gigho, James N. *The Presidency of John F. Kennedy.* 1991.

Hamilton, Nigel. *JFK: Reckless Youth.* 1992.

Kaiser, David E. *American Tragedy: Kennedy, Johnson, and the Origins of the Vietnam War.* 2000.

Manchester, William R. *The Death of a President.* 1967.

Reeves, Richard. *President Kennedy: Profile of Power.* 1993.

Schlesinger, Arthur M. *A Thousand Days.* 1965.

Sorenson, Theodore C. *Kennedy.* 1965.

White, Theodore H. *The Making of the President 1960.* 1961.

Wills, Garry. *The Kennedy Imprisonment.* 1982.

Courtesy of The Library of Congress

Lyndon Baines Johnson

Date of birth—Aug. 27, 1908

Place of birth—Near Stonewall, Tex.

Education—Tutored by mother; attended public schools, Stonewall, Tex., and Johnson City, Tex.; Johnson City High School, graduated 1924; Southwest Texas State College, San Marcos, Tex., bachelor of science degree, Aug. 19, 1930; Georgetown University Law School, 1934–1935

Religion—Disciples of Christ (International Convention of Christian Churches)

Ancestry—English, Scottish, German

Career—Teacher, secretary to U.S. congressman, state director of National Youth Administration, Navy aviation officer in World War II, U.S. congressman, U.S. senator, Vice President, rancher

Political party—Democratic

State represented—Texas

Term of office—Nov. 22, 1963–Jan. 20, 1969 (Johnson succeeded to the presidency on the death of John Fitzgerald Kennedy.)

Term served—5 years, 59 days

Administration—44th, 45th

Congresses—88th, 89th, 90th

Age at inauguration—55 years, 87 days

Lived after term—4 years, 2 days

Occupation after term—Ranching, writing

Date of death—Jan. 22, 1973

Age at death—64 years, 148 days

Place of death—San Antonio, Tex.

Burial place—Stonewall, Tex.

FAMILY

FATHER

Name—Sam Ealy Johnson, Jr.

Date of birth—Oct. 11, 1877

Place of birth—Buda, Tex.

Marriage—Rebekah Baines, Aug. 20, 1907, Fredericksburg, Tex.

Occupation—Farmer, barber, teacher, cotton planter, realtor, laborer; Texas state legislator, magistrate, justice of the peace

Date of death—Oct. 22, 1937

Place of death—Austin, Tex.

Age at death—60 years, 11 days

MOTHER

Name at birth—Rebekah Baines

Date of birth—June 26, 1881

Place of birth—McKinney, Tex.

Marriage—Sam Ealy Johnson, Jr., Aug. 20, 1907, Fredericksburg, Tex.

Date of death—Sept. 12, 1958

Place of death—Austin, Tex.

Age at death—77 years, 78 days

SIBLINGS

Lyndon Baines Johnson was the oldest of five children, two boys and three girls

Children of Sam Ealy Johnson, Jr., and Rebekah Baines Johnson

Lyndon Baines Johnson, b. Aug. 27, 1908; d. Jan. 22, 1973

Rebekah Luruth Johnson, b. Sept. 12, 1910; d. Feb. 4, 1978

Josefa Hermine Johnson, b. May 16, 1912; d. Dec. 25, 1961

Sam Houston Johnson, b. Jan. 31, 1914; d. Dec. 11, 1978

Lucia Huffman Johnson, b. June 20, 1916; d. Nov. 19, 1997

MARRIAGE

Married—Claudia Alta ("Lady Bird") Taylor

Date of marriage—Nov. 17, 1934

Place of marriage—San Antonio, Tex.

Age of wife at marriage—21 years, 330 days

Age of husband at marriage—26 years, 82 days

Years married—39 years, 66 days

CHILDREN

Lynda Bird Johnson, b. Mar. 19, 1944, Washington, D.C.; m. Charles S. Robb, Dec. 9, 1967, at the White House, Washington, D.C.

Luci (originally Lucy) Baines Johnson, b. July 2, 1947, Washington, D.C.; m. Patrick John Nugent, Aug. 6, 1966, Washington, D.C. (annulled 1979); m. Ian Turpin, 1984

THE PRESIDENT'S WIFE

Name at birth—Claudia Alta ("Lady Bird") Taylor

Date of birth—Dec. 22, 1912

Place of birth—Karnack, Tex.

Mother—Minnie Lee Pattillo Taylor

Father—Thomas Jefferson Taylor

Father's occupation—Planter, merchant

Education—local schools, Karnack and Jefferson, Tex.; Marshall High School, Marshall, Tex.; St. Mary's Episcopal School for Girls, Dallas, Tex.; University of Texas, Austin, bachelor of arts degree, 1933; journalism degree, 1934

Marriage—Lyndon Baines Johnson, Nov. 17, 1934, San Antonio, Tex.

Children—Lynda Bird Johnson, b. Mar. 19, 1944; Luci (originally Lucy) Baines Johnson, b. July 2, 1947

Occupation—Owner of radio and television broadcasting companies; manager of family ranch; helped run husband's congressional offices

Date of death—July 11, 2007

Age at death—94 years, 201 days

Place of death—West Lake Hills, Tex.

Burial place—Stonewall, Texas

Years younger than the President—4 years, 107 days

Years she survived the President—34 years, 170 days

Courtesy of the Library of Congress

Claudia "Lady Bird" Johnson, wife of Lyndon Johnson

THE FIRST LADY

Lady Bird Johnson brought to the White House a rich background in political and business activities. A well-known figure in the public and social life of the capital, she had aided her husband in his campaigns for office, helped manage their ranch, and run a newspaper and broadcasting operation.

As First Lady, Mrs. Johnson was particularly identified with the promotion of highway and civic beautification projects around the country.

FIRST WIFE TO HOLD BIBLE AT INAUGURATION

In January 1965, Lady Bird Johnson became the first President's wife to hold the Bible on which her husband took the oath of office. It was the same Bible on which he had taken his oath as Vice President of the United States. It had been given to the Johnsons by Rebekah Baines Johnson and was inscribed "To Lyndon and Lady Bird. Love, Mother."

IMPORTANT DATES IN THE PRESIDENT'S LIFE

Courtesy of The Library of Congress

Lyndon Johnson as Senate Majority Leader

1913, moved to Johnson City, Tex.

1924, graduated from Johnson City High School

1924–1926, worked as laborer in California and Texas

1926–1930, worked his way through college at a variety of jobs, including teaching grade school in Cotulla, Tex.

Aug. 19, 1930, graduated from Southwest Texas State Teachers College, San Marcos, with B.S. degree

1930–1931, taught public speaking and debate at Sam Houston High School, Houston, Tex.

1932–1935, secretary to Representative Richard Mifflin Kleberg (Democrat, Texas)

1935–1937, state director of National Youth Administration for Texas

Apr. 10, 1937, won special election for seat in U.S. House of Representatives to fill vacancy caused by death of James Paul Buchanan (Democrat, Texas); reelected five times and served until Dec. 31, 1948

June 21, 1940, special duty officer, naval intelligence, U.S. Naval Reserve

June 28, 1941, defeated in special election for U.S. Senate

Dec. 1941, obtained consent of the House of Representatives for a leave of absence to enter service in U.S. Naval Reserve (first member of Congress in World War II to enter active duty); commissioned lieutenant commander

July 1942, received Silver Star for gallantry under fire when patrol bomber in which he was flying was attacked by Japanese

June 1, 1948, commissioned commander, U.S.N.R.

Nov. 2, 1948, elected to U.S. Senate (from Texas); reelected in 1954 and 1960

Jan. 2, 1951, Democratic whip (served until 1953)

Jan. 3, 1953, Democratic leader (served until 1961)

July 2, 1955, suffered heart attack

July 13, 1960, nominated for the presidency by Speaker Sam Rayburn at Democratic convention; received 409 votes; defeated by John F. Kennedy

July 14, 1960, nominated for vice presidency by unanimous vote

Nov. 8, 1960, elected Vice President of the United States

Jan. 3, 1961, sworn in as senator from Texas for third term; resigned three minutes after being sworn in

Jan. 20, 1961–Nov. 22, 1963, Vice President under John F. Kennedy

Nov. 22, 1963, in presidential motorcade in Dallas, Tex., at time of President Kennedy's assassination; sworn in as President of the United States after President Kennedy's death

Aug. 24, 1964, nominated for President on Democratic ticket

Nov. 3, 1964, elected President of the United States

Jan. 20, 1965–Jan. 20, 1969, President (second term)

Mar. 31, 1968, President informed the nation in a televised speech that he would not accept the nomination of the Democratic Party for President; decision influenced by country's split over Vietnam war, and strong second-place showing by Senator Eugene McCarthy (Democrat, Minn.), opponent of the war, in the crucial New Hampshire presidential primary

Jan. 20, 1969, first day in 34 years as a private citizen

Apr. 8, 1972, heart attack, Charlottesville, Va.

ELECTIONS

THE ELECTION OF 1964

November 3, 1964

CANDIDATES

Democratic Party (34th Convention)

Aug. 24–26, 1964, Convention Hall, Atlantic City, N.J.

P: Lyndon Baines Johnson, Tex.
VP: Hubert Horatio Humphrey, Minn.

Johnson was nominated unanimously on the first ballot. Humphrey was nominated unanimously for the vice presidency on the first ballot.

Republican Party (28th Convention)

July 13–16, 1964, Grand National Livestock Pavilion (Cow Palace), San Francisco, Calif.

P: Barry Morris Goldwater, Ariz.
VP: William Edward Miller, N.Y.

Goldwater was nominated on the first ballot. Candidates for nomination and the votes they received:
Barry Morris Goldwater, Ariz., 883
William Warren Scranton, Pa., 214
Nelson Aldrich Rockefeller, N.Y., 114
George Wilcken Romney, Mich., 41
Margaret Chase Smith, Me., 27
Walter Henry Judd, Minn., 22
Hiram Leong Fong, Hawaii, 5
Henry Cabot Lodge, Mass., 2
Total number of votes: 1,308
Number necessary for nomination: 655
Nomination made unanimous

Liberal Party of New York State

P: Lyndon Baines Johnson, Tex.
VP: Hubert Horatio Humphrey, Minn.

The nominations were made Sept. 1, 1964, by the State Committee meeting in New York City.

Socialist Party

May 2–3, 1964, Henry Hudson Hotel, New York, N.Y.

P: Eric Hass, N.Y.
VP: Henning A. Blomen, Mass.

Prohibition Party

Aug. 26–27, 1964, Pick Congress Hotel, Chicago, Ill.

P: Earle Harold Munn, Mich.
VP: Mark Shaw, Mass.

Socialist Workers Party

Dec. 28, 1963, New York, N.Y.

P: Clifton De Berry, N.Y.
VP: Edward Shaw, N.Y.

National States' Rights Party

Mar. 2, 1964, Louisville, Ky.

P: John Kasper, Tenn.
VP: J.B. Stoner, Ga.

Constitution Party

July 23–25, 1964, Houston, Tex.

P: Joseph B. Lightburn, W.Va.
VP: Theodore C. Billings, Colo.

Independent States' Rights Party

Oct. 15, 1964, Richmond, Va.

P: Thomas Coleman Andrews, Va.
VP: Thomas H. Werdel, Calif.

Theocratic Party

May 21, 1964, Fulton, Mo.

P: Homer Aubrey Tomlinson, N.Y.

VP: William R. Rogers, Mo.

Universal Party

Aug. 8, 1964, Oakland, Calif.

P: Kirby James Hensley, Calif.

VP: John O. Hopkins, Iowa

1964 POPULAR VOTE

Democratic Party, 42,825,463

Republican Party, 27,175,770

Liberal Party of New York State, 342,432

Socialist Labor Party, 46,642

Prohibition Party, 23,267

Socialist Workers Party, 22,249

National States' Rights Party, 6,957

Blank and void, 199,675

Others, 20,692

Scattering, 9,696

Johnson received 61.05 percent of the popular vote, the highest percentage known to have been won by any president.

1964 ELECTORAL VOTE

There were 538 electoral votes from the 50 states and the District of Columbia.

Johnson received 90.34 percent (486 votes—44 states and D.C.) as follows: Alaska 3; Ark. 6; Calif. 40; Colo. 6; Conn. 8; Del. 3; D.C. 3; Fla. 14; Hawaii 4; Idaho 4; Ill. 26; Ind. 13; Iowa 9; Kan. 7; Ky. 9; Me. 4; Md. 10; Mass. 14; Mich. 21; Minn. 10; Mo. 12; Mont. 4; Neb. 5; Nev. 3; N.H. 4; N.J. 17; N.M. 4; N.Y. 43; N.C. 13; N.D. 4; Ohio 26; Okla. 8; Ore. 6; Pa. 29; R.I. 4; S.D. 4; Tenn. 11; Tex. 25; Utah 4; Vt. 3; Va. 12; Wash. 9; W.Va. 7; Wis. 12; Wyo. 3.

Goldwater received 9.66 percent (52 votes—6 states) as follows: Ala. 10; Ariz. 5; Ga. 12; La. 10; Miss. 7; S.C. 8.

INAUGURATIONS

FIRST TERM

November 22, 1963

Lyndon Baines Johnson took the oath of office as President of the United States on November 22, 1963. The oath was administered by Judge Sarah Tilghman Hughes, District Judge of the North District of Texas, aboard "Air Force One" at Love Field, Dallas, Tex. Mrs. Johnson, Mrs. Kennedy, and 25 others witnessed the ceremony.

SECOND TERM

January 20, 1965

The weather was clear and cold on inauguration day, Wednesday, January 20, 1965, and the bright sun made the temperature rise from 38° to 45° by 3 P.M. The oaths of office were administered to Vice President Hubert Horatio Humphrey by Speaker John William McCormack and to President Lyndon Baines Johnson by Chief Justice Earl Warren. The President's 1,200-word speech, lasting 22 minutes, was spoken softly and

Courtesy of The Library of Congress

Johnson takes the oath of office following the assassination of President Kennedy.

deliberately, drawing applause eleven times. A bullet-proof glass enclosure protected the President.

The Congressional Inaugural Committee sponsored a luncheon in the old Supreme Court chamber in the Capitol. The guests sat at ten circular tables.

The President led the motorcade from the Capitol down Pennsylvania Avenue to the White House, where he and his family and guests watched the 52 bands, 15,000 marchers, and numerous floats pass by until 5:08 P.M. About a million persons lined the streets to watch the two-and-a-half-hour inaugural parade.

At 9:18 P.M., wearing black tie, the President left the White House to attend the five inaugural balls at the Mayflower Hotel, Statler-Hilton Hotel, National Guard Armory, Shoreham Hotel, and Sheraton Park Hotel. (Twenty-eight thousand persons paid twenty-five dollars each for admission to the balls.) The President was accompanied by his wife and the Vice President and his wife. He returned to the White House at 12:21 A.M.

THE VICE PRESIDENT

Name—Hubert Horatio Humphrey (38th V.P.)

Date of birth—May 27, 1911

Place of birth—Wallace, S.D.

Political party—Democratic-Farmer Labor

State represented—Minnesota

Term of office—Jan. 20, 1965–Jan. 20, 1969

Age at inauguration—53 years, 238 days

Occupation after term—Professor of political science, U.S. Senator (from Minnesota)

Date of death—Jan. 13, 1978

Age at death—66 years, 231 days

Place of death—Waverly, Minnesota

Burial place—Lakewood Cemetery, Minneapolis, Minn.

ADDITIONAL DATA ON HUMPHREY

1929, graduated from Doland, S.D., high school

1929–1930, University of Minnesota; left to work in father's drug store

1932–1933, six-month course at Denver College of Pharmacy; graduated with degree

1933–1937, pharmacist, Humphrey Drug Co., Huron, S.D.

1937–1939, University of Minnesota; graduated with A.B. degree; Phi Beta Kappa

1939, M.A., University of Louisiana

1939–1940, assistant instructor, political science, University of Louisiana

1941, administrative staff of Works Progress Administration, later head of Minnesota state division

Courtesy of The Library of Congress

Hubert Humphrey, Vice President to Lyndon Johnson

1942–1943, assistant state supervisor adult education, Minnesota; chief of war services section; director of training reemployment division

1943, assistant regional director, War Manpower Commission

1943–1944, visiting professor of political science, Macalester College

June 11, 1945, elected mayor of Minneapolis; reelected June 9, 1947

Nov. 2, 1948, elected to U.S. Senate from Minnesota; reelected 1954 and 1960

1961–1964, Senate majority whip

Jan. 20, 1965–Jan. 20, 1969, Vice President under Lyndon B. Johnson

Aug. 1968, chosen on first ballot at Chicago convention as Democratic presidential nominee

Nov. 5, 1968, defeated by Richard M. Nixon in a close race for the presidency

1969–1970, visiting professor of political science, Macalester College

Nov. 3, 1970, elected to U.S. Senate from Minnesota; reelected 1976

CABINET

FIRST TERM

November 22, 1963–January 20, 1965

State—(David) Dean Rusk, N.Y., continued from preceding administration

Treasury—(Clarence) Douglas Dillon, N.J., continued from preceding administration

Defense—Robert Strange McNamara, Mich., continued from preceding administration

Attorney General—Robert Francis Kennedy, Mass., continued from preceding administration

Postmaster General—John A. Gronouski, Wis., continued from preceding administration

Interior—Stewart Lee Udall, Ariz., continued from preceding administration

Agriculture—Orville Lothrop Freeman, Minn., continued from preceding administration

Commerce—Luther Hartwell Hodges, N.C., continued from preceding administration

Courtesy of the Lyndon Baines Johnson Presidential Library

President Johnson meets with his cabinet.

Labor—(William) Willard Wirtz, Ill., continued from preceding administration

Health, Education, and Welfare—Anthony Joseph Celebrezze, Ohio, continued from preceding administration

SECOND TERM

January 20, 1965–January 20, 1969

State—(David) Dean Rusk, N.Y., continued from preceding administration

Treasury—(Clarence) Douglas Dillon, N.J., continued from preceding administration; Henry Hamill Fowler, Va., Apr. 1, 1965; Joseph Walker Barr, Ind., Dec. 23, 1968

Defense—Robert Strange McNamara, Mich., continued from preceding administration; Clark McAdams Clifford, Md., Mar. 1, 1968

Attorney General—Robert Francis Kennedy, Mass., continued from preceding administration; Nicholas deBelleville Katzenbach, D.C., Feb. 13, 1965; William Ramsey Clark, Tex., Mar. 10, 1967

Postmaster General—John A. Gronouski, Wis., continued from preceding administration; Lawrence Francis O'Brien, Mass., Nov. 3, 1965; William Marvin Watson, Tex., Apr. 26, 1968

Interior—Stewart Lee Udall, Ariz., continued from preceding administration

Agriculture—Orville Lothrop Freeman, Minn., continued from preceding administration

Commerce—Luther Hartwell Hodges, N.C., continued from preceding administration; John Thomas Connor, N.J., Jan. 18, 1965; Alexander Buel Trowbridge, N.Y., June 14,

1967; Cyrus Rowlett Smith, N.Y., Mar. 6, 1968

Labor—(William) Willard Wirtz, Ill., continued from preceding administration

Health, Education, and Welfare
—Anthony Joseph Celebrezze, Ohio, continued from preceding administration; John

William Gardner, N.Y., Aug. 18, 1965; Wilbur Joseph Cohen, Wis., May 9, 1968

Housing and Urban Development—Robert Clifton Weaver, N.Y., Jan. 18, 1966; Robert Coldwell Wood, Mass., Jan. 7, 1969

Transportation—Alan Stephenson Boyd, Fla., Jan. 16, 1967

CONGRESS

EIGHTY-NINTH CONGRESS

January 3, 1965–January 3, 1967

First session—Jan. 4, 1965–Oct. 23, 1965 (293 days)

Second session—Jan. 10, 1966–Oct. 22, 1966 (286 days)

Vice President—Hubert Horatio Humphrey, Minn.

President pro tempore of the Senate—Carl Hayden, Ariz.

Secretary of the Senate—Felton McLellan Johnston, Miss.; Francis Ralph Valeo, N.Y., elected Oct. 1, 1966

Speaker of the House—John William McCormack, Mass.

Clerk of the House—Ralph R. Roberts, Ind.

NINETIETH CONGRESS

January 3, 1967–January 3, 1969

First session—Jan. 10, 1967–Dec. 15, 1967 (340 days)

Second session—Jan. 15, 1968–Oct. 14, 1968 (274 days)

Vice President—Hubert Horatio Humphrey, Minn.

President pro tempore of the Senate—Carl Hayden, Ariz.

Secretary of the Senate—Francis Ralph Valeo, N.Y.

Speaker of the House—John William McCormack, Mass.

Clerk of the House—William Pat Jennings, Va.

APPOINTMENTS TO THE SUPREME COURT

Associate Justices

Abe Fortas, Tex., Oct. 4, 1965 (replaced Arthur Joseph Goldberg, whom Johnson appointed Ambassador to the United Nations)

Thurgood Marshall, Md., Oct. 2, 1967 (replaced Thomas Campbell Clark)

IMPORTANT DATES IN THE PRESIDENCY

Nov. 27, 1963, President, in address to Congress, pledged to continue President Kennedy's policies and urged action on civil rights and tax cuts

Nov. 29, 1963, President appointed seven-man commission headed by Chief Justice Earl Warren to investigate assassination of President Kennedy

Jan. 8, 1964, President, in State of the Union message to Congress, announced reduction of the federal budget and urged action against poverty and racial discrimination

Jan. 9–10, 1964, riots in Canal Zone brought on by dispute over flying of American flag; Panama demanded revision of Canal Zone treaty and suspended relations with United States

President Johnson signs the Civil Rights Act, with Martin Luther King, Jr. looking on.

Jan. 11, 1964, U.S. Public Health Service issued report on cigarette smoking and cancer

Jan. 23, 1964, ratification of Twenty-fourth Amendment to Constitution, banning poll taxes in federal elections .

Feb. 17, 1964, Supreme Court ruled that congressional districts should be equal in population (known as "one-man, one-vote" decision)

Mar. 16, 1964, President sent antipoverty program to Congress

Apr. 3, 1964, U.S.–Panama relations restored

Apr. 22, 1964, New York City World's Fair opened

June 15, 1964, Supreme Court ruled that state legislatures must have districts substantially equal in population in both houses

July 2, 1964, President signed Civil Rights Act

July 18–21, 1964, racial violence in Harlem and Bedford-Stuyvesant sections of New York City; outbreaks in Rochester, N.Y. (July 24–26)

Aug. 7, 1964, Congressional resolution gave advance approval to President Johnson for any actions in Southeast Asia following U.S. raids on North Vietnamese bases in retaliation for reported attacks on U.S. destroyers in Gulf of Tonkin

Aug. 20, 1964, $974.5 million antipoverty bill signed by President

Sept. 27, 1964, release of Warren Commission report on Kennedy assassination, with conclusion that Oswald was sole assassin

Nov. 3, 1964, President defeated Barry Goldwater in landslide presidential election

Jan. 4, 1965, "Great Society" program proposed by President in State of the Union message

Feb. 7, 1965, U.S. planes bombed North Vietnamese bases after Vietcong attack on U.S. base

Mar. 8–9, 1965, U.S. Marines landed in South Vietnam (first American combat troops there)

Mar. 20, 1965, Alabama National Guard called out to protect Selma-Montgomery Freedom March

Apr. 28, 1965, U.S. Marines landed in Dominican Republic after clashes between rebels and army

May 18, 1965, U.S. raids on North Vietnam resumed after lull had failed to bring about negotiations

May 26, 1965, U.S. Marines on Dominican Republic replaced by patrols of Organization of American States

June 3, 1965, Major Edward H. White first American to walk in space (*Gemini 4* flight)

July 30, 1965, President signed Medicare bill

Aug. 6, 1965, President signed voting rights bill

Aug. 11–16, 1965, 35 killed, 883 injured in six days of rioting, looting, and burning in Watts, African-American section of Los Angeles, Calif.

Aug. 31, 1965, Housing and Urban Affairs cabinet post created

Oct. 9, 1965, President signed $1.785-billion antipoverty bill, doubling previous appropriation.

Nov. 9–10, 1965, electric power failure affecting 25 million persons in Northeast

Nov. 27, 1965, Vietnam peace march on Washington by 15,000 demonstrators

Dec. 15, 1965, successful rendezvous in space of two separately launched manned capsules (*Gemini 6* and *Gemini 7*)

Dec. 24, 1965, beginning of holiday truce and thirty-seven-day suspension of U.S. bombing of North Vietnam

Feb. 4, 1966, President authorized grain shipment to famine-threatened India

Mar. 16, 1966, first "docking" of two orbiting space vehicles (*Gemini 8* and *Agena* target)

Mar. 18, 1966, support of NATO by United States and thirteen other nations reaffirmed despite withdrawal of France from defense system

Apr. 21, 1966, artificial heart pump successfully implanted

Apr. 26, 1966, U.S. automobile industry announced willingness to abide by federal safety standards; reported recall of 8.7 million cars to check possible flaws

May 20, 1966, Atomic Energy Commission reported that China had probably achieved thermonuclear reaction in May 9 test

June 13, 1966, Supreme Court ruled that Fifth Amendment protection against self-incrimination limits interrogation of suspects and use of confessions, and guarantees right to have counsel (known as the "Miranda" ruling)

July 4–9, 1966, convention of National Association for the Advancement of Colored People rejected "black power" doctrine advocated by other African-American organizations

July 7–Aug. 19, 1966, strike of machinists halted major U.S. airlines

July 30, 1966, U.S. planes attacked Communist base in demilitarized zone of South Vietnam

Sept. 9, 1966, President signed bill establishing federal automobile safety standards

Oct. 15, 1966, Department of Transportation established as Cabinet office

Jan. 10, 1967, President asked Congress to enact 6 percent surcharge on income taxes to support war and domestic programs

Jan. 27, 1967, three astronauts killed in fire in spacecraft at Cape Kennedy, Fla., while conducting tests for scheduled launching

Feb. 1967, disclosures of financial backing of numerous private foundations by U.S. Central Intelligence Agency

Feb. 10, 1967, Twenty-fifth Amendment, dealing with presidential disability, ratified

Mar. 21, 1967, President's proposals for peace talks rejected by Ho Chi Minh

Apr. 1967, bombing of North Vietnam intensified

May 1967, demilitarized zone between North and South Vietnam invaded by U.S.-led forces; Hanoi bombed by U.S. planes

June 1967, U.S. pledged neutrality in Middle East war between Arab states and Israel

June 13, 1967, House approved $70 billion defense bill—largest single appropriations bill ever passed by either house

June 23, 25, 1967, President conferred with Soviet Premier Kosygin at Glassboro, N.J.

July 1967, prolonged riots in slums of Newark, N.J., and Detroit exacted heavy toll of life and property; numerous outbreaks of racial violence in other ghetto areas

Jan. 23, 1968, U.S.S. *Pueblo* and 83-man crew seized in Sea of Japan by North Koreans

Mar. 31, 1968, President announced a partial halt to bombing of North Vietnam and that he would not seek a second term

Apr. 4, 1968, Dr. Martin Luther King Jr., assassinated, Memphis, Tenn.

Apr. 4–14, 1968, riots took place in many cities in the United States

June 5–6, 1968, Senator Robert F. Kennedy shot and killed in Los Angeles, Calif., while celebrating his California presidential primary victory

Aug. 1968, violence erupted in Chicago, Ill., at Democratic National Convention with confrontation of antiwar demonstrators and Chicago police

Courtesy of the National Archives and Records Administration

Anti-Vietnam demonstrator offers a flower to a miltary policeman, Arlington, Virginia, October 21, 1967. By S. Sgt. Albert Simpson.

Oct. 31, 1968, President announced complete halt to bombing of North Vietnam

Dec. 22, 1968, U.S.S. *Pueblo* crew released

ADDITIONAL DATA ON JOHNSON

LYNDON BAINES JOHNSON

—was the first President since Andrew Johnson who was a Southerner by birth and residence.

—was the second President born in Texas.

—was the first Democratic President to carry Vermont.

—was the first Democratic President to carry Maine since 1912.

—was the first President to ride in an armored automobile at his inauguration.

—was the first President to review an inaugural parade in a heated reviewing stand.

—was the first President sworn in behind a three-sided bullet-proof glass enclosure.

—was the first President to take the oath of office in an airplane.

—was the first President sworn in by a woman.

—was the first President who took his oath on a Bible held by his wife.

—was the first President inaugurated in a business suit.

—was the first Vice President to witness the assassination of the President whom he succeeded in office.

—was the second Vice President named Johnson to succeed to the presidency on the death of the incumbent.

—was the third Vice President named Johnson

—was the fourth Vice President to become President as the result of assassination.

—was the eighth Vice President to become President as the result of the death of the incumbent.

JOHNSON WELL PREPARED FOR PRESIDENCY

Lyndon Baines Johnson was exceptionally well prepared to succeed to the presidency. As Vice President he had served on the National Security Council and was chairman of the National Aeronautics and Space Council, and he was consulted by President Kennedy on all major policy matters. As chairman of the President's Committee on Equal Employment Opportunity, he was in close touch with two major domestic issues—civil rights and employment. On his trips abroad as Vice President he had conferred with Chancellor Konrad Adenauer of West Germany, President Charles de Gaulle of France, and other leading world figures. An added advantage was his long experience in Congress—nearly 12 years in the House of Representatives and 12 years in the Senate, including seven years as the Senate Democratic leader, a post in which he served with great effectiveness.

JOHNSON'S FIRST PROCLAMATION

President Johnson's first proclamation, on November 23, 1963, was a declaration of a day of national mourning (November 25) as a tribute to his predecessor, John Fitzgerald Kennedy. An extract from the proclamation follows:

He upheld the faith of our Fathers, which is freedom for all men. He broadened the frontiers of that faith, and backed it with the energy and the courage which are the mark of the nation he led. A man of wisdom, strength and peace, he molded and moved the power of our nation in the service of a world of growing liberty and order. All who love freedom will mourn his death. As he did not shrink from his responsibilities, but welcomed them, so he would not have us shrink from carrying on his work beyond this hour of national tragedy. He said it himself: "The energy, the faith, the devotion which we bring to this endeavor will light our country and all who serve it—and the glow from that fire can truly light the world."

Courtesy of the Lyndon B. Johnson Library

Lyndon Johnson meets with the troops in Vietnam.

JOHNSON DECRIED FEAR

Replying to the Secret Service guards who urged President Johnson to ride from the White House to St. Matthew's Cathedral to attend the Kennedy funeral services, instead of walking with the world's great leaders, Johnson said, "I'd rather give my life than be afraid to give it."

SECRET SERVICE AGENTS HONORED

One of President Johnson's first acts was to pay high tribute on December 4, 1963, to Rufus Youngblood, who at the time of President Kennedy's assassination "volunteered his life to save mine." The citation read: "Upon hearing the first shot, Mr. Youngblood instantly vaulted across the front seat of the car, pushed the Vice President to the floor and shielded the Vice President's body with his own."

The previous day, another Secret Service Agent, Clinton J. Hill, was awarded the Treasury Department Medal for "exceptional bravery." In similar manner, he had shielded Mrs. Kennedy.

TWENTY-FOURTH AMENDMENT RATIFIED

The Twenty-fourth Amendment to the Constitution, banning the use of poll taxes as a requirement for voting in federal elections, was acted upon by the House of Representatives on August 27, 1962, when it approved Senate Joint Resolution No. 29, passed March 27, 1962.

The first state to ratify the proposed amendment was Illinois, on November 14, 1962. The required number of votes (38) was reached on January 23, 1964, when South Dakota voted its approval.

Section 1 of the Amendment follows:

The right of citizens of the United States to vote in any primary or other election for President or Vice President, for electors for President or Vice President, or for Senator or Representative in Congress, shall not be denied or abridged by the United States or any state by reason of failure to pay any poll tax or other tax.

HONORARY DEGREES

The first President and his wife to receive honorary degrees simultaneously were President and Mrs. Lyndon Baines Johnson. On May 30, 1964, the University of Texas at Austin awarded the President a Doctor of Laws degree and Mrs. Johnson a Doctor of Letters degree.

WARREN COMMISSION REPORT

A commission to investigate and report on the Kennedy assassination was authorized December 13, 1963, by Senate Joint Resolution 137. The commission consisted of Chief Justice Earl Warren of California, Senator Richard Brevard Russell (Democrat, Georgia), Senator John Sherman Cooper (Republican, Kentucky), Representative Hale Boggs (Democrat, Louisiana), Representative Gerald Rudolph Ford (Republican, Michigan); Allen Welsh Dulles, former director of the Central Intelligence Agency; and John Jay McCloy, former U.S. Military Governor and High Commissioner for Germany.

The report was released September 28, 1964. It contained the following statement: "On the basis of the evidence before the Commission it concludes that Oswald acted alone."

WOMAN CONSIDERED FOR PRESIDENTIAL NOMINATION

The first woman considered for nomination for the presidency by a major political party was Senator Margaret Chase Smith of Maine, whose name was placed in nomination by Senator George David Aiken of Vermont on July 15, 1964, at the Republican National Convention, San Francisco, Calif. She received 27 votes on the first roll call, which was later declared a unanimous vote for Senator Barry Morris Goldwater.

PLANS FOR JOHNSON'S PAPERS

Congress enacted legislation on September 6, 1965 (79 Stat. L. 648), to authorize the Administrator of General Services to enter into an agreement with the University of Texas for the Lyndon Baines Johnson Presidential Archival Depository. The university houses the presidential papers for the National Archives system. The Lyndon Baines Johnson Library and School of Public Affairs, Austin, Tex., was dedicated May 22, 1971.

NEW CABINET POSTS CREATED

The Department of Housing and Urban Development was authorized September 9, 1965 (79 Stat. L. 667). The first secretary was Robert Clifton Weaver of New York, who was appointed on January 13, 1966, and sworn in on January 18, 1966. Weaver was the first African-American ever appointed to a cabinet post.

The Department of Transportation was authorized October 15, 1966 (80 Stat. L. 931) to deal with air, rail, and highway transportation. It comprises thirty-four federal agencies, including the Federal Aviation Agency, the Coast Guard, the Civil Aeronautics Board, the Bureau of Public Roads, and the Interstate Commerce Commission. The first secretary was Alan Stephenson Boyd of Florida, who was appointed in November 1966 and sworn in January 16, 1967.

PAPAL VISIT

The first President to confer in the United States with a Pope was Lyndon Baines Johnson, who called upon Pope Paul VI at the Waldorf Astoria Hotel, New York City, on October 4, 1965, while the Pope was in New York to address the United Nations. As Vice President he had had an audience with Pope John XXIII in Rome.

TWENTY-FIFTH AMENDMENT RATIFIED

The Twenty-fifth Amendment was introduced by Senator Birch Bayh of Indiana on December 12, 1963. It was ratified on February 10, 1967, when the thirty-eighth state voted for its adoption. There is some dispute as to whether North Dakota, Minnesota, or Nevada was the thirty-eighth state, for North Dakota withdrew its original ratifying resolution after discovering it was only the thirty-seventh. The text of the amendment follows:

Section I. In case of the removal of the President from office or his death or resignation, the Vice President shall become President.

Section II. Whenever there is a vacancy in the office of the Vice President, the President shall nominate a Vice President who shall take the office upon confirmation by a majority vote of both houses of Congress.

Section III. Whenever the President transmits to the President pro tempore of the Senate and the Speaker of the House of Representatives his written declaration that he is unable to discharge the powers and duties of his office, and until he transmits to them a written declaration to the contrary, such powers and duties shall be discharged by the Vice President as Acting President.

Section IV. Whenever the Vice President and a majority of either the principal officers of the executive departments, or of such other body as Congress may by law provide, transmit to the President pro tempore of the Senate and the Speaker of the House of Representatives their written declaration that the President is unable to discharge the powers and duties of his office, the Vice President shall immediately assume the powers and duties of the office as Acting President. Thereafter when the President transmits to the President pro tempore of the Senate and the Speaker of the House of Representatives his written declaration that no inability exists, he shall resume the powers and duties of his office unless the Vice President and a majority of either the principal officers of the executive department, or of such other body as Congress may by law provide, transmit within four days to the President pro tempore of the Senate and the Speaker of the House of Representatives their written declaration that the President is unable to discharge the powers and duties of his office. Thereupon Congress shall decide the issue, assembling within 48 hours for that purpose if not in session. If the Congress, within 21 days after receipt of the latter written declaration, or, if Congress is not in session, within 21 days after Congress is required to assemble, determines by two-thirds vote of both houses that the President is unable to discharge the powers and duties of his office, the Vice President shall continue to discharge the same as Acting President; otherwise, the President shall resume the powers and duties of his office.

MARSHALL APPOINTED TO SUPREME COURT

The first African-American appointed to the United States Supreme Court was Thurgood Marshall of Maryland, age 59, the son of a Pullman car steward and great-grandson of a slave. He was appointed June 13, 1967, by President Johnson to succeed Justice Tom C. Clark. On July 13, 1965, Marshall had been appointed United States Solicitor General and on October 6, 1961, judge of the United States Second Circuit Court of Appeals.

L.B.J.

The monogram and initials L.B.J. are closely associated with President Johnson. They were the initials of Lyndon Baines Johnson; of Mrs. Johnson, nicknamed Lady Bird; and of his two daughters, Lynda Bird and Luci Baines. The initials provided the name of his ranch, the LBJ, and were also used for one of his dogs, Little Beagle Johnson.

JOHNSON ANALYZED HIMSELF

In the April 1959 issue of the *Reader's Digest*, in an article reprinted from the *Texas Quarterly*, Vice President Lyndon Johnson wrote:

> I am a free man, an American, a United States Senator, and a Democrat, in that order. I am also a liberal, a conservative, a consumer, a parent, a voter, and not as young as I used to be nor as old as I expect to be—and I am all those things in no fixed order.

Courtesy of the Library of Congress

Thurgood Marshall, the first African-American appointed to the Supreme Court

---

FURTHER READING

Califano, Joseph A. *The Triumph and Tragedy of Lyndon Johnson: The White House Years*. 1991.

Caro, Robert. *The Years of Lyndon Johnson: The Path to Power*. 1982.

———. *Means of Ascent*. 1990.

Dallek, Robert. *Lone Star Rising: Lyndon Johnson and His Times, 1908–1960*. 1991.

———. *Flawed Giant: Lyndon Johnson and His Times, 1961–1973*. 1998.

Dugger, Ronnie. *The Politician*. 1982.

Goldman, Eric F. *The Tragedy of Lyndon Johnson*. 1968.

Goodwin, Doris K. *Lyndon Johnson and the American Dream*. 1976.

White, Theodore H. *The Making of the President 1964*. 1965.

———. *The Making of the President 1968*. 1969.

Woods, Randall B. *LBJ: Architect of American Ambition*. 2006.

Courtesy of the Library of Congress

Richard Milhous Nixon

Date of birth—Jan. 9, 1913

Place of birth—Yorba Linda, Calif.

Education—Attended public schools, Yorba Linda, Calif., and Whittier, Calif.; Fullerton High School; Whittier High School, graduated 1930; Whittier College, bachelor of arts degree in history, June 9, 1934; Duke University Law School, Durham, N.C., graduated June 7, 1937

Religion—Quaker

Ancestry—Scotch-Irish, English, Irish, German

Career—Lawyer, businessman, Navy officer in World War II, U.S. congressman, U.S. senator, Vice President

Political party—Republican

State represented—New York

Term of office—Jan. 20, 1969–Aug. 9, 1974

Term served—5 years, 201 days

Administration—46th, 47th

Congresses—91st, 92nd, 93rd

Age at inauguration—56 years, 11 days

Occupation after term—Author

Date of death—Apr. 22, 1994

Age at death—81 years, 113 days

Place of death—New York, N.Y.

Burial place—Yorba Linda, Calif.

FAMILY

FATHER

Name—Francis Anthony Nixon

Date of birth—Dec. 3, 1878

Place of birth—McArthur, Vinton County, Ohio

Marriage—Hannah Milhous, June 25, 1908

Occupation—Farm worker, streetcar motorman, citrus grower, grocer, gas station owner

Date of death—Sept. 4, 1956

Place of death—Whittier, Calif.

Age at death—78 years, 274 days

MOTHER

Name at birth—Hannah Milhous

Date of birth—Mar. 7, 1885

Place of birth—Butlersville, Jennings County, Ind.

Marriage—Francis Anthony Nixon, June 25, 1908

Date of death—Sept. 30, 1967

Place of death—Whittier, Calif.

Age at death—82 years, 207 days

SIBLINGS

Richard Milhous Nixon was the second child in a family of five sons.

Children of Francis Anthony Nixon and Hannah Milhous Nixon

Harold Samuel Nixon—b. June 1, 1909; d. Mar. 7, 1933

Richard Milhous Nixon—b. Jan. 9, 1913; d. Apr. 22, 1994

Francis Donald Nixon—b. Nov. 23, 1914; d. 1987

Arthur Burdg Nixon—b. May 26, 1918; d. Aug. 10, 1925

Edward Calvert Nixon—b. May 3, 1930

MARRIAGE

Married—Thelma Catherine ("Pat") Ryan

Date of marriage—June 21, 1940

Place of marriage—Riveside, Calif.

Age of wife at marriage—28 years, 97 days

Age of husband at marriage—27 years, 163 days

Years married—53 years, 181 days

CHILDREN

Patricia ("Tricia") Nixon, b. Feb. 21, 1946, San Francisco, Calif.; m. Edward Finch Cox, June 12, 1971, at the White House, Washington, D.C.

Julie Nixon, b. July 5, 1948, Washington, D.C.; m. Dwight David Eisenhower II, Dec. 22, 1968, New York City

THE PRESIDENT'S WIFE

Name at birth—Thelma Catherine ("Pat") Ryan

Date of birth—Mar. 16, 1912

Place of birth—Ely, Nev.

Mother—Katharina Halberstadt Bender Ryan

Father—William Ryan

Education—High school, graduated with honors; Fullerton Junior College, Fullerton, Calif.; University of Southern California, graduated cum laude with master's-level degree in merchandising and teacher's certificate, 1937

Marriage—Richard Milhous Nixon, June 21, 1940, Riverside, Calif.

Children—Patricia ("Tricia") Nixon, b. Feb. 21, 1946; Julie Nixon, b. July 5, 1948

Occupation—High school business teacher, Whitter, Calif.; secretary; price analyst and economic analyst, Office of Price Administration, Washington, D.C.

Date of death—June 23, 1993

Place of death—Park Ridge, N.J.

Burial place—Yorba Linda, Calif.

Years older than the President—299 days

Years the President survived her—303 days

Courtesy of The Library of Congress

Thelma "Pat" Nixon, wife of Richard Nixon

THE FIRST LADY

Pat Nixon became active in politics during her husband's congressional campaigns in California. When he was Vice President under Eisenhower, Mrs. Nixon accompanied her husband on diplomatic and goodwill tours; during his presidency, she accompanied him on his trip to the Soviet Union and on his historic visit to Communist China.

In her youth Mrs. Nixon worked at various jobs to earn money to attend the University of Southern California, from which she graduated with honors in 1937. She taught commercial subjects in Whittier, Calif., and during World War II, while her husband was in the Navy, she was employed as an economist in the Office of Price Administration in San Francisco.

As First Lady, Mrs. Nixon showed interest in educational programs and self-help projects and traveled widely on a number of public missions. She supported her husband throughout the Watergate crisis.

IMPORTANT DATES IN THE PRESIDENT'S LIFE

1920s, worked in father's grocery store

June 9, 1934, graduated from Whittier College

June 7, 1937, graduated from Duke University Law School

1937, admitted to the bar; practiced at Whittier, Calif.

Jan.–Aug. 1942, attorney with Office of Emergency Management, Washington, D.C.

1942–1946, lieutenant, j.g., U.S. Navy; served in South Pacific as aviation ground officer on Bougainville, Vella Lavella, and Green Islands; won two battle stars

1946, joined law firm of Wingert & Bewley in Whittier, Calif. (firm name changed to Wingert, Bewley & Nixon; later, to Bewley, Knoop & Nixon)

Jan. 3, 1947–Nov. 31, 1950, U.S. House of Representatives (from California)

Nov. 7, 1950, elected to U.S. Senate (from California)

Dec. 1, 1950, received interim appointment, after his own election, to replace Senator Sheridan Downey, who resigned several weeks before expiration of term

Jan. 3, 1951–Jan. 20, 1953, U.S. Senate (from California)

July 10, 1952, nominated for vice presidency by Republican Party

Sept. 23, 1952, saved his candidacy by delivering "Checkers" speech on nationwide television, defending his acceptance of $18,000 slush fund

Jan. 20, 1953–Jan. 20, 1961, Vice President under Dwight D. Eisenhower

May 1958, visited South America on goodwill tour; attacked by anti-U.S. demonstrators in Caracas, Venezuela

July 24, 1959, engaged in sharp discussion with Soviet Premier Nikita S. Khrushchev in Moscow during visit to U.S.S.R. ("kitchen debate" in showroom of American exhibition)

July 28, 1960, nominated for presidency by Republican Party

Nov. 8, 1960, lost presidential election to John Fitzgerald Kennedy by 118,574 votes (two tenths of 1 percent of a total 69 million votes

1962, nominated for governorship of California; defeated in election

Mar. 29, 1962, *Six Crises* published

Jan. 1963, joined New York City law firm of Mudge, Stern, Baldwin & Todd (later Nixon, Mudge, Rose, Alexander, Guthrie & Stern)

Aug. 8, 1968, nominated for presidency by Republican party

Nov. 5, 1968, elected President of the United States

Jan. 20, 1969, inaugurated 37th President of the United States

Feb. 1972, visited Communist China

Aug. 23, 1972, nominated for second term

Nov. 7, 1972, reelected President of the United States

Jan. 20, 1973–Aug. 9, 1974, President (second Term)

July 27–30, 1974, House Judiciary Committee voted to recommend impeachment on grounds of obstruction of justice, abuse of power, and contempt of Congress

Aug. 8, 1974, in televised address announced intention to resign

Aug. 9, 1974, resigned; retired to his residence in San Clemente, Calif.

Sept. 18, 1974, accepted pardon from President Ford for all federal offenses that he "committed or may have committed"

Apr. 20, 1975, announced plan for presidential library at University of Southern California

July 8, 1976, disbarred by Appellate Division of the New York State Supreme Court on charges of obstruction of justice connected with Watergate

1978, *RN: The Memoirs of Richard Nixon* published

1980, *The Real War* published

1988, *1999* published

1991, *In the Arena* published

1992, *Seize the Moment* published

1994, *Beyond Peace* published

ELECTIONS

THE ELECTION OF 1968

November 5, 1968

CANDIDATES

Republican Party (29th Convention)

Aug. 5–8, 1968, Convention Hall, Miami Beach, Fla.

P: Richard Milhous Nixon, N.Y.
VP: Spiro Theodore Agnew, Md.

Nixon was nominated on the first ballot. Candidates for nomination and the votes they received:

Richard Milhous Nixon, N.Y., 692
Nelson Aldrich Rockefeller, N.Y., 277
Ronald Reagan, Calif., 182
James Allen Rhodes, Ohio, 55
George Romney, Mich., 50
Clifford Philip Case, N.J., 22
Frank Carlson, Kan., 20
Winthrop Rockefeller, Ark., 18
Hiram Leong Fong, Hawaii, 14
Harold Edward Stassen, Pa., 2
John Vliet Lindsay, N.Y., 1
Total number of votes: 1,333
Number necessary for nomination: 667

Democratic Party (35th Convention)

Aug. 26–29, 1968, International Amphitheater, Chicago, Ill.

P: Hubert Horatio Humphrey, Minn.
VP: Edmund Sixtus Muskie, Me.

Humphrey was nominated on the first ballot. Candidates for nomination and the votes they received:

Hubert Horatio Humphrey, Minn., $1,761^3/_4$
Eugene Joseph McCarthy, Minn., 601
George Stanley McGovern, S.D., $146^1/_2$
Channing Emery Phillips, D.C., $67^1/_2$
Daniel Killian Moore, N.C., $17^1/_2$
Edward Moore Kennedy, Mass., $12^3/_4$
Paul William "Bear" Bryant, $1^1/_2$

George Corley Wallace, Ala., 1
James H. Gray, Ga., $^1/_2$
Total number of votes: 2,622
Number necessary for nomination: 1,312

American Independent Party (Courage Party in New York)

P: George Corley Wallace, Ala.
VP: Curtis Emerson LeMay, Ohio

Samuel Marvin Griffin, Ga., was selected Feb. 14, 1968 as the vice presidential candidate; LeMay was named on Oct. 3, 1968.

Liberal Party

Sept. 24, 1968, Hotel Roosevelt, New York, N.Y.

The Liberal Party endorsed the candidates of the Democratic Party.

Conservative Party of Kansas

The Conservative Party of Kansas endorsed the candidates of the American Independent Party.

Peace and Freedom Party

Aug. 18, 1968, Ann Arbor, Mich.

P: Eldridge Cleaver
VP: Judith Mage, N.Y.

On the first ballot Cleaver received $161^1/_2$ votes, Dick Gregory 54.

Socialist Labor Party

May 5, 1968, Towers Hotel, Brooklyn, N.Y.

P: Henning A. Blomen, Mass.
VP: George Sam Taylor, Pa.

Socialist Workers Party

Aug. 28, 1968, New York, N.Y.

P: Fred Halstead, N.Y.
VP: Paul Boutelle, N.J.

Prohibition Party

June 28–29, 1967, Young Women's Christian Association, Detroit, Mich.

P: Earle Harold Munn, Sr., Mich.
VP: Rolland E. Fisher, Kan.

Communist Party (USA)

July 3–7, 1968, Diplomat Hotel, New York, N.Y.

P: Charlene Mitchell, Calif.
VP: Michael Zagarell, N.Y.
   First national slate since 1940.

Constitution Party

July 18–21, 1968, Denver, Colo.

P: Richard K. Troxell, Tex.
VP: Merle Thayer, Iowa

Freedom and Peace Party

P: Dick Gregory (Richard Claxton Gregory), Ill.

Patriotic Party

July 2–4, 1967

P: George Corley Wallace, Ala.
VP: William Penn Patrick, Calif.

People's Constitutional Party

P: Ventura Chavez, N.M.
VP: Adelicio Moya, N.M.

Universal Party

Denver, Colo.

P: Rev. Kirby James Hensley, Calif.
VP: Roscoe B. MacKenna

Theocratic Party

P: Bishop William R. Rogers, Mo.

1968 POPULAR VOTE

Republican Party, 31,710,470
Democratic Party, 30,898,055
American Independent Party, 9,446,167
Courage Party (N.Y.), 358,864
Liberal Party, 311,622
Conservative Party of Kansas, 88,921
Peace and Freedom Party, 74,014
Socialist Labor Party, 51,962
Socialist Workers Party, 38,011
Prohibition Party, 14,787
Independent Party (Ala.), 10,960
New Party (Ariz., Colo., N.H., Vt.), 5,144
New Politics Party (Mich.), 4,585
Petition Party (Iowa), 3,377
People's Constitutional Party (N.M.), 1,519
New Reform Party (Mont.), 470
Communist Party (Minn., Ohio), 438

Free Ballot Party (Wash.), 377
Industrial Government Party (Minn.), 285
Universal Party (Iowa), 142
Constitution Party (N.D.), 34
Write-in votes, 2,645
Scattering, 3,982

1968 ELECTORAL VOTE

There were 538 electoral votes from the 50 states and the District of Columbia.

Nixon received 55.94 percent (301 votes—32 states) as follows: Alaska 3; Ariz. 5; Calif. 40; Colo. 6; Del. 3; Fla. 14; Idaho 4; Ill. 267; Ind. 13; Iowa 9; Kan. 7; Ky. 9; Mo. 12; Mont. 4; Neb. 5; Nev. 3; N.H. 4; N.J. 17; N.M. 4; N.C. 12; N.D. 4; Ohio 26; Okla. 8; Ore. 6; S.C. 8; S.D. 4; Tenn. 11; Utah 4; Vt. 3; Va. 12; Wis. 12; Wyo. 3.

Humphrey received 35.50 percent (191 votes—13 states and D.C.) as follows: Conn. 8; Hawaii 4; Me. 4; Md. 10; Mass. 14; Mich. 21; Minn. 10; N.Y. 43; Pa. 29; R.I. 4; Tex. 25; Wash. 9; W.Va. 7; D.C. 3.

Wallace received 8.55 percent (46 votes—5 states as follows: Ala. 10; Ark. 6; Ga. 12; La. 10; Miss. 7; N.C. 1.

THE ELECTION OF 1972

November 7, 1972

CANDIDATES

Republican Party (30th Convention)

Aug. 21–23, 1972, Convention Hall, Miami Beach, Fla.

P: Richard Milhous Nixon, Calif.
VP: Spiro Theodore Agnew, Md.

  Nixon was nominated on the first ballot. Candidates for nomination and the votes they received:
Richard Milhous Nixon, Calif., 1,347
Paul Norton McCloskey, Jr., Calif., 1
Total number of votes: 1,348
Number necessary for nomination: 675

Democratic Party (36th Convention)

July 10–13, 1972, Convention Hall, Miami Beach, Fla.

P: George Stanley McGovern, S.D.
VP: Thomas Francis Eagleton, Mo.

Eagleton resigned 19 days later and was replaced on August 8, 1972, by Robert Sargent Shriver, Md., selected by the Democratic National Committee.

McGovern was nominated on the first ballot. Candidates for nomination and the votes they received:

George Stanley McGovern, S.D., 1,864.95
Henry Martin Jackson, Wash., 485.65
George Corley Wallace, Ala., 377.5
Shirley Anita St. Hill Chisholm, N.Y., 101.45
Terry Sanford, N.C., 69.5
Hubert Horatio Humphrey, Minn., 35.0
Wilbur Daigh Mills, Ark., 32.8
Edmund Sixtus Muskie, Me., 20.8
Edward Moore Kennedy, Mass., 10.65
Wayne Levere Hays, Ohio, 5.0
Eugene Joseph McCarthy, Minn., 2.0
Walter Frederick Mondale, Minn., 1.0
Abstentions, 9.7
Total number of votes: 3,016
Number necessary for nomination: 1,509

American Party

Aug. 3–5, 1972, Freedom Hall, Louisville, Ky.

P: John George Schmitz, Calif.
VP: Thomas Jefferson Anderson, Tenn.

Schmitz was nominated on the first ballot. Candidates for nomination and the votes they received:

John George Schmitz, Calif., 329.75
George Lester Garfield, Ga., 55.65
Allen Greer, Fla., 25.5
Thomas Jefferson Anderson, Tenn., 23.6
Richard B. Kay, 16.0

Socialist Workers Party

Detroit, Mich.

P: Linda Jenness, Ga.
VP: Andrew Pulley, Ill.

Both candidates were ineligible as they were under the statutory age.

Socialist Labor Party

Apr. 8–10, 1972, Detroit-Hilton, Detroit, Mich.

P: Louis Fisher, Ill.
VP: Genevieve Gunderson, Minn.

Communist Party

Feb. 18, 1972, New York, N.Y.

P: Gus Hall, N.Y.
VP: Jarvis Tyner

Present at the convention were 275 delegates from 34 states.

Prohibition Party

P: Earle Harold Munn, Sr., Mich.
VP: Marshall Inchapher

Libertarian Party

P: John Hospers, Calif.
VP: Theodora Nathan, Ore.

People's Party

July 27–30, 1972, St. Louis, Mo.

P: Dr. Benjamin McLane Spock
VP: Julius Hobson, Washington, D.C.

America First Party

P: John V. Mahalchik
VP: Irving Homer

Universal Party

P: Gabriel Green
VP: Daniel Fry

1972 POPULAR VOTE

Republican Party, 46,740,323
Democratic Party, 28,901,598
American Party, 993,199
Conservative Party of New York, 368,136
Liberal Party (N.Y.), 183,128
Socialist Workers Party, 96,176
Constitutional Party (Pa.), 70,593
Peace and Freedom Party, 64,098
Socialist Labor Party, 53,617
National Democratic Party (Alaska), 37,815
Communist Party, 25,222
Prohibition Party, 13,444
People's Party (N.J., Wash., Ky.), 9,117
Independent Government Party (Minn.), 2,855
Libertarian Party, 2,691
United Citizen's Party (S.C.), 2,265
America First Party (N.J.), 1,743
Liberty Union Party (Vt.), 1,010
Independent Party (Wis.), 506
Universal Party (Iowa, Calif.), 220
Write-in votes, 10,776

Scattering, 12,915

1972 ELECTORAL VOTE

There were 538 electoral votes from the 50 states and the District of Columbia.

Nixon received 96.6 percent (520 votes—49 states) as follows: Ala. 9; Alaska 3, Ariz. 6; Ark. 6; Calif. 45; Colo. 7; Conn. 8; Del. 3; Fla. 17; Ga. 12; Hawaii 4; Idaho 4; Ill. 26; Ind. 13; Iowa 8; Kan. 7; Ky. 9; La. 10; Me. 4; Md. 10; Mich. 21; Minn. 10; Miss. 7; Mo. 12; Mont. 4; Neb. 5; Nev. 3; N.H. 4; N.J. 17; N.M. 4; N.Y. 41; N.C. 13; N.D. 3; Ohio 25; Okla. 8; Ore. 6; Pa. 27; R.I. 4; S.C. 8; S.D. 4; Tenn. 10; Tex. 26; Utah 4; Vt. 3; Va. 11; Wash. 9; W.Va. 6; Wis. 11; Wyo. 3.

McGovern received 3.4 percent (17 votes—1 state and D.C.) as follows: Mass. 14; D.C. 3.

One delegate from Virginia cast his vote for John Hospers, Libertarian Party.

INAUGURATIONS

FIRST TERM

January 20, 1969

Nixon was inaugurated Monday, January 20, 1969, at 12:15 P.M. The oath of office was administered by Chief Justice Earl Warren. The rain held off, but the air was heavily overcast, and the temperature ranged from 33 to 38 degrees. Nixon made a seventeen-minute inaugural address. About 38,000 reserved seats were sold along the parade route.

At least six past, present, or future Vice Presidents attended the inauguration. They were Nixon himself, outgoing President Lyndon Baines Johnson, Hubert Horatio Humphrey, Spiro Theodore Agnew, Gerald Rudolph Ford, and Nelson Aldrich Rockefeller.

SECOND TERM

January 20, 1973

There was a stiff breeze blowing, with the temperature in the low 40s, when Nixon was sworn in for his second term on Saturday,

Courtesy of The Library of Congress

Nixon takes the oath of office during his first inauguration.

January 20, 1973. He was the thirteenth President sworn in for a second term. The oath was administered by Chief Justice Warren Earl Burger. The theme of the parade was "The Spirit of '76" and the cost exceeded four million dollars. Many protestors expressed disapproval.

The President and Mrs. Nixon attended all six inaugural balls held that evening in the capital.

THE VICE PRESIDENTS

FIRST AND SECOND TERMS

Name—Spiro Theodore Agnew (39th V.P.)

Name at birth—Spiro Theodore Anagnosto-poulos

Date of birth—Nov. 9, 1918

Place of birth—Baltimore, Md.

Political party—Republican

State represented—Maryland

Term of office—Jan. 20, 1969–Oct. 10, 1973

Age at inauguration—51 years, 72 days

Occupation after term—Novelist

Date of death—Sept. 17, 1996

Age at death—77 years, 303 days

Place of death—Ocean City, Md.

Burial place—Timonium, Md.

ADDITIONAL DATA ON AGNEW

1942–1946, World War II company commander with Tenth Armored Division in Europe; recalled for one year during Korean conflict

1947, night school law degree, University of Baltimore Law School

1947–1962, law practice, Baltimore, Md.

1958–1961, chairman, county board of zoning appeals, Baltimore County

1960, ran last in five-way race for circuit judge, Baltimore County

1962, became Baltimore County executive (four-year term)

Nov. 8, 1966, elected governor of Maryland (four-year term; fifth Republican governor in 180 years)

Jan. 25, 1967, inaugurated as governor

Jan. 7, 1969, resigned as governor of Maryland

Jan. 20, 1969–Oct. 10, 1973, Vice President under Richard M. Nixon

Oct. 10, 1973, resigned as Vice President of the United States; later pleaded no contest to charges of income tax evasion before U.S. District Court, Baltimore, Md.; received $10,000 fine and accepted 3 years unsupervised probation

1976, novel, *The Canfield Decision,* published

Courtesy of The Library of Congress

Spiro Agnew, first Vice President to Richard Nixon

1980, *Go Quietly . . . or Else* published
—Apr. 27, 1981, ordered by Maryland judge to pay $247,735 to state to compensate for bribes and kickbacks received while Governor of Maryland and Vice President

SECOND TERM

Name—Gerald Rudolph Ford (40th V.P.)

Political party—Republican

State represented—Michigan

Term of office—Dec. 6, 1973–Aug. 9, 1974

Age at inauguration—60 years, 145 days

Occupation after term—President of the United States

For further biographical information, see the chapter on Gerald Rudolph Ford, 38th President, on page 480.

VICE PRESIDENTIAL VACANCY

The Twenty-fifth Amendment to the Constitution, ratified on February 10, 1967, provides that "whenever there is a vacancy in the office of the Vice President, the President shall nominate a Vice President who shall take office upon confirmation by a vote of both Houses of Congress."

The resignation of Vice President Agnew on October 10, 1973, left the position vacant. President Nixon nominated Gerald Rudolph Ford of Michigan, House Republican leader, in accord with the provisions of the Twenty-fifth Amendment. The nomination was con-firmed by the Senate in a vote of 92 to 3 on November 27, 1973, and by the House of Representatives in a vote of 387 to 35 on December 6, 1973.

Ford was sworn in by Chief Justice Warren E. Burger on December 6, 1973, in the 116-year-old House chamber, as the fortieth Vice President of the United States.

CABINET

FIRST TERM

January 20, 1969–January 20, 1973

State—William Pierce Rogers, Md., Jan. 22, 1969

Treasury—David Matthew Kennedy, Ill., Jan. 22, 1969–Feb. 1, 1971; John Bowden Connally, Jr., Tex., Feb. 11, 1971; George Pratt Shultz, Ill., June 12, 1972

Defense—Melvin Robert Laird, Wis., Jan. 22, 1969

Attorney General—John Newton Mitchell, N.Y., Jan. 22, 1969 (resigned 1972); Richard Gordon Kleindienst, Ariz., June 12, 1972

Postmaster General—Winton Malcolm Blount, Ala., Jan. 22, 1969–July 1, 1971

Interior—Walter Joseph Hickel, Alaska, Jan. 24, 1969–Nov. 25, 1970; Rogers Clark Ballard Morton, Md., Jan. 29, 1971

Agriculture—Clifford Morris Hardin, Neb., Jan. 22, 1969–Nov. 11, 1971; Earl Lauer Butz, Ind., Dec. 2, 1971

Commerce—Maurice Hubert Stans, N.Y., Jan. 22, 1969; Peter George Peterson, Ill., Feb. 21, 1972

Labor—George Pratt Shultz, Ill., Jan. 22, 1969–July 1, 1970; James Day Hodgson, Minn., July 2, 1970

Health, Education, and Welfare—Robert Hutchinson Finch, Calif., Jan. 22, 1969–June 23, 1970; Elliot Lee Richardson, Mass., June 24, 1970

Housing and Urban Development—George Wilcken Romney, Mich., Jan. 22, 1969

Transportation—John Anthony Volpe, Mass., Jan. 22, 1969

Courtesy of the Richard Nixon Library

Richard Nixon, front row center, with his cabinet

SECOND TERM

January 20, 1973–August 9, 1974

State—William Pierce Rogers, Md., continued from preceding administration, resigned Sept. 3, 1973; Henry Alfred Kissinger, Sept. 22, 1973

Treasury—George Pratt Shultz, Ill., continued from preceding administration; William Edward Simon, N.J., May 8, 1974

Defense—Melvin Robert Laird, Wis., continued from preceding administration; Elliot Lee Richardson, Mass., Feb. 2, 1973; James Rodney Schlesinger, Va., July 2, 1973

Attorney General—Richard Gordon Kleindienst, Ariz., continued from preceding administration, resigned Apr. 30, 1973; Elliot Lee Richardson, Mass., May 25, 1973, resigned Oct. 20, 1973; Robert H. Bork (acting), Oct. 21, 1973; William Bart Saxbe, Ohio, Jan. 4, 1974

Interior—Rogers Clark Ballard Morton, Md., continued from preceding administration

Agriculture—Earl Lauer Butz, Ind., continued from preceding administration

Commerce—Peter George Peterson, Ill., continued from preceding administration; Frederick Baily Dent, S.C., Feb. 2, 1973

Labor—James Day Hodgson, Minn., continued from preceding administration; Peter Joseph Brennan, N.Y., Feb. 2, 1973

Health, Education, and Welfare—Elliot Lee Richardson, Mass., continued from preceding administration; Caspar Willard Weinberger, Calif., Feb. 12, 1973

Housing and Urban Development—George Wilcken Romney, Mich., continued from preceding administration; James Thomas Lynn, Ohio, Feb. 2, 1973

Transportation—John Anthony Volpe, Mass., continued from preceding administration; Claude Stout Brinegar, Calif., Feb. 2, 1973

CONGRESS

NINETY-FIRST CONGRESS

January 3, 1969–January 3, 1971

First session—Jan. 3, 1969–Dec. 23, 1969 (355 days)

Second session—Jan. 19, 1970–Jan. 2, 1971 (349 days)

Vice President—Spiro Theodore Agnew, Md.

President pro tempore of the Senate—Richard Brevard Russell, Ga.

Secretary of the Senate—Francis Ralph Valeo, N.Y.

Speaker of the House—John William McCormack, Mass.

Clerk of the House—William Pat Jennings, Va.

NINETY-SECOND CONGRESS

January 3, 1971–January 3, 1973

First session—Jan. 21, 1971–Dec. 17, 1971 (331 days)

Second session—Jan. 18, 1972–Oct. 18, 1972 (275 days)

Vice President—Spiro Theodore Agnew, Md.

President pro tempore of the Senate—Richard Brevard Russell, Ga., d. Jan. 21, 1971; Allen Joseph Ellender, Sr., La., elected Jan. 23, 1971

Secretary of the Senate—Francis Ralph Valeo, N.Y.

Speaker of the House—Carl Bert Albert, Okla.

Clerk of the House—William Pat Jennings, Va.

NINETY-THIRD CONGRESS

January 3, 1973–January 3, 1975

First session—Jan. 3, 1973–Dec. 22, 1973 (354 days)

Second session—Jan. 21, 1974–Dec. 20, 1974 (344 days)

Vice President—Spiro Theodore Agnew, Md., resigned Oct. 10, 1973; Gerald Rudolph Ford, Mich., sworn in Dec. 6, 1973; succeeded to the presidency on the resignation of President Nixon, Aug. 9, 1974

President pro tempore of the Senate —James Oliver Eastland, Miss.

Secretary of the Senate—Francis Ralph Valeo, N.Y.

Speaker of the House—Carl Bert Albert, Okla.

Clerk of the House—William Pat Jennings, Va.

APPOINTMENTS TO THE SUPREME COURT

Chief Justice

Warren Earl Burger, Minn., June 23, 1969 (replaced Earl Warren)

Associate Justices

Harry Andrew Blackmun, Minn., June 9, 1970 (replaced Abe Fortas)

Lewis Franklin Powell, Jr., Va., Jan. 7, 1972 (replaced Hugo LaFayette Black)

William Hubbs Rehnquist, Wis., Jan. 7, 1972 (replaced John Marshall Harlan II)

IMPORTANT DATES IN THE PRESIDENCY

July 20, 1969, first men landed on moon (*Apollo 11* astronauts Neil A. Armstrong and Edwin E. Aldrin, Jr.)

Apr. 8, 1970, Senate rejected nomination of G. Harrold Carswell to Supreme Court (second rejection of Southern conservative; first nominee, Clement F. Haynsworth, Jr., rejected Nov. 21, 1969)

Courtesy of the Richard Nixon Library

President Richard Nixon, right, welcomes the Apollo 11 astronauts aboard the U.S.S. Hornet *on July 24, 1969.*

Apr. 10, 1970, Senate Foreign Relations Committee voted to repeal the 1964 Gulf of Tonkin resolution

Apr. 30, 1970, President announced sending of U.S. troops to Cambodia

May 4, 1970, death of four students killed by gunfire of National Guardsmen at Kent State University (Ohio) during antiwar demonstration touched off nationwide protests

May 14, 1970, two students killed in police gunfire at Jackson State College (Miss.)

June 29, 1970, American ground troops left Cambodia

July 9, 1970, President proposed creation of independent Environmental Protection Agency

Dec. 2, 1970, Senate vetoed supersonic transport aircraft (SST)

Mar. 4, 1971, President declared South Vietnamese drive into Laos successful and promised continued withdrawal of American forces

Mar. 7, 1971, American planes bombed Laos and Cambodia in support of South Vietnamese action

471

Mar. 29, 1971, First Lieutenant William L. Calley found guilty of premeditated murder of 22 South Vietnamese civilians at Songmy (My Lai) in 1968

Apr. 7, 1971, President announced withdrawal of 100,000 American soldiers from South Vietnam by Dec. 1, 1971

Apr. 20, 1971, Supreme Court ruled that busing could be used to achieve desegregation in dual school systems of South

May 2–5, 1971, antiwar demonstrators protested Vietnam War in Washington, D.C.; several thousand arrested

June 10, 1971, President lifted 21-year embargo on trade with Communist China

June 13, 1971, *New York Times* printed excerpts from "Pentagon Papers," classified report on history of U.S. involvement in Vietnam; right to publish material later upheld by Supreme Court

June 28, 1971, Daniel Ellsberg, Defense Department staff member in Johnson Administration, admitted turning over copy of Pentagon Papers to *New York Times*; arraigned on charges of possessing classified material

July 1, 1971, United States Postal Service inaugurated as semi-independent agency

July 5, 1971, President certified Twenty-sixth Amendment lowering voting age from 21 to 18

Aug. 15, 1971, President announced drastic monetary and fiscal program: 90-day wage, price, and rent freeze; "floating" dollar no longer tied to gold; other measures to achieve economic stability

Sept. 3, 1971, secret undercover operatives directed by White House (later exposed as the "plumbers") broke into the office of the psychiatrist of Daniel Ellsberg seeking evidence against Ellsberg

Oct. 23, 1971, UN General Assembly voted to seat Communist China and to expel Nationalist China

Nov. 13, 1971, Phase II of economic stabilization program went into effect with mandatory, flexible controls

Dec. 1971, presidential adviser Henry Kissinger made two trips to Communist China to pave way for President's proposed trip in 1972

Jan. 5, 1972, President approved plans for development of space shuttle

Courtesy of the Richard Nixon Library
President Nixon visits with troops in Vietnam.

Feb. 22, 1972, President conferred with Chinese Premier Chou En-Lai in Beijing

Mar. 22, 1972, Senate approved constitutional amendment banning sex discrimination (subsequent ratification by 38 states required)

May 15, 1972, Governor George Corley Wallace of Alabama, contender for Democratic presidential nomination, wounded in assassination attempt at Laurel, Md., rally

May 22, 1972, President conferred with Communist Party Secretary Leonid I. Brezhnev in Moscow

May 26, 1972, U.S.-Soviet strategic arms control agreements signed (known as "SALT I")

June 17, 1972, five men arrested in burglary of Democratic National Committee headquarters at the Watergate complex, Washington, D.C.

June 29, 1972, Supreme Court declared death penalty unconstitutional

July 8, 1972, President announced $750 million sale of grain to Soviet Union

Aug. 12, 1972, U.S. combat ground troops departed from Vietnam

Oct. 19, 1972, President announced impoundment of funds appropriated by Congress in order to limit Federal spending to $250 billion for fiscal 1973

Dec. 30, 1972, U.S. bombing of Hanoi-Haiphong area halted; resumption of peace talks announced

Jan. 20, 1973, first convictions in Watergate case handed down in U.S. District Court; G. Gordon Liddy and James W. McCord, Jr., were convicted of burglary, conspiracy, eavesdropping, and wiretapping

Jan. 22, 1973, Supreme Court, in the case of *Roe v. Wade,* made abortion legal in all states

Jan. 27, 1973, United States, North Vietnam, South Vietnam, and Viet Cong provisional government signed cease-fire agreement in Paris; end of military draft announced

Feb. 7, 1973, Senate established Select Committee headed by Sam J. Ervin (Democrat, N.C.) to investigate Watergate affair

Feb. 27, 1973, 200 members of American Indian Movement seized Wounded Knee on Oglala Sioux reservation in South Dakota

Apr. 30, 1973, President announced three Watergate-connected resignations (Attorney General Richard G. Kleindienst and chief White House aides John D. Ehrlichman and H. R. Haldeman) and one dismissal (John W. Dean, counsel to President)

May 8, 1973, 70-day occupation of Wounded Knee ended

May 11, 1973, charges against Daniel Ellsberg dismissed because of "conduct of the Government" in the case

May 18, 1973, Archibald Cox named special Watergate prosecutor

July 16, 1973, Alexander P. Butterfield, former presidential appointments secretary, revealed that President had taped all discussions and phone calls in his offices

July 17, 1973, Pentagon revealed that President and Defense Secretary Melvin R. Laird had authorized secret bombing of Cambodia and subsequent falsification of reports

Oct. 2, 1973, energy shortage reached crisis proportions; mandatory fuel allocation announced

Oct. 6, 1973, fourth Arab-Israeli war broke out

Oct. 10, 1973, Vice President Spiro T. Agnew resigned

Oct. 12, 1973, President nominated Gerald R. Ford as Vice President; Ford later confirmed and sworn in (Dec. 6, 1973)

Oct. 14, 1973, President, ordered by Court of Appeals to relinquish tapes to U.S. District Court Judge John J. Sirica, proposed compromise summary of tapes

Oct. 18–21, 1973, Arab countries embargoed oil deliveries in effort to curtail U.S. support to Israel

Oct. 20, 1973, Attorney General Elliot L. Richardson resigned rather than enforce President's order to dismiss special Watergate prosecutor Cox, who had rejected President's compromise on tapes; Assistant Attorney General William Ruckelshaus also resigned

Nov. 5, 1973, Leon Jaworski appointed new special Watergate prosecutor

Nov. 7, 1973, war powers bill, limiting a President's freedom to take military action without congressional approval, enacted by Congress over presidential veto

Nov. 26, 1973, President turned over seven tapes to Judge Sirica

Jan. 4, 1974, President refused to comply with subpoena of Watergate tapes and documents issued by Senate Select [Ervin] Committee

Feb. 6, 1974, House of Representatives authorized Judiciary Committee impeachment inquiry

Feb. 8, 1974, astronauts of *Skylab 3* returned after record space flight of 84 days

Mar. 1, 1974, seven former presidential aides indicted in Watergate cover-up conspiracy: John N. Mitchell, H. R. Haldeman, John D. Ehrlichman, Charles W. Colson (charges dropped June 3, 1974), Robert C. Mardian, Kenneth W. Parkinson (acquitted Jan. 1, 1975), and Gordon Strachan (charges dismissed Mar. 10, 1975); separate sealed report, delivered to House Judiciary Committee, named President as unindicted co-conspirator (disclosure made June 5, 1974)

Mar. 7, 1974, six men indicted on conspiracy charges related to break-in at office of Daniel Ellsberg's psychiatrist

Apr. 11, 1974, House Judiciary Committee subpoenaed tapes and records of White House conversations relating to Watergate

May 2, 1974, former Vice President Agnew disbarred by Maryland Court of Appeals as a result of his *nolo contendere* plea (Oct. 10, 1973) on tax-evasion charge

May 7, 1974, Federal Energy Administration created, replacing Federal Energy Office

May 9, 1974, House Judiciary Committee opened hearings on impeachment

May 16, 1974, former Attorney General Kleindienst pleaded guilty to misdemeanor charge based on inaccurate and incomplete testimony before Senate committee investigating antitrust settlement (first attorney general convicted of criminal offense); felony charges of perjury dropped in return for misdemeanor plea

June 3, 1974, Supreme Court ruled in five-to-three decision that women must receive equal pay for equal work

June 10–19, 1974, President on nine-day tour conferred with Arab and Israeli leaders (first incumbent President to visit Middle East)

July 3, 1974, President signed limited nuclear agreements in Moscow

July 12, 1974, President signed bill curbing executive impoundment of appropriated funds

July 24, 1974, Supreme Court upheld order that presidential tapes and documents be surrendered to the Watergate special prosecutor (first Supreme Court deliberation on criminal case in which President was named as co-conspirator)

July 27–30, 1974, House Judiciary Committee, after months of investigation and nationwide television hearings (July 24–30), recommended to the full house three articles of impeachment: obstruction of justice in the Watergate cover-up, abuse of presidential powers, and contempt of Congress in refusing to supply subpoenaed papers

July 29, 1974, former Secretary of Treasury Connally indicted in milk-support bribery scandal (acquitted Apr. 17, 1975)

July 30, 1974, President surrendered to Judge Sirica 11 subpoenaed tapes that Supreme Court had ordered turned over July 24

July 31, 1974, John D. Ehrlichman, former chief domestic adviser to the President, sentenced after conviction on charges relating to Ellsberg burglary and cover-up

Aug. 2, 1974, former presidential counsel John W. Dean III sentenced on charges relating to his admitted part in Watergate cover-up

Aug. 5, 1974, transcripts of June 23, 1972, White House conversations released, revealing that President had directed FBI to end investigation of Watergate break-in

Aug. 9, 1974, President resigned

ADDITIONAL DATA ON NIXON

RICHARD MILHOUS NIXON

—was the first President to nominate a Vice President under the Twenty-fifth Amendment.

—was the third President against whom articles of impeachment were drawn up.

—was the first President to resign.

—was the first President to be pardoned by his successor for possible offenses against the United States.

—was the first President to visit China while in office.

NIXON'S "CHECKERS" SPEECH

After his nomination to the vice presidency on the Republican ticket in 1952, Senator Nixon came under attack by the Democrats after it was disclosed that he had amassed a secret $18,000 slush fund. The charges were so damaging that Dwight D. Eisenhower, the presidential candidate, considered dropping him from the ticket. To restore his credibility, Nixon bought network television time in the slot after the popular *Milton Berle Show*. In a maudlin but effective performance, he recounted his personal history and struggles, defended his thrift and honesty, and denied accepting any gifts except for a cocker spaniel named Checkers, which he had given to his daughters. As the crowning touch, he added: "I want to say right now that regardless of what they say, we're going to keep it." The speech was a public relations triumph for Nixon and secured his place on the ticket.

FIRST PRESIDENT TO ATTEND LAUNCHING OF A MANNED SPACE FLIGHT

The first President in office to attend the launching of a manned space flight was Richard Milhous Nixon, who viewed the launching of *Apollo 12* at 11:22 A.M., on November 14, 1969, from Pad A at Cape Kennedy, Fla. The crew consisted of Commander Charles Conrad, Jr., Richard Francis Gordon, Jr., in command of the module pilot, and Alan LaVern Bean. The total flight time was 244 hours, 36 minutes, and 25 seconds. All mission objectives were successfully accomplished.

TWENTY-SIXTH AMENDMENT RATIFIED

The Twenty-sixth Amendment to the Constitution enabling individuals eighteen years or older to vote was passed by the Senate (94 to 0) on March 10, 1971, and by the House of Representatives (400 to 19) on March 23, 1971. It was enacted June 30, 1971, when it was passed by Alabama, North Carolina, and Ohio, who were the 36th, 37th, and 38th states to ratify. The first state to ratify was Minnesota, on March 23, 1971. President Richard Milhous Nixon certified the amendment on July 5, 1971.

NIXON VISITED COMMUNIST CHINA

The first President to visit a nation not recognized by the United States was Richard Milhous Nixon, who left the United States on February 17, 1972, and arrived in the People's Republic of China on February 21, 1972, where he conferred with Chairman Mao Tse-tung and Premier Chou En-lai.

THE WATERGATE SCANDAL

On June 17, 1972, five men were arrested for breaking into the Democratic National Committee headquarters at the Watergate hotel and office building complex on the Potomac, in Washington, D.C. At the time of their capture, they were found to be in possession of electronic surveillance devices and cam-

Courtesy of the U.S. Department of State

President Nixon meets with Chairman Mao in China.

eras, all part of an elaborate bugging scheme—devised, it transpired, by agents of the Committee to Re-elect the President.

The break-in was followed by various attempts to cover up the incident on the part of important government officials and chief aides in the Nixon Administration. The full impact of the situation was not felt immediately, but by the end of 1972 the Senate and the press had begun to probe into the Watergate incident. A series of accusations followed, some formal, some implied, concerning covert and illegal activities dealing with campaign sabotage. These activities were said to have been sanctioned directly by White House aides and members of the President's campaign committee.

In total, seven men were indicted by a Federal Grand Jury, on September 15, 1972, on charges related to the bugging and break-in of the Democratic National Committee's offices at Watergate. One conspirator told U.S. District Court Judge John J. Sirica, who presided over the trial of the Watergate Seven, that high-ranking officials were involved in the cover-up.

It became apparent that further examination of the Watergate break-in and cover-up was necessary. On April 17, 1973, President Nixon authorized a new investigation with the appointment of a special Watergate prosecutor, Archibald Cox of Harvard Law School. (He was dismissed by the President, on October 20, 1973, to be replaced by Leon Jaworski; refusal to dismiss Cox led to the resignations of Attorney General Elliot L. Richardson and Deputy Attorney General William D. Ruckelshaus.)

On May 17, 1973, the seven-man Senate Select Committee on Presidential Campaign Activities (better known as the Watergate Committee), headed by Senator Samuel J. Ervin, Jr. (Democrat, North Carolina), reconvened and began a nationally televised inquiry into the events leading up to and following the Watergate incident. The testimony given to the Watergate Committee, by those involved, seriously impaired the credibility of the President. This led to many demands for his impeachment or resignation, and the House Judiciary Committee began an inquiry into possible grounds for impeachment. At the same time, the FBI was investigating an erasure in a White House tape recording of a conversation on Watergate.

The tangled web of scandals collectively known as Watergate continued to dominate the attention of the country during 1974. Constitutional clashes between the Executive and Legislative branches and between the Executive and Judicial branches were given exhaustive coverage by the mass media. Confrontations were reported with accelerating frequency: charges and denials, subpoenas and claims of executive privilege and confidentiality, indictments and sentencings of Cabinet members and presidential aides. Senate and House probes ground on: prosecutors argued their cases in court. Edited transcripts of taped White House conversations, then the tapes themselves—with the unexplained gaps—were made public. Each day brought revelations of political immorality on an unprecedented scale.

Courtesy of Indutiomarus

The Watergate hotel complex as seen from the air

More than twenty-five individuals and many important corporations were involved in court actions stemming from the Watergate affair, from illegal corporation campaign contributions, and from the September 3, 1971, break-in at the California office of the psychiatrist of Daniel Ellsberg, who made public the classified Pentagon Papers. Two former Cabinet members and campaign committee officials—John N. Mitchell, former Attorney General, and Maurice H. Stans, former Secretary of Commerce—and the President's closest aides—H. R. Haldeman, former White House chief of staff, and John D. Ehrlichman, former chief domestic adviser—were among those indicted.

The increasing clamor for resignation or impeachment reflected the turning tide of opinion against the President reelected with the second largest electoral sweep in history. His Vice President had been forced to resign, pleading no contest to tax-evasion charges. What brought about his own downfall was not merely the tapes of the conversations after the Watergate burglary, but a complex of schemes and misconduct at the highest levels. Some of the events predated the June 1972 break-in, some ensued, and all were damaging: the attempt to conceal staff responsibility for the theft; the earlier break-in at the office of Dr. Lewis J. Fielding (psychiatrist of Daniel Ellsberg); the use of domestic surveillance and intelligence operations against political adversaries; the use of the Internal Revenue Service for political benefit; huge undisclosed campaign contributions by large corporations; the secret bombing of Cambodia; the President's questioned income-tax returns; unwarranted federal expenditures for personal homes; the failure to cooperate with congressional investigators and special prosecutors. Two years of "Watergate," of intensifying erosion of popular and congressional support, led to the first resignation from office of a President of the United States.

THE RESIGNATION

On Thursday, August 8, 1974, at 9:00 P.M., Richard Milhous Nixon, the thirty-seventh President of the United States, announced in a nationally televised speech that he would resign, effective at noon on August 9. Refer-

476

ring to his earlier repeated declarations that he would not leave office before his term expired, the President explained his decision:

> Throughout the long and difficult period of Watergate, I have felt it was my duty to persevere, to make every possible effort to complete the term of office to which you elected me.
>
> In the past few days, however, it has become evident to me that I no longer have a strong enough political base in the Congress to justify continuing that effort. . . .
>
> I would have preferred to carry through to the finish whatever the personal agony it would have involved. . . .
>
> I have never been a quitter. To leave office before my term is completed is opposed to every instinct in my body. But as President I must put the interests of America first. America needs a full-time President and a full-time Congress. . . .
>
> To continue to fight through the months ahead for my personal vindication would almost totally absorb the time and attention of both the President and Congress in a period when our entire focus should be on the great issues of peace abroad and prosperity without inflation at home.
>
> Therefore, I shall resign the presidency effective at noon tomorrow.

On the morning of August 9, the President bade farewell to his Cabinet and staff. The Nixon family left immediately for San Clemente, Calif., and did not attend the noon swearing-in of Gerald Rudolph Ford as thirty-eighth President.

ACCEPTANCE OF THE PARDON

In San Clemente, Calif., former President Nixon accepted the pardon granted on September 8, 1974, by President Ford. The unconditional pardon for all federal offenses that he "committed or may have committed or taken part in" while in office precluded any indictment. A statement issued from San Clemente revealed his perspective and mood:

> In accepting this pardon, I hope that his compassionate act will contribute to lifting the burden of Watergate from our country. . . .
>
> Looking back on what is still in my mind a complex and confusing maze of events, decisions, pressures and personalities, one thing I can see clearly now is that I was wrong in not acting more decisively and more forthrightly in dealing with Watergate, particularly when it reached the stage of judicial proceedings and grew from a political scandal into a national tragedy.
>
> No words can describe the depth of my regret and pain at the anguish my mistakes over Watergate have caused the nation and the presidency. . . . I know many fair-minded people believe that my motivations and action in the Watergate affair were intentionally self-serving and illegal. I now understand how my own mistakes and misjudgments have contributed to that belief and seemed to support it. This burden is the heaviest one of all to bear.
>
> That the way I tried to deal with Watergate was the wrong way is a burden I shall bear for every day of the life that is left to me.

(See also The Nixon Pardon on page 480.)

FURTHER READING

Aitken, Jonathan. *Nixon: A Life.* 1993.

Ambrose, Stephen. *Nixon: The Education of a Politician, 1913–1962.* 1987.

———. *Nixon: The Triumph of a Politician, 1962–1972.* 1987.

———. *Nixon: Ruin and Recovery, 1973–1990.* 1991.

Black, Conrad. *Richard M. Nixon: A Life in Full.* 2007.

Emery, Fred. *Watergate: The Corruption of American Politics and the Fall of Richard Nixon.* 1994.

Matusow, Allen J. *Nixon's Economy: Booms, Busts, Dollars, and Votes.* 1998.

Morris, Roger. *Richard Milhous Nixon: The Rise of an American Politician.* 1989.

Perlstein, Rick. *Nixonland: The Rise of a President and the Fracturing of America.* 2008.

Safire, William L. *Before the Fall.* 1975.

White, Theodore H. *Breach of Faith.* 1975.

Wills, Garry. *Nixon Agonistes: The Crisis of the Self-Made Man.* 1970.

Courtesy of The Library of Congress

Gerald R. Ford

Gerald Rudolph Ford

Name at birth—Leslie Lynch King, Jr.

Date of birth—July 14, 1913

Place of birth—Omaha, Neb.

Education—Attended public schools, Grand Rapids, Mich.; South High School, Grand Rapids, graduated 1931; University of Michigan, Ann Arbor, bachelor of science degree in economics and political science, June 27, 1935; Yale Law School, LL.B., June 18, 1941

Religion—Episcopalian

Ancestry—English

Career—Lawyer, Navy officer in World War II, U.S. congressman and House minority leader, Vice President

Political party—Republican

State represented—Michigan

Term of office—Aug. 9, 1974–Jan. 20, 1977

Administration—47th

Congresses—93rd, 94th

Age at inauguration—61 years, 26 days

Occupation after term—Lecturer, author

Date of death—Dec. 26, 2006

Age at death—93 years, 165 days

Place of death—Rancho Mirage, Calif.

Burial place—Grand Rapids, Mich.

FAMILY

FATHER

Name—Leslie Lynch King

Date of birth—July 25, 1882

Place of birth—Shadron, Neb.

First marriage—Dorothy Ayer Gardner, Sept. 7, 1912, Harvard, Ill. (div. 1915)

Second marriage— Margaret Atwood, Jan. 5, 1919, Yuma, Ariz. (b. 1891; 2nd marriage to Roy Mather, 1949)

Occupation—Wool trader

Date of death—Feb. 18, 1941

Place of death—Tucson, Ariz.

Age at death—59 years, 208 days

STEPFATHER

Name—Gerald Rudolff Ford

Date of birth—Dec. 9, 1889

Place of birth—Grand Rapids, Mich.

Occupation—Paint manufacturer; director of county civil defense, civic activist

Marriage—Dorothy Ayer Gardner King, Feb. 1, 1916, Grand Rapids, Mich.

Date of death—Jan. 26, 1962

Place of death—Grand Rapids, Mich.

Age at death—72 years, 48 days

MOTHER

Name at birth—Dorothy Ayer Gardner

Date of birth—Feb. 28, 1892

Place of birth—Harvard, Ill.

First marriage—Leslie Lynch King, Sept. 7, 1912, Harvard, Ill. (div. 1915)

Second marriage—Gerald Rudolff Ford, Feb. 1, 1916, Grand Rapids, Mich.

Date of death—September 17, 1967

Place of death—Grand Rapids, Mich.

Age at death—75 years, 201 days

SIBLINGS

Gerald Rudolph Ford (originally named Leslie Lynch King, Jr.) was the only child of Leslie Lynch King and Dorothy Ayer Gardner King. When he was only a few days old, his mother left home with him in the middle of the night and returned to her parents' house to escape her abusive husband, who had threatened to hurt the baby. Their marriage ended in divorce in 1915. The boy was adopted by his mother's second husband, Gerald Rudolff Ford, and was given the name Gerald Rudolff Ford, Jr. The younger Ford later changed the spelling of his middle name to Rudolph. Ford barely knew his biological father and considered his mother and stepfather to be his true parents.

Ford was the only child of his parents' marriage. Each of his parents remarried and produced additional children, Ford's half-brothers and half-sisters.

Children of Leslie Lynch King and Dorothy Ayer Gardner King

Leslie Lynch King, Jr. (later renamed Gerald Rudolph Ford), b. July 14, 1913, d. Dec. 26, 2006

Children of Gerald Rudolff Ford and Dorothy Ayer Gardner King Ford

Thomas Gardner Ford, b. July 15, 1918, d. Aug. 28, 1995

Richard Addison Ford, b. June 3, 1924

James Francis Ford, b. Aug. 11, 1927, d. Jan. 23, 2001

Children of Leslie Lynch King and Margaret Atwood King

Marjorie B. King, b. 1921, d. Apr. 8, 1993

Leslie Henry ("Bud") King, b. Mar. 28, 1923; d. Dec. 2, 1976

Patricia Jane King, b. 1925

MARRIAGE

Married—Elizabeth Anne ("Betty") Bloomer

Date of marriage—Oct. 15, 1948

Place of marriage—Grand Rapids, Mich.

Age of wife at marriage—30 years, 190 days

Age of husband at marriage—35 years, 93 days

Years married—58 years and 72 days

CHILDREN

Michael Gerald Ford, b. Mar. 14, 1950, Washington, D.C.; m. Gayle Ann Brumbaugh, July 5, 1974, Catonsville, Md.

John ("Jack") Gardner Ford, b. Mar. 16, 1952, Washington, D.C.; m. Juliann Felando, Aug. 29, 1989

Steven Meigs Ford, b. May 19, 1956, Washington, D.C.

Susan Elizabeth Ford, b. July 6, 1957, Washington, D.C.; m. Charles Frederick Vance, Feb. 9, 1979, Palm Desert, Calif. (div.); m. Vaden Bales

THE PRESIDENT'S WIFE

Name at birth—Elizabeth Anne ("Betty") Bloomer

Date of birth—Apr. 8, 1918

Place of birth—Chicago, Ill.

Mother—Hortense Neahr Bloomer

Father—William Stephenson Bloomer (d. 1934)

Father's occupation—Machinery salesman

Stepfather—Arthur Meigs Godwin

Education—Central High School, Grand Rapids, Mich., graduated 1936; Bennington School of the Dance, Bennington, Vt., summers 1936, 1937

First marriage—William C. Warren, 1942 (div. Sept. 22, 1947)

Second marriage—Gerald Rudolph Ford, Oct. 15, 1948, Grand Rapids, Mich.

Children from first marriage—None

Children from second marriage—Michael Gerald Ford, b. Mar. 14, 1950; John Gardner ("Jack") Ford, b. Mar. 16, 1952; Steven Meigs Ford, b. May 19, 1956; Susan Elizabeth Ford, b. July 6, 1957

Occupation—Dancer, teacher of dance, model, department store fashion coordinator

Years younger than the President—4 years, 278 days

THE FIRST LADY

Betty Bloomer Warren Ford was suddenly and dramatically thrust into her position as First Lady in August 1974, just eight months after her husband had assumed office as Vice President.

Before her marriage to Gerald Ford, she had pursued a number of activities. A teenage model at a store in Grand Rapids, Mich., she was later a dance instructor and a student of Martha Graham. After attending the Bennington School of the Dance in Vermont, she moved to New York City to work with the Graham dance group; then, back in Grand Rapids, she became a fashion coordinator and a volunteer teacher of dance to handicapped children.

As the wife of a member of Congress, Mrs. Ford took no direct part in politics, concentrating her efforts on providing a strong and devoted family background for her husband and children. As the President's wife, she became more active; she endorsed the Equal Rights Amendment and lent support to the arts and to programs for handicapped children. Her candor regarding a mastectomy which she underwent on September 28, 1974, was credited with inspiring hundreds of

Courtesy of The Library of Congress

Elizabeth "Betty" Ford, wife of Gerald Ford

women to seek medical advice for symptoms of breast cancer. She was equally candid about her addiction to alcohol and prescription drugs. The treatment center she founded, the Betty Ford Center in Rancho Mirage, Calif., was dedicated on October 3, 1982.

IMPORTANT DATES IN THE PRESIDENT'S LIFE

1917, adopted by Gerald Rudolff Ford

June 1931, graduated from South High School, Grand Rapids, Mich.

1932–1933, linebacker and center on University of Michigan's national championship football teams

1935, graduated from University of Michigan, B.A. degree

1935–1940, boxing coach and assistant varsity football coach, Yale University

June 7, 1941, admitted to Michigan bar

June 18, 1941, graduated from Yale Law School, LL.B. degree

Apr. 20, 1942, enlisted as ensign in U.S. Naval Reserve

June 1943–Dec. 1944, director of physical education, gunnery division officer, and assistant navigator aboard light aircraft carrier, U.S.S. *Monterey*, Pacific theater, World War II

Jan. 1946, discharged with reserve rank of lieutenant commander, with 47 months of active service and ten battle stars

1946–1949, practiced law with firm of Butterfield, Keeney & Amberg in Grand Rapids

Sept. 14, 1948, won Republican nomination for U.S. House of Representatives, defeating four-term incumbent in primary

Jan. 3, 1949–Dec. 6, 1973, served in U.S. House of Representatives (Fifth District, Michigan)

1963–1964, member of Warren Commission

Jan. 4, 1965, elected House minority leader

1965, co-author (with John R. Stiles) of *Portrait of the Assassin,* book about Lee Harvey Oswald

1968, 1972, Permanent Chairman, Republican National Convention

Dec. 6, 1973, confirmed by Congress as Vice President under provisions of the Twenty-fifth Amendment to fill vacancy left by resignation of Vice President Agnew

Dec. 6, 1973–Aug. 9, 1974, Vice President under Richard M. Nixon

Aug. 9, 1974, succeeded to presidency after resignation of Richard M. Nixon

Aug. 9, 1974–Jan. 20, 1977, President

Aug. 18, 1976, nominated for President at Republican National Convention in Kansas City

Nov. 2, 1976, defeated by Jimmy Carter

1979, *A Time to Heal* published

April 27, 1981, dedicated Gerald R. Ford Library in Ann Arbor, Mich.

INAUGURATION

August 9, 1974

Gerald Rudolph Ford was sworn in as the thirty-eighth President on August 9, 1974, at 12:03 P.M. The oath of office was administered by Chief Justice Warren Earl Burger in the East Room of the White House. In his inaugural comments to a nation saddened and stunned by the tumultuous events of the preceding months, he took note of the unprecedented circumstances under which he had succeeded to the presidency:

> The oath I have taken is the same oath that was taken by George Washington and by every President under the Constitution. But I assume the presidency under extraordinary circumstances, never before experienced by Americans. This is an hour of history that troubles our minds and hurts our hearts.
>
> Therefore, I feel it is my first duty to make an unprecedented compact with my countrymen. Not an inaugural speech, not a fireside chat, not a campaign speech, just a little straight talk among friends. And I intend it to be the first of many.

I am acutely aware that you have not elected me as your President by your ballots. So I ask you to confirm me as your President with your prayers. And I hope that such prayers will also be the first of many.

If you have not chosen me by secret ballot, neither have I gained office by any secret promises. I have not campaigned either for the presidency or the vice presidency. I have not subscribed to any partisan platform, I am indebted to no man and only to one woman—my dear wife—as I begin the most difficult job in the world. I have not sought this enormous responsibility, but I will not shirk it. . .

My fellow Americans, our long national nightmare is over. Our Constitution works; our great republic is a government of laws and not of men.

THE VICE PRESIDENT

Name—Nelson Aldrich Rockefeller (41st V.P.)

Date of birth—July 8, 1908

Place of birth—Bar Harbor, Me.

Political party—Republican

State represented—New York

Term of office—December 19, 1974–January 20, 1977

Age at inauguration—66 years, 165 days

Occupation after term—Business, writing

Date of death—January 26, 1979

Age at death—70 years, 202 days

Place of death—New York, N.Y.

Place of burial—North Tarrytown, N.Y.

ADDITIONAL DATA ON ROCKEFELLER

June 17, 1930, graduated from Dartmouth College, A.B., cum laude

1931–1938, director, Rockefeller Center, Inc. (president, 1938–1945, 1948–1951; chairman, 1945–1953, 1956–1958)

1939–1941, 1946–1953, president, Museum of Modern Art, New York City

Aug. 1940, appointed coordinator of Inter-American Affairs by President Roosevelt

1944–1945, assistant secretary of state for American republic affairs

Nov. 1950, appointed chairman of Development Advisory Board, Point IV program, by President Truman

Nov. 1952, appointed chairman of President's Advisory Committee on Government Organization by President Eisenhower

1953–1954, undersecretary, Department of Health, Education, and Welfare

1954, founded Museum of Primitive Art, New York City

1954–1955, special assistant to the President for foreign affairs

1956–1958, chairman, Rockefeller Brothers Funds special studies project, "America at Mid Century"

1956–1959, headed studies of New York State constitution

1958–1973, governor of New York (resigned Dec. 18, 1973)

1972–1974, chairman, National Commission on Water Quality

1973–1974, chairman, Commission on Critical Choices for America

Aug. 20, 1974, nominated as Vice President by President Ford under provisions of the Twenty-fifth Amendment

Courtesy of The Library of Congress

Nelson Rockefeller, Vice President to Gerald Ford

Dec. 19, 1974, confirmed by the Senate and sworn in as Vice President

December 19, 1974–January 20, 1977, Vice President under Gerald R. Ford

Jan. 4, 1975, appointed head of panel to investigate charges of domestic espionage by the CIA

Nov. 3, 1975, announced that he would not run for Vice President in the 1976 election

CABINET

August 9, 1974–January 20, 1977

State—Henry Alfred Kissinger, Mass., continued from preceding administration

Treasury—William Edward Simon, N.J., continued from preceding administration

Defense—James Rodney Schlesinger, Va., continued from preceding administration; Donald Henry Rumsfeld, Ill., Nov. 20, 1975

Attorney General—William Bart Saxbe, Ohio, continued from preceding administration; Edward Hirsch Levi, Ill., Feb. 7, 1975

Interior—Rogers Clark Ballard Morton, Jr., Md., continued from preceding administration; Stanley Knapp Hathaway, Wyo., June 13, 1975; Thomas Savig Kleppe, Oct. 17, 1975

Agriculture—Earl Lauer Butz, Ind., continued from preceding administration; John Albert Knebel, Okla., Nov. 4, 1976

Commerce—Frederick Baily Dent, S.C., continued from preceding administration; Rogers Clark Ballard Morton, Jr., Md., May 1, 1975; Elliot Lee Richardson, Mass., Feb. 2, 1976

Labor—Peter Joseph Brennan, N.Y., continued from preceding administration; John Thomas Dunlop, Mass., Mar. 18, 1975; Willie Julian Usery, Jr., Ga., Feb. 10, 1976

Health, Education, and Welfare—Caspar Willard Weinberger, Calif., continued from preceding administration; Forrest David Matthews, Ala., Aug. 8, 1975

Housing and Urban Development
—James Thomas Lynn, Ohio, continued from preceding administration; Carla Anderson Hills, Calif., Mar. 10, 1975

Transportation—Claude Stout Brinegar, Calif., continued from preceding administration; William Thaddeus Coleman, Jr., Pa., Mar. 7, 1975

CONGRESS

NINETY-FOURTH CONGRESS

January 3, 1975–January 3, 1977

First session—Jan. 14, 1975–Dec. 19, 1975 (340 days)

Second session—Jan. 19, 1976–Oct. 2, 1976 (257 days)

Vice President—Nelson Aldrich Rockefeller, N.Y.

President pro tempore of the Senate —James Oliver Eastland, Mass.

Secretary of the Senate—Francis Ralph Valeo, N.Y.

Speaker of the House—Carl Bert Albert, Okla.

Clerk of the House—William Pat Jennings, Va.

APPOINTMENTS TO THE SUPREME COURT

Associate Justice

John Paul Stevens, Ill., Dec. 19, 1975 (replaced William Orville Douglas)

IMPORTANT DATES IN THE PRESIDENCY

Aug. 12, 1974, President addressed Congress, calling for measures to fight inflation, "public enemy number one"

Sept. 4, 1974, diplomatic relations established with East Germany

Sept. 8, 1974, President granted unconditional pardon to former President Nixon

Sept. 16, 1974, President offered plan granting conditional amnesty to draft evaders and military deserters

Oct. 1, 1974, Watergate cover-up trial of seven former presidential aides began

Oct. 15, 1974, campaign reform legislation enacted, providing for public funding of presidential campaigns

Nov. 1974, mass cutbacks and layoffs announced by automobile manufacturers

Nov. 23–24, 1974, President Ford and Soviet leader Leonid Brezhnev conferred in Vladivostok on limiting the numbers of offensive nuclear weapons

Dec. 19, 1974, Nelson Aldrich Rockefeller confirmed and sworn in as Vice President

Jan. 1, 1975, John N. Mitchell, H. R. Haldeman, John D. Ehrlichman, and Robert C. Mardian convicted in Watergate cover-up trial; Kenneth W. Parkinson acquitted

Jan. 4, 1975, President announced establishment of commission to investigate charges of illegal domestic surveillance by the CIA

Feb. 18, 1975, Supreme Court ruled that former President Nixon had no right to impound funds voted by Congress

Apr. 16, 1975, Cambodian government surrendered to Communist rebel forces

Apr. 17, 1975, former Secretary of the Treasury Connally acquitted in milk-price bribery trial

Apr. 21, 1975, President Nguyen Van Thieu of South Vietnam resigned

Apr. 27, 1975, Saigon shelled and imperiled by approaching Communist forces; President Ford ordered helicopter evacuation of remaining Americans

Apr. 30, 1975, South Vietnam government announced unconditional surrender to the Vietcong

May 1975, unemployment rate at 9.2, highest since 1941, although other signs indicated recession might be ending

May 14, 1975, the American merchantman *Mayaguez*, seized two days before by a Cambodian naval vessel, was retaken by U.S. forces; 15 Americans dead, 3 missing, 50 wounded. American planes sank three Cambodian gunboats and blew up an oil dump on the mainland

June 9, 1975, President made public the report of the Rockefeller Commission, confirming domestic espionage by the CIA

Sept. 27, 1975, Organization of Petroleum Exporting Countries voted a 10-percent rise in price of oil

Oct. 24, 1975, rioting over school integration in South Boston, Mass.

Apr. 28, 1976, Soviet Union agreed to purchase $400 million worth of U.S. grain

May 19, 1976, Senate established a permanent Select Committee on Intelligence

May 28, 1976, U.S. and Soviet Union signed treaty to limit size of underground nuclear explosions; on-site inspection allowed

July 2, 1976, Court ruled death penalty did not constitute cruel and unusual punishment

July 20, 1976, *Viking I* landed on Mars, transmitted pictures and data

Aug. 27, 1976, scientists at MIT synthesized a gene

Oct. 5, 1976, President accepted resignation of Secretary of Agriculture Earl Butz, criticized for racist remark

Jan. 1977, factories, offices, and schools in the East closed because of shortages of natural gas and electricity

ADDITIONAL DATA ON FORD

GERALD RUDOLPH FORD

—was the first President born in Nebraska.

—was the first President to hold the nation's two top posts without being elected to either.

—was the first President to issue a presidential pardon to a former President.

—was the first President to visit Japan while in office.

—was the first President whose parents were divorced.

—was the third left-handed President.

—was the third President in the twentieth century to be denied a second term.

—was the third President to marry a divorced woman.

—was the first Vice President to succeed to the presidency upon the resignation of a President.

—was the first Vice President chosen under the Twenty-fifth Amendment.

—was the ninth Vice President to assume the presidency without being elected to the office.

THE NIXON PARDON

On Sunday morning, September 8, 1974, President Ford startled the nation with his announcement that he had decided to grant his predecessor "a full, free and absolute pardon," explaining his decision as an act of conscience to promote the healing of a troubled nation and to spare the former President and his family further suffering. Public response to the pardon was heated, with many outraged by the President's action and much talk of secret "deals." The President's press secretary, Jerald terHorst, resigned in protest. The pardon was irrevocable, however, and the outcry abated. The text of the proclamation concludes:

Now, therefore, I, Gerald R. Ford, President of the United States, pursuant to the pardon power conferred upon me by Article II, Section 2, of the Constitution, have granted and by these presents do grant a full, free and absolute pardon unto Richard Nixon for all offenses against the United States which he, Richard Nixon, has committed or may

487

have committed or taken part in during the period from January 20, 1969, through August 9, 1974.

In witness whereof, I have hereunto set my hand this 8th day of September in the year of Our Lord Nineteen Hundred Seventy-four, and of the independence of the United States of America the 199th.

FIRST PRESIDENTIAL TEAM IN OFFICE WITHOUT A NATIONAL ELECTION

The first President and Vice President to serve together without being elected to their respective offices were President Gerald Rudolph Ford and Vice President Nelson Aldrich Rockefeller. Both reached office under the provisions of the Twenty-fifth Amendment.

Ford was nominated Vice President by President Nixon on October 12, 1973, two days after the resignation of Spiro Theodore Agnew; on December 6, 1973, Ford was confirmed and sworn in. With the resignation of Nixon on August 9, 1974, Ford succeeded to the presidency.

Rockefeller was nominated Vice President by President Ford on August 20, 1974; on December 19, 1974, after protracted hearings, he was confirmed and sworn in.

Nixon served 56 days without a Vice President; Ford served 132 days without a Vice President.

Courtesy of the Gerald Ford Library

President Ford announces his pardon of Richard Nixon from the Oval Office.

INVESTIGATION AND REFORM OF CIA AND FBI

During the Watergate investigations of 1973–1974, the Central Intelligence Agency and the Federal Bureau of Investigation were found to be implicated in the cover-up scandal, and their involvement was feared to be part of a larger pattern of illegal covert activities. Many abuses were brought to light in investigations held in 1975 and 1976 by the Rockefeller Commission (established by President Ford on January 4, 1975), by congressional committees on intelligence, and by the Justice Department.

The CIA, it was learned, had infiltrated antiwar groups, joined in or originated plots to assassinate foreign political leaders, and conducted drug and bacteria experiments on unsuspecting Americans. The FBI was censured for such acts as violating civil rights while investigating dissident groups, engaging in partisan politics, and conducting a campaign to discredit Martin Luther King, Jr.

For security reasons, the President initially sought to restrict congressional inquiry. When the extent of the abuses became known, however, he attempted to curtail them and restore public confidence in the intelligence services. On November 2, 1975, William E. Colby was dismissed as CIA director and George Bush named in his stead. Secretary of State Kissinger was removed from the post of National Security Advisor. In February 1976, Bush was made chairman of a new intelligence operations coordinating committee under the policy direction of the National Security Council, and an independent oversight board of three was appointed. An executive order limited surveillance of American citizens. A sweeping reorganization of the FBI began in August, but Clarence Kelley was retained as director.

PRESIDENT'S STATEMENT ON VIETNAM EVACUATION

With the military collapse of the Thieu regime in April 1975, President Ford ordered the evacuation of all remaining American personnel in South Vietnam. Reporting on his actions to the nation on April 29, he declared:

During the past week, I had ordered the reduction of American personnel in the United States mission in Saigon to levels that could be quickly evacuated during emergency, while enabling that mission to continue to fulfill its duties.

During the day on Monday, Washington time, the airport at Saigon came under persistent rocket as well as artillery fire and was effectively closed. The military situation in the area deteriorated rapidly.

I therefore ordered the evacuation of all personnel remaining in South Vietnam. The evacuation has been completed. . . .

This action closes a chapter in the American experience. I ask all Americans to close ranks, to avoid recrimination about the past, to look ahead to the many goals we share and to work together on the great tasks that remain to be accomplished.

FORD VETOED LEGISLATION

During his two and a half years in office, President Ford vetoed 66 bills sent to him by Congress (48 by regular veto, 18 by pocket veto). Congress overrode his veto 12 times.

Courtesy of The U.S. Marine Corps

South Vietnamese refugees walk across a U.S. Navy vessel buring Operation Frequent Wind, the final operation in Saigon and the end of the Vietnam War.

ASSASSINATION OF FORD ATTEMPTED TWICE

A threat to the life of President Ford was made on September 5, 1975, by Lynette Alice ("Squeaky") Fromme, aged 27, who pointed a loaded pistol at the President as he moved through a crowd in a park one hundred yards from the California State Capitol in Sacramento. A secret service agent, Larry Beundorf, jammed his hand over the .45-caliber pistol, preventing the weapon from firing. Later it was found that the weapon's chamber was empty.

Fromme, who described herself as a follower of convicted murderer Charles Manson, was charged with attempted assassination. She was tried in the U.S. District Court at Sacramento before Judge Thomas Jamison MacBride, found guilty on November 26, 1975, and sentenced to life imprisonment.

On September 22, 1975, Sara Jane Moore, aged 45, fired a single shot at President Ford as he was leaving the St. Francis Hotel in San Francisco. The bullet, from a .38-caliber revolver, missed him by five feet, striking a taxi driver, who was not seriously wounded. Moore was disarmed by Oliver Sipple, a former Marine, and police officers Tim Hettrich and Gary Lemos.

Charged with attempted assassination, Moore pleaded guilty. Her plea was accepted December 16, 1975, by Judge Samuel Conti of the U.S. District Court in San Francisco, and she was sentenced to life imprisonment.

The day before the shooting, Moore had been arrested for carrying an illegal handgun, questioned by the Secret Service, and released after the weapon was confiscated. She had had ties with radical groups in Berkeley and had been employed by the Federal Bureau of Investigation as an informant.

On February 5, 1979, Moore and another inmate scaled a 12-foot fence and escaped from the Federal Reformatory for Women, a minimum-security prison in West Virginia. The two women were recaptured after four hours.

FORD SUBMITTED HEALTH REPORT

Ford was the first President to release to the public a full report of his medical checkup. He underwent a four-hour examination at the Naval Medical Center, Bethesda, Md., on

January 25, 1975. Rear Admiral William Matthew Lukash, the White House physician, reported, "He is in excellent health. . . The results of all medical tests were normal in every way."

THE BICENTENNIAL

Across the nation, Americans celebrated the 200th anniversary of independence on July 4, 1976, with fireworks, parades, picnics, reenactments of historic moments, and many other commemorative events. President Ford traveled to Independence Hall, Philadelphia, Pa., site of the signing of the Declaration of Independence, and to New York City to review Operation Sail, an international flotilla of sailing ships, from the deck of the carrier *Forrestal*. Then the President returned to the capital to enjoy a brilliant display of fireworks at the Washington Monument.

At 2:00 P.M. eastern daylight time, bells were rung throughout the country in accordance with the White House Bicentennial Independence Day proclamation signed June 29, 1976:

> . . . I, Gerald R. Ford, President of the United States of America, do hereby proclaim that the two hundredth anniversary of the adoption of the Declaration of Independence be observed by the simultaneous ringing of bells throughout the United States at the hour of two o'clock, eastern daylight time, on the afternoon of the Fourth of July, 1976, our Bicentennial Independence Day, for a period of two minutes, signifying our two centuries of independence.
>
> I call upon civic, religious, and other community leaders to encourage public participation in this historic observance. I call upon all Americans, here and abroad, including all United States flag ships at sea, to join in this salute.
>
> As the bells ring in our third century, as millions of free men and women pray, let every American resolve that this nation, under God, will meet the future with the same courage and dedication Americans showed the world two centuries ago. In perpetuation of the joyous ringing of the Liberty Bell in Philadelphia, let us again "proclaim liberty throughout all the land unto all the inhabitants thereof." . . .

FORD DONATED RECORDS

President Ford was the first President while in office to donate to the Federal Government the papers and other historical materials and documents acquired during his career as congressman, Vice President, and President. He declined to accept any tax exemption for this donation. The material is housed in the Gerald R. Ford Library, constructed by the University of Michigan and located on the campus in Ann Arbor.

FORD RECEIVED AWARD FOR NIXON PARDON

On May 21, 2001, former President Gerald Ford received the John F. Kennedy Library's Profile in Courage award for his controversial (and politically costly) pardon of Richard Nixon twenty-seven years previously. The award, named for Kennedy's 1956 book, honors those who have made difficult decisions of conscience. It is symbolized by a silver lantern, which was presented to Ford on this occasion by Caroline Kennedy Schlossberg, the slain President's daughter, at the Kennedy Library in Boston, Mass. Addressing the audience during the ceremony, Senator Edward M. Kennedy of Massachusetts said, "I was one of those who spoke out against his action then. But time has a way of clarifying past events, and now we see that President Ford was right. His courage and dedication to our country made it possible for us to begin the process of healing and put the tragedy of Watergate behind us." Ford said that he was surprised and pleased to be recognized in this way but that historians would probably go on arguing about his decision forever.

A second honoree, Representative John Lewis of Georgia, was cited for his bravery during the civil rights movement of the 1960s and his lifelong commitment to integration.

Each award carried a stipend of $25,000.

PRESIDENT AND STEPFATHER BOTH THIRTY–THIRD–DEGREE MASONS

The thirty-third and highest degree of the Ancient and Accepted Scottish Rite of Freemasonry was conferred on Gerald Rudolff Ford, Sr., on September 30, 1949. The same honorary membership was conferred on Gerald Rudolph Ford, his stepson, on September 26, 1962 (in the Supreme Council for the Northern Masonic Jurisdiction of the United States of America).

FURTHER READING

Firestone, Bernard J. and Ugrinsky, Alexej, eds. *Gerald R. Ford and the Politics of Post-Watergate America.* 1993.

Greene, John Robert. *The Presidency of Gerald R. Ford.* 1995.

Hartmann, Robert T. *Palace Politics.* 1980.

Mollenhoff, Clark. *The Man Who Pardoned Nixon.* 1976.

Reeves, Richard A. *A Ford, Not a Lincoln.* 1975.

Courtesy of The Library of Congress

Jimmy Carter

Name at birth—James Earl Carter, Jr.

Date of birth—Oct. 1, 1924

Place of birth—Plains, Ga.

Education—Attended public schools, Plains, Ga.; Plains High School, graduated 1941; Georgia Southwestern College, Americus, Ga., 1941–1942; Georgia Institute of Technology, 1942–1943; United States Naval Academy, Annapolis, Md., bachelor of science degree, June 5, 1946; Union College, Schenectady, N.Y., degree in nuclear physics, 1952

Religion—Baptist

Ancestry—English, Scotch-Irish

Career—Career naval officer, peanut farmer and broker, chairman of county education board, church deacon, state senator, governor of Georgia

Political party—Democratic

State represented—Georgia

Term of office—Jan. 20, 1977–Jan. 20, 1981

Administration—48th

Congresses—95th, 96th

Age at inauguration—52 years, 111 days

Occupation after term—Lecturing, writing, consultant to Habitat for Humanity, diplomatic and humanitarian missions

FAMILY

FATHER

Name—James Earl Carter

Date of birth—Sept. 12, 1894

Place of birth—Arlington, Ga.

Marriage—(Bessie) Lillian Gordy, Sept. 25, 1923

Occupation—Farmer, soldier, owner of farm supply store, agent for peanut oil mill; Georgia state legislator

Date of death—July 23, 1953

Place of death—Plains, Ga.

Age at death—58 years, 314 days

MOTHER

Name at birth—(Bessie) Lillian Gordy

Date of birth—Aug. 15, 1898

Place of birth—Richland, Ga.

Marriage—James Earl Carter, Sept. 25, 1923

Occupation—Nurse

Date of death—Apr. 30, 1983

Place of death—Americus, Ga.

Age at death—85 years, 76 days

Lillian Gordy Carter was the first mother of a President to be sent on a diplomatic mission. President Carter appointed her, together with his son James Earl ("Chip") Carter III, to head the United States delegation attending the funeral of India's President Fakhruddin Ali Ahmed at New Delhi on February 11, 1977. Mrs. Carter, widely known among Indians for her service as a Peace Corps nurse in the factory town of Vikhroli (1966–1968), was warmly received by both the government and people.

Mrs. Carter joined the Peace Corps at the age of sixty-seven after a busy career as wife, mother, and nurse in Plains, Ga. Prior to joining the Corps, she served as co-chairman of Lyndon Johnson's 1964 campaign in Sumter County, Ga. Long known as a friend of the African-American families in and around Plains—she provided medical help for them when no one else would—she endorsed Johnson's stand in favor of civil rights.

SIBLINGS

Jimmy Carter was the oldest of four children.

Children of James Earl Carter, Sr., and Lillian Gordy Carter

James Earl ("Jimmy") Carter, Jr., b. Oct. 1, 1924

Gloria Carter, b. Oct. 22, 1926, d. 1983

Ruth Carter, b. Aug. 7, 1929, d. 1983

William Alton ("Billy") Carter, 3rd, b. Mar. 29, 1937; d. Sept. 25, 1988

MARRIAGE

Married—(Eleanor) Rosalynn Smith

Date of marriage—July 7, 1946

Place of marriage—Plains, Ga.

Age of wife at marriage—18 years, 323 days

Age of husband at marriage—21 years, 279 days

CHILDREN

John William ("Jack") Carter, b. July 3, 1947, Portsmouth, Va.; m. Juliette Langford, Nov. 20, 1971 (div.); m. Elizabeth Brasfield, May 15, 1992

James Earl ("Chip") Carter, III, b. April. 12, 1950, Honolulu, Hawaii, m. Carol Griffith, June 23, 1973 (div.); m. Ginger Hodges, 1982 (div.); m. Becky Payne

Donnel Jeffrey ("Jeff") Carter, b. Aug. 18, 1952, New London, Conn.; m. Annette Jene Davis, Apr. 6, 1975

Amy Lynn Carter, b. Oct. 19, 1967, Plains, Ga.; m. Michael Antonucci, May 1994, Memphis, Tenn. (div.); m. Jim Wentzel, 1996, Plains, Ga.

THE PRESIDENT'S WIFE

Name at birth—(Eleanor) Rosalynn Smith

Date of birth—Aug. 18, 1927

Place of birth—Botsford, Ga.

Mother—Frances Allethea ("Allie") Murray Smith

Mother's occupation—Seamstress, post office worker

Father—Wilburn Edgar Smith (d. 1940)

Father's occupation—School bus driver, auto-repair shop owner, store clerk, farmer; town councilman

Education—High school, Plains, Ga., graduated (valedictorian), 1944; Georgia Southwestern College, Americus, Ga.

Marriage—James Earl Carter, Jr.

Children—John William ("Jack") Carter, b. July 3, 1947; James Earl ("Chip") Carter, 3rd, b. April. 12, 1950; Donnel Jeffrey ("Jeff") Carter, b. Aug. 18, 1952; Amy Lynn Carter, b. Oct. 19, 1967

Occupation—Businesswoman at family peanut warehouse, political advisor to husband, official U.S. representative on foreign missions

Years younger than the President—2 years, 321 days

Courtesy of The Library of Congress

Rosalynn Carter, wife of Jimmy Carter.

THE FIRST LADY

Rosalynn Smith Carter was a dedicated working associate and supporter of her husband, frequently characterized as one of his few close friends. Before becoming First Lady, she led an active life as a bookkeeper for the family peanut business in Plains, Ga.;

as a political campaigner; and as a governor's wife, with special concern for mental health care.

In the White House, she preferred modest and relatively informal entertainments, and did not consider herself primarily a hostess. She served as Honorary Chairman of the President's Commission on Mental Health and campaigned vigorously for the proposed Equal Rights Amendment.

FIRST FIRST LADY TO MAKE A FOREIGN POLICY TRIP

In the spring of 1977, President Carter made plans to attend the Economic Summit in London, England. Because his schedule, and the schedules of the Vice President and Secretary of State, prevented any of them from undertaking a politically important trip to Latin America, he asked Rosalynn Carter to go as his official representative. From May 30, 1977, to June 12, 1977, she visited the leaders of Jamaica, Costa Rica, Ecuador, Peru, Brazil, Colombia, and Venezuela (a trip of 12,000 miles in all), discussing the Carter administration's foreign policy objectives. She was accompanied by nineteen government officials and 27 journalists.

IMPORTANT DATES IN THE PRESIDENT'S LIFE

1941–1942, attended Georgia Southwestern University, Americus

1942–1943, attended Georgia Institute of Technology, Atlanta (served in naval ROTC)

1943–1946, attended U.S. Naval Academy, Annapolis, Md.

June 5, 1946, graduated from the Naval Academy with a B.S. degree and a naval commission

1946–1953, naval officer, attaining rank of lieutenant commander, serving aboard battleships and submarines

1951, worked under Admiral Hyman G. Rickover on nuclear submarine program

1952, studied nuclear physics at Union College, Schenectady, N.Y., and received postgraduate degree

1953, resigned from Navy to rejoin family farm and warehouse business in Plains, Ga.

1955–1962, chairman of Sumter County, Ga., Board of Education

1963–1966, served two terms in state senate

Sept. 16, 1966, defeated in Georgia Democratic gubernatorial primary

Nov. 3, 1970, elected 76th governor of Georgia (served Jan. 12, 1971–Jan. 12, 1975)

1974, chairman, Democratic National Campaign Committee

Dec. 12, 1974, announced he would seek the Democratic nomination for the presidency

Oct. 1, 1975, *Why Not the Best?* published

Feb. 24, 1976, won New Hampshire presidential primary election, the first of 29 such state contests held in 1976 (Carter entered them all, won 19)

June 16, 1976, chosen presidential candidate by Democratic convention, New York City

Nov. 2, 1976, elected President of the United States

Nov. 15, 1976, was instrumental in persuading congregation of the Baptist Church in Plains, Ga., to drop membership restrictions against blacks

Jan. 20, 1977–Jan. 20, 1981, President

Aug. 14, 1980, renominated for President at the Democratic convention, New York City

Nov. 4, 1980, defeated in presidential election by Ronald Reagan

1982, *Keeping Faith: Memoirs of a President* published

1982, co-founded humanitarian foundation, the Carter Center, in Atlanta, Ga.

1996, *Living Faith* published; a bestseller

Aug. 10, 1999, awarded presidential Medal of Freedom, jointly with Rosalynn Carter

2000, dissociated himself from the Southern Baptist Convention, his longtime denomination, over its increasingly conservative stance

Dec. 10, 2002, awarded the Nobel Peace Prize

ELECTIONS

THE ELECTION OF 1976

November 2, 1976

CANDIDATES

Democratic Party (37th Convention)

July 12–15, 1976, Madison Square Garden, New York, N.Y.

P: Jimmy Carter, Ga.
VP: Walter Frederick Mondale, Minn.

Carter was nominated on the first ballot. Candidates for nomination and the votes they received:

Jimmy Carter, Ga., 2,468$^1/_2$

Morris King Udall, Ariz., 329$^1/_2$

Edmund Gerald Brown, Jr., Calif., 70$^1/_2$

George Corley Wallace, Ala., 57
Ellen McCormack, N.Y, 22
Frank Church, Idaho, 19
Hubert Horatio Humphrey, Minn., 10
Henry Martin Jackson, Wash., 10
Fred Roy Harris, Okla., 9
Milton Shapp, Pa., 2
Robert Carlyle Byrd, W.Va., 1
Cesar Chavez, Wash., 1
Leon Jaworski, Tex., 1
Barbara Charline Jordan, Tex., 1
Edward Moore Kennedy, Mass., 1
Jennings Randolph, W.Va., 1
Fred Stover, Minn., 1
Total number of votes: 3,008
Number necessary for nomination: 1,505

Republican Party (31st Convention)

Aug. 16–19, 1976, Kemper Sports Arena, Kansas City, Mo.

P: Gerald Rudolph Ford, Mich.
VP: Robert Joseph Dole, Kan.

Ford was nominated on the first ballot. Candidates for nomination and the votes they received:
Gerald Rudolph Ford, Mich., 1,187
Ronald Wilson Reagan, Calif., 1,070

Elliott Lee Richardson, Mass., 1
Abstention, 1
Total number of votes: 2,259
Number necessary for nomination: 1,130

Independent candidate (Independence Party)

P: Eugene Joseph McCarthy, Minn.

In some states, McCarthy had to name a running mate in order to appear on the ballot. He had some two dozen running mates in all.

American Independent Party

Aug. 26–28, 1976, Chicago, Ill.

P: Lester Garfield Maddox, Ga.
VP: William E. Dyke, Wis.

In New Jersey only, Christian Larson, N.J., was nominated as President, and Edmund Otto Matzal, N.J., as Vice President.

American Party

P: Thomas J. Anderson, Tenn.
VP: Rufus Shackleford, Fla.

Socialist Workers Party

P: Peter Camejo, N.Y.
VP: Willie Mae Reid, Ill.

Communist Party

June 27–29, 1975, Ambassador West Hotel, Chicago, Ill.

P: Gus Hall, N.Y.
VP: Jarvis Tyner, N.Y.

People's Party

P: Margaret Wright, Calif.
VP: Dr. Benjamin Spock, V.I.

U.S. Labor Party

P: Lyndon Hermyle LaRouche, Jr., N.H.
VP: R. Wayne Evans, Mich.

Libertarian Party

Aug. 25–31, 1975, Statler Hilton Hotel, New York, N.Y.

P: Roger Lea MacBride, Va.
VP: David Bergland, Calif.

Prohibition Party

June 26–27, 1975, Beth Eden Baptist Church, Wheat Ridge, Colo.

P: Benjamin C. Bubar, Me.
VP: Earl F. Dodge, Colo.

Socialist Democrats, U.S.A.

July 17–18, 1976, Americana Hotel, New York, N.Y.

P: Jimmy Carter, Ga.
VP: Walter Frederick Mondale, Minn.

The party was known as the Socialist Party until 1972.

Socialist Labor Party

February 11, 1976, Southfield, Mich.

P: Jules Levin, N.J.
VP: Connie Blomen, Mass.

Socialist Party, U.S.A.

Sept. 1, 1975, Milwaukee, Wis.

P: Frank Paul Zeidler, Wis.
VP: Quinn Brisben, Ill.

1976 POPULAR VOTE

Democratic Party, 40,830,763
Republican Party, 39,147,793
McCarthy (independent candidate), 756,691
Libertarian Party, 173,011
American Independent Party, 170,531
American Party, 160,773
Socialist Workers, 91,314
Communist Party, 58,992
People's Party, 49,024
U.S. Labor Party, 40,043
Prohibition Party, 15,934
Socialist Labor Party, 9,616
Socialist Party, 6,038
Write-in votes (Reagan), 1,260
Scattered write-ins, 36,601
None of these candidates (Nevada), 5,108

1976 ELECTORAL VOTE

Announcement of the electoral vote was made by Vice President Nelson Aldrich Rockefeller on January 6, 1977, before a joint session of Congress. There were 538 electoral votes from the 50 states and the District of Columbia.

Carter received 55.20 percent (297 votes—23 states and District of Columbia) as follows: Ala. 9; Ark. 6; Del. 3; D.C. 3; Fla. 17; Ga. 12; Hawaii 4; Ky. 9; La. 10; Md. 10; Mass. 14; Minn. 10; Miss. 7; Mo. 12; N.Y. 41; N.C. 13; Ohio 25; Pa. 27; R.I. 4; S.C. 8; Tenn. 10; Tex. 26; W.Va. 6; Wis. 11.

Ford received 44.61 percent (240 votes—27 states) as follows: Alaska 3; Ariz. 6; Calif. 45; Colo. 7; Conn. 8; Idaho 4; Ill. 26; Ind. 13; Iowa 8; Kan. 7; Me. 4; Mich. 21; Mont. 4; Neb. 5; Nev. 3; N.H. 4; N.J. 17; N.M. 4; N.D. 3; Okla. 8; Ore. 6; S.D. 4; Utah 4; Va. 12; Vt. 3; Wash. 8; Wyo. 3.

Michael J. Padden, an elector from Washington, cast one of the state's nine electoral votes for Ronald Reagan instead of President Ford. The vote was cast December 13, 1976, at Olympia, Wash.

Courtesy of The Library of Congress

The inauguration of Jimmy Carter

INAUGURATION

January 20, 1977

Jimmy Carter was inaugurated as the thirty-ninth President of the United States at 12:05 P.M on Thursday, January 20, 1977, on a platform erected on the east portico of the Capitol. The weather was clear and cold; snow had been removed from the parade area.

Chief Justice Warren Earl Burger addressed Carter as "Jimmy," and the President-elect, when repeating the oath, stated his name as "Jimmy" instead of "James Earl."

The inaugural address, written largely by Carter himself, was relatively short, taking only 17 minutes to deliver. It drew on a variety of sources, including Jefferson's first inaugural and the words of the Hebrew prophet Micah.

After the ceremony, Carter, accompanied by his wife, Rosalynn, whose left hand he held, walked the mile and a half from the Capitol to the White House, even though a bullet-proof limousine had been assigned to him for the trip. The Carters were later joined by their nine-year-old daughter, Amy, and a group of friends and family members. They entered a solar-heated reviewing stand to watch the inaugural parade, which took two hours to pass by. It included 30 floats, 50 bands, and 400 horses. In the evening, the Carters attended seven inaugural balls given in their honor.

On the occasion of his inauguration President Carter made a special statement that was televised and broadcast to the people of the world.

THE VICE PRESIDENT

Name—Walter Frederick ("Fritz") Mondale (42nd V.P.)

Date of birth—Jan. 5, 1928

Place of birth—Ceylon, Minn.

Political party—Democratic (and, in Minnesota, Democratic-Farmer-Labor)

State represented—Minnesota

Term of office—Jan. 20, 1977–Jan. 20, 1981

Age at inauguration—49 years, 15 days

Occupation after term—Lawyer

ADDITIONAL DATA ON MONDALE

1946–1949, attended Macalester College, St. Paul, Minn.

1948, 2nd Congressional District Manager of Hubert H. Humphrey's successful campaign for U.S. Senate

1951, graduated cum laude from University of Minnesota, B.A. degree

1951–1953, served in U.S. Army, attaining rank of corporal

1953–1956, University of Minnesota Law School, graduating with degree

1958, managed Governor Orville L. Freeman's successful third-term reelection campaign

1956–1960, practiced law with Minneapolis firm

May 1960, appointed Minnesota State Attorney General; elected to that office in Nov. 1960; reelected in 1962

Dec. 30, 1964, appointed to U.S. Senate seat vacated by Hubert H. Humphrey's election as Vice President; elected to Senate in 1966; reelected in 1972

June 18, 1976, chosen vice presidential candidate by the Democratic convention

Nov. 2, 1976, elected Vice President

Jan. 20, 1977–Jan. 20, 1981, Vice President under Jimmy Carter

Jan. 23–Feb. 1, 1977, diplomatic mission to Europe and Japan

Courtesy of The Library of Congress

Walter Mondale, Vice President to Jimmy Carter

Aug. 25–31, 1979, visited China; broadcast an address to the Chinese people

Aug. 14, 1980, renominated for Vice President at Democratic convention

Nov. 4, 1980, defeated in election

July ·18, 1984, nominated for President by Democratic convention, San Francisco, Calif.

Nov. 6, 1984, defeated in election by Ronald Wilson Reagan

CABINET

January 20, 1977–January 20, 1981

State—Cyrus Roberts Vance, N.Y., Jan. 23, 1977; resigned Apr. 21, 1980; Edmund Sixtus Muskie, Me., May 8, 1980

Treasury—Werner Michael Blumenthal, Mich., Jan. 23, 1977; George William Miller, R.I., Aug. 6, 1979

Defense—Harold Brown, Calif., Jan. 23, 1977

Attorney General—Griffin Boyette Bell, Ga., Jan. 26, 1977; Benjamin Richard Civiletti, Aug. 16, 1979

Interior—Cecil Dale Andrus, Idaho, Jan. 23, 1977

Agriculture—Robert Selmer Bergland, Minn., Jan. 23, 1977

Commerce—Juanita Morris Kreps, N.C., Jan. 23, 1977; Philip Morris Klutznick, Ill., Jan. 9, 1980

Labor—Fred Ray Marshall, Tex., Jan. 27, 1977

Health, Education, and Welfare—Joseph Anthony Califano, Jr., D.C., Jan. 25, 1977; Patricia Roberts Harris, D.C., Aug. 3, 1979

Health and Human Services—Patricia Roberts Harris, D.C., Sept. 27, 1979

Housing and Urban Development—Patricia Roberts Harris, D.C., Jan. 23, 1977; Moon Landrieu, La., Sept. 24, 1979

Transportation—Brockman Adams, Wash., Jan. 23, 1977; Neil Edward Goldschmidt, Ore., Sept. 24, 1979

Energy—James Rodney Schlesinger, Va., Oct. 1, 1977; Charles William Duncan, Jr., Tex., Aug. 24, 1979

Education—Shirley Mount Hufstedler, Calif., Dec. 6, 1979

CONGRESS

NINETY–FIFTH CONGRESS

January 3, 1977–January 3, 1979

First session—Jan. 4, 1977–Dec. 15, 1977 (346 days)

Second session—Jan. 19, 1978–Oct. 15, 1978 (270 days)

Vice President—Walter Frederick Mondale, Minn.

President pro tempore of the Senate —James Oliver Eastland, Miss.

Secretary of the Senate—Joseph Stanley Kimmitt, Mont.

Speaker of the House—Thomas Philip O'Neill, Jr., Mass.

Clerk of the House—Edmund Lee Henshaw, Jr., Va.

NINETY–SIXTH CONGRESS

January 3, 1979–January 3, 1981

First session—Jan. 15, 1979–Jan. 3, 1980 (354 days)

Second session—Jan. 3, 1980–Dec. 16, 1980 (349 days)

Vice President—Walter Frederick Mondale, Minn.

President pro tempore of the Senate ·   —Warren Grant Magnuson, Wash.

Secretary of the Senate—Joseph Stanley Kimmitt, Mont.

Speaker of the House—Thomas Philip O'Neill, Jr., Mass.

Clerk of the House—Edmund Lee Henshaw, Jr., Mont.

IMPORTANT DATES IN THE PRESIDENCY

Jan. 21, 1977, President pardoned Vietnam War draft resisters and supported review of desertion cases to upgrade discharges

June 20, 1977, 789-mile Trans-Alaska oil pipeline opened

June 30, 1977, President opposed production of the B-1 strategic bomber, saying that less expensive cruise missiles would be equally effective

Aug. 4, 1977, Department of Energy created

Aug. 10, 1977, U.S. negotiators announced an agreement with Panama on the Canal

Sept. 20, 1977, U.S. and Canada agreed to build a 2,700-mile natural gas pipeline from Alaska to the lower 48 states

Sept. 21, 1977, Bert Lance, Director of the Office of Management and Budget, resigned amid controversy over his personal finances

Nov. 1, 1977, President signed into law a bill that would raise the minimum wage from $2.30 to $3.35 by 1981

Nov. 19, 1977, President Sadat of Egypt arrived in Jerusalem to address the Israeli parliament

Dec. 6, 1977–Mar. 25, 1978, 110-day coal miners' strike, the longest in U.S. history

Jan. 28, 1978, trade deficit for 1977 was reported the biggest ever, principally because of higher prices for imported oil

June 6, 1978, Californians voted to approve Proposition 13, which would cut property taxes in the state 57 percent; beginning of so-called "tax revolt" nationwide

June 16, 1978, President Carter and Brigadier General Omar Torrijos Herrera signed the Panama Canal treaties in Panama City

June 28, 1978, Supreme Court ordered Allan Bakke admitted to the Medical School of the University of California at Davis on grounds that the affirmative-action admissions policy that had excluded the white student was not sufficiently flexible

Aug. 6, 1978, Pope Paul VI died

Sept. 6, 1978, President met with Israeli Prime Minister Begin and Egyptian President Sadat at Camp David

Sept. 17, 1978, Sadat and Begin signed the Camp David accords, virtually ending strife between Egypt and Israel

Sept. 28, 1978, Pope John Paul I died

Oct. 16, 1978, a Polish cardinal, Karol Wojtyla, was elected Pope, taking the papal name of John Paul II

Oct. 24, 1978, President signed Airline Deregulation Act

Nov. 6, 1978, Shah declared martial law throughout Iran after heavy rioting

Nov. 18, 1978, Rep. Leo J. Ryan (D., Calif.) and four others were shot while investigating the People's Temple, an American cult that had emigrated to Guyana. Suicides by over 900 cult members followed

Dec. 17, 1978, OPEC scheduled oil price increases for 1981 of over 14 percent

Jan. 1, 1979, U.S. and China established formal diplomatic ties for the first time since 1949; commercial relations were established Mar. 14, 1979

Jan. 7, 1979, Phnom Penh, capital of Cambodia, fell to an invading army of Vietnamese and exiled Cambodians

Jan. 16, 1979, Shah left Iran after 37 years as ruler

Feb. 1, 1979, Ayatollah Ruholla Khomeini returned to Iran after 15 years of exile; on Feb. 9–11, he took control of the government

Mar. 26, 1979, Israel and Egypt signed a formal peace treaty in Washington

Mar. 28, 1979, nuclear reactor at Three-Mile Island in the Susquehanna River malfunctioned, threatening a meltdown

June 7, 1979, President approved the development of the MX missile

June 1979, gasoline shortage spread around the nation; many states adopted odd-even-day rationing

June 18, 1979, Presidents Carter and Brezhnev signed the SALT II Treaty in Vienna

July 11, 1979, the orbiting space station Skylab disintegrated over Australia and the Indian Ocean

July 17, 1979, President Somoza of Nicaragua resigned and fled the country, as Sandinista guerrillas won the seven-week civil war

July 18, 1979, three Cabinet members dismissed in a shake-up of the administration

Sept. 27, 1979, Department of Education created

Oct. 1, 1979, Panama took control of the Canal Zone from the United States

Oct. 22, 1979, Shah flew to New York City for treatment of cancer

Nov. 3, 1979, Ku Klux Klan killed five demonstrators at an anti-Klan rally in Greensboro, N.C.

Nov. 4, 1979, militants stormed U.S. embassy in Teheran, taking 66 hostages and demanding the return of the Shah

Nov. 19–20, 1979, Iran released thirteen black and women hostages

Nov. 21, 1979, mob attacked the U.S. Embassy in Islamabad, Pakistan, killing four people

Dec. 4, 1979, President announced he would be a candidate for a second term

Dec. 15, 1979, Shah left the U.S. for Panama

Dec. 17, 1979, Senate passed a bill taxing windfall profits in the oil industry

Dec. 21, 1979, Congress granted $1.5 billion in federal loan guarantees to financially imperilled Chrysler Corporation

Dec. 27, 1980, President Hafizullah Amin of Afghanistan was deposed and executed in a coup engineered by the U.S.S.R. and carried out by an invading Soviet army

Jan. 4, 1980, President announced an embargo on sales of technology and a drastic reduction in grain sales to the U.S.S.R.; the administration offered to buy grain off the market to keep the domestic price up

Jan. 25, 1980, Consumer Price Index rose more than 13 percent during 1979, the largest inflation jump since 1946

Feb. 3, 1980, results of FBI Operation Abscam implicated a U.S. senator, seven members of the House, and 31 other public officials

Mar. 24, 1980, Archbishop Oscar Arnulfo Romero assassinated in El Salvador

Apr. 7, 1980, U.S. broke diplomatic relations with Iran

Apr. 17, 1980, President announced that a recession in the U.S. economy had begun

Apr. 22, 1980, U.S. Olympic Committee voted to boycott the Moscow Olympics to protest the Soviet invasion of Afghanistan

Apr. 25, 1980, U.S. helicopter mission to rescue the hostages in Teheran was called off owing to equipment failure; eight died and five were wounded when one of the helicopters collided with a transport plane at a remote staging site in the Iranian desert

Apr. 28, 1980, Cyrus Vance resigned as Secretary of State in protest against the aborted raid on Iran

May 18, 1980, Mount St. Helens in the State of Washington began a series of eruptions

June 6, 1980, unemployment rate rose to 7.8 percent

June 6, 1980, Congress voted to override a presidential veto—the first such override since 1952 by a congress controlled by a president's own political party—thereby killing a proposed fee on imported oil

July 27, 1980, the former Shah of Iran died in Egypt

Aug. 1980, labor unrest spread in Poland as workers went on strike for the right to form independent unions

Sept. 26, 1980, the five-month-long exodus of Cuban refugees to the U.S. ended when the Cuban government closed the port from which the boatlift had been staged

Sept. 22, 1980, war began between Iran and Iraq

Nov. 4, 1980, Ronald Reagan was elected 40th President of the United States

Jan. 18, 1981, the final agreement to exchange the 52 American hostages for billions of dollars of frozen Iranian assets was signed in Teheran by the chief Iranian negotiator and, hours later, by Deputy Secretary of State Warren M. Christopher in Algeria

---

ADDITIONAL DATA ON CARTER

JIMMY CARTER   —was the first President from Georgia.

—was the first President who was a graduate of the U.S. Naval Academy.

—was the first President sworn in using his nickname.

—was the first President to walk from the Capitol to the White House after his inauguration.

—was the first President to appoint three women to the cabinet.

—was the first President to be born in a hospital.

JIMMY WHO?

A response to the queries during the primaries concerning the relatively unknown Jimmy Carter is found in his book *Why Not the Best?*, published in 1975: "I am a Southerner and an American, I am a farmer, an engineer, a father and husband, a Christian, a politician and former governor, a planner, a businessman, a nuclear physicist, a naval officer, a canoeist, and among other things a lover of Bob Dylan's songs and Dylan Thomas's poetry."

THE FORD–CARTER DEBATES

The first public debate between an incumbent President and a rival candidate was held September 23, 1976. Under the sponsorship of the League of Women Voters, three network television companies pooled their resources to telecast President Ford and Jimmy Carter, the Democratic candidate, in a discussion of domestic issues at the Walnut Street Theater, Philadelphia, Pa. A second debate, on foreign policy, took place on October 6, 1976, at the Palace of Fine Arts Theatre in San Francisco, Calif., and a third, unrestricted in subject, took place on October 22, 1976, at Phi Beta Kappa Hall on the campus of the College of William and Mary, Williamsburg, Va. Each debate was ninety minutes long and gave each candidate the opportunity not only to answer questions addressed to him by a panel of journalists but to reply to his opponent's answers.

The first debate between vice presidential candidates, also sponsored by the League of Women Voters, was held October 15, 1976, at the Alley Theatre, Houston, Tex. The Republican candidate, Senator Robert Joseph Dole

of Kansas, and the Democratic candidate, Senator Walter Frederick Mondale of Minnesota, confronted each other during 75 minutes of nationally televised debate on such issues as social programs and the nation's economy.

"ASK PRESIDENT CARTER"

The first presidential phone-in broadcast was presented on March 5, 1977, from the Oval Room of the White House over the CBS television and radio network. Walter Cronkite served as moderator of the "Ask President Carter" show, in which President Jimmy Carter replied to 42 listeners from 26 states who called in questions. More than 9 million callers attempted to reach the President.

THE CARTER ADMINISTRATION AND HUMAN RIGHTS

The Carter administration's policy, first enunciated in his inaugural address, was to consider human rights an integral factor in U.S. relations with other countries. The President addressed the General Assembly of the United Nations on the issue on March 17, 1977, and reemphasized his commitment at meetings of the Organization of American States.

The President carried out his policy by suspending or reducing American aid to nations that chronically violated human rights, including, at one time or another, Argentina, Uruguay, Chile, Nicaragua, Brazil, Venezuela, Ethiopia, and South Africa. He was outspoken in criticizing the Soviet Union and Czechoslovakia for harassing and silencing dissidents—criticism that provoked an angry response from the Soviet Union.

Secretary of State Vance on February 24, 1977, admitted that strategic considerations would cause some inconsistency in the application of the human rights policy, and the President, on July 20, 1978, stated that while he deplored the Soviet campaign against dissidents, he could not intervene directly in the internal affairs of another nation. Nevertheless, he continued to lend moral support to protesters within the Soviet Union and on April 27, 1979, arranged to trade two captured Russian spies for five dissidents.

In national politics, the President supported the proposed Equal Rights Amendment and showed concern over alleged violations of civil liberties by American intelligence agencies.

THE HOSTAGE CRISIS IN IRAN

One event above all others preoccupied, tested, and ultimately frustrated the Carter Administration. The storming of the United States Embassy in Teheran and the capture of 66 Americans on November 4, 1979, began a fourteen-month period in which the United States government searched for some way out of the impasse, for a way to negotiate for the release of the hostages with the various, and sometimes conflicting, segments of political leadership of a divided Iran.

World opinion, the best efforts of the United Nations, diplomatic and economic sanctions, a U.S. military raid, the death of the Shah—none of these in themselves appeared to have an effect on the Iranians' determination to pursue their course of confrontation with the United States. The immediate cause of the Embassy seizure had been the United States' admittance of the former Shah from his political asylum in Mexico for treatment of cancer at a New York hospital. The militants, with the support of the Ayatollah Ruholla Khomeini, had vowed that they would hold the Americans hostage until the Shah was returned to Iran to stand trial on various criminal charges, including torture and murder. However, it gradually became clear that the real motives for the seizure were deeper and more complex, involving the Iranians' image of the United States as a force for evil in Iranian history.

As the months went by, hopes rose and fell with contradictory public statements issued by the Iranian militants, the government, the Parliament, and Ayatollah Khomeini himself. A path to resolution was opened up on September 2, 1980, when the Khomeini announced four conditions for the release of the American hostages. These conditions were accepted by the Iranian parliament on November 2. With Algeria acting as intermediary, the United States and Iran began the complex legal and financial negotiations that would free the American prisoners in exchange for Iranian assets frozen in American banks since the beginning of the crisis,

Courtesy of U.S. Department of Defense

Recently freed Americans held hostage by Iran disembark Freedom One.

the Shah's personal wealth, the cancellation of all U.S. claims against Iran, and a promise from the United States not to interfere in Iranian affairs.

Throughout the last three months of its term in office, the Carter Administration worked to gain the release of the hostages. Demands, counter-proposals, confusions, requests for clarifications dogged the progress of the negotiations up to the last moment. The Iranians dealt a last blow to Carter by waiting to release the hostages until January 20, 1981, just minutes after Ronald Reagan had been sworn in as fortieth President.

THE PANAMA CANAL TREATIES

A major foreign policy achievement of the Carter Administration was the Senate's 1978 ratification of two treaties (signed the previous year by President Carter and Brigadier General Omar Torrigos, Chief of State of Panama) that transferred the control and sovereignty of the Panama Canal to Panama, after almost 75 years as American territory.

The basic treaty, known as the Panama Canal Treaty, called for an increasing Panamanian role in the control, management, and defense of the waterway, culminating in the acquisition by Panama of full sovereignty and control on December 31, 1999. A second treaty, known as the Permanent Neutrality Treaty, guaranteed the canal's neutrality and permitted the United States and Panama to defend the canal after 1999. Negotiations on the two treaties had been going on since 1964.

The biggest obstacle to Senate approval was strong conservative opposition around the country, led by former California Governor Ronald Reagan. Opponents of the treaty argued that retention of the canal was vital to American prestige as well as to national and hemispheric defense, that an American presence in Central America was an important deterrent to Cuban-Soviet influence, and that in any case the waterway and the surrounding strip of land known as the Canal Zone were American territory legitimately acquired, paid for, and defended through the years.

The pro-treaty forces, led by Secretary of State Cyrus R. Vance and buttressed by former President Gerald R. Ford and former Secretary of State Henry A. Kissinger, among many others, maintained that owing to changes in international trade routes and the fact that neither supertankers nor the largest U.S. aircraft carriers could go through the canal, the waterway had lost much of its strategic and commercial importance. Moreover, treaty supporters claimed, transfer of the canal would have a positive effect on U.S. relations not only with Panama but with all of Latin America.

After a prolonged, often bitter national debate and aggressive lobbying by both sides, the Senate approved the Neutrality Treaty on March 16, 1978, by the narrow margin of a 68–32 vote (a two-thirds majority is necessary for any treaty ratification). On April 18, the Senate ratified the basic treaty, again by a 68–32 vote.

On June 16, 1978, President Carter met Brigadier General Torrigos in Panama to exchange the instruments of the treaties' ratification. As of October 1, 1978, the Canal Zone ceased to exist.

EGYPT AND ISRAEL SIGN TREATY

On September 17, 1978, Prime Minister Menachem Begin of Israel and President Anwar Sadat of Egypt signed the Camp David accords, establishing a framework for peace in the Middle East. President Carter, who had been actively involved in the negotiations conducted at his Maryland retreat, signed as a witness.

Reaction in the United States to the news of Camp David was euphoric; however, the Israeli right wing and some of the Arab states were strongly opposed to any attempt to bargain over lands captured by Israel during the 1967 war.

The deadline set in the Camp David accords for a peace treaty came and went, as the Egyptians and Israelis argued and as President Carter and Secretary of State Vance pressured both sides to reach a formal agreement. On March 26, 1979, a treaty was signed in Washington, D.C., ending a 31-year state of war between Egypt and Israel. The treaty implemented the Camp David accords concerning Israeli withdrawal from the Sinai and set a timetable for negotiations on the more difficult questions of Palestinian self-rule, the West Bank, the Gaza Strip, and East Jerusalem. The United States pledged to defend Israel if Egypt broke the treaty and promised aid to both countries.

Although the treaty was acknowledged to be a beginning rather than an end, it was considered a triumph of personal diplomacy for President Carter.

CARTER CREATED CABINET POSTS

On August 4, 1977, the President authorized a Department of Energy and nominated James R. Schlesinger, a former Secretary of

Courtesy of Jimmy Carter Library & Museum

President Carter, center, Anwar Sadat, left, and Prime Minister Menachem Begin join hands to celebrate the signing of the Camp David Accords.

Defense, as its first Secretary. Schlesinger was confirmed by Congress the same day. The Department officially came into existence on October 1, 1977.

On September 27, 1979, the President divided the existing Department of Health, Education, and Welfare into the Department of Health and Human Services and the Department of Education. Patricia Roberts Harris, the Secretary of HEW, continued as Secretary of Health and Human Services, and Shirley M. Hufstedler, a circuit court judge from California, was appointed the first Secretary of Education. She was sworn in on December 6, 1979.

CARTER APPOINTED JUDGES

The Omnibus Judgeship Act (PL 95–486), passed by Congress in 1978 to reduce a huge backlog of cases in the federal court system, created 117 new judgeships on the district courts and 35 on the circuit courts of appeal. This was the greatest expansion of the federal judiciary in the nation's history.

In staffing the new posts and filling the vacancies that occurred during his administration, Carter appointed more women, African-Americans, and Hispanics to the federal bench than any previous President. On the whole, his appointments were well received by the American Bar Association, which rated 62.5 percent of the nominees "well qualified" or "exceptionally well qualified," as compared to 50 percent of Ford's nominees, 49.1 percent of Nixon's, 55.5 percent of Lyndon Baines Johnson's, and 62.2 percent of Kennedy's.

CARTER SIGNED ALASKA CONSERVATION ACT

On December 2, 1980, President Carter signed the Alaska National Interest Lands Conservation Act, adding more than 97 million acres to the national park and wildlife refuge systems in Alaska and placing another 56 million acres of forest, mountain, glacier, and tundra under federal wilderness protection. The act is considered a milestone in conservation history.

POST-PRESIDENTIAL CAREER

After leaving office, Carter and his wife established the Carter Center on the grounds of Emory University in Atlanta, Ga. The organization, operating globally, had two primary components: Peace Programs (including monitoring elections, facilitating negotiations, and promoting the work of human rights activists) and Health Programs (including efforts to improve agriculture and nutrition and to eradicate Third World diseases). Carter's work with the Center, together with his mediation of the Camp David Accords during his presidency, earned him the Nobel Peace Prize in 2002.

Carter was also a prolific writer, and his books tracked the leftward turn of his political thinking over the years. One book in particular, *Palestine: Peace Not Apartheid,* published in 2006, resulted in the departure of 15 members of the Carter Center's advisory board, who tendered their resignations to protest what they said was its bias and inaccuracy. A documentary film about the controversy, *Man from Plains,* premiered in 2007.

FURTHER READING

Bourne, Peter G. *Jimmy Carter: A Comprehensive Biography from Plains to Postpresidency.* 1997.

Brinkley, Douglas. *The Unfinished Presidency: Jimmy Carter's Journey Beyond the White House.* 1998.

Brzezinski, Zbigniew. *Power and Principle.* 1983.

Germond, Jack. *Blue Smoke and Mirrors.* 1981.

Kaufman, Burton Ira. *The Presidency of James Earl Carter, Jr.* 1993.

Morris, Kenneth Earl. *Jimmy Carter: American Moralist.* 1996.

Smith, Gaddis. *Morality, Reason and Power.* 1986.

Courtesy of The Library of Congress

Ronald Reagan

Ronald Wilson Reagan

Date of birth—Feb. 6, 1911

Place of birth—Tampico, Ill.

Education—Tutored by mother; attended public schools, Dixon, Calif.; Dixon High School, graduated 1928; Eureka College, Eureka, Ill., bachelor of arts degree in sociology and economics, June 7, 1932

Religion—Episcopalian

Ancestry—Irish, English, Scottish

Career—Radio announcer, movie and television actor, Army noncombat officer in World War II, president of Screen Actors Guild, spokesman for General Electric, governor of California, radio and newspaper commentator, lecturer

Political party—Republican

State represented—California

Term of office—Jan. 20, 1981–Jan. 20, 1989

Term served—8 years

Administration—49th, 50th

Congresses—97th, 98th, 99th, 100th

Age at inauguration—69 years, 349 days

Occupation after term—Retired, author

Date of death—June 5, 2004

Age at death—93 years, 120 days

Place of death—Los Angeles, Calif.

Burial place—Simi Valley, Calif.

FAMILY

FATHER

Name—John Edward Reagan

Date of birth—July 13, 1883

Place of birth—Fulton, Ill.

Marriage—Nelle Clyde Wilson, 1904, Fulton, Ill.

Occupation—Dry goods store clerk, shoe salesman; head of local welfare office

Date of death—May 18, 1941

Place of death—Hollywood, Calif.

Age at death—57 years, 309 days

MOTHER

Name at birth—Nelle Clyde Wilson

Date of birth—July 24, 1885

Place of birth—Fulton, Ill.

Marriage—John Edward Reagan, 1904, Fulton, Ill.

Date of death—July 25, 1962

Place of death—Santa Monica, Calif.

Age at death—77 years, 1 day

SIBLINGS

Ronald Wilson Reagan was the second of two sons.

Children of John Edward Reagan and Nelle Clyde Wilson Reagan

(John) Neil Reagan, b. Sept. 3, 1909; d. 1996

Ronald Wilson Reagan, b. Feb. 6, 1911; d. June 5, 2004

MARRIAGES

First marriage

Married—Jane Wyman

Date of marriage—January 24, 1940

Place of marriage—Glendale, Calif.

Age of wife at marriage—26 years, 10 days

Age of husband at marriage—28 years, 352 days

Date of divorce—July 19, 1949 (final decree)

Years married—9 years, 176 days

Second marriage

Married—Nancy Davis

Date of second marriage—Mar. 4, 1952

Place of marriage—Los Angeles, Calif.

Age of wife at marriage—30 years, 242 days

Age of husband at marriage—41 years, 26 days

Years married—52 years and 93 days

CHILDREN

Children of Ronald Wilson Reagan and Jane Wyman Reagan

Maureen Elizabeth Reagan, b. Jan. 4, 1941, Los Angeles, Calif.; m. John Filippone, 1961, Washington, D.C.; m. David Sills, Feb. 8, 1964, Beverly Hills, Calif.; m. Dennis Revell, Apr. 25, 1981, Beverly Hills, Calif.; d. Aug. 8, 2001, Sacramento, Calif.

Michael Edward Reagan, b. 1945 (adopted child); m. Pamela Putnam, 1970; m. Colleen Sterns, July 2, 1975, Paris

Christine Reagan, b. June 26, 1947; d. June 27, 1947

Children of Ronald Wilson Reagan and Nancy Davis Reagan

Patricia Ann Reagan (known professionally as Patti Davis), b. Oct. 21, 1952; m. Paul Grilley, Aug. 14, 1984, Los Angeles, Calif.

Ronald Prescott ("Skip," "Ron") Reagan, b. May 20, 1958, Los Angeles, Calif.; m. Doria Palmieri, Nov. 24, 1980, New York City

THE PRESIDENT'S WIVES

First Wife

Name at birth—Sarah Jane Mayfield

Professional name—Jane Wyman

Date of birth—Jan. 5, 1917

Place of birth—St. Joseph, Mo.

Mother—Gladys Hope Christian

Father—Manning Mayfield

Mother's occupation—office worker

Father's occupation—schoolteacher

Adoptive mother—Emme Reise Fulks

Adoptive father—R. D. Fulks

Adoptive father's occupation—police chief

First marriage—Myron Futterman, 1937 (div. 1938)

Second marriage—Ronald Wilson Reagan, January 24, 1940, Glendale, Calif. (div. July 19, 1949)

Third marriage—Fred Karger, 1952 (div.)

Fourth marriage—Fred Karger, 1961 (div. 1965)

Children from first marriage—None

Children from second marriage—Maureen Elizabeth Reagan, b. Jan. 4, 1941; Michael Edward Reagan, b. 1945 (adopted child); Christine, b. June 26, 1947, d. June 27, 1947

Children from third marriage—None

Occupation—Actress

Date of death—Sept. 10, 2007

Age at death—90 years, 248 days

Place of death—Palm Springs, Calif.

Burial place—Cathedral City Calif.

Years younger than the President—5 years, 334 days

Years she outlived the President—3 years, 97 days

Second wife

Name at birth—Anne Frances Robbins

Professional name—Nancy Davis

Date of birth—July 6, 1921

Place of birth—New York, N.Y.

Mother—Edith Luckett Robbins Davis ("Dee Davis")

Father—Kenneth Robbins (div. from mother early 1920s)

Father's occupation—Auto salesman

Stepfather—Dr. Loyal Davis (married Edith Robbins, 1929)

Stepfather's occupation—Neurosurgeon

Education—Girls' Latin School, Chicago, Ill; Smith College, Northampton, Mass., B.A. in drama, 1943

Marriage—Ronald Wilson Reagan, Mar. 4, 1952, Los Angeles, Calif.

Children—Patricia Ann Reagan (known professionally as Patti Davis), b. Oct. 21, 1952; Ronald Prescott ("Skip," "Ron") Reagan, b. May 20, 1958

Occupation—Actress

Years younger than the President—10 years, 120 days

THE FIRST LADY

Nancy Davis Reagan was a stylish and sociable First Lady, with a flair for lavish entertainment and a taste for *haute couture*. She gained valuable experience in public life as the wife of the governor of California; she took up charity work as her project and proved to be a skillful and indefatigable campaigner.

Mrs. Reagan studied drama at Smith College, worked in Broadway theater, and then went to Hollywood. She appeared in eleven films before retiring from movies, though she had roles in three television dramas as late as 1962. She and Ronald Reagan appeared together in *Hellcats of the Navy* (1957), the last motion picture for both of them.

As the First Lady, Mrs. Reagan was prominently involved in the campaign against illegal drugs. She visited drug rehabilitation centers, sponsored drug education programs in public schools, and helped to popularize the slogan "Just Say No," which emphasized the elimination of demand for drugs more than cutting off the sources of their supply.

Although he was an immensely genial man, President Reagan is said to have had only one truly close friend, his wife. Late in the President's second term, Mrs. Reagan

Courtesy of The Library of Congress

Nancy Reagan, wife of Ronald Reagan

was depicted in the press as a wielder of enormous, behind-the-scenes power over the President's White House aides. However, Mrs. Reagan had run-ins with the President's advisors only when she felt that they had deflated his generally upbeat mood or knocked him off his confident stride. Her husband was a consummate political performer and, having been an actress herself, Mrs. Reagan saw it as her duty to keep the President "up" for his public appearances and to nurture his infectiously sunny outlook. Sharing the national stage with him for eight years, she was in many ways the President's unwaveringly loyal "co-star."

IMPORTANT DATES IN THE PRESIDENT'S LIFE

1926–1933, lifeguard at local park

1928, graduated from high school, Dixon, Ill.

June 7, 1932, B.A. degree in sociology and economics from Eureka College, Ill.; was president of student body

1932, hired as sports announcer for Iowa radio station WOC, later part of the NBC network

1932–1937 acquired national reputation as sportscaster

1937, signed $200-a-week contract with Warner Brothers studios

1937, film debut in *Love Is On the Air*

1940, performance in *Knute Rockne—All American* established reputation as serious actor

April 14, 1942, entered U.S. Army as Second Lieutenant of Cavalry in reserve; poor eyesight disqualified him for combat duty

1942–1945, made training films for Army

Dec. 9, 1945, honorable discharge with rank of captain

1945–1962, employed by General Electric Co. as host and program supervisor of *General Electric Theatre*; toured plants as corporate spokesman

1946–1952, Board of Directors, Screen Actors Guild

Nov. 17, 1947–June 1960, president of Screen Actors Guild for five consecutive terms

1947, appeared before House Committee on Un-American Activities as a witness

1948, campaigned for Truman

1949, selected chairman of Motion Pictures Industry Council

1962, switched from Democratic to Republican Party

1962–1965, host and performer on the TV series *Death Valley Days*

1964, campaigned for Goldwater, giving a well-received nationally televised speech for Goldwater that convinced Reagan he might have a future in politics

1965, *Where's the Rest of Me?* published

Jan. 4, 1966, announced candidacy for governor of California

June 7, 1966, won Republican primary

Nov. 8, 1966, defeated Edmund Gerald ("Pat") Brown in gubernatorial election

Jan. 2, 1967, sworn in as governor of California

Jan. 4, 1971, sworn in for second term after defeating Jesse Unruh

1968, 1976, unsuccessful candidate for Republican presidential nomination

July 16, 1980, nominated for President at Republican National Convention in Detroit, Mich.

Nov. 4, 1980, elected President of the United States

Jan. 20, 1981–Jan. 20, 1985, President (first term)

Mar. 30, 1981, shot in the chest by a would-be assassin but was released from hospital in less than two weeks and resumed duties of office.

1982, *Ronald Reagan Talks to America* published

1984, *Abortion and the Conscience of the Nation* published

Nov. 6, 1984, reelected President of the United States, carrying 49 states

Jan. 20, 1985–Jan. 20, 1989, President (second term)

July 13, 1985, underwent surgery for removal of a malignant colon polyp

Jan. 20, 1989, left office with opinion polls showing him to be the most popular President since Franklin D. Roosevelt

Nov. 5, 1994, disclosed diagnosis of Alzheimer's

ELECTIONS

THE ELECTION OF 1980

November 4, 1980

CANDIDATES

Republican Party (32nd Convention)

July 14–17, 1980, Joe Louis Arena, Detroit, Mich.

P: Ronald Wilson Reagan, Calif.
VP: George Herbert Walker Bush, Tex.

   Reagan was nominated on the first ballot. Candidates for nomination and the votes they received:

Ronald Wilson Reagan, Calif., 1,939

John Bayard Anderson, Ill., 37

George Herbert Walker Bush, Tex., 13

Anne Legendre Armstrong, Tex., 1

Abstentions, 4

Total number of votes: 1,994

Number necessary for nomination: 1,130

Democratic Party (38th Convention)

Aug. 11–14, 1980, Madison Square Garden, New York, N.Y.

P: Jimmy Carter, Ga.
VP: Walter Frederick Mondale, Minn.

   Carter was nominated on the first ballot. Candidates for nomination and the votes they received:

Jimmy Carter, Ga., 2,123

Edward Moore Kennedy, Mass., 1,150½ William Proxmire, Wis., 10
Koryne Hobal, Minn., 5
Scott Milne Matheson, Utah, 5
Ronald Vernie Dellums, Calif., 2½
Robert Carlyle Byrd, W.Va., 2
John C. Culver, Iowa, 2
Kent Hance, Tex., 2
Jennings Randolph, W.Va., 2
Warren Spannous, Minn., 2
Alice Tripp, Minn., 2
Edmund Gerald Brown, Jr., Calif., 1
Dale Bumpers, Ark., 1
Hugh Leo Carey, N.Y., 1
Walter Frederick Mondale, Minn., 1
Edmund Sixtus Muskie, Me., 1
Tom Steed, Okla., 1
Uncommitted, 10
Abstentions, 4
Absent, 2
Not voting, 1
Total number of votes: 3,331
Number necessary for nomination: 1,666

Independent Ticket
P: John Bayard Anderson, Ill.
VP: Patrick Joseph Lucey, Wis.

Anderson ran as an independent in some states and as the candidate of the National Unity Party in others.

Libertarian Party
Sept. 7–9, Los Angeles, Calif.
P: Ed Clark, Calif.
VP: David Koch, N.Y.

Citizens Party
Apr. 10–13, 1980, Cleveland, Ohio
P: Barry Commoner, N.Y.
VP: LaDonna Harris, N.M.

Socialist Workers Party
Aug. 14, 1979, Oberlin, Ohio
P: Andrew Pulley, Ill.
VP: Matilde Zimmerman, N.Y.

Andrew Pulley was disqualified because he was under 35 years of age. Clifton De Berry became the candidate in most states where the party was listed; Richard Congress ran in Ohio.

Communist Party
P: Gus Hall, N.Y.
VP: Angela Davis, Calif.

American Independent Party
P: John R. Rarick, La.
VP: Eileen Shearer, Calif.

Independent Ticket
P: Ellen McCormack, N.Y.
VP: Carroll Driscoll, N.J,

McCormack ran as an independent in some states and as the candidate of the Right to Life or Respect for Life Party in others.

Peace and Freedom Party
P: Maureen Smith, Calif.
VP: Elizabeth Cervantes Barron, Calif.

American Party
P: Percy L. Greaves, Jr., N.Y.
VP: Frank Varnum, Calif.

Workers World Party
P: Deirdre Griswold, N.J.
VP: Larry Holmes, N.Y.

National Statesman Party (Prohibition Party)
June 20–21, 1979, Birmingham, Ala.
P: Benjamin C. Bubar, Me.
VP: Earl F. Dodge, Colo.

Socialist Party
Feb. 23–24, 1980, Hotel Wisconsin, Milwaukee, Wis.
P: David McReynolds, N.Y.
VP: Diane Drufenbrock, Wis.

Middle Class Party
P: Kurt Lynen

Down With Lawyers
P: Bill Gahres

Independent Candidate
P: Martin Wendelken

Natural People's League
P: Harley McLain

1980 POPULAR VOTE

Republican Party, 43,901,812
Democratic Party, 35,483,820

Anderson (independent candidate), 5,719,722
Libertarian Party, 921,188
Citizens Party, 234,279
Socialist Workers Party, 50,445
Communist Party, 44,954
American Independent Party, 41,268
McCormack (independent candidate), 32,327
Peace and Freedom Party, 18,116
American Party, 14,338
Workers World Party, 13,300
Nat'l Statesman Party (Prohibition), 7,212
Socialist Party, 6,895
Middle Class, 3,694
Down With Lawyers, 1,718
Wendelken (independent candidate), 923
Natural People's League, 296
Scattered write-ins, 12,796
None of the above, 4,193

1980 ELECTORAL VOTE

Announcement of the electoral vote was made on January 6, 1980, before a joint session of Congress. There were 538 electoral votes from the 50 states and the District of Columbia.

Reagan received 90.89 per cent (489 votes—44 states) as follows; Ala. 9, Alaska 3, Ariz. 6, Ark. 6, Calif. 45, Colo. 7, Conn. 8, Del. 3, Fla. 17, Ida. 4, Ill. 26, Ind. 13, Iowa 8, Kans. 7, Ken. 9. La. 10, Me. 4, Mass. 14, Mich., 21, Miss. 7, Mo. 12, Mon. 4, Neb. 5, Nev. 3, N.H. 4, N.J. 17, N.M. 4, N.Y. 41, N.C. 13, N.D. 3, Ohio 25, Okla. 8, Ore. 6, Pa. 27, S.C. 8, S.D. 4, Tenn. 10, Tex. 26, Utah 4, Vt. 3, Va. 12, Wash. 9, Wis. 11, Wyo. 3

Carter received 9.11 per cent (49 votes—6 states and the District of Columbia) as follows: D.C. 3, Ga. 12, Hawaii 4, Md. 10, Minn. 10, R.I. 4, W.Va. 6

THE ELECTION OF 1984

November 6, 1984

CANDIDATES

Republican Party (33d Convention)
Aug. 20–23, 1984, Dallas Convention Center Dallas, Tex.

P: Ronald Wilson Reagan Calif.

VP: George Herbert Walker Bush, Tex.

Reagan was nominated on the first ballot. Candidates for nomination and the votes they received:
Ronald Wilson Reagan, Calif., 2,233
Abstentions, 2
Total number of votes: 2,235
Number necessary for nomination: 1,500

Democratic Party (39th Convention)
July 16–19, 1984, Moscone Convention Center, San Francisco, Calif.

P: Walter Frederick Mondale, Minn.
VP: Geraldine Anne Ferraro, N.Y.

Mondale was nominated on the first ballot. Candidates for nomination and the votes they received:
Walter Frederick Mondale, Minn., 2,191
Gary Warren Hart, Colo., 1,200$^{1}/_{2}$
Jesse Louis Jackson, Ill., 465$^{1}/_{2}$
Thomas Francis Eagleton, Mo., 18
George Stanley McGovern, S.D., 4
John Herschel Glenn, Jr., Ohio, 2
Joseph Robinette Biden, Jr., Del., 1
Martha Kirkland, Ala., 1
Abstentions, 40
Absent, 10
Total number of votes: 3,933
Number necessary for nomination: 1,967

Libertarian Party
Sept. 3, 1983, New York, N.Y.

P: David Bergland, Calif.
VP: Jim Lewis, Conn.

Independent Democrat
P: Lyndon H. LaRouche, Jr., Va.
VP: Billy Davis, Miss.

Citizens Party
Aug. 10–12, 1984, St. Paul, Minn.

P: Sonia Johnson, Va.
VP: Richard Walton, R.I.

Populist Party
P: Bob Richards, Tex.
VP: Maureen Kennedy Salaman, Calif.

Independent Alliance
P: Dennis L. Serrette, N.J.
VP: Nancy Ross, N.Y.

Communist Party

Jan. 23, 1984, New York, N.Y.

P: Gus Hall, N.Y.
VP: Angela Yvonne Davis, Calif.

Socialist Workers Party

Nov. 1983, New York, N.Y.

P: Mel Mason, Calif.
VP: Andrea González, N.J.

Workers World Party

P: Larry Holmes, N.Y.
VP: Gloria Estella LaRiva, Calif.

In some states, Gavrielle Holmes ran on the Workers World ticket.

American Party

P: Delmar Dennis, Tenn.
VP: Traves Brownlee, Del.

Workers League

P: Ed Winn, Ariz.
VP: Helen Halyard

National Statesman Party (Prohibition Party)

June 22, 1983, Mandan, N.D.

P: Earl F. Dodge, Colo.
VP: Warren C. Martin, N.D.

National Unity Party of Kentucky

P: John D. Anderson

1984 POPULAR VOTE

Republican Party, 54,451,521
Democratic Party, 37,565,334
Libertarian Party, 227,168
Independent Democrat, 78,773
Citizens Party, 71,947
Populist Party, 66,168
Independent Alliance, 58,898
Communist Party, 36,215
Socialist Workers Party, 24,672
Workers World Party, 17,968
American Party, 13,149
Workers League, 14,363
Nat' l Statesman Party (Prohibition), 4,235
National Unity Party of Kentucky, 1,479
None of the above, 1,714
Scattered write-ins and blanks, 17,438

1984 ELECTORAL VOTE

Announcement of the electoral vote was made on January 7, 1985, at a joint session of Congress. There were 538 electoral votes from the 50 states and the District of Columbia.

Reagan received 97.58 per cent (525 votes— 49 states) as follows: Ala. 9, Alaska, 3, Ariz., 7, Ark. 6, Calif. 47, Colo. 8, Conn. 8, Del. 3, Fla. 21, Ga. 12, Hawaii 4, Ida. 4, Ill. 24, Ind. 12, Iowa 8, Kans. 7, Ky. 9, La. 10, Me. 4, Md. 10, Mass. 13, Mich. 20, Miss. 7, Mo. 11, Mon. 4, Neb. 5, Nev. 4, N.H. 4. N.J. 16, N.M. 5, N.Y. 36, N.C. 13, N.D. 3, Ohio 23, Okla. 8, Ore. 7, Pa. 25, R.I. 4, S.C. 8, S.D. 3, Tenn. 11, Tex. 29, Utah 5, Vt. 3, Va. 12, Wash. 10, W. Va. 6, Wis. 11, Wyo. 3.

Mondale received 2.42 percent (13 votes—1 state and the District of Columbia as follows: D.C. 3, Minn. 10.

INAUGURATIONS

FIRST TERM

January 20, 1981

Ronald Wilson Reagan was inaugurated as 40th President of the United States at 11:57 A.M. on Tuesday, January 20, 1981. Chief Justice Warren Earl Burger administered the oath of office. For the first time, the ceremony was held at the West Front of the Capitol, in a symbolic allusion to the new President's western roots. The weather was clear and mild.

The President gave a 20-minute address, calling for "an era of national renewal" and promising to reduce taxes and control government spending. Minutes after, he fulfilled a campaign promise by placing a freeze on government hiring.

As the President finished his address at 12:33 P.M., the Iranian government finally allowed the 52 American hostages to depart from Iran, on the first leg of their journey home. This welcome news added to the festive spirit of the occasion.

The President attended a luncheon at the Capitol and then rode in an open limousine to the White House, waving to spectators and singing the Marine Hymn. From a glass-fronted reviewing stand, he and his family and guests watched a magnificent inaugural parade, including some 8,000 marchers, 450 equestrian teams, Indians in tribal dress, mountain men in coonskin caps, and 25 Alaskan sled dogs. A crowd of more than 300,000 people lined the parade route.

The President and his wife attended all eight inaugural balls held in their honor that evening. The balls were broadcast by cable television to inaugural parties around the nation.

The Reagan inauguration, which cost $8 million, was at the time said to have been the most expensive in American history. Eight years later, however, the cost of President George H. W. Bush's inauguration exceeded $25 million.

SECOND TERM

January 20, 1985

President Reagan was sworn in for his second term by Chief Justice Burger at 11:57 A.M. on January 20, 1985, in the grand foyer of the White House. An outdoor ceremony had been planned, but was canceled when Arctic winds blasted the city and the temperature dropped below zero (–2° F). The inaugural parade down Pennsylvania Avenue was

Courtesy of The Library of Congress

President Reagan takes the oath of office for a second time.

also canceled. (Only one other inaugural parade has ever been canceled—that of Andrew Jackson in 1833.)

In keeping with the tradition that, when the inauguration falls on a Sunday, a second swearing-in ceremony is held on Monday, President Reagan took the oath of office from Chief Justice Burger at 11:48 A.M. in the Rotunda of the Capitol on January 21. His eighteen-minute address called for "a new American Emancipation—a great national drive to tear down economic barriers and liberate the spirit of enterprise in the most distressed areas of the country." In the evening, President and Mrs. Reagan attended nine inaugural balls held in their honor.

THE VICE PRESIDENT

Name—George Herbert Walker Bush (43rd Vice President)
Political party—Republican
State represented—Texas

Term of office—Jan. 20, 1981–Jan. 20, 1989
Age at inauguration—56 years, 223 days

For further biographical information, see chapter on George Herbert Walker Bush, 41st President, on page 473.

CABINET

FIRST TERM

January 20, 1981–January 20, 1985

State—Alexander Meigs Haig, Jr., Conn., Jan. 21, 1981; George Pratt Shultz, Calif., July 16, 1982

Treasury—Donald Thomas Regan, N.J., Jan. 21, 1981

Defense—Caspar Willard Weinberger, Calif., Jan. 20, 1981

Attorney General—William French Smith, Calif., Jan. 22, 1981

Interior—James Gaius Watt, Colo., Jan. 22, 1981; William Patrick Clark, Calif., Nov. 21, 1983

Agriculture—John Rudling Block, Ill., Jan. 22, 1981

Commerce—Malcolm Baldrige, Conn., Jan. 22, 1982

Labor—Raymond Joseph Donovan, N.J., Feb. 3, 1981

Health and Human Services—Richard Schultz Schweiker, Pa., Jan. 21, 1981; Margaret Mary O'Shaughnessy Heckler, Mass., March 9, 1983

Housing and Urban Development—Samuel Riley Pierce, Jr., N.Y., Jan. 22, 1981

Transportation—Drew Lindsay Lewis, Jr., Pa., Jan. 22, 1981; Elizabeth Hanford Dole, Washington, D.C., Feb. 7, 1983

Energy—James Burrows Edwards, S.C., Jan. 22, 1981; Donald Paul Hodell, Ore., Dec. 8, 1982

Education—Terrel Howard Bell, Utah, Jan. 22, 1981

SECOND TERM

January 20, 1985–January 20, 1989

State—George Pratt Shultz, Calif., continued from preceding administration

Treasury—Donald Thomas Regan, N.J., continued from preceding administration; James Addison Baker III, Tex., Feb. 25, 1985; Nicholas Frederick Brady, N.J., Aug. 18, 1988

Defense—Caspar Willard Weinberger, Calif., continued from preceding administration; Frank Charles Carlucci III, Pa., Nov. 21, 1987

Justice—Edward French Smith, Calif., continued from preceding administration; Edwin Meese III, Calif., Feb. 25, 1985; Richard Lewis Thornburgh, Pa., Aug. 12, 1988

Interior—William Patrick Clark, Calif., continued from preceding administration; Donald Paul Hodel, Oreg., Feb. 7, 1985

Agriculture—John Rusling Block, Ill., continued from preceding administration; Richard Edmund Lyng, Calif., Mar. 7, 1986

Commerce—Malcolm Baldrige, Conn., continued from preceding administration;

Calvin William Verity, Jr., Ohio, Oct. 19, 1987

Labor—Raymond James Donovan, N.J., continued from preceding administration; William Emerson Brock III, Tenn., Apr. 29, 1985; Ann Dore McLaughlin, N.J., December 17, 1987

Health and Human Services—Margaret Mary O'Shaughnessy Heckler, Mass., continued from preceding administration; Otis Ray Bowen, Ind., Dec. 13, 1985

Housing and Urban Development—Samuel Riley Pierce, Jr., N.Y., continued from preceding administration

Transportation—Elizabeth Hanford Dole, N.C., continued from preceding administration; James Horace Burnley IV, N.C., Dec. 3, 1987

Energy—Donald Paul Hodel, Ore., continued from preceding administration; John Stewart Herrington, Calif., Feb. 7, 1985

Education—Terrel Howard Bell, Utah, continued from preceding administration; Will-

iam John Bennett, N.C., Feb. 7, 1985; Lauro
Fred Cavazos, Jr., Tex., Sept. 20, 1988

CONGRESS

NINETY-SEVENTH CONGRESS

January 3, 1981–January 3, 1983

First session—Jan. 5, 1981–Dec. 16, 1981
(346 days)

Second session—Jan. 25, 1982–Dec. 23,
1982 (333 days)

Vice President—George Herbert Walker
Bush, Tex.

President pro tempore of the Senate
—(James) Strom Thurmond, S.C.

Secretary of the Senate—William F.
Hildenbrand, Pa.

Speaker of the House—Thomas Philip
O'Neill, Jr., Mass.

Clerk of the House—Edmund Lee Henshaw, Jr., Va.

NINETY-EIGHTH CONGRESS

January 3, 1983–January 3, 1985

First session—Jan. 3, 1983–Nov. 18, 1983
(320 days)

Second session—Jan. 23, 1984–Oct. 12,
1984 (264 days)

Vice President—George Herbert Walker
Bush, Tex.

President pro tempore of the Senate
—(James) Strom Thurmond, S.C.

Secretary of the Senate—William Frye
Hildenbrand, Pa.

Speaker of the House—Thomas Philip
O'Neill, Jr., Mass.

Clerk of the House—Benjamin J. Guthrie,
Md.

NINETY-NINTH CONGRESS

January 3, 1985–January 3, 1987

First session—Jan. 3, 1985–Dec. 20, 1985
(352 days)

Second session—Jan. 21, 1986–Oct. 18,
1986 (278 days)

Vice President—George Herbert Walker
Bush, Tex.

President pro tempore of the Senate
—(James) Strom Thurmond, S.C.

Secretary of the Senate—Jo-Ann L. Coe,
Calif.

Speaker of the House—Thomas Philip
O'Neill, Jr., Mass.

Clerk of the House—Benjamin J. Guthrie,
Md.

ONE HUNDREDTH CONGRESS

January 3, 1987–January 3, 1989

First session—Jan. 6, 1987–Dec. 22, 1987
(351 days)

Second session—Jan. 25, 1988–Oct. 21,
1988 (272 days)

Vice President—George Herbert Walker
Bush, Tex.

President pro tempore of the Senate
—John Cornelius Stennis, Miss.

Secretary of the Senate—Jo-Ann L. Coe,
Calif.

Speaker of the House—James Claude
Wright, Jr., Tex.

Clerk of the House—Benjamin J. Guthrie,
Md.

APPOINTMENTS TO THE SUPREME COURT

Chief Justice

William Hubbs Rehnquist, Wis., Sept. 26,
1986 (replaced Warren Earl Burger)

Associate Justices

Sandra Day O'Connor, Ariz., Sept. 25, 1981
(replaced Potter Stewart)

Antonin Scalia, N.J., Sept. 26, 1986 (replaced William Hubbs Rehnquist)

Anthony McLeod Kennedy, Calif., Feb. 18, 1988 (replaced Lewis Franklin Powell, Jr.)

IMPORTANT DATES IN THE PRESIDENCY

Mar. 30, 1981, President was shot in the chest by a would-be assassin, John Warnock Hinckley, Jr.

Apr. 1, 1981, the U.S. suspended aid to Nicaragua because of the Marxist Sandinista government's alleged assistance to rebels in El Salvador

Apr. 11, 1981, President recovered from gunshot wound and left hospital

July 29, 1981, President's proposal for a three-stage tax cut, the biggest in U.S. history, was approved by Congress

Aug. 5, 1981, President ordered the dismissal of 13,000 air traffic controllers who broke federal law by going on strike

Sept. 25, 1981, Sandra Day O'Connor was sworn in as the first woman justice on the Supreme Court

Oct. 6, 1981, Egyptian President Anwar el-Sadat assassinated by Muslim militants

Apr. 2, 1982, Argentina invaded and seized the British-controlled Falkland Islands

June 5, 1982, Israel launched an invasion of southern Lebanon to eliminate PLO guerrilla bases

June 6, 1982, Reagan addressed meeting of combined Houses of Parliament (first U.S. President to do so) and took Britain's side against Argentina in the Falklands conflict

June 30, 1982, deadline for ratification of the Equal Rights Amendment passed without the necessary votes

Nov. 10, 1982, Soviet leader Leonid Brezhnev died of heart attack

Nov. 12, 1982, Yuri V. Andropov chosen to succeed Brezhnev as general secretary of the Central Committee of the Communist Party

Dec. 2, 1982, first implantation of a permanent artificial heart performed on retired dentist, Barney B. Clark, in Salt Lake City, Utah

Dec. 3, 1982, Labor Department reported the unemployment rate for November as 10.6 percent, the highest since 1940, with nearly 12 million people out of work

Mar. 23, 1983, President urged research and development of the Strategic Defense Initiative

Sept. 1, 1983, South Korean Airlines Flight 007, a passenger plane bound from New York to Seoul, South Korea, shot down by a Soviet fighter plane

Oct. 23, 1983 headquarters of the U.S. Marine Corps force in Beirut blown up by a truck bomb driven into the building's lobby by a Muslim terrorist

Oct. 25, 1983, U.S. invaded Caribbean island of Grenada after a coup by hard-line Marxist members of the government

Oct. 31, 1983, first contingent of U.S. ground-based cruise missiles deployed at Greenham Common Air Base in England in response to an ongoing buildup in Warsaw Pact Countries

Feb. 9, 1984, Soviet leader Yuri V. Andropov died

Feb. 13, 1984, Konstantin U. Chernenko succeeded Andropov as general secretary of the Central Committee of the Communist Party

Apr. 23, 1984, Margaret Heckler, Secretary of Health and Human Services, announced a National Cancer Institute team headed by Dr. Robert Gallo had discovered a viral cause (HIV) for AIDS

May 8, 1984, Soviet Union withdrew from summer Olympic Games

July 28–Aug. 12, 1984, U.S. athletes won record total of 174 medals, including 83 gold, at summer Olympic Games in Los Angeles, Calif.

Oct. 20, 1984, People's Republic of China announced plans to ease state control over the nation's economy and gradually to adopt free-market policies

Oct. 31, 1984, Prime Minister Indira Gandhi of India shot to death by Sikh members of her bodyguard; her son Rajiv succeeded her

Nov. 6, 1984, President reelected

Feb. 6, 1985, with a farm credit crisis posing the greatest threat to U.S. agriculture since the Depression, the administration eased rules governing a $650 million loan-guarantee program, but refused additional funding

Mar. 10, 1985, Soviet leader Konstantin U. Chernenko died

Mar. 11, 1985, Mikhail S. Gorbachev became seventh general secretary of the Central Committee of the Communist Party, at age 54, the youngest Soviet leader since Joseph Stalin

May 5, 1985, President attended a wreath-laying ceremony at Bitburg military cemetery in West Germany, gravesite of nearly 2,000 German soldiers, including 49 Nazis, members of Hitler's SS

July 13, 1985, President had a malignant colon polyp removed; Vice President served as Acting President for eight hours while Reagan was in surgery (first use of Section 3 of the 25th Amendment since ratification in 1967)

Nov. 19-21, 1985, summit meeting between President and Premier Gorbachev in Geneva, Switzerland, the first between Soviet and U.S. heads of state since 1979

Jan. 28, 1986, space shuttle *Challenger* exploded just 74 seconds after liftoff at Cape Canaveral, the worst accident in history of the American space program

Apr. 14, 1986, to deter terrorist strikes against American targets, U.S. mounted air attack on Libya; more than 30 bombers raided desert barracks of Libyan leader Col. Muammar el-Qaddafi and attacked military bases near Tripoli and Benghazi

Courtesy of NASA

The explosion of the space shuttle Challenger

Apr. 28, 1986, Soviet Union reported that the graphite core of a reactor at the Chernobyl Nuclear power plant had caught fire, spewing extraordinarily high levels of radioactive material into the atmosphere

Oct. 22, 1986, President signed into law the most thorough revision of the tax code in more than four decades

Nov. 4, 1986, Democrats won control of the Senate, confronting President with Democratic majorities in both houses of Congress for the first time in Reagan's term of office

Nov. 13, 1986, the White House informed Congressional leaders that U.S. had secretly sold arms to Iran in an attempt to secure the release of Americans held hostage in Lebanon

Nov. 25, 1986, administration admitted that from $10 to $30 million had been diverted from Iranian arms sales and funneled to Nicaraguan *contras* in the form of military aid

Mar. 23, 1987, U.S. offered to protect Kuwaiti tankers in the Persian Gulf, where shipping routes were threatened by Iran

May 5, 1987, congressional hearings investigating Iran-*contra* affair opened

May 6, 1987, CIA Director William Casey died

May 17, 1987, an accidental Iraqi missile attack on the *Stark*, a U.S. Navy frigate in the Persian Gulf, resulted in death of 37 sailors

July 8, 1987, Lieut. Col. Oliver L. North, former National Security Council staff member, testified to Congressional committees investigating Iran-*contra* that former CIA Director William J. Casey had helped provide covert military aid to the *contras*

July 15, 1987, Rear Adm. John M. Poindexter, former chief of the National Security Council, testified to Iran-*contra* committees that he had authorized diversion of profits from Iranian arms sales to contras

Aug. 7, 1987, Central American peace accord signed by the Presidents of Nicaragua, Costa Rica, El Salvador, Honduras, and Guatemala

Aug. 17, 1987, Dow Jones Industrial Average closed above 2,700 for first time

Oct. 19, 1987, stock market convulsed, plunging a record 508 points during a one-day session

Nov. 23, 1987, U.S. and Soviet arms negotiators reached agreement on arms treaty eliminating intermediate-range nuclear missiles

Dec. 7–10, 1987, Gorbachev and Reagan met in Washington, D.C., signing the Intermediate-Range Nuclear Forces Treaty, the first arms treaty to cut the superpowers' nuclear arsenals

Jan. 29, 1988, administration prohibited federally funded family planning centers from discussing abortion with women seeking assistance

Feb. 5, 1988, Panamanian strongman Gen. Manuel Noriega was indicted in Florida on drug trafficking and racketeering charges; U.S. efforts to have him extradited failed

Apr. 14, 1988, accords signed by the U.S.S.R. in Geneva, Switzerland, setting a timetable for the withdrawal of Soviet armed forces from Afghanistan and the creation of a nonaligned Afghan government

May 29–June 1, 1988, President visited the Soviet Union

July 3, 1988, an Iranian jetliner accidentally shot down over Persian Gulf by an American warship; all 290 passengers killed

July 18, 1988, Iran accepted United Nations peace plan calling for a cease-fire in the eight-year-old war between Iran and Iraq

Oct. 3, 1988, space shuttle *Discovery* completed a five-day orbit, making it the first space-shuttle flight since explosion of *Challenger*

Nov. 8, 1988, Vice President Bush was elected President

Dec. 7, 1988, Gorbachev, addressing the United Nations in New York, announced the Soviet Union would reduce the size of its military forces in Warsaw Pact countries

Dec. 14, 1988, State Department lifted a 13-year ban on contacts with the Palestine Liberation Organization after PLO chairman Yasir Arafat renounced terrorism and recognized Israel's right to exist

ADDITIONAL DATA ON REAGAN

RONALD WILSON REAGAN

—was the first President born in Illinois.

—was the first President to have been divorced.

—was the first President to have been head of a union. He was president of the Screen Actors Guild.

—was the oldest President both when he was inaugurated (69 years, 349 days) and when he left office (77 years, 349 days)

—was the eighth President to be the victim of an assassination attempt during his term of office, and the only one to survive a wound.

—was the first President to address a meeting of the combined Houses of Parliament

—was the first President to serve two terms since Eisenhower and only the fourth in the 20th century to serve at least two full terms (the others were Eisenhower, Franklin D. Roosevelt, and Wilson)

REAGAN'S MOVIE DEBUT

Ronald Reagan played a smalltown radio announcer in *Love Is On the Air*, his first film, which was released in 1937. As Andy McLeod, he told too much in his news broadcasts about corrupt local politicians and was demoted to children's programs. But he persevered, exposed the crooks, and won the girl (June Travis). The film was well received.

Reagan's most memorable role was probably that of Drake McHugh, the victim of a sadistic surgeon in *King's Row* (1942), a classic Hollywood film directed by Sam Wood. Reagan also won praise for his portrayal of George Gipp, the football player, in *Knute Rockne—All American* (1940).

REAGAN SAVED LIVES

During the summers of 1927–1932, Ronald Reagan was employed as a lifeguard at the Lowell Park riverside beach near Dixon, Ill. He saved 77 people from drowning, and the town put up a plaque in his honor. The plaque was attached to a wooden log where the lifeguard would notch his "saves"; the log has vanished, but the plaque may still be seen in the Loveland Museum.

REAGAN WAS DIVORCED

Ronald Reagan was the first President to have been divorced. He and Jane Wyman were married on January 24, 1940; they received a final decree of divorce on July 19, 1949. They had two children.

Jane Wyman, a talented, well-known actress, appeared in numerous films and won an Academy Award in 1948 for her portrayal of a girl who can neither hear nor speak in *Johnny Belinda*. She was nominated again for the award in 1951 and 1954. In the 1980s she played a Machiavellian matriarch in *Falcon Crest*, a prime-time television serial.

DAY OF THANKSGIVING

The first formal act of President Reagan was the signing of Joint Resolution Public Law No. 1 designating January 29, 1981, "A Day of Thanksgiving to Honor Our Safely Returned Hostages."

ATTEMPT ON REAGAN'S LIFE

President Reagan was shot in the chest as he left the Washington Hilton Hotel at about 2:30 P.M. on March 30, 1981, after addressing a group of union officials. His assailant, who fired six explosive bullets from a .22-caliber pistol, also wounded the President's press secretary, James Scott Brady; a Secret Service agent, Timothy J. McCarthy; and a District of Columbia policeman, Thomas K. Delahanty.

The President was rushed to nearby George Washington University hospital, where later in the afternoon he underwent surgery to remove a bullet from his left lung. Vice President Bush, cutting short a speaking trip to Texas, flew back to Washington in order to be able to take over the duties of the President should Mr. Reagan be unable to carry them out for even a short period. However, the President's recovery was quick. He joked with his wife and doctors before surgery, and at 7:15 A.M. the next day he signed a piece of legislation. The President returned to the White House April 11, though he remained in considerable pain while continu-

Courtesy of Ronald Reagan Presidential Library Foundation

President Reagan waves to crowd immediately before being shot in an assassination attempt at the Washington Hilton Hotel.

ing to mend from the wound. The other three victims, all severely wounded, survived the attack.

The assailant, John Warnock Hinckley, Jr., 25 years old, of Evergreen, Colo., was overpowered and arrested at the scene of the crime. He had no accomplice. Shortly after midnight, Hinckley was charged with attempting to assassinate the President and shooting the three others. He was sent to Butner Federal Prison near Raleigh, N.C., for psychiatric testing. On June 21, 1982, a jury found Hinckley not guilty by reason of insanity. He was confined for an indefinite period in St. Elizabeth's Hospital, an institution for the mentally ill.

The shooting resulted in lifelong paralysis for James Brady, whose wife became a leader in the handgun-control movement. Continued pressure on Congress, fueled by the frequency of handgun murders and suicides, resulted in the passage of the Brady Bill on November 30, 1993. The bill mandated a five-day waiting period before handgun purchases and set up a computerized system for checking prospective buyers for criminal records.

REAGAN APPOINTS FIRST WOMAN JUSTICE TO THE SUPREME COURT

On July 7, 1981, President Reagan nominated Sandra Day O'Connor, a judge on the Arizona State court of Appeals, to fill the

Supreme Court seat vacated by the retiring Potter Stewart. Although O'Connor was a political conservative, her nomination was opposed by antiabortion activists who considered her voting record in the Arizona Senate, where she served from 1969 to 1974, too liberal. She was confirmed by the Senate by a vote of 99 to 0 and was sworn in on September 25, 1982, becoming the first woman justice in the history of the Supreme Court and the youngest member of the Burger Court.

REAGANOMICS AND THE ECONOMY

President Reagan took office in 1981 during a prolonged period of so-called stagflation. The inflation rate had reached 11.2 percent and interest rates had soared to 20 percent, circumstances that contributed to Reagan's victory over Jimmy Carter. In early 1981 the "misery index," a statistical combination of the unemployment and inflation rates, stood at 20.7 percent.

The President's plan to stimulate the economy while cutting inflation—a version of supply-side economics popularly dubbed "Reaganomics"—combined a three-stage tax cut with a tightened money supply and deep cuts in federal spending for social programs, including funding for health, food, housing, and education. The nation underwent a severe recession, the worst since the Great Depression, and by late 1982 unemployment hit a 42-year high of 10.6 percent, with almost 12 million people out of work. In 1983 the poverty rate reached its highest point in 18 years.

The President supported the tight money policies of Paul Volcker, the head of the Federal Reserve Board, who had been appointed by Jimmy Carter. The harsh medicine prescribed by Volcker helped to cure the ailing economy. By late 1984 inflation was down to 4.3 percent and unemployment stood at 7.4 percent, the same rate it was when Reagan took office. Personal and industrial income had increased substantially and the stock market had reached record heights. Reagan's landslide victory over Walter F. Mondale in 1984 was due in large part to this economic boom. At the end of the President's tenure, the inflation rate was a manageable 4.4 percent and unemployment had fallen to 5.3 percent, the lowest rate since 1974. Moreover,

during an unprecedented peacetime expansion of the economy which began in November 1982, more than 15 million new jobs had been created, and the number of workers earning no more than the minimum wage had been reduced by 22 percent.

Although Reagan had promised to seek a balanced budget during his 1980 election campaign, his policies produced a huge budget deficit that in the view of most economists posed a threat to the long-term stability of the economy. The 1984 deficit rose to $185 billion, a peacetime record, but because of the strong economic recovery, the President made a campaign pledge that he would raise taxes in his second term only as a last resort. At the end of the President's first term, annual interest payments on the federal debt exceeded all the savings in federal spending obtained through cuts in domestic programs.

Nevertheless, the President's belief in supply-side theory—that tax cuts would initially cause a revenue shortfall but also economic growth that would eventually bring revenues into line with expenditures—was unwavering. The average annual deficit in the fiscal years 1982 through 1987 was more than $180 billion, producing total deficits of $1.1 trillion. To forestall being engulfed by this tidal wave of budgetary red ink, the administration borrowed hundreds of billions from foreign countries. Consequently, the U.S., once the world's largest creditor nation, became one of the world's largest debtor nations. The U.S. national debt of $914 billion that Reagan inherited had swollen in 1988 to $2.6 trillion. When Jimmy Carter left office, interest payments of the national debt amounted to $71 billion a year. By 1988 annual debt service had risen to $152 billion—more than the combined budgets of the departments of State, Justice, Agriculture, Transportation, Educaton, Energy, Labor, Interior, and Commerce.

The President's usual response to questions about the deficit was to blame the Congress for wanton social spending and to reiterate his support for a balanced-budget amendment to the Constitution. However, in the six budgets (1981 through 1986) that produced a $1.1 trillion deficit, about 93 percent of the total expenditure was proposed to Congress by the Reagan Administration. Expenditures added by Congress accounted for only one-fourteenth of the deficit.

THE SOVIET UNION AND THE REAGAN DOCTRINE

Relations between the United States and the Soviet Union during the President's first term were mutually distrustful, the two superpowers engaging in proxy confrontations in Central America, the Middle East, Africa, and Asia. The United States launched an unprecedented peacetime buildup of its military, which would ultimately carry a $2.4-trillion price tag, and Reagan's anti-Soviet rhetoric was harsher than that of any recent President. On March 8, 1983, he called the Soviet Union an "evil empire" and Soviet communism "the focus of evil in the modern world." Two weeks later he proposed the Strategic Defense Initiative, a new, laser-beam-operated defensive shield—popularly known as "Star Wars"—that could destroy enemy missiles and warheads in space, although many scientists doubted that the technology for SDI could be perfected.

To counter the Soviet deployment in Warsaw bloc countries of SS-20 medium-range missiles aimed at Western Europe, the United States deployed cruise missiles and medium-range nuclear missiles in five NATO countries during the fall of 1983, despite mass protests in those countries and in the United States. On November 23, 1983, a week after the first cruise missiles were installed in Great Britain, the Soviets withdrew from the arms control negotiations in which they and the United States had been participating since 1981.

As the 1984 presidential election approached and Reagan's reelection seemed certain, he and the Soviets adopted a more conciliatory attitude. Early in 1985 Secretary of State George P. Shultz met with Soviet Foreign Secretary Andrei Gromyko for talks that produced an agreement to begin arms control negotiations in March 1985. And when Mikhail S. Gorbachev was elevated to the position of General Secretary of the Communist Party, President Reagan, who had chosen not to meet with his predecessors Brezhnev, Andropov, or Chernenko, sought a meeting with the new head of the Kremlin.

Economic deterioration in the Soviet Union strengthened Gorbachev's hand with the Central Committee of the Communist Party when he espoused the policies of glasnost, the opening up of Soviet society and a call for the eventual transfer of some power from the Communist Party to popularly elected bodies, and of perestroika, an economic restructuring that lessened state control over agriculture and heavy industry and introduced some free-market practices. Guardedly optimistic about these developments, the Reagan Administration agreed to four superpower summit meetings during his second term. They were held in Geneva, Switzerland; Rejkyavik, Iceland; Washington, D.C.; and Moscow, U.S.S.R.

The most significant result of this thaw in U.S.–Soviet relations took place in Washington, D.C., in December 1987, when Reagan and Gorbachev signed the most sweeping arms control agreement in modern history. The Intermediate-Range Nuclear Force Treaty (INF) eliminating medium-range missiles was the first agreement between the superpowers to reduce their nuclear stockpiles. It led to the destruction of approximately 2,600 warheads over an 18-month period and for the first time permitted the on-site inspection of nuclear missile facilities in the Soviet Union and in the United States.

The Reagan Doctrine was the name given to the President's policy of offering support—covert (CIA aid to anti-Soviet Afghan rebels, for example) as well as overt—to anticommunist insurgencies in the Third World. Since the late 1940s American policy had aimed to contain Soviet expansionism, but Reagan sought to roll back communism in countries where unpopular regimes were propped up by the Soviets or by Soviet client states like Cuba. The forces in the 1980s that coalesced to thwart the spread of totalitarianism had been gathering strength over many years, but the Reagan Doctrine itself produced tangible results. The Soviet Union withdrew from Afghanistan, the Vietnamese began their retreat from Cambodia, and the Cubans agreed to pull out of Angola. At the same time, right-wing dictatorships gave way to democratic rule in the Philippines, South Korea, and Brazil. The ideological component of the Reagan Doctrine stated that social progress is tied to the development of markets, and free markets require political liberty. That argument was forcefully advanced by both the President and his frequent ally in Europe, Prime Minister Margaret Thatcher of Great Britain.

THE INVASION OF GRENADA, THE IRAN-*CONTRA* AFFAIR, AND REAGAN'S POLICIES IN CENTRAL AMERICA

President Reagan ordered a 1,700-man force of U.S. Marines and Army Rangers to invade the Caribbean island of Grenada on October 25, 1983, after the leftist government of Prime Minister Maurice Bishop was overthrown by extremist members of his own party. The administration said that the invasion, called Operation Urgent Fury, was undertaken at the invitation of other Caribbean nations to prevent a takeover by Cuba, and that it had acted to protect more than one thousand American citizens on the island. The death toll in nine days of fighting was 18 American soldiers, 45 Grenadians, and 24 Cubans. The American troops occupied the country until mid-December. A small peacekeeping force remained in Grenada to assist in the establishment of a democratic government. It was the first major armed intervention by the United States in the Western Hemisphere since 1965, when President Johnson ordered the invasion of the Dominican Republic. The U.N. Security Council voted to condemn the invasion, but a majority of the American public supported the President's view that the action was a "rescue mission," not an invasion.

President Reagan's policy in Central America was to contain the spread of communism by both open and covert activities. In El Salvador, the administration sent massive amounts of military and economic aid to the Christian Democratic government of José Napoléon Duarte, which was trying to hold back pressure from right-wing extremists whose death squads murdered thousands of Salvadorans and several American citizens and at the same time suppress a leftist guerrilla rebellion. In Nicaragua, the Reagan administration provided funds, arms, and training to the *contras*, rebels who were dedicated to overthrowing the Marxist Sandinista government. The administration contended that, because of growing Soviet influence in the region, Nicaragua was in danger of being absorbed into the communist bloc.

President Reagan and the Congress often clashed over funding for the *contras*. Congress was willing to support a Central American paramilitary force for the purpose of shutting off the flow of arms from Nicaragua to leftist rebels in El Salvador, but not for the purpose of overthrowing the Sandinistas. Despite calling *contra* leaders the "moral equivalent of our founding fathers," the President was unable to convince the public that Nicaragua posed a serious threat to political stability in Central America.

In December 1983 President Reagan was forced to sign into law the Boland Amendment, which prohibited the expenditure of funds "for the purpose of overthrowing the government of Nicaragua." In 1984, after CIA complicity in the mining of Nicaraguan harbors was proven, Congress cut off all funding for the *contras*. However, CIA Director William Casey arranged for the secret funding of the rebels by Saudi Arabia, which contributed some $15 to $30 million to them. To keep the *contras* from being annihilated by the Nicaraguan military, Congress, in December 1985, provided the rebels with $40 million, most of which was for nonlethal assistance—food, supplies, and transportation. In October 1986 the President prevailed upon the Congress to lift its ban and send the *contras* $100 million in military aid.

Less than a month later, it was revealed that the administration had been secretly selling arms since 1985 to Iran in exchange for Iranian assistance in freeing American hostages from captivity in Lebanon. This arms-for-hostages swap contravened the President's declared policy of never negotiating with terrorists, though Reagan claimed that his Iranian initiative was an attempt to conciliate moderates in Teheran and lay the foundations for an American-Iranian relationship in the post-Khomeini era. But in late November an embarrassing problem blew up into a political crisis for the administration. It came to light in the press that Iran had been overcharged for the weapons and that the profits had been diverted to the *contras* by operatives working on the staff of the National Security Council. In the wake of these revelations, Rear Admiral John Poindexter, chief of the National Security Council, resigned and Lieutenant Colonel Oliver L. North, one of Poindexter's deputies, was dismissed.

A preliminary investigation by Attorney General Edwin Meese disclosed that between $10 and $30 million had been diverted from arms sales profits, though President Reagan claimed not to have known about the scheme. A presidential commission headed by former Senator John Tower was formed to probe into the affair, and joint committees of the House and Senate launched an investigation into Iran-*contra* as well. The Tower Commission found that North had operated a virtual shadow government of clandestine activities from inside the NSC and harshly criticized the President for his lax style of management and for failing to exercise control over his administration's Iran policies.

In testimony before the congressional investigating committees in the summer of 1987, North implicated former CIA chief Casey, who had died on May 6, the day after Congress began its public hearings on Iran-*contra*, in the use of secret funds to finance a guerrilla war. Poindexter testified under oath that he, and not the President, had authorized the diversion of Iranian arms sales profits. Because the operation was potentially explosive politically, he said, he deliberately shielded the President from the decision, which Poindexter insisted would have received presidential approval had Reagan been consulted.

Congressional investigators concluded that in the end only about $3 million in diverted funds actually reached the *contras*, and that another $8 million remained in various bank accounts in Switzerland. With Congress cutting off almost all but humanitarian aid to the *contras*, their potency as a fighting force waned in 1988, when the rebels signed a cease-fire agreement with the Sandinistas. In February 1990 the Nicaraguans held a democratic election for the presidency in which the Sandinistas were defeated.

THE SPACE SHUTTLE AND THE *CHALLENGER* DISASTER

Columbia, the world's first reusable spacecraft, was launched on its maiden flight at 7 A.M. on April 12, 1981, from Cape Canaveral, Florida. The shuttle completed 36 orbits before landing at Edwards Air Force Base in California. Originally budgeted during the Carter administration, the shuttle cost $9.9 billion to develop, and three more shuttlecraft were added to the fleet over the next four years. The first American woman astronaut, Sally Ride, and the first African-American astronaut, Guion Bluford, flew on shuttle flights during 1983.

By the beginning of the President's second term, after an unbroken string of successful flights, the shuttlecraft had become the nation's chief means of putting military, industrial, and scientific payloads into space. The National Aeronautics and Space Administration energetically pursued the goal of making the shuttle a revenue-generating cargo ship, whose missions—such as putting communications satellites into orbit for private industry and ferrying spy satellites to the stratosphere for the Pentagon—ultimately would pay for the costs of the entire shuttle program. Emboldened by success, NASA imposed a demanding schedule of missions on the shuttle program, setting up fifteen flights for the four shuttlecraft in 1986. On the first of these flights, scheduled for January, NASA decided to include a civilian passenger who would be the first private citizen to ride on a shuttle. A competition was held for the privilege and was won by Christa McAuliffe, a high school teacher from New Hampshire. She and six crew members boarded the *Challenger* on the morning of January 28 at the launch pad at Cape Canaveral. At 11:39 A.M., just 74 seconds after liftoff, the *Challenger* exploded in a ball of fire, killing everyone aboard.

In the aftermath of the worst accident in the history of the American space program, President Reagan appointed a commission, headed by William P. Rogers, who had served as Secretary of State under Richard M. Nixon, to study the causes of the *Challenger* explosion and to recommend changes that would make the shuttle program safer.

The President accepted the findings and recommendations of the Rogers Commission in June 1986. The specific cause of the *Challenger* disaster was the failure, due to cold weather on the morning of the launch, of O-rings in the rocket joint to seal in the solid-fuel booster rocket's gases during liftoff. However, the presidential commission found that both the decision to launch the *Challenger* in cold weather and the management of the shuttle program itself were gravely flawed. Warnings by engineers that shuttle launches were unsafe at temperatures lower than 53 degrees Fahrenheit had not been presented to high-level NASA decision-makers. More important, NASA's single-minded, "can-do" determination to meet its own hectic schedule of shuttle flights caused administrators to abandon the safety and quality control standards that had governed the Apollo moon missions of the 1960s and 1970s.

Although a fourth shuttlecraft was built to replace the *Challenger*, the ability of the United States to lift commercial, military, and scientific payloads was crippled for two years. In the meantime, the Reagan administration ordered NASA out of the commercial payload business, directing the agency to use the shuttle for launching military satellites and for space exploration. The first space-shuttle flights since the *Challenger* explosion were conducted in the fall of 1988. On October 3 the *Discovery* completed a five-day orbit. A few weeks later a shuttlecraft completed a spy satellite launching for the Pentagon.

THE TANKER WAR IN THE PERSIAN GULF

In 1987 the seven-year-old war between Iran and Iraq became a threat to commercial shipping in the Persian Gulf, through which flows 60 percent of the noncommunist world's oil. After sustaining a crippling setback in an attack on the Iraqi city of Basra, Iran demanded that Kuwait, a small, oil-rich Gulf sheikdom, cease to provide Iraq with money and port facilities. Thus, in April 1987, when the Soviet Union proposed that three Kuwaiti tankers be placed under the protection of its naval forces, the United States made a higher bid, which Kuwait accepted.

Eleven Kuwaiti oil tankers were re-registered as American vessels, reflagged with the Stars and Stripes, and escorted through the Gulf by U.S. Navy minesweepers and warships. Congressional leaders of both parties feared that American intervention in the Gulf might provoke a war between Iran and the United States, but the Reagan Administration defended its policy by citing three vital interests: one, maintaining the free flow of oil; two, protecting the stability of friendly Gulf States like Saudi Arabia, Oman, Bahrain, and Kuwait; and three, denying political leverage in the Gulf to the Soviets. The administration also wanted to demonstrate to friendly Gulf states and to the European allies that the United States was willing to project its power abroad in the defense of vital interests, that the so-called "Vietnam-induced loss of national nerve" had been overcome.

In May an Iraqi pilot mistook an American frigate for an Iranian warship and launched a missile attack that killed 37 sailors. Commercial shipping was further imperiled in July, when Iran began seeding the Persian Gulf with mines. A long lull in the tanker war was shattered in September, when Iraq launched a series of air attacks against Iranian oil targets. Shortly thereafter, a U.S. Army helicopter destroyed the *Iran Ajr*, an Iranian vessel that had been sowing mines in international waters off the coast of Bahrain. This attack touched off a series of reprisals, including a missile attack on the U.S.-flagged tanker *Sea Isle City*, and culminated, in late October, in the American destruction of two offshore Iranian oil platforms and an answering Iranian missile attack on Kuwait's principal oil terminal.

Rather than retaliate with military force for the missile attack on Kuwait, the United States pressed for an international arms embargo against Iran while continuing to steer Kuwaiti tankers through the Gulf. Over the next six months, U.S. warships escorted Kuwaiti tankers through the embattled Gulf to and from oil ports in the northern end. Despite their overwhelming number, the escort patrols were conducted with all the risks of warfare. And in April 1988, after sustaining a devastating defeat inflicted by Iraq, Iran initiated a new round of mine-sowing that severely damaged a U.S. Navy frigate, the *Samuel B. Roberts*.

When the United States responded by destroying two oil-production platforms, the Iranian Navy launched a quixotic attack on the American fleet. Within a few hours the outcome was settled. In the most significant American naval surface battle since 1944 the United States lost just one helicopter and its two-man crew, whereas 20 percent of the Iranian Navy was destroyed. On April 29 President Reagan ordered American forces in the Gulf to broaden their protection of commercial ships to include all neutral vessels attacked by Iran.

On July 3, 1988, an American warship in the Gulf, the U.S.S. *Vincennes*, shot down an Iranian jetliner that it mistook for hostile aircraft, killing all 290 passengers on board. On

July 19, however, Iran accepted the terms of a United Nations plan that called for a cease-fire in the war with Iraq. President Reagan's policy succeeded in protecting the free flow of oil.

THE OLDEST PRESIDENT

President Reagan, who was 77 years and 349 days old at the conclusion of his second term on January 20, 1989, was the oldest President. Before Reagan, the oldest President was Dwight David Eisenhower, who was 70 years and 98 days old when he left office on January 20, 1961. Reagan also had been the oldest President at the time of his inauguration (he was 69 years and 349 days old on January 20, 1981).

REAGAN'S LAST YEARS

Six years after President Reagan left office, he was diagnosed with Alzheimer's disease, a fatal neurological disorder. On November 5, 1994, he disclosed the diagnosis in a letter to the American people. He continued to live at his home in Los Angeles, Calif., in seclusion.

Courtesy of the U.S. Navy

Former First Lady Nancy Reagan lays her head on the flag-draped coffin of her late husband.

On February 6, 2001, the former President reached his ninetieth birthday, joining John Adams and Herbert Hoover in the ranks of presidential nonagenarians. He had broken his hip in a fall some weeks earlier and was still recovering at the time of his landmark birthday.

FURTHER READING

Barrett, Laurence. *Gambling with History.* 1983.

Brinkley, Douglas, ed. *The Reagan Diaries.* 2007.

Cannon, Lou. *Reagan.* 1982.

Evans, Rowland. *The Reagan Revolution.* 1981.

Fitzgerald, Frances. *Way Out There in the Blue: Reagan, Star Wars, and the End of the Cold War.* 2000.

Pemberton, William E. *Exit with Honor: The Life of President Ronald Reagan.* 1997.

Reagan, Ronald et al. *Reagan, In His Own Hand: The Writings of Ronald Reagan That Reveal His Revolutionary Vision for America.* 2001.

Schaller, Michael. *Reckoning with Reagan: America and Its President in the 1980s.* 1992.

Wills, Garry. *Reagan's America: Innocents at Home.* 1987.

Courtesy of The Library of Congress

41st PRESIDENT

George Herbert Walker Bush

Date of birth—June 12, 1924

Place of birth—Milton, Mass.

Education—Phillips Academy, Andover, Mass., graduated 1941; Yale College, New Haven, Conn., bachelor of arts degree in economics, June 22, 1948

Religion—Episcopalian

Ancestry—English

Career—Navy pilot in World War II, equipment salesman, president and CEO of oil drilling company, U.S. congressman, U.S. ambassador to the United Nations, chairman of Republican National Committee, U.S. liaison chief in Beijing, director of Central Intelligence Agency, professor, Vice President

Political party—Republican

State represented—Texas

Term of office—Jan. 20, 1989–Jan. 20, 1993

Administration—51st

Congresses—101st, 102nd

Age at inauguration—64 years, 223 days

FAMILY

FATHER

Name—Prescott Sheldon Bush

Date of birth—May 15, 1895

Place of birth—Columbus, Ohio

Marriage—Dorothy Walker, Aug. 1921, Kennebunkport, Me.

Occupation—Soldier, investment banker, philanthropist, civic activist; U.S. Senator (from Connecticut)

Date of death—Oct. 8, 1972

Place of death—New York, N.Y.

Age at death—77 years, 147 days

MOTHER

Name at birth—Dorothy Walker

Date of birth—July 1, 1901

Place of birth—Kennebunkport, Me.

Marriage—Prescott Sheldon Bush, Aug. 1921, Kennebunkport, Me.

Date of death—Nov. 19, 1992

Place of death—Greenwich, Conn.

Age at death—91 years, 141 days

SIBLINGS

George Herbert Walker Bush was the second son, the second oldest in a family of four boys and one girl.

Children of Prescott Sheldon Bush, Sr., and Dorothy Walker Bush

Prescott Sheldon Bush, Jr., b. 1922

George Herbert Walker Bush, b. June 12, 1924

Nancy Bush, b. 1926

Jonathan James Bush, b. 1931

William Henry Trotter Bush, b. July 14, 1938

MARRIAGE

Married—Barbara Pierce

Date of marriage—Jan. 6, 1945

Place of marriage—Rye, N.Y.

Age of wife at marriage—19 years, 213 days

Age of husband at marriage—20 years, 209 days

CHILDREN

George Walker Bush, b. July 6, 1946, New Haven, Conn.; m. Laura Welch, Nov. 5, 1977, Midland, Tex.

Pauline Robinson ("Robin") Bush, b. Dec. 20, 1949, Midland, Tex.; d. Oct. 11, 1953, New York, N.Y.

John Ellis ("Jeb") Bush, b. Feb. 2, 1953, Midland, Tex.; m. Columba Garnica, 1974

Neil Mallon Bush, b. Jan. 22, 1955, Midland, Tex.; m. Sharon Smith, 1980

Marvin Pierce Bush, b. Oct. 22, 1956, Midland, Tex.; m. Margaret Molster, 1981

Dorothy Pierce Bush, b. August 18, 1959, Houston, Tex.; m. William LeBlond, 1981; m. Bobby Koch, June 27, 1992

THE PRESIDENT'S WIFE

Name at birth—Barbara Pierce

Date of birth—June 8, 1925

Place of birth—New York, N.Y.

Mother—Pauline Robinson Pierce

Father—Marvin Pierce

Father's occupation—Magazine publisher

Education—Public school to sixth grade; Rye Country Day School; Ashley Hall, Charleston, S.C., graduated June 1943; Smith College, Northampton, Mass., 1943–1944

Marriage—George Herbert Walker Bush, Jan. 6, 1945, Rye, N.Y.

Children:—George Walker Bush, b. July 6, 1946; Pauline Robinson ("Robin") Bush, b. Dec. 20, 1949, d. Oct. 11, 1953; John Ellis ("Jeb") Bush, b. Feb. 2, 1953; Neil Mallon Bush, b. Jan. 22, 1955; Marvin Pierce Bush, b. Oct. 22, 1956; Dorothy Pierce Bush, b. August 18, 1959

Occupation—Author

Years younger than the President—361 days

Barbara Bush, wife of George H. W. Bush

THE FIRST LADY

During her husband's eight-year tenure as Vice President, Barbara Bush flew some one million miles on Air Force Two, visiting the 50 states and 68 countries while serving quietly as the nation's "second lady." Despite her privileged background, Mrs. Bush went on to become one of the most down-to-earth First Ladies since Bess Truman. Her father was president of the corporation that published *McCall's* and *Redbook* magazines and she grew up in wealthy suburban Rye, N.Y., yet Barbara Bush displayed a common touch that made her much admired.

Mrs. Bush's image stood in marked contrast to the public styles cultivated by her recent predecessors. Whereas Rosalynn Carter was an avowed feminist, Barbara Bush never regretted having dropped out of Smith College in her sophomore year to marry George Bush, who was, she said, "the first man I ever kissed." With her matronly figure and white hair, she had none of Nancy Reagan's telegenic glamor. But Mrs. Bush's grandmotherly, but well-tailored, appearance was turned to her husband's advantage in the 1988 presidential race, in which she proved to be an effective campaigner. The palpable sense of accomplishment she derived from raising five children and managing the Bush household while her husband's career had taken the family to homes in 17 different cities lent authenticity to George Bush's claim to be an advocate for the traditional values of conservative, mainstream America.

As First Lady, Mrs. Bush worked for the eradication of illiteracy, an issue that had long concerned her. Calling attention to the fact that approximately 23 million Americans are functionally illiterate and another 35 million semi-illiterate, she established the Barbara Bush Foundation for Family Literacy.

Toward the end of George Bush's term, Barbara Bush was credited with being more popular than the President. She was called "the Republican secret weapon." Her speech to the Republican National Convention in August 1992 was the first major address of a President's wife to a national convention. She reassured women that whether they balanced the demands of jobs and family life or elected to take care of their children and sacrifice careers, their decisions were right.

The author of two best-selling books, Barbara Bush modestly gave her dog Millie credit for *Millie's Book*, as she had previously given the family dog credit for *C. Fred's Story*.

IMPORTANT DATES IN THE PRESIDENT'S LIFE

1941, graduated from Phillips Academy, Andover, Mass.

June 12, 1942, enlisted in U.S. Navy; commissioned as pilot

Sept. 2, 1944, his plane shot down in the Pacific

1945, discharged from U.S. Navy with rank of lieutenant, j.g.; awarded Distinguished Flying Cross and three air medals

1948, graduated with B.A. in economics from Yale University; Phi Beta Kappa

1948–1950, worked as a salesman for Ideco, an oilfield equipment supply company

1950, co-founder of Bush-Overbey Oil Development Co., Inc., which purchased oil leases and royalty rights

Oct. 11, 1953, death of daughter Robin from leukemia

1953, co-founder of Zapata Petroleum Corp., contract drilling firm

1954, founder and president of Zapata Off-Shore Co.

1959, moved to Houston, Tex., when Zapata Off-Shore separated from Zapata Petroleum to become an independent company

1962, elected chairman of Harris County Republican Party; served 1962–1964

1964–1966, chairman of the board and CEO of Zapata Off-Shore

July 13–16, 1964, attended Republican National Convention as a Goldwater delegate

Nov. 3, 1964, defeated in Texas Senate race by Ralph W. Yarborough

Feb. 1966, sold his stock in Zapata Off-Shore to run for Congress

Nov. 8, 1966, elected to House of Representatives from Seventh District in Texas (Houston); reelected 1968

Jan. 3, 1967–Jan. 3, 1971, U.S. congressman (from Texas)

Nov. 5, 1970, defeated in Texas Senate race by Lloyd M. Bentsen, Jr.

Dec. 11, 1970, appointed U.S. ambassador to the United Nations; served 1971–1972

1973–1974, chairman of Republican National Committee

1974–75, chief of U.S. Liaison Office, Beijing, People's Republic of China

1976–1977, director, Central Intelligence Agency

1979, adjunct professor at Rice University, Tex.

Jan. 1980, won Republican presidential primary in Iowa

1980, co-author (with Philip Crane) of *Great Issues 1979–1980: A Forum on Important Questions Facing the American Public,*

July 17, 1980, nominated for Vice President at Republican National Convention

Jan. 20, 1981–Jan. 20, 1989, Vice President under Ronald W. Reagan

1987, *Looking Forward* published

Feb. 1988, won Republican presidential primary in New Hampshire

Aug. 17, 1988, nominated for President at Republican National Convention in New Orleans

Nov. 8, 1988, elected President of the United States

Jan. 20, 1989–Jan. 20, 1993, President

Jan. 3, 2005, joined with former Pres. Clinton in fundraising drive for victims of Indian Ocean tsunami

Sept. 5, 2005, joined with former Pres. Clinton in fundraising drive for victims of Hurricane Katrina

ELECTIONS

THE ELECTION OF 1988

November 8, 1988

CANDIDATES

Republican Party (34th Convention)
Aug. 15–18, 1988, the Superdome, New Orleans, La.

P: George Herbert Walker Bush, Tex.
VP: Dan (James Danforth) Quayle III, Ind.
   Bush was nominated by acclamation on the first ballot.
Total number of votes: 2,263
Number necessary for nomination: 1,132

Democratic Party (40th Convention)
July 18–21, 1988, The Omni, Atlanta, Ga.

P: Michael Stanley Dukakis, Mass.
VP: Lloyd M. Bentsen, Jr., Tex.
   Dukakis was nominated on the first ballot. Candidates for nomination and the votes they received:
Michael Stanley Dukakis, Mass. 2,876.25
Jesse Louis Jackson, Ill. 1,218.5
Total number of votes: 4,136
Number necessary for nomination: 2,069

Libertarian Party
Sept. 5, 1987, Seattle, Wash.

P: Ron Paul, Tex.
VP: Andre Marrou, Alaska

New Alliance Party
Aug. 20–21 1988, New York, N.Y.

P: Lenora B. Fulani, N.Y.
VP: Joyce Dattner, N.Y.

Independent Populist Party
June 1988, Baton Rouge, La.

P: David E. Duke, La.

VP: Trenton Stokes, Ark.

Consumer Party
P: Eugene Joseph McCarthy, Minn.
VP: Susan Gardner, Ill.

American Independent Party
P: Warren Griffin, Ala.
VP: James S. Burnett, Fla.

Independent Party
P: Lyndon Hermyle LaRouche, Jr., Va.
VP: Billy Davis, Miss.

Right To Life Party
Sept. 12–13, Albany, N.Y.

P: William A. Marra, Conn.
VP: Joan Andrews, Ohio

Workers League
P: Ed Winn, Ariz.
VP: Helen Halyard

Socialist Workers Party
Nov. 1987, New York, N.Y.

P: James Mac Warren, N.Y.
VP: Kathleen Mickells, W.Va.

Peace and Freedom Party
P: Herbert Lewin, Vt.
VP: F. Booth Dollarhyde, N.C.

National Statesman Party (Prohibition)
P: Earl F. Dodge, Colo.
VP: Warren C. Martin, N.D.

Workers World Party
Aug. 1987, New York, N.Y.

P: Larry Holmes, N.Y.
VP: Gloria Estella LaRiva, Calif.

Socialist Party
P: Willa Kenoyer

American Party

P: Delmar Dennis

Grassroots Party

P: Jack Herer

Independent Candidate

P: Louie G. Youngkeit

Third World Assembly

P: John G. Martin

1988 POPULAR VOTE

Republican Party, 48,881,278

Democratic Party, 41,805,374

Libertarian Party, 431,616

New Alliance Party, 217,200

Independent Populist Party, 46,910

Consumer Party, 30,903

American Independent Party, 27,818

Independent Party, 25,530

Right to Life Party, 20,497

Workers League Party, 18,662

Socialist Workers Party, 15,603

Peace and Freedom Party, 10,370

National Statesman Party (Prohibition), 8,000

Workers World Party, 7,846

Socialist Party, 3,878

American Party, 3,476

Grassroots Party, 1,949

Youngkeit (independent candidate), 372

Third World Assembly, 236

None of the above, 6,934

Scattered write-ins, 20,368

1988 ELECTORAL VOTE

Announcement of the electoral vote was made on January 4, 1989, before a joint session of Congress. There were 538 electoral votes from the 50 states and the District of Columbia.

Bush received 79.18 percent (426 votes—40 states) as follows: Ala. 9, Alaska 3, Ariz. 7, Ark. 6, Calif. 47, Colo. 8, Conn. 8, Del. 3, Fla. 21, Ida. 4, Ill. 24, Ind. 12, Kans. 7, Ken. 9, La. 10, Me. 4, Mich. 20, Miss. 7, Mo. 11, Mon. 4, Neb. 5, Nev. 4, N.H. 4, N.J. 16, N.M. 5, N.C. 13, N.D. 3, Ohio 23, Okla. 8, Pa. 25, S.C. 8, S.D. 3, Tenn. 11, Tex. 29, Utah 5, Vt. 3, Va. 12, Wyo. 3

Dukakis received 20.63 percent (111 votes—10 states and the District of Columbia) as follows: D.C. 3, Hawaii 4, Iowa 8, Mass. 13, Minn. 10, N.Y. 36, Ore. 7, R.I. 4, Wash. 10, Wis. 11, W.Va. 5 (one for Bentsen) A Democratic elector in W.Va. voted for Lloyd M. Bentsen rather than Dukakis.

INAUGURATION

January 20, 1989

George Herbert Walker Bush was sworn in as the forty-first President on the West Front of the Capitol Building, signifying that Bush, like his fellow Republican predecessor, represented a Western state (Bush, Texas; Reagan, California). Wearing an informal blue business suit rather than the traditional morning coat, Bush took the oath from Chief Justice William Hubbs Rehnquist at 12:03 P.M., three minutes later than the Constitution specifies. Despite occasional gusts of wind the weather was unseasonably mild. Temperatures were in the high 40s and the sky was overcast as the President delivered a well-received 20-minute inaugural address. He renewed the pledge he had made at the Republican National Convention to seek a "kinder, gentler nation" and, using the image

Courtesy of The Library of Congress

The inauguration of George H. W. Bush

of the extended hand, called for a return to the bipartisanship that had characterized relations between the executive branch and the Congress before discord was sown by the Vietnam War.

After attending the traditional post-inauguration luncheon in the Capitol's Statuary Hall, the President and the First Lady rode in a $600,000 armored limousine up Pennsylvania Avenue at the head of the inaugural parade. Three times Mr. and Mrs. Bush emerged from their vehicle to greet the crowd and walk parts of the 1.6-mile route to the White House.

At a record cost of more than $25 million the inaugural festivities were the most lavish in history. The President and the First Lady attended each of the nine inaugural balls, which were held at eleven sites in the capital.

THE VICE PRESIDENT

Name—James Danforth ("Dan") Quayle III (44th V.P.)

Date of birth—Feb. 4, 1947

Place of birth—Indianapolis, Ind.

Political party—Republican

State represented—Indiana

Term of office—Jan. 20, 1989–Jan. 20, 1993

Age at inauguration—41 years, 351 days

ADDITIONAL DATA ON QUAYLE

1969, graduated with a B.A. in political science from DePauw University, Greencastle, Ind.

1974, graduated from law school at Indiana University

Nov. 2, 1976, elected to House of Representatives from Fourth District in Ind.; reelected 1978

Nov. 4, 1980, defeated incumbent Birch Bayh in Indiana Senate race; reelected 1986

Aug. 18, 1988, nominated for Vice President at Republican National Convention in New Orleans, La.

Nov. 8, 1988, elected Vice President of the United States

Courtesy of The Library of Congress

Dan Quayle, Vice President to George H.W. Bush

Jan. 20, 1989–Jan. 20, 1993, Vice President under George Herbert Walker Bush

CABINET

FIRST TERM

January 20, 1989–January 20, 1993

State—James Addison Baker 3rd, Tex., Jan. 25, 1989

Treasury—Nicholas Frederick Brady, N.J., continued from preceding administration

Defense—Richard Bruce Cheney, Wyo., Mar. 21, 1989

Attorney General—Richard Lewis Thornburgh, Pa., continued from preceding administration; William P. Barr, Washington, D. C., Nov. 20. 1991

Interior—Manuel Lujan, Jr., N.M., Feb. 3, 1989

Agriculture—Clayton Keith Yeutter, Neb., Feb. 8, 1989; Edward Madigan, Ill., Mar. 7, 1991

Commerce—Robert Adam Mosbacher, Tex., Feb. 1, 1989

Labor—Elizabeth Hanford Dole, N.C., Jan. 30, 1989

Health and Human Services—Louis Wade Sullivan, Ga., Mar. 1, 1989

Housing and Urban Development—Jack F. Kemp, N.Y., Feb. 6, 1989

Transportation—Samuel K. Skinner, Ill., Feb. 1, 1989; Andrew H. Card, Mass., Jan. 22, 1992

Energy—James David Watkins, Calif., Mar. 1, 1989

Education—Lauro Fred Cavazos, Jr., Tex., continued from preceding administration; Lamar Alexander, Mar. 14, 1991

Veterans Affairs—Edward Joseph Derwinski, Ill., March 15, 1989–Oct. 26, 1992

CONGRESS

ONE HUNDRED AND FIRST CONGRESS

January 3, 1989–January 3, 1991

First session—Jan.3, 1989–Nov. 22, 1989 (324 days)

Second session—Jan. 23, 1990–Oct. 28, 1990 (260 days)

Vice President—James Danforth Quayle III, Ind.

President pro tempore of the Senate —Robert Carlyle Byrd, W.Va.

Secretary of the Senate—Walter J. Stewart, Del

Speaker of the House— James Claude Wright, Tex. (resigned June 6, 1989); Thomas S. Foley, Wash.

ONE HUNDRED SECOND CONGRESS

January 3, 1991–January 3, 1992

First session— Jan. 3, 1991–Jan. 3, 1992 (366 days)

Second session—January 3, 1992–October 9, 1992 (281 days)

Vice President— James Danforth Quayle III, Ind.

President pro tempore of the Senate —Robert Carlyle Byrd, W.Va.

Secretary of the Senate—Walter J. Stewart, Del.

Speaker of the House—Thomas S. Foley, Wash.

Clerk of the House—Donnald K. Anderson, Calif.

APPOINTMENTS TO THE SUPREME COURT

Associate Justices

David Hackett Souter, N.H., Oct. 9, 1990 (replaced William Joseph Brennan)

Clarence Thomas, Ga., Oct. 15, 1991 (replaced Thurgood Marshall)

IMPORTANT DATES IN THE PRESIDENCY

Jan. 23, 1989, Supreme Court ruled that government-sponsored affirmative action programs are in conflict with the equal protection clause of the Constitution

Jan. 27, 1989, President pledged the federal government's backing of deposits in savings and loan associations facing insolvency

Feb. 7, 1989, Congress rejected a 51-percent pay increase for members of Congress and federal judges

Feb. 14, 1989, Iran's Ayatollah Khomeini called for the execution of Salman Rushdie, British author of *The Satanic Verses*, a novel viewed by many Muslims as a blasphemous insult to their religion

Feb. 15, 1989, Soviet troops completed withdrawal from Afghanistan

Feb. 22, 1989, Lieut. Col. Oliver L. North went on trial, facing an array of criminal charges stemming from involvement in the Iran-*contra* affair

Mar. 9, 1989, Senate voted to reject the nomination of former Senator John G. Tower for Secretary of Defense

March 24, 1989, *Exxon Valdez*, oil tanker, ran aground in Prince William Sound, resulting in largest oil spill in U.S. history

May 4, 1989, Oliver L. North convicted of three crimes in the Iran-*contra* affair, including shredding documents; acquitted of nine other charges

May 11, 1989, President announced troop deployments to Panama to help oust General Manuel Noriega

June 1, 1989, Speaker of the House Jim Wright resigned after lengthy public hearings by House ethics committee

June 3, 1989, Chinese troops regained control of Beijing from pro-democracy protesters, killing hundreds of students and workers in Tiananmen Square and restoring the primacy of the Deng Xiaoping regime

August 18, 1989, Solidarity trade union of Poland took control of the government by popular election, ending 40 years of Communist Party rule

Sept. 21, 1989, Hurricane Hugo struck South Carolina coast, causing extensive damage and rendering many homeless. It was the most expensive disaster to date in the United States, with losses estimated at $3.7 billion in South Carolina alone

Oct. 17, 1989, San Francisco and its environs rocked by a powerful earthquake. Federal government promised aid

Oct. 18, 1989, Erich Honecker ousted as East German Communist Party leader

Nov. 12, 1989, destruction of Berlin wall began

Nov. 24, 1989, Czechoslovakia's Communist leadership resigned

Dec. 3, 1989, President met with Soviet President Gorbachev for their first summit, on shipboard off Malta

Dec. 10, 1989, a non-Communist government took power in Czechoslovakia for the first time in 41 years

Dec. 20, 1989, American armed forces invaded Panama and installed a new government

Dec. 25, 1989, Nicolae Ceausescu, longtime leader of Romania, and his wife executed and a new regime installed in Romania, ending the Communist dictatorship

Dec. 29, 1989, Vaclav Havel, noted author, elected President of Czechoslovakia

Jan. 3, 1990, Gen. Manuel Noriega surrendered; brought by United States authorities to Florida to face trial

Courtesy of the U.S. Department of Defense

East and West Germans meet at a breach in the Berlin Wall.

Feb. 11, 1990, Nelson Mandela, leader of the African National Congress, freed after more than 27 years in South African prisons

Feb. 25, 1990, Violeta Barrios de Chamorro elected President of Nicaragua, ending Sandinista rule and improving United States relations with Nicaragua

Feb. 26, 1990, Congressional ban on smoking on domestic flights of less than six hours went into effect

Feb. 27, 1990, Exxon Corporation indicted by a Federal grand jury on charges stemming from the *Exxon Valdez* oil spill

Mar. 11, 1990, Patricio Aylwin inaugurated President of Chile, ending 16-year dictatorship of Augusto Pinochet

Apr. 7, 1990, John M. Poindexter convicted on five charges of lying to and deceiving Congress in order to conceal the Reagan Administration's part in the Iran-*contra* affair; conviction was overturned in November 1991

Apr. 24, 1990, Michael Milken agreed to a guilty plea in the largest securities fraud case in Wall Street history; fine set at $600 million

May 29, 1990, Boris N. Yeltsin elected President of the Russian Republic

June 1, 1990, agreements covering nuclear arms limitations, elimination of most chemical weapons, and normalized economic relations signed by Soviet leader Mikhail Gorbachev and the President in Washington

June 26, 1990, proposed constitutional amendment to outlaw "flag burning," supported by President, defeated in Senate

June 20, 1990, Nelson Mandela arrived for a 10-day U.S. tour, pleading for sanctions against South Africa to remain in place until black majority could gain political rights

Aug. 2, 1990, Iraqi troops invaded and occupied Kuwait. The action, condemned by the United Nations Security Council, set off chain of events leading to the Persian Gulf War

Sept. 18, 1990, Charles Keating, former chairman of Lincoln Savings & Loan in California, symbol of misconduct rampant in the savings and loan industry, indicted on fraud charges and jailed for failure to raise bail

Oct. 3, 1990, Germany reunified

Oct. 22, 1990, President vetoed Civil Rights Act intended to restore job discrimination protections cut by recent Supreme Court decisions

Nov. 15, 1990, President signed Clean Air Act, mandating lower toxic emissions from automobiles, industry and utility smokestacks, and phasing out chlorofluorocarbon use

Nov. 22, 1990, Margaret Thatcher, longest-serving British leader of 20th century, announced resignation as British Prime Minister; John Major assumed Conservative Party leadership and office of Prime Minister Nov. 28

Jan. 12, 1991, both Houses of Congress authorized President to use force against Iraq after two-day debate

Jan. 16–Feb. 28, 1991, code-named Operation Desert Storm, a U.S.-led multinational force launched the Persian Gulf War with air attacks on Iraq and Iraqi-occupied Kuwait, followed by an invasion on Feb. 23 to sweep the Iraqis out of Kuwait; Iraq capitulated to UN demands on Feb. 28 and U.S. military operations ceased

Feb. 27, 1991, Senate Ethics Committee ended probe into "Keating Five," group of Senators who had accepted substantial contributions from Charles Keating, owner of Lincoln Savings and Loan Association; Sen. Alan Cranston of Calif. called culpable in misconduct investigation

Apr. 6, 1991, Iraq accepted UN terms for cease-fire, formally concluding Persian Gulf war; endangered Kurds attempted to flee; no-fly zones established to protect Kurds in north and Shiites in south

Apr. 18, 1991, education initiatives proposed by President include ensuring literacy for all adult Americans

May 4, 1991, President entered hospital with irregular heartbeat; Graves disease, thyroid overactivity, diagnosed

June 12, 1991, Boris N. Yeltsin elected Executive President of Russian Republic in first-ever popular election of Russian leader

June 25, 1991, Croatia and Slovenia announced their independence from Yugoslavia

July 10, 1991, President lifted trade and investment sanctions on South Africa, calling liberalizing actions of de Klerk regime a "profound transformation"

July 24, 1991, House Banking Committee began probe into First American Bank's links with Bank of Credit and Commerce International, announcing Clark Clifford, First American's chairman, as principal witness

July 30–31, 1991, first post–Cold War summit in Moscow attended by President Bush and President Gorbachev of the Soviet Union

Aug. 19, 1991, Soviet hard-liners attempted coup against President Mikhail Gorbachev, but pro-democracy forces led by Russian Republic President Boris Yeltsin restored order by Aug. 21

Aug. 29, 1991, Communist Party outlawed by parliament in Soviet Union

Sept. 6, 1991, President Gorbachev recognized independence of Estonia, Latvia, and Lithuania

Oct. 11–14, 1991, Senate Judiciary Committee conducted televised hearings on charges of sexual harassment against Supreme Court nominee Clarence Thomas by Anita Hill, law professor at the University of Oklahoma and former Thomas staffer; Republican senators and Thomas witnesses attacked Hill's credibility and mental stability; Hill was widely supported by women's groups

Oct. 30, 1991, Middle East peace conference opened in Madrid with the participation of Israel, Syria, Egypt, Lebanon, Jordan, and Palestinians

Nov. 12, 1991, Robert M. Gates sworn in as Central Intelligence Agency chief, replacing William H. Webster who had resigned the previous May

Dec. 15, 1991, last three American hostages held in Lebanon freed

Dec. 19, 1991, President signed bill authorizing $70 billion in new borrowing authority to bail out Federal Deposit Insurance Corporation, hit by large number of bank failures

Dec. 25, 1991, Soviet Union dissolved; Commonwealth of Independent States formed from 11 republics; Gorbachev resigned as

President; Boris Yeltsin, President of the Russian Republic, in command of Soviet nuclear codes

Jan. 31, 1992, many world leaders attended United Nations Security Council Summit Meeting in New York City

Feb. 1, 1992, Presidents Bush and Yeltsin met at Camp David and declared formal end to Cold War

Apr. 6, 1992, President Alberto Fujimori of Peru dictatorially dissolved congress, imposed censorship, and arrested leading politicians in effort to combat Shining Path guerrillas

Apr. 7, 1992, amid civil war in Yugoslavia, European Community and U.S. acknowledged national dissolution and recognized independence of Bosnia and Herzegovina

April 9, 1992, John Major, British Conservative Prime Minister, held his seat after General Elections gave Conservatives a majority in Parliament

Apr. 29, 1992, acquittal of four white police officers who had beaten a black motorist in Los Angeles touched off days of rioting in L.A. and elsewhere, leading to dozens of deaths, thousands of injuries and arrests, and destruction of many businesses and homes

May 30, 1992, UN Security Council voted to impose sanctions against Serbian government in effort to stop attacks on Bosnia and Herzegovina

June 5, 1992, nation's unemployment rate rose to 7.5 percent, the highest in eight years

June 12, 1992, President, attending Earth Summit in Rio de Janeiro, defended administration opposition to major environmental initiatives

July 13, 1992, Labor Party leader Yitzhak Rabin inaugurated as Prime Minister of Israel

July 20, 1992, Vaclav Havel stepped down as President of Czechoslovakia, acknowledging historical forces pulling his country apart

July 29, 1992, Clark M. Clifford, former cabinet member and advisor to Presidents, indicted on corruption charges relating to Bank of Credit and Commerce International

July 29, 1992, Supreme Court in *Planned Parenthood v. Casey* affirmed (5-4) the 1973 *Roe v. Wade* decision that gave women the right to abortion, but then also upheld a state's right to regulate and restrict abortions

Aug. 8, 1992, President called for United Nations aid to protect relief supplies to Bosnia and Herzegovina, amid ongoing civil war

Aug. 24, 1992, Hurricane Andrew battered Florida and Louisiana, becoming the most expensive hurricane in U.S. history; President asked Congress for $7.6 billion for clean-up and sent army units to assist

Sept. 26, 1992, opposition of veterans' groups forced Edward J. Derwinski, Veterans Affairs Secretary, to resign

Nov. 3, 1992, Bill Clinton elected 42nd President of the United States

Nov. 4, 1992, President vetoed $27 billion tax bill to create enterprise zones designed to aid cities as a response to Los Angeles riots; pledge of "no new taxes" renewed

Dec. 4, 1992, President authorized sending 28,000 U.S. troops in an expeditionary force to Somalia to protect delivery of humanitarian aid to starving Somalians

Dec. 9, 1992, Attorney General William Barr rejected Congressional demands for an independent prosecutor to investigate possible criminal involvement by government officials in loans to Iraq by Atlanta branch of Banca Nazionale del Lavoro

Dec. 17, 1992, President signed North American Free Trade Agreement with Canada and Mexico

Dec. 24, 1992, President pardoned six former government officials convicted or indicted on charges of lying to Congress or perjury during the Congressional investigation of the Iran-*contra* scandal

Dec. 30, 1992, President flew to Somalia to spend New Year's with American troops

Jan. 3, 1993, President flew from Somalia to Moscow to sign START II Treaty with President Yeltsin of Russia; treaty greatly reduced permissible numbers of nuclear arms

Jan. 13, 1993, President ordered series of bombing raids on Iraq as a result of Iraq's persistent refusal to comply with Security Council resolutions requiring inspection of Iraqi nuclear sites by UN inspectors and Iraqi incursions into Kuwait to retrieve material from 1991 fighting; bombing continued until the end of Bush's term

Courtesy of the George Bush Presidential Library

The signing of the North American Free Trade Agreement (NAFTA). From left to right: (standing) President Salinas, President Bush, Prime Minister Mulroney (Seated) Jaime Serra Puche, Carla Hills, Michael Wilson.

ADDITIONAL DATA ON BUSH

GEORGE HERBERT WALKER BUSH

—was the first incumbent Vice President to be elected President since Martin Van Buren in 1836.

—was the first President to have been chairman of his political party.

—was the first President to have been Ambassador to the United Nations.

—was the first President to have served as director of the Central Intelligence Agency.

BUSH WAS A DECORATED NAVY PILOT

Of the 42 individuals who have been President, 26 served with the military, 20 of them in the Army. George Bush is only the sixth Navy man to become President, but of the six Presidents who saw combat in World War II, only one, Eisenhower, was in the Army. Kennedy, Johnson, Nixon, Ford, and Bush were in the Navy. (Carter had 11 years of service in the Navy, but did not take part in a war.)

Bush and Kennedy served as lieutenants, junior grade. Johnson and Ford (the only two in the Naval Reserves) and Nixon all left active service having attained the rank of lieutenant commander. Bush was awarded the Distinguished Flying Cross. Johnson, the only other pilot of any service besides Bush, received the Silver Star. Kennedy received the Purple Heart, and the Navy and Marine Corps medal. Ford was awarded ten battle stars.

Bush, who enlisted on his eighteenth birthday, was the youngest aviator in the Navy when he received his wings in 1943. Assigned to a torpedo squadron operating in the Pacific off the carrier *San Jacinto*, Bush flew a TBM Avenger, a relatively slow bomber which carried a three-man crew and a one-ton payload. The name "Barbara" was painted on the Avenger, after his fiancée, Barbara Pierce.

On September 2, 1944, while carrying out a bombing run against gun emplacements on the island of Chichi-Jima, Bush's plane was hit. He delivered four bombs to the target, then bailed out of the burning plane. However, his two crewmates perished. Rescued by a submarine, the U.S.S. *Finback*, Bush rejoined the *San Jacinto* in time to participate in bombing strikes in the Philippines. In December 1945 Bush was ordered home, having flown a total of 58 combat missions and logged 1,228 hours of flight time. In addition to the Distinguished Flying Cross, he was awarded three air medals.

BUSH WAS THE FIRST ACTING PRESIDENT

Ratified in 1967, the Twenty-fifth Amendment to the Constitution dealt with the line of presidential succession, filling vice presidential vacancies and providing for continuity in case of presidential disability. The amendment's third section outlines the method a President, in the event of incapacity, uses to transfer power temporarily to the Vice President, thereby providing the executive branch with unbroken decision-making authority.

The third section gives the Vice President powers of Acting President so that he can make decisions that cannot be postponed. For example, the President's response to a nuclear strike would have to be immediate. Section 3 calls for the chief executive to notify the president pro tempore of the Senate and the Speaker of the House that "he is unable to discharge the powers and duties of his office." When the President is able to resume his duties, he again notifies the president pro tempore and the Speaker with a letter.

On July 13, 1985, President Reagan was operated on for two hours and 53 minutes at the Bethesda Naval Medical Center. Surgeons removed a cancerous polyp from his large intestine, but the President did not awaken from the operation for several more hours. However, just before receiving anesthesia, Reagan transferred the powers of the presidency to his Vice President, George Bush. The text of Reagan's letter to the Senate president pro tempore (Senator Strom Thurmond) and the House Speaker (Representative Thomas P. O'Neill, Jr.) read:

Dear Mr. President (Mr. Speaker):

I am about to undergo surgery during which time I will be briefly and temporarily incapable of discharging the Constitutional powers and duties of the Office of the President of the United States. After consultations with my Counsel and the Attorney General, I am mindful of the provisions of Section 3 of the 25th Amendment to the Constitution and of the uncertainties of its application to such brief and temporary periods of incapacity. I do not believe that the drafters of this Amendment intended its application to situations such as the instant one. Nevertheless, consistent with my longstanding arrangement with Vice President George Bush, and not intending to set a precedent binding anyone privileged to hold this Office in the future, I have determined and it is my intention and direction that Vice President George Bush shall discharge those powers and duties in my stead commencing with the administration of anesthesia to me in this instance. I shall advise you and the Vice President when I determine that I am able to resume the discharge of the Constitutional powers and duties of this Office.

May God bless this Nation and us all.

Sincerely,

RONALD REAGAN

When the President came to, he signed a letter reclaiming his powers of office:

Dear Mr. President (Mr. Speaker):

Following up on my letter to you of this date, please be advised I am able to resume the discharge of the Constitutional powers and duties of the Office of the President of the United States. I have informed the Vice President of my determination and my resumption of those powers and duties.

Sincerely,

RONALD REAGAN

During that time, for seven hours and 54 minutes, Vice President Bush served as Acting President, although in his first letter Reagan did not expressly use that phrase. It was the first time that the third section of the Twenty-fifth Amendment had been applied to a temporarily incapacitated President. (On March 30, 1981, when Reagan was hospitalized after being shot by a would-be assassin, there had not been time to install Bush as Acting President under the provisions of the Twenty-fifth Amendment.)

George Bush is the only Vice President to have exercised the powers of the presidency, resumed the vice presidency, and then gone on to serve as the President in his own right.

THE TOWER NOMINATION

On March 9, 1989, the Senate voted 47-53 to reject President Bush's nominee for Secretary of Defense, John G. Tower, who had formerly served as U.S. senator from Texas, the President's home state. Tower was only the ninth cabinet nominee to be voted down by the Senate, and the first since 1959, when Dwight Eisenhower's nomination of Lewis Strauss as Commerce Secretary was defeated.

The nine potential cabinet members were nominated by six Presidents—Andrew Jackson, John Tyler, Andrew Johnson, Calvin Coolidge, Dwight Eisenhower, and George Bush. The President who had the most cabinet nominees voted down by the Senate was Tyler, who saw four of his candidates spurned in 1843. Tower was the first nominee for Defense Secretary to be rejected.

WAR IN THE GULF

No other event during his years in office showed President Bush's abilities as a leader to better advantage or gained him greater support both at home and around the world than the Persian Gulf War. In August 1990 Iraqi troops invaded Kuwait, seizing control of the country and its rich oil fields, which in combination with Iraq's totaled more than 20 percent of the world's oil reserves. President Bush called the invasion an act of "naked aggression" and vowed, "This will not stand."

The United Nations Security Council, responding to the President's call for action, passed a series of resolutions that required Iraq's withdrawal from Kuwait, backed up the demand with sanctions, and finally, on November 29, authorized the use of force if Iraq did not withdraw by January 15, 1991. In the meantime, conferring with leaders around the world, the President put together a coalition of troops from many nations, including Egypt, Saudi Arabia, Syria, the United Arab Emirates, Britain, France, Italy, Spain, and Canada. Japan and Germany contributed financial backing to the coalition. In the Security Council, the Soviet Union supported the action taken against Iraq, marking the first time since World War II that the Cold War foes were allied on a major international crisis. China, as well, agreed not to block U.N. action with a veto.

The President had issued orders as early as August 7, deploying American troops and naval forces to positions in Saudi Arabia and the Persian Gulf in "Operation Desert Shield." With the buildup of U.S. and coalition forces, there was considerable political debate on the question of whether more time should be allowed for the economic sanctions to work against Iraq before military force was used. This debate culminated in a vote of Congress on January 12, 1991, in which the Senate and the House by narrow margins passed a joint resolution that authorized the President to use military force if Iraq had not complied with the UN resolutions by January 15.

The UN's deadline passed without withdrawal by Iraq, and in the pre-dawn darkness of January 16, coalition air strikes began against Iraqi targets. The air war of massive, round-the-clock bombardments lasted some six weeks until, on February 24th, ground forces moved from Saudi Arabia against Iraqi positions in Kuwait and Iraq itself. Four days later, after the coalition had virtually destroyed the Iraqi army and expelled it from Kuwait, military action by coalition forces ceased. Although antiwar demonstrations took place around the country, including a large one in Washington, D.C., on January 19, the President enjoyed great public support for the action he had initiated. By March 1, 1991, public opinion polls gave him an approval rating of 91 percent, the highest rating of any President and a level that President Bush would never again come close to achieving.

With the brief war over, U.S. troops quickly returned home, but the Iraqi leader Saddam Hussein remained in control of his country despite continued economic sanctions, and managed to put down with great severity rebellions by Kurds in the North and Shiites in the South, who had been encouraged by Saddam's defeat at the hands of the coalition. To afford some measure of protection to these minorities against Saddam's reprisals, the United States established so-called no-fly zones above the 38th and below the 32nd parallels of latitude, in which Iraqi aircraft were not allowed to fly. Against these regulations and the UN's insistence on verifying on-site the destruction of Iraq's nuclear capability, as required by the Security Council resolutions and the terms of the cease-fire, Saddam embarked on a policy of provocative moves designed to test the resolve of the Security Council and the United States. Almost two years to the day from the beginning of the Gulf War, President Bush found it necessary once again to order coalition warplanes to attack Iraqi installations as a message to Saddam that further violations would not be tolerated. It was an unprecedented action for a President to take in the final week of his term.

"READ MY LIPS: NO NEW TAXES"

Even though George Bush had campaigned strongly for the presidency using the slogan, "Read my lips: no new taxes," only a month after taking office he was forced to reveal a plan for the bailout of the crashing American thrift industry that would cost $126.2 billion, with the burden of payment to be shared by the taxpayers and the industry itself.

Although that plan was not accepted by Congress, an alternative rescue package, which included provisions for restructuring the industry, was passed by Congress and signed by the President on August 9, 1989. It was expected to cost more than $300 billion over 30 years, with a $225 billion bill falling on the shoulders of taxpayers.

Then, in the fall of 1990, caught between the demands of deficit reduction and a weakening economy, increased military commitments in the Persian Gulf, and rising costs for the savings and loan bailout, the President made a significant compromise on the budget with Congress in which he agreed to raise taxes. The original compromise bill had been crafted by administration and congressional leaders meeting in secret at Andrews Air Force Base, inciting a revolt among conservative Republican members of the House, who regarded it as a betrayal by the President of his campaign pledge. Forced to reverse himself on his most cherished proposal, a cut in the capital gains tax, Bush signed a budget in order to allow the government to continue functioning.

The final 1991 budget, with provision for expanded Medicaid coverage of poor children and tax credits for working poor families, would have been considered an improvement in social welfare policy, except that the benefits were embedded in a bill to raise taxes and trim dozens of government programs. Increases in gasoline, cigarette, and liquor taxes were termed "regressive" by Democrats, taking a disproportionately larger share of the incomes of the poor.

In March 1992, now campaigning for reelection, Bush repudiated the deal he had made in 1990 on the 1991 budget, saying, "If I had to do all that over, I wouldn't do it. Look at all the flak it's taking." His effort to retrieve his position on the "no new taxes" pledge later led the President to veto an appropriations bill that included provision for enterprise zones to aid cities, but the veto came on November 4, 1992, the day after President Bush lost his bid for reelection.

THE THOMAS-HILL HEARINGS

When Justice Thurgood Marshall, the first African-American to sit on the Supreme Court, announced his retirement in June 1991, President Bush quickly nominated

542

Clarence Thomas, an African-American judge he had previously named to the U.S. Court of Appeals. Thomas had spent his early childhood in rural poverty in Georgia and bore the wounds of discrimination; he was a social conservative who had expressed reservations about affirmative action programs and abortion rights. In the confirmation hearings, however, Thomas refused to divulge his position on these issues to the Senate Judiciary Committee, saying only that he would be impartial as a Justice. His nomination to the Supreme Court was opposed by such organizations as the NAACP and other civil rights groups.

While the hearings were underway, an allegation of sexual harassment made against Judge Thomas by Anita F. Hill, a law professor at the University of Oklahoma and a former Thomas staffer, became public. The subsequent nationally televised testimony before the Judiciary Committee shocked the nation because of the frankness of the testimony. Some witnesses called on behalf of Judge Thomas gave opinions of Dr. Hill's charges that tended to cast severe doubt on her veracity, character, and mental stability. Moreover, in the course of their questioning of witnesses for either side, the all-male committee showed little sympathy for Dr. Hill or the issue she had raised.

On October 15, 1991, the Senate, by a vote of 52 to 48, confirmed the President's nomination of Clarence Thomas to be an Associate Justice of the Supreme Court. The vote was mainly along party lines, with all but two Republican senators voting in favor of the nomination and with enough Southern Democrats joining them to make a majority.

The impact of the televised proceedings was enormous. Sexual harassment in the workplace became a major social and political issue around the nation. More women ran for and were elected to the Senate and the House in 1992 than ever before. Among voters, more women than in any previous election voted and contributed to political campaigns, especially Bill Clinton's campaign, which unseated the President. Ironically, a sexual harassment lawsuit would eventually cause trouble for Clinton, bringing about his impeachment though not his removal from office.

NUCLEAR ARMS CUTS, A HISTORIC TREATY

In a dramatic gesture for the end of a presidential term, George Bush flew to Moscow from Somalia on January 3, 1993, to sign the START II Treaty (Strategic Nuclear Arms Reduction) with Boris N. Yeltsin, the Russian President. Signed in St. Vladimir Hall in the Kremlin, the treaty called for a reduction by about two-thirds of existing nuclear warheads by 2003. Unlike previous nuclear arms limitation and reduction agreements, such as the SALT (Strategic Arms Limitation Treaties) and START I, signed in 1991, which took a decade or more to come to fruition, the START II Treaty was negotiated in only six months.

Yeltsin paid tribute to Bush: "His remarkable personal and political qualities and competence have contributed to a successful transition from the cold war to a new world order." Bush saluted the Russian leader in return, citing his "unwavering commitment to democratic reform."

As President Bush left office on January 20, 1993, the treaty's implementation depended on the likely approval of the U.S. Congress and the far less certain approval of the Russian parliament. In addition, it was not clear whether the new nation of Ukraine would be willing to turn over to Russia for destruction the many nuclear warheads based on its soil by the old Soviet Union. Ukraine had not signed START I, a necessary preliminary to START II.

BUSH FIRST TO SPEND HOLIDAYS WITH TROOPS ABROAD

President Bush spent two holidays in very unusual places. In November 1990, United States troops were deployed in the Persian Gulf area as part of a United Nations multinational force awaiting the onset of action to clear Kuwait of Iraqi occupation. President Bush joined the troops for a Thanksgiving dinner. In fact, he ate several Thanksgiving dinners, taking quick helicopter jaunts from place to place, in Saudi Arabia and offshore. During the course of his two days with the armed forces, Bush made strong speeches condemning Iraq's invasion and occupation of Kuwait, calling Saddam Hussein, the Iraqi President, "a classic bully."

At the close of his term, Bush joined American marines in Somalia for the 1993 New Year's celebration. The American troops were stationed in Somalia to prevent the country's warring factions from looting food supplies intended for the starving populace.

CHRISTMAS EVE PARDONS

On December 24, 1992, President Bush announced that he had granted full pardons to Caspar W. Weinberger and five other former government officials in Ronald Reagan's administration. All six had been indicted on, or convicted of, charges relating to their testimony during the 1988 congressional inquiry into the Iran-*contra* scandal.

Weinberger, Secretary of Defense from 1981 through 1987, was scheduled to go on trial in January 1993 on charges that he had lied to Congress by concealing his knowledge of arms sales to Iran in 1986 and the illegal financing of the Nicaraguan rebels. Also pardoned for similar crimes were Clair E. George, Duane R. Claridge, and Alan G. Fiers, Jr., all former CIA officials; Robert MacFarlane, President Reagan's National Security Advisor; and Elliott Abrams, former Assistant Secretary of State.

President Bush said he had pardoned the six individuals because their motivation was patriotism, none had profited or sought to profit from their action, and all had already "paid a price—in depleted savings, lost careers, anguished families—grossly disproportionate to any misdeeds or errors of judgment they may have committed." Saying that the actions of the men were part of the Cold War, which was now over, the President cited the historical precedents of James Madison's pardon of Jean Lafitte's pirates after the War of 1812, Andrew Johnson's pardon of soldiers who had fought for the Confederacy, and Harry S. Truman's and Jimmy Carter's pardons of those who had evaded the draft during World War II and Vietnam.

BUSH TEAMS UP WITH CLINTON FOR RELIEF EFFORTS

In early January 2005, at the request of President George W. Bush, former Presidents Bush and Clinton started the Bush-Clinton Tsunami Fund to help victims of the Indian Ocean tidal wave that killed 150,000 people on December 26, 2004. The one-time political rivals, who ran against each other in the 1992 election, toured the afflicted region together and made joint appeals for donations. On Sept. 5, 2005, they started a similar fund for the Gulf Coast victims of Hurricane Katrina.

FURTHER READING

Bush, George. *A World Transformed*. 1998.
Graubard, Stephen R. *Mr. Bush's War*. 1992.
Hyams, Joe. *Flight of the Avenger*. 1991.

Parmet, Herbert S. *George Bush: The Life of a Lone Star Yankee*. 1997.
Plimpton, George. *The X Factor*. 1990.
Stinnet, Robert B. *George Bush*. 1992.

Courtesy of The Library of Congress

William Jefferson Clinton

Name at birth—William Jefferson Blythe III

Date of birth—Aug. 19, 1946

Place of birth—Hope, Ark.

Education—Georgetown University, Washington, D.C., bachelor of science degree in international affairs, June 9, 1968; Rhodes Scholar studying politics, New College, Oxford University, England, Oct. 1968–June 1970; Yale Law School, New Haven, Conn., J.D., 1973

Religion—Baptist

Ancestry—English

Career—Law professor, state attorney general, state governor

Political party—Democratic

State represented—Arkansas

Term of office—Jan. 20, 1993–Jan. 20, 2001

Administration—52nd, 53rd

Congresses—103rd, 104th, 105th, 106th

Age at inauguration—46 years, 149 days

Occupation after term—Speaker, author, head of charitable foundation, fundraiser

FAMILY

FATHER

Name—William Jefferson Blythe II

Date of birth—Feb. 21, 1917

Place of birth—Near Sherman, Tex.

Education—Grade school through his early teens

First marriage—Virginia Adele Gash, Sherman, Tex., 1935 (div. 1936);

Second marriage—Maxine Hamilton, Ardmore, Okla., 1938 (div. 1939)

Third marriage—Minnie Fave Gash, Okla., 1940 (div.?)

Fourth marriage—Wahnetta Alexander, Kansas City, Mo., 1941 (div. 1944)

Fifth marriage—Virginia Cassidy, Texarkana, Ark., Sept. 3, 1943

Children—See note under Siblings

Occupation—Traveling salesman of heavy equipment, car salesman

Date of death—May 17, 1946

Place of death—Near Sikeston, Mo.

Place of burial—Hope, Ark.

Age at death—29 years, 85 days

The parents of William Jefferson Blythe II were farmers in rural Texas. The father of the future president was the sixth of their nine children. He left school in his early teens to go to work. After the family's farm was foreclosed, he became a traveling salesman, selling auto parts and heavy equipment and entering into a series of brief marriages. His fifth and last marriage, to Virginia Cassidy, took place seven months before he was divorced from his fourth wife.

During World War II he served as a technician third grade with the 303rd Company, 125th Ordnance Base Auto Maintenance Battalion, earning a Good Conduct Medal. He died in a one-car accident five months after his discharge from the Army.

STEPFATHER

Name—Roger Clinton

Date of birth—July 25, 1909

Place of birth—Dardanelle, Ark.

Education—Grade school, possibly high school

First marriage—Ina Mae Murphy, 1933 (div. 1948)

Second marriage—Virginia Cassidy Blythe, June 19, 1950 (div. 1962)

Third marriage—Virginia Blythe Clinton, Aug. 6, 1962

Children—(from 2d marriage) Roger Cassidy Clinton, b. July 25, 1956

Occupation—Car salesman

Date of death—Nov. 8, 1967

Place of death—Hot Springs, Ark.

Place of burial—Hot Springs, Ark.

Age at death—58 years, 106 days

Bill Clinton was three years old when his widowed mother remarried. His stepfather was Roger Clinton, nicknamed "Dude," an alcoholic who had been divorced by his first wife on grounds of physical abuse. Roger Clinton terrorized his second wife, her son, and his own son until Bill, at age 14, was big enough to stop him. Virginia Clinton divorced Roger in 1962 but remarried him a few months later. The fifth of five children of Eula and Al Clinton, a grocer, he worked most of his life as a parts salesman in his brother's car dealership in Hot Springs, Ark.

MOTHER

Name at birth—Virginia Dell Cassidy

Date of birth—June 6, 1923

Place of birth—Bodcaw, Ark.

Education—Nursing school, Tri-State Hospital, Shreveport, La., 1941–1944; nurse anesthetist training, Charity Hospital, New Orleans, La., 1947–1948

First marriage—William Jefferson Blythe III, Oct. 3, 1943 (d. 1946)

Second marriage—Roger Clinton, June 19, 1950 (div. 1962)

Third marriage—Roger Clinton, Aug. 6, 1962 (d. Nov. 8, 1967)

Fourth marriage—George Jefferson Dwire, Jan. 3, 1969 (d. Aug. 1974)

Fifth marriage—Richard Kelley, Jan. 17, 1982

Children (from 1st marriage)—William Jefferson [Blythe] Clinton, b. Aug. 19, 1946; (from 2d marriage) Roger Cassidy Clinton, b. July 25, 1956

Occupation—Nurse anesthetist

Date of death—Jan. 6, 1994

Place of death—Hot Springs, Ark.

Place of burial—Hope, Ark.

Age at death—70 years, 214 days

Bill Clinton's maternal grandparents were Edith Cassidy, a practical nurse, and Eldridge Cassidy, an ice deliveryman and grocer. Bill lived with them as a toddler when his widowed mother, already licensed as a registered nurse, went to Shreveport, La., to receive training as a nurse anesthetist. For most of her life she lived and worked in Hot Springs, Ark., where, in addition to running her own nurse anesthetist firm, she was a well-known frequenter of the racetrack and the nightclubs. Bill Clinton is said to have received an informal education on racial fairness and other social issues at her kitchen table.

Beginning with his run for Congress in 1974, Bill Clinton received the benefit of his mother's enthusiastic campaigning. When he was nominated for the presidency at the 1992 national convention of the Democratic Party, Virginia Kelley (as she was known after her fifth marriage) was in attendance as part of the Arkansas delegation. When the roll was called, she announced: "Madame Secretary, Arkansas proudly casts our 48 votes for our favorite son—and my son—Bill Clinton!" This was a first for mothers of presidential candidates, and the crowd gave her an ovation when Bill Clinton paid tribute to her in his acceptance speech.

Virginia Kelley's autobiography, *Leading with My Heart* (co-authored by James Morgan), was published posthumously in 1994, after her death from breast cancer.

SIBLINGS

Bill Clinton was his mother's first son, the only child of his parents' marriage.

Child of William Jefferson Blythe II and Virginia Cassidy Blythe

William Jefferson ("Bill") Clinton, b. Aug. 19, 1946

Child of Roger Clinton and Virginia Cassidy Blythe Clinton

Roger Cassidy Clinton, b. July 25, 1956

William Jefferson ("Bill") Clinton—originally named William Jefferson Blythe III—was the only child of William Jefferson Blythe II and Virginia Cassidy Blythe. His father was killed in an automobile accident before his birth. Although Bill's mother refused to allow him to be adopted by her second husband, Roger Clinton, he took his stepfather's last name as a way of showing loyalty to his half-brother, Roger Cassidy Clinton, who was born in 1956.

The younger Roger Clinton dropped out of college and eventually became a cocaine addict and dealer. In 1984, when Bill Clinton was governor of Arkansas, he authorized a police sting operation that resulted in a 13-month prison term for his brother. The 176 grants of clemency issued by President Clinton on his last day in office included a pardon for his brother's conviction. Roger Clinton's memoir, *Growing Up Clinton,* was published in 1995.

William Jefferson Blythe II's previous marriages and liaisons produced a number of children who are also the half-brothers and half-sisters of William Jefferson Clinton. Blythe is named as the father on the birth certificate of Henry Leon Ritzenthaler (born Henry Leon Blythe on Jan. 17, 1938, to Adele Gash, Blythe's former first wife), and on the birth certificate of a girl born in May 1941 to a waitress in Missouri. He was also the father of Sharon Lee Blythe Pettijohn, born in 1941 to Wahnetta Alexander Blythe eight days after their wedding. Blythe's first wife claimed that he married her sister Minnie in 1940 as a way of escaping marriage to another woman who was pregnant with another of his children. Blythe's fifth wife, Virginia Cassidy, was unaware of her husband's previous marriages and children until evidence was unearthed by reporters after her son Bill became President, and in her autobiography she expressed doubt about whether the evidence was valid.

MARRIAGE

Married—Hillary Diane Rodham

Date of marriage—Oct. 11, 1975

Place of marriage—Fayetteville, Ark.

Age of wife at marriage—27 years, 359 days

Age of husband at marriage—29 years, 42 days

CHILDREN

Chelsea Victoria Clinton, b. Feb. 27, 1980, Little Rock, Ark.

THE PRESIDENT'S WIFE

Name at birth—Hillary Diane Rodham

Date of birth—Oct. 26, 1947

Place of birth—Park Ridge, Ill.

Mother—Dorothy Howell

Father—Hugh Ellsworth Rodham (d. Apr. 7, 1993)

Father's occupation—Fabric-store owner

Siblings—Two brothers

Education—Public schools, Park Ridge, Ill.; Wellesley College, Wellesley, Mass., bachelor of arts degree with high honors, 1969; Yale Law School, New Haven, Conn., J.D. 1973

Religion—Methodist

Marriage—William Jefferson Clinton, Fayetteville, Ark., Oct. 11, 1975

Children—Chelsea Victoria Clinton, b. Feb 27, 1980

Occupation—Lawyer, political activist

Years younger than the President—1 year, 68 days

Courtesy of The Library of Congress

Hillary Clinton, wife of Bill Clinton

Additional Data on Hillary Clinton

1973–1974, staff attorney, Children's Defense Fund, Washington, D.C., and Cambridge, Mass.; also, legal counsel, Carnegie Council on Children, New Haven, Conn.

1974, counsel, impeachment inquiry staff, House Judiciary Committee, Washington, D.C.

1974–1977, assistant professor of law and director of Legal Aid Clinic, University of Arkansas, Fayetteville

1977–1992, partner, Rose Law Firm, Little Rock, Ark.

1977, published *Handbook on Legal Rights for Arkansas Women* (new ed. 1987)

1977–1984, founder and board president, Arkansas Advocates for Children and Families

1978–1980, chair, Arkansas Legal Services Corporation

1979–1981, 1983–1993, First Lady of Arkansas

1983–1985, chair, Arkansas Education Standards Committee

1986–1991, chair, Children's Defense Fund, Washington, D.C.

1987–1991, chair, Commission on Women in the Profession, American Bar Association

1993–2001, First Lady of the United States

1993–1994, chair, President's Task Force on National Health Care Reform

1993–2001, honorary chair, Presidential Commission on the Arts and Humanities

Sept. 5–15, 1995, U.S. delegate to United Nations Fourth World Conference on Women, Beijing, China

1995–2001, author of syndicated column, "Talking It Over"

1996, author, *It Takes a Village: And Other Lessons Children Teach Us*

Nov. 7, 2000, elected to the U.S. Senate from New York

June 9, 2003, memoir, *Living History*, published

2008, campaigned for Democratic Party nomination as candidate for President; lost to Barack Obama

Jan. 21, 2009, sworn in as Secretary of State

THE FIRST LADY

Hillary Rodham Clinton presented the American public with a new kind of First Lady. A Yale-trained lawyer who had served on the House Judiciary Committee's legal team during the Watergate crisis, she was an accomplished activist on behalf of liberal causes, specializing in child-welfare issues. She was also an essential part of Bill Clinton's political operation, supplying ambition and ideas that complemented and energized his own. The two of them worked so closely together that they were known by the joint nickname "Billary." The First Lady had a central role in every major event of the Clinton administration, including the crisis over the president's impeachment and trial, and was reported by aides to be as powerful within the White House inner circle as Vice President Al Gore. Indeed, much of the criticism directed at the Clintons originated in widespread concern that an unelected "co-president" was sharing the executive leadership of the nation.

Born and raised in the Chicago suburb of Park Ridge, Hillary Diane Rodham grew up in a middle-class Republican household. Her father was the son of immigrants from Great Britain. She moved to the political left during her college years at Wellesley, where she was a student leader, and came under the influence of child-welfare advocate Marian Wright Edelman, founder of the Children's Defense Fund, while she was studying law at Yale. During the Watergate crisis, she researched impeachment issues for the House Judiciary Committee.

After her marriage in 1975 to Bill Clinton, who had been a fellow student at Yale, she taught at the University of Arkansas Law School, where she set up a legal aid service for poor people. As a member of the prestigious Rose Law Firm in Little Rock and the wife of the Governor of Arkansas, she waged a successful campaign for educational reform, traveling the state to conduct citizens' forums and testifying before the legislature.

Upon taking office, President Clinton named Hillary Rodham Clinton to head his Task Force on National Health Reform, the most powerful official position ever held by a First Lady. She was also the first First Lady to have an office in the West Wing of the White House, where the President's office is located. After the collapse of her overly ambitious health care plan, Mrs. Clinton was not named to any other formal government position, instead working behind the scenes to draft policy speeches by the President, promote White House initiatives and congressional legislation she favored, raise money for the Democratic Party, and plan election strategies. Much of her time was taken up in damage control, as one scandal after another engulfed the White House. Mrs. Clinton herself came under suspicion in the Whitewater real estate fraud case, the firing of the White House Travel Office staff, the disappearance of documents relating to the suicide of deputy White House counsel Vincent Foster, and the relocation to the White House of confidential F.B.I. files on prominent Republicans, but she was never indicted, and her husband's involvement in a lurid adultery case gave her the politically useful image of a wronged but loyal and forgiving wife.

As President Clinton's second term drew to a close, Mrs. Clinton prepared to run for a seat in the Senate. Her campaign was successful and she was sworn in on January 3, 2001.

THE FIRST LADY AS FEDERAL OFFICIAL

Since no previous First Lady came to the White House with the professional qualifications that Hillary Clinton had, there was no precedent for her appointment by the President to the chairmanship of a closed-door task force to revise the national health care system. Her status remained unclear until June 22, 1993, when the U.S. Appeals Court in Washington, D.C., ruled that Mrs. Clinton was a "de facto" federal official.

For more about the health care reform effort, see the section "Additional Data on Bill Clinton" at the end of this chapter.

THE WHITEWATER CASE

On January 22, 1996, Hillary Clinton became the first wife of a sitting president to receive a subpoena to testify in a criminal (or any other) case. The subpoena was issued by Kenneth Starr, the independent federal prosecutor looking into charges that the Clintons had been involved in illegal real estate dealings in Arkansas. Mrs. Clinton testified before a grand jury on January 26.

For an explanation of the origins and outcome of the Whitewater case, see the section "Additional Data on Bill Clinton" at the end of this chapter.

SENATOR HILLARY CLINTON OF NEW YORK

The first First Lady to run for any public office was Hillary Rodham Clinton. On February 6, 2000, after many months of testing the waters for her candidacy, she declared herself in the race for the seat being vacated by the retiring U.S. senator from New York, Daniel Patrick Moynihan. Her Republican opponent was Rick Lazio, a congressman from Long Island. (The presumed original Republican candidate, Rudolph Giuliani, mayor of New York City, dropped out of the race after he was diagnosed with prostate cancer.) The Clintons purchased a home in Chappaqua, N.Y., to enable Mrs. Clinton to qualify as a resident of the state, though she was born in Chicago and lived most of her life in Arkansas or Washington. On November 7, Mrs. Clinton won the election with 55 percent of the vote. She took office the following January 3 as the first woman elected to the Senate from New York. The candidates spent a combined total of more than $60 million, making the race one of the most expensive Senate contests to date.

SECRETARY OF STATE

Senator Clinton was reelected to a second term in the Senate in 2006, taking 67 percent of the vote. During her first term, she began planning a run for the Democratic Party's presidential nomination in 2008. If she had succeeded, she would have been the first woman nominated by a major party. In the course of the primary season, she presented herself as a political veteran with much more experience than her main rival, Barack Obama, the junior senator from Illinois, and became the preferred candidate of many working-class Democrats and women. However, the nomination was won by Obama, and at the Democratic National Convention Mrs. Clinton freed her pledged delegates so that he could be nominated by acclamation. She also campaigned for him during his winning race for the White House against John McCain.

Shortly after his victory, Obama named Senator Clinton to head the State Department in his administration. She was confirmed by the Senate and was sworn in as Secretary of State on Jan. 21, 2009, with her husband, former President Bill Clinton, holding the Bible as she took the oath of office.

IMPORTANT DATES IN THE PRESIDENT'S LIFE

June 9, 1968, graduated from Georgetown University, Washington, D.C., with a degree in international affairs

1968–1970, Rhodes scholar at Oxford University in England

1973, graduated from Yale Law School

1973–1976, professor, University of Arkansas Law School, Fayetteville, and attorney in private practice

1974, defeated in race for House of Representatives, Third District Arkansas, by John Paul Hammerschmidt

1976, directed Jimmy Carter's presidential campaign in Arkansas

1977–1979, Arkansas attorney general

1979–1981, governor of Arkansas

1980, defeated by Frank White for governorship

1981–1982, practiced law in Little Rock with law firm Wright, Lindsey & Jennings

1982, elected governor of Arkansas for two-year term

1983, won passage of controversial education reform act involving teacher testing and increased sales taxes

1984, re-elected governor of Arkansas for newly established four-year term

1985–1986, chair, Southern Growth Policies Board

1986–1987, chair, National Governors Association; chair, Education Commission of the States

1988, reelected governor of Arkansas; made speech nominating Michael Dukakis for President at Democratic National Convention in July 1988 in Atlanta

1989–1990, chair, Lower Mississippi Delta Development Commission

1990–1991, chair, Democratic Leadership Council

July 15, 1992, nominated for President at Democratic National Convention in New York

1992, published (with Al Gore, Jr.) *Putting People First: How We Can All Change America*

Jan. 20, 1993–Jan. 20, 1997, President of the United States (first term)

1995, published *My Plans for a Second Term*

1996, published *Between Hope and History: Meeting America's Challenges for the 21st Century*

Jan. 20, 1997–Jan. 20, 2001, President of the United States (second term)

Dec. 16, 1998, impeached by House of Representatives

Feb. 12, 1999, acquitted in Senate impeachment trial

2001– , head of William J. Clinton Foundation

Nov. 18, 2004, presidential library dedicated

June 22, 2004, autobiography, *My Life*, published

2005–2007, United Nations special envoy for tsunami recovery

Sept. 4, 2007, *Giving: How Each of Us Can Change the World* published

ELECTIONS

THE ELECTION OF 1992

November 3, 1992

CANDIDATES

Democratic Party (41st Convention)

July 13–16, 1992, Madison Square Garden, New York, N.Y.

P: William Jefferson Clinton, Ark.
VP: Albert Arnold Gore, Jr., Tenn.

Clinton was nominated on the first ballot. The rules were suspended during the vote to enable the delegates to nominate him by acclamation. Al Gore was then nominated for vice president by acclamation. Candidates for nomination and the votes they received:

William Jefferson Clinton, Ark., 3,372
Edmund G. ("Jerry") Brown, Calif., 596
Paul E. Tsongas, Mass., 209
Robert P. Casey, Penn., 10
Patricia Schroeder, Colo., 8
Lawrence A. Agran, Calif., 3
Albert Arnold Gore, Jr., Tenn., 1
Joseph Simonetti, 1
Other, 2
Abstentions, 85
Uncommitted, 1
Total number of votes: 4,288
Number necessary for nomination: 2,145

Republican Party (35th Convention)

Aug. 17–20, 1992, Astrodome, Houston, Tex.

P: George Herbert Walker Bush, Tex.
VP: James Danforth Quayle, III, Ind.

Bush was nominated on the first ballot. Candidates for nomination and the votes they received:

George Herbert Walker Bush, Texas, 2,166
Patrick J. Buchanan, Washington, D.C., 18
Howard Phillips, Va., 2
Alan Keyes, Mass., 1
Abstentions, 23*
Total number of delegates: 2,210
Total number of votes: 2,187*
Number necessary for nomination: 2,106

*The 23 votes missing from the total represent the votes of the New Hampshire delegation. President Bush was renominated by acclamation before New Hampshire's votes could be cast.

Independent Ticket

P: (Henry) Ross Perot, Tex.
VP: James Bond Stockdale, Calif.

Perot entered the race on Oct. 1, 1992, after his supporters placed his name on the ballot in every state.

Libertarian Party

Aug. 29–31, 1991, Chicago, Ill.

P: Andre Verne Marrou, Nev.
VP: Nancy Lord, Ga.

Populist/America First Party

May 2–3, 1992, Clark, N.J.

P: James Gordon (Bo) Gritz, Pa.
VP: Cy Minett, Tex.

New Alliance Party

P: Lenora B. Fulani, N.Y.
VP: Maria Elizabeth Muñoz, Calif.

American Independent Party

Aug. 29, 1992, Sacramento, Calif.

P: Howard Phillips, Va.
VP: Albion Williamson Knight, Jr., Md.

The party decided to affiliate with the U.S. Taxpayers Party on the day following the convention.

U.S. Taxpayers Party

Sept. 4–5, 1992, New Orleans, La.

P: Howard Phillips, Va.
VP: (in various states) Stephen Carey Graves, Ark.; Albion Williamson Knight, Jr., Md.; Robert Emmanuel Tisch, Mich.

Phillips also ran on the ticket of the Illinois Taxpayers Party, with Alexander B. Magnus, Jr., of Illinois. as his running mate, and on the ticket of the Tisch Independent Citizens Party, with Robert Emmanuel Tisch as his running mate.

Natural Law Party

P: John Samuel Hagelin, Iowa

VP: Vinton Michael Tompkins, Iowa

The Natural Law Party was founded in Fairfield, Iowa., on Apr. 20, 1992. The candidates were chosen by the executive committee.

Independent Candidate
P: Ron Daniels, Ohio
VP: Asiba Tupahache, N.Y.

Peace and Freedom Party
Aug. 15–16, 1992, San Diego, Calif.
P: Ron Daniels, Ohio
VP: Asiba Tupahache, N.Y.

Freedom for LaRouche Party
P: Lyndon Hermyle LaRouche, Va.
VP: James Luther Bevel, Pa.

Socialist Workers Party
Nov. 1991, Chicago, Ill.
P: James Mac Warren, N.Y.
VP: Willie Mae Reid, Ill.

Independent Candidate
P: Drew Bradford, N.J.

Grassroots Party
P: Jack Herer, Calif.
VP: Derrick P. Grimmer, Mo.

Socialist Party
Sept. 1, 1991, Chicago, Ill.
P: John Quinn Brisben, Ill.
VP: William Davis Edwards, Calif.

Edwards died on Aug. 5, 1992, and Barbara Garson of Mass. was named as his replacement by the party's national committee.

Workers League
P: Helen Halyard, Mich.
VP: Fred Mazelis, N.Y.

Take Back America Party
P: John Yiamouyiannis, Ohio
VP: Allen C. McCone, Mo.

Independent Candidate
P: Delbert L. Ehlers, Iowa
VP: Rick Wendt, Iowa

Prohibition Party
June 24–26, 1991, Minneapolis, Minn.
P: Earl Farwell Dodge, Colo.
VP: George Ormsby, Pa.

Apathy Party
P: James Harlan Boren, Va.
VP: Will Weidman

Third Party
P: Eugene Arthur Hem, Wis.
VP: Joanne Roland, Wis.

Looking Back Party
P: Isabelle Masters, Okla.
VP: Walter Ray Masters, Kan.

American Party
P: Robert Junior Smith, Utah
VP: Doris Feimer, N.D.

Workers World Party
P: Gloria Estella La Riva, Calif.
VP: Larry Holmes, N.Y.

1992 POPULAR VOTE

Democratic Party, 44,909,326 (43.00%)
Republican Party, 39,103,882 (37.45%)
(Henry) Ross Perot, 19,741,657 (18.91%)
Libertarian Party, 291,627
Populist/America First, 107,014
New Alliance Party, 73,714
U.S. Taxpayers Party, 43,434
Natural Law Party, 39,179
Ron Daniels (indep.), 27,961
Freedom for LaRouche Party, 26,333
Socialist Workers Party, 23,096
Drew Bradford (indep.), 4,749
Grassroots Party, 3,875
Socialist Party, 3,057
Workers League, 3,050
John Yiamouyiannis (indep.), 2,199
Delbert Ehlers (indep.), 1,149
Prohibition Party, 961
Apathy Party, 956
Third Party, 405
Looking Back Group, 339
American Party, 292
Workers World, 181
Scattered write-ins, 14,041

None of these candidates (Nev.), 2,537

Total, 104,425,014

1992 ELECTORAL VOTE

Announcement of the electoral vote was made on January 6, 1993, before a joint session of Congress. There were 538 votes from 50 states and the District of Columbia.

Clinton received 69 percent (370 votes—31 states and the District of Columbia) as follows: Ark. 6, Calif. 54, Colo. 8, Conn. 8, Del. 3, D.C. 3, Ga. 13, Haw. 4, Ill. 22, Iowa 7, Ky. 8, La. 9, Me. 4, Md. 10, Mass. 12, Mich. 18, Minn. 10 Mo. 11, Mont. 3, Nev. 4, N.H. 4, N.J. 15, N.M. 5, Ohio 21, Ore. 7, Pa. 23, R.I. 4, Tenn. 11, Vt. 3, Wash. 11, W.Va. 5, Wis. 11

Bush received 31 percent (168 votes—18 states) as follows: Ala. 9, Alas. 3, Ariz. 8, Fla. 25, Ida. 4, Ind. 12, Kan. 6, Miss. 7, Neb. 5, N.C. 14, N.D. 3, Okla. 8, S.C. 8, S.C. 3, Tex. 32, Utah 5, Va. 13, Wyo. 3

THE ELECTION OF 1996

November 5, 1996

CANDIDATES

Democratic Party (42nd Convention)

Aug. 26–29, 1996, United Center, Chicago, Ill.

P: William Jefferson Clinton, Ark.
VP: Albert Arnold Gore, Jr., Tenn.

Bill Clinton was nominated on the first ballot. Candidates for nomination and the votes they received:
William Jefferson Clinton, Ark., 4,277
Abstentions, 12
Total number of votes: 4,289
Number necessary for nomination: 2,146

Republican Party (36th Convention)

Aug. 12–15, 1996, San Diego Convention Center, San Diego, Calif.

P: Robert Joseph Dole, Kan.
VP: Jack Kemp, N.Y.

Bob Dole was nominated on the first ballot. Candidates for nomination and the votes they received:
Robert Joseph Dole, Kan., 1928
Patrick J. Buchanan, D.C., 43

Phil Gramm, Tex., 2
Alan Keyes, Mass., 1
Robert Bork, D.C., 1
Abstentions, 15
Total number of votes: 1990
Number necessary for nomination: 996

Reform Party

Aug. 11, 1996, Long Beach, Calif., private primary by mail (results announced Aug. 17, Valley Forge, Pa.)

P: (Henry) Ross Perot, Tex.
VP: Pat Choate, Okla.

Green Party

Aug. 15–19, 1996, Los Angeles, Calif.

P: Ralph Nader, Conn.
VP: Winona LaDuke, Minn.

Libertarian Party

July 3–7, 1996, Washington, D.C.

P: Harry Browne, Ind.
VP: Joanne M. Jorgensen, S.C.

U.S. Taxpayers Party

Aug. 16–18, 1996, San Diego, Calif.

P: Howard Phillips, Va.
VP: Herb Titus, Va.

Natural Law Party

Aug. 23–24, 1996, Washington, D.C.

P: John Samuel Hagelin, Iowa
VP: Vinton Michael Tompkins, N.C.

Workers World Party

Dec. 2–3, 1995, New York, N.Y.

P: Monica Moorehead, N.Y.
VP: Gloria Estella La Riva, Calif.

Peace and Freedom Party

Aug. 29, 1996, Calif.

P: Marsha Feinland, Calif.
VP: Kate McClatchy, Mass.

Independent Candidate

P: Charles Collins, Ga.
VP: Rosemary Giumarra, Calif.

Socialist Workers Party

P: James E. Harris, Jr., Ga.
VP: Laura Garza, N.Y.

Grassroots Party

May 4, 1996, teleconference

P: Dennis Peron, Calif.
VP: Arlin Troutt, Ariz.

Arlin Troutt was serving time in federal prison on marijuana offenses.

Socialist Party

Oct. 6–9, 1995, Cambridge, Mass.

P: Mary Cal Hollis, Colo.
VP: Eric T. Chester, Arlington, Mass.

Socialist Equality Party (formerly Workers League)

P: Jerome White, Mich.
VP: Fred Mazelis, N.Y.

American Party

Feb. 22–23, 1996, Wichita, Kan.

P: Diane Beall Templin, Calif.
VP: Gary Van Horn, Utah

Prohibition Party

June 29–30, 1995, Denver, Colo.

P: Earl F. Dodge, Colo.
VP: Rachel B. Kelly, Ill.

Independent Party of Utah

P: A. Peter Crane, Utah
VP: Connie Chandler, Utah

America First Party

P: Ralph Forbes, Ark.
VP: Pro-Life Anderson

Independent Grassroots Party

Sept. 1996, Minn.

P: John Birrenbach, Minn.
VP: George McMahon, Iowa

Looking Back Party

P: Isabell Masters, Ark.
VP: Shirley Jean Masters, Ark.

AIDS Cure Party

P: Steve Michaels, D.C.
VP: Anne Northrop, N.Y.

1996 POPULAR VOTE

Democratic Party, 47,402,357 (49.24%)

Republican Party, 39,198,755 (40.71%)
Reform Party, 8,085,402 (8.40%)
Green Party, 685,040
Libertarian Party, 485,798
U.S. Taxpayers Party, 184,658
Natural Law Party, 113,668
Workers World Party, 29,083
Peace and Freedom Party, 25,332
Miscellaneous write-ins, 25,118
Charles Collins (indep.), 8,930
Socialist Workers, 8,476
None of These Candidates (Nev.), 5,608
Grassroots Party, 5,378
Socialist Party, 4,706
Socialist Equality Party, 2,438
American Party, 1,847
Prohibition Party, 1,298
Independent Party of Utah, 1,101
America First Party, 932
Independent Grassroots Party, 787
Looking Back Party, 752
AIDS Cure Party, 408
Total, 96,277,872

This total does not include 123,000 blank votes and write-ins reported by New York State.

1996 ELECTORAL VOTE

Announcement of the electoral vote was made on Jan. 8, 1997, before a joint session of Congress. There were 538 votes from 50 states and the District of Columbia.

Clinton received 49.24 percent (379 votes—31 states and the District of Columbia) as follows: Ariz. 8, Ark. 6, Calif. 54, Conn. 8, Del. 3, D.C. 3, Fla. 25, Haw. 4, Ill. 22, Iowa 7, Ky. 8, La. 9, Me. 4, Md. 10, Mass. 12, Mich. 18, Minn. 10, Mo. 11, Nev. 4, N.H. 4, N.J. 15, N.M. 5, N.Y. 33, Ohio 21, Ore. 7, Pa. 23, R.I. 4, Tenn. 11, Vt. 3, Wash. 11, W.V. 5, Wisc. 11

Dole received 40.71 percent (159 votes—19 states) as follows: Ala. 9, Alas. 3, Colo. 8, Ga. 13, Ida. 4, Ind. 12, Kan. 6, Miss. 7, Mont. 3, Neb. 5, N.C. 14, N.D. 3, Okla. 8, S.C. 8, S.D. 3, Tex. 32, Utah 5, Va. 13, Wyo. 3

INAUGURATIONS

FIRST TERM

January 20, 1993

William Jefferson Clinton was inaugurated forty-second President of the United States on a crisp, clear day of brilliant blue skies with a temperature in the low forties. As his immediate predecessors in office had done, Clinton chose to take the inaugural oath on the West Front of the Capitol. Chief Justice William Hubbs Rehnquist administered the oath at 11:59 A.M. on Wednesday, January 20, 1993.

The inaugural address surprised many by its brevity. In a 14-minute speech, the new President called for renewal, using the metaphor of a "forced spring," and asked for responsibility and sacrifice. "There is nothing wrong with America that cannot be cured by what is right with America," he declared.

Poet Maya Angelou read "On the Pulse of Morning," a poem written for the inauguration.

The inaugural parade, the longest in history, included Ben Nighthorse Campbell of Colorado, the second Native American elected to the Senate, riding his horse in full regalia, and such oddities as a lawn-chair drill team.

The inauguration was preceded by a series of popular events, including a bus trip to Washington from Thomas Jefferson's home, Monticello, by the Clintons and the Gores and a "Faces of Hope" luncheon in the Folger Library, with 50 guests from various walks of life that Clinton had met during his campaign. On the morning of the ceremony, Clinton attended a prayer service at the Metropolitan African Methodist Episcopal Church, an African-American church with ties to the civil rights movement. Lavish balls and gala celebrations continued throughout inaugural week, and the President and Mrs. Clinton attended most of them. Thousands attended an Open House in the White House the day after the inauguration.

Courtesy of The Library of Congress

President Clinton delivers his first inaugural address.

SECOND TERM

January 20, 1997

Before his second inauguration, President Clinton and his wife attended a prayer service at the Metropolitan AME Church, as they had done four years earlier. The President was sworn in at 12:05 P.M. at the West Front of the Capitol by Chief Justice William H. Rehnquist, using the same family Bible that he had used at his first swearing-in ceremony. It was opened to Isaiah 58:12, which reads: "Those from among you / Shall build the old waste place; / You shall raise up the foundations of many generations; / And you shall be called the Repairer of the Breach, / The Restorer of Streets to Dwell In." Clinton made reference to this verse in his 22-minute address, which unfolded a utopian view of the future, though with little mention of specific ways to achieve it.

The invocation was made by the Rev. Billy Graham, participating in his eighth presidential inauguration. Arkansas poet Miller Williams read from his work, and soprano Jessye Norman sang a medley of patriotic hymns. The crowd was estimated at more than

200,000. The temperature was reasonably warm—about 45 degrees—and clouds gave way to sunshine at the start of the ceremony.

The post-inauguration lunch given in the President's honor at the Capitol offered a menu derived from a recipe book that had been used at Thomas Jefferson's home, Monticello, circa 1838. It consisted of shrimp, oyster, and scallop pie; beef à la mode; beggar's pudding; and quince ice cream. The President stayed so long that the start of the inaugural parade was delayed until after 3 P.M., forcing the last marching bands to play in darkness. The parade included Navajo codetalkers from World War II, Vietnam War helicopter pilots, a covered wagon representing the Mormon trek to Utah, synchronized rope jumpers, and a polka float.

The Clintons stayed up all night visiting the 14 official inaugural balls as well as an unofficial ball hosted by a veterans' group.

THE VICE PRESIDENT

Name—Albert Arnold ("Al") Gore, Jr.

Date of birth—Mar. 31, 1948

Place of birth—Washington, D.C.

Mother—Pauline La Fon Gore

Mother's occupation—Lawyer

Father—Albert Gore, Sr.

Father's occupation—Congressman from Tennessee; U.S. Senator, 1953–1971 (Tenn.); chairman, Island Creek Coal Company, Lexington, Ky.

Education—Public elementary schools, Carthage, Tenn.; St. Alban's Episcopal School for Boys, Washington, D.C., grad. 1965; Harvard University, Cambridge, Mass., bachelor of arts degree in government, cum laude, 1969, University Scholar; Vanderbilt University School of Religion, Nashville, Tenn., 1971–1972; Vanderbilt University Law School, 1974–1976

Religion—Baptist

Married—Mary Elizabeth ("Tipper") Aitcheson, May 19, 1970

Children—Karenna, b. Aug. 6, 1973, m. Drew Schiff; Kristin, b. June 5, 1977; Sarah, b. Jan. 7, 1979; Albert III, b. Oct. 19, 1982

Political party—Democratic

State represented—Tennessee

Term of office—Jan. 20, 1993–Jan. 20, 2001

Age at inauguration—44 years, 295 days

Occupation after term—University lecturer

Courtesy of the U.S. Department of Defense

Al Gore, Vice President to Bill Clinton

ADDITIONAL DATA ON GORE

1969, graduated from Harvard cum laude, with a senior thesis entitled "The Impact of Television on the Conduct of the Presidency, 1947–1959"

1969–1971, U.S. Army in Vietnam, where he served as a reporter

1971–1976, investigative reporter and editorial writer for the *Tennessean,* Nashville, Tenn.; also developer, Tanglewood Home Builders Company

1973–, tobacco and livestock farmer

Nov. 2, 1976, elected to House of Representatives; reelected 1978, 1980, 1982; served 1977–1985

Nov. 6, 1984, elected to the Senate; reelected in 1990; served 1985–1993

1988, campaigned for Democratic presidential nomination

1992, chair, Senate delegation to United Nations Earth Summit, Rio de Janeiro, Brazil

1992, author, *Earth in the Balance*, a best-selling book on environmental issues

Jan. 20, 1993–Jan. 20, 1997, elected Vice President of the United States (first term)

Jan. 20, 1997–Jan. 20, 2001, Vice President of the United States (second term)

Aug. 16, 2000, nominated for President at the Democratic National Convention with running mate Senator Joseph Lieberman of Connecticut

Nov. 7, 2000, won popular vote in presidential election

Dec. 12, 2000, lost the electoral college to Republican candidate George W. Bush after a Supreme Court ruling on contested ballots in Florida

2001, taught at Columbia University, the University of California at Los Angeles, Fisk University, and Middle Tennessee State College

2001– , environmental activist and lecturer

2004, founder, Generation Investment Management

2005, winner of Primetime Emmy Award; winner of Webby Award

2006, founder, Alliance for Climate Protection; starred in documentary *An Inconvenient Truth*

Oct. 12, 2007, co-winner of the Nobel Peace Prize

May 22, 2007, *The Assault on Reason* published

2009, *The Path to Survival* published

Al Gore spent a large part of his childhood in Washington, D.C., where his father served many years as congressman and senator from Tennessee. His mother was one of the first woman to earn a law degree from Vanderbilt University. The younger Al Gore attended divinity and law classes at Vanderbilt in the 1970s while he was working as a newspaper reporter, farmer, and home builder. He entered Congress as a representative of Tennessee's Fourth District—his father's former seat—in 1977 and was reelected three times, taking more than 79 percent of the vote each time, before running successfully for the Senate in 1984. He served in the Senate as a member of the Communications, Science, and Transportation committees and the Arms Control Observer Group, and chaired the Science, Technology and Space, Armed Services, and Rules subcommittees, as well as the Joint Economic Committee. Though he ran an aggressive primary campaign for the Democratic presidential nomination in 1988, he lost to Michael Dukakis, but raised his national profile high enough to be picked as Bill Clinton's running mate in 1992.

Gore's expertise in issues of technology and the environment allowed him to function as a valuable advisor to President Clinton but also to develop a separate power base within the White House. Soon after taking office, he gave the administration a much-needed boost by winning a public debate with H. Ross Perot, the Texas oilman and political dabbler, over the merits of the controversial North American Free Trade Agreement, which was subsequently passed by Congress. Gore also headed REGO, the President's plan to increase efficiency by "re-inventing government"; served as a member of the National Security Council; and was an early champion of Internet expansion initiatives.

CAREER AFTER THE VICE PRESIDENCY

The presidential election of 2000 pitted Gore and running mate Joseph Lieberman, Senator from Connecticut, against George W. Bush and Dick Cheney. The outcome on Election Day was too close to call. The subsequent recounting of ballots lasted until December 13, when Gore conceded, having won the popular vote by a small margin only to lose the electoral vote.

(For more details about the 2000 election, see the chapter on George Walker Bush.)

Gore then embarked on a career as an environmental evangelist, touring the United States with a slideshow about catastrophic global warming entitled *An Inconvenient Truth*. A film of the same name, featuring Gore as narrator, won an Academy Award for Best Documentary Feature in 2007, and Gore's companion book reached the top spot on the bestseller lists. He also co-founded and chaired an environment-oriented investment firm and started the Alliance for Climate Protection. These activities earned him the 2007 Nobel Peace Prize, which he shared with the Intergovernmental Panel on Climate Control.

THE SECOND LADY

Name at birth—Mary Elizabeth ("Tipper") Aitcheson

Date of birth—Aug. 19, 1948

Place of birth—Washington, D.C.

Mother—Margaret Carlson

Mother's occupation—Accountant

Father—John Aitcheson

Father's occupation—Plumbing supplier

Education—St. Stephen and St. Agnes School, Alexandria, Va.; Garland Junior College; Boston University, Boston, Mass., bachelor of arts degree 1970; George Peabody College, Vanderbilt University, Nashville, Tenn., master's degree in psychology, 1975

Married—Albert Arnold Gore, Jr., May 19, 1970

Children—Karenna, b. Aug. 6, 1973; Kristin, b. June 5, 1977; Sarah, b. Jan. 7, 1979; Albert III, b. Oct. 19, 1982

Additional Data on Tipper Gore

1970s, freelance photographer, *Tennessean,* Nashville, Tenn.

1978–1979, founder and chair, Congressional Wives Task Force

Courtesy of the U.S. Department of Defense

Mary Elizabeth "Tipper" Gore, wife of Al Gore

1984, founder, Families for the Homeless

1985, founder, Parents Music Resource Center

1987, author, *Raising PG Kids in an X-Rated Society*

1990, founder, Tennessee Voices for Children, mental-health services coalition

1996, author, *Picture This: A Visual Diary*

1996–2001, co-chair, America Goes Back to School Initiative

July 1999, organizer, first White House Conference on Mental Health, Howard University, Washington, D.C.; advisor during Clinton administration on mental health policy

CABINET

FIRST TERM

January 20, 1993–January 20, 1997

State—Warren Minor Christopher, Calif., Jan. 20, 1993

Treasury—Lloyd Millard Bentsen, Jr., Tex., Jan. 20, 1993–Dec. 22, 1994; Robert E. Rubin, N.Y., Jan. 10, 1995

Defense—Leslie Aspin, Jr., Wis., Jan. 20, 1993–Feb. 2, 1994; William James Perry, Calif., Feb. 3, 1994

Justice—Janet Reno, Fla., Mar. 12, 1993

Interior—Bruce Edward Babbitt, Ariz., Jan. 20, 1993

Agriculture—Albert Michael Espy, Miss., Jan. 21, 1993–Dec. 31, 1994; Daniel Glickman, Kansas, Mar. 31, 1995

Commerce—Ronald Harmon Brown, D.C., Jan. 21, 1993, d. Apr. 3, 1996; Mickey Kantor, Calif., ad interim Apr. 12, 1996–Jan. 29, 1997

Labor—Robert Bernard Reich, Mass., Jan. 21, 1993

Health and Human Services—Donna Edna Shalala, Wis., Jan. 22, 1993

Housing and Urban Development —Henry Gabriel Cisneros, Tex., Jan. 21, 1993

Transportation—Federico Fabia Peña, Colo., Jan. 21, 1993

Energy—Hazel Rollins O'Leary, Minn., Jan. 21, 1993

Education—Richard Wilson Riley, S.C., Jan. 21, 1993

Veterans Affairs—Jesse Brown, Ill., Jan. 21, 1993

SECOND TERM

January 20, 1997–January 20, 2001

State—Madeleine Korbel Albright, D.C., Jan. 23, 1997

Treasury—Robert E. Rubin, N.Y., continued from previous administration; Lawrence Summers, Mass., July 2, 1999

Defense—William Sebastian Cohen, Me., Jan. 24, 1997

Justice—Janet Reno, Fla., continued from previous administration

Interior—Bruce Edward Babbitt, Ariz., continued from previous administration

Agriculture—Daniel Glickman, Kansas, continued from previous administration

Commerce—William M. Daley, Ill., Jan. 30, 1997–June 15, 2000; Norman Yoshio Mineta, Calif., July 20, 2000

Labor—Alexis M. Herman, D.C., May 9, 1997

Health and Human Services—Donna Edna Shalala, Wis., continued from previous administration

Housing and Urban Development —Andrew Cuomo, N.Y., Jan. 29, 1997

Transportation—Rodney E. Slater, Ark., Feb. 14, 1997

Energy—Federico Fabia Peña, Colo., Mar. 12, 1997–Apr. 6, 1998; Bill Richardson, N.M., Aug. 18, 1998

Education—Richard Wilson Riley, S.C., Jan. 21, 1993, continued from previous administration

Veterans Affairs—Togo D. West, Jr., N.C., ad interim Jan. 2, 1998–May 5, 1998; Togo Dennis West, Jr., May 5, 1998

Courtesy of The Library of Congress

President Clinton with his cabinet

CONGRESS

ONE HUNDRED THIRD CONGRESS

January 3, 1993–January 3, 1995

First session—Jan. 5, 1993–Nov. 26, 1993 (326 days)

Second session—Jan. 25, 1994–Dec. 1, 1994 (311 days)

Vice President—Albert Arnold Gore, Jr., Tenn.

President pro tempore of the Senate —Robert Carlisle Byrd, W.Va.

Secretary of the Senate—Walter J. Stewart, Del.; (from Apr. 15, 1994) Martha S. Pope

Speaker of the House—Thomas Stephen Foley, Wash.

Clerk of the House—Donnald K. Anderson, Calif.

ONE HUNDRED FOURTH CONGRESS

January 3, 1995–January 3, 1997

First session—Jan. 4, 1995–Jan. 3, 1996 (365 days)

Second session—Jan. 3, 1996–Oct. 4, 1996 (276 days)

Vice President—Albert Arnold Gore, Jr., Tenn.

President pro tempore of the Senate —(James) Strom Thurmond, S.C.

Secretary of the Senate—Sheila P. Burke; (from June 8, 1995) Kelly D. Johnston; (from Oct. 1, 1996) Gary Lee Sisco

Speaker of the House—Newton L. Gingrich, Ga.

Clerk of the House—Robin H. Carle, Ida.

ONE HUNDRED FIFTH CONGRESS

January 3, 1997–January 3, 1999

First session—Jan. 7, 1997–Nov. 13, 1997 (311 days)

Second session—Jan. 27, 1998–Dec. 19, 1998 (312 days)

Vice President —Albert Arnold Gore, Jr., Tenn.

President pro tempore of the Senate —(James) Strom Thurmond, S.C.

Secretary of the Senate—Gary Lee Sisco

Speaker of the House—Newton L. Gingrich, Ga.

Clerk of the House—Robin H. Carle, Ida.

ONE HUNDRED SIXTH CONGRESS

January 3, 1999–January 3, 2001

First session—Jan. 6, 1999–Nov. 22, 1999 (321 days)

Second session—Jan. 24, 2000–Dec. 15, 2000 (327 days)

Vice President—Al Gore, Tenn.

President pro tempore of the Senate —(James) Strom Thurmond, S.C.

Secretary of the Senate—Gary Lee Sisco

Speaker of the House—John Dennis Hastert, Ill.

Clerk of the House—Jeff Trandahl, S.D.

APPOINTMENTS TO THE SUPREME COURT

Associate Justices

Ruth Joan Bader Ginsburg, D.C., Aug. 10, 1993 (replacing Byron R. White)

Stephen Gerald Breyer, Mass., Aug. 3, 1994 (replacing Harry A. Blackmun)

IMPORTANT DATES IN THE PRESIDENCY

Jan. 25, 1993, President appointed the First Lady to head a task force charged with revising the health care system to provide universal coverage

Jan. 29, 1993, President declared his intention to reverse longstanding policy of excluding homosexuals from service in the armed forces. After objections from military leaders and members of Congress, he settled (July 19) on a compromise position known as "don't ask, don't tell"

Feb. 17, 1993, President addressed joint session of Congress on economic recovery and tax increase package

Feb. 26, 1993, six people died and several hundred were injured when a truck bomb blew a 200-foot crater in the parking garage of the World Trade Center in New York City. Radical Islamic cleric Sheik Omar Abdel Rahman and an associate were convicted on Nov. 12, 1997

Feb. 28, 1993, U.S. planes began airlift of humanitarian aid supplies to war-torn Bosnia; President announced creation of national service program in which college students would be able to repay college loans by working in community service after graduation

Mar. 1, 1993, six federal agents were killed when the FBI and the Bureau of Tobacco and Firearms raided the armed compound of the Branch Davidian cult in Waco, TX. The site remained under siege until Apr. 19, when a tear-gas assault by federal agents ended with the burning of the compound and the deaths of 72 cult members; an investigation by special counsel produced a finding in July 2000 that the deaths were caused by the cult's leaders rather than by the federal government

May 19, 1993, seven longtime employees of the White House travel office were fired by the Clinton administration; accusations of political motives in the firings dogged the President and First Lady for the rest of their two terms

Summer 1993, the Mississippi River and its tributaries inundated 8 million acres across nine Midwestern states and Kentucky, in what was called a "hundred-year flood"

June 26, 1993, Clinton, citing evidence that the Iraqi intelligence service had attempted to assassinate former president George Bush, ordered a retaliatory Tomahawk missile attack on its headquarters in Baghdad

July 20, 1993, Vincent Foster, the deputy White House counsel and a close friend of the Clintons, was found dead, an apparent suicide

Aug. 10, 1993, President signed a measure designed to reduce the federal deficit through cuts in spending and additional taxes

Sept. 13, 1993, President hosted a ceremony on the White House lawn for the signing of the Oslo Accords, an agreement setting forth a framework for negotiations between the State of Israel and the Palestine Liberation Organization

Sept. 22, 1993, President unveiled the First Lady's comprehensive plan for reform of the health care system; the plan was scuttled on Sept. 26, 1994, after meeting with widespread criticism

Oct. 3, 1993, 18 American soldiers and hundreds of Somalis died in a firefight in Mogadishu, Somalia, during a mishandled raid to abduct top lieutenants of warlord Mohammed Farah Aidid; the deaths led to the resignation of Defense Secretary Les Aspin

Nov. 30, 1993, President signed the Brady Handgun Violence Prevention Act, providing for background checks for handgun buyers

Dec. 8, 1993, President signed the North American Free Trade Agreement, despite objections by the labor movement

Jan. 10, 1994, President announced a deal in which Ukraine would receive a payment of cash from the United States in return for dismantling its nuclear arsenal, the third largest in the world

Jan. 12, 1994, President requested appointment of a special prosecutor to investigate the Whitewater real estate allegations; congressional hearings into Whitewater began on July 26

Jan. 17, 1994, an earthquake measuring 6.6 on the Richter Scale struck Los Angeles, killing 61 and causing extensive property damage

Feb. 3, 1994, trade embargo against Vietnam lifted after 19 years; accord permitting free trade between Vietnam and United States was signed on July 13, 2000

Feb. 21, 1994, C.I.A. senior official Aldrich Ames and his wife were arrested and charged with espionage for the Soviet Union; Ames was later sentenced to a life term in prison

Apr. 27, 1994, five Presidents (Clinton, Bush, Reagan, Carter, and Ford) attended funeral of President Richard Nixon

May 6, 1994, President named as defendant in sexual harassment lawsuit by Paula Corbin Jones

July 26, 1994, beginning of congressional hearings into Whitewater

Sept. 12, 1994, Clinton told Haitian military regime that the United States would invade Haiti unless ousted president Jean-Bertrand Aristide was restored to power; Aristide returned in October

Nov. 8, 1994, Republicans gained control of both the House and the Senate in the mid-term elections

Dec. 6, 1994, longtime Clinton friend Webster Hubbell pleaded guilty to mail fraud and tax evasion in the Whitewater case; he was later sentenced to 21 months in prison

Jan. 4, 1995, at the opening of the new, Republican-dominated Congress, Newton L. Gingrich, author of the "Contract with America," was elected Speaker of the House; Robert Dole became Senate Majority Leader

Jan. 31, 1995, President used emergency powers to lend $20 billion to Mexico, to stave off financial collapse

Apr. 19, 1995, 168 people died and hundreds were wounded when the Alfred R. Murrah Federal Building in Oklahoma City, OK, was destroyed by a truck bomb planted by Timothy McVeigh and Terry Nichols, militants with ties to the radically antigovernment militia movement; many of the dead were young children in the building's day-care center. They chose the date in retaliation for the federal government's raid on the Branch Davidian cult two years earlier

June 12, 1995, in a 5-4 vote, the Supreme Court, in *Adarand Constructors, Inc., v. Peña,* ordered the Justice Department to evaluate all federal affirmative action programs for compliance with strict constitutional tests

July 11, 1995, U.S. established diplomatic relations with Vietnam

July 18, 1995, beginning of Senate hearings into Whitewater; the committee members, after 13 months of hearings, divided along party lines in their conclusions about the guilt or innocence of the Clintons

Nov. 14, 1995, the federal government was shut down as a result of the impasse in budget negotiations between the White House and Congress; shutdown lasted until Nov. 20

Nov. 15, 1995, start of President's affair with Monica Lewinsky (according to the Starr Report)

Nov. 21, 1995, Dayton Accords signed by presidents of Serbia, Croatia, and Bosnia-Herzegovina; agreement brokered by Clinton administration

Dec. 17, 1995, another budget impasse between President and Congress results in a second government shutdown that lasts until Jan. 6, 1996

Jan. 26, 1996, First Lady testified in the Whitewater case before a federal grand jury

Mar. 12, 1996, President signed a bill tightening the economic embargo against Cuba, after Cuban jets shot down two unarmed planes belonging to a Miami-based exile group (Feb. 24)

Courtesy of NATO

The signing of the Dayton Peace Accords

Apr. 3, 1996, Secretary of Commerce Ron Brown died in a plane crash in Croatia

Apr. 10, 1996, President vetoed bill to ban late-term partial-birth abortions

Apr. 28, 1996, President gave videotaped testimony in trial of the McDougals, his associates in the Whitewater deal; they and Arkansas governor Jim Guy Tucker were subsequently convicted and imprisoned

June 25, 1996, 19 Air Force personnel were killed and hundreds wounded in truck bomb attack on the Khobar Towers military complex near Dhahran, Saudi Arabia, carried out by followers of Islamic terrorist Osama bin Laden

Aug. 22, 1996, President signed bill to reform welfare system though he objected to some of its provisions. The bill set up a new system of block grants to be administered by the states and curtailed federal aid to poor families.

Aug. 29, 1996, President and Vice President renominated at Democratic national convention

Sept. 3, 1996, President ordered missile attack on Baghdad, Iraq, in retaliation for attacks on Kurds by Iraqi forces

Sept. 21, 1996, President signed the Defense of Marriage Act, which defined marriage in federal law as a union between one woman and one man and allowed states to deny recognition to homosexual unions

Nov. 5, 1996, President and Vice President reelected

May 27, 1997, the Supreme Court, in *Jones v. Clinton*, allowed Paula Jones's sexual harassment suit against President to go forward during his term in office; the vote was unanimous

Sept. 1, 1997, the minimum wage was increased from $4.75 to $5.15 per hour

Oct. 29, 1997, summit meeting with Chinese president Jiang Zemin in Washington, D.C.

Jan. 17, 1998, President gave videotaped testimony before judge in the Jones suit; asked many unexpected questions about his relationship with Monica Lewinsky, he testified that they were never alone in the Oval Office and that they did not have sex

Jan. 26, 1998, President assured the nation in a televised press conference, "I did not have sexual relations with that woman, Miss Lewinsky"

Feb. 2, 1998, first balanced budget since 1969 signed by President

Mar. 16, 1998, Johnny Chung, fund-raiser for Democrats, pleaded guilty to charges that he arranged for $20,000 in illegal donations to Clinton reelection campaign

Apr. 10, 1998, Good Friday pact, brokered by former U.S. senator George Mitchell, signed by Protestant and Catholic leaders in Northern Ireland conflict

Aug. 6, 1998, Lewinsky testified before Starr grand jury

Aug. 7, 1998, U.S. embassies in Kenya and Tanzania blown up by car bombs, causing hundreds of deaths; four men—a Tanzanian, a Jordanian, a Saudi Arabian, and a naturalized American citizen—went on trial in U.S. District Court on Feb. 5, 2001, on charges of conspiring with Islamic terrorist Osama bin Laden to carry out the attack

Aug. 17, 1998, President testified before Starr grand jury, then gave televised speech in which he admitted to an affair with Lewinsky and claimed he was the victim of persecution by the special prosecutor

Aug. 20, 1998, President ordered cruise missile strikes against suspected terrorist bases run by bin Laden in Sudan and Afghanistan

Sept. 11, 1998, Starr Report ordered released to the Internet by a 363-63 vote of the House of Representatives; the 445-page report recounted events in the Clinton-Lewinsky affair and suggested four possible grounds for impeachment

Sept. 17, 1998, third government shutdown averted when House approves stopgap spending measures

Sept. 30, 1998, budget surplus announced, the first since 1969

Oct. 8, 1998, House deliberation on possible impeachment began

Nov. 12, 1998, President signed the 1997 Kyoto Protocol, product of a United Nations conference on global warming. The accord set targets for the reduction of "greenhouse gases"; although it was never ratified by the signatory nations, environmentalists considered it an important first step

Nov. 13, 1998, President agreed to settle the Paula Jones lawsuit for $850,000

Dec. 16, 1998, President announced the start of Operation Desert Fox, a 72-hour campaign of American and British air strikes against Iraq in retaliation for its refusal to allow U.N. inspections for weapons of mass destruction

Dec. 19, 1998, President impeached by House on charges of perjury and obstruction of justice

Jan. 3, 1999, Newton L. Gingrich, Republican representative from Georgia and former Speaker of the House, resigned from Congress

Jan. 7, 1999, Senate impeachment trial began with Chief Justice William Rehnquist presiding; President was acquitted on Feb. 12

Mar. 24, 1999, beginning of Operation Allied Force, 78 days of daily NATO bombing raids on Belgrade to force Serbians to abandon assaults on Albanian Muslims in province of Kosovo; air strikes end on June 10

Apr. 12, 1999, President held in contempt of court for giving false testimony in Jan. 1998 during deposition in Jones lawsuit

Sept. 10, 1999, President gave clemency to 11 members of the FALN (Armed Forces of National Liberation) Puerto Rican terrorist group imprisoned for involvement in armed robberies; the act was condemned by the House of Representatives by a vote of 311 to 41 amid charges that the President was trying to court New York's Puerto Rico voters in case the First Lady decided to run for the Senate

Nov. 25, 1999, Elián Gonzalez, six-year-old refugee from Cuba, rescued by fisherman from shipwreck that killed his mother; custody battle between his father in Cuba and his relatives in Miami, Fla., ended on Apr. 22, 2000, with raid by federal agents to seize the boy; he went back to Cuba on June 28

Nov. 28–Dec. 4, 1999, thousands protesting global corporate economic policies disrupted a summit meeting of the World Trade Organization in Seattle, Wash.

Feb. 7, 2000, President submitted to Congress a budget proposal of $1.84 trillion

Mar. 1, 2000, House voted, 422-0, to allow Social Security recipients to earn unlimited income without losing benefits; unanimous vote in the Senate followed on Mar. 22

Mar. 16, 2000, independent counsel's office ended its inquiry into how the White House acquired confidential F.B.I. files of prominent Republicans, saying that there was no evidence of criminal wrongdoing

Mar. 22, 2000, class-action suit against federal government resulted in $508 million settlement; suit was brought by women who worked at the U.S. Information Agency and said they were denied promotions and jobs

Mar. 23, 2000, appointment of first Roman Catholic chaplain in the House of Representatives, Rev. Daniel Coughlin of Chicago, Ill.

Apr. 13, 2000, President refused possible pardon from next President

Apr. 24, 2000, State Department's Bureau of Intelligence and Research disciplined after the disappearance of sensitive information in a missing laptop computer

May 22, 2000, disciplinary committee of Arkansas judicial system recommended the disbarment of President

June 4, 2000, President and Russian president Vladimir Putin agreed to destroy 34 metric tons of plutonium

June 12, 2000, lawsuit by the estate of former President Richard M. Nixon ended with agreement by the Justice Department to pay $18 million as compensation for documents and tape recordings confiscated after Nixon's resignation

June 26, 2000, the Human Genome Project and Celera Genomics announced that together they had completed the "first draft" (over 90 percent) of the human genome sequence

July 8, 2000, plans for a $60-billion missile defense system were undermined when a new high-speed missile interceptor failed in testing; President decided in December to leave decision on building system to his successor

Aug. 5, 2000, President vetoed bill to give tax relief to married couples. An attempt to override the veto in the House failed on Sept. 13

Aug. 16, 2000, Vice President nominated as Democratic candidate for president

Aug. 23, 2000, federal National Institutes of Health reversed ban on medical research involving stem cells from embryonic humans

Aug. 31, 2000, President vetoed bill to repeal the estate tax

Sept. 20, 2000, Whitewater inquiry closed down by special prosecutor Robert W. Ray with no finding of criminal wrongdoing by the President and First Lady

Oct. 10, 2000, President signed law establishing normal trade relations with China, ending policy of annual congressional review

Oct. 12, 2000, in Aden, Yemen, two Islamic suicide bombers rammed an explosive-laden raft into the side of the Navy destroyer *Cole* while it was docked for refueling; 17 Americans died and 37 were wounded. On Dec. 8, Navy inquiry found captain and crew negligent regarding security precautions

Oct. 23, 2000, Secretary of State Albright paid official visit to Communist nation of North Korea, two weeks after President hosted North Korean military official at the White House (Oct. 10)

Nov. 7, 2000, First Lady elected to Senate seat from New York; presidential race inconclusive because of ballot irregularities in Florida

Dec. 12, 2000, after weeks of litigation, U.S. Supreme Court ended Florida recount of disputed ballots, giving victory in presidential race to Republicans

Dec. 28, 2000, Census Bureau declared total U.S. population to be 281,421,906, up 13.2 percent from the census count of 1990

Jan. 19, 2001, President received immunity from further prosecution in all matters previously under investigation in exchange for fine and suspension from bar

Jan. 19, 2001, President issued 140 pardons and 36 sentence commutations to felons and fugitives from justice; in February, Congress began inquiry into legality of some of these grants of clemency

Feb. 7, 2001, the Clintons returned furnishings they had taken from the White House that had been donated to the National Park Service rather than to them

Feb. 8, 2001, the House Government Reform Committee began hearings into whether presidential pardons were sold

ADDITIONAL DATA ON BILL CLINTON

WILLIAM JEFFERSON CLINTON

—was the first President born in Arkansas.

—was the first President who was a Rhodes Scholar.

—was the first President born after World War II.

—was the first President to have worked as a Senate staffer in his college years.

—was the first President to play the saxophone.

—was the first President since 1828 to head an all-Southern ticket.

—was the third youngest President to take office and the head of the youngest combined ticket in history.

—was the first Democratic President after World War II to win a second term in office.

—was the first President since Franklin D. Roosevelt to have had no military service.

—was the first Democratic President elected who did not carry the state of Texas.

—was the first and only President to use the line-item veto.

—was the first President to participate in a live Internet chat.

—was the first President to attend a hockey game.

—was the first President to visit a country on the State Department list of terrorist states.

—was the first President to visit Bulgaria.

—was the first President to appoint his wife the head of a presidential commission.

—was the first President to be named as a defendant in a sexual harassment suit.

—was the first sitting President to give testimony before a grand jury in a matter in which he was himself under investigation.

—was the second President to be impeached.

—was the first elected President to be impeached.

—was the first President to have a legal defense fund set up for him while in office.

—was the first sitting President to be held in contempt of court.

CLINTON'S EARLY TASTE OF POLITICS

Bill Clinton's fascination with the White House began in 1963, when, as a high school senior, he represented Arkansas at the American Legion's Boys Nation conference and shook hands with President John F. Kennedy in the Rose Garden. He also lunched in the Senate Dining Room with Arkansas senator J. William Fulbright, the chairman of the Foreign Relations Committee. Fulbright gave Clinton a job as an intern when he returned to Washington the following year as an undergraduate at Georgetown University.

CLINTON A RHODES SCHOLAR

At his death, Cecil John Rhodes (1853–1902), the British imperialist and business tycoon, left one of the world's largest fortunes, estimated at over three million pounds. Among the many provisions of his will was the establishment of scholarships to allow young men to study for two years at Oxford University in England. Candidates were to be selected on the basis of their "exhibition during school days of moral force of character and instincts to lead." In 1976 women became eligible for the scholarships. Since their inception in 1903, many Americans who later became prominent in politics and public life were Rhodes Scholars, among them Secretary of State Dean Rusk, Speaker of the House Carl Albert, Supreme Court Justices John M. Harlan, Byron R. White, and David H. Souter, and Senator Fulbright of Arkansas. The first Rhodes Scholar to become President is William Jefferson Clinton, who studied for an advanced degree in politics at New College, Oxford University, from October 1968 to June 1970.

FIRST TWO SOUTHERNERS SINCE JACKSON AND CALHOUN

Candidate Clinton's choice of a fellow Southerner as his running mate in 1992 went against conventional wisdom about the need for a geographically balanced ticket. However, he and vice presidential candidate Al Gore succeeded in beating the odds. The last election that was won by a pair of Southerners was the election of November 4, 1828. The winners were the Democratic-Republican candidates, Andrew Jackson of Tennessee and John Caldwell Calhoun of South Carolina.

THE ECONOMIC PENDULUM

During the 1992 campaign, the Clinton team's mantra was, "It's the economy, stupid!" and in fact, a combination of free trade agreements, higher taxes, budget controls, and a steady reduction in the daunting federal deficit prompted an economic recovery during Clinton's first term and a boom during his second. Productivity rose, unemployment fell, and the stock market reached unprecedented heights, buoyed in part by speculation in promising new technologies. The strength of the economy did much to offset concern over the scandals of the administration.

DIVERSITY IN THE CLINTON ADMINISTRATION

During his two terms in office, President Clinton sought to appoint female, African-American, and Latino people to his cabinet in record numbers. Among them were the first woman to head the Department of Energy (Hazel O'Leary); the first woman to head the State Department (Madeleine Korbel Albright); and the first woman to head the Justice Department (Janet Reno, after two other female nominees withdrew). Other "firsts" for Clinton included Norman Y. Mineta, the first person of Asian descent to serve in a presidential cabinet (as secretary of commerce); Terry Edmonds, the first African-American writer on a presidential speech-writing team; and Dee Dee Myers, the first woman to serve as White House press secretary, as well as the appointment of more than 100 openly homosexual people to senior government posts. President Clinton also named Ruth Bader Ginsburg, justice of the U.S. Appeals Court for the District of Columbia, to fill the seat on the Supreme Court vacated by Associate Justice Byron White. Ginsburg was the first Jewish woman to serve on the Court.

AN "ERA OF BAD FEELING"?

Although President Clinton remained popular (even under impeachment), his party suffered serious reverses, losing, in the 1994 congressional elections, control of the House of Representatives for the first time in 42 years. Many of the newly elected Republican representatives were adherents of Newton L. Gingrich's "Contract with America," a militant conservative reform program. Stubborn battles between the White House and Congress over budgets and legislation ensued, leading to a week-long government shutdown in November of 1995. In this increasingly polarized climate, every action—of the President, his Cabinet members, the leaders of Congress, and various appointed officials—was attacked and defended with fierce partisanship. Several senators and representatives of long standing announced plans to retire at the end of their terms, citing the acrimonious atmosphere and the ever-growing demands of fundraising.

CABINET MEMBERS INVESTIGATED

Six of President Clinton's cabinet members came under investigation for wrongdoing. The first was Agriculture Secretary Mike Espy, who resigned his post on Dec. 31, 1994, after independent counsel Donald C. Smaltz was appointed by the Justice Department to investigate whether he had accepted gifts, trips, and other bribes from agriculture companies. Espy was indicted on August 28, 1997, on 39 corruption charges, including witness tampering and mail fraud. Although he was acquitted on Dec. 3, 1998, the investigation resulted in 15 convictions; among those convicted was a top aide of Espy's and several corporations.

Commerce Secretary Ron Brown was accused in May 1995 of collecting donations to the Democratic Party in exchange for seats in Commerce Department trade missions. Daniel Pearson was appointed independent counsel in the case in July 1995, but the probe was closed down after Brown died in a plane crash on April 3, 1996.

Henry Cisneros, secretary of housing and urban development during Clinton's first term, was indicted by a grand jury on December 11, 1997, for lying to the F.B.I. about hush-money payments that he had made to a former mistress; he pleaded guilty and was fined $10,000, while the woman who received the money was given a three-and-a-half-year jail term for lying. Cisneros was among those pardoned on January 20, 2001, by President Clinton.

Interior Secretary Bruce Babbitt came under suspicion of corruption in a case involving the rejection of a casino license for three tribes of Wisconsin Chippewa after the Democratic Party received donations of more than $350,000 from casino-owning tribes interested in suppressing the competition. After a 19-month investigation, independent counsel Carol Elder Bruce announced that there was insufficient evidence to indict Babbitt.

Labor Secretary Alexis M. Herman was accused of accepting kickbacks from a consulting firm and soliciting political contributions from its clients in her previous job as head of the White House public liaison office. On April 5, 2000, Ralph I. Lancaster, the independent counsel in her case, announced, without explanation, that he would not indict her.

Attorney General Janet Reno was heavily criticized for the outcome of the 1993 tear-gas attack on the Branch Davidian compound in Waco, Tex. She was exonerated in September 2000 by special counsel John Danforth and by the federal judge hearing a $675 million wrongful-death lawsuit brought by the cult's survivors; both agreed that the fire that destroyed the compound was caused by cult leader David Koresh and not by the government. Reno was also held in contempt of Congress on August 7, 1998, by a committee of the House because she refused to turn over documents connected to the Justice Department's probe of 1996 fund-raising abuses by the Democratic National Committee.

COMBATTING THE AIDS CRISIS

To intensify government efforts to deal with the epidemic of AIDS (acquired immune deficiency syndrome), President Clinton appointed Kristine M. Gebbie in August 1993 to fill the newly created position of federal AIDS policy coordinator. She was in charge of overseeing the development of a unified federal strategy for fighting AIDS and for ensuring that the strategy was followed by government agencies. Gebbie was replaced on

November 10, 1994, by Patricia S. Fleming, an African-American AIDS activist. President Clinton also established the White House Office of National AIDS Policy to provide policy guidance and leadership on the government's response to the AIDS epidemic. Its first director, Sandra L. Thurman, was appointed on April 7, 1997.

HEALTH CARE

Soon after taking office, President Clinton declared: "All of our efforts to strengthen the economy will fail unless we also take bold steps to reform our health care system." One of his chief goals was universal health insurance coverage. He appointed the First Lady, Hillary Rodham Clinton, to chair a task force on reform of the system. After many months of hearings, proposals, arguments, and media events, the task force settled on an ambitious, complex plan that would have completely reorganized the way in which health services are delivered and paid for, adding new levels of state and federal bureaucratic oversight. The plan was criticized by everyone from doctors to senior citizens to economists to company executives, and its failure to win support in Congress was a major blow to the administration.

NORTH AMERICAN FREE TRADE AGREEMENT SIGNED

The establishment of a regional free market among the three countries of North America was a project of the Reagan and Bush administrations, but was enthusiastically supported by Democratic candidate Bill Clinton during the 1992 campaign. Shortly before he left office, President Bush signed the North American Free Trade Agreement, which committed the United States to participate in a reduced-tariff market with Mexico and Canada. Incoming president Clinton inherited from him the job of selling the idea to Congress. However, NAFTA had raised the ire of an important Democratic constituency, the labor movement, which feared that the agreement's provisions would subvert the hard-won gains of American workers. The White House engaged in a frenzy of wheeling and dealing with congressional representatives on both sides of the aisle and succeeded

Courtesy of the U.S. National Archives and Records Administration

President Clinton signs the North American Free Trade Agreement (NAFTA).

in getting NAFTA passed by a comfortable margin. It was signed into law on Dec. 8, 1993.

THE WHITE HOUSE WEB SITE

The Clinton administration was the first to sponsor a web site for the White House. Entitled "Welcome to the White House," it appeared on October 21, 1994. In its first year of operation, the site provided more than 50 million pages and images to Internet users. A vast variety of presidential documents, speeches, proclamations, and executive orders were posted on the site, which also transmitted e-mail from the public. After the close of the administration, the site was preserved at the National Archives.

CLINTON HOSTED SUMMIT OF THE AMERICAS

The democratically elected leaders of 34 nations from North, Central, and South America met in Miami, Fla., in December 1994. The only American nation that did not send a representative was Cuba. The summit's Declaration of Principles committed signatories to support "open markets, hemispheric integration, and sustainable development" and to "preserve and strengthen our democratic systems for the benefit of all people of the Hemisphere." New international initiatives were launched in the areas of democratic reform, mutual security, trade, drug trafficking, and corruption.

THE LINE-ITEM VETO

The line-item veto, a power sought by presidents since Ulysses S. Grant, enables presidents to strike particular items from newly enacted federal laws without having to veto the entire bill. Congress passed the line-item veto in late March 1996, making it effective for the next administration. It was used for the first time on August 11, 1997, when President Clinton eliminated three provisions from legislation that had been passed by Congress. One provision, deleted from a bipartisan bill to balance the federal budget, would have allowed the state of New York to tax Medicaid funding received by health-care providers. Two other provisions, deleted from a tax-cutting measure, would have allowed special tax deferrals for food-processing plants and financial service companies. The line-item veto was declared unconstitutional by the Supreme Court on June 25, 1998, on grounds that it upset the balance of power between branches of government. While it was legal, Clinton had used it to remove 82 items from 11 different bills.

CLINTON VISITED A TERRORIST NATION

Although Syria was on the State Department's list of nations engaged in international terrorism, President Clinton paid a visit to Damascus on October 27, 1994, to meet with President Hafez al-Assad. Clinton made the visit to urge Assad, a longtime foe of Israel, to take part in the peace process between the Jewish state and neighboring Arab states.

CLINTON ATTENDED A HOCKEY GAME

No President had attended a professional hockey game until May 25, 1998, when President Clinton was present at a National Hockey League playoff game between the Buffalo Sabres and the Washington Capitals at the MCI Center in Washington, D.C. Also

at the game were Vice President Albert Gore, Senator Daniel Patrick Moynihan of New York, and the NHL commissioner, Gary Bettman. Washington won the game 3-2 in overtime.

FOREIGN-POLICY FIRSTS FOR CLINTON

On their way to bomb the Serbs in Kosovo in the spring of 1999, NATO's planes passed through Bulgaria's airspace. President Clinton went to Sofia the following November to thank the Bulgarians for their assistance. On November 22, 1999, he addressed a crowd of 10,000 in the Cathedral of St. Alexander Nevsky—the scene, a decade earlier, of the rallies that led to the downfall of Communist rule in Bulgaria.

Another foreign-policy first took place on October 10, 2000, when a military leader of North Korea came to the White House at the President's invitation to discuss the conflict between North and South Korea. This was the first time that an American president hosted a North Korean official.

CLINTON PARTICIPATED IN LIVE CHAT OVER INTERNET

President Clinton appreciated the political uses of new communications technology. On November 8, 1999, he appeared on what was billed as a "virtual town meeting" on the website Excite@Home, answering questions that were sent to him by e-mail. While he sat on a stage at George Washington University in Washington, D.C., a laptop computer streamed his image to the computer screens of the 50,000 participants, who also received a scrolling text of his remarks, transmitted by means of voice-recognition software. Participants from state and local governments included Jeanne Shaheen, governor of New Hampshire; Kathleen Kennedy Townsend, lieutenant governor of Maryland; Don Cunningham, mayor of Bethlehem, Pa.; Ron Gonzales, mayor of San Jose, Calif.; Antonio Riley, state assemblyman from Wisconsin; and the moderator, Al From, president of the Democratic Leadership Council, which sponsored the event.

EXPANSION OF THE NATIONAL PARK SYSTEM

During his terms in office, President Clinton supported legislation and took executive actions that substantially enlarged the complex system of parks, preserves, wildlife refuges, and national monuments administered by the federal government. The greatest single additions to the system were probably accomplished by the creation, under the California Desert Protection Act of 1994, of a 1.5 million acre preserve in the Mojave Desert and the designation, by executive action in 1996, of 1.9 million acres in Utah as the Grand Staircase–Escalante National Monument. However, the administration also enlarged the system by adding acreage to existing preserves and parks and by filling in gaps in existing chains of protected land (as along the Pacific shoreline). Clinton also moved to increase the level of protection in existing parks, by closing, for example, over 300,000 acres in the Sequoia National Forest to any logging whatsoever. On December 11, 2000, he signed the bipartisan Water Resources Development Act, which included funding for a $7.8 billion plan to redesign Florida's water-flow system for the benefit of the parched Everglades (and an assortment of municipal and business interests).

Smaller parks created included the Tallgrass Prairie National Preserve in Kansas, comprising one of the country's few remaining stands of unbroken prairie, and Agua Fria grasslands in Colorado. Four places were designated national historic sites: the lot where Little Rock Central High, scene of the 1957 school integration crisis, once stood; the Tuskegee Army Airfield, where the "Redtail Angels" trained during World War II; Sand Creek, where Indian women and children were massacred in 1864; and the Washita Battlefield, where in 1868 General George Armstrong Custer led a pre-dawn attack on an encampment of Cheyenne and Arapaho. In urban areas a number of miniature historic parks were established to honor, among other things, New Bedford whaling, New Orleans jazz, and the contributions of women to the defense industry in the 1940s.

THE 1996 ELECTION AND ILLEGAL FUNDRAISING

An investigation by the Senate Governmental Affairs Committee into political-party fundraising in the 1996 election reported on March 6, 1998, that numerous abuses had taken place—most seriously, attempts by the People's Republic of China to influence the election by funneling illegal campaign contributions to the Democrats. A Justice Department probe resulted in the indictments of several people who had acted as fronts or arranged for donations. Although the Vice President, the First Lady's chiefs of staff, and other White House personnel were implicated, Attorney General Janet Reno turned down requests to appoint an independent counsel.

WHITEWATER AND ITS AFTERMATH

The Clintons' legal troubles originated in 1978, when they and two friends, James B. and Susan McDougal, formed the Whitewater Development Corporation for the purpose of building vacation homes in the Ozark Mountains and borrowed $203,000 to purchase the land. Bill Clinton was then the attorney general of Arkansas and Hillary Clinton was a partner in the Rose Law Firm. The partnership lost money and was dissolved in 1992. The Federal Trust Resolution Corporation began looking into the Whitewater scheme that same year after the federal bailout of James McDougal's savings and loan company, Madison Guaranty, for which Hillary Clinton had done legal work. The federal regulators raised questions about improper funneling of depositor money by James McDougal to the political campaigns of Bill Clinton and other Arkansas politicians.

The case threatened to become a major scandal after deputy White House counsel Vincent Foster, a friend of the Clintons, committed suicide in July 1993, soon after filing delinquent Whitewater corporate tax returns. In January 1994, Attorney General Janet Reno agreed to name an independent counsel to investigate Whitewater and appointed Robert B. Fiske, Jr., who was replaced on August 5, 1994, by Kenneth W. Starr, a former U.S. solicitor and federal appeals court judge.

A series of prosecutions ensued, resulting in a number of guilty pleas and convictions. Among them was former associate attorney general Webster Hubbell, Mrs. Clinton's Arkansas law partner, who pleaded guilty on December 6, 1994, to mail fraud and tax evasion; he was sentenced on June 28, 1995, to 21 months in prison. On May 26, 1996, a jury in Little Rock, Ark., convicted the McDougals and Arkansas governor Jim Guy Tucker of various counts of fraud and conspiracy. James McDougal died in prison in 1998; Susan McDougal was jailed for 18 months for contempt of court—some of it in solitary confinement—before starting her two-year sentence, and was pardoned by President Clinton in 2001.

As more of the tangled history of Whitewater was uncovered, the Clintons found themselves defending their actions in court. Mrs. Clinton received a subpoena from Starr on January 22, 1996, and appeared before a grand jury four days later to explain the disappearance of important billing documents from her law firm. On April 28, 1996, the President recorded videotaped testimony in which he denied accusations by another Arkansas associate, David Hale, who said that in 1986 Governor Bill Clinton had pressured him to make a fraudulent $300,000 loan to Susan McDougal. When the U.S. Circuit Court of Appeals ordered the White House to turn over to Starr legal notes that he had subpoenaed, the President's lawyers took their objections to the Supreme Court, which refused (May 2, 1997) to hear the appeal.

The office of the independent counsel eventually found that the Clintons were not guilty of wrongdoing in the Whitewater case, but by that time its investigation had expanded to cover charges of sexual misconduct that ultimately led to the President's impeachment.

CLINTON THE DEFENDANT IN A SEXUAL HARASSMENT LAWSUIT

On May 6, 1994, a civil lawsuit was filed against President Clinton by Paula Corbin Jones, a former employee of the Arkansas Industrial Development Commission. In 1991, when Clinton was governor of Arkansas, she was employed as a hostess for the Arkansas Quality Management Governors' Conference at the Excelsior Hotel in Little Rock, Ark. Jones claimed that on May 8, 1991, Clinton had a state trooper summon her to his hotel room, where he made unwanted sexual advances toward her, and that he later took steps to destroy her career because she had refused him. Clinton categorically denied the charges. An Arkansas judge ruled on December 28, 1994, that the case could not be tried until after the President's term in office, but this ruling was overturned by a federal appeals court and then by the Supreme Court, on May 27, 1997. Jones's $700,000 case was settled on January 12, 1999, when Clinton sent her a check for $850,000 (the higher amount included lawyers' fees). The money was raised from personal accounts and from an insurance policy.

CLINTON'S APOLOGY IN THE LEWINSKY SCANDAL

Independent Counsel Starr, in the course of seeking to discover whether the President had tried to obstruct justice in the Paula Jones case, received evidence suggesting that the President had carried on an extramarital affair with a young White House intern, Monica Lewinsky; had urged her to lie in order to keep the affair a secret; and had used his influence to find her a high-paying job. Testifying under oath in the harassment case in January 1998, the President denied that he had had sexual relations with the intern. He afterwards held a press conference in which he said emphatically, "I did not have sexual relations with that woman, Miss Lewinsky," and solicited public statements of support from his cabinet secretaries and White House aides.

Seven months later, however, the revelation of the existence of DNA evidence linking him to Ms. Lewinsky caused him to reverse himself. On August 17, during more than four hours of questioning before a federal grand jury, he admitted that he had been physically intimate with her in a relationship that lasted over a year. Later that day, Clinton delivered to the nation a brief speech that had been drafted with the help of his wife. Still on the defensive, he refused to offer a real apology, insisting that the matter was private and attacking the independent counsel for persecuting him.

CLINTON'S TESTIMONY BEFORE A GRAND JURY

President Clinton's testimony on August 17, 1998, marked the first time that a sitting president was subpoenaed to testify before a grand jury in a matter in which he himself was under investigation. The grand jury had been convened in Washington, D.C., by special prosecutor Kenneth Starr to determine whether Clinton had lied under oath in earlier testimony given in connection with the Paula Jones case. In the grand jury session, Clinton admitted that he had had "inappropriate intimate physical contact" with White House intern Monica Lewinsky, a fact he had denied both in the Jones testimony and in public. However, Clinton maintained that he had not committed perjury because the "contact"—consisting of oral sex and other forms of sex play short of sexual intercourse—did not fit the definition of sex used by the Jones lawyers.

CLINTON'S IMPEACHMENT AND ACQUITTAL

At 1:22 P.M. on December 19, 1998, the House of Representatives approved by a vote of 228 to 206 the first of four articles of impeachment brought against President Clinton by the House Judiciary Committee, chaired by Henry J. Hyde of Illinois, on recommendation of independent prosecutor Kenneth Starr. The article accused Clinton of committing perjury while testifying before a federal grand jury on August 17, 1998, about his relationship with White House intern Monica S. Lewinsky. In the Republican-dominated House, five Republicans voted against impeachment and five Democrats voted for it. A second article of impeachment charging Clinton with obstruction of justice was approved 221-212, with 12 Republicans voting against impeachment. Two other articles were defeated.

Clinton's trial in the Senate began on January 7, 1999, with Chief Justice William H. Rehnquist as the presiding officer. It lasted until February 12, when he was acquitted. The vote was 55-45 on the perjury charge and 50-50 on the obstruction of justice charge. A two-thirds majority (67 votes) would have been necessary for a conviction.

OPERATION DESERT FOX

On December 16, 1998, in the midst of the crisis over impeachment, President Clinton went on the air to announce that he had ordered air strikes against targets in Iraq. The purpose of the strikes was to punish Iraq's dictator, Saddam Hussein, for preventing United Nations inspectors from searching Iraq to uncover facilities for making and storing weapons of mass destruction, including biological, chemical, and nuclear weapons. The entire campaign, called Operation Desert Fox, lasted for 72 hours, during which an estimated 100 targets were hit by cruise missiles and American and British bomber planes. As he had done previously in Haiti, Sudan, Afghanistan, and other places, President Clinton did not ask for congressional permission to make war, asserting that the use of limited military force was within his power to order as commander in chief of the armed forces.

CLINTON HELD IN CONTEMPT OF COURT

The Paula Jones case had further ramifications for President Clinton on April 12, 1999, when U.S. District Judge Susan Webber Wright ruled that he was in contempt of court for having lied during his deposition before her on January 17, 1998. This was the first time that a sitting President was held to be in contempt of court. Judge Wright found that the President had given "false, misleading and evasive answers that were designed to obstruct the judicial process" and ordered him to pay "any reasonable expenses. . . caused by his willful failure to obey this court's discovery orders." She stopped short of imposing more severe sanctions that would have impaired his ability to carry out his official duties. Her ruling was based on Clinton's testimony of August 17, 1998, before the Starr grand jury, when he gave answers concerning his relations with Monica Lewinsky that factually contradicted the answers he gave to Judge Wright. The judge asked the state's judicial authorities to consider disbarment proceedings against Clinton. The disciplinary committee recommended on May 22, 2000, that Clinton be deprived of his law license.

CLINTON MADE A DEAL TO RECEIVE IMMUNITY FROM PROSECUTION

On the last full day of his term, Clinton signed an agreement with the federal prosecutor's office giving him protection from criminal liability in all matters that had been under investigation in exchange for a five-year suspension of his license to practice law, payment of a $25,000 fine to the Arkansas Bar Association, and a public admission that he had, in fact, given false testimony under oath. He paid the fine on March 21, 2001.

THE CLINTONS' LEGAL DEFENSE FUND

A legal defense fund was established for the Clintons in June 1994, after the Whitewater investigation began to intensify, and took in some $1.3 million to pay legal bills. It was dissolved in December 1997 amid charges that it had accepted unlawful donations and was replaced by a second fund, the Clinton Legal Expense Trust. By the end of his second term, the President and Mrs. Clinton owed some $9 million to private lawyers. After his immunity deal was struck on his last full day in office, Clinton said that he would waive his right to seek reimbursement for legal expenses from the federal government.

CLINTONS RETURNED WHITE HOUSE FURNISHINGS

During 2000, the Clintons moved a number of furnishings worth about $190,000 from the White House to their new home in Chappaqua, N.Y. Although most of these furnishings had been donated to the Clintons for their personal use, some of them, valued at $28,000, had been donated to the National Park Service for use in the White House. The Clintons returned them on February 7, 2001. They also wrote a check for $86,000 to the federal government in payment for other furnishings they wished to keep.

CLINTON'S FINAL DAY: CONTROVERSIAL GRANTS OF CLEMENCY

Just before leaving the White House, Clinton issued 130 pardons and 40 commutations to various felons and fugitives from justice. A number of these were highly controversial. The most notorious among them was the pardon granted to Marc Rich, a financier who had fled the country and renounced his citizenship to avoid facing prosecution on charges of tax evasion and of doing illegal business with Iran. Not only had the pardon been approved without the knowledge of Rich's federal prosecutor, but the Clinton Presidential Library had received donations totaling nearly half a million dollars from his former wife, Denise. A few weeks later came reports that the President's brother, Roger (who himself received a pardon for a 1984 drug conviction), had lobbied for various pardons; that the First Lady's brother, Hugh Rodham, had received a $400,000 fee for brokering the pardons of a cocaine trafficker and a businessman convicted of mail fraud; that the First Lady's Senate campaign treasurer had used his influence to obtain pardons for two felons; and that four commutations had apparently been traded for votes in the First Lady's Senate race. The House Government Reform Committee opened an investigation into the pardons on February 8, 2001, and the office of the U.S. district attorney for New York, Mary Jo White, began a criminal investigation on February 14.

POST-PRESIDENTIAL CAREER

After leaving office, Clinton spent much of his time raising funds for the William J. Clinton Foundation, which he had established to carry out humanitarian activities on a large scale. It sponsored programs to support small-business entrepreneurs; support efforts to reduce global greenhouse gas emissions; promote health and fitness among schoolchildren; expand access to low-cost AIDS drugs in poor nations; improve conditions for farmers in Africa and Latin America; obtain "Commitments to Action" from world leaders for a variety of specific improvements; and maintain the Clinton Presidential Center and Park in Little Rock, Ark.

President Obama's nomination of Senator Hillary Clinton to the post of Secretary of State in November 2008 forced Mr. Clinton to make public the names of his foundation's donors. Among them were numerous foreign governments, with Saudi Arabia heading the list at $25 million, and corporate executives with connections to their countries' political and military leaders. The total amount raised since 1997 was $500 million.

Financial disclosure statements submitted by Secretary Clinton showed that former President Clinton earned several million dollars each year by giving speeches to foreign companies, receiving up to $525,000 per speech. He also raised money for Democratic Party candidates and took a hand in the management of his wife's campaign for the Democratic presidential nomination in 2008.

FURTHER READING

Allen, Charles F. and Jonathan Portis. *The Comeback Kid: The Life and Career of Bill Clinton*. 1992.

Bennett, William J. *The Death of Outrage: Bill Clinton and the Assault on American Ideals*. 1998.

Clinton, Bill. *My Life*. 2004.

Drew, Elizabeth. *On the Edge: The Clinton Presidency*. 1994.

Kurtz, Howard. *Spin Cycle: Inside the Clinton Propaganda Machine*. 1998.

Maraniss, David. *The Clinton Enigma: A Four-and-a-Half Minute Speech Reveals This President's Entire Life*. 1998.

——. *First in His Class: A Biography of Bill Clinton*. 1995.

Meyer, Wayne, ed. *Clinton on Clinton: A Portrait of the President in His Own Words*. 1995.

Moore, Jim and Rick Inde. *Clinton: Young Man in a Hurry*. 1993.

Renshon, Stanley A. *High Hopes: The Clinton Presidency and the Politics of Ambition*. 1998.

Rozell, Mark J. *The Clinton Scandal and the Future of American Government*. 2000.

Stephanopoulos, George. *All Too Human: A Political Education*. 1999.

Woodward, Bob. *The Agenda: Inside the Clinton White House*. 1995.

——. *The Choice: How Clinton Won*. 1997.

Courtesy of The Library of Congress

43rd PRESIDENT

George Walker Bush

Date of birth—July 6, 1946

Place of birth—New Haven, Conn.

Education—Phillips Academy, Andover, Mass.; Yale University, New Haven, Conn., bachelor of arts degree in history, 1968; Harvard University, Cambridge, Mass., Master of Business Administration, 1975

Religion—Methodist

Ancestry—English

Career—Oil businessman, baseball team owner, state governor

Political party—Republican

State represented—Texas

Term of office—Jan. 20, 2001–Jan. 20, 2009

Administration—54th, 55th

Congresses—107th, 108th, 109th, 110th

Age at inauguration—54 years, 198 days

FAMILY

FATHER

Name—George Herbert Walker Bush

Date of birth—June 12, 1924

Place of birth—Milton, Mass.

Occupation—Vice President of the United States, 1981–1988; President of the United States, 1988–1992

For more information, see the chapter on the presidency of George Herbert Walker Bush on page 529.

MOTHER

Name at birth—Barbara Pierce

Date of birth—June 8, 1925

Place of birth—New York, N.Y.

Occupation—Second Lady of the United States, 1981–1988; First Lady of the United States, 1988–1992

For more information, see the chapter on the presidency of George Herbert Walker Bush.

SIBLINGS

George Walker Bush was the eldest of six children.

Children of George Herbert Walker Bush and Barbara Pierce Bush

George Walker Bush, b. July 6, 1946
Pauline Robinson ("Robin") Bush, b. Dec. 20, 1949; d. Oct. 11, 1953
John Ellis ("Jeb") Bush, b. Feb. 11, 1953
Neil Mallon Bush, b. Jan. 22, 1955
Marvin Pierce Bush, b. Oct. 22, 1956
Dorothy Walker Bush, b. Aug. 18, 1959

MARRIAGE

Married—Laura Lane Welch

Date of marriage—Nov. 5, 1977

Place of marriage—Midland, Tex.

Age of wife at marriage—31 years, 1 day

Age of husband at marriage—31 years, 122 days

CHILDREN

Barbara Pierce Bush, b. Nov. 25, 1981, Midland, Tex.
Jenna Welch Bush, b. Nov. 25, 1981, Midland, Tex.; m. Henry Chase Hager, May 10, 2008, Crawford, Tex.

THE PRESIDENT'S WIFE

Name at birth—Laura Lane Welch

Date of birth—Nov. 4, 1946

Place of birth—Midland, Tex.

Mother—Jenna Louise Hawkins

Mother's occupation—Corporate secretary in husband's real estate firm

Father—Harold Bruce Welch (d. Apr. 29, 1995)

Father's occupation—Real estate developer, credit officer

Siblings—None

Education—Public schools, Midland, Tex.; Southern Methodist University, Dallas, Tex., bachelor's degree in education, 1968; University of Texas, Austin, Master of Library Science, 1973

Religion—Methodist

Married—George Walker Bush, Nov. 5, 1977, Midland, Tex.

Children—Barbara Pierce Bush, b. Nov. 25, 1981; Jenna Welch Bush, b. Nov. 25, 1981, Midland, Tex.; m. Henry Chase Hager, May 10, 2008, Crawford, Tex.

Occupation—Schoolteacher, librarian, homemaker

Years younger than the President—121 days

Additional Data on Laura Bush

1968–1977, taught in Texas public schools, Dallas, Houston, and Austin

1995–2000, First Lady of Texas

2001–2009, First Lady of the United States

THE FIRST LADY

The Bushes attended the same junior high school in Midland, Tex., and lived in the same Houston apartment building in their 20s, but did not meet each other until years later, when they were introduced by friends. The day after their wedding, they began campaigning, unsuccessfully, for George W. Bush's election to the House of Representatives. Laura Bush continued her career as an elementary school teacher and school librarian.

Courtesy of the White House

Laura Bush, wife of George W. Bush

When she became First Lady of Texas in 1995, Mrs. Bush's first act was to invite Texas authors to the state capital to read from their work as part of the inaugural week celebrations. She went on to organize the first Texas Book Festival, the Reach Out and Read program, and the First Lady's Family Literacy Initiative for Texas.

Mrs. Bush's campaign to promote literacy continued in the White House, where she started the White House Salute to American Authors Series and joined with the Library of Congress to create the National Book Festival. Her foundation, the Laura Bush Foundation for America's Libraries, has given millions of dollars to school libraries, with particular attention to the rebuilding of hurricane-damaged libraries in the Gulf Coast. She co-hosted the White House Conference on Early Childhood Cognitive Development and the six regional conferences that followed, and started the Ready to Read, Ready to Learn initiative, a family-based child development program that distributed information to needy parents. She was also named

Honorary Ambassador for the United Nations Literacy Decade and hosted the White House Conference on Global Literacy.

In addition to her worldwide travels in support of education, Mrs. Bush made numerous trips, in the United States and abroad, to encourage attention among women to prevention of heart disease and breast cancer and to support the President's international initiatives in malaria reduction and AIDS relief.

In November 2001, Mrs. Bush substituted for President Bush in delivering the weekly presidential radio address, a first for any First Lady. Her subject was the Taliban regime in Afghanistan and its oppression of women. After the Taliban were overthrown by the U.S. armed forces, she became Honor-ary Chair of the U.S.-Afghan Women's Council and made three trips to Afghanistan to promote the rights of women and girls to education and medical services. She also gave support to pro-democracy activists in the police state of Burma.

Other programs for which Mrs. Bush served as leader include the President's Committee on the Arts and Humanities, Preserve America, and the presidential initiative known as Helping America's Youth, a call for adults to provide good parenting and mentoring to children.

The First Lady's winning personality allowed her to accomplish a great deal without making enemies, and her popularity ratings were high even when those of her husband were low.

IMPORTANT DATES IN THE PRESIDENT'S LIFE

1968–1973, pilot in Texas Air National Guard

1975–1983, founder and CEO, Bush Exploration

1977–1978, Republican nominee for Congress from 19th District, Texas

1983–1986, chairman, Spectrum 7 Corporation, Midland, Tex., and director of its successor, Harken Energy Corporation

1986, consultant, Harken Energy Corporation

1987–1988, adviser and speechwriter for presidential campaign of George Herbert Walker Bush

1989–1994, managing general partner, Texas Rangers baseball team

Nov. 8, 1994, elected governor of Texas with 53.5 percent of vote

Nov. 3, 1998, reelected governor with 68.6 percent of vote; first Texas governor elected to consecutive four-year terms

Aug. 3, 2000, nominated for President at the Republican National Convention

Nov. 7–Dec. 18, 2000, elected President of the United States

Jan. 20, 2001–Jan. 20, 2005, President of the United States (first term)

Nov. 2, 2004, reelected President of the United States

Jan. 20, 2005–Jan. 20, 2009, President of the United States (second term)

ELECTIONS

THE ELECTION OF 2000

November 7, 2000–December 18, 2000

CANDIDATES

Republican Party (37th Convention)

July 31–Aug. 3, 2000, Pennsylvania Convention Center, Philadelphia, Pa.

P: George Walker Bush, Tex.

VP: Richard Bruce Cheney, Wyo.

Bush was nominated on the first ballot. Candidates for nomination and the votes they received:

George Walker Bush, Tex., 2,058
Alan Keyes, Mass., 6
John McCain, Ariz., 1
Abstention, 1
Total number of votes cast: 2,066
Number necessary for nomination: 1,034

Democratic Party (43rd Convention)

Aug. 14–Aug. 17, 2000 Staples Center, Los Angeles, Calif.

P: Albert Arnold Gore, Jr., Tenn.
VP: Joseph Isadore Lieberman, Conn.

Gore was nominated on the first ballot. Candidates for nomination and the votes they received:
Albert Arnold Gore, Jr., Tenn., 4,328
Abstentions, 9
Total number of votes: 4,337
Number necessary for nomination: 2,169

Green Party

June 23–25, 2000, Renaissance Hotel, Denver, Colo.

P: Ralph Nader, Conn.
VP: Winona LaDuke, Minn.

Reform Party

Aug. 10–13, 2000, Long Beach Convention Center, Long Beach, Calif.

P: Patrick J. Buchanan, Va.
VP: Ezola Foster, Calif.

On the first day of the Reform Party convention, the delegates split into two groups, one supporting insurgent contender Buchanan and the other supporting John Hagelin, who had been endorsed by the party's founder, Ross Perot. Hagelin's backers left the hall and reassembled at the Los Angeles Performing Center, down the street. A court ruling later affirmed Buchanan as the party's candidate and awarded him campaign funds from the Federal Election Commission. Hagelin ran on the ticket of the Natural Law Party.

Libertarian Party

June 30–July 3, 2000, Anaheim, Calif.

P: Harry Browne, Tenn.
VP: Art Olivier, Calif.

Constitution Party (formerly U.S. Taxpayers Party)

Sept. 3–4, 1999, St. Louis, Mo.

P: Howard Phillips, Va.
VP: J. Curtis Frazier, Mo.

The vice presidential candidate nominated at the party's convention was Joe Sobran of Virginia, who resigned from the ticket on Mar. 31. Frazier was chosen as his replacement at a national committee meeting on Sept. 2.

Natural Law Party (Reform Coalition)

Aug. 31–Sept. 2, 2000, Hilton Alexandria Mark Center, Arlington, Va.

P: John Samuel Hagelin, Iowa
VP: Amos Nathaniel Goldhaber, Calif.

Socialist Party

Oct. 15–17, 1999, Secaucus, N.J.

P: David McReynolds, N.Y.
VP: Mary Cal Hollis, Colo.

Socialist Workers Party

June 25, 2000, New York, N.Y.

P: James E. Harris, Jr., Ga.
VP: Margaret Trowe, Minn.

Libertarian Party (Arizona Libertarian Party)

Sept. 6, 2000

P: L. Neil Smith, Colo.
VP: Vin Suprynowicz, Nev.

Workers World Party

Nov. 6–8, 1999, New York, N.Y.

P: Monica Moorehead, N.Y.
VP: Gloria Estela La Riva, Calif.

Independent Candidate

P: Cathy Gordon Brown, Tenn.

Grassroots Party

P: Denny Lane, Vt.
VP: Dale Wilkinson, Minn.

Independent Candidate

P: Randall Venson, Tenn.

Prohibition Party

June 28–30, 1999, Bird-in-Hand, Pa.

P: Earl F. Dodge, Colo.
VP: Willard Dean Watkins, Ariz.

Unenrolled Candidate

P: Louie G. Youngkeit, Utah

2000 POPULAR VOTE

Democratic Party, 50,999,897 (48.38%)
Republican Party, 50,456,002 (47.87%)

Green Party, 2,882,955 (2.74%)
Reform Party, 448,895
Libertarian Party (Browne), 384,431
Constitution Party, 98,020
Natural Law Party, 83,714
Socialist Workers Party, 7,378
Libertarian Party (Smith), 5,775
Socialist Party, 5,602
Workers World Party, 4,795
None of These Candidates (Nev.), 3,315
Brown (independent), 1,606
Grassroots Vermont Party, 1,044
Venson (independent), 535
Prohibition Party, 208
Youngkeit (independent), 161
write-in votes, 20,767

Total, 105,405,100
This total does not include 132,216 blank, void, and write-in ballots reported by New York State.

2000 ELECTORAL VOTE

Announcement of the electoral vote was made on January 6, 2001, before a joint session of Congress. There were 538 votes from 50 states and the District of Columbia. A total of 270 was needed to win.

Bush received 50.37 percent (271 vote—30 states) as follows: Ala. 9, Alas. 3, Ariz. 8, Ark. 6, Colo. 8, Fla. 25, Ga. 13, Ida. 4, Ind. 12, Kan. 6, Ky. 8, La. 9, Miss. 7, Mo. 11, Mont. 3, Neb. 5, Nev. 4, N.H. 4, N.C. 14, N.D. 3, Ohio 21, Okla. 8, S.C. 8, S.D. 3, Tenn. 11, Tex. 32, Utah 5, Va. 13, W.V. 5, Wyo. 3

Gore received 49.62 percent (266 votes—20 states and the District of Columbia) as follows: Calif. 54, Conn. 8, Del. 3, D.C. 2, Haw. 4, Ill. 22, Iowa 7, Me. 4, Md. 10, Mass. 12, Mich. 18, Minn. 10, N.J. 15, N.M. 5, N.Y. 33, Ore. 7, Pa. 23, R.I. 4, Vt. 3, Wash. 11, Wisc. 11

Although the number of electoral votes for Gore should have totaled 267, he actually received one less. When the electoral college voted on Dec. 18, 2000, one of the three Democratic electors from Washington, D.C., submitted a blank ballot to protest the fact that the District of Columbia is not represented in Congress.

CHRONOLOGY OF THE 2000 ELECTION

Nov. 7, the nation divided virtually evenly between Gore and Bush; the contest was so close that the outcome depended entirely on the 25 electoral votes from the state of Florida. However, neither side could claim victory in Florida on Election Night; the television networks projected that Gore would be the winner, then admitted that the race was still too close to call

Nov. 8, Bush was the apparent winner in Florida; Gore conceded to Bush in a phone call, then called back to retract his concession

Nov. 9, the Florida count, although incomplete, gave Bush a lead of 1,784 votes; Florida's 67 counties were ordered to begin recounting the votes by machine

Nov. 10, the machine recount from 66 counties showed Bush leading by 327 votes; the Democrats asked for a manual recount in four counties—Miami-Dade, Broward, Palm Beach, and Volusia—where there were ballot irregularities; problematic ballots included the "butterfly ballot," a double-page spread with candidates listed alternately on the opposite pages, and punch-card ballots with partially detached parts, dented parts, or two presidential votes recorded

Nov. 11, a manual recount was scheduled for Palm Beach County; the Republicans sued in Federal District Court to prevent manual recounting on the ground that it is less reliable than machine recounting

Nov. 12, recounting began in Volusia County; in Seminole County, there was a dispute over corrections made to absentee ballots by election workers

Nov. 13, Federal District Court allowed manual recounting to continue; Democrats sued to extend next day's deadline for certification of Florida ballots

Nov. 14, deadline for certification was upheld by state judge, who left open the possibility of future recounts; Bush led by 300 votes after completion of statewide machine recount and Volusia County's manual recount

Nov. 15, Broward County began manual recount; requests to include Broward and Palm Beach county recounts in certified total were rejected by Florida secretary of state Katherine Harris

Nov. 16, manual recounting in Broward and Palm Beach counties was upheld by state supreme court

Nov. 17, Leon County Circuit Court judge allowed certification of results without manual recounts; decision was stayed by state supreme court pending appeal by the Democrats

Nov. 18, absentee ballots from overseas, many from men and women in the armed forces, pushed Bush's lead to 930 votes

Nov. 20, the state supreme court heard lawyers for both sides argue the admissibility of manual counts

Nov. 21, the state supreme court unanimously ruled in favor of manual counting and set a new certification deadline of 5 P.M. on Nov. 26

Nov. 22, the Republicans appealed the state supreme court's ruling to the U.S. Supreme Court; the manual recount in Miami-Dade County was canceled for lack of time

Nov. 23, the Democrats applied to the state supreme court to force Miami-Dade to continue its manual recount, but were turned down; hand recounts in other counties continued over Thanksgiving

Nov. 26, Secretary of State Harris certified Florida's vote, in which Bush held a 537-vote margin

Nov. 27, Gore sued to have the certified results thrown out

Nov. 28, Leon County Circuit Court Judge N. Sanders Sauls told the Democrats that a trial must take place before he could order disputed ballots from Miami-Dade and Palm Beach counties to be manually recounted

Nov. 29, Gore appealed to the state supreme court to order the manual recount

Dec. 1, the Republicans argued before the U.S. Supreme Court that the original certification deadline of Nov. 14 should be allowed to stand

Dec. 2, trial before Judge Sauls began

Dec. 4, Judge Sauls rejected Democrats' arguments; U.S. Supreme Court ordered state supreme court to explain the reasoning that led it to extend the deadline

Dec. 6, Gore appealed Judge Sauls's ruling to the state supreme court; the Florida legislature, citing the constitutional requirement of having Electoral College electors in place by Dec. 12, was called into special session to appoint them

Dec. 7, the state supreme court heard arguments in Gore's appeal

Dec. 8, by a vote of 4 to 3, the state supreme court ordered manual recounting of problem ballots on which machines had been unable to discern a vote for a presidential candidate

Dec. 9, U.S. Supreme Court stopped the manual recount after Bush appealed (in *Bush* v. *Gore*)

Dec. 10, lawyers for both sides filed briefs in preparation for oral arguments before the U.S. Supreme Court

Dec. 11, U.S. Supreme Court justices heard from Gore's lawyers that manual recounting was necessary to guarantee that every vote would be counted, and from Bush's lawyers that manual recounting violated the constitutional guarantee of equal protection under law

Dec. 12, the U.S. Supreme Court, by a vote of 5 to 4, overruled the state supreme court and ordered manual recounting to stop; electors pledged to vote for Bush were appointed by the Republican-dominated Florida legislature

Dec. 13, Gore conceded

Dec. 18, the Electoral College met in Washington, D.C. Bush received 271 votes, Gore received 266 votes, and there was one abstention. Bush's electoral majority made him the winner of the presidential contest despite the fact that the popular vote was 50,996,039 for Gore and 50,456,141 for Bush

THE ELECTION OF 2004

November 2, 2004

CANDIDATES

Republican Party (38th Convention)

Aug. 30–Sept. 2, 2004, Madison Square Garden, New York, N.Y.

P: George Walker Bush, Tex.
VP: Richard Bruce Cheney, Wyo.

The incumbent, who had no challengers, was nominated through a roll call of the state delegations. Candidates for nomination and the votes they received:

George Walker Bush, Tex., 2,508
Abstention, 1
Total number of votes: 2,509
Number necessary for nomination: 1,255

Democratic Party (44th Convention)

July 26–29, 2007, FleetCenter, Boston, Ma.

P: John Forbes Kerry, Mass.
VP: John Reid Edwards, N.C.
    Kerry was nominated on the first ballot. Candidates for nomination and the votes they received:

John F. Kerry, Ma., 4,253
Dennis J. Kucinich, Ohio, 43
Abstentions, 26
Total number of votes: 4,322
Number necessary for nomination: 2,162

Reform Party/Independent

Aug. 27–29, 2004, Irving, Tex.

P: Ralph Nader, D.C.
VP: Peter Camejo, Calif.

Libertarian Party

May 27–31, 2004, Atlanta, Ga.

P: Michael Badnarik, Tex.
VP: Richard Campagna, Iowa

Constitution Party

June 23–26, 2004, Valley Forge, Pa.

P: Michael Peroutka, Md.
VP: Chuck Baldwin, Fla

Green Party

June 23–28, 2004, Milwaukee, Wisc.

P: David Cobb, Calif.
VP: Pat LaMarche, Me.

Prohibition Party/Concerns of People Party

Sept. 2003, Fairfield Glade, Tenn.

P: Gene Amondson, Alaska.
VP: Leroy Pletten, Mich.
    A rift in the Prohibition Party produced a rival candidate, Earl Dodge, who ran in Colorado.

Peace & Freedom Party of California

July 31–Aug. 1, 2004, Los Angeles, Calif.

P: Leonard Peltier, Kans.
VP: Janice Jordan, Calif.

Socialist Party

Oct. 17–19, 2003, Chicago, Ill.

P: Walter F. Brown, Ore.
VP: Mary Alice Herbert, Vt.

Christian Freedom Party

P: Thomas Harens, Minn.
VP: Jennfer Ryan, Minn.

Socialist Workers Party

June 10–12, 2004, Oberlin, Ohio

P: Róger Calero, N.Y.
VP: Arrin Hawkins, N.Y.

Socialist Equality Party

Jan. 2004 (announced)

P: Bill Van Auken, N.Y.
VP: Jim Lawrence, Ohio

Workers World Party

May 23, 2004, New York, N.Y.

P: John Parker, Calif.
VP: Teresa Gutierrez, N.Y.

Personal Choice Party

P: Charles Jay, Ind.
VP: Marilyn Chambers Taylor, Calif.

Independent Candidate

P: Stanford E. Andress, Colo.
VP: Irene M. Deasy, Colo.

2004 POPULAR VOTE

Republican Party, 62,040,610 (50.73%)
Democratic Party, 59,028,444 (48.27%)
Reform Party, 465,650
Libertarian Party, 397,265
Constitution Party, 143,630
Green Party, 119,859
Peace & Freedom, 27,607
Socialist/Natural Law, 10,837
Socialist Workers Party (Harris), 7,102
Socialist Workers Party (Calero), 3,689
None of These Candidates (Nev.), 3,688
Christian Freedom, 2,387
Prohibition Party/Concerns of People, 1,944
Socialist Equality, 1,857

Workers World/Liberty Union Party, 1,646
Personal Choice Party, 946
Stanford E. Andress (unaffiliated), 804
Prohibition Party (Dodge), 140
write-in votes, 37,240

Total, 122,280,899

2004 ELECTORAL VOTE

Announcement of the electoral vote was made on December 13, 2004, before a joint session of Congress. There were 538 votes from 50 states and the District of Columbia. A total of 270 was needed to win.

Bush received 53.16 percent (286 votes—31 states) as follows: Ala. 9, Alaska 3, Ariz. 10, Ark. 6, Colo. 9, Fla. 27, Ga. 15, Ida. 4, Ind. 11, Kan. 6, Ky. 8, La. 9, Miss. 6, Mo. 11, Mont. 3, Neb. 5, Nev. 5, N.M. 5, N.C. 15, N.D. 3, Ohio 20, Okla. 7, S.C. 8, S.D. 3, Tenn. 11, Tex. 34, Utah 5, Va. 13, W.V. 5, Wyo. 3.

Kerry received 46.47 percent (250 votes—19 states and the District of Columbia) as follows: Calif. 55, Conn. 7, Del. 3, D.C. 3, Hawaii 4, Ill. 21, Me. 4, Md. 10, Mass. 12, Mich. 17, Minn. 9, N.H. 4, N.J. 15, N.Y. 31, Ore. 7, Pa. 21, R.I. 4, Vt. 3, Wash. 11, Wisc. 10.

Although the number of electoral votes for Kerry should have totaled 251, he actually received one less. Of the 10 electoral votes from Minnesota, nine were cast for Kerry and one for John Edwards.

INAUGURATIONS

FIRST TERM

January 20, 2001

The swearing-in ceremony of George W. Bush was held at the West Front of the Capitol, the same location chosen by his father in 1989, using a family Bible belonging to his mother. The weather was drizzly, and many of the dignitaries on the platform wore plastic rain gear. The oath was administered by Chief Justice William Hubbs Rehnquist. The inaugural address, drafted by speechwriter Mike Gerson, took 14 minutes to deliver and was interrupted by applause 14 times. The new President asked the nation to unite behind common ideals and to adopt an ethic of mutual service and responsibility.

Because of the controversy surrounding the 2000 election, the planners of the inauguration ceremony expected a large contingent of protesters. The ceremony was therefore designated a "national special security event" (the first inauguration to be so designated) so that it could be placed under the supervision of the Secret Service. In addition to all 3,600 members of the District of Columbia's Metropolitan Police Department, the security effort involved police departments from nearby Maryland and Virginia communities, the police forces of the Capitol, Supreme Court, and National Park Service, the F.B.I., and the federal Bureau of Alcohol, Tobacco, and Firearms. Two subway stations were closed off, together with a large section of the Mall, and checkpoints were established where bags could be inspected for weapons.

Prior to the ceremony, the Bush family attended a prayer service at St. John's Church. Following the traditional post-inauguration lunch at the Capitol (at which the President issued a code of ethical conduct to be observed by the executive branch of government), the Bushes traveled down Pennsyl-

Courtesy of the White House

Bush takes the oath of office for the second time.

vania Avenue in a car, getting out towards the end of the route to walk under an umbrella. Eight inaugural balls were held in the evening, and the following day the families of the President and Vice President attended a prayer service at Washington National Cathedral.

The total cost of the inauguration was $30 million, of which $20 million came from private donations. A cap of $100,000 was placed on contributions from individuals and corporations.

SECOND TERM

January 20, 2005

The extensive security arrangements that had been put in place for the President's 2001 inauguration were dwarfed by those for his 2005 inauguration, not least because it was the first presidential swearing-in ceremony since the attacks of September 11, 2001. Overhead, the skies were patrolled by military helicopters and fighter planes. Underground, the subway system was outfitted with sensors to detect the presence of chemical and biological weapons. A large part of downtown Washington was closed to traffic, and the thousands of police officers and soldiers deployed on the city's streets were augmented by surveillance cameras monitored by emergency response personnel.

Inauguration Day was breezy and cold. After attending services at St. John's Episcopal Church, the President took the oath of office at the Capitol's West Front, using the same family Bible as before, with Chief Justice William Hubbs Rehnquist again presiding. The inaugural address was 21 minutes long (about 2,000 words); like the previous one, it had been drafted by Michael Gerson. The subject was freedom and the obligation felt by Americans to assist people of other nations in their efforts to resist tyrannical ideologies and repressive governments. For the United States, the President envisioned the emergence of a society in which "the public interest depends on private character, on integrity, and tolerance toward others, and the rule of conscience in our own lives."

The President and Mrs. Bush returned to the White House, in an armored limousine and then on foot, to view the parade on Pennsylvania Avenue. In the evening, they attended all nine inaugural balls, most of which were held at the Washington Convention Center. The cost of the 2005 inauguration, estimated at $40 to $50 million, was partly defrayed by the sale of tickets to various celebratory events; at least 50 donors paid $250,000 each for the privilege of receiving admittance to nearly all of them. However, the guests at the Commander-in-Chief Ball paid nothing. Most of them had been invited because they were veterans of the Iraq and Afghanistan wars.

THE VICE PRESIDENT

Name—Richard Bruce ("Dick") Cheney
Date of birth—Jan. 30, 1941
Place of birth—Lincoln, Neb.
Mother—Marjorie Lauraine Dickey Cheney
Father—Richard Herbert Cheney
Father's occupation—U.S. government soil conservation agent
Education—Public schools, Casper, Wyo.; Yale University, New Haven, Conn.; Casper College; University of Wyoming, bachelor of arts degree 1965, M.A. 1966; University of Wisconsin, Madison, graduate study in political science, 1966–1968
Religion—Methodist
Married—Lynne Ann Vincent, Aug. 29, 1964

Children—Elizabeth Cheney; Mary Cheney
Political party—Republican
State represented—Wyoming
Term of office—Jan. 20, 2001–Jan. 20, 2009
Age at inauguration—59 years, 356 days

ADDITIONAL DATA ON CHENEY

1965, intern, Wyoming state legislature
1966, staff, Governor of Wisconsin
1968–1969, congressional fellow, office of Representative William Steiger
1969–1970, special assistant to director, Office of Economic Opportunity
1971, deputy to presidential counselor, White House

Courtesy of the White House

Richard "Dick" Cheney, Vice President to George W. Bush

1971–1973, assistant director of operations, Cost of Living Council

1973–1974, in private business as vice president, Bradley-Woods & Co., Washington, D.C.

1974–1975, deputy assistant to President Ford

1975–1977, assistant to the President and White House chief of staff

1978, heart attack; by the time of his Vice Presidency, he would have survived four of these

1979–1989, U.S. Representative from Wyoming

1981–1987, chair, Republican Policy Committee

1987–1988, chair, House Republican Conference

Jan. 3–Mar. 23, 1989, House minority whip in 101st Congress; resigned to accept nomination as Secretary of Defense

Mar. 21, 1989, sworn in as Secretary of Defense in President Bush's cabinet; served through 1993

1993–1995, senior fellow, American Enterprise Institute

1995–2001, president and CEO, Halliburton Company, Dallas, Tex.

Nov. 7–Dec. 18, 2000, elected Vice President of the United States

Nov. 2, 2004, reelected for second term

When George W. Bush was preparing to evaluate potential running mates, he asked his father's former secretary of defense, Dick Cheney, to head the search effort. Within a short time he realized that Cheney himself had the qualities he was looking for in a vice president, particularly expertise in foreign affairs. Cheney had served as chief of staff in the Ford White House and as a ten-year member of the House with a strongly conservative voting record (his committee memberships included the Interior Committee, the Select Committee on Intelligence, and the Select Committee to Investigate Covert Arms Deals with Iran). His nomination to head the Defense Department in 1989 was approved by the Senate by a vote of 92 to 0. In that job, he oversaw a reorganization of the armed forces that resulted in a 25 percent cutback, surprised some fellow conservatives by slashing costly weapons programs, and proved to be a steady opponent of arms control negotiations. One of the chief architects the Gulf War, he was an early advocate of military force against Iraq and was instrumental in convincing Saudi Arabia's King Fahd to allow staging operations on his soil. He also directed Operation Just Cause in Panama. During the Clinton years, Cheney headed a leading manufacturer of oil-field equipment.

His colleagues in the George W. Bush cabinet included Colin Powell, the new secretary of state, who had served as chairman of the Joint Chiefs of Staff during the Gulf War, and Donald Rumsfeld, the new secretary of defense, whom Cheney had replaced as White House chief of staff in 1975. As the President's chief liaison with Congress, the Vice President was the first Vice President to have an office on the House side of Congress as well as the Senate side.

THE SECOND LADY

Name at birth—Lynne Vincent

Date of birth—Aug. 14, 1941

Place of birth—Casper, Wyo.

Mother—Edna Lybyer Vincent

Mother's occupation—Deputy sheriff, Casper

Father—Wayne Vincent

Father's occupation—Engineer, U.S. Bureau of Reclamation

Education—Public schools, Casper, Wyo.; Colorado College, Colorado Springs, B.A. 1963; University of Colorado, Boulder, master of arts degree 1964; University of Wisconsin, Madison, Ph.D. in British literature, 1970

Religion—Methodist

Married—Richard Bruce Cheney, Aug. 29, 1964

Children—Elizabeth Cheney, b. July 28, 1966, m. Philip Perry; Mary Cheney, b. Mar. 16, 1969, partner, Heather Roan Poe

Courtesy of the White House

Lynne Cheney, wife of Richard Cheney

ADDITIONAL DATA ON LYNNE CHENEY

1970–1983, freelance writer

1972–1977, lecturer, George Washington University, Washington, D.C.

1977–1978, lecturer, University of Wyoming, Casper

1982–1983, researcher and writer, Maryland Public Broadcasting, Owings Mills

1983, author (with Dick Cheney) of *Kings of the Hill: Power and Personality in the House of Representatives*

1983–1986, senior editor, *Washingtonian* magazine

1985–1987, member, U.S. Constitution Bicentennial Commission

1986–1993, chairman, National Endowment for the Humanities

1993–1995, Brady fellow, American Enterprise Institute, Washington, D.C.

1996–, senior fellow, American Enterprise Institute

1996–1998, co-host, Sunday edition, "Crossfire" political discussion television program

CABINET

FIRST TERM

January 20, 2001–January 20, 2005

State—Colin Luther Powell, Va., Jan. 20, 2001

Treasury—Paul Henry O'Neill, Pa., Jan. 20, 2001; Kenneth W. Dam, Ill., acting, Dec. 31, 2002–Feb. 3, 2003; John William Snow, Va., Feb. 3, 2003

Defense—Donald Henry Rumsfeld, Md., Jan. 20, 2001

Justice—John David Ashcroft, Mo., Feb. 1, 2001

Interior—Gale Ann Norton, Colo., Jan. 31, 2001

Agriculture—Ann Margaret Veneman, Calif., Jan. 20, 2001

Commerce—Donald Louis Evans, Col., Jan. 20, 2001

Labor—Elaine Lan Chao, Ky., Jan. 31, 2001

Health and Human Services—David Satcher, Tenn., acting, Jan. 20, 2001; Tommy George Thompson, Wisc., Feb. 2, 2001

Housing and Urban Development—Melquiades Rafael Martinez, Fla., Jan. 24,

2001; Alphonso Roy Jackson, Tex., Apr. 1, 2004

Transportation—Norman Yoshio Mineta, Calif., continued from previous administration

Energy—Edmund Spencer Abraham, Mich., Jan. 20, 2001

Education—Roderick Raynor Paige, Tex., Jan. 24, 2001

Veterans Affairs—Anthony Joseph Principi, Calif., Jan. 24, 2001

Homeland Security—Thomas Joseph Ridge, Pa., Jan. 24, 2003

SECOND TERM

January 20, 2001–January 20, 2009

State—Condoleezza Rice, Calif., Jan. 26, 2005

Treasury—John William Snow, Va., continued from previous administration; Robert M. Kimmitt, Va., acting, June 30; Henry M. Paulson, Jr., N.Y., July 10, 2006

Defense—Donald Henry Rumsfeld, Md., continued from previous administration; Robert Michael Gates, Tex., Dec. 18, 2006

Justice—Alberto Recuerdo Gonzales, Tex., Feb. 3, 2005; Paul Drew Clement, D.C., acting, Sept. 17, 2007; Peter D. Keisler, D.C., acting, Sept. 18, 2007; Michael Bernard Mukasey, N.Y., Nov. 9, 2007

Interior—Gale Ann Norton, Colo., continued from previous administration; Dirk Arthur Kempthorne, Idaho, May 26, 2006

Agriculture—Michael Owen Johanns, Neb., Jan. 21, 2005; Edward Thomas Schafer, N.D., Jan. 28, 2008

Commerce—Carlos Miguel Gutierrez, Mich., Feb. 7, 2005

Labor—Elaine Lan Chao, Ky., continued from previous administration

Health and Human Services—Michael Okerlund Leavitt, Utah, Jan. 26, 2005

Housing and Urban Development —Alphonso Roy Jackson, Tex., continued from previous administration; Steven C. Preston, Va., June 5, 2008

Transportation—Norman Yoshio Mineta, Calif., continued from previous administration; Maria Cino, D.C., acting, July 8, 2006; Mary E. Peters, Ariz., Oct. 17, 2006

Energy—Samuel Wright Bodman, Mass., Feb. 1, 2005

Education—Margaret Spellings, Tex., Jan. 31, 2005

Veterans Affairs—Robert James Nicholson, Colo., Feb. 1, 2005; James Benjamin Peake, D.C., Dec. 20, 2007

Homeland Security—James Milton Loy, D.C., acting, Feb. 1, 2005; Michael Chertoff, N.J., Feb. 15, 2005

CONGRESS

ONE HUNDRED SEVENTH CONGRESS

January 3, 2001–January 3, 2003

First session—Jan. 3, 2001–Dec. 20, 2001 (352 days)

Second session—Jan. 23, 2002–Nov. 22, 2002 (304 days)

Vice President—Richard Bruce Cheney, Wyo.

President pro tempore of the Senate —Robert Carlyle Byrd, W.Va., Jan. 3–20, 2001; (James) Strom Thurmond, S.C., Jan.

20, 2001–June 6, 2001; Byrd, June 6, 2001–Jan. 3, 2003. The 2000 congressional elections produced a Senate evenly divided between Republicans and Democrats; majority leadership positions were given to the Republicans because the Senate's presiding officer, Vice President Cheney, was a Republican and could cast a tie-breaking vote. On May 24, 2001, Senator James M. Jeffords of Vermont announced that he would leave the Republican Party and become an independent. The Republicans thus became a minority in the Senate, with 49 seats, and on June 6 the position of president pro tempore and the other majority leadership posts were transferred to the Democrats.

Secretary of the Senate—Gary Lee Sisco, Tenn., to July 11, 2002; Jeri Thomson, Va.

Speaker of the House—John Dennis Hastert, Ill.

Clerk of the House—Jeff Trandahl, S.D.

ONE HUNDRED EIGHTH CONGRESS

January 3, 2003-January 3, 2005

First session—Jan. 7, 2003–Dec. 8, 2003 (336 days)

Second session—Jan. 20, 2004–Dec. 9, 2004 (323 days)

Vice President—Richard Bruce Cheney, Wyo.

President pro tempore of the Senate —Theodore Fulton Stevens, Alaska

Secretary of the Senate—Emily Jayne Reynolds, Tenn.

Speaker of the House—John Dennis Hastert, Ill.

Clerk of the House—Jeff Trandahl, S.D.

ONE HUNDRED NINTH CONGRESS

January 3, 2005-January 3, 2007

First session—Jan. 4, 2005–Dec. 22, 2005 (353 days)

Second session—Jan. 3, 2006–Dec. 8, 2006 (330 days)

Vice President—Richard Bruce Cheney, Wyo.

President pro tempore of the Senate —Theodore Fulton Stevens, Alaska

Secretary of the Senate—Emily Jayne Reynolds, Tenn.

Speaker of the House—John Dennis Hastert, Ill.

Clerk of the House—Jeff Trandahl, S.D.; Karen Lehman Haas, Md.

ONE HUNDRED TENTH CONGRESS

January 3, 2007-January 3, 2009

First session—Jan. 4, 2007–Dec. 29, 2007 (350 days)

Second session—Jan. 3, 2008–Jan. 3, 2009 (368 days)

Vice President—Richard Bruce Cheney, Wyo.

President pro tempore of the Senate —Robert Carlyle Byrd, W.Va.

Secretary of the Senate—Nancy Erickson, S.D.

Speaker of the House—Nancy Patricia D'Alesandro Pelosi, Calif.

Clerk of the House—Karen Lehman Haas, Md.; Lorraine C. Miller, Tex.

APPOINTMENTS TO THE SUPREME COURT

Chief Justice
John Glover Roberts, Jr., Md., Sept. 29, 2005 (replaced William Hubbs Rehnquist)

Associate Justice
Samuel Anthony Alito, Jr., N.J., Jan. 31, 2006 (replaced Sandra Day O'Connor

IMPORTANT DATES IN THE PRESIDENCY

Jan. 22, 2001, President reinstated a ban on use of federal funds for organizations providing abortions in other countries

Jan. 29, 2001, the White House Office of Faith-Based and Community Initiatives was created by executive order

Mar. 18, 2001, President confirms that he will not submit to the Senate the global-warming convention known as the Kyoto Protocol but will propose alternative plans for reduction of carbon dioxide emissions

May 29, 2001, four agents of Al Qaeda were convicted in federal district court of conspiracy in the 1998 car-bomb attacks on the U.S. embassies in Kenya and Tanzania; they were later sentenced to life in prison without parole

June 5, 2001, the Democrats unexpectedly took over as the majority party in the Senate after James M. Jeffords of Vermont left the Republican Party to become an independent

June 7, 2001, President signed a $1.35 trillion tax-cut bill providing immediate refunds to all taxpayers and lowering tax rates over a ten-year period

June 11, 2001, antigovernment militant Timothy McVeigh was executed by lethal injection for killing 168 people in his 1995 truck-bomb attack on the McMurrah Federal Building in Oklahoma City, Okla.

Aug. 9, 2001, President authorized federal funding for medical research using stem cells from human embryos but disallowed creation of additional stem cell lines

Sept. 11, 2001, 19 agents of the Islamic terrorist organization Al-Qaeda hijacked four commercial passenger airplanes to use them as missiles against significant buildings. They destroyed the Twin Towers of New York's World Trade Center and damaged the Pentagon in Washington, D.C. The fourth plane, intended for the Capitol, crashed in a field after the passengers and crew resisted the hijackers. Nearly 3,000 people were killed in the attacks

Sept. 11, 2001, the Federal Aviation Administration shut down all commercial aviation over the United States; all U.S. armed services were placed on maximum alert

Sept. 12, 2001, Congress declared a national day of mourning; President contacted leaders of other nations regarding formation of a multinational antiterror coalition

Sept. 13, 2001, Secetary of State Colin Powell identified Al-Qaeda leader Osama bin Laden, a Saudi Arabian national under the protection of the Taliban regime in Afghanistan, as chief suspect behind the attacks

Sept. 17, 2001, President demanded the surrender of bin Laden by the Taliban; U.S. financial markets, closed since 9/11, reopened

Sept. 18, 2001, Congress passed a joint resolution "to authorize the use of United States Armed Forces against those responsible for the recent attacks launched against the United States"

Oct. 7, 2001, military campaign began with aerial bombardment of Taliban targets by U.S. and British aircraft

Oct. 8, 2001, Tom Ridge was sworn in as director of new federal agency, the Office of Homeland Security

Oct. 26, 2001, President signed the USA PATRIOT Act, giving federal agencies more power to conduct espionage against domestic and foreign terrorism with some curtailment of civil liberties

Dec. 9, 2001, Taliban regime deposed from power in Afghanistan and were replaced by an interim government, with Osama bin Laden still at large

Jan. 8, 2002, President signed the No Child Left Behind Act, an education-reform bill that made federal funding to schools contingent on standardized testing of students and improvements in teacher quality

Jan. 11, 2002, the U.S. naval base at Guantánamo Bay, Cuba, received its first consignment of suspected Taliban and Al Qaeda prisoners captured in Afghanistan

Jan. 23, 2002, Daniel Pearl, a bureau chief for the *Wall Street Journal,* was kidnapped in Pakistan by terrorists; a videotape showing his murder was released on Feb. 20

Mar. 27, 2002, President signed the Bipartisan Campaign Reform Act, which placed limits on contributions to political candidates

Apr. 18, 2002, Senate rejected administration's plan to drill for oil in the Arctic National Wildlife Refuge (ANWR)

July 15, 2002, four suspects were convicted in a Pakistani court of murdering Daniel Pearl

July 24, 2002, House of Representatives expelled James Traficant, Democrat of Ohio, after his racketeering and bribery conviction

Oct. 8, 2002, President intervened in a labor dispute between dockworkers and shipping companies at West Coast ports; first time a President used the Taft-Hartley Act to stop a lockout rather than a strike

Oct. 16, 2002, House and Senate voted to approve a resolution giving President authority to take military action against Iraq if Saddam Hussein evaded UN resolutions on relinquishing weapons of mass destruction

Oct. 29, 2002, President signed the Help America Vote Act, which provided states with $4 billion in federal funds to modernize their voting equipment and practices

Nov. 5, 2002, midterm elections resulted in a Republican majority in the Senate as well as the House

Nov. 14, 2002, Nancy Pelosi of California was elected House minority leader; first time the leadership of a congressional party was female

Nov. 27, 2002, the bipartisan 9/11 Commission was established to investigate the terrorist attacks and to recommend actions for the future

Jan. 24, 2003, Tom Ridge was sworn in as the first secretary of the newly created Department of Homeland Security, consisting of 22 federal agencies

Jan. 27, 2003, chief UN inspector issued report decrying Iraq's refusal to confirm its removal of chemical and biological weapons

Jan. 30, 2003, Richard Reid, a British Muslim trained by Al Qaeda, was sentenced to life in prison by a federal judge; he was captured by the passengers and crew of an airliner in Dec. 2001 as he tried to ignite explosives hidden in his sneakers

Feb. 1, 2003, six American astronauts and one Israeli astronaut died in the explosion of the Space Shuttle *Columbia* in the skies over Texas and Louisiana

Mar. 1, 2003, Al Qaeda leader Khalid Sheikh Muhammad was captured in Pakistan

Mar. 17, 2003, President warned Saddam Hussein to leave Iraq or face invasion

Mar. 19–21, 2003, Operation Iraqi Freedom began; American and British ground troops entered Iraq accompanied by massive nightly aerial bombardment of Baghdad

Apr. 8, 2003, the Iraqi regime collapsed, with Saddam Hussein evading capture

Apr. 30, 2003, President signed bill creating the nationwide Amber Alert communications system to combat abductions of children

Apr. 30, 2003, State Department unveiled a proposal for a "roadmap" toward a negotiated settlement between Israelis and Palestinian Arabs, intended to resolve their conflict in 2005

May 1, 2003, President declared victory in Iraq and Afghanistan but warned that the war on terror is ongoing

Aug. 14, 2003, a blackout caused by mistakes at an Ohio power plant cascaded through eight states and parts of Canada, cutting off electricity to 50 million people

Aug. 15, 2003, Libya admitted responsibility for the explosion of Pan Am Flight 103 in 1988 and offered to pay $10 million to each of the families of the 270 victims in exchange for the removal of sanctions by the UN and United States

Oct. 16, 2003, UN Security Council accepted proposal for a multinational force to keep order in Iraq until a democratically elected government could be instituted

Nov. 5, 2003, President signed the Partial-Birth Abortion Act, prohibiting a particularly controversial late-term abortion procedure; the ban was upheld by the Supreme Court on Apr. 18, 2007

Dec. 13, 2003, American soldiers captured Saddam Hussein after receiving a tip about the location of his underground hideout

Jan. 7, 2004, President outlined a plan to grant temporary guestworker status to illegal immigrants who are already employed and to foreign workers willing to perform menial jobs

Feb. 6, 2004, President created a nine-member commission to examine the effectiveness of U.S. intelligence agencies in assessing Iraq's weapons capabilities

Apr. 4, 2004, Shiite Muslim leader Moqtada al-Sadr initiated guerrilla insurgency against Coalition in Iraq

Apr. 30, 2004, media outlets published photographs taken at Baghdad's Abu Ghraib prison showing American soldiers abusing Iraqi prisoners

May 29, 2004, World War II Memorial was dedicated on Washington's National Mall

June 5, 2004, former president Ronald Reagan died at the age of 93

June 8-10, President chaired G-8 Summit of leaders of industrial democracies

June 28, 2004, coalition forces transferred sovereignty in Iraq to interim government

July 4, 2004, officials unveiled cornerstone of future Freedom Tower on the site of New York City's World Trade Center, destroyed on 9/11

July 22, 2004, final report by 9/11 Commission recommended unification of all intelligence operations under one cabinet-level director

Sept. 9, 2004, Secretary of State Colin Powell informed Senate Foreign Relations Committee of ongoing government-sponsored genocidal attacks on non-Muslims in Sudan's Darfur area

Sept. 29, 2004, two Al Qaeda agents who planned the attack on the U.S. destroyer *Cole* in 2002 were sentenced to death by a court in Yemen; one escaped from prison in 2006 and was later recaptured and released

Oct. 9, 2004, Afghanistan held its first presidential election since the overthrow of the Taliban regime by the United States, electing Hamid Karzai

Nov. 2, 2004, voters reelected incumbent President with 51 percent of the popular vote; the Republican Party retained its majority in the House and Senate

Dec. 31, 2004, President pledged $350 million in aid to countries devastated by the Dec. 26 tsunami in the Indian Ocean

Jan. 1, 2005, U.S. military began using helicopters based on aircraft carriers to deliver food, fresh water, and supplies to tsunami victims in Indonesia

Jan. 20, 2005, President Bush was sworn in for a second term

Jan. 30, 2005, 8.5 million Iraqi voters chose representatives for a national assembly in the country's first free election

Mar. 1, 2005, Supreme Court ruled 5-4 that the death penalty cannot be applied to murderers who killed while they were minors

Mar. 30, 2005, Terri Schiavo, a brain-damaged Florida woman, died of dehydration and starvation after courts allowed her husband to remove her feeding tube

Mar. 31, 2005, presidential commission issued report chastising U.S. intelligence agencies for inadequate comprehension of foreign weapons of mass destruction (WMDs) programs

Aug. 2, 2005, President signed the Central America Free Trade Agreement (CAFTA)

Aug. 29, 2005, Hurricane Katrina, a Category 5 hurricane, devastated the Gulf Coast

Aug. 31, 2005, the entire population of New Orleans, La., was ordered to evacuate the city after Katrina produced catastrophic flooding

Sept. 8, 2005, President signed bill authorizing $51.8 billion to assist victims of hurricanes

Sept. 23–24, 2005, the Gulf Coast was stricken by Hurricane Rita

Oct. 19, 2005, trial of Saddam Hussein commenced before an Iraqi tribunal

Dec. 17, 2005, President confirmed that after 9/11 he ordered warrantless wiretapping of communications between suspected overseas terrorists and U.S. residents

Jan. 3–4, 2006, Washington lobbyist Jack Abramoff pleaded guilty to charges of fraud, bribery, and tax evasion, resulting in the prosecution of several congressional representatives

Mar. 9, 2006, President signed extension of USA PATRIOT Act

Apr. 10, 2006, mass rallies took place in several cities to protest efforts to stop illegal immigration

May 1, 2006, demonstrators in several cities staged a "Day Without Immigrants"

May 4, 2006, a jury delivered a sentence of life imprisonment without parole to 9/11 conspirator Zacarias Moussaoui

June 8, 2006, a U.S. air strike killed Abu Musab al-Zarqawi, Iraqi Al Qaeda leader who specialized in beheading foreigners

June 29, 2006, the Supreme Court ruled 5-3 that suspected foreign terrorists in U.S. custody cannot be tried by military tribunals without congressional approval; a bill granting that approval was signed into law on Oct. 17

July 19, 2006, in his first use of the veto power, President vetoed a bill to appropriate federal funds for the creation of more embryonic stem cell lines; the veto was sustained in a House vote

Oct. 26, 2006, President signed a bill to construct a 700-mile barrier along the border between the United States and Mexico

Nov. 7, 2006, midterm elections gave the Democratic Party a majority in both the House and the Senate

Nov. 16, 2006, Nancy Pelosi was chosen by Democratic representatives to be first female Speaker of the House

Dec. 26, 2006, Saddam Hussein, convicted on Nov. 5 of crimes against humanity, was executed by hanging

Dec. 26, 2006, former President Ford died at the age of 93

Jan. 10, 2007, President explained plan to combat sectarian violence in Iraq with a U.S. troop surge and a set of time-specific goals for the Iraqi government; surge began on Feb. 7

Mar. 2, 2007, Secretary of the Army Francis J. Harvey resigned after allegations that wounded soldiers at Walter Reed Army Medical Center were receiving substandard care

Mar. 6, 2007, White House aide I. Lewis Libby was convicted of lying to investigators looking into the exposure of a CIA agent's identity; his 30-month prison sentence was commuted by President on July 2

Mar. 10, 2007, transcripts of testimony before military tribunal revealed that Al-Qaeda terrorist Khalid Sheikh Mohammed took credit for organizing the 9/11 attacks and for murdering journalist Daniel Pearl in 2002

June 28, 2007, compromise bill on illegal immigration, combining an amnesty plan for illegal immigrants with stricter border controls and a guestworker program, failed in the Senate

July 20, 2007, President signed executive order establishing general guidelines for CIA in interrogating suspected terrorists; torture, though prohibited, was left undefined

Sept. 17, 2007, Attorney General Alberto Gonzalez stepped down after Justice Department was accused of firing federal prosecutors for political reasons

Nov. 27, 2007, Secretary of State hosted conference at Annapolis, MD, to seek common ground in pursuing Arab-Israeli peace negotiations

Dec. 7, 2007, the CIA acknowledged that it had destroyed videotapes showing the intense interrogation of Al Qaeda suspects

Jan. 21, 2008, U.S. economic troubles sent stock markets crashing in foreign cities

Jan. 22, 2008, Jose Padilla was sentenced to a 17-year jail term for conspiring with Al Qaeda to commit murder

Feb. 13, 2008, President signed economic stimulus package of $145 billion, giving rebates of $300 to $600 to eligible taxpayers

Mar. 8, 2008, President vetoed a bill aimed at restricting CIA interrogation methods

Mar. 16, 2008, failing investment bank Bear Stearns was bought by JPMorgan Chase with a loan from the Federal Reserve

Mar. 23, 2008, the death toll for U.S. troops in Iraq reached 4,000

May 14, 2008, the polar bear was added to the Interior Department's list of threatened species

June 5, 2008, the report of the Senate Select Committee on Intelligence faulted the Bush administration for exaggerating the evidence for the weapons of mass destruction in Iraq

June 5, 2008, Khalid Sheikh Mohammed was arraigned at the detention center at Guantanamo Bay for planning the September 11 terrorist attacks

June 12, 2008, the Supreme Court ruled that inmates held at Guantanamo without being charged may petition federal civilian courts for their release

June 26, 2008, the Supreme Court ruled that gun ownership in many circumstances is protected by the Second Amendment

Aug. 6, 2008, in the first military tribunal held at Guantanamo, Osama bin Laden's captured driver was convicted of supporting terrorism

Sept. 1, 2008, the Republican National Convention in Minnesota was slightly delayed as Hurricane Gustav approached New Orleans

Sept. 1, 2008, control of Iraq's Anbar Province, formerly an insurgent stronghold, was transferred from the United States to Iraq

Sept. 3, 2008, U.S. commando troops entered Pakistan to attack an Al Qaeda base

Sept. 7, 2008, the mortgage-underwriting programs Fannie Mae and Freddie Mac were taken over by the Federal Housing Finance Agency in an attempt to stop the credit crisis

Oct. 3, President signed the Emergency Economic Stabilization Act of 2008, to keep failing banks afloat using federal money

Oct. 11, 2008, the State Department removed the designation "State Sponsor of Terrorism" from North Korea after its government agreed to inspections of its nuclear facilities

Nov. 20, 2008, a proposed bailout of Detroit auto manufacturers was rejected by Congress; a second proposal was rejected on Dec. 11

Nov. 23, 2008, a proposed bailout of Citicorp by the U.S. Treasury and the FDIC was approved

Dec. 1, 2008, the National Bureau of Economic Research declared that the U.S. economy entered a recession in December 2007

Dec. 4, 2008, Iraqi government approved the Strategic Framework Agreement, setting a deadline of Jan. 1, 2011, for the departure of U.S. troops

Dec. 8, 2008, Khalid Sheikh Mohammed and four other Al Qaeda members held at Guantanamo for planning the September 11 attacks declared their intention to plead guilty

Dec. 11, 2008, investment manager Bernard Madoff was arrested for running a massive Ponzi scheme

Dec. 19, 2008, President offered a loan of $17.4 billion to Detroit automakers to prevent their immediate collapse

ADDITIONAL DATA ON GEORGE W. BUSH

GEORGE WALKER BUSH

—was the first President to have been born in Connecticut.

—was the first President to have an M.B.A. degree.

—was the second President whose father had served as President before him.

FIRST BILL SIGNED BY PRESIDENT BUSH

The first piece of federal legislation to be signed into law by President Bush was House Joint Resolution 7, honoring former President Ronald Reagan on the occasion of his ninetieth birthday. It was signed on February 15, 2001.

BUSH REINSTATED BAN ON ABORTION FUNDING

On January 22, 2001, President Bush signed an executive order that barred the expenditure of federal funds to overseas organizations providing abortion services and abortion counseling. The ban had been enacted by President Reagan in 1984 and had been lifted by President Clinton in 1993. It

was reinstated on the 28th anniversary of *Roe v. Wade*, the Supreme Court decision that made abortion legal in all 50 states.

THE BUSH TAX CUT

During the 2000 presidential campaign, the parties offered different proposals for managing the expected budget surplus of $5.6 trillion over a ten-year period. The Democrats demanded that the extra money be used to shore up Social Security and other federal entitlement programs; the Republicans announced their intention to return the money to the voters in the form of tax cuts. On February 8, 2001, President Bush submitted his tax-cut plan to Congress. The main part of it passed the House on March 8 by a vote of 230 to 198, and provided for the lowering of tax rates at different income levels, with the highest rate diminishing to 33 percent from 39.6 percent. Other provisions included doubling the child tax credit, elimination of the estate tax, and reduction of the marriage penalty in two-income households.

The House vote was considered a major victory for Bush. In the evenly divided Senate, compromises were inevitable, but there too the bill fared well. To win the support of a dozen Democrats, the bill's sponsors agreed to make a portion of the refund immediate, so as to stimulate the economy, and to reduce the total amount from $1.60 trillion to $1.35 trillion. This was substantially the bill signed by the President on June 7, 2001. It was the largest tax reduction since the Reagan era, and opponents warned that it might well recreate the staggering deficits of that period. Supporters of the bill, however, argued that as a matter of principle any government surplus should be returned directly to the people. The first rebate checks—amounting, as a rule, to $300 per taxpayer—were sent out in the summer of 2001.

BUSH ORDERED NUCLEAR WEAPONS REVIEW

As part of an initiative to reduce the number of nuclear warheads in the U.S. arsenal, President Bush issued a directive on February 9, 2001, ordering military leaders to make a comprehensive review of the nation's nuclear weapons program and its nuclear defense strategies. As of 2000, the United States had 7,519 warheads, a number that was expected to be reduced by more than 5,000. The Bush administration had already announced its intention to build a defensive missile shield to protect against nuclear attack.

BUSH'S ARREST FOR DRUNK DRIVING

On Sept. 4, 1976, Bush was stopped by a state trooper who had noticed his erratic driving. His blood alcohol was measured at .10 and he failed a road sobriety test. He pled guilty in court to driving under the influence and received a fine and a suspension of his driver's license. It took him another ten years to acknowledge that he had an alcohol problem. His wife and the Rev. Billy Graham, a family friend, persuaded him to stop drinking when he turned 40.

NO CHILD LEFT BEHIND

Education reform was a centerpiece of Bush's tenure as governor of Texas. He presented a reform plan to Congress almost immediately after his first inauguration, and one year later, on January 8, 2002, he signed into law the resulting legislation, known as the No Child Left Behind Act (NCLB). This was a revision of the original 1965 law that authorized Congress to give funds to the states for educational programs on the K–12 level.

NCLB offered states a much higher level of federal funding, especially for poor children, in exchange for verifiable improvements. To receive this money, states were required to hold standardized tests in reading and math, provide documentation of results by students in various demographic subgroups, and ensure that all teachers were knowledgeable in their subject areas. Schools were required to meet a set of 37 stringent benchmarks to demonstrate that they were making "adequate yearly progress" toward targeted goals, with penalties imposed on those falling short.

Critics of NCLB said that the penalties were unfair and that the standardized testing programs undermined good teaching practices. In 2005, the National Education Association teachers' union, together with a number of school districts, brought suit against the Department of Education in federal district court for mandating programs without providing full financial support for them, in contravention of the Constitution. The judge rejected the suit, but a federal appeals court reinstated it in January 2008 and sent it back to the trial court. Margaret Spellings, the Secretary of Education, promised to appeal the ruling to the Supreme Court.

Courtesy of the White House

Bush signs the No Child Left Behind Act.

The issue was still in litigation at the end of President Bush's second term.

SEPTEMBER 11, 2001: TERRORIST ATTACKS

During President Clinton's administration, the United States made a variety of efforts to weaken Al Qaeda, the militant Islamist organization that emerged in the 1980s. Led by the Saudi-born multimillionaire Osama bin Laden, Al Qaeda provided funding, training, and equipment to Muslims engaged in a violent form of *jihad*, or religious struggle, in numerous countries. In 1988, bin Laden declared that Muslims have a duty to kill Americans wherever they can be found. Nine months into the administration of George W. Bush, Al Qaeda carried out, in a single day, a series of coordinated attacks on New York City and Washington, DC, that took the lives of 2,998 people—a death toll higher than that of Pearl Harbor in 1941.

The attacks took place on the morning of September 11, 2001. Four teams of Al Qaeda operatives—15 from Saudi Arabia, two from the United Arab Emirates, and one each from Egypt and Lebanon—hijacked four commercial passenger jets shortly after takeoff. Their aim was to fly the planes directly into buildings that symbolized American power. They succeeded in smashing two planes into the twin skyscrapers of New York's World Trade Center, causing fires of such intensity that both 110-story towers collapsed. They flew a third plane into the Pentagon, the Washington, D.C., headquarters of the Department of Defense. In the fourth plane, which was intended to destroy the Capitol or the White House, a group of passengers fought the hijackers until the plane crashed upside-down in a Pennsylvania field.

This event was the first time since the War of 1812 that the United States experienced a large-scale, lethal attack on its home territory by a foreign foe. The catastrophe produced a brief period of unity in which Americans set aside political differences to grieve together and friendly countries proclaimed their solidarity with the United States. The population's sudden sense of vulnerability was mixed with admiration for the heroism that was displayed on 9/11 by the passengers who stopped the hijackers through their resistance; by the New York firefighters who entered the burning Towers to rescue survivors and died in the collapse; by individuals who helped others to safety at the cost of their own lives; and by volunteers who spent months combing through the debris at the World Trade Center in search of human remains. The Bush administration immediately began preparations for a retaliatory strike, and the U.S. war against terror began in earnest.

The country's sense of unity quickly dissolved in bitter debates over the causes of terrorism, the failure of national intelligence agencies to discover and prevent the attacks, the general lack of coordination among emergency responders, the disruptive effects of counterterrorism measures on daily life, and the possibility that such measures might impair civil liberties.

THE BUSH DOCTRINE

In his address to Congress of September 20, 2001, President Bush announced that his new foreign policy would require zero toleration of terrorism: "Every nation in every region now has a decision to make. Either you are with us or you are with the terrorists." This statement, henceforth known informally as the Bush Doctrine, was rejected by many foreign statesmen, who did not find it expedient to choose sides.

THE INVASION OF AFGHANISTAN

The target of the Americans' retaliatory strike was Afghanistan, where Al Qaeda had had its headquarters since 1996. In his September 20 address to Congress, the President demanded that the rulers of Afghanistan—an unelected group of Islamic militants known as the Taliban—turn over Osama bin Laden and other Al Qaeda leaders and shut down the organization's training camps. Following the Taliban's refusal, the United States began its invasion, known as Operation Enduring Freedom, on October 7, 2001. Two months of U.S. air strikes coupled with ground action by Afghanistan's anti-Taliban Northern Alliance militia resulted in the collapse of the Taliban regime in December. It was replaced by a democratic government headed by Hamid Karzai, who was elected president in October 2004 following the adoption of a constitution.

The Taliban, however, continued to operate from bases inside Pakistan and eventually succeeded in re-infiltrating large areas of Afghanistan, recouping enough strength to spring hundreds of their colleagues from a prison in Kandahar in June 2008 in preparation for a major offensive. By the end of President Bush's term in office, some 48,000 troops remained in Afghanistan, along with NATO troops. More than 550 Americans had died there.

Among those who escaped from Afghanistan in 2001 was Osama bin Laden. Periodically he issued video and sound recordings in which he exhorted Muslims to carry on violent *jihad* against the Western nations.

THE INVASION OF IRAQ

Another source of trouble in the Middle East was Iraq, which had been controlled since 1979 by a despotic regime led by Saddam Hussein. During the administration of President Bush's father, the United States had used military force to prevent Iraq from annexing the neighboring nation of Kuwait, but had stopped short of removing its leader from power. In the intervening years, Hussein continued his violent persecution of Iraqi Shiites and Kurds, materially supported Muslim and Arab terrorist activities, and flouted attempts by the United Nations to monitor his regime's weapons aresenal.

The threat was sufficient to prompt a coalition of countries headed by United States and Great Britain to demand Hussein's voluntary departure. When that did not occur, they launched an invasion of Iraq on March 20, 2003. Iraqi defenses quickly collapsed, and all major cities were in coalition hands by mid-April.

This promising beginning was followed by an occupation that lasted for the rest of the President's two terms, during which the coalition tried to establish the conditions for a renewal of democratic government while attempting to end the guerrilla warfare carried on by Iraq's numerous religious and clan-based militia groups, which continually attacked civilians, coalition forces, and each other. Dissatisfaction on the part of American voters with the length of the war was one fac-

Courtesy of the Department of Defense

An American soldier in Iraq

tor in the Democratic Party's gains in Congress in the 2006 midterm election. Rejecting calls to withdraw American troops immediately, the President in early 2007 ordered the deployment of 30,000 more soldiers under the leadership of a new general, David Petraeus. The surge, as this strategy was called, was reasonably successful and coincided with the repudiation of Al Qaeda's influence by many formerly sympathetic Iraqis.

Saddam Hussein was captured in December 2003 and convicted in an Iraqi court of committing crimes against humanity; he was hanged in December 2006. Though the weapons of mass destruction he was believed to possess were not located by the coalition, numerous mass graves containing the bodies of his opponents were found. The warrant for his execution was signed by Prime Minister Nuri al-Maliki, who took office under a constitution that was approved by Iraqi voters in October 2005.

More than 4,200 American soldiers died in the course of the Iraq War from March 2003 through January 2009. The estimated number of deaths of Iraqi civilians range from 90,000 to more than 1 million.

NATIONAL SECURITY VS. CIVIL LIBERTIES

On September 11, the United States found itself dealing with a new kind of enemy—a transnational network of trained operatives, intent on killing mass numbers of civilians, who knew how to make effective use of internet and cell phone communications while exploiting the open nature of American society. Within a month, the President signed the USA PATRIOT Act, a set of initiatives intended to give law enforcement officials better ways to detect and prevent terrorist activity within the United States, including closer checking of financial transactions and visa applications, detention of questionable immigrants for indefinite periods, and quicker sharing of information among agencies. It was passed by Congress with strong bipartisan support. A number of its provisions—for example, the use of "national security letters," a form of subpoena with which federal officials could secretly acquire data on a suspicious person—met with legal challenges from critics who feared that they allowed the government too much freedom to investigate the private lives of its citizens. The Act was reauthorized in March 2006, minus provisions that had been struck down as unconstitutional.

Some of President Bush's plans to counteract terrorism were accomplished through the use of executive orders rather than congressional acts. One of these, which remained secret until described by the *New York Times*, was a program to monitor—without recourse to court-ordered warrants—the financial transactions, emails, and phone calls of Americans with suspected connections to foreign terrorist organizations. Similarly, the President, by executive order, established military tribunals that could designate foreigners captured in battle as "unlawful enemy combatants" who did not have the legal status of prisoners of war and could be held indefinitely. In response to a Supreme Court ruling in 2006, the tribunals received authorization from Congress; nonetheless, the Court ruled 5–4 in 2008 that the inmates of the U.S. detention camp at Guantanamo Bay, Cuba, could petition federal judges for release.

A question much debated in the press was the degree to which force and humiliation could be used against prisoners who might be able to give up valuable information. The debate was sparked by the revelation in 2004 that U.S. personnel had tortured Iraqis held in Baghdad's Abu Ghraib prison and by reports that the CIA used a suffocation technique called "waterboarding" in its interrogations of suspected terrorists. Torture was banned by executive order of the President in 2007, but opinions differed as to whether waterboarding constitutes torture. Among those who are known to have undergone waterboarding was Al Qaeda leader Khalid Sheikh Muhammad, the chief planner of the September 11 attack.

In his final address to the nation, on January 15, 2008, the President made mention of the fact that since September 11 "Amerca has gone seven years without another terrorist attack on our soil."

HURRICANE KATRINA

One of the worst natural disasters in the history of the United States occurred on August 29, 2005, when Hurricane Katrina devastated 90,000 square miles in Louisiana, Mississippi, and Alabama, killing some 2,000 people. The greatest destruction took place in low-lying New Orleans, La., which was covered with deep floodwaters. Most of the city's 462,000 residents had left town in a mass evacuation as the storm approached, but many of the poorest and least mobile were left stranded in horrific conditions.

The federal government's relief operation was run by the Federal Emergency Management Agency (FEMA). Massive help was provided by all branches of the armed services

Courtesy of the U.S. Coast Guard

Flooding in New Orleans after Hurricane Katrina

and several federal departments, together with National Guardsmen, public safety personnel from all parts of the country, and volunteers from humanitarian organizations.

There was considerable criticism of FEMA's slowness in its initial handling of the crisis and of the lack of coordination among the federal, state, and city governments. FEMA's director, Michael Brown, appointed by President Bush, had no experience with disaster relief and had to be replaced within a few days by someone who did; at a congressional hearing he placed the blame on budget cuts that occurred after FEMA was absorbed by the Department of Homeland Security. FEMA functioned better in preparations for Hurricane Rita, which hit Louisiana and Texas on September 24, and during the recovery effort for both hurricanes it distributed some $6 billion in aid. However, a report by the Government Accountability Office, issued in June 2006, found that up to 16 percent of that money had been given to fraudulent claimants.

Two and a half years after the hurricanes, 100,000 people who had lost their homes were still living in FEMA trailers. They were moved into apartments and hotel rooms beginning in February 2008, after the Centers for Disease Control and Prevention announced the trailers appeared to be contaminated with formaldehyde.

SOCIAL SECURITY REFORM

In his first State of the Union speech after his 2004 reelection, President Bush discussed the need to change the federal Social Security program to prevent it from running a deficit in the future. He proposed to allow workers under age 55 to use a portion of their Social Security payroll taxes to open individual retirement accounts, which, under the right market conditions, would compensate them for a reduction in their Social Security retirement benefits. Alternative possibilities, introduced by opponents of the privatization plan, include a wholesale reduction in benefits, an increase in payroll taxes, an increase in the amount of wages subject to taxation, an increase in the age of retirement, or a change in the way benefits are calculated.

The President undertook a 60-day campaign to promote his plan. But despite a general consensus that Social Security was in urgent need of restructuring, Congress was unable to produce legislation that appealed to both the pro- and the anti-privatization camps. The issue was shelved until January 2007, when Treasury Secretary Henry Paulson, under directions from the President, began negotiations with the Senate Budget Committee and the House Ways and Means Committee in search of potential compromises. In the end, it was decided that the next Congress would be in a better position to address the problem.

ROLLER-COASTER RATINGS

President Bush's approval rating, as measured by poll-takers in phone conversations with a sample of respondents, varied tremendously in the course of his two terms. In October 2001, in the aftermath of the September 11 attack by Al Qaeda, his approval score stood at 88 percent, according to the Harris Poll. This is the highest presidential rating ever recorded by the organization, which began polling during the presidency of Lyndon B. Johnson.

By April 2007, the President's rating had dropped 60 points, to 28 percent—only six points higher than the lowest rating ever recorded by the Harris Poll, which was earned by Jimmy Carter in 1980. However, just before he left office, he equalled Carter's 22 percent rating in a CBS News/*New York Times* poll.

Another polling organization, Associated Press-Ipsos, found that the President's approval rating stood at 30 percent in February 2008. But the approval rating for Congress stood even lower, at 22 percent.

STEM CELL RESEARCH

Stem cells are unspecialized cells that can develop into specialized cells; they are potentially useful in treating a variety of medical conditions. They occur as somatic ("adult") stem cells, found in body tissues, and as embryonic stem cells, found only in embryos. Federal funding has long been available for research using the first type, but not the second. A law known as the Dickey Amendment bars the federal government from giving taxpayer money to scientific research projects that involve creating or destroying human embryos. Since the collection of embryonic stem cells always results in the embryo's destruction, this research cannot, by law, receive federal support.

Upon taking office in 2001, President Bush was asked to make use of a loophole in the law that would have permitted federal funding to be disbursed as long as the actual destruction of the embryos was done by personnel who were paid with private funds. He rejected that idea, but on August 9, 2001, he announced that he was willing to authorize the use of federal money on condition that the stem cells were already in existence on the date of the announcement and that they had been collected from embryos created for fertility treatments but no longer needed for that purpose. In response to complaints that the existing cell lines were insufficient, Congress passed a bill that would have allowed the creation of additional lines from unused embryos; it was the subject of the President's first veto, on July 19, 2006. A year later, he vetoed a similar bill.

Research into the use of "adult" stem cells has resulted in treatments for heart-attack damage and for blood and bone cancers. In November 2007, two different research teams announced that they had developed techniques that transform human skin cells into the equivalent of embryonic stem cells, opening the way to medical treatments using cells taken from the patient's own body.

ILLEGAL IMMIGRATION

As of March 2008, an estimated 11.9 million illegal immigrants were living in the United States, with hundreds of thousands arriving each year, mostly from Mexico and Central America, in search of work in agriculture, domestic service, and other low-skill industries. A revamping of the malfunctioning immigration system was high on President Bush's agenda when he took office, but was postponed by the 9/11 attack and its aftermath.

Chaotic conditions caused by human smuggling, drug smuggling, and violent crime along the 2,000-mile U.S.-Mexican border prompted the governors of Arizona and New Mexico to declare states of emergency in affected counties in August 2005. In the course of the ensuing year, both houses of Congress passed bills combining an official guest-worker program—an essential part of

the President's plan—with a more forceful campaign to stop the flow of immigrants, including the reclassification of illegal entry as a criminal felony. In response, protest rallies were held in cities across the country. The bills failed for lack of a consensus on granting some form of amnesty to illegal immigrants, and the only piece of legislation to be signed was one authorizing construction of a 700-mile barrier along the border.

A comprehensive reorganization bill that would have authorized the distribution of permanent visas to all illegal aliens currently living in the United States appeared poised for enactment in the Senate in June 2007, but it likewise failed to pass.

The departments of Justice and Homeland Security announced in early 2008 that employers of illegal immigrants would face higher fines and a greater likelihood of prosecution under newly promulgated rules. They also announced that a high-tech surveillance system using sensors, cameras, radar, and aerial drones had been installed along part of the border, but it could not be deployed immediately because of technical difficulties.

DEPARTMENT OF HOMELAND SECURITY

The creation of the Department of Homeland Security was a consequence of Al Qaeda's attack on September 11, 2001. Six months previously, in February 2001, the Defense Department's Commission on National Security/21st Century had recommended that all federal operations related to homeland security should be consolidated under a single agency. The shock of the 9/11 terror attack prompted President Bush to establish the White House Office of Homeland Security in October 2001, with Tom Ridge as its chief.

A bill supported by both national parties expanded the office into a full-fledged department of the executive branch, headed by a secretary with cabinet-level status. It commenced operations on January 24, 2003. Tom Ridge served as its first secretary, followed by Michael Chertoff, who took office in February 2005.

The introduction of the new department required the biggest reorganization of the executive branch since the creation of the Defense Department in 1947. The Secret Service, the Coast Guard, the Customs Service, and the Federal Emergency Management Agency were among the many agencies that were reassigned to the DHS. Other operations were taken over from the departments of Agriculture, Defense, Energy, Health and Human Services, Justice, Transportation, and Treasury, as well as the FBI and the General Services Administration. Most of these were divided among four directorates: Border and Transportation Security, Emergency Preparedness and Response, Science and Technology, and Information Analysis and Infrastructure Protection. This made the DHS one of the largest federal departments, with more than 200,000 employees.

ECONOMIC RECESSION AND GOVERNMENT BAILOUT

During President Bush's second term, the United States entered an economic crisis that pulled other nations along with it into recession. The crisis originated in the 1990s with the growth of high-risk subprime mortgages, which were then used by financial institutions as backing for widely sold securities. Defaults by subprime-mortgage holders were thus able to set off a chain reaction that led to the collapse of the credit market in 2008 and the disappearance of some of the country's longstanding financial powerhouses, including Countrywide Financial, Lehman Brothers, Merrill Lynch, Bear Stearns, and Washington Mutual (the biggest bank failure in American history). Some, like the insurance company AIG and the mortgage firms known as Fannie Mae and Freddie Mac, survived only through timely federal loans or outright takeovers. Stocks and consumer savings plummeted in value, gross domestic product fell, house prices dropped, and employee layoffs rose, with the loss of 2.6 million jobs in the last year of the Bush administration.

Congress and the President made an attempt, early in 2008, to stimulate the economy through a modest tax rebate. On October 3, the President signed a much more ambitious law, the Emergency Economic Stabilization Act of 2008 (commonly referred to as "the bailout"), which gave Treasury Secretary Henry Paulson the authority to buy up the assets of shaky financial institutions using $700 billion of taxpayer funds.

In January 2008, just before the end of President Bush's second term, the Congressional Budget Office announced that the federal budget deficit would rise from $455 billion in the 2008 budget year to $1.2 trillion in the 2009 budget year.

FURTHER READING

Barnes, Fred. *Rebel in Chief: Inside the Bold and Controversial Presidency of George W. Bush*. 2006.

Deadlock: The Inside Story of America's Closest Election. Compiled and edited by the political staff of the *Washington Post*. 2001.

Dietrich, John W., ed. *The George W. Bush Foreign Policy Reader: Presidential Speeches with Commentary*. 2005.

Dionne, E.J., Jr., and William Kristol, eds. *Bush v. Gore: The Court Cases and the Commentary*. 2001.

Frum, David. *The Right Man: The Surprise Presidency of George W. Bush*. 2003.

Jacobson, Gary C. *A Divider, Not a Uniter: George W. Bush and the American People*. 2006.

McMahon, Kevin J., David M. Rankin, and Jon Kraus. *Transformed by Crisis: The Presidency of George W. Bush and American Politics*. 2004.

Minutaglio, Bill. *First Son: George W. Bush and the Bush Family Dynasty*. 1999.

Woodward, Bob. *Bush at War*. 2002.

——— . *Plan of Attack*. 2004.

——— . *State of Denial*. 2006.

——— . *The War Within*. 2008.

Courtesy of The U.S. Senate

44th PRESIDENT

Barack Hussein Obama

Name at birth—Barack Hussein Obama, Jr.

Birthdate—Aug. 4, 1961

Birthplace—Honolulu, Hawaii

Education—Franciscus Assisi Primary School, Jakarta, Indonesia; Besuki Menteng public elementary school, Jakarta; Punahou School, Honolulu, Hawaii, grad. 1979; Occidental College, Los Angeles, Calif., 1979–81; Columbia University, New York, N.Y., bachelor's degree in political science, 1983; Harvard Law School, J.D., magna cum laude, 1991

Religion—United Church of Christ

Ancestry—Kenyan, English, Irish, Dutch

Occupation—community organizer, state senator , U.S. Senator

Political party—Democrat

State represented—Illinois

Term of office—Jan. 20, 2009–

Administration—56th

Congresses—111th

Age at inauguration—47 years, 169 days

FAMILY

FATHER

Name—Barack Hussein Obama

Date of birth—1936

Place of birth—Nyangoma Kogela, Siaya District, Kenya; member of Luo tribe

Education—Gendia Primary School; Ngiya Intermediate School; Maseno National School; University of Hawaii at Manoa, grad. 1962; Harvard University, Cambridge, Mass., master's degree, 1965

First marriage—Kezia, in a Luo tribal ceremony in Kenya

Second marriage concurrent with first
—Stanley Ann Dunham, Maui, Hawaii, Feb. 2, 1961 (div. 1964)

Third marriage concurrent with first—Ruth Nidesand, Kenya, ca. 1965 (div.)

Children—See note under Siblings

Occupation—government economist

Date of death—November 24, 1982

Place of death—Nairobi, Kenya

Place of burial—Nyangoma Kogelo, Kenya

Age at death—46 years

MOTHER

Name at birth—Stanley Ann Dunham

Date of birth—Nov. 29, 1942

Place of birth—Fort Leavenworth, Kan.

Education—Mercer Island High School, Mercer Island, Wash.; University of Washington; University of California, Berkeley; University of Hawaii at Manoa, B.A. in math, Aug. 6, 1967; University of Hawaii, M.A. in anthropology, Dec. 18, 1983, Ph.D. in anthropology, Aug. 9, 1992

First marriage—Barack Hussein Obama, Maui, Hawaii, Feb. 2, 1961 (div. 1964)

Second marriage—Lolo Soetoro, 1967 (div. 1980)

Children (from 1st marriage)—Barack Hussein Obama, Jr., b. Aug. 4, 1961; **(from 2nd marriage)** Maya Kassandra Soetoro, b. Aug. 15, 1970

Occupation—cultural anthropologist and antipoverty activist in Third World countries

Date of death—Nov. 7, 1995

Place of death—Honolulu, Hawaii

Place of burial—ashes scattered from Oahu, Hawaii, over Pacific Ocean

Age at death—52 years, 343 days

SIBLINGS

Barack Obama was his mother's first son, the only child of his parents' marriage.

Child of Stanley Ann Dunham Obama and Barack Hussein Obama, Sr.

Barack Hussein Obama, Jr., b. Aug. 4, 1961

Child of Stanley Ann Dunham Soetoro and Lolo Soetoro

Maya Kassandra Soetoro, b. Aug. 15, 1970

Barack Hussein Obama, Jr., is the elder of two children born to his mother. From his mother's second marriage, to an Indonesian geologist, he has one half–sister, Maya Soetoro–Ng.

On his father's side, the situation is much more complicated. His father, Barack Hussein Obama, Sr., was born into a polygamous family in Kenya. When he was 18, he married a young woman named Kezia in a Luo tribal ceremony. Their son Malik Abongo Obama was born in 1957. A daughter, Auma Obama, was born in 1960, but during his wife's pregnancy, Obama left Kenya to study at the University of Hawaii. The following year he married Stanley Ann Dunham, an 18–year–old college student who had become pregnant with his child. Their son, born in 1961, was Barack Hussein Obama, Jr., the future President.

When Obama was a toddler, Obama Sr. left this second family and moved across the country to Massachusetts, where he entered Harvard University as a graduate student. He and Ann Dunham Obama were divorced in 1964. Returning to Kenya, he married Ruth Nidesand, whom he had met at Harvard. This third marriage produced two sons, Mark and David Ndesandjo, before it too ended in divorce.

In the meantime, Obama Sr. had resumed his relationship with his original wife, Kezia, who gave birth to their son Abo Obama in 1968. Kezia Obama gave birth to a fourth child, Bernard Obama, in 1970, but it is unclear whether Obama Sr. was his biological father. The last child fathered by Barack Obama, Sr., was George Hussein Onyango Obama, born in 1982 to Jael Otiengo. Barack Obama, Sr., was killed in a car crash that same year. His son by Stanley Ann Dunham, Barack Obama, Jr., was a college student at the time.

Thus, President Obama has two half–sisters, one from his mother and one from his father. He also has five and perhaps six half–brothers on his father's side, birthed by three different women. His half–brother David Ndesandjo died in a motorcycle accident in the 1980s.

MARRIAGE

Married—Michelle LaVaughn Robinson

Date of marriage—Oct. 3, 1992

Place of marriage—Chicago, Ill.

Age of wife at marriage—28 years, 260 days

Age of husband at marriage—31 years, 60 days

CHILDREN

Malia Ann Obama, b. July 4, 1998, Chicago, Ill.

Natasha (Sasha) Obama, b. June 10, 2001, Chicago, Ill.

THE PRESIDENT'S WIFE

Name at birth—Michelle LaVaughn Robinson

Date of birth—Jan. 17, 1964

Place of birth—Chicago, Ill.

Mother—Marian Shields Robinson

Mother's occupation—secretary

Father—Fraser Robinson III (d. 1991)

Father's occupation—city water plant pump operator; Democratic precinct captain

Siblings—Craig Robinson, b. April 21, 1962

Education—Whitney Young Magnet High School, Chicago, Ill., grad. 1981; Princeton University, Princeton, N.J., A.B. in sociology, cum laude, 1985; Harvard Law School, Cambridge, Mass., J.D. 1988

Religion—United Church of Christ

Married—Barack Hussein Obama, Oct. 3, 1992, Chicago, Ill.

Children—Malia Ann Obama, b. July 4, 1998, Chicago, Ill.; Natasha Obama, b. June 10, 2001, Chicago, Ill.

Occupation—attorney, executive for city of Chicago, hospital administrator

Years younger than the President—2 years, 166 days

Additional Data on Michelle Obama

1988–1991, associate, law firm of Sidley Austin, Chicago

1992–1993, mayoral assistant, then assistant commissioner of planning and development, City of Chicago

1993–1996, executive director, Chicago office of nonprofit organization Public Allies

1996–2002, associate dean of students, University of Chicago

2002–2005, executive director of community affairs, University of Chicago Hospitals

2005–2008, vice president for community and external affairs, University of Chicago Hospitals

2009– , First Lady of the United States

THE FIRST LADY

Michelle Robinson Obama has the distinction of being the first African-American First Lady, as well as the first member of a Presidential family to be descended from slaves. She was born to a working-class family in Chicago, where her father was a precinct captain for the Democratic Party. After graduat-

Courtesy of the U.S. Department of Defense

Michelle Obama, wife of Barack Obama

ing from Princeton University and Harvard Law School, she was admitted to the Illinois bar in May 1989.

By the time her husband launched his presidential campaign, Mrs. Obama had years of experience as a high-level executive in the public sector. (Her 2006 salary as an executive of the University of Chicago Hospitals was $273,618.) She delivered an address at the Democratic National Convention.

IMPORTANT DATES IN THE PRESIDENT'S LIFE

1985–1988, director, Developing Communities Project, Chicago, Ill.

1988–1991, student at Harvard Law School; editor, 1989–1990, and president, 1990–1991, *Harvard Law Review*

1992, director, Project Vote, Illinois

1992–1996, lecturer, and 1996–2004, senior lecturer in constitutional law, University of Chicago Law School

1993–1996, associate, and 1996–2004, of counsel, Davis, Miner, Barnhill & Galland law firm, Chicago, Ill.

1997–2004, Illinois state senator

2000, defeated in Democratic primary election for U.S. House of Representatives

July 27, 2004, delivered keynote speech at Democratic National Convention, Boston

Nov. 2, 2004, elected to U.S. Senate from Illinois

Aug. 27, 2008, nominated for President at the Democratic National Convention, Denver

Nov. 4, 2008, elected President of the United States

Nov. 16, 2008, resigned Senate seat

ELECTIONS

THE ELECTION OF 2008

November 4, 2008

CANDIDATES

Democratic Party (45th Convention)

Aug. 25–28, 2008, Pepsi Center and INVESCO Field at Mile High, Denver, Colo.

P: Barack Hussein Obama, Ill.
VP: Joseph Robinette Biden, Del.

Obama was nominated on the first ballot. While the verbal roll call of the states was still in progress, Senator Clinton offered a motion to suspend it and to nominate Senator Obama by acclamation. The motion was accepted. A paper ballot was then taken. Candidates for nomination and the votes they received on the paper ballot:

Hillary Rodham Clinton, N.Y., 1,010.5
Barack Hussein Obama, Ill., 3,188.5
Votes not cast, 219
Abstention, 1
Total number of votes: 4,419
Number necessary for nomination: 2,210

Republican Party (39th Convention)

Sept. 1–4, 2008, Xcel Center, St. Paul, Minn.

P: John Sidney McCain, Ariz.
VP: Sarah Heath Palin, Alaska

McCain was nominated on the first ballot. Candidates for nomination and the votes they received:

John Sidney McCain, Ariz., 2,343
Ron Paul, 15
Mitt Romney, 2
Votes not cast, 20
Total number of votes cast: 2,380
Number necessary for nomination: 1,191

Prohibition Party

Sept. 13–14, 2007, Indianapolis, Ind.

P: Gene Amondson, Alaska
VP: Leroy Pletten, Mich.

Socialist Party USA

Oct. 19–21, 2007, St. Louis, MO

P: Brian Patrick Moore, Fla.

VP: Stewart A. Alexander, Calif.

Libertarian Party of New Hampshire

Nov. 2007

P: George Phillies, Mass.

Socialist Workers Party

Jan. 14, 2008 (announced)

P: Róger Calero, N.Y.
VP: Alyson Kennedy, N.J.

Party for Socialism and Liberation

Jan. 18, 2008 (candidates announced)

P: Gloria Estela La Riva, Calif.
VP: Eugene Puryear, D.C.

Independent candidate

Feb. 4, 2008 (announced)

P: Ralph Nader, D.C.
VP: Matt Gonzalez, Calif.

Constitution Party

Apr. 23–26, 2008, Kansas City Marriott Hotel Downtown, Kansas City, Mo.

P: Chuck Baldwin, Fla.
VP: Darrell Castle, Tenn.

Libertarian Party

May 23–26, 2008, Denver, Colo.

P: Bob Barr, Ga.
VP: Wayne Allyn Root, Nev.

Objectivist Party

May 25, 2008, Denver, Colo.

P: Thomas Robert Stevens, N.Y.
VP: Alden Link, N.Y.

Green Party

July 10–13, 2008, Blackstone Hotel and Chicago Theatre, Chicago, Ill.

P: Cynthia McKinney, Ga.
VP: Rosa Clemente, N.Y.

Reform Party USA

July 18–20, 2008, Dallas, Tex.

P: Ted C. Weill, Miss.
VP: Frank Edward McEnulty, Calif.

America's Independent Party

Aug. 20, 2008, online

P: Alan Keyes, Md.
VP: no nomination

Boston Tea Party

P: Charles Jay, Ind.

Campaign for Liberty

Ron Paul, Tex.

New Party

P: John Joseph Polachek, Ill.

U.S. Pacifist Party

P: Bradford Lyttle, Ill.
VP: Abraham Bassford

Independent candidate

P:Jonathan Edward Allen
VP: Jeffrey D. Stath, Calif.

Independent candidate

P: Jeffrey Boss, N.J.
VP: Andrea Marie Psoras

Independent candidate

P: Richard Duncan, Ohio
VP: Ricky Johnson, Pa.

Independent candidate

P: Frank Edward McEnulty, Calif.
VP: David Mangan

Independent candidate

P: Jeffrey J. Wamboldt, Wisc.

VP: David J. Klimis

2008 POPULAR VOTE

Democratic Party, 69,456,897 (52.92%)
Republican Party, 59,934,814 (45.66%)
Nader (independent), 738,475
Libertarian Party, 523,686
Constitution Party, 199,314
Green Party, 161,603
America's Independent, 47,694
Campaign for Liberty, 42,426
Socialist Workers Party, 7,551
Party for Socialism and Liberation, 6,808
Socialist Party USA, 6,528
None of These Candidates (Nev.), 6,267
Duncan (independent), 3,902
Boston Tea Party, 2,422
New Party, 1,149
McEnulty (independent), 828
Wamboldt (independent), 764
Objectivist Party, 755
Prohibition Party, 653
Boss (independent), 639
Libertarian Party of N.H., 531
Reform Party, 481
Allen (independent), 477
U.S. Pacifist Party, 110
write-ins, 112,554

Total, 131,257,328

INAUGURATION

January 20, 2009

The inauguration of the first African-American President in the nation's history was a cathartic moment for millions of people, and the day's proximity to Martin Luther King Day (January 19) lent it even more emotional power, particularly after the President-elect asked Americans to honor King by using the holiday as an opportunity for volunteer service.

Additional symbolism was provided by Obama's tributes to Abraham Lincoln on the occasion of the bicentennial of his birth. Obama arrived in Washington by train along part of the route taken by Lincoln for his own inauguration in 1861 and swore his oath of office on the same Bible that Lincoln used. The first event of his inaugural celebration, a concert on Sunday, took place at the Lincoln Memorial, where the Rev. King had delivered his "I Have a Dream" speech some 45 years before.

Although the weather on January 20 was frigid, the National Mall—open to the public for the first time ever during an inauguration—began filling up with people before dawn. Many of them treated the occasion as an outdoor festival, with spontaneous dancing and singing. By noon, the crowd con-

609

tained an estimated 1.5 million people, most of whom watched the proceedings on huge television screens.

Following traditional protocol, the Obamas attended a prayer service at St. John's Episcopal Church on the morning of the inauguration and paid a visit to the Bushes at the White House before the noon-time ceremony. A brief moment of confusion took place when Chief Justice John Glover Roberts, administering the oath of office, mis-spoke and put an adverb out of place. (As a precaution, the oath was repeated at the White House on the following day.) President Obama then delivered an inaugural address, drafted by chief speechwriter Jon Favreau, that combined a sober assessment of the diffi-culties facing the nation with his trademark call for a fresh sense of optimism, confidence, and trans-partisan cooperation.

The Lincoln connection was carried over to the postinaugural lunch at the Capitol, which was served on replicas of Lincoln's chinaware and featured seafood stew, breast of duck, and other dishes Lincoln is said to have liked.

The Obama family then watched the long inaugural parade from a viewing stand. In the evening, the President and First Lady danced at ten inaugural balls.

Courtesy of the U.S. Department of Defense

Barack Obama takes the oath of office.

The level of security enforcement required for the 2009 inauguration was so high and so costly that President Bush, in advance of the fact, declared the existence of a three-day state of emergency, which qualified the capi-tal city for millions of additional dollars in federal funds.

THE VICE PRESIDENT

Name—Joseph Robinette "Joe" Biden, Jr.

Date of birth—Nov. 20, 1942

Place of birth—Scranton, Pa.

Mother—Catherine Eugenia Finnegan Biden

Mother's occupation—homemaker

Father—Joseph Robinette Biden, Sr.

Father's occupation—automobile and real estate salesman

Siblings—eldest of four; two brothers, one sister

Education—Archmere Academy, Claymont, Del., grad. 1961; University of Delaware, Newark, Del., B.A. in history and political science, 1965; Syracuse University College of Law, Syracuse, N.Y., J.D. 1968

Religion—Roman Catholic

Married—(1) Neilia Hunter, Aug. 27, 1966 (d. Dec. 18, 1972)

Children from first marriage—Joseph Robinette "Beau" Biden III; Robert Hunter Biden; Naomi Christina (d. Dec. 18, 1972)

Married—(2) Jill Tracy Jacobs, June 17, 1977

Child from second marriage—Ashley Blazer Biden

Political party—Democratic

State represented—Delaware

Term of office—Jan. 20, 2009–

Age at inauguration—66 years, 61 days

ADDITIONAL DATA ON BIDEN

1968–1972, law practice, Wilmington, Del.

1970–1972, councilman, New Castle County, Del.

1973–2009, U.S. senator from Delaware

1988, defeated in Democratic primary elec-tions for presidential candidate

Courtesy of the White House

Joe Biden, Vice President to Barack Obama

1991–, adjunct professor of constitutional law, Widener University School of Law, Wilmington, Del.

2008, defeated in Democratic primary elections for presidential candidate

Nov. 4, 2008, elected Vice President of the United States

Biden entered the Senate in 1973, only a few weeks after his wife and baby daughter were killed in an automobile accident. He took his oath of office in the hospital where he was keeping watch over his two young sons, both of whom were recovering from injuries sustained in the accident.

During his 36 years in the Senate, Biden served as chairman of the Senate Committee on the Judiciary (1987–1995) and the Senate Committee on Foreign Relations (2001–2003 and 2007–2009). All his Senate election campaigns were managed by his sister, Valerie Biden Owens.

THE SECOND LADY

Name at birth—Jill Tracy Jacobs

Date of birth—June 5, 1951

Place of birth—Hammonton, N.J.

Mother—Bonny Jean Jacobs

Mother's occupation—homemaker

Father—Donald C. Jacobs (d. 1999)

Father's occupation—head of savings and loan institution

Siblings—eldest of five daughters

Education—Upper Moreland High School, Willow Grove, Pa.; University of Delaware, B.A., 1975; West Chester University, West Chester, Pa., master's in education with specialty in reading, 1981; Villanova University, Villanova, Pa., master's in English, 1987; University of Delaware, Ed.D., 2006

Religion—Roman Catholic

Married—(1) brief marriage during college (2) Joseph Robinette Biden, June 17, 1977

Children from first marriage—None

Children from second marriage—Ashley Blazer Biden, b. June 8, 1981

ADDITIONAL DATA ON JILL BIDEN

Jill Biden was for 13 years a teacher of English and reading in the public schools and at a psychiatric hospital program for adolescents. In 1993, she became an English professor at Delaware Technical and Community College in Stanton, Del. She founded the Biden Breast Health Initiative for high–school girls and Book Buddies, a reading–promotion organization for poor children. Her doctoral dissertation was entitled *Student Retention at the Community College: Meeting Students' Needs.*

CABINET

FIRST TERM

January 20, 2009–

State—Hillary Rodham Clinton, N.Y., Jan. 21, 2009

Treasury—Timothy Franz Geithner, N.Y., Jan. 26, 2009

Defense—Robert Michael Gates, Tex., continued from previous administration

Justice—Eric Himpton Holder, D.C., Feb. 2, 2009

Interior—Kenneth Lee Salazar, Colo., Jan. 21, 2009

Agriculture—Thomas James Vilsack, Iowa, Jan. 21, 2009

Commerce—Judd Alan Gregg, N.H. (nom.)

Labor—Hilda L. Solis, Calif. (nom.)

Health and Human Services—vacant

Housing and Urban Development—Shaun Donovan, N.Y. , Jan. 26, 2009

Transportation—Raymond H. LaHood, Ill., Jan. 22, 2009

Energy—Steven Chu, Calif., Jan. 21, 2009

Education—Arne Duncan, Ill., Jan. 21, 2009

Veterans Affairs—Eric Ken Shinseki, Tex., Jan. 21, 2009

Homeland Security—Janet Napolitano, Ariz., Jan. 21, 2009

Two the federal departments—Commerce and Labor—did not have secretaries at the time this book went to press. The Labor nominee, Hilda L. Solis of California, had completed her Senate hearings, but her confirmation had been stalled by a procedural hold. Senator Judd Alan Gregg was nominated for Commerce in early February but was not yet confirmed.

ADDITIONAL DATA ON BARACK OBAMA

BARACK HUSSEIN OBAMA

—was the first African-American President.

—was the first biracial President.

—was the first President born outside the continental United States.

—was the first President to spend part of his childhood in Asia.

—was the first President to spend part of his childhood in a Muslim country.

—was the first President born in the second half of the twentieth century.

—was the first African-American editor of the *Harvard Law Review*.

—was the first presidential candidate to raise substantial amounts of money on the Internet.

—was the first President to have a parent who was a citizen of a different country.

—was the first President to have a weekly broadcast on YouTube.

THE FIRST AFRICAN-AMERICAN PRESIDENT

The election of Barack Obama signaled a milestone in the evolution of race relations and racial-identity politics in the United States. Exit polls indicated that Obama was able to appeal to both white and African-American voters in large numbers. That he took approximately 95 percent of the black vote was not surprising. At the same time, however, he took 41 percent of the white male vote, which is higher than any of the previous five Democratic presidential nominees received. He also won the votes of nearly half of white independent voters. In general any racial backlash against Obama was effectively offset by those who voted for him precisely because of the historic nature of his candidacy. Obama himself set the tone of the election in regard to race politics in a speech entitled "A More Perfect Union" that he delivered at the Constitution Center in Philadelphia, Pennsylvania, on March 18, 2008. In that speech he addressed two concerns: "On one end of the spectrum, we've heard the implication that my candidacy is somehow an exercise in affirmative action; that it's based solely on the desire of wide-eyed liberals to purchase racial reconciliation on the cheap. On the other end, we've heard my former pastor, Reverend Jeremiah Wright, use incendiary language to express views that have the potential not only to widen the racial divide, but views that denigrate both the greatness and the goodness of our nation; that rightly offend white and black alike." The speech, which dealt unflinchingly with the question of race in American politics and in American life, effectively quelled the issue for the duration of the presidential campaign.

The emotional impact of Obama's election was felt especially by older African Americans who remembered segregation in the South. In some states blacks had even been prevented from voting in many circumstances. Obama, who was still a small child in Hawaii at the time of the Civil Rights Movement, was reluctant to claim the mantle of the leaders of that movement but at the same time eagerly acknowledged their greatness. He delivered his acceptance speech at the Democratic National Convention on the 45th anniversary of Martin Luther King's famous "I Have a Dream" speech of August 28, 1963. In his acceptance speech Obama quoted King but referred to him only as "the preacher." It went unsaid that for many Obama's candidacy was to some degree the fulfillment of that dream.

POSTINAUGURAL PRAYER SERVICE

The custom of having the new President attend church "to hear divine service" originated with a congressional resolution passed before Washington's inaugural in 1789. A worship service for President Obama was held at the National Cathedral the day after his inauguration. Prayers were offered by Roman Catholic and Greek Orthodox clergy as well as by representatives of numerous Protestant groups. A way was found to allow Hindu, Muslim, and Jewish leaders to participate by having them lead brief sections of a responsive reading. The sermon was given by the Rev. Dr. Sharon Watkins of the Disciples of Christ, marking the first time that a woman preached the sermon at the postinaugural service.

OBAMA'S FIRST TELEVISED INTERVIEW

President Obama's first White House interview was broadcast on the Arabic-language television channel Al Arabiya on Jan. 27, 2009. It had been taped the previous day. The interviewer was Hisham Melhem, the channel's Washington bureau chief. The President spoke of his own Muslim connections, including his years attending school in Indonesia (where his mother had gone to live with her second husband) and his own Muslim relatives on his father's side of the family.

EARLY EXECUTIVE ORDERS

In the first week of his presidency President Obama issued several executive orders reversing policies of the Bush administration. Among the more controversial of these was his order of Jan. 22, requiring the prison at Guantanamo Bay, Cuba, to be shut within a year and establishing a commission to determine what to do with the 245 known and suspected Islamic terrorists still detained there. (Shortly after the order was issued, it was reported that a number of Saudi Arabians who had been released from Guantanamo were now in Yemen working for Al Qaeda.) Another order banned all U.S. officials, including the Central Intelligence Agency, from using waterboarding and similar techniques to extract information from suspected terrorists.

On Jan. 23, President Obama reversed the policy of refusing taxpayer funding to nongovernmental health-care organizations operating in other countries if they provide abortions or encourage abortion as a form of birth control. This policy, originally instituted by President Reagan, had been reversed by President Clinton and reinstated by President George W. Bush.

OBAMA'S STIMULUS PACKAGE

President Obama took office in the midst of an economic recession and immediately began preparing a comprehensive stimulus package to present to Congress. This ambitious plan included proposals for a public works program, similar to that of the New Deal, to rebuild roads, bridges, and schools, creating millions of jobs in the process. Other proposals involved massive federal investment in alternative energy sources, electronic health records, and technology research, as well as expansion of the social "safety net" for people hurt by the recession, an influx of federal money to the states, and a tax cut for individuals and businesses. The total cost of the various proposals was estimated at nearly $900 billion.

President Obama boards Air Force One *for the first time.*

OBAMA AND THE CLINTON CONNECTION

The first primary of the 2008 election took place on Jan. 8, 2008, in New Hampshire. It was won by Hillary Clinton with 39 percent of the vote to Barack Obama's 36 percent. For the remainder of the primary season, the two Senators engaged in a hard-fought campaign that Obama eventually won. Many of Clinton's supporters were irate when the second place on the ticket went to Joseph Biden rather than to her. Soon after the election, however, she accepted Obama's offer of the post of secretary of state. She was confirmed by the Senate and sworn in on Jan. 21, 2009.

In picking his staff, Obama relied heavily on veterans of Bill Clinton's administration. Posts filled by experienced Clinton hands included White House counsel, White House chief of staff, vice presidential chief of staff,

attorney general, most of the members of the Transition Advisory Board, and the head of the National Economic Council.

OBAMA'S BESTSELLERS

Obama's memoir *Dreams from My Father: A Story of Race and Inheritance* was published in 1995. It was republished in 2004 to take advantage of the interest in Obama generated by his delivery of the keynote address at that year's Democratic National Convention.

That speech was also the basis for Obama's *The Audacity of Hope: Thoughts on Reclaiming the American Dream*. Published in November 2006, it remained on the bestseller list for 30 months.

THE MULTIRELIGIOUS OBAMA FAMILY

The extended Obama family encompasses four major religions. Barack and Michelle Obama, and most of their American relatives, are Christians. The President's father was the son of a Kenyan convert to Islam, and some of his descendants are Muslims, including the President's half-brother Malik. President Obama's half-sister, Maya Soetoro-Ng, is a Buddhist. Michelle Obama's first cousin once removed, Rabbi Capers C. Funnye, Jr., converted to Judaism and leads Chicago's Beth Shalom B'nai Zaken Ethiopian Hebrew Congregation.

OBAMA HAD EARLY SECRET SERVICE PROTECTION

Secret Service protection for Barack Obama began in May 2007, well before the usual time for a presidential candidate or prospective candidate. Protection was already in place for Hillary Clinton because she had been a First Lady.

FURTHER READING

The American Journey of Barack Obama. By the editors of Life magazine. 2008.

The Essential Barack Obama: The Grammy Award-Winning Recordings (audiobook), 2008.

Freddoso, David. *The Case Against Barack Obama*. 2008.

Ignatius, Adi, ed. *President Obama: The Path to the White House*. 2008.

Niven, Steven J. *Barack Obama: A Pocket Biography of Our 44th President*. 2009.

Obama, Barack. *Dreams from My Father: A Story of Race and Inheritance.* 2004.
———. *The Audacity of Hope: Thoughts on Reclaiming the American Dream.* 2006.
———. *Change We Can Believe In.* 2008.

Part II

Comparative Data

The Presidents

Chronology, Family History, and Personal Background

PRESIDENTS OF THE UNITED STATES—YEARS SERVED

1. George Washington 1789–1797
2. John Adams 1797–1801
3. Thomas Jefferson 1801–1809
4. James Madison 1809–1817
5. James Monroe 1817–1825
6. John Quincy Adams 1825–1829
7. Andrew Jackson 1829–1837
8. Martin Van Buren 1837–1841
9. William Henry Harrison 1841
10. John Tyler 1841–1845
11. James Knox Polk 1845–1849
12. Zachary Taylor 1849–1850
13. Millard Fillmore 1850–1853
14. Franklin Pierce 1853–1857
15. James Buchanan 1857–1861
16. Abraham Lincoln 1861–1865
17. Andrew Johnson 1865–1869
18. Ulysses Simpson Grant 1869–1877
19. Rutherford Birchard Hayes 1877–1881
20. James Garfield 1881
21. Chester Alan Arthur 1881–1885
22. Grover Cleveland 1885–1889
23. Benjamin Harrison 1889–1893
24. Grover Cleveland 1893–1897
25. William McKinley 1897–1901
26. Theodore Roosevelt 1901–1909
27. William Howard Taft 1909–1913
28. Woodrow Wilson 1913–1921
29. Warren Gamaliel Harding 1921–1923
30. Calvin Coolidge 1923–1929
31. Herbert Clark Hoover 1929–1933
32. Franklin Delano Roosevelt 1933–1945
33. Harry S. Truman 1945–1953
34. Dwight David Eisenhower 1953–1961
35. John Fitzgerald Kennedy 1961–1963
36. Lyndon Baines Johnson 1963–1969
37. Richard Milhous Nixon 1969–1974
38. Gerald Rudolph Ford 1974–1977
39. Jimmy Carter 1977–1981
40. Ronald Wilson Reagan 1981–1989
41. George Herbert Walker Bush 1989–1993
42. William Jefferson Clinton 1993–2001
43. George Walker Bush 2001–2009
44. Barack Hussein Obama 2009–

BIRTH AND DEATH DATES

Washington 1732–1799
J. Adams 1735–1826
Jefferson 1743–1826
Madison 1751–1836
Monroe 1758–1831
J. Q. Adams 1767–1848
Jackson 1767–1845
Van Buren 1782–1862
W. H. Harrison 1773–1841
Tyler 1790–1862
Polk 1795–1849
Taylor 1784–1850
Fillmore 1800–1874
Pierce 1804–1869
Buchanan 1791–1868
Lincoln 1809–1865
A. Johnson 1808–1875
Grant 1822–1885
Hayes 1822–1893
Garfield 1831–1881
Arthur 1829–1896

Cleveland   1837–1908
B. Harrison   1833–1901
McKinley   1843–1901
T. Roosevelt   1858–1919
Taft   1857–1930
Wilson   1856–1924
Harding   1865–1923
Coolidge   1872–1933
Hoover   1874–1964
F. D. Roosevelt   1882–1945
Truman   1884–1972
Eisenhower   1890–1969
Kennedy   1917–1963
L. B. Johnson   1908–1973
Nixon   1913–1994
Ford   1913–2006
Carter   1924–
Reagan   1911–2004
G. Bush   1924–
Clinton   1946–
G. W. Bush   1946–
Obama   1961–

STATES REPRESENTED AND PARTY AFFILIATIONS

Washington   Virginia, Federalist
J. Adams   Massachusetts, Federalist
Jefferson   Virginia, Democratic–Republican
Madison   Virginia, Democratic–Republican
Monroe   Virginia, Democratic–Republican
J. Q. Adams   Massachusetts, Democratic–Republican
Jackson   Tennessee, Democrat (Democratic–Republican)
Van Buren   New York, Democrat (Democratic–Republican)
W. H. Harrison   Ohio, Whig
Tyler   Virginia, Whig
Polk   Tennessee, Democrat
Taylor   Louisiana, Whig
Fillmore   New York, Whig
Pierce   New Hampshire, Democrat
Buchanan   Pennsylvania, Democrat
Lincoln   Illinois, Republican

A. Johnson   Tennessee, Democrat (but nominated and elected with Lincoln on Republican ticket)
Grant   Illinois, Republican
Hayes   Ohio, Republican
Garfield   Ohio, Republican
Arthur   New York, Republican
Cleveland   New York, Democrat
B. Harrison   Indiana, Republican
McKinley   Ohio, Republican
T. Roosevelt   New York, Republican
Taft   Ohio, Republican
Wilson   New Jersey, Democrat
Harding   Ohio, Republican
Coolidge   Massachusetts, Republican
Hoover   California, Republican
F. D. Roosevelt   New York, Democrat
Truman   Missouri, Democrat
Eisenhower   New York, Republican
Kennedy   Massachusetts, Democrat
L. B. Johnson   Texas, Democrat
Nixon   New York, Republican
Ford   Michigan, Republican
Carter   Georgia, Democrat
Reagan   California, Republican
G. Bush   Texas, Republican
Clinton   Arkansas, Democrat
G. W. Bush   Texas, Republican
Obama   Illinois, Democrat

DATES AND PLACES OF BIRTH

Washington   Feb. 22, 1732, Westmoreland County, Va.
J. Adams   Oct. 30, 1735, Braintree (now Quincy), Mass.
Jefferson   Apr. 13, 1743, Shadwell, Va.
Madison   Mar. 16, 1751, Port Conway, Va.
Monroe   Apr. 28, 1758, Westmoreland County, Va.
J. Q. Adams   July 11, 1767, Braintree, Mass.
Jackson   Mar. 15, 1767, Waxhaw, S.C.
Van Buren   Dec. 5, 1782, Kinderhook, N.Y.
W. H. Harrison   Feb. 9, 1773, Berkeley, Va.
Tyler   Mar. 29, 1790, Greenway, Va.
Polk   Nov. 2, 1795, Mecklenburg County, N.C.

Taylor   Nov. 24, 1784, Orange County, Va.

Fillmore   Jan. 7, 1800, Cayuga County, N.Y.

Pierce   Nov. 23, 1804, Hillsborough, N.H.

Buchanan   Apr. 23, 1791, Cove Gap, Pa.

Lincoln   Feb. 12, 1809, Hardin County, Ky.

A. Johnson   Dec. 29, 1808, Raleigh, N.C.

Grant   Apr. 27, 1822, Point Pleasant, Ohio

Hayes   Oct. 4, 1822, Delaware, Ohio

Garfield   Nov. 19, 1831, Orange, Ohio

Arthur   Oct. 5, 1829, Fairfield, Vt.

Cleveland   Mar. 18, 1837, Caldwell, N.J.

B. Harrison   Aug. 20, 1833, North Bend, Ohio

McKinley   Jan. 29, 1843, Niles, Ohio

T. Roosevelt   Oct. 27, 1858, New York, N.Y.

Taft   Sept. 15, 1857, Cincinnati, Ohio

Wilson   Dec. 29, 1856, Staunton, Va.

Harding   Nov. 2, 1865, Corsica (now Blooming Grove), Ohio

Coolidge   July 4, 1872, Plymouth, Vt.

Hoover   Aug. 10, 1874, West Branch, Iowa

F. D. Roosevelt   Jan. 30, 1882, Hyde Park, N.Y.

Truman   May 8, 1884, Lamar, Mo.

Eisenhower   Oct. 14, 1890, Denison, Tex.

Kennedy   May 29, 1917, Brookline, Mass.

L. B. Johnson   Aug. 27, 1908, near Stonewall, Tex.

Nixon   Jan. 9, 1913, Yorba Linda, Calif.

Ford   July 14, 1913, Omaha, Neb.

Carter   Oct. 1, 1924, Plains, Ga.

Reagan   Feb. 6, 1911, Tampico, Ill.

G. Bush   June 12, 1924, Milton, Mass.

Clinton   Aug. 19, 1946, Hope, Ark.

G. W. Bush   July 6, 1946, New Haven, Conn.

Obama   August 4, 1961, Honolulu, Hawaii

Two Presidents were born in 1767: Jackson (March 15) and John Quincy Adams (July 11). Two were born in 1822: Grant (April 27) and Hayes (October 4). Two were born in 1913: Nixon (January 9) and Ford (July 14). Two were born in 1924: Carter (October 1) and George Bush (June 12). Two were born in 1946: Clinton (August 19) and George W. Bush (July 6).

Two Presidents were born on November 2: Polk in 1795 and Harding in 1865. Two were born on December 29: Andrew Johnson in 1808 and Wilson in 1856.

One President, Coolidge, was born on a national holiday, July 4, 1872.

The first President born outside the original thirteen states was Lincoln.

The first President born west of the Mississippi River was Hoover.

The first President born outside the continental United States was Barack Hussein Obama, in Honolulu, Hawaii.

The President born farthest north was Arthur, in Fairfield, Vt.

The Presidents born farthest east were John Adams and John Quincy Adams, in Braintree (now Quincy), Mass.

The President born farthest south was Lyndon Baines Johnson, near Stonewall, Tex.

The President born farthest west was Barack Hussein Obama, in Honolulu, Hawaii

The President born farthest west in the continental United States was Richard Milhous Nixon, in Yorba Linda, Calif.

Only four Presidents were born in large cities: Taft in Cincinnati, Ohio; Theodore Roosevelt in New York City; Ford in Omaha, Neb.; and Obama in Honolulu, Hawaii.

Only four Presidents were born in a hospital: Jimmy Carter, Bill Clinton, George W. Bush, and Barack Obama.

PRESIDENTS BORN BRITISH SUBJECTS

Eight Presidents were British subjects at birth even though they were born in North America: Washington, John Adams, Jefferson, Madison, Monroe, John Quincy Adams, Jackson, and William Henry Harrison. The first President not born a British subject was Van Buren.

THE PRESIDENTS OF CHARLES CITY COUNTY

Charles City County, Va., is noted as the birthplace of two men who were simultaneously elected President and Vice President of the United States. They were William Henry Harrison and John Tyler, elected November 3, 1840, and inaugurated March 4, 1841.

The careers of the two men who became the ninth and the tenth Presidents had much in common. Both had been governors, Harrison the territorial governor of Indiana and Tyler the state governor of Virginia. Each had served in the House of Representatives and the Senate.

THREE SUCCESSIVE OHIO PRESIDENTS

The 18th, 19th, and 20th Presidents—Grant, Hayes, and Garfield—were Republicans, born in Ohio, and generals in the Union Army.

EIGHT OF LAST FOURTEEN PRESIDENTS BORN WEST OF THE MISSISSIPPI RIVER

Herbert Clark Hoover, the 31st President, born August 10, 1874, in West Branch, Iowa, was the first President born west of the Mississippi River. Harry S. Truman, the 33rd President, was born May 8, 1884, in Lamar, Mo.; Dwight David Eisenhower, the 34th President, was born October 14, 1890, in Denison, Tex.; Lyndon Baines Johnson, the 36th President, was born August 27, 1908, near Stonewall, Tex; Richard Milhous Nixon, the 37th President, was born Jan. 9, 1913, in Yorba Linda, Calif.; Gerald Rudolph Ford, the 38th President, was born July 14, 1913, in Omaha, Neb.; and William J. Clinton, the 42nd President, was born August 19, 1946, in Hope, Ark; Barack Hussein Obama, the 44th President, was born August 4, 1961, in Honolulu, Hawaii.

BIRTHDAYS

January

7, 1800, Fillmore
9, 1913, Nixon
29, 1843, McKinley
30, 1882, F. D. Roosevelt

February

6, 1911, Reagan
9, 1773, W. H. Harrison
12, 1809, Lincoln
22, 1732, Washington

March

15, 1767, Jackson

16, 1751, Madison
18, 1837, Cleveland
29, 1790, Tyler

April

13, 1743, Jefferson
23, 1791, Buchanan
27, 1822, Grant
28, 1758, Monroe

May

8, 1884, Truman
29, 1917, Kennedy

June

12, 1924, G. Bush

July

4, 1872, Coolidge
6, 1946, G. W. Bush
11, 1767, J. Q. Adams
14, 1913, Ford

August

4, 1961, Obama
10, 1874, Hoover
19, 1946, Clinton
20, 1833, B. Harrison
27, 1908, L. B. Johnson

September

15, 1857 Taft

October

1, 1924, Carter
4, 1822, Hayes
5, 1829, Arthur
14, 1890, Eisenhower
27, 1858, T. Roosevelt
30, 1735, J. Adams

November

2, 1795, Polk
2, 1865, Harding
19, 1831, Garfield
23, 1804, Pierce
24, 1784, Taylor

December

5, 1782, Van Buren
29, 1808, A. Johnson
29, 1856, Wilson

PRESIDENTS' ZODIACAL SIGNS

Aries (March 21–April 19)

Tyler (Mar. 29)
Jefferson (Apr. 13)

Taurus (April 20–May 20)

Buchanan (Apr. 23)
Grant (Apr. 27)
Monroe (Apr. 28)
Truman (May 8)

Gemini (May 21–June 21)

Kennedy (May 29)
G. Bush (June 12)

Cancer (June 22–July 22)

Coolidge (July 4)
G. W. Bush (July 6)
J. Q. Adams (July 11)
Ford (July 14)

Leo (July 23–August 22)

Obama (Aug. 4)
Hoover (Aug. 10)
Clinton (Aug. 19)
B. Harrison (Aug. 20)

Virgo (August 23–September 22)

L. B. Johnson (Aug. 27)
Taft (Sept. 15)

Libra (September 23–October 23)

Carter (Oct. 1)
Hayes (Oct. 4)
Arthur (Oct. 5)
Eisenhower (Oct. 14)

Scorpio (October 24–November 21)

T. Roosevelt (Oct. 27)
J. Adams (Oct. 30)
Polk (Nov. 2)
Harding (Nov. 2)
Garfield (Nov. 19)

Sagittarius (November 22–December 21)

Pierce (Nov. 23)
Taylor (Nov. 24)
Van Buren (Dec. 5)

Capricorn (December 22–January 19)

A. Johnson (Dec. 29)
Wilson (Dec. 29)
Fillmore (Jan. 7)

Nixon (Jan. 9)

Aquarius (January 20–February 18)

McKinley (Jan. 29)
F. D. Roosevelt (Jan. 30)
Reagan (Feb. 6)
W. H. Harrison (Feb. 9)
Lincoln (Feb. 12)

Pisces (February 19–March 20)

Washington (Feb. 22)
Jackson (Mar. 15)
Madison (Mar. 16)
Cleveland (Mar. 18)

BIRTHPLACES

Only 21 of the 50 states have been the birthplaces of Presidents.

Virginia (8): Washington, Jefferson, Madison, Monroe, W. H. Harrison, Tyler, Taylor, Wilson

Ohio (7): Grant, Hayes, Garfield, B. Harrison, McKinley, Taft, Harding

Massachusetts (4): J. Adams, J. Q. Adams, Kennedy, G. Bush

New York (4): Van Buren, Fillmore, T. Roosevelt, F. D. Roosevelt

North Carolina (2): Polk, A. Johnson

Texas (2): Eisenhower, L. B. Johnson

Vermont (2): Arthur, Coolidge

Arkansas (1): Clinton

California (1): Nixon

Connecticut (1): G. W. Bush

Georgia (1): Carter

Hawaii (1): Obama

Illinois (1): Reagan

Iowa (1): Hoover

Kentucky (1): Lincoln

Missouri (1): Truman

Nebraska (1): Ford

New Hampshire (1): Pierce

New Jersey (1): Cleveland

Pennsylvania (1): Buchanan

South Carolina (1): Jackson

ANCESTRY

Washington English
J. Adams English
Jefferson Scottish, English, Welsh
Madison English

623

Monroe   Scottish

J. Q. Adams   English

Jackson   Scotch-Irish

Van Buren   Dutch

W. H. Harrison   English

Tyler   English

Polk   Scotch-Irish

Taylor   English

Fillmore   English

Pierce   English

Buchanan   Scotch-Irish

Lincoln   English

A. Johnson   English, Scottish, Irish

Grant   English, Scottish

Hayes   Scottish, English

Garfield   English, French

Arthur   Scotch-Irish, English

Cleveland   English, Irish

B. Harrison   English

McKinley   Scotch-Irish

T. Roosevelt   Dutch, Scottish, French, English

Taft   English

Wilson   Scotch-Irish, English, Scottish

Harding   English, Scottish, Irish, Dutch

Coolidge   English, Scottish, Welsh

Hoover   Swiss-German, English

F. D. Roosevelt   Dutch, French

Truman   English, Irish, German

Eisenhower   Swiss-German

Kennedy   Irish

L. B. Johnson   English, Scottish, German

Nixon   Scotch-Irish, English, Irish, German

Ford   English

Carter   English, Scotch-Irish

Reagan   Irish, English, Scottish

G. Bush   English

Clinton   English

G. W. Bush   English

Obama   Kenyan, English, Irish, Dutch

PRESIDENTS WHO WERE RELATED

The most closely related Presidents were John Adams and John Quincy Adams, father and son, and George Herbert Walker Bush and George Walker Bush, father and son.

William Henry Harrison was the grandfather of Benjamin Harrison.

James Madison and Zachary Taylor were second cousins.

Franklin Delano Roosevelt, genealogists have shown, was remotely related to eleven former Presidents, five by blood and six by marriage. He was a fifth cousin of Theodore Roosevelt.

George Herbert Walker Bush was credited with 15 provable kinships with other Presidents, including Franklin Pierce. Since his wife, Barbara Pierce Bush, was herself related to Pierce—she was his fourth cousin four times removed—their son, George Walker Bush, had 16 such kinships.

On his mother's side, Obama shared ancestors with Presidents Madison, Truman, L. B. Johnson, Ford, George H. W. Bush, and George W. Bush, as well as Vice President Dick Cheney, Confederate general Robert E. Lee, and British prime ministers Winston Churchill and Harold Macmillan.

NAMES OF PRESIDENTS' PARENTS

Full names of fathers and full maiden names of mothers follow:

Washington

Augustine Washington and Mary Ball

J. Adams

John Adams and Susanna Boylston

Jefferson

Peter Jefferson and Jane Randolph

Madison

James Madison and Nelly Rose Conway

Monroe

Spence Monroe and Elizabeth Jones

J. Q. Adams

John Adams and Abigail Smith

Jackson

Andrew Jackson and Elizabeth Hutchinson

Van Buren

Abraham Van Buren and Maria Hoes (Van Alen)

W. H. Harrison

Benjamin Harrison and Elizabeth Bassett

Tyler

John Tyler and Mary Marot Armistead

Polk

Samuel Polk and Jane Knox

Taylor

Richard Taylor and Sarah Dabney Strother

Fillmore

Nathaniel Fillmore and Phoebe Millard

Pierce

Benjamin Pierce and Anna Kendrick

Buchanan

James Buchanan and Elizabeth Speer

Lincoln

Thomas Lincoln and Nancy Hanks (step-mother: Sarah Bush Johnston)

A. Johnson

Jacob Johnson and Mary McDonough

Grant

Jesse Root Grant and Hannah Simpson

Hayes

Rutherford Hayes and Sophia Birchard

Garfield

Abram Garfield and Eliza Ballou

Arthur

William Arthur and Malvina Stone

Cleveland

Richard Falley Cleveland and Anne Neal

B. Harrison

John Scott Harrison and Elizabeth Ramsey Irwin

McKinley

William McKinley and Nancy Campbell Allison

T. Roosevelt

Theodore Roosevelt and Martha Bulloch

Taft

Alphonso Taft and Louise Maria Torrey

Wilson

Joseph Ruggles Wilson and Jessie Janet Woodrow

Harding

George Tryon Harding and Phoebe Elizabeth Dickerson

Coolidge

John Calvin Coolidge and Victoria Josephine Moor

Hoover

Jesse Clark Hoover and Hulda Randall Minthorn

F. D. Roosevelt

James Roosevelt and Sara Delano

Truman

John Anderson Truman and Martha Ellen Young

Eisenhower

David Jacob Eisenhower and Ida Elizabeth Stover

Kennedy

Joseph Patrick Kennedy and Rose Elizabeth Fitzgerald

L. B. Johnson

Sam Ealy Johnson, Jr., and Rebekah Baines

Nixon

Francis Anthony Nixon and Hannah Milhous

Ford

Leslie Lynch King and Dorothy Ayer Gardner (stepfather: Gerald Rudolff Ford)

Carter

James Earl Carter and Lillian Gordy

Reagan

John Edward Reagan and Nelle Clyde Wilson

G. Bush

Prescott Sheldon Bush and Dorothy Walker

Clinton

William Jefferson Blythe II and Virginia Cassidy (stepfather: Roger Clinton)

G. W. Bush

George Herbert Walker Bush and Barbara Pierce

Obama

Barack Hussein Obama and Stanley Ann Dunham (stepfather: Lolo Soetoro)

OCCUPATIONS OF PRESIDENTS' FATHERS

At various times the fathers of the Presidents were engaged in different occupations—in some cases two or more at the same time.

Washington

Augustine Washington, farmer, planter, iron exporter, sheriff, justice of the peace

J. Adams

John Adams, farmer, shoe- and harness-maker, public official (church deacon, tithingman, tax collector, city councilman)

Jefferson

Peter Jefferson, farmer, planter, soldier, surveyor, mapmaker, magistrate, colonial legislator, justice of the peace

Madison

James Madison, farmer, planter, soldier (commander of King's militia), public official (church vestryman, tax collector, sheriff, city lieutenant, county magistrate), justice of the peace; active in Revolution

Monroe

Spence Monroe, farmer, carpenter, circuit judge; active in Revolution

J. Q. Adams

John Adams, teacher, farmer, lawyer, diplomat, founder of the Republic, framer of the Constitution, Vice President, President of the United States; active in Revolution

Jackson

Andrew Jackson, farmer, linen weaver

Van Buren

Abraham Van Buren, farmer, captain in the militia, innkeeper, tavernkeeper, town clerk

W. H. Harrison

Benjamin Harrison V, planter, legislator (House of Burgesses, Speaker of House of Delegates), governor of Virginia; active in Revolution, signer of Declaration of Independence

Tyler

John Tyler, planter, soldier, lawyer, legislator (Speaker of House of Delegates), state and federal judge, governor of Virginia; active in Revolution

Polk

Samuel Polk, farmer, planter, surveyor, land speculator, businessman, newspaper founder, bank director, magistrate

Taylor

Richard Taylor, farmer, planter, soldier, port collector, justice of the peace, magistrate, state legislator, presidential elector; active in Revolution, delegate to state constitutional convention

Fillmore

Nathaniel Fillmore, tenant farmer, magistrate, justice of the peace

Pierce

Benjamin Pierce, farmer, soldier, innkeeper, tavernkeeper, sheriff, state legislator, presidential elector, member of governor's council, governor of New Hampshire; served nine years in Revolutionary War, delegate to state constitutional convention

Buchanan

James Buchanan, farmer, storekeeper, magistrate, justice of the peace

Lincoln

Thomas Lincoln, farmer, soldier, carpenter, woodcutter, wheelwright, laborer

A. Johnson

Jacob Johnson, soldier, sexton, jack of all trades (porter, constable, miller, horse tender, barbeque caterer, town bell-ringer)

Grant

Jesse Root Grant, leather tanner, factory manager, livery stable owner, merchant, postmaster

Hayes

Rutherford Hayes, farmer, storekeeper, distiller

Garfield

Abram Garfield, farmer, canal constructor

Arthur

William Arthur, teacher, author, editor, Baptist minister

Cleveland

Richard Falley Cleveland, teacher, Congregational minister, district secretary of missionary organization

B. Harrison

John Scott Harrison, farmer, U.S. congressman from Ohio

McKinley

William McKinley, iron manufacturer

T. Roosevelt

Theodore Roosevelt, glass importer, merchant, wealthy philanthropist, active in civic organizations

Taft

Alphonso Taft, lawyer, justice of state supreme court, U.S. ambassador to Austria-Hungary, U.S. Secretary of War, U.S. Attorney General

Wilson

Joseph Ruggles Wilson, teacher, Presbyterian minister, university and seminary professor, church officer

Harding

George Tryon Harding, farmer, soldier, teacher, homeopathic physician, realtor, trader, insurance salesman, newspaper owner

Coolidge

John Calvin Coolidge, farmer, soldier, storekeeper, carpenter, cabinetmaker, buggy maker, mason, blacksmith, notary public, public officer (school superintendent, deputy sheriff, selectman, tax collector, road commissioner), Vermont state legislator and state senator

Hoover

Jesse Clark Hoover, blacksmith, owner of farm implement business

F. D. Roosevelt

James Roosevelt, gentleman farmer, lawyer, financier, coal-mine owner, railroad vice president, church vestryman and senior warden; active in civic organizations

Truman

John Anderson Truman, farmer, livestock dealer, watchman, road overseer

Eisenhower

David Jacob Eisenhower, creamery mechanic, gas company manager, storekeeper, director of employee savings plan

Kennedy

Joseph Patrick Kennedy, bank examiner, investment banker, financier, stock manipulator, chairman of Securities and Exchange Commission, wartime shipyard manager, liquor distributor, real estate executive, movie studio executive, U.S. ambassador to Great Britain

L. B. Johnson

Sam Ealy Johnson, Jr., farmer, barber, teacher, cotton planter, realtor, laborer, Texas state legislator, magistrate, justice of the peace

Nixon

Francis Anthony Nixon, farm worker, streetcar motorman, citrus grower, grocer and gasoline station owner

Ford

Leslie Lynch King, wool trader.

Gerald Rudolff Ford (stepfather), paint manufacturer, county civil defense director, active in civic organizations

Carter

James Earl Carter, farmer, soldier, businessman (farm supply store, agent for peanut oil mill), Georgia state legislator

Reagan

John Edward Reagan, dry goods store clerk, shoe salesman, head of local welfare office

G. Bush

Prescott Sheldon Bush, soldier, investment banker, U.S. Senator from Connecticut, wealthy philanthropist; active in civic organizations

Clinton

William Jefferson Blythe II, soldier, traveling salesman of automobile parts and heavy equipment.

Roger Clinton (stepfather), automobile dealer, manager of auto dealership parts department

G. W. Bush

George Herbert Walker Bush, oil businessman, C.I.A. director, U.S. ambassador to United Nations, Vice President and President of United States

Obama

Barack Obama Sr., economist. Lolo Soetoro (stepfather), geologist

Twenty-four of the forty-three Presidents were sons of farmers or planters.

Thirteen of the fathers served in the armed forces, including two as militia officers.

Thirteen of the fathers served as law officers—judge, magistrate, sheriff, or justice of the peace.

Seven of the fathers held local public office.

Eight of the fathers served in colonial or state legislatures.

Five Presidents were sons of prominent statesmen: William Henry Harrison, whose father was one of the signers of the Declaration of Independence; John Quincy Adams, whose father had been President and Vice President of the United States; William Howard Taft, whose father had been a cabinet officer; George Herbert Walker Bush, whose father was U.S. Senator from Connecticut; and the latter's son, George Walker Bush, whose father had been President and Vice President of the United States. Benjamin Harrison's grandfather was W. H. Harrison, the ninth President.

OCCUPATIONS OF PRESIDENTS' MOTHERS

Until the twentieth century, most mothers of Presidents had as their main occupation the rearing of their children and the running of their homes, as well as assisting their husbands in their own occupations.

The mothers of two Presidents from the early years of the Republic—John Quincy Adams and his successor, Andrew Jackson—form a striking contrast. Adams's mother was Abigail Adams, wife of the statesman and President John Adams, who took over the management of the family farm during her husband's long absences on political business and accompanied him on his diplomatic missions in France and England; she was also the first woman to be in charge of the White House and was an advisor to her husband in political matters. Jackson's mother, Elizabeth Jackson, was a barely literate immigrant from Ireland and a poor widow whose husband died while she was pregnant with the future President; during the Revolutionary War, she volunteered to go aboard a British prisoner-of-war ship to tend American soldiers who were sick with cholera and died of it herself.

Like many poor women during the nineteenth century who needed to earn money, Nancy Hanks Lincoln and Eliza Garfield were seamstresses; Mary Johnson was a weaver. The more middle-class women were often occupied with church work, including Sophia Hayes and Nancy McKinley. Hulda Hoover, a schoolteacher before her marriage and a seamstress after she was widowed, was a Quaker Sunday School teacher and minister. Nelle Reagan, too, taught Sunday School, and headed the missionary society at her Disciples of Christ church. Jessie Wilson was the wife of a Presbyterian minister.

Another schoolteacher before marriage, Louisa Taft, was the first presidential mother to attend college classes, at Mount Holyoke Female Seminary. The first to have a professional career was Phoebe Harding, a midwife and homeopathic physician. Rebekah Baines Johnson, a graduate of Baylor Female College, gave elocution lessons and wrote for local newspapers. Hannah Nixon helped her husband run his grocery store and baked the pies that were sold there. Dorothy Ford worked in real estate, Lillian Carter was a nurse (and, in her late sixties, a Peace Corps volunteer), and Virginia Clinton was a nurse anesthetist.

Sara Delano Roosevelt, Rose Kennedy, and Dorothy Bush were the wealthy matriarchs of political families. Barbara Bush, the mother of George W. Bush, organized campaigns to promote literacy.

Ann Obama Soetoro was the first presidential mother to earn a doctorate and the first to spend most of her adult life abroad (in Indonesia, where she worked as a cultural anthropologist.)

PRESIDENTS' PARENTS WHO WERE NOT AMERICAN-BORN

According to the Constitution, the President must be a native of the United States and cannot be a foreign-born, naturalized citizen. However, the parents of several Presidents were born elsewhere and came to America as settlers or immigrants. Jackson's mother and father were both born in Ireland, as were Buchanan's father (County Donegal) and Arthur's (County Antrim). Jefferson's mother was born in London, and Wilson's in the northern English city of Carlisle. Hoover's mother came from a small town in Ontario, Canada. Van Buren's parents, though native to America, lived in a predominantly Dutch (and Dutch-speaking) community, making him the first President to have had a bilingual upbringing. It is said that when Van Buren returned to Kinderhook, N.Y., after his term in office, he made a point of visiting people he had known as a child and set them at ease by chatting sociably in Dutch.

Barack Obama is the only President to have a parent who was neither a native-born American nor an immigrant. His father was born and raised in Kenya and returned there permanently after studying in the United States.

THREE MINISTERS' SONS ELECTED TO THE PRESIDENCY

The fathers of Chester Alan Arthur, Grover Cleveland, and Woodrow Wilson were ministers. William Arthur was a Baptist clergyman; Richard Falley Cleveland was a Congregational clergyman; and Joseph Ruggles Wilson was a Presbyterian clergyman.

THREE GOVERNORS' SONS ELECTED TO THE PRESIDENCY

The fathers of three Presidents had served their respective states as governors.

William Henry Harrison's father, Benjamin Harrison, served as governor of Virginia from November 30, 1781, to November 30, 1784.

John Tyler's father, John Tyler, also served as governor of Virginia. He served from December 12, 1808, to January 15, 1811.

Franklin Pierce's father, Benjamin Pierce, served two terms as the constitutional executive of New Hampshire, 1827–1828 and 1829–1830.

TWO PRESIDENTS' SONS ELECTED TO THE PRESIDENCY

Two Presidents were themselves the sons of Presidents: John Quincy Adams, the sixth President, whose father was John Adams, the second President; and George Walker Bush, the forty-third President, whose father was George Herbert Walker Bush, the forty-first President. Between the end of John Adams's administration in 1801 and the inauguration of John Quincy Adams in 1825, there was a span of 24 years that encompassed the administrations of three Presidents (Jefferson, Madison, and Monroe), each of whom served two terms. Between the end of George Herbert Walker Bush's administration in 1993 and the inauguration of George Walker Bush in 2001, there was a span of eight years that encompassed the two terms of a single President, Bill Clinton.

NUMBER OF CHILDREN IN THE PRESIDENTS' FAMILIES

Four Presidents—Ford, Franklin D. Roosevelt, Clinton, and Obama—were the only children of their parents' marriages. However, Ford was brought up with three younger half-brothers from his mother's second marriage; Roosevelt had one grown half-brother from his father's first marriage, and Clinton had one younger half-brother from his mother's second marriage. Obama grew up with one younger half-sister from his mother's second marriage. From his father's multiple relationships with women in Kenya, he had one older half-brother, one older half-sister, and four or possibly five younger half-brothers (the paternity of one half-brother is unclear).

Three Presidents came from families of more than ten children: Benjamin Harrison (13), Madison (12), and Buchanan (11).

Four Presidents came from families of ten children: Washington, Jefferson, Polk, and Taft.

Seven came from families of nine children: Taylor, Fillmore, Pierce, Arthur, Cleveland, McKinley, and Kennedy.

Two came from families of eight children: Tyler and Harding.

Two came from families of seven children: William Henry Harrison and Eisenhower.

Two came from families of six children: Grant and George Walker Bush.

Eight Presidents came from families of five children: Monroe, John Quincy Adams, Van Buren, Hayes, Garfield, Lyndon Baines Johnson, Nixon, and George Bush.

Four Presidents came from families of four children: Theodore Roosevelt, Wilson, Ford, and Carter.

Five Presidents came from families of three children: John Adams, Jackson, Lincoln, Hoover, and Truman.

Six Presidents came from families of two children: Andrew Johnson, Coolidge, Franklin Delano Roosevelt, Reagan, Clinton, and Obama.

Summing up, the families of the forty-three Presidents included a total of 263 children (not counting the Kenyan half-siblings of Obama, who were unknown to him during his childhood).

POSITION IN FAMILY AND NUMBER OF BROTHERS AND SISTERS

Each of the following fourteen Presidents was the family's firstborn child and eldest son: John Adams, Madison, Monroe, Polk, Grant, Harding, Coolidge, Truman, Lyndon Baines Johnson, Ford, Carter, Clinton, George Walker Bush, and Obama.

Each of the following twelve Presidents was the second child in the family: John Quincy Adams, Fillmore, Buchanan, Lincoln, and Theodore Roosevelt (each the eldest son);

and Andrew Johnson, Hoover, Franklin Delano Roosevelt, Kennedy, Nixon, Reagan, and George Bush (each the second son).

Six Presidents occupied the position of third child in the family.

Six Presidents occupied the position of fifth child in the family.

One President occupied the position of sixth child in the family.

Four Presidents occupied the position of seventh child in the family.

Seven Presidents occupied the position of youngest child in the family: Jackson, W. H. Harrison, A. Johnson, Hayes, Garfield, F. D. Roosevelt, and Reagan.

Washington was the fourth son, the fifth child in a family of ten children (seven boys and three girls).

John Adams was the first son, the first child in a family of three boys.

Jefferson was the first son, the third child in a family of ten (four boys and six girls).

Madison was the first son, the first child in a family of twelve (eight boys and four girls).

Monroe was the first son, the first child in a family of five (four boys and one girl).

John Quincy Adams was the first son, the second child in a family of five (three boys and two girls).

Jackson was the third son, the third child in a family of three boys.

Van Buren was the second son, the third child in a family of five (four boys and one girl).

William Henry Harrison was the third son, the seventh child in a family of seven (three boys and four girls).

Tyler was the second son, the sixth child in a family of eight (three boys and five girls).

Polk was the first son, the first child in a family of ten (six boys and four girls).

Taylor was the third son, the third child in a family of nine (six boys and three girls).

Fillmore was the first son, the second child in a family of nine (six boys and three girls).

Pierce was the fourth son, the seventh child in a family of nine (five boys and four girls).

Buchanan was the first son, the second child in a family of eleven (five boys and six girls).

Lincoln was the first son, the second child in a family of three (two boys and one girl).

Andrew Johnson was the second son, the second child in a family of two boys.

Grant was the first son, the first child in a family of six (three boys and three girls).

Hayes was the third son, the fifth child in a family of five (three boys and two girls).

Garfield was the third son, the fifth child in a family of five (three boys and two girls).

Arthur was the first son, the fifth child in a family of nine (three boys and six girls).

Cleveland was the third son, the fifth child in a family of nine (four boys and five girls).

Benjamin Harrison was the third son, the fifth child in a family of thirteen (eight boys and five girls).

McKinley was the third son, the seventh child in a family of nine (four boys and five girls).

Theodore Roosevelt was the first son, the second child in a family of four (two boys and two girls).

Taft was the sixth son, the seventh child in a family of ten (eight boys and two girls).

Wilson was the first son, the third child in a family of four (two boys and two girls).

Harding was the first son, the first child in a family of eight (three boys and five girls).

Coolidge was the first son, the first child in a family of two (one boy and one girl).

Hoover was the second son, the second child in a family of three (two boys and one girl).

Franklin Delano Roosevelt was the second son, the second child in a family of two boys.

Truman was the first son, the first child in a family of three (two boys and one girl).

Eisenhower was the third son, the third child in a family of seven boys.

Kennedy was the second son, the second child in a family of nine (four boys and five girls).

Lyndon Baines Johnson was the first son, the first child in a family of five (two boys and three girls).

Nixon was the second son, the second child in a family of five boys.

Ford was the first son, the first child in a family of four boys.

Carter was the first son, the first child in a family of four (two boys and two girls).

Reagan was the second son, the second child in a family of two boys.

George Bush was the second son, the second child in a family of five (four boys and one girl).

Clinton was the first son, the first child in a family of two boys.

George W. Bush was the first son, the first child in a family of six (four boys and two girls).

Obama was the first son, the first child in a family of two (one boy and one girl).

AGE OF PRESIDENTS AT DEATH OF FATHER AND DEATH OF MOTHER

In the following list the name of each President is followed by (1) his age when his father died and (2) his age when his mother died.

Washington   11 years, 49 days; 57 years, 184 days

J. Adams   25 years, 207 days; 61 years, 169 days

Jefferson   14 years, 126 days; 32 years, 352 days

Madison   49 years, 348 days; 77 years, 301 days

Monroe   about 16 years; about 68 years.

J. Q. Adams   59 years, 358 days; 51 years, 109 days

Jackson   born posthumously; about 14 years

Van Buren   34 years, 124 days; 34 years, 73 days

W. H. Harrison   18 years, 74 days; about 19 years

Tyler   22 years, 283 days; about 7 years

Polk   32 years, 3 days; survived by mother

Taylor   41 years, 56 days; 38 years, 19 days

Fillmore   63 years, 80 days; 31 years, 115 days

Pierce   34 years, 129 days; about 34 years

Buchanan   30 years, 49 days; 42 years, 21 days

Lincoln   41 years, 339 days; 9 years, 235 days

A. Johnson   3 years, 6 days; 47 years, 46 days

Grant   51 years, 63 days; 61 years, 14 days

Hayes   born posthumously; 44 years, 26 days

Garfield   1 year, 170 days; survived by mother

Arthur   46 years, 22 days; 39 years, 103 days

Cleveland 16 years, 197 days; 45 years, 123 days

B. Harrison 44 years, 278 days; 16 years, 360 days

McKinley 49 years, 299 days; 54 years, 317 days

T. Roosevelt 19 years, 105 days; 25 years, 110 days

Taft 33 years, 248 days; 50 years, 84 days

Wilson 46 years, 23 days; 31 years, 107 days

Harding survived by father; 44 years, 199 days

Coolidge 53 years, 257 days; 12 years, 253 days

Hoover 6 years, 124 days; 9 years, 196 days

F. D. Roosevelt 18 years, 312 days; 59 years, 220 days

Truman 30 years, 179 days; 63 years, 79 days

Eisenhower 51 years, 147 days; 55 years, 332 days

Kennedy survived by father and mother

L. B. Johnson 29 years, 56 days; 50 years, 16 days

Nixon 43 years, 239 days; 54 years, 264 days

Ford 27 years, 219 days (father); 48 years, 196 days (stepfather); 54 years, 65 days (mother)

Carter 28 years, 296 days; 59 years, 29 days

Reagan 30 years, 101 days; 51 years, 151 days

G. Bush 48 years, 119 days; 68 years, 160 days

Clinton born posthumously (father); 21 years, 8 days (stepfather); 50 years, 140 days (mother)

Obama 21 years, 112 days (father); 25 years, 210 days (stepfather); 34 years, 95 days (mother)

AGE OF PRESIDENTS AT DEATH OF MOTHER

Three Presidents were less than 10 years of age when their mother died.

Seven Presidents were under 21 when their mothers died.

Twenty-three Presidents were over 40 when their mother died.

Eighteen Presidents were over 50 when their mothers died.

Six Presidents were over 60 when their mothers died.

Only one President was over 70 when his mother died.

Only three Presidents were survived by their mothers.

The following is a comparative list:

Tyler 7 years

Hoover 9 years, 196 days

Lincoln 9 years, 235 days

Coolidge 12 years, 253 days

Jackson 14 years

B. Harrison 16 years, 360 days

W. H. Harrison 19 years

T. Roosevelt 25 years, 110 days

Wilson 31 years, 107 days

Fillmore 31 years, 115 days

Jefferson 32 years, 352 days

Pierce 34 years

Van Buren 34 years, 73 days

Obama 34 years, 95 days

Taylor 38 years, 19 days

Arthur 39 years, 103 days

Buchanan 42 years, 21 days

Hayes 44 years, 26 days

Harding 44 years, 199 days

Cleveland 45 years, 123 days

A. Johnson 47 years, 46 days

L. B. Johnson 50 years, 16 days

Taft 50 years, 84 days

Clinton 50 years, 140 days

J. Q. Adams 51 years, 109 days

Reagan 51 years, 151 days

Ford 54 years, 65 days

Nixon 54 years, 264 days

McKinley 54 years, 317 days

Eisenhower 55 years, 332 days

Washington 57 years, 184 days

Carter 59 years, 29 days

F. D. Roosevelt 59 years, 220 days

Grant 61 years, 14 days

J. Adams 61 years, 169 days

Truman 63 years, 79 days

Monroe 68 years

G. Bush   68 years, 160 days
Madison   77 years, 332 days
Polk   survived by mother
Garfield   survived by mother
Kennedy   survived by mother

AGE OF PRESIDENTS AT DEATH OF FATHER

Three Presidents were born after their fathers' deaths: Jackson, Hayes, and Clinton.

Two Presidents were survived by their fathers: Harding and Kennedy.

The following is a comparative list:

Jackson   born after his father's death

Hayes   born after his father's death

Clinton   born after his father's death

Garfield   1 year, 170 days

A. Johnson   3 years, 6 days

Hoover   6 years, 124 days

Washington   11 years, 49 days

Jefferson   14 years, 126 days

Monroe   16 years

Cleveland   16 years, 197 days

W. H. Harrison   18 years, 74 days

F. D. Roosevelt   18 years, 313 days

T. Roosevelt   19 years, 105 days

Clinton   21 years, 8 days (stepfather)

Obama   21 years, 112 days (father)

Tyler   22 years, 283 days

J. Adams   25 years, 207 days

Obama   25 years, 210 days (stepfather)

Ford   27 years, 219 days (father)

Carter   28 years, 296 days

L. B. Johnson   29 years, 56 days

Buchanan   30 years, 49 days

Reagan   30 years, 101 days

Truman   30 years, 179 days

Polk   32 years, 3 days

Taft   33 years, 248 days

Van Buren   34 years, 124 days

Pierce   34 years 129 days

Taylor   41 years, 56 days

Lincoln   41 years, 339 days

Nixon   43 years, 239 days

B. Harrison   44 years, 278 days

Arthur   46 years, 22 days

Wilson   46 years, 23 days

G. Bush   48 years, 119 days
Ford   48 years, 196 days (stepfather)
McKinley   49 years, 299 days
Madison   49 years, 348 days
Grant   51 years, 63 days
Eisenhower   51 years, 147 days
Coolidge   53 years, 257 days
J. Q. Adams   59 years, 358 days
Fillmore   63 years, 80 days
Harding   survived by father
Kennedy   survived by father

PRESIDENTS SURVIVED BY PARENTS

The only President survived by both parents was Kennedy.

Two Presidents—Harding and Kennedy—were survived by their fathers.

Three Presidents—Polk, Garfield, and Kennedy—were survived by their mothers.

PARENTS OF PRESIDENTS ALIVE AT INAUGURATION

Both parents alive at inauguration

Both parents of three Presidents were living when their sons took office:

Ulysses Simpson Grant was inaugurated on March 4, 1869; his father, Jesse Root Grant, who attended the ceremony, died on June 29, 1873; his mother, Hannah Simpson Grant, who did not attend, died on May 11, 1883.

John Fitzgerald Kennedy was inaugurated on January 20, 1961; his father, Joseph Patrick Kennedy, and his mother, Rose Fitzgerald Kennedy, both attended the ceremony. President Kennedy was assassinated on November 23, 1963; his father died on November 18, 1969; his mother died on January 22, 1995.

George Walker Bush was inaugurated on January 20, 2001; his father, George Herbert Walker Bush, and his mother, Barbara Pierce Bush, both attended the ceremony.

Father alive at inauguration

Four fathers, in addition to those of Grant, Kennedy, and George W. Bush, lived to see their sons take office as President:

John Quincy Adams was inaugurated on March 4, 1825; his father, John Adams, died on July 4, 1826.

Millard Fillmore took office on July 10, 1850; his father, Nathaniel Fillmore, died on May 28, 1863.

Warren Gamaliel Harding was inaugurated on March 4, 1921; his father, George Tryon Harding, died on November 19, 1928.

Calvin Coolidge took office on August 3, 1923; his father, John Calvin Coolidge, died on March 18, 1926.

Mother alive at inauguration

Eleven mothers, in addition to those of Grant, Kennedy, and George Herbert Walker Bush, lived to see their sons take office as President:

George Washington was inaugurated on April 30, 1789; his mother, Mary Ball Washington, died on August 25, 1789.

John Adams was inaugurated on March 4, 1797; his mother, Susanna Boylston Adams, died on April 17, 1797.

James Madison was inaugurated on March 4, 1809; his mother, Nelly Rose Conway Madison, died on February 11, 1829.

James Knox Polk was inaugurated on March 4, 1845; his mother Jane Knox Polk, died on January 11, 1852.

James Abram Garfield was inaugurated on March 4, 1881; his mother, Eliza Ballou Garfield, died on January 21, 1888.

William McKinley was inaugurated on March 4, 1897; his mother, Nancy Allison McKinley, died on December 12, 1897.

Franklin Delano Roosevelt was inaugurated on March 4, 1933; his mother, Sara Delano Roosevelt, died on September 7, 1941.

Harry S. Truman took office on April 12, 1945; his mother, Martha Ellen Young Truman, died on July 26, 1947.

Jimmy Carter was inaugurated on January 20, 1977; his mother Lillian Gordy Carter, died on October 30, 1983.

George Herbert Walker Bush was inaugurated on January 20, 1989; his mother, Dorothy Walker Bush, died on November 19, 1992.

William Jefferson Clinton was inaugurated on January 20, 1993; his mother, Virginia Kelley, died on January 6, 1994.

PRESIDENTS' FATHERS WHO REMARRIED

The fathers of twelve Presidents remarried. Six of them remarried after the birth of their President-sons.

Millard Fillmore was 31 years and 114 days old when his mother, Phoebe Millard Fillmore, died on May 2, 1831. His father married Eunice Love on May 2, 1834.

Abraham Lincoln was 9 years and 235 days old when his mother, Nancy Hanks Lincoln, died on October 5, 1818. His father married Sarah Bush Johnston on December 2, 1819.

Warren Gamaliel Harding was 44 years and 198 days old when his mother, Phoebe Elizabeth Dickerson Harding, died on May 20, 1910. His father married Eudora Adella Kelley Luvisi on November 23, 1911; was divorced from her in 1916; and married Mary Alice Severns on August 11, 1921.

Calvin Coolidge was 12 years and 253 days old when his mother, Victoria Josephine Moor Coolidge, died on March 14, 1885. His father married Caroline A. Brown on September 9, 1891.

Gerald Rudolph Ford was 2 years old when his father, Leslie Lynch King, and his mother, Dorothy Ayer Gardner King were divorced, in 1915. His father married Margaret Atwood on January 5, 1919. Ford remained with his mother, who married Gerald Rudolff Ford on February 1, 1916.

Barack Hussein Obama, Jr., was 3 years old when his mother, Stanley Ann Dunham Obama, divorced his father, Barack Hussein Obama, Sr. His father, who was still married to his original wife in Kenya, then contracted another marriage with Ruth Nidesand, who afterwards divorced him.

Six Presidents were the sons of their fathers' second marriages. They were Washington, Pierce, Benjamin Harrison, Taft, Franklin Delano Roosevelt, and Obama.

One President, Clinton, was the son of his father's fifth marriage.

PRESIDENTS' MOTHERS WHO REMARRIED

The mothers of six Presidents remarried. Five of them remarried after the birth of their President-sons.

John Adams was 25 years and 207 days old when his father, John Adams, died on May 25, 1761. His mother, Susanna Boylston Adams, married John Hall in 1766.

Andrew Johnson was 3 years and 6 days old when his father, Jacob Johnson, died on Jan. 4, 1812. His mother, Mary McDonough Johnson, was remarried to Turner Dougherty.

Gerald Rudolph Ford was about 2 years old when his mother, Dorothy Gardner King, divorced his father, Leslie Lynch King, in 1915. On Feb. 1, 1916, she married Gerald Rudolff Ford, who adopted her child.

William Jefferson Clinton was not yet born when his father, William Jefferson Blythe II, died in 1946. His mother, Virginia Cassidy Clinton, was married on June 19, 1950, to Roger Clinton, whom she divorced in 1962 and remarried a short while later. After his death in 1967, she was married to George Jefferson Dwire from 1969 until his death in 1974. She then married Richard Kelley, who survived her.

Barack Hussein Obama was about 3 years old when his mother, Stanley Ann Dunham Obama, divorced his father, Barack Hussein Obama, Sr. His mother married Lolo Soetoro in 1967 and divorced him in 1980.

One President, Martin Van Buren, was the son of his mother's second marriage.

WIVES OF THE PRESIDENTS— DATES OF BIRTH, MARRIAGE, AND DEATH

Washington

Martha Dandridge, b. June 21, 1731; m. Custis 1749; m. Washington Jan. 6, 1759; d. May 22, 1802

J. Adams

Abigail Smith, b. Nov. 11, 1744; m. Oct. 25, 1764; d. Oct. 28, 181

Jefferson

Martha Wayles, b. Oct. 19, 1748; m. Skelton Nov. 20, 1766 (d.); m. Jefferson Jan. 1, 1772; d. Sept. 6, 1782

Madison

Dolley Dandridge Payne, b. May 20, 1768; m. Todd Jan. 7, 1790 (d.); m. Madison Sept. 15, 1794; d. July 12, 1849

Monroe

Elizabeth Kortright, b. June 30, 1768; m. Feb. 16, 1786; d. Sept. 23, 1830

J. Q. Adams

Louisa Catherine Johnson, b. Feb. 12, 1775; m. July 26, 1797; d. May 14, 1852

Jackson

Rachel Donelson, b. June 15 (?), 1767; m. Robards Mar. 1, 1785 (div.); m. Jackson Aug. 1791 and Jan. 17, 1794; d. Dec. 22, 1828

Van Buren

Hannah Hoes, b. Mar. 8, 1783; m. Feb. 21, 1807; d. Feb. 5, 1819

W. H. Harrison

Anna Tuthill Symmes, b. July 25, 1775; m. Nov. 25, 1795; d. Feb. 25, 1864

Tyler

Letitia Christian, b. Nov. 12, 1790; m. Mar. 29, 1813; d. Sept. 10, 1842

Julia Gardiner, b. May 4, 1820; m. June 26, 1844; d. July 10, 1889

Polk

Sarah Childress, b. Sept. 4, 1803; m. Jan. 1, 1824; d. Aug. 14, 1891

Taylor

Margaret Mackall Smith, b. Sept. 21, 1788, m. June 21, 1810; d. Aug. 18, 1852

Fillmore

Abigail Powers, b. Mar. 13, 1798; m. Feb. 5, 1826; d. Mar. 30, 1853

Caroline Carmichael, b. Oct. 21, 1813; m. McIntosh Nov. 1832 (d.); m. Fillmore Feb. 10, 1858, d. Aug. 11, 1881

Pierce

Jane Means Appleton, b. Mar. 12, 1806; m. Nov. 10, 1834; d. Dec. 2, 1863

Lincoln

Mary Todd, b. Dec. 13, 1818; m. Nov. 4, 1842; d. July 16, 1882

A. Johnson

Eliza McCardle, b. Oct. 4, 1810; m. May 17, 1827; d. Jan. 15, 1876

Grant

Julia Boggs Dent, b. Jan. 26, 1826; m. Aug. 22, 1848; d. Dec. 14, 1902

Hayes

Lucy Ware Webb, b. Aug. 28, 1831; m. Dec. 30, 1852; d. June 25, 1889

Garfield

Lucretia Rudolph, b. Apr. 19, 1832; m. Nov. 11, 1858; d. Mar. 14, 1918

Arthur

Ellen Lewis Herndon, b. Aug. 30, 1837; m. Oct. 25, 1859; d. Jan. 12, 1880

Cleveland

Frances Folsom, b. July 21, 1864; m. Cleveland June 2, 1886; m. Preston Feb. 10, 1913; d. Oct. 29, 1947

B. Harrison

Caroline Lavinia Scott, b. Oct. 1, 1832; m. Oct. 20, 1853; d. Oct. 25, 1892

Mary Scott Lord, b. Apr. 30, 1858; m. Dimmick July 4, 1856 (d.); m. Harrison Apr. 6, 1896; d. Jan. 5, 1948

McKinley

Ida Saxton, b. June 8, 1847; m. Jan. 25, 1871; d. May 26, 1907

T. Roosevelt

Alice Hathaway Lee, b. July 29, 1861; m. Oct. 27, 1880; d. Feb. 14, 1884

Edith Kermit Carow, b. Aug. 6, 1861; m. Dec. 2, 1886; d. Sept. 30, 1948

Taft

Helen Herron, b. Jan. 2, 1861; m. June 19, 1886; d. May 22, 1943

Wilson

Ellen Louise Axson, b. May 15, 1860; m. June 24, 1885; d. Aug. 6, 1914

Edith Bolling, b. Oct. 15, 1872; m. Galt Apr. 30, 1896; m. Wilson Dec. 18, 1915; d. Dec. 28, 1961

Harding

Florence Kling, b. Aug. 15, 1860; m. DeWolfe 1880; m. Harding July 8, 1891; d. Nov. 21, 1924

Coolidge

Grace Anna Goodhue, b. Jan. 3, 1879; m. Oct. 4, 1905; d. July 8, 1957

Hoover

Lou Henry, b. Mar. 29, 1874; m. Feb. 10, 1899; d. Jan. 7, 1944

F. D. Roosevelt

(Anna) Eleanor Roosevelt, b. Oct. 11, 1884; m. Mar. 17, 1905; died Nov. 7, 1962

Truman

Elizabeth Virginia ("Bess") Wallace, b. Feb. 13, 1885; m. June 28, 1919; d. Oct. 18, 1982

Eisenhower

Mamie Geneva Doud, b. Nov. 14, 1896; m. July 1, 1916; d. Nov. 1, 1979

Kennedy

Jacqueline Lee Bouvier, b. July 28, 1929; m. Kennedy Sept. 12, 1953; m. Onassis Oct. 20, 1968; d. May 19, 1994

L. B. Johnson

Claudia Alta ("Lady Bird") Taylor, b. Dec. 22, 1912; m. Nov. 17, 1934

Nixon

Thelma Catherine ("Pat") Ryan, b. Mar. 16, 1912; m. June 21, 1940; d. June 23, 1993

Ford

Elizabeth Anne ("Betty") Bloomer, b. Apr. 18, 1918; m. Warren 1942 (div.); m. Ford Oct. 15, 1948

Carter

Rosalynn Smith, b. Aug. 18, 1927; m. July 7, 1946

Reagan

Jane Wyman (Sarah Jane Mayfield, Sarah Jane Fulks), b. Jan. 5, 1917; m. Futterman June 29, 1937 (div.); m. Reagan Jan. 24, 1940 (div.); m. Karger 1952 (div.); m. Karger 1961 (div.); d. Sept. 10, 2007

Nancy Davis (Anne Frances Robbins), b. July 6, 1921; m. Mar. 4, 1952

G. Bush

Barbara Pierce, b. June 8, 1925; m. Jan. 6, 1945

Clinton

Hillary Rodham, b. Oct. 25, 1947; m. Oct. 11, 1975

G. W. Bush

Laura Welch. b. Nov. 4, 1946, m. Nov. 5, 1977

Obama

Michelle LaVaughn Robinson, b. Jan. 17, 1964, m. Aug. 3, 1992

BIRTHPLACES OF PRESIDENTS' WIVES

Martha Washington   New Kent County, Va.

Abigail Adams   Weymouth, Mass.

Martha Jefferson   Charles City County, Va.

Dolley Madison   Guilford County, N.C.

Elizabeth Monroe   New York, N.Y.

Louisa Adams   London, England

Rachel Jackson   Halifax County, Va.

Hannah Van Buren   Kinderhook, N.Y.

Anna Harrison   Morristown, N.J.

Letitia Tyler   New Kent County, Va.

Julia Tyler   Gardiners Island, N.Y.

Sarah Polk   Murfreesboro, Tenn.

Margaret Taylor   Calvert County, Md.

Abigail Fillmore   Stillwater, N.Y.

Carolina Fillmore   Morristown, N.J.

Jane Pierce   Hampton, N.H.

Mary Lincoln   Lexington, Ky.

Eliza Johnson   Leesburg, Tenn.

Julia Grant   St. Louis, Mo.

Lucy Hayes   Chillicothe, Ohio

Lucretia Garfield   Hiram, Ohio

Ellen Arthur   Culpeper Court House, Va.

Frances Cleveland   Folsomville, N.Y.

Caroline Harrison   Oxford, Ohio

Mary Harrison   Honesdale, Pa.

Ida McKinley   Canton, Ohio

Alice Roosevelt   Chestnut Hill, Mass.

Edith Roosevelt   Norwich, Conn.

Helen Taft   Cincinnati, Ohio

Ellen Wilson   Savannah, Ga.

Edith Wilson   Wytheville, Va.

Florence Harding   Marion, Ohio

Grace Coolidge   Burlington, Vt.

Lou Hoover   Waterloo, Iowa

Eleanor Roosevelt   New York, N.Y.

Bess Truman   Independence, Mo.

Mamie Eisenhower   Boone, Iowa

Jacqueline Kennedy   Southampton, N.Y.

Lady Bird Johnson   Karnack, Tex.

Pat Nixon   Ely, Nev.

Betty Ford   Chicago, Ill.

Rosalynn Carter   Botsford, Ga.

Jane (Wyman) Reagan   St. Joseph, Mo.

Nancy Reagan   New York, N.Y.

Barbara Bush   New York, N.Y.

Hillary Clinton   Park Ridge, Ill.

Laura Bush   Midland, Tex.

Michelle Obama   Chicago, Ill.

BIRTHPLACES OF PRESIDENTS' WIVES (ARRANGED BY LOCATION)

New York (9)

Elizabeth Monroe, Hannah Van Buren, Julia Tyler, Abigail Fillmore, Frances Cleveland, Eleanor Roosevelt, Jacqueline Kennedy, Nancy Reagan, Barbara Bush

Ohio (6)

Lucy Hayes, Lucretia Garfield, Caroline Harrison, Ida McKinley, Helen Taft, Florence Harding

Virginia (6)

Martha Washington, Martha Jefferson, Rachel Jackson, Letitia Tyler, Ellen Arthur, Edith Wilson

Missouri (3)

Julia Grant, Bess Truman, Jane (Wyman) Reagan

Georgia (2)

Ellen Wilson, Rosalynn Carter

Illinois (3)

Betty Ford, Hillary Clinton, Michelle Obama

Iowa (2)

Lou Hoover, Mamie Eisenhower

Massachusetts (2)

Abigail Adams, Alice Roosevelt

New Jersey (2)

Anna Harrison, Caroline Fillmore

Tennessee (2)

Sarah Polk, Eliza Johnson

Texas (2)

Lady Bird Johnson, Laura Bush

Connecticut (1)

Edith Roosevelt

Kentucky (1)

Mary Lincoln

Maryland (1)

Margaret Taylor

Nevada (1)

Pat Nixon

New Hampshire (1)

Jane Pierce

North Carolina (1)

Dolley Madison

Pennsylvania (1)

Mary Harrison

Vermont (1)

Grace Coolidge

London, England (1)

Louisa Adams

NAMES OF WIVES' PARENTS

Full name of father and maiden name of mother are given below. Further data may be found under the names of the Presidents' wives in Part I.

Martha Washington

John Dandridge and Frances Jones

Abigail Adams

William Smith and Elizabeth Quincy

Martha Jefferson

John Wayles and Martha Eppes

Dolley Madison

John Payne and Mary Coles

Elizabeth Monroe

Lawrence Kortright and Hannah Aspinwall

Louisa Adams

Joshua Johnson and Catherine Nuth

Rachel Jackson

John Donelson and Rachel Stockley

Hannah Van Buren

John Hoes and Maria Quackenboss

Anna Harrison

John Cleves Symmes and Anna Tuthill

Letitia Tyler

Robert Christian and Mary Brown

Julia Tyler

David Gardiner and Juliana McLachlan

Sarah Polk

Joel Childress and Elizabeth Whitsitt

Margaret Taylor

Walter Smith and Ann Mackall

Abigail Fillmore

Lemuel Powers and Abigail Newland

Caroline Fillmore

Charles Carmichael and Temperance Blachley

Jane Pierce

Jesse Appleton and Elizabeth Means

Mary Lincoln

Robert Smith Todd and Eliza Ann Parker

Eliza Johnson

John McCardle and Sarah Phillips

Julia Grant

Frederick Dent and Ellen Wrenshall

Lucy Hayes

James Webb and Maria Cook

Lucretia Garfield

Zebulon Rudolph and Arabella Green Mason

Ellen Arthur

William Lewis Herndon and Frances Elizabeth Hansbrough

638

Frances Cleveland

Oscar Folsom and Emma Cornelia Harmon

Caroline Harrison

John Witherspoon Scott and Mary Potts Neal

Mary Harrison

Russell Farnham Lord and Elizabeth Scott

Ida McKinley

James Asbury Saxton and Catherine Dewalt

Alice Roosevelt

George Cabot Lee and Caroline Haskell

Edith Roosevelt

Charles Carow and Gertrude Elizabeth Tyler

Helen Taft

John Williamson Herron and Harriet Collins

Ellen Wilson

Samuel Edward Axson and Margaret Hoyt

Edith Wilson

William Holcombe Bolling and Sallie White

Florence Harding

Amos H. Kling and Louisa M. Bouton

Grace Coolidge

Andrew Issachar Goodhue and Lemira Barrett

Lou Hoover

Charles Delano Henry and Florence Ida Weed

Eleanor Roosevelt

Elliott Roosevelt and Anna Livingston Hall

Bess Truman

David Willock Wallace and Madge Gates

Mamie Eisenhower

John Sheldon Doud and Elivera Carlson

Jacqueline Kennedy

John Vernou Bouvier III and Janet Norton Lee

Lady Bird Johnson

Thomas Jefferson Taylor and Minnie Lee Pattillo

Pat Nixon

William Ryan and Katharine Halberstadt Bender

Betty Ford

William Stephenson Bloomer and Hortense Neahr

Rosalynn Carter

Wilburn Edgar Smith and Frances Allethea ("Allie") Murray

Jane (Wyman) Reagan

Manning Jefferies Mayfield and Gladys Hope Christian (Richard D. Fulks and Emme Reise, adoptive parents)

Nancy Reagan

Kenneth Robbins and Dee Dee (Edith) Luckett (Dr. Loyal Davis, stepfather)

Barbara Bush

Marvin Pierce and Pauline Robinson

Hillary Rodham Clinton

Hugh Rodham and Dorothy Howell

Laura Bush

Harold Bruce Welch and Jenna Louise Hawkins

Michelle Obama

Fraser Robinson III and Marian Shields

OCCUPATIONS OF WIVES' FATHERS

The names of wives whose fathers' occupations are not definitely known are omitted.

Martha Washington

Colonel Dandridge, planter

Abigail Adams

William Smith, Congregational minister

Martha Jefferson

John Wayles, planter, lawyer

Dolley Madison

John Payne, farmer, planter

Elizabeth Monroe

Captain Lawrence Kortright, former British army officer

Louisa Adams
Joshua Johnson, U.S. consul

Rachel Jackson
Colonel John Donelson, surveyor

Anna Harrison
John Cleves Symmes, judge

Letitia Tyler
Colonel Robert Christian, planter

Julia Tyler
David Gardiner, senator

Sarah Polk
Captain Joel Childress, planter

Margaret Taylor
Walter Smith, planter

Abigail Fillmore
Lemuel Powers, Baptist minister

Jane Pierce
Jesse Appleton, Congregational minister

Mary Lincoln
Robert Smith Todd, banker

Julia Grant
Frederick Dent, judge

Lucy Hayes
Dr. James Webb, physician

Lucretia Garfield
Zebulon Rudolph, farmer

Ellen Arthur
Captain William Lewis Herndon, U.S. naval officer

Frances Cleveland
Oscar Folsom, lawyer

Caroline Harrison
John Witherspoon Scott, Presbyterian minister

Mary Harrison
Russell Farnham Lord, canal engineer

Ida McKinley
James Asbury Saxton, banker

Helen Taft
John Williamson Herron, judge

Ellen Wilson
Samuel Edward Axson, Presbyterian minister

Edith Wilson
William Holcombe Bolling, judge

Florence Harding
Amos H. Kling, banker

Lou Hoover
Charles Delano Henry, banker

Eleanor Roosevelt
Elliott Roosevelt, coal mining interests

Bess Truman
David Willock Wallace, farmer

Mamie Eisenhower
John Sheldon Doud, meat packer

Jacqueline Kennedy
John Vernou Bouvier, stockbroker

Lady Bird Johnson
Thomas Jefferson Taylor, planter, merchant

Pat Nixon
William Ryan, miner

Betty Ford
William Stephenson Bloomer, industrial supplies salesman

Rosalynn Carter
Wilburn Edgar Smith, mechanic, school-bus driver

Jane (Wyman) Reagan
R. D. Fulks, mayor, civic official

Nancy Reagan
Kenneth Robbins, auto salesman (father); Loyal Davis, neurosurgeon (stepfather)

Barbara Bush
Marvin Pierce, magazine publisher

Hillary Rodham Clinton
Hugh Rodham, drapery business owner

Laura Bush

Harold Bruce Welch, real estate developer, credit officer

Michelle Obama

Fraser Robinson III, city water plant pump operator, Democratic precinct captain

FIVE PRESIDENTS MARRIED MINISTERS' DAUGHTERS

Five Presidents married the daughters of ministers. They were John Adams, Millard Fillmore, Franklin Pierce, Benjamin Harrison, and Woodrow Wilson.

John Adams married Abigail Smith, daughter of William Smith, a Congregational minister who was ordained on November 4, 1729, at Norwich, Conn.

Millard Fillmore married Abigail Powers, daughter of Lemuel Powers, a Baptist clergyman.

Franklin Pierce married Jane Means Appleton, daughter of Jesse Appleton, a Congregational minister.

Benjamin Harrison married Caroline Scott, daughter of John Witherspoon Scott, ordained a clergyman in 1830 in the Presbyterian church. Scott was also a professor and served at Washington College, Miami University, and Oxford Female College.

Woodrow Wilson married Ellen Louise Axson, daughter of Samuel Edward Axson, a Presbyterian minister.

EDUCATION OF THE PRESIDENTS' WIVES

It is difficult to appraise the education of the wives of the Presidents as most of the earlier First Ladies had no formal schooling. Since the requirements and the standards of the institutions they did attend varied considerably, and since the curricula are not known in most instances, it is possible to give only a brief summary.

The first wife of a President who is known to have regularly attended school was Anna Harrison (the wife of William Henry Harrison); she attended the Clinton Academy at Easthampton, Long Island, N.Y., and Mrs. Graham's Boarding School for Young Ladies at No. 1 Broadway, New York City.

Julia Tyler went to Chegary Institute, New York City.

Sarah Polk attended the Moravian Female Academy, Salem, N.C.

Mary Lincoln studied at the academy conducted by John Ward, and at Mme. Mentelle's school, Lexington, Ky., where she studied French.

Julia Grant attended a boarding school.

Lucretia Garfield was a pupil at Geauga Seminary and at Hiram College, Hiram, Ohio.

Caroline Harrison, the first wife of Benjamin Harrison, attended the Oxford Female Seminary.

Mary Harrison, the second wife of Benjamin Harrison, attended Mrs. Moffat's School in Princeton, N.J., and Elmira College, Elmira, N.Y.

Ida McKinley went to Brook Hall Seminary, Media, Pa.

Edith Roosevelt attended Miss Comstock's private school in New York City.

Helen Taft went to Miss Nourse's private school in Cincinnati, Ohio, and Miami University in Oxford, Ohio; she subsequently studied music in Cincinnati.

Ellen Wilson went to private schools and the Female Seminary in Rome, Ga.; she also took courses at the Art Students' League, New York City.

Edith Bolling Wilson attended Martha Washington College, Abington, Va., and Powell's School, Richmond, Va.

Florence Harding took courses at the Cincinnati Conservatory of Music.

Eleanor Roosevelt was tutored as a child and attended the Allenwood School in London, England, between the ages of 15 and 18.

Bess Truman graduated from high school at Independence, Mo., and attended the Barstow School for Girls, Kansas City, Mo.

The first wife of a President to graduate from college was Lucy Hayes, who graduated from Wesleyan Female Seminary in Cincinnati, Ohio, in 1850.

Frances Cleveland graduated from Wells College, Aurora, N.Y., in June 1885, receiving a B.A. degree.

Grace Coolidge graduated from the University of Vermont in 1902, receiving a bachelor of philosophy degree.

Lou Hoover received a B.A. degree in 1898 from Leland Stanford University, Stanford, Calif.

Jacqueline Kennedy attended the Holton-Arms School, Washington, D.C., 1942–1944, and Miss Porter's School, Farmington, Conn., 1944–1947. She entered Vassar College in 1947, spent her junior year at the Sorbonne in Paris, and received a B.A. degree from George Washington University in 1951.

Lady Bird Johnson graduated from Marshall High School and St. Mary's Episcopal School for Girls. She received a B.A. degree in 1933 and a journalism degree in 1934 from the University of Texas.

Pat Nixon graduated from the University of Southern California in 1937.

Betty Ford graduated from Central High School, Grand Rapids, Mich. She attended summer sessions of the Bennington School of the Dance in 1936 and 1937.

Rosalynn Carter was valedictorian of her Plains, Ga., high school class. She completed a two-year secretarial course at Georgia Southwestern College and later studied accounting and Spanish.

Nancy Reagan graduated from Girls' Latin School, Chicago, and received a B.A. degree in Drama from Smith College in 1943.

Barbara Bush graduated from Ashley Hall, a preparatory school in Charleston, S.C., and dropped out of Smith College in her sophomore year when she married George Bush.

Hillary Rodham Clinton graduated in 1969 from Wellesley College, Wellesley, Mass., where she was the college's first student commencement speaker. She received a law degree from Yale Law School, New Haven, Conn., in 1973.

Laura Bush attended public schools in Midland, Tex. She earned a bachelor's degree in education from Southern Methodist University, Dallas, Tex., in 1968, and an M.L.S. from the University of Texas, Austin, in 1973.

Michelle Obama attended public schools in Chicago, Ill. She earned a bachelor's degree in sociology from Princeton University in 1985 and a J.D. from Harvard Law School in 1988.

OCCUPATIONS AND ACCOMPLISHMENTS OF WIVES

In the eighteenth and early nineteenth centuries, most of the Presidents' wives were occupied full-time with running their homes and rearing their children. Many of them also helped run their family farms and other businesses. Once their husbands were in office, most of them also took on the social duties of the White House.

The list of presidential wives who carried on careers begins in 1845 with Sarah Polk, who assisted her husband as his personal secretary and political adviser. Abigail Fillmore and Lucretia Garfield were schoolteachers; so was Laura Bush, who also worked as a school librarian. Grace Coolidge taught at a school for deaf children.

Lady Bird Johnson, the wife of Lyndon Baines Johnson, bought a small Austin radio station in 1943 with a legacy from her mother and built it into a major broadcasting concern. Betty Ford was a model and a dancer with the Martha Graham troupe; later she worked as a fashion coordinator for a department store in Grand Rapids, organized her own dance troupe, and taught dance to handicapped people. Nancy Reagan acted on Broadway and in films. Pat Nixon worked her way through college as a salesclerk and movie extra, and subsequently taught commercial courses in high school. During World War II, she was employed by the Office of Price Administration in San Francisco as a price and economic analyst. Jacqueline Kennedy conducted an "inquiring photographer" column for a Washington newspaper before her marriage; in later years she worked as a book editor and took on various cultural projects, such as the exhibitions of costumes at the Metropolitan Museum of Art and the preservation and maintenance of Grand Central Terminal and other historic buildings

Caroline Harrison, Ellen Wilson, and Jacqueline Kennedy studied painting. Polly Jefferson owned and presumably played a pianoforte, Caroline Harrison played the piano, and Ellen Arthur, who had a fine contralto voice, sang in a church choir.

Several wives worked in their husbands' businesses. Edith Wilson took over the management of her husband's jewelry store after his death. Florence Harding was the circulation manager of the *Daily Star* in Marion, Ohio. Lou Hoover, a geologist who learned five languages, received Belgium's Cross of Chevalier for her work in her husband's relief efforts during World War I; she was later active in the scouting movement, serving for a time as president of the Girls Scouts of America. Rosalynn Carter did the bookkeeping at the Carter peanut warehouse. Bess Truman served as her husband's secretary while he was in the Senate, and Lady Bird Johnson managed Lyndon Johnson's congressional office after he joined the Navy in World War II, and again in 1955, when he was recovering from a heart attack. She also helped run the LBJ Ranch.

When Lucy Hayes was first lady, she did much charitable work, visiting prisons, reform schools, and asylums. She strongly supported the temperance movement. Edith Roosevelt, the second wife of Theodore Roosevelt, was active in the Needlework Guild, which supplied clothing to the poor. Ellen Wilson was an exhibiting painter who also campaigned for better housing in the slums of the capital, and Caroline Harrison, wife of Benjamin Harrison, raised money for Johns Hopkins University, on condition that the medical school admit women.

The first active and independent First Lady was Eleanor Roosevelt, wife of Franklin Delano Roosevelt. She traveled widely, spoke, gave press conferences, and wrote a syndicated newspaper column. Though at first a controversial figure, she ultimately won international renown. In 1945, 1947–1952, and 1961, she served as a U.S. delegate to the United Nations, and from 1946 to 1951, she headed the UN Commission on Human Rights.

Hillary Rodham Clinton, wife of Bill Clinton, was the first First Lady to graduate from law school. She was active as an advocate of children's rights and chaired the national Children's Defense Committee in 1973 and 1974. She served as a counsel to the House Judiciary Committee's subcommittee on Nixon's impeachment, and went on to have a distinguished career as an attorney, joining the Rose Law Firm in Little Rock, Ark., and earning more money than her husband for all but one year of their marriage before he became President. Toward the end of her husband's second term, she was elected to the U.S. Senate from New York State. She served in the Senate for eight years. In the 2008 presidential race, she came close to winning the nomination of the Democratic Party. She was then named to the post of Secretary of State by President-elect Obama.

Michelle Obama was the second First Lady to graduate from law school. Before her husband's election, she was an attorney for the University of Chicago Hospitals.

In the White House, Jacqueline Kennedy was primarily identified with cultural programs, Lady Bird Johnson with highway and civic beautification efforts, Pat Nixon with social voluntarism, Betty Ford with aid to handicapped children, Rosalynn Carter with programs to aid the mentally ill, and Nancy Reagan with anti-drug-use campaigns. Barbara Bush and Laura Bush campaigned for the eradication of illiteracy. Both Nancy Reagan and Jacqueline Kennedy were trendsetting devotees of high fashion. Rosalynn Carter was the first President's wife to visit foreign nations alone, as an official representative of the administration. Hillary Rodham Clinton was the first President's wife to chair a presidential commission: the Task Force on Health Reform. Other wives accompanied their husbands on state visits and represented them at ceremonial and political functions within the United States. At least one wife did considerably more: During Woodrow Wilson's last term, after he had suffered a paralytic stroke, Edith Wilson, his second wife, performed many of the duties of the presidency. Hillary Rodham Clinton was her husband's political partner, had her own office in the West Wing of the White House, and wielded enormous influence in the Clinton administration.

Presidents' wives who have written books include Helen Taft, Edith Wilson, Eleanor Roosevelt, Lady Bird Johnson, Rosalynn Carter, Barbara Bush, Hillary Clinton, and Laura Bush. The letters Abigail Adams exchanged with her husband, John Adams, though not written for publication, have appeared in several editions. Lou Hoover was co-translator with her husband of a classic Renaissance text on metallurgy.

PRESIDENTS' MARRIAGES

Noted under the name of each President in the following list are:

(1) his age at marriage;

(2) his wife's age at marriage; and
(3) the duration of the marriage.

Washington

26 years, 318 days
27 years, 199 days
40 years, 329 days

J. Adams

28 years, 360 days
19 years, 348 days
54 years, 3 days

Jefferson

28 years, 263 days
23 years, 74 days
10 years, 248 days

Madison

43 years, 183 days
26 years, 118 days
41 years, 286 days

Monroe

27 years, 294 days
17 years, 231 days
44 years, 219 days

J. Q. Adams

30 years, 15 days
22 years, 164 days
50 years, 212 days

Jackson

about 24 years
about 24 years
about 37 years

Van Buren

24 years, 78 days
23 years, 350 days
11 years, 349 days

W. H. Harrison

22 years, 289 days
20 years, 123 days
45 years, 130 days

Tyler (first wife)

23 years
22 years, 137 days
29 years, 165 days

Tyler (second wife)

54 years, 89 days

24 years, 53 days
17 years, 206 days

Polk

28 years, 60 days
20 years, 119 days
25 years, 165 days

Taylor

25 years, 209 days
21 years, 273 days
40 years, 18 days

Fillmore (first wife)

26 years, 29 days
27 years, 329 days
27 years, 53 days

Fillmore (second wife)

58 years, 34 days
44 years, 112 days
16 years, 36 days

Pierce

29 years, 352 days
28 years, 243 days
29 years, 22 days

Lincoln

33 years, 265 days
23 years, 326 days
22 years, 162 days

A. Johnson

18 years, 139 days
16 years, 225 days
48 years, 75 days

Grant

26 years, 117 days
22 years, 208 days
36 years, 335 days

Hayes

30 years, 87 days
21 years, 124 days
40 years, 18 days

Garfield

26 years, 357 days
26 years, 206 days
22 years, 312 days

Arthur

30 years, 20 days

22 years, 56 days
20 years, 79 days

Cleveland

49 years, 76 days
21 years, 316 days
22 years, 22 days

B. Harrison (first wife)

20 years, 61 days
21 years, 19 days
39 years, 5 days

B. Harrison (second wife)

62 years, 229 days
37 years, 341 days
4 years, 341 days

McKinley

27 years, 361 days
23 years, 231 days
30 years, 232 days

T. Roosevelt (first wife)

22 years, 0 days
19 years, 82 days
3 years, 110 days

T. Roosevelt (second wife)

28 years, 36 days
25 years, 118 days
32 years, 35 days

Taft

28 years, 277 days
25 years, 168 days
43 years, 262 days

Wilson (first wife)

28 years, 177 days
25 years, 48 days
29 years, 43 days

Wilson (second wife)

58 years, 354 days
43 years, 64 days
8 years, 47 days

Harding

25 years, 248 days
30 years, 327 days
32 years, 25 days

Coolidge

33 years, 92 days

26 years, 274 days
27 years, 93 days

Hoover

24 years, 184 days
24 years, 318 days
44 years, 331 days

F. D. Roosevelt

23 years, 46 days
20 years, 157 days
40 years, 26 days

Truman

35 years, 51 days
34 years, 135 days
53 years, 181 days

Eisenhower

25 years, 260 days
19 years, 229 days
52 years, 270 days

Kennedy

36 years, 106 days
24 years, 46 days
10 years, 71 days

L. B. Johnson

26 years, 82 days
21 years, 330 days
39 years, 66 days

Nixon

27 years, 163 days
28 years, 97 days
53 years, 2 days

Ford

35 years, 93 days
30 years, 190 days
58 years, 72 days

Carter

21 years, 279 days
18 years, 323 days

Reagan (first wife)

28 years, 332 days
26 years, 20 days
9 years, 176 days

Reagan (second wife)

41 years, 26 days
30 years, 242 days

52 years, 93 days

G. Bush

20 years, 208 days
19 years, 213 days

Clinton

29 years, 42 days
27 years, 359 days

G. W. Bush

31 years, 122 days
31 years, 1 day

Obama

31 years, 60 days
28 years, 260 days

MARRIAGE TO WIDOWS

Six Presidents married widows, including three of the first four Presidents.

George Washington married Martha Dandridge Custis, the widow of Colonel Daniel Parke Custis, on January 6, 1759. In June 1749, at the age of 17, she had married Custis, who was 20 years her senior. He died in 1757 of tuberculosis and she became a widow at the age of 25.

Thomas Jefferson married Martha Wayles Skelton, widow of Bathurst Skelton, on January 1, 1772. She had married Skelton on November 20, 1766. He died on September 30, 1768.

James Madison married Dolley Payne Todd, widow of John Todd, Sr., on September 15, 1794. She had married Todd on January 7, 1790, in the Friends Meeting House, Pine Street, Philadelphia, Pa.

The other three Presidents who married widows were widowers:

Millard Fillmore married Caroline Carmichael McIntosh, the widow of Ezekiel C. McIntosh, on February 10, 1858, in Albany, N.Y.

Benjamin Harrison married Mary Scott Lord Dimmick, the widow of Walter Erskine Dimmick, a New York lawyer, on April 6, 1896, in New York City.

Woodrow Wilson married Edith Bolling Galt, the widow of Norman Galt, a Washington, D.C., jeweler, on December 18, 1915, in the capital. She had married Galt on April 30, 1896. Galt died on January 28, 1908.

MARRIAGES TO DIVORCÉES

Andrew Jackson married Rachel Donelson Robards, who had been married to Captain Lewis Robards. Robards had sued for divorce, but technically the status of the divorce was in question—a fact the Jacksons were not aware of at the time of their marriage. Jackson had a second wedding ceremony performed three years after the first to eliminate all possible doubts concerning the legality of his marriage.

Warren Gamaliel Harding married Florence Kling DeWolfe, who had been married to Henry DeWolfe. Her marriage to Harding took place after the death of her former husband.

Gerald Rudolph Ford married Betty Bloomer, who had been married to William C. Warren.

Ronald Wilson Reagan married Jane Wyman, who had been married to Myron Futterman.

MARRIAGES ENDING IN DIVORCE

Ronald Wilson Reagan and Jane Wyman were married on January 24, 1940; they were divorced July 19, 1949.

WIVES WITH CHILDREN BY FORMER HUSBANDS

Martha Washington was the mother of four children by her marriage to Daniel Parke Custis. The children were Patsy and Jackey Custis, who had died in infancy; Martha Parke Curtis, who died in 1774 at the age of sixteen; and John Parke Custis, who died in 1781 at the age of twenty-five, leaving four children, two of whom were raised by Martha and George Washington.

Martha Jefferson was the mother of one son by her marriage to Bathurst Skelton, who had died before she was twenty. Her son, John Skelton, born November 7, 1767, had died June 10, 1771.

Dolley Madison was the mother of two sons by her marriage to John Todd. Her sons were John Payne Todd, born February 29, 1792, and William Temple Todd, who had died in infancy in 1792.

Florence Harding was the mother of one son by her marriage in 1880 to Henry DeWolfe—a marriage which ended in divorce. Her son, (Eugene) Marshall DeWolfe, died in young adulthood of tuberculosis.

AGE AT WHICH WIVES BECAME FIRST LADIES

Anna Harrison   (Mrs. W. H. Harrison) 65 years, 222 days

Barbara Bush   (Mrs. George H. W. Bush) 64 years, 227 days

Abigail Fillmore   62 years, 111 days

Florence Harding   60 years, 202 days

Margaret Taylor   60 years, 164 days

Bess Truman   60 years, 57 days

Nancy Reagan   59 years, 198 days

Elizabeth Monroe   58 years, 247 days

Martha Washington   57 years, 313 days

Pat Nixon   56 years, 310 days

Caroline Harrison   (Mrs. Benjamin Harrison) 56 years, 141 days

Mamie Eisenhower   56 years, 68 days

Lou Hoover   54 years, 340 days

Eliza Johnson   (Mrs. Andrew Johnson) 54 years, 151 days

Laura Bush   (Mrs. George W. Bush) 54 years, 78 days

Betty Ford   53 years, 123 days

Ellen Wilson   52 years, 293 days

Abigail Adams   (Mrs. John Adams) 52 years, 113 days

Lady Bird Johnson   (Mrs. Lyndon B. Johnson) 50 years, 335 days

Letitia Tyler   50 years, 145 days

Louisa Adams   (Mrs. John Quincy Adams) 50 years, 20 days

Ida McKinley   49 years, 269 days

Rosalynn Carter   49 years, 155 days

Lucretia Garfield   48 years, 320 days

Eleanor Roosevelt   (Mrs. Franklin D. Roosevelt) 48 years, 144 days

Helen Taft   48 years, 61 days

Jane Pierce   46 years, 357 days

Hillary Rodham Clinton   46 years, 86 days

Lucy Hayes   45 years, 188 days

Michelle Obama   45 years, 3 days

Grace Coolidge   44 years, 212 days

Edith Wilson   43 years, 64 days

Julia Grant   43 years, 37 days

Mary Lincoln   42 years, 81 days

Sarah Polk   41 years, 181 days

Dolley Madison   40 years, 288 days

Edith Roosevelt   (Mrs. Theodore Roosevelt) 40 years, 39 days

Jacqueline Kennedy   31 years, 176 days

Julia Tyler   24 years, 53 days

Frances Cleveland   21 years, 226 days

Martha Jefferson, Rachel Jackson, Hannah Van Buren, Ellen Arthur, and Alice Roosevelt (Mrs. Theodore Roosevelt) died before their husbands became President. Jane Wyman was divorced from Ronald Reagan before he became President.

Millard Fillmore and Benjamin Harrison married second wives after completing their terms in office.

LIFE SPAN OF PRESIDENTS' WIVES

Five wives died before their husbands became President:

Martha Jefferson

Rachel Jackson

Hannah Van Buren

Ellen Arthur

Alice Roosevelt (1st wife)

Three wives died while their husbands were in office:

Letitia Tyler (1st wife)

Caroline Harrison (1st wife)

Ellen Wilson (1st wife)

Thirty-three wives died after their husbands' terms:

Martha Washington

Abigail Adams

Dolley Madison

Elizabeth Monroe

Louisa Adams

Anna Harrison

Julia Tyler (2nd wife)

Sarah Polk

Margaret Taylor

Abigail Fillmore (1st wife)

Caroline Fillmore (2nd wife)

Jane Pierce

Mary Lincoln

Eliza Johnson
Julia Grant
Lucy Hayes
Lucretia Garfield
Frances Cleveland
Mary Harrison (2nd wife)
Ida McKinley
Edith Roosevelt (2nd wife)
Edith Wilson (2nd wife)
Helen Taft
Florence Harding
Grace Coolidge
Lou Hoover
Eleanor Roosevelt
Mamie Eisenhower
Bess Truman
Jacqueline Kennedy
Lady Bird Johnson
Pat Nixon
Jane Wyman (Reagan's 1st wife)

AGE OF WIVES AT DEATH

Bess Truman   97 years, 247 days
Lady Bird Johnson   94 years, 201 days
Jane Wyman (Reagan)   90 years, 248 days
Mary Harrison   89 years, 250 days
Edith Wilson   89 years, 64 days
Anna Harrison   88 years, 215 days
Sarah Polk   87 years, 344 days
Edith Roosevelt   87 years, 45 days
Lucretia Garfield   85 years, 329 days
Frances Cleveland   83 years, 100 days
Mamie Eisenhower   82 years, 352 days
Helen Taft   82 years, 140 days
Pat Nixon   81 years, 99 days
Dolley Madison   81 years, 53 days
Grace Coolidge   78 years, 186 days
Eleanor Roosevelt   78 years, 27 days
Louisa Adams   77 years, 91 days
Julia Grant   76 years, 322 days
Abigail Adams   73 years, 351 days
Martha Washington   70 years, 335 days
Lou Hoover   69 years, 284 days
Julia Tyler   69 years, 67 days
Caroline Fillmore   67 years, 294 days
Eliza Johnson   65 years, 103 days

Jacqueline Kennedy   64 years, 295 days
Florence Harding   64 years, 98 days
Margaret Taylor   63 years, 331 days
Mary Lincoln   63 years, 215 days
Elizabeth Monroe   62 years, 85 days
Rachel Jackson   61 years, 190 days
Caroline Harrison   60 years, 24 days
Ida McKinley   59 years, 352 days
Lucy Hayes   57 years, 301 days
Jane Pierce   57 years, 265 days
Abigail Fillmore   55 years, 17 days
Ellen Wilson   54 years, 83 days
Letitia Tyler   51 years, 302 days
Ellen Arthur   42 years, 135 days
Hannah Van Buren   35 years, 334 days
Martha Jefferson   33 years, 322 days
Alice Roosevelt   22 years, 192 days

LONGEVITY OF THE PRESIDENTS' WIVES

Of the forty-eight Presidents' wives, seven are living (2009): Betty Ford, Rosalynn Carter, Nancy Reagan, Barbara Bush, Hillary Rodham Clinton, Laura Bush, and Michelle Obama.

Fourteen of the forty-one wives no longer living were 81 years of age or older when they died: Dolley Madison, Anna Harrison, Sarah Polk, Lucretia Garfield, Frances Cleveland, Mary Harrison (second wife), Edith Roosevelt (second wife), Helen Taft, Edith Wilson (second wife), Bess Truman, Mamie Eisenhower, Pat Nixon, Lady Bird Johnson, and Jane Wyman (Reagan's first wife).

Twenty of the forty-one wives were 70 or older when they died. In addition to the fourteen mentioned above, they were Martha Washington, Abigail Adams, Louisa Adams, Julia Grant, Grace Coolidge, and Eleanor Roosevelt.

Thirty-one of the forty-one wives were 60 or older when they died.

Thirty-seven of the forty-one wives were 50 or older when they died.

The wife who died at the most advanced age was Bess Truman, who was 97 years and 247 days old when she died.

The wife who died at the earliest age was the first wife of Theodore Roosevelt, who was only 22 years and 192 days old when she died.

PLACES OF DEATH AND BURIAL OF PRESIDENTS' WIVES

Martha Washington

Mount Vernon, near Alexandria, Va.; Mount Vernon

Abigail Adams

Quincy, Mass.; Quincy, Mass.

Martha Jefferson

Monticello, near Charlottesville, Va.; Monticello

Dolley Madison

Washington, D.C.; Montpelier, near Charlottesville, Va.

Elizabeth Monroe

Oak Hill, near Leesburg, Va.; Richmond, Va.

Louisa Adams

Washington, D.C.; Quincy, Mass.

Rachel Jackson

The Hermitage, near Nashville, Tenn.; The Hermitage

Hannah Van Buren

Albany, N.Y.; Kinderhook, N.Y.

Anna Harrison

North Bend, Ohio; North Bend, Ohio

Letitia Tyler

Washington, D.C.; Cedar Grove, Va.

Julia Tyler

Richmond, Va.; Richmond, Va.

Sarah Polk

Nashville, Tenn.; Nashville, Tenn.

Margaret Taylor

Pascagoula, Miss; Louisville, Ky.

Abigail Fillmore

Washington, D.C.; Buffalo, N.Y.

Caroline Fillmore

Buffalo, N.Y.; Buffalo, N.Y.

Jane Pierce

Andover, Mass.; Concord, N.H.

Mary Lincoln

Springfield, Ill.; Springfield, Ill.

Eliza Johnson

Greene County, Tenn.; Greeneville, Tenn.

Julia Grant

Washington, D.C.; New York, N.Y.

Lucy Hayes

Fremont, Ohio; Fremont, Ohio

Lucretia Garfield

Pasadena, Calif.; Cleveland, Ohio

Ellen Arthur

Albany, N.Y.; Albany, N.Y.

Frances Cleveland

Baltimore, Md.; Princeton, N.J.

Caroline Harrison

Washington, D.C.; Indianapolis, Ind.

Mary Harrison

New York, N.Y.; Indianapolis, Ind.

Ida McKinley

Canton, Ohio; Canton, Ohio

Alice Roosevelt

New York, N.Y.; Cambridge, Mass.

Edith Roosevelt

Oyster, Bay, N.Y.; Oyster Bay, N.Y.

Helen Taft

Washington, D.C.; Arlington, Va.

Ellen Wilson

Washington, D.C.; Rome, Ga.

Edith Wilson

Washington, D.C.; Washington, D.C.

Florence Harding

Marion, Ohio; Marion, Ohio

Grace Coolidge

Northampton, Mass.; Plymouth, Vt.

Lou Hoover

New York, N.Y.; Palo Alto, Calif., reinterred West Branch, Iowa

Eleanor Roosevelt

New York, N.Y.; Hyde Park, N.Y.

Bess Truman

Independence, Mo.; Independence, Mo.

Mamie Eisenhower

Washington, D.C.; Abilene, Kan.

Jacqueline Kennedy

New York, N.Y.; Arlington, Va.

Pat Nixon

Park Ridge, N.J.; Yorba Linda, Calif.

Lady Bird Johnson

West Lake Hills, Tex.; Stonewall, Tex.

Jane Wyman (Reagan)

Rancho Mirage, Calif.; Cathedral City, Calif.

WIDOWS OF PRESIDENTS GRANTED FREE USE OF THE MAILS

An act of Congress of April 3, 1800—"an act to extend the privilege of franking letters and packages to Martha Washington" (2 Stat L. 19)—granted the widow of George Washington the free use of the mails for her natural life. The act of Congress that formalized the granting of the franking privilege was the Former Presidents Act of 1958, which became law in December 1973. Presidential widows to whom the franking privilege had been extended by special acts of Congress were the following:

Dolley Madison, July 2, 1836
Anna Harrison, September 9, 1841
Louisa Adams, March 9, 1848
Sarah Polk, January 10, 1850
Margaret Taylor, July 18, 1850
Mary Lincoln, February 10, 1866
Lucretia Garfield, December 20, 1888
Julia Grant, June 28, 1886
Ida McKinley, January 22, 1902
Mary Harrison, February 1, 1909
Frances Cleveland, February 1, 1909
Edith Roosevelt, October 27, 1919

Florence Harding, January 25, 1924
Edith Wilson, March 4, 1924
Helen Taft, June 14, 1930
Grace Coolidge, June 16, 1934
Eleanor Roosevelt, May 7, 1945
Jacqueline Kennedy, December 11, 1963
Mamie Eisenhower, April 25, 1969

PENSIONS TO PRESIDENTIAL WIDOWS

Pensions of varying amounts were paid to presidential widows of specific acts of Congress. The first to receive a pension was Anna Harrison (Mrs. William Henry Harrison). On June 30, 1841, Congress passed "an act for the relief of Mrs. Harrison, widow of the late President of the United States." She was granted the sum of $25,000, equivalent to a President's salary.

A similar award of $25,000 was made to Mary Lincoln on December 21, 1865, and on July 14, 1870, Congress passed "an act granting a pension to Mary Lincoln" which provided "that the Secretary of the Interior be, and is hereby authorized to place the name of Mary Lincoln, widow of Abraham Lincoln, deceased, late President of the United States, on the pension roll." It authorized a pension of $3,000 a year. An act of February 2, 1882, awarded her an annual pension of $5,000.

An act of March 31, 1882—"an act granting pensions to Lucretia R. Garfield, Sarah Childress Polk and Julia Gardiner Tyler"—directed the Secretary of the Interior to place their names "on the pension roll and pay each of them a pension during their respective natural lives at the rate of $5,000 a year from and after the 19th day of September 1881." It also specified that the pension of $5,000 granted by this act to Julia Tyler should be in lieu of the pension previously granted her by Congress.

On July 27, 1882, Congress passed an act awarding Lucretia Garfield the sum of $50,000.

Annual pensions of $5,000 were also awarded to the following:

Julia Grant, December 26, 1885 (24 Stat. L. 653)
Ida McKinley, April 17, 1902 (32 Stat. L. 1328)
Edith Roosevelt, February 25, 1919 (40 Stat. L. 1530)

Edith Wilson, February 28, 1929 (45 Stat. L. 2338)

Grace Coolidge, January 14, 1937 (50 Stat. L. 923)

Helen H. Taft, May 22, 1937 (50 Stat. L. 973)

Mary Harrison, May 24, 1938 (52 Stat. L. 1318)

Frances Folsom Cleveland Preston, November 25, 1940 (54 Stat. L. 1396) (Mrs. Cleveland had remarried in 1913.)

On August 25, 1958 (72 Stat. L. 838) Congress passed an act granting annual pensions of $10,000 to the widows of Presidents. Entitled to this pension have been Edith Wilson, Eleanor Roosevelt, Bess Truman, Mamie Eisenhower, and Jacqueline Kennedy.

On January 8, 1971 (84 Stat. L. 1963) the pension to widows of Presidents was increased to $20,000. The pension terminated if the widow remarried before reaching the age of sixty. In 2009, the only surviving presidential widows were Nancy Reagan and Betty Ford, neither of whom accepted the pension.

PRESIDENT'S WIDOW IN EXECUTIVE CAPACITY

The first President's widow to serve the federal government in an executive capacity was Anna Eleanor Roosevelt, who was appointed on December 19, 1945, by President Harry S. Truman, to the United States delegation to the United Nations General Assembly. (The other delegates appointed at the same time were Edward Riley Stettinius and Senators Tom Connally and Arthur Hendrick Vandenberg.) On April 29, 1946, she was elected to lead the preliminary United Nations Human Rights Commission, which again elected her as its leader upon its formal establishment on January 27, 1947.

"FIRST LADY"

The term "first lady" as a synonym for the wife of a President is believed to have been used for the first time in 1877 by Mary Clemmer Ames in an article in the *Independent* describing the inauguration of President Rutherford Birchard Hayes on Monday, March 5, 1877.

The term became popular when a comedy about Dolley Madison by Charles Nirdlinger entitled *The First Lady in the Land* was produced by Henry B. Harris at the Gaiety Theatre, New York City, on December 4, 1911. It featured Elsie Ferguson, Clarence Handyside, Luke Martin, David Todd, and Beatrice Noyes.

MARRIAGE STATISTICS

Forty-two of the forty-three Presidents married. (James Buchanan was the only President who did not marry.) Five Presidents remarried after the death of their first wives, and one remarried after divorce.

The President who married at the earliest age was Andrew Johnson, who married Eliza McCardle when he was 18 years and 139 days old.

The President who married for the first time at the most advanced age was Grover Cleveland, who married Frances Folsom when he was 49 years and 76 days old. She was 21 years and 316 days old.

Benjamin Harrison was married for a second time when he was 62 years and 229 days old, a little more than three years after he retired from the presidency.

The youngest of the six Presidents to remarry was Theodore Roosevelt, who married Edith Kermit Carow when he was 28 years and 36 days old.

The greatest age difference between a President and his wife existed between John Tyler and his second wife, Julia Gardiner. Tyler was 54 years and 89 days old on their wedding day; his wife was 24 years and 53 days old.

The next greatest age difference between a President and his wife was that of Grover Cleveland, who was 49 years and 76 days old at marriage, and Frances Folsom, who was 21 years and 316 days old.

Presidents who celebrated golden anniversaries were John Adams, his son John Quincy Adams, Harry S. Truman, Dwight David Eisenhower, Richard M. Nixon, Gerald Ford, Jimmy Carter, Ronald Reagan, and George Bush. John Adams was married 54 years and 3 days and John Quincy Adams was married 50 years and 112 days. Truman was married 53 years and 181 days, Eisenhower was married 52 years and 270 days, Nixon was married 53 years and 2 days, Ford was married 58 years and 72 days, and Reagan was married to his second wife 52 years and 93 days. Jimmy and Rosalynn Carter celebrated their fiftieth wedding anniversary in 1996. George and Barbara Bush were 20 and 19 years old, respectively, when they were married on January 6, 1945; on January 20, 2001, at the inauguration of their son George W. Bush, they had been married 56 years and 14 days.

The shortest marriage was that of Theodore Roosevelt and his first wife, Alice Hathaway Lee, who had been married only 3 years and 110 days when she died.

The wife who married at the earliest age was Eliza McCardle, who married Andrew Johnson when she was 16 years and 225 days old.

The oldest to marry a President was Caroline Carmichael McIntosh, who married Millard Fillmore, her second husband, when she was 44 years and 112 days old.

The oldest to marry for the first time was Bess Wallace, who married Harry S. Truman when she was 34 years and 135 days old.

Six Presidents married women older than they: Washington, Harding, Fillmore, Benjamin Harrison, Hoover, and Nixon. Washington was 246 days younger than his wife, and Harding was 5 years and 79 days younger. Both Mrs. Washington and Mrs. Harding survived their husbands. Fillmore was 1 year and 300 days younger than his wife, and Harrison was 323 days younger. Both Fillmore and Harrison survived their wives and remarried. Hoover was 134 days younger than his wife, and Nixon was 1 year and 66 days younger than his wife. Both Hoover and Nixon survived their wives, but did not remarry.

TWO PRESIDENTS MARRIED ON THEIR BIRTHDAYS

Two Presidents were married on their birthdays. John Tyler married Letitia Christian, his first wife, on March 29, 1813, his twenty-third birthday. Theodore Roosevelt married Alice Hathaway Lee, his first wife, on October 27, 1880, his twenty-second birthday.

WIDOWERS IN THE WHITE HOUSE

Two widowers were elected President: Thomas Jefferson, whose wife had died on September 6, 1782, almost 19 years before his inauguration on March 4, 1801, and Martin Van Buren, whose wife had died on February 5, 1819, more than 18 years before his inauguration on March 4, 1837.

Andrew Jackson's wife died on December 22, 1828. She lived to see him elected but died before he was inaugurated on March 4, 1829.

Chester Alan Arthur was a widower when he succeeded to the presidency. His wife had died on January 12, 1880, before he was elected Vice President in November 1880.

When Theodore Roosevelt was elected Vice President in 1900, he had already married his second wife, his first wife having died in 1884.

SECOND MARRIAGES

Theodore Roosevelt and Reagan remarried before they became President. Tyler and Wilson remarried while they were in office. Fillmore and Benjamin Harrison remarried after their terms as President.

With the exception of Theodore Roosevelt, who was 2 years and 293 days older than his second wife, these Presidents married women considerably younger than they were. Reagan was 10 years and 150 days older than his second wife, Fillmore was 13 years and 287 days older, Wilson was 15 years and 291 days older, Harrison was 24 years and 253 days older, and Tyler was 30 years and 36 days older.

Four of the six Presidents who remarried had children by both wives: John Tyler, Benjamin Harrison, Theodore Roosevelt, and Ronald Reagan.

Millard Fillmore and Woodrow Wilson had children by their first marriages but none by their second.

Three of the six wives, Mrs. Fillmore, Mrs. Harrison, and Mrs. Wilson, were widows when they married.

Five of the wives survived their husbands.

PRESIDENTS' WIDOWS REMARRIED

The widows of two former Presidents remarried after the deaths of the Presidents.

Frances Folsom Cleveland, widow of Grover Cleveland, married Professor Thomas Jex Preston, Jr., in Princeton, N.J., on February 10, 1913. Cleveland had died on June 24, 1908.

Jacqueline Lee Bouvier Kennedy, widow of John Fitzgerald Kennedy, married Aristotle Socrates Onassis on the island of Skorpios, Greece, on October 20, 1968. Kennedy had died on November 22, 1963.

CHILDREN OF THE PRESIDENTS

Washington   None
J. Adams   3 boys, 2 girls
Jefferson   1 boy, 5 girls
Madison   None
Monroe   1 boy, 2 girls
J. Q. Adams   3 boys, 1 girl
Jackson   None
Van Buren   4 boys
W. H. Harrison   6 boys, 4 girls
Tyler   (by first wife) 3 boys, 5 girls
Tyler   (by second wife) 5 boys, 2 girls
Polk   None
Taylor   1 boy, 5 girls
Fillmore   (by first wife) 1 boy, 1 girl
Fillmore   (by second wife) None
Pierce   3 boys
Buchanan   None
Lincoln   4 boys
A. Johnson   3 boys, 2 girls
Grant   3 boys, 1 girl
Hayes   7 boys, 1 girl
Garfield   5 boys, 2 girls
Arthur   2 boys, 1 girl
Cleveland   2 boys, 3 girls
B. Harrison   (by first wife) 1 boy, 1 girl
B. Harrison   (by second wife) 1 girl
McKinley   2 girls
T. Roosevelt   (by first wife) 1 girl
T. Roosevelt   (by second wife) 4 boys, 1 girl
Taft   2 boys, 1 girl
Wilson   (by first wife) 3 girls
Wilson   (by second wife) None
Harding   None
Coolidge   2 boys
Hoover   2 boys
F. D. Roosevelt   5 boys, 1 girl
Truman   1 girl

Eisenhower   2 boys
Kennedy   2 boys, 1 girl
L. B. Johnson   2 girls
Nixon   2 girls
Ford   3 boys, 1 girl
Carter   3 boys, 1 girl
Reagan   (by first wife) 1 boy, 1 girl
Reagan   (by second wife) 1 boy, 1 girl
G. Bush   4 boys, 2 girls
Clinton   1 girl
G. W. Bush   2 girls
Obama   2 girls
Total number of boys: 89
Total number of girls: 65

Six of the forty-three Presidents had no children. They were Washington, Madison, Jackson, Polk, Harding, and Buchanan, who was a bachelor. However, Washington served as father to his wife's two surviving children from her first marriage and to two of her grandchildren; Madison likewise served as father to his wife's surviving child from her first marriage; and Jackson adopted one of his wife's nephews. Harding, though he had no children with his wife, fathered a daughter out of wedlock.

The remaining thirty-seven Presidents had a total of 153 children—89 boys and 65 girls. Eight of the Presidents had girls and no boys—McKinley, Wilson, Truman, Lyndon Baines Johnson, Nixon, Clinton, George W. Bush, and Obama. Six had boys and no girls—Van Buren, Pierce, Lincoln, Coolidge, Hoover, and Eisenhower. One—George Walker Bush—had twins.

Jefferson is widely thought to have fathered additional children, after his wife's death, during a long-term relationship with his wife's half sister, who was a slave in his household. Cleveland, before his marriage, accepted responsibility for a son born out of wedlock and paid child support to the mother, though in all likelihood he was not the boy's father.

The President who had the greatest number of children was John Tyler, the father of fifteen. He had three sons and five daughters by his first wife, Letitia Christian. He married Julia Gardiner while he was President. After leaving the White House, they had seven children, five sons and two daughters.

The President who had the greatest number of children prior to his election was William Henry Harrison, who had ten children, four of whom were alive when he became President.

CHILDREN BORN IN FOREIGN COUNTRIES

George Washington Adams, the son of John Quincy Adams, was the first child of a President born in a foreign country. He was born on April 13, 1801, in Berlin, Germany. His youngest sister, Louisa Catherine Adams, was born ten years later in St. Petersburg, Russia. Their father was serving the United States abroad on diplomatic assignments.

Both of President Hoover's sons were born in London, England. Herbert Clark Hoover, Jr., was born on August 4, 1903, and Allan Henry Hoover on July 17, 1907.

Franklin Delano Roosevelt, Jr., was born at Campobello, New Brunswick, Canada, on August 17, 1914.

CHILDREN WHO DIED WHILE THEIR FATHERS WERE IN OFFICE

Charles Adams, son of John Adams, 30 years old, died Nov. 30, 1800

Mary Jefferson, 26 years old, died April 17, 1804

William Wallace Lincoln, 11 years old, died Feb. 20, 1862

Calvin Coolidge, Jr., 16 years old, died July 7, 1924

Patrick Bouvier Kennedy, 2 days old, died Aug. 9, 1963

PRESIDENTS' CHILDREN AT THE UNITED STATES MILITARY ACADEMY, WEST POINT

Abraham Van Buren, graduated 1827; 37th in a class of 38

Frederick Dent Grant, graduated June 12, 1871; 37th in a class of 41

John Sheldon Doud Eisenhower, graduated June 6, 1944; 138th in a class of 474

PRESIDENTS' CHILDREN IN MILITARY SERVICE

Second Seminole War

Abraham Van Buren

Texas War for Independence

Son of William Henry Harrison

Benjamin Harrison (uncle of President Benjamin Harrison), served in Texas Army; wounded and captured

Mexican War

Abraham Van Buren

John Tyler, Jr., obtained commission but saw no action

Richard Taylor, accompanied his father as military secretary

Civil War—Union

Robert Todd Lincoln, briefly served as non-combatant officer

Frederick Dent Grant, accompanied his father, wounded at Vicksburg

Charles Johnson, Army surgeon

Robert Johnson

Civil War—Confederacy

David Gardiner Tyler

John Alexander Tyler, later served with Saxon Army in Franco-Prussian War

Tazewell Tyler, army surgeon

Richard Taylor, lieutenant general, succeeded to command of J. B. Hood's army Nov. 1864

Spanish-American War and Philippine Insurrection

James Webb Cook Hayes, won Medal of Honor in the Philippines campaign (Dec. 4, 1899, Vigan action); also served in the Boxer Rebellion expeditionary force and the Mexican Border campaign, as well as in World War I

Son of Benjamin Harrison

Russell B. Harrison

World War I

James Webb Cook Hayes

Richard Folsom Cleveland

Charles Phelps Taft

Sons of Theodore Roosevelt

Archibald B. Roosevelt

Kermit Roosevelt

Quentin Roosevelt, shot down in aerial combat in France, died July 14, 1918

Theodore Roosevelt, Jr.

World War II

Sons of Theodore Roosevelt

Archibald B. Roosevelt

Kermit Roosevelt, died on duty in Alaska

Theodore Roosevelt, Jr., died of a heart attack July 12, 1944, in Normandy, France; posthumously awarded Medal of Honor for his part in the invasion

Sons of Franklin Delano Roosevelt

Elliott Roosevelt

Franklin Delano Roosevelt, Jr.

James Roosevelt

John Aspinwall Roosevelt

Korean War

John Sheldon Doud Eisenhower

PRESIDENTS' CHILDREN WHO SERVED IN PRESIDENTIAL CABINETS

John Quincy Adams, Secretary of State (Monroe)

Robert Todd Lincoln, Secretary of War (Garfield)

James Rudolph Garfield, Secretary of the Interior (T. Roosevelt)

Herbert Clark Hoover, Jr., Under Secretary of State (Eisenhower)

Franklin Delano Roosevelt, Jr., Under Secretary of Commerce (L. B. Johnson)

PRESIDENTS' CHILDREN PROPOSED FOR THE PRESIDENCY

John Quincy Adams, son of John Adams; the candidate of one faction of the Democratic-Republican Party in 1824, he won the presidency

John Scott Harrison, son of William Henry Harrison; proposed by the Whigs in 1856, he declined (his own son, Benjamin Harrison, was elected President in 1888)

John Van Buren, proposed by the Free Soil Democrats in 1848; he declined in favor of his father, Martin Van Buren, who was defeated in the election by Zachary Taylor

Robert Todd Lincoln, a contender for the nomination at the Republican conventions in 1884 and 1888

Robert Alphonso Taft, a leading contender at the 1940, 1948, and 1952 Republican conventions

George Walker Bush, son of George Bush; the candidate of the Republican Party in 2000, he won the presidency

PRESIDENTS' CHILDREN WHO SERVED IN CONGRESS

Senate and House of Representatives

John Quincy Adams, Mass. (son of John Adams)

Senate, Mar. 4, 1803–June 6, 1808

House of Representatives, (22nd–30th Congresses, Mar. 4, 1831–Feb. 23, 1848)

Senate

Robert Alphonso Taft, Ohio (son of William Howard Taft)

Jan. 3, 1939–July 31, 1953

House of Representatives

Charles Francis Adams, Mass. (son of John Quincy Adams)

36th–37th Congresses, Mar. 4, 1859–May 1, 1861

John Scott Harrison, Ohio (son of William Henry Harrison)

33rd–34th Congress, Mar. 4, 1853–Mar. 3, 1857

David Gardiner Tyler, Va. (son of John Tyler)

53rd–54th Congresses, Mar. 4, 1893–Mar. 3, 1897

Franklin Delano Roosevelt, Jr., N.Y. (son of Franklin Delano Roosevelt)

81st–82nd–83rd Congresses, June 14, 1949–Jan. 2, 1955

James Roosevelt, Calif. (son of Franklin Delano Roosevelt)

84th–85th–86th Congresses, Jan. 3, 1955–Sept. 30, 1965

WHITE HOUSE WEDDINGS

1812

Mar. 29, Mrs. Lucy Payne Washington, sister of Mrs. James Madison and widow of George Steptoe Washington, a nephew of George Washington, to Thomas Todd, Associate Justice, U.S. Supreme Court; the Reverend Mr. McCormick officiated

1820

Mar. 9, Maria Hester Monroe, youngest daughter of President Monroe, to Samuel Lawrence Gouverneur; the Reverend Mr. Hawley officiated

1828

Feb. 25, Mary Catherine Hellen, niece of Mrs. John Quincy Adams, to John Adams, son of President John Quincy Adams; the Reverend Mr. Hawley officiated

1832

Apr. 10, Mary A. Eastin, niece of President Andrew Jackson, to Lucien J. Polk; the Reverend Mr. Hawley officiated

Nov. 29, Delia Lewis, daughter of William B. Lewis of President Jackson's "kitchen cabinet," to Alphonse Joseph Pageot, secretary of the French legation

1842

Jan. 31, Elizabeth Tyler, daughter of President John Tyler, to William Nevison Waller; the Reverend Mr. Hawley officiated

1874

May 21, Nellie Grant, daughter of President Ulysses Simpson Grant, to Algernon Charles Frederick Sartoris of the British legation; the Reverend Dr. Tiffany officiated

1878

June 19, Emily Platt, niece of President Rutherford Birchard Hayes, to Colonel Russell Hastings; Bishop Jagger officiated

1886

June 2, Frances Folsom to President Grover Cleveland; the Reverend Dr. Sunderland officiated

1906

Feb. 17, Alice Roosevelt, daughter of President Theodore Roosevelt, to Representative Nicholas Longworth; the Right Reverend Mr. Satterlee officiated

1913

Nov. 25, Jessie Woodrow Wilson, daughter of President Woodrow Wilson, to Francis Bowes Sayre; the Reverend Dr. Beach officiated

1914

May 7, Eleanor Wilson, daughter of President Woodrow Wilson, to William Gibbs McAdoo, Secretary of the Treasury in President Wilson's cabinet; the Reverend Dr. Beach officiated

1918

Aug. 7, Alice Wilson, niece of President Woodrow Wilson, to the Reverend Isaac Stuart McElroy, Jr.; the Reverend Isaac Stuart McElroy, Sr., officiated

1942

July 30, Mrs. Louise Gill Macy to Harry L. Hopkins, Secretary of Commerce in President Franklin Delano Roosevelt's second administration; the Reverend Mr. Clinchy officiated

1967

Dec. 9, Lynda Bird Johnson, daughter of President Lyndon Baines Johnson, to Charles Spittal Robb; the Reverend Gerald McAllister officiated

1971

June 12, Patricia (Tricia) Nixon, daughter of President Richard Milhous Nixon, to Edward Ridley Finch Cox; the Reverend Edward Gardiner Latch officiated

1994

May 28, Nicole Boxer, daughter of Senator Barbara Boxer of California, to Tony Rodham, younger brother of First Lady Hillary Rodham Clinton; Judge Peter Capua officiated

THE PRESIDENTS' DESCENDANTS

The President with the greatest number of children was John Tyler, who had 15 children by his two wives. William Henry Harrison led with the greatest number of grandchildren and great-grandchildren. He had 48 grandchildren and 106 great-grandchildren.

With the deaths of Presidents Washington, Madison, Jackson, Polk, Pierce, Buchanan, McKinley, and Harding, their direct lines ceased.

PRESIDENTS' DESCENDANTS MARRIED

On June 30, 1853, Mary Louise Adams married William Clarkson Johnson. Both were descendants of President John Adams, and she was also descended from President John Quincy Adams. He was born on August 16, 1823, in Utica, N.Y. and she was born on December 2, 1828, in Washington, D.C. It was his second marriage.

On November 16, 1961, Newell Garfield, Jr., great-grandson of President Garfield, married (Mary) Jane Harrison Walker, great-granddaugher of President Benjamin Harrison. She was born November 3, 1929, and he was born July 8, 1923. It was his second marriage.

On December 22, 1968, Julie Nixon, daughter of President Nixon, married David Eisenhower, grandson of President Eisenhower. She was born July 5, 1948, in Washington, D. C., and he was born March 31, 1948, in West Point, N.Y. They were childhood acquaintances, Nixon having served as Vice President during the Eisenhower administration.

THE PRESIDENTS' NAMES

Nine Presidents bore the same given names as their fathers: John Adams, James Madison, Andrew Jackson, John Tyler, James Buchanan, William McKinley, Theodore Roosevelt, Jimmy Carter (whose given name was James Earl Carter, Jr.), and Barack Hussein Obama. Gerald Ford was given the same name as his father, Leslie Lynch King, but took the name of his adoptive father instead. President Clinton also was given the same name as his father, William Jefferson Blythe, but took the last name of his stepfather.

Two pairs of fathers and sons were elected to the Presidency. In each case, the father and son shared their first and last names, but were distinguished by different middle names. They were John Adams and John Quincy Adams, and George Herbert Walker Bush and George Walker Bush.

Eight Presidents had family names ending in "–son": Jefferson, Madison, Jackson, William Henry Harrison, Andrew Johnson, Benjamin Harrison, Wilson, and Lyndon Baines Johnson.

Four Presidents had the same family names as the four earlier Presidents to whom they were related: John Quincy Adams, son of John Adams; Benjamin Harrison, grandson of William Henry Harrison; Franklin Delano Roosevelt, a fifth cousin of Theodore Roosevelt; and George Walker Bush, son of George Herbert Walker Bush.

Andrew Johnson and Lyndon Baines Johnson bore the same family name but were not related.

Seventeen of the forty-three Presidents were not given a middle initial or name. They were George Washington, John Adams, Thomas Jefferson, James Madison, James Monroe, Andrew Jackson, Martin Van Buren, John Tyler, Zachary Taylor, Millard Fillmore, Franklin Pierce, James Buchanan, Abraham Lincoln, Andrew Johnson, Benjamin Harrison, William McKinley, and Theodore Roosevelt. (Harry Truman had only the middle initial "S.")

Twenty-two of the forty-three Presidents were given biblical names. Six were named James—the name most frequently given: Madison, Monroe, Polk, Buchanan, Garfield (whose middle name, Abram, was also biblical), and Carter. Five were named John: John Adams, John Quincy Adams, Tyler, Coolidge (originally John Calvin), and Kennedy. Two were named Andrew: Jackson and Johnson. Two were named Thomas: Jefferson and Wilson (originally Thomas Woodrow). One—Lincoln—was named Abraham. One—Harrison—was named Benjamin. Also given biblical names were Harding, whose middle name was Gamaliel; Eisenhower, who transposed his names from David Dwight to Dwight David; Taylor, whose first name, Zachary, was an adaptation of Zachariah;

Grant, who dropped his original first name, Hiram; and Cleveland, who dropped his original first name, Stephen.

Obama's first and middle names are Arabic in origin.

Seven Presidents were given at birth first names that they later changed. Hiram Ulysses Grant became Ulysses Simpson Grant, Stephen Grover Cleveland became Grover Cleveland, Thomas Woodrow Wilson became Woodrow Wilson, John Calvin Coolidge became Calvin Coolidge, and David Dwight Eisenhower became Dwight David Eisenhower. Gerald Ford was born Leslie Lynch King and assumed the name of his adoptive father. William Jefferson Blythe took his stepfather's name and became Bill Clinton.

Barack Obama was known as Barry Soetoro while his mother was married to Lolo Soetero, her second husband.

The last names of five Presidents began with the letter H: William Henry Harrison, Rutherford Birchard Hayes, Benjamin Harrison, Warren Gamaliel Harding, and Herbert Clark Hoover. The second most common initial letters have been C, J, and T.

NICKNAMES AND SOBRIQUETS

Many of the Presidents have been known by nicknames and sobriquets, a few of which are given below. In some instances, malcontents have applied epithets to those whom they disliked intensely.

Washington

American Fabius, Atlas of America, Cincinnatus of the West, Deliverer of America, Farmer President, Father of His Country, Father of Pittsburgh, Old Fox, Sage of Mount Vernon, Savior of His Country, Stepfather of His Country, Surveyor President, Sword of the Revolution

J. Adams

Atlas of Independence, Colossus of Debate, Colossus of Independence, Duke of Braintree, Father of American Independence, Father of the American Navy, His Rotundity, Old Sink or Swim, Partisan of Independence

Jefferson

Father of the Declaration of Independence, Father of the University of Virginia, Long Tom, Man of the People, Pen of the Revolution, Philosopher of Democracy, Red Fox, Sage of Monticello, Scribe of the Revolution

Madison

Father of the Constitution, Sage of Montpelier

Monroe

Era of Good Feeling President, Last of the Cocked Hats

J. Q. Adams

Accidental President, Old Man Eloquent, Second, John

Jackson

Duel Fighter, Hero of New Orleans, King Andrew the First, Land Hero of 1812, Mischievous Andy, Old Hickory, People's President, Pointed Arrow, Sage of the Hermitage, Sharp Knife

Van Buren

American Talleyrand, Enchanter, Flying Dutchman, Fox, Kinderhook Fox, King Martin the First, Little Magician, Little Van, Machiavellian Belshazzar, Mistletoe Politician, Old Kinderhook, Petticoat Pet, Red Fox of Kinderhook, Sage of Kinderhook, Sage of Lindenwald, Whiskey Van, Wizard of Kinderhook, Wizard of the Albany Regency

W. H. Harrison

Farmer President, Hero of Tippecanoe, Log Cabin President, Old Granny, Old Tip, Old Tippecanoe, Tippecanoe, Washington of the West

Tyler

Accidental President, His Accidency, Young Hickory

Polk

First Dark Horse, Napoleon of the Stump, The People's Choice, Young Hickory

Taylor

Old Buena Vista, Old Rough and Ready, Old Zach

Fillmore

Accidental President, American Louis Philippe, His Accidency, Wool-Carder President

Pierce

Handsome Frank, Purse, Young Hicko of the Granite Hills, Young Hickory

Buchanan

Bachelor President, Old Buck, Old Public Functionary, Sage of Wheatland, Ten-cent Jimmy

Lincoln

Ancient, Buffoon, Caesar, Father Abraham, Flatboat Man, Grand Wrestler, Great Emancipator, Honest Abe, Illinois Baboon, Jester, Long 'Un, Man of the People, Martyr President, Railsplitter, Sage of Springfield, Sectional President, Tycoon, Tyrant, Uncle Abe

A. Johnson

Daddy of the Baby, Father of the Homestead Act, His Accidency, King Andy the First, Old Andy, Old Veto, Sir Veto, Tennessee Tailor, Veto President

Grant

American Caesar, Butcher from Galena, Butcher Grant, Galena Tanner, Great Hammerer, Great Peacemaker, Hero of Appomattox, Hero of Fort Donelson, Old Three Stars, Silent Man, Tanner President, Texas, Uncle Sam, Unconditional Surrender, Union Safeguard, United States, Unprecedented Strategist, Unquestionably Skilled, Useless S. Grant

Hayes

Dark Horse President, Fraud President, Granny Hayes, Hero of '77, His Fraudulency, Old Eight to Seven, President De Facto

Garfield

Canal Boy, Martyr President, Preacher President, Teacher President

Arthur

America's First Gentleman, Arthur the Gentleman, Dude President, Elegant Arthur, First Gentleman of the Land, His Accidency, Our Chet, Prince Arthur

Cleveland

Buffalo Hangman, Buffalo Sheriff, Claimant, Dumb Prophet, Grover the Good, Hangman of Buffalo, Man of Destiny, Old Grover, Old Veto, People's President, Perpetual Candidate, Pretender, Reform Governor, Sage of Princeton, Stubborn Old Grover, Stuffed Prophet, Uncle Jumbo, Veto Governor, Veto Mayor, Veto President

B. Harrison

Centennial President, Chinese Harrison, Grandfather's Hat, Grandpa's Grandson, Kid Gloves Harrison, Little Ben, Son of His Grandfather

McKinley

Idol of Ohio, Napoleon of Protection, Prosperity's Advance Agent, Stocking-foot Orator, Wobbly Willie

T. Roosevelt

Bull Moose, Driving Force, Dynamo of Power, Four Eyes, Great White Chief, Happy Warrior, Haroun-al-Roosevelt, Hero of San Juan Hill, Man on Horseback, Meddler, Old Lion, Rough Rider, T.R., Teddy, Telescope Teddy, Trust Buster, Typical American

Wilson

Coiner of Weasel Words, Phrasemaker, Professor, Schoolmaster in Politics

Coolidge

Red, Silent Cal

Hoover

Chief, Friend of Helpless Children, Grand Old Man, Hermit Author of Palo Alto, Man of Great Heart

F. D. Roosevelt

Boss, F.D.R., Houdini in the White House, Sphinx, Squire of Hyde Park, That Man in the White House

Truman

Give 'Em Hell Harry, Haberdasher Harry, High Tax Harry, Man from Missouri, Man of Independence

Eisenhower

General Ike, Ike

Kennedy

J.F.K., Jack

L. B. Johnson

L.B.J., Landslide Lyndon, Light Bulb Johnson

Nixon

Tricky Dick

Ford

Jerry, Junie

Carter

Grits, Jimmy, Dhimmi Jimmy

Reagan

Dutch, Gipper, Great Communicator, Ronnie, Teflon President

G. Bush

Résumé Candidate, Poppy

Clinton

Bill, Bubba, Comeback Kid, Slick Willie

G. W. Bush

The Decider, Dubya, Junior, Shrub

Obama

Bam, The One, Barry O'Bomber (his nickname as a high school basketball player)

Education and Career

PRESIDENTS WHO ATTENDED COLLEGE

The following is a list of Presidents who attended college, the institutions attended, and the dates of graduation:

J. Adams   Harvard, July 16, 1755

Jefferson   William and Mary, Apr. 25, 1762

Madison   Princeton, Sept. 25, 1771; Princeton, postgrad. studies, 1771–1772

Monroe   William and Mary, left before graduation 1776

J. Q. Adams   Harvard, July 18, 1787

W. H. Harrison   Hampden-Sydney, left before graduation; University of Pennsylvania Medical School, 1791

Tyler   William and Mary, July 4, 1807

Polk   North Carolina, June 4, 1818

Pierce   Bowdoin, Sept. 1, 1824

Buchanan   Dickinson, Sept. 27, 1809

Grant   U.S. Military Academy, July 1, 1843

Hayes   Kenyon, Aug. 3, 1842; Harvard Law School, graduated Jan. 1845

Garfield   Williams, Aug. 6, 1856

Arthur   Union, July 1848

B. Harrison   Miami (Ohio), June 24, 1852

McKinley   Allegheny, left before graduation; Albany Law School (N.Y.), 1866–1867

T. Roosevelt   Harvard, June 30, 1880; Columbia Law School, 1880–1881

Taft   Yale, June 27, 1878; University of Cincinnati Law School, graduated May 1, 1880

Wilson   Princeton, June 18, 1879; University of Virginia Law School, 1879–1880; Johns Hopkins, Ph. D. in political science, 1886

Harding   Ohio Central, 1882

Coolidge   Amherst, June 26, 1895

Hoover   Stanford, May 29, 1895

F. D. Roosevelt   Harvard, June 24, 1904; Columbia Law School, 1904–1907

Truman   Kansas City Law School (Mo.), 1923–1925

Eisenhower   U.S. Military Academy, June 12, 1915; Command and General Staff School (Fort Leavenworth, Kans.), 1925–1926; Army War College, 1928–1929

Kennedy   Harvard, June 20, 1940

L. B. Johnson   Southwest Texas State, Aug. 19, 1930; Georgetown University Law School, 1934–1935

Nixon   Whittier, June 9, 1934; Duke Law School, June 7, 1937

Ford Michigan, June 27, 1935; Yale Law School, June 18, 1941

Carter U.S. Naval Academy, June 5, 1946; Union, postgrad.

Reagan Eureka (Illinois), June 7, 1932

G. Bush Yale, June 22, 1948

Clinton Georgetown, June 22, 1968; Oxford (Eng.); Yale Law School, 1973

G. W. Bush Yale, 1968; Harvard Business School, June 12, 1975

Obama Occidental College; Columbia University, 1983; Harvard Law School, 1991

COLLEGES OF THE PRESIDENTS

Albany McKinley (law school)

Allegheny McKinley

Amherst Coolidge

Army War College Eisenhower

Bowdoin Pierce

Cincinnati Taft (law school)

Columbia T. Roosevelt (law school), F. D. Roosevelt (law school), Obama

Command and General Staff School Eisenhower

Dickinson Buchanan

Duke Nixon (law school)

Eureka Reagan

Georgetown L. B. Johnson (law school), Clinton

Hampden-Sydney W. H. Harrison

Harvard J. Adams, J. Q. Adams, Hayes (law school), T. Roosevelt, F. D. Roosevelt, Kennedy, G. W. Bush (business school), Obama (law school)

Johns Hopkins Wilson

Kansas City Truman (law school)

Kenyon Hayes

Miami (Ohio) B. Harrison

Michigan Ford

North Carolina Polk

Occidental Obama

Ohio Central Harding

Oxford (England) Clinton (Rhodes Scholar)

Pennsylvania W. H. Harrison (medical school)

Princeton Madison, Wilson

Southwest Texas State L. B. Johnson

Stanford Hoover

Union Arthur, Carter

U.S. Military Academy Grant, Eisenhower

U. S. Naval Academy Carter

Whittier Nixon

William and Mary Jefferson, Monroe, Tyler

Williams Garfield

Virginia Wilson (law school)

Yale Taft, Ford (law school), G. Bush, Clinton (law school), G. W. Bush

PRESIDENTS WHO DID NOT ATTEND COLLEGE

Washington
Jackson
Van Buren
Taylor
Fillmore
Lincoln
A. Johnson
Cleveland

OCCUPATIONS OF THE PRESIDENTS

Twenty-six of the forty-three Presidents were admitted to the bar as attorneys, having fulfilled the legal requirements. However, they were not all graduates of law schools.

The seventeen Presidents who were not lawyers were Washington and William Henry Harrison, who were farmers and soldiers; Hoover, an engineer; Taylor, Grant, and Eisenhower, professional soldiers; Andrew Johnson, Theodore Roosevelt, Harding, Truman, Kennedy, Lyndon Baines Johnson, Carter, Reagan, George Bush, and George W. Bush, who were public officials. George Bush and George W. Bush had also been successful businessmen before entering public service. Madison, Theodore Roosevelt, and Harding studied law but did not become lawyers.

CAREERS PRIOR TO PRESIDENCY

Washington Surveyor, planter, soldier; colonial legislator, delegate to Continental Congress, commander in chief of Continental Army, president of Constitutional Convention

J. Adams   Lawyer, colonial legislator, delegate to Continental Congress, delegate to state constitutional convention, minister to France, the Netherlands, and Great Britain

Jefferson   Lawyer, colonial legislator, delegate to Continental Congress and state constitutional convention, author of the Declaration of Independence, state legislator, governor of Virginia, minister to France, Secretary of State, Vice President

Madison   Lawyer, delegate to state constitutional convention, state legislator, member of state council and executive council, delegate to Continental Congress, delegate to Constitutional Convention, chief author of the Constitution, U.S. congressman, author of the Virginia Resolutions, Secretary of State

Monroe   Lawyer, officer in Continental Army, military commissioner of Virginia, state legislator, member of state council, delegate to Continental Congress, U.S. senator, minister to France, Great Britain, and Spain, governor of Virginia, Secretary of State, Secretary of War

J. Q. Adams   Lawyer, private secretary, minister to the Netherlands, Portugal, Prussia, Russia, and Great Britain, state senator, U.S. senator, treaty negotiator, Secretary of State

Jackson   Lawyer, saddler, owner of racing stable, delegate to state constitutional convention, U.S. congressman, U.S. senator, justice of state superior court, state senator, Army general in War of 1812 and First Seminole War, military governor of Florida

Van Buren   Lawyer, county surrogate, state senator, state attorney general, U.S. senator, governor of New York, Secretary of State, Vice President

W. H. Harrison   Army officer, secretary of Northwest Territory, territorial delegate to U.S. House, governor of Indiana Territory, Army general in War of 1812, U.S. representative, state senator, U.S. senator, minister to Colombia

Tyler   Lawyer, state legislator, member of state council, U.S. congressman, governor of Virginia, U.S. senator, Vice President

Polk   Lawyer, officer in militia cavalry, state legislator, U.S. congressman, Speaker of the House, governor of Tennessee

Taylor   Farmer, army officer rising to general in Mexican War

Fillmore   Wool comber, lawyer, state legislator, U.S. congressman, state comptroller, Vice President

Pierce   Lawyer, state legislator and house speaker, U.S. congressman, U.S. senator, delegate to state constitutional convention, chairman of state Democratic party, U.S. district attorney, Army general in Mexican War

Buchanan   Lawyer, volunteer in War of 1812, state legislator, U.S. congressman, minister to Russia and Great Britain, U.S. senator, Secretary of State

Lincoln   Farmer, store clerk, soldier, postmaster, rail-splitter, surveyor, lawyer, state legislator, U.S. congressman

A. Johnson   Tailor, alderman, mayor, state legislator, state senator, U.S. congressman, governor of Tennessee, U.S. senator, military governor, Vice President

Grant   Farmer, army officer, rising to general in Civil War; Secretary of War

Hayes   Lawyer, city solicitor, general in Civil War, U.S. congressman, governor of Ohio

Garfield   Teacher, canal driver, lawyer, state senator, general in Civil War, U.S. congressman

Arthur   Teacher, lawyer, inspector general and quartermaster general in state militia in Civil War, state Republican chairman, customhouse collector of Port of New York, Vice President

Cleveland   Lawyer, assistant district attorney, sheriff, mayor of Buffalo, governor of New York

B. Harrison   Lawyer, city attorney, Army general in Civil War, state supreme court reporter, member of Mississippi River Commission, U.S. senator

McKinley Army officer in Civil War, lawyer, county prosecutor, U.S. congressman, governor of Ohio

T. Roosevelt Officer in state national guard, state legislator, member of U.S. Civil Service Commission, New York City police commissioner, Army colonel in Spanish-American War, assistant Secretary of the Navy, governor of New York, Vice President

Taft Lawyer, assistant county prosecutor, tax collector, assistant county solicitor, judge of Cincinnati Superior Court, U.S. solicitor general, judge of Sixth U.S. Circuit Court, law professor and law school dean, commissioner and governor-general of the Philippines, Secretary of War

Wilson Lawyer, college professor, historian and political scientist, president of Princeton University, governor of New Jersey

Harding Insurance salesman, reporter, newspaper publisher, state senator, state lieutenant governor, U.S. senator

Coolidge Lawyer, city councilman, city solicitor, state legislator, mayor, state senator and senate president, state lieutenant governor, governor of Massachusetts, Vice President

Hoover Mining engineer, relief administrator during World War I, member of federal and international economic organizations, Secretary of Commerce

F. D. Roosevelt Lawyer, state senator, assistant Secretary of the Navy, governor of New York

Truman Bank and mailroom clerk, farmer, Army officer in World War I, haberdasher, county administrative judge, U.S. senator, Vice President

Eisenhower Army officer, rising to Supreme Allied Commander and five-star general in World War II; president of Columbia University, supreme commander of North Atlantic Treaty Organization

Kennedy Naval officer in World War II, journalist, U.S. congressman, U.S. senator, author

L. B. Johnson Teacher, secretary to U.S. congressman, state director of National Youth Administration, Navy aviation officer in World War II, rancher, U.S. congressman, U.S. senator, Vice President

Nixon Lawyer, businessman, Navy officer in World War II, rancher, U.S. congressman, U.S. senator, Vice President

Ford Lawyer, Navy officer in World War II, U.S. congressman and House minority leader, Vice President

Carter Career naval officer, peanut farmer and broker, chairman of county education board, church deacon, state senator, governor of Georgia

Reagan Radio announcer, movie and television actor, Army noncombat officer in World War II, president of Screen Actors Guild, spokesman for General Electric corporation, governor of California, radio and newspaper commentator, lecturer

G. Bush Navy pilot in World War II, equipment salesman, president and CEO of oil drilling company, U.S. congressman, U.S. ambassador to the United Nations, chairman of Republican National Committee, U.S. liaison chief in Beijing, director of Central Intelligence Agency, professor, Vice President

Clinton Lawyer, law professor, state attorney general, governor of Arkansas

G. W. Bush Head of oil drilling companies, owner of baseball team, governor of Texas

Obama Social activist, lawyer, state senator, U.S. senator

OCCUPATIONS AFTER TERMS

Four Presidents engaged in governmental activities after completing their terms: John Quincy Adams served in the House of Representatives, Andrew Johnson became a Senator, Taft served as Chief Justice of the Supreme Court, and Hoover was active on various government commissions. Carter served as a mediator in several international disputes, but in an extra-governmental capacity.

Grant, Theodore Roosevelt, Hoover, Truman, Eisenhower, L. B. Johnson, Nixon, and Carter devoted considerable time to writing; Roosevelt, Hoover, Truman, and Eisenhower were also active as public speakers; Carter became strongly identified with humanitarian causes.

John Adams, Pierce, and Buchanan retired from public life and avoided public appearances.

Five Presidents were active as farmers or planters: Washington, Jefferson, Madison, Jackson, and Hayes. Washington was also active as commander in chief of the army.

Benjamin Harrison was a professor of international law at Leland Stanford University.

Six Presidents traveled extensively after their terms: Van Buren, Fillmore, Polk, Pierce, Grant, and Theodore Roosevelt.

Truman, Eisenhower, L. B. Johnson, Ford, and Carter devoted much time to developing the libraries named for them.

POLITICAL EXPERIENCE

Presidents who had not revealed administrative ability prior to election or proved their vote-getting power were those famed for their military exploits, namely Washington, Taylor, Grant, and Eisenhower. Grant, however, had served in Andrew Johnson's cabinet as secretary of war ad interim.

The following is a list of the various capacities in which Presidents served and the number of Presidents who served in each:

Mayors of home towns—3

Ministers and ambassadors to foreign countries—8

Governors of states—17

Territorial governors—2

Vice Presidents—14

Members of presidential cabinets—9

U.S. Representatives—19

U. S. Senators—16

Members of both the House and Senate—10

Some Presidents served in more than one capacity.

MAYORS OF HOME TOWNS

A. Johnson   Greeneville, Tenn., 1830–1834
Cleveland   Buffalo, N.Y., 1882
Coolidge   Northampton, Mass., 1910–1911

MINISTERS AND AMBASSADORS TO FOREIGN COUNTRIES (8)

J. Adams   Netherlands, Great Britain
Jefferson   France
Monroe   France
J. Q. Adams   The Netherlands, Portugal, Prussia, Russia, Great Britain
Van Buren   Great Britain
W. H. Harrison   Colombia
Buchanan   Great Britain
G. Bush   People's Republic of China

STATE GOVERNORS (17)

Jefferson   Virginia
Monroe   Virginia
Van Buren   New York
Tyler   Virginia
Polk   Tennessee
Hayes   Ohio
A. Johnson   Tennessee
Cleveland   New York
McKinley   Ohio
T. Roosevelt   New York
Wilson   New Jersey
Coolidge   Massachusetts
F. D. Roosevelt   New York
Carter   Georgia
Reagan   California
Clinton   Arkansas
G. W. Bush   Texas

TERRITORIAL GOVERNORS (2)

Jackson   Florida
W. H. Harrison   Indiana

PRESIDENTS WHO SERVED AS VICE PRESIDENTS (14)

J. Adams
Jefferson
Van Buren
Tyler
Fillmore
A. Johnson
Arthur
T. Roosevelt
Coolidge

664

Truman
Nixon
L. B. Johnson
Ford
G. Bush

PRESIDENTS WHO SERVED IN PRESIDENTIAL CABINETS

Secretary of State

Jefferson (under Washington), Sept. 26, 1789–Mar. 3, 1797 (entered upon duties Mar. 22, 1790)

Madison (under Jefferson), Mar. 5, 1808–Mar. 3, 1801 (entered upon duties May 2, 1801)

Monroe (under Madison), Apr. 2, 1811–Mar. 3, 1817 (entered upon duties Apr. 6, 1811)

J. Q. Adams (under Monroe), Mar. 5, 1817–Mar. 3, 1825 (entered upon duties Sept. 22, 1817)

Van Buren (under Jackson), Mar. 6, 1829–May 23, 1831 (entered upon duties Mar. 28, 1829)

Buchanan (under Polk), Mar. 6, 1845–Mar. 3, 1849 (entered upon duties Mar. 10, 1845)

Buchanan (under Taylor), Mar. 4, 1849–Mar. 6, 1849

Secretary of War

Monroe (under Madison), ad interim Jan. 1, 1813–Jan. 13, 1813

Monroe (under Madison), ad interim Aug. 30, 1814–Mar. 14, 1815

Grant (under Johnson), ad interim Aug. 12, 1867–Jan. 13, 1868

Taft (under T. Roosevelt), Jan. 11, 1904–June 29, 1908 (to take effect Feb. 1, 1904)

Secretary of Commerce

Hoover (under Harding), Mar. 5, 1921–Aug. 2, 1923

Hoover (under Coolidge), Aug. 3, 1923–Aug. 21, 1928

PRESIDENTS WHO SERVED IN CONGRESS—STATES REPRESENTED AND TERMS OF OFFICE

Washington—Virginia

Continental Congress, 1774–1775

J. Adams—Massachusetts

Continental Congress 1774–1778

Jefferson—Virginia

Continental Congress, 1775–1776; 1783–1785

Madison—Virginia

Continental Congress, 1780–1783; 1786–1788

U.S. House of Representatives, 1st–4th Congresses, Mar. 4, 1789–Mar. 3, 1797

Monroe—Virginia

Continental Congress, 1783–1786

U.S. Senate, Nov. 9, 1790–May 27, 1794

J. Q. Adams—Massachusetts

U.S. Senate, Mar. 4, 1803–June 8, 1808

U.S. House of Representatives, 22nd–30th Congresses, Mar. 4, 1831–Feb. 23, 1848

Jackson—Tennessee

U.S. House of Representatives, 4th Congress, Dec. 5, 1796–Mar. 3, 1797

U.S. Senate, Nov. 1797–Apr. 1798; Mar. 4, 1823–Oct. 14, 1825

Van Buren—New York

U.S. Senate, Mar. 4, 1823–Oct. 14, 1825

W. H. Harrison—Ohio

U.S. House of Representatives, a delegate from the Territory Northwest of the River Ohio, Mar. 4, 1799–May 14, 1800

U.S. House of Representatives, 14th Congress, Oct. 8, 1816–Mar. 3, 1819, took his seat Dec. 2, 1816

U.S. Senate, Mar. 4, 1825–May 20, 1828

Tyler—Virginia

U.S. House of Representatives, 16th Congress, Dec. 16, 1817–Mar. 3, 1821

U.S. Senate, Mar. 4, 1827–Feb. 29, 1836

Polk—Tennessee

U.S. House of Representatives, 19th–25th Congresses, Mar. 4, 1825–Mar. 3, 1839

Fillmore—New York

U.S. House of Representatives, 23rd Congress, Mar. 4, 1833–Mar. 3, 1834

Pierce—New Hampshire

U.S. House of Representatives, 23rd–24th Congresses, Mar. 4, 1833–Mar. 3, 1837

U.S. Senate, Mar. 4, 1837–Feb. 28, 1842

Buchanan—Pennsylvania

U.S. House of Representatives, 17th–21st Congresses, Mar. 4, 1821–Mar. 3, 1831

U.S. Senate, Dec. 6, 1834–Mar. 5, 1845

Lincoln—Illinois

U.S. House of Representatives, 30th Congress, Mar. 4, 1847–Mar. 3, 1849

A. Johnson—Tennessee

U.S. House of Representatives, 28th–32nd Congresses, Mar. 4, 1843–Mar. 3, 1853

U.S. Senate, Oct. 8, 1857–Mar. 4, 1862; Mar. 4, 1875–July 31, 1875

Hayes—Ohio

U.S. House of Representatives, 40th–42st Congresses, Mar. 4, 1865–July 20, 1867

Garfield—Ohio

U.S. House of Representatives, 38th—46th Congresses, Mar. 4, 1863–Nov. 8, 1880

U.S. Senate (elected to the Senate, but declined Dec. 23, 1880, having been elected president of the United States)

B. Harrison—Indiana

U.S. Senate, Mar. 4, 1881–Mar. 3, 1887

McKinley—Ohio

U.S. House of Representatives, 45th–47th Congresses, Mar. 4, 1877–Mar. 3, 1883; 48th Congress, Mar. 4, 1883–May 27, 1884; 49th–51st Congresses, Mar. 4, 1885–Mar. 3, 1891

Harding—Ohio

U.S. Senate, Mar. 4, 1915–Jan. 13, 1921

Truman—Missouri

U.S. Senate, Jan. 3, 1935–Jan. 17, 1945

Kennedy—Massachusetts

U.S. House of Representatives, 80th–82nd Congresses, Jan. 3, 1947–Jan. 3, 1953

U.S. Senate, Jan. 3, 1953–Dec. 22, 1960

L. B. Johnson—Texas

U.S. House of Representatives, 75th–80th Congresses, Apr. 10, 1937–Jan. 3, 1949

U.S. Senate, Jan. 3, 1949–Jan. 3, 1961

Nixon—California

U.S. House of Representatives, 80th–81st Congresses, Jan. 3, 1947–Nov. 1950

U.S. Senate, Dec. 1, 1950–Jan. 3, 1953

Ford—Michigan

U.S. House of Representatives, 81st–93rd Congresses, Jan. 3, 1949–Dec. 5, 1973

G. Bush—Texas

U.S. House of Representatives, 90th–91st Congresses, Jan. 3, 1967–Jan. 3, 1971

Obama—Illinois

U.S. Senate, Jan. 3, 2005–Nov. 16, 2008

PRESIDENTS WHO SERVED IN BOTH HOUSES OF CONGRESS (10)

J. Q. Adams
Jackson
W. H. Harrison
Tyler
Pierce
Buchanan
A. Johnson
Kennedy
L. B. Johnson
Nixon

PRESIDENTS WHO SERVED ONLY IN THE HOUSE OF REPRESENTATIVES (9)

Madison
Polk
Fillmore
Lincoln
Hayes
Garfield (also elected to Senate, but did not serve)
McKinley
Ford
G. Bush

PRESIDENTS WHO SERVED ONLY IN THE SENATE (6)

Monroe
Van Buren
B. Harrison
Harding
Truman
Obama

PRESIDENTS WHO DID NOT SERVE IN CONGRESS (18)

Washington
J. Adams
Jefferson
Taylor
Grant
Arthur
Cleveland
T. Roosevelt
Taft
Wilson
Coolidge
Hoover
F. D. Roosevelt
Eisenhower
Carter
Reagan
Clinton
G. W. Bush

MILITARY SERVICE

The Constitution (Article II, section 2) provides that "the President shall be Commander in Chief of the Army and Navy of the United States, and of the Militia of the several states, when called into the actual Service of the United States."

Twenty-eight of the forty-three Presidents served in the nation's armed forces. They are listed below under the wars in which they served, with an asterisk preceding the name of each of the Presidents who served in two or more wars. (The dates of service are listed in the individual biographies in Part I.) Though Madison and Reagan went to war, neither served in a theater of operations.

Revolutionary War

Washington
Madison
Monroe

*Jackson

Northwest Territory Wars

*W. H. Harrison

Shawnee Confederation Conflict

*W. H. Harrison

Creek War

*Jackson

War of 1812

*Jackson
*W. H. Harrison
*Taylor
Tyler
Buchanan

Seminole War

*Jackson
*Taylor

Frontier Militia

Polk

Black Hawk War

*Taylor
Lincoln

Mexican War

*Taylor
Pierce
*Grant

Civil War

A. Johnson
*Grant
Hayes
Garfield
Arthur
B. Harrison
McKinley

Spanish-American War

T. Roosevelt

World War I

Truman
*Eisenhower

World War II

*Eisenhower
Kennedy
L. B. Johnson

667

Nixon
Ford
Reagan
G. Bush

Madison was the only President to come under enemy fire and to exercise active command over forces while in office. In 1814, during the War of 1812, President Madison assumed command of a unit known as "Barney's Battery" in an attempt to prevent British troops from reaching Washington, D.C.

The following were professional military officers:

Washington
Jackson
W. H. Harrison
Taylor
Grant
Eisenhower
Carter

Carter had eleven years of military service but did not take part in a war. He was a midshipman at the U.S. Naval Academy during World War II and an officer in the Navy's nuclear submarine program during the Korean War.

The following had no military service:

J. Adams
Jefferson
J. Q. Adams
Van Buren
Fillmore
Cleveland
Taft
Wilson
Harding
Coolidge
Hoover
F. D. Roosevelt
Clinton
G. W. Bush
Obama

PRESIDENTS WOUNDED IN ACTION

James Monroe was wounded in the shoulder at the battle of Trenton, N.J., on December 26, 1776, in the Revolutionary War.

Franklin Pierce was injured when his horse fell during the battle of Contreras on August 19, 1847, in the Mexican War.

Rutherford Birchard Hayes was wounded four times while serving in the Union army. On May 10, 1862, a shell wounded his right knee at Giles Court House, Va. He was wounded in the left arm by a musket ball on September 14, 1862, at the battle of South Mountain, Md. On September 19, 1864, while at Winchester, Va., he was wounded in his head and shoulder by a musket ball. At the battle of Cedar Creek, Va., October 19, 1864, he was wounded in the ankle, his horse was shot from under him, and he was erroneously reported dead. The following day, he was promoted to brigadier general.

John Fitzgerald Kennedy received the Purple Heart for injuries sustained in action off the Solomon Islands on August 2, 1943. Following the ramming and sinking of his PT boat, he personally rescued three of his men, one of whom was seriously wounded.

TWO FUTURE PRESIDENTS IN SAME REGIMENT DURING CIVIL WAR

The 23rd Ohio Regiment, which was organized in June 1861, had on its roster the names of two soldiers who later became Presidents of the United States. On June 23, 1861, William McKinley, age 18, was enrolled as a private. He was promoted to commissary sergeant on April 15, 1862, and commissioned as a second lieutenant on September 23, 1862, and as a first lieutenant on February 7, 1863. He became a captain on July 25, 1864. On March 13, 1865, he was brevetted a major of volunteers for gallantry and meritorious service during the campaign in West Virginia and in the Shenandoah Valley. He was mustered out July 26, 1865.

Rutherford Birchard Hayes, age 38, was commissioned a major on June 27, 1861; he advanced to lieutenant colonel on October 24, 1861, and to colonel on October 24, 1862. He was made a brigadier general of volunteers on October 19, 1864, and was brevetted major general of volunteers on March 13, 1865, for gallantry and distinguished service during the campaign of 1864 in West Virginia, and particularly at the battles of Fisher's Hill and Cedar Creek, Va. He resigned June 8, 1865.

RELIGIOUS AFFILIATION

The religious affiliation of Presidents often differed from that of their parents, since some of them adopted other religious faiths.

Episcopalian (12)

Washington, Madison, Monroe, W. H. Harrison, Tyler, Taylor, Pierce, Arthur, F. D. Roosevelt, Ford, Reagan, G. Bush

Presbyterian (6)

Jackson, Buchanan, Cleveland, B. Harrison, Wilson, Eisenhower

Unitarian (4)

J. Adams, J. Q. Adams, Fillmore, Taft

Baptist (4)

Harding, Truman, Carter, Clinton

Methodist (4)

Polk, Grant, McKinley, G. W. Bush

Disciples of Christ (2)

Garfield, L. B. Johnson

Dutch Reformed (2)

Van Buren, T. Roosevelt

Society of Friends (Quaker) (2)

Hoover, Nixon

Congregationalist (1)

Coolidge

Roman Catholic (1)

Kennedy

United Church of Christ (1)

Obama

Christian—no specific denomination (4)

Jefferson, Lincoln, A. Johnson, Hayes

THREE PRESIDENTS WON THE NOBEL PEACE PRIZE

Three Presidents were awarded the Nobel Peace Prize—two during their terms in office and one afterwards.

Theodore Roosevelt won the Prize in 1906 for his successful efforts to negotiate an end to the Russo-Japanese War. He declined to receive it while still in office and asked an emissary to deliver his speech in his stead on Dec. 10, 1906. He collected the award personally in 1910 on a visit to Norway. The money was distributed to the Red Cross and other humanitarian organizations during World War I. This was the first Nobel Prize awarded to an American.

Woodrow Wilson won the Prize in 1919 for his expression of the Fourteen Points that formed the basis for Germany's surrender in World War I and for his efforts to avoid future wars through the establishment of the League of Nations. He was too ill to travel to Norway to receive the Prize, which was accepted on his behalf by the American ambassador on Dec. 10, 1920.

More than 20 years after leaving office, Jimmy Carter was awarded the 2002 Nobel Peace Prize for his work with the Carter Center, the human rights organization he co-founded with his wife Rosalynn in 1982.

MEMBERS OF PHI BETA KAPPA—YEAR OF ELECTION, CHAPTER, AND TYPE OF MEMBERSHIP

J. Q. Adams   1787, Harvard, in course
Van Buren   1830, Union, honorary
Pierce   1825, Bowdoin, alumnus
Hayes   1880, Kenyon, alumnus
Garfield   1864, Williams, alumnus
Arthur   1848, Union, in course
Cleveland   1907, Princeton, honorary
T. Roosevelt   1880, Harvard, in course
Wilson   1889, Wesleyan, honorary
Coolidge   1921, Amherst, alumnus
F. D. Roosevelt   1929, Harvard, alumnus; 1929, Hobart, honorary
G. Bush   1948, Yale, in course
Clinton   1968, Georgetown, in course
Carter   1991, Kansas State, honorary

Members in course are elected from candidates for degrees in liberal arts and sciences, generally from the upper tenth of the graduating class.

Alumni members are elected from the alumni body of the sheltering institution; ordinarily they have been graduated at least ten years and are thought to merit recognition for scholarly accomplishment.

Honorary members are elected from outside the student and alumni bodies of the sheltering institution, and are chosen on substantially the same basis as alumni members. Of honorary members the chapters now elect severally an average of not more than one in each triennium.

PRESIDENTS WHO WERE MASONS

Washington   Aug. 4, 1753, Fredericksburg Lodge No. 4, Fredericksburg, Va.

Monroe   1775, Williamsburg Lodge No. 6, Williamsburg, Va.

Jackson   1800, Harmony Lodge No. 1, Nashville, Tenn.

Polk   Sept. 4, 1820, Columbia Lodge No. 31, Columbia, Tenn.

Buchanan   Jan. 24, 1817, Lodge No. 43, Lancaster, Pa.

A. Johnson   1851, Greeneville Lodge No. 119, Greeneville, Tenn.

Garfield   Nov. 22, 1864, Magnolia Lodge No. 20, Columbus, Ohio

McKinley   May 3, 1865, Hiram Lodge No. 21, Winchester, Va.

T. Roosevelt   Apr. 24, 1901, Matinecock Lodge No. 806, Oyster Bay, N.Y.

Taft   Feb. 18, 1909, affiliated with Kilwinning Lodge No. 356, Cincinnati, Ohio

Harding   Aug. 27, 1920, Marion Lodge No. 70, Marion, Ohio

F. D. Roosevelt   Nov. 28, 1911, Holland Lodge No. 8, Hyde Park, N.Y.

Truman   Mar. 9, 1909, Belton Lodge No. 450, Belton, Mo.

L. B. Johnson   Oct. 30, 1937, Johnson City Lodge No. 561, Johnson City, Tex.

Ford   May 18, 1951, Malta Lodge No. 465, Grand Rapids, Mich.

BOOKS WRITTEN BY THE PRESIDENTS

Practically all of the Presidents distinguished themselves as writers. Perhaps the most prolific were John Quincy Adams, Theodore Roosevelt, and Herbert Hoover.

Many of the books contained addresses and speeches and were compiled by editors. Others were extracts from famous speeches and addresses. Many of the famous speeches were published separately in deluxe editions. Many were not written for publication, but eventually were published.

The following list contains most of the books (of 36 or more pages) written by the Presidents. Posthumous collections of letters, speeches, and papers are listed after works prepared specifically for publication by the Presidents themselves. Many collected works containing letters, papers, messages, etc. have also been printed.

George Washington

The letters and papers of George Washington have been published in many collections.

John Adams

Thoughts on Government, 1776

History of the Dispute with America from Its Origin in 1754, 1784

Defence of the Constitutions of Government of the United States of America (3 volumes), 1787–1788

Discourses on Davila, 1805

Correspondence Between the Hon. John Adams and the Late William Cunningham, 1823

Familiar Letters of John Adams and His Wife Abigail Adams During the Revolution, 1876

Thomas Jefferson

A Dissertation on Canon and Feudal Law, 1765

Notes on the State of Virginia, 1785

Kentucky Resolutions, 1798

Manual of Parliamentary Practice, 1801

Proceedings of the Government of the United States in Maintaining the Public Right to the Beach of the Mississippi, 1812

Essay Towards Facilitating Instruction. . . [in the English language], 1851

Writings of Thomas Jefferson (9 volumes), 1853–54

Calendar of Correspondence of Thomas Jefferson (3 volumes), 1894–1903

Jeffersonian Cyclopedia, 1900

Jefferson's Germantown Letters, 1906

Autobiography of Thomas Jefferson, 1914

James Madison

Letters of Helvidius, 1796

Examination of the British Doctrine, 1806

670

Papers of James Madison (3 volumes), 1840

Letters and Other Writings of James Madison (4 volumes), 1865

Calendar of the Correspondence of James Madison, 1894

Writings of James Madison (9 volumes), 1900–1910

James Monroe

View of the Conduct of the Executive in the Foreign Affairs of the United States, 1798

Calendar of the Correspondence of James Monroe, 1891

Writings of James Monroe (7 volumes), 1898–1903

John Quincy Adams

Jubilee of the Constitution, 1789

An Answer to Paine's Rights of Man, 1793

Letters on Silesia, 1804

Letter to Hon. Harrison Gray Otis, 1808

Lectures on Rhetoric and Oratory, 1810

Duplicate Letters, the Fisheries and the Mississippi. Documents Relating to Transactions at the Negotiation of Ghent, 1822

Eulogy on the Life and Character of James Monroe, 1831

Dermot MacMorrogh, or the Conquest of Ireland, 1834

Oration on the Life and Character of Gilbert Motier de La Fayette, 1835

Eulogy on the Life and Character of James Madison, 1836

Letters from John Quincy Adams to His Constituents of the Twelfth Congressional District in Massachusetts, 1937

Oration Before the Inhabitants of Newburyport, 1837

Discourse on Education, 1840

Social Compact, 1842

New England Confederacy of 1648, 1843

Life of General Lafayette, 1847

Letters of John Quincy Adams to His Son on the Bible, 1850

Lives of James Madison and James Monroe, 1850

Letters and Opinions of the Masonic Fraternity, 1851

Poems of Religion and Society, 1854

Memoirs of John Quincy Adams (12 volumes), 1847–1877

Letters and Addresses on Freemasonry, 1875

Life in a New England Town (Diary of J. Q. A.), 1903

Diary of John Quincy Adams, 1929

Andrew Jackson

Correspondence of Andrew Jackson (7 volumes), 1926–1935

Martin Van Buren

Inquiry into the Origin and Course of Political Parties in the United States, 1867

Autobiography of Martin Van Buren, 1920

William Henry Harrison

Discourse on the Aborigines of the Valley of Ohio, 1840

John Tyler

Lecture Delivered Before the Maryland Institute for the Promotion of the Mechanic Arts, 1855

James Knox Polk

Diary of James Knok Polk (4 volumes), 1910

Letters of James K. Polk to Cave Johnson, 1915

Zachary Taylor

Letters of Zachary Taylor, 1908

Millard Fillmore

Early Life of Hon. Millard Fillmore, 1880

Millard Fillmore Papers (2 volumes), 1907

James Buchanan

The Administration on the Eve of the Rebellion, 1865

Works of James Buchanan (12 volumes), 1908–1911

Abraham Lincoln

Legacy of Fun, 1865

Lincoln's Anecdotes, 1867

Abraham Lincoln's Complete Works (2 volumes), 1894

Autobiography of Abraham Lincoln, 1905

Writings of Abraham Lincoln (8 volumes), 1905–1906

Life and Works of Abraham Lincoln (9 volumes), 1907

Uncollected Letters of Abraham Lincoln, 1917

Abraham Lincoln's Don'ts, 1918

Andrew Johnson

Speeches of Andrew Johnson, 1866

Ulysses Simpson Grant

Personal Memoirs (2 volumes), 1885–1886
General Grant's Letters to a Friend, 1897

Rutherford Birchard Hayes

Diary and Letters of R. B. Hayes (5 volumes), 1922

James Abram Garfield

Great Speeches of James Abram Garfield, 1881

Grover Cleveland

Principles and Purposes of Our Form of Government, 1892
Writings and Speeches of Grover Cleveland, 1892
Self Made Man in American Life, 1897
Independence of the Executive, 1900
Presidential Problems, 1904
Fishing and Shooting Sketches, 1906
Good Citizenship, 1908
Addresses—State Papers, 1909
Venezuelan Boundary Controversy, 1913
Letters of Grover Cleveland, 1933

Benjamin Harrison

Constitution and Administration of the U.S.A., 1897
This Country of Ours, 1897
Views of an Ex-President, 1901

William McKinley

Life and Speeches of William McKinley, 1896
The Tariff, 1904

Theodore Roosevelt

Naval War of 1812, 1882
Hunting Trip of a Ranchman, 1885
Personal Experiences of Life on a Cattle Ranch, 1885
Thomas Hart Benton, 1887
Ranch Life and the Hunting-Trail, 1888
Winning of the West, 1889
History of New York City, 1891
The Wilderness Hunter, 1893
Hero Tales from American History (with Henry Cabot Lodge), 1895
Gouverneur Morris, 1896

American Ideals and Other Essays, 1897
Rough Riders, 1899
Oliver Cromwell, 1900
Strenuous Life, 1900
Outdoor Pastimes of an American Hunter, 1905
Good Hunting, 1907
True Americanism, 1907
African and European Addresses, 1910
African Game Trails, 1910
New Nationalism, 1910
Conservation of Womanhood and Childhood, 1912
Realizable Ideals, 1912
History as Literature and Other Essays, 1913
Progressive Principles, 1913
Theodore Roosevelt, An Autobiography, 1913
Life-Histories of African Game Animals (with Edmund Heller), 1914
Through the Brazilian Wilderness, 1914
America and the World War, 1915
Book-Lover's Holiday in the Open, 1916
Fear God and Take Your Own Part (articles from the *Metropolitan*), 1916
The Foes of Our Own Household, 1917
Great Adventure, 1918
National Strength and International Duty, 1918
Theodore Roosevelt's Letters to His Children, 1919
Letters to Anna Roosevelt Cowles, 1870–1918, 1924
Who Should Go West, 1927
Theodore Roosevelt's Diaries of Boyhood and Youth, 1928
Letters to Kermit Roosevelt, 1902–1908, 1946

William Howard Taft

Four Aspects of Civic Duty, 1906
Present Day Problems, Addresses, 1908
Political Issues and Outlooks, 1909
Popular Government, 1913
Anti-Trust Act and the Supreme Court, 1914
United States and Peace, 1914
Ethics in Service, 1915
Our Chief Magistrate and His Powers, 1916
Liberty Under Law, 1922

Woodrow Wilson

Congressional Government, 1885
The State, 1889

State and Federal Governments of the United States, 1889

Division and Re-union, 1893

George Washington, 1896

Mere Literature and Other Essays, 1896

When a Man Comes to Himself, 1901

History of the American People (5 volumes), 1902

Constitutional Government, 1911

New Freedom, 1913

On Being Human, 1916

International Ideals, 1919

Robert E. Lee, an Interpretation, 1924

Public Papers of Woodrow Wilson (6 volumes), 1925–1927

Warren Gamaliel Harding

Rededicating America, 1920

Our Common Country, 1921

Calvin Coolidge

Have Faith in Massachusetts, 1919

Price of Freedom, 1924

America's Need for Education, 1925

Foundations of the Republic, 1926

Autobiography of Calvin Coolidge, 1929

Herbert Clark Hoover

Principles of Mining, 1909

American Individualism, 1922

New Day, 1928

Boyhood in Iowa, 1931

Hoover After Dinner, 1933

Challenge to Liberty, 1934

Addresses Upon the American Road (8 volumes), 1938–1961

America's Way Forward, 1940

Shall We Send Our Youth to War? 1940

America's First Crusade, 1942

Problems of Lasting Peace, 1942

Memoirs—Volume I, *Years of Adventure, 1874–1920,* 1951; Volume II, *The Cabinet and the Presidency, 1920–1933,* 1952; Volume III, *The Great Depression, 1929–1942,* 1952

Ordeal of Woodrow Wilson, 1958

An American Epic, 1959–1961

On Growing Up, 1962

Fishing for Fun—And to Wash Your Soul, 1963

Franklin Delano Roosevelt

Happy Warrior, Alfred E. Smith, 1928

Records of the Town of Hyde Park, 1928

Government, Not Politics, 1932

Looking Forward, 1933

On Our Way, 1934

Public Papers and Addresses of F. D. Roosevelt (13 volumes), 1938–1950

Records of Crum Elbow Precinct, Dutchess County, 1940

Harry S. Truman

Memoirs—Volume I, *Year of Decision,* 1955; Volume II, *Years of Trial and Hope,* 1956

Plain Speaking: An Oral Biography (by Merle Miller), 1974

Dwight David Eisenhower

Crusade in Europe, 1951

The White House Years—Volume I, *Mandate for Change, 1953–1956,* 1963; Volume II, *Waging Peace, 1956–1961,* 1965

At Ease, Stories I Tell to Friends, 1967

In Review: Pictures I've Kept, 1969

The Eisenhower Diaries, edited by R. H. Ferrell, 1981

John Fitzgerald Kennedy

Why England Slept, 1940

As We Remember Joe, 1945

Profiles in Courage, 1956 (Pulitzer Prize for biography, 1957)

A Nation of Immigrants, 1959

The Strategy of Peace, 1960

To Turn the Tide, 1962

The Burden and the Glory, 1964

Lyndon Baines Johnson

My Hope for America, 1964

A Time for Action, 1964

This America, 1966

The Vantage Point, Perspectives of the Presidency, 1971

Richard Milhous Nixon

Six Crises, 1962

RN: The Memoirs of Richard Nixon, 1978

The Real War, 1980

Leaders, 1982

Real Peace, 1983

No More Vietnams, 1985

1999, 1988

From: The President, 1989

In the Arena: A Memoir of Victory, Defeat, and Renewal, 1990

Seize the Moment: America's Challenge in a One-Superpower World, 1992

Beyond Peace, 1994

Gerald Rudolph Ford

Portrait of the Assassin (coauthor John R. Stiles), 1965

A Time to Heal, 1979

Jimmy Carter

Why Not the Best?, 1975

A Government as Good as Its People, 1977

Keeping Faith, 1982

Negotiation: The Alternative to Hostility, 1984

The Blood of Abraham, 1985

Everything to Gain: Making the Most of the Rest of Your Life (with Rosalynn Carter), 1987

An Outdoor Journal, 1988

Turning Point: A Candidate, a State, and a Nation Come of Age, 1992

Talking Peace: A Vision for the Next Generation, 1993

Always a Reckoning, 1995

The Little Baby Snoogle-Fleejer, 1995

Living Faith, 1996

Sources of Strength: Meditations on Scripture for a Living Faith, 1997

The Virtues of Aging, 1998

An Hour Before Daylight, 2001

Christmas in Plains: Memories, 2001

The Hornet's Nest: A Novel of the Revolutionary War, 2003

Sharing Good Times, 2004

Our Endangered Values: America's Moral Crisis, 2005

Palestine: Peace Not Apartheid, 2006

Beyong the White Houase; Waging Peace, Fighting Disease, Building Hope, 2008

A Remarkable Mother, 2008

We Can Have Peace in the Holy Land: A Plan That Will Work, 2009

Ronald Reagan

Where's the Rest of Me? 1965

Abortion and the Conscience of the Nation, 1984

An American Life, 1990

In His Own Hand: The Writings of Ronald Reagan That Reveal His Revolutionary Vision for America, 2001

George Herbert Walker Bush

Looking Forward: An Autobiography, 1987

National Security Strategy of the United States 1989–1990, 1989

(with Brent Scowcroft) *A World Transformed*, 1998

"All the Best, George Bush": My Life in Letters and Other Writings, 1999

William Jefferson Clinton

Putting People First: How We Can All Change America (with Al Gore, Jr.), 1993

My Plans for a Second Term, 1995

Between Hope and History: Meeting America's Challenges for the 21st Century 1996

Preface to the Presidency: Selected Speeches of Bill Clinton, 1974–1992, 1996

Clinton on Clinton: A Portrait of the President in His Own Words (ed. by Wayne Meyer), 1999

The Clinton Foreign Policy Reader: Presidential Speeches with Commentary (with others), 2000

My Life, 2004

Giving: How Each of Us Can Change the World, 2007

George Walker Bush

A Charge to Keep: My Journey to the White House (with Karen Hughes), 1999

Barack Obama

Dreams from My Father: A Story of Race and Inheritance, 2004

The Audacity of Hope: Thoughs on Reclaiming the American Dream, 2006

Change We Can Believe In, 2008

PRESIDENTS' SPORTS AND HOBBIES

Sports and recreations indulged in by Presidents while in office are listed below. Some Presidents were real enthusiasts, other participated mildly.

Baseball—G. W. Bush (as team owner)

Basketball—Obama

Billiards—J. Q. Adams, Garfield

Boating—G. Bush

Bowling—Nixon

Boxing—T. Roosevelt

Bridge—Eisenhower

Canoeing—Carter

Croquet—Hayes

Driving—Hayes

Fishing—Washington, Jefferson, Arthur, Cleveland, Coolidge, Eisenhower, L. B. Johnson, Carter, G. Bush

Golf—Taft, Wilson, Harding, Coolidge, Eisenhower, Nixon, Ford, G. Bush, Clinton

Hooverball—Hoover (his own invention)

Horseshoes—G. Bush

Horticulture—Jefferson

Hunting—B. Harrison, T. Roosevelt, Eisenhower, L. B. Johnson, G. Bush

Indian clubs—Coolidge

Jogging—Ford, Carter, G. Bush, Clinton, George W. Bush

Jujitsu—T. Roosevelt

Mechanical horse—Coolidge

Medicine ball—Hoover

Mountain biking—George W. Bush

Painting—Eisenhower

Piano—Truman, Nixon

Pitching hay—Coolidge

Poker—Harding, Truman

Riding—Washington, Jefferson, Jackson, Van Buren, Taylor, McKinley, T. Roosevelt, Taft, Wilson, Harding, L. B. Johnson, Reagan

Sailing—F. D. Roosevelt, Kennedy, Ford

Saxophone—Clinton

Shooting—Hayes, T. Roosevelt, Ford

Skiing—Ford, Carter

Softball—Carter

Stamp collecting—F. D. Roosevelt

Swimming—J. Q. Adams, Grant, McKinley, Wilson, F. D. Roosevelt, Truman, Kennedy, Ford, Carter, Reagan

Tennis—T. Roosevelt, Carter, G. Bush

Touch football—Kennedy, Clinton

Townball—Lincoln

Trapshooting—Coolidge

Violin—Jefferson, Tyler

Walking—J. Q. Adams, Jefferson, Lincoln, McKinley, Wilson, Truman

Weight training—Obama

Wrestling—Lincoln, T. Roosevelt

Several Presidents participated in sports at college. Gerald R. Ford, who played linebacker and center on the University of Michigan's championship football teams in 1932 and 1933, was voted Most Valuable Player in 1934. He received offers from several professional teams. Dwight D. Eisenhower played football for the U.S. Military Academy at West Point. Known as the "Kansas Cyclone," he ran seventy yards in a game against Yale in 1912. Jimmy Carter was a cross-country runner at the U.S. Naval Academy, and John F. Kennedy was a member of the Harvard varsity swimming team. George Bush was team captain and "good field, fair hit" first baseman for the varsity Yale baseball team. He hit for an average of .280 in his senior year, when Yale lost in the College World Series to the University of Southern California.

PRESIDENTS' MUSICAL ACCOMPLISHMENTS

Very few Presidents had musical training or the ability to play instruments. Jefferson and Tyler played the violin, Truman and Nixon the piano, and Coolidge the harmonica. As a young man, Harding played the alto horn and the cornet. Clinton played the saxophone and performed at a public ball the evening of his inauguration.

PRESIDENTIAL PETS

The Presidents and their families, particularly the children, have had a collection of pets that for its diversity would have been the envy of many a zoological park. At one time or another, the White House sheltered nearly everything that can walk, crawl, swim, or fly. Zebras, coyotes, badgers, guinea pigs, hyenas, alligators, lizards, snakes, turtles, tropical fish, and birds—not to mention innumerable horses and ponies, and of course cats and dogs—have shared the Executive Mansion and its manicured grounds.

The pets were brought to the White House by the presidential families, purchased by them during the Presidents' tenures, or given to them by foreign dignitaries or by admiring or self-seeking constituents. No complete tabulation of pets has been made, but some of the creatures were described by Margaret Truman in her book *White House Pets* (New York: McKay, 1969).

Dolley Madison had a macaw, John Quincy Adams raised silkworms, Andrew Johnson kept white mice, and Theodore Roosevelt had a young lion and several bear cubs. During the Taft administration, a cow, Pauline Wayne, grazed on the White House lawn, which was periodically patrolled by Enoch Gander. McKinley kept a Mexican yellow parrot and briefly, roosters, to the consternation of the other White House residents.

Dogs seem to have been the favorites of the media. Franklin D. Roosevelt's Scottie, Fala, was almost as famous as the President himself. The Trumans had an Irish setter named Mike, and the Nixons had one named King Timahoe (the better-known Checkers, a cocker spaniel, lived at the vice presidential home). Harding had an Airedale, Laddie Boy, and Lyndon Baines Johnson owned the beagles Him and Her, to whom dog lovers rallied when the President picked them up by their ears (L. B. J. believed that this was the proper way to lift dogs). One of the beagles (Him) attended Johnson's inaugural parade. Liberty, the golden retriever belonging to the Ford family, gave birth to nine puppies in the White House.

The Reagans had two dogs, Lucky and Rex. Lucky, a Bouvier des Flandres, was transferred to the Reagans' California ranch after she misbehaved in the White House. Rex, a King Charles spaniel, was a gift from William F. Buckley, Jr.

The elder Bushes were fond of springer spaniels. Barbara Bush wrote two books, *C. Fred's Story* and *Millie's Book,* about the family dogs. George and Laura Bush entered the White House with a springer spaniel named Spot, who was one of Millie's daughters (born in the White House on March 17, 1989), and a Scottish terrier named Barney. They also had an American Shorthair cat named India.

India was preceded as First Cat by Socks Clinton, who belonged to Chelsea Clinton, both the senior Clintons being allergic. After Chelsea went to college, the Clintons found another home for Socks and acquired a dog, a golden retriever named Buddy.

The National Zoological Park in Washington, D.C., has been the recipient of many exotic animals sent to Presidents or to the American people by foreign governments. In 1972, following Nixon's visit to the People's Republic of China, the Chinese government gave two giant pandas—Ling-Ling and Hsing-Hsing—to the zoo in exchange for two musk oxen.

PRESIDENTS' FAVORITE FOODS

Many aspects of life have changed from President Washington's time to the era of President Obama. One of the things that has generally remained constant, however, is the Presidents' appreciation of ice cream. George Washington was said to have spent $200 in one summer on ice cream; Thomas Jefferson acquired a taste for the delight and a recipe in France; Dolley Madison served "pink" ice cream; and the Lyndon Johnson family had peaches shipped from home for their Texas peach ice cream.

Other staple presidential favorites have been pancakes and spoon breads. Jefferson indulged in these, and so did Jackson, who liked buckwheat and cornmeal pancakes; Coolidge, who came from Vermont and liked plenty of maple syrup on his buckwheat pancakes; Franklin Roosevelt, who enjoyed buttered pancakes with maple syrup; and Lyndon Johnson, a giant who liked tiny pancakes for breakfast, often topped with Mrs. Johnson's peach preserves. Washington preferred fish to meat, perhaps because of his ill-fitting dentures. Franklin Roosevelt liked fish for breakfast, and Kennedy was fond of New England fish chowder. Lyndon Johnson, despite the Texas barbecue image he presented, liked seafood and also spinach souffles. Clinton, though partial to fast-food snacks, emphasized vegetables for the White House table; in this he was preceded by Jefferson, who advocated fresh vegetables and salads and instructed the public on the health benefits of a produce-laden diet. (George Bush, however, declared that freedom from broccoli was a perk of office.) One favorite vegetable has been cabbage, in its pickled form as sauerkraut, which was enjoyed with pork by Presidents Buchanan, Harding, and F. D. Roosevelt. Another favorite has been sweet potatoes topped with tiny toasted marshmallows. That dish was served to and admired by Presidents Hoover, F. D. Roosevelt, Eisenhower, and L. B. Johnson.

The Presidents with the smallest appetites were Kennedy, Arthur, and Lincoln. Lincoln liked to dine on fruit salad, cheese, and crackers. The fattest President, Taft, enjoyed the elaborate multi-course dinners popular in his time, and one of his favorite dishes was turtle soup.

George W. Bush favored Mexican food and pizza with cheeseburger toppings. Obama was also known as a pizza fan, though when cooking at home he specialized in chili.

Residence

RESIDENT STATES OF THE PRESIDENTS

The Presidents, when inaugurated, were residents (though not necessarily natives) of the states listed below.

New York (8): Van Buren, Fillmore, Arthur, Cleveland, T. Roosevelt, F. D. Roosevelt, Eisenhower, Nixon

Ohio (6): W. H Harrison, Hayes, Garfield, McKinley, Taft, Harding

Virginia (5): Washington, Jefferson, Madison, Monroe, Tyler

Massachusetts (4): J. Adams, J. Q. Adams, Coolidge, Kennedy

Tennessee (3): Jackson, Polk, A. Johnson

Texas (3): L. B. Johnson, G. Bush, G. W. Bush

California (2): Hoover, Reagan

Illinois (3): Lincoln, Grant, Obama

Arkansas (1): Clinton

Georgia (1): Carter

Indiana (1): B. Harrison

Louisiana (1): Taylor

Michigan (1): Ford

Missouri (1): Truman

New Hampshire (1): Pierce

New Jersey (1): Wilson

Pennsylvania (1): Buchanan

PRESIDENTS WHO RESIDED IN STATES OTHER THAN THEIR BIRTHPLACES

The twenty Presidents listed below were residents of states other than their native states. The name of each is followed by (1) the state in which he resided and (2) the state in which he was born.

Jackson   Tennessee, South Carolina

W. H. Harrison   Ohio, Virginia

Polk   Tennessee, North Carolina

Taylor   Louisiana, Virginia

Lincoln   Illinois, Kentucky

A. Johnson   Tennessee, North Carolina

Grant   Illinois, Ohio

Arthur   New York, Vermont

Cleveland   New York, New Jersey

B. Harrison   Indiana, Ohio

Wilson   New Jersey, Virginia

Coolidge   Massachusetts, Vermont

Hoover   California, Iowa

Eisenhower   New York, Texas

Nixon   New York, California

Ford   Michigan, Nebraska

Reagan   California, Illinois

G. Bush   Texas, Massachusetts

G. W. Bush   Texas, Connecticut

Obama   Illinois, Hawaii

FAMOUS PRESIDENTIAL HOMES

Many of the Presidents were born in or lived in homes which have become famous. Some of the more famous homes or estates follow:

Washington   Mount Vernon, near Alexandria, Va.

Jefferson   Monticello, near Charlottesville, Va.

Madison   Montpelier, near Charlottesville, Va.

Monroe   Ash Lawn, Oak Hill, near Leesburg, Va.

Jackson   The Hermitage, near Nashville, Tenn.

Van Buren   Lindenwald, Kinderhook, N.Y.

Tyler   Sherwood Forest, Charles City County, Va.

Buchanan   Wheatland, Pa.

Hayes   Spiegel Grove, near Fremont, Ohio

T. Roosevelt   Sagamore Hill, Oyster Bay, N.Y.

F. D. Roosevelt   Springwood, Hyde Park, N. Y.

Coolidge   The Beeches, Northampton, Mass.

L. B. Johnson   The LBJ Ranch, near Johnson City, Tex.

There are other well-known residences, such as the Eisenhower farm at Gettysburg, Pa., but they are not known by any special names.

Physical Characteristics

PHYSICAL APPEARANCE

There is much interest in comparing the physical characteristics of the Presidents at the time when they were inaugurated or assumed office.

As contemporary reports vary and as writers interpret according to their own impressions, many conflicting reports exist. The description of a Republican President by a Democrat may differ from one by a Republican, and even without bias due to politics, personal appraisals by different people may vary.

The following is a list of known characteristics:

Washington   Height, 6 feet 2 inches; weight, 175 pounds; brown sandy hair, powdered, under powdered wig; blue eyes; high brow, scar on left cheek, black mole under right ear, pock-marks on nose and cheeks; strongly pointed chin; false teeth; powerful physique; broad sloping shoulders

J. Adams   Height, 5 feet 7 inches; corpulent; bald; expanded eyebrows

Jefferson   Height, 6 feet 2½ inches; sandy, reddish hair; prominent cheekbones and chin; large hands and feet

Madison   Height, 5 feet 6 inches at most; some sources say 5 feet 4 (shortest President); weight about 100 pounds; blond hair; blue eyes; weak speaking voice

Monroe   Height, 6 feet; rugged physique; blue-gray eyes, well shaped nose, broad forehead; stooped shoulders

J. Q. Adams   Height, 5 feet 7 inches; bald

Jackson   Height; 6 feet 1 inch; thin; weight, 140 pounds; bushy iron-gray hair, brushed high above forehead; clear, dark blue eyes; prominent eyebrows

Van Buren   Height, 5 feet 6 inches; small, erect, plump; red and graying hair, bald spot; deep wrinkles

W. H. Harrison   Height, 5 feet 8 inches; long, thin face, irregular features

Tyler   Height, 6 feet; thin; light brown hair; blue eyes; light complexion; high-bridged nose

Polk   Height, 5 feet 8 inches; nearly white hair, worn long; sharp gray eyes; high forehead, thin, angular brow

Taylor   Height, 5 feet 8 inches; weight, 170 pounds; black hair; gray eyes, squint; ruddy complexion; short legs in proportion to body

Fillmore   Height, 5 feet 9 inches; finely proportioned body; thin, grayish hair; blue eyes; light complexion; smooth forehead; well-developed chest

Pierce   Height, 5 feet 10 inches; erect bearing; penetrating dark gray eyes;

678

light complexion; smooth forehead; well-developed chest

Buchanan Height, 6 feet; imperfect vision; light complexion; protruding chin; short neck; muscular appearance

Lincoln Height, 6 feet 4 inches (tallest President); weight, 180 pounds; beard; black hair; gray eyes

A. Johnson Height, 5 feet 10 inches; stocky; brown hair, worn long; light eyes; high forehead

Grant Height, 5 feet $8^1/_2$ inches; beard; square straight brows; large head; heavy nostrils; firm-set mouth

Hayes Height, 5 feet $8^1/_2$ inches; weight, 170 pounds; dark brown hair; sandy red beard; deeply set blue eyes; large head, high forehead, straight nose, circling brows; mild but very audible voice

Garfield Height, 6 feet; light brown, graying hair, receding hair line; beard; blue eyes; large head, high forehead; strong frame, broad shoulders

Arthur Height, 6 feet 2 inches; full side whiskers and mustache; handsome appearance; well-proportioned body

Cleveland Height, 5 feet 11 inches; weight, 260 pounds, corpulent; graying hair, growing bald; heavy, drooping mustache; short neck

B. Harrison Height, 5 feet 6 inches; blond, graying hair; full beard; small, bright blue eyes; short neck; short legs

McKinley Height, 5 feet 7 inches; high forehead, receding hair line; prominent chin; broad forehead

T. Roosevelt Height, 5 feet 10 inches; pince-nez eyeglasses with thick lenses; prominent teeth; bushy eyebrows; drooping mustache; high voice

Wilson Height, 5 feet 11 inches; weight, 170 pounds; eyeglasses; clean-cut, ascetic face

Harding Height, 6 feet; high forehead; graying hair; bushy eyebrows

Coolidge Height, 5 feet 10 inches; large, clear forehead; thin nose; tightly set lips

Hoover Height, 5 feet 11 inches; square-faced; ruddy complexion

F. D. Roosevelt Height, 6 feet 2 inches; weight, 188 pounds; high forehead; graying hair; wore braces on his legs

Truman Height, 5 feet 9 inches; weight, 167 pounds; receding steel-gray hair, parted on left; hazel eyes; eyeglasses with thick lenses

Eisenhower Height, 5 feet $10^1/_2$ inches; weight, 168–173 pounds; bald, with fringe of sandy, graying hair; blue eyes; ruddy complexion; engaging smile

Kennedy Height, 6 feet; weight, 170–175 pounds; reddish-brown hair; handsome appearance

L. B. Johnson Height, 6 feet 3 inches; weight, 200 pounds; large ears; mobile, expressive face

Nixon Height, 5 feet $11^1/_2$ inches; receding hair line; bushy eyebrows; upswept nose; jutting jaw

Ford Height, 6 feet; weight, 195 pounds; square jaw; receding sandy hair; contact lenses; left-handed; ambidextrous; athletic build

Carter Height, 5 feet $9^1/_2$ inches; weight, 160 pounds; graying reddish-brown hair; blue eyes; prominent teeth; soft voice

Reagan Height, 6 feet 1 inch; weight, 185 pounds; dark brown hair; blue eyes; contact lenses; hearing aids in both ears

G. Bush Height, 6 feet 2 inches; weight, 195 pounds; brown hair; blue eyes; trim, athletic build

Clinton Height, 6 feet 2 inches; weight, 230 pounds; sandy, graying hair; blue eyes; ruddy complexion

G. W. Bush Height, 5 feet 11 inches; weight, 190 pounds; brown, graying hair; blue eyes; trim, athletic build

Obama Height, 6 feet $1^1/_2$ inches; weight, 180 pounds; dark hair; brown eyes; lean and fit; brown skin; prominent ears; melodious voice

LEFT-HANDED PRESIDENTS

The Presidents who are known to have been left-handed are Truman, Reagan, G. Bush, Clinton, and Obama. Truman and Reagan wrote with their right hands because they had been trained to do so in childhood; they used their left hands for other activities.

Gerald Ford was ambidextrous; he used his right hand for sports and his left hand for writing. James Garfield is also rumored to have been ambidextrous, but it cannot be confirmed.

The inclusion of Herbert Hoover on most lists of left-handed Presidents is an error. Hoover was right-handed, according to the archival staff at the Herbert Hoover Presidential Library and Museum.

In the presidential election of 1992, the candidates of both major parties—George H. W. Bush and Bill Clinton—were left-handed; so was Ross Perot, their independent challenger. The 2008 election was another contest between two left-handed candidates—Barack Obama and John McCain. Since Gerald Ford succeeded to the presidency in 1974, the occupants of the Oval Office have either been left-handed or ambidextrous, with only two exceptions: Jimmy Carter and George W. Bush.

Death and Burial

DATE OF DEATH, AGE AT DEATH, PLACE OF DEATH, AND PLACE OF BURIAL OF THE PRESIDENTS

Washington   Dec. 14, 1799; 67 years, 295 days; Mount Vernon, near Alexandria, Va.

J. Adams   July 4, 1826; 90 years, 247 days; Quincy, Mass.

Jefferson   July 4, 1826; 83 years, 82 days; Monticello, near Charlottesville, Va.

Madison   June 28, 1836; 85 years, 104 days; Montpelier, near Charlottesville, Va.

Monroe   July 4, 1831; 73 years, 67 days; New York, N.Y.; buried at Richmond, Va.

J. Q. Adams   Feb. 23, 1848; 80 years, 227 days; Washington, D.C.; buried at Quincy, Mass.

Jackson   June 8, 1845; 78 years, 85 days; The Hermitage, near Nashville, Tenn.

Van Buren   July 24, 1862; 79 years, 231 days; Kinderhook, N.Y.

W. H. Harrison   Apr. 4, 1842; 68 years, 54 days; Washington, D.C.; buried at North Bend, Ohio

Tyler   Jan. 18, 1862; 71 years, 295 days; Richmond, Va.

Polk   June 15, 1849, 53 years, 225 days; Nashville, Tenn.

Taylor   July 9, 1850; 65 years, 227 days; Washington, D.C.; buried at Louisville, Ky.

Fillmore   Mar. 8, 1874; 74 years, 60 days; Buffalo, N.Y.

Pierce   Oct. 8, 1869; 64 years, 319 days; Concord, N.H.

Buchanan   June 1, 1868; 77 years, 40 days; Lancaster, Pa.

Lincoln   Apr. 15, 1865; 56 years, 62 days; Washington, D.C., buried at Springfield, Ill.

A. Johnson   July 31, 1875; 66 years, 214 days; Carter's Station, Tenn.; buried at Greeneville, Tenn.

Grant   July 23, 1885; 63 years, 87 days; Mt. McGregor, N.Y.; buried at New York, N.Y.

Hayes   Jan. 17, 1893; 70 years, 105 days; Fremont, Ohio

Garfield   Sept. 19, 1881; 49 years, 304 days; Elberon, N.J.; buried at Cleveland, Ohio

Arthur   Nov. 18, 1886; 57 years, 44 days; New York, N.Y.; buried at Albany, N.Y.

Cleveland   June 24, 1908; 71 years, 98 days; Princeton, N.J.

B. Harrison   Mar. 13, 1901; 67 years, 205 days; Indianapolis, Ind.

McKinley   Sept. 14, 1901; 58 years, 228 days; Buffalo, N.Y.; buried at Canton, Ohio

T. Roosevelt   Jan. 6, 1919; 60 years, 71 days; Oyster Bay, N.Y.

Taft   Mar. 8, 1930; 72 years, 174 days; Washington, D.C.; buried at Arlington National Cemetery, Arlington, Va.

Wilson   Feb. 3, 1924; 67 years, 36 days; Washington, D.C.

Harding   Aug. 2, 1923; 57 years, 273 days; San Francisco, Calif., buried at Marion, Ohio

Coolidge   Jan. 5, 1933; 60 years, 185 days; Northampton, Mass.; buried at Plymouth, Vt.

Hoover   Oct. 20, 1964; 90 years, 71 days, New York, N.Y.; buried at West Branch, Iowa

F. D. Roosevelt   Apr. 12, 1945; 63 years, 72 days; Warm Springs, Ga.; buried at Hyde Park, N.Y.

Truman   Dec. 26, 1972; 88 years, 232 days; Kansas City, Mo.; buried at Independence, Mo.

Eisenhower   Mar. 28, 1969; 78 years, 165 days; Washington, D.C.; buried at Abilene, Kan.

Kennedy   November 22, 1963; 46 years, 177 days; Dallas, Tex.; buried at Arlington National Cemetery, Arlington, Va.

L. B. Johnson   Jan. 22, 1973; 64 years, 148 days; San Antonio, Tex.; buried at Stonewall, Tex.

Nixon   Apr. 22, 1994; 81 years, 113 days; New York, N.Y.; buried at Yorba Linda, Calif.

Ford   Dec. 26, 2006; 93 years, 165 days; Rancho Mirage, Calif.; buried at Grand Rapids, Mich.

Reagan   June 5, 2004; 93 years, 120 days; Los Angeles, Calif.; buried at Simi Valley, Calif.

DEATH DATES ARRANGED BY MONTHS OF THE YEAR

January

5, 1933—Coolidge
6, 1919—T. Roosevelt
17, 1893—Hayes
18, 1862—Tyler
22, 1973—L. B. Johnson

February

3, 1924—Wilson
23, 1848—J. Q. Adams

March

8, 1874—Fillmore
8, 1930—Taft
13, 1901—B. Harrison
28, 1969—Eisenhower

April

4, 1842—W. H. Harrison
12, 1945—F. D. Roosevelt
15, 1865—Lincoln
22, 1994—Nixon

June

1, 1868—Buchanan
5, 2004—Reagan
8, 1845—Jackson
15, 1849—Polk
24, 1908—Cleveland
28, 1836—Madison

July

4, 1826—J. Adams
4, 1826—Jefferson
4, 1831—Monroe
9, 1850—Taylor
23, 1885—Grant
24, 1862—Van Buren
31, 1865—A. Johnson

August

2, 1923—Harding

September

14, 1901—McKinley
19, 1881—Garfield

October

8, 1869—Pierce
20, 1964—Hoover

November

18, 1886—Arthur
22, 1963—Kennedy

December

14, 1799—Washington
26, 1972—Truman
26, 2006—Ford

PRESIDENTS' DEATHS

Of the thirty-eight Presidents no longer living in 2009, eight died in office and thirty survived their terms.

Three Presidents died on July 4: John Adams and Thomas Jefferson in 1826, and James Monroe in 1831.

Both of the Presidents who were elected as Whigs—William Henry Harrison and Zachary Taylor—died in office.

Two Democratic Presidents died in office: Franklin Delano Roosevelt, who died during his fourth term, and John Fitzgerald Kennedy, who was assassinated.

Four Republican Presidents died in office: Abraham Lincoln, James Abram Garfield, and William McKinley, who were assassinated, and Warren Gamaliel Harding. Lincoln and McKinley were serving their second terms.

PRESIDENTS WHO DIED IN OFFICE

Eight Presidents died in office:

William Henry Harrison died on Apr. 4, 1842, at Washington, D.C.; served 1 month; unexpired term of 3 years and 11 months filled by John Tyler

Zachary Taylor died on July 9, 1850, at Washington, D.C.; served 1 year, 4 months, and 5 days; unexpired term of 2 years, 7 months, and 26 days filled by Millard Fillmore

Abraham Lincoln died on Apr. 15, 1865, at Washington, D.C.; served 1 month and 10 days of second term; unexpired term of 3 years, 10 months, and 20 days filled by Andrew Johnson

James Abram Garfield died on Sept. 19, 1881, at Elberon, N.J.; served 6 months and 15 days; unexpired term of 3 years, 5 months, and 15 days filled by Chester Alan Arthur

William McKinley died on Sept. 14, 1901, at Buffalo, N.Y.; served 6 months and 10 days of second term; unexpired term of 3 years, 5 months, and 20 days filled by Theodore Roosevelt.

Warren Gamaliel Harding died on Aug. 2, 1923, at San Francisco, Calif.; served 2 years, 4 months, and 29 days; unexpired term of 1 year, 7 months, and 2 days filled by Calvin Coolidge

Franklin Delano Roosevelt died on Apr. 12, 1945, at Warm Springs, Ga.; served 2 months and 23 days of fourth term; unexpired term of 3 years, 9 months, and 7 days filled by Harry S. Truman

John Fitzgerald Kennedy died on Nov. 22, 1963, at Dallas, Tex.; served 2 years, 10 months 2 days; unexpired term of 1 year, 1 month, and 29 days filled by Lyndon Baines Johnson

The presidency of the United States has been held for a total of 23 years and 11 months by men who were not elected to the office but who obtained it through the death of the incumbent.

THE TWENTY-YEAR JINX— BROKEN BY THE OLDEST PRESIDENT

The Presidents elected every twenty years from 1840 through 1960 all died in office.

William Henry Harrison, the ninth president, was elected on November 3, 1840, and died in office on April 4, 1842.

Abraham Lincoln, the sixteenth president, was elected on November 6, 1860. He was assassinated, dying in office on April 15, 1865.

James Abram Garfield, the twentieth president, was elected on November 2, 1880. He was assassinated, dying in office on September 19, 1881.

William McKinley, the twenty-fifth president, was elected on November 6, 1900. He was assassinated, dying in office on September 14, 1901.

Warren Gamaliel Harding, the twenty-ninth president, was elected on November 2, 1920, and died in office on August 2, 1923.

Franklin Delano Roosevelt, the thirty-second president, was elected on November 5, 1940, and died in office on April 12, 1945.

John Fitzgerald Kennedy, the thirty-fifth president, was elected on November 8, 1960. He was assassinated, dying in office on November 22, 1963.

Despite this "jinx," more than a dozen candidates vied for the presidency in 1980. The victor was Ronald Reagan. Early in his first term, Reagan was shot in the chest by a would-be assassin in front of the Washington Hilton Hotel. However, surgeons removed the bullet from Reagan's left lung and he made a swift recovery, remarkably swift for a 70-year-old man. Ronald Reagan, the oldest man to be elected President, broke the 20-year jinx.

LENGTH OF LIFE AFTER COMPLETION OF TERM

Of the thirty-eight Presidents who are no longer living, thirty survived their terms of office. The following list shows the number of years lived after retirement from the presidency:

Polk   103 days
Arthur   1 year, 260 days
Washington   2 years, 285 days
Wilson   2 years, 337 days
Coolidge   3 years, 308 days
L. B. Johnson   4 years, 2 days
Monroe   6 years, 122 days
A. Johnson   6 years, 149 days
Buchanan   7 years, 89 days
B. Harrison   8 years, 9 days
Eisenhower   8 years, 67 days
Jackson   8 years, 96 days
Grant   8 years, 142 days
T. Roosevelt   9 years, 309 days
Cleveland   11 years, 112 days (after second term)
Hayes   11 years, 319 days
Pierce   12 years, 218 days
Reagan   15 years, 137 days
Tyler   16 years, 320 days
Taft   17 years, 4 days
Jefferson   17 years, 122 days
J. Q. Adams   18 years, 356 days
Cleveland   19 years, 112 days (after first term)
Madison   19 years, 116 days
Nixon   19 years, 246 days
Truman   19 years, 340 days
Fillmore   21 years, 4 days
Van Buren   21 years, 142 days
J. Adams   25 years, 122 days
Ford   29 years, 340 days
Hoover   31 years, 231 days

AGE AT DEATH

The average life span of the thirty-eight Presidents who are no longer living was 70 years and 312 days. The following list shows the relative longevity of the Presidents:

Ford   93 years, 165 days
Reagan   93 years, 120 days
J. Adams   90 years, 247 days
Hoover   90 years, 71 days
Truman   88 years, 232 days
Madison   85 years, 104 days
Jefferson   83 years, 82 days
Nixon   81 years, 113 days
J. Q. Adams   80 years, 227 days
Van Buren   79 years, 231 days
Eisenhower   78 years, 165 days
Jackson   78 years, 85 days
Buchanan   77 years, 40 days
Fillmore   74 years, 60 days
Monroe   73 years, 67 days
Taft   72 years, 174 days
Tyler   71 years, 295 days
Cleveland   71 years, 98 days
Hayes   70 years, 98 days
W. H. Harrison   68 years, 54 days
Washington   67 years, 295 days
B. Harrison   67 years, 205 days
Wilson   67 years, 36 days
A. Johnson   66 years, 214 days
Taylor   65 years, 227 days
Pierce   64 years, 319 days
L. B. Johnson   64 years, 148 days
Grant   63 years, 87 days
F. D. Roosevelt   63 years, 72 days
Coolidge   60 years, 185 days
T. Roosevelt   60 years, 71 days
McKinley   58 years, 228 days
Harding   57 years, 273 days
Arthur   57 years, 44 days
Lincoln   56 years, 62 days
Polk   53 years, 225 days
Garfield   49 years, 304 days
Kennedy   46 years, 177 days

RELATIVE LONGEVITY OF THE PRESIDENTS AND THEIR PARENTS

The following list notes the age at death:
(1) of each President;
(2) of his father; and
(3) of his mother.

Washington

67 years, 295 days

about 49 years
81 years

J. Adams

90 years, 247 days
70 years, 106 days
98 years, 43 days

Jefferson

83 years, 82 days
49 years, 170 days
56 years, 50 days

Madison

85 years, 104 days
77 years, 337 days
98 years, 33 days

Monroe

73 years, 67 days
unknown
unknown

J. Q. Adams

80 years, 227 days
90 years, 247 days
73 years, 351 days

Jackson

78 years, 85 days
unknown
unknown

Van Buren

79 years, 231 days
80 years, 40 days
about 70 years

W. H. Harrison

68 years, 54 days
65 years, 19 days
about 62 years

Tyler

71 years, 295 days
65 years, 312 days
about 36 years

Polk

53 years, 225 days
55 years, 123 days
75 years, 57 days

Taylor

65 years, 227 days

84 years, 291 days
61 years, 364 days

Fillmore

74 years, 60 days
91 years, 343 days
about 51 years

Pierce

64 years, 319 days
81 years, 97 days
about 70 years

Buchanan

77 years, 40 days
about 60 years
about 66 years

Lincoln

56 years, 62 days
73 years, 11 days
34 years, 242 days

A. Johnson

66 years, 214 days
about 33 years
72 years, 211 days

Grant

63 years, 87 days
79 years, 167 days
84 years, 169 days

Hayes

70 years, 105 days
35 years, 197 days
74 years, 198 days

Garfield

49 years, 304 days
33 years, 126 days
86 years, 122 days

Arthur

57 years, 44 days
78 years, 326 days
66 years, 262 days

Cleveland

71 years, 98 days
49 years, 104 days
76 years, 165 days

B. Harrison

67 years, 205 days

73 years, 233 days
40 years, 28 days

McKinley

58 years, 228 days
85 years, 9 days
88 years, 234 days

T. Roosevelt

60 years, 71 days
46 years, 140 days
49 years, 221 days

Taft

72 years, 174 days
80 years, 197 days
80 years, 88 days

Wilson

67 years, 36 days
80 years, 327 days
61 years, 110 days

Harding

57 years, 273 days
84 years, 160 days
66 years, 159 days

Coolidge

60 years, 185 days
80 years, 352 days
40 years

Hoover

90 years, 71 days
34 years, 112 days
35 years, 294 days

F. D. Roosevelt

63 years, 72 days
72 years, 145 days
86 years, 351 days

Truman

88 years, 232 days
62 years, 333 days
94 years, 243 days

Eisenhower

78 years, 165 days
79 years, 168 days
84 years, 78 days

Kennedy

46 years, 177 days

81 years, 73 days
104 years, 184 days

L. B. Johnson

64 years, 148 days
60 years, 11 days
77 years, 78 days

Nixon

81 years, 113 days
78 years, 274 days
82 years, 207 days

Ford

93 years, 165 days
59 years, 208 days
75 years, 201 days

Reagan

93 years, 120 days
57 years, 309 days
77 years, 1 day

RELATIVE LONGEVITY OF THE PRESIDENTS AND THEIR WIVES

It is often stated that the presidency is a killing job, but over half of the Presidents who are no longer living had greater life spans than their respective wives (though they did not necessarily survive their wives). Most of these Presidents lived in the 18th and 19th centuries. The following list shows the number of years by which the President's life span exceeded that of his wife:

J. Adams   16 years, 261 days
Jefferson   49 years, 125 days
Madison   4 years, 51 days
Monroe   10 years, 347 days
J. Q. Adams   3 years, 136 days
Jackson   16 years, 260 days
Van Buren   43 years, 262 days
Tyler (first wife)   19 years, 358 days
Tyler (second wife)   2 years, 228 days
Taylor   1 year, 261 days
Fillmore (first wife)   19 years, 43 days
Fillmore (second wife)   6 years, 131 days
Pierce   7 years, 54 days
A. Johnson   1 year, 111 days
Hayes   12 years, 169 days

685

Arthur   14 years, 274 days
B. Harrison (first wife)   7 years, 181 days
T. Roosevelt (first wife)   37 years, 244 days
Wilson (first wife)   12 years, 319 days
Hoover   21 years, 152 days
Nixon   14 days
Reagan (first wife)   2 years, 237 days

The following is a list of wives whose life spans were greater than those of their husbands:

Mrs. Washington   3 years, 40 days
Mrs. W. H. Harrison   20 years, 161 days
Mrs. Polk   34 years, 119 days
Mrs. Lincoln   7 years, 153 days
Mrs. Grant   13 years, 235 days
Mrs. Garfield   36 years, 25 days
Mrs. Cleveland   12 years, 12 days
Mrs. B. Harrison (second wife)   22 years, 45 days
Mrs. McKinley   1 year, 124 days
Mrs. T. Roosevelt (second wife)   26 years, 340 days
Mrs. Taft   9 years, 331 days
Mrs. Wilson (second wife)   22 years, 27 days
Mrs. Harding   3 years, 190 days
Mrs. Coolidge   18 years, 1 day
Mrs. F. D. Roosevelt   24 years, 320 days
Mrs. Truman   9 years, 15 days
Mrs. Eisenhower   4 years, 187 days
Mrs. Kennedy   18 years, 118 days
Mrs. L. B. Johnson   30 years, 53 days

PRESIDENTS WHO SURVIVED THEIR WIVES

Of the thirty-eight Presidents who are no longer living, fifteen became widowers. The following list shows the number of years each lived after the death of his wife:

J. Adams   7 years, 249 days
Jefferson   43 years 301 days
Monroe   284 days
Jackson   16 years, 168 days
Van Buren   43 years, 169 days
Tyler (first wife)   19 years, 130 days
Fillmore (first wife)   20 years, 343 days

Pierce   5 years, 310 days
Hayes   3 years, 206 days
Arthur   6 years, 310 days
B. Harrison (first wife)   8 years, 140 days
T. Roosevelt (first wife)   34 years, 326 days
Wilson (first wife)   9 years, 181 days
Hoover   20 years, 286 days
Nixon   303 days

PRESIDENTS' WIVES WHO SURVIVED THEIR HUSBANDS

Of the forty Presidents' wives who are no longer living (not counting Jane Wyman, whose marriage to Ronald Reagan ended in divorce), twenty-five became widows. The following list shows the number of years each lived after the death of her husband:

Mrs. Washington   2 years, 159 days
Mrs. Madison   13 years, 14 days
Mrs. J. Q. Adams   4 years, 80 days
Mrs. W. H. Harrison   22 years, 327 days
Mrs. Tyler (second wife)   27 years, 173 days
Mrs. Polk   42 years, 60 days
Mrs. Taylor   2 years, 40 days
Mrs. Fillmore (second wife)   7 years, 156 days
Mrs. Lincoln   17 years, 92 days
Mrs. A. Johnson   168 days
Mrs. Grant   17 years, 144 days
Mrs. Garfield   36 years, 176 days
Mrs. Cleveland   40 years, 127 days
Mrs. B. Harrison (second wife)   46 years, 298 days
Mrs. McKinley   5 years, 254 days
Mrs. T. Roosevelt (second wife)   29 years, 267 days
Mrs. Taft   13 years, 75 days
Mrs. Wilson (second wife)   37 years, 328 days
Mrs. Harding   1 year, 111 days
Mrs. Coolidge   24 years, 184 days
Mrs. F. D. Roosevelt   17 years, 209 days
Mrs. Truman   9 years, 296 days
Mrs. Eisenhower   10 years, 217 days
Mrs. Kennedy   30 years, 178 days
Mrs. L. B. Johnson   34 years, 170 days

CAUSES OF DEATH

The exact causes of death of many Presidents are not known, since medical and death certificates were not always filed. Furthermore, in many instances there were complications, and the direct causes of death could not be ascertained. There may also be differences in terminology; in the past, illnesses were grouped under generic headings, whereas today the same illnesses would be described in specific terms.

Washington Pneumonia

J. Adams Debility

Jefferson Diarrhea

Madison Debility

Monroe Debility

J. Q. Adams Paralysis

Jackson Consumption, dropsy

Van Buren Asthma

W. H. Harrison Pleurisy, pneumonia

Tyler Bilious fever

Polk Diarrhea

Taylor Bilious fever, typhoid fever, cholera morbus

Fillmore Debility, paralysis

Pierce Stomach inflammation

Buchanan Rheumatic gout

Lincoln Assassination

A. Johnson Paralysis

Grant Cancer (carcinoma of the tongue and tonsils)

Hayes Heart disease

Garfield Assassination

Arthur Bright's disease, apoplexy (cerebral hemorrhage)

Cleveland Debility, coronary sclerosis

B. Harrison Pneumonia

McKinley Assassination

T. Roosevelt Inflammatory rheumatism

Taft Debility

Harding Apoplexy (rupture of brain artery), pneumonia, enlargement of the heart, high blood pressure

Wilson Apoplexy, paralysis

Coolidge Heart failure (coronary thrombosis)

Hoover Bleeding from upper gastrointestinal tract; strained vascular system

F. D. Roosevelt Cerebral hemorrhage

Truman Minor lung congestion, complexity of organic failures, collapse of cardiovascular system

Eisenhower Heart disease

Kennedy Assassination

L. B. Johnson Heart failure

Nixon Cerebral hemorrhage

Ford Arteriosclerotic cerebrovascular disease and diffuse arteriosclerosis

Reagan Alzheimer's Disease

ASSASSINATIONS AND ATTEMPTED ASSASSINATIONS

Four Presidents—Lincoln, Garfield, McKinley, and Kennedy—were assassinated while in office.

Attempts were made against the lives of Presidents Jackson, Truman, Ford (twice), and Reagan. Attempts were made also against Lincoln and Franklin Delano Roosevelt when they were Presidents-elect, and against former President Theodore Roosevelt when he was campaigning for reelection. Details are given in the respective biographical chapters in Part I.

On August 28, 1965, Congress enacted a law (79 Stat. L. 580) making it a federal crime to kill, kidnap, or assault the President, Vice-President, or President-elect. It is also a crime to threaten these officials with death or bodily harm.

LAST WORDS

Since emotion and grief are important factors in death scenes, there is variance in the reported accounts. The generally accepted last words of the Presidents follow:

Washington "It is well. I die hard, but I am not afraid to go."

J. Adams "Thomas Jefferson still survives."

Jefferson "Is it the fourth?" (A reference to the Fourth of July); "I resign my spirit to God, my daughter to my country."

Madison "I always talk better lying down."

J. Q. Adams "This is the last of earth. I am content."

Jackson "I hope to meet each of you in heaven. Be good children, all of you, and

687

strive to be ready when the change comes."

Van Buren "There is but one reliance."

W. H. Harrison "Sir, I wish you to understand the true principles of government. I wish them carried out. I ask nothing more." (Spoken in delirium to Vice President Tyler)

Tyler "Doctor, I am going . . . perhaps it is best."

Polk "I love you, Sarah, for all eternity, I love you."

Taylor "I am about to die. I expect the summons very soon. I have tried to discharge all my duties faithfully. I regret nothing, but am sorry that I am about to leave my friends."

Fillmore "The nourishment [food] is palatable."

Buchanan "O Lord, God Almighty, as Thou wilt."

A. Johnson "Oh, do not cry. Be good children and we shall meet in Heaven."

Grant "Water."

Hayes "I know that I am going where Lucy is." (His wife)

Garfield "The people my trust." "Oh, Swaim, there is a pain here . . . oh, oh, Swaim." (Spoken to David Gaskill Swaim, his chief of staff)

Cleveland "I have tried so hard to do right."

B. Harrison "Are the doctors here?" "Doctor . . . my lungs."

McKinley "It is God's way. His will be done, not ours." "We are all going, we are all going, we are all going. Oh, dear."

T. Roosevelt "Please put out the light."

Wilson "Edith." (His wife) "I'm a broken machine, but I'm ready."

Harding "That's good. Go on, read some more." (Spoken to his wife, who was reading to him)

F. D. Roosevelt "I have a terrific headache."

Eisenhower "I've always loved my wife. I've always loved my children. I've always loved my grandchildren. And I have always loved my country."

Kennedy "My God, I've been hit." (This is what Kennedy is reputed to have said,

although one of the Secret Service officers riding in the car when the President was shot has said that Kennedy made no remarks after he was struck.)

No last words have been reported for Presidents Nixon, Ford, and Reagan, the last of whom suffered from Alzheimer's Disease and was unable to speak.

BURIAL SITES

Washington Mount Vernon, near Alexandria, Va., family vault

J. Adams Quincy, Mass. First Unitarian Church

Jefferson Monticello, near Charlottesville, Va., family plot

Madison Montpelier, near Charlottesville, Va., family plot

Monroe Richmond, Va., Hollywood Cemetery

J. Q. Adams Quincy, Mass., First Unitarian Church

Jackson The Hermitage, near Nashville, Tenn., burial plot

Van Buren Kinderhook, N.Y., Kinderhook Cemetery

W. H. Harrison North Bend, Ohio, William Henry Harrison Memorial State Park

Tyler Richmond, Va., Hollywood Cemetery

Polk Nashville, Tenn., State Capitol grounds

Taylor Louisville, Ky., Zachary Taylor National Cemetery

Fillmore Buffalo, N.Y., Forest Lawn Cemetery

Pierce Concord, N.H., Old North Cemetery

Buchanan Lancaster, Pa., Woodward Hill Cemetery

Lincoln Springfield, Ill., Oak Ridge Cemetery

A. Johnson Greeneville, Tenn., Andrew Johnson National Cemetery

Grant New York, N.Y., Grant's Tomb

Hayes Fremont, Ohio, Spiegel Grove State Park

Garfield Cleveland, Ohio, Lake View Cemetery

Arthur Albany, N.Y., Rural Cemetery

Cleveland Princeton, N.J., Princeton Cemetery

B. Harrison Indianapolis, Ind., Crown Hill Cemetery

McKinley Canton, Ohio, near Westlawn Cemetery

T. Roosevelt Oyster Bay, N.Y., Young's Memorial Cemetery

Taft Arlington, Va., Arlington National Cemetery

Wilson Washington, D.C., National Cemetery

Harding Marion, Ohio, Marion Cemetery

Coolidge Plymouth, Vt., Notch Cemetery

Hoover West Branch, Iowa, Herbert Hoover Library and Birthplace

F. D. Roosevelt Hyde Park, N.Y., family plot

Truman Independence, Mo., Harry S. Truman Library Institute

Eisenhower Abilene, Kan., Eisenhower Center Library and Museum

Kennedy Arlington, Va., Arlington National Cemetery

L. B. Johnson Stonewall, Tex., family plot at LBJ ranch

Nixon Yorba Linda, Calif., Richard Nixon Library and Birthplace

Ford Grand Rapids, Mich., Gerald R. Ford Presidential Museum

Reagan Simi Valley, Calif., Ronald Reagan Presidential Library and Museum

PRESIDENTS BURIED AT ARLINGTON

The first President buried in the National Cemetery at Arlington, Va., was William Howard Taft, interred on March 11, 1930. On November 25, 1963, President John Fitzgerald Kennedy was buried at Arlington. His widow, Jacqueline Kennedy Onassis, was buried next to him in May 1994.

PRESIDENTS BURIED IN THE SAME CHURCH

Two Presidents are buried in the same church: John Adams, the second president, who died on July 4, 1826, and his son, John Quincy Adams, the sixth president, who died on February 23, 1848. Their burial place is the First Unitarian Church, Quincy, Mass.

THE PRESIDENTS' ESTATES

There has always been interest in comparing the estates of Presidents. In order to obtain an accurate impression, there are certain basic facts to consider. Appraisals of the same estate by different people often result in different valuations, especially concerning real property and personal possessions. The real market value of a piece of property cannot be ascertained unless it is sold.

When comparing the monetary value of Presidents' estates, one must consider the purchasing power of the dollar in the years under consideration. For example, it might now take over $20 million to acquire Washington's real estate, which was valued at $530,000. (It may be noted that Washington was "land poor." Although his land holdings were worth a great deal, he was sometimes hard-pressed for cash.)

Even if the figures given are exact to the penny, they are not always accurate estimates of the Presidents' wealth because many Presidents, while living, made appreciable gifts and donations to their families. Often estates were divided and distributed before death to avoid the imposition of excise and inheritance taxes.

The figures below indicate the total value of the estates, not solely cash and securities. They are estimates and are likely to vary from the final amounts reported by the administrators or filed with the surrogates.

Washington $530,000 ("land poor")

J. Adams $30,000

Jefferson owed $40,000

Madison value unknown

Monroe none

J. Q. Adams $60,000

Jackson value unknown ("land poor")

Van Buren value unknown

W. H. Harrison in debt

Tyler value unknown

Polk $100,000 to $150,000

Taylor $142,000

Fillmore value unknown

Pierce $70,000

Buchanan value unknown

Lincoln $83,000 (net estate of $83,343 increased by the administrators to $110,974)

A. Johnson $50,000

Grant   none (left manuscript of book which brought in approximately $500,000)

Hayes   value unknown

Garfield   value unknown

Arthur   value unknown

Cleveland $250,000

B. Harrison $375,000

McKinley $215,000

T. Roosevelt $811,000

Taft $475,000

Harding $487,000

Wilson $600,000

Coolidge $500,000

Hoover   value unknown (in the millions)

F. D. Roosevelt $1,085,500

Truman   exact value unknown

Eisenhower   exact value unknown

Kennedy   value unknown (in the millions)

Johnson   exact value unknown (most likely in the millions)

Nixon   value undisclosed

Ford   value undisclosed

Reagan   value undisclosed

Four Presidents left no wills. Those who died intestate were Abraham Lincoln, Andrew Johnson, Ulysses Simpson Grant, and James Abram Garfield.

Calvin Coolidge made the shortest will: "Not unmindful of my son John, I give all my estate both real and personal to my wife Grace Coolidge, in fee simple. Home at Washington, District of Columbia, this twentieth day of December a.d. nineteen hundred and twenty six, signed by me on the date in the presence of the testator and of each other as witnesses to said will and the signature thereof, Calvin Coolidge."

PRESIDENTIAL LIBRARIES

Most of the recent Presidents have founded libraries to house their presidential papers, gifts, and memorabilia, as well as films, tapes, and clippings relating to their terms in office. The libraries were all planned and built by private organizations using private funds. The federal government operates them through the National Archives and Records Service, usually with the assistance of a private foundation. The research collections are open to scholars by appointment, and the general collections are open daily to the public.

The Franklin D. Roosevelt Library at the President's childhood home in Hyde Park, N.Y., was dedicated on July 4, 1940, by the President, who also designed it. Besides its extensive collection of documents, it contains a small naval museum and many family mementos. Roosevelt was the first President to plan a library while in office, and the arrangements he made provided the basis for future repositories, via the Presidential Libraries Act of 1955.

The Truman Library in Independence, Mo., was dedicated on July 6, 1957. Along with the presidential papers, it contains a large mural and several paintings by Thomas Hart Benton, one of Truman's favorite artists. The President is buried in the courtyard of the building.

The Lyndon Baines Johnson Library is situated on the Austin campus of the University of Texas, in a building constructed by the university. The library was dedicated on May 22, 1971, by the former President. It is the only presidential library to offer free admission, and at 134,695 square feet, it is the largest of the libraries.

The Eisenhower Center is a complex of buildings in Abilene, Kan. One of them is a nondenominational chapel that is also the burial place of the President. Another building, the Dwight D. Eisenhower Library, houses the presidential papers. Memorabilia from Eisenhower's military career and from the White House are displayed in a museum. The library was dedicated on May 1, 1972.

The Herbert Hoover Library was dedicated on August 10, 1972, and is located in West Branch, Iowa, the birthplace of the President. The library contains the records of Hoover's long career in public service, rare books, his fishing tackle, and a collection of valuable Chinese porcelain.

The John Fitzgerald Kennedy Library was dedicated on October 20, 1979. It is housed in a building designed by I. M. Pei on the Columbia Point promontory in Boston, near the University of Massachusetts.

The Gerald R. Ford Library was dedicated on April 27, 1981, at Ann Arbor, Mich., on the University of Michigan campus. Ford's papers, including many from his years in the House of Representatives, are preserved here.

The Jimmy Carter Presidential Library is located in Atlanta, Georgia. It was dedicated in September 1986. Associated with Emory University, it contains the Carter Presidential Center, which organizes efforts to expand voter rights and improve public health.

The Richard M. Nixon Library is located in Yorba Linda, Calif. Designed as a Mediterranean villa, it was dedicated on July 19, 1990, in the presence of President George Bush and former Presidents Nixon, Ford, and Reagan and their wives. The Nixon presidential archives are located in College Park, Md.

The Ronald Reagan Presidential Library in Simi Valley, Calif., was dedicated on Nov. 4, 1991. The dedication was attended by the largest gathering of Presidents and their wives and widows ever assembled. Present were President and Mrs. George Bush, former Presidents Carter, Ford, Nixon, and Reagan and their wives, and Lady Bird Johnson, the widow of Lyndon Baines Johnson.

George Bush established his presidential library and museum on the campus of Texas A&M University in College Station. It opened to the public on November 7, 1997. The site also housed the Bush School of Government and Public Service. When the library reopened in 2007 after a renovation, the 83-year-old former President marked the occasion with a parachute jump, assisted by an Army paratrooper.

The Clinton Presidential Center is part of the University of Arkansas in Little Rock and houses the university's Clinton School of Public Service, as well as the presidential library and museum and the headquarters of the William J. Clinton Foundation.

The George W. Bush Presidential Center will be built on the campus of Southern Methodist University, Dallas, Tex.

PRESIDENTS PAST AND FUTURE

Between the years 1822 and 1826, there were eighteen men living who had held the office of President, were in office, or were destined to hold office—the greatest number alive at any four-year period in history. The following is a list of those eighteen Presidents, with dates of birth and death:

J. Adams 1735–1826
Jefferson 1743–1826
Madison 1751–1836
Monroe 1758–1831
J. Q. Adams 1767–1848
Jackson 1767–1845
Van Buren 1782–1862
W. H. Harrison 1773–1842
Tyler 1790–1862
Polk 1795–1849
Taylor 1784–1850
Fillmore 1800–1874
Pierce 1804–1869
Buchanan 1797–1868
Lincoln 1809–1865
A. Johnson 1808–1875
Grant 1822–1885
Hayes 1822–1893

A similar compilation of Vice Presidents appears in the section VICE PRESIENTS PAST AND FUTURE on page 767.

FORMER PRESIDENTS ALIVE WHEN NEW PRESIDENT TOOK OFFICE

J. Adams 1797—Washington
Jefferson 1801—J. Adams
Madison 1809—J. Adams, Jefferson
Monroe 1817—J. Adams, Jefferson, Madison
J. Q. Adams 1825—J. Adams, Jefferson, Madison, Monroe
Jackson 1829—Madison, Monroe, J. Q. Adams; 1833 (second term)—Madison, J. Q. Adams
Van Buren 1837—J. Q. Adams, Jackson
W. H. Harrison 1842—J. Q. Adams, Jackson, Van Buren
Tyler 1842—J. Q. Adams, Jackson, Van Buren
Polk 1845—J. Q. Adams, Jackson, Van Buren, Tyler
Taylor 1849—Van Buren, Tyler, Polk
Fillmore 1850—Van Buren, Tyler
Pierce 1853—Van Buren, Tyler, Fillmore
Buchanan 1857—Van Buren, Tyler, Fillmore, Pierce

Lincoln 1861—Van Buren, Tyler, Fillmore, Pierce, Buchanan

A. Johnson 1865—Fillmore, Pierce, A. Johnson

Grant 1869—Fillmore, Pierce, A. Johnson

Hayes 1877—Grant

Garfield 1881—Grant, Hayes

Arthur 1881—Grant, Hayes

Cleveland 1885—Grant, Hayes, Arthur

B. Harrison 1889—Hayes, Cleveland

Cleveland 1893—B. Harrison

McKinley 1897—Cleveland, B. Harrison

T. Roosevelt 1901—Cleveland

Taft 1909—T. Roosevelt

Wilson 1913—T. Roosevelt, Taft

Harding 1921—Taft, Wilson

Coolidge 1923—Taft, Wilson

Hoover 1929—Taft, Coolidge

F. D. Roosevelt 1933—Hoover

Truman 1945—Hoover

Eisenhower 1953—Hoover, Truman

Kennedy 1961—Hoover, Truman, Eisenhower

L. B. Johnson 1963—Hoover, Truman, Eisenhower; 1965 (second term)—Truman, Eisenhower

Nixon 1969—Truman, Eisenhower, Johnson; 1973 (second term)—Johnson

Ford 1974—Nixon

Carter 1977—Nixon, Ford

Reagan 1981—Nixon, Ford, Carter

G. Bush 1989—Nixon, Ford, Carter, Reagan

Clinton 1993—Nixon, Ford, Carter, Reagan, G. Bush; 1997 (second term)—Ford, Carter, Reagan, G. Bush

G. W. Bush 2001—Ford, Carter, Reagan, G. Bush, Clinton; 2005 (second term)—Ford, Carter, G. Bush, Clinton

Obama 2009—Carter, G. Bush, Clinton, G. W. Bush

PERIODS IN WHICH THERE WERE NO LIVING FORMER PRESIDENTS

There were five periods in United States history during which no former Presidents were alive.

The first period was December 14, 1799–March 4, 1801, during the administration of John Adams. George Washington, the first and only former President, died on December 14, 1799.

The second period was July 31, 1875–March 4, 1877, during the administration of Ulysses S. Grant. Andrew Johnson died on July 31, 1875.

The third period was June 24, 1908–March 4, 1909, during the administration of Theodore Roosevelt. Grover Cleveland died on June 24, 1908.

The fourth period was January 5, 1933–March 4, 1933, during the administration of Herbert Hoover. Calvin Coolidge died on January 5, 1933.

The fifth period was January 22, 1973–August 9, 1974, during the second term of Richard Milhous Nixon. Harry S. Truman died on December 26, 1972, and L. B. Johnson died on January 22, 1973.

Commemoratives

PRESIDENTS DEPICTED ON COINS

The first President depicted on a U.S. coin (excluding commemorative currency) was Abraham Lincoln, shown on the bronze penny issued during the centennial of his birth. The new design for the bronze one-cent piece was adopted in April 1909, and coinage began in May 1909, at the mint in Philadel-phia, Pa. The first delivery of the coins was made on June 30, 1909, to the Cashier of the Mint. No coins were paid out until after the close of the fiscal year, the distribution beginning on August 2, 1909.

The second President depicted on a U.S. coin was George Washington, shown on a twenty-five-cent silver coin, the bicentennial quarter commemorating the bicentennial of his birth. The first coins were struck on June 4, 1932, at the Philadelphia mint.

The third President depicted on a U.S. coin was Thomas Jefferson, shown on the five-cent piece of 1938. The first coins were ordered cast on October 1, 1938, and were released to the public on November 15, 1938. They were coined at the mints at Philadelphia, Pa., Denver, Colo., and San Francisco, Calif.

The fourth President depicted on a U.S. coin was Franklin Delano Roosevelt, shown on a ten-cent silver piece. Production of the coins commenced on January 16, 1946. They were coined at Denver and San Francisco and were issued on January 30, 1946, Roosevelt's birthday.

The fifth President depicted on a U.S. coin was John Fitzgerald Kennedy, shown on a fifty-cent piece. The coins were authorized by Congress on December 30, 1963 (77 Stat. L. 843) to replace the Franklin half-dollars. They were minted at Denver and Philadelphia and were first offered for public distribution on March 24, 1964. About 70 million coins were minted.

The sixth President depicted on a U.S. coin was Dwight David Eisenhower, shown on a silver dollar minted from 1971 through 1978.

A NEW VIEW OF JEFFERSON

The first U.S. coin to show a President in any view other than profile was a redesign of the Jefferson nickel, released on January 12, 2006. Based on a portrait by the painter Rembrandt Peale, it shows a three-quarter view of Jefferson, together with the word "Liberty" in his handwriting. The obverse was a picture of Monticello.

THE PRESIDENTIAL DOLLARS

A series of one-dollar gold coins depicting all the Presidents was launched by the U.S. Mint on February 15, 2007. The dollars were released at the rate of four a year. The reverse of each coin showed the Statue of Liberty.

Running concurrently with this program was the First Spouse Gold Coin series, depicting the Presidents' wives on $10 gold pieces. Each one showed a portrait of the First Lady on the obverse and an image related to her

life on the reverse. For Presidents who were widowers or bachelors during their terms of office, the substitute coin showed a contemporary image of Liberty.

LINCOLN BICENTENNIAL PENNIES

On February 12, 2009, the bicentennial of Lincoln's birth, the U.S. Mint released a new version of the hundred-year-old Lincoln penny, showing the traditional portrait of Lincoln on the obverse and one of four new designs on the reverse. These designs showed his log cabin in Kentucky, Lincoln as a young Indiana railsplitter, Lincoln as a lawyer in Illinois, and the Capitol building with its dome under construction as it looked during Lincoln's presidency.

PRESIDENTS DEPICTED ON PAPER CURRENCY

Portraits of Presidents appear on U.S. paper currency on the following denominations: Washington, one dollar; Jefferson, two dollars; Lincoln, five dollars; Jackson, twenty dollars; Grant, fifty dollars; McKinley, five hundred dollars; Cleveland, one thousand dollars; Madison, five thousand dollars; Wilson, one hundred thousand dollars.

PRESIDENTS DEPICTED ON POSTAGE STAMPS

The Presidents have served as subjects on postage stamps since the first issue on July 1, 1847, when a 10-cent black stamp depicting George Washington went on sale in New York City, together with a five-cent stamp depicting Benjamin Franklin. Washington and Franklin were featured repeatedly in subsequent issues, joined by Jefferson in 1851 and eventually by other individuals who had held the office of president.

It was not until 1938 that all the Presidents were depicted in a single issue. This series, known as "The Prexies," showed likenesses of all the Presidents from Washington to Coolidge, arranged in accordance with their tenure of office. The following list names the President, the denomination and color of the stamp, and the date of issue in 1938:

Washington   1-cent green, Apr. 25

J. Adams   2-cent red, June 3

Jefferson 3-cent purple, June 16
Madison 4-cent pink, July 1
Monroe 5-cent blue, July 21
J. Q. Adams 6-cent red-orange, July 28
Jackson 7-cent sepia, Aug. 4
Van Buren 8-cent olive, Aug. 11
W. H. Harrison 9-cent pink, Aug. 18
Tyler 10-cent salmon, Sept. 2
Polk 11-cent blue, Sept. 8
Taylor 12-cent lavender, Sept. 14
Fillmore 13-cent green, Sept. 22
Pierce 14-cent blue, Oct. 6
Buchanan 15-cent gray, Oct. 13
Lincoln 16-cent black, Oct. 20
Johnson 17-cent crimson, Oct. 27
Grant 18-cent brown, Nov. 3
Hayes 19-cent lilac, Nov. 10
Garfield 20-cent green, Nov. 10
Arthur 21-cent steel blue, Nov. 22
Cleveland 22-cent copper red, Nov. 22
B. Harrison 24-cent gray, Dec. 2
McKinley 25-cent burgundy, Dec. 2
T. Roosevelt 30-cent blue, Dec. 8
Taft 50-cent lavender, Dec. 8
Wilson $1 lavender and black, Aug. 29
Harding $2 green and black, Sept. 29
Coolidge $5 red and black, Nov. 17

Various individual Presidents were depicted as part of the Liberty series in 1954, the Prominent American series in 1965, and the Great Americans series in 1980.

George Washington's portrait has been shown on far more stamp issues than that of any other President. He has appeared more than 250 times on American stamps and more than 200 times on the stamps of other nations.

THE PRESIDENTIAL MEDALS

Each of the Presidents of the United States is commemorated by official bronze medals. Available in two sizes, 3-inch diameter and 15/16-inch diameter, the medals are designed by prominent designers and sold on a non-profit basis by the United States Mint in Philadelphia, Pa.

PRESIDENTS IN THE HALL OF FAME

The Hall of Fame for Great Americans on the campus of Bronx Community College of the City University of New York (formerly the campus of New York University) displays busts of thirteen Presidents.

At the first Hall of Fame election in 1900, five Presidents were elected: Washington, John Adams, Jefferson, Lincoln, and Grant.

In 1905, two more Presidents were elected: Madison and John Quincy Adams.

Five years later, Jackson was elected. In 1930, Monroe was elected, and in 1935, Cleveland. Both Wilson and Theodore Roosevelt were elected in 1950. Franklin D. Roosevelt was elected in 1969, but 19 years elapsed while $25,000 was collected to pay for the sculptor's commission.

One of the qualifications for election is that 25 years must have passed between the death of the nominee and the election.

PRESIDENTS IN STATUARY HALL

Statuary Hall, established by act of July 2, 1864, permits each state to place in Statuary Hall, in the House of Representatives, two statues honoring their distinguished citizens. The statues of three Presidents have been placed in the rotunda: Garfield by Ohio, Jackson by Tennessee, and Washington by Virginia.

STATES AND STATE CAPITALS NAMED FOR PRESIDENTS

Only one state, Washington, bears the name of a President. The capital cities of four states were named for Presidents; Jackson, Miss.; Jefferson City, Mo.; Lincoln, Neb.; and Madison, Wis.

COUNTIES NAMED FOR PRESIDENTS

The following is a list of counties named for Presidents. (A number of similarly named counties commemorate other individuals who bore the same names as certain Presidents.)

Washington—31

Ala., Ark., Colo., Fla., Ga., Idaho, Ill. Ind., Iowa, Kan., Ky., La., Me., Md., Minn., Miss., Mo., Neb., N.Y., N.C., Ohio, Okla., Ore., Pa., R.I., Tenn., Tex., Utah, Vt., Va., Wis.

Jefferson—26

Ala., Ark., Colo., Fla., Ga., Idaho, Ill., Ind., Iowa, Kan., Ky., La., Miss., Mo., Mont., Neb., N.Y., Ohio, Okla., Ore., Pa., Tenn., Tex., Wash., W.Va., Wis.

Jackson—22

Ala., Ark., Colo., Fla., Ill., Ind., Iowa, Kan., Ky., La., Mich., Miss., Mo., N.C., Ohio, Okla., Ore., S.D., Tenn., Tex., W. Va., Wis.

Madison—19

Ala., Ark., Fla., Ga., Idaho, Ill., Ind., Iowa, Ky., La., Miss., Mo., Mont., N.Y., N.C., Ohio, Tenn., Tex., Va.

Lincoln—16

Ark., Colo., Idaho, Kan., La., Minn., Miss., Neb., Nev., N.M., Okla., Ore., S.D., Wash., W.Va., Wyo.

Monroe—14

Ala., Ark., Fla., Ga., Ill., Ind., Ky., Mich., Miss., Mo., N.Y., Ohio, Tenn., W.Va.

Grant—12

Ark., Kan., La., Minn., Neb., N.M., N.D., Okla., Ore., S.D., Wash., W.Va.

Polk—11

Ark., Fla., Ga., Iowa., Minn., Mo., Neb., Ore., Tenn., Tex., Wis.

J. Adams—7

Idaho, Miss., Neb., Ohio, Pa., Wash., Wis.

Garfield—6

Colo., Mont., Neb., Okla., Utah, Wash.

J. Q. Adams—4

Ill., Ind., Iowa, N.D.

Van Buren—4

Ark., Iowa, Mich., Tenn.

W. H. Harrison—4

Ind., Iowa, Miss., Ohio

Taylor—4

Fla., Ga., Iowa, Ky.

Pierce—4

Ga., Neb., Wash., Wis.

Buchanan—3

Iowa, Mo., Va.

Tyler—2

Texas, W.Va.

Fillmore—2

Minn., Neb.

Cleveland—2

Ark., Okla.

T. Roosevelt—2

Mont., N.M.

Hayes—1

Neb.

McKinley—1

N.M.

Arthur—1

Neb.

Harding—1

N.M.

No counties have been named for Andrew Johnson, Benjamin Harrison, Taft, or Wilson, or for the Presidents following Harding.

THE PRESIDENTIAL MOUNTAIN RANGE

The Presidential Range of the White Mountains in New Hampshire includes a group of peaks named for Presidents: Mount Washington (6,288 feet), Mount Adams (5,798 feet), Mount Jefferson (5,715 feet), Mount Pierce (4,312 feet), and Mount Jackson (4,052 feet). Mount Quincy Adams, a spur of Mount Adams, is 5,470 feet.

OTHER MOUNTAINS NAMED FOR PRESIDENTS

There are two mountains named for Presidents in the Franconia Range in New Hampshire: Mount Garfield (4,488 feet) and Mount Lincoln (5,108 feet). There is also a Mount Lincoln (4,013 feet) in Vermont.

Mount McKinley (20,320 feet; the highest peak in North America) and Mount Hayes (13,740 feet) are both in the Alaska Range.

Mount Cleveland (5,680 feet) in the Aleutian Islands is a live volcano, which last erupted in 1951.

The Lewis Range in Montana includes Mount Cleveland (10,448 feet) and Mount Jackson (10,003 feet).

Mount Adams (12,307 feet) and Mount Jefferson (10,495 feet) are both in the Cascade Range, in Washington and Oregon, respectively.

There is a Mount Lincoln in the Park Range in Colorado (14,284 feet) and there are two peaks called Mount Grant in Nevada, one in the Clan Alpine Mountains (11,247 feet) and the other in the Wassuk Range (11,303 feet).

There is a Mount Jackson, formerly Mount Andrew Jackson, in Antarctica. It is 13,745 feet high.

Three mountains in Canada bear the names of U.S. Presidents: Mount Roosevelt (9,500 feet) in British Columbia, named for F. D. Roosevelt; Mount Eisenhower (9,400 feet) in Alberta, named for the General in 1946; and Mount Kennedy (13,095 feet) in the Yukon. Mount Kennedy was climbed for the first time in 1965, by a team that included the President's brother, Robert Francis Kennedy.

RIVERS NAMED FOR PRESIDENTS

The Jefferson River and the Madison River are located in Montana. They come together with the Gallatin River to form the Missouri.

The Rio Roosevelt, in the Amazon Basin in Brazil, was named for Theodore Roosevelt, who explored the area in 1914.

General Statistics

BIRTHS

8 of 43 Presidents were born in Virginia

15 of 43 were born in Ohio, New York, or Massachusetts

4 of 43 were born in a hospital

6 of 43 were born in October

PARENTS AND ANCESTORS OF THE PRESIDENTS

28 of 43 Presidents were of English or part English ancestry

1 of 43 was partly of African ancestry

21 of 43 had fathers who were farmers or planters

4 of 43 had fathers who were lawyers

4 of 43 had fathers who were judges, magistrates, or justices of the peace

3 of 43 had fathers who were ministers

1 of 43 had a father who was a physician

3 of 43 had fathers who were state governors

1 of 43 had a father who was a U.S. Senator

2 of 43 had a father who was President

1 of 43 had a grandfather who was President

3 of 43 were born after the death fo their fathers

13 of 43 lost their fathers before they were 21

7 of 43 lost their mothers before they were 21

12 of 43 had fathers who married twice

2 of 43 had fathers who married more than than

5 of 43 had mothers who married twice

1 of 43 had a mother who married more than once

7 of 43 had fathers living at their inaugurations

14 of 43 had mothers living at their inaugurations

3 of 43 had both parents living at their inaugurations

SIBLINGS OF THE PRESIDENTS

7 of 43 Presidents had 9 or more brothers and sisters

14 of 43 had 8 or more brothers and sisters

16 of 43 had 7 or more brothers and sisters

18 of 43 had 6 or more brothers and sisters

20 of 43 had 5 or more brothers and sisters

14 of 43 were the first-born in their families

5 of 43 were the second-born, the first sons in their families

7 of 43 were the second-born, the second sons, in their families

19 of 43 were the eldest sons in their families

4 of 43 were the only children of their parents' marriages

MARRIAGES AND WIVES OF THE PRESIDENTS

42 of 43 Presidents married

6 of 43 Presidents married widows

4 of 43 Presidents married divorcees

2 of 43 Presidents married on their birthdays

9 of 43 Presidents celebrated golden wedding anniversaries

5 of 43 Presidents were widowed before they were inaugurated

3 of 43 Presidents were widowed while in office

1 of 43 Presidents was divorced

6 of 43 Presidents remarried

1 of 48 wives was not born in the United States

21 of 48 wives were born in New York, Ohio or Virginia

12 of 48 wives were college graduates

6 of 48 wives were older than their husbands

4 of 48 wives had children by former husbands

7 of 48 wives are living (2009)

41 of 48 wives are deceased (2009)

20 of 48 wives lived to be over 70

14 of 48 wives lived to be over 80

10 of 48 wives died in Washington, D.C.

CHILDREN OF THE PRESIDENTS

37 of 43 Presidents had children

6 of 37 had no daughters

8 of 37 had no sons

1 of 37 had 15 children

1 of 37 had twins

2 of 37 had a son who became President

2 of 37 had sons who became senators

5 of 37 had sons who became representatives

1 of 37 had a son who served in both houses of Congress

DEATHS OF THE PRESIDENTS

5 of 43 Presidents are living (2009)

38 of 43 are deceased (2009)

19 of 38 lived to be over 70

8 of 38 died in July

3 of 38 died on July 4

8 of 38 died in office

5 of 38 died during their first and only term

2 of 38 died during their second term

1 of 38 died during his fourth term

4 of 38 were assassinated

34 of 38 died a natural death

2 of 38 were survived by their fathers

3 of 38 were survived by their mothers

CULTURAL, VOCATIONAL, AND GEOGRAPHICAL BACKGROUND OF THE PRESIDENTS

12 of 43 Presidents were Episcopalians

31 of 43 were college graduates

14 of 43 were members of Phi Beta Kappa

15 of 43 were Masons

26 of 43 had military service

27 of 43 were lawyers

6 of 43 served as secretary of state

9 of 43 served in presidential cabinets

14 of 43 served as Vice President

25 of 43 were elected to Congress

17 of 43 served as senators

19 of 43 served as representatives

11 of 43 served in both houses of Congress

8 of 43 served as ambassadors

17 of 43 served as state governors

8 of 43 were residents of New York

15 of 43 were residents of Ohio, Virginia, or Massachusetts

20 of 43 were residents of states other than their native states

COMMEMORATIVES

13 of 43 Presidents were elected to the Hall of Fame

4 of 43 are honored by statues in Statuary Hall

25 of 43 had counties named for them

4 of 43 had capital cities named for them

1 of 43 had a state named for him

ELECTIONS, TENURE, AND AGES OF THE PRESIDENTS

2 of 43 were Federalists

4 of 43 were Whigs

18 of 43 were Democrats

19 of 43 were Republicans

1 of 43 is currently in office

14 of 43 were elected for only one term

16 of 43 were elected for a second term

1 of 43 was elected for a third and a fourth term

10 of 43 served less than one term

12 of 43 served one full term

12 of 43 served two full terms

3 of 43 began second terms but did not complete them

2 of 43 were impeached

1 of 43 resigned

4 of 43 succeeded to the presidency and were subsequently elected in their own right

5 of 43 succeeded to the presidency and were never elected in their own right

18 of 43 did not receive a majority of the popular vote

9 of 43 were in their forties when they took office

24 of 43 were in their fifties when they took office

10 of 43 were in their sixties when they took office

The Presidency

Elections

The following Constitutional provisions apply to presidential elections:

ARTICLE II, SECTION 1. The executive Power shall be vested in a President of the United States of America. He shall hold his Office during the Term of four Years, and, together with the Vice-President, chosen for the same Term, be elected, as follows:

Each State shall appoint, in such Manner as the Legislature thereof may direct, a Number of Electors, equal to the whole Number of Senators and Representatives to which the State may be entitled in the Congress: but no Senator or Representative, or Person holding an Office of Trust or Profit under the United States, shall be appointed an Elector.

[The Electors shall meet in their respective States, and vote by Ballot for two persons, of whom one at least shall not be an Inhabitant of the same State with themselves. And they shall make a List they shall sign and certify, and transmit sealed to the Seat of the Government of the United States, directed to the President of the Senate. The President of the Senate shall, in the Presence of the Senate and House of Representatives, open all the Certificates, and the Votes shall then be counted. The Person having the greatest Number of Votes shall be the President, if such Number be a Majority of the whole number of Electors appointed; and if there be more than one who have such Majority, and have an equal Number of Votes, then the House of Representatives shall immediately chuse by Ballot one of them for President; and if no Person have a Majority, then from the five highest on the List the said House shall in like Manner chuse the President. But in chusing the Presi-

dent, the Votes shall be taken by States, the Representation from each State having one Vote; A quorum for this purpose shall consist of a Member or Members from two-thirds of the States, and a Majority of all the States shall be necessary to a Choice. In every Case, after the Choice of the President, the Person having the greatest Number of Votes of the Electors shall be the Vice-President. But if there should remain two or more who have equal Votes, the Senate shall chuse from them by Ballot the Vice-President.][1] The Congress may determine the Time of chusing the Electors, and the Day on which they shall give their Votes; which Day shall be the same throughout the United States. (*Constitution ratified Sept. 17, 1787.*)

AMENDMENT XII. The electors shall meet in their respective states and vote by ballot for President and Vice-President, one of whom, at least, shall not be an inhabitant of the same state with themselves; they shall name in their ballots the person voted for as President, and in distinct ballots the person voted for as Vice-President, and they shall make distinct lists of all persons voted for as President, and of all persons voted for as Vice-President, and of the number of votes for each, which lists they shall sign and certify, and transmit sealed to the seat of the government of the United States, directed to the President of the Senate;—The President of the Senate shall, in presence of the Senate and House of Representatives, open all the certificates and the votes shall then be counted;—The person having the greatest number of votes for President, shall be the President, if such number be a majority of the whole number of Electors appointed; and

---

[1]   Superseded by Amendment XII

if no person have such majority, then from the persons having the highest numbers not exceeding three on the list of those voted for as President, the House of Representatives shall choose immediately, by ballot, the President. But in choosing the President, the votes shall be taken by states, the representation from each state having one vote; a quorum for this purpose shall consist of a member or members from two-thirds of the states, and a majority of all the states shall be necessary to a choice. And if the House of Representatives shall not choose a President whenever the right of choice shall develop upon them, [before the fourth day of March next following,][2] then the Vice-President shall act as President, as in the case of the death or other constitutional disability of the President;—The person having the greatest number of votes as Vice-President, shall be the Vice-President, if such a number be a majority of the whole number of electors appointed, and if no person have a majority, then from the two highest numbers on the list, the Senate shall choose the Vice-President; a quorum for the purpose shall consist of two-thirds of the whole number of Senators, and a majority of the whole number shall be necessary to a choice. But no person constitutionally ineligible to the office of President shall be eligible to that of Vice-President of the United States. (*Amendment XII ratified 1804.*)

AMENDMENT XX. SECTION 1. The terms of the President and Vice-President shall end at noon on the 20th day of January, and the terms of Senators and Representatives at noon on the 3rd day of January, of the years in which such terms would have ended if this article had not been ratified; and their terms of their successors shall then begin.

SECTION 3. If, at the time fixed for the beginning of the term of the President, the President elect shall have died, the Vice-President elect shall become President. If a President shall not have been chosen before the time fixed for the beginning of his term, or if the President elect shall have failed to qualify, then the Vice-President elect shall act as President until a President shall have qualified; and the Congress may by law provide for the case wherein neither a President elect nor a Vice-President elect shall have qualified, declaring who shall then act as President, or the manner in which one who is to act shall be selected, and such person shall act accordingly until a President or Vice-President shall have qualified.

SECTION 4. The Congress may by law provide for the case of the death of any of the persons from whom the House of Representatives may choose a President whenever the right of choice shall have devolved upon them, and for the case of the death of any of the persons from whom the Senate may choose a Vice-President whenever the right of choice shall have devolved upon them. (*Amendment XX ratified Jan. 23, 1933.*)

AMENDMENT XXII. SECTION 1. No person shall be elected to the office of the President more than twice, and no person who has held the office of President, or acted as President, for more than two years of a term to which some other person was elected President shall be elected to the office of the President more than once. But this Article shall not apply to any person holding the office of President when this Article was proposed by the Congress, and shall not prevent any person who may be holding the office of President, or acting as President, during the term within which this Article becomes operative from holding the office of President or acting as President during the remainder of such term. (*Amendment XXII ratified Feb. 27, 1951.*)

AMENDMENT XXV. SECTION 1. In case of the removal of the President from office or of his death or resignation, the Vice-President shall become President.

SECTION 2. Whenever there is a vacancy in the office of the Vice-President, the President shall nominate a Vice President who shall take office upon confirmation by a majority vote of both Houses of Congress.

---

[2] Superseded by Amendment XX

SECTION 3. Whenever the President transmits to the President pro tempore of the Senate and the Speaker of the House of Representatives his written declaration that he is unable to discharge the powers and duties of his office, and until he transmits to them a written declaration to the contrary, such powers and duties shall be discharged by the Vice-President as Acting President.

SECTION 4. Whenever the Vice-President and a majority of either the principal officers of the executive departments or of such other body as Congress may by law provide, transmit to the President pro tempore of the Senate and the Speaker of the House of Representatives their written declaration that the President is unable to discharge the powers and duties of his office, the Vice-President shall immediately assume the powers and duties of the office as Acting President.

Thereafter, when the President transmits to the President pro tempore of the Senate and the Speaker of the House of Representatives his written declaration that no inability exists, he shall resume the powers and duties of his office unless the Vice-President and a majority of either the principal officers of the executive department or of such other body as Congress may by law provide, transmit within four days to the President pro tempore of the Senate and the Speaker of the House of Representatives their written declaration that the President is unable to discharge the powers and duties of his office. Thereupon Congress shall decide the issue, assembling within forty-eight hours for that purpose if not in session. If the Congress, within twenty-one days after receipt of the latter written declaration, or, if Congress is not in session, within twenty-one days after Congress is required to assemble, determines by two-thirds vote of both Houses that the President is unable to discharge the powers and duties of his office, the Vice-President shall continue to discharge the same as Acting President; otherwise the President shall resume the powers and duties of his office.

The Conventions

NOMINATING CONVENTION FIRST HELD BY ANTI-MASONIC PARTY

Until the election of 1832, candidates for the presidency and the vice presidency were selected by caucuses generally held in secret by the various political parties.

The first convention at which national nominating was the feature was held by the newly formed Anti-Masonic Party on September 26, 1831, at the Athenaeum, Baltimore, Md. The presiding officer at this convention was John Spencer of New York. Two tellers—Abner Phelps of Massachusetts and Thaddeus Stevens of Pennsylvania—were appointed. They sat in the center of the hall where the delegates, when their names were called, deposited their ballots in an open box. The first ballot for the presidency showed 111 votes cast, of which 108 were for William Wirt of Maryland, 1 for Richard Rush of Pennsylvania, and two blanks. As only 84 votes were necessary for the choice, it was moved that the nomination be made unanimous. Wirt thus became the first presidential candidate nominated by a national nominating convention.

OTHER FIRST CONVENTIONS

Both the National Republicans and the Democrats held their first nominating conventions in preparation for the 1832 election, and both conventions took place in the Athenaeum in Baltimore, Md. The National Republicans met in December 1831, the Democrats (then known as the Democratic-Republicans) in May 1832. The Democrats unanimously nominated Andrew Jackson of Tennessee on the first ballot, and the

National Republicans unanimously nominated Henry Clay of Kentucky on the first ballot.

THE TWO-THIRDS RULE

The two-thirds rule requiring presidential and vice presidential nominees to obtain two thirds of the votes cast at the nominating convention was first adopted May 22, 1832, at the Democratic National Convention held at Baltimore, Md. The rule was an extension of a provision adopted in 1831:

> Resolved: That each state be entitled in the nomination to be made of a candidate for the vice presidency to a number of votes equal to the number to which they will be entitled in the electoral college, under the new apportionment, in voting for the President and the Vice President; and that two thirds of the whole number of the votes in the convention shall be necessary to constitute a choice.

THE TWO-THIRDS RULE ABROGATED

On June 25, 1936, at the sixth session of the Democratic National Convention in Philadelphia, Pa., Bennett Champ Clark of Missouri brought in the Report of the Committee on Rules and Order of Business. The report stated that "all questions, including the question of nomination of candidates for President of the United States and Vice President of the United States, shall be determined by a majority vote of the delegates to the convention, and the rule heretofore existing in Democratic conventions requiring a two-thirds vote in such cases is hereby abrogated."

PRESIDENTS NOMINATED IN CHURCHES

Two Presidents were nominated by their parties at conventions held in churches. Three unsuccessful presidential candidates were also nominated in churches.

Martin Van Buren was nominated on May 20, 1835, by the Democrats at a convention held in the First Presbyterian Church, Baltimore, Md. William Henry Harrison was nominated on December 4, 1839, by the Whigs at a convention held at the First Lutheran (or Zion) Church, Baltimore, Md.

The three unsuccessful candidates nominated in churches were Henry Clay, nominated on May 1, 1844, by the Whigs in convention at the Universalist church, Baltimore, Md.; Lewis Cass, nominated on May 22, 1848, by the Democrats at the Universalist Church, Baltimore, Md.; and John Bell, nominated by the Constitutional Union Party on May 9, 1860, in the First Presbyterian Church, Baltimore, Md.

NATIONAL POLITICAL CONVENTIONS HELD BY MAJOR PARTIES

The following is a list of conventions from 1856 through 2008. The date on which each convention started is followed by the duration, the city in which the convention was held, and the presidential nominee. The winning party is listed above the defeated party.

1856

Democratic, June 2, 5 days, Cincinnati, Ohio, James Buchanan

Republican, June 17, 3 days, Philadelphia, Pa., John Charles Frémont

1860

Republican, May 16, 3 days, Chicago, Ill., Abraham Lincoln

Democratic, Apr. 23, 10 days, Charleston, S.C. (adjourned to Baltimore)

Democratic, June 18, 6 days, Baltimore, Md., Stephen Arnold Douglas

1864

Republican, June 7, 2 days, Baltimore, Md., Abraham Lincoln

Democratic, Aug. 29, 3 days, Chicago, Ill., George Brinton McClellan

1868

Republican, May 20, 2 days, Chicago, Ill., Ulysses Simpson Grant

Democratic, July 4, 6 days, New York, N.Y., Horatio Seymour

1872

Republican, June 5, 2 days, Philadelphia, Pa., Ulysses Simpson Grant

Democratic, June 9, 2 days, Baltimore, Md., Horace Greeley

1876

Republican, June 14, 3 days, Cincinnati, Ohio, Rutherford Birchard Hayes

Democratic, June 27, 3 days, St. Louis, Mo., Samuel Jones Tilden

1880

Republican, June 2, 6 days, Chicago, Ill., James Abram Garfield

Democratic, June 22, 3 days, Cincinnati, Ohio, Winfield Scott Hancock

1884

Democratic, July 8, 4 days, Chicago, Ill., Grover Cleveland

Republican, June 3, 4 days, Chicago, Ill., James Gillespie Blaine

1888

Republican, June 19, 6 days, Chicago, Ill., Benjamin Harrison

Democratic, June 5, 3 days, St. Louis, Mo., Grover Cleveland

1892

Democratic, June 21, 3 days, Chicago, Ill., Grover Cleveland

Republican, June 7, 4 days, Minneapolis, Minn., Benjamin Harrison

1896

Republican, June 16, 3 days, St. Louis, Mo., William McKinley

Democratic, July 7, 5 days, Chicago, Ill., William Jennings Bryan

1900

Republican, June 19, 3 days, Philadelphia, Pa., William McKinley

Democratic, July 4, 3 days, Kansas City, Mo., William Jennings Bryan

1904

Republican, June 21, 3 days, Chicago, Ill., Theodore Roosevelt

Democratic, July 6, 4 days, St. Louis, Mo., Alton Brooks Parker

1908

Republican, June 16, 4 days, Chicago, Ill., William Howard Taft

Democratic, July 8, 3 days, Denver, Colo., William Jennings Bryan

1912

Democratic, June 25, 7 days, Baltimore, Md., Woodrow Wilson

Republican, June 18, 5 days, Chicago, Ill., William Howard Taft

1916

Democratic, June 14, 3 days, St. Louis, Mo., Woodrow Wilson

Republican, June 7, 4 days, Chicago, Ill., Charles Evans Hughes

1920

Republican, June 8, 5 days, Chicago, Ill., Warren Gamaliel Harding

Democratic, June 28, 8 days, San Francisco, Calif., James Middleton Cox

1924

Republican, June 10, 3 days, Cleveland, Ohio Calvin Coolidge

Democratic, June 24, 14 days, New York, N.Y., John William Davis

1928

Republican, June 12, 4 days, Kansas City, Mo., Herbert Hoover

Democratic, June 26, 4 days, Houston, Tex., Alfred Emanuel Smith

1932

Democratic, June 27, 3 days, Chicago, Ill., Franklin Delano Roosevelt

Republican, June 14, 3 days, Chicago, Ill., Herbert Hoover

1936

Democratic, June 23, 5 days, Philadelphia, Pa., Franklin Delano Roosevelt

Republican, June 9, 4 days, Cleveland, Ohio, Alfred Mossman Landon

1940

Democratic, July 15, 4 days, Chicago, Ill., Franklin Delano Roosevelt

Republican, June 24, 5 days, Philadelphia, Pa., Wendell Lewis Willkie

1944

Democratic, July 19, 3 days, Chicago, Ill., Franklin Delano Roosevelt

Republican, June 26, 3 days, Chicago, Ill., Thomas Edmund Dewey

1948

Democratic, July 12, 3 days, Philadelphia, Pa., Harry S. Truman

Republican, June 21, 5 days, Philadelphia, Pa., Thomas Edmund Dewey

1952

Republican, July 7, 5 days, Chicago, Ill., Dwight David Eisenhower

Democratic, July 21, 6 days, Chicago, Ill., Adlai Ewing Stevenson

1956

Republican, Aug. 20, 4 days, San Francisco, Calif., Dwight David Eisenhower

Democratic, Aug. 13, 4 days, Chicago, Ill., Adlai Ewing Stevenson

1960

Democratic, July 11, 5 days, Los Angeles, Calif., John Fitzgerald Kennedy

Republican, July 25, 4 days, Chicago, Ill., Richard Milhous Nixon

1964

Democratic, Aug. 24, 3 days, Atlantic City, N.J., Lyndon Baines Johnson

Republican, July 13, 4 days, San Francisco, Calif., Barry Morris Goldwater

1968

Republican, Aug. 5, 4 days, Miami Beach, Fla., Richard Milhous Nixon

Democratic, Aug. 26, 4 days, Chicago, Ill., Hubert Horatio Humphrey

1972

Republican, Aug. 21, 3 days, Miami Beach, Fla., Richard Milhous Nixon

Democratic, July 10, 4 days, Miami Beach, Fla., George Stanley McGovern

1976

Democratic, July 12, 4 days, New York, N.Y., Jimmy Carter

Republican, Aug. 16, 4 days, Kansas City, Kan., Gerald Rudolph Ford

1980

Republican, July 14, 4 days, Detroit, Mich., Ronald Wilson Reagan

Democratic, Aug. 11, 4 days, New York, N.Y., Jimmy Carter

1984

Republican, Aug. 20, 4 days, Dallas, Tex., Ronald Wilson Reagan

Democratic, July 16, 4 days, San Francisco, Calif., Walter Frederick Mondale

1988

Republican, Aug. 15, 4 days, New Orleans, La., George Herbert Walker Bush

Democratic, July 18, 4 days, Atlanta, Ga., Michael Stanley Dukakis

1992

Democratic, July 13, 4 days, New York, N.Y., William Jefferson Clinton

Republican, Aug. 17, 4 days, Houston, Tex., George Herbert Walker Bush

1996

Democratic, Aug. 26, 4 days, Chicago, Ill., William Jefferson Clinton

Republican, Aug. 12, 4 days, San Diego, Calif., Robert Dole

2000

Republican, July 31, 4 days, Philadelphia, Pa., George Walker Bush

Democratic, Aug. 14, 4 days, Los Angeles, Calif., Albert Arnold Gore, Jr.

2004

Republican, Aug. 30, 4 days, New York, N.Y., George Walker Bush

Democratic, July 26, 4 days, Boston, Mass., John Forbes Kerry

2008

Democratic, Aug. 25, 4 days, Denver, Colo., Barack Hussein Obama

Republican, Sept. 1, 4 days, St. Paul, Minn., John Sidney McCain

CONVENTION CITIES— 1856-2008

The following lists show the number of conventions held in each city. Dates in bold-face indicate years in which the party was victorious.

Republican Conventions

Chicago, Ill., 14—**1860**, **1868**, **1880**, 1884, **1888**, **1904**, **1908**, 1912, 1916, **1920**, 1932, 1944, **1952**, 1960
Philadelphia, Pa., 6—1856, **1872**, **1900**, 1940, 1948, **2000**
Cleveland, Ohio, 2—**1924**, 1936
Kansas City, Mo., 2—**1928**, 1976
Miami Beach, Fla., 2—**1968**, **1972**
San Francisco, Calif. 2—**1956**, 1964
Baltimore, Md., 1—**1864**
Cincinnati, Ohio, 1—**1876**
Dallas, Texas, 1—**1984**
Detroit, Mich., 1—**1980**
Houston, Texas, 1—1992
Minneapolis, Minn., 1—1892
New Orleans, La., 1—**1988**
New York, N.Y., 1—**2004**
St. Louis, Mo., 1—**1896**
St. Paul, Minn., 1—2008
San Diego, Calif., 1—1996

Democratic Conventions

Chicago, Ill., 11—1864, **1884**, **1892**, 1896, **1932**, **1940**, **1944**, 1952, 1956, 1968, **1996**
New York, N.Y., 5—1868, 1924, **1976**, 1980, **1992**
St. Louis, Mo., 4—1876, 1888, 1904, **1916**
Baltimore, Md., 3—1860, 1872, **1912**
Cincinnati, Ohio, 2—**1856**, 1880
Denver, Colo., 2—1908, **2008**
Los Angeles, Calif., 2—**1960**, 2000
Philadelphia, Pa., 2—**1936**, **1948**
San Francisco, Calif., 2—1920, 1984
Atlanta, Ga., 1—1988
Atlantic City, N.J., 1—**1964**
Boston, Mass., 1—2004
Charleston, S.C., 1—1860
Houston, Tex., 1—1928
Kansas City, Mo., 1—1900
Miami Beach, Fla., 1—1972

PRESIDENTS NOMINATED IN CHICAGO

Eleven of the forty-three Presidents were nominated in Chicago, Ill.

The Republicans nominated fourteen candidates in Chicago. Eight were elected: Lincoln, 1860; Grant, 1868; Garfield, 1880; Benjamin Harrison, 1888; Theodore Roosevelt, 1904; Taft, 1908; Harding, 1920; and Eisenhower, 1952. Six were unsuccessful: Blaine, 1884; Taft, 1912; Hughes, 1916; Hoover, 1932; Dewey, 1944; and Nixon, 1960.

The Democrats at eleven conventions in Chicago nominated seven individuals as candidates. Three were elected: Cleveland, 1884 and 1892; Franklin D. Roosevelt, 1932, 1940, and 1944; Clinton, 1996. Four were unsuccessful: McClellan, 1864; Bryan, 1896; Stevenson, 1952 and 1956; and Humphrey, 1968.

CONVENTION FAILED TO SELECT NOMINEES

The only nominating convention of a major party which did not decide upon a presidential candidate was the Democratic convention of 1860, which met at the Hall of the South Carolina Institute, Charleston, S.C., on April 23, 1860. After ten days in session, during which 57 indecisive ballots were taken, and several fistfights broke out, the convention adjourned to meet at Baltimore, Md., on June 18, 1860. In a six-day session at the Front Street Theatre in Baltimore, Stephen Arnold Douglas of Illinois was nominated on the second ballot.

ADMISSION CHARGED AT CONVENTION

The first political convention at which admission was charged was the Progressive Party Convention, held at Convention Hall, Philadelphia, Pa., July 23–25, 1948. The public also paid to hear the candidates' acceptance speeches at Shibe Park, the grounds of the Philadelphia Athletics baseball team. Approximately $15,000 was received to defray campaign expenses.

CONVENTION RULES

There is no set rule which governs every convention although there is a more or less standard procedure. Conventions usually open with an invocation. Credentials and committee rules are reported upon. A temporary chairman is selected. The keynote speech is delivered. Accredited delegates vote for a permanent chairman. The reports of committees are voted upon and a platform is adopted. A presidential nominee is chosen. A vice presidential nominee is chosen. Committees are appointed to notify the selected nominees. A new national committee is selected to act for the party and carry on the campaign and the work of the party until the next convention.

CONVENTION DELEGATES

Each political party has the right and privilege to determine the qualifications and number of its delegates. Conventions adopt their own regulations and procedures, and these are subject to change.

The apportionment of delegates varies from convention to convention in accordance with the current rules. The methods of selecting delegates—chiefly caucuses and primary elections—vary according to the regulations of the state organizations.

In recent years, the Democratic Party has used a complicated system that includes "superdelegates," who are entitled to vote at the national convention owing to their status as PLEOs ("party leaders and elected officials").

CONVENTION NOMINATIONS—1832–2008

Since the first nominating convention in 1832, there have been 90 conventions held by the major political parties (the Democratic-Republicans, afterwards known as the Democrats; the National Republicans, afterwards known as the Whigs; and the Republicans). At these 90 conventions, 62 presidential nominations were made by acclamation or on the first ballot. (Franklin Delano Roosevelt was renominated in 1936 by acclamation and no vote was taken.) Of the 62 candidates so nominated, 32 were elected—18 Republicans and 14 Democrats; of the 30 losers who were nominated on the first ballot, 15 were Democrats, 13 were Republicans, and two were Whigs.

The President who required the greatest number of ballots at a nominating convention was Franklin Pierce, Democrat, who did not receive the nomination until the 49th ballot. Woodrow Wilson, Democrat, was a runner-up, requiring 46 ballots before he was nominated in 1912. The Republican who required the greatest number of ballots in order to win a nomination was James Abram Garfield, who was nominated on the thirty-sixth ballot in 1880.

The longest nominating convention ever held was the Democratic convention of 1924, in session 14 days, which required 103 ballots before a presidential nominee was agreed upon. On the first ballot, William Gibbs McAdoo of California had 431 votes, nearly twice as many as the next highest candidate, Alfred Emanuel Smith of New York, who had 241 votes. As 731 votes were necessary for choice, the balloting continued and 103 ballots were taken before one candidate received the necessary number. John William Davis of West Virginia, who had only 31 votes on the first ballot, won the nomination on the 103rd ballot, receiving 844 votes.

The development of the presidential primary process, which thins out the field of candidates over the course of several months, has obviated the need for multiple ballots at conventions.

Often a candidate is nominated without opposition and receives a unanimous vote. Occasionally no tally of votes is made, the nomination being by acclamation. In many cases, after a vote is recorded a motion is offered to make the nomination unanimous. Since this involves no change in the selection of candidates and since it shows a solid and united party, many nominations are declared unanimous even though the candidate does not receive all the votes on the earlier ballots. It often happens at conventions that after the vote has been tabulated and recorded, states change their votes from one candidate to another. For this reason, there is sometimes a disparity in the returns, and as a result the amended vote differs from the original vote.

REPUBLICAN PRESIDENTIAL CANDIDATES NOMINATED ON THE FIRST BALLOT—1856–2008

(Elections won by Republicans are indicated by asterisks.)

  1856 John Charles Frémont, Calif.
***1864** Abraham Lincoln, Ill.
***1868** Ulysses Simpson Grant, Ill.
***1872** Ulysses Simpson Grant, Ill.
  1892 Benjamin Harrison, Ind.
***1896** William McKinley, Ohio
***1900** William McKinley, Ohio
***1904** Theodore Roosevelt, N.Y.
***1908** William Howard Taft, Ohio
  1912 William Howard Taft, Ohio
***1924** Calvin Coolidge, Mass.

*1928 Herbert Clark Hoover, Calif.
1932 Herbert Clark Hoover, Calif.
1936 Alfred Mossman Landon, Kan.
1944 Thomas Edmund Dewey, N.Y.
*1952 Dwight David Eisenhower, N.Y.
*1956 Dwight David Eisenhower, N.Y.
1960 Richard Milhous Nixon, Calif.
1964 Barry Morris Goldwater, Ariz.
*1968 Richard Milhous Nixon, N.Y.
*1972 Richard Milhous Nixon, Calif.
1976 Gerald Rudolph Ford, Mich.
*1980 Ronald Wilson Reagan, Calif.
*1984 Ronald Wilson Reagan, Calif.
*1988 George Herbert Walker Bush, Tex.
1992 George Herbert Walker Bush, Tex.
1996 Robert Joseph Dole, Kan.
*2000 George Walker Bush, Tex.
*2004 George Walker Bush, Tex.
2008 John Sidney McCain, Ariz.

DEMOCRATIC PRESIDENTIAL CANDIDATES NOMINATED ON THE FIRST BALLOT—1832–2008

(Elections won by Democrats are indicated by asterisks.)

*1832 Andrew Jackson, Tenn.
*1836 Martin Van Buren, N.Y.
1840 Martin Van Buren, N.Y.
1864 George Brinton McClellan, N.J.
1872 Horace Greeley, N.Y.
1888 Grover Cleveland, N.Y.
*1892 Grover Cleveland, N.Y.
1900 William Jennings Bryan, Neb.
1904 Alton Brooks Parker, N.Y.
1908 William Jennings Bryan, Neb.
*1916 Woodrow Wilson, N.J.
1928 Alfred Emanuel Smith, N.Y.
*1936 Franklin Delano Roosevelt, N.Y.
*1940 Franklin Delano Roosevelt, N.Y.
*1944 Franklin Delano Roosevelt, N.Y.
*1948 Harry S. Truman, Mo.
1956 Adlai Ewing Stevenson, Ill.
*1960 John Fitzgerald Kennedy, Mass.
*1964 Lyndon Baines Johnson, Tex.
1968 Hubert Horatio Humphrey, Minn.
1972 George Stanley McGovern, S.D.
*1976 Jimmy Carter, Ga.
1980 Jimmy Carter, Ga.
1984 Walter Frederick Mondale, Minn.
1988 Michael Stanley Dukakis, Mass.
*1992 William Jefferson Clinton, Ark.
*1996 William Jefferson Clinton, Ark.

2000 Albert Arnold Gore, Jr., Tenn.
2004 John Forbes Kerry, Mass.
*2008 Barack Hussein Obama, Ill.

WHIG PRESIDENTIAL CANDIDATES

The Whig Party nominated six candidates for the presidency (1832–1852), of whom two were elected.

One candidate was nominated twice and elected once. This candidate was William Henry Harrison.

One candidate was nominated twice and defeated both times. This candidate was Henry Clay.

One candidate was nominated once and elected once. This candidate was Zachary Taylor.

One candidate was nominated once but was not elected. This candidate was Winfield Scott.

A remnant of the dissolved Whig Party met in convention in Baltimore, Md., in 1856 and endorsed the candidate already nominated by the American Party, former President Millard Fillmore, who was not reelected.

REPUBLICAN PRESIDENTIAL CANDIDATES

The Republican Party nominated 39 candidates for the presidency (1856–2008), of whom 23 were elected.

One candidate was nominated three times and elected twice. This candidate was Nixon.

Six candidates were nominated twice and elected both times. They were Lincoln, Grant, McKinley, Eisenhower, Reagan, and George W. Bush.

Four candidates were nominated twice, elected for one term, and defeated when they ran for reelection. They were B. Harrison, Taft, Hoover, and George Bush.

One candidate was nominated twice and defeated both times. This candidate was Dewey.

Six candidates were nominated once and elected once. They were Hayes, Garfield, T. Roosevelt, Harding, and Coolidge.

Nine candidates were nominated once but were not elected. They were Frémont, Blaine, Hughes, Landon, Willkie, Goldwater, Ford, Dole, and McCain.

DEMOCRATIC PRESIDENTIAL CANDIDATES

The Democratic Party nominated 45 candidates for the presidency (1832–2008), of whom 20 were elected.

One candidate was nominated four times and elected four times. This candidate was F. D. Roosevelt.

One candidate was nominated three times and elected twice. This candidate was Cleveland.

One candidate was nominated three times and defeated three times. This candidate was Bryan.

Two candidates were nominated twice and elected both times. They were Wilson and Clinton.

Two candidates were nominated twice, elected for one term, and defeated when they ran for reelection. They were Van Buren and Carter.

One candidate was nominated twice and defeated twice. This candidate was Stevenson.

Seven candidates were nominated once and elected once. They were Jackson, Polk, Pierce, Buchanan, Truman, Kennedy, and Johnson. (However, Jackson had already been nominated and elected once before, in 1828, when both he and his opponent, incumbent President John Quincy Adams, represented different factions of the Democratic-Republicans, the predecessor to the Democratic Party.)

Seventeen candidates were nominated once but were not elected. They were Cass, Douglas, McClellan, Seymour, Greeley, Tilden, Hancock, Parker, Cox, Davis, Smith, Humphrey, McGovern, Mondale, Dukakis, Gore, and Kerry.

The current President, Barack Obama, was nominated and elected in 2008.

PRESIDENTIAL "DARK HORSES"

Numerous "dark horses"—little-known but unexpectedly strong candidates—have made spectacular, hardly believable runs to secure nominations. The first dark horse to win his party's nomination was Polk, in 1844; he also won the election. Three other dark horses achieved similar victories: Pierce in 1852, Garfield in 1880, and Harding in 1920. Two dark horses won nomination but were not elected: Seymour in 1868 and Bryan in 1896.

BROTHERS NOMINATED FOR THE PRESIDENCY

At the eighth Republican convention, held at Exposition Hall, Chicago, Ill., on June 3–6, 1884, the names of two brothers were placed in nomination for the presidency. One was John Sherman, U.S. Senator from Ohio; the other, General William Tecumseh Sherman. The former received thirty votes on the first ballot, the latter two votes.

William Tecumseh Sherman, who succeeded Grant as general and commander of the army, retired from military service in 1884. In a letter to his brother, Senator John Sherman, dated St. Louis, Mo., May 7, 1884, General Sherman wrote:

> Why should I, at sixty-five years of age, with a reasonable provision for life, not a dollar of debt, and with the universal respect of my neighbors and countrymen, embark in the questionable game of politics? The country is in a state of absolute peace, and it would be a farce to declare that any man should sacrifice himself to a mere party necessity.

The Candidates

WOMAN PRESIDENTIAL CANDIDATES

The first woman to be nominated for President was Victoria Claflin Woodhull of New York, who was nominated by the People's Party (also known as the National Radical Reformers and later as the Equal Rights Party) on May 10, 1872, in New York City, after the group seceded from the National

Woman Suffrage Association. She was nominated by Judge Carter of Cincinnati, Ohio. Frederick Douglass was the vice presidential nominee.

The first women to be nominated for President in the 20th century were Ventura Chavez of New Mexico and Charlene Mitchell of California, both of whom were nominated in 1968. Chavez, who was also the first Latina to run for President, was nominated by the People's Constitutional Party and received 1,519 votes in New Mexico on Election Day. Her running mate, Adelicio Moya, was the first Latino to be nominated for Vice President. Mitchell, who was also the first African-American woman to run for President, was nominated by the Communist Party in July 1968 in New York, N.Y. She and her running mate, Michael Zagarell, received 438 votes—415 votes in Minnesota and 23 in Ohio—on Election Day.

The first woman to be proposed for the presidential nomination at the convention of a major political party was Margaret Chase Smith of Maine, who was nominated by Senator George David Aiken of Vermont on July 15, 1964, at the Republican National Convention in San Francisco, Calif. She received 27 votes on the first and only ballot. The nomination was won by Barry Morris Goldwater, who lost the election to Lyndon Baines Johnson.

Hillary Rodham Clinton, U.S. senator from New York and former First Lady, was the first woman to be a serious contender for the presidential nomination of a major party. During the 2008 Democratic primaries, she won 1,640 pledged delegates and 286 super-delegates; her opponent, Barack Obama, won 1,763 pledged delegates and 395 superdelegates, resulting in his nomination at the Democratic convention in August 2008.

AFRICAN-AMERICAN PRESIDENTIAL CANDIDATES

The first African-American to be nominated for President was Clennon King, who was nominated by the Independent Afro-American Party in 1960. His running mate was Reginald Carter. Both candidates were from Georgia. The party received 1,485 votes on Election Day.

The first African-American to be proposed for the presidential nomination at the convention of a major political party was Frederick Douglass of New York, who received one vote on June 23, 1888, on the fourth ballot of the Republican national convention at Chicago, Ill. On the eighth ballot, the convention nominated Benjamin Harrison, who was elected as the twenty-third president. The first to be proposed by a major party in the twentieth century was the Rev. Channing Emery Phillips of Washington, D.C., who was proposed on August 28, 1968, at the Democratic Convention in Chicago, Ill. The nomination was eventually won by Hubert Horatio Humphrey, who lost the election to Richard Milhous Nixon.

The first African-American candidate to be nominated for President by a major party was Barack Hussein Obama, who was nominated by the Democratic Party in 2008. He won 52.9 percent of the popular vote and 67.8 percent of the electoral vote, making him the first U.S. President of African descent. He was also the first biracial President, having been born to a white mother and a black father.

CATHOLIC CANDIDATES

The first Catholic to be nominated for President was Charles O'Conor of New York, who was nominated at Louisville, Ky., on September 3, 1872, by the Straight-out Democratic Party, an offshoot of the Democrats. O'Conor declined the nomination, but his name nevertheless was listed and he received approximately 30,000 votes from 23 states.

The first Catholic to be nominated for President by a major political party was the governor of New York, Alfred Emanuel Smith, who was nominated by the Democratic Party on June 28, 1928, in Houston, Tex.; he accepted on August 22. The election was won by his Republican opponent, Herbert Clark Hoover.

The first Catholic to be elected President was John Fitzgerald Kennedy of Massachusetts, nominated by the Democratic Party in 1960.

The first Catholic to be elected Vice President was Joseph Robinette Biden, nominated by the Democratic Pary in 2008.

GENERALS VERSUS ADMIRALS FOR THE PRESIDENCY

Despite the many sea battles in which United States naval heroes have been engaged, no admiral has been nominated for the presidency. The preference has been entirely in favor of the generals.

The Presidents who had been generals were Washington, Jackson, William Henry Harrison, Taylor, Pierce, Grant, Hayes, Garfield, Benjamin Harrison, and Eisenhower. Andrew Johnson was a military governor with the rank of general.

Nominated by their respective parties but unsuccessful in the contest for the presidency were Generals Winfield Scott, George B. McClellan, Benjamin Franklin Butler, John Charles Fremont, Winfield Scott Hancock, and Douglas MacArthur.

Although Theodore Roosevelt was not a general, he had served with distinction in the Spanish-American War.

OPPOSING CANDIDATES FROM THE SAME STATES

Illinois presented two presidential candidates in 1860, Abraham Lincoln and Stephen Arnold Douglas. Lincoln received 180 electoral votes and Douglas 12 electoral votes.

Illinois had two presidential nominees in 1872. Ulysses Simpson Grant received 286 electoral votes and David Davis received 1 electoral vote.

In 1904, Theodore Roosevelt and Alton Brooks Parker were the candidates, both from New York. Roosevelt received 336 electoral votes, and Parker received 140 electoral votes.

Ohio had two candidates for the presidency in 1920, Warren Gamaliel Harding and James Middleton Cox, the former receiving 404 electoral votes, the latter 127 electoral votes.

In 1940 the two presidential candidates were Franklin Delano Roosevelt of New York and Wendell Lewis Willkie of New York. Roosevelt received 449 electoral votes and Willkie received 82 electoral votes.

New York again in 1944 presented two presidential candidates. Franklin Delano Roosevelt received 432 electoral votes and Thomas Edmund Dewey received 99 electoral votes.

DEFEATED PRESIDENTIAL CANDIDATES RENOMINATED

The first presidential candidate renominated by the Republicans after being defeated was Thomas Edmund Dewey of New York. After being defeated in the election of 1944 by incumbent President Franklin Delano Roosevelt, Dewey was renominated by the Republicans at their 1948 convention in Philadelphia, Pa., but was defeated by Harry S. Truman. Richard Milhous Nixon was defeated in 1960 by John Fitzgerald Kennedy but was renominated in 1968 and 1972 and was elected both times.

Among the Democratic candidates, incumbent President Grover Cleveland was defeated in 1888 by Benjamin Harrison but was renominated in 1892, again with Harrison as his opponent, and was reelected. William Jennings Bryan was nominated three times but lost the elections of 1896 and 1900 to William McKinley and that of 1908 to William Howard Taft. Adlai Ewing Stevenson was defeated by Dwight David Eisenhower in 1952; he was renominated in 1956 and was again defeated by Eisenhower.

DEFEATED PRESIDENTIAL CANDIDATES RETURNED TO THE SENATE

Senators who were returned to the Senate after being defeated as presidential candidates were: Henry Clay of Kentucky, Whig Party candidate defeated on November 5, 1844, who returned to the Senate on March 4, 1849; Barry Morris Goldwater of Arizona, Republican Party candidate defeated on November 3, 1964, who returned to the Senate on January 3, 1969; and Hubert Horatio Humphrey of Minnesota, Democratic Party candidate defeated on November 5, 1968, who returned to the Senate on January 3, 1971. Three other Senators who ran unsuccessfully for President returned immediately to the Senate, where they continued their terms: George Stanley McGovern, Democratic Party candidate defeated on November 7, 1972; John Forbes Kerry, Democratic Party candidate defeated on November 2, 2004; and John Sidney McCain, Republican Party candidate defeated on November 4, 2008.

OLDEST PRESIDENTIAL CANDIDATE

The oldest presidential candidate was Peter Cooper, born February 12, 1791, in New York City, who was 85 years and 94 days old when he was nominated on May 17, 1876, by the Greenback Party in convention at Indianapolis, Ind. He received 81,737 votes in the November 7, 1876 election.

PERSISTENT PRESIDENTIAL CANDIDATES

The most persistent presidential candidate was Norman Mattoon Thomas, who was nominated six times by the Socialist Party and defeated at each election. In 1928, he received 267,420 votes as a candidate against Herbert Hoover. As a contestant in the elections won by Franklin Delano Roosevelt he received 884,782 votes in 1932, 187,512 votes in 1936, 116,798 votes in 1940, and 74,757 votes in 1944. He was also a candidate in 1948, receiving 95,908 votes in the election won by Harry S. Truman.

Harold Edward Stassen of Minnesota attempted to gain the Republican nomination for President in 1948, 1952, 1964, 1968, 1976, 1980, 1984, 1988, and 1992, each time in vain.

CANDIDATES WHO WERE DIVORCED

Candidates from major parties who had been divorced and remarried were: James Middleton Cox, the Democratic candidate defeated by Warren Gamaliel Harding in 1920; Ronald Wilson Reagan, the Republican candidate who defeated Jimmy Carter in 1980 and Walter Frederick Mondale in 1984; John Forbes Kerry, the Democratic candidate defeated by George W. Bush in 2004; and John Sidney McCain, the Republican candidate defeated by Barack Obama in 2008.

Adlai Ewing Stevenson, the Democratic candidate defeated by Dwight David Eisenhower in 1952 and 1956, was divorced, but had not remarried.

AUTOMOBILE USED IN CAMPAIGN

The first presidential candidate to ride in an automobile was William Jennings Bryan, who, accompanied by his wife, was given a ride in 1896 at Decatur, Ill., in an automobile made by the Mueller Manufacturing Company. There were only ten automobiles in the United States at that time.

PRESIDENTIAL CANDIDATES WHO SERVED PRISON TERMS

Eugene Victor Debs of Indiana, the Socialist candidate for the presidency in 1900, 1904, 1908, 1912, and 1920, was in jail when he was nominated on May 13, 1920. Sentenced to ten years in federal prison for violation of the Espionage Act, he had begun his sentence on April 13, 1919, and was in prison when he received over 917,000 votes in the November 2, 1920 election. He was pardoned December 25, 1921. He had also served a six-month jail term in the 1890s.

On August 28, 1952, the American Labor Party nominated as its presidential candidate Vincent Hallinan of California, who had been released from the McNeil Island Federal Penitentiary on August 17, 1952, after serving six months for contempt of court in connection with his defense of Harry Bridges, the labor leader.

Farrell Dobbs, presidential candidate of the Socialist Workers Party in 1948, 1952, 1956, and 1960, was sent to prison on December 31, 1943, having been convicted on December 8, 1941, on charges of advocating the overthrow of the government by force and violence.

John Kasper of Tennessee, presidential nominee of the National States' Rights Party in 1964, served three terms in jail on charges of having interfered with court-ordered desegregation in Tennessee.

Gus Hall of New York, presidential nominee of the Communist Party in 1972, 1976, and 1980, was jailed for 90 days in 1940 for election irregularities in an Ohio race. On trial for conspiring to teach the violent overthrow of the U.S. government, he was jailed for contempt of court from May 1947 to October 1949; found guilty October 14, 1949, he was imprisoned from October 8, 1951, to March 30, 1957.

PRESIDENTIAL CANDIDATE WHO WAS A PRISONER OF WAR

John Sidney McCain, U.S. Senator from Arizona and the Republican candidate for President in 2008, was a naval aviator during the Vietnam Conflict. He was shot down over Hanoi in 1967 and spent the next five and a half years in captivity, two of them in solitary confinement. The North Vietnamese refused to allow medical treatment for the broken limbs he sustained in the crash and subjected him to frequent torture. As the son of an American admiral, he was offered repatriation as a propaganda gesture; despite the knowledge that his decision meant additional torture, he rejected the offer because other prisoners had been waiting longer. He was released in March 1973.

PRESIDENTIAL CANDIDATE WHO WAS CONVICTED IN A FEDERAL CRIMINAL CASE

Lyndon LaRouche ran for president in 1976 on the U.S. Labor Party ticket and continued to do the same in subsequent elections. On December 16, 1988, he was convicted of mail fraud and tax evasion. He was sentenced to 15 years in federal prison, of which he served five years before his release on parole in 1994.

PRESIDENTIAL CANDIDATE KILLED IN ATTEMPT TO RESCUE DROWNING BOY

Frank T. Johns, of Portland, Ore., Socialist Labor presidential candidate in 1924 and 1928, was campaigning at Bend, Ore., on the bank of the Deschutes River, on May 21, 1928, when his speech was interrupted by a cry for help. Charles Rhodes, an 11-year-old, was being drawn into deep water about 75 feet from the shore. Johns rushed to the boy's rescue and brought him to about 10 feet from the shore when he collapsed and they both drowned. Johns was 39 years of age.

To fill the vacancy caused by the death of Johns, the party nominated Verne L. Reynolds.

PRESIDENCY SEEKERS ASSASSINATED

Joseph Smith, the leader of the Church of Jesus Christ of Latter-day Saints (the Mormons), declared himself a candidate for President in February 1844. On June 27, 1844, in Carthage, Ill, Smith and his brother Hyrum were taken from the city jail by a mob of armed men and murdered. They had been imprisoned on charges of treason after Smith ordered the destruction of a printing press run by church dissenters. The church's doctrine of plural marriage had already earned Smith numerous enemies.

Senator Robert Francis Kennedy of New York was assassinated by Sirhan Bishara Sirhan on June 5, 1968, at the Biltmore Hotel, Los Angeles, Calif., while campaigning for the Democratic presidential nomination. He died on June 6, 1968.

PRESIDENTIAL CANDIDATES WOUNDED

While campaigning for the presidency on the Progressive or "Bull Moose" ticket, Theodore Roosevelt was shot in the chest, at about 8 P.M. on October 14, 1912, in Milwaukee, Wis. He was scheduled to deliver a speech that evening and he did deliver it, in spite of the wound.

Governor George Corley Wallace of Alabama was shot on May 15, 1972, in Laurel, Md., while campaigning for the Democratic presidential nomination. He was partially paralyzed as a result.

PROVISIONS FOR DEATH OF CANDIDATE OR PRESIDENT-ELECT

If a presidential nominee should die before election day, his party would select a new candidate in his place. It could be anyone and would not necessarily be the vice presidential nominee. The Democrats require the choice to be made by the Democratic National Committee, each state having the same number of votes. The person with the majority would be nominated for the presidency. The Republicans allow the choice to be made either by the Republican National Committee (the committee members having the same number of votes as their states at the national convention) or by another convention if time permits.

If the President-elect should die after election day but before the meeting of the electoral college, the electors could vote as they desire. They are not obliged to select the Vice President-elect. If both President-elect and Vice President-elect should die, the electoral college could choose any two persons for the offices, with or without the consent of the political party.

If the President-elect should die after receiving the votes of the electoral college, the Vice President would be sworn in as President. If both the President and the Vice President should die, the rule of succession would be invoked: the Speaker of the House, the president pro tempore of the Senate, the Secretary of State, the Secretary of the Treasury, and so forth.

DEATH OF PRESIDENTIAL
CANDIDATE GREELEY

Only once in the history of the United States has a presidential candidate died shortly after an election. Horace Greeley of New York, the Liberal Republican and Democratic candidate defeated by Ulysses Simpson Grant in 1872, died on November 29, after election day but before the electoral college assembled. His death released his 66 electors;

with complete freedom of choice, they voted as follows: 42 for Thomas Andrews Hendricks of Indiana, 18 for Benjamin Gratz Brown of Missouri (Greeley's vice presidential running mate), 2 for Charles J. Jenkins of Georgia, 1 for David Davis of Illinois, and 3 for the deceased Greeley. By resolution of the House, the votes for Greeley were not counted.

Before his nomination, Greeley had held one legislative office. Filling a vacancy in the House of Representatives, he had served as a Whig congressman from New York from December 4, 1848, to March 3, 1849. In 1872 the Democrats accepted him as their candidate with great reluctance. Greeley, an abolitionist and one of the founders of the Republican Party, had never voted the Democratic ticket. (On the other hand, Grant, the Republican nominee, had never voted the Republican ticket; it is believed that Grant had voted only once before—casting his ballot for the Democrat Buchanan in the election of 1856.)

Greeley was the object of much abuse during the campaign. In a letter dated November 5, 1872, he complained: "I have been so bitterly assailed that I hardly know whether I am running for the presidency or the penitentiary." He was physically and mentally exhausted by the campaign, and lived only three weeks after his defeat.

Election Returns

POPULAR ELECTION
RETURNS

Unlike the official electoral vote count, popular election return figures vary from source to source because there is no uniformity of selection in the tabulations. Many charts use estimated returns, preliminary returns, or incomplete returns, which are derived from newspapers, press associations, political parties, and the candidates themselves. These figures are subject to recount, to the addition of absentee ballots and the

soldier vote, and to final revision. They are also subject to human error in recording and to the ever-present possibility of typographical errors.

Since official figures are not always available from the secretary of state of each state, and since some official figures are interspersed with nonofficial figures, the popular election returns are not always 100 percent correct. Most of the figures in this book have been obtained from official federal publications.

PRESIDENTIAL ELECTORS

The Constitution, which went into effect on June 21, 1788, when it was ratified by New Hampshire, the ninth of the original thirteen states, provided for a President and Vice President and specified the manner in which they were to be elected. Article II, Section 1, provided for election by electors and designated the number of electors, the method by which they were to be chosen, and their electoral function:

Each State shall appoint, in such Manner as the Legislature thereof may direct, a Number of Electors, equal to the whole number of Senators and Representatives to which the State may be entitled in the Congress: but no Senator or Representative, or person holding an Office of Trust or Profit under the United States, shall be appointed an Elector.

The Electors shall meet in their respective States, and vote by Ballot for two Persons, of whom one at least shall not be an inhabitant of the same State with themselves.

On September 13, 1788, the Continental Congress directed that each state choose its own electors in the manner it saw fit and that these electors be chosen on the first Wednesday in January (January 7) 1789. These electors were directed to cast their ballots on the first Wednesday in February (February 4) 1789.

Each elector was entitled to cast two ballots, one for the Vice President. There was no distinction between the two offices on the ballot. According to the Constitution:

The Person having the greatest Number of Votes shall be the President, if such Number be a Majority of the whole Number of electors appointed; and if there be more than one who have such Majority, and have an equal Number of Votes, then the House of Representatives shall immediately chuse by Ballot one of them for President; and if no Person have a Majority, then from the five highest on the List the said House shall in like Manner chuse the President. But in chusing the President, the votes shall be taken by States, the Representation from each state having one Vote; a quorum for this Purpose shall consist of a Member or Members from two thirds of the States, and a Majority of all the States shall be necessary to a Choice. In every Case, after the Choice of the President, the Person having the greatest Number of Votes of the Electors shall be the Vice President. But if there should remain two or more who have equal Votes, the Senate shall chuse from them by Ballot the Vice President.

This method was found to have several objections and to meet them the Twelfth Amendment was drawn up. The Amendment, declared in force on September 25, 1804, made the following provision:

The Electors shall meet in their respective states, and vote by ballot for President and Vice President, one of whom, at least, shall not be an inhabitant of the same state with themselves; they shall name in their ballots the person voted for as President, and in distinct ballots the person voted for as Vice President, and they shall make distinct lists of all persons voted for as President, and of all persons voted for as Vice President, and of the number of votes for each, which lists they shall sign and certify, and transmit sealed to the seat of the government of the United States, directed to the President of the Senate;—The President of the Senate shall, in the presence of the Senate and the House of Representatives, open all the certificates and the votes shall then be counted;—The person having the greatest number of votes for President, shall be the President, if such number be a majority of the whole number of electors appointed. . . .

On March 1, 1792, an act of Congress (1 Stat. L. 239) fixed the meeting of electors within thirty-four days preceding the first Wednesday in December.

The act of February 3, 1887 (24 Stat. L. 373) provided that the electors should meet on the second Wednesday in February.

An act of Congress of June 5, 1934 (48 Stat. L. 879) fixed the time and place for the meeting of the presidential electors as the sixth day of January, when the votes are counted in the presence of the two houses. Congress now requires the vote to be made on January 6 or another day close to that date.

The electors meet in their respective states (at their state capitals) on the first Monday after the second Wednesday in December.

The electors are equal to the number of representatives and senators (531 in the election of 1956, 537 in the election of 1960, and 538 in the elections since 1964; since 1961 the total has included three electors from the District of Columbia). The group is known as the "electoral college" and exists for the sole purpose of casting two ballots, one for President and one for Vice President.

The result is recorded in triplicate; one copy is sent to the President of the Senate by mail; one copy is sent to him by messenger; and one copy is deposited with the Federal judge of the district in which the electors meet.

THE ELECTORAL COLLEGE TODAY

With the emergence of political parties in the early nineteenth century, the electoral college began to function in the way it does now—a way quite different from that intended by the framers of the Constitution. The President is elected by the mechanism of *electoral votes* (derived from popular votes) rather than by the will of the *electors*. In accordance with the provisions of the Constitution, electors still choose the President. But the electors are chosen by means of the popular votes registered for the party candidates. By casting ballots for specified party candidates, voters choose the party electors, who in turn go through the formality of voting for the party candidates when the electoral college convenes. The machinery by which the electors are chosen varies from state to state—in many states the names of the electors do not even appear on the ballot—but in most states the party candidate with the highest number of popular votes receives all of the state's electoral votes. The exceptions are Maine and Nebraska, which have adopted a plan that allows each congressional district to vote for its own elector, with the statewide winner receiving two at-large electors.

SELECTION OF ELECTORS

There is no uniform law governing the selection of presidential electors. Each state has its own method of choice. The most favored method is election by party convention; the second most favored, appointment by party committee. Other states resort to party primaries. Some states have adopted individualistic and unusual ways of choosing electors.

The individuals who serve as electors are generally designated by political groups and usually are persons who have contributed heavily to the party coffers or who have served the party with distinction. The honor is available to all citizens except those excluded by the Constitution: senators and representatives and persons "holding an Office of Trust or Profit under the United States."

ELECTIONS DEVOLVING UPON THE HOUSE AND SENATE

In the event that a presidential candidate does not receive a majority of the electoral votes, the House of Representatives chooses a President from the three leading contenders. Each state is entitled to one vote, and the winning candidate must receive a majority. Should the House of Representatives fail to choose a President, the Vice President-elect becomes President.

The House was called into action twice, in 1801 and in 1825, when Thomas Jefferson and John Quincy Adams were elected respectively.

If the vice presidential candidate does not receive a majority of the electoral votes, the Senate, voting as individuals, selects the Vice President from the two highest candidates. The only time the Senate was called upon to exercise this privilege was in 1837, when it elected Richard Mentor Johnson.

THE ELECTORAL VOTE FOR PRESIDENT

The following list shows the total number of electoral votes cast for President in each election from 1789 through 2008.

1789	69
1792	132
1796, 1800	138

1804	176
1808	175
1812	217
1816	217
1820	235
1824, 1828	261
1832	286
1836, 1840	294
1844	275
1848	290
1852, 1856	296
1860	303
1864	233
1868	294
1872	352
1876, 1880	369
1884, 1888	401
1892	444
1896, 1900	447
1904	476
1908	483
1912–1956	531
1960	537
1964–2008	538

In 1789, there were 69 electors, each of whom had two votes, one for President and one for Vice President. The candidate with the greatest number of votes was elected President, the second highest became Vice President. George Washington of Virginia received 69 votes. Other votes were cast as follows: John Adams, Mass., 34; John Jay, N.Y., 9; Robert Hanson Harrison, Md., 6; John Rutledge, S.C., 6; John Hancock, Mass., 4; George Clinton, N.Y., 3; Samuel Huntington, Conn., 2; John Milton, Ga., 2; James Armstrong, Pa., 1; Benjamin Lincoln, Mass., 1; Edward Telfair, Ga., 1.

In 1792, the second term, George Washington of Virginia received 132 votes. Others for whom votes were cast were: John Adams, Mass., 77; George Clinton, N.Y., 50; Thomas Jefferson, Va., 4; Aaron Burr, N.Y., 1.

In 1796, the third term, votes were cast as follows: John Adams, Mass., 71; Thomas Jefferson, Va., 68; Thomas Pinckney, S.C., 59; Aaron Burr, N.Y., 30; Samuel Adams, Mass., 15; Oliver Ellsworth, Conn., 11; George Clinton, N.Y., 7; John Jay, N.Y., 5; James Iredell, N.C., 3; John Henry, Md., 2; Samuel Johnston, N.C., 2; George Washington, Va., 2; Charles Cotesworth Pinckney, S.C., 1.

In 1800, the fourth term, votes were cast as follows; Thomas Jefferson, Va., 73; Aaron Burr, N.Y., 73; John Adams, Mass., 65; Charles Cotesworth Pinckney, S.C., 64; John Jay, N.Y., 1.

Since in 1800 Jefferson and Burr (both representing the same party) received equal numbers of votes and the election had to be decided by the House, subsequent elections were divided into two parts. First the electors voted for a President, then for a Vice President.

In 1804, the fifth term, votes for President were cast as follows: Thomas Jefferson, Va., 162; Charles Cotesworth Pinckney, S.C., 14.

In 1808, the sixth term, votes were cast as follows: James Madison, Va., 122; Charles Cotesworth Pinckney, S.C., 47; George Clinton, N.Y., 6.

In 1812, the seventh term, the votes were cast as follows: James Madison, Va., 128; De Witt Clinton, N.Y., 89.

In 1816, the eighth term, votes were cast as follows: James Monroe, Va., 183; Rufus King, N.Y., 34.

In 1820, the ninth term, votes were cast as follows: James Monroe, Va., 231; John Quincy Adams, Mass., 1. (Senator William Plumer, N.H., cast the vote for Adams.)

In 1824, the tenth term, votes were cast as follows: Andrew Jackson, Tenn., 99; John Quincy Adams, Mass., 84; William Harris Crawford, Ga., 41; Henry Clay, Ky., 37 (One of New York's 36 electors deserted Henry Clay to vote for Jackson.)

After 1824, the popular vote increasingly became an important element in the electoral vote, as more and more states opted to choose presidential electors according to the results of the popular vote rather than through balloting in the state legislature.

ELECTORS WHO SWITCHED VOTES

Each elector chosen by the citizenry on Election Day is morally committed to vote for the candidate of the party with which he or she is affiliated. On occasion, electors have ignored that commitment and have voted for a different candidate. This is not illegal under federal law, but it is illegal in the District of Columbia and in 29 states.

On March 25, 1969, Maine became the first state to require its presidential electors to cast their ballots for the ticket of the political party for which they were chosen.

The following electors switched their votes:

In 1796, Samuel Miles, a Pennsylvania Federalist, voted for Thomas Jefferson instead of John Adams.

In 1820, a New Hampshire Democratic-Republican elector, William Plumer, Sr., voted for John Quincy Adams instead of James Monroe.

In 1948, Preston Parks of Sommerville, one of the twelve electors from Tennessee, voted for James Strom Thurmond of South Carolina, the States' Rights (Dixiecrat) candidate, instead of Harry S. Truman.

In 1956, W. F. Turner of Montgomery, one of the eleven electors of Alabama, voted for Walter Burgwyn Jones, a circuit court judge of Montgomery, Ala., instead of Adlai Ewing Stevenson.

In 1960, Henry D. Irwin of Bartlesville, one of the electors of Oklahoma, cast his vote for Senator Harry Flood Byrd of Virginia instead of Richard Milhous Nixon.

In 1968, Dr. Lloyd W. Bailey of Rocky Mount, one of the 13 Republican electors from North Carolina, voted for George Corley Wallace instead of Richard Milhous Nixon.

In 1972, Roger L. MacBride of Charlottesville, Va., voted for John Hospers of Oregon, candidate of the Libertarian Party, instead of Richard Milhous Nixon. MacBride later ran for President on the Libertarian ticket.

In 1976, Mike Padden of Spokane, a Republican elector, cast one of Washington's nine electoral votes for Ronald Wilson Reagan instead of Gerald Rudolph Ford.

In 1988, Margaret Leach, a Democratic elector from West Virginia, cast her vote for Lloyd M. Bentsen, Jr., instead of Michael Stanley Dukakis.

In 2000, Barbara Lett-Simmons, a Democratic elector from Washington, D.C., submitted a blank ballot, rather than a ballot for Albert Arnold Gore, Jr., to protest the fact that the District of Columbia is not represented in Congress.

In 2004, a Democratic elector from Minnesota cast one of Minnesota's nine electoral votes for John Edwards instead of John Forbes Kerry.

ELECTORAL ODDITIES

It would have been possible for a presidential candidate to win any election from 1912 through 1956 without receiving a single vote in 36 states.

A presidential candidate with the electoral votes of only 12 states could have won the election. The combined electoral vote of New York (45), Pennsylvania (32), California (32), Illinois (27), Ohio (25), Texas (24), Michigan (20), Massachusetts (16), New Jersey (16), North Carolina (14), Indiana (13), and Missouri (13), amounted to 277 votes, whereas only 266 votes were required for victory.

In 1956, for example, the total vote cast in the 12 states mentioned above was 39,768,470. Under the unit or block system by which the candidate with the highest vote receives the entire electoral vote of a state, a candidate with 20,000,000 votes could have carried the twelve vital states. Thus a candidate with the votes of only 12.5 percent of the population of the United States (more than 160,000,000) could conceivably have been elected President of the United States.

In 1980, a candidate could have won the election by gaining the greater part of the popular vote in 11 states—California, New York, Pennsylvania, Illinois, Texas, Ohio, Michigan, Florida, New Jersey, Massachusetts, and Indiana. The candidate would then have won 272 electoral votes, and only 269 were needed for victory.

Only four Presidents have been elected without carrying both New York and Pennsylvania: Wilson in 1916, Truman in 1948, Nixon in 1968, and G. W. Bush in 2000 and 2004.

FIRST ELECTORAL VOTE CAST FOR A WOMAN

The first electoral vote for a woman was cast by Roger L. MacBride of Charlottesville, Va., whose vote for Theodora Nathan of Oregon, vice presidential candidate of the Libertarian Party, was counted on January 6, 1973.

PRESIDENTS ELECTED WITHOUT A MAJORITY OF THE POPULAR VOTE

Only four Presidents were elected with fewer popular votes than an opponent: J. Q. Adams in 1824, Hayes in 1876, B. Harrison in 1888, and G. W. Bush in 2000 (although the popular vote of 1824 is considered dubious, as it was counted in only 18 of the 24 states and different candidates appeared on the various ballots). However, many presidents have been elected without receiving a majority (more than 50 percent) of the votes cast. Listed below are the 18 elections in which the winning candidate failed to receive a majority of the popular vote.

The names of the candidates are followed by the percentage of the popular vote received. Winning candidates in each election are listed first.

1824

John Quincy Adams, Dem.-Rep., 30.54
Andrew Jackson, Dem.-Rep., 43.13
Henry Clay, Dem.-Rep., 13.24
William Harris Crawford, Dem.-Rep., 13.09

1844

James Knox Polk, Dem., 49.56
Henry Clay, Whig, 48.13
James Gillespie Birney, Liberty, 2.31

1848

Zachary Taylor, Whig, 47.35
Lewis Cass, Dem., 42.52
Martin Van Buren, Free Soil, 10.13

1856

James Buchanan, Dem., 45.63
John Charles Fremont, Rep., 33.27
Millard Fillmore, American, 21.08
Others, 0.02

1860

Abraham Lincoln, Rep., 39.80
Stephen Arnold Douglas, Dem., 29.40
John Cabell Breckinridge, Nat. Dem., 18.20
John Bell, Constitutional, 12.60

1876

Rutherford Birchard Hayes, Rep., 48.04
Samuel Jones Tilden, Dem., 50.99
Peter Cooper, Greenback, 0.97

1880

James Abram Garfield, Rep., 48.32
Winfield Scott Hancock, Dem., 48.21
James Baird Weaver, Greenback Labor, 3.35
Others, 0.12

1884

Grover Cleveland, Dem., 48.53
James Gillespie Blaine, Rep., 48.24
Benjamin Franklin Butler, Anti-Monopoly, 1.74
John Pierre St. John, Prohibition, 1.49

1888

Benjamin Harrison, Rep., 47.86
Grover Cleveland, Dem., 48.66
Clinton Bowen Fisk, Prohibition, 2.19
Alson Jenness Streeter, Union Labor, 1.29

1892

Grover Cleveland, Dem., 46.04
Benjamin Harrison, Rep., 43.01
James Baird Weaver, People's 8.53
Others, 2.42

1912

Woodrow Wilson, Dem., 41.85
Theodore Roosevelt, Progressive, 27.42
William Howard Taft, Rep., 23.15
Others, 7.58

1916

Woodrow Wilson, Dem., 49.26
Charles Evans Hughes, Rep., 46.12
Allan Louis Benson, Socialist, 3.16
Others, 1.46

1948

Harry S. Truman, Dem., 49.51
Thomas Edmund Dewey, Rep., 45.13
James Strom Thurmond, States' Rights, 2.40
Henry Agard Wallace, Progressive, 2.38
Others, 0.58

1960

John Fitzgerald Kennedy, Dem., 49.71
Richard Milhous Nixon, Rep., 49.55
Others, 0.74

1968

Richard Milhous Nixon, Rep., 43.42
Hubert Horatio Humphrey, Dem., 42.72

George Corley Wallace, American Independent, 13.53
Others, 0.33

1992

William Jefferson Clinton, Dem., 43.00
George Herbert Walker Bush, Rep., 37.45
H. Ross Perot, Ind., 18.91
Others, 0.64

1996

William Jefferson Clinton, Dem., 49.24
Robert Joseph Dole, Rep., 40.71
H. Ross Perot, Reform, 8.40
Others, 1.66

2000

George Walker Bush, Rep., 47.87
Albert Arnold Gore, Jr., Dem., 48.38
Ralph Nader, Green, 2.73
Others, 1.02

ELECTORAL VOTES CAST FOR BROTHERS IN 1796

In the election of 1796, before the President and the Vice President were separately voted upon, the electors voted for two brothers, Thomas and Charles Cotesworth Pinckney of South Carolina.

Thomas Pinckney received 59 of the electoral votes. (John Adams, who received 71 votes, was elected President, and Thomas Jefferson, who received 68 electoral votes, was elected Vice President.) Pinckney served as minister to Great Britain from 1792 to 1796 and in 1794–1795 was envoy extraordinary to Spain.

Charles Cotesworth Pinckney, governor of South Carolina, received one electoral vote in 1796. He also received 64 electoral votes in the election of 1800 and 14 in the election of 1804 (elections won by Jefferson). In the election of 1808 (won by Madison), he received 47 electoral votes.

VICE PRESIDENT DECLARED HIMSELF ELECTED PRESIDENT

On Wednesday, February 8, 1797, John Adams, Vice President of the United States, acting as presiding officer of the Senate, at the joint session of the Senate and the House of Representatives, said after the tally of votes of the electoral college, "In obedience to the Constitution and Law of the United States and to the commands of both Houses of Congress expressed in their resolution passed in the present session, I declare that John Adams is elected President of the United States for four years, to commence with the fourth day of March next; and that Thomas Jefferson is elected Vice President of the United States for four years to commence with the fourth of March next. And may the Sovereign of the Universe, the ordainer of civil government on earth, for the preservation of liberty, justice and peace, among men, enable both to discharge the duties of these offices conformably to the Constitution of the United States with conscientious diligence, punctuality and perseverance."

There were 138 electoral votes cast, a majority of 70 votes being required for election. No distinction was made as to the office of President and the Vice President. The candidate with the largest number of votes was elected President, and the candidate with the second largest was elected Vice President. (It was thus possible for the President and the Vice President to belong to different parties.)

POPULAR AND ELECTORAL VOTES AFTER 1824

After 1824, the popular vote had a direct influence on the electoral vote, through the process of choosing electors. But the two votes are not identical. Usually the electoral vote magnifies the margin of victory, as in the four close elections of 1880, 1884, 1960, and 1968, where a margin of less than one percent of the popular vote separated the winner from the loser.

		Percentage of Popular Vote	Percentage of Electoral Vote			Percentage of Popular Votes	Percentage of Electoral Votes
1880	Garfield	48.32	57.99	1920	Harding	60.30	76.08
	Hancock	48.21	42.01		Cox	34.17	23.92
1884	Cleveland	48.53	54.61	1936	Roosevelt	60.79	98.49
	Blaine	48.24	45.39		Landon	36.54	1.51
1960	Kennedy	49.71	56.43	1964	Johnson	61.05	90.34
	Nixon	49.55	40.78		Goldwater	38.47	9.66
1968	Nixon	43.42	55.94	1972	Nixon	60.69	96.6
	Humphrey	42.72	35.50		McGovern	37.53	3.4
				1984	Reagan	58.77	97.58
					Mondale	40.54	2.42

In the similarly close election of 1888, the electoral vote reversed the popular vote. Cleveland won 48.66 percent of the popular vote but only 41.90 percent of the electoral vote. Harrison won the election with 58.10 percent of the electoral vote, although he had only 47.86 of the popular vote. In the election of 1876, neither candidate had a majority in the electoral college, although Tilden had gained 50.99 percent of the popular vote against Hayes's 48.04 percent.

Another reversal of the popular vote occurred in 2000, when Gore took 48.38 percent of the popular vote and G. W. Bush took 47.87 percent. In the electoral college, however, Bush received 50.37 percent and Gore took 49.62.

In the landslide elections of 1920, 1936, 1964, 1972, and 1984, the electoral and popular vote percentages were as follows:

Thus, Johnson in 1964 won the greatest percentage of the popular vote, but Roosevelt in 1936 won a higher percentage of the electoral vote.

THE SUPREME COURT AND THE 2000 ELECTION

The election of November 7, 2000, was the only one to involve the Supreme Court. The two candidates, George Walker Bush for the Republicans and Albert Arnold Gore, Jr., for the Democrats, emerged from Election Night in a dead heat, with neither one able to claim a majority of the electoral vote. The winner of the popular vote in Florida, and thus of the state's 25 electoral votes, could not be determined immediately because of balloting irregularities in several counties, although Bush maintained a slim lead. Both parties sent legal teams into the state court system to argue the validity of machine recounts versus manual recounts in the hope of gaining an advantage; the resulting rulings were appealed to the U.S. Supreme Court. On December 12 the Supreme Court ordered the manual recounts to stop. The popular vote certified by the Florida secretary of state showed Bush to be the winner by a margin of only 537 votes. The Republican-controlled legislature of Florida proceeded to appoint electors for Bush, which gave him a majority of the electoral college. Gore conceded on December 13.

Although Democrats charged that the election had been stolen, an independent ballot review sponsored by three news organizations early in 2001 showed that further recounts would probably not have changed the results.

The irregularities in Florida, which involved confusing ballots, antiquated voting machines, and arbitrary decisions by officials, were by no means unique to that state. After the election, there was widespread demand for reforms at the local level to ensure that every vote would be recognized and counted.

PERCENTAGE OF VOTERS VOTING

The greatest percentage of eligible voters cast their ballots in the election of 1860—81.2 percent. The smallest percentage voted in 1824—26.9 percent.

1900	73.2
1904	65.2
1908	65.4
1912	58.8
1916	61.6
1920	49.2
1924	48.9
1928	56.9
1932	56.9
1936	61.0
1940	62.5
1944	55.9
1948	53.0
1952	63.3
1956	60.6
1960	64.0
1964	61.7
1968	60.6
1972	55.4
1976	56.5
1980	53.9
1984	53.1
1988	50.1
1992	55.2
1996	48.9
2000	51.2
2004	56.7
2008	60.7

THE POPULAR VOTE OF THE THIRD PARTIES

Between 1832 and 2008, the only third party to receive more than 25 percent of the popular vote was the Progressive Party, whose candidate, Theodore Roosevelt, received 27.4 percent of the popular vote in 1912, putting him in second place, ahead of the Republican candidate. Millard Fillmore, the candidate of the American Party in 1856, received 21.5 percent of the popular vote. Independent candidate Henry Ross Perot received 18.9 percent of the popular vote in 1992.

THIRD-PARTY ELECTORAL VOTES

The two-party system has been dominant since 1932. With one exception (the Progressive Party in 1912), the strength of third parties has been of little consequence.

Third parties have won electoral votes in only nine elections since 1832.

In 1832, William Wirt, presidential candidate of the Anti-Masonic Party, received Vermont's seven electoral votes, out of a total of 286 (2.5 percent). John Floyd, presidential candidate of the National Republican Party (predecessor of the Whig Party), received South Carolina's 11 electoral votes (3.9 percent).

In 1836, the Whig Party nominated four regional candidates in hopes of drawing votes from the Democrats. Willie Person Mangum received 11 electoral votes, Daniel Webster 14, Hugh Lawson White 26, and William Henry Harrison 73. Their combined votes totaled 124 out of 294 (42.2 percent).

In 1856, Millard Fillmore, presidential candidate of the American Party, received eight of the 296 electoral votes (2.7 percent).

In 1860, John Bell, presidential candidate of the Constitutional Union Party, received 39 of the 303 electoral votes (12.87 percent).

In 1892, James Baird Weaver, presidential candidate of the People's Party, received 22 of the 444 electoral votes (4.95 percent).

In 1912, Theodore Roosevelt, presidential candidate of the Progressive Party, received 88 of the 531 electoral votes (16.57 percent).

In 1924, Robert Marion La Follette, presidential candidate of the Progressive Party, received 13 of the 531 electoral votes (2.45 percent).

In 1948, James Strom Thurmond, presidential candidate of the States' Rights Democratic Party, received 39 of the 531 electoral votes (7.35 percent).

In 1968, George Corley Wallace, presidential candidate of the American Independent Party, received 46 of the 538 electoral votes (8.55 percent).

In addition, in 1960, Harry Flood Byrd, though not nominated by any party, received 15 of the 537 electoral votes (2.79 percent).

DEFEATED CANDIDATES LATER ELECTED TO PRESIDENCY

Many candidates defeated in one election for the presidency or the vice presidency were later elected to the presidency.

In the election of 1792, George Washington was unanimously reelected President by the electors. Four other men contended for the vice presidency. John Adams received the highest number of electoral votes, 77, and was elected Vice President. Thomas Jefferson came in third with four votes.

In the election of 1796, Thomas Jefferson received 68 electoral votes and John Adams 71 electoral votes. Adams, who had the highest number of votes, was elected President, and Jefferson, who had the next highest number, was automatically elected Vice President. In the election of 1800, the situation was reversed: Jefferson and Aaron Burr tied with 73 votes each, and Adams received 65. It took the House of Representatives thirty-six ballots to decide on Jefferson for President and Burr for Vice President.

In the election of 1808, both James Madison and James Monroe received three electoral votes in the voting for Vice President. Madison won the voting for President; the winner of the vote for Vice President was George Clinton. Monroe went on to win the Presidency in 1820 with 231 electoral votes. John Quincy Adams received one electoral vote that year.

In the election of 1824, John Quincy Adams defeated Andrew Jackson for the presidency. Jackson received a larger number of electoral votes, but not a majority. The House of Representatives voted by states and elected Adams. In the same year Jackson also received 13 electoral votes for the vice presidency and Martin Van Buren received nine; the office was won by John Calhoun. Jackson returned in 1828 to defeat Adams, taking 178 electoral votes to Adams's 84 votes. Calhoun continued to serve as Vice President in Jackson's first term, but was replaced in his second term by Van Buren.

In the election of 1836, Van Buren, with 170 electoral votes, was elected President. He defeated William Henry Harrison, who received 73 electoral votes. John Tyler, who received 47 electoral votes, was defeated for the vice presidency by Richard Mentor Johnson. Harrison came back to win the Presidency in 1840, defeating Van Buren with an electoral vote of 234 to 60; Tyler was elected as Harrison's running mate. Also in that year, one electoral vote was cast for James Knox Polk.

Tyler became President in 1841 after Harrison's sudden death. Although the Whigs refused to renominate him in 1844, he was nominated by the National Democratic Tyler Convention, but received no electoral votes. The election was won by James Knox Polk, who received 170 electoral votes.

In the election of 1888, incumbent President Grover Cleveland was defeated for reelection by Benjamin Harrison. Their electoral ratio was 168 to 233. Cleveland regained the presidency in the election of 1892 by defeating Harrison, 277 electoral votes to 145.

In the election of 1920, Calvin Coolidge was elected Vice President on the same ticket with Warren Gamaliel Harding. They received 404 electoral votes. The Democratic ticket of James Middleton Cox and Franklin Delano Roosevelt received 127 electoral votes. Roosevelt was elected President in 1932 with 472 electoral votes, 1936 with 523 electoral votes, 1940 with 449 electoral votes, and 1944 with 432 electoral votes.

Richard Milhous Nixon was elected Vice President in 1952 and 1956 under Dwight David Eisenhower. He ran for President in 1960, but lost to John Fitzgerald Kennedy, taking 219 electoral votes to Kennedy's 303. Nixon went on to win the elections of 1968 with 301 electoral votes and 1972 with 520 electoral votes.

ELECTIONS IN WHICH PRESIDENTS WERE RENOMINATED BUT NOT REELECTED

1796 George Washington (not a candidate for reelection), 2 electoral votes; John Adams elected, 71 electoral votes

1800 John Adams, 65 electoral votes; defeated by Thomas Jefferson and Aaron Burr, each with 73 electoral votes (tie decided by House of Representatives)

1828 John Quincy Adams, 83 electoral votes; defeated by Andrew Jackson, 178 electoral votes

1840 Martin Van Buren, 60 electoral votes; defeated by William Henry Harrison, 234 electoral votes

1856 Millard Fillmore, 8 electoral votes; defeated by James Buchanan, 174 electoral votes

1888 Grover Cleveland, 168 electoral votes; defeated by Benjamin Harrison, 233 electoral votes

1892 Benjamin Harrison, 145 electoral votes; defeated by Grover Cleveland, 277 electoral votes

1912 Theodore Roosevelt, 88 electoral votes; William Howard Taft, 8 electoral votes; defeated by Woodrow Wilson, 435 electoral votes

1932 Herbert Clark Hoover, 59 electoral votes; defeated by Franklin Delano Roosevelt, 472 electoral votes

1976 Gerald Rudolph Ford, 240 electoral votes; Ronald Wilson Reagan, 1 electoral vote; defeated by Jimmy Carter, 297 electoral votes

1980 Jimmy Carter, 49 electoral votes; defeated by Ronald Wilson Reagan, 489 electoral votes

1992 George Bush, 168 electoral votes; defeated by Bill Clinton, 370 electoral votes

Some Presidents had also been defeated when they ran for office prior to their successful elections.

FIVE PRESIDENTS DENIED RENOMINATION

Of the five Presidents denied renomination by their political party, four had become President only through the death of the previous Chief Executive.

John Tyler, who became the tenth President after the death of William Henry Harrison, and served from April 6, 1841 to March 4, 1845, was not renominated by the Whig Party, which convened on May 1, 1844, in Baltimore, Md. Henry Clay was nominated for the presidency on the first ballot by acclamation. Tyler was nominated by a breakaway group, the National Democratic Tyler Convention.

Millard Fillmore became the thirteenth President on July 10, 1850, after the death of Zachary Taylor, and served until March 4, 1853. When the Whig Party convened at Baltimore, Md., on June 17–20, 1852, Fillmore received 133 votes and Winfield Scott received 131 votes. On the fifty-third ballot, Scott received 159 votes and was declared the nominee of the Whig Party. Fillmore received 112 votes and Daniel Webster received 21 votes.

Andrew Johnson became the seventeenth President on April 15, 1865, after the assassination of Abraham Lincoln. Johnson served to March 4, 1869. The Democratic Party convention held in New York City on July 4–9, 1868, did not support Johnson. Instead, the nomination went to Horatio Seymour, who was nominated on the twenty-second ballot.

Chester Alan Arthur, who served as the twenty-first President from September 20, 1881, to March 4, 1885, after the death of James Abram Garfield, failed to receive the presidential nomination at the Republican Party convention that met in Chicago, Ill., on June 3–6, 1884. James Gillespie Blaine, Arthur's secretary of state, was nominated on the fourth ballot with 541 votes; Arthur received only 207 votes.

Tyler, Fillmore, A. Johnson, and Arthur were Vice Presidents who succeeded to the presidency after to the death of the incumbent.

Franklin Pierce was nominated for the presidency by the Democratic Party in convention in Baltimore, Md., on June 1–5, 1852, and was elected to the White House. Four years later, at the Democratic Party convention in Cincinnati, Ohio, June 2–6, 1856, the Democrats declined to renominate Pierce. On the first ballot, he received 122.5 votes to 135.5 for James Buchanan. Buchanan took all 296 votes on the seventeenth ballot and was elected President on Election Day.

POLITICAL PARTIES AND ELECTIONS

The forty-three Presidents belonged to four political parties.

Two were Federalists: Washington and J. Adams.

Four were Whigs: W. H. Harrison, Tyler, Taylor, and Fillmore.

Eighteen were Democratic-Republicans or, after 1832, Democrats: Jefferson, Madison, Monroe, J. Q. Adams, Jackson, Van Buren, Polk, Pierce, Buchanan, Cleveland, Wilson, F. D. Roosevelt, Truman, Kennedy, L. B. Johnson, Carter, Clinton, and Obama.

Nineteen were Republicans: Lincoln, A. Johnson (a Democrat, but elected Vice President on the Republican ticket), Grant, Hayes, Garfield, Arthur, B. Harrison, McKinley, T. Roosevelt, Taft, Harding, Coolidge, Hoover, Eisenhower, Nixon, Ford, Reagan, G. Bush, and G. W. Bush.

Federalists

Federalists won three (37.5 percent) of eight elections. (Elections won by Federalists are indicated by asterisks.)

*1789	Washington
*1792	Washington
*1796	J. Adams
1800	J. Adams
1804	Pinckney
1808	Pinckney
1812	Clinton
1816	King

Democrats

Democrats (and their predecessors, the Democratic-Republicans) have won 28 (50 percent) of 56 elections. (Elections won by Democrats are indicated by asterisks.)

1796	Jefferson
*1800	Jefferson
*1804	Jefferson
*1808	Madison
*1812	Madison
*1816	Monroe
*1820	Monroe
*1824	J. Q. Adams
*1828	Jackson
*1832	Jackson
*1836	Van Buren
1840	Van Buren
*1844	Polk

1848	Cass
*1852	Pierce
*1856	Buchanan
1860	Douglas
1864	McClellan
1868	Seymour
1872	Greeley
1876	Tilden
1880	Hancock
*1884	Cleveland
1888	Cleveland
*1892	Cleveland
1896	Bryan
1900	Bryan
1904	Parker
1908	Bryan
*1912	Wilson
*1916	Wilson
1920	Cox
1924	Davis
1928	Smith
*1932	F. D. Roosevelt
*1936	F. D. Roosevelt
*1940	F. D. Roosevelt
*1944	F. D. Roosevelt
*1948	Truman
1952	Stevenson
1956	Stevenson
*1960	Kennedy
*1964	L. B. Johnson
1968	Humphrey
1972	McGovern
*1976	Carter
1980	Carter
1984	Mondale
1988	Dukakis
*1992	Clinton
*1996	Clinton
2000	Gore
2004	Kerry
*2008	Obama

Whigs

Whigs (originally known as National Republicans) won two (28.6 percent) of six elections. (Elections won by Whigs are indicated by asterisks.) By 1856 the Whigs were defunct; a small remnant held a convention and endorsed the candidates of the American (Know-Nothing) Party.

1832	Clay
1836	W. H. Harrison
*1840	W. H. Harrison
1844	Clay

724

*1848 Taylor
1852 Scott
1856 Fillmore

Republicans

Republicans have won 23 (60 percent) of 39 elections from 1856 through 2008. (Elections won by Republicans are indicated by asterisks.)

1856 Frémont
*1860 Lincoln
*1864 Lincoln
*1868 Grant
*1872 Grant
*1876 Hayes
*1880 Garfield
1884 Blaine
*1888 B. Harrison
1892 B. Harrison
*1896 McKinley
*1900 McKinley
*1904 T. Roosevelt
*1908 Taft
1912 Taft
1916 Hughes
*1920 Harding
*1924 Coolidge
*1928 Hoover
1932 Hoover
1936 Landon
1940 Willkie
1944 Dewey
1948 Dewey
*1952 Eisenhower
*1956 Eisenhower
1960 Nixon
1964 Goldwater
*1968 Nixon
*1972 Nixon
1976 Ford
*1980 Reagan
*1984 Reagan
*1988 G. Bush
1992 G. Bush
1996 Dole
*2000 G. W. Bush
*2004 G. W. Bush
2008 McCain

NOMINATIONS AND ELECTIONS—1832–2008

In the 45 presidential elections from 1832 through 2008, the Whigs (from 1832 through 1852) and the Republicans (since 1856) won 25 elections and lost 20 elections. The Whigs and Republicans nominated a total of 32 individuals as presidential candidates in these 45 elections, some of them more than once. Of these 32 individuals, a total of 19 were elected President; 12 were elected once, and 7 were elected twice.

In the 20 elections lost by the Whig and Republican parties, a total of 18 individuals were nominated. Three of them had already been elected once (B. Harrison, Taft, G. Bush); two of them went on to be elected later (W. H. Harrison, Nixon). Two (Clay, Dewey) lost twice.

In the 45 elections since 1832, the Democrats won 20 elections and lost 25 elections. The party nominated a total of 32 individuals in these 45 elections, some of them more than once. Of these 32 individuals, a total of 15 were elected President; ten were elected once (though Jackson, elected in 1832, had already served one term), four were elected twice, and one was elected four times.

In the 25 elections lost by the Democratic Party, a total of 22 individuals were nominated. Three of them had already been elected once (Van Buren, Cleveland, Carter); one of them went on to be elected later (Cleveland). One (Bryan) lost three times, and one (Stevenson) lost twice.

REPUBLICAN VERSUS DEMOCRATIC ADMINISTRATIONS

The Republican Party ran its first presidential candidate, John Charles Frémont, in 1856. In the years 1856–2008, the Republicans have elected 16 individuals, some of them twice, for a total of 23 terms.

The Republican administrations have been those of Lincoln (and Andrew Johnson), 8 years; Grant, 8 years; Hayes, 4 years; Garfield (and Arthur), 4 years; Benjamin Harrison, 4 years; McKinley (and Theodore Roosevelt), 8 years; T. Roosevelt, 4 years; Taft, 4 years; Harding (and Coolidge), 4 years; Coolidge, 4 years; Hoover, 4 years; Eisenhower, 8 years; Nixon (and Ford), 8 years; Reagan, 8 years; G. Bush, 4 years; G. W. Bush, 8 years. This is a total of 92 years.

In the years 1856–2008 the Democrats have elected ten individuals for a total of 16 terms.

The Democratic administrations have been those of Buchanan, 4 years; Cleveland, 8 years (two non-consecutive terms); Wilson, 8 years; Franklin Delano Roosevelt (and Truman), 16 years; Truman, 4 years; Kennedy (and Lyndon Baines Johnson), 4 years; Johnson, 4 years; Carter, 4 years; Clinton, 8 years; Obama, 4 years. This is a total of 64 years.

ADMINISTRATION CHANGES

In the 56 presidential elections from 1789 through 2008, 22 Presidents have succeeded Presidents of a different political party:

Thomas Jefferson (Dem.-Rep.) followed John Adams (Fed.)

Andrew Jackson (Dem.) followed John Quincy Adams (Dem.-Rep.)

William Henry Harrison (Whig) followed Martin Van Buren (Dem.)

James Knox Polk (Dem.) followed John Tyler (Whig)

Zachary Taylor (Whig) followed James Knox Polk (Dem.)

Franklin Pierce (Dem.) followed Millard Fillmore (Whig)

Abraham Lincoln (Rep.) followed James Buchanan (Dem.)

Grover Cleveland (Dem.) followed Chester Alan Arthur (Rep.)

Benjamin Harrison (Rep.) followed Grover Cleveland (Dem.)

Grover Cleveland (Dem.) followed Benjamin Harrison (Rep.)

William McKinley (Rep.) followed Grover Cleveland (Dem.)

Woodrow Wilson (Dem.) followed William Howard Taft (Rep.)

Warren Gamaliel Harding (Rep.) followed Woodrow Wilson (Dem.)

Franklin Delano Roosevelt (Dem.) followed Herbert Hoover (Rep.)

Dwight David Eisenhower (Rep.) followed Harry S. Truman (Dem.)

John Fitzgerald Kennedy (Dem.) followed Dwight David Eisenhower (Rep.)

Richard Milhous Nixon (Rep.) followed Lyndon Baines Johnson (Dem.)

Jimmy Carter (Dem.) followed Gerald Rudolph Ford (Rep.)

Ronald Wilson Reagan (Rep.) followed Jimmy Carter (Dem.)

William Jefferson Clinton (Dem.) followed George Bush (Rep.)

George Walker Bush (Rep.) followed William Jefferson Clinton (Dem.)

Barack Hussein Obama (Dem.) followed George Walker Bush (Rep.)

THE LONGEST POLITICAL REGIME

The Democratic-Republicans, considered the forerunners of the present-day Democrats, had the longest uninterrupted term of office. On March 4, 1801, Thomas Jefferson took office and served eight years. He was followed by James Madison, who served eight years; James Monroe, who served eight years; and John Quincy Adams, who served four years. The party had been in power for 28 years, from March 4, 1801, to March 4, 1829, when Andrew Jackson (usually considered the first Democrat in the present sense) was inaugurated.

The longest Republican regime began on March 4, 1861, when Abraham Lincoln was inaugurated. Lincoln was reelected and after his death Andrew Johnson completed the remainder of his term. Grant was elected twice and served eight years. Rutherford B. Hayes served four years. James A. Garfield was elected and after his death Chester A. Arthur completed the remainder of his term. The Republicans had been in power for 24 years, from March 4, 1861, to March 4, 1885, when Grover Cleveland, a Democrat, was inaugurated.

In modern times, the longest uninterrupted term of office held by a party began with Franklin D. Roosevelt's inauguration on March 4, 1933, and lasted 20 years, until Dwight D. Eisenhower's inauguration on January 20, 1953.

ALPHABETICAL LIST OF PRESIDENTIAL AND VICE PRESIDENTIAL CANDIDATES

1789–1824

The candidates on the following list ran for the presidency before a formal political party structure developed in the United States. Until 1804 each elector cast one vote for each of two individuals; the runner-up in the balloting became Vice President. Beginning in 1804, candidates were named separately for the vice presidency and voted for separately by the electors.

Adams, John   1789, 1792, 1796, 1800
Adams, John Quincy   1820, 1824
Adams, Samuel   1796
Armstong, James   1789
Burr, Aaron   1792, 1796, 1800
Calhoun, John Caldwell   1824–VP, 1828–VP
Clay, Henry   1824
Clinton, De Witt   1812
Clinton, George   1789, 1792, 1796, 1804–VP, 1808–VP
Crawford, William Harris   1816, 1824
Ellsworth, Oliver   1796
Gerry, Elbridge   1812–VP
Hancock, John   1789
Harper, Robert Goodloe   1816–VP, 1820–VP
Harrison, Robert Hanson   1789
Henry, John   1796
Howard, John Eager   1816–VP
Huntington, Samuel   1789
Ingersoll, Jared   1812–VP
Iredell, James   1796
Jackson, Andrew   1824
Jay, John   1789, 1796, 1800
Jefferson, Thomas   1792, 1796, 1800, 1804
Johnson, Samuel   1796
King, Rufus   1804–VP, 1808–VP, 1816
Langdon, John   1808–VP
Lincoln, Benjamin   1789
Macon, Nathaniel   1824–VP
Madison, James   1808, 1812
Marshall, John   1816–VP
Milton, John   1789
Monroe, James   1808–VP, 1816, 1820
Pinckney, Charles Cotesworth   1796, 1800, 1804, 1808
Pinckney, Thomas   1796
Rodney, Daniel   1816–VP, 1820–VP
Ross, James   1816–VP
Rush, Richard   1820–VP
Rutledge, John   1789
Sanford, Nathan   1824–VP
Stockton, Richard   1820–VP

Telfair, Edward   1789
Tompkins, Daniel D.   1816–VP, 1820–VP
Van Buren, Martin   1824–VP
Washington, George   1789, 1792, 1796

1828–2008

The abbreviation VP following the year indicates a vice presidential candidacy for the year specified.

Adams, Charles Francis   1848–VP, Free Soil
Adams, Charles Francis Jr.   1872–VP, Straight-Out Democratic
Adams, John Quincy   1828, Federalist
Agnew, Spiro Theodore   1968–VP, 1972–VP, Republican
Aiken, John W.   1932–VP, 1936, 1940, Socialist Labor
Albaugh, Arla A.   1944–VP, Socialist Labor
Alexander, Stewart A.   2008, Socialist
Allen, Seymour E.   1932, National
Amondson, Gene   2004, Prohibition/Concerns of People; 2008, Prohibition
Anderson, John Bayard   1980, Independent (National Unity)
Anderson, John D.   1984, National Unity Party of Kentucky
Anderson, Pro-Life   1996–VP, America First
Anderson, Thomas Jefferson   1972–VP, American Independent; 1976, American
Andress, Stanford E.   2004, independent
Andrews, Joan   1988–VP, Right to Life
Andrews, Thomas Coleman   1956, States' Rights; 1964, Independent States' Rights
Arthur, Chester Alan   1880–VP, Republican
Babson, Roger Ward   1940, Prohibition
Badnarik, Michael   2004, Libertarian
Baldwin, Chuck   2004–VP, 2008 Constitution
Banks, Nathaniel Prentice   1856, North American
Barker, Wharton   1900, People's
Barkley, Alben William   1948–VP, Democratic
Barnum, R. G.   1920–VP, Single Tax
Barr, Bob   2008, Libertarian

Barron, Elizabeth Cervantes 1980–VP, Peace and Freedom

Bass, Charlotta A. 1952–VP, American Labor, Progressive

Bass, Willie Isaac 1952–VP, Church of God

Bell, John 1860, Constitutional Union

Bennington, Wesley Henry 1928–VP, Greenback

Benson, Allan Louis 1916, Socialist

Bentley, Charles Eugene 1896, National

Bentsen, Lloyd Millard, Jr. 1988–VP, Democratic

Bergland, David 1976–VP, 1984, Libertarian

Bevel, James Luther 1992–VP, Freedom for LaRouche

Bidwell, John 1892, Prohibition

Biden, Joseph Robinette 2008–VP, Democratic

Billings, Theodore C. 1964–VP, Constitution

Birney, James Gillespie 1840, 1844, Liberty

Birrenbach, John 1996, Independent Grassroots

Black, James 1872, Prohibition

Blaine, James Gillespie 1884, Republican

Blair, Francis Preston 1868–VP, Democratic

Blomen, Connie 1976–VP, Socialist Labor

Blomen, Henning A. 1964–VP, 1968, Socialist Labor

Boren, James Harlan 1992, Apathy

Bouck, William 1924–VP, Farmer Labor

Boutelle, Paul 1968–VP, Socialist Workers

Bradford, Drew 1992, independent

Breckinridge, John Cabell 1856–VP, Democratic; 1860, Independent Democratic, Southern Democratic

Brehm, Marie Caroline 1924–VP, Prohibition

Bricker, John William 1944–VP, Republican

Brisben, Quinn 1976–VP, 1992, Socialist

Brooks, John Anderson 1888–VP, Prohibition

Browder, Earl Russell 1936, 1940, Communist

Brown, Benjamin Gratz 1872–VP, Democratic, Liberal Republican, Liberal Republican Convention of Colored Men

Brown, Cathy Gordon 2000, independent

Brown, Walter F. 2004, Socialist

Browne, Harry 1996, 2000, Libertarian

Brownlee, Traves 1984–VP, American

Bryan, Charles Wayland 1924–VP, Democratic

Bryan, William Jennings 1896, Democratic, National Silver, Populist; 1900, Democratic, People's Silver Republican; 1908, Democratic

Bubar, Benjamin C. 1976, Prohibition; 1980, National Statesman

Buchanan, James 1856, Democratic

Buchanan, Patrick J. 2000, Reform

Buckner, Simon 1896–VP, National Democratic

Burnett, James S. 1988–VP, American Independent

Bush, George Herbert Walker 1980–VP, 1984–VP, 1988, 1992, Republican

Bush, George Walker 2000, 2004, Republican

Butler, Benjamin Franklin 1884, Anti-Monopoly, Greenback

Butler, William Orlando 1848–VP, Democratic

Byrd, Harry Flood 1952–VP, America First, Constitution; 1956, States' Rights, South Carolinians for Independent Electors

Caffery, Donelson 1900, National

Calero, Róger 2004, 2008, Socialist Workers

Calhoun, John Caldwell 1828–VP, Democratic

Camejo, Peter 1976, Socialist Workers; 2004–VP, Reform/Independent

Campagna, Richard 2004–VP, Libertarian

Carlson, Grace 1948–VP, Socialist Workers

Carroll, George W. 1904–VP, Prohibition

Carter, Jimmy 1976, 1980, Democratic, Social Democrats

Carter, Reginald   1960–VP, Independent Afro-American

Cary, Samuel Fenton   1876–VP, Greenback

Cass, Lewis   1848, Democratic

Castle, Darrell   2008–VP, Constitution

Chafin, Eugene Wilder   1908, 1912, Prohibition

Chambers, Benjamin J.   1880–VP, Greenback Labor

Chandler, Connie   1996–VP, Independent Party of Utah

Chavez, Ventura   1968, People's Constitutional

Cheney, Richard Bruce   2000–VP, 2004–VP, Republican

Chester, Eric T.   1996–VP, Socialist

Choate, Pat   1996–VP, Reform

Christensen, Parley Parker   1920, Farmer Labor

Clark, Ed   1980, Libertarian

Clay, Henry   1832, National Republican; 1844, Whig

Cleaver, Eldridge   1968, Peace and Freedom

Clemente, Rosa   2008–VP, Green

Cleveland, Grover   1884, 1888, 1892, Democratic

Clinton, William Jefferson   1992, 1996, Democratic

Cobb, David   2004, Green

Cochrane, John   1864–VP, Independent Republican

Coffin, Lorenzo S.   1908–VP, United Christian

Coiner, C. Benton   1960, Conservative (Va.)

Colfax, Schuyler   1868–VP, Republican

Collins, Charles   1996, independent

Colvin, David Leigh   1920–VP, 1936, Prohibition

Colvin, John   1888–VP, Industrial Reform

Commoner, Barry   1980, Citizens

Conant, John A.   1884–VP, American Prohibition

Congress, Richard   1980, Socialist Workers

Coolidge, Calvin   1920–VP, 1924, Republican

Cooper, Peter   1876, Greenback

Corregan, Charles Hunter   1904, Socialist Labor

Courtney, Kent H.   1960–VP, Conservative (N.J.)

Cowdery, Robert Hall   1888, United Labor

Cox, James Middleton   1920, Democratic

Cox, James Renshaw   1932, Jobless

Cox, William Wesley   1904–VP, 1920, Socialist Labor

Coxey, Jacob Sechler   1932–VP, Farmer Labor

Cozzini, Georgia   1956–VP, 1960–VP, Socialist Labor

Crane, A. Peter   1996, Independent Party of Utah

Cranfill, James Britton   1892–VP, Prohibition

Crommelin, John Geraerdt   1960–VP, National States' Rights

Crowley, Jeremiah D.   1928–VP, Socialist Labor

Cunningham, Charles E.   1888–VP, Union Labor

Curtis, Charles   1928–VP, 1932–VP, Republican

Curtis, James Langdon   1888, American

Curtis, Merritt Barton   1960, Constitution (Wash.); 1960–VP, Tax Cut

Dallas, George Mifflin   1844–VP, Democratic

Daly, Lar   1960, Tax Cut

Daniel, William   1884–VP, Prohibition

Daniels, Ron   1992, independent

Dattner, Joyce   1988–VP, New Alliance

Davis, Angela Yvonne   1980–VP, 1984–VP, Communist

Davis, Billy   1984–VP, Independent

Davis, David   1872, Labor Reform

Davis, Henry Gassaway   1904–VP, Democratic

Davis, John William   1924, Democratic

Dawes, Charles Gates   1924–VP, Republican

Dayton, William Lewis   1856–VP, Republican

De Berry, Clifton   1964, 1980, Socialist Workers

Deasy, Irene M. 2004–VP, independent

Debs, Eugene Victor 1900, Social-Democratic; 1904, 1908, 1912, 1920, Socialist

Dennis, Delmar 1984, 1988, American

Decker, Rutherford Losey 1960, Prohibition

Dewey, Thomas Edmund 1944, 1948, Republican

Dobbs, Farrell 1948, 1952, 1956, 1960, Socialist Workers

Dodge, Earl Farwell 1976–VP, 1992, 1996, 2000, 2004 (Colo.), Prohibition; 1980–VP, 1984, 1988, National Statesman

Dole, Robert Joseph 1976–VP, 1996, Republican

Dollarhyde, F. Booth 1988–VP, Peace and Freedom

Donelson, Andrew Jackson 1856–VP, American, Whig

Donnelly, Ignatius 1900–VP, People's

Douglass, Frederick 1872–VP, Equal Rights

Douglas, Stephen Arnold 1860, Democratic

Dow, Neal 1880, Prohibition

Driscoll, Carroll 1980–VP, Independent (Right to Life)

Drufenbrock, Diane 1980–VP, Socialist

Dukakis, Michael Stanley 1988, Democratic

Duke, David E. 1988, Independent Populist

Dyke, William E. 1976–VP, American Independent

Earle, Thomas 1840–VP, Liberty

Edgerton, James Arthur 1928–VP, Prohibition

Edwards, John Reid 2004–VP, Democratic

Ehlers, Delbert L. 1992, independent

Eisenhower, Dwight David 1952, 1956, Republican

Ellis, Seth Hockett 1900, Union Reform

Ellmaker, Amos 1832–VP, Anti-Masonic

Emery, Stephen 1948–VP, Socialist Labor

Evans, R. Wayne 1976–VP, U.S. Labor

Everett, Edward 1860–VP, Constitution

Fairbanks, Charles Warren 1904–VP, 1916–VP, Republican

Faris, Herman Preston 1924, Prohibition

Faubus, Orval Eugene 1960, National States' Rights

Feimer, Doris 1992–VP, American

Feinland, Marsha 1996, Peace and Freedom

Ferguson, James Edward 1920, American

Ferraro, Geraldine Anne 1984–VP, Democratic

Field, James Gaven 1892–VP, People's

Fillmore, Millard 1848–VP, Whig; 1856, American, Whig

Fisher, Louis 1972, Socialist Labor

Fisher, Rolland E. 1968–VP, Prohibition

Fisk, Clinton Bowen 1888, Prohibition

Floyd, John 1832, Independent

Foote, Charles C. 1848–VP, National Liberty

Forbes, Ralph 1996, America First

Ford, Gerald Rudolph 1976, Republican

Ford, James William 1932–VP, 1936–VP, 1940–VP, Communist

Foster, Ezola 2000–VP, Reform

Foster, William Zebulon 1924, 1928, Workers (Communist); 1932, Communist

Frazier, J. Curtis 2000–VP, Constitution

Frelinghuysen, Theodore 1844–VP, Whig

Frémont, John Charles 1856, Republican; 1864, Independent Republican

Friedman, Samuel Herman 1952–VP, 1956–VP, Socialist

Fry, Daniel 1972–VP, Universal

Fulani, Lenora B. 1988, 1992, New Alliance Party

Gahres, Bill 1980, Down With Lawyers

Gardner, Susan 1988–VP, Consumer

Garfield, James Abram 1880, Republican

Garner, John Nance 1932–VP, 1936–VP, Democratic

Garvin, Florence 1936–VP, National Greenback

Garson, Barbara 1992–VP, Socialist

Garza, Laura 1996–VP, Socialist Workers

Gian-Cursio, Christopher 1960–VP,
  Vegetarian

Gillhaus, August 1908, 1912–VP, 1920–
  VP, Socialist Labor

Gitlow, Benjamin 1924–VP, 1928–VP,
  Workers (Communist)

Giumarra, Rosemary 1996–VP,
  independent (with Collins)

Goldhaber, Amos Nathaniel 2000–VP,
  Natural Law

Goldwater, Barry Morris 1964,
  Republican

Gonzalez, Andrea 1984–VP, Socialist
  Workers

Gonzalez, Matt 2008–VP, independent
  (with Nader)

Gore, Albert Arnold, Jr. 1992–VP, 1996–
  VP, 2000, Democratic

Gould, Symon 1948–VP, 1952–VP, 1956–
  VP, American Vegetarian; 1960,
  Vegetarian

Graham, William Alexander 1852–VP,
  Whig

Granger, Francis 1836–VP, Whig

Grant, Ulysses Simpson 1868,
  Republican; 1872, National Working
  Men, Republican

Graves, John Temple 1908–VP,
  Independence

Graves, Stephen Carey 1992–VP, U.S.
  Taxpayers

Greaves, Percy L. 1980, American

Greeley, Horace 1872, Democratic,
  Liberal Republican, Liberal Republican
  Convention of Colored Men

Green, Gabriel 1972, Universal

Gregory, Dick 1968–VP, Freedom and
  Peace

Griffin, Warren 1988, American
  Independent

Grimmer, Derrick P. 1992–VP,
  Grassroots

Griswold, Deirdre 1980, Workers World

Gritz, James Gordon (Bo) 1992,
  Populist/America First

Groesbeck, William Slocum 1872,
  Independent Liberal Republican

Gunderson, Genevieve 1972–VP,
  Socialist Labor

Gutierrez, Teresa 2004–VP, Workers
  World

Hagelin, John Samuel 1992, 1996, 2000,
  Natural Law

Hale, John Parker 1848, Liberty; 1852,
  Free Soil

Hall, Gus 1972, 1976, 1980, 1984,
  Communist

Hallinan, Vincent William 1952,
  American Labor, Progressive

Halstead, Fred 1968, Socialist Workers

Halyard, Helen 1984–VP, 1988–VP, 1992,
  Workers League

Hamblen, Stuart 1952, Prohibition

Hamlin, Hannibal 1860–VP, Republican

Hancock, Winfield Scott 1880,
  Democratic

Hanford, Benjamin 1904–VP, 1908–VP,
  Socialist

Hanly, James Franklin 1916, Prohibition

Harding, Warren Gamaliel 1920,
  Republican

Harens, Thomas 2004, Christian Freedom

Harriman, Job 1900–VP, Social-
  Democratic

Harris, James E. 1996, 2000, Socialist
  Workers

Harris, LaDonna 1980–VP, Citizens

Harrison, Benjamin 1888, 1892,
  Republican

Harrison, Caleb 1916–VP, Socialist Labor

Harrison, William Henry 1836, 1840,
  Whig

Harrop, Roy M. 1924–VP, Greenback

Harvey, William Hope 1932, Liberty

Hass, Eric 1952, 1956, 1960, 1964,
  Socialist Labor

Hawkins, Arrin 2004–VP, Socialist
  Workers

Hayes, Maximilian Sebastian 1920–VP,
  Farmer Labor

Hayes, Rutherford Birchard 1876,
  Republican

Hem, Eugene Arthur 1992, Third

Hemenway, Frank B. 1932–VP, Liberty

Hendricks, Thomas Andrews 1876–VP,
  1884–VP, Democratic

Hensley, Kirby James 1964, 1968,
  Universal

Herbert, Mary Alice   2004–VP, Socialist

Herer, Jack   1988, 1992, Grassroots

Hisgen, Thomas Louis   1908, Independence

Hobart, Garret Augustus   1896–VP, Republican

Hobson, Julius   1972–VP, People's

Holcomb, Austin   1904, Continental

Holdridge, Herbert Charles   1956–VP, Prohibition

Hollis, Mary Cal   1996, 2000–VP, Socialist

Holmes, Larry   1980–VP, 1984, 1988, 1992–VP, Workers World

Holtwick, Enoch Arden   1952–VP, 1956, Prohibition

Homer, Irving   1972–VP, America First

Hoopes, Darlington   1944–VP, 1952, Socialist

Hoover, Herbert Clark   1928, 1932, Republican

Hopkins, John O.   1964–VP, Universal

Hospers, John   1972, Libertarian

Howe, Archibald Murray   1900–VP, National

Hughes, Charles Evans   1916, Republican

Humphrey, Hubert Horatio   1964–VP, Democratic, Liberal (N.Y.); 1968, Democratic

Inchapher, Marshall   1972–VP, Prohibition

Jackson, Andrew   1828, 1832, Democratic

Jay, Charles   2004, Personal Choice

Jenner, William Ezra   1956, Texas Constitution; 1956–VP, States' Rights (Ky.)

Jenness, Linda   1972, Socialist Workers

Johns, Frank T.   1924, Socialist Labor

Johnson, Andrew   1864–VP, Republican

Johnson, Andrew   1944–VP, Prohibition

Johnson, Hale   1896–VP, Prohibition

Johnson, Herschel Vespasian   1860–VP, Democratic

Johnson, Hiram Warren   1912–VP, Progressive

Johnson, Lyndon Baines   1960–VP, 1964, Democratic, Liberal (N.Y.)

Johnson, Richard Mentor   1836–VP, 1840–VP, Democratic

Johnson, Sonia   1984, Citizens

Johnson, William Freame   1856–VP, North American

Jordan, Janice   2004–VP, Peace and Freedom

Jorgensen, Joanne M.   1996–VP, Libertarian

Julian, George Washington   1852 VP, Free Soil

Kasper, John   1964, National States' Rights

Kefauver, Estes   1956–VP, Democratic, Liberal

Kelly, Rachel B.   1996–VP, Prohibition

Kemp, Jack   1996–VP, Republican

Kennedy, Alyson   2008–VP, Socialist Workers

Kennedy, John Fitzgerald   1960, Democratic

Kenoyer, Willa   1988, Socialist

Kern, John Worth   1908–VP, Democratic

Kerry, John Forbes   2004, Democratic

Keyes, Alan   2008, America's Independent

King, A.   1904–VP, Continental

King, Clennon   1960, Independent Afro-American

King, Leicester   1848, Liberty

King, William Rufus Devane   1852–VP, Democratic

Kirby, Edward   1956–VP, Greenback

Kirkpatrick, Donald   1876–VP, American National

Kirkpatrick, George Ross   1916–VP, Socialist

Knight, Albion Williamson, Jr.   1992–VP, U.S. Taxpayers

Knox, Frank   1936–VP, Republican

Koch, David   1980, Libertarian

Krajewski, Henry   1956, American Third

Krueger, Maynard C.   1940–VP, Socialist

La Follette, Robert Marion   1924, Progressive, Socialist

La Riva, Gloria Estella   1984–VP, 1988–VP, 1992, 1996–VP, 2000, Workers World; 2008, Party for Socialism and Liberation

LaDuke, Winona   1996–VP, 2000–VP, Green

LaMarche, Pat   2004–VP, Green

Landon, Alfred Mossman   1936, Republican

Landrith, Ira   1916–VP, Prohibition

Lane, Denny   2000, Grassroots

Lane, Joseph   1860–VP, Independent Democrat, Southern Democrat

Langer, William   1956, Pioneer

LaRouche, Lyndon Hermyle   1976, U.S. Labor; 1984, Independent Democrat; 1988, Independent; 1992, Freedom for LaRouche

Lawrence, Jim   2004–VP, Socialist Equality

Learn, Dale   1948–VP, Prohibition

Lee, Henry   1832–VP, Independent

Lee, Joseph Bracken   1956–VP, Texas Constitution; 1960, Conservative (N.J.)

Leeke, Granville B.   1948–VP, Greenback

LeMay, Curtis Emerson   1968–VP, American Independent, Courage

Lemke, William   1936, Union

Leonard, Jonah Fitz Randolph   1900, United Christian

Levering, Joshua   1896, Prohibition

Levin, Jules   1976, Socialist Labor

Lewin, Herbert   1988, Peace and Freedom

Lewis, Jim   1984–VP, Libertarian

Lieberman, Joseph Isadore   2000–VP, Democratic

Lightburn, Joseph B.   1964, Constitution

Lincoln, Abraham   1860, 1864, Republican

Lincoln, John Cromwell   1924–VP, Commonwealth Land

Lockwood, Belva Ann Bennett   1884, 1888, People's (Equal Rights)

Lodge, Henry Cabot   1960–VP, Republican

Logan, John Alexander   1884–VP, Republican

Lord, Nancy   1992–VP, Libertarian

Love, Alfred Henry   1888–VP, People's (Equal Rights)

Lucey, Patrick Joseph   1980–VP, Independent (National Unity)

Lynen, Kurt   1980, Middle Class

MacArthur, Douglas   1952, America First, Constitution

Macauley, Robert Colvin   1920, Single Tax

MacBride, Roger Lea   1976, Libertarian

MacKenna, Roscoe B.   1968–VP, Universal

Maddox, Lester Garfield   1976, American Independent

Mage, Judith   1968–VP, Peace and Freedom

Maguire, Matthew   1896–VP, Socialist Labor

Mahalchik, John V.   1972, America

Malloney, Joseph Francis   1900, Socialist Labor

Marra, William A.   1988, Right to Life

Marrou, Andre Verne   1988–VP, 1992, Libertarian

Marshall, Thomas Riley   1912–VP, 1916–VP, Democratic

Martin, David H.   1900–VP, United Christian

Martin, John G.   1988, Third World Assembly

Martin, Warren C.   1984–VP, 1988–VP, National Statesman

Mason, Mel   1984, Socialist Workers

Masters, Isabelle   1992, 1996, Looking Back

Masters, Shirley Jean   1996–VP, Looking Back

Masters, Walter Ray   1992–VP, Looking Back

Matchett, Charles Horatio   1896, Socialist Labor

Mauer, James Hudson   1928–VP, 1932–VP, Socialist

Maxwell, John   1948, Vegetarian

Mazelis, Fred   1992–VP, Workers League; 1996–VP, Socialist Equality

McCain, John Sidney   2008, Republican

McCarthy, Eugene Joseph   1976, independent; 1988, Consumer

McClatchy, Kate   1996–VP, Peace and Freedom

McClellan, George Brinton   1864, Democratic

McCloskey, Burr   1956–VP, Pioneer

McCone, Allen C.   1992–VP, Take Back America

McCormack, Ellen   1980, Independent
   (Right To Life)

McDonald, Duncan   1924, Farmer Labor

McEnulty, Frank Edward   2008–VP,
   Reform

McGovern, George Stanley   1972,
   Democratic

McKinley, William   1896, 1900,
   Republican

McKinney, Cynthia   2008, Green

McLain, Harley   1980, National People's
   League

McMahon, George   1996–VP, Independent
   Grassroots

McNary, Charles Linza   1940–VP,
   Republican

McReynolds, David   1980, 2000, Socialist

Meador, Edward Kirby   1956–VP,
   Greenback

Metcalf, Henry Brewer   1900–VP,
   Prohibition

Michaels, Steve   1996, AIDS Cure

Mickells, Kathleen   1988–VP, Socialist
   Workers

Miller, William Edward   1964–VP,
   Republican

Minett, Cy   1992–VP, Populist/America
   First

Mitchell, Charlene   1968, Communist

Mondale, Walter Frederick   1976–VP,
   1980–VP, 1984, Democratic

Moore, Brian P.   2008, Socialist

Moorehead, Monica   1996, 2000, Workers
   World

Moorman, Edgar V.   1940–VP, Prohibition

Morris, Thomas   1844–VP, Liberty

Morton, Levi Parsons   1888–VP,
   Republican

Moya, Adelicio   1968–VP, People's
   Constitutional

Munn, Earle Harold   1960–VP, 1964,
   1968, 1972, Prohibition

Muñoz, Maria Elizabeth   1992–VP, New
   Alliance

Munro, Donald L.   1908–VP, Socialist
   Labor

Murphy, Daniel J.   1952, American
   Vegetarian

Muskie, Edmund Sixtus   1968–VP,
   Democratic

Nader, Ralph   1996, 2000, Green; 2004,
   Reform/Independent; 2008, independent

Nathan, Theodora   1972–VP, Libertarian

Nations, Gilbert Owen   1924, American

Nelson, George A.   1936–VP, Socialist

Nicholson, Samuel T.   1900–VP, Union
   Reform

Nixon, Richard Milhous   1952–VP, 1956–
   VP, 1960, 1968, 1972, Republican

Northrop, Anne   1996–VP, AIDS Cure

O'Brien, Thomas Charles   1936–VP,
   Union

O'Conor, Charles   1872, Straight-Out
   Democratic

Obama, Barack Hussein   2008,
   Democratic

Olivier, Art   2000–VP, Libertarian

Olmsted, Frederick Law   1872–VP,
   Independent Liberal Republican

Orange, Aaron M.   1940–VP, Socialist
   Labor

Ormsby, George   1992–VP, Prohibition

Palin, Sarah Heath   2008–VP, Republican

Palmer, John McAuley   1896, National
   Democratic

Parker, Alton Brooks   1904, Democratic

Parker, Joel   1872–VP, Labor Reform

Parker, John   2004, Workers World

Parker, John Milliken   1916–VP,
   Progressive

Paul, Ron   1988, Libertarian; 2008,
   independent

Peltier, Leonard   2004, Peace and
   Freedom

Pendleton, George Hunt   1864–VP,
   Democratic

Peron, Dennis   1996, Grassroots

Perot, Henry Ross   1992, independent;
   1996, Reform

Peroutka, Michael   2004, Constitution

Phelps, John Wolcott   1880, American

Phillips, Howard   1992, U.S. Taxpayers,
   Illinois Taxpayers, Tisch Independent
   Citizens; 1996, U.S. Taxpayers, Right to
   Life (N.Y.); 2000, Constitution

Pierce, Franklin   1852, Democratic

Pletten, Leroy   2004–VP, Prohibition/
Concerns of People; 2008–VP,
Prohibition

Polk, James Knox   1844, Democratic

Pomeroy, Samuel Clarke   1880–VP,
American; 1884, American Prohibition

Proehl, Frederick C.   1956, Greenback

Pulley, Andrew   1972–VP, 1980, Socialist
Workers

Quayle, James Danforth, 3rd   1988–VP,
1992–VP, Republican

Randall, Charles Hiram   1924–VP,
American

Rarick, John R.   1980, American
Independent

Reagan, Ronald Wilson   1980, 1984,
Republican

Redstone, Albert E.   1888, Industrial
Reform

Regan, Frank Stewart   1932–VP,
Prohibition

Reid, Whitelaw   1892–VP, Republican

Reid, Willie Mae   1976–VP, 1992–VP,
Socialist Workers

Reimer, Arthur Elmer   1912, 1916,
Socialist Labor

Remmel, Valentine   1900–VP, Socialist
Labor

Reynolds, Verne L.   1924–VP, 1928, 1932,
Socialist Labor

Richards, Bob   1984, Populist

Robinson, Joseph Taylor   1928–VP,
Democratic

Rogers, William R.   1964–VP, 1968,
Theocratic

Roland, Joanne   1992–VP, Third

Romer, Henry A.   1944–VP, America First;
1948–VP, Christian Nationalist

Roosevelt, Franklin Delano   1920–VP,
1932, 1936, 1940, 1944, Democratic

Roosevelt, Theodore   1900–VP, 1904,
Republican; 1912, Progressive

Root, Wayne Allyn   2008–VP, Libertarian

Ross, Nancy   1984–VP, Independent
Alliance

Rush, Richard   1828–VP, Federalist

Russell, John   1872–VP, Prohibition

Ryan, Jennifer   2004–VP, Christian
Freedom

St. John, John Pierce   1884, Prohibition

Schmitz, John George   1972, American
Independent

Scott, John G.   1948, Greenback

Salaman, Maureen Kennedy   1984–VP,
Populist

Scott, Winfield   1852, Whig

Seidel, Emil   1912–VP, Socialist

Sergeant, John   1832–VP, National
Republican

Serrette, Dennis L.   1984, Independent
Alliance

Sewall, Arthur   1896–VP, Democratic,
National Silver

Seymour, Horatio   1868, Democratic

Shackleford, Rufus   1976–VP, American

Shaw, Edward   1964–VP, Socialist
Workers

Shaw, Mark   1964–VP, Prohibition

Shearer, Eileen   1980–VP, American
Independent

Shelton, Frank   1980, American

Shelton, Herbert M.   1956, American
Vegetarian

Sherman, James Schoolcraft   1908–VP,
1912–VP, Republican

Shriver, Robert Sargent   1972–VP,
Democratic

Silverman, Edward M.   1960–VP,
Conservative (Va.)

Slocomb, Whitney Hart   1960, Greenback

Smith, Alfred Emanuel   1928, Democratic

Smith, Gerald Lyman Kenneth   1944,
America First; 1948, Christian
Nationalist

Smith, Gerrit   1848, National Liberty

Smith, Green Clay   1876, Prohibition

Smith, L. Neil   2000, Libertarian (Ariz.)

Smith, Maureen   1980, Peace and
Freedom

Smith, Robert Junior   1992, American

Smith, Tucker Powell   1948–VP, Socialist

Southgate, James Haywood   1896–VP,
National

Sparkman, John Jackson   1952–VP,
Democratic

Spock, Benjamin McLane   1972, 1976–
VP, People's

Stedman, Seymour   1920–VP, Socialist

Stevenson, Adlai Ewing 1891–VP, Democratic; 1900–VP, Democratic, People's, Silver Republican

Stevenson, Adlai Ewing 1952, 1956, Democratic; 1956, Liberal

Stewart, Gideon Tabor 1876–VP, Prohibition

Stockdale, James Bond 1992–VP, independent (with Perot)

Stokes, Trenton 1988–VP, Independent Populist

Stoner, J. B. 1964–VP, National States' Rights

Streeter, Alson Jennes 1888, Union Labor

Sullivan, Charles Loten 1960, Constitution (Tex.)

Suprynowicz, Vin 2000–VP, Libertarian (Ariz.)

Swallow, Silas Comfort 1904, Prohibition

Taft, William Howard 1908, 1912, Republican

Taylor, George Sam 1968–VP, Socialist Labor

Taylor, Glen Hearst 1948–VP, Progressive

Taylor, Marilyn Chambers 2004–VP, Personal Choice

Taylor, Zachary 1848, Whig

Teague, Raymond L. 1960–VP, Theocratic

Teichert, Edward A. 1944, 1948, Socialist Labor

Teichert, Emil F. 1936–VP, Socialist Labor

Templin, Diane Beall 1996, American

Thayer, Merle 1968–VP, Constitution

Thomas, Norman Mattoon 1928, 1932, 1936, 1940, 1944, 1948, Socialist

Thompson, Henry Adams 1880–VP, Prohibition

Thurman, Allen Granberry 1888–VP, Democratic

Thurmond, James Strom 1948, States' Rights

Tibbles, Thomas Henry 1904–VP, People's

Tilden, Samuel Jones 1876, Democratic

Tisch, Robert Emmanuel 1992–VP, U.S. Taxpayers, Tisch Independent Citizens

Tisdal, V. C. 1932–VP, Jobless

Titus, Herb 1996–VP, U.S. Taxpayers, Right to Life (N.Y.)

Tomlinson, Homer Aubrey 1952, Church of God; 1960, 1964, Theocratic

Tompkins, Vinton Michael 1992–VP, 1996–VP, Natural Law

Troutt, Arlin 1996–VP, Grassroots

Trowe, Margaret 2000–VP, Socialist Workers

Troxell, Richard K. 1968, Constitution

Truman, Harry S. 1944–VP, 1948, Democratic

Turner, Daniel Braxton 1908, United Christian

Tupahache, Asiba 1992–VP, independent (with Daniels)

Tyler, John 1840–VP, Whig; 1844, National Democratic

Tyner, Jarvis 1972–VP, 1976–VP, Communist

Upshaw, William David 1932, Prohibition

Van Auken, Bill 2004, 2008–VP, Socialist Equality

Van Buren, Martin 1832–VP, 1836, 1840, Democratic; 1848, Free Soil

Van Horn, Gary 1996–VP, American

Varney, William Frederick 1928, Prohibition

Varnum, Frank 1980–VP, American

Venson, Randall 2000, independent

Verseen, Will 1928–VP, Farmer Labor

Wakefield, William H. T. 1888–VP, United Labor

Walker, James B. 1876, American National

Wallace, George Corley 1968, American Independent, Courage (N.Y.)

Wallace, Henry Agard 1940–VP, Democratic; 1948, Progressive

Wallace, William J. 1824, Commonwealth Land

Walton, Richard 1984–VP, Citizens

Warren, Earl 1948–VP, Republican

Warren, James Mac 1988–VP, 1992, Socialist Workers

Watkins, Aaron Sherman 1908–VP, 1912–VP, Prohibition

Watkins, Willard Dean   2000–VP, Prohibition

Watson, Claude A.   1944, 1948, Prohibition

Watson, Thomas Edward   1896–VP, Populist; 1904, 1908, People's

Weaver, James Baird   1880, Greenback Labor; 1892, People's

Webb, Frank Elbridge   1928, 1932, Farmer Labor

Weidman, Will   1992–VP, Apathy

Weill, Ted   2008, Reform

Weiss, Myra Tanner   1952–VP, 1956–VP, 1960–VP, Socialist Workers

Wendelken, Martin   1980, independent

Wendt, Rick   1992–VP, independent (with Ehlers)

Werdel, Thomas Harold   1956–VP, States' Rights; 1964–VP, Independent States' Rights

West, Absolom Madden   1884–VP, Anti-Monopoly, Greenback

Wheeler, Burton Kendall   1924–VP, Progressive, Socialist

Wheeler, William Almon   1876–VP, Republican

White, Jerome   1996, 2008, Socialist Equality

Wigginton, Peter Dinwiddie   1888–VP, American

Wilkinson, Dale   2000–VP, Grassroots

Willkie, Wendell Lewis   1940, Republican

Williams, Samuel   1908–VP, People's

Wilson, Henry   1872–VP, Republican, National Working Men

Wilson, Woodrow   1912, 1916, Democratic

Winn, Ed   1984, 1988, Workers League

Wing, Simon   1892, Socialist Labor

Wirt, William   1832, Anti-Masonic

Woodhull, Victoria Claflin   1872, People's (Equal Rights)

Woolley, John Granville   1900, Prohibition

Wright, Fielding Lewis   1948–VP, States' Right

Wright, Margaret   1976, People's

Yates, James Elmer   1940–VP, Greenback

Yiamouyiannis, John   1992, Take Back America

York, Alvin   1936–VP, Prohibition

Youngkeit, Louie G.   1988, 2000, independent

Zagarell, Michael   1968–VP, Communist

Zahnd, John   1924, 1928, 1936, 1940, Greenback

Zeidler, Frank Paul   1976, Socialist

Zimmerman, Matilde   1980–VP, Socialist Workers

The Office

PRESIDENTIAL OATH OF OFFICE

The following oath of office is prescribed by Article II, section 1 of the Constitution:

I do solemnly swear (or affirm) that I will faithfully execute the Office of President of the United States, and will to the best of my ability, preserve, protect and defend the Constitution of the United States.

The President-elect takes the oath of office with his hand upon a Bible, which is open to a passage that he has selected.

INAUGURAL OATHS

Listed below under the names of the Presidents elected to office are the dates on which the oaths were taken and the names of the administering officials (Chief Justice of the United States unless otherwise identified).

Washington

Thurs., Apr. 30, 1789; Robert R. Livingston, chancellor of New York State

Mon., Mar. 4, 1793; William Cushing, Associate Justice of the Supreme Court

J. Adams

Sat., Mar. 4, 1797; Oliver Ellsworth

Jefferson

Wed., Mar. 4, 1801; John Marshall
Mon., Mar. 4, 1805; Marshall

Madison

Sat., Mar. 4, 1809; Marshall
Thurs., Mar. 4, 1813; Marshall

Monroe

Tues., Mar. 4, 1817; Marshall
Mon., Mar. 5, 1821; Marshall

J. Q. Adams

Fri., Mar. 4, 1825; Marshall

Jackson

Wed., Mar. 4, 1829; Marshall
Mon., Mar. 4, 1833; Marshall

Van Buren

Sat., Mar. 4, 1837; Roger Brooke Taney

W. H. Harrison

Thurs., Mar. 4, 1841; Taney

Polk

Tues., Mar. 4, 1845; Taney

Taylor

Mon., Mar. 5, 1849; Taney

Pierce

Fri., Mar. 4, 1853; Taney

Buchanan

Wed., Mar. 4, 1857; Taney

Lincoln

Mon., Mar. 4, 1861; Taney
Sat., Mar. 4, 1865; Salmon Portland Chase

Grant

Thurs., Mar. 4, 1869; Chase
Tues., Mar. 4, 1873; Chase

Hayes

Sat., Mar. 3, 1877 (private); Morrison Remick Waite
Mon., Mar. 5, 1877 (public); Morrison Remick Waite

Garfield

Fri., Mar. 4, 1881; Waite

Cleveland

Wed., Mar. 4, 1885; Waite

B. Harrison

Mon., Mar. 4, 1889; Melville Weston Fuller

Cleveland

Sat., Mar. 4, 1893; Fuller

McKinley

Thurs., Mar. 4, 1897; Fuller
Mon., Mar. 4, 1901; Fuller

T. Roosevelt

Sat., Mar. 4, 1905; Fuller

Taft

Thurs., Mar. 4, 1909; Fuller

Wilson

Tues., Mar. 4, 1913; Edward Douglass White
Mon., Mar. 5, 1917; White

Harding

Fri., Mar. 4, 1921; White

Coolidge

Wed., Mar. 4, 1925; William Howard Taft

Hoover

Mon., Mar. 4, 1929; Taft

F. D. Roosevelt

Sat. Mar. 4, 1933; Charles Evans Hughes
Wed., Jan. 20, 1937; Hughes
Mon., Jan. 20, 1941; Hughes
Sat., Jan. 20, 1945; Harlan Fiske Stone

Truman

Thurs., Jan. 20, 1949; Frederick Moore Vinson

Eisenhower

Tues., Jan. 20, 1953; Vinson
Sun., Jan. 20, 1957 (private); Earl Warren
Mon., Jan. 21, 1957 (public); Earl Warren

Kennedy

Fri., Jan. 20, 1961; Warren

L. B. Johnson

Wed., Jan. 20, 1965; Warren

Nixon

Mon., Jan. 20, 1969; Warren
Sat., Jan. 20, 1973; Warren Earl Burger

Carter

Thurs., Jan. 20, 1977; Burger

Reagan

Tues., Jan. 20, 1981; Burger
Sun., Jan. 20, 1985 (private); Burger
Mon., Jan. 21, 1985 (public); Burger

G. Bush

Fri., Jan. 20, 1989; William Hubbs Rehnquist

Clinton

Wed., Jan. 20, 1993; Rehnquist
Mon., Jan. 20, 1997; Rehnquist

G. W. Bush

Sat., Jan. 20, 2001; Rehnquist
Thurs., Jan. 20, 2005; Rehnquist

Obama

Tues., Jan. 20, 2009 (public); John Glover Roberts
Wed., Jan. 21, 2009 (private); John Glover Roberts

The following took their oaths after succeeding to the presidency on the death or resignation of their predecessors:

Tyler

Tues., Apr. 6, 1841; William Cranch, Chief Justice, U.S. Circuit Court, District of Columbia

Fillmore

Wed., July 10, 1850; Cranch

A. Johnson

Sat., Apr., 15, 1865; Salmon Portland Chase

Arthur

Tues., Sept. 20, 1881 (private); John R. Brady, Justice, New York Supreme Court
Thurs., Sept. 22, 1881 (public); Morrison Remick Waite

T. Roosevelt

Sat., Sept. 14, 1901; John R. Hazel, Justice, U.S. District Court

Coolidge

Fri., Aug. 3, 1923; John Calvin Coolidge, notary public
Tues., Aug. 21, 1923; Adolph August Hoehling, Justice, District of Columbia Supreme Court

Truman

Thurs., Apr. 12, 1945; Harlan Fiske Stone

L. B. Johnson

Fri., Nov. 22, 1963; Sarah Tilghman Hughes, District Judge of the North District of Texas

Ford

Fri., Aug. 9, 1974; Warren Earl Burger

DOUBLE INAUGURATIONS

Six Presidents have had reason to take the inaugural oath twice within a short time.

Rutherford Birchard Hayes was sworn in at the White House by Chief Justice Morrison Remick Waite on Saturday, March 3, 1877. Because of the peculiar circumstances of his election (the result of a deal between the Democrats and Republicans), he had been advised to take the oath immediately and not to wait until the following Monday, when the formal inauguration was scheduled. Waite administered the oath to him a second time on March 5 in a public ceremony at the Capitol.

Chester Alan Arthur succeeded to the presidency after the death of James Abram Garfield, who had been shot by an assassin many weeks before. Arthur was in New York City when he received the news. The oath was administered to him privately at his home by John R. Brady, justice of the state supreme court, on September 20, 1881. Two days later, he repeated the oath before Chief Justice Waite.

Calvin Coolidge succeeded to the presidency after the sudden death of Warren Gamaliel Harding, who died while on a trip to California. Coolidge was at his parents' home in Vermont when he received the news on August 3, 1923. He was sworn in by his father, John Calvin Coolidge, a notary public.

On August 21, he repeated the oath in Washington, D. C., before Adolph August Hoehling, justice of the Supreme Court of the District of Columbia.

Two Presidents took the oath privately when January 20 fell on a Sunday and repeated the oath in a public ceremony held on the following day. Dwight David Eisenhower took the oath for his second term on Sunday, January 20, 1957, in a private ceremony in the East Room of the White House, with Chief Justice Earl Warren presiding. Warren presided again at Eisenhower's formal inauguration on January 21. Ronald Wilson Reagan took the oath for his second term on the terrace of the West Front of the Capitol on Sunday, January 20, 1985, and again at his formal inauguration on January 21. Chief Justice Warren Burger presided at both ceremonies.

At his inauguration on Tuesday, January 20, 2009, Barack Hussein Obama took the oath of office with one word out of place, the result of a moment's confusion between the new President and Chief Justice John Glover Roberts, who was administering the oath. Instead of pledging "that I will faithfully execute the office of President of the United States," Obama pledged "that I will execute the office of President of the United States faithfully." Although the rearrangement did not change the meaning of the sentence and did not affect Obama's status as President, the wording of the oath is prescribed in the Constitution, and the President's legal advisers thought it prudent to have Chief Justice Roberts administer the oath a second time. That ceremony took place the following evening, January 22, 2009, at 7:35 p.m., in the Map Room of the White House, in the presence of the White House photographer and a small group of aides. A Bible was used in the first oath but not the second.

PRESIDENTIAL INAUGURAL OATHS ADMINISTERED BY CHIEF JUSTICES OF THE UNITED STATES

Chief Justice John Marshall administered the oath nine times to five Presidents: Jefferson twice, Madison twice, Monroe twice, J. Q. Adams once, and Jackson twice.

Chief Justice Roger Brooke Taney administered the oath to more Presidents than anyone—seven times to seven men: once each to Van Buren, W. H. Harrison, Polk, Taylor, Pierce, Buchanan and Lincoln.

Chief Justice Melville Weston Fuller swore in six Presidents: B. Harrison, Cleveland, T. Roosevelt, Taft, and McKinley twice.

Chief Justice Warren Earl Burger swore in five Presidents: Nixon (second term), Ford, Carter, and Reagan twice.

Chief Justice William Hubbs Rehnquist also administered the oath five times: once to G. Bush, twice to William Jefferson Clinton, and twice to G. W. Bush.

Chief Justice Earl Warren administered the oath four times, once each to Eisenhower, Kennedy, L. B. Johnson and Nixon.

Chief Justices who administered the inaugural oath three times each were Salmon Portland Chase, Charles Evans Hughes, Morrison Remick Waite, and Edward Douglass White. Chase swore in Lincoln once and Grant twice. Hughes administered the oath to F. D. Roosevelt three times. Waite swore in Hayes, Garfield, and Cleveland. White swore in Wilson twice and Harding once.

Those Chief Justices who administered the oath twice were William Howard Taft, Harlan Fiske Stone, and Frederick Moore Vinson. Taft swore in Coolidge and Hoover. Stone swore in F. D. Roosevelt and Truman. Vinson swore in Truman and Eisenhower.

Chief Justice Oliver Ellsworth administered the oath to John Adams.

Only three of the nine men who succeeded to the presidency because of a President's death or resignation had the inaugural oath administered by the Chief Justice of the United States. Salmon Portland Chase gave the oath to Andrew Johnson, Harlan Fiske Stone to Harry S. Truman, and Warren Earl Burger to Gerald Rudolph Ford.

Chief Justice John Glover Roberts administered the oath to Obama twice—once in the public ceremony on January 20, 2009, the second time in private on January 21, 2009.

OATHS ADMINISTERED BY OTHERS

The presidential oath of office is not required to be administered by the Chief Justice of the United States. The following Presidents of the United States were not sworn in by the Chief Justice:

George Washington, Apr. 30, 1789, oath administered by Robert R. Livingston, Chancellor of New York State.

George Washington, Mar. 4, 1793, by William Cushing, Associate Justice of the Supreme Court.

John Tyler, Apr. 6, 1841, by William Cranch, Chief Justice of the United States Circuit Court of the District of Columbia.

Millard Fillmore, July 10, 1850, by William Cranch, Chief Justice of the United States Circuit Court of the District of Columbia.

Chester Alan Arthur, Sept. 20, 1881, by John R. Brady, Justice of the New York Supreme Court. Arthur was sworn in two days later by Chief Justice Morrison Remick Waite.

Theodore Roosevelt, Sept. 14, 1901, by John R. Hazel, of the United States District Court.

Calvin Coolidge, Aug. 3, 1923, by his father, John Calvin Coolidge, a notary public. The oath was repeated on Aug. 21, 1923, before Adolph August Hoehling of the District of Columbia Supreme Court.

Lyndon Baines Johnson, Nov. 22, 1963, by Sarah Tilghman Hughes, District Judge of the North District of Texas.

No specific requirements exist as to the place where the oath must be administered. The following Presidents took their oaths in cities other than Washington, D.C.:

George Washington, 1789, New York City

George Washington, 1793, Philadelphia, Pa.

John Adams, 1797, Philadelphia, Pa.

Chester Alan Arthur, 1881, New York City

Theodore Roosevelt, 1901, Buffalo, N.Y.

Calvin Coolidge, 1923, Plymouth, Vt.

Lyndon Baines Johnson, 1963, Dallas, Tex.

HISTORIC BIBLES USED AT INAUGURATIONS

George Washington took his first oath of office upon a 10-pound Bible that belonged, and still belongs, to the St. John's No. 1 Lodge of the Free and Accepted Masons of the State of New York, located in downtown Manhattan. It is an illustrated edition of the King James Version, printed in London in 1767. Five later Presidents brought this historic Bible to the capital for use in their own inaugurations. They were: Harding, Eisenhower, Carter, G. Bush, and G. W. Bush in 2001, although the younger President Bush was forced to substitute a closed family bible because the weather on Inauguration Day was so wet that the Washington Bible could not safely be taken outdoors. Much ceremony surrounds the Bible itself, the Lodge requiring that it be transported by land and escorted on its journey by three member officers. It is on permanent display at Federal Hall on Wall Street.

For his 2009 inauguration, Barack Obama borrowed from the Library of Congress the Bible that Abraham Lincoln used in 1861 at his first swearing-in ceremony. It is a small velvet-covered edition, bought for the occasion by William Thomas Carroll, who was then the Clerk of the Supreme Court.

SUNDAY INAUGURATION DATES

Only four of the thirty-seven March inaugurations fell on Sunday—in 1821, 1849, 1877, and 1917. In those years the public ceremonies were postponed until the following day.

James Monroe, the fifth President, postponed taking his oath of office for his second term until Monday, March 5, 1821.

Zachary Taylor, the twelfth President, did not take his oath of office until Monday, March 5, 1849 (a circumstance which has caused many to assert that David Rice Atchison, president pro tempore of the Senate, was President for one day between the outgoing James Knox Polk and the incoming Zachary Taylor).

Rutherford Birchard Hayes, the nineteenth President, did not wait for March 4, but took the oath on Saturday, March 3, 1877, at a private ceremony in the White House. He took it again on Monday, March 5, at a public ceremony.

Woodrow Wilson, the twenty-eighth President, postponed taking his second oath of office until Monday, March 5, 1917.

Only two of the seventeen January inaugurations have fallen on Sunday: those of Dwight David Eisenhower in 1957 and Ronald Wilson Reagan in 1985. Both of them were sworn in on Sunday, January 20, and again on the following Monday, as described above.

Inauguration Day (January 20) will fall on Sunday only two times in the next hundred years: in 2013 and 2041.

INAUGURAL SITES

Thirty-six of the 56 inaugurations of the elected presidents were held at the east portico of the Capitol. The other twenty inaugurations were held at the following places:

Federal Hall, Wall Street, New York, N.Y.

1789—George Washington

Congress Hall, Sixth and Chestnut Streets, Philadelphia, Pa.

1793—George Washington
1797—John Adams

Senate chamber, Washington, D.C.

1801—Thomas Jefferson
1805—Thomas Jefferson
1909—William Howard Taft

House of Representatives, Washington, D.C.

1809—James Madison
1813—James Madison
1821—James Monroe
1825—John Quincy Adams
1833—Andrew Jackson

South portico, White House, Washington, D.C.

1945—Franklin Delano Roosevelt

West front, Capitol, Washington, D.C.

1981—Ronald Wilson Reagan
1989—George Herbert Walker Bush
1993—William Jefferson Clinton
1997—William Jefferson Clinton
2001—George Walker Bush
2005—George Walker Bush
2009—Barack Hussein Obama

Rotunda, Capitol, Washington, D.C.

1985—Ronald Wilson Reagan

INAUGURAL WEATHER

Of the 56 presidential inaugurations between 1789 and 2009, there were 38 held in clear or partly cloudy weather, eleven in rain, and seven in snow, the weather reported being the weather at noon.

Contemporary reports on the weather often disagree as the weather was not always the same during the entire day. For example, when Hayes was inaugurated in 1877, it rained until 7 A.M on March 5 (inauguration day) but it was clear the rest of the day. On the day Garfield was inaugurated, March 4, 1881, it snowed and rained until 10 A.M., and then it cleared, much of the snow having disappeared by the time of the inaugural parade. When Taft was inaugurated in 1909, temperatures were about freezing; more than nine inches of snow had fallen on March 3 and until 12:30 P.M. on March 4, and the afternoon of March 4 was windy and cloudy.

The rainy days were in 1845, 1865, 1869, 1873, 1889, 1901, 1929, 1933, 1937, 1957, and 2001.

The snowy days were in 1817, 1821, 1833, 1841, 1853, and 1909.

Details of the weather at the January 20 inaugurations follow: 1937, raining, 33 degrees; 1941, clear, 29 degrees; 1945, cloudy, 35 degrees; 1949, clear, 38 degrees; 1953, partly cloudy, 49 degrees; 1957, overcast, 43 degrees; 1961, crisp, cold, 28 degrees; 1965, clear, 38 degrees–45 degrees; 1969; overcast, 33 degrees–38 degrees; 1973, windy, low 40s; 1977, clear, cold; 1981, clear, 56 degrees; 1985, clear, windy, and frigid, 7 degrees; 1989, cloudy, warm, high 40s; 1993, clear, crisp, low 40s; 1997, windy and partly sunny, 34 degrees; 2001, overcast and rainy with southerly gusts, 36 degrees; 2005, windy and cloudy, 35 degrees; 2009, windy and sunny, 28 degrees with a wind chill of 18 degrees.

RETIRING PRESIDENTS AT SWEARING-IN CEREMONIES OF SUCCESSORS

All but four retiring presidents have attended the swearing-in ceremonies of their successors. John Adams was not present when Thomas Jefferson was inaugurated, John Quincy Adams was not present when Andrew Jackson was inaugurated, Andrew Johnson was not present when Ulysses Simpson Grant was inaugurated, and Richard Milhous Nixon was not present when Gerald Rudolph Ford took the oath of office.

PRESIDENTIAL TRANSITION ACT

"To promote the orderly transfer of the executive power in connection with the expiration of the term of office of a President and the inauguration of a new President" is the full title of the Presidential Transition Act of 1963 (78 Stat. L. 153), enacted March 7, 1964. The act provides funds and authority for the new President.

AGE AT INAUGURATION OR SUCCESSION

The oldest President inaugurated was Ronald Wilson Reagan, who was 69 years and 349 days old when he was inaugurated and 77 years and 349 days old when he stepped down.

The youngest President elected to office was John Fitzgerald Kennedy, who was 43 years and 236 days old when he was inaugurated. Theodore Roosevelt was 42 years and 322 days old when he succeeded to the presidency.

The average age at which the 43 Presidents were first inducted into office is 55 years, 34 days.

The oldest at the time of his inauguration or succession was Ronald Wilson Reagan, who took office when he was 69 years and 349 days old; the youngest was Theodore Roosevelt, who became President when he was 42 years and 322 days old.

Ten Presidents were over sixty when they took office: William Henry Harrison, Buchanan, Taylor, Eisenhower, Jackson, John Adams, Truman, Ford, Reagan, and G. Bush.

Nine Presidents were under fifty when they became chief executive: Polk, Garfield, Pierce, Cleveland (first term), Grant, Theodore Roosevelt, Kennedy, Clinton, and Obama.

The range in age, from oldest to youngest, is indicated in the following list:

Reagan   69 years, 349 days
W. H. Harrison   68 years, 23 days
Buchanan   65 years, 315 days
G. Bush   64 years, 223 days
Taylor   64 years, 100 days

Eisenhower   62 years, 98 days
Jackson   61 years, 354 days
J. Adams   61 years, 125 days
Ford   61 years, 26 days
Truman   60 years, 339 days
Monroe   58 years, 310 days
Madison   57 years, 353 days
Jefferson   57 years, 325 days
J. Q. Adams   57 years, 236 days
Washington   57 years, 67 days
A. Johnson   56 years, 107 days
Wilson   56 years, 65 days
Nixon   56 years, 11 days
B. Harrison   55 years, 196 days
Harding   55 years, 122 days
L. B. Johnson   55 years, 87 days
Hoover   54 years, 206 days
G. W. Bush   54 years, 198 days
Hayes   54 years, 151 days
Van Buren   54 years, 89 days
McKinley   54 years, 34 days
Carter   52 years, 111 days
Lincoln   52 years, 20 days
Arthur   51 years, 350 days
Taft   51 years, 170 days
F. D. Roosevelt   51 years, 33 days
Coolidge   51 years, 30 days
Tyler   51 years, 8 days
Fillmore   50 years, 184 days
Polk   49 years, 122 days
Garfield   49 years, 105 days
Pierce   48 years, 101 days
Cleveland   47 years, 351 days
Obama   47 years, 169 days
Grant   46 years, 311 days
Clinton   46 years, 149 days
Kennedy   43 years, 236 days
T. Roosevelt   42 years, 322 days

INAUGURAL ADDRESS

George Washington, who was inaugurated for a second term on March 4, 1793, at Philadelphia, Pa., used only 133 words in his inaugural address. The longest inaugural address was delivered during a snowfall by William Henry Harrison, who employed 8,445 words, almost twice as many as any other president.

He used the personal pronoun *I* 45 times, a record. The only president who did not use *I* in his inaugural address was Theodore Roosevelt.

The average number of words in the 56 inaugurals is 2,330. The following list shows the number of words used by the Presidents in their inaugural addresses:

Washington   1,419 (first), 133 (second)
J. Adams   2,318
Jefferson   1,721 (first), 2,151 (second)
Madison   1,174 (first), 1,210 (second
Monroe   3,366 (first), 4,456 (second)
J. Q. Adams   2,911
Jackson   1,125 (first), 1,172 (second)
Van Buren   3,832
W.H. Harrison   8,445
Polk   4,801
Taylor   1,087
Pierce   3,329
Buchanan   2,822
Lincoln   3,628 (first), 698 (second)
Grant   1,122 (first), 1,337 (second)
Hayes   2,481
Garfield   2,975

Cleveland   1,681 (first)
B. Harrison   4,392
Cleveland   2,012 (second)
McKinley   3,964 (first), 2,215 (second)
T. Roosevelt   983
Taft   5,426
Wilson   1,699 (first), 1,526 (second)
Harding   3,326
Coolidge   4,054
Hoover   3,801
F. D. Roosevelt   1,880 (first), 1,808 (second), 1,340 (third), 559 (fourth)
Truman   2,273
Eisenhower   2,446 (first), 1,655(second)
Kennedy   1,364
L. B. Johnson   1,492
Nixon   2,123 (first), 1,668 (second)
Ford   850
Carter   1,288
Reagan   2,463 (first), 2,564 (second)
G. Bush   2,283
Clinton   1,580 (first), 2,155 (second)
G. W. Bush   1,571 (first), 2,065 (second
Obama   2,396

The Executive Office

REQUIREMENTS FOR THE PRESIDENCY

There are no legal requirements for the presidency except for one paragraph in Article II, section 1 of the Constitution:

No Person except a natural born Citizen, or a Citizen of the United States, at the time of the Adoption of this Constitution, shall be eligible to the Office of President; neither shall any Person be eligible to that Office who shall not have attained to the Age of thirty five Years, and been fourteen Years a Resident within the United States.

PRESIDENTIAL DUTIES AND POWERS

The duties and powers of the President are specifically enumerated in the Constitution:

ARTICLE II, SECTION 2. The President shall be Commander in Chief of the Army and Navy of the United States, and of the Militia of the several States, when called into the actual Service of the United States; he may require the Opinion, in writing, of the principal Officer in each of the Executive Departments, upon any Subject relating to the Duties of their respective Offices, and he shall have the Power to grant Reprieves and Pardons for Offences against the United States, except in Cases of Impeachment. He shall have Power, by and with the

Advice and Consent of the Senate, to make Treaties, provided two thirds of the Senators present concur; and he shall nominate, and by and with the Advice and Consent of the Senate, shall appoint Ambassadors, other public Ministers and Consuls, Judges of the Supreme Court, and all other Officers of the United States, whose Appointments are not herein otherwise provided for, and which shall be established by Law; but the Congress may by Law vest the Appointment of such inferior Officers, as they think proper, in the President alone, in the Courts of Law, or in the Heads of Departments. The President shall have Power to fill up all Vacancies that may happen during the Recess of the Senate, by granting Commissions which shall expire at the End of their next Session.

SECTION 3. He shall from time to time give to the Congress Information of the State of the Union, and recommend to their Consideration such Measures as he shall judge necessary and expedient; he may, on extraordinary Occasions, convene both Houses, or either of them, and in Case of Disagreement between them, with Respect to the Time of Adjournment, he may adjourn them to such Time as he shall think proper; he shall receive Ambassadors and other public Ministers; he shall take Care that the Laws be faithfully executed, and shall Commission all the Officers of the United States.

STATE OF THE UNION MESSAGES

Presidential messages are not required in any specific form or at any specified time. The annual State of the Union messages are either read to Congress or delivered by the President in person. Presumably, they fulfill the requirement of Article II, section 3 of the Constitution, which provides that the President "shall from time to time give to the Congress Information of the State of the Union." The term "State of the Union Message" came into use on January 6, 1941; before then, the messages were generally called "annual messages."

William Henry Harrison and James Abram Garfield did not prepare annual messages. Harrison served only 32 days and Garfield only 199 days.

George Washington did not prepare a message during the calendar year 1789, but delivered two messages in 1790, one on January 8 and one on December 8.

Washington and John Adams established the custom of Presidents reading their messages aloud to a joint session of Congress in the chamber of the House of Representatives. Jefferson thought this custom smacked of monarchy; he sent his messages to Congress to be read by a clerk. Future Presidents continued Jefferson's practice until 1913, when Wilson returned to the precedent set by the Federalists. Since that time, most, but not all, of the State of the Union messages have been delivered by the Presidents in person.

Until the administration of Franklin Delano Roosevelt in 1933, there were 144 messages. Of these 128 were delivered in December, 1 in January, 1 in September, 3 in October, and 11 in November.

Since the inauguration date was changed to January, 77 messages have been delivered (through January of 2009): 68 in January and 9 in February.

The longest State of the Union message was sent to Congress in 1946 by President Harry S. Truman and consisted of more than 25,000 words, but it also included his annual budget message.

It is generally conceded that most presidential speeches are prepared by writers, presumably carrying out the wishes and thoughts of the executives. It is estimated that President Lyndon Baines Johnson's speech of January 8, 1964, consisting of 3,059 words, required the services of some twenty-four writers, who took about six weeks to draft the speech, with ten to sixteen major revisions.

In the twentieth century, technological developments enabled the Presidents to use the State of the Union Message to address the citizenry as well as Congress. Coolidge's 1923 address was the first to be broadcast on radio. Television broadcasts began with Truman's 1947 address. The first State of the Union message to reach the public as a live webcast was George W. Bush's speech of 2002.

State of the Union messages were given on these dates:

Washington

Jan. 8, 1790
Dec. 8, 1790
Oct. 25, 1791
Nov. 6, 1792
Dec. 3, 1793
Nov. 19, 1794
Dec. 8, 1795
Dec. 7, 1796

J. Adams

Nov. 22, 1797
Dec. 8, 1798
Dec. 3, 1799
Nov. 22, 1800

Jefferson

Dec. 8, 1801
Dec. 15, 1802
Oct. 17, 1803
Nov. 8, 1804
Dec. 3, 1805
Dec. 2, 1806
Oct. 27, 1807
Nov. 8, 1808

Madison

Nov. 29, 1809
Dec. 5, 1810
Nov. 5, 1811
Nov. 4, 1812
Dec. 7, 1813
Sept. 20, 1814
Dec. 5, 1815
Dec. 3, 1816

Monroe

Dec. 2, 1817
Nov. 16, 1818
Dec. 7, 1819
Nov. 14, 1820
Dec. 3, 1821
Dec. 3, 1822
Dec. 2, 1823
Dec. 7, 1824

J. Q. Adams

Dec. 6, 1825
Dec. 5, 1826
Dec. 4, 1827
Dec. 2, 1828

Jackson

Dec. 8, 1829
Dec. 6, 1830
Dec. 6, 1831
Dec. 4, 1832
Dec. 3, 1833
Dec. 1, 1834
Dec. 7, 1835
Dec. 5, 1836

Van Buren

Dec. 5, 1837
Dec. 3, 1838
Dec. 2, 1839
Dec. 5, 1840

Tyler

Dec. 7, 1841
Dec. 6, 1842
Dec. 5, 1843
Dec. 3, 1844

Polk

Dec. 2, 1845
Dec. 8, 1846
Dec. 7, 1847
Dec. 5, 1848

Taylor

Dec. 4, 1849

Fillmore

Dec. 2, 1850
Dec. 2, 1851
Dec. 6, 1852

Pierce

Dec. 5, 1853
Dec. 4, 1854
Dec. 31, 1855
Dec. 2, 1856

Buchanan

Dec. 8, 1857
Dec. 6, 1858
Dec. 19, 1859
Dec. 3, 1860

Lincoln

Dec. 3, 1861
Dec. 1, 1862
Dec. 8, 1863
Dec. 6, 1864

A. Johnson

Dec. 4, 1865
Dec. 3, 1866
Dec. 3, 1867
Dec. 9, 1868

Grant

Dec. 6, 1869
Dec. 5, 1870
Dec. 4, 1871
Dec. 2, 1872
Dec. 1, 1873
Dec. 7, 1874
Dec. 7, 1875
Dec. 5, 1876

Hayes

Dec. 3, 1877
Dec. 2, 1878
Dec. 1, 1879
Dec. 6, 1880

Arthur

Dec. 6, 1881
Dec. 4, 1882
Dec. 4, 1883
Dec. 1, 1884

Cleveland—1st Admin.

Dec. 8, 1885
Dec. 6, 1886
Dec. 6, 1887
Dec. 3, 1888

B. Harrison

Dec. 3, 1889
Dec. 1, 1890
Dec. 9, 1891
Dec. 6, 1892

Cleveland—2nd Admin.

Dec. 4, 1893
Dec. 3, 1894
Dec. 2, 1895
Dec. 7, 1896

McKinley

Dec. 6, 1897
Dec. 5, 1898
Dec. 5, 1899
Dec. 3, 1900

T. Roosevelt

Dec. 3, 1901
Dec. 2, 1902
Dec. 7, 1903
Dec. 6, 1904
Dec. 5, 1905
Dec. 3, 1906
Dec. 3, 1907
Dec. 8, 1908

Taft

Dec. 7, 1909
Dec. 6, 1910
Dec. 5, 1911
Dec. 3, 1912

Wilson

Dec. 2, 1913
Dec. 8, 1914
Dec. 7, 1915
Dec. 5, 1916
Dec. 4, 1917
Dec. 2, 1918
Dec. 2, 1919
Dec. 7, 1920

Harding

Dec. 4, 1921
Dec. 8, 1922

Coolidge

Dec. 6, 1923
Dec. 3, 1924
Dec. 8, 1925
Dec. 7, 1926
Dec. 6, 1927
Dec. 4, 1928

Hoover

Dec. 3, 1929
Dec. 2, 1930
Dec. 8, 1931
Dec. 6, 1932

F. D. Roosevelt

Jan. 3, 1934
Jan. 4, 1935
Jan. 3, 1936
Jan. 6, 1937
Jan. 3, 1938
Jan. 4, 1939
Jan. 3, 1940
Jan. 6, 1941
Jan. 6, 1942
Jan. 7, 1943
Jan. 11, 1944
Jan. 6, 1945

Truman

Jan. 22, 1946
Jan. 6, 1947
Jan. 7, 1948
Jan. 5, 1949
Jan. 4, 1950
Jan. 8, 1951
Jan. 9, 1952
Jan. 7, 1953

Eisenhower

Feb. 2, 1953
Jan. 7, 1954
Jan. 6, 1955
Jan. 5, 1956
Jan. 10, 1957
Jan. 9, 1958
Jan. 9, 1959
Jan. 7, 1960
Jan. 12, 1961

Kennedy

Jan. 30, 1961
Jan. 11, 1962
Jan. 14, 1963

L. B. Johnson

Jan. 8, 1964
Jan. 4, 1965
Jan. 12, 1966
Jan. 10, 1967
Jan. 17, 1968
Jan. 14, 1969

Nixon

Jan. 22, 1970
Jan. 22, 1971
Jan. 20, 1972
Feb. 2, 1973
Jan. 30, 1974

Ford

Jan. 15, 1975
Jan. 19, 1976
Jan. 12, 1977

Carter

Jan. 19, 1978
Jan. 23, 1979
Jan. 23, 1980
Jan. 16, 1981

Reagan

Jan. 26, 1982
Jan. 25, 1983

Jan. 25, 1984
Feb. 4, 1985
Feb. 4, 1986
Jan. 27, 1987
Jan. 25, 1988
Jan. 11, 1989

G. Bush

Jan. 31, 1990
Jan. 29, 1991
Jan. 28, 1992

Clinton

Feb. 17, 1993
Jan. 25, 1994
Jan. 24, 1995
Jan. 23, 1996
Feb. 4, 1997
Jan. 27, 1998
Jan. 19, 1999
Jan. 27, 2000

G. W. Bush

Feb. 27, 2001
Jan. 29, 2002
Jan. 28, 2003
Jan. 20, 2004
Feb. 2, 2005
Jan. 31, 2006
Jan. 23, 2007
Jan. 28, 2008

THE PRESIDENTIAL VETO

Article I, Section 7 of the Constitution contains the following provisions:

Every Bill which shall have passed the House of Representatives and the Senate, shall, before it becomes a Law, be presented to the President of the United States; if he approve he shall sign it, but if not he shall return it, with his Objections to that House in which it shall have originated, who shall enter the Objections at large on their Journal, and proceed to reconsider it. If after such Reconsideration two thirds of that House shall agree to pass the bill, it shall be sent, together with the Objections, to the other House, by which it shall likewise be reconsidered, and if approved by two thirds of that House, it shall become a Law. . . . If any Bill shall not be returned by the President within ten Days (Sundays excepted) after it shall have been presented to him, the Same shall be a Law, in like Manner as if he had signed it, unless the Congress by their Adjournment prevent its Return, in which case it shall not be a Law.

Every Order, Resolution, or Vote to which the Concurrence of the Senate and House of Representatives may be necessary (except on a question of Adjournment) shall be presented to the President of the United States; and before the Same shall take Effect, shall be approved by him, or being disapproved by him, shall be repassed by two thirds of the Senate and House of Representatives, according to the Rules and Limitations prescribed in the Case of a Bill.

The Constitution thus provides not only for a regular veto, which Congress may override by a two-thirds majority of both Houses, but also for a "pocket veto"—if the President opposes a bill sent to him ten days before the adjournment of Congress, he can, instead of vetoing it, merely ignore it, or "pocket" it, and prevent it from becoming a law.

The following list shows the number of bills vetoed by each President. Noted in parenthesis after each total are the number of regular vetoes, the number of pocket vetoes, the number of vetoes sustained by Congress, and the number of vetoes overridden by Congress.

Washington   2 (2, 0; 2, 0)
J. Adams   0
Jefferson   0
Madison   7 (5, 2; 7, 0)
Monroe   1 (1, 0; 1, 0)
J. Q. Adams   0
Jackson   12 (5, 7; 12, 0)
Van Buren   1 (0, 1; 1, 0)
W.H. Harrison   0
Tyler   10 (6, 4; 9, 1)
Polk   3 (2, 1; 3, 0)
Taylor   0
Fillmore   0
Pierce   9 (9, 0; 4, 5)
Buchanan   7 (4, 3; 7, 0)
Lincoln   7 (2, 5; 7, 0)
A. Johnson   29 (21, 8; 14, 15)
Grant   93 (45, 48; 89, 4)

Hayes   13 (12, 1; 12, 1)
Garfield   0
Arthur   12 (4, 8; 11, 1)
Cleveland (1st term)   414 (304, 110; 412, 2)
B. Harrison   44 (19, 25; 43, 1)
Cleveland (2nd term)   170 (42, 128; 165, 5)
McKinley   42 (6, 36; 42, 0)
T. Roosevelt   82 (42, 40; 81, 1)
Taft   39 (30, 9; 38, 1)
Wilson   44 (33, 11; 38, 6)
Harding   6 (5, 1; 6, 0)
Coolidge   50 (20, 30; 46, 4)
Hoover   37 (21, 16; 34, 3)
F. D. Roosevelt   635 (372, 263; 626, 9)
Truman   250 (180, 70; 238, 12)
Eisenhower   181 (73, 108; 179, 2)
Kennedy   21 (12, 9; 21, 0)
L. B. Johnson   30 (16, 14; 30, 0)
Nixon   43 (26, 17; 36, 7)
Ford   66 (48, 18; 54, 12)
Carter   31 (13, 18; 29, 2)
Reagan   78 (39, 39; 69, 9)
G. Bush   44 (29, 15; 43, 1)
Clinton   37 (36, 1; 35, 2)
G. W. Bush   10 (10, 0; 7, 3)
Total   2,560 (1,494, 1,066; 2,451, 109)

The first veto occurred on April 5, 1792, when Washington rejected a new plan of apportionment on the grounds that it violated the provisions of the Constitution. The pocket veto was first used by James Madison, in 1812, against House of Representatives Bill 170, on a uniform rule of naturalization.

Franklin D. Roosevelt holds the record for having vetoed the greatest number of bills—635—but this embraced a twelve-year period. During a two-term period, Grover Cleveland vetoed 584 bills.

The President who had the largest number of vetoes overridden—15—was Andrew Johnson.

From August 11, 1997, to June 25, 1998, President Clinton had the use of the line-item veto, enabling him to strike particular items from newly enacted laws without vetoing entire bills. He vetoed 82 items from 11 different bills during the ten months that the line-item veto was in effect, before it was struck down as unconstitutional by the Supreme Court.

On two occasions, George W. Bush made pocket vetoes, but Congress deemed them invalid on procedural grounds and the bills were enacted into law.

PRESIDENTIAL SALARIES

Article II, Section 1 of the Constitution contains the following provision:

> The President shall, at stated Times, receive for his Services, a Compensation, which shall neither be increased nor diminished during the Period for which he shall have been elected, and he shall not receive within that Period any other Emolument from the United States, or any of them.

On September 24, 1789, the First Congress fixed the salary of the President of the United States at $25,000 a year, to be paid quarterly, "in full consideration for his respective service with the use of the furniture and other effects now in his possession."

The congressional act of March 3, 1873, raised the salary of the President to $50,000. The law became effective with the new term that began the next day. Consequently, President Grant served his first term at a salary of $25,000 and his second term at $50,000.

On June 23, 1906, Congress authorized an additional sum not exceeding $25,000 for the traveling expenses of the President, "such sum when appropriated to be expended in the discretion of the President and accounted for on his certificate solely."

The act of March 4, 1909, raised the salary of the President to $75,000. The first President to receive $75,000 was Taft.

The act of June 25, 1948, increased the President's traveling expenses to $40,000 a year.

The act of January 19, 1949, authorized a salary of $100,000 a year for the President, to be paid monthly, and an additional expense allowance of $50,000 a year "to assist in defraying expenses relating to or resulting from the discharge of his official duties, for which expense allowance no tax liability shall accrue and for which no accounting shall be made by him." Truman was the first President to receive the $100,000 yearly salary.

The President's expense allowance was made subject to income taxes in 1953 but was restored to its tax-exempt status in 1979. (The Vice President's expense account, however, has been subject to taxes since 1953.)

The act of January 17, 1969, raised the salary of the President to $200,000 and provided him with a $100,000 travel allowance and a $12,000 entertainment allowance, both tax exempt, in addition to the $50,000 expense allowance. President Nixon was the first President to receive the $200,000 yearly salary. The Consolidated Appropriations Act, signed into law by President Clinton on December 21, 2000, went into effect on January 1, 2001. It increased the President's salary to $400,000. It also specified that any part of the $50,000 expense account that remained unused would be returned to the Treasury. The first President to receive the $400,000 yearly salary was George W. Bush.

PRESIDENTS' PENSIONS

A presidential pension was authorized by act of August 25, 1958 (7 Stat. L. 838). Under the act, former Presidents received a monetary allowance of $25,000 a year for life; adequate office space, appropriately furnished and equipped; a sum not to exceed $50,000 a year for office help; and unlimited free mailing privileges.

Subsequent legislation has established that the pension shall always be equivalent to the annual base salary of a cabinet secretary. This amounted to $151,800 per year in 1998 and $161,200 in 2001. In 2009, his first year after leaving office, President George W. Bush received $191,300. Cost-of-living increases are also factored into the calculation of the pension.

A President who resigns is entitled to a pension; a president who is impeached and convicted is not.

Former Presidents also receive free mailing privileges, free office space, $96,000 a year for office help, and, during the first thirty months after their term of office has ended, up to $150,000 for staff assistance. In 1993, Congress, faced with budget constraints, passed a bill to end subsidies for the five living ex-Presidents (Nixon, Ford, Carter, Reagan, and George Bush) as of October 1, 1998, and to limit the number of years that future ex-Presidents could receive the subsidies (to four and a half years). The law was repealed in October 1997 as part of a Treasury spending bill and the subsidies continued. The total amount paid in allowances that year was about $1.6 million. For 2008, the allowances came to about $2.5 million. Former President Clinton claimed nearly half the total amount, including $516,000 for rental payments and $79,000 for telephone costs.

PRESIDENTS' SECRETARIES

The salary of the secretaries of the Presidents was paid by the Presidents from their private funds until 1857.

On March 3, 1857, the 34th Congress enacted a law (11 Stat. L. 228) which provided "that the President of the United States be and is hereby authorized to appoint or employ, in his official household, one private secretary at an annual salary of $2,500."

The first private secretary to a President to be recognized as such and to be paid a salary was James Buchanan Henry, who served President James Buchanan from 1857 to 1859.

The first "Secretary to the President" was authorized by the 56th Congress on April 17, 1900 (31 Stat. L. 97). The salary of the secretary was set at $5,000 and that of each of two assistant secretaries at $2,800.

Staff assistance and administrative services are now provided to the President through the White House Office. In 2008, top-level members of the White House office staff, such as the chief of staff and press secretary, received an annual salary of $172,200.

In fiscal year 2008, Congress appropriated more than $187 million to pay for salaries and expenses in the White House Office and Executive Residence.

OTHER PERQUISITES OF THE PRESIDENCY

In addition to his salary, a President is the beneficiary of many perquisites, which may vary from time to time. He and his family live rent-free at the White House, assisted by a 90-member resident staff, and are guarded by Secret Service agents paid by the Department of Homeland Security. The Air Force maintains two customized Boeing 747 jet aircraft for his use; he travels in an armored Cadillac and is entitled to use military helicopters and boats. He is attended by a personal physician supplied by the armed forces and has access to any of the Army and Navy hospitals. Health care for his family is free as well. A library, supplied by booksellers, is at his disposal in the White House. The presidential retreat at Camp David, in the Maryland mountains, is available at all times.

GIFTS TO PRESIDENTS

Gifts to the Presidents are governed by the Constitution, Article I, Section 9: "No person holding any office of profit or trust, under them, shall, without the consent of the Congress, accept of any present, emolument, office, or title, of any kind whatever, from any king, prince, or foreign state." Gifts are often made to Presidents and their families by individuals and companies.

THE PRESIDENTS AND THE COURTS

A misconception prevails that the President may not be summoned to court and is immune from arrest. Actually, the President may be summoned to court and is liable to arrest. Nothing in the Constitution grants him immunity.

Thomas Jefferson was summoned on June 10, 1807, to appear as a witness in the trial of Aaron Burr for treason, but refused to attend. (See the chapter on Jefferson.) This action established a precedent but did not bind future Presidents.

In the course of the Watergate investigation, both Special Prosecutor Archibald Cox and the Senate Select Committee on Presidential Campaign Activities subpoenaed tapes and documents belonging to President Richard Milhous Nixon. Nixon refused to release the materials, claiming executive privilege and invoking the doctrine of separation of powers, as Jefferson had done. On July 24, 1974, the Supreme Court ruled 8-0 that the President must turn over the subpoenaed tapes and documents.

President Clinton and his wife were the subjects of criminal investigations throughout the President's two terms in office, and had a legal defense fund organized in 1994. (See the chapter on Clinton.) During his term, he was named as the defendant in a sexual harassment lawsuit, which the Supreme Court allowed to proceed while he was still in office. He was called to give depositions before a U.S. district judge and before a grand jury in connection with this lawsuit, and was held in contempt of court by the judge for giving false testimony. He was impeached on charges of perjury and obstruction of justice, but was acquitted in a Senate trial. Just before leaving office, Clinton received a grant of immunity in exchange for a fine and a five-year disbarment.

SECRET SERVICE PROTECTION

Following the assassination of President McKinley in 1901, Congress asked the Treasury Department's Secret Service to provide agents for the protection of the President. Since that time, the number of persons given Secret Service protection has steadily expanded. In addition to the President and Vice President, the list includes their immediate families; visiting dignitaries and heads of state; Presidents who have left office, together with their spouses (formerly for life, but beginning with George W. Bush for a maximum of 10 years); children of former Presidents; presidential candidates of the major parties; and the President- and Vice President-elect.

PROTECTION AGAINST THREATS

On June 25, 1948, Congress enacted a law (62 Stat. L. 740) which made threats by mail against the President punishable by a thousand-dollar fine or imprisonment for not more than five years or both. On June 1, 1955 (69 Stat. L. 80), this protection was extended to the President-elect and to the Vice President.

Legislation proving "penalties for the assassination of the President or the Vice President" was enacted August 28, 1965 (79 Stat. L. 580). It provided that "whoever kills any individual who is the President of the United States, the President-elect, the Vice President. . . whoever kidnaps any individual as designated above shall be punished by imprisonment for any term of years or for life. . . or by death or imprisonment for any term of years or for life if death results to such individual. . . whoever attempts to kill or kidnap any individual. . . shall be punished by imprisonment for any term of years or for

life. . . . The Attorney General of the United States is authorized to pay an amount not to exceed $100,000 for information and services concerning a violation of this section." Assistance may be requested from any Federal, State or local agency, including the Army, Navy and Air Force.

THE PRESIDENT'S SEAL

The seal of the President, shown on page 322, consists of his coat of arms encircled by fifty stars and the words SEAL OF THE PRESIDENT OF THE UNITED STATES. The coat of arms is described in heraldic terms as follows: "Shield—Paleways of thirteen pieces argent and gules, and chief azure, upon the breast of an American eagle displayed holding in his dexter talon an olive branch proper and in his sinister a bundle of thirteen arrows gray, and in his beak a gray scroll inscribed E PLURIBUS UNUM sable. Crest—Behind and above the eagle a radiating glory or, on which appears an arc of thirteen cloud puffs gray, and a constellation of thirteen mullets gray." This differs only slightly from the coat of arms on the Great Seal of the United States.

The eagle on the coat of arms used to face left, but President Truman had the seal redesigned so that the eagle would face right, the heraldic direction of honor, and look toward the olive branch of peace.

THE PRESIDENT'S FLAG

Before 1916 several Presidents had flags, but these were not official and were really nothing but emblems.

The official President's flag—the President's seal in bronze upon a blue background with a large white star in each corner—was adopted on May 29, 1916, by President Wilson's Executive Order No. 2,390.

President Truman, by executive order No. 9,646, dated October 25, 1945, made several further changes and increased the number of stars to 48, one for each state.

President Eisenhower's Executive Order No. 10,798, dated January 3, 1959, increased the number of stars on the flag to 49 to provide for Alaska. On August 21, 1959, the President revoked this order and increased the number of stars to 50 to provide for Hawaii.

SALUTE TO THE PRESIDENT

The President is customarily honored with a twenty-one-gun salute. The twenty-one-gun salute is given also to former Presidents, sovereigns, members of a royal family, and Presidents of other republics. It is claimed that the twenty-one-gun salute commemorates the year 1776, and for that reason salutes are often fired thus: one-seven-seven-six.

THE PRESIDENTIAL YACHTS

Lincoln, though he did not have an official presidential yacht, made trips on the *Silver Queen,* a steamer leased by the War Department.

The first President to have the benefit of a presidential yacht was Hayes, who traveled in the U.S.S. *Despatch*. It was followed by the U.S.S. *Dolphin, Sylph,* and *Mayflower*, the latter a Scottish-built gunboat that had seen service in Cuba during the Spanish-American War (and was afterwards used to carry Jewish survivors of the Holocaust to Israel).

The U.S.S. *Potomac* was a favorite of F. D. Roosevelt. Unable to climb stairs owing to the effects of polio, he used an elevator hidden in a false smokestack to go between decks. The *Potomac,* replaced by the U.S.S. *Williamsburg* for the administrations of Truman and Eisenhower, is currently moored at the FDR Pier in Oakland, Calif.

The yacht *Lenore* was seized by the federal government from the chairman of Montgomery Ward in a revenue dispute. It was called the *Barbara Ann* by Eisenhower, the *Honey Fitz* by Kennedy, and the *Tricia* by Nixon. A smaller yacht was the *Margie,* so named by Truman, and later dubbed the *Susie E.* by Eisenhower, the *Patrick J.* by Kennedy, and the *Julie* by Nixon.

The last presidential yacht in service was the U.S.S. *Sequoia*, the site of numerous historic events, including Truman's decision to use the atomic bomb against Japan and Nixon's negotiations with Soviet leaders over the terms of the Strategic Arms Limitation Treaty. The boat was ordered sold by Jimmy Carter. Its current owner now makes it available to paying guests for cruises on the Potomac. In 1987 it was designated a National Historic Landmark.

TERMS OF OFFICE

Twenty-two Presidents served no more than one term.

Twelve Presidents served one full four-year term: John Adams, John Quincy Adams, Van Buren, Polk, Pierce, Buchanan, Hayes, Benjamin Harrison, Taft, Hoover, Carter, and George Bush.

Ten Presidents served less than one full term. Five died during their first term: William Henry Harrison, Taylor, Garfield, Harding, and Kennedy. Five succeeded to the presidency, filled the unexpired portion of a term, and were not subsequently elected in their own right: Tyler, Fillmore, Andrew Johnson, Arthur, and Ford.

Twenty Presidents served more than one term.

One—Franklin Delano Roosevelt—served three terms and part of a fourth.

Twelve served two full terms: Washington, Jefferson, Madison, Monroe, Jackson, Grant, Cleveland (non-consecutive), Wilson, Eisenhower, Reagan, Clinton, and George W. Bush.

Three began a second term but did not complete it: Lincoln, McKinley, and Nixon.

Four succeeded to the presidency, filled the unexpired portion of a term, and were then elected to a full term: Theodore Roosevelt, Coolidge, Truman, and Lyndon Baines Johnson.

The following list shows the length of service of past Presidents:

W. H. Harrison   32 days

Garfield   199 days

Taylor   1 year, 128 days

Harding   2 years, 151 days

Ford   2 years, 164 days

Fillmore   2 years, 236 days

Kennedy   2 years, 306 days

Arthur   3 years, 166 days

A. Johnson   3 years, 322 days

Tyler   3 years, 332 days

J. Adams   4 years

J. Q. Adams   4 years

Van Buren   4 years

Polk   4 years

Pierce   4 years

Buchanan   4 years

Hayes   4 years

B. Harrison   4 years

Taft   4 years

Hoover   4 years

Carter   4 years

G. Bush   4 years

Lincoln   4 years, 43 days

McKinley   4 years, 194 days

L. B. Johnson   5 years, 59 days

Nixon   5 years, 201 days

Coolidge   5 years, 213 days

T. Roosevelt   7 years, 171 days

Truman   7 years, 283 days

Washington   7 years, 308 days (first term began Apr. 30 instead of Mar. 4)

Jefferson   8 years

Madison   8 years

Monroe   8 years

Jackson   8 years

Grant   8 years

Cleveland   8 years (two nonconsecutive terms)

Wilson   8 years

Eisenhower   8 years

Reagan   8 years

Clinton   8 years

George W. Bush   8 years

F. D. Roosevelt   12 years, 39 days (first term ended Jan. 20 instead of Mar. 3)

TERMS OF OFFICE—THE EARLY YEARS

In the first 50 years of United States history (1789–1839), three Presidents were not reelected for a second term: John Adams, John Quincy Adams, and Van Buren. The Presidents who were elected for two terms during this period were Washington, Jefferson, Madison, Monroe, and Jackson.

THE ONE-TERM TRADITION

After Andrew Jackson's second term, which ended in 1837, a one-term presidential policy prevailed until 1865, when Abraham Lincoln was sworn in for a second term he did not live to complete.

Presidents who for various reasons served one term or less during this period were Van Buren, William Henry Harrison, Tyler, Polk, Taylor, Fillmore, Pierce, and Buchanan.

PRESIDENTS WHO SUCCEEDED THEMSELVES IN OFFICE

George Washington   Apr. 30, 1789–Mar. 3, 1793; Mar. 4, 1793–Mar. 3, 1797

Thomas Jefferson   Mar. 4, 1801–Mar. 3, 1805; Mar. 4, 1805–Mar. 3, 1809

James Madison   Mar. 4, 1809–Mar. 3, 1813; Mar. 4, 1813–Mar. 3, 1817

James Monroe   Mar. 4, 1817–Mar. 3, 1821; Mar. 4, 1821–Mar. 3, 1825

Andrew Jackson   Mar. 4, 1829–Mar. 3, 1833; Mar. 4, 1833–Mar. 3, 1837

Abraham Lincoln   Mar. 4, 1861–Mar. 3, 1865; Mar. 4, 1865–Apr. 15, 1865

Ulysses Simpson Grant   Mar. 4, 1869–Mar. 3, 1873; Mar. 4, 1873–Mar. 3, 1877

William McKinley   Mar. 4, 1897–Mar. 3, 1901; Mar. 4, 1901–Sept. 14, 1901

Theodore Roosevelt   Sept. 14, 1901–Mar. 3, 1905, succession; Mar. 4, 1905–Mar. 3, 1909

Woodrow Wilson   Mar. 3, 1913–Mar. 3, 1917; Mar. 4, 1917–Mar. 3, 1921

Calvin Coolidge   Aug. 3, 1924–Mar. 3, 1925, succession; Mar. 4, 1925–Mar. 3, 1929

Franklin Delano Roosevelt   Mar. 4, 1933–Jan. 20, 1937; Jan. 20, 1937–Jan. 20, 1941; Jan. 20, 1941–Jan. 20 1945; Jan. 20, 1945–Apr. 12, 1945

Harry S. Truman   Apr. 12, 1945–Jan. 20, 1949, succession; Jan. 20, 1949–Jan. 20, 1953

Dwight David Eisenhower   Jan. 20, 1953–Jan. 20, 1957; Jan. 20, 1957–Jan. 20, 1961

Lyndon Baines Johnson   Nov. 22, 1963–Jan. 20, 1965, succession; Jan. 20, 1965–Jan. 20, 1969

Richard Milhous Nixon   Jan. 20, 1969–Jan. 20, 1973; Jan. 20, 1973–Aug. 9, 1974

Ronald Wilson Reagan   Jan. 20, 1981–Jan. 20, 1985; Jan. 20, 1985–Jan. 20, 1989

William Jefferson Clinton   Jan. 20, 1993–Jan. 20, 1997; Jan. 20, 1997–Jan. 20, 2001

George Walker Bush   Jan. 20, 2001–Jan. 20, 2005; Jan. 20, 2005–Jan. 20, 2009

THE CABINET

The cabinet is an advisory body; the members hold office at the pleasure of the President. It is customary for cabinet members to submit their resignations when a new administration enters into power.

There is nothing in the Constitution that specifically provides for a cabinet, nor are there any laws regulating the qualifications or duties of those designated as members of the cabinet.

The first cabinet office of the newly formed government was authorized by act of Congress of July 27, 1789 (1 Stat. L. 28) "establishing an executive department to be denominated the Department of Foreign Affairs." Later, it was redesignated the Department of State. John Jay of New York was Secretary of Foreign Affairs under the Confederation, and continued to act, at the request of President Washington, until Thomas Jefferson of Virginia entered upon his duties on March 22, 1790.

The second department created was the War Department, authorized by act of August 7, 1789 (1 Stat. L. 49) "to establish an executive department to be denominated the Department of War." The first Secretary of War was Henry Knox of Massachusetts, who took office on September 12, 1789.

The third department was the Treasury Department, authorized by act of September 2, 1789 (1 Stat. L. 65) "to establish the Treasury Department." On September 11, 1789, Alexander Hamilton of New York assumed his duties as the first Secretary of the Treasury.

These three departments constituted the first cabinet. The annual salary for the Secretary of War was $3,000, and for the Secretary of State and the Secretary of the Treasury $3,500 each.

The Attorney General and the Postmaster General served as members of the cabinet although neither was the head of a department at that time. Their compensation was $1,500 a year (September 24, 1789, 1 Stat. L. 93). On September 26, 1789, Samuel Osgood of Massachusetts became the Postmaster General and on the same date Edmund Randolph of Virginia was appointed Attorney General, assuming his duties on February 2, 1790.

The sixth cabinet post was that of Secretary of the Navy. The act of April 30, 1798 (1 Stat. L. 553), established "an executive department to be denominated the Department of the Navy." The Secretary received an annual salary of $3,000. The first Secretary of the Navy was Benjamin Stoddert of Maryland, who entered upon his duties on June 18, 1798, during the administration of President John Adams.

These six posts constituted the cabinet from 1798 to 1849.

On March 3, 1849, "an act to establish the Home Department" was passed (9 Stat. L. 395). President Zachary Taylor appointed Thomas Ewing of Ohio as the first Secretary of the Home Department. He took office on March 8, 1849. The name of the department was later changed to Department of the Interior.

Forty years later, on February 13, 1889, an eighth cabinet post was created. Norman Jay Colman of Missouri was appointed Secretary of Agriculture by President Grover Cleveland. He assumed his duties on February 13, 1889. (He had been Commissioner of Agriculture from April 4, 1885, to February 12, 1889).

The Attorney General, one of the first cabinet group, was given departmental power on June 22, 1870, by "an act to establish the Department of Justice" (16 Stat. L. 162). This act placed the Attorney General at the head of the Department of Justice.

On June 8, 1872, the Post Office Department was created by "an act to revise, consolidate, and amend the statute relating to the Post Office Department" (17 Stat. L. 283). This act gave a department to the Postmaster General, who had been given equal cabinet status in 1829 by President Andrew Jackson.

The ninth cabinet post was that of Secretary of Commerce and Labor, established by act of February 14, 1903 (32 Stat. L. 826), "to establish the Department of Commerce and Labor." The first incumbent was George Bruce Cortelyou of New York, who took office on February 16, 1903, at a salary of $8,000 a year during the first term of President Theodore Roosevelt.

During President Taft's administration, the cabinet post of Secretary of Commerce and Labor was discontinued and in its stead two cabinet posts were created, the Department of Commerce and the Department of

Labor, under authority of the act of March 4, 1913 (37 Stat. L. 736). The first Secretary of Commerce was William Cox Redfield of New York and the first Secretary of Labor was William Bauchop Wilson of Pennsylvania. They were appointed by President Woodrow Wilson and took office on March 5, 1913.

On July 26, 1947, the National Security Act of 1947 (61 Stat. L. 495) was passed "to promote the National Security by providing for a Secretary of Defense." The Secretary of Defense was to be head of the National Military Establishment, consisting of the Department of the Army, the Department of the Navy, and the Department of the Air Force, together with all other agencies created under Title II of the act. The first Secretary of Defense was James Vincent Forrestal of New York. At this time the cabinet posts of Secretary of War and Secretary of the Navy were discontinued.

The next change in the organization of the cabinet was made in the administration of President Dwight David Eisenhower, who appointed Oveta Culp Hobby of Texas as the first Secretary of Health, Education, and Welfare. She took office on April 11, 1953.

Two new cabinet positions were created by President Lyndon Baines Johnson. The Department of Housing and Urban Development was authorized on September 9, 1965 (79 Stat. L. 667). The first incumbent was Robert Clifton Weaver of New York, who was sworn in on January 18, 1966. The Department of Transportation was authorized on October 15, 1966 (80 Stat. L. 931) to deal with air, rail, and highway transportation. The first director was Alan Stephenson Boyd of Florida, who was sworn in on January 16, 1967.

The cabinet position of Postmaster General was abolished on July 1, 1971. Winton Malcolm Blount was the last Postmaster General to be a cabinet member.

Under President Jimmy Carter, a new Department of Energy was authorized, on August 4, 1977. James R. Schlesinger of Virginia, Secretary of Defense during the Nixon and Ford Administrations, was appointed Secretary of Energy, confirmed by the Senate the same day, and sworn in on October 1, 1977, when the department came into existence. On September 27, 1979, the Department of Health, Education, and Welfare was divided into the Department of Health and Human Services and the Department of Education. Patricia Roberts Harris of Washington, D.C., the Secretary of HEW, continued as Secretary of Health and Human Services, and Shirley M. Hufstedler of California, a circuit court judge, was appointed the first Secretary of Education. She was sworn in on December 6, 1979.

Under President George Bush's direction, the cabinet position of Secretary for Veterans Affairs was created on March 15, 1989, with Edward Joseph Derwinski as the first incumbent.

The Department of Homeland Security came into being on January 24, 2003, as part of a massive reorganization of federal agencies under President George W. Bush. Its first secretary, sworn in on the same day, was Thomas Joseph Ridge, former governor of Pennsylvania and former Assistant to the President for Homeland Security.

CABINET CHANGES DURING PRESIDENTIAL ADMINISTRATIONS

Three of the Presidents who did not live to complete their terms in the White House retained their original cabinets during their incumbency. They were William Henry Harrison, Taylor, and Garfield. Except for ad interim appointments and appointees carried over from the preceding administrations for a few days, these Presidents had only one cabinet officer for each post.

The only President to retain a cabinet for a full four-year period was Franklin Pierce. John Quincy Adams, with two different Secretaries of War, had the next closest retaining record.

The President who had the greatest number of changes in his administration was John Tyler, who succeeded to the presidency upon the death of William Henry Harrison. When Tyler became President in 1841, the consensus of the six-man cabinet was that he be designated "Acting President." This suggestion angered Tyler, and a few months after taking office he caused all of the members of his cabinet to resign, with the exception of Daniel Webster, who finally resigned in 1843. In less than four years in office, Tyler made 26 changes in his cabinet. In all fairness to him, however, it should be noted that 6 of the changes were made to replace appointees of Harrison, 11 were interim appointments, several others were occasioned by death, and still others were necessitated by the transfer of cabinet members to different departments. Tyler himself appointed two Secretaries of State, three Secretaries of the Treasury, three Secretaries of War, two Attorneys General, one Postmaster General, and four Secretaries of the Navy. His ad interim appointments included four Secretaries of State, three Secretaries of the Treasury, one Secretary of War, two Secretaries of the Navy, and one Postmaster General.

CABINET OFFICERS WHO SERVED IN TWO OR MORE POSITIONS

Many cabinet members have held two or more different positions in presidential cabinets. The following list shows under the name of the appointing President (1) the name of the cabinet officer; (2) the position and the date of appointment, and (3) the cabinet officer's prior position and the date of that appointment (with the name of the earlier appointing President, if any).

Washington

Timothy Pickering—State, 1795; ad interim, War, 1795

Edmund Randolph—State, 1794; Attorney General, 1789

Adams

Samuel Dexter—War, 1801; Treasury, 1801

Jefferson

Henry Dearborn—ad interim, Navy, 1801; War, 1801

Levi Lincoln—Attorney General, 1801; ad interim, State, 1801

Madison

William Harris Crawford—Treasury, 1816; War, 1815

James Monroe—ad interim, War, 1814; State, 1811

Robert Smith—State, 1809; Navy, 1801 (appointed by Jefferson)

Monroe

Richard Rush—ad interim, State, 1817; Attorney General, 1814 (appointed by Madison)

J. Q. Adams

Samuel Lewis Southard—War, 1828; ad interim, Treasury, 1825; Navy, 1823 (appointed by Monroe)

Jackson

Benjamin Franklin Butler—ad interim, War, 1836; Attorney General, 1833

Louis McLane—State, 1833; Treasury, 1831

Roger Brooke Taney—Treasury, 1833; Attorney General, 1831; ad interim, Attorney General, 1831

Levi Woodbury—Treasury, 1834; Navy, 1831

Tyler

John Caldwell Calhoun—State, 1844; War, 1817 (appointed by Monroe)

John Nelson—ad interim, State, 1844; Attorney General, 1843

Abel Parker Upshur—State, 1843; Navy, 1841

Polk

John Young Mason—Attorney General, 1845; Navy, 1844 (appointed by Tyler)

Pierce

William Learned Marcy—State, 1853; War, 1845 (appointed by Polk)

Buchanan

Jeremiah Sullivan Black—State, 1860; Attorney General, 1857

Lewis Cass—State, 1857; War, 1831 (appointed by Jackson)

Joseph Holt—War, 1861; Postmaster General, 1859

Isaac Toucey—Treasury, 1860; Navy, 1857; Attorney General, 1848 (appointed by Polk)

Lincoln

Edwin McMasters Stanton—War, 1862; Attorney General, 1860 (appointed by Buchanan)

Grant

Alphonso Taft—War, 1876; Attorney General, 1876

Hayes

William Maxwell Evarts—State, 1877; Attorney General, 1868 (appointed by A. Johnson)

Arthur

Walter Quintin Gresham—Treasury, 1884; Postmaster General, 1883

Cleveland

Richard Olney—State, 1895; Attorney General, 1893

William Freeman Vilas—Interior, 1888; Postmaster General, 1885

McKinley

John Sherman—State, 1897; Treasury, 1877 (appointed by Hayes)

T. Roosevelt

Charles Joseph Bonaparte—Attorney General, 1906; Navy, 1905

George Bruce Cortelyou—Treasury, 1907; Postmaster General, 1905; Commerce and Labor, 1903

Victor Howard Metcalf—Navy, 1906; Commerce and Labor, 1904

William Henry Moody—Attorney General, 1904; Navy, 1902

Elihu Root—State, 1905; War, 1899 (appointed by McKinley)

Taft

Philander Chase Knox—State, 1909; Attorney General, 1901 (appointed by McKinley)

George von Lengerke Meyer—Navy, 1909; Postmaster General, 1907 (appointed by T. Roosevelt)

Harding

Hubert Work—Interior, 1923; Postmaster General, 1922

Hoover

Henry Lewis Stimson—State, 1929; War, 1911 (appointed by Taft)

F. D. Roosevelt

Henry Agard Wallace—Commerce, 1945; Agriculture, 1933

Truman

James Vincent Forrestal—Defense, Sept. 17, 1947; Navy, May 18, 1944 (appointed by F. D. Roosevelt)

George Catlett Marshall—Defense, 1950; State, 1947

Ford

Rogers Clark Ballard Morton, Jr.—Commerce, 1975; Interior, 1971 (appointed by Nixon)

Elliott Lee Richardson—Commerce, 1976; Attorney General, May 25, 1973; Defense, Feb. 2, 1973; Health, Education, and Welfare, June 24, 1970 (the latter three appointments by Nixon)

Carter

Patricia Roberts Harris—Health and Human Services, Sept. 1979; Health, Education, and Welfare, July 1979; Housing and Urban Development, 1977

James Rodney Schlesinger—Energy, 1977; Defense, 1973 (appointed by Nixon)

Reagan

Caspar Willard Weinberger—Defense, 1981; Health, Education, and Welfare, 1973 (appointed by Nixon)

George Pratt Shultz—State, 1982; Labor, 1969 (appointed by Nixon)

G. Bush

James Addison Baker 3rd—State, 1989; Treasury, 1985 (appointed by Reagan)

Cavazos, Lauro Fred, Jr.—Education, 1989; Education, 1988 (appointed by Reagan) Elizabeth Hanford Dole—Labor, 1989; Transportation, 1983 (appointed by Reagan)

G. W. Bush

Norman Yoshio Mineta—Transportation, 2001; Commerce, 2000 (appointed by Clinton)

Donald Henry Rumsfeld—Defense, 2001; Defense, 1975 (appointed by Ford)

Obama

Robert Michael Gates—Defense, 2009; Defense, 2006 (appointed by G. W. Bush)

CABINET OFFICERS WHO WON THE NOBEL PRIZE

Five Secretaries of State have been awarded the Nobel Prize for Peace.

McKinley (and Roosevelt)

Administration—Republican

57th Congress (1901–1903)

　　Senate—R 56; D 29; others 3; vacant 2
　　House—R 198; D 153; others 5; vacant 1

T. Roosevelt

Administration—Republican

58th Congress (1903–1905)

　　Senate—R 58; D 32
　　House—R 207; D 178; vacant 1

59th Congress (1905–1907)

　　Senate—R 58; D 32
　　House—R 250; D 136

60th Congress (1907–1909)

　　Senate—R 61; D 29; vacant 2
　　House—R 222; D 164

Taft

Administration—Republican

61st Congress (1909–1911)

　　Senate—R 59; D 32; vacant 1
　　House—R 219; D 172

62nd Congress (1911–1913)

　　Senate—R 49; D 42; vacant 1
　　House—D 228; R 162; others 1

Wilson

Administration—Democratic

63rd Congress (1913–1915)

　　Senate—D 51; R 44; others 1
　　House—D 290; R 127; others 18

64th Congress (1915–1917)

　　Senate—D 56; R 39; others 1
　　House—D 231; R 193; others 8, vacant 3

65th Congress (1917–1919)

　　Senate—D 53; R 42; others 1
　　House—R 216; D 210; others 9

66th Congress (1919–1921)

　　Senate—R 48; D 47; others 1
　　House—R 237; D 191; others 7

Harding

Administration—Republican

67th Congress (1921–1923)

　　Senate—R 59; D 37
　　House—R 300; D 132; others 1; vacant 2

Coolidge

Administration—Republican

68th Congress (1923–1925)

　　Senate—R 51; D 43; others 2
　　House—R 225; D 207; others 3

69th Congress (1925–1927)

　　Senate—R 54; D 40; others 1; vacant 1
　　House—R 247; D 183; others 5

70th Congress (1927–1929)

　　Senate—R 48; D 47; others 1
　　House—R 237; D 195; others 3

Hoover

Administration—Republican

71st Congress (1929–1931)

　　Senate—R 56; D 39; others 1
　　House—R 267; D 163; others 1; vacant 4

72nd Congress (1931–1933)

　　Senate—R 48; D 47; others 1
　　House—R 218; D 216; others 1;

F. D. Roosevelt

Administration—Democratic

73rd Congress (1933–1935)

　　Senate—D 59; R 36; others 1
　　House—D 313; R 117; other 5

74th Congress (1935–1937)

　　Senate—D 69; R 25; others 2
　　House—D 322; R 103; others 10

75th Congress (1937–1939)

　　Senate—D 75; R 17; others 4
　　House—D 333; R 89; others 13

76th Congress (1939–1941)

　　Senate—D 69; R 23; others 4
　　House—D 262; R 169; others 4

77th Congress (1941–1943)

　　Senate—D 66; R 28; others 2
　　House—D 267; R 162; others 6

78th Congress (1943–1945)

　　Senate—D 57; R 38; others 1
　　House—D 222; R 209, others 4

F. D. Roosevelt (and Truman)

Administration—Democratic

79th Congress (1945–1947)

　　Senate—D 57; R 38; others 1
　　House—D 243; R 190; others 2

Truman

Administration—Democratic

80th Congress (1947–1949)
  Senate—R 51; D 45
  House—R 246; D 188; others 1
81st Congress (1949–1951)
  Senate—D 54; R 42
  House—D 263; R 171; others 1
82nd Congress (1951–1953)
  Senate—D 48; R 47; others 1
  House—D 234; R 199; others 2

Eisenhower

Administration—Republican

83rd Congress (1953–1955)
  Senate—R 48; D 46; others 2
  House—R 221; D 213; others 1
84th Congress (1955–1957)
  Senate—D 48; R 47; others 1
  House—D 232; R 203
85th Congress (1957–1959)
  Senate—D 49; R 47
  House—D 234; R 201
86th Congress (1959–1961)
  Senate—D 64; R 34
  House—D 283; R 153

Kennedy

Administration—Democratic

87th Congress (1961–1963)
  Senate—D 65; R 35
  House—D 261; R 176

Kennedy (and L. B. Johnson)

Administration—Democratic

88th Congress (1963–1965)
  Senate—D 67; R 33
  House—D 258; R 176, vacant 1

L. B. Johnson

Administration—Democratic

89th Congress (1965–1967)
  Senate—D 67; R 33
  House—D 295; R 140
90th Congress (1967–1969)
  Senate—D 64; R 36
  House—D 248; R 187

Nixon

Administration—Republican

91st Congress (1969–1971)
  Senate—D 57; R 43
  House—D 243; R 192
92nd Congress (1971–1973)
  Senate—D 54; R 45; vacant 1
  House—D 255; R 180

Nixon (and Ford)

Administration—Republican

93rd Congress (1973–1975)
  Senate—D 56; R 42; others 2
  House—D 242; R 192; others 1
94th Congress (1975–1977)
  Senate—D 61; R 37; others 2
  House—D 291; R 144

Carter

Administration—Democratic

95th Congress (1977–1979)
  Senate—D 61; R 38; others 1
  House—D 292; R 143
96th Congress (1979–1981)
  Senate—D 58; R 41; others 1
  House—D 277; R 158

Reagan

Administration—Republican

97th Congress (1981–1983)
  Senate—R 53; D 46; others 1
  House—D 243; R 192
98th Congress (1983–1985)
  Senate—R 54; D 46
  House—D 268; R 167
99th Congress (1985–1987)
  Senate—R 53; D 47
  House—D 253; R 182
100th Congress (1987–1989)
  Senate—D 54; R 46
  House—D 258; R 177

G. Bush

Administration—Republican

101st Congress (1989–1991)
  Senate—D 55; R 45
  House—D 260; R 175
102nd Congress (1991–1993)

Senate—D 57; R 43
House—D 267; R 167; others 1

Clinton

Administration—Democratic

103rd Congress (1993–1995)

Senate—D 57; R 43
House—D 258; R 176; others 1

104th Congress (1995–1997)

Senate—R 52; D 48 (at end of Congress: R 53, D 47)
House—R 230; D 204; others 1

105th Congress (1997–1999)

Senate—R 55; D 45
House—R 228; D 206; others 2

106th Congress (1999–2001)

Senate—R 55; D 45 (at end of Congress: R 54, D 46)
House—R 222, D 211; others 2

G. W. Bush

Administration—Republican

107th Congress (2001–2003)

Senate—R 50; D 50 (at end of Congress: D 50; R 49; others 1)
House—R 221; D 212; others 2

108th Congress (2003–2005)

Senate—R 51; D 48; others 1
House—R 229; D 204; others 1; vacant 1

109th Congress (2005–2007)

Senate—R 55; D 44; others 1
House—R 232; D 202; others 1

110th Congress (2007–2009)

Senate—D 49; R 49; others 2
House—D 233; R 202

Obama

Administration—Democratic

111th Congress (2009–2011)

Senate—D 56; R 41; others 2; vacant 1
House—D 256; R 178; vacant 1

PRESIDENTS WITH OPPOSITION MAJORITIES IN CONGRESS

Each elected President since 1789 came to office with a Senate majority of his own party, with the exception of Taylor, Eisen-hower in his second term, Nixon, George Bush, Clinton in his second term, and George W. Bush.

Each elected President came to office with a House of Representatives majority of his own party, with the following exceptions:
Washington (1793—second term)
Taylor (1849)
Hayes (1876)
Cleveland (1885)
Wilson (1917—second term)
Eisenhower (1957—second term)
Nixon (1969—first term; 1973—second term)
Reagan (1981—first term; 1985—second term)
G. Bush (1989)
Clinton (1997—second term)

Several elected Presidents came to office with a majority of their own party in one or both houses of Congress, but lost that majority in the course of the term. These Presidents were:
Washington (1791)
Polk (1847)
Pierce (1855)
Buchanan (1859)
Grant (1875)
Hayes (1879)
B. Harrison (1891)
Cleveland (1895)
Taft (1911)
Wilson (1919)
Eisenhower (1955)
Reagan (1987)
Clinton (1995)
G. W. Bush (2007)

In addition, three Presidents who succeeded to office lost a majority in one or both houses of Congress before the completion of the term—Tyler (1843), Arthur (1883), and Truman (1947). Two Presidents—Fillmore and Ford—succeeded to office with opposition majorities in both the House and the Senate.

REMOVAL FROM OFFICE

Provisions for removing the President from office are contained in Article II, section 4 of the Constitution:

The President, Vice President and all Officers of the United States, shall be removed from Office on Impeachment for, and Conviction of, Treason, Bribery, or other high Crimes and Misdemeanors.

If the President is unable to perform the duties of office, the Vice President can step in as Acting President, according to the provisions of the Twenty-fifth Amendment (see page 394). However, the President is not removed from office in such a case, and may resume the functions of the presidency at a later date.

IMPEACHMENT

Two Presidents have been impeached, that is, formally charged with serious misconduct in office and tried by the Senate on those charges. Both of them were tried and acquitted in the Senate.

On February 24, 1868, the House passed a resolution of impeachment against Andrew Johnson, who was charged with usurpation of the law, corrupt use of the veto power, interference at elections, and misdemeanors. His Senate trial began on March 13, 1868, and ended on May 26, 1868, when he was acquitted by a margin of one vote (a two-thirds majority is necessary for conviction). He completed his term. Had he been found guilty, he would have been removed from office. Johnson succeeded to the presidency after the murder of Abraham Lincoln and was never elected to it in his own right.

The first elected President to be impeached was William Jefferson Clinton. Two articles of impeachment, accusing Clinton of perjury and obstruction of justice in a sexual harassment lawsuit in which he was the defendant, were approved by the House on December 19, 1998. His Senate trial began on January 7, 1999, and ended with his acquittal on February 12, 1999. The Senate vote was 55-45 on the perjury charge and 50–50 on the obstruction charge. After he had received immunity from further prosecution, Clinton admitted to having given false testimony; he paid a fine and accepted temporary disbarment.

On January 10, 1843, a resolution to impeach President John Tyler was introduced in the House of Representatives, but it was voted down.

On July 27–30, 1974, the Judiciary Committee of the House of Representatives recommended three articles of impeachment to the full House, against President Richard Milhous Nixon. Before any action was taken, the President resigned, on August 9, 1974.

RESIGNATION PROCEDURE

The only evidence of a refusal to accept, or of a resignation of the office of President or Vice President, shall be an instrument in writing, declaring the same, and subscribed by the person refusing to accept or resigning, as the case may be, and delivered into the office of the Secretary of State. (June 25, 1948, 62 Stat. L. 678, ch. 644)

RESIGNATION

Only one President resigned from office. Richard Milhous Nixon, the thirty-seventh President, resigned on August 9, 1974, under threat of impeachment, the charges stemming from his role in the Watergate affair and other administration scandals. Nixon had completed 1 year and 201 days of his second term. He was succeeded by Vice President Gerald Rudolph Ford.

PRESIDENTIAL SUCCESSION

Article II, Section 1 of the Constitution of the United States provided for presidential succession as follows:

In Case of the Removal of the President from Office, or of his death, Resignation, or Inability to discharge the Powers and Duties of the said Office, the Same shall devolve on the Vice President, and the Congress may by Law provide for the Case of Removal, Death, Resignation or Inability, both of the President and Vice President, declaring what Officer shall then act as President, and such Officer shall act accordingly, until the Disability be removed, or a President shall be elected.

A law was enacted by Congress on March 1, 1792 (1 Stat. L. 239), which provided that

In case of the removal, death, resignation, or disability of both the President and the Vice President of the United States, the President of the Senate pro tempore, and in case there shall be no President of the Senate, then the Speaker of the House of Representatives for the time being shall act as President of the United States until such disability be removed or until a President be elected.

Although the Twelfth Amendment, ratified in 1804, did not change the order of presidential succession, it provided that both the President and the Vice President be elected separately, voiding the system whereby the presidential candidate with the second largest vote became Vice President and thus eligible to succeed to the presidency.

No change was made in the order of succession from 1792 until the Presidential Succession Act of January 19, 1886 (24 Stat. L. 1) was passed during Grover Cleveland's administration. This act, entitled "An Act to provide for the performance of the duties of the office of President in case of the removal, resignation or inability both of the President and the Vice President," provided that the succession should devolve upon the departmental secretaries according to the order of the creation of their respective departments. The order was State, Treasury, War, Attorney General, Postmaster General, Navy, Interior, Agriculture, Commerce, and Labor (easily remembered by the mnemonic *St. Wapniacl*). Actually, the order of succession was incorrect as the Department of War was established prior to the Treasury Department.

The Presidential Succession Act of July 18, 1947 (61 Stat. L. 380)—"to provide for the performance of the duties of the office of President in case of the removal, resignation, death or inability both of the President and the Vice President"—established the succession as follows: the Vice President, the Speaker of the House of Representatives, the President pro tempore of the Senate, the Secretary of War, the Attorney General, the Postmaster General, the Secretary of the Navy, the Secretary of the Interior, the Secretary of Agriculture, the Secretary of Commerce, and the Secretary of Labor.

The act of July 26, 1947 (61 Stat. L. 509) substituted the Secretary of Defense for the Secretary of War and eliminated the Secretary of the Navy.

As additional departments of the executive branch were established, their secretaries were added to the order of succession. The Postmaster General was dropped from the list in 1971 after the creation of the U.S. Postal Service as a separate federal agency without Cabinet-level respresentation. By 2000, the list of cabinet officers had been extended to include the Secretaries of Health and Human Services, Housing and Urban Development, Transportation, Energy, Education, and Veterans Affairs. Postmasters General, however, ceased to be cabinet officials in 1971 and are no longer in the line of succession.

The Twenty-fifth Amendment, adopted February 10, 1967, was designed to fill vice presidential vacancies and provide for continuity in case of disability. The text follows:

Section 1. In case of the removal of the President from office or his death or resignation, the Vice President shall become President.

Section 2. Whenever there is a vacancy in the office of the Vice President, the President shall nominate a Vice President who shall take the office upon confirmation by a majority vote of both houses of Congress.

Section 3. Whenever the President transmits to the President pro tempore of the Senate and the Speaker of the House of Representatives his written declaration that he is unable to discharge the powers and duties of his office, and until he transmits to them a written declaration to the contrary, such powers and duties shall be discharged by the Vice President as Acting President.

Section 4. Whenever the Vice President and a majority of either the principal officers of the executive departments, or of such other body as Congress may by law provide, transmit to the President pro tempore of the Senate and the Speaker of the House of Representatives their written declaration that the President is unable to discharge the powers and duties of his office as Acting President.

Thereafter when the President transmits to the President pro tempore of the Senate and the Speaker of the House of Representatives his written declaration that no inability exists, he shall resume the powers and duties of his office unless the Vice President and a majority of either the principal officers of the executive department, or of such other body as Congress may by law provide, transmit within four days to the President pro tempore of the Senate and the Speaker of the House of Representatives their written declaration that the President is unable to discharge the powers and duties of his office. Thereupon Congress shall decide this issue, assembling within 48 hours for that purpose if not in session. If the Congress, within 21 days after receipt of the latter written declaration, or, if Congress is not in session, within 2 days after Congress is required to assemble, determines by two-thirds vote of both houses that the President is unable to discharge the powers and duties of his office, the Vice President shall continue to discharge the same as Acting President; otherwise, the President shall resume the powers and duties of his office.

No President and Vice President have both died during the same administration, and no cabinet officer or Congressional leader has succeeded to the presidency thereby. Statisticians have calculated that the death from natural causes of both President and Vice President in the same administration is not likely to occur more than once in 840 years.

During President Nixon's second term, both he and Vice President Agnew resigned. However, they did not resign simultaneously, and no congressional leader succeeded to either post. President Nixon appointed a new Vice President after Agnew resigned, in 1973; the appointment was confirmed by the Congress; and the appointed Vice President (Ford) then succeeded to the Presidency upon Nixon's resignation, in 1974. President Ford subsequently appointed Nelson Rockefeller Vice President.

The Presidents and Their Vice Presidents

VICE PRESIDENT'S OATH

I do solemnly swear that I will support and defend the Constitution of the United States against all enemies, foreign and domestic, that I will bear true faith and allegiance to the same: that I take this obligation freely, without any mental reservation or purpose of evasion, and I will well and faithfully discharge the duties of the office on which I am about to enter. So help me God.

PRESIDENTS AND VICE PRESIDENTS

There have been 44 Presidents (with Grover Cleveland counted twice since his two terms were not consecutive), of whom only 40 had Vice Presidents. Four of the eight men who succeeded to the presidency did not appoint a Vice President to take their place and were not subsequently elected to the presidency in their own right. Each of the four other men who succeeded to the presidency served out his predecessor's term without appointing a Vice President, but was then elected in his own right along with a vice presidential running mate. Seven of the 36 remaining Presidents had two different Vice Presidents, and one had three, so there have been 49 separate teams. However, only 47 individuals have held the office of Vice President: George Clinton and John Caldwell Calhoun each served under two different Presidents.

The following is a list of the Presidents and their Vice Presidents. Biographical material on each Vice President may be found in Part I in the appropriate presidential section.

Washington

John Adams (first and second terms)

J. Adams

Thomas Jefferson

Jefferson

Aaron Burr (first term)
George Clinton (second term)

Madison

George Clinton (first term)
Elbridge Gerry

Monroe

Daniel D. Tompkins (first and second terms)

J. Q. Adams

John Caldwell Calhoun

Jackson

John Caldwell Calhoun (first term)
Martin Van Buren (second term)

Van Buren

Richard Mentor Johnson

W. H. Harrison

John Tyler

Tyler

————

Polk

George Mifflin Dallas

Taylor

Millard Fillmore

Fillmore

————

Pierce

William Rufus Devane King

Buchanan

John Cabell Breckinridge

Lincoln

Hannibal Hamlin (first term)
Andrew Johnson (second term)

A. Johnson

————

Grant

Schuyler Colfax (first term)
Henry Wilson (second term)

Hayes

Williams Almon Wheeler

Garfield

Chester Alan Arthur

Arthur

————

Cleveland (first term)

Thomas Andrews Hendricks

B. Harrison

Levi Parsons Morton

Cleveland (second term)

Adlai Ewing Stevenson

McKinley

Garrett Augustus Hobart (first term)
Theodore Roosevelt (second term)

T. Roosevelt

————(first term)
Charles Warren Fairbanks (second term)

Taft

James Schoolcraft Sherman

Wilson

Thomas Riley Marshall (first and second terms)

Harding

Calvin Coolidge

Coolidge

————(first term)
Charles Gates Dawes (second term)

Hoover

Charles Curtis

F. D. Roosevelt

John Nance Garner (first and second terms)
Henry Agard Wallace (third term)
Harry S. Truman (fourth term)

Truman

————(first term)
Alben William Barkley

Eisenhower

Richard Milhous Nixon (first and second terms)

Kennedy

Lyndon Baines Johnson

L. B. Johnson

————(first term)
Hubert Horatio Humphrey (second term)

Nixon

Spiro Theodore Agnew (first term; resigned October 10, 1973, after serving 10 months of his second term)

Gerald Rudolph Ford, Jr. (second term; December 6, 1973, sworn in, filling vacancy left by resignation of Spiro Agnew)

Ford

Nelson Aldrich Rockefeller (sworn in December 19, 1974)

Carter

Walter Frederick Mondale

Reagan

George Herbert Walker Bush (first and second terms)

G. Bush

James Danforth Quayle III

Clinton

Albert Arnold Gore, Jr. (first and second terms)

G. W. Bush

Richard Bruce Cheney (first and second terms)

Obama

Joseph Robinette Biden

VICE PRESIDENTS—TERMS OF OFFICE AND PRESIDENTS SERVED

1. John Adams

1789–1797, Washington

2. Thomas Jefferson

1797–1801, J. Adams

3. Aaron Burr

1801–1805, Jefferson

4. George Clinton

1805–1809, Jefferson
1809–1812, Madison

5. Elbridge Gerry

1813–1814, Madison

6. Daniel D. Tompkins

1817–1825, Monroe

7. John Caldwell Calhoun

1825–1829, J. Q. Adams
1829–1832, Jackson

8. Martin Van Buren

1833–1837, Jackson

9. Richard Mentor Johnson

1837–1841, Van Buren

10. John Tyler

1841, W. H. Harrison

11. George Mifflin Dallas

1845–1849, Polk

12. Millard Fillmore

1849–1850, Taylor

13. William Rufus Devane King

1853, Pierce

14. John Cabell Breckinridge

1857–1861, Buchanan

15. Hannibal Hamlin

1861–1865, Lincoln

16. Andrew Johnson

1865, Lincoln

17. Schuyler Colfax

1869–1873, Grant

18. Henry Wilson

1873–1875, Grant

19. William Almon Wheeler

1877–1881, Hayes

20. Chester Alan Arthur

1881, Garfield

21. Thomas Andrews Hendricks

1885, Cleveland (first term)

22. Levi Parsons Morton

1889–1893, B. Harrison

23. Adlai Ewing Stevenson

1893–1897, Cleveland (second term)

24. Garret Augustus Hobart

1897–1899, McKinley

25. Theodore Roosevelt

1901, McKinley

26. Charles Warren Fairbanks

1905–1909, T. Roosevelt

27. James Schoolcraft Sherman

1909–1912, Taft

28. Thomas Riley Marshall

1913–1921, Wilson

29. Calvin Coolidge

1921–1923, Harding

30. Charles Gates Dawes

1925–1929, Coolidge

31. Charles Curtis

1929–1933, Hoover

32. John Nance Garner

1933–1941, F. D. Roosevelt

33. Henry Agard Wallace

1941–1945, F. D. Roosevelt

34. Harry S. Truman

1945, F. D. Roosevelt

35. Alben William Barkley

1949–1953, Truman

36. Richard Milhous Nixon

1953–1961, Eisenhower

37. Lyndon Baines Johnson

1961–1963, Kennedy

38. Hubert Horatio Humphrey

1965–1969, L. B. Johnson

39. Spiro Theodore Agnew

1969–1973, Nixon

40. Gerald Rudolph Ford, Jr.

1973–1974, Nixon

41. Nelson Aldrich Rockefeller

1974–1977, Ford

42. Walter Frederick Mondale

1977–1981, Carter

43. George Herbert Walker Bush

1981–1989, Reagan

44. James Danforth Quayle III

1989–1993, G. Bush

45. Albert Arnold Gore, Jr.

1993–2001, Clinton

46. Richard Bruce Cheney

2001–2009, G. W. Bush

47. Joseph Robinette Biden

2009– , Obama

PRESIDENTS AND VICE PRESIDENTS—NUMERICAL POSITION

Although the President and the Vice President are inaugurated at the same ceremony, it does not follow that their numerical position with regard to their offices is the same. As some Vice Presidents have served two Presidents and as some Presidents have had two Vice Presidents (three, in the case of F. D. Roosevelt), and as some Vice Presidents have succeeded to the presidency without a corresponding Vice President, there is often little relationship in the numerical positions of the Presidents and their Vice Presidents.

The following list shows the numerical order of the Presidents and Vice Presidents whose numbers were the same:

1. Washington, Adams
2. J. Adams, Jefferson
3. Jefferson (first term), Burr
4. Madison, Clinton (second term)
7. Jackson (first term), Calhoun (second term)
11. Polk, Dallas
12. Taylor, Fillmore
16. Lincoln, A. Johnson
18. Grant (second term), Wilson
19. Hayes, Wheeler
20. Garfield, Arthur
25. McKinley (second term), T. Roosevelt
26. T. Roosevelt (second term), Fairbanks
27. Taft, Sherman
28. Wilson, Marshall
29. Harding, Coolidge
30. Coolidge (second term), Dawes
31. Hoover, Curtis

32. F. D. Roosevelt (first and second terms), Garner

VICE PRESIDENTS—STATES REPRESENTED AND PARTY AFFILIATIONS

Adams   Massachusetts, Federalist

Jefferson   Virginia, Democratic-Republican

Burr   New York, Democratic-Republican

G. Clinton   New York, Democratic-Republican

Gerry   Massachusetts, Democratic-Republican

Tompkins   New York, Democratic-Republican

Calhoun   South Carolina, Democratic-Republican

Van Buren   New York, Democrat

R. M. Johnson   Kentucky, Democrat

Tyler   Virginia, Whig

Dallas   Pennsylvania, Democrat

Fillmore   New York, Whig

King   Alabama, Democrat

Breckinridge   Kentucky, Democrat

Hamlin   Maine, Republican

A. Johnson   Tennessee, Democrat (but nominated and elected with Lincoln on Republican ticket)

Colfax   Indiana, Republican

Wilson   Massachusetts, Republican

Wheeler   New York, Republican

Arthur   New York, Republican

Hendricks   Indiana, Democrat

Morton   New York, Republican

Stevenson   Illinois, Democrat

Hobart   New Jersey, Republican

T. Roosevelt   New York, Republican

Fairbanks   Indiana, Republican

Sherman   New York, Republican

Marshall   Indiana, Democrat

Coolidge   Massachusetts, Republican

Dawes   Illinois, Republican

Curtis   Kansas, Republican

Garner   Texas, Democrat

Wallace   Iowa, Democrat

Truman   Missouri, Democrat

Barkley   Kentucky, Democrat

Nixon   California, Republican

L. B. Johnson   Texas, Democrat

Humphrey   Minnesota, Democrat

Agnew   Maryland, Republican

Ford   Michigan, Republican

Rockefeller   New York, Republican

Mondale   Minnesota, Democrat

G. Bush   Texas, Republican

Quayle   Indiana, Republican

Gore   Tennessee, Democrat

Cheney   Wyoming, Republican

Biden   Delaware, Democrat

VICE PRESIDENTS—DATES AND PLACES OF BIRTH

J. Adams   Oct. 30, 1735, Braintree (now Quincy), Mass.

Jefferson   Apr. 13, 1743, Shadwell, Va.

Burr   Feb. 6, 1756, Newark, N.J.

Clinton   July 26, 1739, Little Britain, N.Y.

Gerry   July 17, 1744, Marblehead, Mass.

Tompkins   June 21, 1774, Fox Meadows (now Scarsdale), N.Y.

Calhoun   Mar. 18, 1782, Abbeville District, S.C.

Van Buren   Dec. 5, 1782, Kinderhook, N.Y.

R. M. Johnson   Oct. 17, 1780, Floyd's Station, Ky.

Tyler   Mar. 29, 1790, Charles City County, Va.

Dallas   July 10, 1792, Philadelphia, Pa.

Fillmore   Jan. 7, 1800, Summerhill, N.Y.

King   Apr. 7, 1786, Sampson County, N.C.

Breckinridge   Jan. 21, 1821, Lexington, Ky.

Hamlin   Aug. 27, 1809, Paris, Me.

A. Johnson   Dec. 29, 1808, Raleigh, N.C.

Colfax   Mar. 23, 1823, New York, N.Y.

Wilson   Feb. 16, 1812, Farmington, N.H.

Wheeler   June 30, 1819, Malone, N.Y.

Arthur   Oct. 5, 1829, Fairfield, Vt.

Hendricks   Sept. 7, 1819, Muskingum County, Ohio

Morton   May 16, 1824, Shoreham, Vt.

Stevenson   Oct. 23, 1835, Christian County, Ky.

Hobart   June 3, 1844, Long Branch, N.J.

T. Roosevelt   Oct. 27, 1858, New York, N.Y.

Fairbanks   May 11, 1852, Unionville Center, Ohio

Sherman   Oct. 24, 1855, Utica, N.Y.

Marshall   Mar. 14, 1854, North Manchester, Ind.

Coolidge   July 4, 1872, Plymouth, Vt.

Dawes   Aug. 27, 1865, Marietta, Ohio

Curtis   Jan. 25, 1860, Topeka, Kan.

Garner   Nov. 24, 1877, Graves County, Ky.

Wallace   Oct. 7, 1888, Adair County, Iowa

Truman   May 8, 1884, Lamar, Mo.

Barkley   Nov. 24, 1877, Graves County, Ky.

Nixon   Jan. 9, 1913, Yorba Linda, Calif.

L. B. Johnson   Aug. 27, 1908, Stonewall, Tex.

Humphrey   May 27, 1911, Wallace, S.D.

Agnew   Nov. 9, 1918, Baltimore, Md.

Ford   July 14, 1913, Omaha, Neb.

Rockefeller   July 8, 1908, Bar Harbor, Me.

Mondale   Jan. 5, 1928, Ceylon, Minn.

G. Bush   June 12, 1924, Milton, Mass.

Quayle   Feb. 4, 1947, Indianapolis, Ind.

Gore   Mar. 31, 1948, Washington, D.C.

Cheney   Jan. 30, 1941, Lincoln, Neb.

Biden   Nov. 20, 1942, Scranton, Pa.

VICE PRESIDENTS PAST AND FUTURE

As a rule there are not a great many living Vice Presidents in any single year. In 1824, 1864, 1865, and 1868, however, at least 18 individuals were living who had held the office of Vice President, were in office, or were destined to be elected to the office.

The following is a list of the 19 Vice Presidents alive in 1824, with dates of birth and death:

Adams   1735–1826

Jefferson   1743–1826

Burr   1756–1836

Tompkins   1774–1825

R. M. Johnson   1780–1850

Calhoun   1782–1850

Van Buren   1782–1862

King   1786–1853

Tyler   1790–1862

Dallas   1792–1864

Fillmore   1800–1874

A. Johnson   1808–1875

Hamlin   1809–1891

Wilson   1812–1875

Wheeler   1819–1885

Hendricks   1821–1875

Breckinridge   1821–1875

Colfax   1823–1885

Morton   1824–1920

The following is a list of the eighteen Vice Presidents alive in 1864, with dates of birth and death:

Dallas   1792–1864

Fillmore   1800–1874

A. Johnson   1808–1875

Hamlin   1809–1891

Wilson   1812–1875

Wheeler   1819–1887

Hendricks   1819–1885

Breckinridge   1821–1875

Colfax   1823–1885

Morton   1824–1920

Arthur   1830–1886

Stevenson   1835–1914

Hobart   1844–1899

Fairbanks   1852–1918

Marshall   1854–1925

Sherman   1855–1912

T. Roosevelt   1858–1919

Curtis   1860–1936

The death of Dallas in 1864 was offset by the birth of Dawes (1865–1951), and the number remained the same in 1865. The birth of Garner (1868–1967) brought the number to 19 in 1868.

A similar compilation of PRESIDENTS PAST AND FUTURE appears on page 612.

VICE PRESIDENTS— BIRTHPLACES

New York (8):   Clinton, Tompkins, Van Buren, Fillmore, Colfax, Wheeler, T. Roosevelt, Sherman

Kentucky (4):   R. M. Johnson, Breckinridge, Stevenson, Barkley

Massachusetts (3):   Adams, Gerry, G. Bush

Ohio (3): Hendricks, Fairbanks, Dawes
Vermont (3): Arthur, Morton, Coolidge
Indiana (2): Marshall, Quayle
Maine (2): Hamlin, Rockefeller
Nebraska (2): Ford, Cheney
New Jersey (2): Burr, Hobart
North Carolina (2): King, A. Johnson
Pennsylvania (2): Dallas, Biden
Texas (2): Garner, L. B. Johnson
Virginia (2): Jefferson, Tyler
California (1): Nixon
Iowa (1): Wallace
Kansas (1): Curtis
Maryland (1): Agnew
Minnesota (1): Mondale
Missouri (1): Truman
New Hampshire (1): Wilson
South Carolina (1): Calhoun
South Dakota (1): Humphrey
Washington, D.C. (1): Gore

NEW YORK STATE THE BIRTHPLACE OF EIGHT VICE PRESIDENTS

The number of Vice Presidents born in New York State has been greater than the number born in any two other states combined. The eight Vice Presidents born in New York were George Clinton (who served under Jefferson and Madison), Daniel D. Tompkins (under Monroe), Martin Van Buren (under Jackson), Millard Fillmore (under Taylor), Schuyler Colfax (under Grant), William Almon Wheeler (under Hayes), Theodore Roosevelt (under McKinley), and James Schoolcraft Sherman (under Taft). Three of the eight succeeded to the presidency: Van Buren, Fillmore, and Theodore Roosevelt.

YOUNGEST AND OLDEST VICE PRESIDENTS FROM KENTUCKY

The two Vice Presidents who were the youngest and the oldest at their respective inaugurations were both natives of Kentucky. The youngest was John Cabell Breckinridge, born at Lexington, Ky., who was 36 years and 42 days old when he was inaugurated Vice President under President James Buchanan in 1857. The oldest was Alben William Bark-ley, born near Lowes, in Graves County, Ky., who was 71 years and 57 days old when he was inaugurated Vice President under President Harry S. Truman in 1949.

RESIDENT STATES OF THE VICE PRESIDENTS

The Vice Presidents, upon taking office, were residents (though not necessarily natives) of the following states:

New York (11): Burr, Clinton, Tompkins, Van Buren, Fillmore, Wheeler, Arthur, Morton, T. Roosevelt, Sherman, Rockefeller
Indiana (5): Colfax, Hendricks, Fairbanks, Marshall, Quayle
Massachusetts (4): Adams, Gerry, Wilson, Coolidge
Kentucky (3): R. M Johnson, Breckinridge, Barkley
Texas (3): Garner, L. B. Johnson, G. Bush
Illinois (2): Stevenson, Dawes
Minnesota (2): Humphrey, Mondale
Tennessee (2): A. Johnson, Gore
Virginia (2): Jefferson, Tyler
Alabama (1): King
California (1): Nixon
Delaware (1): Biden
Iowa (1): Wallace
Kansas (1): Curtis
Maine (1): Hamlin
Maryland (1): Agnew
Michigan (1): Ford
Missouri (1): Truman
New Jersey (1): Hobart
Pennsylvania (1): Dallas
South Carolina (1): Calhoun
Wyoming (1): Cheney

VICE PRESIDENTS RESIDING IN STATES OTHER THAN THEIR BIRTHPLACES

The eighteen Vice Presidents listed below were residents of states other than their native states. The name of each is followed by (1) the state of which he was a resident and (2) the state in which he was born:

Burr New York, New Jersey
King Alabama, North Carolina

A. Johnson   Tennessee, North Carolina

Colfax   Indiana, New York

Wilson   Massachusetts, New Hampshire

Hendricks   Indiana, Ohio

Morton   New York, Vermont

Stevenson   Illinois, Kentucky

Fairbanks   Indiana, Ohio

Coolidge   Massachusetts, Vermont

Dawes   Illinois, Ohio

Humphrey   Minnesota, South Dakota

Ford   Michigan, Nebraska

Rockefeller   New York, Maine

G. Bush   Texas, Massachusetts

Gore   Tennessee, District of Columbia

Cheney   Wyoming, Nebraska

Biden   Delaware, Pennsylvania

VICE PRESIDENT'S RESIDENCE

Legislation establishing an official residence for the Vice President was enacted April 9, 1966 (80 Stat. L. 106), "authorizing the planning, design, construction, furnishing, and maintenance of an official residence" on the site of the United States Naval Observatory, Washington, D.C. The money for this project was never appropriated, and no construction was undertaken. The Admiral's House, an 81-year-old building on a 12-acre section of the 72-acre lot, was designated July 12, 1974 (88 Stat. L. 340) as the official residence upon the termination of the incumbent Chief of Naval Operations. The first occupant of the renovated building was Vice President Walter Frederick Mondale, who moved in January 20, 1977.

THE VICE PRESIDENT'S SEAL AND FLAG

The seal of the Vice President bears the same coat of arms as that of the President, but encircled by the words SEAL OF THE VICE PRESIDENT OF THE UNITED STATES. The Vice President's flag is a white rectangle, with his seal in the center and a blue star in each corner. Both the seal and the flag were established by Presidential Executive Order Number 11,884, dated October 7, 1975, which superseded all previous directives on the matter. The seal was redrawn at the request of Vice President Rockefeller, who wanted an energetic-looking eagle. The eagle on the old seal, he said, resembled "a wounded quail."

DESCENDANT OF NATIVE AMERICANS ELECTED VICE PRESIDENT

Senator Charles Curtis of Kansas was Vice President of the United States from March 4, 1929, to March 3, 1933, under President Hoover. His maternal grandmother was a member of the Kaw tribe and the granddaughter of the Osage chief Pawhuskie.

JOHNSONS SOUGHT VICE PRESIDENTIAL OFFICE

Five unrelated men named Johnson were important contenders for the vice presidency. Three of the five were elected: Richard Mentor Johnson, who served under Van Buren; Andrew Johnson, who served during Lincoln's second term and succeeded to the presidency upon the death of Lincoln; and Lyndon Baines Johnson, who served under Kennedy, succeeded to the presidency upon the death of Kennedy, and was then elected to the presidency in his own right. The two defeated Johnsons were Herschel Vespasian Johnson of Georgia, who ran on the Democratic ticket in 1860 under Stephen Arnold Douglas, and Hiram Warren Johnson of California, who was the running mate of Theodore Roosevelt in 1912 on the Progressive ticket.

VICE PRESIDENTS WITH PRESIDENTS' NAMES

In addition to the three Vice President Johnsons, three other Vice Presidents also bore the names of Presidents. Henry Wilson, Vice President in Grant's second administration was not related to President Woodrow Wilson. He was born Jeremiah Jones Colbaith and changed his name legally to Wilson. George Clinton, Vice President in Jefferson's second administration and Madison's first administration, was not related to President Bill Clinton. Theodore Roosevelt, Vice President under President William McKinley, was a fifth cousin of Franklin D. Roosevelt.

VICE PRESIDENTIAL ASPIRANT ELECTED PRESIDENT OF CONFEDERATE STATES

Jefferson Davis of Mississippi became president of the Confederate States of America on February 18, 1861. Nine years earlier, he had been a contender for the vice presidential nomination at the Democratic national convention held at the Maryland Institute, Baltimore, Md., June 1–5, 1852. On the first ballot New York cast two votes for Davis; on the second ballot, Illinois cast eleven votes for him.

OCTOGENARIAN NOMINATED FOR VICE PRESIDENCY

The oldest nominee for the vice presidency by a major party was Henry Gassaway Davis of West Virginia, a former senator, who was 80 years and 235 days old when he was nominated at the Democratic convention at St. Louis, Mo., in July 1904.

VICE PRESIDENT WAS GRANDFATHER OF PRESIDENTIAL CANDIDATE

Three men with the name Adlai Ewing Stevenson played roles in national politics. The first, born in Kentucky in 1835, represented Illinois in the House of Representatives and served as Vice President in Cleveland's second administration (1893–1897). His grandson, born in California in 1900, had a distinguished diplomatic and political career and was elected governor of Illinois in 1948. He ran for President on the Democratic ticket in 1952 and 1956, losing both times to Dwight David Eisenhower. Adlai Ewing Stevenson III, his son, served as U.S. senator from Illinois.

WOMAN VICE PRESIDENTIAL CANDIDATES

The first woman to be nominated for Vice President was Marietta Lizzie Bell Stow of California, who was nominated by the People's Party (also known as the National Radical Reformers and later as the Equal Rights Party) on September 20, 1884, at San Francisco, Calif. Her running mate was Belva Ann Bennett Lockwood of Washington, D.C.

The first woman to be nominated for Vice President in the 20th century was Marie Caroline Brehm of California, who was nominated by the Prohibition Party on June 6, 1924, at Columbus, Ohio. Brehm and her running mate, Herman Preston Faris of Missouri, received 57,520 votes on Election Day.

The first woman to be proposed for the vice presidential nomination of a major political party was Mrs. Leroy Springs of Lancaster, S.C., a former schoolteacher. She attended the 1924 Democratic National Convention in New York City as delegate at large and national committeewoman of South Carolina. On July 9, 1924, she received eighteen votes, the votes of the South Carolina delegation. The candidate nominated for Vice President was Charles Wayland Bryan of Nebraska.

The first woman to be nominated for Vice President by a major political party was Geraldine Anne Ferraro, congressional representative from New York State. She was chosen by Democratic presidential nominee Walter F. Mondale as his running mate on July 12, 1984, at the Democratic National Convention. They lost the election to incumbent President Ronald Reagan and Vice President George Bush. The first female vice presidential nominee from the Republican Party was Sarah Heath Palin, the governor of Alaska, who had second place on the ticket of John Sidney McCain in 2008; they were defeated by Barack Obama and Joseph R. Biden.

AFRICAN-AMERICAN VICE PRESIDENTIAL CANDIDATES

The first African-American to be proposed for the vice presidential nomination of a major political party was Blanche Kelso Bruce, U.S. Senator from Mississippi, who received eleven votes in the balloting for the vice presidency at the Republican convention held in Chicago, Ill., in June 1880. The nomination went to Chester Alan Arthur.

The first African-American to be nominated for Vice President was Frederick Douglass of New York, who was nominated on May 10, 1872, by the People's Party (also known as the National Radical Reformers and later as the Equal Rights Party). The presidential nominee was Victoria Claflin Woodhull.

The first African-American to be nominated for Vice President in the twentieth century was James William Ford of New York, who was nominated on May 28, 1932, in Chicago, Ill., by the Communist Party. William Zebulon Foster of Illinois was the presidential nominee. They received 102,785 votes on Election Day. Ford was twice renominated as Vice President by the Communist Party, both times with Earl Russell Browder as the presidential nominee: in 1936, when they received 80,159 votes, and in 1940, when they received 46,251 votes.

The first African-American woman to be nominated for Vice President was Charlotta A. Bass of New York, who was nominated on July 5, 1952, in Chicago, Ill, by the Progressive Party and on August 28 in New York City by the American Labor Party. Her running mate on both tickets was Vincent William Hallinan. The Progressive ticket received 135,007 votes on Election Day.

JEWISH VICE PRESIDENTIAL CANDIDATE

The first Jew to be nominated for Vice President by a major political party was Senator Joseph Isadore Lieberman of Connecticut (the first Orthodox Jewish senator), who was selected on August 8, 2000, to be the running mate of the Democratic candidate, Albert Arnold Gore, Jr. They were defeated by their Republican opponents, George Walker Bush and Richard Bruce Cheney, on Election Day.

VICE PRESIDENTIAL TERMS

Nineteen of the forty-six past Vice Presidents were elected once to that office and served full four-year terms. They were Thomas Jefferson, Aaron Burr, Martin Van Buren, Richard Mentor Johnson, George Mifflin Dallas, John Cabell Breckinridge, Hannibal Hamlin, Schuyler Colfax, William Almon Wheeler, Levi Parsons Morton, Adlai Ewing Stevenson, Charles Warren Fairbanks, Charles Gates Dawes, Charles Curtis, Henry Agard Wallace, Alben William Barkley, Hubert Horatio Humphrey, Walter Frederick Mondale, and Dan Quayle.

Sixteen Vice Presidents served less than one full term, as follows:

Eight were elected to office but did not complete their terms because they succeeded to the presidency. They were John Tyler, Millard Fillmore, Andrew Johnson, Chester Alan Arthur, Theodore Roosevelt, Calvin Coolidge, Harry S. Truman, and Lyndon Baines Johnson. (Four of the eight—Roosevelt, Coolidge, Truman, and Lyndon Baines Johnson—were also elected to the presidency in their own right.)

Two were appointed to the Vice Presidency to fill the unexpired portion of a term, under the provisions of the Twenty-fifth Amendment. Gerald Rudolph Ford served 246 days as Vice President before succeeding to the presidency and Nelson Aldrich Rockefeller served 2 years and 32 days.

Six were elected to office but died before completing their four-year terms. They were William Rufus Devane King, who served 25 days; Thomas Andrews Hendricks, 266 days; Elbridge Gerry, 1 year and 26 days; Henry Wilson, 2 years and 263 days; Garret Augustus Hobart, 2 years and 262 days; and James Schoolcraft Sherman, 3 years and 240 days.

Eleven Vice Presidents were elected twice. They were John Adams, George Clinton, John Caldwell Calhoun, Daniel D. Tompkins, Thomas Riley Marshall, John Nance Garner, Richard Milhous Nixon, Spiro Theodore Agnew, George Bush, Albert Arnold Gore, Jr., and Richard Bruce Cheney.

Of the eleven who were reelected, two served their second terms under different Presidents: George Clinton under Jefferson and Madison, and Calhoun under John Quincy Adams and Jackson. Neither Clinton nor Calhoun completed his second term. Clinton was reelected to serve under James Madison from 1809 to 1813, but he died on April 20, 1812, leaving the nation without a Vice President for 318 days. Calhoun was reelected to serve under Jackson from 1829 to 1833, but he resigned on December 28, 1832, after his election to the Senate to fill the vacancy caused by the resignation of Robert Young Hayne of South Carolina. Calhoun served 82 days less than eight full years.

Agnew did not serve eight full years. He resigned October 10, 1973, having served 263 days of his second term.

Technically, only six of the forty-six past Vice Presidents served eight full years in office. They were Tompkins, who served under Monroe; Marshall, who served under

Wilson; Nixon, who served under Eisenhower; George Bush, who served under Reagan; Gore, who served under William Jefferson Clinton; and Cheney, who served under George W. Bush. Two other Vice Presidents served two full terms without serving eight full years: John Adams served 47 days less than eight full years because he did not assume office until April 21, 1789 (nine days before George Washington was inaugurated). Garner served 43 days less than eight full years because his second term under Franklin D. Roosevelt expired on January 20, instead of the previous March 4 date.

John Adams, Nixon, and George Bush were the only Vice Presidents who had completed two full terms of service in that office before attaining the presidency.

RESIGNATION OF
VICE PRESIDENT CALHOUN

John Caldwell Calhoun, of South Carolina, who served as Vice President under President John Quincy Adams from March 4, 1825, to March 4, 1829, was reelected Vice President to serve under Andrew Jackson from March 4, 1829, to March 4, 1833. Political differences between Calhoun and Jackson, especially over the tariff policy, developed into a personal feud, and Jackson decided to replace Calhoun with Martin Van Buren. Calhoun resigned December 28, 1832, having been elected on December 12 to fill the vacant seat of Robert Y. Hayne, who had been elected governor of South Carolina. Calhoun served as Senator from December 29, 1832, to March 3, 1843, in the 22nd and the seven succeeding Congresses. He also served as Senator from November 26, 1845, until his death on March 31, 1850.

RESIGNATION OF
VICE PRESIDENT AGNEW

Spiro Theodore Agnew, of Maryland, who served as Vice President under President Richard Milhous Nixon from January 20, 1969, to October 10, 1973, resigned because of charges brought against him by the Internal Revenue Service concerning the violation of income tax laws. He pleaded no contest, and other charges of bribery, extortion, and conspiracy were dismissed. Agnew was placed on probation and fined $10,000.

On April 27, 1981, a civil suit brought by Maryland taxpayers resulted in a judgment against Agnew, who was ordered to pay the State of Maryland $248,735 to compensate for bribes allegedly taken while he was Governor of Maryland and Vice President. Agnew appealed the decision, which was upheld. He paid $270,000 to the State of Maryland on January 4, 1983.

PRESIDENTIAL AND
VICE PRESIDENTIAL TEAMS
SELDOM REELECTED

Only nine of the fifty-six elections from 1789 through 2008 resulted in the reelection of a President and his Vice President. In fourteen elections Presidents were reelected for a second consecutive term.

The nine presidents who carried their Vice Presidents into office for a second term were Washington (1789–1797), Monroe (1817–1825), Wilson (1913–1921), Franklin Delano Roosevelt (1933–1941), Eisenhower (1953–1961), Nixon (1969–1973), Reagan (1981–1989), Clinton (1993–2001), and George W. Bush (2001–2009). The Vice Presidents elected with them were respectively J. Adams, Tompkins, Marshall, Garner, Nixon, Agnew, George Bush, Gore, and Cheney. (Roosevelt's Vice Presidents for his third and fourth terms were Wallace and Truman.)

In 1804, when Jefferson was elected for a second term, Burr was replaced by George Clinton. At this election, the President and the Vice President were on separate ballots and it would have been possible to elect one and not the other.

Four Presidents had different Vice Presidents during their second terms because of the death or resignation of their Vice Presidents. Clinton, who had served as Vice President during the second term of Jefferson, died in office during the first term of Madison, and Gerry was elected to serve during Madison's second term. Hobart died during the first term of McKinley, and Theodore Roosevelt was selected for the second term. Calhoun resigned during the first term of Jackson, and Van Buren served as Vice President during Jackson's second term. Agnew resigned during the second term of Nixon, and Nixon promptly nominated Representative Gerald Rudolph Ford, Jr., to fill the vacancy, in accordance with the Twenty-fifth

Amendment. This nomination depended on confirmation by a majority vote of both houses of Congress. Ford was sworn in as the fortieth Vice President of the United States on December 6, 1973.

Lincoln had two Vice Presidents, Hamlin and Andrew Johnson. Grant's Vice Presidents were Colfax and Wilson.

Cleveland was elected for two nonconsecutive terms (1885–1889 and 1893–1897), and he had a different Vice President each term. Hendricks died while in office during the first term, and Stevenson served during the second.

REPUBLICAN AND DEMOCRATIC PRESIDENTS AND VICE PRESIDENTS

Four Republican presidential and vice presidential teams have been elected twice: Eisenhower and Nixon; Nixon and Agnew; Reagan and George Bush; George W. Bush and Cheney

Three Democratic teams were elected for second terms: Wilson and Marshall; Franklin Delano Roosevelt and Garner; Clinton and Gore.

The only Republican Vice Presidents elected to the presidency were Theodore Roosevelt, Coolidge, Nixon, and George Bush. The only Democratic Vice Presidents elected to the presidency were Van Buren, Truman, and Lyndon Baines Johnson.

The only presidential and vice presidential teams defeated for a second term were Van Buren and Richard Mentor Johnson (D, 1840), Hoover and Curtis (R, 1932), Carter and Mondale (D, 1980), and George Bush and Quayle (R, 1992). Several other Presidents were defeated for reelection, but each had a different vice presidential running mate.

VICE PRESIDENTIAL CANDIDATE RESIGNED

The first and only vice presidential candidate of a major political party to resign was Senator Thomas Francis Eagleton of Missouri, who was nominated on July 13, 1972, at the Democratic National Convention held at Miami Beach, Florida. In accepting the nomination, he failed to inform his running mate, George Stanley McGovern, of previous treatment for mental illness, a history soon made public by the press. Annoyed by Eagleton's lack of candor and fearing that he would prove a political liability, McGovern insisted that he resign. Eagleton submitted his resignation on August 1, 1972, and the National Democratic Committee nominated Robert Sargent Shriver of Maryland.

VACANCIES IN THE OFFICE OF VICE PRESIDENT

In the 220 years between 1789 and 2009, there was no Vice President for 37 years and 290 days, about one sixth of the time.

Of the forty-six past Vice Presidents, nineteen did not serve a full four-year term.

Seven Vice Presidents died in office and did not complete their terms:

George Clinton, the fourth Vice President, took office on March 4, 1809, and died on April 20, 1812. He served 3 years and 47 days, the office remaining vacant 318 days.

Elbridge Gerry, the fifth Vice President, took office on March 4, 1813, and died on November 23, 1814. He served 1 year and 264 days, the office remaining vacant 2 years and 101 days.

William Rufus Devane King, the 13th Vice President, took office on March 4, 1853, and died on April 18, 1853. He served 45 days, the office remaining vacant 3 years and 320 days.

Henry Wilson, the 18th Vice President, took office on March 4, 1873, and died on November 22, 1875. He served 2 years and 263 days, the office remaining vacant 1 year and 2 days.

Thomas Andrews Hendricks, the 21st Vice President, took office on March 4, 1885, and died on November 25, 1885. He served 266 days, the office remaining vacant 3 years and 99 days.

Garret Augustus Hobart, the 24th Vice President, took office on March 4, 1897, and died on November 21, 1899. He served 2 years and 262 days, the office remaining vacant 1 year and 103 days.

James Schoolcraft Sherman, the 27th Vice President, took office on March 4, 1909, and died on October 30, 1912. he served 3 years and 240 days, the office remaining vacant 125 days.

Two Vice Presidents resigned:

John Caldwell Calhoun, the seventh Vice President, resigned on December 28, 1832. The office remained vacant 66 days.

Spiro Theodore Agnew, the 39th Vice President, resigned on October 10, 1973. The office remained vacant 57 days until Congress confirmed Gerald Rudolph Ford, Jr., on December 6, 1973, on which date he was sworn in.

Ten Vice Presidents succeeded to the presidency:

John Tyler, the tenth Vice President, succeeded William Henry Harrison, who died in office, and the office remained vacant 3 years and 332 days.

Millard Fillmore, the twelfth Vice President, succeeded Zachary Taylor, who died in office, and the office remained vacant 2 years and 238 days.

Andrew Johnson, the sixteenth Vice President, succeeded Abraham Lincoln, who was assassinated, and the office remained vacant 3 years and 323 days.

Chester Alan Arthur, the twentieth Vice President, succeeded James Abram Garfield, who was assassinated, and the office remained vacant 3 years and 166 days.

Theodore Roosevelt, the twenty-fifth Vice President, succeeded William McKinley, who was assassinated, and the office remained vacant 3 years and 171 days.

Calvin Coolidge, the twenty-ninth Vice President, succeeded Warren Gamaliel Harding, who died in office, and the office remained vacant 1 year and 214 days.

Harry S. Truman, the thirty-fourth Vice President, succeeded Franklin Delano Roosevelt, who died in office, and the office remained vacant 3 years and 283 days.

Lyndon Baines Johnson, the thirty-seventh Vice President, succeeded John Fitzgerald Kennedy, who was assassinated, and the office remained vacant 1 year and 59 days.

Gerald Rudolph Ford, the fortieth Vice President, succeeded Richard Milhous Nixon, who resigned the presidency, and the office remained vacant 132 days.

Nelson Aldrich Rockefeller was confirmed by the Congress and sworn in as the 41st Vice President on December 19, 1974.

The Twenty-fifth Amendment, adopted in 1967, was designed to eliminate lengthy vice presidential vacancies. Section 2 of the Amendment provides that whenever there is a vacancy, "the President shall nominate a Vice President who shall take office upon confirmation by a majority vote of both houses of Congress." Both Ford and Rockefeller were appointed under the provisions of this amendment.

VICE PRESIDENTS IN THE PRESIDENCY

Fourteen of the Vice Presidents went on to serve as chief executive.

Four Vice Presidents were elected to the presidency at the conclusion of their vice presidential terms: John Adams, Thomas Jefferson, Martin Van Buren, and George Bush. Of these, only Jefferson was elected to a second term.

Richard Milhous Nixon was the first Vice President to be elected President several years after his vice presidential term. Nixon was Vice President from January 20, 1953, to January 20, 1961, under President Dwight David Eisenhower. Nixon was not in government service again until January 20, 1969, when he was inaugurated President. In the intervening years, he ran unsuccessfully for political office, practiced law, and wrote a book.

Nine Vice Presidents succeeded to the presidency upon the death or resignation of the Presidents under whom they had served:

Tyler, 3 years and 332 days

Fillmore, 2 years and 238 days

Andrew Johnson, 3 years and 323 days

Arthur, 3 years and 166 days

Theodore Roosevelt, 3 years and 171 days

Coolidge, 1 year and 214 days

Truman, 3 years and 283 days

Lyndon Baines Johnson, 1 year and 59 days

Gerald Rudolph Ford, 2 years and 164 days

—a total of 26 years and 123 days during which the country was run by men who had not been elected to presidential office.

Four of the nine who succeeded to the presidency were elected for additional four-year terms: Theodore Roosevelt, Calvin Coolidge, Harry S. Truman, and Lyndon Baines Johnson.

Five former Vice Presidents ran for President and were defeated. John Cabell Breckenridge served under Buchanan and was the Independent Democratic/Southern Democratic candidate in 1860; Henry Agard Wallace served in F. D. Roosevelt's third term and was the Progressive candidate in 1948; Hubert Horatio Humphrey served under L. B. Johnson and was the Democratic candidate in 1968; Walter Frederick Mondale served under Carter and was the Democratic candidate in 1984; and Albert Arnold Gore, Jr., served under Clinton and was the Democratic candidate in 2000.

VICE PRESIDENTS—STATUS AFTER HOLDING OFFICE

Many Vice Presidents have retired to private life after the completion of their terms. Farming, business, law, writing, lecturing, and teaching have been their occupations.

There have been a number of notable exceptions, including the Vice Presidents who became President through succession or election, as described above.

Six Vice Presidents served in the Senate after their vice presidential terms: John Caldwell Calhoun (who resigned as Vice President to serve in the Senate), John Cabell Breckinridge, Hannibal Hamlin, Andrew Johnson (who was elected to the Senate after serving as President), Alben William Barkley, and Hubert Horatio Humphrey. Hamlin was minister to Spain as well as Senator, and Breckinridge served as Secretary of War for the Confederacy after being expelled from the Senate.

Other Vice Presidents who remained in public service were Richard Mentor Johnson, who served in the Kentucky legislature; George Mifflin Dallas, who was minister to Great Britain; Levi Parsons Morton, who was elected Governor of New York; Adlai Ewing Stevenson, who was active in Illinois politics; Charles Gates Dawes, who was ambassador to Great Britain; and Aaron Burr, who was tried for treason for attempting to form a government of his own in the Louisiana Territory. He was acquitted.

Seven Vice Presidents died in office: George Clinton (who died during his second term), Elbridge Gerry, William Rufus De Vane King, Henry Wilson, Thomas Andrews Hendricks, Garret Augustus Hobart, and James Schoolcraft Sherman.

TWO VICE PRESIDENTS WON THE NOBEL PEACE PRIZE

In 1925, during his term in office, Charles Gates Dawes, Vice President under Coolidge, received the Nobel Peace Prize for work he had done previously in attempting to stabilize Germany's economy in the aftermath of World War I. He shared the prize with Sir Austen Chamberlain.

In 2007, Albert Arnold Gore, Jr., Vice President under Clinton, won the Nobel Peace Prize for his crusade against global warming, with which he had been occupied since leaving office in 2001. He shared the prize with the Intergovernmental Panel on Climate Change.

VICE PRESIDENT ON A POSTAGE STAMP

The only Vice President to be honored with a postage stamp (apart from Vice Presidents who later became Presidents) was Hubert Horatio Humphrey, Vice President under Lyndon Baines Johnson. A 52-cent stamp bearing his likeness was issued on June 3, 1991, as part of the Great American series.

EIGHTH AND TENTH VICE PRESIDENTS BECAME THE EIGHTH AND TENTH PRESIDENTS

Martin Van Buren, who was the eighth Vice President (March 4, 1833–March 4, 1837), was elected to the presidency and served as the eighth President (March 4, 1837–March 4, 1841

John Tyler, who was the tenth Vice President (March 4, 1841–April 4, 1841) succeeded to the presidency when William Henry Harrison died, and thus became the tenth President.

VICE PRESIDENTIAL SALARIES

The Vice President's salary was fixed by the First Congress at $5,000 per year in its act of September 24, 1789. That figure remained in force until March 3, 1873, when Congress doubled it. The Vice President's salary was raised to $12,000 in 1906 and to $20,000 in 1946.

The act of January 19, 1949, provided that the Vice President's salary be increased to $30,000 and authorized an expense allowance of $10,000 "for which no tax liability shall occur or accounting be made." Another increase, to $35,000, was made in 1951. The expense allowance was made subject to income taxes in 1953.

The Federal Employees Salary Act of 1964, enacted on August 14, 1964, raised the Vice President's salary to $43,000.

The act of September 14, 1969, raised the Vice President's salary from $43,000 to $62,500. In common with U.S. congressional representatives and senators, the Vice President receives an annual cost-of-living increase. By 1993, the Vice President was entitled to receive a salary of $94,600. Congress changed the Vice President's base pay to $171,000 in 1994.

The Vice President's salary as of January 1, 2008, was $221,100.

VICE PRESIDENTS' PENSIONS

The Vice President receives a pension under the congressional pension plan, calculated according to his years of service, with intermittent cost-of-living increases. In 2009, his first year after leaving office, Vice President Cheney received a pension of $132,451, based on his 10 years in Congress and eight years as Vice President.

VICE PRESIDENTS—AGE UPON ASSUMING OFFICE AND AGE AT DEATH

Adams

53 years, 174 days; 90 years, 247 days

Jefferson

53 years, 325 days; 83 years, 82 days

Burr

45 years, 26 days; 80 years, 82 days

G. Clinton

65 years, 221 days; 72 years, 268 days

Gerry

68 years, 230 days; 70 years, 129 days

Tompkins

42 years, 256 days; 50 years, 355 days

Calhoun

42 years, 351 days; 68 years, 13 days

Van Buren

50 years, 89 days; 79 years, 231 days

R. M. Johnson

56 years, 138 days; 70 years, 33 days

Tyler

50 years, 340 days; 71 years, 295 days

Dallas

52 years, 237 days; 72 years, 174 days

Fillmore

49 years, 56 days; 74 years, 60 days

King

66 years, 331 days; 67 years, 11 days

Breckinridge

36 years, 42 days; 54 years, 116 days

Hamlin

51 years, 189 days; 81 years, 311 days

A. Johnson

56 years, 65 days; 66 years, 214 days

Colfax

45 years, 346 days; 61 years, 296 days

Wilson

61 years, 16 days; 63 years, 279 days

Wheeler

57 years, 247 days; 67 years, 339 days

Arthur

51 years, 150 days; 57 years, 44 days

Hendricks

65 years, 178 days; 66 years, 79 days

Morton

64 years, 292 days; 96 years

Stevenson

57 years, 132 days; 78 years, 234 days

Hobart

52 years, 274 days; 55 years, 171 days

T. Roosevelt

42 years, 128 days; 60 years, 71 days

Fairbanks

52 years, 297 days; 66 years, 24 days

Sherman

53 years, 131 days; 57 years, 6 days

Marshall

58 years, 355 days; 71 years, 79 days

Coolidge

48 years, 243 days; 60 years, 185 days

Dawes

59 years, 189 days; 85 years, 239 days

Curtis

69 years, 38 days; 76 years, 14 days

Garner

64 years, 102 days; 98 years, 351 days

Wallace

52 years, 105 days; 77 years, 42 days

Truman

60 years, 257 days; 88 years, 232 days

Barkley

71 years, 57 days; 78 years, 157 days

Nixon

40 years, 11 days; 81 years, 113 days

L. B. Johnson

52 years, 146 days; 64 years, 148 days

Humphrey

53 years, 238 days; 66 years, 231 days

Agnew

51 years, 72 days; 77 years, 303 days

Ford

60 years, 145 days; 93 years, 165 days

Rockefeller

66 years, 165 days; 70 years, 202 days

Mondale

49 years, 15 days

G. Bush

56 years, 223 days

Quayle

41 years, 352 days

Gore

44 years, 232 days

Cheney

59 years, 356 days

Biden

66 years, 61 days

The average age of the Vice Presidents upon taking office was 54 years and 284 days.

The oldest Vice President to succeed to the presidency upon the death or resignation of the President was Truman, who was 60 years and 339 days old when he became President after the death of Franklin D. Roosevelt.

The youngest Vice President to succeed to the presidency upon the death or resignation of the President was Theodore Roosevelt, who was 42 years and 322 days old when he became President after the death of McKinley.

The average age at death of the 41 Vice Presidents who are no longer living was 73 years and 234 days.

COMPARATIVE AGES OF THE PRESIDENTS AND THEIR VICE PRESIDENTS ON INAUGURATION DAY

The following list shows the age at inauguration of each President and Vice President. Omitted from the list of Presidents are Tyler, Fillmore, Andrew Johnson, and Arthur, who had no Vice Presidents since they succeeded to the presidency but were not elected for additional terms in their own right, as were Theodore Roosevelt, Coolidge, Truman, and Lyndon Baines Johnson.

Seven Presidents had two Vice Presidents: Jefferson—Burr and Clinton; Madison—Clinton and Gerry; Jackson—Calhoun and Van Buren; Lincoln—Hamlin and Johnson; Grant—Colfax and Wilson; McKinley—Hobart and Roosevelt; Nixon—Agnew and Ford (Ford was not inaugurated with Nixon). Franklin Delano Roosevelt had three Vice Presidents—Garner, Wallace, and Truman.

Where a President and a Vice President were inaugurated together twice, only their age at the first inauguration is shown.

Washington 57 years, 67 days; **J. Adams** 53 years, 174 days

Adams 61 years, 125 days; **Jefferson** 53 years, 325 days

Jefferson 57 years, 325 days; **Burr** 45 years, 26 days

Jefferson 61 years, 325 days; **Clinton** 65 years, 221 days

Madison 57 years, 353 days; **Clinton** 69 years, 221 days

Madison 61 years, 353 days; **Gerry** 68 years, 230 days

Monroe 58 years, 310 days; **Tompkins** 42 years, 256 days

J. Q. Adams 57 years, 236 days; **Calhoun** 42 years, 351 days

Jackson 61 years, 354 days; **Calhoun** 46 years, 351 days

Jackson 65 years, 354 days; **Van Buren** 50 years, 89 days

Van Buren 54 years, 89 days; **R. M. Johnson** 56 years, 138 days

W. H. Harrison 68 years, 23 days; **Tyler** 50 years, 340 days

Polk 49 years, 122 days; **Dallas** 52 years, 237 days

Taylor 64 years, 100 days; **Fillmore** 49 years, 56 days

Pierce 48 years, 101 days; **King** 66 years, 331 days

Buchanan 65 years, 315 days; **Breckinridge** 36 years, 42 days

Lincoln 52 years, 20 days; **Hamlin** 51 years, 189 days

Lincoln 56 years, 20 days; **A. Johnson** 56 years, 65 days

Grant 46 years, 311 days; **Colfax** 45 years, 346 days

Grant 50 years, 311 days; **H. Wilson** 61 years, 16 days

Hayes 54 years, 151 days; **Wheeler** 57 years, 247 days

Garfield 49 years, 105 days; **Arthur** 51 years, 150 days

Cleveland 47 years, 351 days; **Hendricks** 65 years, 178 days

B. Harrison 55 years, 196 days; **Morton** 64 years, 292 days

Cleveland 55 years, 351 days; **Stevenson** 57 years, 132 days

McKinley 54 years, 34 days; **Hobart** 52 years, 274 days

T. Roosevelt 46 years, 128 days; **Fairbanks** 52 years, 297 days

Taft 51 years, 170 days; **Sherman** 53 years, 131 days

Wilson 56 years, 65 days; **Marshall** 58 years, 355 days

Harding 55 years, 122 days; **Coolidge** 48 years, 243 days

Coolidge 52 years, 243 days; **Dawes** 59 years, 189 days

Hoover 54 years, 206 days; **Curtis** 69 years, 38 days

F. D. Roosevelt 51 years, 33 days; **Garner** 64 years, 102 days

F. D. Roosevelt 58 years, 355 days; **Wallace** 52 years, 105 days

F. D. Roosevelt 62 years, 355 days; **Truman** 60 years, 257 days

Truman 64 years, 257 days; **Barkley** 71 years, 57 days

Eisenhower 62 years, 98 days; **Nixon** 40 years, 11 days

Kennedy 43 years, 236 days; **L. B. Johnson** 52 years, 146 days

Johnson 56 years, 146 days; **Humphrey** 53 years, 238 days

Nixon 56 years, 11 days; **Agnew** 51 years, 72 days; Ford 60 years, 145 days (age upon taking office; Nixon was 186 days older than Ford)

Ford 61 years, 26 days (age upon taking office); **Rockefeller** 66 years, 165 days (age upon taking office; Rockefeller was 5 years and 7 days older than Ford)

Carter 52 years, 111 days; **Mondale** 49 years, 15 days

Reagan 69 years, 349 days; **G. Bush** 56 years, 223 days

G. Bush 64 years, 223 days; **Quayle** 41 years, 352 days

Clinton 46 years, 149 days; **Gore** 44 years, 232 days

G. W. Bush 54 years, 198 days; **Cheney** 59 years, 356 days

Obama 47 years, 169 days; **Biden** 66 years, 61 days

The following Presidents were older than their Vice Presidents: Washington, John Adams, Jefferson (first Vice President), Monroe, John Quincy Adams, Jackson (first and second Vice Presidents), William Henry Harrison, Taylor, Buchanan, Lincoln (first Vice President), Grant (first Vice President), McKinley (first and second Vice Presidents), Harding, Franklin Delano Roosevelt (second and third Vice Presidents), Eisenhower, Lyndon Baines Johnson, Nixon (first and second Vice Presidents), Carter, Reagan, George Bush, and Clinton.

The following Presidents were younger than their Vice Presidents: Jefferson (second Vice President), Madison (first and second Vice Presidents), Van Buren, Polk, Pierce, Lincoln (second Vice President), Hayes, Garfield, Cleveland (first and second Vice Presidents), Benjamin Harrison, Theodore Roosevelt, Taft, Wilson, Coolidge, Hoover, Franklin Delano Roosevelt (first Vice President), Truman, Kennedy, Ford, George W. Bush, and Obama.

The average age of the Vice Presidents at inauguration was 54 years and 284 days, that of the Presidents at inauguration or succession 55 years and 34days.

VICE PRESIDENTS DECLARE THEIR OPPONENTS ELECTED PRESIDENT

On Wednesday, February 13, 1861, John Cabell Breckinridge of Kentucky, Vice President under James Buchanan, presided in the House of Representatives over a joint session of Congress that had assembled to count the electoral votes in the election of 1860. It was his duty to announce that "Abraham Lincoln, of Illinois, having received a majority of the whole number of electoral votes, is elected President of the United States for four years, commencing the fourth of March 1861. Hannibal Hamlin, of Maine, having received a majority of the whole number of electoral votes, is duly elected Vice President of the United States for four years commencing the fourth of March. The business for which the two Houses were assembled having been finished, the Senate will now return to its own Chamber."

Breckinridge had been Lincoln's opponent in the election. The electoral votes for President were cast as follows: Abraham Lincoln of Illinois 180 votes, John Cabell Breckinridge of Kentucky 72 votes, John Bell of Tennessee 39 votes, and Stephen Arnold Douglas of Illinois 12 votes.

On January 6, 1961, Richard Milhous Nixon, Vice President under Dwight David Eisenhower, had to fulfill the same responsibility as Breckinridge. Presiding over a joint session of Congress assembled for the counting of the 1960 electoral votes, it was his duty to announce that the tally stood at 303 votes for John Fitzgerald Kennedy, Democrat of Massachusetts; 219 votes for Richard Milhous Nixon, Republican of California; and 15 votes for Harry Flood Byrd. (A majority of 269 of the 537 votes was necessary to win.) After announcing that his opponent was elected, Nixon said, "In our campaigns, no matter how hard they may be, no matter how close the election may turn out to be, those who lose accept the verdict and support those who won."

In January 1969, the same situation occurred with Hubert Horatio Humphrey, Vice President under L. B. Johnson. Humphrey had run as the Democratic candidate in the 1968 presidential election but had lost to Richard Milhous Nixon. Humphrey escaped the necessity of announcing his own defeat because he had to travel to Norway to represent the United States at the funeral of former United Nations Secretary-General Trygve Lie. Senator Richard Brevard Russell presided over the counting of the electoral votes instead and made the announcement in Humphrey's place.

On January 6, 1981, Walter Frederick Mondale, Vice President under Jimmy Carter and vice presidential candidate in 1980, was required to declare that Ronald Wilson Reagan and George Herbert Walker Bush had received 489 electoral votes, while the incumbents, Carter and Mondale, had received 49.

On January 8, 2001, the task of announcing his own defeat fell to Albert Arnold Gore, Jr., Vice President under William Jefferson Clinton, who declared to a joint session of Congress that the electors had cast 266 votes for himself and 271 votes for his Republican opponent, George W. Bush.

VICE PRESIDENTS IN CONGRESS

Thirty-three of the forty-seven Vice Presidents served in Congress before becoming Vice President.

Fourteen served in both the House of Representatives and the Senate: Calhoun, Richard Mentor Johnson, Tyler, King, Breckinridge, Hamlin, Andrew Johnson, Hendricks, Curtis, Barkley, Nixon, Lyndon Baines Johnson, Quayle, and Gore.

Nine served only in the Senate: Burr, Van Buren, Dallas, Wilson, Fairbanks, Truman, Humphrey, Mondale, and Biden.

Eleven served only in the House of Representatives: Gerry, Fillmore, Colfax, Wheeler, Morton, Stevenson, Sherman, Garner, Ford, George Bush, and Cheney.

Fourteen Vice Presidents never served in either house of Congress: John Adams, Jefferson, George Clinton, Tompkins (who was elected to the House of Representatives but did not serve), Arthur, Hobart, Marshall, Theodore Roosevelt, Coolidge, Dawes, Wallace, Agnew, and Rockefeller. However, three of these fourteen did serve in the Continental Congress: John Adams, Jefferson, and Clinton. One Vice President, Gerry, served in both the Continental Congress and later in the House of Representatives.

Four Vice Presidents served in the Continental Congress: John Adams, Jefferson, Clinton, and Gerry. Gerry was later a member of the House of Representatives.

The following is a list of the Vice Presidents elected to Congress, with the states they represented and their terms of office:

J. Adams—Massachusetts

Continental Congress, 1774–1778

Jefferson—Virginia

Continental Congress, 1775–1776; 1783–1785

Burr—New York

U.S. Senate, Mar. 4, 1791–Mar. 3, 1797

Clinton—New York

Continental Congress, May 15, 1775–July 8, 1777

Gerry—Massachusetts

Continental Congress, 1776–1781; 1782–1785

U.S. House of Representatives, 1st–2nd Congresses, Mar. 4, 1789–Mar. 3, 1793

Tompkins—New York

U.S. House of Representatives, elected to 9th Congress, but resigned before term

Calhoun—South Carolina

U.S. House of Representatives, 12th–15th Congresses, Mar. 4, 1811–Nov. 3, 1817

U.S. Senate, Dec. 29, 1832–Mar. 3, 1843; Nov. 26, 1845–Mar. 31, 1850

Van Buren—New York

U.S. Senate, Mar. 4, 1821–Dec. 20, 1828

R. M. Johnson—Kentucky

U.S. House of Representatives, 10th–15th Congresses, Mar. 4, 1807–Mar. 3, 1819

U.S. Senate, Dec. 10, 1819–Mar. 3, 1829

Tyler—Virginia

U.S. House of Representatives, 14th–16th Congresses, Dec. 16, 1817–Mar. 3, 1821

U.S. Senate, Mar, 4, 1827–Feb. 29, 1836

King—North Carolina; Alabama

U.S. House of Representatives, 12th–14th Congresses, Mar. 4, 1811–Nov. 4, 1816

U.S. Senate, Dec. 14, 1819–Apr. 15, 1844; July 1, 1848–Dec. 20, 1852

Dallas—Pennsylvania

U.S. Senate, Dec. 13, 1831–Mar. 3, 1833

Fillmore—New York

U.S. House of Representatives, 23rd Congress, Mar. 4, 1833–Mar. 3, 1835; 25th–27th Congresses, Mar. 4, 1837–Mar. 3, 1843

Breckinridge—Kentucky

U.S. House of Representatives, 32nd–33rd Congresses, Mar. 4, 1851–Mar. 3, 1855

U.S. Senate, Mar. 4, 1861 (expelled by resolution of Dec. 4, 1861)

Hamlin—Maine

U.S. House of Representatives, 28th–29th Congresses, Mar. 4, 1843–Mar. 3, 1847

U.S. Senate, June 8, 1848–Jan. 7, 1857; Mar. 4, 1857–Jan. 17, 1861; Mar. 4, 1869–Mar. 3, 1881

A. Johnson—Tennessee

U.S. House of Representatives, 28th–32nd Congresses, Mar. 4, 1843–Mar. 3, 1853

U.S. Senate, Oct. 8, 1857–Mar. 4, 1862; Mar. 4, 1875–July 31, 1875

Colfax—Indiana

U.S. House of Representatives, 34th–40th Congresses, Mar. 4, 1855–Mar. 3, 1869

Wilson—Massachusetts

U.S. Senate, Jan. 31, 1855–Mar. 3, 1873

Wheeler—New York

U.S. House of Representatives, 37th Congress, Mar. 4, 1861–Mar. 3, 1863; 41st–44th Congresses, Mar. 4, 1869–Mar. 3, 1877

Hendricks—Indiana

U.S. House of Representatives, 32nd–33rd Congresses, Mar. 4, 1851–Mar. 3, 1855
U.S. Senate, Mar. 4, 1863–Mar. 3, 1869

Morton—New York

U.S. House of Representatives, 46th–47th Congresses, Mar. 4, 1879–Mar. 21, 1881

Stevenson—Illinois

U.S. House of Representatives, 44th Congress, Mar. 4, 1875–Mar. Mar. 3, 1877; 46th Congress, Mar. 4, 1879–Mar. 3, 1881

Fairbanks—Indiana

U.S. Senate, Mar. 4, 1897–Mar. 3, 1905

Sherman—New York

U.S. House of Representatives, 50th–51st Congresses, Mar. 4, 1887–Mar. 3, 1891; 53rd–60th Congresses, Mar. 4, 1893–Mar. 3, 190

Curtis—Kansas

U.S. House of Representatives, 53rd–59th Congresses, Mar. 4, 1893–Jan. 28, 1907
U.S. Senate, Jan. 29, 1907–Mar. 3, 1913; Mar. 4, 1915–Mar. 3, 1929

Garner—Texas

U.S. House of Representatives, 58th–73rd Congresses, Mar. 4, 1903–Mar. 3, 1933

Truman—Missouri

U.S. Senate, Jan. 3, 1935–Jan. 17, 1945

Barkley—Kentucky

U.S. House of Representatives, 63rd–69th Congresses, Mar. 4, 1913–Mar. 3, 1927
U.S. Senate, Mar. 4, 1927–Jan. 19, 1949; Jan. 3, 1955–Apr. 30, 1956

Nixon—California

U.S. House of Representatives, 80th–81st Congresses, Jan. 3, 1947–Jan. 3, 1951
U.S. Senate, Jan. 3, 1951–Jan. 20, 1953

L. B. Johnson—Texas

U.S. House of Representatives, 75th–80th Congresses, Apr. 10, 1937–Jan. 3, 1949
U.S. Senate, Jan. 3, 1949–Jan. 3, 1961

Humphrey—Minnesota

U.S. Senate, Jan. 3, 1949–Dec. 29, 1964; Jan. 21, 1971–Jan. 13, 1978

Ford—Michigan

U.S. House of Representatives, 81st–93rd Congresses, Jan. 3, 1949–Dec. 6, 1973

Mondale—Minnesota

U.S. Senate, Jan. 4, 1965–Jan. 20, 1977

G. Bush—Texas

U.S. House of Representatives, 90th–91st Congresses, Jan. 10, 1967–Jan. 2, 1971

Quayle—Indiana

U.S. House of Representatives, 95th–96th Congresses, Jan. 3, 1977–Jan. 3, 1981
U.S. Senate, Jan. 5, 1981–Jan. 3, 1989

Gore—Tennessee

U.S. House of Representatives, 94th–98th Congresses, Jan. 3, 1975–Jan. 3, 1985
U.S. Senate, Jan. 3, 1985–Jan. 5, 1993

Cheney—Wyoming

U.S. House of Representatives, 96th–101st Congresses, Jan. 3, 1979–Mar. 23, 1989

Biden—Delaware

U.S. Senate, 93rd–111th Congresses, Jan. 3, 1973–Jan. 15, 2009

VICE PRESIDENTS WHO WERE STATE GOVERNORS

The following Vice Presidents served as governors of their respective states: Jefferson, Va.; G. Clinton, N.Y.; Gerry, Mass.; Tompkins, N.Y.; Van Buren, N.Y.; Tyler, Va.; Hamlin, Me.; A. Johnson, Tenn.; Hendricks, Ind.; Morton, N.Y. (after term); T. Roosevelt, N.Y.; Marshall, Ind.; Coolidge, Mass.; Agnew, Md.; and Rockefeller, N.Y.

VICE PRESIDENTS—DATE OF DEATH, PLACE OF DEATH, AND PLACE OF BURIAL

J. Adams   July 4, 1826; Quincy, Mass.; Quincy, Mass.

Jefferson   July 4, 1826; Monticello, Va.; Monticello, Va.

Burr   Sept. 14, 1836; Staten Island, N.Y.; Princeton, N.J.

Clinton   Apr. 20, 1812; Washington, D.C.; Kingston, N.Y.

Gerry   Nov. 23, 1814; Washington, D.C.; Washington, D.C.

Tompkins   June 11, 1825; Staten Island, N.Y.; New York, N.Y.

Calhoun   Mar. 31, 1850; Washington, D.C.; Charleston, S.C.

Van Buren   July 24, 1862; Kinderhook, N.Y.; Kinderhook, N.Y.

R. M. Johnson   Nov. 19, 1850; Frankfort, Ky.; Frankfort, Ky.

Tyler   Jan. 18, 1862; Richmond, Va.; Richmond, Va.

Dallas   Dec. 31, 1864; Philadelphia, Pa.; Philadelphia, Pa.

Fillmore   Mar. 8, 1874; Buffalo, N.Y.; Buffalo, N.Y.

King   Apr. 18, 1853; Cahaba, Ala.; Selma, Ala.

Breckinridge   May 17, 1875; Lexington, Ky.; Lexington, Ky.

Hamlin   July 4, 1891; Bangor, Me.; Bangor, Me.

A. Johnson   July 31, 1875; Carter's Station, Tenn.; Greeneville, Tenn.

Colfax   Jan. 13, 1885; Mankato, Minn.; South Bend, Ind.

Wilson   Nov. 22, 1875; Washington, D.C.; Natick, Mass.

Wheeler   June 4, 1887; Malone, N.Y.; Malone, N.Y.

Arthur   Nov. 18, 1886; New York, N.Y.; Albany, N.Y.

Hendricks   Nov. 25, 1885; Indianapolis, Ind.; Indianapolis. Ind.

Morton   May 16, 1920; Rhinebeck, N.Y.; Rhinebeck, N.Y.

Stevenson   June 14, 1914; Chicago, Ill.; Bloomington, Ill.

Hobart   Nov. 21, 1899; Paterson, N.J.; Paterson, N.J.

T. Roosevelt   Jan. 6, 1919; Oyster Bay, N.Y.; Oyster Bay, N.Y.

Fairbanks   June 4, 1918; Indianapolis, Ind.; Indianapolis, Ind.

Sherman   Oct. 30, 1912; Utica, N.Y.; Utica, N.Y.

Marshall   June 1, 1925; Washington, D.C.; Indianapolis, Ind.

Coolidge   Jan. 5, 1933; Northampton, Mass.; Plymouth, Vt.

Dawes   Apr. 23, 1951; Evanston, Ill.; Chicago, Ill.

Curtis   Feb. 8, 1936; Washington, D.C.; Topeka, Kan.

Garner   Nov. 7, 1967; Uvalde, Tex.; Uvalde, Tex.

Wallace   Nov. 18, 1965; Danbury, Conn; Des Moines, Iowa

Truman   Dec. 26, 1972; Kansas City, Mo.; Independence, Mo.

Barkley   Apr. 30, 1956; Lexington, Va.; Paducah, Ky.

Nixon   Apr. 22, 1994; New York, N.Y.; Yorba Linda, Calif.

L. B. Johnson   Jan. 22, 1973; San Antonio, Tex.; Stonewall, Tex.

Humphrey   Jan. 13, 1978; Waverly, Minn.; Minneapolis, Minn.

Agnew   Sept. 17, 1996; Ocean City, Md.; Timonium, Md.

Rockefeller   Jan. 26. 1979; New York, N.Y.; North Tarrytown, N.Y.

Ford   Dec. 26, 2006; Rancho Mirage, Calif.; Grand Rapids, Mich.

PENSION TO VICE PRESIDENT'S WIDOW

On January 25, 1929, Congress passed an act (45 Stat. L. 2041) awarding an annual pension of $3,000 to Lois I. Marshall, widow of Vice President Thomas Riley Marshall, who had served under President Wilson. This was the first pension awarded to the widow of a Vice President. This is the only instance in which a Vice President's widow has been awarded a pension.

VICE PRESIDENTS
APPOINTED

The first Vice President to be appointed rather than elected to office was Gerald Rudolph Ford, the fortieth Vice President. He was nominated by President Nixon to fill the vacancy caused by the resignation of Vice President Agnew, confirmed by both houses of Congress according to the provisions of the Twenty-fifth Amendment, and sworn in on December 6, 1973.

After Ford succeeded to the presidency, he appointed Nelson Aldrich Rockefeller as the 41st Vice President. Rockefeller was sworn in on December 19, 1974, having been confirmed by Congress. Ford and Rockefeller were the only Vice Presidents chosen in this manner. Before the Twenty-fifth Amendment was ratified in 1967, no procedures existed for filling a vacancy in the office.

THREE VICE PRESIDENTS IN
FOURTEEN MONTHS

Between October 10, 1973, and December 19, 1974, the United States had three Vice Presidents. Spiro Theodore Agnew resigned on October 10, 1973; on December 6, 1973, Gerald Rudolph Ford was sworn in as Vice President. When President Nixon resigned on August 9, 1974, Ford became President. On December 19, 1974, Nelson Aldrich Rockefeller was sworn in as Vice President. In 14 months (436 days) the country had had three Vice Presidents and the office had been vacant for 189 days—57 days after Agnew's resignation and 132 after Ford's advancement.

FIRST VICE PRESIDENT TO
MARRY IN OFFICE

Alben William Barkley, Vice President to Harry S. Truman, was the first Vice President to marry in office. He married Elizabeth Jane Rucker Hadley on November 18, 1949, in St. Louis Mo. She was born in Keytesville, Mo., and died on September 6, 1964, at Washington, D.C. She was the widow of Carleton S. Hadley, who died on February 17, 1945.

"THE VEEP"

Alben William Barkley was the first Vice President to be called (and to call himself) "The Veep." The nickname was coined from the abbreviation V.P. and it has persisted as a colloquial term for Vice President.

VICE PRESIDENT SWORN IN
BY HOUSE SPEAKER

Lyndon Baines Johnson was sworn in as Vice President of the United States on January 20, 1961, at 12:41 P.M., by Speaker of the House Sam Rayburn. This was the first time that a Vice President was sworn in by a Speaker of the House. Both were Texans. The legendary Rayburn served nearly 49 years in the House, 17 of them as Speaker.

VICE PRESIDENT CHAIRED
THE UNITED NATIONS
SECURITY COUNCIL

For some 40 minutes on January 10, 2000, Vice President Al Gore presided over a Security Council session on the AIDS epidemic. He promised that the United States would contribute an additional 150 million dollars to fight AIDS worldwide, with a focus on bringing treatments to African nations ravaged by the disease. This was the first time that an American Vice President had been invited to chair a meeting of the U.N. Security Council.

TWENTY-SEVEN COUNTIES
NAMED FOR VICE
PRESIDENTS

Calhoun—11

Ala., Ark., Fla., Ga., Ill., Iowa, Mich., Miss., S.C., Tex., W.Va.

R. M. Johnson—5

Ill., Iowa, Ky., Mo., Neb.

Dallas—4

Ark., Iowa, Mo., Tex.

Clinton—2

N.Y., Ohio

Colfax—2

Neb., N.M.

Tompkins—1

N.Y.

King—1

Wash.

Hamlin—1

S.D.

Index